J2EE

DEVELOPER'S HANDBOOK

ETS
TM

J2EE

DEVELOPER'S HANDBOOK

Paul J. Perrone
Venkata S. R. "Krishna" R. Chaganti
Tom Schwenk

DEVELOPER'S LIBRARY

Sams Publishing, 201 West 103rd Street, Indianapolis, Indiana 46290

J2EE Developer's Handbook

International Standard Book Number: 0-67232-348-6

Library of Congress Catalog Card Number: 2002100928

Printed in the United States of America

First Printing: June 2003

06 05 04 03 4 3 2 1

Trademarks

Warning and Disclaimer

Bulk Sales

Sams Publishing offers excellent discounts on this book when ordered in quantity for bulk purchases or special sales. For more information, please contact

U.S. Corporate and Government Sales
1-800-382-3419
corpsales@pearsontechgroup.com

For sales outside of the U.S., please contact

International Sales
1-317-581-3793
international@pearsontechgroup.com

Associate Publisher
Michael Stephens

Acquisitions Editor
Todd Green

Development Editor
Songlin Qiu

Managing Editor
Charlotte Clapp

Project Editor
Elizabeth Finney

Copy Editor
Cheri Clark

Indexer
Chris Barrick

Proofreader
Suzanne Thomas

Technical Editors
Eileen Boer
Robert Byrom
Nazir Faisal
Mike Kopack
Craig Pfeifer
Stephen Potts
Lowell Thomas

Team Coordinator
Cindy Teeters

Cover Designer
Alan Clements

Graphics
Tammy Graham
Laura Robbins

Paul J. Perrone:

To my wife, Janie Perrone.

Venkata S. R. "Krishna" R. Chaganti:

For my love and best friend, Geetha.

Tom Schwenk:

To my parents.

Contents at a Glance

Table of Contents

About the Lead Author

Paul J. Perrone: Paul J. Perrone is the Founder, President, and CTO at Assured Technologies, Inc. (`www.assuredtech.com`). Through Assured Technologies, Paul provides software architecture and development consulting, mentoring, and training related to J2EE, XML, Web services, and object-oriented technologies. Paul has been involved with the architecture, design, and development of numerous large-scale enterprise systems and products for both Fortune 500 and medium-sized organizations. Paul also has co-authored *Building Java Enterprise Systems with J2EE* and *Java Security Handbook*; has published articles on Java; and has spoken at conferences such as JavaOne and Web Services Edge. He has an MS from the University of Virginia and a BS from Rutgers University. He is a member of the IEEE and ACM, has served as chapter chair for the Northern Virginia IEEE Computer Society, has helped in the startup of the Northern Virginia Java User's Group (NOVAJUG), and chairs the NOVAJUG's enterprise SIG (`www.novajig.org/novajug`). Paul is also an avid Java-based robot and AI tinkerer. Paul can be reached at `pperrone@assuredtech.com` or 703-669-4054.

About the Co-Authors

Venkata S. R. "Krishna" R. Chaganti: Krishna is a senior software-engineering consultant and has been developing commercial applications software for the past 12 years. Krishna has cross-platform background in designing and developing Internet-based distributed systems across a wide range of technologies, including DCE, CORBA, EJB, Web Services using Java, and C/C++ programming languages. Krishna's experience also includes development of GUI-based applications using Swing, JSP, Servlets, and so on. Krishna has also been teaching and speaking Java and related technologies for five years. He has an MSEE in Computer Engineering and an MSEE in Electrical Engineering from the University of Alabama in Huntsville. He also has a B.Tech in Electronics and Communications Engineering from Nagarjuna University, A.P., India. Krishna can be reached at `chaganti@erols.com`.

Tom Schwenk: Tom Schwenk is a Senior Software Consultant with Assured Technologies, Inc. Since 1995, he has been working with Java, specializing in highly scalable, distributed application design and development. He has been involved in the design and implementation of Java enterprise and e-commerce applications for both Fortune 500 and smaller companies. He holds a BS in Electrical Engineering and an ME in Biomedical Engineering, both from the University of Virginia. Tom can be reached at `tschwenk@assuredtech.com`.

Acknowledgments

This book has been a major undertaking that has consumed a considerable amount of time both to write and to develop supporting code examples. Although three authors have been involved with the book's writing, the division of labor was undertaken in a logically partitioned fashion in order to ensure consistency. Paul Perrone has drawn upon his communications and architecture skills to write much of the initial material, create the supporting diagrams, assist with the example code design and implementation, and oversee the book's development. Krishna Chaganti has drawn upon his software development skills to develop much of the supporting sample software, help define what technologies should be covered, and test the various code samples. Tom Schwenk has drawn upon his software development skills to also develop supporting sample software, write some of the material, define the steps and scripts for building and executing the software, perform testing, and help verify the technical accuracy of the manuscript.

The Sams Publishing staff has been absolutely fabulous and instrumental in making this a successful project. Todd Green deserves many thanks for managing the overall creation of this book and working closely with us on numerous issues. Songlin Qiu also deserves many thanks for so enthusiastically managing the development side of this book with the utmost attention to detail and perfection. We'd also like to thank Michael Stephens for working with us early on to help promote this project and having vision with its inception. Thanks also to Craig Pfeifer, Eileen Boer, and Rob Byrom as the key folks who have been involved with the tech editing of this book and have been second to none in ensuring that the material is technically accurate, as well as testing the supporting sample code. Numerous thanks also go to Elizabeth Finney and Cheri Clark for their editing prowess. Last but not least, an effort as large as this one would all be for naught if developers were not made aware of its existence, and for that we thank Amy Sorokas, Kim Spilker, and Randi Roger, as well as the other Sams marketing and public relations folks who work very hard to get the word out there about this book.

In what follows, we would like to individually acknowledge those who have helped us make this project a reality in their own way.

Paul J. Perrone:

Writing a book like this one can consume a lot of time that would otherwise be spent with family and friends. To begin, I owe many thanks to Janie Perrone for providing love, patience, and understanding, and for managing both our lives. I also thank my parents, Don and Judy Perrone, for being great parents and always supporting me; my brother and sister-in-law, Don and Denise Perrone; my nieces/goddaughters, Allison, Julia, and "not yet born niece" Perrone; my grandmother Catherine Stiles; my parents-in-law, Reid and Margaret Vance; the Heilmann, Izzo, Lawless, and in general my large extended family. Finally, I owe much gratitude to my late grandfather Anthony Perrone and uncle Louis Perrone.

Many friends and colleagues also make work both educational and fun. Of course, my friends and co-authors, Krishna Chaganti and Tom Schwenk, deserve many thanks for their truly extraordinary technical talent and unwavering dedication to making this book come to fruition. I also thank friends, fellow Assured Technologies employees, lawyers, and colleagues alike (to name a few), including Peter Thaggard, Craig Prall, Chris Craig, Eileen Boer, John Drum, Hunter Ware, Dave Remkes, Raymond Karrenbauer, Ken Isaacson, Robert Lagerman, Babu Kuttala, Heidi Koenig, Steven Sandler, Dana Krochmal, Julio Barros, Karen Eglin, Gary Miller, Andy Stauffer, Jim Wamsley, Anup Ghosh, Paul Kirkitelos, Jeff Ebert, Charles Choi, Doug Szajda, Heather Hoch, Geoff Hoekstra, Mike Woosley, Tom Hubbard, Frank Baglivio, Richard Hatch, John Duffin, John Mottola, Steve Wynne, Chris Ryan, Mike Carr, Fred Ingham, Catherine "McGill" Longo, Ben Collingsworth, Barry Clinger, Roy Tharpe, John Rollins, Malcolm McRoberts, Mark Thomas, Joe Hoff, Kent Banks, Stefan Buchanan, Denise Taylor, Barry Johnson, Michael Bushnell, Richard Mammone, Alan Polivka, Danielle Williams, Larry Rosenthal, Michael Jakes, Michael Raschid, Michael McKenzie and all of the members of the Northern Virginia Java User's Group. Finally, thanks to "Cappy."

Krishna Chaganti

There are many people to thank who have helped me in some way to make this book possible, including family, friends, and co-workers. First and foremost, I would like to thank Geetha, my wife and friend, for all of her love, support, encouragement, and patience. I would also like to thank my parents, who have been pillars of strength and laid the foundation for my life, and special thanks to my Mom for her amazing patience and help all the time. I would like to thank my son, Abhijith, for his understanding, for not complaining about his dad being attached to the computer, and for relaxing me by asking lot of questions about how the book is published.

It has been my privilege to work again with my friend and co-author Paul, whose guidance and firm leadership helped this project through its often-turbulent course. I would like to thank my other friend Tom, whose contribution helped make this book finish on time. I would also like to thank all of my friends and co-workers who have helped me along the way, including David Remkes, Karen Eglin, Gary Miller, Doug Smith, Denise Anezin, Peter Haynes, Dana Krochmal, Dan Estepp, Tom Dickey, Peter Dahlstrom, Chris Tran, Weimin Shi, Doug Kister, Odysseas Pentakalos, Dr. Ponaka N. Reddy, Dr. Remata S. Reddy, Alok Nigam, Dr. Ray Emami, Dr. Nagendra Singh, Dr. B.J.Beyer, Clay Gabler, Tommy and Raji Erskine, and many others. Finally, I would like to thank the almighty God, who has been the true guide in my life.

Tom Schwenk

There are many people I would like to thank for helping to make this book possible. Without the patience, assistance, and support of many friends, family, and colleagues, I would never have been able to do this. First of all, I would like to thank my co-authors, Paul and Krishna, whose diligence and commitment were truly remarkable throughout the entire process.

I would also like to mention just a few of the many colleagues I have worked with who have given me the opportunity to learn and grow in this field, including Allen Cunningham, Temple Fennell, Julann Griffin, Maureen Roberts, Rajesh Thakkar, Chris Goebel, Suresh Raman, Eric Rath, Del Wood, Hunter Ware, John Leech, Rob Ridings, Greg Mowery, Jeff Sweeting, Daniel Shifflett, and Lloyd Wilson. Trent Thurston, Ben Hernandez, Jen Neal, and Dorothy Sullenberger also deserve thanks for keeping me sane during this process.

Finally, I would like to give special thanks to Kathryn Cunningham for all of her love, support, and patience. And last but not least, thank you again to my parents, who, in addition to being great parents, bought me my first computer over 20 years ago.

We Want to Hear from You!

As the reader of this book, *you* are our most important critic and commentator. We value your opinion and want to know what we're doing right, what we could do better, what areas you'd like to see us publish in, and any other words of wisdom you're willing to pass our way.

As an associate publisher for Sams Publishing, I welcome your comments. You can email or write me directly to let me know what you did or didn't like about this book—as well as what we can do to make our books better.

Please note that I cannot help you with technical problems related to the *topic* of this book. We do have a User Services group, however, to which I will forward specific technical questions related to the book.

When you write, please be sure to include this book's title and author, as well as your name, email address, and phone number. I will carefully review your comments and share them with the author and editors who worked on the book.

Email: `feedback@samspublishing.com`
Mail: Michael Stephens
Associate Publisher
Sams Publishing
201 West 103rd Street
Indianapolis, IN 46290 USA

For more information about this book or another Sams Publishing title, visit our Web site at `www.samspublishing.com`. Type the ISBN (excluding hyphens) or the title of a book in the Search field to find the page you're looking for.

Foreword

Very Big Real-World Enterprise Problems

As many of the readers of this book will probably already know and have experienced, in the real world, enterprise application development problems are often more complex and tangled than they might seem on the surface and as a project evolves. These problems are not unique nor are they terribly different in the financial services industry. However, in my experience, the enterprise application development problems that arise for large international financial services organizations involve just about every possible problem that can hamper the path of most any enterprise application development effort.

In fact, many organizations in the financial services industry are challenged with keeping enterprise applications very current and very competitive. The users of these applications are of myriad types and often participate at some particular point along a path in a demand-and-supply chain of information. The end result is attempting to support a complex matrix of applications that have increasingly rapid lifecycles with a user base that is shifting as fast as the demands of the financial markets.

No stranger to such demands and a global leader in the financial services industry, ING Group originated in 1990 from the merger between National-Nederlanden and NMB Postbank Groep. The organization has experienced a decade of ambitious business expansion, primarily through autonomous growth and international acquisitions. Most recently, ING Group has acquired major financial services companies such as Reliastar and Aetna Financial Services (United States), Seguros Comercial America (Mexico), and Zurich Financial (Canada), which comprise organizations within the Americas region of its operations. The collective portfolio of mergers and acquisitions has transformed ING Group into one of the 50-largest organizations in the world. The pre-implementation organizations grew from subsequent merger and acquisitions during the 1990s, thus making the resulting ING Group technology architecture and portfolio exponentially complex.

In what follows, I provide a brief background about my role in a large multinational enterprise such as ING and highlight how J2EE technology, this book's authors, and this book help solve the enterprise application development problem.

Navigating the Enterprise Problem

For the past few years, I've been the Chief Technology Officer (CTO) for ING Americas–Technology Management Office (TMO). I've been responsible for leading enterprise architecture, information security, shared application infrastructure/services, information management, and technology direction setting across the ING Americas region. As CTO, I've been involved with the delivery and support of an adaptive approach to business and technology, which exploits the importance of time-to-market opportunities. Vital to our business has been the need for an open and adaptive architecture that allows various enterprise application modules and services from third-party vendors as well as from custom development to plug-and-play with our massively diverse enterprise-wide platforms.

The need for extraordinarily adaptable enterprise architecture is not new for industry and has been a common enterprise "needs" theme that has been apparent to me throughout my career as an enterprise technologist and advisor. On a global basis, I've been an active member of the ING Group IT Architecture Council (ITAC), IT Standards Council (ITSC), Strategic Infrastructure Council (SIC), and Information Security Strategy Council (ISSC), which compose the global IT governance forums. Before joining ING in 2001, I led the information technology organization at Cyberian Outpost. Within two years' tenure in this role, I was responsible for leading the development of a world-class enterprise technology service delivery infrastructure that supported several industry-leading retailers, accelerating them into the knowledge-rich world of multichannel and customer interaction enabling technologies. Prior to this role, I served as Vice President of Meta Group and also served as a managing partner in several professional services firms. In my professional services managing partner roles, I developed consulting models, products, and solutions that provided clients such as Wal-Mart, Hewlett-Packard, AT&T, Total Fina Elf S.A., Volkswagen, Coca-Cola, Delta Airlines, Kroger, AOL Time Warner, International Monetary Fund, and ABN Amro with technology solutions that identified, valued, and transformed their business, utilizing best-in-class and latest industry practices, processes, and principles.

Using J2EE to Solve the Enterprise Problem

Working in these various capacities, the need to solve the enterprise application development problem in an efficient and "total" fashion yielding a massively adaptable architecture has been paramount to being successful. Java and J2EE technologies have been instrumental in ensuring such success and making the solutions to such problems even possible in more recent years. At ING, J2EE has become the software platform on which all our mission-critical enterprise applications have been and continue to be ported and developed. J2EE's modular and adaptable enterprise interoperability features have been essential to our ability to integrate various data warehouses and legacy applications across the entire organization. The tremendous ease with which we've been able to develop and deploy J2EE applications that not only are rich with features, but also scale and adapt to different platforms and enterprise environments is like nothing experienced prior to this juncture in time for the financial services industry. The modular, open, and widely supported architecture of J2EE enabling adaptability across application modules, services, and servers has finally come along and addressed those age-old business needs for adaptable architecture like I've seen no other solution in the past or present. It is for these reasons that J2EE has been "the" platform on which all our applications are being developed and deployed to allow us optimal and rapid adaptability vital to ING's success in the financial services industry.

Furthermore, J2EE is no longer a technology untested by industry and without a positive history. In fact, in my own experiences, prior to ING, my work at Cyberian Outpost also reaped the benefits of J2EE. J2EE-based technology was used to help us rapidly port much of our existing infrastructure over to a more stable and higher performing clustered J2EE environment. Additionally, J2EE-based technology was used to provide adaptability, reuse, and rapid development across different Web sites being developed to support multiple e-commerce storefronts. Aside from such inter-application adaptability and reuse, much intra-application adaptability and reuse was leveraged to more rapidly roll out new features onto our existing primary Web site.

Using This Book to Solve Your Enterprise Problems

I first encountered Paul Perrone, the lead author for this *J2EE Developer's Handbook*, after reading his *Building Java Enterprise Systems with J2EE* book published in 2000 with co-author Krishna Chaganti. Paul eventually got involved as a software director for my technology group at Cyberian Outpost to architect the very foundation of J2EE-based infrastructure and deploy J2EE-based applications as described earlier. Paul and other members at his company Assured Technologies came aboard and employed J2EE-based technology and enterprise-class J2EE vendor products at Cyberian Outpost. I subsequently brought Paul and Assured Technologies into ING to also help us define our J2EE-based architecture infrastructure across the entire organization.

It is through these experiences and prior books that I can now attest and reflect upon firsthand that Paul's ability to communicate how to build Java enterprise systems with J2EE in his writing clearly translated into his ability to communicate on the job. This very synergy between communicating by writing and communicating in practice is what in fact strikes me as something that makes a book such as this one so genuine and unique. As a practitioner, I've seen Paul entrench himself in every technical detail, leaving no stone unturned, and bring to the table an extraordinary wealth of knowledge about every aspect of J2EE and Java technology. As a writer, I've seen how Paul scours the guts of J2EE and Java technology, writes about it in clear and complete terms, and brings a rigorous practitioner's view to his writing that I've not often seen in many publications.

I've also had the pleasure of working with this book's co-authors, Tom Schwenk at Cyberian Outpost and ING, and Krishna Chaganti at ING. Their software development skills and well-rounded software development knowledge further ensure the success of such a book as this one in providing code examples straight from the trenches. In fact, I recall the numerous occasions on which we had to bring Tom in to quickly and decisively solve a technical problem deep inside of a J2EE server that we otherwise would've banged our heads against for weeks on end. Together, Paul, Tom, and Krishna are what I call hard-core architecture and development types who all possess straightforward personalities which ensure that the job gets done and carry that professionalism and knowledge into their writing.

When I first learned that their "battle cry" for this *J2EE Developer's Handbook* was for the book to be a comprehensive, cohesive, and practical guide for building enterprise applications using J2EE, I wasn't surprised that their "war" in writing this book would be won. I've had the pleasure of reading their earlier books on J2EE, as well as working with them directly in the trenches at companies such as ING and Cyberian Outpost. Their work as authors has enabled them to explore and communicate just about every dark corner of J2EE technology. Their work as J2EE architects and developers has enabled them to ensure that the rubber meets the road and that they put into practice various J2EE development approaches in the workplace.

In closing, I see how their hard work in practice benefits from a rich understanding of J2EE, while their hard work in authoring books such as this one benefits not only from a rich understanding of J2EE but also from employing J2EE in practice. Lastly, well-written material, illustrative diagrams, and real-world code examples make this book not only informative but also enjoyable and fun to read.

by Raymond Karrenbauer, Chief Technology Officer,
ING Americas—Technology Management Office

Introduction

If you can read this writing...you are closer than you think to understanding all the glorious and exciting technology that is embodied by the Java 2 Platform, Enterprise Edition (J2EE)! ;)

YOU ARE ABOUT TO EMBARK ON AN ODYSSEY that will explore Java- and XML-based enterprise technologies from the ground up that can be used to build just about any application deployable throughout an enterprise that you can imagine ranging from the simple to the complex and from the very functional to the very cool. Accessing data in databases, parsing and manipulating XML data and messages, sending and receiving messages over the most common distributed communication network types, looking up and discovering services on a network or over the Internet, ensuring the integrity and security of applications and data, hosting and deploying applications over the Web, building highly scalable enterprise workhorse applications, and integrating with just about any application and system possible are all discussed by example throughout this book.

Before you delve into the contents of a huge tome such as this one, it is a good idea to first acquire an understanding of the problem you are trying to solve. In this way, you can best ensure that our book is addressing your needs. Furthermore, you should be aware of the topics to be presented that address such problems, to ensure that our book's material is relevant to your technology interests. This introduction describes the problem being solved by this book, an overview of the topics discussed, the target audience addressed, and our basic approach for presenting the material.

This Is Your Enterprise on Caffeine!

Let's first acquire a brief overview of the scope and problems being addressed by this book. As with any software architect or developer, we too have been in numerous situations in which tight deadlines must be met and/or the need for a solid software release must be produced. As software development professionals who've provided numerous enterprise system solutions and who've used the technologies described in this book under the pressure of deadlines and schedules, we share your pain and very much wish we had a book like this at our disposal a long time ago. Of course, such a book must also reflect the current technologies being used to build enterprise systems. We thus consider this book to be an extremely market-driven and technology-driven book directly addressing the needs of enterprise system developers. We begin this section by defining the mission statement and battle cry that have both initiated this book's effort and that have driven the course of its development along the way. We then specifically address the type of problems we are trying to solve, and describe how information technology and the Java enterprise solution can be infused throughout the veins of an enterprise.

Scope of the Book, Mission Statement, and Battle Cry

> *J2EE Developer's Handbook* provides a comprehensive, cohesive, and practical guide for building scalable, secure, assured, Web-enabled, and distributed enterprise systems with the Java 2 Platform, Enterprise Edition (J2EE). The technologies presented in this book can be used to rapidly build any enterprise system and integration solution that you can imagine. We describe these enterprise technologies from the ground up, leaving you with a thorough and in-depth understanding of the Java enterprise application stack.

Problem to Be Solved

Enterprise systems encompass those distributed, scalable, multiuser, and business-critical systems that are intimately related to enhancing the productivity of a corporate or organizational enterprise via information technology. We are deep into an information and knowledge technology revolution that has catapulted economies and ways of life far beyond those that even the industrial revolution wrought. A primary engine of automation and productivity enhancement behind this revolution is the enterprise system. More and more, corporations and organizations are tying themselves into a complex informational network in an effort to further enhance the productivity of their operations for competitive and cost-reduction reasons. E-commerce, Internet/Web enabling, business-to-business (B2B) connectivity, enterprise application integration (EAI), and data mining are just a few of the requirements that must be satisfied by enterprise system designs.

This is why effective means for building enterprise systems that address the unique problems and high demand for enterprise software development effectiveness are always being sought by enterprise system development teams. Corporations and organizations more and more look for enterprise-class developers and engineers who can solve a broad range of enterprise system problems. Java enterprise technologies, Web services, and the J2EE provide an approach for more rapidly and effectively building enterprise systems that address the needs for producing enterprise software that is reusable, scalable, distributable, maintainable, secure, reliable, and available.

This Is the Book to Address Your Needs!

This book is partitioned into six major parts and a set of appendixes. The structure of the book and each part's technologies described are listed here so that you can better understand what to expect from each major part of the book. You can thus tailor how you'll approach reading the book and perhaps determine those chapters that cover material with which you are already familiar. We also discuss some of the software used and included with the book so that you can more concretely understand the type of enterprise software with which you will come into contact as well as create yourself while using this book. Finally, in this section, we also describe the diagram and notation conventions used within the chapter text.

Part I: Enterprise Systems

This part of the book defines and describes the following concepts and technologies:

- ***Enterprise system problem:*** Scope for the problem to be solved with enterprise system development (Chapter 1).
- ***Enterprise system architecture:*** Basic reference architecture for understanding enterprise system solutions (Chapter 1).
- ***Java enterprise system architecture:*** Basic architecture of Java and Web services–based enterprise system solutions (Chapter 1).
- ***J2EE:*** Overview architecture of J2EE-based technologies (Chapter 1).
- ***Java enterprise technologies:*** Overview of where other non-J2EE Java enterprise technologies fit into the picture (Chapter 1).
- ***Web services:*** Overview of Web services technology included within the J2EE (Chapter 1).

Part II: Enterprise Data Enabling

This part of the book defines and describes the following concepts and technologies by example:

- ***Enterprise data representation:*** How data can be represented, parsed, manipulated, and validated (Chapters 2–4).
- ***XML:*** How to represent data in a standard fashion (Chapter 3).
- ***XML DTDs:*** How to describe the structure of XML documents (Chapter 3).
- ***XML Schema:*** How to describe the structure and semantics of XML documents (Chapter 3).
- ***XSLT:*** How to automatically transform XML documents to and from one form of an XML document to another (Chapter 3).
- ***SAX:*** Standard to parse XML documents (Chapter 4).
- ***DOM:*** Standard to read and write XML documents (Chapter 4).
- ***JAXP:*** API used to parse, read, write, validate, and translate XML documents (Chapter 4).
- ***Enterprise data access:*** How data can be read, written, updated, and deleted from a database (Chapters 2, 5–6).
- ***JDBC:*** API used to access data in a database (Chapters 5–6).

Part III: Enterprise Communications Enabling

This part of the book defines and describes the following concepts and technologies by example:

- ***Distributed object communications:*** How object-based computing platforms can communicate in a distributed fashion (Chapters 7–9).
- ***CORBA:*** Used to build platform- and language-independent distributed object clients and servers (Chapter 8).
- ***GIOP/IIOP:*** Used as the underlying communications transport protocols of CORBA (Chapter 8).
- ***IDL:*** Standard language-independent means for describing CORBA interfaces (Chapter 8).
- ***Java IDL:*** API provided by the Java platform for building CORBA applications (Chapter 8).
- ***RMI:*** API for building Java-based distributed object clients and servers (Chapter 9).
- ***RMI/IIOP:*** Adapted version of RMI to use IIOP as the underlying communications protocol (Chapter 9).
- ***Web service communications:*** How XML-based messages can be communicated between clients and services via the Web in a standard fashion (Chapters 7, 10).
- ***SOAP:*** Standard means to represent requests and responses in a Web services communications paradigm (Chapter 10).
- ***SAAJ:*** API used to parse and manipulate SOAP messages with attachments to such messages (Chapter 10).
- ***WSDL:*** Standard means for describing Web service interfaces via XML (Chapter 10).
- ***JWSDL:*** API used to parse and manipulate WSDL documents (Chapter 10).
- ***JAX-RPC:*** API used to build Web service clients and servers (Chapter 10).
- ***WS-I:*** Standard used to collect individual Web services standards into a cohesive profile (Chapter 10).

Part IV: Common Enterprise Services

This part of the book defines and describes the following concepts and technologies by example:

- ***Naming services:*** How names are used to register and look up distributed objects (Chapter 11).
- ***Directory services:*** How names and attributes are used to register and look up distributed objects (Chapter 12).

- ***Trading services:*** How names, attributes, and types are used to register and look up distributed objects (Chapter 12).
- ***Web services lookup:*** How names and attributes are used to register and look up Web services (Chapter 13).
- ***JNDI:*** API used to encapsulate naming and directory services (Chapters 11–12).
- ***CORBA Naming:*** Standard naming service approach for CORBA-based applications (Chapter 11).
- ***RMI Naming:*** Standard naming service approach for RMI-based applications (Chapter 11).
- ***LDAP:*** Standard lightweight directory service protocol (Chapter 12).
- ***DSML:*** Standard directory service protocol using XML as a data format (Chapter 12).
- ***Jini:*** API for a Java-based dynamic trading service (Chapter 12).
- ***ebXML Registries:*** Standard for Web service registration and lookup (Chapter 13).
- ***UDDI:*** Another standard for Web service registration and lookup (Chapter 13).
- ***JAXR:*** API to encapsulate Web service registration and lookup (Chapter 13).
- ***Transaction services:*** Means for guaranteeing the atomicity and reliability of distributed computing operations (Chapter 14).
- ***JTA:*** API for transaction management (Chapter 14).
- ***JTS:*** API for lower-level interoperable distributed transaction management (Chapter 14).
- ***Messaging services:*** Means for providing asynchronous, loosely coupled, and distributed communications (Chapter 15).
- ***JMS:*** API for messaging service implementations (Chapter 15).
- ***JAXM:*** API for asynchronous Web service messaging (Chapter 15).
- ***JavaMail:*** API for sending and receiving e-mail (Chapter 16).
- ***Assurance services:*** Services providing the reliability, availability, maintainability, security, and perhaps safety of a system (Chapter 17).
- ***Security services:*** Services providing for confidentiality, privacy, integrity, user identification, authentication, access control, auditing, and nonrepudiation associated with security-critical operations (Chapter 17).
- ***Java security:*** Broad range of APIs used to secure Java applications (Chapter 17).

Part V: Enterprise Web Enabling

This part of the book defines and describes the following concepts and technologies by example:

- ***Web components and servers:*** Describes how applications are exposed and accessed via the Web in a managed environment (Chapter 18).
- ***Java Servlets:*** API used to encapsulate the server-side processing of a request and response via the Web (Chapter 19).
- ***JavaServer Pages (JSP):*** Used to encapsulate the server-side processing of a request and response via the Web using elements and tags mixed with HTML content (Chapter 20).
- ***JSP tags:*** Standard and custom defined tags mixed with HTML that provide a means for encapsulating software-based actions on the server side (Chapters 20–21).
- ***JSTL:*** Standard expression language for describing variables and flow inside of a JSP (Chapter 20).
- ***Web services with Web components:*** Standard means for deploying J2EE Web components as Web services (Chapter 22).

Part VI: Enterprise Applications Enabling

This part of the book defines and describes the following concepts and technologies by example:

- ***Enterprise application components and servers:*** Describes how large-scale enterprise applications are constructed and deployed in a managed environment (Chapter 23).
- ***Enterprise JavaBeans (EJB):*** API used to build components that operate inside of a standard application server environment as well as declaratively configured and deployed using standard XML-based deployment descriptors (Chapters 24–28).
- ***Stateless session EJB:*** API and deployment standards used to build components that encapsulate coarse-grained business interactions with clients in a stateless fashion (Chapter 25).
- ***Stateful session EJB:*** API and deployment standards used to build components that encapsulate coarse-grained business interactions with clients whereby the conversational state with the client is maintained (Chapter 25).
- ***BMP entity EJB:*** API and deployment standards used to build components that encapsulate hand-coded object-to-relational mappings with a persistent store (Chapter 26).

- ***CMP entity EJB:*** API and deployment standards used to build components that encapsulate container-generated object-to-relational mappings with a persistent store (Chapter 26).
- ***EJB QL:*** Standard language used to describe how the container queries for objects in a persistent store when using CMP entity EJBs (Chapter 26).
- ***Message-driven EJB:*** API and deployment standards used to build components that encapsulate asynchronous consumers of messages (Chapter 27).
- ***EJB transactions:*** Means for programmatically or declaratively defining transaction management for EJBs (Chapter 28).
- ***EJB security:*** Means for programmatically or declaratively securing EJBs (Chapter 28).
- ***JAAS:*** API to encapsulate authentication and authorization mechanisms (Chapter 28).
- ***EJB clustering:*** Means for deploying EJBs in redundant servers for load-balancing and failover purposes (Chapter 28).
- ***EAI:*** Means for enterprise application integration of legacy and auxiliary application clients and servers with J2EE components and containers (Chapter 29).
- ***J2EE Connector Architecture:*** API and system interfaces for integrating J2EE applications with external enterprise information systems (Chapter 29).
- ***JACC:*** Standard interfaces for integrating J2EE containers with third-party security service providers (Chapter 29).
- ***J2EE Management and JMX:*** Standard interfaces for integrating J2EE containers with tools used to observe and manage J2EE components (Chapter 29).
- ***J2EE Deployment:*** Standard interfaces for integrating J2EE containers with tools used to configure and deploy J2EE components (Chapter 29).
- ***Web services with EJB:*** Standard means for deploying EJBs as Web services (Chapter 30).

Appendixes

Appendixes are found on the CD-ROM. They include supporting material used as a reference and allow for further elaboration of concepts outside of the book's most imminent scope. However, many of the topics discussed in this book rely upon your basic knowledge of the material contained in these appendixes. The appendixes are as listed here:

A ***Software Configuration:*** Where to obtain, how to install, how to configure, and how to run the third-party software and example software used throughout this book. This is a very important appendix to review up front and consult throughout the book because much of the example software configuration discussion is deferred to this appendix. Also note that this appendix is subject to the most change as new third-party software versions are released that affect the running of example code. Refer to the Web site `www.assuredtech.com/j2eedev.htm` for updates to this appendix and the software configuration for the book's examples.

B *JavaBeans:* API used to encapsulate components that can be inspected and invoked according to a standard interface model. Many J2EE APIs assume a basic understanding of the JavaBeans API and interface standards.

C *Database Concepts and SQL:* Standard database concepts and reference for SQL commands. Development with JDBC often requires that developers know how to formulate SQL statements.

D *TCP/IP Communications:* Standard TCP/IP communications stack and Java socket–based programming concepts. Many J2EE and J2SE communications standards assume a basic conceptual understanding of TCP/IP and Java socket programming.

E *HTTP Communications:* Standards revolving around the HTTP protocol and Web communications. Many J2EE and J2SE Web communications standards assume a basic conceptual understanding of HTTP and Java HTTP abstractions.

F *HTML:* Reference for basic HTML syntax. Development with Java Servlets and JSP often requires that developers know basic HTML.

G *Enterprise Software Development:* Basic object-oriented and component-based development concepts, as well as UML primer. The J2EE APIs described throughout the book use UML as a graphical means to more quickly convey their design.

H *Additional Resources:* References and Web links to specifications, standards, and other information referenced in the book.

Software Used with This Book

The various J2EE and Java enterprise technologies described throughout this book include supporting examples. Appendix A, "Software Configuration," describes how to locate, install, configure, and run the examples associated with this book. It is very important that you consult that appendix early on and that you refer to it throughout the book. Furthermore, because the third-party software used to run the examples is subject to the most change, the Web site `www.assuredtech.com/j2eedev.htm` has been established and should be consulted for any updates to Appendix A's instructions and the book's examples. You'll also want to refer to Appendix A to determine which software you need to download and how to download it. To run a particular chapter's example may require that you download, install, and configure not only software from third-party vendors, but also software associated with examples from other chapters in the book.

Many of the examples have been run on platforms implemented by enterprise-class commercial vendors such as BEA, Iona, and Borland. In fact, the J2EE container examples described throughout this book have been run against the commercial-grade BEA WebLogic server and Oracle database. Additionally, the J2EE reference implementation provided by Sun Microsystems and the MySQL database were used to run many of the examples. Finally, some of the examples were also executed against open source product profiles. In addition to the various profiles against which the examples in this book can be run, the book also includes ANT build scripts to compile, package, deploy, and run the examples on either a Windows platform or a Unix- and Linux-based platform.

Thus, the various profiles used throughout this book demonstrate how truly platform-independent Java and the J2EE are. By running the examples in this book, you are also able to expose yourself to the experience of using a commercial-grade platform profile such as the BEA WebLogic server and Oracle database on Unix, a bleeding-edge development-grade profile such as the J2EE reference implementation and Cloudscape database on Windows, or an open source profile with the MySQL database and Linux. We include configuration files for the commercial-grade and development-grade profiles included with this book's code and as described in Appendix A. Also refer to the Web site `www.assuredtech.com/j2eedev.htm` for updates to the appendix, additional software configuration notes, and new profiles against which the book's examples may be run. Furthermore, you'll want to stay tuned to that Web site to learn about and participate in the growing community of support involved with this book and providing/downloading additional platform profile configurations, as well as new information and updates related to J2EE and supporting technologies.

Design Conventions

Throughout this book, we use UML to describe the design of the various J2EE APIs. UML diagrams provide a graphical way to more quickly mentally absorb the class structure, method signatures, and class relationships associated with the J2E API. Whereas other books may include an entire API for reference, we've taken the time to present these APIs in a fashion that lets you immediately understand the relationships of particular J2EE API classes, as well as the methods defined on those classes. Such diagrams also are useful as a reference guide long after you finish reading a particular chapter.

It is for these reasons that we've taken care to include as much of the J2EE APIs and their method signatures as possible in UML diagrams. When encountering a new aspect of J2EE, you are first presented with a UML diagram illustrating its design. The chapter text then describes that API in the context of the diagram. Examples that illustrate and reinforce the design concepts are then presented. It will thus also behoove you to refer to Appendix G, "Enterprise Software Development," early on to understand the particular UML design conventions we employ throughout the book.

Notation Conventions

Throughout this book, we also use certain notation conventions when presenting the material. The conventions used throughout the book can assume different meanings depending on the context in which they are used. For example, conventions used to describe artifacts of code or programming can differ from those used in textual descriptions. Although these conventions are often intuitive and easily understood when used in context, we list the conventions here for your reference:

- Three consecutive dots, ..., in text refers to additional text that naturally follows.
- Three consecutive dots, `. . .`, in code refers to code that has been left out of a code listing.
- Square brackets, `[ ]`, in directory names or filenames can serve as placeholders for information that should be replaced with an actual directory name or filename.
- Square brackets, `[ ]`, in text or code encapsulate information that is optional and can be replaced with some other data.
- Angle brackets, < >, used in text or code encapsulate information that is required and should be replaced with some other data.
- Italicized words in artifacts of code and programming also can be used to identify information that is required and should be replaced with some other data.
- Italicized words in plain text can be used to simply accentuate particular words to focus on.
- Boldface words in code and generic file formats accentuate key words or terms.
- The character sequence *`XXX`* is sometimes used inside of class names and method names to indicate that the *`XXX`* may be substituted for an actual character sequence.
- Some code that is inserted into a chapter from sample code is most often inserted as it was in the code with any indentation left as is to preserve consistency between the manuscript and the code as much as possible.

Other Conventions Used in This Book

This book uses different typefaces to differentiate between code and regular English, and also to help you identify important concepts.

Text that you type and text that should appear on your screen is presented in `monospace` type:

```
It will look like this to mimic the way text looks on your screen.
```

An arrow (➥) at the beginning of a line of code means that a single line of code is too long to fit on the printed page. Continue typing all characters after the ➥ as though they were part of the preceding line.

Note

A Note presents interesting pieces of information related to the surrounding discussion.

A Sidebar provides you with additional information on a topic somewhat outside of the scope but related to the surrounding discussion.

Tip

A Tip offers advice or teaches an easier way to do something.

Caution

A Caution advises you about potential problems and helps you steer clear of disaster.

This Is Your Brain After Reading This Book!

Now that you've seen the problems this book addresses and an outline of the topics discussed that help solve these problems, we want to describe the intended audience for this material and describe what you will have learned after reading the book. We also take the opportunity here to describe our specific approach to presenting the material.

Intended Audience

J2EE Developer's Handbook will be of interest to professional software engineers fulfilling roles such as software developer, designer, and architect. The formally trained software developer, designer, and architect with a background in object-oriented software development and basic Java who has a demand for acquiring enterprise-level development skills using Java is the primary target audience for this book. However, some background material in the book's appendixes provides an overview and refresher of some core concepts and technologies on top of which enterprise-level Java technologies are built. As a side benefit of this overview and refresher material, formally trained and experienced software engineers who have little Java background but who have been thrust into an enterprise software development project using Java may also benefit from reading this book.

Approach of the Book

Although some of the Java enterprise technologies that we use in this book have been around for some time, the J2EE platform integrates these technologies into one cohesive platform. The J2EE itself in fact has grown to include a significantly comprehensive platform enabling you to create just about any enterprise application you can imagine, solely using J2EE technology. Although J2EE is indeed extensive and a centerpiece technology, J2EE-based containers alone do not currently solve all Java enterprise problems. Consequently, we also describe a few other Java-based technologies in this book that round out the Java enterprise development picture.

We in fact are incorporating into this book a lot of practical and real-world experience with these technologies. Therefore, at times we stray from purist views in the interest of describing practical enterprise development solutions. Since this book's inception, our battle cry has been to provide a cohesive, comprehensive, and practical guide for building Java enterprise systems with J2EE as a centerpiece. To this end we not only provide detailed coverage of Java enterprise architectural and design concepts, but also illustrate much of the material with practical examples and code. We focus on describing how to build Java enterprise applications via illustration of how to use core APIs and how to configure your Java enterprise system applications. However, we do from time to time also try to keep certain examples simple and deviate from pure object-oriented abstraction techniques and style in the interest of more quickly and directly demonstrating how to use specific APIs for pedagogic reasons.

Because the J2EE and auxiliary Java enterprise APIs are extremely rich with features, we start from the ground up and avoid "description anachronisms" in the book. That is, we make every attempt in the book to first describe those concepts, technologies, and APIs that are utilized and assumed by subsequent chapters in the book. For example, before we describe EJB, we describe JNDI used to look up EJB handles. Before we describe JNDI's use with CORBA naming services and EJB's CORBA-based interoperability, we describe CORBA. In such a way, you learn about the J2EE and Java enterprise technologies from the ground up, whereby technology A is described before technology B if technology B depends upon and uses technology A.

Furthermore, as another way of looking at the approach taken by this book, you might consider the book's scope in the context of a Model-View-Controller (MVC) architecture view of a system. Because we focus on those aspects of a system that are utilized by middle-tier server-side applications, you might say that we are primarily interested in the "C" aspect of an MVC system. We are largely only interested in describing how to enable the "V" to be realized (user interface and Web enabling), as well as in encapsulating, representing, and enabling access to the "M" (data enabling).

Finally, whereas other books may focus on a particular technology such as EJB, JDBC, JMS, Web services, or some other J2EE API, one might think that this book only covers a few topics lightly because we cover so much inside of the J2EE umbrella. To allay this concern, for one, we encourage you to simply take a look at the size of this book. Its size alone is indicative of the amount of material we've packed into the book. And, no, we do not repeat the words "all work and no play makes us dull developers" over and over again after page 300, hoping that you'll never get past that point. All of the pages in this book are jam-packed and loaded with J2EE information and examples.

What's more, other books that focus on technologies like EJB often end up spending half of the book discussing those aspects of JNDI, JDBC, JMS, Web Services, and other technologies needed to understand how to build EJB applications. They may even end up doing so very lightly. And the mere fact that such technologies need be addressed is indicative of the fact and supports the belief of this book's authors that all such technologies really do need to be explained in a cohesive fashion for you to actually be able to apply these technologies in the real world. Moreover, some books also end up consuming a significant number of pages including JavaDocs for APIs in the book. This book's ground-up approach, size of the book, and use of UML design diagrams all complement one another to allow this book to live up to its cohesive, comprehensive, and practical mission to describe J2EE by example.

The End Result

In summary, after reading this book, you will walk away with a deep knowledge of how to apply and use J2EE and Java enterprise technologies for enterprise data enabling, communications, rapid development, assurance provisioning, Web enabling, Web services, and scalable applications enabling. Your knowledge will be comprehensive and practical by nature. Knowledge of the J2EE and other Java enterprise technologies will then serve as your primary toolkit for building enterprise systems.

So pour yourself a warm cup of joe, sit back, and enjoy the rest of the book as we describe for you how to build enterprise systems with *J2EE Developer's Handbook* at your side. We sincerely hope that you enjoy, learn, and provide us with any feedback (visit `www.assuredtech.com/j2eedev.htm`).

I

Enterprise Systems

1

Enterprise Development with J2EE

THIS CHAPTER INTRODUCES YOU TO THE BASIC concepts involved in understanding what an enterprise system is and how the Java 2 Platform, Enterprise Edition (J2EE) provides a comprehensive and cohesive implementation of enterprise system needs. We first provide an overview of what constitutes an enterprise system, the enterprise system development problem, and the basic categories of enterprise systems solutions. We then describe the J2EE enterprise systems solution in the context of the basic enterprise system solution categories. We describe those object-oriented and component-based technologies that can be used to build enterprise systems using J2EE. The J2EE model, means for data access and representation, distributed communications enabling, systems assurance, Web enabling, and applications enabling are considered part of an overall enterprise architecture. In addition to describing what the J2EE currently provides for developing enterprise systems, we also highlight a few key technologies used for building Java enterprise systems that fall outside the realm of current J2EE environments.

In this chapter, you will learn:

- An overview of the enterprise system problem, basic needs, and general solutions.
- A model for developing enterprise applications using the J2EE.
- A top-level architecture for building Java enterprise applications with the J2EE.
- The core standards and J2EE APIs involved in enabling access and representation of enterprise data.
- The core standards and J2EE APIs involved in enabling communications among distributed enterprise applications.
- The core standards and J2EE APIs involved in providing common distributed enterprise and assurance services for enterprise applications.

- The core standards and J2EE APIs involved in enabling enterprise applications to expose themselves and to communicate via the Web.
- The core standards and J2EE APIs involved in enabling enterprise applications to scale, integrate, interoperate, and be managed.

Enterprise Systems Overview

In its most generic form, the term *enterprise* can simply refer to an organization that has set out to accomplish certain goals. The organization may be a small-, medium-, or large-scale commercial corporation; a nonprofit institution; or perhaps a government organization. In some contexts, including the context of this book, the term *enterprise* is typically used to refer to a large organization. It is usually assumed that enterprises have a desire to grow and expand their operations and human/inter-enterprise associations over time. It is also often assumed that pursuit of the enterprise's goals are essential both for survival of the enterprise and for growth of the enterprise.

Enterprise Assets

Figure 1.1 depicts the main assets of an enterprise that are used to help the enterprise accomplish its goals. Physical resources and assets are one asset type of an enterprise utilized to accomplish enterprise goals. For example, computing equipment, manufacturing facilities, product supplies, and corporate accounts are all examples of resources and physical assets that are essential to the operations of an enterprise. People and users are another fundamental asset of an enterprise, with customers, employees, contractors, and partners (with other enterprises) forming the core of those classes of people who help the enterprise accomplish its goals. Finally, enterprise information and enterprise knowledge are also key assets used to help further the goals of an enterprise.

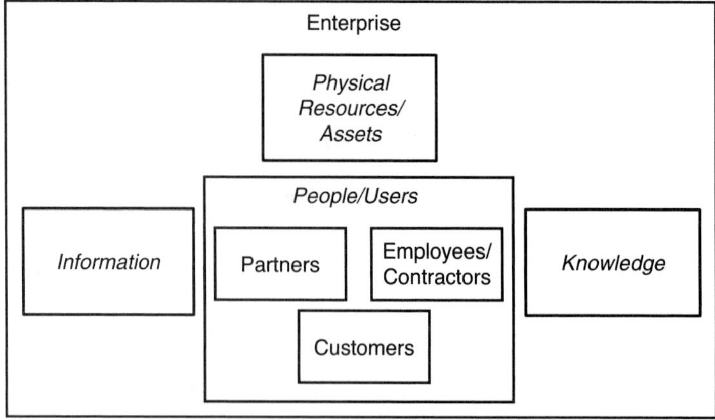

Figure 1.1 Enterprise assets.

Because the various enterprise assets help an enterprise accomplish its goals, they offer some value to the enterprise. It is in the best interest of an enterprise to preserve, protect, grow, make accessible, make efficient, and be sensitive to change in the value offered by the various enterprise assets. These interests and primary objectives of an enterprise are to foster such desirable outcomes as these:

- Growth of a customer base
- Preservation of a customer base
- Sensitivity to a changing customer base
- Growth of an employee base
- Efficiency of an employee base
- Growth of a partnership base
- Growth of physical resources/assets
- Preservation of physical resources/assets
- Protection of physical resources/assets
- Accessibility of physical resources/assets
- Sensitivity to a change in physical resources/assets
- Growth of information and business knowledge
- Preservation of information and business knowledge
- Protection of information and business knowledge
- Accessibility of information and business knowledge
- Sensitivity to changes in information and knowledge

Enterprise System Problem

Given those assets of an enterprise that have some value to the enterprise and the pursuit of an enterprise's interest in these valued assets, Figure 1.2 presents the type of system a modern enterprise will strive to incorporate into its operations to maximize its goals. Figure 1.2 thus highlights the various problems needing to be addressed in developing and deploying an enterprise system. These are the general categories of problems needing to be addressed:

- *Distributed Enterprise Communications:* A means for connecting the various distributed components of an enterprise system must be provided.
- *Enterprise Data (representation):* A means for representing the data that flows throughout the distributed enterprise must be provided.
- *Enterprise Data (access):* A means for storing and accessing data for the enterprise must be provided.
- *Legacy Intra-Enterprise Applications:* A means for interfacing and interoperating with various legacy applications internal to the enterprise must be provided.

- *Auxiliary Intra-Enterprise Applications:* A means for interfacing and interoperating with various third-party applications and applications being developed independently but yet internal to the enterprise must be provided.
- *Embedded Intra-Enterprise Applications:* A means for interfacing and interoperating with various embedded applications and communication points internal to the enterprise must be provided.
- *External Inter-Enterprise Applications:* A means for interfacing and interoperating with various applications provided by business partners external to the enterprise must be provided.
- *Scalable and Integrated Enterprise Application Logic:* A means for exposing an integrated view and control point for enterprise applications and data to enable a unified and scalable means for providing distributed access to such functionality and information often must be provided.
- *Enterprise Web Connectivity Logic:* A means for exposing enterprise applications and data via the Web often must be provided.
- *Enterprise Web Presentation Content:* A means for presenting enterprise content and providing a lightweight user interface via the Web often must be provided.
- *Enterprise Applications Presentation Content:* A means for presenting enterprise content and providing a heavyweight user interface via thick clients often must be provided.

An enterprise generally attempts to develop and deploy these elements of an enterprise system given the interests it has in striving to achieve its goals, such as in the case of the following examples:

- Growth of a customer base can lead an enterprise to provide Internet/Web connectivity perhaps in the form of a business-to-consumer (B2C) e-commerce or enterprise portal application to open up the opportunity for more customers to patronize the enterprise. Furthermore, a growing customer base will also require the provision of a scalable Web and application connectivity solution.
- Preservation of a customer base may be accomplished by streamlining connectivity to legacy distribution supply chains such that customer satisfaction remains high due to the speed with which an enterprise can satisfy customers' orders.
- Sensitivity to a changing customer base can also be facilitated via a tailored presentation interface for different Web-based customers depending on customer profiles persisted in an enterprise database.
- Growth of an employee base can be managed by a streamlined and scalable human resources Enterprise Resource Planning (ERP) application.
- Efficiency of an employee base can be offered via direct connection to enterprise applications through a distributed enterprise client application over an intranet.

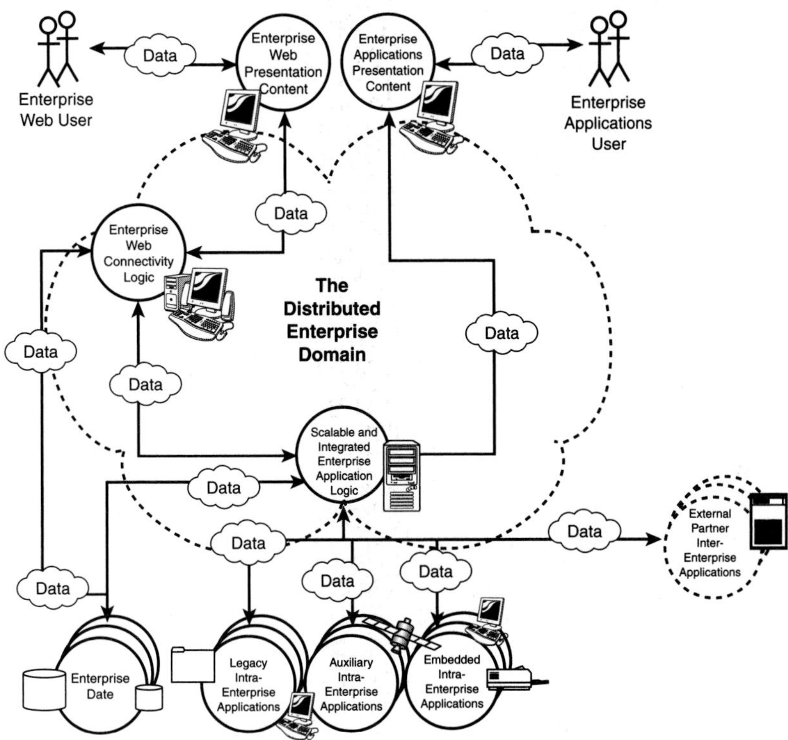

Figure 1.2 Enterprise system problem.

- Growth of a partnership base can be managed via the establishment of secure business-to-business (B2B) application logic and transaction handling.
- Growth and preservation of resources/assets can be managed and provided via Enterprise Application Integration (EAI) with legacy applications, distributed enterprise applications, and connectivity to embedded resources.
- Protection of resources/assets can be provided via the establishment of a security domain to protect valued resources distributed on an enterprise network.
- Accessibility of resources/assets can be provided via use of various distributed communications technologies to connect resources to the enterprise.
- Growth and preservation of information and knowledge can be efficiently managed in an enterprise database management system (DBMS).
- Protection of information and knowledge can also be managed in an enterprise database as well as by provision of assurance techniques to provide information and knowledge security and reliability.
- Accessibility of information and knowledge can also be provided via Web connectivity and various distributed communications paradigms.

Enterprise System Solution

In attempting to solve such a broad category of enterprise system problems, enterprise information technology is employed. Information technology employed by an enterprise system can itself be broadly classified along the lines of the various enabling and service technologies depicted in Figure 1.3. These various enterprise enablers and services drive the very outline and approach taken by this book. The Java enterprise technologies described throughout the book can all be categorized according to the generic enterprise system architecture of Figure 1.3. These generic enterprise system architecture technology classifications are as listed here:

- *Enterprise User Interfacing:* Provides a means to present content to both Web-based and standard applications-based users of an enterprise system. Because enterprise user interfacing is outside the scope of this book, we only highlight user-interface development techniques via brief discussions of how client-side enterprise technologies interface with the various enterprise server-side technologies discussed throughout this book.
- *Enterprise Data Enabling—Representation:* Provides a means to represent and manipulate enterprise information and knowledge using standard data representation techniques. Such a service is considered a global service that permeates every aspect of a distributed enterprise system. Part II of this book, "Enterprise Data Enabling," contains a dedicated discussion of data representation enabling using XML technology.
- *Enterprise Data Enabling—Access:* Provides a means to access, store, and manage enterprise information and knowledge via enterprise databases. Part II contains a dedicated discussion of data access enabling using JDBC technology.
- *Enterprise Communications Enabling:* Provides a means to access information and applications throughout a distributed enterprise system. Such a service is considered a global service that permeates every aspect of a distributed enterprise system. Part III, "Enterprise Communications Enabling," is dedicated to a discussion of communications enabling via such technologies as CORBA, RMI, and Web services.
- *Common Enterprise Services:* Provides a set of common services used by distributed object communications paradigms. Also provides for the secure, reliable, available, maintainable, and safe qualities of an enterprise system. Such services are also considered global services that permeate every aspect of a distributed enterprise system. Part IV, "Common Enterprise Services," is dedicated to a discussion of higher-level communications services and systems assurance with a focus on naming and directory services via JNDI, Web services lookup via JAXR, transaction services using JTA and JTS, messaging services via JMS and JAXM, email services with JavaMail, and assurance and Java security services.

- *Enterprise Web Enabling:* Provides for the connectivity of the enterprise to the Internet/Web, as well as for generating Web-based presentation content. Part V, "Enterprise Web Enabling," is dedicated to a Web-enabling discussion with a detailed discussion of Java Servlets, JSP, and Web services using Web components.
- *Enterprise Applications Enabling:* Provides for the integrated middle tier of scalable application logic management with the connectivity to legacy enterprise application logic, the provision of new enterprise application logic, connectivity to distributed enterprise applications and embedded devices, and business-to-business connectivity with enterprise partners. Part VI, "Enterprise Applications Enabling," is dedicated to an applications enabling discussion with a focus on EJB and various Java-based EAI techniques.

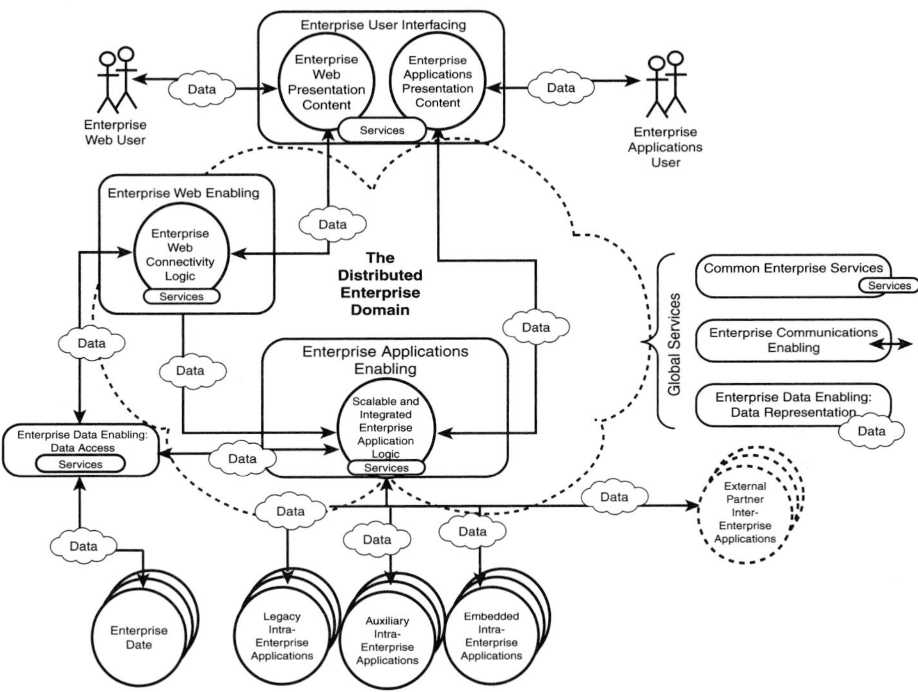

Figure 1.3 Enterprise system solution.

J2EE Enterprise System Solution Model

Now that we have a basic conceptual overview of what constitutes an enterprise system solution, let's turn our attention to how the Java enterprise model comprehensively and cohesively implements this solution. Before there was a formal Java enterprise model of development, the Java Development Kit (JDK) versions 1.0 and 1.1 were the original standard platforms defined by Sun to create standalone Java-based applications and Web-based Java applets. The JDK did indeed offer many advantages for use in enterprise development projects by providing an easy-to-use and platform-independent approach to rapidly building enterprise systems. In addition to the core JDK platform support, a collection of enterprise APIs emerged, some of which were part of the JDK and others of which were offered as standard extensions to the Java platform. Java APIs useful to enterprise applications, such as those for database connectivity and distributed communications, were employed by developers wanting to rapidly build enterprise applications with Java.

The use of Java to build enterprise systems was catching on. In addition to the standard Java platform and standard Java extension APIs, many third-party Java-based APIs began to enter the market. In particular, Java-based COTS implementations of the CORBA distributed computing platform further stimulated interest in developing enterprise applications with Java. Although Sun was originally touting Java as the platform for the World Wide Web and focusing on Java applets, the explosion in back-end server-side enterprise usage of Java by industry soon aligned Sun's marketing efforts to consider the enterprise application of Java more formally and seriously.

Marketers originally coined the terms *Java Technologies for the Enterprise (JTE)* and *Java Platform for the Enterprise (JPE)* to refer to a collection of APIs that were extensions to the Java platform and had direct relevance to enterprise applications. However, the APIs were often developed by different groups and at times grew apart from one another. Furthermore, it was not always clear to developers just how these APIs could relate to one another and how they could be used to keep their systems open for use with different underlying vendor implementations of the various enterprise services. This is where the Java 2 Platform, Enterprise Edition (J2EE) entered the picture and attempted to address these needs. The J2EE was introduced by Sun Microsystems in June 1999 as a standard platform and environment for building enterprise systems using Java. The J2EE is now at version J2EE v1.4 and serves as the basis for this book's material and examples.

J2EE Features

The J2EE is defined as an umbrella platform and programming model for building Java enterprise systems for use with different underlying vendor implementations of an enterprise system infrastructure. The J2EE (`http://java.sun.com/j2ee`) is most accurately defined and scoped according to five standard documents and software libraries:

- *Specification:* The J2EE specification defines the requirements that a J2EE vendor product implementation must satisfy.
- *Design Guidelines:* The design guidelines and programming model is cast in the form of a developer's guide explaining how application developers might use

various aspects of the J2EE. The guide is primarily described at a conceptual and high level along with a sample application.

- *Platform:* The J2EE platform is the set of integrated enterprise API library software and development tools.
- *Reference Implementation:* The J2EE reference implementation is a sample implementation of the underlying services utilized by the J2EE platform APIs. It is primarily meant for use in early development and prototyping environments.
- *Compatibility Test Suite:* The compatibility test suite is used by vendors to determine whether their implementation of the J2EE services satisfies the J2EE specification requirements.

J2EE Component-Container Architecture

The J2EE model for enterprise application development involves an enterprise component-container approach to development. An enterprise component is an encapsulation of a certain body of code utilized in an enterprise application. An enterprise container represents an environment in which a component operates. The container itself may offer a set of services that components may tap in a standard fashion. Appendix G, "Enterprise Software Development," discusses such a generic model in more detail.

Specific to the J2EE environment, however, a J2EE v1.4 container essentially offers services as illustrated in Figure 1.4 and described here:

- *J2SE Platform:* The Java 2 Platform, Standard Edition (J2SE) atop of which J2EE applications operate. Includes the J2SE's hardware and operating-system platform-independence feature offered by the Java runtime environment. Also includes the various common programming and distributed communication services offered by the J2SE APIs.
- *J2EE Interfaces:* A collection of standard Java enterprise API versions. Provides independence across database, Web, and application server platforms for J2EE enterprise components that are implemented to these standard interfaces.
- *Java Interface Implementations:* A Java enterprise service provider implementation of the Java enterprise APIs.
- *Resource Management Services:* Resource management services offered by the container for providing an efficient, scalable, and dependable computing environment. Used also for the management of resources associated with connecting to distributed databases or external system processes.
- *Deployment/Configuration Services:* An environment for configurably and portably deploying J2EE components.

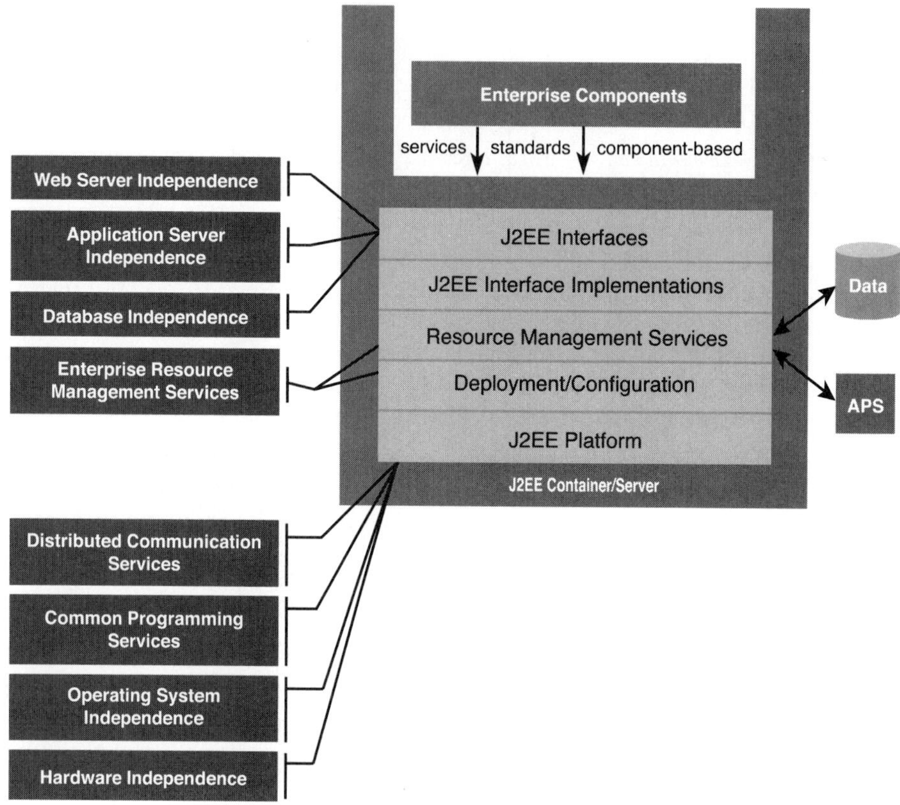

Figure 1.4 J2EE enterprise system solution.

J2EE Component-Container Types

Five major classes of components and four container types are defined within the J2EE specification. These component-container classifications, depicted in Figure 1.5, can be classified according to whether they are client-oriented or server-oriented and whether they are Web-oriented or purely application-oriented. Figure 1.5 also depicts the most common client/server relationships between the various component/container types represented as dotted arrows in the diagram. The five J2EE component models are described here:

- *EJB Application Servers:* Enterprise JavaBean components represent application-specific components built by a developer or third party to operate inside of an EJB application container environment. EJB container environments are implemented by third-party vendors to offer scalable application services to EJB component developers. EJBs can be exposed to clients using standard communication protocols such as CORBA and Web services. A J2EE EJB application can contain one or more J2EE EJBs and are configured according to a J2EE EJB deployment descriptor (EJB DD).

- *Web Application Servers:* Web components come in two flavors: Java Servlets and JavaServer Pages (JSPs). Web components represent application-specific handling of requests received by a Web server and generate Web responses. Web components can be exposed to clients using standard communication protocols such as HTTP and Web services. A J2EE Web application can contain one or more J2EE Web components and are configured according to a J2EE Web application deployment descriptor (Web DD).
- *Applet Clients:* Applets are Java applications that can run inside of a Web browser and offer a GUI inside of a Web browser. The J2EE specification outlines a methodology for hosting applets inside of a standardized applet container environment with added support for acting as J2EE-based clients to J2EE-based servers.
- *Application Clients:* Application clients are Java-based clients that typically run on a user desktop or workstation and offer a GUI. The J2EE specification outlines a methodology for hosting application clients inside of a standardized application client container environment with added API support for acting as J2EE-based clients to J2EE-based servers. A J2EE application client is configured according to a J2EE application client deployment descriptor (Ap Client DD).
- *Resource Adapters:* A resource adapter serves as a component type that provides connectivity resources to a resource manager for an enterprise system external to a J2EE container. A resource adapter accomplishes this by either implementing a standard J2EE API (for example, JDBC) or via the implementation of an API specific to a particular type of external resource (for example, an ERP system). A resource adapter component is deployed along with an associated set of J2EE Web or EJB components to the containers for those respective component types. A J2EE resource adapter is configured according to a J2EE resource adapter deployment descriptor (RA DD).

J2EE Component Assembly

The five classes of components depicted in Figure 1.5 can be deployed inside of a J2EE container in various ways. For one, J2EE application clients, Web components, and EJB components can all be packaged inside of a Java archive (JAR) type file and deployed inside of their respective containers as J2EE modules. Another type of J2EE module can be deployed that includes only a resource adapter. Each JAR file is packaged along with a deployment descriptor describing how the contained component(s) are to be configured and deployed. The deployment descriptor associated with a module and its encapsulating JAR file describes configurable properties of container services and components utilized by a particular deployed instance of its associated components (for example, security levels, transactions semantics, initialization parameters).

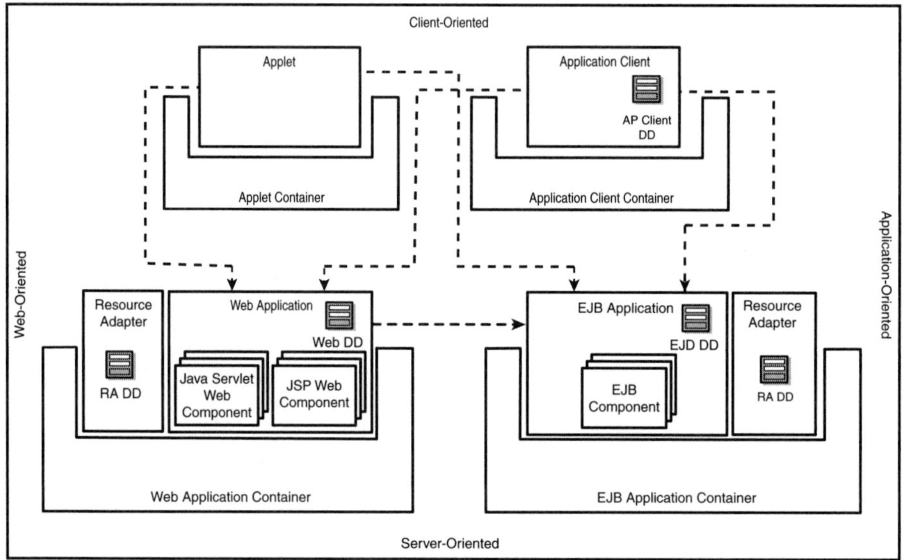

Figure 1.5 J2EE component and container types.

These are the four J2EE module and associated JAR file types:

- *EJB Module:* One or more J2EE EJB components have their associated class files and an XML-based deployment descriptor packaged inside of an EJB JAR file with a `.jar` file extension.
- *Web Module:* One or more J2EE Web components (Java servlets or JSPs) have their associated class files and an XML-based deployment descriptor packaged inside of a WAR file (that is, JAR file specific to a Web application) with a `.war` file extension.
- *Application Client Module:* A J2EE application client can have its associated class files and an XML-based deployment descriptor packaged inside of an application client JAR file with a `.jar` file extension.
- *Resource Adapter Module:* A resource adapter can have its associated class files and an XML-based deployment descriptor packaged inside of an RAR file (that is, Jar file specific to resource adapters) with a `.rar` file extension.

In addition to deploying J2EE modules independently, a collection of one or more modules may be assembled into a single enterprise application to run inside of a unified J2EE container environment. Each module file is assembled into a cohesive enterprise application to allow all the components within the modules to interoperate inside of the same container environment. This J2EE enterprise application is packaged inside of an EAR file (that is, JAR file specific to a J2EE enterprise application) with a `.ear` file extension. Additionally, the EAR file also includes an enterprise application deployment descriptor describing how the enterprise application as a whole is to be configured and deployed.

J2EE Restrictions

Because J2EE container environments include an underlying J2SE platform and Java enterprise APIs, without further restrictions, J2EE components could simply perform all the operations that an application in a standalone J2SE environment could perform. However, this would violate the fundamental component-container model of the J2EE and affect a container's capability to provide management services for its components. This is why the J2EE specification defines a minimum set of permissions that scope which operations a J2EE-based component can invoke on its underlying J2SE and Java enterprise API environment. Although certain J2EE product service providers may allow for a wider set of permissions, J2EE-based component application developers are at a minimum restricted to the following set of permissions:

- *EJB Application Servers:* EJB application components can queue print jobs, create socket connections as a client (but not server connections), and read system properties.
- *Web Application Servers:* Web components can also queue print jobs, create socket connections as a client, and read system properties. Additionally, Web components can load external libraries and can read and write files.
- *Applet Clients:* Applet components can only connect to the server defined within its `CODEBASE` and can read a limited set of properties.
- *Application Clients:* Application client components have the most freedom out of all J2EE-component types. Application clients can create socket connections as a client and accept and listen for socket connections as a server on a local machine's ports above and including port 1024. Application clients can also read system properties, queue print jobs, exit a JVM process, and load external libraries. Application clients can also perform various security-sensitive GUI operations such as accessing a clipboard, accessing an event queue, and displaying a window without a warning banner.

J2EE Architecture

Although the J2EE is a centerpiece of Java enterprise development as well as the focus of this book, this book discusses more than just the development of components that operate inside of J2EE-based containers. We also describe many of the Java enterprise APIs that are part of the J2EE in general such that they can also be used in standalone Java environments and not necessarily be used from within the context of a J2EE container having J2EE restrictions. In addition to the standard Java enterprise APIs that are incorporated by the J2EE, we occasionally mention and cover a few other Java-based technologies that can be used to facilitate the practical construction of enterprise systems. Although such auxiliary technologies are currently outside of the J2EE scope, we suspect, and in certain cases are already aware of the fact, that in due time such technologies will become integrated with the J2EE platform.

There are many advantages to the approach taken by this book. For one, not all fully integrated J2EE-based features may always be immediately available and offered by a particular vendor's product that you are using. Furthermore, many real-world enterprise system applications still have widely distributed and disparate legacy system and application needs that may make it difficult to invest in J2EE-based environments for all distributed enterprise server scenarios. Rather, a standalone Java enterprise application may be just fine for certain lower-end enterprise system deployment scenarios. It is also certainly the case that some legacy Enterprise Application Integration (EAI) solutions will still need to consider use of standalone Java application environments until their specific EAI connector technologies are made available. For all of these reasons, we describe many of the J2EE APIs that can be used in standalone Java applications in a largely unrestricted fashion early in the book. We then focus on Web-enabling and applications-enabling technologies later in the book in the context of using J2EE containers. Furthermore, we also describe how use of such J2EE environments can greatly simplify usage of the Java enterprise APIs that are described throughout this book. After all, the aim of this book is to turn you into a well-rounded and well-informed J2EE enterprise systems developer.

J2EE Architecture Overview

Figure 1.3 presented a broad classification of the various enabling services needed to create enterprise systems. Figure 1.6 shows the more concrete architecture solution components advocated by this book for building enterprise systems using J2EE technologies. The diagram in Figure 1.6 is primarily logical by nature and is not meant to depict a physical architecture for enterprise systems. Rather, the diagram depicts the various logical needs for construction of an enterprise system and the various Java enterprise technologies used to support such needs. The logical architecture defined within Figure 1.6 actually has many physical architecture permutations.

As you'll see in subsequent sections of this chapter, all the enterprise APIs specified within the J2EE are represented in Figure 1.6. Figure 1.6 also identifies a few technologies that we describe in this book that currently fall outside of the J2EE scope. Each logical enterprise component depicted in Figure 1.6 has a corresponding enterprise technology solution provided in the following fashion:

- *Enterprise User Interfacing:* Web-based Java applets and desktop Java application clients can be built using Java-based GUI techniques and can be hosted in standalone J2SE environments or inside J2EE container environments. Traditional non-Java–oriented Web browsing applications can also be used with J2EE-based Web servers. Additionally, non-Java–based clients can also interface with server-side components using distributed communication technologies such as CORBA, Web services, and TCP/IP. Coverage of client-side enterprise user interfacing development is beyond the scope of this book. However, we do discuss how server-side enterprise applications are developed to support such clients.

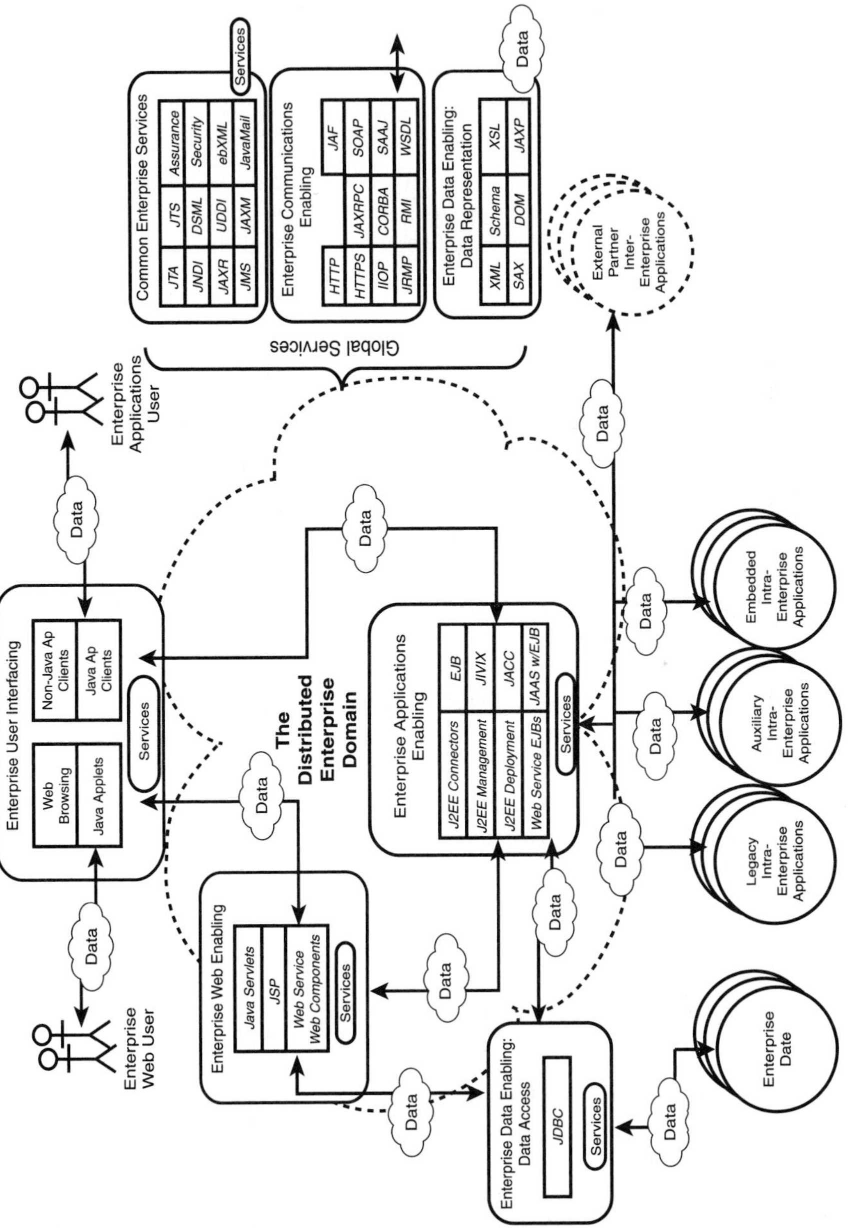

Figure 1.6 J2EE logical architecture.

- *Enterprise Data Enabling:* XML, XML Schema, XSL, SAX, and DOM are standards used in the representation and manipulation of data. JAXP is a Java API defined to encapsulate such standards. JDBC is used to access data in databases. J2EE Web, EJB application, and application client containers all utilize the JAXP and JDBC APIs. Standalone Java enterprise applications running outside of a J2EE environment can also be used with JAXP and JDBC.
- *Enterprise Communications Enabling:* Protocols and standards for distributed communications such as CORBA, IIOP, JRMP, TCP/IP, HTTP, HTTPS, SOAP, WSDL, and Web services are all possible within Java enterprise environments, whether they're embedded in Web servers, application servers, standalone Java applications, or enterprise user interface clients. Java APIs exist to enable such communications including Java IDL (for CORBA), RMI with JRMP and IIOP, SAAJ, JWSDL, and JAX-RPC. All such communication paradigms also assume their own means to activate objects in memory based on network request or may leverage the standard activation framework provided by JAF.
- *Common Enterprise Services:* A host of communication services are possible within Java enterprise environments. Naming and directory services, such as DSML, enable the lookup of objects across a network and are encapsulated by the JNDI API. Web service–based lookup standards such as UDDI and ebXML registries are encapsulated by the JAXR API. Services to manage distributed transactions are encapsulated by the JTA and JTS APIs. Asynchronous messaging can be achieved in a message-oriented-middleware fashion using JMS, via Web services using JAXM, or via lightweight email processing using JavaMail. Various properties of systems assurance such as reliability, availability, maintainability, safety, and security are more inherent properties of a system as opposed to a distinct service. However, Java-based enterprise environments encapsulate many security services with distinct APIs.
- *Enterprise Web Enabling:* Java Servlets and Java Server Pages are the standard J2EE-based mechanisms for receiving Web-based requests and for generating Web-based responses. Web-enabled applications can also take advantage of the various global services for distributed communications, communication services, and assurance services. Furthermore, Web-enabled applications can also be exposed as Web services for broader interoperability across the Internet.
- *Enterprise Applications Enabling:* EJBs are the primary means defined within the J2EE to create server-side application business logic. Various enterprise application integration and management technologies are also a part of application enabling such as the J2EE Connector Architecture (a.k.a. J2EE Connectors), J2EE Management, JMX, J2EE Deployment, JACC, and JAAS w/EJB. Enterprise-enabled applications can also take advantage of the various global services for distributed communications, communication services, and assurance services. Furthermore, scalable EJB applications can be exposed as Web services for broader interoperability across the Internet.

J2EE and WS-I

As referenced thus far, Web services is a standard distributed communications paradigm. For requests and responses, XML-based messages (that is, SOAP messages) are employed. A means for communicating such messages in a remote-procedure calling fashion is also detailed within the SOAP standards. Various individual standards are defined and used to realize Web services, such as XML, XML Schema, SOAP, WSDL, UDDI, and HTTP. The J2EE v1.4 provides considerable support for Web services via its inclusion of various Web services–related APIs that provide Java-based realizations of Web services and their individual standards, such as JAXP, SAAJ, JAX-RPC, JWSDL, JAXR, JAXM, and J2EE component-based Web services.

As discussed previously, the J2EE serves to define a standard profile to coagulate a set of standard APIs and services used to build enterprise applications. Similarly, specifications created by the Web Services Interoperability Organization (WS-I) serve to define standard profiles to coagulate sets of Web service standards used to build interoperable Web services. In fact, the J2EE v1.4 is compliant with the WS-I Basic Profile. The WS-I Basic Profile defines a profile for XML, XML Schema, SOAP, WSDL, UDDI, and HTTP. Hence, by virtue of implementing Web services using J2EE-compliant APIs and containers, you are also implementing Web services that are compliant with WS-I standards. We discuss WS-I, its contained standards, and their J2EE realizations throughout this book.

J2EE Enterprise Data Enabling

The eXtensible Markup Language (XML) is a flexible and extendible type of language first integrated into Web environments as an extension to HTML. XML documents can represent data in a hierarchical form and can be accompanied by Document Type Definitions (DTDs) or XML schemas, which describe the structure and semantics of a particular class of documents. Although XML has grown out of the World Wide Web, it also has a much broader application to the generic representation of data in general. Thus, data exchanged or stored via a particular medium can be described using the standard syntax of XML.

In fact, J2EE deployment descriptors are described and stored in a standard XML format. Furthermore, XML is also used to represent message requests and responses sent between distributed applications. This is one reason why XML document parsing libraries have been wholly incorporated into the J2SE and J2EE. The Java API for XML Parsing (JAXP) is a standard Java extension that is used to parse and build XML-based documents adhering to the constraints of DTDs and XML schemas.

Enterprise information and knowledge are most often managed inside of a database management system (DBMS). Such data is often accumulated over many years and also is often heavily depended on by legacy applications. It should come as no surprise that such data is thus highly valued by an enterprise. Enterprises also end up creating strong dependencies and ties to particular vendor DBMS implementations. For all of these reasons, it is important to have a DBMS-independent solution for accessing enterprise data in a fashion that enables enterprise applications to remain stable despite changes in DBMS vendor product selections.

The Java Database Connectivity (JDBC) API is an enterprise API that provides a means for accessing and managing enterprise data stored in a DBMS. The JDBC API is defined in a fashion that permits DBMS-independent construction of commands to access the database using a DBMS command language known as the Structured Query Language (SQL). As with most Java enterprise APIs, an underlying Service Provider Interface (SPI) allows a particular DBMS vendor interface to be adapted for use with the JDBC libraries and permit enterprise applications to use the same JDBC API.

J2EE Enterprise Communications Enabling

Enabling applications for distributed communications is a fundamental necessity when building an enterprise system. An enterprise application may need to offer its services in a distributed server mode, or it may need to tap the services of a distributed server and act as a distributed client. Both modes of operation require an interface to some distributed communications code for enabling an application to communicate over a network.

The technologies described in this book involve two main approaches for enabling an enterprise application to utilize distributed communications. One approach involves use of a standalone Java enterprise environment that uses an underlying distributed communications API and implementation. Another approach advocates use of an underlying communications infrastructure embedded into a J2EE container environment that offers distributed communication services transparently to J2EE components.

Regardless of the approach, a particular methodology of communications and underlying protocol must be selected to enable clients and servers to communicate with one another. These are the primary approaches adopted in this book:

- *TCP/IP:* The Transmission Control Protocol/Internet Protocol (TCP/IP), is a standard protocol suite used on the Internet, and it serves as the underlying protocol for all distributed computing paradigms discussed in this book. Java provides a set of libraries that allow an application to communicate directly via TCP/IP and is thus equipped with the J2EE by virtue of its inclusion with the J2SE.
- *HTTP/HTTPS:* The Hypertext Transfer Protocol (HTTP) is the protocol over TCP/IP used for communicating between Web browsers and servers. APIs for communicating directly via HTTP are provided by the J2SE. Furthermore, HTTP requests and responses are encapsulated by higher-level abstractions for use by programmers in J2EE Web-container environments. The use of a Secure Socket Layer (SSL) protocol must also be available for use with HTTP to enable secure Web communications via HTTPS.
- *CORBA/IIOP:* The Common Object Request Broker Architecture (CORBA) is an industry-standard and language-independent distributed object communications paradigm that transparently handles the mapping of object method calls to and from an underlying communications message data representation. The Internet

Inter-ORB Protocol (IIOP), which is the underlying communications protocol used by CORBA, operates above TCP/IP.

- *Java IDL:* Java IDL is a Java-based API and implementation of the CORBA communications paradigm, and is equipped with the J2EE by virtue of its inclusion with the J2SE. However, although creating CORBA clients in a J2EE environment is possible for EJB, Web, and application client containers, only application client components can create their own CORBA server instances.
- *RMI/JRMP:* Remote Method Invocation (RMI) is the distributed object communications paradigm that was developed for use with Java. Java Remote Method Protocol (JRMP) is the original protocol used by RMI for communications beneath the RMI interface and also operates above TCP/IP. RMI/JRMP is equipped with the J2EE by virtue of its inclusion with the J2SE.
- *RMI/IIOP:* RMI has also been adapted to operate over IIOP. With RMI/IIOP, Java-based applications that use the RMI distributed object communications interface can communicate with CORBA-based applications. RMI/IIOP adds a few API features to RMI that must be included by J2EE EJB, Web, and application client environment vendors.
- *SOAP:* The Simple Object Access Protocol (SOAP) defines a set of standards for XML document formats that represent requests and responses associated with distributed object calls (that is, Web services). SOAP, along with its support for using attachments (for example, images and document files associated with a SOAP message), is a requirement of the J2EE.
- *SAAJ:* The SOAP with Attachments API for Java (SAAJ) is a standard API used to encapsulate the parsing and creation of SOAP messages and is required for inclusion with the J2EE.
- *WSDL:* The Web Services Description Language (WSDL) defines an XML-based approach for describing Web services and their SOAP interfaces.
- *JWSDL:* JWSDL is a Java API defined for reading, writing, and manipulating WSDL data, but it is not included with the J2EE.
- *JAX-RPC:* The Java API for XML-based Remote Procedure Calls (JAX-RPC) defines a standard API used to expose server-side Java objects as Web services communicating via SOAP, as well as for building Java clients to Web services.

Finally, an activation service is a component of software responsible for bringing other software from an inactive dormant state into an active in-memory state based on a network request. We discuss the various activation models implicit in each distributed communications paradigm throughout this book. The JavaBeans Activation Framework (JAF) is a framework for building applications that can automatically activate objects that can manipulate data received via an input stream. We describe the JAF in this book as well.

J2EE Common Enterprise Services

Use of the aforementioned distributed communications paradigms alone enables one to build distributed application clients and servers. However, a set of common services hosted atop a distributed communications paradigm makes creating distributed enterprise applications an easier task. Furthermore, the infusion of assurance and security into an enterprise application enables such applications to be dependable and secure. The core common enterprise services discussed in this book are listed here:

- *Naming Services and JNDI:* Naming services are used to reference and look up distributed objects on a network in terms of a human-readable name. The Java Naming and Directory Interface (JNDI) is used to provide a common Java API to various underlying naming service implementations and types. A file system, an RMI registry, and a CORBA Naming Service are all examples of specific naming services accessible via JNDI.
- *Directory Services and JNDI:* Directory services are a type of naming service that add the capability to reference and search for distributed objects on a network in terms of descriptive attributes about the object. JNDI is also used to provide a common Java API to various underlying directory service implementations and types. NIS, NDS, LDAP, DSML, and DNS are all examples of directory services with JNDI-based interfaces.
- *Transaction Services with JTA and JTS:* A transaction service provides a mechanism for encapsulating inseparable operations performed over a distributed network into an atomic operation. The CORBA Object Transaction Service (OTS) is mapped to Java by virtue of the Java Transaction Service (JTS). The Java Transaction API (JTA) is a higher-level framework for managing transactions and resources from Java enterprise applications.
- *Messaging Services and JMS:* Messaging services provide an asynchronous means for sending and receiving messages over a network. The Java Message Service (JMS) API provides a standard interface to such messaging services and is part of J2EE EJB, Web, and application client environments.
- *JAXM:* The Java API for XML Messaging (JAXM) is a standard API primarily used for enabling asynchronous communications between Web services and clients via SOAP. The JAXM is not currently part of the J2EE.
- *JavaMail:* The JavaMail API for sending and receiving email messages is also part of J2EE EJB, Web, and application client environments.
- *Assurance and Security Services:* The security, reliability, availability, maintainability, and perhaps safety of your system indicate its level of assurance. Various implied and explicit features of J2EE address such needs. In particular, the J2SE and J2EE include a rather rich suite of APIs specifically geared for creating secure enterprise applications.

J2EE Enterprise Web Enabling

Enterprise Web connectivity involves providing a solution for handling Web requests and generating Web responses via a Web server. A Web server tier is often best thought of as a middle-tier layer whose responsibility is to handle Web-based client interface requests and to generate a new Web presentation interface for the Web client. Web server tiers often delegate to an enterprise application serving tier for any scalable business logic, transaction-based, secured, or widely integrated processing that must be performed. J2EE Web containers enable two types of Web components: Java Servlets and JavaServer Pages (JSP).

Java Servlets is a Java API that encapsulates HTTP requests, HTTP responses, and HTTP session management interfaces. The J2EE allows Java Servlet components to operate inside of a J2EE Java Servlet Web container. The Web container handles the mapping of requests to specific servlet instances and handles transforming request and response objects to and from the underlying HTTP I/O stream.

JSPs are documents written in a scripting-based language. JSPs can interact with Java code and actually are described using a syntax considered to be familiar and easily comprehended by Web developers. JSPs are constructed to manage Web requests and responses as are servlets. JSPs are actually converted into Java Servlets by a J2EE JSP Web container environment when the JSP is first loaded or referenced. JSP tags provide a way for JSPs to interact with back-end business logic and data access software using taglike structures most appropriate for embedding into dynamic Web presentation templates.

J2EE Web components may expose themselves as Web services. That is, a J2EE Web component may be deployed in such a way that it exposes a set of interfaces as a Web service. Thus, J2EE Web components can be deployed in such a way that they transparently receive SOAP requests and generate SOAP responses. The J2EE Web container does all the work translating between SOAP messages and Java object types handled by the J2EE Web component interfaces.

J2EE Enterprise Applications Enabling

Writing server-side enterprise applications can be significantly more difficult than writing client-side applications. Enterprise applications must be scalable, be secure, handle a large number of client requests, manage server-side resources, and manage external resources, among many other multiple client/application/resource management duties.

Standalone Java enterprise applications are applications written on top of the Java platform that take advantage of standard Java enterprise API extensions. Standalone Java applications offer maximum flexibility in terms of choices for COTS and the capability to support many types of client connectivity paradigms. J2EE-based EJB container environments are also used to build enterprise applications. The container environment offers a vendor-independent interface to a host of enterprise services for building scalable enterprise applications. J2EE EJB container services reduce the amount of infrastructure hand-coding required of the developer and allow developers to concentrate on the development of business logic embedded within EJB components.

However, the direct instantiation of distributed communication server instances (for example, RMI and CORBA) by application components in J2EE EJB application servers is not permitted by the container environment. You thus have to rely on those distributed communications server types that can be created by the J2EE container environment. J2EE EJB container environments are required only to support RMI/IIOP-based implementations. Some vendors may provide full IIOP-based connectivity, however.

New to the J2EE is the fact that certain J2EE EJB components may expose themselves as Web services. That is, an EJB may be deployed such that its interfaces are exposed as a Web service. Thus, as is the case with J2EE Web components, EJBs can now be deployed to transparently receive SOAP requests and generate SOAP responses with the EJB container doing all the translation to and from SOAP messages and object-oriented interfaces defined on the EJB.

Enabling your J2EE-based servers to support connectivity from different distributed communication paradigm clients is thus standardized for RMI/IIOP and Web service communication paradigms. Other supported communication paradigms are currently a function of your particular J2EE vendor's offering. Standalone Java enterprise applications can, of course, support many types of client connectivity. Although creating and managing distributed server instances in standalone environments can require more hand-coding, it may be your only choice for certain client connectivity solutions in some cases. Furthermore, the scalability requirements and complexity of a particular enterprise application may not warrant the investment in a J2EE-based COTS EJB application server. For many other moderate- to large-scale and complex enterprise application cases, however, use of a J2EE-based EJB application server will be your only option given your time-to-market needs, cost limitations, and human-resource availability.

In addition to building J2EE-based EJBs or standalone Java enterprise applications, the enabling of legacy and embedded applications for access by the enterprise will also be a key consideration in enterprise application enabling. Enterprise application integration techniques require the provision of a means to integrate a legacy, auxiliary, or embedded application into your Java enterprise application environment. Technologies such as CORBA, JMS, XML, Web services, and J2EE Connector Architecture are all examples of technologies usable for EAI in some fashion. JMS, XML, Web services, and CORBA are particularly important for enterprise applications to interoperate with other enterprise applications in business-to-business (B2B) integration scenarios. B2B integration may occur between separately managed business units within an enterprise or with partner businesses external to an enterprise.

Last but not least, the management and deployment of your enterprise applications must be carefully considered. J2EE now provides standard APIs to allow for such management and deployment in a fashion allowing greater portability and interoperability with vendor-supplied tools for such services.

Conclusions

Enterprises achieve their goals with the use of valued resources and assets, information, knowledge, and people. In an effort to preserve, protect, grow, make accessible, make efficient, and be sensitive to change of such enterprise components, modern enterprises pursue the use of information technology to build enterprise systems that help them effectively foster their goals and objectives. Information technology is used to build enterprise systems that provide user interfacing, data enabling, communications enabling, communications services, assurance services, Web enabling, and applications enabling. Java enterprise technologies with the J2EE provide standard means for covering all such bases of an enterprise system architecture's needs.

This chapter presented an overview of the J2EE model for building enterprise systems. Given the defined set of enterprise-system needs, this chapter demonstrated how J2EE technologies can satisfy those needs. You learned that although J2EE container environments provide many advantages for Web and application enabling, certain application scenarios and needs may not warrant use of a J2EE container environment. In such cases, many of the Java enterprise APIs that form the core of J2EE will indeed still be of use. They may, however, be useful only in certain standalone Java application configurations. Additionally, many other non-J2EE but Java-based enterprise APIs are also useful in building enterprise systems.

Nevertheless, the J2EE is a centerpiece of current and future Java enterprise development. This chapter presented a Java enterprise system architecture useful in many different enterprise system scenarios. Solutions for enterprise database connectivity, distributed communications, communication services, systems assurance, Web enabling, and application enabling were all discussed in this chapter. Lo and behold…all enterprise system problems have solutions that can use J2EE technology.

II

Enterprise Data Enabling

2

Enterprise Data

INTERFACING WITH ENTERPRISE DATA IS ONE of the most important steps involved in building an enterprise system. Knowledge of how to represent data in a standard fashion to ensure maximum interoperability among enterprise applications is a key consideration when building an enterprise system. General database concepts and issues, as well as concepts and issues specific to relational and object database management systems, are also very important for the enterprise systems developer to understand. Knowing basic architectural constructs for such database systems helps one more easily grasp how to interface with enterprise data. Most significant to this book, understanding how to represent and interface with enterprise data from Java is important. The options available to the enterprise Java developer and knowing which of these options is most important help one to focus on more rapidly assembling an enterprise data-enabling solution.

This chapter describes the basic concepts involved in enterprise data representation, enterprise databases, and the options for interfacing to databases from within the enterprise Java programming paradigm. In this chapter, you will learn:

- The terminology and concepts behind enterprise data management.
- The concepts of enterprise data representation and the standards of most importance to enterprise Java developers.
- The concepts and architecture of database management systems.
- The concepts and architecture of relational database management systems, SQL, and the basic steps behind using object/relational mapping products.
- The concepts and architecture of object database management systems.
- An introduction to key data access technologies available to the enterprise Java developer.

Enterprise Data Overview

Information is one of the most significant assets of any enterprise. Information must flow into and out of an enterprise, flow through an enterprise, and be manipulated by an enterprise. Information must be easily disseminated to the right people at the right time. Information also has security constraints that mandate access control based on the type and content of the information. Information is plentiful and tends to grow exponentially in time and with the growth of an enterprise.

When information is transformed by Information Technology (IT) into a form that an enterprise system can manipulate, the information becomes "data" from an IT perspective. Thus the information that exists in the ethereal world of our minds and external to the realm of enterprise systems is captured as data at that boundary between the human world and the internal world of enterprise systems. When inside the enterprise computing world, such data is distributed, manipulated, copied, destroyed, and often retransformed into information presented back to the human world.

As the data is distributed throughout the realm of enterprise systems, it manifests itself in various forms. But as with the human world and human languages, the enterprise computing world must agree on common forms for such data in order to communicate and interoperate. Thus, common forms for representing data must be agreed on and defined carefully for enterprise applications to communicate and interoperate. We introduce the core concepts behind enterprise data representation forms in this chapter.

Furthermore, many different people in an enterprise often must concurrently access the same data at a given time. Clearly, data is extremely important to an enterprise; it must be persisted in such a way that it is not lost and must be efficiently and easily retrieved and updated. A database management system (DBMS) is precisely the IT component used by enterprises to efficiently retrieve, update, and generally solve the problem of managing enterprise data. The collection of data managed by a DBMS is often referred to as a database. However, the term *database* also is often used to refer to the DBMS itself. We also introduce the core concepts behind enterprise databases and how to access data stored inside databases in this chapter.

Data Representation

As we just discussed, it is very important to define schemes for representing data such that various enterprise applications can communicate and interoperate. A few key considerations in determining how to represent data such that enterprise applications can interoperate are listed here:

- Is the data represented in binary or ASCII form?
- What is the structure of the data?
- How do you constrain the structure of the data?
- How do you enable extensibility in structuring the data?
- How do you enable it to be efficient to communicate in a distributed fashion?

- How do you enable it to be efficient to store and access?
- How do you enable it to be self-contained either with data values and/or with references to data such that it can be used in a distributed enterprise environment?

Data Representation Standards

With such a core problem to be solved by computing systems, it should come as no surprise that many solutions have been defined to solve such a problem over the years. But while many different solutions may have been defined, what is of most importance to enterprise systems development is that a solution be the most widely adopted. Widely adopted data representation solutions are of paramount importance to enterprise systems simply because of the size of most systems and the need to assemble a heterogeneous collection of components to compose the system. To guarantee optimal selectability and interoperability of disparate components, the lingua franca of such components must be the same.

Historically, it hasn't been easy to get different organizations to agree on such standards to ensure an optimally widely adopted form. The reason is that very often enterprise system components and applications are developed without considering the need for interoperability or with their own proprietary data representation formats in mind. Such actions are driven by cost considerations, business strategies, politics, and sometimes just plain ignorance. Regardless of the reasons and motives, we enterprise developers are of course concerned with the task of building enterprise systems as efficiently and effectively as possible so that we may shine in our jobs.

Many widely adopted data representation standards have arisen out of the need to enable distributed communications between enterprise systems. We discuss the most important of such standards in Part III, "Enterprise Communications Enabling." However, such standards have naturally focused on representing data for communication between distributed enterprise applications and for communication over a communications medium in a binary format. Thus, there is often a disparity between how the enterprise applications represent and access data locally versus how it is communicated in a distributed fashion. As a result, interoperability is limited to coarser-grained distributed enterprise applications. Such standards do not address data representation formats for the assembly or configuration of enterprise components, interoperability of enterprise components, or representation of persisted data for use by different enterprise applications.

HTML for Data Representation?

Along came the birth and growth of the World Wide Web. The Hypertext Markup Language (HTML) was used on the Web to define a common data representation format for presenting a user interface over the distributed Internet. As the popularity of the Web quickly caught on, organizations scrambled to offer Web-enabled interfaces to their enterprise systems both for external and internal usage purposes. As a result, HTML immediately became a de facto lingua franca standard for representing data.

However, organizations struggled to make HTML represent their enterprise data in ways for which HTML wasn't designed. This occurred because organizations sought to minimize the need for translating data to and from one format, either as stored in databases or in a form local to their enterprise applications, to and from the format of HTML. Organizations thus attempted to cram the representation of business data, such as orders or customers, into an HTML format such that the presentation of such data via the Web would be simplified. But such efforts were limited by the lack of extensibility of HTML and the fact that HTML was designed for presenting versus representing data.

XML for Data Representation!

This is where the eXtensible Markup Language (XML) entered the picture. XML was designed to specifically address such shortcomings of HTML and to be the core way to represent enterprise data in general. And indeed it has become what it was designed to be, which is the de facto data representation standard.

XML provides a standard way to represent data that is exchanged between applications implemented in any language, on any platform, and via any communications protocol. XML's data structure definition thus fulfills a role similar to the role fulfilled by Java's underlying object serialization format definition. However, Java's object serialization format is Java-language specific albeit platform and communications-protocol independent. By using XML formats to represent data, Java applications can now communicate serialized object information to and from applications implemented in other languages.

As more enterprise software products are developed using XML data representations for data interchange and as standard types of XML documents are defined, Java enterprise systems can integrate with and take advantage of these software products and standard releases. Despite XML's language independence, we of course advocate the development of enterprise applications using Java for all the reasons stemming from Java's advantages and features touted throughout this book. However, from a practical perspective, not all enterprise software vendors will want to offer interfaces to their products that permit only Java-based product clients.

In fact, as you'll see in subsequent chapters, the term "Web Services" applies to those applications built to interoperate over standard protocols using XML documents as the message format. It is for this reason that the Java specification initiatives focused on developing Java APIs for XML and J2EE v1.4's complete embrace of Web Services and XML have become paramount to further ensuring Java's success in the marketplace. The Java APIs for XML specifications, or "JAX" specifications, are currently plentiful and growing. There are JAX specifications for serializing Java objects to/from XML representations, for parsing, for messaging, and for implementing XML-based Web Services. The JAX specifications surrounding Web Services are particularly important to consider for enterprise Java applications. We discuss all such JAX specifications throughout this book in dedicated chapters as their description and supporting examples become relevant in each section of the book. Chapter 3, "XML," and Chapter 4, "JAXP," describe XML in depth, how to enforce its structure, how to parse XML, and how to automatically translate XML to and from different formats. As a reference, Appendix F, "HTML," provides more information about HTML's structure and how to create and interpret HTML-based documents.

Database Basics

Another key consideration for enterprise systems development is how to coagulate, store, and enable efficient access to voluminous amounts of enterprise data by a large enterprise user base. This is where use of DBMSs (that is, databases) comes into play. Databases serve as central repositories for enterprise data and play a crucial role in allowing proper dissemination and management of that data. Because such enterprise data is often critical to the business of the enterprise, the creation, modification, deletion, and management of data in a database is a serious matter, and it behooves enterprise developers to have a reasonable amount of knowledge regarding how databases work and of course how to access enterprise data within enterprise databases. The remainder of this chapter describes database concepts in more detail. Appendix C, "Database Concepts and SQL," provides auxiliary information about databases in the context of a reference for SQL, the standard database query language.

Data Model Abstraction Levels

When one is referring to databases, it is important to understand the different levels of abstraction at which people think about databases. Database designers sometimes think of databases at the lowest level of abstraction in terms of a physical data model used to represent storage of data on physical media, including how the data is structurally related. A higher level of abstraction describes a logical data model (aka a conceptual data model) wherein logical-data-model entities correspond to one or more underlying physical-data-model entities and their relationships. Logical data models describe data in terms of what is stored in the database, such as "customer information" or "order information." The logical data model typically relates to an object model and is largely used to describe specific database designs to an enterprise programmer. The logical data model is thus the level of modeling employed by this book. The highest level of data abstraction is referred to as a *view* and corresponds to a specific customization of a logical data model for use by a particular enterprise user class. Data from the logical model is eliminated from the view level, and new information is derived from the logical level for the view level. Many different views can exist above the logical-data-model level.

A different way to describe the database generally exists at all three levels of database abstraction. The description of the database structure at each abstraction level is called the *database scheme*. At the physical level of abstraction, the database is described in terms of an internal scheme. At the logical level, a database is described in terms of a conceptual scheme. Views of the database are described in terms of an external scheme or subscheme. Although a database scheme at each level describes the structure of the database, the term *database instance* is typically used to describe a particular instantiation of a database scheme. Thus, database A on a host machine X and database B on a host machine Y may adhere to the same database scheme but represent two separate database instances.

General DBMS Architecture

Figure 2.1 depicts a generic architecture for DBMSs and databases. The DBMS is broken out separately from the database in this diagram. The database represents the physical storage of actual allocated file space for all data and structures being managed by the DBMS. Although we have made a distinction between the database and DBMS, we should note that the terms DBMS and database are sometimes individually used to mean both the DBMS and the database.

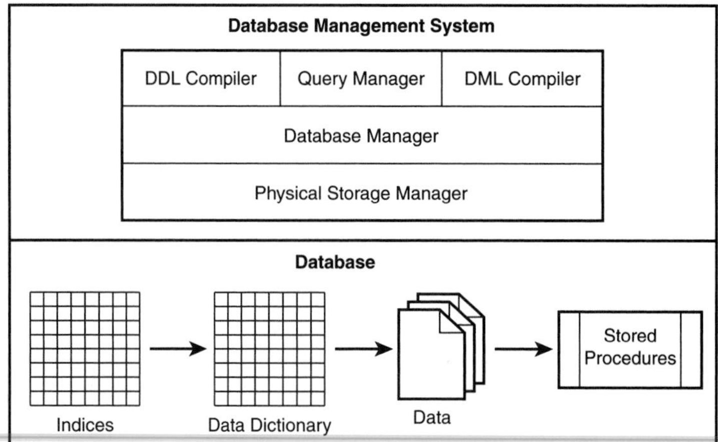

Figure 2.1 Generic DBMS and database architectural diagram.

The database itself contains the physical manifestation of all data files, data dictionaries, indices, and stored procedures. Data files are used for storing the actual enterprise information values (for example, credit-card numbers, employee names, and so on). A data dictionary stores all meta-data about the enterprise data, including data attribute names, relationships between data, and data value constraints. Indices are used to provide indexing of information stored in the data dictionary for faster access of the associated data. Stored procedures are predefined and user-defined functional code stored in the database to operate directly on the data stored in the database.

Technically speaking, the term *DBMS* encompasses all the software that rests atop the physical database layer. A DBMS will make use of a physical storage manager to allocate and deallocate physical file space for data, meta-data, indices, and procedures to be stored. The higher-level database manager provides a layer of abstraction for manipulating data, meta-data, and stored procedures related to a way that higher-level DBMS components desire to view the database. DDL compilers map database schemes described in a database definition language (DDL) into lower-level calls that create and delete new structures and data types in the database. A query manager maps high-level statements described in some query language into lower-level calls that can retrieve data from the database. DML compilers use a data manipulation language (DML) to map high-level database access and update calls into lower-level calls according to a particular data model. Although a query language technically corresponds to a subset of DML pertaining to data retrieval, the term *query language* is very often used to refer to functionality provided by a DML as well.

Transactions

The inherent distributed nature of DBMSs and databases is not apparent from the generic logical architecture of DBMSs and databases depicted in Figure 2.1. Not only are databases and DBMSs often physically distributed, but client applications to these DBMSs are typically plentiful, especially in enterprise environments. These inherent distribution facets of DBMSs and databases raise a set of concurrent access issues around which a whole science has developed, known as *transaction management*.

When a sequence of processing steps either must all take place or must have no individual step take place at all, we say that such a sequence of steps represents a transaction. When all steps occur as an inseparable operation, we say that the transaction may be committed. When no steps are allowed to occur because one or more steps failed, we say that the transaction must be rolled back (to the original system state). The classic example illustrating a transaction is the example involving a withdrawal from one bank account that must be followed by a deposit to another account. If both steps occur, the transaction can be committed. If one step fails, neither must be allowed to occur and the transaction is rolled back (aborted).

Transactions must be managed such that they are governed by what the ISO/IEC calls ACID principles. ACID is an acronym standing for atomicity, consistency, isolation, and durability. Atomicity of a transaction means that any failure occurring during a transaction will result in an undoing of all changes made during the transaction. Consistency means that all data affected by a transaction is restored to its original state before the transaction in the event of a failure during the transaction. Isolation means that any data changes made during a transaction are not visible to other transactions until the transaction is complete. Durability means that all committed data is saved such that, in the event of a failure, the state of the data will be correct.

A distributed transaction is a transaction that involves operations being performed by multiple distributed applications, as well as perhaps involving multiple distributed databases. Guaranteeing that transactions can adhere to the ACID principles in a distributed transaction processing environment can be difficult, by and large due to the heterogeneous nature of both distributed applications invoking the transactions and the distributed databases involved with the transactions. Such complexity affecting heterogeneous environments has led to some key standards that have been developed to handle distributed transaction processing (DTP). One such DTP standard has been developed by the Open Group (aka X/Open). The X/Open DTP standard defines the DTP model utilized by the J2EE.

Figure 2.2 depicts the most basic view of the X/Open DTP model. The X/Open DTP model is composed of transaction managers (TM), resource managers (RM), communication resource managers (CRM), and application programs (AP). The DTP standard specifies standard roles for these components and standard interfaces between the components. In addition to these components, we depict a resource adapter between APs and RMs to be described shortly.

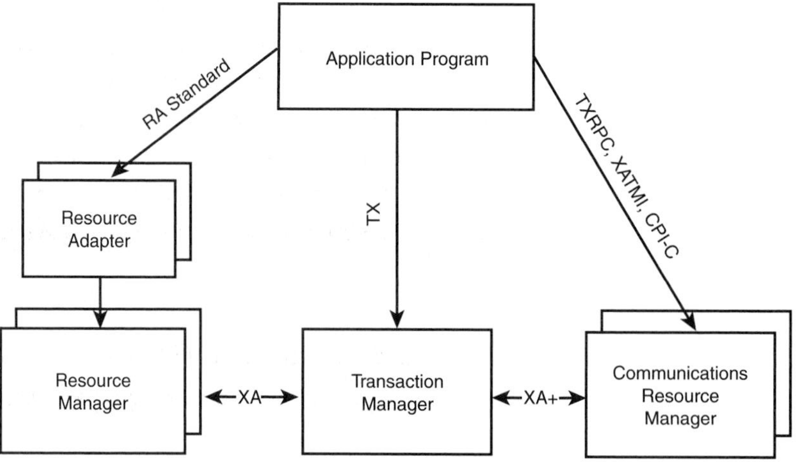

Figure 2.2 X/Open distributed transaction processing model.

The X/Open term *resource manager* is used to describe a management process for any shared resource, but it is most often used to mean a DBMS. Although the interface between application programs and resource managers is RM-specific under the X/Open DTP model, a resource adapter can be used as an interface to provide a common means for communicating with various resource manager types. Thus, database interfaces such as ODBC and JDBC can be thought of as resource adapters.

Transaction managers represent the heart of the X/Open DTP model and are the modules responsible for coordinating transactions among the various distributed entities. Resource managers participate in distributed transactions by implementing a transaction resource interface (XA) to communicate information needed by transaction managers for coordinating transactions. Using information from the distributed resource managers, the transaction manager can ensure that all steps in a transaction are atomically completed. A commit protocol (that is, two-phase commit) implemented by transaction managers helps guarantee ACID principles by ensuring that all resource managers commit to transaction completion or rollback to an original state in the event of a failure. The TX interface between application programs and transaction managers enables applications to initiate the begin, commit, and rollback of transactions, as well as to obtain the status of transactions. A middle-tier server, sometimes referred to as a transaction monitor, can help provide support for communicating with transaction managers, as well as resource managers. Use of transaction monitors can help reduce the amount of knowledge needed by applications programmers for managing transactions.

Transaction managers are often configured to manage a particular domain of distributed resource managers and applications. Communication resource managers provide a standard means for connecting distributed transaction managers to propagate transaction information among different transaction domains for more widely distributed transactions. The standard interface between transaction managers and communication resource managers is defined by an XA+ interface, whereas communication-resource-manager to application-program interfaces are defined by three different interfaces known as TxRPC, XATMI, and CPI-C.

Relational Databases

R&D and commercial developments have produced a few general architectural approaches for DBMSs over the years. Nevertheless, the relational database management system (RDBMS) architecture has clearly been the most successful architecture used in the most popular of DBMS products on the commercial market today. As a result, much of today's legacy enterprise data is hosted inside of RDBMSs. This fact alone makes a basic understanding of RDBMS principles key for any serious enterprise systems developer. The fact that RDBMSs are also the assumed underlying DBMS model for J2EE data connectivity makes understanding RDBMSs even more critical for the Java enterprise systems developer.

RDBMS Architecture

Figure 2.3 depicts the general architecture for an RDBMS in terms of its primary logical components. A table in an RDBMS serves to group a collection of attribute values for a type of logical entity. A table actually contains the collection of element attributes in what are called rows of a database. Each row corresponds to one instance of a particular entity. The columns of a table correspond to particular attributes of the entity that the table represents. Thus, for example, Figure 2.4 shows a database table called Customer that has one row per customer instance in the table. Each column of the table corresponds to an attribute of a particular customer.

One or more columns per table can be used to uniquely identify a row entry in a table. These one or more columns taken together form what is called the table's primary key. No two rows in a table can have the same primary key value. Some tables can also have columns containing foreign keys, which are primary key values from other tables. Foreign keys are used to explicitly relate one table to another. For example, if a Customer table uses the Account Number as a primary key, then an Order table used to capture the details for a particular customer order may have a foreign key containing the Account Number column value for the customer associated with a particular order. Tables are organized into schemas, whereby a schema encapsulates a collection of tables. Catalogs can also be used to group schemas. Catalogs and schemas help organize tables as well as other entities such as views into groups such that access control and maintenance policies can be defined at the group level. With catalogs and schemas, data can also be scoped by referring to data in a format such as `<Catalog>.<Schema>.<Table>.<Column>`. Not all RDBMSs support grouping of tables into catalogs and schemas, and the separator used to delimit the scope of data can also vary between DBMS vendors.

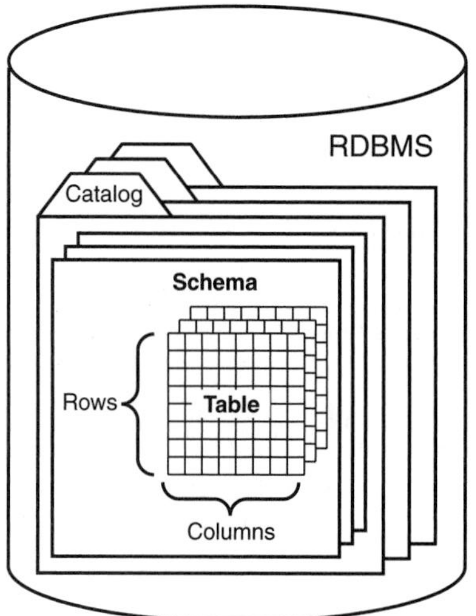

Figure 2.3 RDBMS architecture.

Customer Table

Last Name	First Name	Account Number	
Shorr	Pauly	149-6423-00	
Dooley	Stax	149-6425-00	
⋮	⋮	⋮	
Ziemba	Jack	111-2763-00	

Figure 2.4 Table entries in an RDBMS.

SQL

Structured Query Language (SQL) is the most widely used query language for RDBMSs. Even though it is called a *query language*, SQL is used for much more than just data retrieval. SQL is also used to create and define database structures like a DDL and to update data like a DML. SQL was created by IBM in the 1970s and became standardized in the 1980s. Although a few standard versions of SQL exist, the version of SQL used by the J2EE database connectivity solution is the American National Standards Institute's (ANSI) SQL-92, as well as some extensions to SQL via the SQL3 standard. Within such standards, different levels of compliance are defined.

We will discuss mappings between SQL data types and Java types in subsequent chapters. However, if you are unfamiliar with SQL, Appendix C, "Database Concepts and SQL," may be of some benefit to you because it presents descriptions of core SQL types, concepts, and examples. SQL examples are given for how to create, delete, and modify tables and rows in a table. SQL examples are also given for issuing queries and yielding a set of results. The nature and formulation of SQL queries is perhaps the most important concept in SQL to understand because it typically has the most significant ramifications for performance of your enterprise applications. SQL queries also embody concepts that form the basis of other query-like mechanisms used by Java enterprise APIs.

Object/Relational Mappings

Because many enterprises already make use of RDBMSs hosting legacy enterprise data, object-oriented developers are usually stuck with more programming overhead than they care to have. Mapping object-oriented classes and relationships to RDBMS tables and relations can be a tedious and complex task. However, tools now exist to facilitate relational/object translations.

Many RDBMS vendors are now providing hybrid object/relational back-end database architecture solutions. Additionally, a host of object/relational mapping solutions is now on the market to provide an OO layer above an RDBMS. Object/relational mapping products usually either generate object models from relational schemas or create relational models for you from preexisting object models. Object/relational mapping products can be purchased separately or are sometimes found integrated with other enterprise products. Data-aware GUI JavaBeans, for example, implicitly map GUI components to RDBMS database calls according to GUI-based customizers used by the developer to define such mappings. More sophisticated and general-purpose object/relational mapping products are also now being integrated into middle-tier products with particular applicability in Enterprise JavaBeans, as you'll see in later chapters.

Mapping Java objects to RDBMS tables involves an object/relational mapping tool analyzing Java class relationships and then generating an associated relational model. Each class will often map to a table. Class attributes that correspond to fundamental SQL types map to table columns. Classes having references to other class objects map to a table with a foreign key to another table that represents the referenced class.

However, given the prevalence of legacy RDBMSs in the world, the most common object/relational mapping scenario encountered by the enterprise developer is to map an existing RDBMS schema into an object model. An example process for mapping an RDBMS schema into an object model is as shown here:

1. Open your object/relational mapping tool.
2. Provide your tool with the schema name for which the object-relational mapping must be performed.
3. The tool displays all the tables contained by that schema.
4. Select the tables from which you want to create Java classes.
5. Select each table name and provide a class name to which you want it to be mapped. Many tools use the table name as the default name for the class but in a Java language format. For example, the Customer table by default maps to a public class named `Customer` in a `Customer.java` source file.
6. Depending on the particular mapping tool, the generated Java class might be extended from some sort of persistable class or perhaps implement some persistable interface. For example, a mapped object may be produced in this way:

```
public class Customer extends Persistable
{
  int customerId;
  String firstName;
  String lastName;
  String middleInitial;
  String address1;
  String address2;
  String city;
  State  state;
  String zip;
  String phone;
     ..
     ..
// Generated getter/setter methods for the columns
public void setXXX()
{
}
public XXX getXXX()
{
}
// For one to one relationship with other tables, we have...
public XXX getXXX()
{
}
// For one to many relationship with other tables, we have...
public Enumeration getXXX()
{
}
```

```
// To select a particular Customer from the database, we might have...
public static Customer selectElement(String predicate)
{
}
// To select one or more Customers from the database, we might have...
public static Enumeration select(String predicate)
{
}
```

7. Use the generated classes as regular Java objects by your Java application code. The underlying RDBMS queries, inserts, deletes, and updates are transparent to the Java application programmer. For example:

```
Customer c = Customer.selectElement("customerID=1");
String firstName = c.getFirstName();
String lastName = c.getLastName();
State  state = c.getState();
String stateCode = c.getStateCode();
String stateName = c.getStateName();
    ...
c.setState("VA");

// Updates the state of customer to VA to persistent store
c.updateCustomer();
    ...
Enumeration customers = Customer.select("state = VA");
```

8. Compile the code and run your application.

Data Model Diagram Conventions

Because the data model abstraction pursued in this book is at a logical/conceptual level, the data model diagramming convention used in this book closely resembles the object-oriented model diagramming convention described in Appendix G, "Enterprise Software Development." The modeling convention also employs some features that closely follow typical data modeling conventions. The data model used here can actually be thought of as a subset of a general object model. Nonetheless, we take a few liberties in describing data models in this book to bridge the gap between traditional data modeling and object modeling without resorting to explaining a completely new modeling paradigm. The simple set of conventions used for data model diagrams in this book and their UML object model diagram analogues are described here:

- Tables are represented by squares much like classes are represented in object diagrams.
- Columns are represented as elements of the table much like attributes in classes are represented in object diagrams.

- Columns are defined according to the following general form:

```
[<<optional_key_stereotype>>] column_name : column_type //
column_description
```

- Primary keys and foreign keys appear as stereotypes for a particular column.
- Column types are defined in terms of SQL types.
- Two forward slashes are used after a `column_type` to delineate the beginning of a column description.
- Table relations are represented by lines much like lines are used to represent relationships in object diagrams.
- The same multiplicity notation at the end of a relationship is used for data models here as is used for object models.
- Directionality of a relationship indicates how one table explicitly references another table via a foreign key (this is different from object modeling conventions).
- Roles are used at each end of a directional relation to indicate which primary or foreign keys are involved in the explicit relationship.
- No directionality of a relationship indicates how one table implicitly relates to another table.

Object Databases

Relational data models are used to describe an RDBMS design for storing and relating data. Because storing and relating data is precisely the problem that RDBMSs attempt to solve, relational data models are well suited for their intended purpose. However, the types of systems that evolve from using relational data models are much more limited than the types of systems that evolve from object-oriented and component-based models. Wouldn't it be nice if we could continue to model our scalable enterprise systems using the object-oriented and component-based models that we've grown to love and then simply be able to indicate what elements of state in those models should be persisted? Enter the object database management system (ODBMS).

Object database management systems are DBMSs that allow one to directly store and retrieve objects to and from a database. An ODBMS stores class attributes and relations in such a way that database operations can be accomplished in a manner that is most natural to the object-oriented programmer. Thus, in the case of Java, Java objects can be saved to an ODBMS by one JVM and later retrieved by another JVM.

ODBMS Architecture

ODBMS architectures for Java typically include a tool to map Java class references to database calls. This mapping tool is usually either baked into a modified JVM or external to a JVM and used as a post-compiler. Although using a modified JVM is undesirable for some applications, post-compilation tools can normally be used only on user-defined classes. User-defined persistable Java objects can automatically store and retrieve any persistable Java objects they reference during database operations.

The Object Data Management Group (ODMG) is a standards body that has defined a standard model for ODBMSs. The basic model consists of an Object Definition Language (ODL) for defining object databases and an Object Query Language (OQL) for ODBMS querying. Language-specific APIs are used for manipulating objects. An Object Interchange Format (OIF) is used for importing and exporting objects between different ODBMSs.

The ODMG standard defines a `Database` class used to open and close database connections, bind objects to names, and look up objects' given names. Java collection types are extended by the standard's `DCollection`, `DList`, `DArray`, `DSet`, and `DBag` interfaces to allow persistable versions of a collection of objects. The classes `ListOfObject`, `SetOfObject`, and `BagOfObject` implement these extended persistable interfaces. One typically must bind a collection to a name so that it can be used to query, update, insert, and delete objects from such collections using a name. The creation of a `Transaction` object creates a transaction that the current thread joins. You can also call `join()` on a `Transaction` object passed in from another thread to join the current thread to that transaction. Standard transaction `begin()`, `commit()`, and `abort()` methods also exist on a `Transaction` object.

The ODMG's OQL is to ODBMSs as SQL is to RDBMSs. Calls to `select()`, `selectElement()`, and `query()` on `DCollection` objects can be used to issue queries in a manner much like `SQL SELECT` clauses are formulated. An `Iterator.next()` call can then be used to obtain query results in the form of objects by executing such OQL calls.

RDBMSs Versus ODBMSs

For most enterprise development situations, the question of whether you should use an ODBMS or a RDBMS is usually moot. For one thing, the database to which you must provide connectivity may be a legacy database for which exist many configuration scripts or perhaps much in-house knowledge, or most certainly the product has already been purchased and you have a maintenance/upgrade contract established with the vendor. And even if a legacy database is not already in place, the question of purchasing a new database may still be skewed by political or business factors such as preestablished vendor relationships, previous engineering staff and management product familiarity, or flat-out blind dislike of "new" ODBMS technologies or "old" RDBMS technologies. Regardless of such business, political, or personal realities, it is important to compare and contrast RDBMS and ODBMS technologies from a pure and unbiased technical and economical perspective.

ODBMSs indeed do provide a database platform that more closely maps to the types of object models the Java developer uses. However, replacement of long-lived RDBMSs can be a futile endeavor. Enterprise data is typically plentiful, and converting legacy

RDBMS data into a form exportable by ODBMSs can be time-consuming and can possibly require more effort than would be required by developers' RDBMS-to-OO hand-coding. Furthermore, the enterprise-class capabilities of certain ODBMSs over RDBMSs are still questionable for certain application demands. Projects defining new databases may be in a position to consider ODBMSs but should evaluate vendor offerings very carefully to ensure enterprise-class applicability. Given the relative youth of the current ODBMS standards, such standards will need to be evolved to help ensure vendor portability.

We believe that ODBMSs will be the DBMS of choice in the future when vendor offerings become more suitable to handle the full gamut of enterprise-class applications, as well as when the standards mature enough to the point of helping ensure true cross-platform portability. Most RDBMS vendors have seen this as a potential direction of industry as well and thus have been evolving their back-end architectures appropriately toward supporting the needs of object-oriented (and in particular Java) programming paradigms. A new breed of object/relational hybrid databases and data-mapping products now on the market clearly highlights the trend from relational to object-oriented data modeling.

Java Data Access Technologies

So how does one talk with a DBMS from Java? This section provides a brief overview of those core and underlying technologies that an enterprise Java developer will use in accessing data in a DBMS. Other chapters throughout this book expand on such means for accessing data in much greater detail.

CLIs

A Call Level Interface (CLI) represents a functional call API to a database. CLIs provided for the various RDBMS vendor solutions are often proprietary and have a native SQL API implementation. Typically, C language–based APIs are provided, but bindings for Cobol and FORTRAN are also common. CLI calls can be made directly to an underlying database driver or can be remotely invoked over a network.

The Open Group has specified the X/Open SQL CLI standard for interfacing to databases via a CLI. The X/Open SQL CLI interfaces define function calls at the level of allocating and deallocating system resources, controlling database connections, obtaining database status information, executing dynamic SQL statements, and controlling transactions. The X/Open SQL CLI specification was published as an addendum to the SQL-92 standard and is now also part of the ISO standard. X/Open SQL CLI support for SQL3 features is also being considered.

Embedded SQL

SQLJ offers one standard created by key DBMS industry players such as Oracle, Sybase, and IBM for embedding SQL directly into Java applications. Java source code containing embedded SQL commands is run through a SQLJ preprocessor to generate new Java source code with the appropriate database calls (mainly JDBC calls). During the precompilation process, the SQLJ runtime engine can access the database to determine whether all the tables, columns, and SQL statements are syntactically correct with respect to the database. Certain security restrictions can also be checked at this time. The main utility of SQLJ is that a significant set of SQL errors can be caught at compile time rather than during runtime as with other Java database connectivity solutions such as JDBC.

By embedding SQL directly into a Java program, SQLJ extends the Java API with a whole new set of programming interfaces. Each embedded SQL command in the Java code begins with a `#sql` token. A colon in an embedded SQL statement is placed before a Java variable used as either input or output in a SQL command. A database connection can be created using the expression `#sql context` *`ContextName`*`;`. The context is compiled into a Java class having a set of constructors with arguments used to create database connections. Some vendor solutions also read Java properties files to obtain connection-related information.

Iterators are used to map SQL results from queries into Java objects. Iterators can be defined using the command `#sql [`*`modifiers`*`] iterator` *`IteratorType`* `(`*`colType1`*`, ...,` *`colTypeN`*`);`. Such a form is used to retrieve query result values by an index number in the result set and subsequently map these result values to an associated Java object. Optional Java modifiers such as `static` and `public` can be used to modify the visibility and semantics of the iterator. An iterator of the preceding type is declared using the regular Java variable declaration syntax *`IteratorType myIterator`*. The command `#sql` *`myIterator`* `= {` *`SQL_Command`* `};` is used to populate *`myIterator`* with the result of a query. The mapping of iterator results to a Java object is then accomplished using `#sql {FETCH :` *`myIterator`* `INTO :`*`JavaVar1`*`, ... , :`*`JavaVarN`*`};`. Here, the *`JavaVarX`* values refer to regular Java attributes in a Java class. Iterators can also be defined to retrieve database values by name such as this: `#sql [`*`modifiers`*`] iterator` *`IteratorType`* `(`*`colType1 JavaVar1`*`, ...,` *`colTypeN JavaVarN`*`);`. After declaring your iterator instance and querying the database as before, you can then use regular Java calls such as `myIterator.JavaVarX()` to obtain values from the query result by name.

ODBC

In addition to embedding SQL directly into programs, a more common solution for standard database connectivity involves use of a standard API for making database calls. In an effort to alleviate developers from database vendor dependence and use of vendor-specific database protocols to communicate with databases, Microsoft defined the open database connectivity (ODBC) solution. ODBC is based on SQL/CLI standards and has been widely supported since its introduction.

ODBC applications depend only on the ODBC API and the SQL standard. SQL statements are submitted to ODBC API calls, and results are retrieved using standard ODBC API constructs. The ODBC API is defined in terms of the C programming language. Given the C language dependence, ODBC requires that API libraries be pre-installed on client machines.

The ODBC API communicates with an underlying ODBC driver manager that loads an appropriate ODBC driver as specified by the ODBC API client application. ODBC drivers are code libraries that adhere to a standard ODBC service-provider interface. The ODBC service-provider interface is implemented by ODBC driver vendors to map standard ODBC calls to database-vendor–specific calls. ODBC drivers may call the database directly via a CLI or via some networking protocol.

JDBC

Providing a Java binding for the ODBC API would have required some modifications to the ODBC API because not all C-based constructs (for example, pointers) have decent corresponding Java analogues. Thus, Sun has created the Java Database Connectivity (JDBC) solution as Java's answer to database-vendor interface independence. JDBC provides a database connectivity solution for Java applications just as ODBC provides for C and Microsoft applications. As you'll see in subsequent chapters, JDBC has a basic architecture philosophy similar to the ODBC architecture. That is, JDBC has a standard JDBC API that communicates with a JDBC driver manager that loads JDBC drivers. JDBC drivers implement a JDBC service-provider interface and map standard JDBC calls into database-vendor–specific calls.

To better understand why Sun created a Java-specific database connectivity solution, consider the fact that client-side installs of ODBC API libraries would have made it difficult to run Java anywhere (that is, such as within Web-based applets). Regardless, ODBC was still an attractive database-connectivity solution when JDBC was created, largely due to widespread ODBC driver implementations. To make JDBC a viable Java-based database connectivity solution, Sun created a JDBC-ODBC bridge to solve the temporary problem of JDBC driver unavailability while enabling Java applications to capitalize on the use of ODBC driver availability.

Of all methods for data-enabling your enterprise using Java technologies, JDBC is the preferred solution utilized by the J2EE. For one, in light of the widespread RDBMS database vendor solutions available, JDBC's gearing for RDBMSs makes it a commercial-ready solution. ODBMS databases and Java binding standards are still in their relative enterprise-class infancy. Because ODBC cannot map directly to Java, Java bindings for ODBC are not possible. Because embedded SQL for Java requires a post-compiler and clutters Java code, it is also not as desirable a solution for database connectivity.

Object/relational mapping tools are a very good idea and can off-load much of the model mapping hand-coding work for you. Nevertheless, some object/relational mapping tools are not suitable for use in many enterprise-class applications. Thus, knowledge of JDBC as a solution for interacting with databases is key for any serious enterprise developer and architect. JDBC is by far the most common way to interact with databases, and JDBC drivers exist for most database vendor solutions. Finally, if you are still wondering why understanding JDBC is important, consider the fact that JDBC provides a very rich set of database connectivity features available to Java enterprise applications and is an integral part of the J2EE.

JDO

A Java Data Objects (JDO) standard has been developed via the Java Community Process (`www.jcp.org`) to specify a more object-oriented–based approach to persisting data. JDO follows the same approach as JDBC and ODBC in that the developer uses a standard API and a separate underlying driver handles the actual mapping to a particular database. With JDO, the application developer is offered a way to work directly with the Java business entity objects and allow the translations from objects to database to be specified in a separate fashion. In the case of an RDBMS, a JDO driver implements an object/relational mapping to the particular RDBMS.

JDO is not currently covered beneath the umbrella of J2EE technologies. JDO was also in its relative infancy for usage in an enterprise environment at the time of this book's writing. It is, however, an important standard to watch and to see whether and how it may be integrated with a future J2EE specification. More information on JDO can be found at `http://java.sun.com/products/jdo`.

Conclusions

Clearly, the development of an enterprise system will involve connecting to enterprise data from within your enterprise applications. RDBMSs currently have the most significant market presence of any database architecture. Even though ODBMSs have less presence now, RDBMS vendors are evolving their architectures toward the more object-oriented interfacing needs of enterprise developers. Capitalizing on this shortcoming, object/relational mapping products bridge the gap from relational data models of RDBMS demand to object-oriented models of enterprise applications development demand.

Many database connectivity solutions for DBMSs have been around for some time. SQL CLIs and ODBC represent two approaches and standards for interfacing with DBMSs from non-Java applications. SQLJ offers one means to interface with DBMSs from Java programs, but it requires more overhead in terms of development. The Java Database Connectivity solution is the J2EE-recommended means for enterprise Java data connectivity. Just about every object/relational mapping tool available for Java maps Java objects to JDBC calls. Whether you are using JDBC directly, using an object/relational mapping tool, or creating object/relational mappings yourself, an understanding of JDBC is key for the enterprise Java architect and developer. Chapter 5, "Core JDBC," and Chapter 6, "Advanced JDBC," cover JDBC from the basics to fairly advanced topics to arm you with the knowledge you need to successfully connect your enterprise data to your enterprise Java applications.

3

XML

THE EXTENSIBLE MARKUP LANGUAGE (XML) QUICKLY caught on in the industry as the most widely adopted standard for describing and exchanging data in a platform-, language-, and protocol-independent fashion. XML and its auxiliary specifications are used to describe data representations in the form of XML documents, describe constraints for XML document types, describe links between XML documents and resources, and describe automated transformations and formatting of XML documents. This chapter describes the format of XML documents, and how Document Type Definitions (DTDs) and XML Schema can be used to describe XML document structure and semantics, as well as other core XML standards used in enterprise application development environments. Subsequent chapters in this book describe how J2EE technologies encapsulate such XML standards via APIs that make it easier for the enterprise Java developer to work with XML standards.

In this chapter, you will learn:

- An overview of what XML is and the standards defined to support it.
- The basic structure of well-formed XML documents.
- The structure and usage of a Document Type Definition (DTD) to validate XML documents.
- The structure and usage of XML Schema to validate and define semantic constraints associated with XML documents.
- The basic utility behind the XML Stylesheet Language (XSL) for automated transformations of XML documents, as well as automated formatting of XML documents.
- The basic utility behind the XML Linking Language (XLink) and the XML Pointer Language (XPointer) for linking XML document data to external resources, as well as other XML document data.

Overview of the World of XML

XML is a markup language used to describe how data should be represented. An XML document is a block of data structured according to the rules of XML syntax. As depicted in Figure 3.1, an XML document is often thought of with respect to its transfer between applications. An application sending an XML message may create an XML document directly or utilize a special XML document builder to produce an XML document that is sent over a network in a communications-protocol–independent fashion. A receiving application may then take advantage of an XML parser to parse the XML document stream into a form that can be easily manipulated by the application. The application may be less likely, although it is possible, to parse the document sans any XML parser by reading and interpreting the XML data directly from an I/O stream. A key point to note here is that XML documents can be exchanged between applications regardless of the application's implementation language and host platform. Reiterating the main point here, XML is simply a way to represent data.

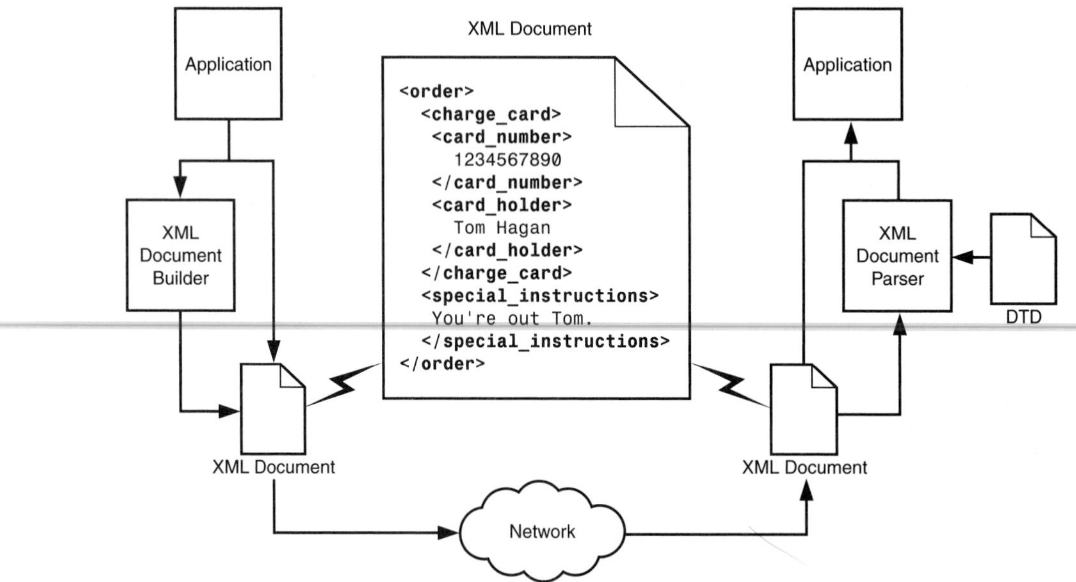

Figure 3.1 Basic XML usage.

In addition to a standard syntax for describing document data representation, a standard way to define the basic structure of a particular type of XML document is also possible via an XML Document Type Definition. A DTD describes the basic structure and rules for particular XML document classifications. Thus, whereas XML document syntax rules are akin to an underlying data serialization format, a DTD is akin to a schema definition of the document data. As an example, the contents of an XML document may contain a hierarchical set of order data in an online e-commerce application, but a DTD defines the standard structure that must be adhered to by an XML document that contains order data.

While DTDs define the basic structure and rules for particular XML document classifications, actual use of DTDs in industry has accentuated a few glaring deficiencies of DTDs to ascribe semantic meaning to XML documents. It is for this reason that a new standard referred to as "XML Schema" has been an important work in progress. XML Schema further imbues semantics into use of XML documents by providing a means to specify constraints for an XML document's constituent parts.

The World Wide Web Consortium (W3C) is the standards body that works to define the syntax of XML documents, DTDs, and XML schemas (`www.w3.org/XML/`). XML is defined as a simplified subset of the more complicated Standard Generalized Markup Language (SGML). XML's markup tag syntax has a similar appearance to HTML, but it provides a much richer, more flexible, and extensible set of language conventions. The W3C also defines a set of supporting standards that augment the capabilities offered by use of XML. These are the most significant W3C standard specifications:

- *eXtensible Markup Language (XML):* Defines the basic syntax of XML and DTDs (`www.w3.org/TR/REC-xml`).
- *XML Schema:* Defines constraints to be evaluated when processing XML documents (`www.w3.org/XML/Schema`).
- *XML Linking Language (XLink):* Defines how resources are referenced from within XML documents (`www.w3.org/TR/xlink/`).
- *XML Pointer Language (XPointer):* Defines a mechanism for addressing different portions of an XML document (`www.w3.org/TR/xptr`).
- *eXtensible Stylesheet Language (XSL):* Defines how XML documents can be transformed into other document types, as well as how XML documents should be formatted (`www.w3.org/TR/xsl`).
- *eXtensible Hypertext Markup Language (XHTML):* Defines HTML v4.0 in terms of an XML application (`www.w3.org/TR/xhtml1`).

Above and beyond the general language-oriented specifications, the W3C also maintains a standard API definition for interfacing with XML documents via the Document Object Model (DOM) specification. An independent industry group has also defined an API model for XML document interfacing known as the Simple API for XML (SAX) standard.

In addition to the broadly defined standards for XML and auxiliary specifications, many other organizations are involved in defining standard DTDs and XML schemas for specific vertical markets. The Organization for the Advancement of Structured Information Standards (OASIS) in particular is involved in promoting the adoption of XML standards within specific industries. In fact, OASIS and the United Nations Centre for Trade Facilitation and Electronic Business (UN/CEFACT) have teamed up to define a suite of XML-based processes specific to eBusiness known as ebXML. Similarly, an organization known as RosettaNet has also defined open eBusiness standards and XML-based eBusiness interaction schemes. Finally, the Java Community Process has defined standard DTDs and XML schemas for use with the J2EE and continues to integrate XML standards into the J2EE platform.

XML Document Structure

Now let's investigate XML in more detail. An XML document is a structured collection of text-based markup tags. Each tag either defines some information used to describe how the document is to be interpreted or describes some data contained within the document. The basic generically described structure and syntax of an XML document is shown here:

```
<?xml version="1.0" encoding="ISO-8859-1" standalone="yes" ?>

<!-- A comment -->

<!-- Begin root document element scope below -->
<RootElement>

  <!-- Begin sub-element scope below -->
  <SubElement1>
    <!-- A sub-element value -->
    SubElement1_Value
  </SubElement1>
  <!-- Close sub-element scope -->

  <!-- Begin sub-element with attributes in tag below -->
  <SubElement2 attribute1="value1" attribute2="value2">
    <!-- Another sub-element value -->
    SubElement2_Value
  </SubElement2>
  <!-- Close another sub-element scope -->

  <!-- Begin another sub-element scope below-->
  <SubElement3>

    <!-- A sub-element value with entity references -->
    &quot; Foo &#38; Bar &CorpAddress; &quot;

    <!-- A processing instruction with data -->
    <?ProcessingInstructionName SomeData MoreData?>
```

```
    <!-- Unparsed character data -->
    <![CDATA[ Don't Parse This Stuff ]]>

  </SubElement3>
  <!-- Close another sub-element scope -->

  <!-- An empty marker element below -->
  <EmptyElement1/>

  <!-- Another empty marker element below -->
  <EmptyElem2></EmptyElem2>

</RootElement>
<!-- Close root document element scope -->
```

> **Note**
>
> Throughout this book, we refer to an example of an e-commerce site called Beeshirts.com. The code samples in this section are excerpts from an XML document that contains the data associated with an order placed on that site. The document contains not only order-related data, but also an ordered item sub-element and a charge-card sub-element.
>
> A collection of sample files associated with this chapter can be located per the instructions in Appendix A, "Software Configuration," and is associated with the `examples\src\ejava\xml` directory. The files in the `examples\src\ejava\jaxp` directory contain a cohesive collection of the XML document snippets used in this chapter.

Comments

Comments represent information useful to someone examining the source document only and are not interpreted by XML tools. Comments are added to XML documents between the `<!--` and `-->` character sequences. Comments can be placed anywhere in the XML document.

Here's an example of a comment:

```
<!-- Definition of order data follows below -->
```

XML Declaration

An XML declaration is added to identify the associated block of data as an XML document. XML declarations are defined between the `<?xml` and `?>` case-sensitive character sequences. The XML standard version number is identified within the declaration using `version="versionNumber"`. Furthermore, the text encoding format of the document can optionally be defined within the declaration using `encoding="encodingFormat"`, and the dependence on any other documents defined external to the current document can also optionally be defined with the declaration using `standalone="yes/no"`. The XML declaration must be the first thing in an XML file, appearing before any other characters, including whitespace.

As an example of a most basic XML declaration, we might have this:

```
<?xml version="1.0"?>
```

Namespaces

The basic concept of a namespace for XML is not much unlike namespaces for other computer science constructs. A namespace used in an XML document simply defines the context within which names are unique. These "names" are used to identify components of the XML document. The "context" is simply another name structure that uniquely identifies a realm of names in a more global space.

To make an analogy, the package names in Java define a namespace for class names. For example, the name `Policy` belongs to a package namespace `java.security` in the J2SE. That name `Policy` also belongs to the `javax.security.auth` and `org.omg.CORBA` package namespaces inside the J2SE v1.4. Without a package namespace context, the name `Policy` would conflict with the other definitions of `Policy` in the J2SE. This desire to avoid naming conflicts is also a key reason for using namespaces in XML as well. In XML, however, the namespace is identified by a URI reference.

Most commonly, a namespace will first be declared in an XML document with the identifier `xmlns`, followed by a colon (`:`), followed by a user-defined identifier, followed by an equal sign (`=`), followed by a quoted URI. For example:

```
xmlns:ati="http://assuredtech.com/schema"
```

Thus, the namespace is defined by the URI `http://assuredtech.com/schema` and associated with the shorthand identifier `ati`. That identifier may then be used in conjunction with various components of the XML document to indicate that those components are defined within that particular namespace. For example, we might see a component in an XML document used as follows:

```
<ati:orderDescription/>
```

This indicates that the element named `orderDescription` belongs to the namespace identified by `ati`. In later sections of this chapter, we will see how to apply the concept of namespaces to elements and attributes of XML documents.

Elements

Container elements contain data values or other XML elements. Elements have a case-sensitive name that is defined within < and > characters, such as `<ElementName>`.

Element boundaries are defined within a start tag, such as `<ElementName>`, and an end tag, such as `</ElementName>`. Element names begin with a letter, underscore (_), or colon (:). Element names are subsequently constructed with letters, numbers, underscores (_), colons (:), hyphens (-), or periods (.). Elements can be nested within one another but cannot overlap. An XML document can have only one root element that contains all other elements.

As an example of a base order element containing order data and a nested order item element, we have this (note that the three dots [. . .] in such snippets is our way of excluding irrelevant detail):

```
<order>
    <order_id> 123 </order_id>
    <customer_id> 101 </customer_id>
    <order_date> 10/19/02 </order_date>
    <ship_instruct>Leave stuff at back door if no answer</ship_instruct>
    <ship_date> 11/10/02 </ship_date>
    <ship_charge> $3.80 </ship_charge>
    <paid_date> 11/01/02 </paid_date>

  <item>
    <item_id> 1001 </item_id>
    <quantity> 10    </quantity>
    <total_price> $78.99 </total_price>
  </item>
    ...
</order>
```

Empty element names are defined within < and /> characters. Empty elements can also be defined within a start tag followed immediately by an end tag with no data between the tags.

For example, adding an empty element to our order data, we might have this:

```
<order>
       ...
  <ship_weight/>
       ...
</order>
```

In addition to the standard context of an XML element, a namespace may be ascribed to an XML element as well. A namespace when used with XML elements is simply a way to provide context for an element much like a package provides context for a class and thus avoid name collisions. Namespaces of XML element context may be separated with colons (:) between each namespace.

For example, we could have first declared two namespaces for our XML document as shown here:

```
<ati:order
           xmlns:ati="http://assuredtech.com/schema"
           xmlns:beeshirts="http://beeshirts.com/b2c"
```

```
>
    ...
</ati:order>
```

Then, we could have referenced various sub-elements of our order element from various namespaces as exemplified here:

```
  <ati:order_id> 123 </ati:order_id>
      ...
  <ati:paid_date> 11/01/02 </ati:paid_date>

  <beeshirts:item>
    <beeshirts:item_id> 1001 </beeshirts:item_id>
      ...
    <beeshirts:total_price> $78.99 </beeshirts:total_price>
  </beeshirts:item>
```

Note that we can leave off the namespace identifier for elements if we want to assume that first namespace defined for that element or its parent is to be used as the default namespace. For example:

```
<order
           xmlns:ati="http://assuredtech.com/schema"
           xmlns:beeshirts="http://beeshirts.com/b2c"
>
  <order_id> 123 </order_id>
      ...
  <paid_date> 11/01/02 </paid_date>

  <beeshirts:item>
    <beeshirts:item_id> 1001 </beeshirts:item_id>
      ...
    <beeshirts:total_price> $78.99 </beeshirts:total_price>
  </beeshirts:item>
</order>
```

Thus, `order`, `order_id`, and `paid_date` in the preceding example are all in the default `ati` namespace.

Attributes

Attributes are name-value pairs associated with elements, and they serve to describe some information about the element. Attributes are defined within the start tag of an element as one or more whitespace-separated sequences of *`name="value"`* pairs. Attribute values must be within quotation marks, and attribute names within the same element start tag must be unique.

As an example, a charge-card sub-element of an order element may define a card type attribute:

```
<order>
             ...
```

```
  <charge_card card_type="credit">
    <card_number> 12345678901234 </card_number>
    <expired_date> 10/10/2004 </expired_date>
    <card_confirmation_number> 0987654321 </card_confirmation_number>
      ...
  </charge_card>
</order>
```

Namespaces of XML attributes may also be separated with colons (:) between each namespace. For example, the attribute `card_type` may be defined to belong to the `beeshirts` namespace as exemplified here:

```
<order
           xmlns:ati="http://assuredtech.com/schema"
           xmlns:beeshirts="http://beeshirts.com/b2c"
>
               ...
  <beeshirts:charge_card beeshirts:card_type="credit">
    <beeshirts:card_number> 12345678901234 </beeshirts:card_number>
      ...
  </beeshirts:charge_card>
</order>
```

Entity References

Entity references are special identifiers and character sequences that refer to a value that is expanded by an XML parser whenever the entity is referenced (in a fashion similar to a C/C++ macro). Certain predefined entity references have special identifiers reserved and are used within the `&` and `;` characters. For example, `&` defines an ampersand, `'` defines an apostrophe, `"` defines a quotation mark, `<` defines a less-than symbol, and `>` defines a greater-than symbol. To reference a special character in an XML document, you can also refer to that character using its Unicode decimal representation between `&#` and `;` characters. Hexadecimal representations of Unicode characters can be defined within `&#x` and `;` characters. For example:

```
<!-- The tilde (~) symbol in hexadecimal and decimal form     -->
<!--                         &#x007E         &#126            -->

<!-- The medical Rx symbol in hexadecimal and decimal form    -->
<!--                         &#x211E         &#8478           -->

<!-- The less than (<) symbol in hexadecimal and decimal form -->
<!--                           &#x003C         &#60           -->
```

A user-defined entity is an XML mechanism that associates an identifier with some user-defined data to be expanded. A user-defined entity reference in an XML document can refer to a user-defined entity with the entity identifier incorporated within `&` and `;` characters. The entity reference acts to replace every instance of an entity reference within an XML document with the data associated with the user-defined entity. An entity must be declared within a DTD before it is referenced. We discuss entity declaration in the next section on DTDs.

For example, if we assume that a set of card-name entities, such as `VISA`, `MC`, and `AMEX`, has been defined in a DTD, our sample charge card may reference one of these entities within a card name as shown here:

```
<order>
              ...
  <charge_card card_type="credit">
    <card_name> &VISA; </card_name>
              ...
  </charge_card>
</order>
```

Processing Instructions

A processing instruction embedded in an XML document can be used by an application to tell it to perform some operation and use some optional data during that operation. A processing instruction is defined within `<?` and `?>` character sequences. Within such a tag, a processing instruction name identifier may be optionally followed by processing instruction parameter data. Processing instruction names should not begin with the reserved word `xml`.

For example, if we assume that our XML order document wants to trigger an external application to validate an order passing in credit-check and check-customer flags, we might have this:

```
<order>
              ...
  <?OrderValidation creditCheck checkCustomer?>
</order>
```

Unparsed Character Data

Because all character data within an XML document is parsed by an XML document parser, a special notation must be used when it is necessary to tell the XML document parser not to parse certain data in the document and pass it directly to an application. Unparsed character data is contained within `<![CDATA[` and `]]>` character sequences. Thus, such CDATA, to which it is often referred, is purposely not parsed but is exposed to the application so that it can read the data.

For example, our charge-card data may want to embed binary data representing a customer signature directly into the document stream as shown here:

```
<order>
              ...
  <charge_card card_type="credit">
              ...
    <card_signature> <![CDATA[0xA72938B72F79C8DE]]> </card_signature>
```

```
  </charge_card>
</order>
```

Well-Formed XML Documents

A document that adheres to the syntax of XML per the XML specification is said to be "well-formed." The basic syntax of an XML document is defined according to the basic formatting rules presented thus far. If a document is not well-formed, it is not considered to be an XML document. Unlike some other markup languages, such as HTML, that have somewhat looser restrictions on syntax, XML requires that documents strictly conform to the rules of the language. In much the same sense that a Java program with syntax errors will not compile, a malformed XML document will not be understood by an application. Thus, the requirements for creating XML documents are more stringent than those for creating HTML documents. Our `dtdAndXmlDocument.xml` file included with this chapter's code is an example of a well-formed XML document, but the lackadaisical fashion in which HTML documents can be specified is not permitted for XML documents. For example, this would not be well-formed XML document body syntax, but a Web browser would read and parse it as HTML correctly:

```
<HTML>
  <BODY>
    <H1>I'll use proper tags here.</H1>
    <H2>Here I will not.
    <H3>But here I will again.</H3>
<!-- I won't close the BODY and HTML tags either -->
```

We make the analogy here between a Java file and an XML file. If you adhere to the syntax rules of Java, you will be able to successfully compile your code. If not, you will receive a compiler error when you attempt to compile such code and will have to fix the syntax errors in your code for it to be well-formed Java source code. Similarly, you will have to fix a syntax error in your XML file for it to be considered a well-formed XML document.

Document Type Definitions (DTDs)

The fact that a document can be defined as a well-formed XML document simply indicates that the document follows the rules of XML syntax. But what about structure? That is, although the sample order document of the preceding section may be a well-formed XML document, what must be the structure of that document? We could just as easily replace the root element name `order` with the name `customer`, and the document would still be a well-formed XML document. But an application that reads such data would certainly want to distinguish between a `customer` and an `order`. After all, a `customer` object may be manipulated by an e-commerce application to maintain customer address information and data for use in delivering an order. An `order` object, on the other hand, may be manipulated to induce the actual order of a set of items and may additionally require that a customer's credit card be associated with the order data.

A Document Type Definition (DTD) is a structured collection of ASCII-based declarations which partially define constraints that apply to a particular type of XML document. More specifically, a DTD is essentially meta-information that defines the required structure and characteristics of an XML document for the document to be considered a valid type of particular XML document. The tags required, relationships among tags, valid attribute values, and named entities are all defined within a DTD.

The basic top-level structure of a DTD with its four types of DTD declarations is shown here:

```
<!DOCTYPE RootElementName SYSTEM "URL" [
  <!--  DTD elements inserted below -->

  <!-- DTD Element Declarations -->
  <!ELEMENT ... >

  <!-- DTD Attribute Declarations -->
  <!ATTLIST ... >

  <!-- DTD Entity Declarations -->
  <!ENTITY ... >

  <!-- DTD Notation Declarations -->
  <!NOTATION ... >

]>
<!-- End Root Element DTD -->
```

DTDs and Semantics

Although some literature seems to indicate otherwise, it should be highlighted that a DTD does not completely define the semantics or meaning of an XML document. However, it does partially define an XML document's meaning by defining the required structure and composition of the document. We'll make another analogy here to clarify this point. Hydrogen (H) atoms and oxygen (O) atoms represent fundamental atomic elements. A molecule, such as water (H_2O), corresponds to a description of a specific structural composition of such atoms. In essence, the symbols H_2O are analogous to a DTD specification, whereas specific instances of water molecules are analogous to XML document instances. The symbols H_2O do indeed convey partial meaning to us as to what water is in terms of its structure. But what water really means to us as human beings is best understood by examining how water is used by the environment external (that is, context) to such molecules. Similarly, the true meaning of an XML document cannot be fully understood by examining a DTD, but rather the meaning will best be understood when analyzing or developing the application environment that is external to such structures and that operates on such structures. Thus, application context for such XML documents in addition to a DTD is key to understanding the semantics or meaning of an XML document.

As a simple first example, suppose that an order management application was designed to assume that any order identifiers it generates and reads uniquely identify an order in that system. Now suppose that a centralized order fulfillment application assumes that an order identifier generated from that order management application and a store identifier are what uniquely identify an order in its context. This may be important to the order fulfillment application because it must deal with many different order management applications. Thus, defining `order_id` as an element in an XML document to uniquely identify an order will depend on the context of applications reading that element.

A slightly more complex example revolves around shipping and handling charges. An order management application may treat shipping charges and handling charges separately, whereas a legacy order fulfillment application assumes that shipping charges are the combination of both handling and shipping charges because their distinction was irrelevant when the order fulfillment application was designed. Very often such gaps in meaning as applied to XML documents need to be dealt with via mechanisms external to DTDs. It is almost as if another layer of interpretation or filtering is applied atop the raw meaning described by a DTD.

Document Type Definition Header

Now that we have a basic understanding of what a DTD is supposed to be, let's begin examining the details of a DTD document itself and how they are used. A DTD, if present, must be declared in the beginning of an XML document after the XML declaration. The root-containing element name for the XML document is used to identify the XML document type for which the DTD defines structure and characteristics. The `<!DOCTYPE` and `>` characters delimit the boundaries of the DTD's definition. A DTD and root element name are thus defined using the following delimiters:

```
<!DOCTYPE RootElementName [...]>
```

A DTD stored at some external URL may also be referenced with a system identifier and utilized by the current DTD using the following general form:

```
<!DOCTYPE RootElementName SYSTEM "SystemURL"[...]>
```

A public identifier may also be used with a system identifier to reference an external DTD. The public identifier may be used by an application to determine the alternative location of the DTD. Otherwise, the application will use the system identifier URL. This is the general form of use for public identifiers with system identifiers:

```
<!DOCTYPE RootElementName PUBLIC "PublicIdentifier" "SystemURL"[...]>
```

Element Declarations

An element declaration within a DTD defines the characteristics of a named element as it should exist within the XML document. Element declarations are defined within `<!ELEMENT` and `>` characters and have one of the following general forms:

- *Empty Content:* The named element is defined to have no content and is therefore an empty element if it has this form:

  ```
  <!ELEMENT ElementName EMPTY>
  ```

- *Any Content:* The named element is defined to have any content, and therefore the DTD allows any content defined for the named element if it has the following form:

  ```
  <!ELEMENT ElementName ANY>
  ```

- *Content Model:* A particular content model is defined to constrain the contents of the named element with an appended question mark (?) designating that the model is optional, an appended asterisk (*) designating that the model may contain zero or more of the model elements, and an appended plus symbol (+) designating that the model may contain one or more of the model elements. The basic format for the content model is this:

  ```
  <!ELEMENT ElementName (exactly_one_content_model)>
                <!-- OR -->
  <!ELEMENT ElementName (optional_content_model)?>
                <!-- OR -->
  <!ELEMENT ElementName (zero_or_more_content_model)*>
                <!-- OR -->
  <!ELEMENT ElementName (one_or_more_content_model)+>
  ```

The content model definition within an element declaration itself has various valid formats and may employ the following format conventions:

- A single element, such as `SubElement`, can be defined to indicate that an element contains one other element:

  ```
  <!ELEMENT ElementName (SubElement)>
  ```

- Commas between named elements indicate that the elements must be contained in the sequence specified:

  ```
  <!ELEMENT ElementName (SubElement1, SubElement2, SubElement3)>
  ```

- A plus symbol (+) can be used to indicate that an element contains one or more elements named `SubElement`:

  ```
  <!ELEMENT ElementName (SubElement+)>
  ```

- An asterisk (*) can be used to indicate that an element contains zero or more elements named `SubElement`:

  ```
  <!ELEMENT ElementName (SubElement*)>
  ```

- A question mark (?) can be used to indicate that an element optionally contains an element named *SubElement*:

```
<!ELEMENT ElementName (SubElement?)>
```

- Optional character data within an element that can be parsed is indicated as shown here:

```
<!ELEMENT ElementName (#PCDATA)*>
```

- An OR relation symbol (|) can be used to indicate that zero or more elements (as well as possibly parsed character data) can be contained within an enclosing element:

```
<!ELEMENT ElementName (#PCDATA | SubElement1 | SubElement2)*>
```

Notation Declarations

A notation declaration is used to define a specific type of data external to an XML document. A named data type is associated with a data type value. The format for a notation declaration follows this form:

```
<!NOTATION DataTypeName SYSTEM "DataTypeValue">
```

Entity Declarations

An entity declaration is used to associate an entity name with data. Entity declarations are defined within `<!ENTITY` and `>` characters and have the following basic forms:

- *Internal Entity:* A defined entity name can be associated with some data value that is used in an XML document to replace each user-defined entity reference of the form `&EntityName;` with the *EntityDataValue*. The internal entity declaration has the following form:

```
<!ENTITY EntityName "EntityDataValue">
```

- *External XML Entity:* A defined entity name can be associated with an XML document defined at some external URL to replace each entity reference of the form `&EntityName;` with the XML document at the URL. The external XML document entity is parsed when read. The external XML entity declaration has this form:

```
<!ENTITY EntityName SYSTEM "URL">
```

- *External Binary Entity:* A defined entity name can be associated with a binary block of data defined at some external URL to replace each entity reference of the form `&EntityName;` with the binary data defined at the URL of the data type defined in a data type name. For example, if the data type name has a defined value of

GIF87A, a GIF file may be referenced at the URL. The external binary entity is not parsed by the XML parser and may only be referenced in an element's attribute. The external binary entity declaration has this form:

```
<!ENTITY EntityName SYSTEM "URL" NDATA DataTypeName>
```

- *Parameter Entity:* A defined DTD entity name can be associated with a value that is used only within a DTD (as opposed to an XML document). The DTD entity name is preceded by a percent sign (%) and is referenced within the DTD using %*DTDEntityName*; to expand the entity to its associated entity data value within the DTD. The parameter entity has the following form:

```
<!ENTITY % DTDEntityName "DTDEntityDataValue">
```

Attribute Declarations

Attribute declarations define the characteristics of attributes that are associated with a named element. The attribute name along with an attribute type and default value may all be specified for an attribute. One or more attributes can be characterized within <!ATTLIST and > characters according to this general form:

```
<!ATTLIST ElementName
  AttributeName1 AttributeType1 DefaultAttributeValue1
  AttributeName2 AttributeType2 DefaultAttributeValue2
                           ...
  AttributeNameN AttributeTypeN DefaultAttributeValueN
  >
```

Each attribute associated with a named element, such as *ElementName*, must be identified by its name, such as *AttributeName1* and *AttributeName2*. The attribute type may be defined according to one of the following general forms:

- *Identifiers:* An ID attribute value is an identifier that is unique throughout an XML document. Only one ID attribute can exist per element.
- *Identifier References:* An IDREF attribute value refers to an ID attribute value elsewhere in an XML document. An IDREFS attribute value refers to one or more whitespace-separated ID attribute values in the document.
- *Entities:* An ENTITY attribute value must be the name of an entity. ENTITIES are whitespace-separated ENTITY values.
- *Character Data:* A CDATA attribute value is a string of text that may be expanded from embedded markup data in the string.
- *Name Tokens:* An NMTOKEN attribute value is a single string word with no expanded markup data in the string. NMTOKENS are whitespace-separated NMTOKEN values.
- *Enumerated Types:* An enumerated type can define the set of valid values that an attribute may assume within parentheses. Value options are separated within the

parentheses by an `OR` symbol (|). For example: `(Value1 | Value2 | Value3)`.

Default attribute values are defined according to one of the following general forms:

- *Required Values:* An attribute must have a defined value in the document if the `#REQUIRED` identifier is defined as the default value.
- *Implied Values:* An attribute does not need to have a defined value in the document if the `#IMPLIED` identifier is defined as the default value.
- *Defined Default Values:* An attribute value will have the default value defined between quotation marks, such as `"AttributeValue"`, if a value is not defined in the document.
- *Fixed Values:* An attribute value does not need to be defined but must have the fixed value defined within quotation marks in the expression `#FIXED "AttributeValue"`.

Valid XML Documents

A valid XML document is one that satisfies the rules defined within the DTD. This, of course, presumes that both the XML document and the DTD have a well-formed syntax. Validity may apply to only the declarations defined within the XML document, to both external and internal declarations, or to none at all.

DTD Example

In this section, we present a concrete example of a DTD that can be used to validate an XML order document. Note that we have a `DOCTYPE` header at the top of our XML order document instance to reference a DTD defined externally at a URL. Here, the URL simply references an `order.dtd` file presumed to be in the current working directory. The `dtdAndXmlDocument.xml` file contains a reference to the external `order.dtd` file and must designate that the XML document no longer stands alone in the XML declaration. The `dtdAndXmlDocument.xml` file is shown in Listing 3.1.

> **Note**
>
> All the example XML files, schemas, and DTDs shown in this chapter may be obtained by following the instructions in Appendix A and will be extracted to the `examples/src/ejava/jaxp` directory.

Listing 3.1 **XML Order Document with DTD Reference** (`dtdAndXmlDocument.xml`)

```
<?xml version="1.0" standalone="no"?>

<!-- DTD of Order Document follows below -->
<!DOCTYPE order SYSTEM "file:order.dtd">
```

Listing 3.1 **Continued**

```
<!-- Definition of order data follows below -->
<order>
    <order_id> 123 </order_id>
    <customer_id> 101 </customer_id>
    <order_date> 10/19/02 </order_date>
    <ship_instruct>Leave stuff at back door if no answer</ship_instruct>
    <ship_date> 11/10/02 </ship_date>
    <ship_charge> $3.80 </ship_charge>
    <paid_date> 11/01/02 </paid_date>
    <ship_weight/>
    <item>
        <item_id> 1001 </item_id>
        <quantity> 10 </quantity>
        <total_price> $78.99 </total_price>
    </item>
    <charge_card card_type="credit">
        <card_name> &VISA; </card_name>
        <card_number> 12345678901234 </card_number>
        <expired_date> 10/10/2004 </expired_date>
        <card_confirmation_number> 0987654321</card_confirmation_number>
        <card_signature>
            <![CDATA[0xA72938B72F79C8DE]]>
        </card_signature>
    </charge_card>
    <?OrderValidation creditCheck checkCustomer?>
</order>
```

Listing 3.2 presents our sample `order.dtd` DTD file used to validate an order XML document, such as the one in our `dtdAndXmlDocument.xml` file. Note first that we've defined top-level element content models for an `order`, an `item`, and a `charge_card`. Note that the order element contains both the `item` and the `charge_card` element. The `card_signature` element in our `charge_card` element is optional.

We've also defined entities for `VISA`, `MC`, and `AMEX` credit-card strings, as well as a parameter entity for `PD` that is referenced within the `charge_card` element definition. Most entities have parseable data values identified by the `#PCDATA` type. A couple of key things should also be noted about the elements within the order document. The `ship_weight` element within our `order` element optionally has content. Finally, note that our `charge_card` element has a required `card_type` attribute.

Listing 3.2 **XML Order DTD** (`order.dtd`)

```
<!-- Define Top-Level Element for order -->
<!ELEMENT order (order_id, customer_id, order_date, ship_instruct,
                 ship_date, ship_charge, paid_date, ship_weight, item,
```

Listing 3.2 **Continued**

```
                charge_card )>
<!ELEMENT item (item_id, quantity, total_price)>
<!ELEMENT charge_card (card_name, card_number, expired_date,
                      card_confirmation_number, card_signature?)>

<!-- Define entities -->
<!ENTITY VISA "Visa Credit Card">
<!ENTITY MC "Master Card Credit Card">
<!ENTITY AMEX "American Express Credit Card">
<!ENTITY % PD "(#PCDATA)">

<!-- Define Elements for order -->
<!ELEMENT order_id (#PCDATA)>
<!ELEMENT customer_id (#PCDATA)>
<!ELEMENT order_date (#PCDATA)>
<!ELEMENT ship_instruct (#PCDATA)>
<!ELEMENT ship_date (#PCDATA)>
<!ELEMENT ship_charge (#PCDATA)>
<!ELEMENT paid_date (#PCDATA)>
<!ELEMENT ship_weight (#PCDATA)*>

<!-- Define Elements for Item -->
<!ELEMENT item_id (#PCDATA)>
<!ELEMENT quantity (#PCDATA)>
<!ELEMENT total_price (#PCDATA)>

<!-- Define elements for charge card and use PD entity -->
<!ELEMENT card_type %PD;>
<!ELEMENT card_name %PD;>
<!ELEMENT card_number %PD;>
<!ELEMENT expired_date %PD;>
<!ELEMENT card_confirmation_number %PD;>
<!ELEMENT card_signature %PD;>

<!-- define attributes for charge_card -->
<!ATTLIST charge_card card_type CDATA  #REQUIRED>
```

XML Schema

An XML schema is a document (an XML document, in fact) that is used to describe the structure and certain semantics of an XML document. It is a replacement for DTDs. It provides a much richer and extensible system for describing the required structure of an XML document than does the DTD standard. Furthermore, because XML schemas are themselves created as XML documents, you are not required to learn a new syntax like you are required when learning DTD syntax. However, although the syntax for XML schemas is the same as that for XML documents, an XML schema has a very large range of specific components that are required to be understood when working with them. It is in fact because of its richness and extensibility that XML Schema is a fairly difficult and complicated standard to grasp.

This section is by no means a comprehensive and in-depth study of XML Schema. Rather, the intention of this section is to convey to the reader what XML schemas are, how to create them, and how to interpret them. The goal here is to arm you with the capability to understand XML Schema enough so that you can be proficient when working with XML schemas as you encounter them in your Java enterprise development efforts.

Much like XML documents are associated with a DTD by an appropriate header reference in the XML document, XML documents are associated with XML schemas with the referencing mechanism defined in the next section. An XML schema validator is used to parse the XML schema and ensure that the XML document associated with the XML schema is a valid XML document conforming to that schema. This section describes the basic structure of XML schemas and how they can be created and associated with XML documents. Validation of XML documents against XML schemas can be performed using an XML schema validator on examples in this section and the next chapter on JAXP.

Naming and Referencing XML Schemas

To stipulate that an XML document conforms to a particular schema, one needs a way to refer to that XML schema from within an XML document. Only a few things must be taken into consideration when referring to XML schemas. Namespaces for schemas must first be considered so that the correct schema can be referenced. Then there is the matter of understanding the syntax used for actually referring to the schema from within an XML document. Finally, mechanisms also exist for including, importing, and redefining schemas. This section describes all of these important initial considerations when working with XML schemas.

> **Note**
>
> To better illustrate the concepts within this chapter, snippets of XML schemas and associated XML documents will be presented as their individual component parts become relevant. Many of the examples list a snippet of an XML schema, followed by a snippet of an XML document which relates to that schema.

Namespaces for XML Schemas

Earlier in this chapter, we described the concept of namespaces for elements and attributes of an XML document. Note, however, that there was no namespace to be associated with the types defined inside of a DTD. XML Schema, on the other hand, does allow you to define namespaces for the type names defined inside of the schema. To begin with, because an XML schema is itself an XML document, it is declared to belong to a particular namespace, namely the XML schema namespace. Thus, an XML schema has an outermost element defined as exemplified here:

```
<?xml version="1.0"?>
<xsd:schema xmlns:xsd="http://www.w3.org/2001/XMLSchema">
    ...
</xsd:schema>
```

Thus, the preceding XML schema is defined to belong to the standard W3C namespace `http://www.w3.org/2001/XMLSchema` as identified with the conventional `xsd` identifier. Thus, all standard components of the W3C standard XML Schema are prefixed with the conventional `xsd` identifier and indicate that each such component belongs to the W3C standard XML Schema namespace.

While the vocabulary of the XML schema definition itself is defined by the `xsd` namespace, the vocabulary for user-defined types that compose an XML schema is associated with another namespace. This namespace is referred to as the target namespace and is declared at the beginning of the XML schema document as exemplified here:

```
<xsd:schema
    xmlns:xsd="http://www.w3.org/2001/XMLSchema"
    xmlns="http://www.beeshirts.com/schema"
    targetNamespace="http://www.beeshirts.com/schema"
>
    ...
</xsd:schema>
```

The preceding declaration indicates that the elements defined inside of this schema belong to the `http://www.beeshirts.com/schema` namespace by default. If we want to identify multiple namespaces within a schema or refer to the target namespace using an identifier, we can declare a namespace identifier that matches the target namespace URI as exemplified here:

```
<xsd:schema
    xmlns:xsd="http://www.w3.org/2001/XMLSchema"
    xmlns:beeshirts="http://www.beeshirts.com/schema"
    targetNamespace="http://www.beeshirts.com/schema"
>
    ...
</xsd:schema>
```

By default, any XML documents that conform to the XML schema previously defined do not require elements or attributes that are explicitly qualified with this schema's namespace. However, if the syntax

```
<xsd:schema
    xmlns:xsd="http://www.w3.org/2001/XMLSchema"
    xmlns:beeshirts="http://www.beeshirts.com/schema"
    xmlns:ati="http://www.assuredtech.com/schema"
```

```
    targetNamespace="http://www.beeshirts.com/schema"
    elementFormDefault="qualified"
    attributeFormDefault="qualified"
>
    ...
</xsd:schema>
```

is used, then the XML document conforming to this schema must have elements and attributes that are qualified with this schema's namespace identifier. That is, for example, if an element named `order` is defined inside this schema that requires elements to be `qualified`, then an XML document instance reference to that `order` type must be prefixed as such: `beeshirts:order`. Note also that the namespace `http://www.assuredtech.com/schema` may also be used within this schema when pre-pending user-defined schema components with the `ati` identifier.

Referencing XML Schemas from XML Documents

How does an XML document declare that it conforms to an XML schema? The XML document must declare that its elements used come from a particular namespace. This may be accomplished via an identified namespace as exemplified here:

```
<?xml version="1.0"?>
<order xmlns:beeshirts="http://www.beeshirts.com/schema">
    ...
</order>
```

Or it may be accomplished via a namespace with no identifier, and thus the declared namespace is the default for the document as exemplified here:

```
<?xml version="1.0"?>
<order xmlns="http://www.beeshirts.com/schema">
    ...
</order>
```

An XML document may also define a mapping between a schema namespace location and a corresponding XML schema document at that location, and declare that the syntax used to reference an XML schema uses the standard W3C schema referencing syntax. An example best illustrates this point. Imagine first that the `beeshirts` schema is stored at `http://www.beeshirts.com/schema` and in the schema named `order.xsd`. An XML document wanting to conform to this schema type would declare itself as such:

```
<?xml version="1.0"?>
<order
      xmlns="http://www.beeshirts.com/schema"
      xmlns:xsi="http://www.w3.org/2001/XMLSchema-instance"
      xsi:schemaLocation="http://www.beeshirts.com/schema
                          http://www.beeshirts.com/schema/order.xsd"
>
    ...
</order>
```

The default namespace for this XML document is thus defined to be `http://www.beeshirts.com/schema`, the standard W3C schema referencing syntax is declared via `xmlns:xsi="http://www.w3.org/2001/XMLSchema-instance"`, and the location to find the `http://www.beeshirts.com/schema` namespace is defined to exist at `http://www.beeshirts.com/schema/order.xsd` using the standard `xsi:schemaLocation` identifier.

> **Note**
>
> Note that a parser using an XML schema validator will use the `schemaLocation` mapping defined in an XML document only if your application does not tell it otherwise. That is, if your server application instructs your XML parser and schema validator to utilize schemas defined at some other location, the `schemaLocation` directive in the XML document will be ignored. Actually, it should be ignored as a matter of security.

When an XML schema is defined without associating elements to a namespace, the XML schema is defined without a `targetNamespace`. This simply means that all the elements defined in this schema will be used only in this type of document, and cannot be included in other schemas. XML instance documents that want to conform to that XML schema may then declare that no schema location is defined, using this syntax example:

```
<order
      xmlns:xsi="http://www.w3.org/2001/XMLSchema-instance"
      xsi:noNamespaceSchemaLocation
                ="http://www.beeshirts.com/schema/order.xsd"
>
   ...
</order>
```

Include, Import, and Redefine

Special elements also exist that allow you to utilize other components from other schemas in your schema. A special `include` element lets you use components from other schemas in the same namespace as your schema. The common general form of `include` is

```
<xsd:include schemaLocation="SomeSchemaURI"/>
```

where *`SomeSchemaURI`* is the URI for the schema with a component that you want to include. For example:

```
<?xml version="1.0" encoding="UTF-8"?>
<xsd:schema targetNamespace="http://www.beeshirts.com/schemas"
          xmlns:xsd="http://www.w3.org/2001/XMLSchema"
          xmlns:beeshirts="http://www.beeshirts.com/schemas"
          elementFormDefault="qualified">
     <xsd:include schemaLocation="order.xsd"/>
```

```
<xsd:include schemaLocation="dispatcher.xsd"/>
<xsd:include schemaLocation="delivery-information.xsd"/>
```

When accessing schemas from different namespaces, a special `import` element can be used. The common general form of `import` is

```
<xsd:import namespace="SomeNamespaceURI" schemaLocation="SomeSchemaURI"/>
```

where *`SomeSchemaURI`* is the URI for the schema with a component from *`SomeNamespaceURI`* that you want to import. For example:

```
<xsd:schema targetNamespace="http://www.beeshirts.com/schemas"
           xmlns:xsd="http://www.w3.org/2001/XMLSchema"
           xmlns:beeshirts="http://www.beeshirts.com/schemas"
           xmlns:dispatchers="http://www.ups.com/dispatchers"
           xmlns:suppliers="http://www.suppliers.com/suppliers"
           elementFormDefault="qualified">
    <xsd:import namespace="http://www.beeshirts.com/schemas"
               schemaLocation="order.xsd"/>
    <xsd:import namespace="http://www.ups.com/dispatchers"
               schemaLocation="dispatcher.xsd"/>
    <xsd:import namespace="http://www.suppliers.com/suppliers"
               schemaLocation="delivery-information.xsd"/>
```

Now suppose that you want to include an element from another schema, but add slightly to its structure. This is called redefining. The general form of a redefine element is as follows:

```
<xsd:redefine schemaLocation="SomeSchemaURI">
   RedefinedDataTypes
</xsd:redefine>
```

As an example of a base type, consider the following:

```
<?xml version="1.0"?>
<xsd:schema targetNamespace="http://www.beeshirts.com/schemas"
            xmlns="http://www.beeshirts.com/schemas"
            xmlns:xsd="http://www.w3.org/2001/XMLSchema"
            elementFormDefault="qualified">

    <xsd:complexType name="item">
        <xsd:sequence>
            <xsd:element name="item_id" type="xsd:long"/>
            <xsd:element name="quantity" type="xsd:int"/>
            <xsd:element name="total_price" type="xsd:double"/>
        </xsd:sequence>
    </xsd:complexType>
</xsd:schema>
```

And here is an example of a redefined type:

```
<?xml version="1.0"?>
<xsd:schema targetNamespace="http://www.beeshirts.com/schemas"
            xmlns:xsd="http://www.w3.org/2001/XMLSchema"
            xmlns="http://www.beeshirts.com/schemas"
            elementFormDefault="qualified">

    <xsd:redefine schemaLocation="item.xsd">
        <xsd:complexType name="item">
          <xsd:complexContent>
            <xsd:extension base="item">
              <xsd:sequence>
                <xsd:element name="shirt_size" type="xsd:string"/>
                <xsd:element name="shirt_color" type="xsd:string"/>
              </xsd:sequence>
            </xsd:extension>
          </xsd:complexContent>
        </xsd:complexType>
    </xsd:redefine>

    <xsd:element name="order_item" type="item"/>
</xsd:schema>
```

And here is a sample snippet of a corresponding XML document:

```
<?xml version="1.0"?>
<order_item xmlns="http://www.beeshirts.com/schemas"
            xmlns:xsi="http://www.w3.org/2001/XMLSchema-instance"
            xsi:schemaLocation="http://www.beeshirts.com redefine.xsd">
    <item_id>1001</item_id>
    <quantity>12</quantity>
    <total_price>90.88</total_price>
    <shirt_size> XL </shirt_size>
    <shirt_color> BLACK </shirt_color>
</order_item>
```

Core Components of XML Schemas

There are a few fundamental components involved in the creation of most XML schemas. Of these components, the means for defining elements and attributes to be included inside XML documents is obviously of central importance. Furthermore, a means for defining annotation comments and notations is also a key consideration. This section defines how such fundamental components are specified in XML schemas, as well as providing examples of such components.

Elements

Elements of XML documents are declared inside of XML schemas using XML schema element declarations. The general form for such declaration is

```
<xsd:element SomeAttributes />
```

for elements with no content, or in the form

```
<xsd:element SomeAttributes > SomeContent </xsd:element>
```

for elements with content.

In addition to user-defined attributes of an element, a standard set of attributes may be used to further describe the element. Many of these standard attributes will be described in subsequent sections, but a few basic attributes are described here:

- A name for the element

  ```
  <xsd:element name="order" ... >
  ```

  that is referenced in an XML document:

  ```
  <order> ... </order>
  ```

- Reference to an element definition within the same or another schema is accomplished via a `ref` attribute. If no namespace is associated with the `ref` value, the default namespace for that schema is assumed; otherwise, another namespace may be referenced as shown here:

  ```
  <xsd:element ref="beeshirts:order"...>
  ```

- A type for the element

  ```
  <xsd:element ... type="xsd:string" ... >
  ```

  that is used to assign a type to the element. We'll see specific examples of types later in this chapter.

- A minimum (default is 1) and/or maximum (default is 1) number of occurrences for the element in an associated XML document:

  ```
  <xsd:element ... minOccurs="0" maxOccurs="unbounded" ... >
  ```

- A default element value string

  ```
  <xsd:element name="cardName"... default="VISA" ...>
  ```

  such that when referenced in an XML document, if the element is empty, the default value is assumed.

- A fixed element value string

  ```
  <xsd:element name="cardName"... fixed="VISA" ...>
  ```

  such that when referenced in an XML document, the fixed value is always assumed and no other value is possible.

- An indication as to whether the element must be `qualified` with a namespace prefix, or `unqualified` (the default case) in an associated XML document:

  ```
  <xsd:element ... form="qualified" ...>
  ```

- An indication as to whether the element is allowed to take an empty ("nil") value:

```
<xsd:element name="orderPrefix"... nillable="true" ...>
```

- Nillable elements in an XML document may thus have no value (similar to `null` Java values) and indicate this by setting an attribute `xsi:nil="true"`:

```
<orderPrefix xsi:nil="true"/>
```

If elements in an XML schema are defined immediately within the scope of `<xsd:schema ...> ... </xsd:schema>`, those elements are considered global elements. Global elements can be referenced within the same schema and by other schemas. Local elements are those defined inside of the scope of other elements aside from `xsd:schema`. Local elements cannot be referenced by the same or other schemas. Thus, given the snippet

```
<?xml version="1.0"?>
<xsd:schema xmlns:xsd="http://www.w3.org/2001/XMLSchema">
  <xsd:element name="order" ... >
     ...
     <xsd:element name="orderType" ... />
     ...
  </xsd:element>
  <xsd:element name="orderAddress"... >
    ...
  </xsd:element>
</xsd:schema>
```

the `order` and `orderAddress` elements are global and can be referenced (that is, reused) within this same or other schemas. However, the `orderType` element is local to the `order` element and thus is not a candidate for reuse within this or other schemas.

Attributes

Attributes of XML documents are declared inside of XML schemas using XML schema attribute declarations. The general form for such declaration is

```
<xsd:attribute SomeAttributes />
```

for attributes with no content, or in the form

```
<xsd:attribute SomeAttributes > SomeContent </xsd:attribute>
```

for attributes with content. Attributes are associated with element declarations and are defined after the main components of the element declaration. For example:

```
  <xsd:element name="order" ... >
     ...
     <xsd:element name="orderType" ... />
     ...
     <xsd:attribute ... > ... </xsd:attribute>
  </xsd:element>
```

In addition to user-defined attributes of a schema attribute, a standard set of attributes may be used to further describe the attribute. The majority of these attributes follow the same convention as those in the element declaration just discussed. Specifically, they are as listed here:

- A name for the attribute

  ```
  <xsd:element name="creditCard" ... >
        ...
      <xsd:attribute name="cardName" ... />
        ...
  </xsd:element>
  ```

  that is referenced in an XML document:

  ```
  <creditCard cardName="VISA" ...> ... </creditCard>
  ```

- Reference to an attribute definition within the same or another schema through the `ref` attribute. If no namespace is associated with the `ref` value, the default namespace for that schema is assumed; otherwise, another namespace may be referenced as shown here:

  ```
  <xsd:attribute ref="beeshirts:cardName".../>
  ```

- A type for the attribute

  ```
  <xsd:attribute ... type="xsd:string" ... />
  ```

  that is used to ascribe a type to the attribute. We'll see specific examples of types later in this chapter.

- A default attribute value string

  ```
  <xsd:attribute name="cardName"... default="VISA" ...>
  ```

  such that when referenced in an XML document, if the attribute is empty, the default value is assumed.

- A fixed attribute value string

  ```
  <xsd:attribute name="cardName"... fixed="VISA" ...>
  ```

  such that when referenced in an XML document, the fixed value is always assumed and no other value is possible.

- An indication as to whether the attribute must be `qualified` with a namespace prefix, or `unqualified` (the default case) in an associated XML document:

  ```
  <xsd:attribute ... form="qualified" ...>
  ```

- An optional indication of how the attribute is to be used in terms of whether it is `optional`, `required`, or `prohibited`:

  ```
  <xsd:attribute ... use="required" ...>
  ```

If attributes in an XML schema are defined immediately within the scope of `<xsd:schema ...> ... </xsd:schema>`, those attributes are considered global attributes. Global attributes can be referenced within the same schema and by other schemas. Local attributes are those defined inside of the scope of other attributes aside from `xsd:schema`. Local attributes cannot be referenced by the same or other schemas.

Annotations

Annotations in XML schema provide documentation for the schema that can be useful to humans as well as applications. The general form of an `annotation` element is

```
<xsd:annotation>
  <xsd:appinfo> ... </xsd:appinfo>
  <xsd:documentation> .. </xsd:documentation>
</xsd:annotation>
```

where information inserted between the `appinfo` elements represents well-formed XML documentation useable by applications, and information between the `documentation` elements is string information presentable to humans.

For example:

```
<?xml version="1.0"?>
<xsd:schema xmlns:xsd="http://www.w3.org/2001/XMLSchema"
            elementFormDefault="qualified">
    <xsd:element name="order">
      <xsd:annotation>
        <xsd:documentation>
          order is the root element for the order schema
        </xsd:documentation>
      </xsd:annotation>
    </xsd:element>
</xsd:schema>
```

There are a few other simple notes about annotations. For one, annotations can be used throughout an XML schema but are generally located before or after global elements or at the beginning of global elements.

It should also be noted that an optional source attribute may also be associated with an `appinfo` and `documentation` element to indicate a URI where more information may be found.

Notations

"Annotations" in XML Schema are not to be confused with "notations." XML Schema `notation` elements are similar to `NOTATION` elements in DTDs. That is, the `notation` element helps define a specific type of data type value according to the common general form

```
<xsd:notation name="NotationName"
    public="IdentifierURI" system="LocationURI"/>
```

where *IdentifierURI* is a URI for the type of data defined and *LocationURI* is a URI for the location of that data. For example:

```
<?xml version="1.0" encoding="UTF-8"?>
<xsd:schema xmlns:xsd="http://www.w3.org/2001/XMLSchema"
            elementFormDefault="qualified"
            attributeFormDefault="unqualified">

    <xsd:notation name="gif" public="image/gif"
                  system="Imageviewer.exe "/>
    <xsd:notation name="jpeg" public="image/jpeg"
                  system="imageviewer.exe "/>

    <xsd:simpleType name="imageType">
      <xsd:restriction base="xsd:NOTATION">
        <xsd:enumeration value="gif"/>
        <xsd:enumeration value="jpeg"/>
      </xsd:restriction>
    </xsd:simpleType>

    <xsd:complexType name="scannedSignature">
      <xsd:attribute name="imageType" type="imageType" use="required"/>
    </xsd:complexType>

    <xsd:element name="recordedAgreement"
                 type="scannedSignature"
                 minOccurs="0"/>
</xsd:schema>
```

Here is a sample snippet of a corresponding XML document:

```
<?xml version="1.0"?>
<recordedAgreement
    xmlns:xsi="http://www.w3.org/2001/XMLSchema-instance"
    xsi:noNamespaceSchemaLocation="notation.xsd"
    imageType="gif"/>
```

Facets of XML Schema Components

XML Schema features a sophisticated type system. A data type in XML Schema is defined by the values it may assume (value space), by the set of lexical representations it may assume (lexical space), and by a set of characteristics or constraints (facets) for the value space.

Facets are perhaps of primary importance to developers when trying to understand XML schema data types. Facets define those characteristics or constraints for the space of values that may be assumed by a particular data type. For example, you may have a string data type that you want to use to represent Social Security numbers. A facet of a newly defined "Social Security number" type may attempt to impose an order to the string such that the string assumes a value like "*nnn-nnn-nnnn*" where *n* is a number between 0 and 9.

Although we describe types in more detail in subsequent sections, it is useful not only to understand the basic concept of facets but also to understand their general format when described inside of XML schemas. This general form is as shown here:

```
<xsd:SomeFacetName
    value="SomeFacetValue"
    fixed="TrueOrFalse"
/>
```

A facet with some `SomeFacetName` will thus have `SomeFacetValue`. Some facets may have an attribute that indicates whether it is a `fixed` value ("`true`") or not ("`false`").

The built-in facets are defined here:

- `length` is used to define the number of units in length for the units inside of a particular data type:

  ```
  <xsd:length value="64"/>
  ```

- `minLength` and `maxLength` are used to define the minimum and maximum number of units in length for the units inside of a particular data type, respectively:

  ```
  <xsd:minLength value="1"/>
  <xsd:maxLength value="1000"/>
  ```

- `totalDigits` is a positive number indicating the maximum number of digits in length allowed for the digits inside a decimal data type:

  ```
  <xsd:totalDigits value="10"/>
  ```

- `fractionDigits` is a non-negative number indicating the maximum number of digits in length allowed for the digits inside the fractional part of a decimal data type:

  ```
  <xsd:fractionDigits value="2"/>
  ```

- `enumeration` establishes the valid set of values allowed to be assumed by a particular data type:

  ```
  <xsd:enumeration value="red"/>
  <xsd:enumeration value="green"/>
  <xsd:enumeration value="blue"/>
  ```

- `minInclusive` and `maxInclusive` are used to define the minimum and maximum values, including those values that may be assumed for a particular data type, respectively:

  ```
  <xsd:minInclusive value="-128"/>
  <xsd:maxInclusive value="127"/>
  ```

- `minExclusive` and `maxExclusive` are used to define the minimum and maximum values, excluding those values, that may be assumed for a particular data type, respectively:

```
<xsd:minExclusive value="-129"/>
<xsd:maxExclusive value="128"/>
```

- `whiteSpace` normalizes string values replacing tabs, line feeds, and carriage returns with spaces when `value="replace"`; normalizes strings and collapses multiple spaces to single spaces when `value="collapse"`; and does not normalize at all when `value="preserve"`:

```
<xsd:whiteSpace value="preserve"/>
<xsd:whiteSpace value="replace"/>
<xsd:whiteSpace value="collapse"/>
```

- `pattern` defines a regular expression that constrains the value space for a particular data type:

```
<xsd:pattern value="[A-Z]"/>
```

Of all the facets defined in the preceding text, the `pattern` facet stands out as both the most complicated and often the most useful. A regular expression is a sequence of characters that can be used to define a set of valid value combinations that may be assumed by a particular data type.

The most important aspects of regular expressions used in XML schemas are outlined here:

- *Regular Characters:* Letters and digits are atomic regular expressions that may be matched:

```
<xsd:pattern value="Java"/>
```

- *Escaped Characters:* Meta-characters that have meaning in regular expressions and other characters such as line feed, tab, and carriage return may be escaped with a \ character:

```
<xsd:pattern value="\n\r\t\\"/>
```

- *Character List:* Lists of valid characters in which any character in the list is a valid match may be expressed between `[` and `]`, such as allowing 0, 1, or 2 here:

```
<xsd:pattern value="[012]"/>
```

- *Negation:* A caret, ^, preceding a character group indicates to not match any expression in that group:

```
<xsd:pattern value="[^012]"/>
```

- *Quantifiers:* A component of a regular expression may be followed by a quantifier indicating how many of that component are allowed: `?` meaning 0 or 1, `*` meaning

0 or more, + meaning 1 or more, {`n`} meaning exactly *n*, {`n,m`} meaning between and including *n* to *m*, {`n,`} meaning *n* or more, or {`,m`} meaning up to and including *m*:

```
<xsd:pattern value="[012]?"/>
<xsd:pattern value="[012]*"/>
<xsd:pattern value="[012]+"/>
<xsd:pattern value="[012]{3,5}"/>
<xsd:pattern value="[012]{2,}"/>
```

- *Character Ranges:* ASCII ranges of characters can be identified using a - (hyphen) between the characters as shown here:

```
<xsd:pattern value="[0-9]"/>
```

- *Expression Grouping:* A grouping of expressions may be embedded inside parentheses:

```
<xsd:pattern value="(Tom)"/>
```

- *Expression OR-ing:* Indicating that any one of a set of expressions may match, we use the symbol | as shown here:

```
<xsd:pattern value="(Tom | Thomas)"/>
```

- *Expression Categories:* Certain special categories of characters may be expressed using a syntax of \p{*`CharacterProperty`*} (or the inverse \P{*`CharacterProperty`*}), where *`CharacterProperty`* is one of the more popular properties as listed here:

```
<xsd:pattern value="\p{L}"/>                (All letters)
<xsd:pattern value="\p{Lu}"/>               (Uppercase letters)
<xsd:pattern value="\p{Ll}"/>               (Lowercase letters)
<xsd:pattern value="\p{N}"/>                (All numbers)
<xsd:pattern value="\p{Nd}"/>               (Decimal numbers)
<xsd:pattern value="\p{P}"/>                (All punctuation marks)
<xsd:pattern value="\p{Z}"/>                (All separators)
<xsd:pattern value="\p{Zs}"/>               (Space)
<xsd:pattern value="\p{Zl}"/>               (Line)
<xsd:pattern value="\p{Zp}"/>               (Paragraph)
<xsd:pattern value="\p{S}"/>                (All symbols)
```

- *Shorthand Categories:* Shorthand notation may be used for the most common expression characters as shown here:

```
<xsd:pattern value="."/>    (All characters except newline and return)
<xsd:pattern value="\s"/>   (Whitespace)
<xsd:pattern value="\S"/>   (Not whitespace)
<xsd:pattern value="\d"/>   (Decimal numbers)
```

```
<xsd:pattern value="\D"/>    (Not decimal numbers)
<xsd:pattern value="\w"/>    (Characters sans punctuation & separators)
<xsd:pattern value="\W"/>    (Line)
<xsd:pattern value="\c"/>    (Name characters)
<xsd:pattern value="\C"/>    (Not name characters)
<xsd:pattern value="\i"/>    (Initial name characters)
<xsd:pattern value="\I"/>    (Not initial name characters)
```

Here are a few examples of regular expression patterns, with strings that match those expressions:

- <xsd:pattern value="[0-9]{3}-[A-Z]{4}"/> matches "324-FILM" but not "324-3456".
- <xsd:pattern value="Fred .*Jones"/> matches "Fred Jones" or "Fred works for Mr. Jones". (The * applies to the pattern immediately before it, in this case the period, which is any character.)
- xsd:pattern value="Fred \p{L}+|\p{Lu}\. Jones"/> matches "Fred Irving Jones" or "Fred I. Jones" but not "Fred Jones".

Built-in Types

There are various built-in data types you should familiarize yourself with when using XML schemas. There are built-in primitive types and built-in derived types that serve various purposes.

The built-in **numeric types** are as listed here:

- float: IEEE single-precision 32-bit float such as 18.9E3, infinity (INF or -INF), or not a number (NAN).
- double: IEEE double-precision 64-bit float such as 18.9E3, infinity (INF or -INF), or not a number (NAN).
- decimal: A decimal number such as 23.9 or -1202.87.
- integer: A decimal that is an integer in the range {... -2, -1, 0, 1, 2, ...}.
- nonPositiveInteger: An integer in the range {... -2, -1, 0}.
- negativeInteger: An integer in the range {... -2, -1}.
- nonNegativeInteger: An integer in the range {0, 1, 2, ...}.
- positiveInteger: An integer in the range {1, 2, ...}.
- long: An 8-byte integer.
- int: A 4-byte integer.
- short: A 2-byte integer.
- byte: A single-byte integer.
- unsignedLong: A non-negative 8-byte integer.

- `unsignedInt`: A non-negative 4-byte integer.
- `unsignedShort`: A non-negative 2-byte integer.
- `unsignedByte`: A non-negative single-byte integer.

The built-in **logical and binary encoded related types** are as listed here:

- `boolean`: Boolean values of `true` or `false`.
- `hexBinary`: Hex-encoded binary data such as `AF32`.
- `base64Binary`: Base 64–encoded binary data such as ABXCFK4D.

The built-in **time and date related types** are as listed here:

- `duration`: ISO duration of time in the form `PaYbMcDTdHeMfS`, where *a* = number of years, *b* = number of months, *c* = number of days, *d* = number of hours, *e* = number of minutes, and *f* = number of seconds, such as the example `P1Y2M3DT4H40M30S` (1 year, 2 months, 3 days, 4 hours, 40 minutes, and 30 seconds), or `-P1DT30M` (- 1 day and 30 minutes).
- `time`: ISO instant of time in the form *hh:mm:ss.sss-HH:MM*, where *hh* = hour, *mm* = minute, *ss* = seconds, *sss* = milliseconds, *HH* = time-zone hours, and *MM* = time-zone minutes, such as 12:30:00 (12:30 p.m.), or `14:15:00-05:00` (2:15 p.m. eastern standard time).
- `date`: A calendar date in the form *CCYY-MM-DD*, where *CC* is the century, *YY* is the year in that century, *MM* is the month, and *DD* is the day, such as `1968-11-27` (November 27, 1968).
- `dateTime`: A concatenation of date and time in the form *CCYY-MM-DDThh:mm:ss.sss-HH:MM*, such as `1943-09-08T01:00:00` (September 8, 1943, at 1:00 a.m.).
- `gYear`: A calendar year in the form *CCYY*, such as `1972`.
- `gMonth`: A calendar month in the form *--MM--*, such as `--02--` (February).
- `gDay`: A calendar day in the form *---DD*, such as `---01`.
- `gMonthDay`: A concatenated month and day in the form *--MM-DD*, such as `--02-01`.
- `gYearMonth`: A concatenated year and month in the form *CCYY-MM*, such as `1972-02`.

The built-in **string related types** are as listed here:

- `string`: A string type such as `"Buy Beeshirts!"`.
- `normalizedString`: A `string` with no carriage return, no line feed, and no tab characters.
- `token`: A `normalizedString` with no leading spaces, no trailing spaces, and no sequences of more than one space.

The built-in **XML name and token related types** are as listed here:

- QName: A name that is qualified with a namespace such as beeshirts:order.
- NOTATION: A specific type of data external to an XML document similar to the NOTATION component in a DTD.
- language: A token that has an xml:lang value such as en, en-US, or de.
- NMTOKEN and NMTOKENS: A token or whitespace-separated tokens that have no expanded markup data similar to NMTOKEN and NMTOKENS defined in a DTD, respectively.
- Name and NCName: A token that is a valid XML name and non-colonized XML name, respectively.
- ID, IDREF, and IDREFS: Non-colonized names that correspond to XML DTD ID, IDREF, and IDREFS, respectively.
- ENTITY and ENTITIES: Non-colonized names that correspond to XML DTD ENTITY and ENTITIES, respectively.

Finally, a built-in **URI related type** is as follows:

- anyURI: A URI such as http://www.assuredtech.com.

Simple Types

The built-in types just listed are all examples of simple types used in XML schemas. There will be many times when the built-in types themselves satisfy the need to describe a particular piece of data in an XML document. However, there will also be times when you want to ascribe more structure and constraints to the built-in types without creating a completely new complex type. The simpleType definition mechanism in XML Schema satisfies this need.

A common general form of the simpleType is shown here:

```
<xsd:simpleType name="SomeSimpleTypeName">
  <xsd:restriction base="SomeSuperTypeName">
    <xsd:SomeFacetName value="SomeFacetValue"/>
    <xsd:AnotherFacetName value="AnotherFacetValue"/>
      ...
  </xsd:restriction>
</xsd:simpleType>
```

The name *SomeSimpleTypeName* simply defines the name for the simple type. The restriction base *SomeSuperTypeName* defines a super type on which this simple type is based. The facet names and values define constraints for this particular simple type. We will explain the concept of restriction in more detail later in this chapter, but it may help clarify the concept to show an example first. Here's an example of a simpleType:

```
<?xml version="1.0"?>
<xsd:schema targetNamespace="http://www.beeshirts.com/schemas"
```

```
            xmlns:xsd="http://www.w3.org/2001/XMLSchema"
            elementFormDefault="qualified">
    <xsd:element name="quantity">
      <xsd:simpleType>
        <xsd:restriction base="xsd:integer">
          <xsd:minInclusive value="1"/>
          <xsd:maxInclusive value="100"/>
        </xsd:restriction>
      </xsd:simpleType>
    </xsd:element>
</xsd:schema>
```

And here is a sample snippet of a corresponding XML document:

```
<?xml version="1.0"?>
<quantity
    xmlns="http://www.beeshirts.com/schemas"
    xmlns:xsi="http://www.w3.org/2001/XMLSchema-instance"
    xsi:schemaLocation="http://www.beeshirts.com/schemas quantity.xsd">
50
</quantity>
```

A `simpleType` may also be defined as a list of simple values using the following general form:

```
<xsd:simpleType name="SomeSimpleTypeName">
  <xsd:list itemType="SomeTypeName"/>
</xsd:simpleType>
```

Here, the `list itemType` *SomeTypeName* defines a type on which this new simple list type is based. Lists can be composed only of simple types and not of other lists or complex types. When the list of elements in the XML document is defined, each element is separated by whitespace. Here is an example:

```
<?xml version="1.0"?>
<xsd:schema targetNamespace="http://www.beeshirts.com/schemas"
            xmlns:xsd="http://www.w3.org/2001/XMLSchema"
            elementFormDefault="qualified">
    <xsd:element name="emailList">
      <xsd:simpleType>
        <xsd:list itemType="xsd:string"/>
      </xsd:simpleType>
    </xsd:element>
</xsd:schema>
```

And here is a sample snippet of a corresponding XML document:

```
<?xml version="1.0"?>
<emailList
  xmlns="http://www.beeshirts.com/schemas"
  xmlns:xsi="http://www.w3.org/2001/XMLSchema-instance"
```

```
  xsi:schemaLocation="http://www.beeshirts.com/schemas emailList.xsd">
 john.doe@hotmail.com jdoe@yahoo.com jdoe@beeshirts.com
</emailList>
```

Finally, a `simpleType` may also be defined as a union of other simple types. The union concept here is similar to the union concept in the C programming language. A union type can take on one of the types that comprise it. Unions are defined using the following general form:

```
<xsd:simpleType name="SomeSimpleTypeName">
  <xsd:union memberTypes="SomeTypeName AnotherTypeName OneMoreTypeName"/>
</xsd:simpleType>
```

Here, the `union memberTypes` *`SomeTypeName`*, *`AnotherTypeName`*, and *`OneMoreTypeName`* define those types of which this new simple type is a union. For example, we have following `simpleType union`:

```
<?xml version="1.0"?>
<xsd:schema targetNamespace="http://www.beeshirts.com/schemas"
            xmlns:xsd="http://www.w3.org/2001/XMLSchema"
            xmlns:beeshirts="http://www.beeshirts.com/schemas"
            elementFormDefault="qualified">
    <xsd:simpleType name="by_pounds">
      <xsd:restriction base="xsd:double"/>
    </xsd:simpleType>
    <xsd:simpleType name="by_package_type">
      <xsd:restriction base="xsd:string">
        <xsd:enumeration value="envelope"/>
        <xsd:enumeration value="small package"/>
        <xsd:enumeration value="medium package"/>
        <xsd:enumeration value="large package"/>
        <xsd:enumeration value="extra large package"/>
      </xsd:restriction>
    </xsd:simpleType>
    <xsd:simpleType name="weight">
      <xsd:union
          memberTypes="beeshirts:by_package_type beeshirts:by_pounds"/>
    </xsd:simpleType>
    <xsd:element name="ship_weight" type="beeshirts:weight"/>
</xsd:schema>
```

And here is a sample snippet of a corresponding XML document:

```
<?xml version="1.0"?>
<ship_weight
    xmlns="http://www.beeshirts.com/schemas"
    xmlns:xsi="http://www.w3.org/2001/XMLSchema-instance"
    xsi:schemaLocation="http://www.beeshirts.com/schemas union.xsd">
  envelope
</ship_weight>
<ship_weight
```

```
    xmlns="http://www.beeshirts.com/schemas"
    xmlns:xsi="http://www.w3.org/2001/XMLSchema-instance"
    xsi:schemaLocation="http://www.beeshirts.com/schemas union.xsd">
37.5
</ship_weight>
```

As a final note, simple types may also be declared within attributes according to this general form:

```
<xsd:attribute ...>
  <xsd:simpleType ...> ... </xsd:simpleType>
</xsd:attribute>
```

Here is an example:

```
<xsd:attribute name="card_type" default="Visa Credit Card">
    <xsd:simpleType>
       <xsd:restriction base="xsd:string">
           <xsd:enumeration value="Visa Credit Card"/>
           <xsd:enumeration value="Master Card Credit Card"/>
           <xsd:enumeration value="American Express Credit Card"/>
       </xsd:restriction>
    </xsd:simpleType>
</xsd:attribute>
```

And here is a sample snippet of a corresponding XML document:

```
<?xml version="1.0" ?>
<charge_card
    xmlns="http://www.beeshirts.com/schemas"
    xmlns:xsi="http://www.w3.org/2001/XMLSchema-instance"
    xsi:schemaLocation="http://www.beeshirts.com/schemas attrib.xsd"
    card_type="Visa Credit Card"/>
```

Complex Types

Simple types may satisfy a requirement to represent data from time to time, but very often more complicated structures are needed. The `complexType` element in XML Schema addresses this need by allowing one to define more complicated data types whereby sub-elements and attributes of that type are desired. Such complex types are thus more similar to a class's type definition and its fields.

A common general form of the `complexType` is shown here:

```
<xsd:complexType name="SomeComplexTypeName">
  <xsd:sequence>
    <xsd:element name="SomeElementName" ...>...</xsd:element>
    <xsd:element name="AnotherElementName" ...>...</xsd:element>
       ...
   </xsd:sequence>
</xsd:complexType>
```

That is, a complexType named *SomeComplexTypeName* is used to define a data type that has a sequence of sub-elements named *SomeElementName*, *AnotherElementName*, and so on. These sub-elements can be built-in types, simple types, or other complex types. Thus, an arbitrarily complicated structure can be defined. Here's an example:

```
<?xml version="1.0"?>
<xsd:schema
      targetNamespace="http://www.beeshirts.com/schemas"
      xmlns:beeshirts="http://www.beeshirts.com/schemas"
      xmlns:xsd="http://www.w3.org/2001/XMLSchema"
      elementFormDefault="qualified">

  <xsd:element name="charge_card" type="beeshirts:charge_card_type"/>
  <xsd:complexType name="charge_card_type">
    <xsd:sequence>
      <xsd:element name="card_name" type="xsd:string"/>
      <xsd:element name="card_number"
                   type="beeshirts:card_number_type"
                   nillable="false"/>
      <xsd:element name="expired_date"
                   type="xsd:dateTime"
                   nillable="false"/>
      <xsd:element name="card_confirmation_number"
                   type="beeshirts:confirmation_num_type"
                   nillable="false"/>
      <xsd:element name="card_signature"
                   type="beeshirts:signature_type"
                   nillable="false"/>
    </xsd:sequence>
  </xsd:complexType>
  <xsd:simpleType name="card_number_type">
    <xsd:restriction base="xsd:string">
      <xsd:pattern value="\d{14}"/>
    </xsd:restriction>
  </xsd:simpleType>
  <xsd:simpleType name="confirmation_num_type">
    <xsd:restriction base="xsd:string">
      <xsd:pattern value="\d{4}-\d{3}-\d{6}"/>
    </xsd:restriction>
  </xsd:simpleType>
  <xsd:complexType name="signature_type">
    <xsd:sequence>
      <xsd:element name="header" type="xsd:string"/>
      <xsd:element name="content"
                   type="xsd:base64Binary"
```

```
                    nillable="false"/>
    </xsd:sequence>
  </xsd:complexType>
</xsd:schema>
```

And here is a sample snippet of a corresponding XML document:

```
<?xml version="1.0"?>
<charge_card
  xmlns="http://www.beeshirts.com/schemas"
  xmlns:xsi="http://www.w3.org/2001/XMLSchema-instance"
  xsi:schemaLocation="http://www.beeshirts.com/schemas complextype.xsd">
  <card_name>VISA</card_name>
  <card_number>12345678901234</card_number>
  <expired_date>2004-09-08T01:05:00</expired_date>
  <card_confirmation_number>1234-123-123244</card_confirmation_number>
  <card_signature>
    <header>gif</header>
    <content>103434055axDx98590dfhABCder</content>
  </card_signature>
</charge_card>
```

XML Schema Type System

The type system of XML Schema is actually quite a rich and extensible type system. Consequently, it also can be quite complicated and difficult to understand. The best advice we can give the reader who is trying to quickly understand XML Schema and who already is armed with an object-oriented background is to try to cast the concepts embodied in XML Schema into the light of an object-oriented type system. In this way, the grasping of concepts embedded into XML Schema becomes easier. This section, in fact, describes the remaining key points of the XML Schema type system. Concepts from object-oriented paradigms such as anonymous types, type inheritance hierarchies, type substitutions, abstract types, any types, collections, ordered collections, and identity constraints are all described in this section in the context of their embodiment into XML Schema.

Named Versus Anonymous Types

In the previous sections, we saw examples of named types. That is, the simple and complex data types that we defined had names. These names could then be referenced by other types and therefore reused throughout or external to the XML schema. Simple and complex types can also be declared inline with an element declaration and made anonymous. Using an anonymous type can make the schema easier to read and understand for less complicated type definitions, and also allows an element to keep its type definition "private" from other elements that are in the schema or that may include this schema.

The general form of the complexType that uses an anonymous element declaration is shown here:

```
<xsd:element name="SomeComplexTypeName">
  <xsd:complexType>
    <xsd:sequence>
      <xsd:element name="SomeElementName" ...>...</xsd:element>
      <xsd:element name="AnotherElementName" ...>...</xsd:element>
         ...
     </xsd:sequence>
  </xsd:complexType>
</xsd:element>
```

For example, compare the following anonymous complex type to the complex type defined in the preceding section:

```
<?xml version="1.0"?>
<xsd:schema targetNamespace="http://www.beeshirts.com/schemas"
            xmlns:beeshirts="http://www.beeshirts.com/schemas"
            xmlns:xsd="http://www.w3.org/2001/XMLSchema"
            elementFormDefault="qualified">
  <xsd:element name="charge_card" >
  <xsd:complexType>
    <xsd:sequence>
      <xsd:element name="card_name" type="xsd:string"/>
      <xsd:element name="card_number" nillable="false">
        <xsd:simpleType>
          <xsd:restriction base="xsd:string">
            <xsd:pattern value="\d{14}"/>
          </xsd:restriction>
        </xsd:simpleType>
      </xsd:element>
      <xsd:element name="expired_date"
                   type="xsd:dateTime"
                   nillable="false"/>
      <xsd:element name="card_confirmation_number" nillable="false">
        <xsd:simpleType>
          <xsd:restriction base="xsd:string">
            <xsd:pattern value="\d{4}-\d{3}-\d{6}"/>
          </xsd:restriction>
        </xsd:simpleType>
      </xsd:element>
      <xsd:element name="card_signature" minOccurs="0">
        <xsd:complexType>
          <xsd:sequence>
            <xsd:element name="header" type="xsd:string"/>
            <xsd:element name="content"
                         type="xsd:base64Binary"
```

```
                         nillable="false"/>
          </xsd:sequence>
        </xsd:complexType>
      </xsd:element>
    </xsd:sequence>
  </xsd:complexType>
  </xsd:element>
</xsd:schema>
```

And here is a sample snippet of a corresponding XML document:

```
<?xml version="1.0"?>
<charge_card
   xmlns="http://www.beeshirts.com/schemas"
   xmlns:xsi="http://www.w3.org/2001/XMLSchema-instance"
   xsi:schemaLocation="http://www.beeshirts.com/schemas anoncomplex.xsd">
  <card_name>VISA</card_name>
  <card_number>12345678901234</card_number>
  <expired_date>2004-09-08T01:05:00</expired_date>
  <card_confirmation_number>1234-123-123244</card_confirmation_number>
  <card_signature>
    <header>gif</header>
    <content>103434055axDx98590dfhABCder</content>
  </card_signature>
</charge_card>
```

Type Hierarchies

The most fundamental of all simple and complex types is the anyType (or "ur-type") at the root of the type tree. The anyType simply means that the type specified is of any type in the type system. It is the root type of all simple and complex types akin to java.lang.Object in the Java type system. When no type is specified in an element declaration, the anyType is in fact assumed. Thus, the following two declarations are identical:

```
<xsd:element name="order" type="xsd:anyType"> ... </xsd:element>

<xsd:element name="order"> ... </xsd:element>
```

XML Schema also allows for a sub-typing mechanism with data types. Thus, some of the same benefits that can be yielded from sub-classing in Java can also be yielded from sub-typing in XML Schema. The two ways to subtype in XML Schema are by extension and by restriction. Sub-typing by extension involves extending the parent type by adding more components to the derived type. Sub-typing by restriction involves a derivation of the parent type whereby the values or instances of the parent type are restricted with the derived type. We examine both sub-typing mechanisms in this section.

When it is desired to add components to a parent type, the common general form for sub-typing by extension is as shown here:

```
<xsd:complexType name="SomeNewSubTypeName">
  <xsd:complexContent>
    <xsd:extension base="SomeParentTypeName" >
      <xsd:sequence>
        <xsd:element name="SomeNewElementName" type="SomeType"/>
        <xsd:element name="AnotherElementName" type="AnotherType"/>
        ...
      </xsd:sequence>
    </xsd:extension>
  </xsd:complexContent>
</xsd:complexType>
```

For example:

```
<?xml version="1.0"?>
<xsd:schema targetNamespace="http://www.beeshirts.com/schemas"
            xmlns:beeshirts="http://www.beeshirts.com/schemas"
            xmlns:xsd="http://www.w3.org/2001/XMLSchema"
            elementFormDefault="qualified">
  <xsd:element name="item" type="beeshirts:shirt_item "/>
  <xsd:complexType name="base_item">
    <xsd:sequence>
      <xsd:element name="item_id" type="xsd:long"/>
      <xsd:element name="quantity" type="xsd:integer"/>
      <xsd:element name="total_price" type="xsd:double"/>
    </xsd:sequence>
  </xsd:complexType>
  <xsd:complexType name="shirt_item ">
    <xsd:complexContent>
      <xsd:extension base="beeshirts:base_item">
        <xsd:sequence>
          <xsd:element name="shirt_size" type="xsd:string"/>
          <xsd:element name="shirt_color" type="xsd:string"/>
        </xsd:sequence>
      </xsd:extension>
    </xsd:complexContent>
  </xsd:complexType>
</xsd:schema>
```

And here is a sample snippet of a corresponding XML document:

```
<?xml version="1.0"?>
<item
    xmlns="http://www.beeshirts.com/schemas"
    xmlns:xsi="http://www.w3.org/2001/XMLSchema-instance"
    xsi:schemaLocation="http://www.beeshirts.com/schemas extension.xsd">
  <item_id>1001</item_id>
  <quantity>10</quantity>
  <total_price>78.99</total_price>
```

```
  <shirt_size>XL</shirt_size>
  <shirt_color>Green</shirt_color>
</item>
```

When it is desired to create a new derived type with a more restrictive structure than its parent type, a subtype by restriction element may be used. When sub-typing by restriction, all the declarations from the parent type that have been declared to have one or more occurrences need to be replicated inside of the new restricted type. The common general form for sub-typing by restriction is as follows:

```
<xsd:complexType name="SomeNewSubTypeName">
  <xsd:complexContent>
    <xsd:restriction base="SomeParentTypeName" >
      <xsd:sequence>
        <xsd:element name="SomeNewElementName" type="SomeType"/>
        <xsd:element name="AnotherElementName" type="AnotherType"/>
        ...
      </xsd:sequence>
    </xsd:restriction>
  </xsd:complexContent>
</xsd:complexType>
```

Here's an example:

```
<?xml version="1.0"?>
<xsd:schema
    targetNamespace="http://www.beeshirts.com/schemas"
    xmlns:xsd="http://www.w3.org/2001/XMLSchema"
    xmlns:beeshirts="http://www.beeshirts.com/schemas"
    elementFormDefault="qualified">
  <xsd:element name="legacy_item" type="beeshirts:legacy_item"/>
  <xsd:element name="item" type="beeshirts:item_description"/>
  <xsd:complexType name="base_item">
    <xsd:sequence>
      <xsd:element name="item_id" type="xsd:long"/>
      <xsd:element name="quantity" type="xsd:integer"/>
      <xsd:element name="total_price" type="xsd:double"/>
    </xsd:sequence>
  </xsd:complexType>
  <xsd:complexType name="item_description">
    <xsd:complexContent>
      <xsd:extension base="beeshirts:base_item">
        <xsd:sequence>
          <xsd:element name="shirt_size" type="xsd:string"/>
          <xsd:element name="shirt_color" type="xsd:string"/>
        </xsd:sequence>
      </xsd:extension>
    </xsd:complexContent>
  </xsd:complexType>
```

```
  <xsd:complexType name="legacy_item">
    <xsd:complexContent>
      <xsd:restriction base="beeshirts:base_item">
        <xsd:sequence>
          <xsd:element name="item_id"
                       type="xsd:long"
                       maxOccurs="unbounded"/>
          <xsd:element name="quantity"
                       type="xsd:integer"
                       maxOccurs="unbounded"/>
          <xsd:element name="total_price" type="xsd:double"/>
          <xsd:element name="shirt_size" type="xsd:string"/>
          <xsd:element name="shirt_color" type="xsd:string"/>
        </xsd:sequence>
      </xsd:restriction>
    </xsd:complexContent>
  </xsd:complexType>
</xsd:schema>
```

And here is a sample snippet of a corresponding XML document:

```
<?xml version="1.0"?>
<legacy_item
   xmlns="http://www.beeshirts.com/schemas"
   xmlns:xsi="http://www.w3.org/2001/XMLSchema-instance"
   xsi:schemaLocation=
        "http://www.beeshirts.com/schemas restrictextension.xsd">
  <item_id>1001</item_id>
  <item_id>1002</item_id>
  <item_id>1003</item_id>
  <quantity>1</quantity>
  <quantity>12</quantity>
  <quantity>31</quantity>
  <total_price>900.99</total_price>
  <shirt_size>XL</shirt_size>
  <shirt_color>Green</shirt_color>
</legacy_item>
```

It should be noted that when the parent type is a `complexType`, the content of the derived `complexType` must be declared as `complexContent` as illustrated here:

```
<xsd:complexType name="SomeNewSubTypeName">
  <xsd:complexContent>
    <xsd:extension base="SomeComplexParentTypeName" >
      ...
    </xsd:extension>
  </xsd:complexContent>
</xsd:complexType>
```

When the parent type is a `simpleType`, the content of the derived `complexType` must be declared as `simpleContent` as illustrated here:

```
<xsd:complexType name="SomeNewSubTypeName">
  <xsd:simpleContent>
    <xsd:extension base="SomeSimpleParentTypeName" >
      ...
    </xsd:extension>
  </xsd:simpleContent>
</xsd:complexType>
```

For those parent types that you may not want to be extended and/or restricted, a special attribute of the type may be defined in one of the following forms:

```
<xsd:complexType name="SomeUnextendableType" final="extension" ...>
<xsd:complexType name="SomeUnrestrictableType" final="restriction" ...>
<xsd:complexType name="SomeUnderiveableType" final="#all" ...>
```

Similar to complex types that refuse to allow themselves to be extended or restricted by declaring themselves `final`, elements can also refuse to allow themselves to be extended or restricted as shown here:

```
<xsd:element name="Bla" type="SomeUnextendableType" final="extension"...>
<xsd:element name="Bla" type="SomeUnrestrictableType" final="restriction"...>
<xsd:element name="Bla" type="SomeUnderiveableType" final="#all"...>
```

Substitution Groups

At times you may want to use a synonym for types in XML Schema. That is, if you define some type `A`, you can specify that another type name `B` actually is a substitution group (that is, "synonym") for `A`. This comes in most handy when you already have a type defined but simply want to use a different name for that type in different XML document contexts. This is the general structure for declaring such a synonym for an element:

```
<xsd:element name="B" substitutionGroup="A" type="SomeType"/>
```

The specification of a `type` attribute is necessary for the substitution group only if the type is different from the type for which it is substituted. Of course, the type for the substitution group must always be the same as or derived from the type for which it is substituted.

Similar to types that refuse to allow themselves to be extended or restricted by declaring themselves `final`, elements can also refuse to allow themselves to be substituted by blocking as shown here:

```
<xsd:element name="A" type="SomeType" block="substitution"/>
```

Abstract Types

By now you may have figured out that the XML Schema type system has many features similar to object-oriented type systems (sans methods and logic). Well, XML Schema also has the concept of "abstract" types. You can in fact declare an element to be an abstract element as such:

```
<xsd:element name="order" type="Order" abstract="true"> ... </xsd:element>
```

The abstract element is simply an element that may be referenced and used by other elements in the XML schema. An XML document may not reference that element directly. However, an element that is a substitution group for an abstract element may appear in an XML document. In this way, the abstract element serves as a template for other elements.

Complex types can also be declared as abstract and thus not directly used within an XML document. The general form for declaring a complex type abstract is as follows:

```
<xsd:complexType name="order" abstract="true"> ... </xsd:complexType>
```

Derived types from the complex type may, however, be used within an XML document. Thus, by declaring a complex type as abstract, it serves as a template for derived types.

any **Elements and Attributes**

Suppose you want the author of XML documents to be able to extensibly add new elements or attributes to the document that aren't necessarily specified in a schema. The any element addresses this problem for elements by allowing one to declare additional elements in an XML document when the any element is defined inside the XML schema. The common general form of this element is as shown here:

```
<xsd:complexType ... >
   ...
   <xsd:any maxOccurs=MaxNumberOfElements minOccurs=MinNumberOfElements
      namespace=SomeNameSpaceURI processContents=laxORskipORstrict />
   ...
</xsd:complexType>
```

The defaults for each attribute of the any element are one maximum and minimum occurrence, any namespace, and a `strict` policy for processing contents. If `skip` is specified for processing contents, the element must simply be well-formed XML. If `lax` is specified, the element will be validated against its declaration, if it exists. If `strict` is specified for an element, a declaration for the item must exist and be validated.

Here is an example:

```
<?xml version="1.0"?>
<xsd:schema targetNamespace="http://www.beeshirts.com/schemas"
            xmlns:beeshirts="http://www.beeshirts.com/schemas"
            xmlns:xsd="http://www.w3.org/2001/XMLSchema"
            elementFormDefault="qualified">
  <xsd:element name="item">
    <xsd:complexType>
      <xsd:sequence>
        <xsd:element name="item_id" type="xsd:long"/>
        <xsd:element name="quantity" type="xsd:int"/>
```

```
        <xsd:element name="total_price" type="xsd:double"/>
        <xsd:any minOccurs="0"/>
      </xsd:sequence>
    </xsd:complexType>
  </xsd:element>
  <xsd:element name="item_description">
  <xsd:complexType>
    <xsd:sequence>
      <xsd:element name="shirt_size" type="xsd:string"/>
      <xsd:element name="shirt_color" type="xsd:string"/>
    </xsd:sequence>
  </xsd:complexType>
  </xsd:element>
</xsd:schema>
```

And here is a sample snippet of a corresponding XML document:

```
<?xml version="1.0"?>
<item
    xmlns="http://www.beeshirts.com/schemas"
    xmlns:xsi="http://www.w3.org/2001/XMLSchema-instance"
    xsi:schemaLocation="http://www.beeshirts.com/schemas anyelement.xsd">
  <item_id>1001</item_id>
  <quantity>12</quantity>
  <total_price>900.9</total_price>
  <item_description>
    <shirt_size>XL</shirt_size>
    <shirt_color>Green</shirt_color>
  </item_description>
</item>
```

Similar to extensible elements, the anyAttribute declaration allows one to add attributes to an XML document that weren't specified in a schema according to the following common general form:

```
<xsd:complexType ... >
    ...
   <xsd:anyAttrbute namespace=SomeNameSpaceURI
                    processContents=laxORskipORstrict />
    ...
</xsd:complexType>
```

Here is an example:

```
<?xml version="1.0" encoding="UTF-8"?>
<xsd:schema
    targetNamespace="http://www.beeshirts.com/schemas"
    xmlns:xsd="http://www.w3.org/2001/XMLSchema"
    xmlns:beeshirts="http://www.beeshirts.com/schemas"
  elementFormDefault="qualified">
```

```
  <xsd:element name="charge_card">
    <xsd:complexType>
      <xsd:anyAttribute/>
    </xsd:complexType>
  </xsd:element>
  <xsd:attribute name="card_type" default="Visa Credit Card">
    <xsd:simpleType>
      <xsd:restriction base="xsd:string">
        <xsd:enumeration value="Visa Credit Card"/>
        <xsd:enumeration value="Master Card Credit Card"/>
        <xsd:enumeration value="American Express Credit Card"/>
      </xsd:restriction>
    </xsd:simpleType>
  </xsd:attribute>
</xsd:schema>
```

And here is a sample snippet of a corresponding XML document:

```
<?xml version="1.0"?>
<chage_card
    xmlns="http://www.beeshirts.com/schemas"
    xmlns:xsi="http://www.w3.org/2001/XMLSchema-instance"
    xsi:schemaLocation="http://www.beeshirts.com/schemas attribute.xsd"
  card_type="Visa Credit Card"/>
```

Element Ordering

Sub-elements specified inside types can be specified as a group adhering to some ordered collection. Such element ordering specification refers to a particular type of XML schema "model group." For example, we previously saw illustrations of how the sequence element can be used to require that elements in a schema be specified in a particular order. That is, the XML schema

```
<?xml version="1.0"?>
<xsd:schema
    targetNamespace="http://www.beeshirts.com/schemas"
    xmlns:beeshirts="http://www.beeshirts.com/schemas"
    xmlns:xsd="http://www.w3.org/2001/XMLSchema"
    elementFormDefault="qualified">
  <xsd:element name="charge_card" type="beeshirts:charge_card_type"/>
  <xsd:complexType name="charge_card_type">
    <xsd:sequence>
      <xsd:element name="card_name" type="xsd:string"/>
      <xsd:element name="card_number"
                   type="xsd:string"
                   nillable="false" />
      <xsd:element name="expired_date"
                   type="xsd:dateTime"
                   nillable="false"/>
```

```
      <xsd:element name="card_confirmation_number"
                   type="xsd:string"
                   nillable="false" />
      <xsd:element name="card_signature"
                   type="xsd:base64Binary"
                  minOccurs="0" />
    </xsd:sequence>
  </xsd:complexType>
</xsd:schema>
```

requires that the elements inside the specified type appear in sequences inside an associated XML document as exemplified here:

```
<?xml version="1.0"?>
<charge_card
    xmlns="http://www.beeshirts.com/schemas"
    xmlns:xsi="http://www.w3.org/2001/XMLSchema-instance"
    xsi:schemaLocation="http://www.beeshirts.com/schemas sequence.xsd">
  <card_name>VISA</card_name>
  <card_number>12345678901234</card_number>
  <expired_date>2004-09-08T01:05:00</expired_date>
  <card_confirmation_number>1234-123-123244</card_confirmation_number>
  <card_signature>103434055axDx98590dfhABCder</card_signature>
</charge_card>
```

To allow any order of elements, the `all` element may be used. For example, this `all` element inside the XML schema

```
<?xml version="1.0"?>
<xsd:schema
    targetNamespace="http://www.beeshirts.com/schemas"
    xmlns:beeshirts="http://www.beeshirts.com/schemas"
    xmlns:xsd="http://www.w3.org/2001/XMLSchema"
    elementFormDefault="qualified">
  <xsd:element name="charge_card" type="beeshirts:charge_card_type"/>
  <xsd:complexType name="charge_card_type">
    <xsd:all>
      <xsd:element name="card_name" type="xsd:string"/>
      <xsd:element name="card_number"
                   type="xsd:string"
                   nillable="false" />
      <xsd:element name="expired_date"
                   type="xsd:dateTime"
                   nillable="false"/>
      <xsd:element name="card_confirmation_number"
                   type="xsd:string"
                   nillable="false" />
      <xsd:element name="card_signature"
                   type="xsd:base64Binary"
```

```
                  minOccurs="0" />
    </xsd:all>
  </xsd:complexType>
</xsd:schema>
```

allows any order to be specified for the elements referenced inside an associated XML document as exemplified here:

```
<?xml version="1.0"?>
<charge_card
    xmlns="http://www.beeshirts.com/schemas"
    xmlns:xsi="http://www.w3.org/2001/XMLSchema-instance"
    xsi:schemaLocation="http://www.beeshirts.com/schemas all.xsd">
  <card_signature>103434055axDx98590dfhABCder</card_signature>
  <card_name>VISA</card_name>
   <expired_date>2004-09-08T01:05:00</expired_date>
  <card_number>12345678901234</card_number>
  <card_confirmation_number>1234-123-123244</card_confirmation_number>
</charge_card>
```

Finally, to express a choice among elements, the `choice` element can be used inside types. For example, this `choice` element inside the XML schema

```
<?xml version="1.0"?>
<xsd:schema
      targetNamespace="http://www.beeshirts.com/schemas"
      xmlns:xsd="http://www.w3.org/2001/XMLSchema"
      xmlns:beeshirts="http://www.beeshirts.com/schemas"
      elementFormDefault="qualified">
  <xsd:element name="charge_card" type="beeshirts:charge_card_type"/>
  <xsd:complexType name="charge_card_type">
    <xsd:sequence>
      <xsd:element name="card_name" type="xsd:string"/>
      <xsd:element name="card_number" type="xsd:string"
                   nillable="false"/>
      <xsd:element name="expired_date" type="xsd:dateTime"
                   nillable="false"/>
      <xsd:element name="card_confirmation_number" type="xsd:string"
                   nillable="false"/>
      <xsd:element name="card_signature">
       <xsd:complexType>
        <xsd:choice>
         <xsd:element name="signature" type="xsd:base64Binary"/>
         <xsd:element name="password" type="xsd:string" />
        </xsd:choice>
      </xsd:complexType>
      </xsd:element>
    </xsd:sequence>
  </xsd:complexType>
</xsd:schema>
```

requires that only one of the specified elements be referenced inside an associated XML document as exemplified here:

```
<?xml version="1.0"?>
<charge_card
    xmlns="http://www.beeshirts.com/schemas"
    xmlns:xsi="http://www.w3.org/2001/XMLSchema-instance"
    xsi:schemaLocation="http://www.beeshirts.com/schemas choice.xsd">
  <card_name>VISA</card_name>
  <card_number>12345678901234</card_number>
  <expired_date>2004-09-08T01:05:00</expired_date>
  <card_confirmation_number>1234-123-123244</card_confirmation_number>
  <card_signature>
    <signature>103434055axDx98590dfhABCder</signature>
  </card_signature>
</charge_card>
```

Or perhaps it could be referenced this way:

```
<?xml version="1.0"?>
<charge_card
    xmlns="http://www.beeshirts.com/schemas"
    xmlns:xsi="http://www.w3.org/2001/XMLSchema-instance"
    xsi:schemaLocation="http://www.beeshirts.com/schemas choice.xsd">
  <card_name>VISA</card_name>
  <card_number>12345678901234</card_number>
  <expired_date>2004-09-08T01:05:00</expired_date>
  <card_confirmation_number>1234-123-123244</card_confirmation_number>
  <card_signature>
    <password>*****</password>
  </card_signature>
</charge_card>
```

Element and Attribute Groups

Groups of elements and attributes may also be specified in an XML schema. The general form for grouping together elements is accomplished via the group element. The common general form for the group element is

```
<xsd:group name="SomeGroupName">
   <xsd:sequence> ... </xsd:sequence>
</xsd:group>
```

which then may be referenced inside a type as shown here:

```
<xsd:complexType ... >
    ...
   <xsd:group ref="SomeGroupName" />
    ...
</xsd:complexType>
```

Here is an example:

```
<?xml version="1.0"?>
<xsd:schema targetNamespace="http://www.beeshirts.com/schemas"
            xmlns:xsd="http://www.w3.org/2001/XMLSchema"
            xmlns:beeshirts="http://www.beeshirts.com/schemas"
            elementFormDefault="qualified">
  <xsd:element name="charge_card" type="beeshirts:charge_card_type"/>
  <xsd:complexType name="charge_card_type">
    <xsd:sequence>
      <xsd:group  ref="beeshirts:card_type_elements"  />
      </xsd:sequence>
  </xsd:complexType>
  <xsd:group name="card_type_elements" >
    <xsd:sequence>
     <xsd:element name="card_name" type="xsd:string"/>
      <xsd:element name="card_number"
                   type="xsd:string"
                   nillable="false"/>
      <xsd:element name="expired_date"
                   type="xsd:dateTime"
                   nillable="false"/>
      <xsd:element name="card_confirmation_number"
                   type="xsd:string"
                   nillable="false"/>
      <xsd:element name="card_signature"
                   type="xsd:base64Binary"
                   minOccurs="0"/>
    </xsd:sequence>
  </xsd:group>
</xsd:schema>
```

And here is a sample snippet of a corresponding XML document:

```
<?xml version="1.0"?>
<charge_card
    xmlns="http://www.beeshirts.com/schemas"
    xmlns:xsi="http://www.w3.org/2001/XMLSchema-instance"
    xsi:schemaLocation="http://www.beeshirts.com/schemas group.xsd">
  <card_name>VISA</card_name>
  <card_number>12345678901234</card_number>
  <expired_date>2004-09-08T01:05:00</expired_date>
  <card_confirmation_number>1234-123-123244</card_confirmation_number>
  <card_signature>103434055axDx98590dfhABCder</card_signature>
</charge_card>
```

Similarly, grouping of attributes may be accomplished via a special `attributeGroup` element. The common general form for the `attributeGroup` element is as follows:

```
<xsd:attributeGroup name="SomeGroupName">
   <xsd:attribute> ...   </xsd:attribute>
</xsd:attributeGroup >
```

Also note that another `attributeGroup` or `anyAttribute` can be used instead of an `attribute` sub-element to the `attributeGroup`. Regardless, the attribute group may then be referenced as shown here:

```
<xsd:complexType ... >
    ...
   <xsd:attributeGroup ref="SomeGroupName" />
    ...
</xsd:complexType>
```

For example:

```
<?xml version="1.0"?>
<xsd:schema targetNamespace=http://www.beeshirts.com/schemas
            xmlns:beeshirts="http://www.beeshirts.com/schemas"
            xmlns:xsd="http://www.w3.org/2001/XMLSchema"
            elementFormDefault="qualified">
  <xsd:element name="charge_card" type="beeshirts:charge_card_type"/>
  <xsd:complexType name="charge_card_type">
     <xsd:attributeGroup ref="beeshirts:card_type_attributes"/>
  </xsd:complexType>
  <xsd:attributeGroup name="card_type_attributes">
     <xsd:attribute name="card_name" type="xsd:string"/>
     <xsd:attribute name="card_number" type="xsd:string" />
     <xsd:attribute name="expired_date" type="xsd:dateTime" />
     <xsd:attribute name="card_confirmation_number" type="xsd:string"/>
     <xsd:attribute name="card_signature" type="xsd:base64Binary"/>
  </xsd:attributeGroup>
</xsd:schema>
```

And here is a sample snippet of a corresponding XML document:

```
<?xml version="1.0"?>
<charge_card
    xmlns="http://www.beeshirts.com/schemas"
    xmlns:xsi="http://www.w3.org/2001/XMLSchema-instance"
    xsi:schemaLocation="http://www.beeshirts.com/schemas groupattr.xsd"
    card_name="VISA"
    card_number="12345678901234"
    expired_date="2004-09-08T01:05:00"
    card_confirmation_number="1234-123-123244"
    card_signature="103434055axDx98590dfhABCder"/>
```

Identity Constraints

A uniqueness constraint for an element in a schema defines particular elements that must be unique in the associated XML document. The general form for this `unique` element is

```
<xsd:element ...>
   ...
   <xsd:unique name="SomeIDName">
     <xsd:selector xpath="SelectorOfElementsExpression"/>
     <xsd:field xpath="UniqueFieldElement"/>
        ...
     <xsd:field xpath="UniqueFieldElement"/>
   </xsd:unique>
</xsd:element>
```

where the `selector` element is an XPath expression (see sidebar) that indicates the elements for which the uniqueness constraint applies, and the `field` element specifies those field elements or attributes that are to be unique.

> **XPath Expressions**
>
> XPath (XML Path) is a simple expression language devised to provide a pathlike addressing scheme to the elements and attributes within an XML document, and is a standard building block of XML Schema and XSL. In the interest of brevity, the basics of the language can be learned by example:
>
> - `item/quantity` refers to the `quantity` sub-element of `item`.
> - `order/item[3]` refers to the third `item` sub-element of the `order` element.
> - `charge_card/@card_type` refers to the `card_type` attribute of `charge_card`.
> - `charge_card[@card_type="credit"]` refers to the `charge_card` element whose `card_type` attribute has the value `"credit"`.

For example:

```
<?xml version="1.0"?>
<xsd:schema targetNamespace="http://www.beeshirts.com/schemas"
            xmlns:xsd="http://www.w3.org/2001/XMLSchema"
            xmlns:beeshirts="http://www.beeshirts.com/schemas"
            elementFormDefault="qualified">
  <xsd:element name="order">
    <xsd:complexType>
      <xsd:sequence>
        <xsd:element name="item" maxOccurs="unbounded">
          <xsd:complexType>
            <xsd:sequence>
              <xsd:element name="item_id" type="xsd:long"/>
              <xsd:element name="quantity" type="xsd:int"/>
              <xsd:element name="total_price" type="xsd:double"/>
              <xsd:any minOccurs="0"/>
```

```
          </xsd:sequence>
        </xsd:complexType>
      </xsd:element>
    </xsd:sequence>
  </xsd:complexType>
  <xsd:unique name="item_id_unique">
    <xsd:selector xpath="beeshirts:item"/>
    <xsd:field xpath="beeshirts:item_id"/>
  </xsd:unique>
</xsd:element>
</xsd:schema>
```

And here is a sample snippet of a corresponding XML document:

```
<?xml version="1.0"?>
<order
    xmlns="http://www.beeshirts.com/schemas"
    xmlns:xsi="http://www.w3.org/2001/XMLSchema-instance"
    xsi:schemaLocation="http://www.beeshirts.com/schemas unique.xsd">
  <item>
    <item_id>1001</item_id>
    <quantity>10</quantity>
    <total_price>99.88</total_price>
  </item>
  <item>
    <item_id>1002</item_id>
    <quantity>12</quantity>
    <total_price>108.34</total_price>
  </item>
  <item>
    <item_id>1003</item_id>
    <quantity>14</quantity>
    <total_price>120.46</total_price>
  </item>
</order>
```

A key for an element in a schema defines a particular sub-element within that element that must be unique in the XML document *and* must always be present when that parent element is referenced. The general form for this key element is

```
<xsd:element ...>
   ...
   <xsd:key name="SomeKeyName">
     <xsd:selector xpath="SelectorOfElementsExpression"/>
     <xsd:field xpath="KeyFieldElement"/>
        ...
     <xsd:field xpath="KeyFieldElement"/>
   </xsd:key>
</xsd:element>
```

where the `selector` element is an expression that indicates the elements for which the key applies, and the `field` element specifies those field elements or attributes that define the key. For example:

```
<?xml version="1.0"?>
<xsd:schema targetNamespace="http://www.beeshirts.com/schemas"
            xmlns:xsd="http://www.w3.org/2001/XMLSchema"
            xmlns:beeshirts="http://www.beeshirts.com/schemas"
            elementFormDefault="qualified">
  <xsd:element name="order">
    <xsd:complexType>
      <xsd:sequence>
        <xsd:element name="item" maxOccurs="unbounded">
          <xsd:complexType>
            <xsd:sequence>
              <xsd:element name="item_id" type="xsd:long"/>
              <xsd:element name="quantity" type="xsd:int"/>
              <xsd:element name="total_price" type="xsd:double"/>
              <xsd:any minOccurs="0"/>
            </xsd:sequence>
          </xsd:complexType>
        </xsd:element>
      </xsd:sequence>
    </xsd:complexType>
    <xsd:key name="item_id_key">
      <xsd:selector xpath="beeshirts:item"/>
      <xsd:field xpath="beeshirts:item_id"/>
    </xsd:key>
  </xsd:element>
</xsd:schema>
```

And here is a sample snippet of a corresponding XML document:

```
<?xml version="1.0"?>
<order
    xmlns="http://www.beeshirts.com/schemas"
    xmlns:xsi="http://www.w3.org/2001/XMLSchema-instance"
    xsi:schemaLocation="http://www.beeshirts.com/schemas unique.xsd">
  <item>
    <item_id>1001</item_id>
    <quantity>10</quantity>
    <total_price>99.88</total_price>
  </item>
  <item>
    <item_id>1002</item_id>
    <quantity>12</quantity>
    <total_price>108.34</total_price>
  </item>
```

```
  <item>
    <item_id>1003</item_id>
    <quantity>14</quantity>
    <total_price>120.46</total_price>
  </item>
</order>
```

A `keyref` element may be used to indicate that an element in an XML document must refer to an element defined by a particular `key`. The general form for the `keyref` element is

```
<xsd:element ...>
   ...
   <xsd:keyref name="SomeKeyrefName" refer="SomeKeyName">
     <xsd:selector xpath="SelectorOfElementsExpression"/>
     <xsd:field xpath="KeyFieldElement"/>
        ...
     <xsd:field xpath="KeyFieldElement"/>
   </xsd:key>
</xsd:element>
```

where the `selector` element is an expression that indicates the elements for which the key reference applies, and the `field` element specifies those field elements or attributes that define the key. For example:

```
<?xml version="1.0"?>
<xsd:schema targetNamespace="http://www.beeshirts.com/schemas"
            xmlns:xsd="http://www.w3.org/2001/XMLSchema"
            xmlns:beeshirts="http://www.beeshirts.com/schemas"
            elementFormDefault="qualified">
  <xsd:element name="order">
    <xsd:complexType>
      <xsd:sequence>
        <xsd:element name="item"
                     type="beeshirts:item_description"
                     maxOccurs="unbounded"/>
        <xsd:element name="canceled_item"
                     type="beeshirts:item_description"
                     minOccurs="0"/>
      </xsd:sequence>
    </xsd:complexType>
    <xsd:key name="item_id_key">
      <xsd:selector xpath="beeshirts:item"/>
      <xsd:field xpath="beeshirts:item_id"/>
    </xsd:key>
    <xsd:keyref name="item_id_ref" refer="item_id_key">
      <xsd:selector xpath="beeshirts:canceled_item/beeshirts:item"/>
      <xsd:field xpath="beeshirts:item_id"/>
    </xsd:keyref>
```

```
  </xsd:element>
  <xsd:complexType name="item_description">
    <xsd:sequence>
      <xsd:element name="item_id" type="xsd:long"/>
      <xsd:element name="quantity" type="xsd:int"/>
      <xsd:element name="total_price" type="xsd:double"/>
      <xsd:any minOccurs="0"/>
    </xsd:sequence>
  </xsd:complexType>
</xsd:schema>
```

And here is a sample snippet of a corresponding XML document:

```
<?xml version="1.0"?>
<order
    xmlns="http://www.beeshirts.com/schemas"
    xmlns:xsi="http://www.w3.org/2001/XMLSchema-instance"
    xsi:schemaLocation="http://www.beeshirts.com/schemas keyref.xsd">
  <item>
    <item_id>1001</item_id>
    <quantity>10</quantity>
    <total_price>99.88</total_price>
  </item>
  <item>
    <item_id>1002</item_id>
    <quantity>12</quantity>
    <total_price>108.34</total_price>
  </item>
  <item>
    <item_id>1003</item_id>
    <quantity>14</quantity>
    <total_price>120.46</total_price>
  </item>
  <canceled_item>
    <item_id>1001</item_id>
    <quantity>10</quantity>
    <total_price>99.88</total_price>
  </canceled_item>
</order>
```

eXtensible Stylesheet Language (XSL)

The eXtensible Stylesheet Language (XSL) is an XML-based language for creating stylesheets. XSL is used to describe how XML documents can be transformed into new XML documents or other document formats (such as HTML or text), as well as to describe how XML documents should be formatted on a given presentation medium, such as a Web browser or paper and ink. Thus, its role is to keep the data of a system (the

XML file) independent from its presentation. The specification for XSL is managed by a separate working group within the W3C.

> **Caution**
>
> Although XSL is beyond the scope of this book, we at least want to give you an idea of the nature of XSL transformations and XSL formatting. You will certainly run across XSL terminology in the course of understanding how to use XML in an enterprise environment.

XSL stylesheets are themselves XML documents that contain a set of rules, called "templates." Templates are associated with patterns designed to match the various elements in the input XML document. The patterns are written as XPath expressions. When an element or attribute matching a given template's pattern is encountered during the processing of the document, the rules contained within that template will be applied, and the results will be sent to the output. The rules contained within the templates themselves fall into two general categories: transformations and formatting.

XSL transformations (XSLT) define a set of rules to apply when transforming an XML document into another format or type of XML document. XSLT borrows heavily from the concept of stylesheets used in HTML documents. Stylesheets, such as Cascading Style Sheets (CSS), are a collection of rules attached to HTML documents that affect how its fonts, borders, backgrounds, and other style properties are displayed within a Web browser.

Similarly, an application capable of reading XML and XSL reads an XML document and an XSL stylesheet and then produces a new XML document based on the instructions present within the XSL stylesheet. XSL applications parse the source XML document into a hierarchical tree-based description of the document and build another tree-based description of the target document. XSL applications can also be specialized to produce non-XML documents such as HTML and plain-text documents.

The XSL stylesheet root XML element has a name of `xsl:stylesheet` and a version attribute defined using an `xmlns:xsl` attribute. Template rules within an XSL stylesheet document are defined within the `xsl:template` element. The `xsl:match` attribute inside of the `xsl:template` element defines the pattern to be matched against the input. Instructions for processing a particular matched template are described as sub-elements of the `xsl:template` element with names that begin with the prefix `xsl:`. All other contents of an `xsl:template` element are the XML syntax and data that is output to the target XML document stream. An XSL stylesheet document may thus follow this basic form:

```
<?xml version="1.0"?>
<xsl:stylesheet xmlns:xsl="http://www.w3.org/1999/XSL/Transform">

  <xsl:template match="elementName">
    <!-- Action for element named elementName -->
      <!-- Select sub-elements named myElement -->
      <xsl:apply-template select="myElement"/>
```

```
    <!-- Insert output style in here -->
  </xsl:template>

</xsl:stylesheet>
```

As a more elaborate example, Listing 3.3 shows an XSL stylesheet that could transform our example order XML file into HTML:

Listing 3.3 **XSL Stylesheet for XML to HTML Conversion** (`order2html.xsl`)

```
<?xml version="1.0" encoding="ISO-8859-1"?>

<xsl:stylesheet  xmlns:xsl="http://www.w3.org/1999/XSL/Transform" version="1.0">

  <xsl:output method="html"/>

  <xsl:template match="order">
    <html>
      <head><title>Your Order
      </title>
      </head>
    <body bgcolor='#FFFFFF'>
    <TABLE cellpadding='4' cellspacing='0' border='1'>
        <xsl:apply-templates/>
    </TABLE>
    </body></html>
  </xsl:template>

  <xsl:template match="order_id">
     <tr>
      <td>Order ID</td>
      <td><xsl:apply-templates/></td>
     </tr>
  </xsl:template>

  <xsl:template match="customer_id">
     <tr>
      <td>Customer ID</td>
      <td><xsl:apply-templates/></td>
     </tr>
  </xsl:template>

  <xsl:template match="order_date">
     <tr>
      <td>Order Date</td>
      <td><xsl:apply-templates/></td>
     </tr>
  </xsl:template>
```

Listing 3.3 **Continued**

```
<xsl:template match="ship_date">
   <tr>
    <td>Date Shipped</td>
    <td><xsl:apply-templates/></td>
   </tr>
</xsl:template>

<xsl:template match="paid_date">
   <tr>
    <td>Date Paid</td>
    <td><xsl:apply-templates/></td>
   </tr>
</xsl:template>

<xsl:template match="ship_charge">
   <tr>
    <td>Shipping Cost</td>
    <td><xsl:apply-templates/></td>
   </tr>
</xsl:template>

<xsl:template match="charge_card">
   <tr>
     <td>Payment Method: <xsl:value-of select="@card_type"/>
     </td>
     <td>
      <table>
       <tr>
        <td><xsl:apply-templates select="card_name"/>
        </td>
       </tr>
       <tr>
        <td><xsl:apply-templates select="card_number"/>
        </td>
       </tr>
       <tr>
        <td><xsl:apply-templates select="expired_date"/>
        </td>
       </tr>
      </table>
     </td>
   </tr>
</xsl:template>

<xsl:template match="item">
```

Listing 3.3 **Continued**

```
    <tr>
      <td>Item: <xsl:apply-templates select="item_id"/>
      </td>
      <td>
       <table>
        <tr>
         <td>Count: <xsl:apply-templates select="quantity"/>
         </td>
        </tr>
        <tr>
         <td>Total cost: <xsl:apply-templates select="total_price"/>
         </td>
        </tr>
       </table>
      </td>
    </tr>
  </xsl:template>

  <xsl:template match="ship_instruct">
   <tr>
    <td colspan='2'><b><xsl:apply-templates/></b></td>
   </tr>
  </xsl:template>

</xsl:stylesheet>
```

A source XML document can designate a particular XSL stylesheet to use in transforming itself via a processing instruction declaration of the following form:

```
<?xml version="1.0"?>
<?xml-stylesheet type="text/xml" href="XSLdocumentName.xsl"?>
<!-- Rest of XML document description below -->
            ...
```

XSL formatting is defined using a collection of XSL formatting objects and properties. Formatting objects tell an application that can understand XSL formatting notation where to place XML document portions in a cohesive XML-based page. Formatting objects and properties are standard names for elements and attributes of elements that can be read by a formatting application. You can recognize XSL formatting object notation in a document if you see any elements that begin with the `fo:` namespace prefix. For example:

```
<fo:block font-weight="bold">
   This is bold text
</fo:block>
```

XML Linking

Hyperlinking in XML involves the association of URLs to resources (for example, images and XML documents), as well as defining the relationship between resources. Linking specifications in XML was once referred to as the eXtensible Linking Language (XLL) and is now divided into two separate specifications: XLink and XPointer. The XML Linking Language (XLink) defines how resources are referenced from within XML documents and is embodied within an evolving W3C specification (`www.w3.org/TR/xlink/`). The XML Pointer Language (XPointer) defines a mechanism for addressing different portions of an XML document and is also embodied within an evolving W3C specification (`www.w3.org/TR/xptr`).

> **Caution**
>
> Both the XLink and the XPointer specifications are currently evolving and subject to much change. Although a detailed discussion of XML linking is beyond the scope of this book, we at least want to give you an idea of the nature of XLinks and XPointers. You will certainly run across such terminology in the course of understanding how to use XML in an enterprise environment, and you may even run across concrete examples of their usage.

XLinks

Central to the topic of linking in XML is the concept of a resource. A resource is an addressable piece of information such as the type of information addressed by a URL (for example, files, images, and applications). A link is a relationship between resources. A local resource is a resource embedded inside of an XML link element. A remote resource is the actual resource information pointed to by an XML link.

Linking elements are XML elements that include links. A linking element defines a link as an attribute using the `xlink:type` attribute name. XLink defines several standard `xlink:type` attribute values:

- `simple`: Defines an association between a local resource and a remote resource.
- `extended`: Defines associations among multiple resources.
- `locator`: Defines addresses to remote resources. An extended link must have at least one `locator` element type defined.
- `arc`: Defines rules for traversing between the links contained by an extended link element.
- `title`: Defines a human-readable description of an extended link.
- `resource`: Defines the local resources for an extended link. If an extended link defines a `resource` element type, it is called an inline link.

Simple Links

A simple link associates a local resource with a remote resource. Simple link information is embedded inside of an XML element akin to the way an attribute is embedded inside of an element. The form of the link (that is, "simple") and URL reference are both embedded into the XML element. This is the general form of a simple link:

```
<ElementName xlink:type="simple" xlink:href="URL"> ...</ElementName>
                  <!-- OR -->
<ElementName xlink:type="simple" xlink:href="URL"/> <!-- Empty -->
```

The `xlink:type` attribute of an element is thus defined as "simple" and the URL of the resource is defined after an `xlink:href` attribute. For example:

```
<homepage xlink:type="simple" xlink:href="http://www.beeshirts.com/">
  BeeShirts Home
</homepage>

<beeShirtsLogo xlink:form="simple" xlink:href="images/beeshirts.gif"/>
```

Simple links thus have a familiar HTML flavor. A simple link can be associated with XML element data such that, when it's viewed by an application such as a Web browser, clicking on the link can induce a reference to the remote resource. Likewise, a simple link to a remote resource, such as an image, may be used by an application to display the resource directly within (that is, "inline") the viewed XML document page.

Link Semantics and Behavior Attributes

In addition to defining a link attribute and its associated URL, the title and role of a remote resource may optionally be described as attributes. The `xlink:title` attribute describes the remote resource's title in a human-readable fashion. The `xlink:role` attribute describes the purpose of the remote resource in a fashion useful to an application.

The behavior of a link may also optionally be defined as an attribute inside the element. An `xlink:show` attribute is used to describe how an endpoint resource is to be displayed when referenced. If the `xlink:show="new"` value is specified, a new window will be created to display the remote resource. If the `xlink:show="replace"` value is specified, the window used to load the current link is used to display the remote resource. If the `xlink:show="embed"` value is specified, the window used to load the current link is used to display the remote resource inline.

An `xlink:actuate` attribute is used to describe the latency between parsing of a link and the actual reference of the remote resource. If the `xlink:actuate="onLoad"` value is specified, the application should immediately load the remote resource upon loading of the link. If the `xlink:actuate="onRequest"` value is specified, the application should load the remote resource upon activation of the link (for example, a click on the link).

Extended Links

Simple links have a single association between a local resource and a remote resource. Extended links are more generic links that can associate multiple resources with one another. If one of the links is local, the extended link is said to be inline. If all the links are remote, the extended link is said to be out-of-line.

An extended link is identified within an XML element using the "extended" value for an xlink:type attribute. A local resource is embedded inside of an extended link as an element whose xlink:type attribute value is equal to "resource". A remote resource that exists outside of an extended link (perhaps in another XML document) is represented as an extended link element's sub-element with an xlink:type attribute value of "locator". Such locator-type elements can identify a remote resource URL as an xlink:href attribute, as well as include the other standard attributes used with links, including link semantic and behavior attributes.

For example, a sweaters XML document that defines a local resource sweater advertisement may be associated with three different remote resources that target a particular sweater-style homepage URL. An application may use xlink:role attributes to determine which target remote resource to reference depending on some particular customer preference criteria. Customer profile data may indicate a preference for "classic" or "sporty" styles of sweaters, and the application will select a suitable target remote reference based on this knowledge. An XML document supporting such extended link functionality might look like this:

```
<sweaters xlink:type="extended" xlink:title="BeeShirts.com Sweaters">
  <sweaterAd xlink:type="resource" xlink:role="sweaters">
    BeeShirts.com has sweater styles to suit you
  </sweaterAd>
  <default
    xlink:type="locator"
    xlink:href="http://www.beeshirts.com/sweaters/standard/"
    xlink:role="standard"/>
  <option
    xlink:type="locator"
    xlink:href="http://www.beeshirts.com/sweaters/classic/"
    xlink:title="Classic Sweater Style"
    xlink:role="classic"/>
  <option
    xlink:type="locator"
    xlink:href="http://www.beeshirts.com/sweaters/sports/"
    xlink:title="Sporty Sweater Style"
    xlink:role="sports"/>
</sweaters>
```

Extended links have many traversal possibilities among the resources they identify. The xlink:type attribute with a value of "arc" can be defined within a sub-element of an extended link element to identify a particular traversal rule. Link traversal behavior for an arc-type element can be defined with the link behavior xlink:show and xlink:actuate attributes. Arcs also define xlink:from and xlink:to attributes to identify the "from" resource and "to" resource directionality of link traversal. The values of xlink:from and xlink:to attributes are the values that have been assigned to a defined resource's xlink:role attribute. For example, we might define a set of arcs identifying the traversal from a local resource selection to a particular remote resource selection inside of our sweaters XML document such as the one shown here:

```
<sweaters xlink:type="extended" xlink:title="BeeShirts.com Sweaters">
    ...
  <selection
    xlink:type="arc"
    xlink:from="sweaters"  xlink:to="classic"
    xlink:show="replace" xlink:actuate="onRequest"/>
</sweaters>
```

XPointers

Extended pointers (XPointers) define a means for identifying and addressing sections of an XML document. HTML defines a means for tagging portions of a document and then referencing those internal relative links within a URL by using the convention evident in `http://www.beeshirts.com/myPage.html#myRelativeLink`. XPointers provide a means to reference XML documents in a much more resolute and flexible form. XPointers also provide a way to reference ranges of XML document data.

A particular element with an `ID` attribute type can be referenced using an XPointer syntax of `xpointer(id("`*`MyElementID`*`"))` or simply using *`MyElementID`*. For example, an element named `order` with an `ID` attribute of `jshmoe4867` can be referenced as

```
http://www.beeshirts.com/orders/BoaShirts.xml#jshmoe4867
```

or as

```
http://www.beeshirts.com/orders/BoaShirts.xml#xpointer(id("jshmoe4867"))
```

Nested sub-elements may also be referenced in various ways. For example, the 16th child element of the 3rd child element may be discovered using this:

```
http://www.beeshirts.com/orders/BoaShirts.xml#/3/16
```

Conclusions

XML is used to describe how data should be represented. Such a standard data representation format enables open exchange of information between disparate applications implemented in different languages, on different platforms, and over various communication protocols. DTDs define a standard way to define a standard type of XML document. XML Schema has begun to usurp the role of DTDs to provide a much richer albeit more complicated means for defining standard XML document structures and semantics. XML Linking has been defined to describe standard linking mechanisms between XML documents and resources. XSL defines standard automated transformations and formatting of XML documents. Java's integration with XML is thus of primary significance if Java and the J2EE are to be useful in integrating with enterprise applications in a standard fashion. As you'll learn in subsequent chapters, Java and the J2EE standards have completely embraced XML and Web Services as a key means for achieving openness and interoperability.

4

JAXP

IN THE PRECEDING CHAPTER, WE LOOKED at how XML documents are defined and validated using DTDs and XML Schema. Although such standards are specified in an application-independent fashion, the standards would be for naught if there were not simple and useful ways for applications to actually read XML documents. JAXP provides two methods, in fact. The first is the Simple API for XML (SAX), which defines a set of standard interfaces for applications to use when parsing XML documents. SAX works on an event-driven model, which requires applications to implement handlers for the specific data-parsing events they want to process. The other is the Document Object Model (DOM), which creates a hierarchical representation of the XML document in memory, which an application can access and modify as it needs in a procedural fashion. JAXP also provides an interface to XSL Transformations (XSLT), which allows an application to transform an XML document according to rules set out in an XSL stylesheet.

In this chapter, you will learn:

- An overview of SAX and the architecture of JAXP SAX
- The core abstractions inside of JAXP SAX
- What JAXP SAX event handlers are and how to use them
- How to induce the parsing of an XML document using JAXP SAX
- The architecture and usage of the Document Object Model API for interfacing with XML parsers and documents using the JAXP
- An overview of DOM and the architecture of JAXP DOM
- The JAXP DOM means for representing generic nodes in a DOM encapsulation of an XML document
- The JAXP DOM means for representing concrete nodes in a DOM encapsulation of an XML document
- How to induce the parsing of an XML document using JAXP DOM and implement an application tying together the use of JAXP DOM
- Transforming XML documents using JAXP and XSL Transformations

XML Parsing with SAX

The Simple API for XML (SAX) is used for parsing XML documents via a programmatic interface implemented using a standard set of parse event listeners. SAX is an API standard that was originally developed by a community of individuals participating in an XML-DEV mailing list group and now hosted by the OASIS standards body. The standard interfaces to SAX are defined in the `org.xml.sax`, `org.xml.sax.helpers`, and `org.xml.sax.ext` Java packages. The Java API for XML Parsing (JAXP) v1.1 is a standard component of the J2SE, starting with JDK version 1.4. The JDK provides a reference implementation of these standard interfaces. JAXP also defines a small abstraction layer to these interfaces in the `javax.xml.parsers` package. The classes included in this package are primarily factory classes that create instances of the parsers that the application will use. The J2EE v1.4 requires use of JAXP v1.2 inside J2EE EJB containers, Web containers, and application clients. JAXP v1.2 serves as a maintenance revision to the JAXP v1.1 to support a standard way for enabling XML Schema validation.

SAX1 was the standard API for XML parsing that was supported with the JAXP v1.0 API. SAX1 did not have full support for use of XML namespaces, among other features. SAX2, the current version, does support XML namespaces and adds many new API features. SAX2 is supported by the JAXP v1.1/1.2 APIs and is the SAX version around which the material in this chapter is primarily constructed. Although JAXP v1.1/1.2 still supports many of the APIs of SAX1, these APIs have been deprecated. Although we will occasionally refer to these deprecated interfaces, we will not focus on their use or full description throughout this chapter because the preferred JAXP usage means is to use SAX2-compliant features.

> **Note**
>
> Throughout the sample code in this chapter, we assume the use of the JAXP v1.2 implementation. This is the version that is currently being shipped with J2EE v1.4–compliant containers. A separately bundled reference implementation of JAXP v1.2 can be downloaded from `http://java.sun.com/xml/downloads/jaxp.html` as part of the Java XML Pack. The `sax.jar`, `dom.jar`, `xercesImpl.jar`, `xalan.jar`, and `xsltc.jar` files from the `jaxp-1.2` directory in that bundle are needed to run these examples. Because the J2SE v1.4 comes equipped with JAXP v1.1, you'll need to use these newer JAXP v1.2 libraries with the examples. These newer libraries can be placed under your J2SE v1.4 home directory at `<JAVA_HOME>/jre/lib/endorsed` as a default or wherever else you've set your `java.endorsed.dirs` system property to allow. By placing the JARs in that directory, you can override use of JAXP v1.1 in favor of the JAXP v1.2 libraries with your J2SE v1.4 runtime. Appendix A, "Software Configuration," contains comprehensive information on how to locate, install, and configure software with the examples in the book.

JAXP SAX Architecture Overview

Figure 4.1 depicts the top-level architecture of the main Java-based SAX abstractions. The JAXP SAX exceptions, helper classes, extension interfaces, and deprecated abstractions are not depicted in this diagram. Most classes and interfaces in the diagram come from the standard `org.xml.sax` package. Two additional classes defined in the javax.xml.parsers package are also utilized to define a provider-independent means for creating parser handles as well as a non-SAX-standard parser helper class.

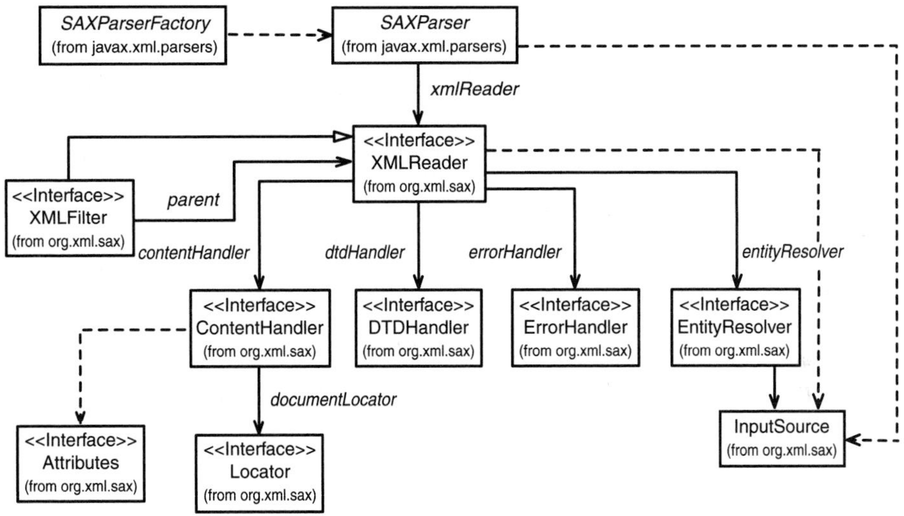

Figure 4.1 Top-level SAX class architecture.

An XMLReader interface defines a standard interface to a SAX parser for initiating the parsing of XML documents. The SAX XMLReader interface can notify parse event-handler objects during the parsing of XML documents and the generation of parse events. Standard SAX abstractions also exist for an XML document content input source, XML element attribute collection, and XML document event location information.

Core SAX Abstractions

Before we delve into the primary application interfaces, let's look at a few of the core and most basic SAX standard objects. The most basic elements can be partitioned into the basic SAX exceptions, a document event location helper, a document element attribute list, an XML namespace helper abstraction, and a document content input source abstraction. These core abstractions are contained in both the org.xml.sax base SAX package and the org.xml.sax.helpers SAX helpers package. The base SAX package provides a home for the primary public interface to these SAX abstractions. The SAX helpers package provides a home for default implementations of many interfaces.

SAX Exceptions

One set of core JAXP SAX abstractions consists of the exception types that may be thrown during SAX parsing. Figure 4.2 depicts the basic exception hierarchy associated with JAXP SAX parsing. The SAXException class encapsulates a generic SAX error condition containing a nested root exception. All exceptions to be thrown by SAX objects inherit from this base exception type.

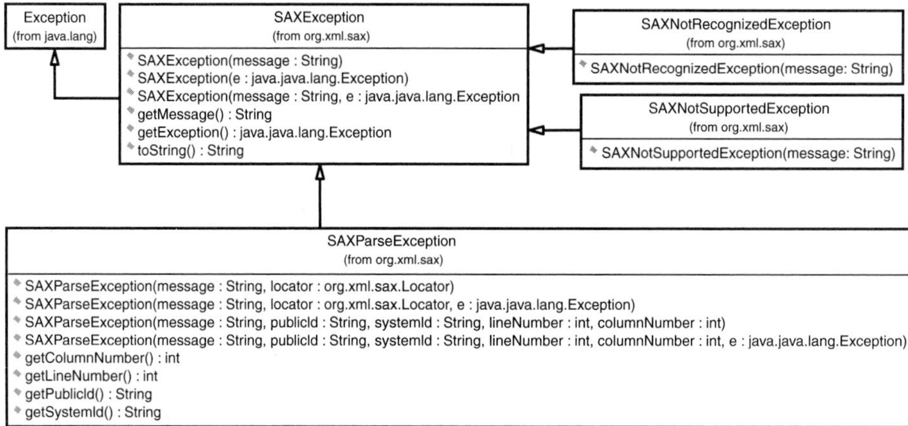

Figure 4.2 SAX exception hierarchy.

The `SAXParseException` class encapsulates a generic error during parsing of an XML document. Information about the location of the error can also be obtained from a `SAXParseException` object. The `SAXParserException` offers getter methods to obtain the approximate location of the parsing exception in the XML document being parsed. Information about the location of an exception in a document can be obtained using appropriately named methods, including retrieval of a public identifier of the element, a system identifier (for example, URL), and the approximate line and column numbers in the document.

The `SAXNotRecognizedException` is thrown when an unrecognized identifier is encountered during SAX parsing. The `SAXNotSupportedException` is thrown when a particular identifier is recognized but cannot be properly handled during SAX parsing.

SAX Event Locator

Figure 4.3 depicts these key abstractions involved with locating a SAX event within an XML document. The `Locator` interface represents the location of some event in an XML document. Information about the location of an event in a document can be obtained from a `Locator`, including a public identifier of the element, a system identifier (for example, URL), and the approximate line and column numbers in the document. This information makes the `Locator` particularly useful in pinpointing syntax or other errors within an XML document.

The `LocatorImpl` class is a helper class that provides a default implementation of the `Locator` interface. The `LocatorImpl` can be constructed with no data present or with the copied contents of another `Locator` object. In addition to implementations of the Locator getter methods, the LocatorImpl class also provides a corresponding set of setter methods.

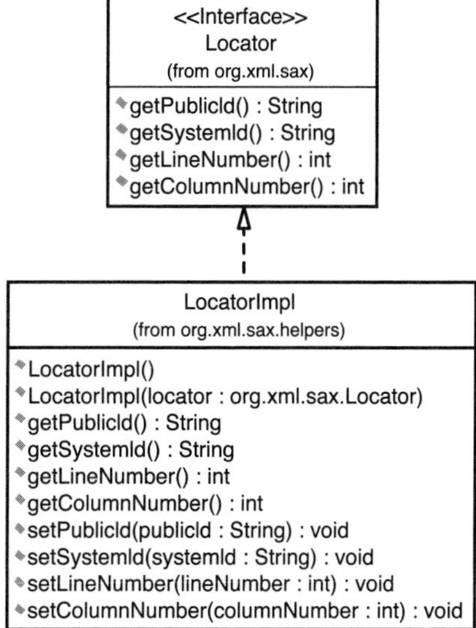

Figure 4.3 SAX Locator object.

SAX Attributes

Figure 4.4 depicts the core abstractions involved with representing attributes in a parsed XML document. The Attributes interface is implemented by a parser provider and describes an interface to an XML element's list of attributes. The Attributes class is now used in JAXP v1.1/1.2 in favor over the deprecated AttributeList class, which did not fully support XML namespaces. The AttributesImpl class provides a default implementation of the Attributes interface. Similarly, the AttributeListImpl is deprecated in favor of the AttributesImpl class.

The Attributes.getLength() method returns the number of attributes contained by the list, although the order of attributes in an Attributes object is arbitrary. An attribute in the Attributes object has a name, type, and value. A String version of the attribute's local name, fully qualified name, or namespace URI may be obtained via calls to getLocalName(int), getQName(int), and getURI(int) methods, respectively, on the Attributes object and by passing in the index number of the attribute in the list. That is, for the XML document snippet

```
<order
          xmlns:ati="http://assuredtech.com/schema"
          xmlns:beeshirts="http://beeshirts.com/b2c"
>
```

```
        ...
  <beeshirts:charge_card beeshirts:card_type="credit">
    <beeshirts:card_number> 12345678901234 </beeshirts:card_number>
      ...
  </beeshirts:charge_card>
</order>
```

the attribute associated with the `charge_card` element has the local name of `card_type`, the `Qname` of `beeshirts:card_type`, and the namespace URI of `http://beeshirts.com/b2c`. If no value is defined or namespace processing is not employed, the name getter methods may return a null `String` value (`""`). An out-of-bounds index number will return a `null` value.

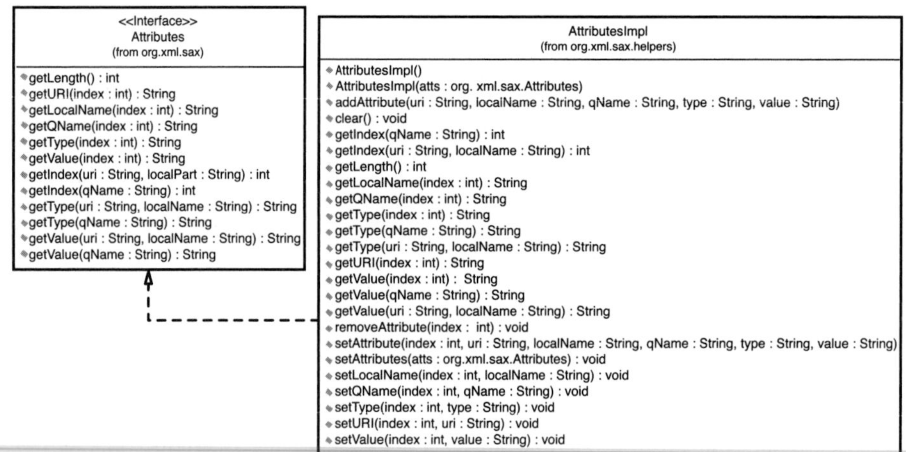

Figure 4.4 `SAX Attributes.`

The actual index value of the attribute may be retrieved from the `Attributes` object using the `getIndex(String qname)` method with the attribute's qualified name `String` or via the `getIndex(String uri, String localName)` with the attribute's namespace URI and local name. A `-1` index value is returned if the attribute is not in the list.

Attributes may also have a type, such as `CDATA`, `ENTITY`, `ENTITIES`, `NMTOKEN`, `NMTOKENS`, `ID`, `IDREF`, `IDREFS`, or `NOTATION`, defined in Chapter 3, "XML." If no attribute type is declared or known, the type value is assumed to be a `CDATA` type. The `String` value of such types for an attribute can be returned via invoking the `Attributes` object's `getType(int index)` method using an index parameter, the `getType(String qname)` method using a qualified name `String` parameter, or the `getType(String uri, String localName)` method using namespace URI and local name `String` parameters. The actual value of the attributes may be retrieved in `String` form from the `Attributes` object via invoking the `getValue(int index)` method using an index parameter, the getValue(String qname) method using a qualified name String parameter, or the getValue(String uri, String localName) method using namespace URI and local name String parameters.

When the attribute value is actually a list itself, the elements of the list are returned as a space-separated concatenated String. The AttributesImpl class provides a default helper implementation of the Attributes interface. In addition to the Attributes interface getters, the AttributesImpl class also provides a set of corresponding setter methods. Removal of attributes in the list is enabled by the AttributesImpl.removeAttribute(int) method providing the index of the attribute to be removed or via clearing of the entire attribute list's contents via the clear() method. Finally, the addition of an attribute to the list can be performed using the addAttribute() method and passing in the String form of the attribute's namespace URI, local name, qualified name, type, and value.

Input Sources and Namespace Support

Figure 4.5 illustrates the composition and operation signatures that exist for the SAX InputSource class and NamespaceSupport helper class. The InputSource class encapsulates a source of XML document data input. Public identifiers, system identifiers, a byte stream, a character stream, and encoding all have appropriately named associated setters and getters on the InputSource class. Public and system identifiers of an input source are optional and have semantics that are specific to an application. A character stream representation of the XML content takes preference over use of a byte-stream representation if both are specified. The system identifier is used as a URI in creating an input stream connection if neither a character stream nor a byte stream is specified. Finally, the encoding format of an input stream can also be specified.

The NamespaceSupport helper class represents the means for processing namespace declarations in XML documents being parsed. Namespace resolution in XML works in a similar fashion to variable scopes in Java; names defined within a scope are valid within that scope, and when that scope is exited, the previous namespace is brought back. NamespaceSupport implements this by pushing and popping information from a stack. The pushContext() method is used to signal a new context for a namespace. This method is invoked when encountering each XML element. Conversely, the popContext() method is invoked after completing parsing of an XML element to restore context to the prior namespace scope. If you want to reuse the same NamespaceContext object to parse another document, the reset() method will clear that object's state and context.

After encountering an element and establishing a new namespace context, you can declare one or more element prefixes by invoking the declarePrefix() method one or more times. You accomplish this by passing a prefix identifier and associated URI for the namespace into the declarePrefix(String prefix, String uri) method. The prefix name will remain valid until the current context is popped from the stack. A raw (unprefixed) XML element name in that context may be looked up using the processName() method call. The processName() method accepts as parameters a qualified name of an XML element or attribute, a String array of at least three String objects used to contain results, and a boolean flag indicating whether the name refers to an XML attribute. The String array passed as an input parameter is actually used to contain results from the call, including the namespace URI for the element or attribute, the local name of the element or attribute, and the original name read from the XML document. Additionally, the String array will also be returned from the method call.

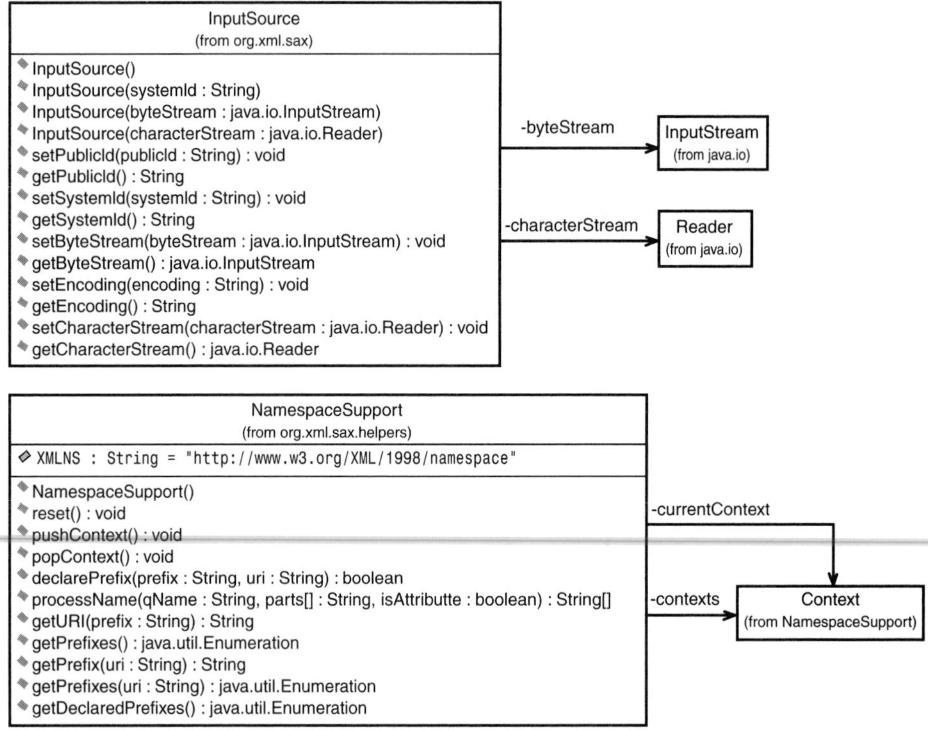

Figure 4.5 InputSource and NamespaceSupport.

A set of getters on the NamespaceSupport class also enables you to obtain information about the current namespace context. An Enumeration of prefix identifiers in the current context can be returned via the getDeclaredPrefixes() call. An Enumeration of prefix identifiers in the current and parent contexts can be returned via the getPrefixes() call. Given a namespace URI, the getPrefix(String) and getPrefixes(String) methods can return a prefix identifier or Enumeration of such identifiers. Conversely, the namespace URI given a prefix can be returned via a call to getURI(String).

SAX Event Handlers

Figure 4.6 represents the abstractions used by applications to receive notification of XML document parsing events from a SAX XML document parser. The four interfaces shown represent interfaces that are implemented by applications to receive such events. Object implementations of these interfaces are registered with an XML parser. A default implementation of these interfaces is defined within the `com.xml.sax.helpers.DefaultHandler` class.

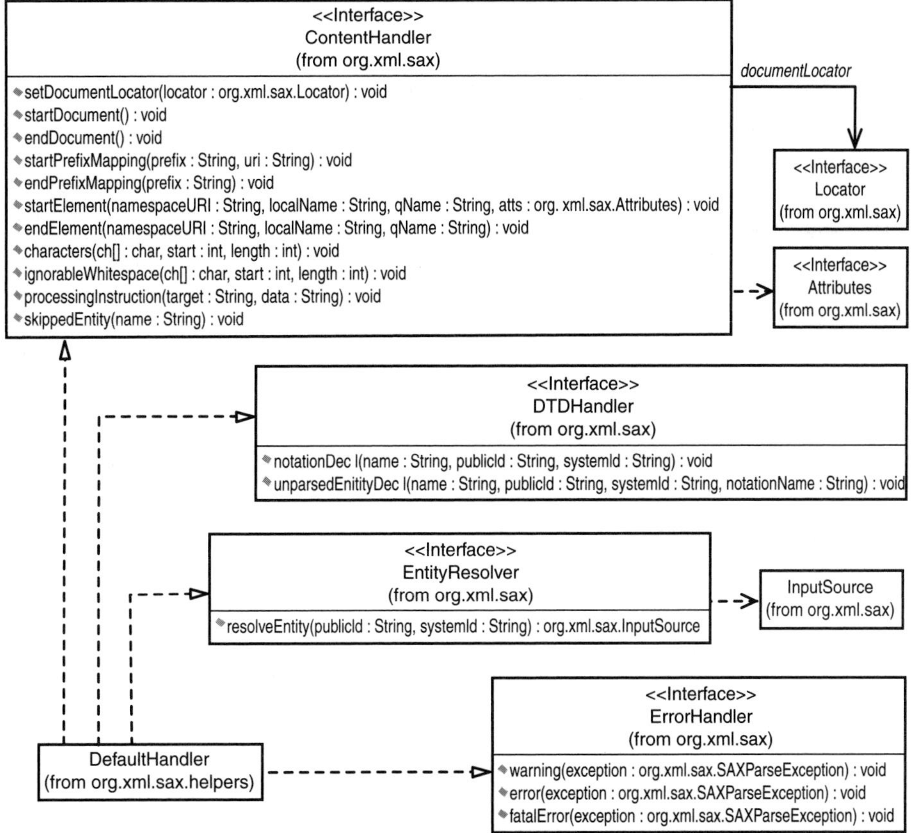

Figure 4.6 SAX event handlers.

The `DTDHandler` is implemented by application classes that handle events related to DTD processing. Specifically, events related to notation and unparsed entity declarations can be received, and the associated information can be stored for later reference when parsing an associated XML document. The `DTDHandler.notationDecl()` method is implemented to receive notification of the declaration of a notation in a parsed DTD. An application uses this information for later reference and includes the name of the notation, an optional public identifier for the notation, and an optional system identifier (for example, URL). The `DTDHandler.unparsedEntityDecl()` method can be implemented to receive notification of a declaration of an unparsed entity in the DTD. The unparsed entity's name, optional public identifier, optional system identifier, and associated notation name may be passed into this method.

> **Note**
>
> Refer to Appendix A for instructions on how to obtain a complete copy of the example listings in this chapter. Instructions on how to build and run the example programs are also available in Appendix A.

Listing 4.1 shows a sample `DTDHandler` implementation via a `SampleDTDHandler` class that simply prints information when its implemented methods are called.

Listing 4.1 **DTD Handler (`SampleDTDHandler.java`)**

```
package ejava.jaxp;

import org.xml.sax.DTDHandler;
import org.xml.sax.SAXException;

/**
  * implements DTDHandler to receive DTD events from parser
  */
public class SampleDTDHandler implements DTDHandler
{

  /**
  * receive information about DTD entity information.
  */
  public void notationDecl(String name, String publicID,
    String systemID)
    throws SAXException
  {
    System.out.println("DTD Handling...");
    System.out.println(" Notation Name :" +name + " publicID :"
      +publicID + "System ID : " +systemID);
  }

  /**
  * receive information about a DTD unparsed entity
  */
  public void unparsedEntityDecl(String name, String publicID,
    String systemID, String notationName)
    throws SAXException
  {
```

Listing 4.1 **Continued**

```
    System.out.println("DTD Handling...");
    System.out.println(" Entity :" + name +" public ID :" + publicID +
      "System ID :" +systemID + "Notation Name :" + notationName);
  }
 }
```

The EntityResolver interface is implemented by application classes that resolve external entities. The single EntityResolver.resolveEntity() method is implemented to receive a public identifier and system identifier of the external entity being referenced. The application creates and returns an InputSource object associated with the external XML content. If a null value is returned, it is assumed that the system identifier URL form can be used to identify the external entity location. A parser calls this method before it attempts to open an external entity. Listing 4.2 shows a sample EntityResolver implementation via a SampleEntityResolver class that simply prints information when its implemented methods are called.

Listing 4.2 **Entity Resolver (SampleEntityResolver.java)**

```
package ejava.jaxp;

import org.xml.sax.EntityResolver;
import org.xml.sax.SAXException;
import org.xml.sax.InputSource;
import org.xml.sax.SAXParseException;

import java.io.IOException;
import java.net.URL;
import java.io.InputStream;

/**
  * Implements EntityResolver. If it sees a specific
  * systemID, it creates a different InputSource to
  * read data.
  */

public class SampleEntityResolver implements EntityResolver
{

  /**
  * to resolve each entity, resolveEntity is called by parser
  */
  public InputSource resolveEntity(String publicID,
                                   String systemID)
    throws SAXException, IOException
```

Listing 4.2 **Continued**

```
  {
    System.out.println("Entity Resolver Public ID :" + publicID);
    System.out.println("Entity Resolver System ID :" + systemID);

    // Modify this value to induce reading from another input source
    String urlString =
    "http://localhost/examples/src/ejava/jaxp/dtdAndXmlDocument.xml";

    if (systemID.equals(urlString)) {
       // return a new input source
       URL url = new URL(urlString);
       InputStream inputStream = url.openStream();
       return new InputSource(inputStream);
     } else {
       // return null and require us of default systemID
       return null;
     }
  }
 }
```

The `ErrorHandler` interface is implemented by applications that need to handle warnings, errors, and fatal errors that can occur during XML parsing. A parser passes a `SAXParseException` during a call to an appropriate `ErrorHandler` method, and the application decides how to handle the exception. Such errors reported may be warning of a questionable condition but to continue processing the document, a clearly defined error in the validity of the document and to continue processing, or a fatal error with the validity of the document and to assume the document is not capable of being parsed further. The application itself may also throw a `SAXException` when one of these methods is called. Listing 4.3 shows a sample `ErrorHandler` implementation via a `SampleErrorHandler` class that simply prints information when its implemented methods are called.

Listing 4.3 **Error Handler (`SampleErrorHandler.java`)**

```
package ejava.jaxp;

import org.xml.sax.ErrorHandler;
import org.xml.sax.SAXException;
import org.xml.sax.SAXParseException;

/**
  * implements Error Handler
  */

public class SampleErrorHandler implements ErrorHandler
```

Listing 4.3 **Continued**

```
{

  /**
  * it receives the errors of type recoverable Errors
  */
  public void error(SAXParseException saxParseException)
    throws SAXException
  {
    System.out.println("ERROR ...");
    printException(saxParseException);
  }

  /**
  * to receive the Fatal or non recoverable Error
  */
  public void fatalError(SAXParseException saxParseException)
    throws SAXException
  {
    System.out.println("FATAL ERROR ...");
    printException(saxParseException);
  }

  /**
  * to receive warnings from the parser
  */
  public void warning(SAXParseException saxParseException)
    throws SAXException
  {
    System.out.println("WARNING ...");
    printException(saxParseException);
  }

  private void printException(SAXParseException saxParseException)
  {
    System.out.println(saxParseException);
    System.out.println("Error Handler Column # :"
                     + saxParseException.getColumnNumber());
    System.out.println("Error Handler Line # : "
                     + saxParseException.getLineNumber());
    System.out.println("Error Handler System ID :"
                     + saxParseException.getSystemId());
    System.out.println("Error Handler Public ID :"
                     +saxParseException.getPublicId());
  }
 }
```

The `ContentHandler` interface is the primary interface implemented by applications that need to handle most XML document parsing–related events. The `ContentHandler` provides SAX2-compliant interfaces and replaces the deprecated `DocumentHandler` interface defined for SAX1. The `ContentHandler.startDocument()` method is called when parsing of an XML document begins, and `ContentHandler.endDocument()` is called when parsing ends. When the parser encounters the start tag of an XML document element, the `ContentHandler.startElement()` method is called. The element name in the form of a namespace URI, local name, and qualified name, as well as the element's attribute contents, will be passed as parameters to the `startElement()` method. Any `IMPLIED` attribute values will be omitted from the `Attributes` object passed into `startElement()`. For each `startElement()` method call, a `ContentHandler.endElement()` method will be called with an element name, also in the form of a namespace URI, local name, and qualified name, indicating that the end of the element was parsed. The `endElement()` method is also called for empty elements.

In certain cases, a parser will invoke the `startPrefixMapping()` and `endPrefixMapping()` methods for the benefit of the application. These cases include situations in which prefixes are used in character data, attribute values, or other places where they cannot be expanded safely by the SAX parser, which by default expands element and attribute namespace prefixes. In such cases XML entity prefix identifier and namespace URI will be handed off to the application sometime prior to reading the entity (`startPrefixMapping`) and after reading the entity (`endPrefixMapping`). Although mappings that expand the prefix with the namespace URI generally occur transparent to the application, the parser may elect to invoke these methods for cases in which such mappings cannot occur safely without further application-specific intervention. Furthermore, for certain parsers that do not validate the XML document against an external DTD or schema as it parses the document, the parser may skip certain entities as it encounters them. In such cases, the `skippedEntity()` method is invoked by the parser and indicates the name of the entity skipped.

A host of other methods on the `ContentHandler` object also report important event information to an application as the parser parses an XML document. The `ContentHandler.setDocumentLocator()` method can be used by an application to obtain a `Locator` object from a parser with the `ContentHandler`. This will allow the location of events in an XML document, within the scope of element boundaries, to be inferred. The `ContentHandler.characters()` method is called by a parser to notify an application of an array of characters that have been retrieved from an XML document element's character data. The `ContentHandler.ignorableWhitespace()` method is used to report whitespace characters read from an XML document element. Any processing instructions embedded in an XML document can be received by an application using the `ContentHandler.processingInstruction()` method. The processing instruction name and associated parameter data are passed as parameters to the `processingInstruction()` method. Listing 4.4 shows a sample `ContentHandler` implementation via a `SampleContentHandler` class that simply prints information when its implemented methods are called.

Listing 4.4 **Content Handler (`SampleContentHandler.java`)**

```
package ejava.jaxp;

import org.xml.sax.ContentHandler;
import org.xml.sax.SAXException;
import org.xml.sax.Locator;
import org.xml.sax.Attributes;
import org.xml.sax.SAXParseException;

import java.io.File;

/**
 * An example document handler
 */
public class SampleContentHandler  implements ContentHandler
{

  /**
   * Receives the character data for each element
   */
  public void characters(char[] value, int start, int length)
      throws SAXException
  {
    String newValue = new String(value);
    System.out.println(" Present Char Chunk :" +
      newValue.substring(start,start+length) );
  }

  /**
   * Receives notification of end of document
   */
  public void endDocument()
    throws SAXException
  {
    System.out.println("End of Document ");
  }

  /**
   * Receives information about end of an element
   */
  public void endElement(String namespaceURI,
                         String localName, String qName)
    throws SAXException
```

Listing 4.4 **Continued**

```
{
  System.out.println(" End of Element :");
  System.out.println("   namespaceURI = " + namespaceURI);
  System.out.println("   localName    = " + localName);
  System.out.println("   qName        = " + qName);
}

/**
 * Ends the scope of a prefix-URI Namespace mapping.
 * Called after the corresponding endElement.
 */
public void endPrefixMapping(String prefix) throws SAXException
{
  System.out.println(" End prefix:");
  System.out.println("    prefix = " + prefix);
}

/**
 * Receives notification of ignorable whitespace in element content.
 */
public void ignorableWhitespace(char[] value, int start , int length)
  throws SAXException
{
  String newValue = new String(value);
  if(length > 0){
   System.out.println(" ignorable Value is :"
                     + newValue.substring(start,start+length-1));
  }
}

/**
 * The XMLReader will invoke this method once for each processing
 * instruction found
*/
public void processingInstruction(String target, String data)
  throws SAXException
{
  System.out.println("Processing Instruction Target :"+target);
  System.out.println("Processing Instruction data :"+data);
}

/**
 * Receives a handle to the XMLReader's Locator object
 */
public void setDocumentLocator(Locator locator)
```

Listing 4.4 **Continued**

```
{
  System.out.println("Received locator");
}

/**
 * Receives notification of a skipped entity
 */
public void skippedEntity(String name) throws SAXException
{
    System.out.println("Skipped entity = " + name);
}

/**
 *  Receives the startDocument notification
 */
public void startDocument()
  throws SAXException
{
  System.out.println(" The parser started parsing document :");
}

/**
 * Info about the new element being parsed, including
 * namespace, local and qualified names of the element,
 * and the list of attributes.
 */
public void startElement(String namespaceURI, String localName,
                         String qName, Attributes attributes)
  throws SAXException
{
  System.out.println(" Start of Element :");
  System.out.println("     namespaceURI = " + namespaceURI);
  System.out.println("     localName    = " + localName);
  System.out.println("     qName        = " + qName);

  int totalAttributes = attributes.getLength();
  for(int i = 0; i < totalAttributes; i++){
    String name = attributes.getLocalName(i);
    String type = attributes.getType(i);
    String value = attributes.getValue(i);
    System.out.println(" Attribute Name :" + name +
      " Type : "+ type +" Value :" +value);
  }
}
```

Listing 4.4 **Continued**

```
  /**
   * Begins the scope of a prefix-URI Namespace mapping.
   * Called before the corresponding startElement.
   */
  public void startPrefixMapping(String prefix, String uri)
     throws SAXException
  {
    System.out.println(" Start prefix:");
    System.out.println("      prefix = " + prefix);
    System.out.println("      uri    = " + uri);
  }
 }
```

Lastly, the `org.xml.sax.helpers.DefaultHandler` class provides a default implementation of the `ContentHandler`, `DTDHandler`, `EntityResolver`, and `ErrorHandler` all within a single abstraction. All the methods of these parent interfaces are provided a dummy implementation inside the `DefaultHandler` (the `DefaultHandler` interfaces are implied but not shown in Figure 4.6). Applications can thus subclass the `DefaultHandler` and implement only those parts of the super-interfaces relevant to that application and its related XML documents to be parsed.

The `DefaultHandler` class by virtue of its `ContentHandler` implementation provides SAX2-compliant features and replaces the SAX1-defined `HandlerBase` class. Although parsers that do not conform to the SAX2 standards may support only SAX1-style interfaces, the `DocumentHandler` interface and `HandlerBase` class are deprecated and thus may not be supported in the future. As we mentioned earlier, all of our examples and material in this chapter focus on SAX2-compliant interfaces.

SAX Parser Interfaces

Figure 4.7 depicts the detail for those interfaces implemented by SAX parser providers. The `XMLReader` interface is the SAX2-standard interface for reading and parsing XML documents. An `XMLReader` is the abstraction responsible for reading an XML document from an input stream, parsing its contents, and inducing the invocation of appropriate SAX handler methods. The `XMLReader` may also be configured to recognize certain features and properties in an XML document and invoke either standard SAX extension objects from the `org.xml.sax.ext` package or other application-defined property objects.

The `XMLReader` interface is implemented by SAX parser providers. Applications register `ContentHandler`, `DTDHandler`, `EntityResolver`, and `ErrorHandler` objects with the `XMLReader` object's appropriately named setter methods. The `XMLReader.parse()` methods are called to ask the `XMLReader` to begin parsing an XML document either from an `InputSource` or from a URL `String`, depending on the version of the `parse()` method that is called.

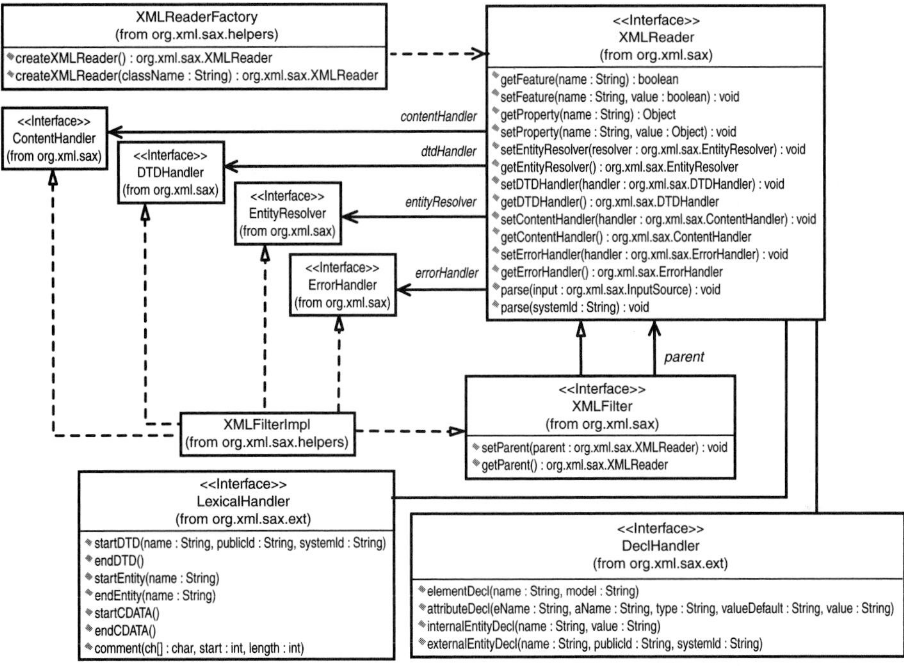

Figure 4.7 SAX parser interfaces.

Different parser vendors will want to enable or disable different features for applications that use their parser implementations. However, all SAX2-compliant parsers must enable the use of namespaces and disable the use of the older-style use of namespace prefixes only. The `XMLReader` interface supports the notion of enabling and disabling features by providing a `setFeature(String featureName, boolean featureOnOffFlag)` method. This method takes the `String` URI name of a feature and a `boolean` value indicating whether the feature is to be enabled (`true`) or disabled (`false`). Thus, all SAX2 parsers have the `http://xml.org/sax/features/namespaces` features set to `true` and the `http://xml.org/sax/features/namespace-prefixes` set to `false`. Determination of feature support is achieved through use of the `getFeature(String featureName)` method, which returns the `boolean` value indicating whether the feature is turned on or off. If an application attempts to get or set a feature not supported by the parser, the `getFeature()`/`setFeature()` method calls return an appropriate SAX exception.

A parser vendor may also support special parser properties as special handler extensions not part of the core SAX handler APIs. The `setProperty(String name, Object propertyObject)` method allows one to associate one of these property objects with the parser given the property's fully qualified URI name. The `getProperty(String name)` returns a handle to such objects. If an application attempts to get or set a property not supported by the parser, the `getProperty()/setProperty()` method calls return an appropriate SAX exception.

> **Note**
>
> The JAXP v1.2 reference implementation that's run with the examples in this chapter requires that two properties be set for proper XML schema validation. A property defining the XML schema language to use and a property pointing to the source location of the XML schema file must be declared as exemplified here:
>
> ```
> XMLReader p = ... // get SAX parser handle
> String schemaFileName = ... // get schema filename
> p.setProperty("http://java.sun.com/xml/jaxp/properties/schemaLanguage",
>               "http://www.w3.org/2001/XMLSchema");
> p.setProperty("http://java.sun.com/xml/jaxp/properties/schemaSource",
>               new File(schemaFileName));
> ```

Two special property extensions are defined in the `org.xml.sax.ext` package. The `DeclHandler` abstraction in that package can be associated with the `XMLReader` object using `http://xml.org/sax/properties/declaration-handler` as its property name. When invoked, the application can receive special information about DTD declarations when encountered in an XML document. Appropriately named methods exist to report information related to the declaration of an element, attribute, external entity, or internal entity. The `LexicalDecl` abstraction can be used to report certain lexical events when parsing an XML document via methods appropriately named for reporting encountering of a comment, the start and end of a `CDATA` section, the start and end of a DTD declaration, and the start and end of an internal or external entity. One approach to creating an `XMLReader` instance is to use the `XMLReaderFactory` class shown in Figure 4.7. The `XMLReaderFactory` class's static `createXMLReader(String className)` method takes the fully qualified class name `String` and instantiates an instance of the associated factory (assuming that it is on the `CLASSPATH` and is of the type `XMLReader`). If the `parameterless` form of `createXMLReader()` is invoked, the class name of the `XMLReader` is obtained from the `org.xml.sax.driver` system property.

Finally, chaining of `XMLReader` objects can be accomplished by using the `XMLFilter` abstraction. An `XMLFilter` is simply a type of `XMLReader` that is associated with a parent `XMLReader`. The `XMLFilter` can be used to parse an XML document and preprocess certain events before delegating the call to its parent `XMLReader`. The `setParent()` and `getParent()` methods on `XMLFilter` can be used to set and get the parent `XMLReader`, respectively. This gives the `XMLFilter` the rather useful capability to receive its parsing events from another `XMLReader`, instead of from a primary `InputSource`. Any number of `XMLFilters` can be chained together in this manner to allow for modular processing components to be developed. A default implementation of an `XMLFilter` that delegates all calls automatically to its parent `XMLReader` is provided by the `XMLFilterImpl` class. Applications can use such a class as a convenience and implement only those methods for which it desires to provide preprocessing filtering behavior.

SAX Parser Factory

The `SAXParser` class depicted in Figure 4.8 is a helper class that wraps a regular `XMLReader` object and provides a set of methods that implement a more convenient way of initiating the parsing of an XML document. Aside from methods for getting and setting parser properties, determining XML namespace awareness, and determining DTD validation capability, the `SAXParser` also defines various methods that help initiate the parsing of a document. The `SAXParser.parse()` methods all take a `DefaultHandler` object as an argument along with a reference to an XML document content stream in the form of a `File` reference, an `InputStream`, an `InputStream` and a system ID `String` for resolving relative URIs, an `InputSource`, or a URL `String` location. The `SaxParser.getXMLReader()` method can be used to obtain a reference to the underlying standard `XMLReader` interface object.

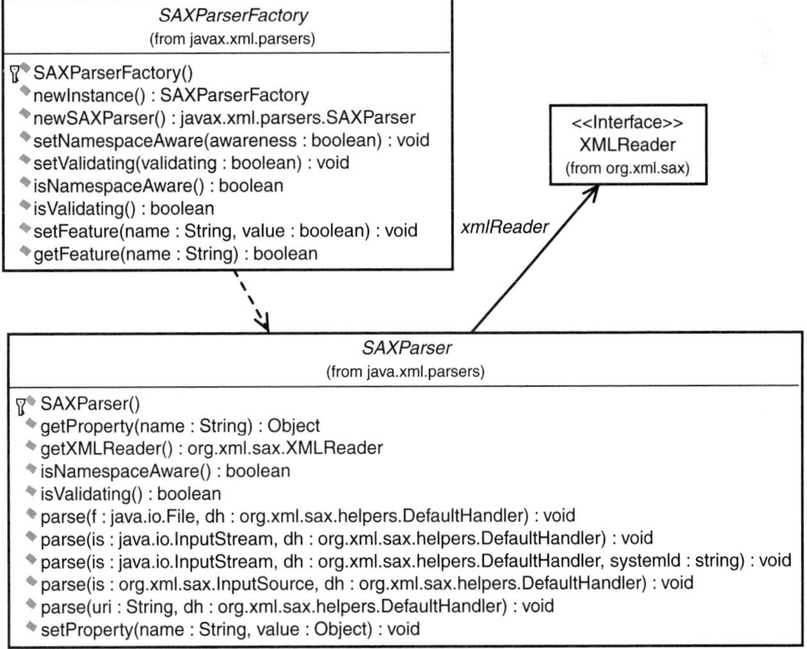

Figure 4.8 SAX parser factory interfaces.

The `SAXParserFactory` abstract class shown in Figure 4.8 can be used to configure and create `SAXParser` objects. A SAX parser provider supplies a concrete implementation of the `SAXParserFactory` class, and the definition of this class is most often defined via the `javax.xml.parsers.SAXParserFactory` system property or inside the JRE's `lib/jaxp.properties` directory. The `static SAXParserFactory.newInstance()` method is used to return an instance of this concrete factory implementation. DTD validation capability, XML namespace awareness, and the supported features of parsers can all also be set and gotten using appropriately named methods on a `SAXParserFactory` object instance. Finally, new instances of `SAXParser` objects can be created by calling the `newSAXParser()` method.

Listing 4.5 presents a SAX sample driver class to tie together a complete sample usage of SAX. The `SaxExample` class takes an XML document filename from the command line via a `main()` method and induces the parsing of this document. A `SaxParserFactory` is first created and then used to create a validating `SAXParser` object. The `SAXParser` object is then used to obtain a handle to the standard `XMLReader` object. The handlers that the application defines are then set onto the `XMLReader`. Lastly, the `XMLReader` is told to parse the XML document.

Listing 4.5 **SAX Example (`SaxExample.java`)**

```
package ejava.jaxp;

import org.xml.sax.SAXException;
import org.xml.sax.Locator;
import org.xml.sax.Attributes;
import org.xml.sax.XMLReader;
import org.xml.sax.SAXParseException;
import javax.xml.parsers.SAXParserFactory;
import javax.xml.parsers.SAXParser;
import java.io.*;

/**
  * An example to induce the parsing of an XML document
  */
public class SaxExample
{

  static final String SCHEMA_PROP =
            "http://java.sun.com/xml/jaxp/properties/schemaLanguage";
  static final String SCHEMA_PROP_VALUE =
            "http://www.w3.org/2001/XMLSchema";
  static final String SCHEMA_SOURCE_PROP =
            "http://java.sun.com/xml/jaxp/properties/schemaSource";

  public static void main(String[] argv)
  {
    if(argv.length < 1){
      System.out.print("Usage: Specify XML and optional schema file.");
      System.out.println("java ejava.jaxp.SaxExample <xml> [schema]");
      System.exit(0);
    }
    try {
      String xmlFileURI = "file:" + new File(argv[0]).getAbsolutePath();
```

Listing 4.5 **Continued**

```
      // Get Parser Factory
      SAXParserFactory saxParserFactory =
          SAXParserFactory.newInstance();
      // set Document Validation true
      saxParserFactory.setValidating(true);
      // set Namespace Awareness true
      saxParserFactory.setNamespaceAware(true);

      // get SAX parser from Factory
      SAXParser saxParser = saxParserFactory.newSAXParser();

      // if using a schema for validation, then set schema
      // property and source
      if(argv.length == 2){
          saxParser.setProperty(SCHEMA_PROP, SCHEMA_PROP_VALUE);
          saxParser.setProperty(SCHEMA_SOURCE_PROP, new File(argv[1]));
      }

      // get an XMLReader from SAX parser
      XMLReader reader = saxParser.getXMLReader();
      // set Content Handler to receive document Handler Events
      reader.setContentHandler(new SampleContentHandler());
      // set DTD Handler to receive DTD events from Parser
      reader.setDTDHandler(new SampleDTDHandler());
      // set EntityResolver to receive EntityResolver Events.
      reader.setEntityResolver(new SampleEntityResolver());
      // set ErrorHandler to receive Errors and warnings.
      reader.setErrorHandler(new SampleErrorHandler());
      // parse document
      reader.parse(xmlFileURI);
    }
    catch (SAXParseException saxParseException) {
      System.out.println (" Parsing error"
             + ", at line " + saxParseException.getLineNumber ()
             + ", in file  " + saxParseException.getSystemId ());
      System.out.println("   " + saxParseException.getMessage ());
      saxParseException.printStackTrace();
    }
    catch (SAXException saxException) {
      saxException.printStackTrace ();
    }
    catch (Throwable throwable) {
      throwable.printStackTrace ();
    }
  }
 }
```

> **Note**
>
> The ANT `all` target defined in the `build.xml` file associated with this chapter's code will compile the source code and generate a `runsax.bat` shell script for Windows platforms or a `runsax.sh` script for Unix platforms. These scripts will run the example as described next.

The `SaxExample` can be executed to parse either an XML document with a DTD or an XML document with an XML schema. Two such examples are included with this chapter's code in the `examples/src/ejava/jaxp` directory. To run the example to be parsed with a DTD, execute the following on the command line:

```
java ejava.jaxp.SaxExample dtdAndXmlDocument.xml
```

This will parse the `dtdAndXmlDocument.xml` XML document using the `order.dtd` file DTD associated with this chapter.

To run the example to be parsed with an XML schema, execute the following on the command line:

```
java ejava.jaxp.SaxExample schemaAndXmlDocument.xml order.xsd
```

This will parse the `schemaAndXmlDocument.xml` XML document using the `order.xsd` file XML schema associated with this chapter.

XML Parsing with DOM

We have just examined how JAXP uses SAX to parse and validate XML documents by making callbacks onto SAX interfaces as the document is parsed. We will now take a look at parsing XML documents via use of the Document Object Model (DOM). DOM provides an object-oriented representation of a parsed XML document. After parsing a document using JAXP DOM, the developer may traverse the XML document structure represented via DOM abstractions.

DOM Overview

The Document Object Model (DOM) was developed by the W3C to provide a standard set of language-independent interfaces to manipulate XML and HTML documents. We are mainly interested in the DOM Level 2 Core Specification (`www.w3.org/TR/DOM-Level-2-Core/`) in terms of the definitions it provides for a set of basic interfaces to manipulate XML documents. These interfaces are defined using the OMG CORBA IDL notation (see Chapter 8, "CORBA Communications"). A Java binding for such interfaces is also presented in the specification and is the style of interface we focus on in this section.

DOM Level 1 was the Document Object Model API that was supported with the JAXP v1.0 API. DOM Level 1 did not have full support for use of XML namespaces among other features. DOM Level 2 is the current version that does support XML namespaces. DOM Level 2 is supported by the JAXP v1.1/1.2 APIs and is the DOM version around which the material in this chapter is primarily constructed. As was mentioned in the preceding chapter, version 1.2 of the JAXP API is now implemented as a standard component of the J2EE version 1.4. It contains the standard interfaces to DOM, which are defined in the `org.w3c.dom` Java package. It also includes some convenient Factory classes in the `javax.xml.parsers` package.

As we learned earlier in the chapter, SAX is a lightweight and straightforward mechanism for reading and processing XML data in a serial fashion. What DOM provides is the additional capability to create, manipulate, and store XML data in a random-access fashion. Figure 4.9 shows how DOM represents an XML document. A DOM parser maps an XML document into a treelike hierarchical structure of nodes in the form of a document object model. Each node in a DOM corresponds to some abstraction of an XML document component (for example, an element, a comment, CDATA). DOM permits applications to access such a model in terms of either a flat or an object-oriented view. In an object-oriented view, applications access each node in terms of a type-safe abstraction of actual components of an XML document (that is, `Element`, `Comment`, `CDATA`). In a flat view, applications access each node in terms of a generic representation of each node (that is, some generic `Node` abstraction).

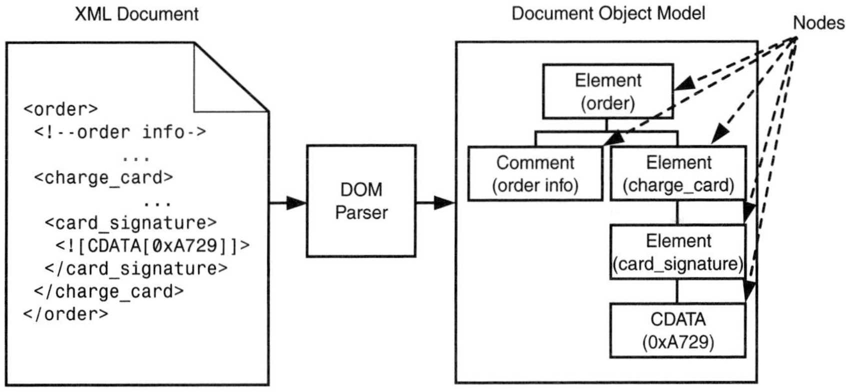

Figure 4.9 The Document Object Model.

DOM Architecture

Figure 4.10 depicts the top-level architecture of Java-based DOM classes and interfaces. Most classes and interfaces come from the `org.w3c.dom` package. Two additional classes defined in the `javax.xml.parsers` package are also utilized to define a provider-independent means for creating parser handles as well as a non-DOM-standard parser class. The `DocumentBuilder` DOM parser is created by a `DocumentBuilderFactory` and is used to create an XML `Document` object encapsulation from an XML content stream. After that, the `Document` and various types of DOM `Node` objects can be used to access the XML document contents in terms of XML document components.

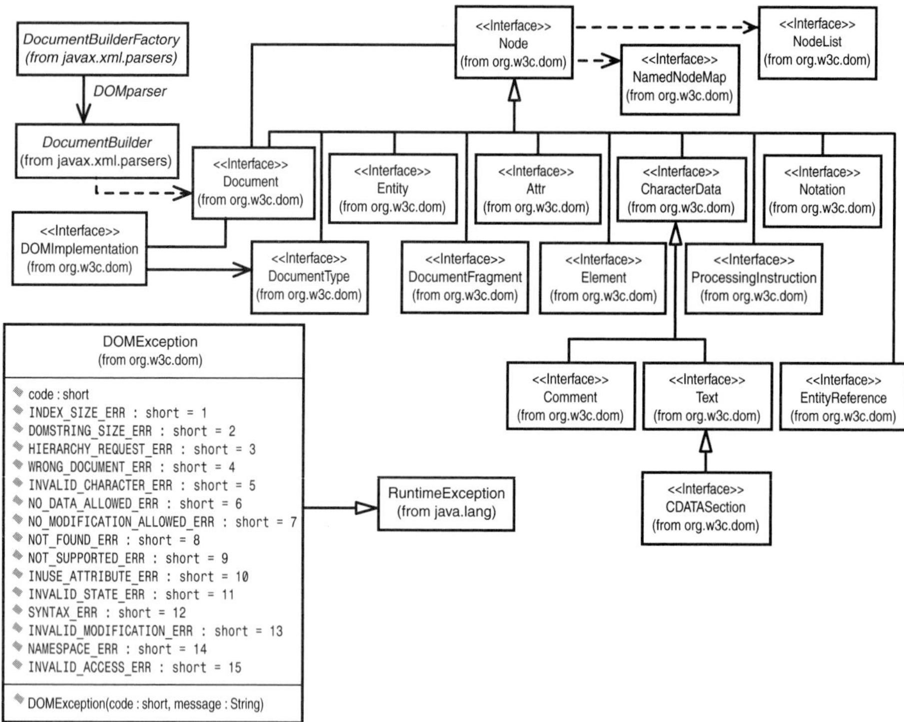

Figure 4.10 The DOM class architecture.

Also shown in this diagram is the only standard abstraction defined for DOM exceptions. The `DOMException` abstract class is a base class for exceptions thrown by the DOM objects. In addition to a message `String`, a `DOMException` can be created with `short` value exception code assigned according to one of the predefined `DOMException static short` constant values.

Generic DOM Nodes

Figure 4.11 depicts the main abstractions involved in generic DOM nodes. A node interface and two node collection interfaces serve as the base generic interfaces for manipulating DOM in a flat-view fashion. Nodes also provide a handle to the object-oriented XML document that they contain and serve as the base interface for object-oriented XML document components.

The `Node` interface is the base interface for all DOM nodes and can be used as the generic abstraction for all nodes in a hierarchical document object model. Nodes are contained inside of XML documents, and the `Node.getOwnerDocument()` method returns a handle to a `Document` object that represents the XML document containing the node. The `Node` also provides interfaces to get the node name `String` using `getNodeName()` such as the element or attribute name for element or nodes; or `#comment` for comment nodes. For nodes that are either element or attribute nodes, their namespace URI, prefix, and local name can be retrieved via the `getNamespaceURI()`, `getPrfix()`, and `getLocalName()` method calls, respectively. The `setPrefix()` call can also be made to set the namespace prefix for the current `Node`.

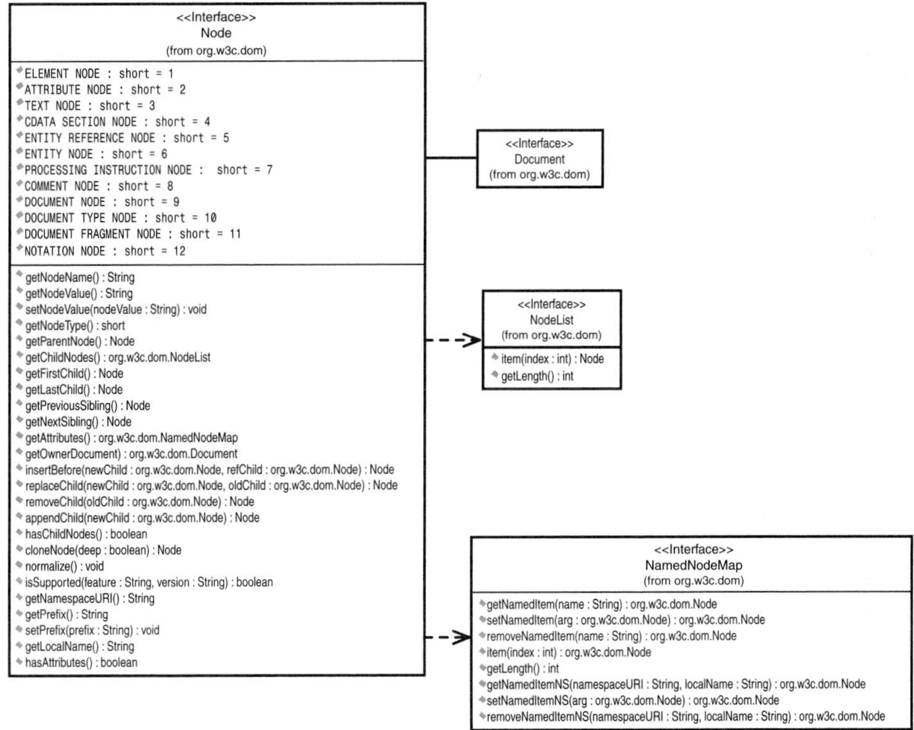

Figure 4.11 DOM nodes.

You can also get and set the node value in the form of a `String` by using `getNodeValue()` and `setNodeValue()`. The value returned or set for a node will, of course, depend on the specific type of node and is relevant only to those node types that have content such as CDATA, comment, text, processing instruction, and attribute node types. Other node types have `null` as their value in the `Node` object. The `getNodeType()` method returns a `short` value code that identifies the type of `Node` according to one of the `static short` constant values defined by the `Node` interface.

The parent node of a `Node` object can be obtained using the `Node.getParentNode()` method. The `Node.getChildNodes()` method returns a `NodeList` object containing a collection of `Node` objects that represent the children of a node. The

NodeList interface provides a simple means for traversing a list of nodes, with a getLength() method returning the length of the list and an item(int) method returning an individual indexed Node. The Node.getFirstChild() and Node.getLastChild() methods return the first and last child node objects, respectively. Children of the node can also be inserted, removed, replaced, and appended using appropriately named Node methods. The existence of any child nodes can be tested using the hasChildNodes() method. The Node object's sibling nodes immediately preceding and following it in its parent's child node list can be retrieved using the getPreviousSibling() and getNextSibling() calls.

As an example, the following method illustrates some sample usage of a Node interface when invoked:

```
/**
 * This method prints the Node Name and Node Value
 */
 public static void printNodeNameAndValue(Node node)
   throws DOMException
 {
  System.out.println("Name :" + node.getNodeName());
  System.out.println("Value :"+ node.getNodeValue());
  if(node.hasChildNodes()){
   NodeList nodeList = node.getChildNodes();
   // print all child node information.
   for(int i = 0; i< nodeList.getLength(); i++){
     Node item = nodeList.item(i);
     System.out.println(" Node Name :"+item.getNodeName());
     System.out.println(" Node Value :" +item.getNodeValue());
     PrintNodeNameAndValue(item);
   }
  }
 }
```

Child Node objects can also be inserted, replaced, removed, and appended within parent Node objects. Given a handle to an existing child Node object, a new child Node can be inserted before the referenced Node using the insertBefore() method or used to replace the referenced Node via the replaceChild() method. A referenced child Node can be removed by calling removeChild() on the parent, and a new child can be appended using the appendChild() method. Copies of Node objects can be returned by calling cloneNode(boolean) on the Node object, which returns a deep copy of that node's structure if true is passed as a parameter to the method.

The attributes of a node can be returned using the Node.getAttributes() method, and it can be determined whether any exist for this node using the Node.hasAttributes() method call. A returned NamedNodeMap object from the getAttributes() method call represents a collection of Node objects that can be referenced via a String name. The NamedNodeMap also allows its elements to be referenced by an index number or via a namespace URI and local name.

Different DOM Level 2 parser vendors will support different features for applications that use their parser implementations. The `Node.isSupported(String feature, String version)` method returns a `boolean` value indicating whether a particular feature is supported. The version indicates whether the feature is relevant to a DOM Level 1 (`1.0`) or DOM Level 2 (`2.0`) feature. Feature name examples include `core` if the parser supports DOM Level 2 core features or `stylesheets` if the parser supports XSL stylesheet processing.

Concrete DOM Node Types

Figure 4.12 presents the various interface extensions to the base `Node` extension. All the sub-interfaces of `Node` are concrete type-safe interfaces to some component of an XML document. Object instances that implement these interfaces can be used to access and manipulate the various parts of an XML document in terms of an object-oriented abstraction. The `Node` sub-interfaces are defined here with accompanying code-snippet methods to illustrate usage taken from the `DOMExample` file:

- `Notation`: Encapsulates a notation in a DTD. A public identifier and system identifier may be obtained via this interface. For example:

  ```
  public static void printNotationInformation(Notation notation)
  {
      System.out.println("Notation System ID :"
                          + notation.getSystemId());
      System.out.println("Notation Public ID :"
                          + notation.getPublicId());
  }
  ```

- `Entity`: Encapsulates an XML entity with getters for any associated public identifier, system identifier, and notation name. For example:

  ```
  public static void printEntityInformation(Entity entity)
  {
      System.out.println("Entity Name :"+ entity.getNotationName());
      System.out.println("Entity System ID :" + entity.getSystemId());
      System.out.println("Entity Public ID :"+entity.getPublicId());
  }
  ```

- `EntityReference`: A marker interface for an entity reference.
- `ProcessingInstruction`: Encapsulates a processing instruction whose target name and data can be read. Additionally, data can also be set for the instruction. For example:

  ```
  public static void printProcessingInstructionInformation(
      ProcessingInstruction processingInstruction)
  {
      System.out.println("Data   :"
                          + processingInstruction.getData());
      System.out.println("Target   :"
  ```

```
                         + processingInstruction.getTarget());
}
```

- `CharacterData`: Encapsulates character data read from the document. Operations for getting, setting, adding, deleting, inserting, and replacing data in the character data stream are provided. For example:

```
public static void printCharacterData(
    CharacterData charData)
{
    System.out.println("Character Data  :"+ charData.getData());
}
```

- `Comment`: A type of character data extended as a marker interface for a comment in an XML document.
- `Text`: A type of character data that can be broken up into two regions of textual content.
- `CDATASection`: A type of textual character data extended as a marker interface for textual CDATA content.
- `Attr`: Encapsulates an attribute in an element, including the retrieval of the attribute's name and value. Additionally, the attribute can be set. If the attribute was originally set in the parsed XML document, the `getSpecified()` method returns `true`. The `Element` to which the attribute is attached can also be retrieved via `getOwnerElement()`. For example:

```
public static void printAttributeInformation(Attr attribute)
{
    System.out.println("Attibute Name :" + attribute.getName());
    System.out.println("Is it specified :" + attribute.getSpecified());
    System.out.println("Attribute Value :" + attribute.getValue());
    System.out.println("Owning Element Local Name :"
             + attribute.getOwnerElement().getLocalName());
}
```

- `Element`: Represents an element in an XML document. An `Element` can be used to retrieve a tag name and get, set, and remove element attribute values named either with a namespace URI and local name or with its DOM Level 1 style name. Additionally, a list of sub-elements returned in a `NodeList` object can be obtained from an `Element`. The `Document.getDocumentElement()` method returns the root element for an XML document. The `Document.getElementsByTagName()` and `Document.getElementsByTagNameNS()` methods return a node list of elements matching a specified tag or namespace-qualified name in a document. The `normalize()` method inherited from the `Node` interface is used to transform any `Text` nodes within an `Element` into a normal format in which only XML document component markup separates `Text` data.

- DocumentType: The Document.getDocumentType() method retrieves a DocumentType object that encapsulates information related to a top-level DTD description. The qualified name, external entities, public ID, system ID, internal subset, and notations defined within a DTD can all be accessed from the DocumentType object. A new DocumentType object can be created using the DOMImplementation.createDocumentType() method given the qualified name, public ID, and system ID for the DTD. As an example for manipulating a DocumentType object:

```
public static void printDocumentTypeInformation(DocumentType
    documentType) throws SAXParseException
{
    String documentName = documentType.getName();
    System.out.println("Document Name :"+ documentName);
    //get all the entities that are defined for document.
    NamedNodeMap entities = documentType.getEntities();
    printNameNodeMap(entities); // to be defined later in section
}
```

- Document: A handle to an XML document. Provides a set of create*XXX*() methods to create instances of other components of an XML document. Where necessary, both regular and namespace-aware versions of these methods are provided for creating elements and attributes. For example,

  ```
  createElement(String tagName)
  ```

  creates a new element of the given name, whereas

  ```
  createElementNS(String namespaceURI, String qualifiedException)
  ```

  creates an element with the qualified name with respect to the given namespace. The DOMImplementation.createDocument() method can be used to create a new Document object given its namespace URI, qualified name, and optional DocumentType object. Additionally, a set of getters is used to retrieve some of the top-level XML document components. For example:

```
public static void printDocument(Document document)
   throws SAXParseException
{

    DocumentType documentType = document.getDoctype();
    printDocumentTypeInformation(documentType);
    Element element = document.getDocumentElement();
    printNodeNameAndValue(element) ;
    NamedNodeMap attributes = element.getAttributes();
    printNameNodeMap(attributes); // to be defined later in section
}
```

- DocumentFragment: A marker interface used to encapsulate a portion of an XML document tree.

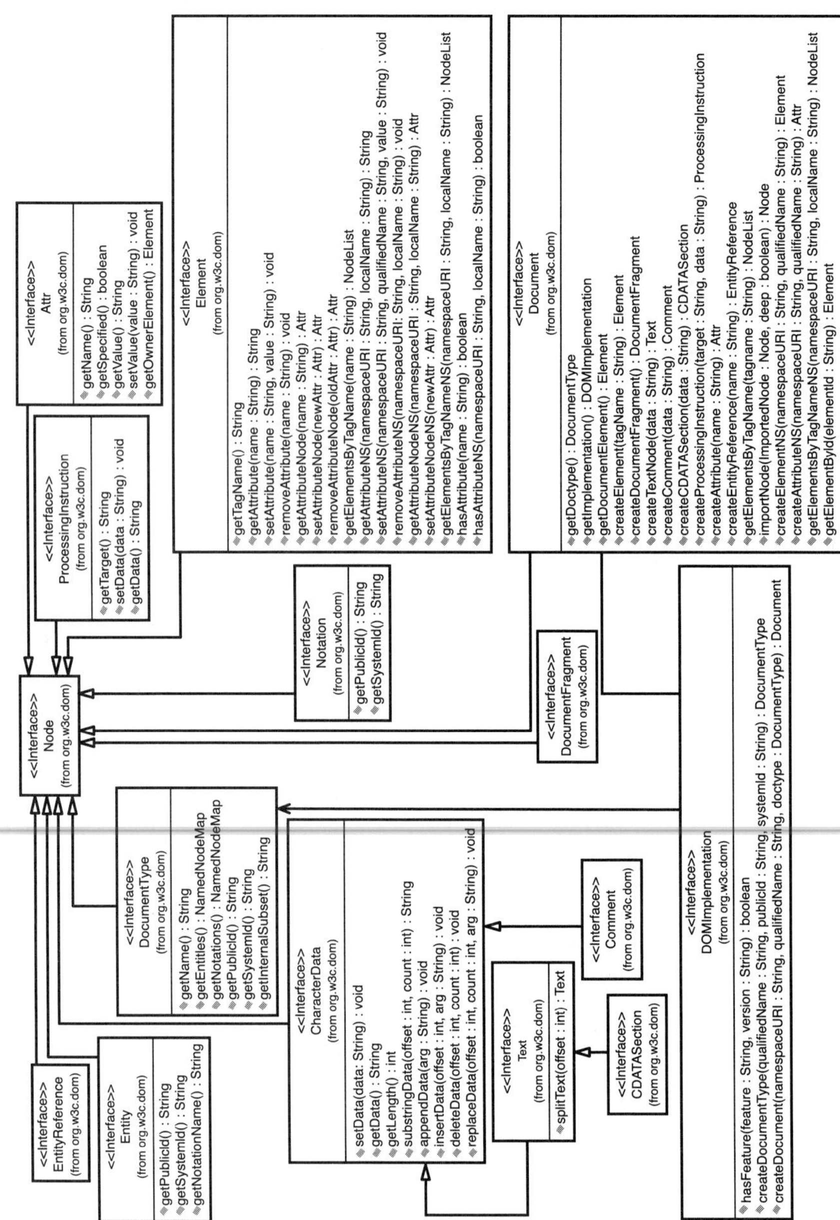

Figure 4.12 DOM node types.

In addition to the various `Node` sub-interfaces, we also show the `DOMImplementation` object in Figure 4.12. In addition to the two `createXXX()` methods described previously, the DOMImplementation interface has a method that is used to determine whether a particular feature was implemented by the DOM parser provider. This hasFeature() method is used identically to the Node.isSupported() method. The hasFeature() method thus takes a feature String name (for example, XML or HTML) and a DOM specification version String (for example, 2.0) and expects a boolean value indicating whether the feature is supported for the particular specification version.

A few of the Node sub-interface snippets that were presented utilized a DOMExample.printNameNodeMap() method. The DOMExample.printNameNodeMap() method cycles through a NameNodeMap and, depending on the Node type, will print some descriptive information about the specific Node instance. The printNameNodeMap() method is defined here:

```
public static void printNameNodeMap(NamedNodeMap values)
        throws SAXParseException
{
  int length = values.getLength();

  for(int i = 0; i < length; i++) {
    Node  node     = values.item(i);
    short nodeType = node.getNodeType();

    switch(nodeType) {

    case Node.ATTRIBUTE_NODE : {
      System.out.println(" This is an attribute :");

      Attr attribute = (Attr) node;

      printAttributeInformation(attribute);
      printNodeNameAndValue(node);

      break;
    }
    case Node.CDATA_SECTION_NODE : {
      System.out.println("This is a CDATA section :");

      CDATASection cdataSection = (CDATASection) node;

      printCharacterData(cdataSection);
      printNodeNameAndValue(cdataSection);

      break;
    }
    case Node.COMMENT_NODE : {
      System.out.println("This is a comment :");
```

```
      Comment comment = (Comment) node;

      printCharacterData(comment);
      printNodeNameAndValue(comment);

      break;
    }
    case Node.DOCUMENT_FRAGMENT_NODE : {
      DocumentFragment documentFragment = (DocumentFragment) node;

      System.out.println("This is a document fragment :");
      printNodeNameAndValue(node);

      break;
    }
    case Node.DOCUMENT_NODE : {
      System.out.println("This is a document :");

      Document document = (Document) node;

      printNodeNameAndValue(node);

      break;
    }
    case Node.DOCUMENT_TYPE_NODE : {
      System.out.println("This is a document type :");

      DocumentType documentType = (DocumentType) node;

      printNodeNameAndValue(node);

      break;
    }
    case Node.ELEMENT_NODE : {
      System.out.println("This is an element :");

      Element element = (Element) node;

      printNodeNameAndValue(node);

      break;
    }
    case Node.ENTITY_NODE : {
      System.out.println("This is an entity :");

      Entity entity = (Entity) node;

      printEntityInformation(entity);
```

```
    printNodeNameAndValue(node);

    break;
  }
  case Node.ENTITY_REFERENCE_NODE : {
    System.out.println("This is an entity reference :");

    EntityReference entityReference = (EntityReference) node;

    printNodeNameAndValue(node);

    break;
  }
  case Node.NOTATION_NODE : {
    System.out.println(" This is a notation :");

    Notation notation = (Notation) node;

    printNotationInformation(notation);
    printNodeNameAndValue(node);

    break;
  }
  case Node.PROCESSING_INSTRUCTION_NODE : {
    System.out.println("This is a processing instruction :");

    ProcessingInstruction processingInstruction =
      (ProcessingInstruction) node;

    printProcessingInstructionInformation(processingInstruction);
    printNodeNameAndValue(node);

    break;
  }
  case Node.TEXT_NODE : {
    System.out.println("This is text :");

    Text text = (Text) node;

    printNodeNameAndValue(node);

    break;
  }
  default : {
    System.out.println("This is not a defined node.");

    break;
```

```
            }
        }
    }
}
```

DOM Parsing

Figure 4.13 depicts the main entities involved in creating and initiating DOM parsing. A DOM parser factory is used to create parser instances. The parser is then used to parse a particular data stream and generate an XML document object. The DOM parser factory and parser are both from the `javax.xml.parsers` package, which is part of the JAXP API.

The `DocumentBuilder` abstract class is extended by DOM parser service providers to parse data streams into XML documents encapsulated by the `Document` interface. Aside from methods for determining XML namespace awareness, as well as DTD and XML Schema validation capability, the `DocumentBuilder` also defines some methods that help initiate the parsing of a document. The `DocumentBuilder.parse()` methods all take an XML document content stream in the form of a `File` reference, an `InputStream`, an `InputSource`, or a URL `String` location and return an XML `Document` object instance. A `parse()` method also exists to take an `InputStream` and root system ID `String` used to resolve relative URIs. The `newDocument()` method simply creates an empty instance of a new `Document` object. A SAX `ErrorHandler` and `EntityResolver` may also be associated with a `DocumentBuilder` and subsequently invoked when parsing the XML document associated with the `DocumentBuilder` object.

The `DocumentBuilderFactory` abstract class can be used to configure and create DOM parser `DocumentBuilder` objects. A DOM parser provider provides a concrete implementation of the `DocumentBuilderFactory` class. The concrete implementation class is most often defined via the `javax.xml.parsers.DocumentBuilderFactory` system property or inside the JRE's `lib/jaxp.properties` directory. The `static DocumentBuilderFactory.newInstance()` method is used to return an instance of this concrete factory implementation. DTD validation capability and XML namespace awareness of parsers can all be set and checked using appropriately named methods on a `DocumentBuilderFactory` object instance.

In addition, XML Schema validation of documents is possible by setting certain attributes of the `DocumentBuilderFactory` object. XML Schema validation and other particular attributes of a parser may be set as special attribute handler objects on the DOM parser. The `setAttribute(String name, Object value)` method allows one to associate one of these parser attributes with the parser given the attribute's name. The `getAttribute(String name)` returns a handle to such objects. If an application attempts to get or set an attribute not supported by the parser, the `getAttribute()/setAttribute()` method calls throw a `java.lang.IllegalArgumentException`.

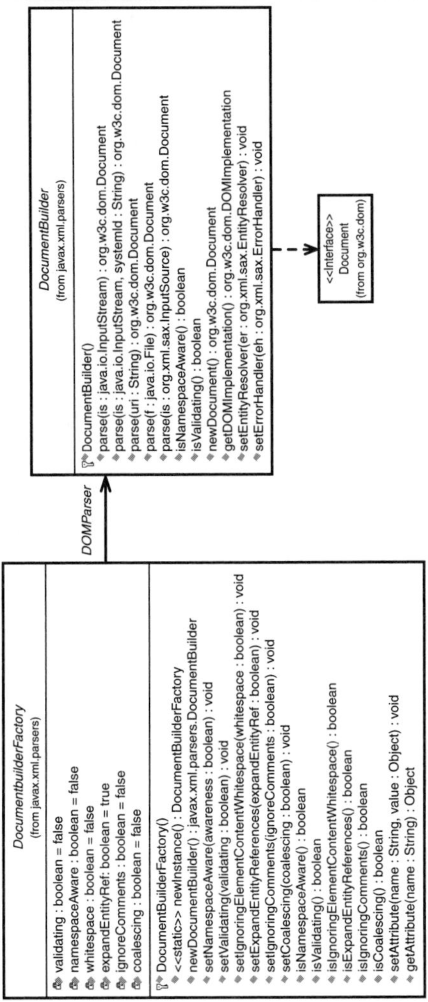

Figure 4.13 DOM parser interfaces.

Note

The JAXP v1.2 reference implementation that is run with the examples in this chapter requires that two attributes be set for proper XML schema validation. A property defining the XML schema language to use and a property pointing to the source location of the XML schema file must be declared as exemplified here:

```
DocumentBuilderFactory p = ... // get DOM parser handle
String schemaFileName = ... // get schema file name
p.setAttribute("http://java.sun.com/xml/jaxp/properties/schemaLanguage",
              "http://www.w3.org/2001/XMLSchema");
```

```
p.setAttribute("http://java.sun.com/xml/jaxp/properties/schemaSource",
            new File(schemaFileName));
```

As depicted in Figure 4.13, a `DocumentBuilderFactory` object also exposes the capability to turn on or off specific attributes of the DOM parser via a series of `setXXX(boolean)` methods. Furthermore, a `DocumentBuilderFactory` object allows one to determine whether such attributes are set via a set of `isXXX()` methods. These methods involve such attributes of a parser as whether or not the parser validates the XML document, considers namespaces, ignores whitespace, ignores comments, expands entity references, and coalesces `CDATA` into text nodes.

As an illustration of how to kick off DOM parsing, the `main()` method of the `DOMExample` should be invoked when `DOMExample` is being executed from the command line with a sample XML document. The `DOMExample.main()` method then creates a new instance of a `DocumentBuilderFactory` object, creates a new `DocumentBuilder` object, turns on parser validation, and induces the parsing of the XML document stream. After the root document element is normalized, the document is told to print itself via a call to `DOMExample.printDocument()`. A set of static constants used by the `DOMExample.main()` method is shown here:

```
static final String SCHEMA_PROP =
            "http://java.sun.com/xml/jaxp/properties/schemaLanguage";
static final String SCHEMA_PROP_VALUE =
            "http://www.w3.org/2001/XMLSchema";
static final String SCHEMA_SOURCE_PROP =
            "http://java.sun.com/xml/jaxp/properties/schemaSource";
```

The `DOMExample.main()` method itself is shown here:

```
public static void main(String[] argv)
{
  if(argv.length < 1) {
   System.out.print("Usage: Specify XML and optional schema file.");
   System.out.println("java ejava.jaxp.DOMExample <xml> [schema]");
   System.exit(0);
  }

  try {
    String xmlFileURI = "file:" + new File(argv[0]).getAbsolutePath();

    // get new instance of Document Factory
    DocumentBuilderFactory domFactory
          = DocumentBuilderFactory.newInstance();
    // set namespace awareness true
    domFactory.setNamespaceAware(true);
```

```
    // set document validation true
    domFactory.setValidating(true);

    // if using a schema for validation, then set schema
    // property and source
    if(argv.length == 2){
       domFactory.setAttribute(SCHEMA_PROP, SCHEMA_PROP_VALUE);
       domFactory.setAttribute(SCHEMA_SOURCE_PROP, new File(argv[1]));
    }

    // get new Document Builder
    DocumentBuilder documentBuilder = domFactory.newDocumentBuilder();
    // parse the document
    Document document = documentBuilder.parse(xmlFileURI);
    // normalize the document
    document.getDocumentElement().normalize();
    // print out the document
    System.out.println("Root element is "
                     + document.getDocumentElement().getNodeName());
    printDocument(document);
  } catch(SAXParseException saxParseException) {
    System.out.println(" Parsing error" + ", at line "
                      + saxParseException.getLineNumber()
                      + ", in file  "
                      + saxParseException.getSystemId());
    System.out.println("    " + saxParseException.getMessage());
    saxParseException.printStackTrace();
  } catch(DOMException domParseException) {
    System.out.println(" Parsing error ");
    System.out.println(domParseException.getMessage());
    domParseException.printStackTrace();
  } catch(Exception e) {
    e.printStackTrace();
  }
}
```

XSL Transformations (XSLT)

In addition to providing the tools needed to read and write XML files, JAXP supports the transformation of XML documents through XSL stylesheets. This allows a single XML document to take on many different presentations, such as an HTML page, a word-processing document format, or another XML file conforming to another schema, while leaving the original source file unchanged. Transforms also provide the capability to move XML documents through a system, such as from an in-memory representation to a disk or byte stream, and vice versa.

XSLT Architecture

The XSL transformation API for Java is contained within the `javax.xml.transform` package and subpackages. It is designed to be a platform- and implementation-independent interface, to allow for maximum interoperability. Figure 4.14 provides a class diagram of the transform API components.

At the core is the `Transformer` object, which does the bulk of the work involved in transforming an XML document. An application acquires a handle to the `Transformer` through the `newTransformer()` method of `TranformerFactory`, which takes an optional `Source` argument specifying the XSL stylesheet. The application will then typically call `transform()` on the `Transform` object, passing in the source XML document as a `Source`, and a `Result` object to receive the resulting transformation.

The `Transformer` object has several other methods that can be useful. The `setOutputProperty()` and `setOutputProperties()` methods can be used to set or override any of the attributes set in the `<xsl:output>` element of the stylesheet. The `getOutputProperty()` and `getOutputProperties()` methods return these values. The `setErrorListener()` method sets an application-defined `ErrorListener` implementation to the `Transformer`, to provide custom error handling. The `getErrorListener()` method returns the `ErrorListener`. The `setURIResolver()` method is used to register an application-defined `URIResolver` implementation, which will be invoked by the transformer when an `<xsl:include>`, `<xsl:import>`, or `document()` function is encountered in the stylesheet. The `URIResolver` will resolve the given URI reference into a `Source` object. The `getURIResolver()` method returns the `URIResolver`. Finally, the `setParameter()` method can be used to add a parameter to the transformation, which can be passed as a parameter to a template, or passed on to an extension. The `getParameter()` method returns the value of the parameter with the specified name, and `clearParameters()` removes all parameters.

As was mentioned before, the `TransformerFactory` class is responsible for creating the `Transformer` objects that perform the XSL transformations. The creation of the `TransformerFactory` implementation class itself is governed by the system property `javax.xml.transform.TransformerFactory`. The J2SE v1.4 comes with a default implementation, but the user could override this property with a `-D` flag on the `java` command line to use an alternative implementation. The method `TransformerFactory.newInstance()` is used to get a handle to the `TransformerFactory` implementation.

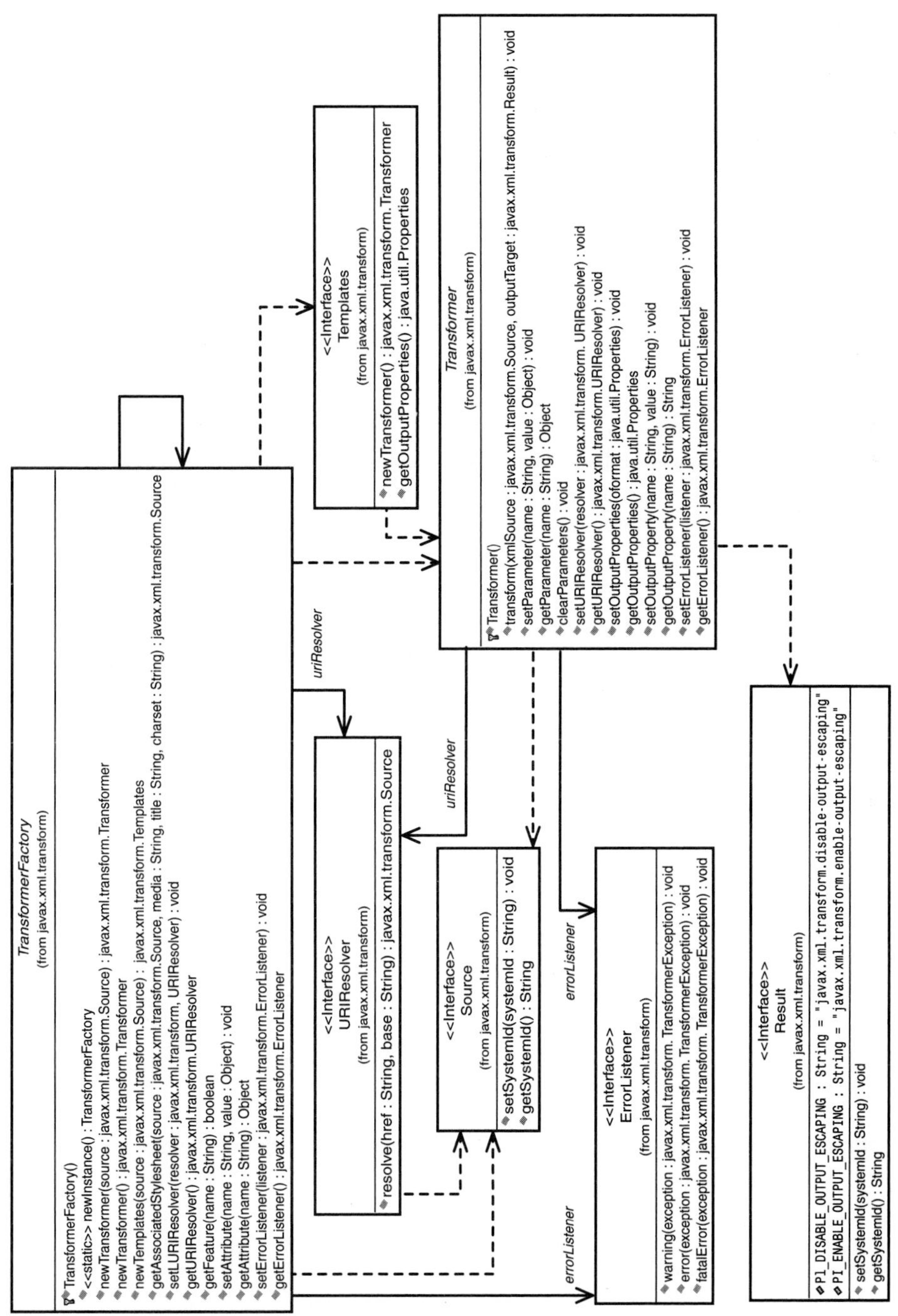

Figure 4.14 XSL transform API interfaces.

TransformerFactory defines some additional useful methods. There are setters and getters for ErrorListener and URIResolver, which work the same as in the Transformer class. The setAttribute() and getAttribute() methods can set or get attributes on the underlying implementation object. The getAssociatedStylesheet() method can be used to locate an XSL Source based on the attributes set in an xml-stylesheet processing instruction in an XML source document. Finally, the newTemplates() method can be used to create a Templates implementation, given a precompiled transformation as its source. The newTransformer() method on the returned Templates implementation will return the appropriate Transformer instance.

The Source and Result interfaces provide convenient adapters to the various sources and sinks of XML data. Each concrete implementation of these interfaces is defined in its own subpackage. DOM inputs and outputs are handled by DOMSource and DOMResult, respectively, in the javax.xml.transform.dom package. Similarly, SAX inputs and outputs are handled by SAXSource and SAXResult, and streamed inputs and outputs are handled by StreamSource and StreamResult in the javax.xml.transform.sax and javax.transform.xml.stream packages, respectively.

Figure 4.15 shows the core Exception abstractions that deal with unexpected problems in transforming XML. The base class javax.xml.transform.TransformerException is used to represent a generic Exception within the XML transformation process. To assist in debugging such problems, it can be created with a SourceLocator object, which holds the public ID, system ID, line number, and column number of the XML file where the transformation process encountered the error. The getLocator() method of TransformationException returns a handle to this object. The getLocationAsString() method returns the same information, packaged as a String. The TransformerException can also be created with a Throwable argument to the constructor, allowing it to "wrap" another exception condition. If it's not constructed in this manner, the initCause() method can be called, at most once, to set the underlying exception. This object can be retrieved through the getCause() or getException() method. A thrown TransformerException will also be passed to any registered implementation of ErrorListener, through its error(), fatalError(), and warning() methods. The TransformerException object also overrides the printStackTrace() method of Throwable, allowing the stack trace to be printed to a user-defined PrintStream or PrintWriter.

The TransformerConfigurationException is a subclass of TransformerException that is used to indicate a serious configuration error in the XML transform package. It is thrown from any of the factory methods of TransformerFactory.

Figures 4.16, 4.17, and 4.18 show detailed class diagrams of the DOM, SAX, and Stream implementations of the various XSL Transform interfaces discussed previously. By and large, these implementation classes are created and used by the underlying implementation, and they are typically isolated from direct communication with the calling program. The two exceptions to this rule are the implementations of the `Source` and `Result` interfaces, which are typically chosen and created specifically by an application depending on its needs.

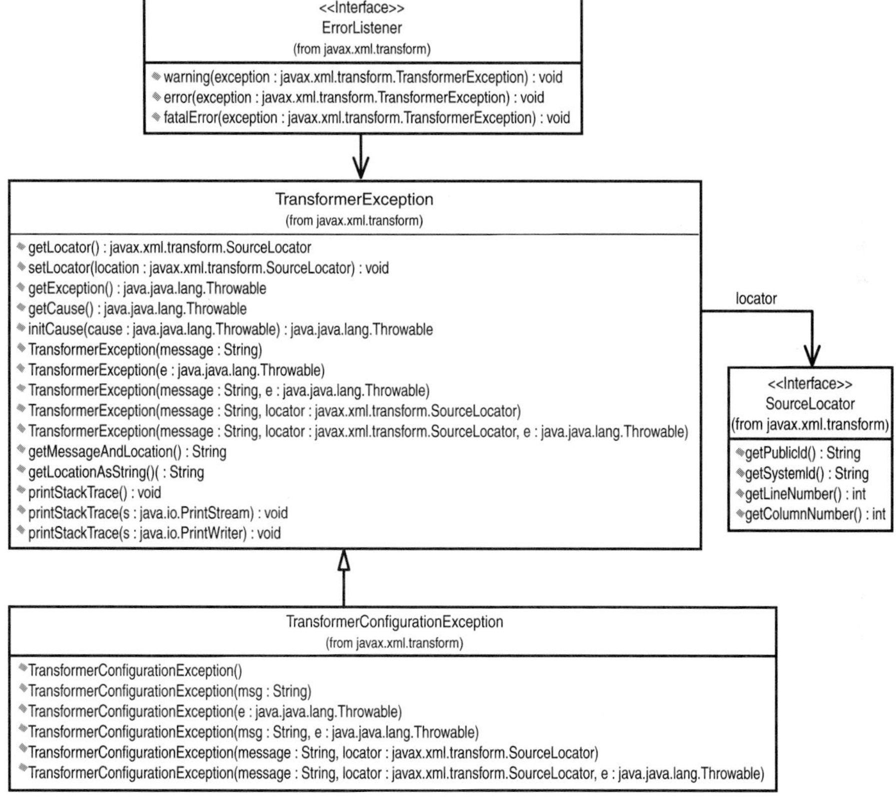

Figure 4.15 XSL transform error abstractions.

The DOM implementations of `Source` and `Result`, `DOMSource` and `DOMResult`, are shown in Figure 4.16. In addition to implementing the required `getSystemId()` and `setSystemId()` methods, they each provide a `getNode()` and `setNode()` method, which allows access to the DOM `Node` that will be the source or the result of the transformation. The package also provides `DOMLocator`, which implements the `SourceLocator` interface. It provides a `getOriginatingNode()` method, which allows access to the DOM `Node` where the error occurred.

The `javax.xml.transform.sax` package defines SAX-specific transform implementation classes. Figure 4.17 shows the relationship between these classes. The interfaces `TemplatesHandler` and `TransformerHandler` extend the org.xml.sax.ContentHandler interface, and will receive and process the SAX events necessary to transform a source into a result, when created through a call to SAXTransformerFactory.newTemplatesHandler() or newTransformerHandler(). SAXTransformerFactory also provides a newXMLFilter() method, which allows a transform object to be used as part of a SAX XMLFilter chain. The SAXSource class provides getters and setters for its underlying XML source, either an org.xml.sax.InputSource or an org.xml.sax.XMLReader object. Similarly, the SAXResult class provides access to its SAX event handlers through getHandler() and setHandler() for the org.xml.sax.ContentHandler instance, and getLexicalHandler() and setLexicalHandler() for the org.xml.sax.ext.LexicalHandler instance.

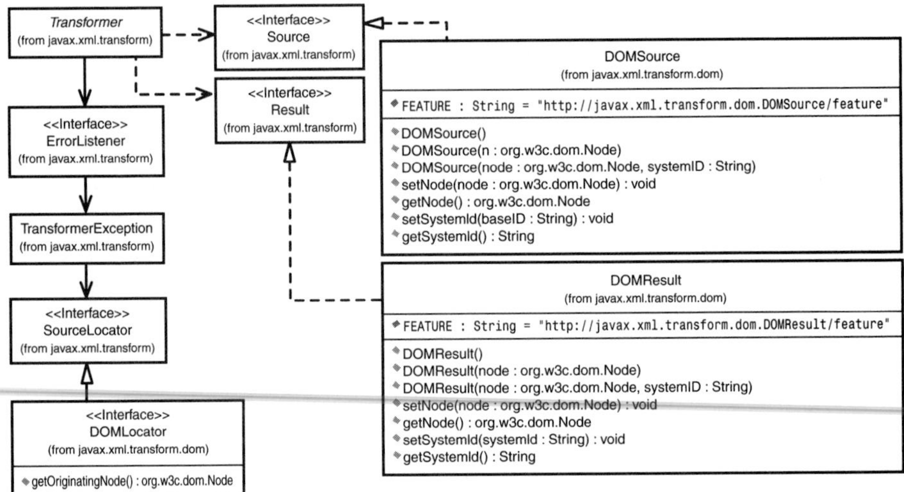

Figure 4.16 javax.xml.transform.dom implementation classes.

The javax.xml.transform.stream package contains only the StreamSource and StreamResult classes, as shown in Figure 4.18. The StreamSource can be created from a java.io.InputStream, java.io.Reader, or java.io.File object as its underlying data source. Similarly, the StreamResult class will direct its output to a java.io.OutputStream, java.io.Writer, or java.io.File class.

Listing 4.6 shows a simple program that transforms an XML document according to the given stylesheet. It reads both a source XML file and an XSL stylesheet as StreamSources. It then constructs a Transformer from a TransformerFactory, sets an output property, and then performs the transformation, sending the output to a File through the StreamResult object.

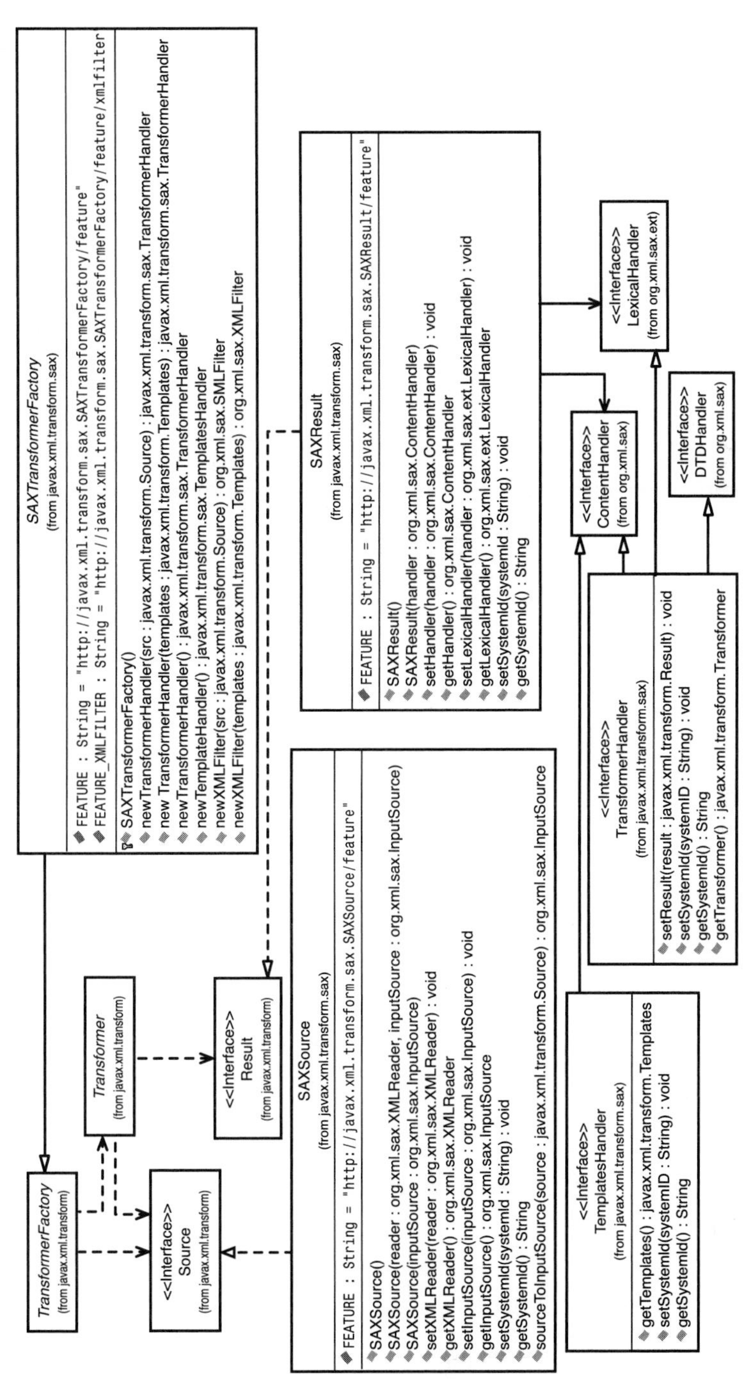

Figure 4.17 `javax.xml.transform.sax` implementation classes.

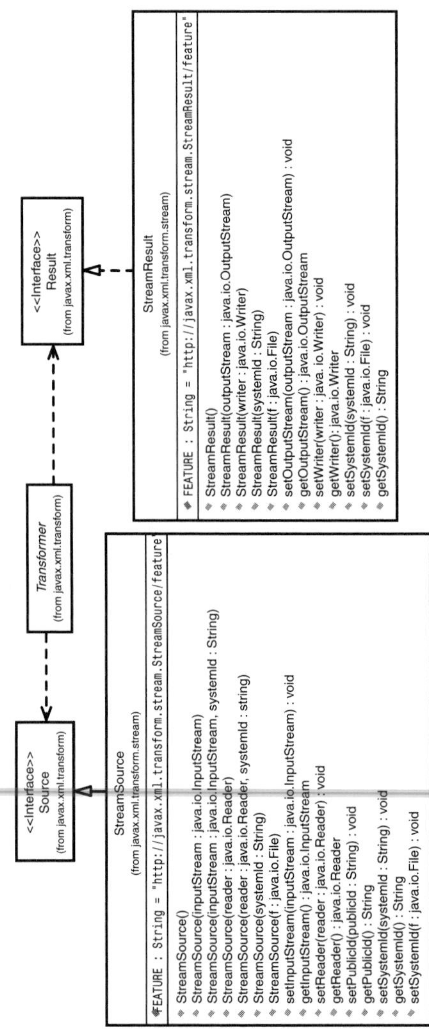

Figure 4.18 `javax.xml.transform.stream` implementation classes.

Listing 4.6 **XSL Transformation Example** (`XMLTransformApp.java`)

```
package ejava.jaxp;

import java.io.File;

import javax.xml.transform.Transformer;
import javax.xml.transform.TransformerException;
import javax.xml.transform.TransformerFactory;
```

Listing 4.6 **Continued**

```
import javax.xml.transform.OutputKeys;
import javax.xml.transform.stream.StreamSource;
import javax.xml.transform.stream.StreamResult;

import javax.xml.transform.OutputKeys;

/**
 *  Takes input file names of
 *     XSL stylesheet,
 *     XML source document,
 *     output file
 *  and applies the transformation
 */

public class XmlTransformApp
{

    public XmlTransformApp()
    {
    }

    public static void main(String[] args)
    {
        TransformerFactory factory = TransformerFactory.newInstance();

        File styleSheet = new File(args[0]);
        File inputFile  = new File(args[1]);
        File outputFile = new File(args[2]);

        StreamSource styleSrc =  new StreamSource(styleSheet);
        StreamSource inputSrc =  new StreamSource(inputFile);
        StreamResult result = new StreamResult(outputFile);

        try
        {
            Transformer transformer = factory.newTransformer(styleSrc);
            transformer.setOutputProperty(OutputKeys.INDENT, "yes");
            transformer.transform(inputSrc, result);
        }
        catch (TransformerException te)
        {
            System.out.println("Error = " + te.toString());
        }
    }
  }
```

Conclusions

The SAX API provides a simple and portable framework for reading and using XML data. It is lightweight, and easy to extend, while still providing needed support for newer XML features such as namespaces and XML schema. Because SAX reads XML documents into memory as a stream and parses content on the fly, SAX proves to be efficient when working with large XML documents or when working with numerous XML documents for multiple concurrent client requests. As such, it is an excellent choice when the XML parsing application is a server-side application needing to handle a large number of client requests.

In contrast, DOM provides a means for representing an XML document using objects encapsulating each component (that is, node) of an XML document's structure. DOM thus provides an interface to an XML document that preserves the hierarchical nature of the data inside of an XML document. This can be useful when an application needs to manipulate XML data, or to traverse data in a random-access fashion. For example, a GUI editing tool that provides a treelike interface to view and edit an XML document might opt to use DOM in its implementation. DOM implementations may, however, be more memory intensive than SAX implementations due to the need to encapsulate each artifact of an XML document inside of a separate object. The efficiency of a SAX or DOM implementation is, of course, a function of the underlying vendor parser implementation. Nevertheless, JAXP incorporates both SAX and DOM approaches to parsing XML documents and allows the developer to choose which API suits the particular application's needs.

JAXP also provides the capability to perform XML transformations, which can serve various purposes. One can apply an "identity" transform that preserves the exact structure of a document, but changes its actual representation, say, from an in-memory DOM tree to a text file on disk. The document itself can also be transformed by applying a set of XSL formatting rules. In addition, the output of one transformation can be piped into another, allowing the capability to write modular, reusable data filtering services.

5

Core JDBC

DATABASE CONNECTIVITY REPRESENTS ONE OF THE MOST fundamental problems that enterprise system need to solve. Because enterprise data is often plentiful, must be archived, and must be shared among many distributed users, it is key for distributed enterprise systems to provide a scalable, reliable, and highly available means for accessing and updating data. Furthermore, the complexity inherent with communicating to a wide variety of DBMS vendor solutions and legacy data models presents a time-to-market impediment that also often hampers the enterprise system solutions provider. The creators of the Java platform have realized these problems and have provided the Java Database Connectivity (JDBC) solution incorporated as part of both the J2SE and the J2EE platforms. JDBC represents the standard means for connecting to DBMSs from Java applications in a fashion that is largely DBMS-independent and enables connectivity to both legacy and newly defined enterprise data. This chapter presents the architecture of JDBC and basic JDBC driver configuration, as well as the programmatic interfaces that applications can use to create database connections, execute queries, read result sets, and retrieve meta-data about the database.

In this chapter, you will learn:

- The architecture of JDBC as the standard means for connecting to databases from Java applications
- A classification of JDBC driver types and their pros and cons for usage
- The steps involved in configuring various JDBC driver types
- The mechanisms for establishing database connections via JDBC
- The creation and execution of regular SQL statements via JDBC
- The creation and execution of prepared SQL statements via JDBC
- The handling of query results and obtaining information about query results via JDBC
- The mappings between core SQL data types and Java types

- How to call database functions and user-defined stored procedures from JDBC
- Obtaining information about databases and database drivers via JDBC

JDBC Architecture

The Java Database Connectivity architecture represents the de facto standard means for connecting to databases from Java applications. JDBC is both an API for Java programmers and an interface model for service providers who implement connectivity to databases. As an API, JDBC provides a standard interface for Java applications to interact with multiple types of databases. As an interface model for service providers, JDBC provides a standard way for database vendors and third-party middleware vendors to implement connectivity to databases. JDBC leverages off of existing SQL standards and provides support for bridging to other database connectivity standards such as ODBC. JDBC accomplishes all of these standards-oriented goals with an interface that is simple, strongly typed, and capable of high-performance implementation.

JDBC version 1.0 was initially offered separately from the JDK 1.0 platform but was integrated with the JDK 1.1 platform in the `java.sql` package. The JDBC 1.0 version contains most of the core and commonly used features of JDBC. Sun then introduced the JDBC 2 version, which was partitioned into two separate categories: the JDBC 2 Core API and the JDBC 2 Standard Extension API. The JDBC 2 Core API included all the functionality contained in the JDBC 1.0 version plus a host of new features that included query result enhancements, enhancements for updating batches of data, persistence of Java objects, and support for a whole slew of new SQL types. The JDBC 2 Core API was packaged in the `java.sql` package common to the J2SE v1.2/v1.3 and J2EE v1.2/v1.3. The JDBC 2 Standard Extension API offered a range of more sophisticated enterprise features such as a simpler paradigm for connecting to databases in a three-tier architecture, support for connection pooling, distributed transactions, and enhanced management of query result sets. The JDBC 2 Standard Extension API was incorporated into the J2EE v1.2/v1.3 in the `javax.sql` package.

In a consolidation effort, the JDBC Core and Standard Extension APIs were unified with the release of the JDBC 3.0 standard. The JDBC 3.0 API is included with the J2SE v1.4 and thus also is part of the J2EE v1.4. A host of relatively minor changes were made to the JDBC API with the release of JDBC v3.0, including better integration with the J2EE Connector Architecture.

Because the JDBC 1.0 API specification has been around longer, support for this API by driver vendors is more prevalent than support for every feature defined in the JDBC 3.0 API. Sun maintains a thorough and searchable list of JDBC driver–compliant vendors for all JDBC versions on its Web site at `http://industry.java.sun.com/products/jdbc/drivers`.

The conceptual diagram in Figure 5.1 depicts a high-level view of the JDBC architecture. Here we see a Java application using the core part of JDBC 3.0 API via usage of the `java.sql` and `javax.sql` packages. The interfaces in these packages are implemented by a JDBC driver vendor. JDBC driver implementations provide Java-based wrappers to one or more DBMS interfaces. We will go into the various types of DBMS interfaces shortly, but suffice it to say that a DBMS interface represents an existing method for connecting to a database provided either in a vendor-specific way or via some vendor-independent means for interfacing with the database. Many JDBC driver implementations will connect only to a single type of database, but some middleware vendor driver implementations actually allow for connectivity to various database types.

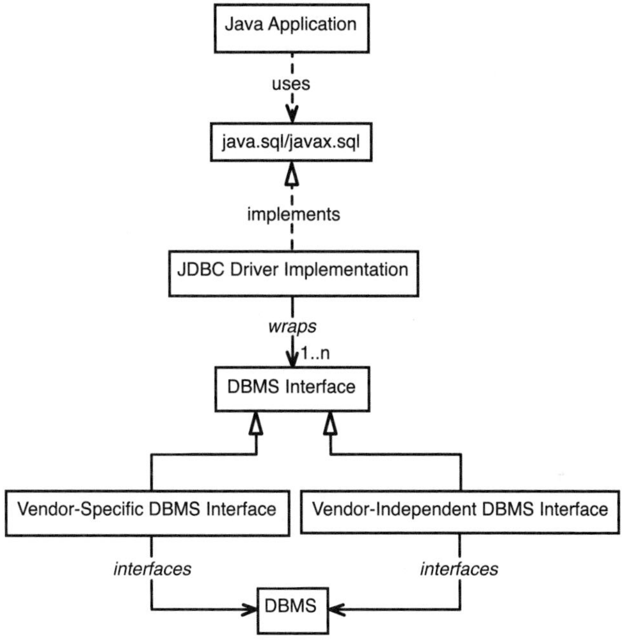

Figure 5.1 A JDBC architecture conceptual diagram.

One of the first steps a Java application will need to take when using JDBC is to obtain a handle to a database connection. A handle to a connection can be obtained in one of two ways. The Java application can first load a JDBC driver into memory. JDBC API database commands from the Java application are then delegated to the loaded JDBC driver implementation. The JDBC driver implementation talks to the vendor-specific or vendor-independent DBMS interface, and calls to this DBMS interface are then routed to the specific DBMS in use.

Alternatively, the Java application may look up a handle to a data source object that is registered with a distributed naming service. The means for accomplishing this is for the JDBC client to use the Java Naming and Directory Interface (JNDI) to look up a handle to a `javax.sql.DataSource` object. The `DataSource` object can then be used to obtain a handle to a JDBC connection. Although this is the preferred means for obtaining handles to JDBC connections, we defer discussion and examples of such a technique until later chapters. The reasoning behind this is to allow you to grasp the core concepts behind JDBC via more simplified client/server examples until we can introduce the concepts behind container-managed JDBC and JNDI.

The class diagram in Figure 5.2 depicts a set of classes, interfaces, exceptions, and key relations for the most basic subset of JDBC. The diagram is partitioned into three groupings showing the core JDBC classes and interfaces, the basic exceptions, and a set of key helper classes used to wrap and identify SQL types. The additional classes, interfaces, and exceptions added to the JDBC 2.0 and 3.0 APIs are not shown in this diagram because the advanced functionality contained in those APIs will be discussed later.

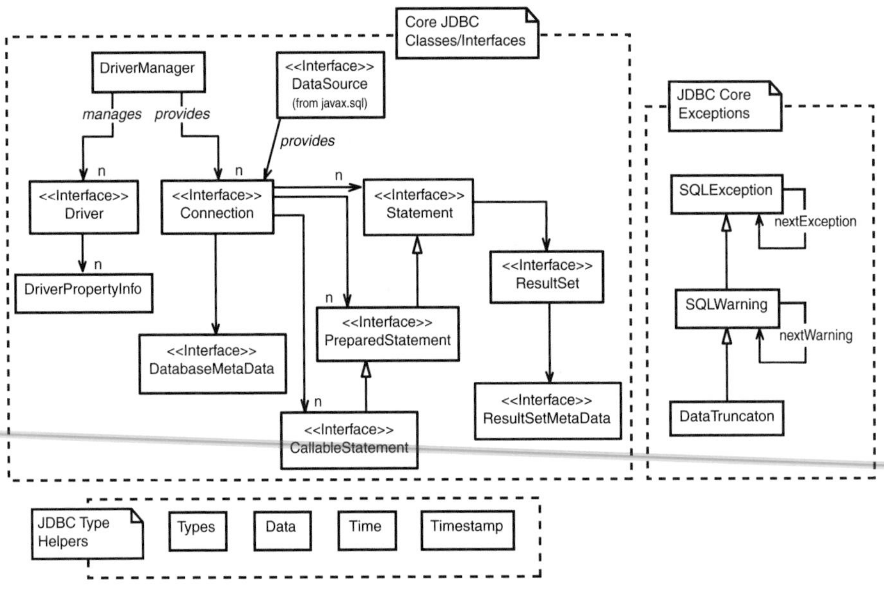

Figure 5.2 A basic JDBC class diagram.

You can see from the diagram that the `DriverManager` is at the top of the JDBC API composition serving as the basic class for managing zero or more JDBC drivers. Such JDBC drivers must implement the `Driver` interface, which is obligated to return a `DriverPropertyInfo` instance to allow an IDE or application to discover information about the driver. The `DriverManager` is also used to manage and return `Connection` objects to the Java application and represent connection sessions with the database. Figure 5.2 also illustrates the relationship between the `DataSource` interface and the `Connection` interface. Handles to `DataSource` objects are obtained from JNDI lookups and are described in more detail in later chapters.

The `Connection` object may then be consulted to obtain meta-data information about the particular database via the `DatabaseMetaData` interface. The `Connection` object's main usage involves creating statements to execute commands against the associated database. Static SQL statements (`Statement` interface), precompiled SQL statements (`PreparedStatement` interface), and stored SQL procedures (`CallableStatement` interface) may all be created and used to execute database commands. Database queries issued against such statements will return a `ResultSet` object reference that corresponds to zero or more query results from the database query. The `ResultSet` is used to obtain the desired query results and may also be used to obtain `ResultSetMetaData` to find out information about the properties of the returned result set.

A hierarchy of exceptions may be thrown during usage of the various JDBC API calls. `SQLExceptions` are the basic types of exceptions that return information regarding database access errors. Because more than one exception may be thrown by the database during certain calls, a chain of `SQLException` objects is returned and the `SQLException` class enables traversal of such exceptions. `SQLException` thus has a `setNextException()` method to chain exceptions and a `getNextException()` method to traverse chained exceptions. `SQLExceptions` can also return vendor-specific error-code information via a `getErrorCode()` call and SQL state information via a `getSQLState()` call. The `SQLWarning` exception is a special type of `SQLException` returning information regarding a database access warning. `SQLWarnings` also have `setNextWarning()` and `getNextWarning()` calls for chaining and traversing `SQLWarnings`. Finally, the `DataTruncation` exception returns information regarding a database read or write warning when the JDBC driver truncates a value returned from or sent to the database.

The JDBC type helpers of Figure 5.2 will be used throughout this and the following chapter. They represent the basic type helpers in JDBC 1.0 for identifying and managing data types submitted to and returned from the database through JDBC. A major enhancement in JDBC 2.0 was its provision of a much richer set of data types. The `java.sql.Types` class is simply a container of constants used to identify SQL types. The values used by the `Types` class are taken from the X/Open standard and are used to uniquely identify SQL standard types (for example, `VARCHAR`, `INTEGER`, `FLOAT`, `DATE`). A mapping between these types and Java types is presented later in this chapter.

JDBC Drivers and Their Types

The basic JDBC architecture presented in the preceding section described two broad categories of DBMS interfaces with which JDBC driver implementations may interact. These interfaces were classified according to interface openness as vendor-specific and vendor-independent DBMS interfaces. Sun has in fact come up with a classification scheme for JDBC drivers that is even more specific. Although the distinction by Sun is still made between JDBC drivers that speak to vendor-specific interfaces and those that speak to vendor-independent interfaces, an additional discriminator is employed to offer four distinct types of drivers. This discriminator indicates whether the JDBC driver talks with an interface that has a native platform implementation or with an interface that has a remote network listener with which the JDBC driver communicates. We refer to this additional classification discriminator as interface locality. Table 5.1 shows each JDBC driver type number and name in the context of how they are classified according to interface openness and interface locality. It should be noted that this classification of the four driver types according to interface openness and interface locality is not a formally defined classification scheme but one presented here for you to more rapidly grasp the fundamental and most common distinctions among the four driver types.

Table 5.1 **JDBC Driver Types**

		Interface Openness	
		Vendor-Independent	**Vendor-Specific**
Interface Locality	**Client-Side Native**	`Type 1`: JDBC -ODBC Bridge	`Type 2`: Native-API Partly Java Technology-Enabled
	Remote Network Listener	`Type 3`: Net-Protocol Fully Java Technology-Enabled	`Type 4`: Native-Protocol Fully Java Technology-Enabled

The J2EE and JDBC Driver Type Selection

Selection of JDBC drivers per the instructions of this section are relevant only to standalone Java enterprise applications. As you'll see later in the book, J2EE container environments shift JDBC driver type selection from the application developer's concern to the concern of the J2EE container providers and application deployers.

Figure 5.3 illustrates a typical configuration for type 1 JDBC drivers. Type 1 JDBC-ODBC Bridge drivers provide a means for Java applications to make JDBC calls that in turn are mapped to ODBC calls. An ODBC driver thus must be installed on the client side typically as a set of native libraries. Because ODBC is a popular DBMS interface standard for which there exists many ODBC drivers already available to talk with a wide variety of databases, and because JDBC is designed with ODBC in mind, Sun provides a JDBC/ODBC driver implementation with the J2SE. Sun's implementation of the `java.sql.Driver` interface for the JDBC-ODBC bridge driver is encapsulated by the `sun.jdbc.odbc.JdbcOdbcDriver` class. Use of this bridge is typically not recommended in production environments but is useful as a way to perhaps bootstrap your enterprise development efforts.

Figure 5.4 illustrates a typical configuration for type 2 JDBC drivers. Type 2 Native-API Partly Java Technology-Enabled drivers provide a mechanism for Java applications to make JDBC calls that are directly mapped to vendor-specific DBMS native library interface calls. Thus the JDBC driver is specifically designed to call native client libraries provided for DBMSs such as Oracle, Sybase, or Informix. Most database vendors now ship JDBC type 2 drivers with their databases. Such type 2 drivers will most typically offer better performance than using a JDBC/ODBC bridge because they bypass the ODBC intermediate layer.

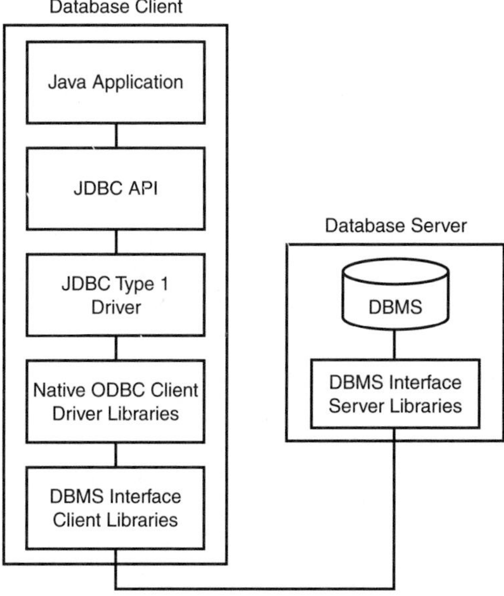

Figure 5.3 Typical type 1 JDBC driver configuration.

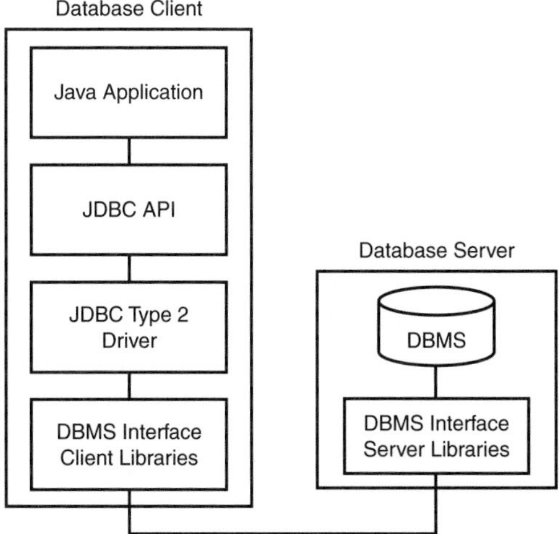

Figure 5.4 Typical type 2 JDBC driver configuration.

Figure 5.5 illustrates a typical configuration for type 3 JDBC drivers. Type 3 Net-Protocol Fully Java Technology-Enabled drivers provide a mechanism for Java applications to make JDBC calls that are mapped to calls embodied in some DBMS vendor-independent network protocol. These over-the-wire calls are then mapped to a specific DBMS vendor's interface calls. This vendor-independent remote listener is typically implemented by a middleware vendor offering support for connecting to various back-end database types. Thus the Java client application is freed from any dependence on having a set of native libraries installed on the client and has a very flexible means for communicating with various database types. The configuration of vendor-specific DBMS interfaces is thus localized to the middleware database server. Although the choice of network protocol for communicating to the middleware listener is left up to the middleware listener vendor, many vendors have been implementing fairly open solutions that are usable in Internet and intranet environments.

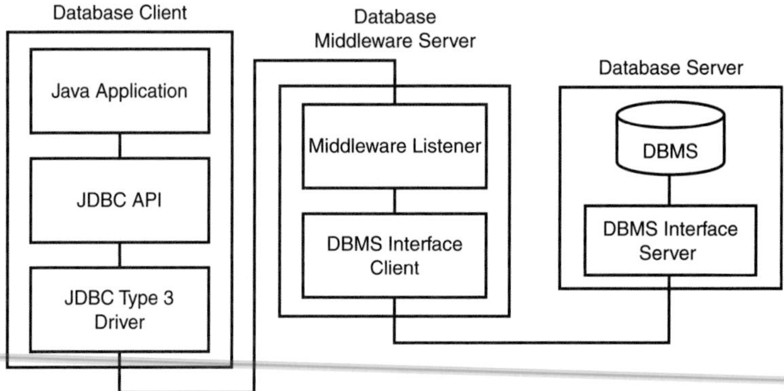

Figure 5.5 Typical type 3 JDBC driver configuration.

Figure 5.6 illustrates a typical configuration for type 4 JDBC drivers. Type 4 Native-Protocol Fully Java Technology-Enabled drivers provide a mechanism for Java applications to make JDBC calls that are mapped to calls embodied in a DBMS vendor's specific remote network listener protocol, which in turn are used to directly access that vendor's database. As with the type 3 drivers, type 4 drivers enable a Java client application to be freed from dependence on the loading of a set of native client-side libraries. However, because these drivers are vendor specific, this driver type solution does make for a less-flexible configuration on the client side because clients can now talk only with that vendor's DBMS.

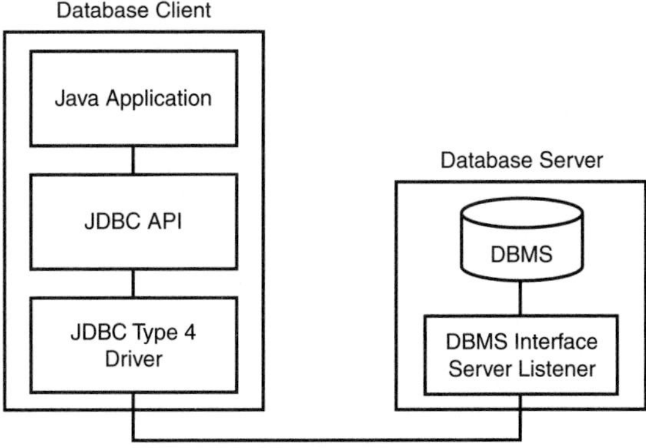

Figure 5.6 Typical type 4 JDBC driver configuration.

Driver Assessment

Choosing a driver for an enterprise application is an important step that affects performance, reliability, flexibility, and maintainability. Different drivers will have different performance characteristics, but some general assumptions and trade-offs are typically made when considering the various driver classes:

- Client-side native drivers (types 1 and 2) are usually more appropriate in networks in which client-side native libraries can be easily installed and configured or in situations in which a middle tier is assumed to provide intermediate database access on behalf of the client tier.
- Client-side native drivers are difficult to configure for Web clients and usually involve trusted applets and client-side library installs.
- Remote network listener-based drivers (types 3 and 4) result in thinner, pure Java clients.
- Type 1 drivers offer more database vendor independence, and type 2 drivers provide higher performance.
- Type 3 drivers offer greater database vendor-independence, and type 4 drivers yield better performance.

Such driver comparisons based on type are indeed gross comparisons. Evaluations of drivers should be performed on an individual basis because drivers will vary in performance according to specific features, databases in use, and other system environment factors. System environment factors such as client usage, client-side platforms, network bandwidth and usage, and server-side platforms all affect the performance of an application. Because driver implementation details are often not known a priori, information about the performance in a particular environment is not always obvious until it's evaluated in a simulated or actual system environment. Other issues such as security and level of JDBC compliance are also worthwhile attributes of a particular JDBC driver vendor to take into consideration.

JDBC Driver Configuration

Now that you know what a JDBC driver is and the various types available, it is important to know how to configure a JDBC driver for use in a standalone enterprise application. Figure 5.7 depicts a class diagram of the key entities involved in configuration of a JDBC driver when not accessing a `DataSource` object via JNDI. Note that although Figure 5.7 shows many of the core JDBC 1.0–style operations, a few JDBC 2.0–style operations are also shown.

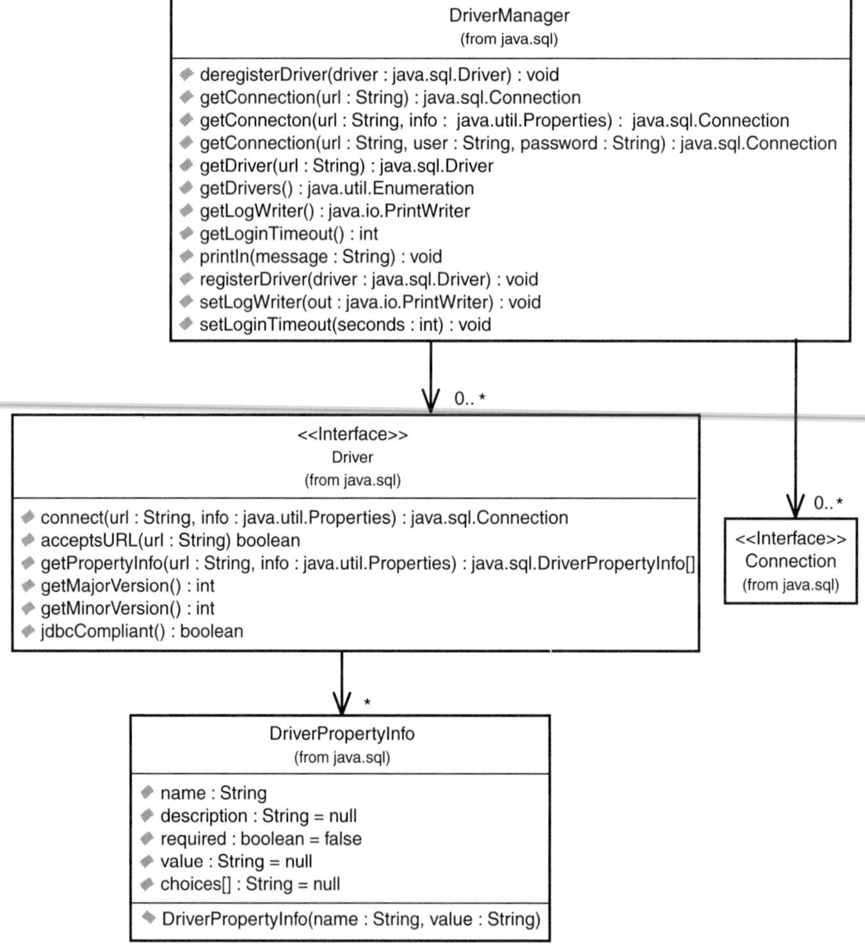

Figure 5.7 Driver management class diagram.

The `java.sql.DriverManager` class represents a primary interface to the JDBC API user for directly loading and managing JDBC drivers. The `DriverManager` can either load the driver classes implicitly by setting the system property `jdbc.drivers` or load them explicitly with calls to `Class.forName()`. The `DriverManager` is also used when creating new connections associated with the pool of loaded drivers.

> **The J2EE and JDBC Driver Configuration**
>
> Configuration of JDBC drivers per the instructions of this section are relevant only to standalone Java enterprise applications that don't use JNDI to access `DataSource` object handles. As you'll see in later chapters, use of the `DataSource` object and J2EE container environments shift JDBC driver configuration from the application developer's concern to the concern of J2EE application assemblers and deployers, as well as J2EE container providers.

To implicitly load a set of drivers, simply specify the driver class names separated by a colon (`:`) in the `jdbc.drivers` system property. Note that the driver class name specified must, of course, be in your `CLASSPATH`. For example:

```
java -Djdbc.drivers=sun.jdbc.odbc.JdbcOdbcDriver:
➥com.assuredtech.jdbc.JdbcDriver MyProgram
```

To explicitly load a driver, use the `Class.forName()` method in your Java program as shown here:

```
Class.forName("com.assuredtech.jdbc.JdbcDriver");
Class.forName("sun.jdbc.odbc.JdbcOdbcDriver");
```

A flexible scheme for configuring a set of drivers for your application may be to provide a set of JDBC driver names in a file adhering to a format readable by a `java.util.Properties` object and then load these driver names and call `Class.forName()` for each driver. The example presented in the next section demonstrates how to accomplish this task.

As a final note on driver configuration, the constructors of some drivers are occasionally used for driver registration. Although this scheme lacks flexibility because you are now rendered with a hard-wired driver name in your code, it is exemplified here for completeness:

```
com.assuredtech.jdbc.JdbcDriver driver
    = new com.assuredtech.jdbc.JdbcDriver();
// Note: com.assuredtech.jdbc.JdbcDriver() calls
//          DriverManager.registerDriver(Driver);
```

Note that the `com.assuredtech.jdbc.JdbcDriver` shown here would have to implement the `java.sql.Driver` interface as all JDBC drivers must. The `Driver` interface specifies the need to return a `DriverPropertyInfo` object that may be used to get and set properties for a connection associated with the driver. The JDBC API user rarely needs to interact with the `Driver` interface and the `java.sql.DriverPropertyInfo` class. Rather, the JDBC API user usually has the `DriverManager` class as the point of contact with the loaded JDBC drivers.

General Configuration Steps per Driver Type

The general steps for configuring type 1 JDBC-ODBC bridge drivers are detailed here:

1. Install the native DBMS interface client libraries and ODBC client driver for the DBMS to which you want to connect according to your DBMS vendor's instructions. It should be noted that Microsoft Windows often comes pre-installed with many Microsoft-related ODBC drivers ready to connect to Microsoft databases such as MS Access and SQL Server.
2. Find and double-click on the ODBC icon (the Data Source Administrator window pops up). The ODBC icon is accessible from the Start Menu's Administrative Tools submenu on newer Windows platforms and via the Control Panel on older Windows platforms.
3. Select the System DSN tab.
4. Click the Add button (the Create New Data Source window pops up).
5. Select the driver for the database with which you want to communicate.
6. Click the Finish button (an ODBC window specific to the selected driver pops up).
7. Type the data source name, fill in a description, and select or type the information regarding the database instance to which you want to connect.
8. Load the type 1 JDBC driver class (in your `CLASSPATH`) from your Java client application according to the instructions described previously in this section.

The general steps for configuring type 2 Native-API Partly Java Technology-Enabled drivers are detailed here:

1. Install the native DBMS interface client libraries for the DBMS to which you want to connect according to your DBMS vendor's instructions.
2. Load the type 2 JDBC driver class (in your `CLASSPATH`) from your Java client application according to the instructions described previously in this section.

The general steps for configuring type 3 Net-Protocol Fully Java Technology-Enabled drivers are detailed here:

1. You may first have to install the native DBMS interface client libraries for the DBMS to which you want to connect according to your DBMS vendor's instructions on your middleware server.
2. Install the middleware component libraries for your middleware remote network listener according to your middleware vendor's instructions.
3. Configure the middleware vendor's remote network listener to use one or more natively installed DBMS interfaces with a JDBC type 1 or JDBC type 2 driver or perhaps a JDBC type 4 driver for connection to a database vendor's remote network listener.

4. Load the middleware vendor's type 3 JDBC driver class (in your `CLASSPATH`) from your Java client application according to the instructions described previously in this section.

The general step for configuring type 4 Native-Protocol Fully Java Technology-Enabled drivers is detailed here:

1. Load the type 4 JDBC driver class (in your `CLASSPATH`) from your Java client application according to the instructions described previously in this section.

Such steps serve as simple guidelines for configuring JDBC drivers. Different drivers may have additional configuration needs than others. Furthermore, pay special attention to release notes for drivers and compatibility issues that may arise from time to time when configuring drivers in different environments. In general, however, database driver configuration is very much simplified relative to other technology paradigms due to the standard support offered by JDBC.

JDBC Connections

Now that we have covered the basic architecture of JDBC and discussed how to configure a JDBC driver, we can now begin to examine what kinds of things you can do programmatically with JDBC. The initial starting point is usually acquiring a handle to a database connection from the JDBC driver. A database connection represents a communications session in which a communications channel is opened and SQL commands are executed between a database client and the database server. The `java.sql.Connection` interface represents this database connection. A database connection is closed when the database session between the database client and the database is terminated (that is, via `Connection.close()`).

The J2EE and JDBC Connections

Configuration and creation of JDBC connections per the instructions of this section are relevant only to Java enterprise applications that don't use JNDI to access `DataSource` object handles. As we'll see later in the book, use of the `DataSource` object and J2EE container environments shift JDBC connection creation from the concern of the application developer to that of the J2EE container provider. Connections are yielded from a connection pool for application code in a J2EE container environment. J2EE assembly and deployment descriptors configure any specific connection information on behalf of the application code.

Configuring the BeeShirts.com Example Data Model

Before we dive into the details behind utilizing the JDBC API, we first need to obtain a basic understanding of the data model we reference within the example JDBC code. That is, to demonstrate how to data-enable an enterprise application with JDBC, we use an actual database and some sample data. The sample data and associated data model define a commercial retail T-shirt business model that we will continue to enable for distributed access, Web-based access, and EJB-based access throughout the remainder of this book. After reading this book, you will have gone through all the key enterprise-enabling steps to be considered in building a distributed Java-based e-commerce enterprise system known as BeeShirts.com.

If you don't already have a database available, you can follow the steps outlined in Appendix A, "Software Configuration," for installing the underlying database that we have used to create these examples. Appendix A also demonstrates how to configure the database with the BeeShirts.com data model and data used throughout this book. You of course can configure and populate your own database with the BeeShirts.com data.

Throughout the book, we incrementally introduce parts of the BeeShirts.com data model as its elements become relevant to understanding the example code that utilizes the model. We take this approach so that you are not plagued with attempting to understand a complete data model before parts of it are even utilized or relevant. Appendix A describes the full-blown example data model used in the example BeeShirts.com application for the reader interested in understanding the data model now, before proceeding.

As described in Appendix G, "Enterprise Software Development," we use a UML-like type notation and SQL type names from the `java.sql.Types` class for describing the data models throughout the book. Figure 5.8 depicts the most basic subset of the BeeShirts.com data model relevant to the examples of this chapter. The item table includes the information related to a particular item (that is, a T-shirt) that may be purchased. The item table is related to an actual order via an order number. The orders table contains the order information for a particular set of items. The orders table is related to a customer table via a customer number. The customer table includes all information related to a potential or existing BeeShirts.com customer. An auxiliary state table contains the mapping from a two-character state code to a complete state name.

Database URLs

A database Uniform Resource Locator (URL) represents a fully qualified database connection name identifying the database and database driver to which you are connecting. To fully describe a connection name, one needs to know information such as the type of database driver, the type of database, the type of database connection, and some connection-instance information such as the username, password, and IP address of the database instance. The database URL is represented as a `String` in the form

```
jdbc:subprotocol:subname
```

in which

- `jdbc` is a database driver type keyword used in the URL for all JDBC database URLs.
- *`subprotocol`* represents the type of database to which one desires connectivity.
- *`subname`* provides additional information needed by the database type for establishing connectivity.

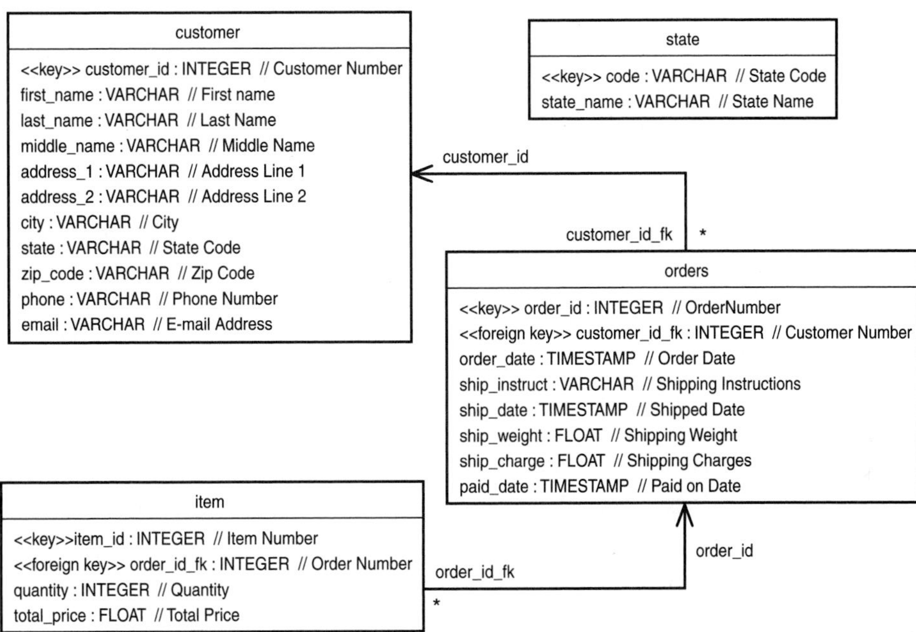

Figure 5.8 BeeShirts.com customer, orders, and items basic data model.

The *`subprotocol`* and *`subname`* to use for a particular database instance should be described in your JDBC driver vendor's documentation, but some examples are listed here for different driver types:

- Type 1: JDBC-ODBC Bridge Driver URLs

```
jdbc:odbc:customer;UID:dba;pwd:dba
jdbc:odbc:customer;CacheSize=100
jdbc:odbc:<datasource name>;param=value;param=value;....
```

- Type 2: Native-API Partly Java Technology-Enabled Driver URL

```
jdbc:oracle:oci7:@SQLNETinstance Name
```

- Type 3: Net-Protocol Fully Java Technology-Enabled Driver URLs

```
jdbc:dbAnywhere:1529
```

- Type 4: Native-Protocol Fully Java Technology-Enabled Driver URLs

```
jdbc:oracle:thin:@<machine name>:<port Number>:<DBMS instance name>
```

Creating Connections

To create a connection object instance using the `DriverManager`, one of the `DriverManager`'s `getConnection()` methods must be invoked with the database

URL as a parameter. When invoking this method, DriverManager first finds a driver from its pool of loaded drivers that can accept the database URL and then asks the driver to connect to the database with the associated database URL. A Connection object is then returned to the object that invoked DriverManager.getConnection(). Three forms of getConnection() exist on the DriverManager class as shown in Figure 5.7:

- getConnection(String url) simply attempts to connect given the database URL.
- getConnection(String url, String user, String password) attempts to connect given the database URL, a database username, and the database user's password.
- getConnection(String url, java.util.Properties info) attempts to connect given the database URL and a set of properties used as connection arguments. Sometimes, a user and password property are passed in via the Properties object.

As an option, the DriverManager.setLoginTimeout() method may be invoked to specify the timeout in seconds for a driver to wait while attempting to connect to a database.

Example: Connecting to a Database

This next example demonstrates how to establish a connection to the database. The example code is contained in the ejava.jdbc.core.ConnectToDatabase class and has the following definition:

```
public class ConnectToDatabase{ ... }
```

> **Note**
>
> All source code associated with this chapter can be located as described in Appendix A and is extracted to the examples\src\ejava\jdbc\core directory, whereas the code execution script templates are extracted to the examples\config\execscripts\ejava\jdbc\core directory. The build.xml ANT script is used to build and run the examples. The code is compiled, preferences are set, and process execution templates are generated using the default all ANT target. As described in Appendix A and later in this chapter, you must also set your database configuration properties as appropriate in the global.properties file in the examples directory. Refer to Appendix A for general database configuration instructions.
>
> The following complete code example uses the ConnectToDatabase.java file in the ejava\jdbc\core source directory. Some exception handling and other handling mechanisms have been left out of the chapter here for simplicity but can be found in the complete examples. A runconnecttodb example script file that can be used to execute the example is generated into the examples\src\ejava\jdbc\core directory after running the ANT execscripts target. Note also that the ANT prefs target will read Preference values via our

ejava.util.ant.PreferenceSetterTask class that are configured in the build.xml file and read from properties in the local build.properties file and global global.properties file.

The main() method of ConnectToDatabase is invoked like this:

```
java ejava.jdbc.core.ConnectToDatabase
```

The main() method then reads the preferences set for this example into a Preferences object. Subsequently, main() instantiates a new ConnectToDatabase object and calls getConnection() to return the Connection object. A series of exceptions are handled and the status of the connection attempt is returned. The key elements of the main() function are shown here:

```
public static void main(String[] args)
{
  Preferences preferences =
  ➥ Preferences.userNodeForPackage(ConnectToDatabase.class);

  ConnectToDatabase connectionToDatabase = new ConnectToDatabase();

    . . .
    Connection connection = connectionToDatabase.getConnection();
    . . .
    // Catch exceptions.
    . . .
    // Else print results of successful connection attempt.
    . . .
}
```

The following member variables of the ConnectToDatabase class are used to maintain the relevant variables used in this example:

```
private String driverClass; // Driver class name
private String dbURL; // Database URL
private Connection connection; // A database connection object
```

Note

As described in Appendix A, we generally use Java preferences (from the java.util.prefs package) throughout the book for most of our examples to enable you to experiment with the examples via setting preferences with different values. The ANT scripts with each chapter have targets that invoke an ANT task defined in our ejava.util.ant.PreferenceSetterTask class. The ANT build.xml script induces the reading properties from the chapter's local build.properties file and from a global global.properties file in the examples/ directory. These properties are then associated with keys in the ANT task for use by the PreferenceSetterTask class. The PreferenceSettertask delegates the actual setting of Java preferences using our ejava.util.prefs.PreferenceSetter class. After the execution scripts are generated and run, these preferences will be thus available to our Java examples.

In this example, we read preferences such as the driver class and database URL, which you will probably have and want to change to run with your particular configuration and database. We will also usually provide you with some variations that may be set for each property that you may comment or uncomment according to your desired experiment. The relevant preferences and properties for this example from the `global.properties` file are illustrated here:

```
# This is an example build properties file.
# You should change the build properties in this file with respect
# to the environment on your system.

# Username and password for database access
db.username=TSHIRTS
db.password=TSHIRTS

# Oracle Database Directories and Libraries
oracle.path=C:/Tools/oracle/ora9i
db.driver.class=oracle.jdbc.driver.OracleDriver
db.driver.location=${oracle.path}/jdbc/lib/classes12.jar;
➥${oracle.path}/jdbc/lib/nls_charset12.jar
db.url=jdbc:oracle:thin:@localhost:1521:TSHIRTS

# Cloudscape Database Directories and Libraries
#cloudscape.dir=C:/Tools/j2sdkee1.4
#db.driver.class=COM.cloudscape.core.JDBCDriver
#db.driver.location=${cloudscape.dir}/lib/system/cloudscape.jar
#db.url=jdbc:cloudscape:${cloudscape.dir}/cloudscape/TSHIRTS

# MySQL Database Directories and Libraries
#db.driver.location=C:/Tools/mysql/lib/
➥mysql-connector-java-3.0.6-stable-bin.jar
#db.driver.class=com.mysql.jdbc.Driver
#db.url=jdbc:mysql://localhost/TSHIRTS
```

The `ConnectToDatabase.getConnection()` method called from `main()` first extracts the driver class name (`driverClass`), database URL (`dbURL`), username (`userName`), and password (`password`) from the `preferences` object. The driver class name is then used to call `Class.forName()` to load the driver. Finally, the database URL, username, and password are used to create a connection via `DriverManager.getConnection()`. Depending on whether you include a `db.username` and `db.password` set of values in the `global.properties` file, you induce the example code to use a particular `DriverManager.getConnection()` method. The key elements of the `getConnection()` method are shown here:

```
public Connection getConnection()
  throws ClassNotFoundException, SQLException, Exception
{
  if(connection != null){
    return this.connection;
  }
```

```
  Preferences preferences =
    Preferences.userNodeForPackage(ConnectToDatabase.class);
  // Get connection properties from preferences
  driverClass = preferences.get("DRIVER_CLASS", null);
  dbURL   = preferences.get("DATABASE_URL",null);
  String userName = preferences.get("USER_NAME",null);
  String password = preferences.get("PASSWORD",null);

  if(driverClass == null || dbURL == null){
    throw new Exception("Driver Class or Driver"+
➥  " URL should not be null");
  }

  System.out.println("Registering driver : "+driverClass);
  // Load driver
  Class.forName(driverClass);

    // Create connection in one of two ways depending on whether or
    //not a username and password were in preferences
    if( (userName == null ) && (password == null)){
      System.out.println("Connecting to Database :"+dbURL);
      connection = DriverManager.getConnection(dbURL);
    }
    else{
      System.out.println("Connecting to DataBase :"+dbURL+
            " UserName :"+userName +"Password :"+password);
      connection =
          DriverManager.getConnection(dbURL, userName, password);
    }
  return connection;
}
```

Connection Interfaces

After a connection to a database is opened, a Java application typically makes actual use of the connection via the creation and execution of a series of SQL commands. These SQL commands are executed as database statements that perform such operations as querying for data, updating data, inserting data, and deleting data. The `java.sql.Statement`, `java.sql.PreparedStatement`, and `java.sql.CallableStatement` interfaces shown in Figure 5.9 encapsulate various forms of database statements that are created by a `Connection` object and that can be issued to the database. We will not cover use of all the methods on the `Connection` interfaces in this section, but throughout the rest of this chapter and continuing into the next, most of the functionality that demonstrates the use of this interface will be presented.

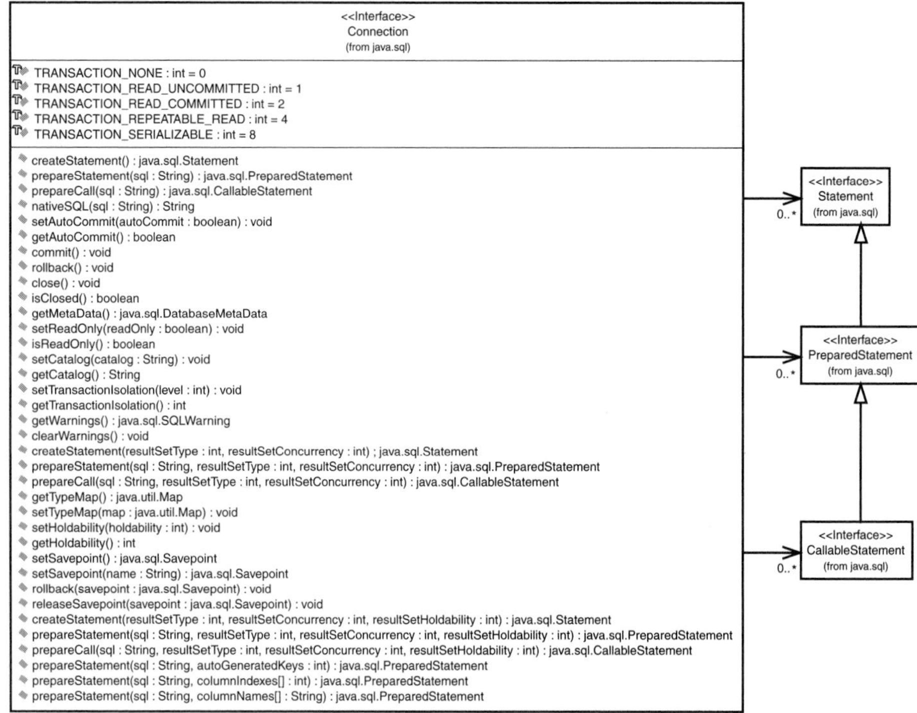

Figure 5.9 Connection class diagram.

The `Connection` object provides a front-line interface to much of the operations that one desires to perform with a database. Creation of handles to the various types of query statements are obtained through the connection interface. The management of resources associated with the creation and execution of such statements is hidden behind the interface of a `Connection` object. Other features associated with the database can also be obtained from the `Connection` object, including obtaining meta-data descriptions of the database itself and managing type mappings. We'll continue to see examples of the `Connection` object's methods throughout this and the next chapter as they become relevant, so be prepared to refer to Figure 5.9 as the occasion arises.

JDBC Statements

With a `Connection` object in hand, you can now begin to execute queries. The JDBC statements mentioned earlier are used to accomplish this task. Figure 5.10 depicts the base `Statement` abstraction created by a `Connection` object. The `Statement` interface represents a basic SQL statement that can be executed. We also will not cover use of all the methods on the statement interface in this section, but throughout the rest of this and the next chapter, most of the functionality that demonstrates use of its methods will be presented.

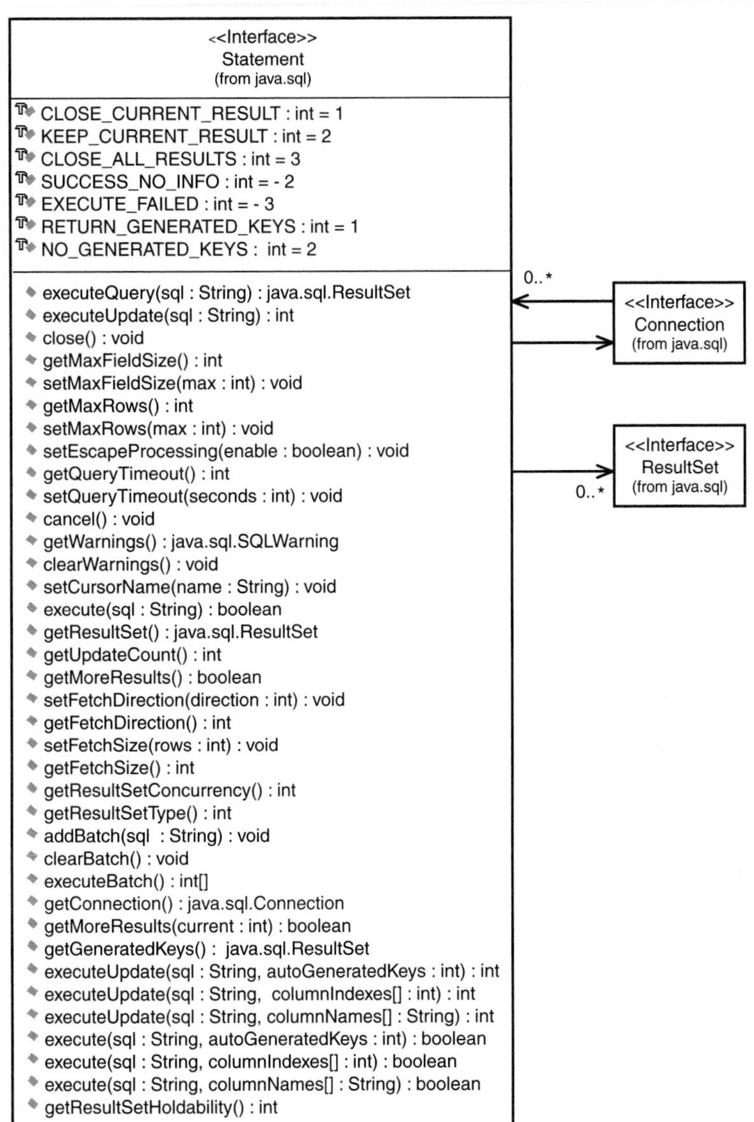

Figure 5.10 Statement class diagram.

SQL commands are contained in Java `String` objects passed to JDBC calls. These `String` objects simply contain SQL commands as described in Appendix C, "Database Concepts and SQL." A regular `Statement` object can be created by invoking `createStatement()` on a `Connection` object. Such nonprepared types of statements will be useful for infrequent queries because they are not precompiled for efficiency, as are `PreparedStatement` objects. You can create a `Statement` object as shown here:

```
Statement statement = connection.createStatement();
```

The `Statement` object is then called upon to execute an actual SQL command using one of three most commonly used methods:

- `ResultSet executeQuery(String sql)` allows one to execute SQL queries and obtain a `ResultSet` object. For example:

  ```
  ResultSet rs = statement.executeQuery("SELECT * FROM CUSTOMER");
  ```

- `int executeUpdate(String sql)` allows one to execute SQL inserts, deletes, and updates and then obtain a count of updated rows. For example:

  ```
  int nValues = statement.executeUpdate("INSERT INTO CUSTOMER VALUES"
    + " ('129','Sam','Cheng','s','123 Sam St.', '12','Baltimore','MD',"
    + "'20222', '(410)444-4444' ,'sc@scheng.com') ");
  ```

- `boolean execute(String sql)` is the most generic type of execute call allowing one to execute SQL DDL commands and then obtain a `boolean` value indicating whether a `ResultSet` was returned. For example:

  ```
  boolean returnValue = statement.execute("SELECT * FROM CUSTOMER" );
  ```

Additionally and new to JDBC 3.0, a feature has been added for indicating that query results may include those columns which contain auto-generated keys. Auto-generated keys are simply those columns that have been populated with key information generated by the database. Most often, you'll configure a database to populate such columns with information such as sequence numbers or identifiers used to uniquely index associated data (for example, an auto-generated order number or account identifier). The `Statement` object can be called upon when executing a SQL `INSERT` command to indicate the allowed retrieval of auto-generated keys. Flags used to respectively indicate whether auto-generated keys should be returned are `Statement.RETURN_GENERATED_KEYS` and `Statement.NO_GENERATED_KEYS`. One of the following `execute` methods may be used to indicate the return of such keys during issuance of a SQL `INSERT`:

- `boolean execute(String sql, int autoGeneratedKeysFlag)` allows one to indicate whether auto-generated keys should be made available for retrieval.
- `boolean execute(String sql, int[] columns)` allows one to indicate that those columns with the indices provided and containing auto-generated keys should be made available for retrieval.
- `boolean execute(String sql, String[] columns)` allows one to indicate that those columns with the names provided and containing auto-generated keys should be made available for retrieval.

Querying with Joins, Outer Joins, and LIKE Clauses

Aside from queries, inserts, deletes, updates, and DDL commands that operate on a single table as in the code snippets shown previously, joins in queries are used when data from more than a single table needs to be returned with a value in one table equaling a value in another table. As an example join that may be issued on the example database, we have this:

```
String joinStatement = "SELECT CUSTOMER.*, ORDERS.* FROM "
   + "CUSTOMER, ORDERS WHERE CUSTOMER.CUSTOMER_ID = ORDERS.CUSTOMER_ID_FK";
Statement statement = connection.createStatement();
ResultSet rs = statement.executeQuery(joinStatement);
```

Outer joins are used when we are trying to join tables that have data in one table that has no cross-reference in the other table yet we still want to return its value from the resultant query. Joins are executed in JDBC statements like any other SQL command, but outer joins may take a different syntax. One database vendor's syntax for outer joins may differ from another vendor's syntax. For example, an outer join `String` in Microsoft Access may be formulated this way:

```
String joinStatement= "SELECT C.* , S.* FROM CUSTOMER C OUTER JOIN"
                        + "STATE S on C.STATE = S.CODE";
```

The same outer join in Oracle may be formulated like this:

```
String joinStatement = "SELECT C.*, S.* FROM CUSTOMER C, STATE S "
    + "WHERE C.STATE(+) = S.CODE(+)";
```

There are also differences for issuing SQL statements with an embedded `LIKE` clause. For example, a Microsoft Access SQL `String` with a `LIKE` clause in it may be formulated like this:

```
String sqlString = " SELECT * FROM CUSTOMER
➥WHERE FIRST_NAME like '*R*' ";
```

The same `LIKE` clause for Oracle is formulated this way:

```
String sqlString = " SELECT * FROM CUSTOMER
➥WHERE FIRST_NAME like '%R%' ";
```

There does exist a standard JDBC escape syntax for handling such outer joins and `LIKE` clause anomalies, but the level of particular support for such features from many driver implementations remains minimal.

Example: Creating and Executing Statements

This next example demonstrates how to create and execute a series of simple statements. The example code is contained in the `ejava.jdbc.core.SimpleStatementExample` class. This example builds off of the previous database-connection example. In fact, the `SimpleStatementExample` class extends the `ConnectToDatabase` class:

```
public class SimpleStatementExample extends ConnectToDatabase{...}
```

> **Note**
> This example uses the `SimpleStatementExample.java`, `ConnectToDatabase.java`, and `build.properties` files. Some exception handling and other handling mechanisms have been left out of the book here for simplicity but can be found in the complete examples. Additionally, a `runsimplestatement` example script file is generated in the `examples\src\ejava\jdbc\core` directory after running ANT, and can be used to execute this example. See Appendix A for more information on general database and example code configuration procedures.

The `main()` method of `SimpleStatementExample` is invoked as shown here:

```
java ejava.jdbc.core.SimpleStatementExample
```

The `main()` method reads preferences and calls `getConnection()` on the example class as it did in the `ConnectToDatabase` example to load the preference information and establish the database connection. However, now we also create a `Statement` object and attempt to execute two regular queries, an update, a join query, an outer join query, and a query with a `LIKE` clause. We also close the associated `Statement` object after all the example statements are executed. A series of exceptions are handled, and the status of each command executed is reported but left out of the following listing:

```
public static void main(String[] args)
{
  Preferences preferences =
  ➥Preferences.userNodeForPackage(ConnectToDatabase.class);

  SimpleStatementExample simpleStatementExample =
  ➥ new SimpleStatementExample();
   . . .
  Connection connection = simpleStatementExample.getConnection();
  . . .
  String sqlString = preferences.get("SQL_QUERY_STATEMENT",null);
  . . .
  boolean executionStatus =
  ➥simpleStatementExample.execute(sqlString);
  . . .
  ResultSet resultSet =
  ➥simpleStatementExample.executeQuery(sqlString);
  . . .
  sqlString =
  ➥preferences.get("SQL_UPDATE_STATEMENT",null);
  . . .
  int count = simpleStatementExample.executeUpdate(sqlString);
  . . .
  String joinStatement =
  ➥preferences.get("SQL_QUERY_STATEMENT_JOIN",null);
  . . .
```

```
   resultSet = simpleStatementExample.executeQuery(joinStatement);
   String outerJoinStatement =
   ➥preferences.get("SQL_QUERY_STATEMENT_OUTER_JOIN",null);
   . . .
   resultSet =
   ➥simpleStatementExample.executeQuery(outerJoinStatement);
   . . .
   String likeStatement =
   ➥preferences.get("SQL_QUERY_STATEMENT_WITH_LIKE",null);
   . . .
   resultSet = simpleStatementExample.executeQuery(likeStatement);
   simpleStatementExample.closeStatement();
   . . .
     . . .
}
```

In addition to the state implicitly inherited from `ConnectToDatabase`, we have added another attribute to this class for containing a reference to the `Statement` object:

```
private Statement  statement; // Statement object
```

Each query or update `String` issued is read from the preferences as initialized in the `build.properties` file for this chapter. You of course can modify this properties file to demonstrate different types of queries, but you will have to run the ANT target `prefs` again. These are the properties that are relevant to the preceding example and located in the `build.properties` file:

```
#SQL Query
sql.statement.query=SELECT * FROM CUSTOMER

# SQL Update, if you run this program multiple times please change the
#  id and email field values each time
sql.statement.update=INSERT INTO CUSTOMER VALUES
➥ ('129','Sam','Cheng','S','123 Sam St.', 'C3','Baltimore',
➥ 'MD','20222','4104444444' ,'sc@scheng.com')

# Join STATEMENT
sql.query.statement.join=SELECT CUSTOMER.*,
➥ ORDERS.* FROM CUSTOMER, ORDERS
➥ WHERE CUSTOMER.CUSTOMER_ID = ORDERS.CUSTOMER_ID_FK

# OUTER JOIN for ORACLE
sql.query.statement.outer.join=SELECT CUSTOMER.*
➥ FROM CUSTOMER,STATE WHERE CUSTOMER.STATE = STATE.CODE(+)
# OUTER JOIN for MSACCESS
#sql.query.statement.outer.join = SELECT C.* , S.*
➥ FROM  CUSTOMER C  OUTER JOIN STATE S on C.STATE = S.CODE
# OUTER JOIN for Cloudscape
```

```
#sql.query.statement.outer.join=SELECT C.* , S.*
FROM  CUSTOMER C  LEFT OUTER JOIN STATE S
➥ on C.STATE = S.CODE

# SQL Statement with Like for ORACLE and Cloudscape
sql.query.statement.like=SELECT * FROM CUSTOMER
➥ WHERE FIRST_NAME LIKE  '%R%'
# SQL Statement with Like for MSACCESS
#SQL_QUERY_STATEMENT_WITH_LIKE = SELECT CUSTOMER.*
➥ FROM CUSTOMER WHERE CUSTOMER.FIRST_NAME LIKE  \'*R*\'
```

When each type of example execute statement is invoked on the `SimpleStatementExample` object, each method attempts to retrieve the `Statement` object. Each method does this by calling a `createStatement()` method that retrieves the connection object from the base class and creates the `Statement` if it does not already exist. The `createStatement()` method is defined as shown here:

```
protected void createStatement()
  throws SQLException, Exception
{
    if(statement == null){
      Connection connection = super.getConnection();
      statement = connection.createStatement();
    }
}
```

Each type of execute command on a `Statement` object is demonstrated from the `SimpleStatementExample`'s `main()` method by calling one of the following three methods on the `SimpleStatementExample` object:

```
public boolean execute(String sqlString)
    throws SQLException, Exception
  {
    if(statement == null){
      createStatement();
    }

    boolean returnValue = statement.execute(sqlString);
    return returnValue;
  }

public ResultSet executeQuery(String sqlString)
    throws SQLException, Exception
  {
    if(statement == null){
      createStatement();
    }
```

```
    ResultSet rs = statement.executeQuery(sqlString);
    return rs;
  }

public int executeUpdate(String sqlString)
    throws SQLException, Exception
  {
    if(statement == null){
      createStatement();
    }

    int returnValue = statement.executeUpdate(sqlString);
    return returnValue;
  }
```

We finally close the statement with this:

```
public void closeStatement()
    throws SQLException
  {
    if(statement != null){
      statement.close();
      statement = null;
    }
  }
```

Prepared Statements

Although each `Statement` object used in the preceding set of examples represents a SQL statement that must be compiled each time it is executed, a prepared statement represents a precompiled SQL statement and is identified by the `java.sql.PreparedStatement` interface as shown in Figure 5.11.

A `PreparedStatement` has advantages over a regular `Statement` in that it is created with a parameterized SQL statement. Each `PreparedStatement`'s SQL command parameter is indicated by a question mark (?) in the SQL `String` and represents an input (`IN`) variable that can be dynamically set before the statement is executed. Because only the values of each parameter need to be set after the statement is created, the statement itself can be compiled when the statement is created (assuming that the database or driver or both fully support this feature). This provides an obvious benefit when sending SQL commands to the database that have the same basic command structure but differ only in the `IN` values used by each submitted command. A `PreparedStatement` is created with the `prepareStatement()` method on the `Connection` object as shown here:

```
PreparedStatement statement = connection.
➥prepareStatement("SELECT * FROM CUSTOMER WHERE CUSTOMER_ID= ?");
```

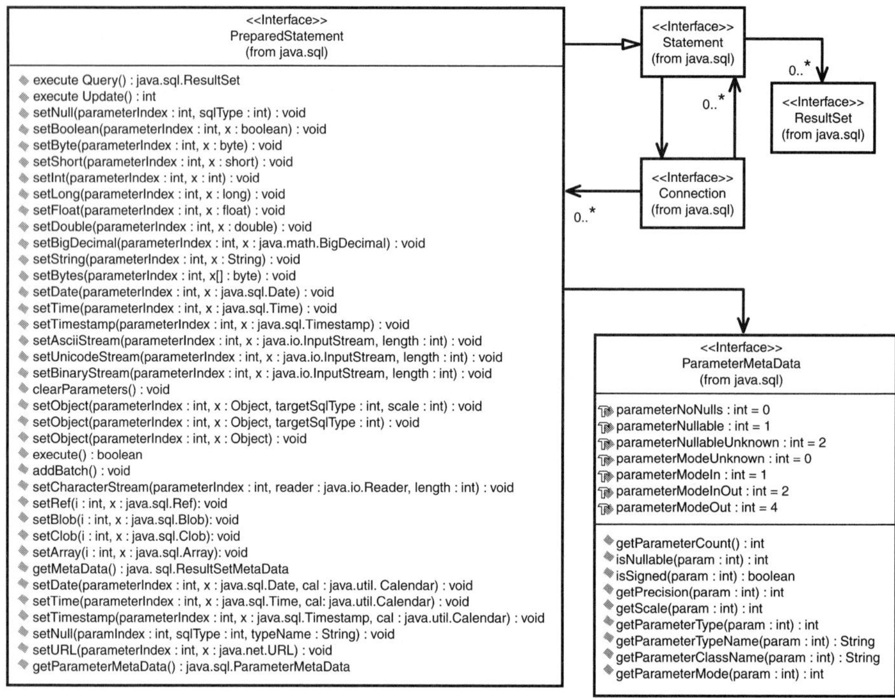

Figure 5.11 Prepared statement class diagram.

New to JDBC 3.0, a feature has been added for indicating that query results from prepared statement executions may include those columns that contain auto-generated keys. Flags used to respectively indicate whether auto-generated keys should be returned are `Statement.RETURN_GENERATED_KEYS` and `Statement.NO_GENERATED_KEYS`. One of the following `prepareStatement()` methods on the `Connection` object may be used to indicate the return of such keys during issuance of a SQL `INSERT` using the returned `PreparedStatement` object:

- `prepareStatement(String sql, int autoGeneratedKeysFlag)` allows one to indicate whether auto-generated keys should be made available for retrieval.
- `prepareStatement(String sql, int[] columns)` allows one to indicate that those columns with the indices provided and containing auto-generated keys should be made available for retrieval.
- `prepareStatement(String sql, String[] columns)` allows one to indicate that those columns with the names provided and containing auto-generated keys should be made available for retrieval.

After a prepared statement is created, the `IN` values must be set. This is accomplished via use of the various `setXXX()` methods that exist on the `PreparedStatement` object. The basic format for each `setXXX()` method is

```
void setXXX(int parameterIndex, XXX value);
```

where *XXX* is the type of object being inserted into the parameterized prepared statement at the index specified by `parameterIndex`. The various `set`*XXX*`()` methods available to a `PreparedStatement` are shown in Figure 5.11. For example, one way to set the parameter for the select clause created in the preceding `PreparedStatement` object would be as follows:

```
statement.setInt(1, new Integer(1295 ));
```

After each `set`*XXX*`()` method is called for each `IN` parameter in the `PreparedStatement`, the statement may be executed. This is accomplished via a call to one of three parameterless execute methods on the `PreparedStatement` object as defined here:

- `ResultSet executeQuery();` to execute SQL queries and obtain a `ResultSet` object
- `int executeUpdate();` to execute SQL updates and obtain a count of updated rows
- `boolean execute();` to execute SQL DDL commands and obtain a `boolean` value indicating whether a `ResultSet` was created

Example: Creating and Executing Prepared Statements

This next example demonstrates how to create and execute a series of `PreparedStatement` objects. The example code is contained in the `ejava.jdbc.core.SimplePreparedStatementExample` class. This example also builds off of the database connection example with the `SimplePreparedStatementExample` class extending the `ConnectToDatabase` class:

```
public class SimplePreparedStatementExample extends ConnectToDatabase{...}
```

> **Note**
>
> The following example may be run by executing the `runsimplepreparedstatement` script in the `examples\src\ejava\jdbc\core` directory, after running the ANT target. See Appendix A for additional information on building and running the examples.

The `main()` method of `SimplePreparedStatementExample` is invoked like this:

```
java ejava.jdbc.core.SimplePreparedStatementExample
```

The `main()` method reads preferences and invokes `getConnection()` on the example class as it did in the `ConnectToDatabase` example to load the preferences and establish the database connection. Here we also create `PreparedStatement` objects to execute queries and an update. For each type of execute command, a parameterized prepared SQL `String` and a `Vector` of `IN` parameter values are read from the properties file and submitted to the execution method. A special helper method for converting the `IN` parameters read from the property files as a `String` into a `Vector` object is also provided. A series of exceptions are handled, and the status of each attempt are reported but left out of the following listing:

```
public static void main(String[] args)
{
  Preferences preferences =
  ➥ Preferences.userNodeForPackage(ConnectToDatabase.class);

  SimplePreparedStatementExample simplePreparedStatementExample
  ➥ = new SimplePreparedStatementExample();
  . . .
    // Establish properties from preferences and get connection
  Connection connection =
  ➥ simplePreparedStatementExample.getConnection();
  . . .
  // Get SQL statements from preferences and execute them...
  String sqlString  =
  ➥ preferences.get("PREPARED_SQL_QUERY_STATEMENT",null);
  String parameters =
  ➥ preferences.get("PREPARED_SQL_QUERY_STATEMENT_VALUES",null);
  System.out.println("Executing statement :"+sqlString);
  Vector values =
   ➥ simplePreparedStatementExample.
   ➥ parseStringToVector(parameters);
  // Issue an execute() command
  boolean executionStatus =
  ➥  simplePreparedStatementExample.execute(sqlString,values);
  . . .
    // Set SQL insert string and values
  String insertString =
  ➥ preferences.get("PREPARED_SQL_INSERT_STATEMENT",null);
  System.out.println("Executing statement :"+insertString);
  String insertValuesString =
  ➥ preferences.get("PREPARED_SQL_INSERT_STATEMENT_VALUES",null);
  values = simplePreparedStatementExample.
  ➥ parseStringToVector(insertValuesString);

  // Issue an executeUpdate command
  int nResults = simplePreparedStatementExample.
  ➥ executeUpdate(insertString, values);
  . . .
  // Set SQL update string and values
  String updateString =
  ➥ preferences.get("PREPARED_SQL_UPDATE_STATEMENT",null);
  System.out.println("Executing statement :"+updateString);
```

```
    String updateValuesString =
    ➥ preferences.get("PREPARED_SQL_UPDATE_STATEMENT_VALUES",null);
    values = simplePreparedStatementExample.
    ➥ parseStringToVector(updateValuesString);

    // Issue an executeUpdate command
    nResults = simplePreparedStatementExample.
    ➥ executeUpdate(updateString, values);
    . . .
    String sqlString =
    ➥ preferences.get("PREPARED_SQL_QUERY_STATEMENT",null);
    String parameters =
    ➥ preferences.get("PREPARED_SQL_QUERY_STATEMENT_VALUES",null);
    System.out.println("Executing statement :"+sqlString);
    Vector values =
    ➥ simplePreparedStatementExample.
    ➥ parseStringToVector(parameters);
    ResultSet rs = simplePreparedStatementExample.
    ➥ executeQuery(sqlString,values);
    . . .
      // Close the statement
    simplePreparedStatementExample.closeStatement();
}
```

In addition to the state inherited from `ConnectToDatabase`, another private variable is used to store a `PreparedStatement` object:

```
private PreparedStatement statement; // PreparedStatement object
```

In addition to the properties contained in the `build.properties` file used for the `ConnectToDatabase` example, the following properties from the `build.properties` file are now used for this example:

```
# Prepared QUERY Statement
sql.query.prepared.statement = SELECT *
➥ FROM CUSTOMER WHERE FIRST_NAME = ?
sql.query.prepared.statement.values = Roy

# Prepared Insert, if you run this program multiple times
# please change the id and email field values each time
sql.query.prepared.statement.insert = INSERT INTO
➥ CUSTOMER VALUES(?,?,?,?,?,?,?,?,?,?,?)
sql.query.prepared.statement.insert.values =130,John,Hiller,Miller,125
➥ S St.,C6,Baltimore,MD,20100,4104444444,jh@jhiller.com

# Prepared Update
sql.query.prepared.statement.update = UPDATE STATE
➥ SET STATE_NAME = 'California' WHERE CODE = ?
sql.query.prepared.statement.update.values =CA
```

When each prepared statement is executed, a new `PreparedStatement` object is created and stored locally in this example using the `createStatement()` method as shown here:

```
protected void createStatement(String sqlString)
    throws SQLException, Exception
  {
    Connection connection = super.getConnection();
    statement = connection.prepareStatement(sqlString);
  }
```

Three types of SQL command executions are performed in the `execute()`, `executeQuery()`, and `executeUpdate()` methods. For each method, a `PreparedStatement` is created and the SQL `String` and `Vector` of `IN` values passed into the method are used to call `setObject()` for each prepared statement value. Finally, the appropriate command execution method on the `PreparedStatement` object is called. These three execute method variations are shown here:

```
public boolean execute(String sqlString, Vector values)
  throws SQLException, Exception
{

  createStatement(sqlString);
  for(int i = 1; i <= values.size(); i++){
    statement.setObject(i,values.elementAt(i-1));
  }
  boolean returnValue = statement.execute();
  return returnValue;
}

public ResultSet executeQuery(String sqlString, Vector values)
  throws SQLException, Exception
{

  createStatement(sqlString);

  for(int i = 1; i <= values.size(); i++){
    statement.setObject(i,values.elementAt(i-1));
  }
  ResultSet rs = statement.executeQuery();
  return rs;
}


public int executeUpdate(String sqlString, Vector values)
  throws SQLException, Exception
{
```

```
  createStatement(sqlString);

  for(int i = 1; i <= values.size(); i++){
    statement.setObject(i,values.elementAt(i-1));
  }
  int returnValue = statement.executeUpdate();
  return returnValue;
}
```

Obtaining Information About Prepared Statement Parameters

JDBC 3.0 now also provides an abstraction to obtain information about the type and characteristics of the parameters inside of `PreparedStatement` objects. As shown in Figure 5.11, this abstraction is referred to as the `ParameterMetaData` interface and can be obtained from a `PreparedStatement` object via its `getParameterMetaData()` method. As an example:

```
PreparedStatement prepreatedStatement = connection.prepareStatement(
    "SELECT * FROM CUSTOMER WHERE CUSTOMER_ID = ?");
ParameterMetaData parameterMetaData = pstmt.getParameterMetaData();
```

The actual number of parameters in the prepared statement can be determined from `getParameterCount()`. Subsequently, given the index of the parameter in the `PreparedStatement` (that is, 1, 2, 3, and so on), a set of `ParameterMetaData` methods return certain information about the parameter. The state of a parameter's mode can be determined via the `getParameterMode(int)` method. A set of `static public` constants are used to indicate the state of a parameter's mode (that is, `IN`, `INOUT`, `OUT`, unknown, nonsupporting of nulls, supporting nulls, or having unknown null supportability).

Other appropriately named methods will return such things as whether or not the parameter is nullable or a signed number, the precision in number of decimal digits, the scale of number of digits to the right of the decimal point, the SQL type name, the database-specific type name, and the fully-qualified Java class name mapped to the parameter. As a simple example:

```
int parameterCount = parameterMetaData.getParameterCount();
for(int i = 0; i<parameterMetaData.getParameterCount();i++){
  int paramterType = parameterMetaData.getParameterType(i);
    switch(parameterType){
      case Types.CHAR:
      case Types.VARCHAR:
      case Types.LONGVARCHAR:
        preparedStatement.setString(i,aStringValue);
        break;

      case Types.BIT:
```

```
            preparedSTatement.setBoolean(i,aBooleanValue);
            break;
            ....
        }
}
preparedStatement.executeQuery();
```

Result Sets

Creating statements and executing SQL queries would be of little value if there were not a way to actually retrieve the results of your database query. The `java.sql.ResultSet` interface encapsulates an object that represents zero or more results from a database query. Each result in a `ResultSet` represents a database row that can span one or more tables (which could be the result of a join). Figures 5.12a through 5.12c present a class diagram depicting the `ResultSet` interface. Because the `ResultSet` class has an absolutely enormous number of methods, we have to resort to spanning the interface across three figures. Although most of the methods are simply type-safe `get`*`XXX`*`()` and `update`*`XXX`*`()` methods, the total number of methods on the JDBC 3.0 `ResultSet` interface amounts to approximately 140 methods!

Manipulating Result Sets

A `ResultSet` object is returned from the `executeQuery()` method call on the `Statement` interface or one of its sub-interfaces. If auto-generated keys were allowed to be returned, then the `getGeneratedKeys()` method will return such values as a separate `ResultSet`. A `ResultSet` object may also be returned to the `Statement` object when `execute()` is called on the `Statement` object, but it is not directly returned from the method call. Rather, the `Statement` method `getResultSet()` may be called to obtain a handle on the returned `ResultSet` object. A null value is returned from `getResultSet()` if there is no result set object or if an update count was returned instead due to a SQL update command.

Because a SQL statement executed with the `execute()` statement may sometimes produce more than one `ResultSet` object, the `getMoreResults()` method on the `Statement` interface may be called to move to the next `ResultSet` and return a true `boolean` value indicating that a `ResultSet` was returned. Any existing result sets that were returned from `getResultSet()` are closed when the `getMoreResults()` method is called. The `execute()` command may also produce multiple updates and the method `getMoreResults()` will return `false` if the current result was an update. Thus, if `getResultSet()` returns a null and `getMoreResults()` returns `false`, the method `getUpdateCount()` may be used to return the number of updates present for the current result.

```
<<Interface>>
ResultSet
(from java.sql)

FETCH_FORWARD : int = 1000
FETCH_REVERSE : int = 1001
FETCH_UNKNOWN : int 1002
TYPE_FORWARD_ONLY : int = 1003
TYPE_SCROLL_INSENSITIVE : int = 1004
TYPE_SCROLL_SENSITIVE : int = 1005
CONCUR_READ_ONLY : int = 1007
CONCUR_UPDATABLE : int = 1008
HOLD_CURSORS_OVER_COMMIT : int = 1
CLOSE_CURSORS_AT_COMMIT : int = 2

absolute(row : int) : boolean
afterLast() : void
beforeFirst() : void
cancelRowUpdates() : void
clearWarnings() : void
close() : void
deleteRow() : void
findColumn(columnName : String) : int
first() : boolean
getArray(colName : String) : java.sql.Array
getArray(i : int) : java.sql.Array
getAsciiStream(columnIndex : int) : java.io.InputStream
getAsciiStream(columnName : String) : java.io.InputStream
getBigDecimal(columnIndex : int) : java.math.BigDecimal
getBigDecimal(columnName : String) : java.math.BigDecimal
getBinaryStream(columnIndex : int) : java.io.InputStream
getBinaryStream(columnName : String) : java.io.InputStream
getBlob(colName : String) : java.sql.Blob
getBlob(i : int) : java.sql.Blob
getBoolean(columnIndex : int) : boolean
getBoolean(columnName : String) : boolean
getByte(columnIndex : int) : byte
getByte(columnName : String) : byte
getBytes(columnIndex : int) : byte[]
getBytes(columnName : String) : byte[]
getCharacterStream(columnIndex : int) : java.io.Reader
getCharacterStream(columnName : String) : java.io.Reader
getClob(colName : String) : java.sql.Clob
getClob(i : int) : java.sql.Clob
getConcurrency() : int
getCursorName() : String
getDate(columnIndex : int) : java.sql.Date
getDate(columnIndex : int, cal : java.util.Calendar) : java.sql.Date
getDate(columnName : String) : java.sql.Date
getDate(columnName : String, cal : java.util.Calendar) : java.sql.Date
getDouble(columnIndex : int) : double
getDouble(columnName : String) : double
getFetchDirection() : int
getFetchSize() : int
getFloat(columnIndex : int) : float
getFloat(columnName : String) : float
getInt(columnIndex : int) : int
getInt(columnName : String) : int
getLong(columnIndex : int) : long
getLong(columnName : String) : long
```

Figure 5.12a Result set interface.

- getMetaData() : java.sql.ResultSetMetaData
- getObject(colName : String, map : java.util.Map) : Object
- getObject(columnIndex : int) : Object
- getObject(columnName : String) : Object
- getObject(i : int, map : java.util.Map) : Object
- getRef(colName : String) : java.sql.Ref
- getRef(i : int) : java.sql.Ref
- getRow() : int
- getShort(columnIndex : int) : short
- getShort(columnName : String) : short
- getStatement() : java.sql.Statement
- getString(columnIndex : int) : String
- getString(columnName : String) : String
- getTime(columnIndex : int) : java.sql.Time
- getTime(columnIndex : int, cal : java.util.Calendar) : java.sql.Time
- getTime(columnName : String) : java.sql.Time
- getTime(columnName : String, cal : java.util.Calendar) : java.sql.Time
- getTimestamp(columnIndex : int) : java.sql.Timestamp
- getTimestamp(columnIndex : int, cal : java.util.Calendar) : java.sql.Timestamp
- getTimestamp(columnName : String) : java.sql.Timestamp
- getTimestamp(columnName : String, cal : java.util.Calendar) : java.sql.Timestamp
- getType() : int
- getURL(columnIndex : int) : java.net.URL
- getURL(columnName : String) : java.net.URL
- getWarnings() : java.sql.SQLWarning
- insertRow() : void
- isAfterLast() : boolean
- isBeforeFirst() : boolean
- isFirst() : boolean
- isLast() : boolean
- last() : boolean
- moveToCurrentRow() : void
- moveToInsertRow() : void
- next() : boolean
- previous() : boolean
- refreshRow() : void
- relative(rows : int) : boolean
- rowDeleted() : boolean
- rowInserted() : boolean
- rowUpdated() : boolean
- setFetchDirection(direction: int) : void
- setFetchSize(rows : int) : void

Figure 5.12b Result set interface (continued).

Alternatively and new to JDBC 3.0, the `getMoreResults(int)` method may be invoked on a `Statement` object to also get the next result set, but may also specify how to deal with the current `ResultSet` object according to a flag passed into the method call. The `Statement.CLOSE_CURRENT_RESULT` flag is used to indicate that the current result set should be closed when moving to the next result set object as is with the case of calling this method's parameterless form. The `Statement.KEEP_CURRENT_RESULT` flag will keep the current result set open when moving to the next result set. The `Statement.CLOSE_ALL_RESULTS` flag will close any open result sets when moving to the next result set.

```
updateArray(columnIndex : int, x : java.sql.Array) : void
updateArray(columnName : String, x : java.sql.Array) : void
updateAsciiStream(columnIndex : int, x : java.io.InputStream, length : int) : void
updateAsciiStream(columnName : String, x : java.io.InputStream, length : int) : void
updateBigDecimal(columnIndex : int, x : java.math.BigDecimal) : void
updateBigDecimal(columnName : String, x : java.math.BigDecimal) : void
updateBinaryStream(columnIndex : int, x : java. io.InputStream, length : int) : void
updateBinaryStream(columnName : String, x : java.io.InputStream, length : int) : void
updateBlob(columnIndex : int, x : java.sql.Blob) : void
updateBlob(columnName : String, x : java.sql.Blob) : void
updateBoolean(columnIndex : int, x : boolean) : void
updateBoolean(columnName : String, x : boolean) : void
updateByte(columnIndex : int, x : byte) : void
updateByte(columnName : String, x : byte) : void
updateBytes(columnIndex : int, x [] : byte) : void
updateBytes(columnName : String, x[] : byte) : void
updateCharacterStream(columnIndex : int, x : java.io.Reader, length : int) : void
updateCharacterStream(columnName : String, reader : java.io.Reader, length : int) : void
updateClob(columnIndex : int, x : java.sql.Clob) : void
updateClob(columnName : String, x : java.sql.Clob) : void
updateDate(columnIndex : int, x : java.sql.Date) : void
updateDate(columnName : String, x : java.sql.Date) : void
updateDouble(columnIndex : int, x : double) : void
updateDouble(columnName : String, x : double) : void
updateFloat(columnIndex : int, x : float) : void
updateFloat(columnName : String, x : float) : void
updateInt(columnIndex : int, x : int) : void
updateInt(columnName : String, x : int) : void
updateLong(columnIndex : int, x : long) : void
updateLong(columnName : String, x : long) : void
updateNull(columnIndex : int) : void
updateNull(columnName : String) : void
updateObject(columnIndex : int, x : Object) : void
updateObject(columnIndex : int, x : Object, scale : int) : void
updateObject(columnName : String, x : Object)  : void
updateObject(columnName : String, x : Object, scale : int) : void
updateRef(columnIndex : int, x : java.sql.Ref) : void
updateRef(columnName : String, x : java.sql.Ref) : void
updateRow() : void
updateShort(columnIndex : int, x : short) : void
updateShort(columnName : String, x : short) : void
updateString(columnIndex : int, x : String) : void
updateString(columnName : String, x : String) : void
updateTime(columnIndex : int, x : java.sql.Time) : void
updateTime(columlnName : String, x : java.sql.Time) : void
updateTimestamp(columnIndex : int, x : java.sql.Timestamp) : void
updateTimestamp( columnName : String, x : java.sql.Timestamp) : void
wasNull() : boolean
```

Figure 5.12c Result set interface (continued).

Many times you will want to specify that only one `ResultSet` instance (which maps to an underlying cursor) can be open at a time for a particular statement. Whenever a new query is issued on a `Statement`, or a new `ResultSet` is obtained via the `getResultSet()` method on the `Statement` object, the existing `ResultSet` instance and associated cursor will then be closed. Of course, multiple statements may be created so that more than one cursor can be open at a time. However, different database configurations will limit the number of cursors that can be openly associated with a single connection. It should also be noted that different ResultSet driver implementations embody different design decisions for populating the ResultSet with data. Implementations may perhaps dynamically consult the database for data as the ResultSet is scrolled forward, may perhaps build up an entire set of data at once and contain this on the client-side ResultSet buffer, or may implement some hybrid of these two extremes.

After a handle to a ResultSet object is obtained, you will typically want to retrieve the column data from each row, scroll forward to the next row, retrieve its data, and then continue this sequence until there is no more data to retrieve from the ResultSet. The methods used to accomplish this task are the get*XXX*() series of methods and the next() method on the ResultSet object. When a ResultSet is returned, the cursor is initially positioned before the first row. When the next() method is called, a boolean value is returned indicating whether there is a next row and then positions itself on that row. Thus, if at least one row is returned in a ResultSet, the first call to next() will return true and be positioned on the first row. Calls to one of the get*XXX*() methods are then to be made to retrieve data from the current row. There are additional methods with JDBC 3.0 that allow for bidirectional and positional scrolling through result sets, but this topic is deferred until Chapter 6, "Advanced JDBC."

Two general forms of get*XXX*() exist. One form takes a column index int, and the other form takes a column name String as an input parameter. Each form of get*XXX*() returns a type corresponding to the actual *XXX* type asked for in the get*XXX*() call. The next section lists the various Java types that are mapped from SQL types via the get*XXX*() methods available to the API programmer. As an example, to obtain the FIRST_NAME in the second column from the CUSTOMER query SELECT * FROM CUSTOMER, you can use either call on a ResultSet object named resultSet:

```
String firstName = resultSet.getString(2);
        // or
String firstName = resultSet.getString("FIRST_NAME");
```

Obtaining Information About Result Sets

The java.sql.ResultSetMetaData interface provides information about the ResultSet such as the types and properties of the columns returned from the query. As shown in Figure 5.13, a ResultSetMetaData object is obtained from the ResultSet object via its getMetaData() method. The ResultSetMetaData object can then be used to provide dynamic information about the returned ResultSet object.

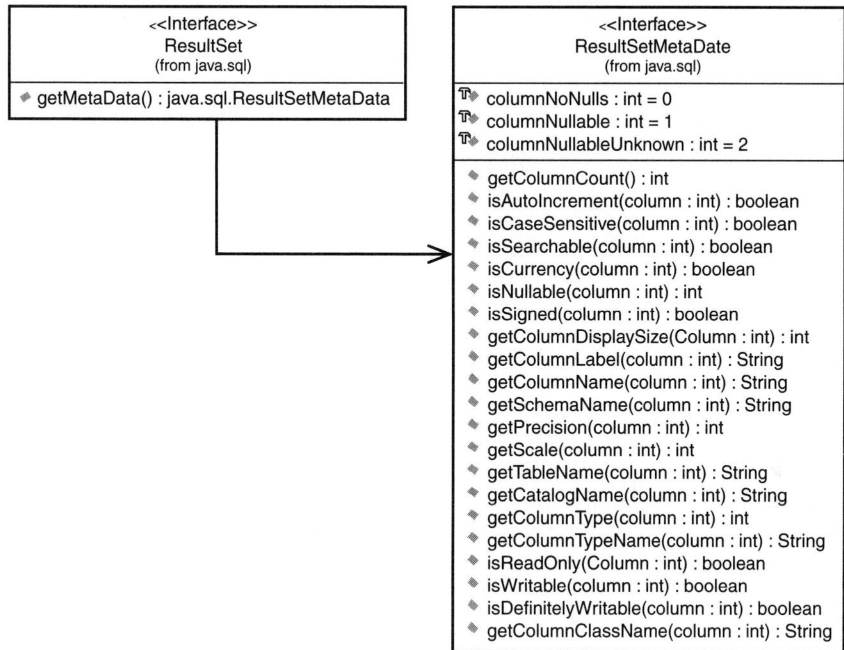

Figure 5.13 Result set meta-data.

With the `ResultSetMetaData` object, the following key types of calls can be made:

- `int getColumnCount()` returns the number of columns associated with this `ResultSet` object.
- `String getColumnName(int column)` returns the name of a column.
- `String getColumnClassName(int column)` returns the class name of a column.
- `String getColumnLabel(int column)` returns the column label recommended for display purposes.
- `int getColumnDisplaySize(int column)` returns the column's maximum character width.
- `int getColumnType(int column)` returns the `java.sql.Types` constant value of a particular column.
- `String getColumnTypeName(int column)` returns a column's type name specific to the database.
- `String getSchemaName(int column)` returns the table's schema name associated with a column.

- `String getCatalogName(int column)` returns a column's table catalog name given a column number.
- `String getTableName(int column)` returns the table name associated with a column.
- `int getPrecision(int column)` returns the column's number of decimal digits.
- `int getScale(int column)` returns the column's number of digits to the right of the decimal point.
- `boolean isCaseSensitive(int column)` indicates whether the column is case-sensitive.
- `boolean isReadOnly(int column)` indicates whether the column is read-only.
- `boolean isWritable(int column)` indicates whether it is possible for this column to be writable.
- `boolean isDefinitelyWritable(int column)` indicates whether a write will absolutely succeed on this column.
- `int isNullable(int column)` indicates whether the column is able to be null.
- `int isSigned(int column)` indicates whether the column represents a signed number.
- `int isCurrency(int column)` indicates whether the column represents a cash value.
- `boolean isSearchable(int column)` indicates whether the column can be used in a `where` clause.

Example: Manipulating Result Sets and Result Set Meta-Data

This next example demonstrates how to use `ResultSet` and `ResultSetMetaData` objects. The example code is contained in the `ejava.jdbc.core.ResultSetExample` class. This example actually builds off of the simple statement example with the `ResultSetExample` class extending the `SimpleStatementExample` class:

```
public class ResultSetExample extends SimpleStatementExample{...}
```

> **Note**
>
> As with earlier examples, this example code can be run using the `runresultset` script file, which can be found in the `examples\src\ejava\jdbc\core` directory after running the ANT target.

The `main()` method of `ResultSetExample` is invoked as

```
java ejava.jdbc.core.ResultSetExample
```

The `main()` method reads preferences and invokes `getConnection()` on the example object as it did in the `ConnectToDatabase` example to load the preferences and establish the database connection. A simple SQL query `String` is read from the loaded preferences and then used to execute a simple SQL statement on the `ResultSetExample` object's inherited `executeQuery()` method. The returned `ResultSet` is then used to analyze the meta-data of the `ResultSet` and then parse and display the entire `ResultSet` structure. The key elements of the `main()` function are shown here:

```
public static void main(String[] args)
{
  Preferences preferences =
  ➥ Preferences.userNodeForPackage(
  ➥ ejava.jdbc.core.ConnectToDatabase.class);
  ResultSetExample resultSetExample = new ResultSetExample();
  . . .
  Connection connection = resultSetExample.getConnection();
  // Get SQL from preferences, execute, get and view results...
  String sqlString = preferences.get("SQL_QUERY_STATEMENT",null);
  ResultSet resultSet = resultSetExample.executeQuery(sqlString);
  // wait for user input.
  ResultSetExample.analyzeMetaData(resultSet);
  System.out.println("Enter when Ready to see the ResultSet "+
  ➥ " Results and each field type for statement :"+sqlString);
  . . .
  ResultSetExample.parseResultData(resultSet);
  resultSetExample.closeStatement();

    . . .
}
```

The `ResultSetExample` class also has one additional member variable to store the `ResultSet` object in addition to the state its base class maintains:

```
private ResultSet resultSet; // ResultSet Object
```

The `analyzeMetaData()` call on `ResultSetExample` obtains a handle to the `ResultSet` object's `ResultSetMetaData` and displays some key information about the result set columns such as the column name, column label, and column type name. A special helper function called `getColumnClass()` is also provided here to demonstrate how you might deduce the column class with the column `java.sql.Types` information. The `analyzeMetaData()` and `getColumnClass()` methods are shown here:

```
public static void analyzeMetaData(ResultSet resultSet)
    throws SQLException
{
```

```
  ResultSetMetaData rMetaData = resultSet.getMetaData();

  for(int i = 1; i<= rMetaData.getColumnCount(); i++){
    System.out.println("Column Name : "+
      rMetaData.getColumnName(i));
    System.out.println("Column Label :  "+
       rMetaData.getColumnLabel(i));
    System.out.println("Column Display Size : "+
       rMetaData.getColumnDisplaySize(i));
    int type = rMetaData.getColumnType(i);
    System.out.println("Column Java Type :   " +
      getColumnClass(type));
    System.out.println("Column Type Name :   " +
      rMetaData.getColumnTypeName(i));
    System.out.println("Null Value Allowed :   " +
      rMetaData.isNullable(i));
    System.out.println("Is Read Only :   " +
      rMetaData.isReadOnly(i));
  }
}


public static Class getColumnClass(int type)
{
      switch(type) {
        case Types.CHAR:
        case Types.VARCHAR:
        case Types.LONGVARCHAR:
            return String.class;

        case Types.BIT:
            return Boolean.class;

        case Types.TINYINT:
        case Types.SMALLINT:
        case Types.INTEGER:
            return Integer.class;

        case Types.BIGINT:
            return Long.class;

        case Types.FLOAT:
        case Types.DOUBLE:
            return Double.class;
```

```
        case Types.DATE:
            return java.sql.Date.class;

        default:
            return Object.class;
      }
}
```

Finally, the rather long `parseResultData()` call on `ResultSetExample` demonstrates how to scroll through a `ResultSet` object and use the `getXXX()` methods to obtain the values from the column of interest. The `parseResultData()` method is generalized such that for each column index in the row, we obtain the `java.sql.Types` information about the column, output the mapping from `java.sql.Types` value to the Java type, and then print the column value. The `parseResultData()` method is shown here:

```
public static void parseResultData(ResultSet resultSet)
    throws SQLException
  {
    ResultSetMetaData rMetaData = resultSet.getMetaData();
    int nColumns = rMetaData.getColumnCount();

    while(resultSet.next()){
      for(int i = 1; i <= nColumns; i++ ){
         int type =  rMetaData.getColumnType(i);
         switch(type) {
            case Types.CHAR:
                 System.out.print("(CHAR->String "+
➥resultSet.getString(i) + "):");
                 break;
            case Types.VARCHAR:
                 System.out.print("(VARCHAR->String " +
➥resultSet.getString(i) + "):");
                 break;
            case Types.LONGVARCHAR:
                 System.out.print("(LONGVARCHAR->String " +
➥resultSet.getString(i) + "):");
                 break;
            case Types.BIT:
                  System.out.print("(BIT->byte " +
➥resultSet.getByte(i)+ "):");
                  break;
            case Types.TINYINT:
                  System.out.print("(TINYINT->int " +
➥resultSet.getInt(i)+ "):");
                  break;
            case Types.SMALLINT:
                  System.out.print("(SMALLINT->int " +
```

```
➥resultSet.getInt(i)+ "):");
                        break;
                case Types.INTEGER:
                        System.out.print("(INTEGER->int " +
➥resultSet.getInt(i)+ "):");
                        break;
                case Types.BIGINT:
                        System.out.print("(BIGINT->long " +
➥resultSet.getLong(i)+ "):");
                        break;
                case Types.FLOAT:
                        System.out.print("(FLOAT->float " +
➥resultSet.getFloat(i)+ "):");
                        break;
                case Types.DOUBLE:
                        System.out.print("(DOUBLE->double " +
➥resultSet.getDouble(i)+ "):");
                        break;
                case Types.DATE:
                        System.out.print("(DATE->Date " +
➥resultSet.getDate(i)+ "):");
                        break;
                case Types.TIME:
                        System.out.print("(TIME->Time " +
➥resultSet.getTime(i)+ "):");
                        break;
                case Types.TIMESTAMP:
                        System.out.print("(TIMESTAP->Timestamp " +
➥resultSet.getTimestamp(i)+ "):");
                        break;
                default:
                        System.out.print("(<other type>->Object " +
➥resultSet.getObject(i)+ "):");
                        break;
            }
        }
        System.out.println();
    }
  }
```

SQL and Java Mappings

We have seen some examples in this chapter demonstrating how to obtain column data from a `ResultSet` as Java types. Database vendors may at times instruct you to use their type names when coding your applications, but a much more portable means for manipulating data is possible when you stick with the JDBC standard SQL and Java mappings.

Table 5.2 shows the standard and most commonly used mappings for SQL types to Java types, and Table 5.3 shows the standard and most commonly used mappings for Java types to SQL types. The next chapter presents mappings for more advanced types.

Table 5.2 **SQL Type to Java Type Mapping**

From SQL Type	To Java Language Type
CHAR	java.lang.String
VARCHAR	java.lang.String
LONGVARCHAR	java.lang.String
BIT	boolean
BOOLEAN	boolean
BINARY	byte[ ]
VARBINARY	byte[ ]
LONGVARBINARY	byte[ ]
TINYINT	byte
SMALLINT	short
INTEGER	int
BIGINT	long
REAL	float
FLOAT	double
DOUBLE	double
NUMERIC	java.lang.math.BigDecimal
DECIMAL	java.lang.math.BigDecimal
DATE	java.sql.Date
TIME	java.sql.Time
TIMESTAMP	java.sql.Timestamp

Table 5.3 **Java Type to SQL Type Mapping**

From Java Language Type	To SQL Type
String	CHAR, VARCHAR, or LONGVARCHAR
boolean	BIT or BOOLEAN
byte [ ]	BINARY, VARBINARY or LONGVARBINARY
byte	TINYINT
short	SMALLINT
int	INTEGER
long	BIGINT
float	REAL
double	DOUBLE

Table 5.3 **Continued**

From Java Language Type	To SQL Type
java.math.BigDecimal	NUMERIC
java.sql.Date	DATE
java.sql.Time	TIME
java.sql.Timestamp	TIMESTAMP

When a `String` is mapped to a SQL type, it typically maps to a `VARCHAR`. However, a `String` can also map to a `CHAR` or to a `LONGVARCHAR` if the `String`'s size is below or exceeds some driver-specific length limit. Similarly, `byte` arrays map to a `BINARY`, a `VARBINARY`, or a `LONGVARBINARY`, depending on the driver's length limits. Fixed-length SQL strings read from the database are usually read in as a `String` of the same length but with some padded spaces at the end. `LONGVARCHAR`s that are excessively long may be retrieved from the database using an input stream `get`*`XXX`*`()` function such as `getAsciiStream()` on the `ResultSet` object. Similarly, the `LONGVARBINARY` value can also be retrieved as an input stream.

The `DECIMAL` and `NUMERIC` types are used when absolute precision is needed. Thus, database values for currency are typically returned as either `DECIMAL` or `NUMERIC` types. These types can also be retrieved as `String`s using `getString()` on the `ResultSet` object.

The `java.util.Date` class does not provide enough granularity for certain database timestamp values and also includes both date and time information that is not suitable for how the SQL types delineate date and time as separate entities. To this end, three classes that extend `java.util.Date` are employed as basic JDBC type helpers. These are the `java.sql.Date`, `java.sql.Time`, and `java.sql.Timestamp` types:

- `java.sql.Date` truncates any non–date-related time information by storing the hour, second, and millisecond fields of `java.util.Date` as zero.
- `java.sql.Time` truncates any date information by storing the year, month, and day of `java.util.Date` as the "zero date" of January 1, 1970.
- `java.sql.Timestamp` adds nanosecond precision to the time provided by `java.util.Date`.

Stored Procedures

Most databases provide a set of helper functions that database programmers can use to operate on data while it is in the database versus retrieving it, computing some result, and possibly updating the database with the new value. The main benefits of such database functions are the performance enhancements involved with avoiding data retrieval and storage. This is particularly apparent when many small functions need to be performed.

Most databases also allow for the definition of user-defined functions that can also be used to operate on data without a remote retrieval or storage call. Such user-defined database functions are called stored procedures because they are functions that are actually stored in the database. Although there may be performance enhancements associated with changing the state of data due to some function call directly within the database, there are many disadvantages as well. Maintainability and code portability are often the two key problem areas associated with using stored procedures. Stored procedures become a maintenance issue when it comes time to provide enhanced or altered functionality. Portability is an issue when you try to relocate stored procedures to another database. The trend in enterprise development has been to move as much of the business logic as possible out of a database and into the middle tier. Nevertheless, at times use of stored procedures is justified, and there will certainly be cases when enterprise systems developers must interface with legacy databases containing stored procedures. Because of these reasons, JDBC has provided support for interfacing with stored procedures since version 1.0 of the specification.

Predefined Database Functions

A few key types of function calls are identified by JDBC for potential (although not required) support by your JDBC driver. They are numeric functions, string manipulation functions, time and date functions, and a few system functions. It is the driver's responsibility to make sure that any supported functions can be mapped from the JDBC syntax for accessing such functions to the underlying database calls for executing the functions. The basic syntax for calling a function from within a JDBC `Statement` is of this general form:

```
"{ fn FCN_NAME( ARGS ) }"
```

For example:

```
ResultSet resultSet = statement.executeQuery("{fn RAND("+ num + ")}");
```

To determine which functions are supported by your database and driver, a series of calls can be made on the `java.sql.DatabaseMetaData` object (obtained by calling a `Connection` object's `getMetaData()` method):

- `String getNumericFunctions()` returns the list of names identifying supported mathematical functions separated by commas.
- `String getStringFunctions()` returns the list of names identifying supported string manipulation functions separated by commas.
- `String getSystemFunctions()` returns the list of names identifying supported system functions separated by commas.
- `String getTimeDateFunctions()` returns the list of names identifying supported time and date functions separated by commas.

Creating Stored Procedures

Manipulating database stored procedures is accomplished via the `java.sql.CallableStatement` interface. The `CallableStatement` interface and a few of its key call signatures are shown in Figure 5.14a and Figure 5.14b. The `CallableStatement` interface extends the `PreparedStatement` interface, which in turn extends the `Statement` interface. `CallableStatement` objects are created by calling `prepareCall()` on a `Connection` object. `Connection.prepareCall()` is invoked with a stored procedure call `String` of the following general form:

```
"{ call PROCEDURE_NAME (?,?,...,?) }"
```

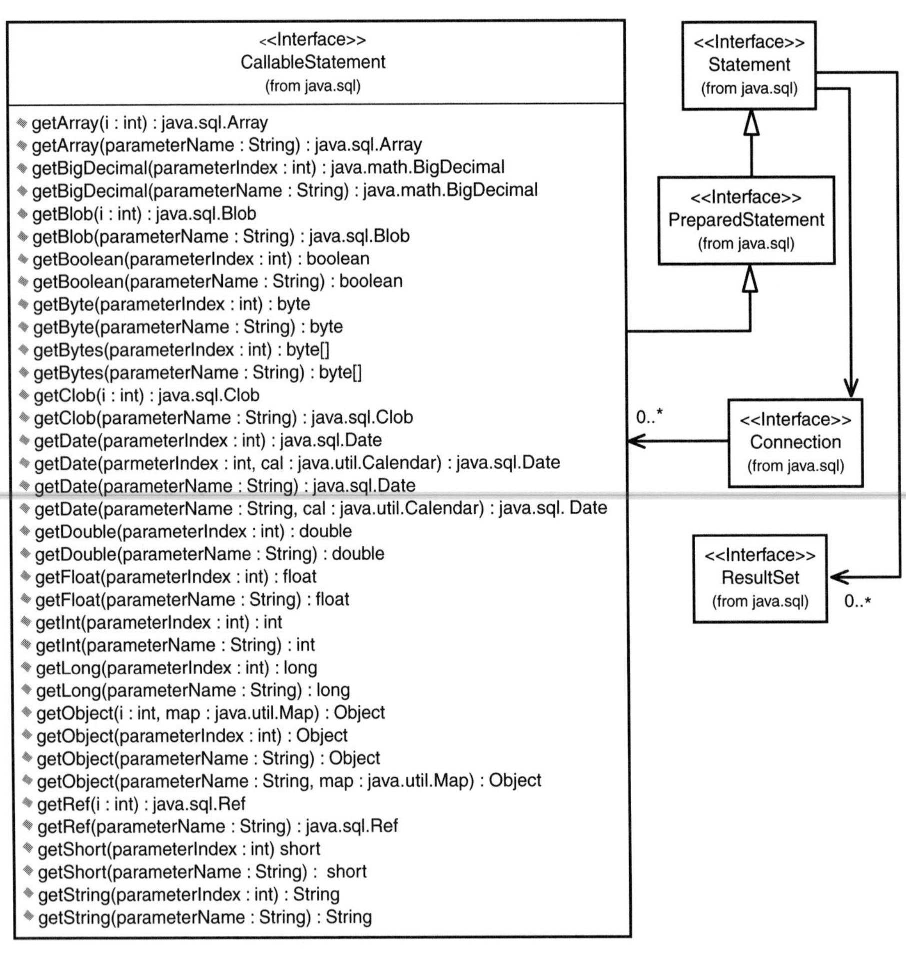

Figure 5.14a Callable statement interface.

```
◆ getTime(parameterIndex : int) : java.sql.Time
◆ getTime(parameterIndex : int, cal : java.util.Calendar) : java.sql.Time
◆ getTime(parameterName : String) : java.sql.Time
◆ getTime(parameterName : String, cal : java.util.Calendar) : java.sql.Time
◆ getTimestamp(parameterIndex : int) : java.sql.Timestamp
◆ getTimestamp(parameterIndex : int, cal : java.util.Calendar) : java.sql.Timestamp
◆ getTimestamp(parameterName: String) : java.sql.Timestamp
◆ getTimestamp(parameterName : String, cal : java.util.Calendar) : java.sql.Timestamp
◆ getURL(parameterIndex : int) : java.net.URL
◆ getURL(parameterName : String) : java.net.URL
◆ registerOutParameter(paramIndex : int, sqlType : int, TypeName : String) : void
◆ registerOutParameter(parameterIndex : int, sqlType : int) : void
◆ registerOutParameter(parameterIndex : int, sqlType : int, scale : int) : void
◆ registerOutParameter(parameterName : String, sqlType : int) : void
◆ registerOutParameter(parameterName : String, sqlType : int, scale : int) : void
◆ registerOutParameter(parameterName : String, sqlType : int, TypeName : String) : void
◆ setAsciiStream(parameterName : String, x : java.io.InputStream, length : int) : void
◆ setBigDecimal(parameterName : String, x : java.math.BigDecimal) : void
◆ setBinaryStream(parameterName : String, x : java.io.InputStream, length : int) : void
◆ setBoolean(parameterName : String, x : boolean) : void
◆ setByte(parameterName : String, x : byte) : void
◆ setBytes(parameterName : String, x [] : byte) : void
◆ setCharacterStream(parameterName : String, reader : java.io.Reader, length: int) : void
◆ setDate(parameterName : String, x : java.sql.Date ) : void
◆ setDate(parameterName : String, x : java.sql.Date, cal : java. util.Calendar) : void
◆ setDouble(parameterName : String, x : double) : void
◆ setFloat(parameterName : String, x : float) : void
◆ setInt(parameterName : String, x : int) : void
◆ setLong(parameterName : String, x : long) : void
◆ setNull(parameterName : String, sqlType : int) : void
◆ setNull(parameterName : String, sqlType : int, typeName : String) : void
◆ setObject(parameterName : String, x : Object) : void
◆ setObject(parameterName : String, x : Object, targetSqlType : int) : void
◆ setObject(parameterName : String, x : Object, targetSqlType : int, scale : int) : void
◆ setShort(parameterName : String, x : short) : void
◆ setString(parameterName : String, x : String) : void
◆ setTime(parameterName : String, x : java.sql.Time) : void
◆ setTime(parameterName : String, x : java.sql.Time, cal : java.util.Calendar) : void
◆ setTimestamp(parameterName : String, x : java.sql.Timestamp) : void
◆ setTimestamp(parameterName : String, x : java.sql.Timestamp, cal : java.util.Calendar) : void
◆ setURL(parameterName : String, val : java.net.URL) : void
◆ wasNull() : boolean
```

Figure 5.14b Callable statement interface (continued).

Given a stored procedure name, you can create a stored procedure `String` with a set of input parameters (`IN`), output parameters (`OUT`), or input/output parameters (`INOUT`) by using the question mark (`?`) for each parameter in the `String`. Stored procedures that return values may also potentially be called with the following syntax:

```
"{ ? = call PROCEDURE_NAME (?,?,...,?) }"
```

Stored procedure syntax is by no means always standard across JDBC driver and database vendors. For example, a stored procedure in Oracle may be created as in this example:

```
String sqlStatement = "begin ? := getTotalPriceForOrder(1001);end;";
CallableStatement callableStatement
      = getCallableStatement(sqlStatement);
callableStatement.registerOutParameter(1, Types.INTEGER);
```

The `IN` and `INOUT` parameters used in a `CallableStatement` can be set in the same fashion as input parameters are set on the extended `PreparedStatement` interface. Thus, a call to some `setXXX(int)` (inherited from the `PreparedStatement` interface) given the parameter index and the actual value of some *XXX* type must be called for each `IN` and `INOUT` parameter. Aside from use of parameter indices, JDBC 3.0 has introduced a new convention for setting parameters in `CallableStatement` objects. The `setXXX(String)` style of calls can be invoked to set parameters of some *XXX* type using its name in `String` form.

Return parameters, `OUT`, and `INOUT` parameters must have their SQL type defined by calling one of the following three methods on the `CallableStatement` object:

- `void registerOutParameter(int index, int type)` registers the parameter in the index position to be of the `java.sql.Types` type specified. The `java.sql.Types.OTHER` type should be used if this type is specific to the database.
- `void registerOutParameter(int index, int type, int scale)` registers the parameter in the index position to be of the `java.sql.Types` type specified. This method form should be used if the type is a `Numeric` or `Decimal` type. The scale value defines the number of digits on the right side of the decimal point.
- `void registerOutParameter(int index, int type, String typeName)` registers the parameter in the index position to be of the `java.sql.Types` type specified. This JDBC 2.0 method form is used for `REF` types or user-defined types such as named arrays, `JAVA_OBJECT`s, `STRUCT`s, and `DISTINCT`s. The `typeName` is the complete SQL type name being registered.

If a return value is generated from a stored procedure of the form `{ ? = call` *`PROCEDURE_NAME`* `(?,?,...,?) }`, the parameter index for this value should be registered as position number 1. Furthermore, JDBC 3.0 also provides three versions of the preceding `registerOutParameter()` methods whereby you can use the `String` name of the parameter instead of its index number.

Executing Stored Procedures

Executing a stored procedure is accomplished by calling one of the execute methods on the `CallableStatement` object. Because a stored procedure may return more than one `ResultSet`, you'll have to scroll through the entire result set before you can obtain any values returned to the statement's `OUT` and `INOUT` parameters. On scrolling through the entire result set, a series of `getXXX(int)` calls on the `CallableStatement` must be made to obtain the OUT and INOUT values returned from the stored procedure given the parameter's index number. Aside from use of parameter indices, JDBC 3.0 has introduced a new convention for getting parameters in CallableStatement objects using a String name via the get*XXX*(String) style of calls. Calls for get*XXX*() exist for various *XXX* types as shown in Figure 5.14a and Figure 5.14b, shown previously.

Creating a Few BeeShirts.com Stored Procedures

The BeeShirts.com database has a few stored procedures in it to compute the total price for a particular order, retrieve a customer's phone number, and obtain the total sum for a set of orders. The SQL statements used to create these functions in the database are as shown here:

```
-- Create procedure for getting total price for the order

CREATE OR REPLACE
FUNCTION getTotalPriceForOrder (vorder_id IN NUMBER )
RETURN NUMBER
IS
    vtotal_value NUMBER;
BEGIN
    SELECT I.total_price INTO vtotal_value
    FROM orders O,item I
    WHERE O.order_id =vorder_id AND O.order_id = I.order_id_fk;
  RETURN vtotal_value;
END;

/

-- Create getCustomerPhoneNumber function

 CREATE OR REPLACE FUNCTION getCustomerPhoneNumber(
    vcustomer_id IN NUMBER)
   RETURN VARCHAR
 IS
   vphone VARCHAR(12);
 BEGIN
    SELECT phone
     INTO  vphone
    FROM customer
    WHERE customer_id = vcustomer_id;
    return vphone;
 END getCustomerPhoneNumber;
/

--  Create procedure for getTotalOrders
```

```
CREATE OR REPLACE PROCEDURE getTotalOrders(
    vcustomer_id_fk IN ORDERS.CUSTOMER_ID_FK%TYPE,
    vtotal_items OUT NUMBER)
  IS
  BEGIN
    SELECT sum(I.quantity) INTO vtotal_items
    FROM item I, orders O
    WHERE O.order_id = I.order_id_fk AND
          O.customer_id_fk = vcustomer_id_fk;
  END getTotalOrders;
/
```

Example: Calling Stored Procedures

This next example demonstrates how to call stored procedures in the database. The example code is contained in the `ejava.jdbc.core.CallableStatementExample` class, which extends the `ejava.jdbc.core.ConnectToDatabase` class:

```
public class CallableStatementExample extends ConnectToDatabase { ... }
```

> **Note**
>
> The following example can be run by executing the `runcallablestatement` script, in the `examples\src\ejava\jdbc\core` directory. This script file is generated in the same manner as in the previous examples. It should also be noted that not all databases support stored procedures. The examples presented in this section are known to work with an Oracle database.

The `main()` method of `CallableStatementExample` is invoked as

```
java ejava.jdbc.core.CallableStatementExample
```

The `main()` method reads in system preferences and instantiates a new `CallableStatementExample` object. Subsequently, the `main()` method calls all three stored procedures in the BeeShirts.com database:

```
  public static void main(String[] args)
{
  Preferences preferences =
  ➥ Preferences.userNodeForPackage(ConnectToDatabase.class);

  CallableStatementExample callStExample =
  ➥  new CallableStatementExample();
  ...
    callStExample.executeGetCustomerPhoneNumberFunction();
    callStExample.executeGetTotalPriceFunction();
    callStExample.executeTotalOrdersFortheCustomer();
```

```
...
      callStExample.setProperties(fileName);
      callStExample.executeGetCustomerPhoneNumberFunction();
      callStExample.executeGetTotalPriceFunction();
      callStExample.executeTotalOrdersFortheCustomer();
}
```

A new `getCallableStatement()` method is defined here for the various `executeXXX()` methods for creating a `CallableStatement` given a SQL `String`:

```
protected CallableStatement getCallableStatement(String sqlStatement)
  throws SQLException, Exception
{
  Connection connection = super.getConnection();
  CallableStatement statement =
    connection.prepareCall(sqlStatement);
  return statement;
}
```

These are the three `executeXXX()` methods used for executing queries against the stored procedures from BeeShirts.com using an Oracle stored procedure call syntax:

```
public void executeGetTotalPriceFunction()
  throws SQLException, Exception
{
  String sqlStatement
    = "begin ? := getTotalPriceForOrder( 1001);end;";

  CallableStatement callableStatement =
    getCallableStatement(sqlStatement);
    callableStatement.registerOutParameter(1, Types.FLOAT);
  callableStatement.execute();
  System.out.println("Total price :" + callableStatement.getFloat(1));
}

public void executeGetCustomerPhoneNumberFunction()
  throws SQLException,Exception
{
  String sqlStatement ="begin ? := getCustomerPhoneNumber(101); end;";
  CallableStatement callableStatement =
    getCallableStatement(sqlStatement);
  callableStatement.registerOutParameter(1, Types.VARCHAR);
  callableStatement.execute();

  System.out.println("Phone #  :" + callableStatement.getString(1) +
      " for Customer_id 101");
}
```

```
public void executeTotalOrdersFortheCustomer()
  throws SQLException,Exception
{
  String sqlStatement = "begin  getTotalOrders(104, ?); end;";
  CallableStatement callableStatement =
    getCallableStatement(sqlStatement);
  callableStatement.registerOutParameter(1, Types.INTEGER);
  callableStatement.execute();

  System.out.println("Total Orders #  :" +
    callableStatement.getInt(1) + " for Customer_id 104");
}
```

JDBC Meta-Data

It is sometimes necessary to obtain information about the database to which you are connected. Information such as the table descriptions, level of SQL support, and stored procedure listings is sometimes useful in creating your Java applications. Sometimes certain databases and database drivers are able to support certain JDBC calls but others are not. This becomes problematic when attempting to offer seamless portability across databases and database drivers. Although you can log exceptions thrown when such support is not offered, it may make more sense to determine a priori what support is provided before a call is even made. The `java.sql.DatabaseMetaData` class shown in Figures 5.15a through 5.15c can provide such database, table schema, and driver support information. However, some drivers will not even support certain `DatabaseMetaData` calls. Such calls typically result in a `SQLException` being thrown.

Obtaining Information About Databases and Drivers

A `DatabaseMetaData` object handle is obtained by calling a `Connection` object's `getMetaData()` method. Some `DatabaseMetaData` calls return information in the form of `ResultSet` objects. Thus, the `ResultSet.getXXX()` methods can be used to obtain information from the `ResultSet` as you would with a regular SQL query. We do not intend to cover the complete set of `DatabaseMetaData` calls here because it too has an enormous number of methods and many of them are very specialized. However, the most key types of methods to examine are listed here:

- `ResultSet getSchemas()` returns a set of schema names available in the database.
- `ResultSet getCatalogs()` returns the catalog names used in the database.
- `ResultSet getTables(String catalog, String schemaPattern, String tableNamePattern, String[] types)` returns a set of tables available in a particular catalog.

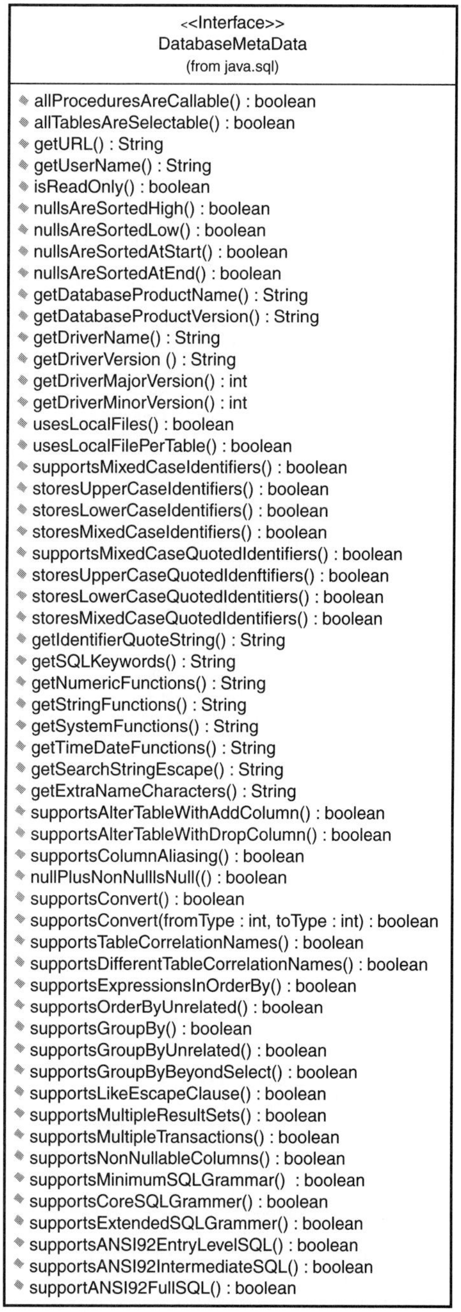

```
<<Interface>>
DatabaseMetaData
(from java.sql)

allProceduresAreCallable() : boolean
allTablesAreSelectable() : boolean
getURL() : String
getUserName() : String
isReadOnly() : boolean
nullsAreSortedHigh() : boolean
nullsAreSortedLow() : boolean
nullsAreSortedAtStart() : boolean
nullsAreSortedAtEnd() : boolean
getDatabaseProductName() : String
getDatabaseProductVersion() : String
getDriverName() : String
getDriverVersion () : String
getDriverMajorVersion() : int
getDriverMinorVersion() : int
usesLocalFiles() : boolean
usesLocalFilePerTable() : boolean
supportsMixedCaseIdentifiers() : boolean
storesUpperCaseIdentifiers() : boolean
storesLowerCaseIdentifiers() : boolean
storesMixedCaseIdentifiers() : boolean
supportsMixedCaseQuotedIdentifiers() : boolean
storesUpperCaseQuotedIdenftifiers() : boolean
storesLowerCaseQuotedIdentitiers() : boolean
storesMixedCaseQuotedIdentifiers() : boolean
getIdentifierQuoteString() : String
getSQLKeywords() : String
getNumericFunctions() : String
getStringFunctions() : String
getSystemFunctions() : String
getTimeDateFunctions() : String
getSearchStringEscape() : String
getExtraNameCharacters() : String
supportsAlterTableWithAddColumn() : boolean
supportsAlterTableWithDropColumn() : boolean
supportsColumnAliasing() : boolean
nullPlusNonNullIsNull(() : boolean
supportsConvert() : boolean
supportsConvert(fromType : int, toType : int) : boolean
supportsTableCorrelationNames() : boolean
supportsDifferentTableCorrelationNames() : boolean
supportsExpressionsInOrderBy() : boolean
supportsOrderByUnrelated() : boolean
supportsGroupBy() : boolean
supportsGroupByUnrelated() : boolean
supportsGroupByBeyondSelect() : boolean
supportsLikeEscapeClause() : boolean
supportsMultipleResultSets() : boolean
supportsMultipleTransactions() : boolean
supportsNonNullableColumns() : boolean
supportsMinimumSQLGrammar()  : boolean
supportsCoreSQLGrammer() : boolean
supportsExtendedSQLGrammer() : boolean
supportsANSI92EntryLevelSQL() : boolean
supportsANSI92IntermediateSQL() : boolean
supportANSI92FullSQL() : boolean
```

Figure 5.15a The `java.sql.DatabaseMetaData` class.

- supportsIntegrityEnhancementFacility() : boolean
- supportsOuterJoins() : boolean
- supportsFullOuterJoins() : boolean
- supportsLimitedOuterJoins() : boolean
- getSchemaTerm() : String
- getProcedureTerm(() : String
- getCatalogTerm() : String
- isCatalogAtStart() : boolean
- getCatalogSeparator() : String
- supportsSchemasInDataManipulation() : boolean
- supportsSchemasInProcedureCalls() : boolean
- supportsSchemasInTableDefinitions() : boolean
- supportsSchemasInIndexDefinitions() : boolean
- supportsSchemasInPrivilegeDefinitions() : boolean
- supportsCatalogsInDataManipulation() : boolean
- supportsCatalogsInProcedureCalls() : boolean
- supportsCatalogsInTableDefinitions() : boolean
- supportsCatalogsInIndexDefinitions() : boolean
- supportsCatalogsInPrivilegeDefinitions() : boolean
- supportsPositionedDelete() : boolean
- supportsPositionedUpdate() : boolean
- supportsSelectForUpdate() : boolean
- supportsStoredProcedures(): boolean
- supportsSubqueriesInComparisons() : boolean
- supportsSubqueriesInExists() : boolean
- supportsSubqueriesInIns() : boolean
- supportsSubqueriesInQuantifieds() : boolean
- supportsCorrelatedSubqueries() : boolean
- supportsUnion() : boolean
- supportsUnionAll() : boolean
- supportsOpenCursorsAcrossCommit() : boolean
- supportsOpenCursorsAcrossRollback() : boolean
- supportsOpenStatementsAcrossCommit() : boolean
- supportsOpenStatementsAcrossRollback() : boolean
- getMaxBinaryLiteralLength() : int
- getMaxCharLiteralLength() : int
- getMaxColumnNameLength() : int
- getMaxColumnsInGroupBy() : int
- getMaxColumnsInIndex() : int
- getMaxColumnsInOrderBy() : int
- getMaxColumnsInSelect() : int
- getMaxColumnsInTable() : int
- getMaxConnections() : int
- getMaxCursorNameLength() : int
- getMaxIndexLength() : int
- getMaxSchemaNameLength() : int
- getMaxProcedureNameLength() : int
- getMaxCatalogNameLength() : int
- getMaxRowSize() : int
- doesMaxRowSizeIncludeBlobs() : boolean
- getMaxStatementLength() : int
- getMaxStatements() : int
- getMaxTableNameLength() : int
- getMaxTablesInSelect() : int
- getMaxUserNameLength() : int
- getDefaultTransactionIsolation() : int
- supportsTransactions() : boolean
- supportsTransactionIsolationLevel(level : int) : boolean
- supportsDataDefinitionAndDataManipulationTransactions() : boolean
- supportsDataManipulationTransactionsOnly() : boolean

Figure 5.15b The `java.sql.DatabaseMetaData` class (continued).

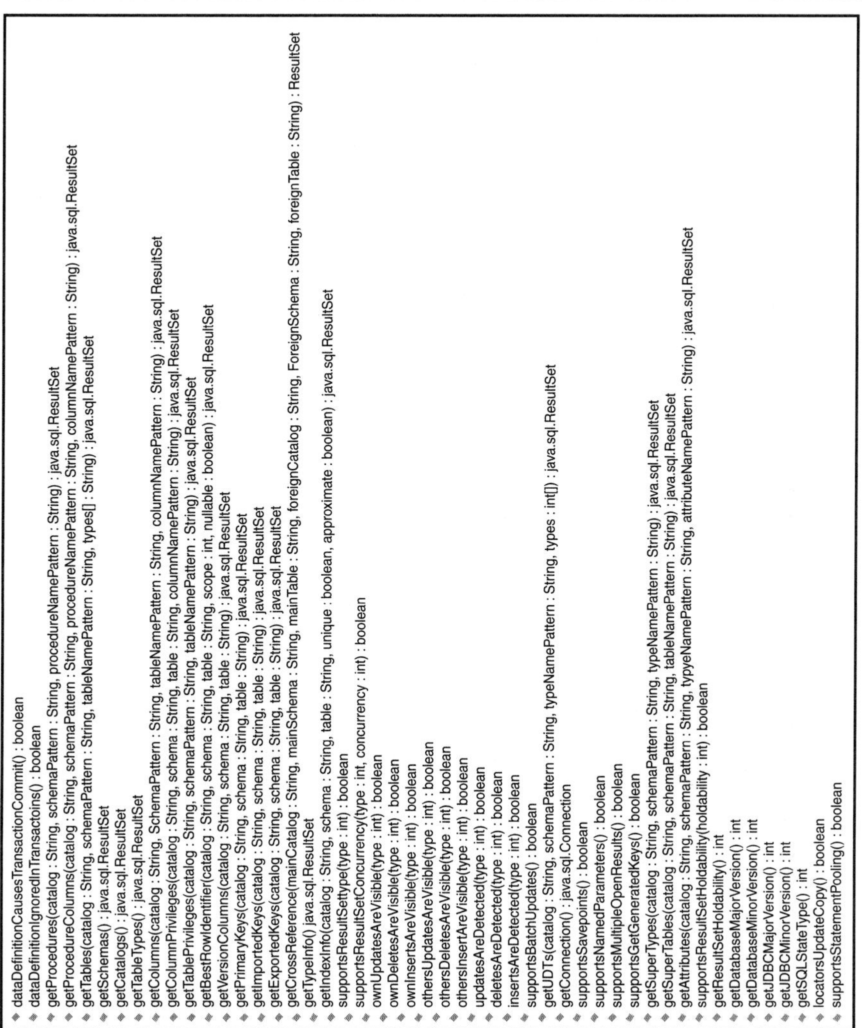

Figure 5.15c The `java.sql.DatabaseMetaData` class (continued).

- `ResultSet getTableTypes()` returns the set of table types available in the database.
- `String getCatalogSeparator()` returns the separator value between catalog and table names.
- `ResultSet getTablePrivileges(String catalog, String schemaPattern, String tableNamePattern)` returns a set of access permissions for each table in this database.

- `ResultSet getColumnPrivileges(String catalog, String schema, String table, String columnNamePattern)` returns the access permissions for a table's columns.
- `ResultSet getColumns(String catalog, String schemaPattern, String tableNamePattern, String columnNamePattern)` returns a description of the table's columns.
- `ResultSet getPrimaryKeys(String catalog, String schema, String table)` retrieves information describing this table's primary keys.
- `ResultSet getExportedKeys(String catalog, String schema, String table)` retrieves information describing which foreign keys reference this table's primary keys.
- `ResultSet getImportedKeys(String catalog, String schema, String table)` retrieves information describing which primary keys are referenced by this table's foreign keys.
- `String getDatabaseProductName()` returns the database product name.
- `String getDatabaseProductVersion()` returns the database product version.
- `String getDriverName()` returns the JDBC driver's name.
- `String getDriverVersion()` returns the JDBC driver's version.
- `String getURL()` returns the database URL.
- `String getUserName()` returns the username associated with this connection.
- `Connection getConnection()` returns the connection object associated with this meta-data (JDBC 2.0).
- `int getMaxConnections()` returns the maximum number of connections allowed.
- `int getMaxStatements()` returns the maximum number of statements allowed to be open at one time.
- `ResultSet getTypeInfo()` returns a list of standard SQL types supported by the database.
- `boolean supportsANSI92EntryLevelSQL()` indicates whether it is ANSI92 entry-level SQL compliant.
- `boolean supportsANSI92IntermediateSQL()` indicates whether it is ANSI92 intermediate-level SQL compliant.
- `boolean supportsANSI92FullSQL()` indicates whether it is fully ANSI92 SQL compliant.
- `boolean supportsMinimumSQLGrammar()` indicates whether it is ODBC minimum SQL compliant.

- boolean supportsCoreSQLGrammar() indicates whether it is ODBC core SQL compliant.
- boolean supportsExtendedSQLGrammar() indicates whether it is ODBC extended SQL compliant.
- boolean supportsOuterJoins() indicates whether it has some outer join support.
- boolean supportsLimitedOuterJoins() indicates whether it has limited outer join support.
- boolean supportsFullOuterJoins() indicates whether full nested outer joins are supported.
- boolean supportsLikeEscapeClause() indicates whether it supports LIKE clauses.

Example: Simple Database Meta-Data Usage

This next example demonstrates a few uses of the DatabaseMetaData object. The example code is contained in the ejava.jdbc.core.DatabaseMetaDataExample class. This DatabaseMetaDataExample class extends the ConnectToDatabase example class:

```
public class DatabaseMetaDataExample extends ConnectToDatabase{...}
```

> **Note**
>
> The following example can be run by executing the runmetadata script, in the examples\src\ejava\jdbc\core directory. This script file is generated in the same manner as in the previous examples.

The main() method of DatabaseMetaDataExample is invoked as

```
java ejava.jdbc.core.DatabaseMetaDataExample
```

The main() method reads preferences and invokes getConnection() on the example class to load the preference information and establish the database connection. The schemas, tables, columns, and keys in the database are then retrieved and listed. The key elements of the main() method are defined here:

```
public static void main(String[] args)
{

  Preferences preferences =
    Preferences.userNodeForPackage(ConnectToDatabase.class);

    DatabaseMetaDataExample databaseMetaDataExample =
         new DatabaseMetaDataExample();
```

```
. . .
    Connection connection = databaseMetaDataExample.getConnection();
    // Induce analysis of meta-data in various ways...
    databaseMetaDataExample.printAvailableSchemas();
    databaseMetaDataExample.printTablesInAllSchemas();
    String schemaName = preferences.get("SCHEMA_NAME",null);

    databaseMetaDataExample.printTablesInASchema(schemaName);
    databaseMetaDataExample.printColumnsInATable(schemaName,
➥"CUSTOMER");
    databaseMetaDataExample.printPrimaryKeysInATable(schemaName,
➥"CUSTOMER");
    . . .
}
```

The `DatabaseMetaDataExample` also maintains one `DatabaseMetaData` object:

```
private DatabaseMetaData dbMetaData; // Database MetaData Object
```

This example also makes use of one additional preference that is set in the `build.properties` file:

```
# Database schema name
schema.name =TSHIRTS
```

All the example methods called from `main()` need first to create the `DatabaseMetaData` handle from `getDatabaseMetaData()`:

```
public void getDatabaseMetaData()
  throws SQLException, Exception
{
   if(dbMetaData == null){
    Connection connection = super.getConnection();
    dbMetaData = connection.getMetaData();
   }

}
```

The `printAvailableSchemas()` method on the `DatabaseMetaDataExample` illustrates obtaining and displaying the database schema information. This example uses `ResultSetExample` to parse and display the returned `ResultSet`. The `printAvailableSchemas()` method is defined as shown here:

```
public void printAvailableSchemas()
  throws SQLException, Exception
{
  if(dbMetaData == null){
    getDatabaseMetaData();
  }

  ResultSet resultSet = dbMetaData.getSchemas();
```

```
  ResultSetExample.parseResultData(resultSet);
  resultSet.close();
}
```

The `printTablesInAllSchemas()` method on the `DatabaseMetaDataExample` retrieves and displays all the tables and views available in the database. After obtaining the schemas available as a `ResultSet` object using the `DatabaseMetaData.getSchemas()` call, we retrieve the schema name from each `ResultSet` element. The schema name in addition to a catalog, table name pattern, schema pattern, and table type specification are used to retrieve a list of all the tables and views in the database using `DatabaseMetaData.getTables()`. A `null` is used to indicate no catalog preference, and a null is also used for the table name pattern to indicate that all tables in the current schema should be retrieved. Finally, we use the `TABLE` and `VIEW` types to indicate that database table and database view descriptions should be retrieved. The `printTablesInAllSchemas()` method is defined here:

```
public  void printTablesInAllSchemas()
  throws SQLException, Exception
{
  if(dbMetaData == null){
    getDatabaseMetaData();
  }

  ResultSet resultSet = dbMetaData.getSchemas();

  while(resultSet.next()){
    String schemaName = resultSet.getString(1);
    String catalog = null;
    String schemaPattern = schemaName;
    String tableNamePattern = null;
    String types[]  = {"TABLE", "VIEW"};

    ResultSet tableInformation = dbMetaData.getTables(catalog,
➥schemaPattern,tableNamePattern, types);
    ResultSetExample.parseResultData(tableInformation);
  }
}
```

The `printTablesInASchema()` method on the `DatabaseMetaDataExample` illustrates how to obtain information about a particular schema in the database. The schema name is passed in from a value read from the property file. The `printTablesInASchema()` method is shown here:

```
public  void printTablesInASchema(String schemaName)
  throws SQLException, Exception
{
  if(dbMetaData == null){
```

```
    getDatabaseMetaData();
  }

  String catalog = null;
  String schemaPattern = schemaName;
      String tableNamePattern = null;
  String types[]  = {"TABLE", "VIEW"};

  ResultSet tableInformation = dbMetaData.getTables(catalog,
➥schemaPattern,tableNamePattern, types);
  ResultSetExample.parseResultData(tableInformation);
}
```

The `printColumnsInATable()` method on `DatabaseMetaDataExample` illustrates how to obtain a description of the columns in a database for a particular table. The `printColumnsInATable()` method is defined here:

```
public void printColumnsInATable(String schemaName, String tableName)
  throws SQLException , Exception
{

  if(dbMetaData == null){
    getDatabaseMetaData();
  }

  String catalogName = null;
  String columnPattern = null;

  ResultSet resultSet = dbMetaData.getColumns(catalogName,
➥schemaName,tableName, columnPattern);
  ResultSetExample.parseResultData(resultSet);
}
```

Finally, the `printPrimaryKeysInATable()` method demonstrates how to obtain information regarding the primary keys associated with a particular schema name and table name. Here, we read the schema name from a file and pass in the value `CUSTOMER` for the table name. The `printPrimaryKeysInATable()` method is defined as shown here:

```
public  void printPrimaryKeysInATable(String schemaName, String tableName)
  throws SQLException, Exception
{
  if(dbMetaData == null){
    getDatabaseMetaData();
  }

  String catalog = null;
```

```
  String schemaPattern = schemaName;

  ResultSet tableInformation = dbMetaData.getPrimaryKeys(catalog,
➥schemaPattern,tableName);
  ResultSetExample.parseResultData(tableInformation);
}
```

Conclusions

JDBC offers a database-independent means for performing some of the most important types of operations needed in enterprise systems to enable enterprise data for use in Java applications. The JDBC architecture provides simplicity and flexibility for creating database connections and using different types of drivers. JDBC also provides a set of core interfaces for working with a database to retrieve, insert, delete, and update data. JDBC offers such services via simple interfaces for configuring different types of drivers, establishing database connections, executing SQL statements, executing prepared statements, executing stored procedures, manipulating query results, and obtaining meta-data about the database itself. In the next chapter, we will examine more advanced features of JDBC that can be used in building your enterprise applications.

6

Advanced JDBC

IN THE PRECEDING CHAPTER, YOU LEARNED the basic steps for configuring and using JDBC to enable your enterprise data for use within enterprise applications. This chapter builds upon the preceding one with advanced material describing some of the more sophisticated and finer-grained features of JDBC. These JDBC features are covered from the perspective of how you, the enterprise developer, will be able to utilize the features in your enterprise applications. In this chapter, you will learn:

- The definition and use of scrollable result sets with JDBC.
- The basic interfaces offered to the JDBC developer for working with database transactions.
- The definition and use of updateable result sets with JDBC.
- The submission of a batch of SQL update statements with JDBC.
- The use of custom and more advanced SQL types with JDBC.
- The concepts behind JDBC row sets and how they can be used in enterprise applications.
- An overview of what it means to access a database through a middle-tier container via JDBC.
- The connection of JDBC clients to a database through a middle tier via JDBC data sources and JNDI.
- The concepts and architecture behind middle-tier JDBC connection pooling.
- The concepts and architecture behind distributed transaction handling in the middle tier with JDBC.

Scrollable Result Sets

The preceding chapter demonstrated how to view the data returned from a query result via use of a `java.sql.ResultSet` object instance. After reading a row from the

ResultSet object, you were shown how to make a call to ResultSet.next() to advance to the next row and retrieve any of that row's data. This model of scrolling forward in a ResultSet to retrieve its data via calls to next() was the only scroll model possible in JDBC 1.0. The JDBC 2.0 API extended the scrolling model for ResultSet objects by adding the capability to scroll backward as well as forward in a ResultSet. Furthermore, the capability to indicate which row you want to point to in the ResultSet can also be indicated in terms of an absolute position as well as a position relative to the current row to which you are pointing.

In light of this expanded model for result set scrollability, the JDBC API specification distinguishes result sets according to types:

- Forward-only
- Scroll-insensitive
- Scroll-sensitive

Forward-only result sets allow one to advance forward only using ResultSet.next(). This was the only scroll model allowed in JDBC 1.0. A static public final int identifier is defined in the ResultSet class to identify forward-only result set types:

```
ResultSet.TYPE_FORWARD_ONLY
```

Scroll-insensitive result sets allow one to scroll forward and backward and also allow for absolute and relative positioning. However, the state of the query result values returned from a query remains the same throughout the lifetime of the returned ResultSet object instance. Thus it can be said that this ResultSet type is insensitive to any database update operations performed because the result set no longer interacts with the database after it is created. This is the ResultSet static public final int field to identify scroll-insensitive result set types:

```
ResultSet.TYPE_SCROLL_INSENSITIVE
```

Scroll-sensitive result sets also allow one to scroll forward and backward and allow for absolute and relative positioning. However, these result set types permit one to dynamically view changes that are made to the underlying data. Thus it can be said that this ResultSet type is sensitive to any database operations performed because the result set interacts with the database even after it is created. This is the static public final int in ResultSet for identifying scroll-sensitive result set types:

```
ResultSet.TYPE_SCROLL_SENSITIVE
```

Creating Scrollable Result Sets

When calling createStatement() or prepareStatement() on a Connection object, the default scroll model assumed for the ResultSet that is returned by such a Statement or PreparedStatement is forward-only. JDBC allows for a Statement and PreparedStatement to be created specifying a preferred ResultSet type identifier as a parameter to the `createStatement()` and `prepareStatement()` methods. These methods also take a parameter for specifying concurrency type used when working with updateable result sets. Updateable result sets will be covered in the next section, but for now we will always assume a non-updateable result set type with a `ResultSet.CONCUR_READ_ONLY` parameter value. After creating a statement with a specified result set type, the `executeQuery()` and `execute()` methods may be called as usual to generate `ResultSet` objects. The significance of using the `ResultSet.CONCUR_READ_ONLY` type for the examples in this section simply indicates that the result set objects returned from executed statements are read-only and cannot be used to update the database, as will be demonstrated in the next section describing updateable result sets. However, the returned `ResultSet` is now specialized according to whether it is a forward-only, scroll-insensitive, or scroll-sensitive result set type.

The signatures for creating `Statement` objects and `PreparedStatement` objects from a `Connection` object with a preferred result set type are defined here:

```
public Statement createStatement(int resultSetType,
➥int resultSetConcurrency) throws SQLException;
public PreparedStatement prepareStatement(String sql,
➥int resultSetType, int resultSetConcurrency) throws SQLException;
```

The following code snippets illustrate a few options now available to the JDBC API programmer for creating statements that can return different result set types:

```
Connection connection = ...// Get a connection as usual.
String sql = "SELECT * FROM CUSTOMER";

// Return forward-only result sets
Statement s1 = connection.createStatement();
ResultSet r1= s1.executeQuery(sql);

// Also returns forward-only result sets
Statement s2 =
    connection.createStatement(ResultSet.TYPE_FORWARD_ONLY,
                               ResultSet.CONCUR_READ_ONLY);
ResultSet r2= s2.executeQuery(sql);

// Return scroll insensitive result sets
Statement s3 =
    connection.createStatement(ResultSet.TYPE_SCROLL_INSENSITIVE,
                                 ResultSet.CONCUR_READ_ONLY);
ResultSet r3= s3.executeQuery(sql);

// Returns scroll sensitive result sets
PreparedStatement ps1 =
       connection.prepareStatement(sql, ResultSet.TYPE_SCROLL_SENSITIVE,
                                   ResultSet.CONCUR_READ_ONLY);
ResultSet r4 = ps1.executeQuery();
```

Scrolling Around Result Sets

After creating a `Statement` or `PreparedStatement` object sensitized to returning a scrollable result set (that is, either scroll-insensitive or scroll-sensitive), you will have to call `executeQuery()` or `execute()` with a SQL query command on the `Statement` or `PreparedStatement` object so that you can obtain a handle to a `ResultSet`. After you have this `ResultSet` object, you can use the JDBC API calls for scrolling through the result set. The API calls for supporting scrollable result sets are indicated in the following list. Note that, though not shown here, each call can throw a `SQLException`. For all calls, except for `next()`, that attempt to move the cursor, a `SQLException` may be thrown if the `ResultSet` is a forward-only type. These are the key method calls on the `ResultSet` class that can be used for scrolling around result sets:

- `boolean next()` moves the cursor to the next row from the current position.
- `boolean previous()` moves the cursor to the previous row from the current position.
- `boolean first()` positions the cursor on the first row.
- `boolean isFirst()` returns `true` if the cursor is positioned on the first row.
- `void beforeFirst()` positions the cursor before the first row.
- `boolean isBeforeFirst()` returns `true` if the cursor is positioned before the first row.
- `boolean last()` positions the cursor on the last row.
- `boolean isLast()` returns `true` if the cursor is positioned on the last row.
- `void afterLast()` positions the cursor after the last row.
- `boolean isAfterLast()` returns `true` if the cursor is positioned after the last row.
- `boolean absolute(int rowNumber)` positions the cursor on the row identified by `rowNumber`. Positive `rowNumbers` position the cursor relative to the beginning of the result set. Negative `rowNumbers` position the cursor relative to the end of the result set. Position numbers can result in a cursor being placed before the first row or after the last row, but they return a `false` value to indicate that the cursor is not on the result set.
- `boolean relative(int rowNumber)` positions the cursor on the row identified by `rowNumber` relative to the current cursor position. Positive `rowNumbers` position the cursor forward relative to the current cursor position. Negative `rowNumbers` position the cursor backward relative to the current cursor position. Position numbers can result in a cursor being placed before the first row or after the last row, but they return a `false` value to indicate that the cursor is not on the result set.
- `int getRow()` returns the row number where the cursor is currently positioned.

As an example, the following call sequence (exception handling not shown) can be used on a scrollable result set to freely move around a result set in a fashion that was previously not supported in JDBC 1.0. You may recall from Chapter 5, "Core JDBC," that an `executeQuery()` invocation on a `Statement` object returns a `ResultSet` object whose cursor is positioned before the first row. A call to `next()` on the `ResultSet` object then positions the cursor on the first row, and scrolling around the result set can proceed via some of the new scrollable result set calls, as shown here:

```
Connection connection = ... // Get connection as usual
Statement statement =
connection.createStatement(ResultSet.TYPE_SCROLL_INSENSITIVE,
                           ResultSet.CONCUR_READ_ONLY);
ResultSet rs = statement.executeQuery("SELECT * FROM CUSTOMER");
rs.next(); // Cursor is on first row
rs.absolute(10); // Cursor is on 10th row
rs.previous(); // Cursor is on 9th row
rs.relative(-3); // Cursor is on 6th row
rs.relative(4); // Cursor is on 10th row again
rs.relative(3); // Cursor is on 13th row
rs.absolute(-2); // Cursor is on 2nd to last row
rs.first(); // Cursor is on first row again
```

Driver Support for Scrollable Result Sets

Support by your JDBC driver vendor for result set scrollability may be dynamically determined by passing in the result set type identifier to a `supportsResultSetType()` call on `DatabaseMetaData` as exemplified here:

```
DatabaseMetaData databaseMetaData
                        = ... // Obtain database meta data handle
boolean supportsFwdOnly = databaseMetaData.supportsResultSetType(
➥ResultSet.TYPE_FORWARD_ONLY);
boolean supportsScrollIns = databaseMetaData.supportsResultSetType(
➥ResultSet.TYPE_SCROLL_INSENSITIVE);
boolean supportsScrollSens = databaseMetaData.supportsResultSetType(
➥ResultSet.TYPE_SCROLL_SENSITIVE);
```

Applications may still attempt to make calls that pertain only to scrollable result sets even if the driver does not support this feature. In the event that an application attempts to create a scrollable result set not supported by an underlying driver, the driver is expected to throw a `SQLWarning` when the `Connection` object attempts to create a statement that is supposed to return result sets of the specified scrollable type. The driver is then expected to create a statement capable of returning a supported result. If an application requests use of a scrollable result set type not supported by the driver, the driver should first attempt to use some other scrollable result type that it does support; otherwise, it should use a forward-only result set type.

Even if a driver does support scrollable result sets and can create statements with a scrollable result set type, certain SQL queries may be executed on that statement object that cannot return a scrollable result set. In these cases, a `SQLWarning` should be thrown by the call, and the driver should select a result set type it can support for that specific SQL query. The returned result set type may then be dynamically determined by calling `getType()` on the `ResultSet` object itself to return the result set type identifier (that is, `ResultSet.TYPE_`*`XXX`*).

You may also attempt to give your driver hints about how your application will use the result set returned. This allows the driver vendor implementation to dynamically optimize decisions that affect cache sizes and communications with the database. One such hint is the `setFetchDirection()` call on the `ResultSet` object. After a `ResultSet` object is returned, `setFetchDirection()` with a result set type identifier (that is, `ResultSet.Type_`*`XXX`*) may be used to tell the driver in which direction your application will attempt to access the result set rows. The method `getFetchDirection()` on the `ResultSet` object will return a result set type identifier defining in which direction the result set is currently optimized to return rows.

The `setFetchSize()` call on `ResultSet` may also be made to set the number of rows the driver should attempt to fetch from the database when it needs to retrieve more rows. The `getFetchSize()` call can be used to return the result set's current fetch size.

Example: Scrollable Result Sets

This next example demonstrates how to use the JDBC scrollable result set features. The example code is contained in the `ejava.jdbc.advanced.ScrollableResultSetExample` class, which extends the `ejava.jdbc.advanced.ConnectToDatabase`, which is identical to Chapter 5's `ConnectToDatabase` class:

```
public class ScrollableResultSetExample extends ConnectToDatabase { ... }
```

Note

The complete set of code examples for the `ScrollableResultSetExample` can be located as described in Appendix A and extracted to the `examples\src\ejava\jdbc\advanced` and `examples\config\execscripts\ejava\jdbc\advanced` directories. Some exception handling and other handling mechanisms have been left out of the book here for simplicity but can be found in the example code.

The ANT `build.xml` script associated with this chapter will compile the source code, set preferences, and generate scripts for executing the examples. The properties specified in the `build.properties` file for this chapter establish a set of query statements that will be used when executing the examples. These properties and the properties read from the `examples/global.properties` file are used to set Java preferences during execution of the ANT prefs target. A `runscrollableresultset` script generated during the ANT build for this chapter can be used to execute this example. Appendix A, "Software

Configuration," describes the general build procedures for all examples in the book and specifies those common environment variables that must be set to execute our example scripts.

Note that at the time of this writing, support for scrollable results sets was not fully adopted by all database and JDBC driver vendors. Consult Appendix A for more information on support and the vendor product with which you can test the `ScrollableResultSetExample`.

The main() method of ScrollableResultSetExample is invoked as

```
java ejava.jdbc.advanced.ScrollableResultSetExample
```

The main method then reads the preferences for this example and instantiates a new `ScrollableResultSetExample` object. The remaining code in `main()` then demonstrates the three types of `ResultSet` scroll models available in JDBC. The method `executeQueryScrollSensitiveReadOnly()` will demonstrate the creation of a scroll-sensitive result set, the method `executeQueryScrollInsensitiveReadOnly()` will demonstrate the creation of a scroll-insensitive result set, and the `executeQueryScrollForwardOnly()` will demonstrate forward-only result sets for completeness. We will also call two versions of the `executeQueryScrollInsensitiveReadOnly()` method to demonstrate how both a `Statement` and a `PreparedStatement` can be used to create different `ResultSet` types. Each result set type returned is then traversed in various ways according to a set of static `print`*`XXX`*`()` methods defined on the `ScrollableResultSetExample` class. The `ScrollableResultSetExample.main()` method is shown here:

```
public static void main(String[] args)
{
  // Read preferences and create example object
  Preferences preferences
      = Preferences.userNodeForPackage(
          ejava.jdbc.advanced.ConnectToDatabase.class);

  ScrollableResultSetExample scrollableResultSetExample
      = new ScrollableResultSetExample();
   ...
  // Execute and print results for scroll insensitive
  // and read only result set example
    String sqlString
          = preferences.get("SCROLLABLE_SQL_STATEMENT",null);

    ResultSet rs = scrollableResultSetExample
      .executeQueryScrollInsensitiveReadOnly(sqlString);

    scrollableResultSetExample
      .printResultSetRowsInForwardDirection(rs);
```

```
    scrollableResultSetExample
      .printResultSetRowsInReverseDirection(rs);
    scrollableResultSetExample.printResultSetNthRow(rs, 3);
    scrollableResultSetExample.printNthMinusIthRow(rs, 4, 2);
  ...
  // Execute and print results for scroll sensitive
  // and read only result set example

    String sqlString =
      preferences.get("SCROLLABLE_SQL_STATEMENT",null);

    ResultSet rs =
      scrollableResultSetExample
      .executeQueryScrollSensitiveReadOnly(sqlString);

    scrollableResultSetExample
      .printResultSetRowsInForwardDirection(rs);
    scrollableResultSetExample.printResultSetNthRow(rs, 3);
    scrollableResultSetExample.printNthMinusIthRow(rs, 4, 2);
  ...
  // Execute and print results for scroll sensitive
  // and read only result set from a PreparedStatement example

    String sqlString =
      preferences.get("SCROLLABLE_SQL_PREPARED_STATEMENT",null);
    Vector vector = new Vector();
    vector.addElement(preferences
         .get("SCROLLABLE_SQL_PREPARED_STATEMENT_VALUES",null));

    ResultSet rs =
      scrollableResultSetExample
      .executeQueryScrollInsensitiveReadOnly(sqlString, vector);

    scrollableResultSetExample
      .printResultSetRowsInForwardDirection(rs);
    scrollableResultSetExample
      .printResultSetRowsInReverseDirection(rs);
    scrollableResultSetExample.printResultSetNthRow(rs, 3);
    scrollableResultSetExample.printNthMinusIthRow(rs, 4, 2);
  ...
  // Execute and print results for scroll forward result set

    String sqlString =
      preferences.get("SCROLLABLE_SQL_STATEMENT",null);

    ResultSet rs =
```

```
      scrollableResultSetExample
      .executeQueryScrollForwardOnly(sqlString);

    scrollableResultSetExample
      .printResultSetRowsInForwardDirection(rs);
   ...
}
```

In addition to the database driver properties read in from the `global.properties` file as in Chapter 5, this class also reads in a SQL statement used in regular `Statement` queries, as well as a parameterized statement and input values for use in a `PreparedStatement` from the local `build.properties` file. These SQL statements defined in the `build.properties` file are shown here:

```
#Simple SQL Statement
sql.scrollable.statement = SELECT * FROM CUSTOMER

#SQL Statement for Prepared Statement
sql.scrollable.prepared.statement = SELECT * FROM CUSTOMER
➥ WHERE CUSTOMER.FIRST_NAME LIKE  ?
sql.scrollable.prepared.statement.values = %R%
```

The three types of result set scrolling features used in this example first call one of two methods on the example object instance to create either a `Statement` or a `PreparedStatement` object. Each statement-creation method first creates a connection object. One `getStatement()` method returns a regular `Statement` given a result set type identifier and a concurrency type identifier. Don't worry about that the concurrency type for now because it is described in the next section.

A second `getStatement()` method returns a `PreparedStatement` given a prepared statement SQL string, a result set type identifier, and a concurrency type identifier. Both `getStatement()` methods are defined here:

```
protected Statement getStatement(int scrollType, int updateType)
  throws SQLException, Exception
{
  Connection connection = super.getConnection();
  Statement statement =
    connection.createStatement(scrollType, updateType);

  return statement;
}


protected PreparedStatement getStatement(String sqlString,
  int scrollType, int updateType)
  throws SQLException,Exception
{
```

```
    Connection connection = super.getConnection();
    PreparedStatement preparedStatement =
      connection.prepareStatement(sqlString, scrollType, updateType);

    return preparedStatement;
  }
```

The four forms of `executeXXX()` called on the `ScrollableResultSetExample` object by `main()` simply demonstrate how to create an appropriate statement, execute a query on the statement, and return the result set object:

```
public ResultSet executeQueryScrollForwardOnly(String sqlString)
  throws SQLException, Exception
{
  Statement statement =
    getStatement(ResultSet.TYPE_FORWARD_ONLY,
                 ResultSet.CONCUR_READ_ONLY);
  ResultSet rs = statement.executeQuery(sqlString);

  return rs;
}

public ResultSet executeQueryScrollSensitiveReadOnly(
                                             String sqlString)
  throws SQLException, Exception
{
  Statement statement =
    getStatement(ResultSet.TYPE_SCROLL_SENSITIVE,
                 ResultSet.CONCUR_READ_ONLY);
  ResultSet rs = statement.executeQuery(sqlString);

  return rs;
}

public ResultSet executeQueryScrollInsensitiveReadOnly(
                                             String sqlString)
  throws SQLException, Exception
{
  Statement statement =
    getStatement(ResultSet.TYPE_SCROLL_INSENSITIVE,
                 ResultSet.CONCUR_READ_ONLY);

  ResultSet rs = statement.executeQuery(sqlString);

  return rs;
}

public ResultSet executeQueryScrollInsensitiveReadOnly(
```

```
                              String sqlString,   Vector values)
  throws SQLException, Exception
{
  PreparedStatement preparedStatement =
    getStatement(sqlString,
                 ResultSet.TYPE_SCROLL_INSENSITIVE,
                 ResultSet.CONCUR_READ_ONLY);

  for (int i = 1; i <= values.size(); i++) {
    preparedStatement.setObject(i, values.elementAt(i - 1));
  }
  ResultSet rs = preparedStatement.executeQuery();

  return rs;
}
```

The `printResultSetRowsInForwardDirection()` method is called from `main()` after each `executeXXX()` method is called in order to simply demonstrate how one can scroll forward in a result set as shown here:

```
public void printResultSetRowsInForwardDirection(ResultSet rs)
   throws SQLException
{
  ResultSetMetaData rMetaData = rs.getMetaData();
  int nColumns = rMetaData.getColumnCount();

  for (int i = 1; i < nColumns; i++) {
    System.out.print(rMetaData.getColumnName(i) + " : ");
  }
  System.out.println(rs.getString(nColumns));

  while (rs.next()) {
    for (int i = 1; i < nColumns; i++) {
      System.out.print(rs.getString(i) + " : ");
    }
    System.out.println(rs.getString(nColumns));

  }
}
```

The `printResultSetRowsInReverseDirection()` is called from `main()` after the `executeXXX()` methods that return scrollable result sets are called. The `printResultSetRowsInReverseDirection()` method then demonstrates how to obtain information about the type of result set returned, positions the cursor after the last row in the result set, and then scrolls backward in the result set from there using the `previous()` method on `ResultSet`. The `printResultSetRowsInReverseDirection()` method is shown here:

```
public void printResultSetRowsInReverseDirection(ResultSet rs)
  throws SQLException
{
  int rsType = rs.getType();

  if (rsType == ResultSet.TYPE_FORWARD_ONLY
          || rsType == ResultSet.TYPE_SCROLL_SENSITIVE) {
    System.out.println(
              "Error : ResultSet is not TYPE_SCROLL_INSENSITIVE");

    return;
  }

  ResultSetMetaData rMetaData = rs.getMetaData();
  int nColumns = rMetaData.getColumnCount();

  for (int i = 1; i < nColumns; i++) {
    System.out.print(rMetaData.getColumnName(i) + " : ");
  }
  System.out.println(rMetaData.getColumnName(nColumns));

  int fetchDirection = rs.getFetchDirection();

  if (fetchDirection == ResultSet.FETCH_FORWARD) {
    System.out
      .println("Result Set is  set to Fetch Forward Direction ");
  }

  rs.afterLast();

  while (rs.previous()) {
    for (int i = 1; i <nColumns; i++) {
      System.out.print(rs.getObject(i) + " : ");
    }
   System.out.println(rs.getObject(nColumns));

  }
}
```

The `printResultSetNthRow()` method is also called from `main()` after `executeXXX()` methods that return scrollable result sets are called. This method positions the cursor at the row position passed to the method as a parameter, verifies that the row is located at the correct position via a call to `getRow()`, and then reports a true or false status resulting from indications of the cursor's position in the result set. The `printResultSetNthRow()` method is shown here:

```
public void printResultSetNthRow(ResultSet rs,int nthRow)
 throws SQLException
{
  int rsType = rs.getType();

  if (rsType == ResultSet.TYPE_FORWARD_ONLY
         || rsType == ResultSet.TYPE_SCROLL_SENSITIVE) {
    System.out
      .println("Error : ResultSet is not TYPE_SCROLL_INSENSITIVE");

    return;
  }

  int fetchDirection = rs.getFetchDirection();

  if (fetchDirection != ResultSet.FETCH_FORWARD) {
    System.out
      .println("Result Set is not set to Fetch Forward Direction ");

    return;
  }

  ResultSetMetaData rMetaData = rs.getMetaData();
  int nColumns = rMetaData.getColumnCount();

  rs.absolute(nthRow);

  int rowNumber = rs.getRow();

  System.out.println(" it is " + nthRow + "th Row in Result Set");

  if (rs.isAfterLast()) {
    System.out.println(" the Present Row is after last Row");
  }

  if (rs.isBeforeFirst()) {
    System.out.println(" The present Row is before first Row");
  }

  if (rs.isFirst()) {
    System.out.println("The present Row is Ist row");
  }

  if (rs.isLast()) {
    System.out.print(" The present Row is last Row");
  }
```

```
    for (int i = 1; i <nColumns; i++) {
      System.out.print(rMetaData.getColumnName(i) + " : ");
    }
    System.out.println(rMetaData.getColumnName(i));

    for (int i = 1; i < nColumns; i++) {
      System.out.print(rs.getObject(i) + " : ");
    }
    System.out.println(rs.getObject(i));

  }
```

Basic Transaction Interfaces

When you're making updates to a database, it is important to understand how these updates are propagated to other views of the data, as well as understand when you can view updates made by others. Understanding update visibility issues such as these requires an understanding of database transactions. Transaction concepts are briefly described in Appendix C, "Database Concepts and SQL," and Java-based transaction services are discussed in depth in Chapter 14, "Transaction Services with JTA and JTS." Nevertheless, the JDBC API offers some support for interfacing with transaction services, and we briefly cover these features in this section and in the section on distributed transactions in the next chapter.

Commits and Rollbacks

It is sometimes important to ensure that with a set of changes to the database, either all occur or none occurs. For example, it would be bad for the BeeShirts.com business if we charged a customer before actually taking the order for delivery to his home. We can avoid this problem in our enterprise data-enabling efforts by encapsulating any database operations that change customer charge-related data and those that change customer order-related data into a single database transaction.

The most simplistic view of a transaction from a JDBC programmer's point of view is to understand the significance of beginning, committing, and rolling back a transaction. The `Connection` object is the point of contact for database transaction interfacing in JDBC. Referring to the preceding chapter, in Figure 5.9, we see that the `Connection` class has a `setAutoCommit()` method. This method takes a `boolean` value indicating whether you want that particular database connection to automatically commit transactions after each update-related SQL statement is submitted to the database. By default, a `Connection` object is created in auto commit mode. However, you can also turn auto commit mode off by calling `setAutoCommit(false)` on the `Connection` object.

If you turn off auto commit, you are obligated to either call `commit()` on the `Connection` object if the group of update operations sent to the database was successful or call `rollback()` on the `Connection` object if one of the desired database operations failed. For example:

```
Connection connection = ... // Get connection as usual.
String chargeCustomerSQLString = ... ;
String placeCustomerOrderSQLString = ...;
try{
  connection.setAutoCommit(false);
  Statement s1 = connection.createStatement();
  Statement s2 = connection.createStatement();
  s1.executeUpdate( chargeCustomerSQLString );
  s2.executeUpdate( placeCustomerOrderSQLString );
  connection.commit();
  s1.close();
  s2.close();
}
catch( SQLException e){
  try{
    connection.rollback();
  }
  catch(SQLException e){
    // bla
  }
}
```

Transaction Isolation Levels

All updates within a transaction are visible to objects associated with the transaction itself. Because the `Connection` object represents where a transaction is managed from a JDBC programmer's point of view and because a `Connection` object can create more than one statement, a transaction can thus be associated with multiple statements. Thus a transaction can also be associated with multiple result sets, because each statement can potentially have a result set open.

You can view changes made by other transactions in accordance with a transaction's isolation level. You can think of the term *isolation level* to mean the degree to which a viewpoint of the data is isolated from changes in the data. A transaction isolation level can be set by calling `setTransactionIsolation()` on the `Connection` object with one of the `Connection` class's `static public final` identifiers for isolation levels. The transaction levels are described here in order from least-restrictive isolation levels to most-restrictive isolation levels:

- `TRANSACTION_NONE`: Transactions are not supported at all when identified by this isolation level.
- `TRANSACTION_READ_UNCOMMITTED`: This level allows other transactions to see row updates made by this transaction before a commit has been issued.

- TRANSACTION_READ_COMMITTED: This level does not allow other transactions to see row updates made by this transaction until a commit has been issued (that is, it does not allow "dirty reads").
- TRANSACTION_REPEATABLE_READ: In addition to TRANSACTION_READ_COMMITTED level support, this level also does not allow a transaction to read a row more than once and observe different data values because some other transaction made data updates to that row in the meantime (that is, it does not allow "nonrepeatable reads" or "dirty reads").
- TRANSACTION_SERIALIZABLE: In addition to TRANSACTION_REPEATABLE_READ level support, this level does not allow a transaction to read a collection of rows more than once, satisfying a particular WHERE clause. Furthermore, this level does not allow a transaction to observe a newly inserted row because some other transaction inserted a row satisfying that WHERE clause in the meantime (that is, it does not allow "phantom reads," "nonrepeatable reads," or "dirty reads").

Transaction Savepoints

JDBC 3.0 has also introduced a new capability for recording an intermediate point within a transaction to which the transaction can be rolled back. Thus, in the event that a transaction cannot be processed to completion, rather than rolling all the way back to the beginning of a transaction, the transaction will roll back only to the last "savepoint." Although not all drivers and databases will support savepoints immediately, you can determine whether your JDBC driver and database support savepoints by invoking DatabaseMetaData.supportsSavepoints().

The Connection interface thus defines a savepoint() method that can be used to indicate the point in your code where a savepoint may be made and to which the transaction can return in the event of an encountered rollback. Alternatively, a savepoint(String) method can also take a String as the name of a particular savepoint. The savepoint() methods may be invoked when the Connection is not in auto-commit mode.

The savepoint() and savepoint(String) methods both return a java.sql.Savepoint object when invoked. If the associated savepoint was an unnamed savepoint, the Savepoint.getSavepointId() method may be invoked to return an int form of the savepoint identifier. If the savepoint is a named savepoint, the Savepoint.getSavepointName() method may be invoked to retrieve the name given to the savepoint. The rollback(Savepoint) method on the Connection object can then be used to roll back to a particular savepoint given a Savepoint object handle.

Here's an example:

```
// Get a connection as usual
Connection connection = ...
```

```
// Establish some SQL commands
String blaSQLString = "INSERT bla INTO bladdybla";
String fooSQLString = "INSERT foo INTO bar";

// Connection set to non auto commit mode
connection.setAutoCommit(false);

// do some work...

Statement s1 = connection.createStatement();
s1.executeUpdate( blaSQLString );

// Set named savepoint
Savepoint blaSP =  connection.setSavepoint("blaSavepoint");

// do some more work...

// Roll back to first savepoint if neccessary
if(some error situation...){
  System.out.println("Error in savepoint named "
                    + blaSP.getSavepointName());
  connection.rollback(blaSP);
}

Statement s2 = connection.createStatement();
s2.executeUpdate( fooSQLString );

// Set unnamed savepoint
Savepoint fooSP = connection.setSavepoint();

// do even more work...

// Roll back to second savepoint if neccessary
if(another error situation...){){
  System.out.println("Error in savepoint with ID "
                    + fooSP .getSavepointId());
  connection.rollback(fooSP);
}

connection.commit();
s1.close();
s2.close();
}
```

After a transaction has been committed, all savepoints recorded within the transaction are released and thus become invalid. When a transaction rolls back to a particular savepoint, all savepoints created after that savepoint also become invalid. You can induce the release of a savepoint and thus remove it as a candidate for rollback by invoking the `Connection.releaseSavepoint(Savepoint)` method.

Holdable Result Sets

After calling `commit()` on a `Connection`, the underlying JDBC implementation is free to close any `ResultSet` objects associated with their transactions. There may, however, be situations in which you'd like to keep the `ResultSet` objects around after a commit. Primarily, for certain commercial infrastructure environments, by inducing a commit before closing the `ResultSet`, advantages may be yielded in performance. The need for this new JDBC 3.0 feature is thus clearly driven by vendors that want to enable their products to better perform inside Java application environments.

Result sets may thus be further classified according to two types:

- Held After Commit
- Closed After Commit

The default holdability of `ResultSet` objects with your particular JDBC driver and database can be determined by invoking the `DatabaseMetaData.getResultSetHoldability()` method. This method may return an `int` having the value of constant `ResultSet.HOLD_CURSORS_OVER_COMMIT` which indicates that `ResultSet` objects will not be closed after a commit. The value of `ResultSet.CLOSE_CURSORS_AT_COMMIT` indicates that `ResultSet` objects will be closed upon a commit. Each type of holdability support may be determined by invoking the `DatabaseMetaDeta.supportsResultSetHoldability(int)` method and passing in one of the constants just defined.

If supported, the current holdability of `ResultSet` objects associated with a `Connection` can be determined from a call to `Connection.getHoldability()`, which returns one of the aforementioned constant values. You can induce a particular holdability policy by calling `Connection.setHoldability(int)` and passing in one of the constant values. For more fine-grained control over a particular statement's holdability, the Connection object's `createStatement()`, `prepareStatement()`, and `prepareCall()` methods can all be invoked to indicate the holdability for each particular statement type. As depicted in Figure 5.9, the result set holdability constant can be passed into each method indicating its holdability level. The holdability of a particular `Statement` type can then be queried via a call to its `getResultSetHoldability()` method.

Updateable Result Sets

In addition to scrollable result sets, JDBC provides a feature for manipulating result sets not previously possible with JDBC 1.0. Updateable result sets in JDBC now allow for the update of rows, insertion of rows, and deletion of rows in a result set all through the `ResultSet` interface itself, whereas JDBC 1.0 previously returned only result sets that were read-only.

Result sets may thus be further classified according to two types:

- Read-only
- Updateable

This new additional result set discriminator is referred to as the *concurrency type* of the result set. Read-only result sets are the result sets you were used to using in JDBC 1.0 that offered you only a view of the data returned from the database. Updates, inserts, and deletes were exclusively accomplished via execution of SQL update, insert, or delete commands using the `executeUpdate()` or `execute()` methods on a statement object. In JDBC 2.0 and 3.0, this work can now be done conveniently from the `ResultSet` handle that you obtained after a query if that `ResultSet` object is updateable. Read-only result sets are identified by the `java.sql.ResultSet.CONCUR_READ_ONLY static public final int` value. Updateable result sets are identified by the `java.sql.ResultSet.CONCUR_UPDATABLE static public final int` value.

Creating Updateable Result Sets

The `Statement` and `PreparedStatement` objects may be created to use read-only result set types using the `Connection.createStatement()` and `Connection.prepareStatement(String sqlCommand)` methods as usual. As you've seen in the preceding section, a form for each method is provided on the `Connection` interface to support passing in result set type identifiers and result set concurrency type identifiers as well. Although you can use these two methods to create read-only result sets using the `ResultSet.CONCUR_READ_ONLY` identifier, you can also request usage of the updateable types as shown here:

```
Connection connection = ... // Get connection as usual
String sqlString = "SELECT * FROM CUSTOMER";
Statement statement =
     connection.createStatement(ResultSet.TYPE_SCROLL_SENSITIVE,
                                ResultSet.CONCUR_UPDATABLE);
ResultSet rs1 = statement.executeQuery(sqlString);
PreparedStatement preparedStatement =
    connection.preparedStatement(sqlString, ResultSet.TYPE_FORWARD_ONLY,
                                 ResultSet.CONCUR_UPDATABLE);
ResultSet rs2 = preparedStatement.executeQuery();
```

After calling `executeQuery()` or `execute()` with a SQL query command on a statement object created to return updateable result sets, an updateable `ResultSet` object may then be returned. A series of `updateXXX()` methods on the `ResultSet` interface are then called to update individual columns associated with the current cursor row.

Updating Rows

Two general forms of updateXXX() exist. One form takes a column index int, and the other form takes a column name String as an input parameter, as with the getXXX() methods described in Chapter 5. However, each updateXXX() method also takes a second parameter value corresponding to the actual XXX type you intend to update in the associated column. For example:

```
int columnIndexFirstName = resultSet.findColumn ("FIRST_NAME");
resultSet.updateString(columnIndexFirstName ,"Tony");
        or
resultSet.updateString("FIRST_NAME","Tony");
```

These updateXXX() calls don't actually update the database row when called. Rather a call to the ResultSet object's updateRow() method must be made to induce the actual change. You of course can then use getXXX() on the result set to see the change. Thus we have a call such as this:

```
resultSet.updateRow();
```

Canceling Updates

If you don't call updateRow() before you move the cursor to another row, the updates made using the updateXXX() calls will be cancelled. You can also explicitly cancel a row update before calling updateRow() using the cancelRowUpdates() method call:

```
resultSet.cancelRowUpdates();
```

Inserting Rows

Inserting a row into the database may be done directly from a ResultSet handle. First call moveToInsertRow() to position the cursor on a special insert row location. This creates a temporary buffer that will contain the contents of all new column information to place in the new row. The updateXXX() method must then be called for each column in the new row that does not allow null values. The values for each column will remain undefined until they are set with an updateXXX() call. Finally, a call to insertRow() is made to commit the insert to the database. If a non-null column value was left undefined by not calling updateXXX() for that column, the insertRow() call will throw a SQLException. By calling moveToCurrentRow() after calling moveToInsertRow() and inserting the row, you can move back to the row that was current just before you inserted the new row. The basic sequence for inserting a row is illustrated here:

```
resultSet.moveToInsertRow();
resultSet.updateInt("CUSTOMER_ID_FK", 101);
resultSet.updateString("SHIP_INSTRUCT", " Deliver to offc if not home");
    ...
```

```
// Call other updateXXX() methods
    ...
resultSet.insertRow();
```

Deleting Rows

Deleting a row from the database is also fairly straightforward after you have a `ResultSet` handle. With a call to `deleteRow()` on the `ResultSet`, the current row pointed to by the cursor will be deleted from the `ResultSet` as well as from the database. A call to this method will throw a `SQLException` if you are positioned on the insert row buffer (that is, after a call to `moveToInsertRow()`):

```
resultSet.deleteRow();
```

Visibility into Database Changes

For updateable result sets, the type of result set, in addition to the isolation level, is important to consider when you're trying to understand update visibility. After a scroll-insensitive updateable result set is opened, no changes from other transactions or even result sets in the same transaction are visible to the holder of the scroll-insensitive result set. Although updates to scroll-sensitive updateable result sets made by other transactions or result sets in the same transaction are visible to the holder of the scroll-sensitive result set, inserts and deletes may not be visible. Despite these general rules for visibility according to result set type, actual support is ultimately a function of what your database and driver vendor supports. You can find out the level of visibility of changes from within a `ResultSet` object made either by other result sets or by your own result set by calling one of the `othersXXXVisible()` or `ownXXXVisible()` calls on the `DatabaseMetaData` object:

- `boolean othersUpdatesAreVisible(int type)` returns `true` if updates made by other result sets for the `ResultSet.TYPE_XXX` identifier are visible.
- `boolean othersInsertsAreVisible(int type)` returns `true` if inserts made by other result sets for the `ResultSet.TYPE_XXX` identifier are visible.
- `boolean othersDeletesAreVisible(int type)` returns `true` if deletes made by other result sets for the `ResultSet.TYPE_XXX` identifier are visible.
- `boolean ownUpdatesAreVisible(int type)` returns `true` if updates made by your own result set for the `ResultSet.TYPE_XXX` identifier are visible.
- `boolean ownInsertsAreVisible(int type)` returns `true` if inserts made by your own result set for the `ResultSet.TYPE_XXX` identifier are visible.
- `boolean ownDeletesAreVisible(int type)` returns `true` if deletes made by your own result set for the `ResultSet.TYPE_XXX` identifier are visible.

After you've determined whether you can even view updates, inserts, and deletes for `ResultSet` objects, before using a `ResultSet`, you can also determine whether a specific `ResultSet` row was updated, inserted, or deleted by calling one of the `rowXXX()` methods on the `ResultSet` object as defined here:

- `boolean rowUpdated()` returns `true` if the current row has been updated.
- `boolean rowInserted()` returns `true` if the current row has experienced a database insert.
- `boolean rowDeleted()` returns `true` if the current row has been deleted.

To complicate matters, the indications returned by the `ResultSet.rowXXX()` methods may not even be possible to determine by your driver. A set of `XXXAreDetected()` methods has been added to the `DatabaseMetaData` interface to support your attempt to determine whether the `ResultSet.rowXXX()` methods are supported:

- `boolean updatesAreDetected(int type)` returns `true` if updates for the `ResultSet.TYPE_XXX` type identifier can be determined when calling `ResultSet.rowUpdated()`.
- `boolean insertsAreDetected(int type)` returns `true` if inserts for the `ResultSet.TYPE_XXX` type identifier can be determined when calling `ResultSet.rowInserted()`.
- `boolean deletesAreDetected(int type)` returns `true` if deletes for the `ResultSet.TYPE_XXX` type identifier can be determined when calling `ResultSet.rowDeleted()`.

When all else fails, simply call `refreshRow()` on the `ResultSet` object to refresh the current row with the most up-to-the-minute updates in the database. Of course, calling this method will hamper performance because the database is accessed for each call. Some caveats also exist for calling `refreshRow()` during updates or inserts. Calling `refreshRow()` when in the midst of updating a row before calling `updateRow()` will cause you to lose all updates made. Furthermore, a `SQLException` will be thrown when you call `refreshRow()` while on the insert row.

Driver Support for Updateable Result Sets

You can call `supportsResultSetConcurrency()` on the `DatabaseMetaData` interface with the `ResultSet.CONCUR_XXX` identifier to determine whether your driver will support that type of concurrency model. However, if an application attempts to create a statement with the `ResultSet.CONCUR_UPDATABLE` concurrency model and the driver cannot support this model, then the driver should throw a `SQLWarning` when attempting to create such a statement. The driver should then fall back to using the read-only concurrency model.

As with the dynamic determination of a result set type for certain calls even when a particular result set type is supported, the concurrency type may also have to be determined dynamically. In such a case, if a statement was created to use updateable result sets, when the `ResultSet` object is generated during an `execute()` or `executeQuery()`

call on that statement, a `SQLWarning` should be thrown and a read-only result set should be generated instead. It may help you at times to call `getConcurrency()` on the `ResultSet` object in JDBC to determine its concurrency type. Selection of a result set type has precedence over selection of a concurrency type if neither the result set type nor the concurrency type is supported.

Example: Updateable Result Sets

This next example demonstrates how to use some of the JDBC updateable result set features. The example code is contained in the `ejava.jdbc.advanced.UpdateableResultSetExample` class, which extends `ejava.jdbc.advanced.ConnectToDatabase`:

```
public class UpdateableResultSetExample extends ConnectToDatabase { ... }
```

> **Note**
>
> The complete set of code examples for the `UpdateableResultSetExample` can be found on the CD-ROM and extracted to the `examples\src\ejava\jdbc\advanced` directory. Some exception handling and other handling mechanisms have been left out of the book here for simplicity but can be found in the complete examples. The `runupdateableresultset` script generated from the ANT build process can be used to execute this example. Appendix A describes the general build procedures for all examples in the book and specifies those common environment variables that must be set to execute our example scripts. Note that the query `String` values defined in `build.properties` for this example need to be changed after each execution of the example in order to not violate unique row identity constraints in the database.

The `main()` method of `UpdateableResultSetExample` is invoked like this:

```
java ejava.jdbc.advanced.UpdateableResultSetExample
```

The `main()` method reads in application preferences and then instantiates a new `UpdateableResultSetExample` object as with the other examples. The `main()` method demonstrates the update of result sets using forward-only and scroll-insensitive concurrency types. Two `executeXXX()` methods are called on an `UpdateableResultSetExample` instance to return a `ResultSet` of a particular concurrency type. This `ResultSet` is then manipulated in various ways using a host of methods that demonstrate the nature of updateable result sets. The `main()` method is defined here:

```
public static void main(String[] args)
{
  // Set preferences and create new example object
  Preferences preferences = Preferences.userNodeForPackage(
                            ejava.jdbc.advanced.ConnectToDatabase.class);
  String sqlString
      = preferences.get("UPDATEABLE_SQL_STATEMENT",null);
```

```
  UpdateableResultSetExample example
      = new UpdateableResultSetExample();

      ...
    // Show example of scroll insensitive updateable result set
    System.out.println("Scroll Insensitive Updateable ResultSet ");
    // Execute query
    ResultSet rs
      = example.executeQueryScrollInsensitiveUpdateable(sqlString);
    // print results
    example.printResultSetRowsInForwardDirection(rs);
    // insert new rows using column Names
    example.insertNewRowIntoOrdersTableUsingColumnNames(rs);
    // update a random row in the results
    example.updateNthRowIthColumnValue(rs, 1, 4, "Office delivery");

    // Show example of forward only updateable result set
    System.out.println("Forward Only Updateable ResultSet ");
    // Execute query
    rs = example.executeQueryScrollForwardOnlyUpdateable(sqlString);
    // insert using column indexes of the resultSet
    example.insertNewRowIntoOrdersTableUsingColumnIndexes(rs);
    // print results
    example.printResultSetRowsInForwardDirection(rs);
      ...
}
```

A SQL statement used to generate an updateable result set is set as a Java preference after being read from the local `build.properties` file:

```
#Updateable SQL STATEMET
sql.statement.for.updateable.statement = SELECT   CUSTOMER_ID_FK,
➥ORDER_ID ,ORDER_DATE ,SHIP_INSTRUCT ,SHIP_DATE , SHIP_WEIGHT,
➥SHIP_CHARGE  ,  PAID_DATE FROM ORDERS
```

A `getStatement()` method is used here as with the `ScrollableResultSetExample` to create a SQL statement with the associated scroll type and concurrency type:

```
protected Statement getStatement(int scrollType, int updateType)
  throws SQLException, Exception
{
  Connection connection = super.getConnection();
  Statement statement
      = connection.createStatement(scrollType, updateType);
  return statement;
}
```

The execute*XXX*() method called from main() actually calls the getStatement() method to return a Statement of the appropriate concurrency type and then executes the sqlString query passed in as a parameter. An execute*XXX*() demonstration method exists for returning scroll-insensitive result sets and scroll forward-only result sets:

```
public ResultSet executeQueryScrollInsensitiveUpdateable(
                                                  String sqlString)
  throws SQLException, Exception
{
  Statement statement = getStatement(
                                ResultSet.TYPE_SCROLL_INSENSITIVE,
                                ResultSet.CONCUR_UPDATABLE);
   // Execute a SQL statement that returns a single ResultSet.
  ResultSet rs = statement.executeQuery(sqlString);
  return rs;
}

public ResultSet executeQueryScrollForwardOnlyUpdateable(
                                                  String sqlString)
  throws SQLException, Exception
{
   Statement statement = getStatement(
                                     ResultSet.TYPE_FORWARD_ONLY,
                                     ResultSet.CONCUR_UPDATABLE);
   // Execute a SQL statement that returns a single ResultSet.
   ResultSet rs = statement.executeQuery(sqlString);
   return rs;
}
```

Two methods for inserting a row into an updateable result set exist in this example and are called from main(). One method inserts a row into our BeeShirts.com ORDERS table using the column names in ResultSet.update*XXX*() calls. Another method inserts a row into the ORDERS table using column indices instead of column names. These methods are defined here:

```
public void insertNewRowIntoOrdersTableUsingColumnNames(
  ResultSet rs)
  throws SQLException
{
  rs.moveToInsertRow();
  rs.updateInt("CUSTOMER_ID_FK", 101);
  rs.updateInt("ORDER_ID", 5001);
  rs.updateDate("ORDER_DATE",  new Date(System.currentTimeMillis()));
  rs.updateString("SHIP_INSTRUCT", "deliver to office if not home");
  rs.updateDate("SHIP_DATE", new Date(System.currentTimeMillis()));
  rs.updateFloat("SHIP_WEIGHT", 22.0f);
```

```
  rs.updateFloat("SHIP_CHARGE", 44.56f);
  rs.updateDate("PAID_DATE", new Date(System.currentTimeMillis()));
  rs.insertRow();
}

public void insertNewRowIntoOrdersTableUsingColumnIndexes(
  ResultSet rs)
  throws SQLException
{
  rs.moveToInsertRow();
  // In the table 1 Column index for ORDER_ID and 2 for
  // CUSTOMER_ID_FK and so on.
  rs.updateInt(1, 101);
  rs.updateInt(2, 5005);
  rs.updateDate(3, new Date(System.currentTimeMillis()));
  rs.updateString(4, "deliver to office if not home");
  rs.updateDate(5, new Date(System.currentTimeMillis()));
  rs.updateFloat(6, 22.0f);
  rs.updateFloat(7, 44.56f);
  rs.updateDate(8, new Date(System.currentTimeMillis()) );
  rs.insertRow();
}
```

Finally, an update method is also called from `main()` to demonstrate how a particular column in a specified row of an updateable result set can be updated with a new value:

```
public void updateNthRowIthColumnValue(ResultSet rs,
  int nThRow, int iThColumn, Object value) throws SQLException
{
  ResultSetMetaData rMetaData = rs.getMetaData();
  int type    =  rMetaData.getColumnType(iThColumn);
  String colName = rMetaData.getColumnName(iThColumn);
  rs.absolute(nThRow);

  switch(type) {
    case Types.CHAR:
    case Types.VARCHAR:
    case Types.LONGVARCHAR:
      rs.updateString(colName, value.toString());
      break;
    case Types.BIT:
      rs.updateByte(colName,
        Byte.valueOf(value.toString()).byteValue());
      break;
    case Types.TINYINT:
    case Types.SMALLINT:
    case Types.INTEGER:
```

```
      rs.updateInt(colName,
        Integer.valueOf(value.toString()).intValue());
      break;
    case Types.BIGINT:
      rs.updateLong(colName,
        Long.valueOf(value.toString()).longValue());
      break;
    case Types.FLOAT:
      rs.updateFloat(colName,
        Float.valueOf(value.toString()).floatValue());
      break;
    case Types.DOUBLE:
      rs.updateDouble(colName,
        Double.valueOf(value.toString()).doubleValue());
      break;
    case Types.DATE:
      rs.updateDate(colName,
        Date.valueOf(value.toString()));
      break;
    case Types.TIME:
      rs.updateTime(colName,
        Time.valueOf(value.toString()));
      break;
    case Types.TIMESTAMP:
      rs.updateTimestamp(colName,
        Timestamp.valueOf(value.toString()));
      break;
    default:
      rs.updateObject(colName, value);
      break;
  }
  rs.updateRow();
}
```

Batch Updates

When submitting updates to the database using JDBC 1.0, you could submit only one update at a time using either the `executeUpdate()` or the `execute()` method calls on a `Statement` interface or one of its sub-interfaces. The JDBC 2.0 API introduced a feature that enabled you to create a batch of update commands associated with a statement and subsequently submit the entire batch of commands to the database in a single call. The database can then process all the updates at once, offering a significant performance enhancement over submitting the same set of updates individually. Whether or not such batch updates are supported is a function of both the database and the driver vendor implementation. You can determine whether batch updates are supported in your database and driver configuration by calling supportsBatchUpdates() on a DatabaseMetaData object that returns a boolean true or false indication.

Creating Batch Updates

Before creating a batch update, you must first turn off auto commit on the Connection object by calling Connection.setAutoCommit(false). Your code, as the JDBC API client, now determines when to commit a transaction during the submission of multiple updates. You then must create a Statement object or one of its sub-interface instances as usual. Each SQL update command is then added to a Statement using the new addBatch(String command) method on the Statement interface. If you have created a PreparedStatement, you should call the setXXX() methods on the PreparedStatement to set each parameterized value and then call addBatch() on the PreparedStatement object. For example:

```
Connection connection = ... // Create connection as usual
connection.setAutoCommit(false);

Statement statement = this.getStatement();
statement.addBatch("INSERT INTO STATE VALUES(\'VA\', \'VIRGINIA')");
statement.addBatch("INSERT INTO STATE VALUES(\'MD\', \'MARYLAND')");


PreparedStatement preparedStatement =
        connection.prepareStatement("INSERT INTO STATE VALUES (?,?)");
preparedStatement.setString(1,"CA");
preparedStatement.setString(2,"California");
preparedStatement.addBatch();
preparedStatement.setString(1,"OH");
preparedStatement.setString(2,"Ohio");
preparedStatement.addBatch();
```

Executing a Batch Update

Executing a batch after it has been created is a simple matter of calling executeBatch() on the Statement interface or a sub-interface. The executeBatch() method takes no parameters and returns an int[] array of update counts in the order in which updates were added to the batch. If the integer constant value of Statement.SUCCESS_NO_INFO (equals -2) is returned instead of an update count value, then even though the update was a success, the number of rows in the database affected by the update cannot be determined. You can use the clearBatch() call on the Statement interface to clear any commands added to a batch.

A SQLException is thrown after executing a batch if any one of the SQL commands added to the batch attempts to generate a ResultSet. A BatchUpdateException is thrown if any of the update commands fails. The

BatchUpdateException has a getUpdateCounts() method to return the number of updates that were executed. If the behavior of the particular database being used requires the JDBC driver to continue processing the remaining updates in the event of a failure, an integer value of Statement.EXECUTE_FAILED (equals -3) may be returned inside the array generated by getUpdateCounts() and associated with those rows not processed. For example:

```
Connection connection = ... // Create connection as usual
connection.setAutoCommit(false);
Statement statement = this.getStatement();
try{
  statement.addBatch("INSERT INTO STATE VALUES(\'VA\', \'VIRGINIA')");
  statement.addBatch("INSERT INTO STATE VALUES(\'MD\', \'MARYLAND')");
  int[] nResults = statement.executeBatch();
  connection.commit();
}
catch(BatchUpdateException bupdateException){
  System.out.println("SQL STATE:" + bupdateException.getSQLState());
  System.out.println("Message:" + bupdateException.getMessage());
  System.out.println("Vendor Code:" + bupdateException.getErrorCode());
  System.out.println(" Update Counts :" );
  int[] nRowsResult = bupdateException.getUpdateCounts();
  for(int i = 0; i < nRowsResult.length; i++){
    System.out.println("Result "+ i +":" + nRowsResult[i]);
  }
  statement.clearBatch();
}
catch(Exception e){
  // Handle other exceptions here
}
```

Example: Batch Updates

This next example demonstrates how to use a few JDBC batch update features. The example code is contained in the ejava.jdbc.advanced.BatchUpdatesExample class, which extends the ejava.jdbc.advanced.ConnectToDatabase class:

```
public class BatchUpdatesExample extends ConnectToDatabase { ... }
```

> **Note**
>
> The complete set of code examples for the BatchUpdatesExample can be found on the CD-ROM and extracted to the examples\src\ejava\jdbc\advanced directory. Some exception handling and other handling mechanisms have been left out of the book here for simplicity but can be found in the complete examples. The runbatchupdates script generated during the ANT build process can be used to execute this example. Appendix A describes the general build procedures for all examples in the book and

> specifies those common environment variables that must be set to execute our example scripts. Consult Appendix A for more information on support and the vendor product with which you can test the `BatchUpdatesExample`. Note that even though certain database and JDBC driver combinations may successfully allow processing of batch updates, the number of updates successfully processed may not be determinable.

The `main()` method of `BatchUpdatesExample` is invoked as

```
java ejava.jdbc.advanced.BatchUpdatesExample
```

The `main()` method first reads in Java preferences for the example and instantiates a new `BatchUpdatesExample` object as with the other examples. The `main()` method for the `BatchUpdatesExample` calls two methods on a `BatchUpdatesExample` instance to demonstrate how a batch of rows can be inserted into the database for both regular statements and prepared statements as shown here:

```
public static void main(String[]  args){
...
  BatchUpdatesExample example = new BatchUpdatesExample();
...
  example.insertBatchofRowsUsingStatement();
  example.insertBatchofRowsUsingPreparedStatement();
...
}
```

The `insertBatchofRowsUsingStatement()` method calls `getStatement()` to obtain a reference to a regular `Statement` object. After checking to see whether batch updates are supported, two regular SQL statements are added to the batch and then executed. Likewise, the `insertBatchofRowsUsingPreparedStatement()` goes through a similar sequence using a `PreparedStatement`. Both methods are shown here:

```
public void insertBatchofRowsUsingStatement()
  throws SQLException, BatchUpdateException, Exception
{
  Connection connection = super.getConnection();
  DatabaseMetaData dbMetaData = connection.getMetaData();
  // check if driver supports batch updates
  if (dbMetaData.supportsBatchUpdates()) {
      ...
      connection.setAutoCommit(false);
      Statement statement = this.getStatement();
      // insert some rows
      statement.addBatch("INSERT INTO STATE VALUES(\'VA\', "
                        + "\'VIRGINIA')");
      statement.addBatch("INSERT INTO STATE VALUES(\'MD\',"
                        + " \'MARYLAND')");
```

```
        int[] nResults = statement.executeBatch();
        // commit
        connection.commit();

        // print results
        for (int i = 0; i < nResults.length; i++) {
          if(nResults[i] >= 0){
              System.out.println(i + "th statement executed with "+
                                     nResults[i] + " results");
          }
          else{
              System.out.println(i + "th statement executed with an"
                    + " indeterminable number of results."
                    + " return value = " + nResults[i]);
          }
        ...
        }
}

public void insertBatchofRowsUsingPreparedStatement()
  throws SQLException, Exception
{
  Connection connection = super.getConnection();
  DatabaseMetaData dbMetaData = connection.getMetaData();
  // check whether driver supports batchupdates
  if (dbMetaData.supportsBatchUpdates()) {
      ...
      connection.setAutoCommit(false);
      // get prepared statement
      PreparedStatement preparedStatement =
        this.getStatement("INSERT INTO STATE VALUES (?,?)");
      // set some statement data
      preparedStatement.setString(1, "CA");
      preparedStatement.setString(2, "California");
      preparedStatement.addBatch();
      preparedStatement.setString(1, "OH");
      preparedStatement.setString(2, "Ohio");
      // start batch
      preparedStatement.addBatch();
      // execute batch
      int[] nResults = preparedStatement.executeBatch();
      // commit batch
      connection.commit();

      // print results
      for (int i = 0; i < nResults.length; i++) {
```

```
            if(nResults[i] >= 0){
                System.out.println(i + "th statement executed with "+
                                     nResults[i] + " results");
            }
            else{
                System.out.println(i + "th statement executed with an"
                      + " indeterminable number of results."
                      + " return value = " + nResults[i]);
            }
        }
        ...
    }
}
```

Advanced Data Types

The JDBC API includes a rich set of advanced data types that may be used to map complex database structures to and from Java objects. Persistable Java object types enable a means for storing and retrieving entire Java objects to and from the database, as well as defining meta-data about these objects. Java mappings for SQL99 types such as BLOBs, CLOBs, Arrays, Distincts, Structs, Refs, and Datalinks are also now possible. Along these lines, custom user-defined database type to Java type mappings are also a possibility with JDBC. Although the JDBC specification standardizes on this support, driver support for these advanced typing features varies from vendor to vendor.

Java Object Types

The JDBC API defines a standard for storing and retrieving Java objects to and from the database. Such persistable Java object support results in databases that become a sort of Java-relational database. The Java object may be serialized to the database or stored in some vendor-dependent fashion. There is no special JDBC-defined storage format as of yet.

Storing a persistable Java object can be straightforward. A regular Java object type is simply first referenced in a SQL update or insert statement and subsequently supplied to the database by calling `setObject()` on that statement. For example, if we attempt to insert some new customer into the database, we might have this:

```
Customer cust = new Customer();
cust.setName("Sam", "Cheng");
  ...
  // Set other customer values
  ...
PreparedStatement statement =
  connection.preparedStatement("INSERT CUSTOMER SET Customer = ?");
statement.setObject(1, cust);
statement.executeUpdate();
```

Retrieving the Java object is equally straightforward. A regular Java type is referenced in the SQL query statement and then retrieved from the database by a call to `getObject()` on the `ResultSet`. For example:

```
ResultSet resultSet = statement.executeQuery(
            "SELECT Customer FROM CUSTOMER WHERE LAST_NAME = Cheng");
resultSet.next();
Customer cust = (Customer) resultSet.getObject(1);
```

The `java.sql.Types` class defines `JAVA_OBJECT` as a type identifier for persistable Java objects. If you are uncertain whether your database and driver support persistable Java objects, a call to `DatabaseMetaData.getTypeInfo()` will return a `ResultSet` that can be used to determine whether `JAVA_OBJECT` types are supported.

You can then call `DatabaseMetaData.getUDTs()` to obtain a `ResultSet` object that describes those user-defined types defined in a particular schema of interest. A catalog `String`, a schema pattern `String`, a type name pattern `String`, and an `int` array with `java.sql.Types.JAVA_OBJECT` as an element are all taken as parameters for the `getUDTs()` method. The `ResultSet` of user-defined types known to the database contains a row per supported type, each with the following column of `Strings`:

- `TYPE_CAT` identifying the catalog.
- `TYPE_SCHEM` identifying the schema.
- `TYPE_NAME` identifying the type name.
- `CLASS_NAME` identifying the associated Java class name.
- `DATA_TYPE` identifying the `java.sql.Types` (for example, `JAVA_OBJECT`).
- `REMARKS` containing optional comments about the type.

SQL99 Types

The SQL99 standard introduces a set of new data types usable in Java environments incorporated by the JDBC 3.0 API specification. For each new type, an identifier was added to the `java.sql.Types` class. Support for each SQL99 type by your database and driver vendors can be determined by calling `DatabaseMetaData.getTypeInfo()` and looking for the type of interest as identified by a `java.sql.Types` identifier in the returned `ResultSet`. These were the new SQL99 types targeted by the JDBC specification:

- BLOBs (Binary Large OBjects) represent a very large set of binary data (`java.sql.Types.BLOB` identifier).
- CLOBs (Character Large OBjects) represent a very large set of character data (`java.sql.Types.CLOB` identifier).
- Reference types represent references to persisted data (`java.sql.Types.REF` identifier).

- Arrays represent simple arrays of data (`java.sql.Types.ARRAY` identifier).
- Structured types represent simple collections of attributes (`java.sql.Types.STRUCT` identifier).
- Datalink types represent URLs to a file existing physically outside of a database (`java.sql.Types.DATALINK` identifier).
- Distinct types represent new type name aliases for existing type names (`java.sql.Types.DISTINCT` identifier).

The `ResultSet` interface has also been embellished to now be more Java SQL99 type-aware by supporting a host of new `get`*`XXX`*`()` methods that serve to return objects from the result set in a type-safe fashion. Recall that `get`*`XXX`*`()` type methods such as `getString()` for `String` types and `getDouble()` for `double` types already exist on the `ResultSet` interface. The `get`*`XXX`*`(int)` method style retrieves objects from a `ResultSet` by column number, and the `get`*`XXX`*`(String)` method style retrieves objects from a `ResultSet` by column name. Thus, as we'll soon see, `get`*`XXX`*`()` methods for a few SQL99 types can be used to retrieve SQL99 types from the `ResultSet` object by column number using `get`*`XXX`*`(int)` type methods or by column name using `get`*`XXX`*`(String)` type methods.

The `PreparedStatement` interface's `set`*`XXX`*`()` type methods have also been extended to set some of the new SQL99 types in a type-safe fashion into indexed parameters of a prepared statement (see the Chapter 5 discussion on the `PreparedStatement` interface). Thus, much like a method `setBoolean(int, boolean)` exists to set a `boolean` value into a prepared statement parameter indexed by the associated `int` parameter to `setBoolean()`, a set of `set`*`XXX`*`()` methods is also now available for a few core SQL99 types, as you'll soon see.

SQL BLOBs and CLOBs

Manipulating database data as a `BLOB` or `CLOB` type is useful when you want to defer the actual transfer of large binary (`BLOB`) or large character (`CLOB`) data between a Java application and the database until it is needed. Thus you might see a `BLOB` type in a returned `ResultSet`, but the actual data for this `BLOB` is not downloaded to your Java application from the database until you explicitly ask for it.

JDBC has incorporated `Blob` and `Clob` Java interfaces to the `java.sql` package. Instances of these types are valid only for the lifetime of the transaction in which they were created. These are the `java.sql.Blob` interface methods:

- `long length()`: Returns the number of bytes in the BLOB.
- `byte[] getBytes(long startPosition, int byteLength)`: Returns `byteLength` number of bytes of the BLOB data as a byte array starting at `startPosition` in the BLOB.
- `int setBytes(long startPosition, byte[] bytes)`: Writes bytes into the BLOB starting at the given position within the BLOB and returns the number of bytes written.

- `int setBytes(long startPosition, byte[] bytes, int offset, int length)`: Writes bytes into the BLOB starting at the given position within the BLOB, starting at the given byte array offset, using the given length of bytes, and returns the number of bytes written.
- `InputStream getBinaryStream()`: Returns a binary `InputStream` reference of this `BLOB`.
- `OutputStream setBinaryStream(long position)`: Obtains a stream handle for writing `BLOB` to output starting at a particular position in the `BLOB`.
- `void truncate(long length)`: Truncate the `BLOB` to the number of bytes in length.
- `long position(Blob blobPattern, long startPosition)`: Starting at the `startPosition` location in this `BLOB`, the position in the `BLOB` is returned where the associated `blobPattern` begins.
- `long position(byte[] bytePattern, long startPosition)`: Starting at the `startPosition` location in this `BLOB`, the position in the `BLOB` is returned where the associated `bytePattern` begins.

An analogous set of `Clob` methods exists in `java.sql.Clob`:

- `long length()`: Returns the number of characters in the `Clob`.
- `String getSubString(long startPosition, int charLength)`: Returns a `charLength` string of `CLOB` data as a `String` starting at `startPosition` in the `CLOB`.
- `int setString(long startPosition, String string)`: Writes a string into the `CLOB` starting at a particular `CLOB` position and returns the number of characters written.
- `int setString(long startPosition, String string, int offset, int length)`: Writes a string into the `CLOB` starting at a particular `CLOB` position, starting at the particular string offset, using the particular length of characters, and returns the number of characters written.
- `InputStream getAsciiStream()`: Returns an ASCII `InputStream` reference of this `CLOB`.
- `OutputStream setAsciiStream(long position)`: Obtains an ASCII stream handle for writing the `CLOB` to output starting at a particular position in the `CLOB`.
- `Reader getCharacterStream()`: Returns a Unicode Reader stream reference of this `CLOB`.
- `Writer setCharacterStream(long position)`: Obtains a Unicode writer handle for writing the `CLOB` to output starting at a particular position in the `CLOB`.

- `void truncate(long length)`: Truncates the `CLOB` to the number of characters in length.
- `long position(Clob clobPattern, long startPosition)`: Starting at the `startPosition` location in this `CLOB`, the position in the `CLOB` is returned where the associated `clobPattern` begins.
- `long position(String stringPattern, long startPosition`: Starting at the `startPosition` location in this `CLOB`, the position in the `CLOB` is returned where the associated `stringPattern` begins.

Retrieving `BLOB` or `CLOB` data from the database, through the `Blob` and `Clob` interfaces, is a simple matter of calling the `getBlob(int)`, `getBlob(String)`, `getClob(int)`, or `getClob(String)` methods on a `ResultSet` object when a particular set of `Blob` or `Clob` data is returned from the database. These methods are additions to the `ResultSet` class. For example:

```
Blob myBlob = resultSet.getBlob(1);
Blob myOtherBlob = resultSet.getBlob("BIG_PICTURE_FILE");
Clob myClob = resultSet.getClob(3);
Clob myOtherClob = resultSet.getClob("BIG_TEXT_FILE");
```

Storing `BLOB` or `CLOB` data is also a simple matter, using the `Blob` and `Clob` interfaces. By calling the `setBlob()` or `setClob()` methods on a `PreparedStatement`, you can submit a `Blob` or `Clob` update to the database. You can also use the `setBinaryStream()` or `setObject()` methods to set `Blob`s and the `setAsciiStream()`, `setUnicodeStream()`, or `setObject()` methods to set `Clob`s on a `PreparedStatement` object. Here's an example for setting `Blob`s and `Clob`s on some `PreparedStatement` object that was created to take four input parameters:

```
preparedStatement.setBlob(1, myBlob);
preparedStatement.setBinaryStream(2, myOtherBlob.getBinaryStream(),
➥myOtherBlob.length());
preparedStatement.setClob(3, myClob);
preparedStatement.setAsciiStream(4, myOtherClob.getAsciiStream(),
➥myOtherClob.length());
```

JDBC 3.0 lets you also update BLOB or CLOB data. By calling the setter methods on a `Blob` or `Clob`, you can submit a `Blob` or `Clob` update. You can determine whether `Blob` and `Clob` updates are allowed by your driver and database by calling the `DatabaseMetaData.locatorsUpdateCopy()` method, which returns `true` if such updates are allowed. Here's an example for updating a `Clob` using one of the aforementioned setter methods:

```
if(databaseMetaData.locatorsUpdateCopy()){
  // First retrieve a Clob in the form of a report
  String sqlString = "SELECT  REPORT  FROM CH06TYPES.CREDIT WHERE"+
➥ "CUSTOMER_ID_FK =101 AND ORDER_ID_FK = 1001 ";
```

```
    Statement statement = connection.createStatement();
    ResultSet rs = statement.executeQuery(sqlString);
    String settingMoreValue = "This is added to existing CLOB";
    boolean result = rs.next();
    // Now get the Clob handle
    Clob clob = null;
    if(result){
       clob = rs.getClob(1);
    }
    // Update the Clob as such
    clob.setString(clob.length(), settingMoreValue);
    rs.close();
    statement.close();
}
```

Updates to those columns in the database that are Blobs or Clobs can also be induced via use of new JDBC 3.0 methods added to updateable result sets. Thus, the `ResultSet.updateBlob(int columnIndex, Blob blob)` or `ResultSet.updateBlob(String columnName, Blob blob)` methods may be called to update `Blobs` given a `ResultSet` handle. Similarly, the `ResultSet.updateClob(int columnIndex, Clob clob)` or `ResultSet.updateClob(String columnName, Clob clob)` methods may be called to update `Clobs` given a `ResultSet` handle.

SQL Arrays

SQL arrays can also be manipulated in JDBC. SQL arrays are simply arrays of data, the lifetime of which is also bound to the enclosing transaction. An `Array` interface exists in the `java.sql` package to encapsulate the SQL array type. Type information about the SQL array elements can be obtained from the `getBaseType()` and `getBaseTypeName()` methods on the `Array` interface:

- `int getBaseType()` returns the `java.sql.Types` identifier identifying the elements of this SQL array.
- `String getBaseTypeName()` returns the SQL type name associated with the elements of this SQL array.

The `Array` interface can also be used to map the SQL array into a form usable by Java programs. The array may thus be retrieved as an `Object` referencing a regular Java array or as a `ResultSet` object in which each row in the `ResultSet` corresponds to an element in the SQL array. Either the entire array contents can be retrieved for each of these Java types or a subset of the SQL array can be retrieved with a given start index of the array and a desired array length. The `Object` and `ResultSet` types of arrays can be retrieved completely or as a subset of the SQL array also by passing in a `java.util.Map` object, which specifies how each SQL type name maps to a Java class.

When no `java.util.Map` object is provided, a default SQL type to Java mapping is assumed. These methods are defined here:

- `Object getArray()` returns the Java `Object` form of array.
- `ResultSet getResultSet()` returns the Java `ResultSet` form of array.
- `Object getArray(long startElement, int arraySize)` returns a subset of the Java `Object` form of array beginning at the `startElement` index and for an `arraySize` number of elements.
- `ResultSet getResultSet(long startElement, int arraySize)` returns a subset of the Java `ResultSet` form of the array beginning at the `startElement` index and for an `arraySize` number of elements.
- `Object getArray(Map map)` returns the Java `Object` form of the array according to the `Map` object.
- `ResultSet getResultSet(Map map)` returns the Java `ResultSet` form of the array according to the `Map` object.
- `Object getArray(long startElement, int arraySize, Map map)` returns a subset of the Java `Object` form of array beginning at the `startElement` index, for an `arraySize` number of elements, and according to the `Map` object translating between SQL type names and Java classes to which they map.
- `ResultSet getResultSet(long index, int count, Map map)` returns a subset of the Java `ResultSet` form of the array beginning at the `startElement` index, for an `arraySize` number of elements, and according to the `Map` object translating between SQL type names and Java classes to which they map.

You can obtain a reference to a SQL array retrieved from a database query from the `ResultSet` class's `getArray()` methods. For example, to obtain `Array` objects from columns 1 and 2 in a `ResultSet`, you would use this:

```
Array myArray = resultSet.getArray(1);
Array myOtherArray = resultSet.getArray(2);
```

You can store such arrays using the `setArray()` method on the `PreparedStatement` or the `setObject()` method. For example:

```
preparedStatement.setArray(1, myArray);
```

You can also update arrays using the `updateArray()` methods added to `ResultSet` in JDBC 3.0:

```
resultSet.updateArray("PAGE_HITS, myArray);
```

SQL Structures

SQL structured types provide a C++ or IDL-like means for encapsulating a collection of data types into a unified structure. Such a structure becomes a new type in and of itself.

In Java-land, we can think of a structured type as a Java class with only public member variables. SQL structured types are encapsulated by a `java.sql.Struct` interface in JDBC. The methods on the `Struct` interface are quite simple:

- `String getSQLTypeName()` returns the name of the SQL type represented by this `Struct` object.
- `Object[] getAttributes()` returns an `Object` array of attribute values from this `Struct` object. This method assumes a default mapping of SQL types to Java types for each element returned in the `Object` array.
- `Object[] getAttributes(Map map)` returns an `Object` array with each array element containing a Java class instance that is mapped according to the `java.util.Map` object specifying how each SQL type maps to a Java class.

Structured types are retrieved from `ResultSet` objects using `getObject()` and are persisted to the database using `setObject()` on `PreparedStatement` objects. For example:

```
Struct ipHostStruct = (Struct) resultSet.getObject("IP_HOST_STRUCTURE");
    ...
preparedStatement.setObject(1, ipHostStruct);
```

The `DatabaseMetaData.getUDTs()` method can be used to obtain a description of the `Struct` types that are currently defined in the database given a catalog name, a schema name pattern, a type name pattern, and an `int` array with the `java.sql.Types.STRUCT` identifier as an element.

SQL Distinct Types

As mentioned previously, `Distinct` types are useful when you want to alias SQL types with another type name. There is no specific `Distinct` interface added to the JDBC interface. Distinct types may be created in the database using a SQL statement of the form `CREATE TYPE <DISTINCT_ALIAS_NAME> AS <EXISTING_SQL_NAME>`. For example:

```
statement.execute("CREATE TYPE CITY AS VARCHAR(25)");
```

A `Distinct` type can be retrieved from a database query `ResultSet` via the `get`*`XXX`*`()` method for whatever type the `Distinct` type aliases. Likewise, a `Distinct` type can be used in a database update statement making the appropriate `set`*`XXX`*`()` calls on a `PreparedStatement`. For example:

```
String myCity = resultSet.getString("CITY");
    ...
preparedStatement.setString("CITY", myCity);
```

The `DatabaseMetaData.getUDTs()` method can be used to obtain a description of the `Distinct` types that are currently defined in the database given a catalog name, a schema name pattern, a type name pattern, and an `int` array with the `java.sql.Types.DISTINCT` identifier as an element.

SQL References

SQL99 references to persistent data are encapsulated by the `Ref` interface in the `java.sql` package. The `Ref` interface has a method called `getBaseTypeName()`, which returns a `String` that identifies the SQL type it references. `Ref` objects can be retrieved from a `ResultSet` object using the `getRef()` method. The data associated with this reference is not retrieved until the reference is dereferenced. Reference objects are valid for the lifetime of the connection in which they were created. A `Ref` object may also be persisted to the database using the `setRef()` method on a `PreparedStatement`.

The object referenced by the `Ref` object can be dereferenced and converted from a SQL structured type into a Java `Object` via a call to `Ref.getObject()`. The conversion may be driven by either a type map defined inside the `Connection` object (as we'll soon learn about in the section on "Custom Types"), or by default to a `java.sql.Struct` object. Alternately, a `Ref.getObject(Map)` method can be used to drive such a conversion with a `java.util.Map` of SQL type names mapped to Java classes. The referenced data may also be set into the Ref object as a SQL structured type by invoking the `Ref.setObject(Object)` method. Finally, an updateable result set may update a `Ref` object via calls to a `ResultSet` object's `updateRef(int, Ref)` or `updateRef(Sting, Ref)` methods.

SQL Datalinks

SQL99 allows one to define a datalink type that represents a link to a file existing outside of the database. Such links are commonly represented as `java.net.URL` objects when retrieved from a database. Thus, the `ResultSet.getURL()` methods let you obtain handles to such links as returned `URL` objects. The `ResultSet.getString()` methods may also be used to provide a `String` form of the datalink value. Datalinks may be stored inside of a database, and the `setURL(int, URL)` or `setString(int, String)` methods on `PreparedStatement` objects expose a way to do this when using prepared statements.

Custom Types

The SQL99 types supported by JDBC offer a means for mapping user-defined SQL types that are stored to and retrieved from a relational database to types that can be used by your Java applications. When describing custom types to the database via JDBC, the `java.util.Map` class is used to map user-defined SQL types to Java classes. Each SQL type name is mapped to a `java.lang.Class` instance. If you want to override the standard type mappings from SQL type to Java type, you can do this at the connection level by calling `setTypeMap()` on the connection object with the desired type mapping. The map for that connection may be retrieved by calling `getTypeMap()`. Various statement and result set calls associated with the connection may override the connection's mapping.

When creating a new Java class that is mapped to the database in this custom fashion, that class must implement the `java.sql.SQLData` interface. The `SQLData` interface requires that a `getSQLTypeName()` method, `readSQL()` method, and `writeSQL()` method be implemented. The `getSQLTypeName()` method must simply return a user-defined SQL type name represented by the Java class.

Third-party vendors will ideally provide the automated mapping of SQL types to Java classes given a user-defined mapping. Such tools would use a design-time set of properties to create the actual `java.util.Map` object and automatically generate the user-defined Java classes that implement the `SQLData` interface. As JDBC 2.0 and 3.0 compliance becomes more widespread and as IDE vendors provide greater levels of support for the Java 2 platform, such automated processes will become more prevalent. In lieu of that level of support, we briefly describe and subsequently demonstrate how to implement the `SQLData` interface for a user-defined class.

The `writeSQL()` method of the `SQLData` interface takes a `SQLOutput` stream object as a parameter. This method is called when the custom class is being dumped to a SQL data stream (that is, during persistence of the Java object to the database). The Java class-specific `writeSQL()` method must make a series of `write`*`XXX`*`()` calls on the `SQLOutput` stream to write each fundamental element of the class to the stream. A different `write`*`XXX`*`()` method exists on the `SQLOutput` interface for all the most fundamental Java to SQL type mappings that exist in JDBC (for example, `writeString()` and `writeBlob()`). For Java classes that contain Java class field members whose SQL type mappings represent a nonfundamental SQL type, it too must implement the `SQLData` interface, and `writeSQL()` must be called on it when writing the parent class to the stream. This all must be done in the order in which the types are defined in the SQL type structure.

The `readSQL()` method on the `SQLData` interface takes a `SQLInput` object and `String` object as input parameters. This method is used to stream the database data into the user-defined Java object implementing this method. The `String` object passed into this method simply identifies the SQL type for which the associated `SQLInput` stream is containing. The actual streaming of data from `SQLInput` into the Java object is accomplished by calling a series of `read`*`XXX`*`()` methods on the `SQLInput` object according to the order in which each SQL type is defined in the SQL structure. In addition to the `read`*`XXX`*`()` methods defined on the `SQLInput` interface, a `wasNull()` method is defined that can be used to return a `boolean` value indicating whether the last value read from the stream was null. A class implementing `readSQL()` calls `read`*`XXX`*`()` on the `SQLInput` object for all fundamental JDBC SQL types or `readSQL()` on a member object that is not a fundamental JDBC type.

A database may also perform its own mapping of underlying data to a particular returned application type. Such database-provided mappings are referred to as "transform groups" and are now supportable in JDBC 3.0. Thus, if no mapping has been provided for such a custom type, the `ResultSetMetaData.getColumnClassName()` method can return a `String` name for the fully qualified Java class type based on the mapping information provided by the database's transform group.

Extending the BeeShirts.com Example Data Model

To demonstrate some of the neat newer features of the JDBC data types, we've extended the BeeShirts.com data model. Figure 6.1 depicts this new model. Here we see that three new entities have been added to the model. First we see a `TSHIRT` table added, which provides extra information specific to T-shirts above and beyond the `ITEM` table. The `TSHIRT` table references the `ITEM` table that it extends with extra data. The `TSHIRT` table contains two SQL `BLOB` types that refer to pictures to be contained on the front and back of a T-shirt. The `CREDIT` table represents credit information related to a customer's particular order. This `CREDIT` table contains a `CHARGE_CARD_TYPE` to be defined as a new SQL type in the database. The `CHARGE_CARD_TYPE` contains information related to a charge card used in a purchase.

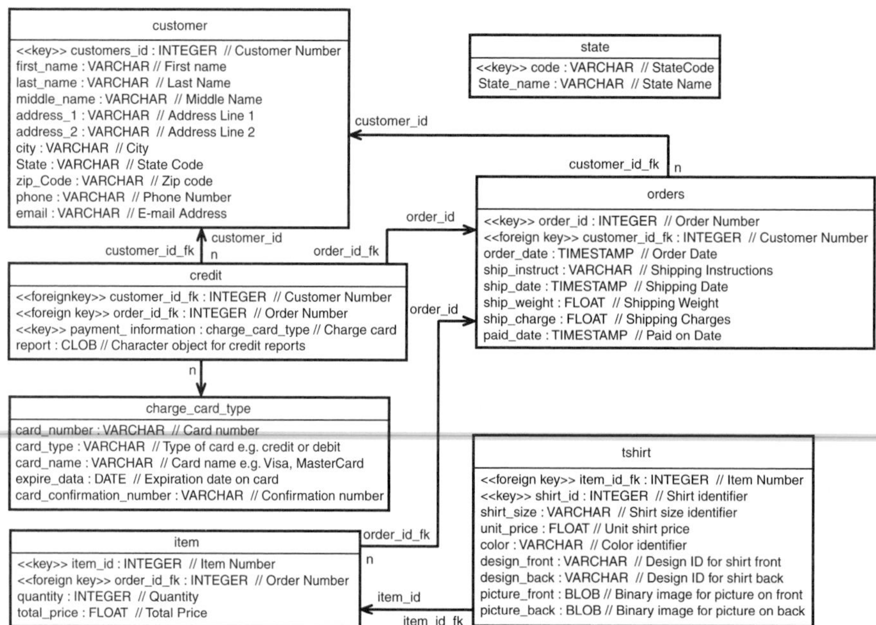

Figure 6.1 The BeeShirts.com customer, orders, items, T-shirt, credit, and charge-card data model.

As an example to illustrate advanced types, the `CHARGE_CARD_TYPE` might be configured in your database to illustrate custom SQL types with the following command:

```
CREATE OR REPLACE TYPE CH06TYPES.CHARGE_CARD_TYPE AS OBJECT(
   CARD_TYPE VARCHAR2(6) ,
   CARD_NAME VARCHAR2(8) ,
   CARD_NUMBER VARCHAR2(20) ,
   EXPIRE_DATE DATE ,
```

```
   CARD_CONFIRMATION_NUMBER VARCHAR2(20)
   )
```

The CREDIT table may then use this new type and also incorporate a CLOB via the following SQL command:

```
CREATE TABLE "CH06TYPES"."CREDIT"(
   "CUSTOMER_ID_FK" NUMBER(8),
   "ORDER_ID_FK" NUMBER(8),
   "REPORT" CLOB,
   "PAYMENT_INFORMATION" "CH06TYPES"."CHARGE_CARD_TYPE"
   ) TABLESPACE "USERS";
```

Finally, the TSHIRT table may be constructed to illustrate use of Blobs via the following SQL command:

```
--- CREATE TABLE TSHIRT
CREATE TABLE "CH06TYPES"."TSHIRT"
   ("ITEM_ID_FK" NUMBER(8),
   "SHIRT_ID" NUMBER(8),
   "SIZE" VARCHAR2(5),
    UNIT_PRICE FLOAT,
   "COLOR" VARCHAR2(10),
   "DESIGN_FRONT" VARCHAR2(10),
   "DESIGN_BACK" VARCHAR2(10),
   "PICTURE_FRONT" BLOB,
   "PICTURE_BACK" BLOB,
  "SUPPLIER_ID_FK" NUMBER(8),
    PRIMARY KEY("SHIRT_ID")
   )  TABLESPACE "USERS";
```

Note

Figure 6.1 depicts the BeeShirts.com data model used to illustrate a few of the advanced data types described in this chapter. Appendix A provides instructions for configuring a database to utilize such a model. However, because of limited JDBC driver support for such features at the time of this writing, the actual data model assumed for use by the remaining chapters in this book differs slightly from the one presented in Figure 6.1. Thus, the TSHIRT, CREDIT, and CHARGE_CARD_TYPE database structures used in the examples that follow all are defined inside of a separate database schema namespace referred to as CH06TYPES.

One key difference is that the CHARGE_CARD_TYPE used for this chapter's examples is configured as a regular database table for use in other chapters, whereas for this chapter it is configured as a SQL structure. The CREDIT table thus maintains a foreign key to the CHARGE_CARD_TYPE table. Another key difference is this chapter's assumption that the TSHIRT table defines BLOB types for the PICTURE_FRONT and PICTURE_BACK columns. Other chapters assume that these two columns are of the VARCHAR type defining filenames of binary image data rather than containing the binary image data itself in the form of a BLOB type. Furthermore, this chapter also assumes that the CREDIT table defines a CLOB type for the REPORT column, whereas this column is neither defined nor used in other chapters.

Appendix A provides an overview of the complete data model assumed by the BeeShirts.com examples used throughout the remaining chapters of this book. Appendix A also describes how to configure a database to work with this chapter's advanced JDBC examples.

Example: Using the Advanced SQL Types with JDBC

This next example demonstrates how to use a few JDBC advanced data type features. The example code is contained in the `ejava.jdbc.advanced.NewSQLTypeExample` class, which extends the `ejava.jdbc.advanced.ConnectToDatabase` class, and the `ejava.jdbc.advanced.ChargeCard.java` class:

```
public class NewSQLTypeExample extends ConnectToDatabase { ... }
```

Note

The complete set of code examples for the `NewSQLTypeExample` and `ChargeCard` can be located as described in Appendix A and extracted to the `examples\src\ejava\jdbc\advanced` directory. Some exception handling and other handling mechanisms have been left out of the book here for simplicity but can be found in the complete examples. The `runnewsqltypes` example script generated during the ANT build can be used to execute this example. Appendix A describes the general build procedures for all examples in the book and specifies those common environment variables that must be set to execute our example scripts.

Note that at the time of this writing, support for advanced SQL types was not fully adopted by all database and JDBC driver vendors. Consult Appendix A for more information on support and the vendor product with which you can test the `NewSQLTypeExample`.

The `main()` method of `NewSQLTypeExample` is invoked like this:

```
java ejava.jdbc.advanced.NewSQLTypeExample
```

The `main()` method reads Java preferences and instantiates a new `NewSQLTypeExample` object. The `main()` method calls `NewSQLTypeExample` instance methods that demonstrate how to insert and retrieve a `BLOB`, how to insert and retrieve a structured type, how to insert and retrieve a `CLOB`, and the manipulation of a custom type that handles `SQLData`:

```
public static void main(String[] args)
{
  Preferences preferences = Preferences.userNodeForPackage(
                    ejava.jdbc.advanced.ConnectToDatabase.class);

  NewSQLTypeExample newSqlTypeExample = new NewSQLTypeExample();
    ...
    System.out.println(" Blob Type Insert Example ");
    String blobTypeInsert =
```

```
    preferences.get("INSERT_A_BLOB_TYPE_STATEMENT",null);
  newSqlTypeExample.insertABLOBtype(blobTypeInsert);

  System.out.println(" Blob Type Retrieval Example ");
  String blobTypeRetrieve =
    preferences.get("RETRIEVE_A_BLOB_TYPE_STATEMENT",null);
  newSqlTypeExample.retrieveBLOBtype(blobTypeRetrieve);

  System.out.println(" Struct Type Insert Example ");
  String structTypeInsert =
    preferences.get("INSERT_STRUCT_TYPE_STATEMENT",null);
  newSqlTypeExample.insertAStructTypeData(structTypeInsert);

  System.out.println(" Struct Type Retrieval Example ");
  String structTypeRetrieve =
    preferences.get("RETRIEVE_STRUCT_TYPE_STATEMENT",null);
  newSqlTypeExample.retrieveAStructTypeData(structTypeRetrieve);

  System.out.println(" Clob Type Insert Example ");
  String clobTypeInsert =
    preferences.get("INSERT_A_CLOB_TYPE_STATEMENT",null);
  newSqlTypeExample.insertACLOBtype(clobTypeInsert);

  System.out.println(" Clob Type Retrieval Example ");
  String clobTypeRetrieve =
    preferences.get("RETRIEVE_A_CLOB_TYPE_STATEMENT",null);
  newSqlTypeExample.retrieveCLOBtype(clobTypeRetrieve);

  System.out.println(" ChargeCard Type Mapping Example");
  newSqlTypeExample.mapCardClassToSQLTypes();

  System.out.println(" ChargeCard Type Insertion Example ");
  newSqlTypeExample.insertCardTypeData();

  System.out.println(" ChargeCard Type Retrieval Example ");
  newSqlTypeExample.retrieveCardTypeData();

  ...
}
```

The `build.properties` file has properties used by the `NewSQLTypeExample` for the advanced SQL type insert and retrieval SQL statements:

```
# Insert a BLOB Type
sql.insert.blob.type = UPDATE CH06TYPES.TSHIRT SET PICTURE_FRONT = ?
➥ WHERE SHIRT_ID = 10
```

```
# Retrieve a BLOB Type
sql.retrieve.blob.type = SELECT   PICTURE_FRONT FROM  CH06TYPES.TSHIRT
➥ WHERE SHIRT_ID = 10

# Insert a STRUCT Type
sql.insert.sqlObject.type = INSERT INTO CH06TYPES.CREDIT VALUES
➥ ('101', '1001', EMPTY_CLOB(),CH06TYPES.CHARGE_CARD_TYPE
➥ ('CREDIT','VISA','1234567890123456','11-Oct-2003',
➥ '1234567890123456') )

# Retrieve a STRUCT TYPE
sql.retrieve.sqlObject.type = SELECT * FROM CH06TYPES.CREDIT
➥ WHERE CUSTOMER_ID_FK =101 AND ORDER_ID_FK = 1001

# Insert a CLOB TYPE
sql.insert.clob.type = UPDATE CH06TYPES.CREDIT SET REPORT = ?
➥ WHERE CUSTOMER_ID_FK =101 AND ORDER_ID_FK = 1001

# Retrieve a CLOB TYPE
sql.retrieve.clob.type =SELECT  REPORT  FROM CH06TYPES.CREDIT
➥ WHERE CUSTOMER_ID_FK =101 AND ORDER_ID_FK = 1001
```

The `insertABLOBType()` method takes an update `String` that was read from the properties file and sets a large binary image onto a prepared statement. The prepared statement is then executed. Later, when the `retrieveBLOBType()` method is called, the BLOB is gotten from the result set and restored to a file. BLOB inserts and retrievals are shown here:

```
public void insertABLOBtype(String updateString)
  throws SQLException, Exception
{
  PreparedStatement preparedStatement = getStatement(updateString);
  byte[] dataInFile = readFile("blobExample.gif");
  preparedStatement.setBytes(1,dataInFile);
  boolean result = preparedStatement.execute();
}

private byte[] readFile(String fileToRead)
  throws Exception
{
  File f = new File(fileToRead);
  int lengthofFile = (int) f.length();
  byte[] dataInFile = new byte[lengthofFile];
  FileInputStream fin = new FileInputStream(f);
  fin.read(dataInFile);
  return dataInFile;
}
```

```
public void retrieveBLOBtype(String queryString)
  throws SQLException, Exception
{
  Statement statement = getStatement();
  ResultSet rs = statement.executeQuery(queryString);

  while (rs.next()) {
    Blob blob = rs.getBlob(1);
    InputStream inputStream = blob.getBinaryStream();

    // open the stream to read data from Blob reference
    long length = blob.length();

    // Write Blob to file
    byte[] x = new byte[LOB_DATA_BUFFER_SIZE];
    int lengthRead = 0;
    String blobFile = "blobExample1.gif";
    FileOutputStream outputStream = new FileOutputStream(blobFile);
    while ((lengthRead =  inputStream.read(x)) != -1) {
      outputStream.write(x,0, lengthRead);
    }
    inputStream.close();
    outputStream.close();

    // Display Blob (see our simple ImageReader class)
    System.out.println(" About to display Blob ");
    (new ImageReader()).render("blobExample1.gif");
  }
}
```

Inserting structured types is demonstrated via a call to the `insertAStructTypeData()` method from `main()`. The subsequent retrieval of a structured type from `retrieveAStructTypeData()` illustrates how to reconstruct the restored `Struct` from the database. Both insert and retrieval are shown here:

```
public void insertAStructTypeData(String insertString)
  throws SQLException, Exception
{
  Statement statement = getStatement();
  int nRows = statement.executeUpdate(insertString);
  System.out.println(" Number rows written: " + nRows);
}

public void retrieveAStructTypeData(String queryString)
  throws SQLException, Exception
{
  Statement statement = getStatement();
```

```
  ResultSet rs = statement.executeQuery(queryString);
  ResultSetMetaData rsMetaData = rs.getMetaData();

  while (rs.next()) {
    for (int i = 1 ; i <= rsMetaData.getColumnCount(); i++) {
      int type = rsMetaData.getColumnType(i);

      switch (type) {

        case Types.STRUCT:
          System.out.println("Struct Type Value is :");
          Struct s = (Struct) rs.getObject(i);
          String structTypeName = s.getSQLTypeName();
          Object[] contents = s.getAttributes();
          for (int j = 0; j < contents.length; j++) {
            System.out.println(contents[j]);
          }

          break;
        default:
          System.out.println("Non Struct Type Value :"+
                                      rs.getObject(i));
          break;
      }
    }
  }
}
```

The `insertACLOBType()` method takes an update `String` that was read from the properties file and sets a large character image onto a prepared statement. The prepared statement is then executed. Later, when the `retrieveCLOBType()` method is called, the CLOB is gotten from the result set and restored to a file. CLOB inserts and retrievals are shown here:

```
public void insertACLOBtype(String updateString)
  throws SQLException, Exception
{
  PreparedStatement preparedStatement = getStatement(updateString);
  byte[] dataInFile = readFile("clobExample.txt");
  preparedStatement.setBytes(1,dataInFile);
  boolean result = preparedStatement.execute();
}
public void retrieveCLOBtype(String queryString)
  throws SQLException, Exception
{
  Statement statement = getStatement();
  ResultSet rs = statement.executeQuery(queryString);
```

```
  for(int i = 0; rs.next(); ++i) {
    Clob c = rs.getClob(1);
    InputStream inputStream = c.getAsciiStream();

    // open the stream to read data from Clob reference
    long length = c.length();

    byte[] x = new byte[LOB_DATA_BUFFER_SIZE];

    // Create byte array to hold the clob data
    int lengthRead = 0;     // Number of bytes read

    String clobFile = "clobExample" + i + ".txt";
    FileOutputStream outputStream = new FileOutputStream(clobFile);

    while ((lengthRead = inputStream.read(x)) != -1) {
      outputStream.write(x);
    }

    inputStream.close();
    outputStream.close();
  }
}
```

To illustrate the use of a custom type with the database, we have provided a simple `ChargeCard` type. `ChargeCard` defines methods for returning its SQL type name, reading SQLData streams, and writing SQLData streams. The `ChargeCard` class is shown here:

```
public class ChargeCard implements SQLData
{
  public String cardType;
  public String cardName;
  public String cardNumber;
  public Date   expireDate;
  public String cardConfirmationNumber;
  public String sqlType;

  public ChargeCard()
  {
  }

  public ChargeCard(String sqlType, String cardType,
             String cardName, String cardNumber,
             Date expireDate , String cardConfirmationNumber )
  {
    this.cardType = cardType;
```

```
    this.cardName = cardName;
    this.cardNumber = cardNumber;
    this.expireDate = expireDate;
    this.cardConfirmationNumber = cardConfirmationNumber;
    this.sqlType = sqlType;
  }
  public String getSQLTypeName()
  {
    return sqlType;
  }

  public void readSQL(SQLInput stream, String type)
    throws SQLException
  {
    cardType = stream.readString();
    cardName = stream.readString();
    cardNumber = stream.readString();
    expireDate = stream.readDate();
    cardConfirmationNumber = stream.readString();
    sqlType = type;
  }

  public void writeSQL(SQLOutput stream)
    throws SQLException
  {
    stream.writeString(cardType);
    stream.writeString(cardName);
    stream.writeString(cardNumber);
    stream.writeDate(expireDate);
    stream.writeString(cardConfirmationNumber);
  }

  public String toString()
  {
    String rString = " ChargeCard Type contents = { "
      + "cardType :" + cardType + "cardName :" + cardName
      + "cardNumber" + cardNumber + "expireDate :"
      + expireDate + "cardConfirmationNumber :"
      + cardConfirmationNumber + " }";
  }
}
```

Such a custom `ChargeCard` type is registered with the connection from within the `NewSQLTypeExample` `mapCardClassToSQLTypes()` method. A `ChargeCard` instance is inserted into the database from the `insertCardTypeData()` method.

Finally, `ChargeCard` data is retrieved from the database from within the `retrieveCardTypeData()` method. Each custom type demonstration method is shown here:

```
public void mapCardClassToSQLTypes()
  throws SQLException, Exception
{
  Connection connection = super.getConnection();
  Map map = connection.getTypeMap();

  map.put("CH06TYPES.CHARGE_CARD_TYPE",
          Class.forName("ejava.jdbc.advanced.ChargeCard"));
}

public void insertCardTypeData()
  throws SQLException, Exception
{
  String insertString =
    "INSERT INTO CH06TYPES.CREDIT VALUES( 200, 2002 , "+
    "'EMPTY_CLOB()', ?) ";
  Date expirationDate = Date.valueOf("2004-10-10");
  ChargeCard chargeCard =
    new ChargeCard("CH06TYPES.CHARGE_CARD_TYPE", "CREDIT", "VISA",
                   "123456789012", expirationDate,
                   "123456789012");
  PreparedStatement preparedStatement = getStatement(insertString);
  preparedStatement.setObject(1, chargeCard, Types.STRUCT);
  boolean result = preparedStatement.execute();
}

public void retrieveCardTypeData()
  throws SQLException, Exception
{
  String retrieveData =
    "SELECT * FROM CH06TYPES.CREDIT WHERE"
    + " CUSTOMER_ID_FK =101 AND ORDER_ID_FK = 1001 ";
  Statement statement = getStatement();
  ResultSet rs = statement.executeQuery(retrieveData);

  while (rs.next()) {
    ChargeCard c = (ChargeCard) rs.getObject(4);
    System.out.println(c);
  }
}
```

Row Sets

The JDBC 2.0 specification first introduced the `javax.sql.RowSet` interface. The `RowSet` interface encapsulates a set of rows retrieved from a relational database akin to a `ResultSet`. The `RowSet` interface actually extends the `ResultSet` interface and adds the capability to be used as a JavaBean in an IDE environment. Arguably, this capability to be manipulated as a JavaBean is the sole distinction between a `RowSet` and a `ResultSet`.

Row Set Architecture

The diagram in Figure 6.2 depicts the main relations and methods involved with `RowSet` interfaces in the `javax.sql` package. As you can see from the diagram, `RowSet` interfaces extend the `ResultSet` interface and can return or be initialized with meta-data about its contents via a `RowSetMetaData` interface that extends the `ResultSetMetaData` interface. `RowSetMetaData` is used to initialize the state of a `RowSet` if it offers a `RowSetInternal` handle on its interior state. Readers and writers of row sets from and to data sources implement the `RowSetReader` and `RowSetWriter` interfaces, respectively, and use the `RowSetInternal` interface to accomplish their task. Finally, `RowSet` objects can have zero or more `RowSetListener` objects associated with them to listen for row set events encapsulated by `RowSetEvent` objects.

When using `RowSet` objects in an IDE environment, you can associate a series of design-time Bean properties with a `RowSet`. Properties such as SQL to Java type maps, data sources, database URLs, and transaction isolation levels can all be set and associated with a `RowSet` Bean during design time. For such properties, JavaBeans-compliant `getter` and `setter` methods must be present on the `RowSet`. `RowSetListener` objects can be added to a `RowSet` using the `RowSet.addRowSetListener()` method. Three types of `RowSetEvent` objects are of interest to objects implementing the `RowSetListener` interface. Row set change events signify that an entire `RowSet` has changed, whereas row change events signify a change in only one row of the row set. Cursor movement events signify that the cursor in a row set has moved to another row in the row set.

`RowSet` objects may also be used during runtime as a key point of interface for JDBC API clients. The `RowSet` may be used in such a way that `Statement` objects and `ResultSet` objects become irrelevant to the JDBC programmer. SQL commands may be set on the `RowSet`, executed via the `RowSet`, retrieve any command execution results to populate the `RowSet`, and subsequently provide an interface to traverse the data in a `RowSet`.

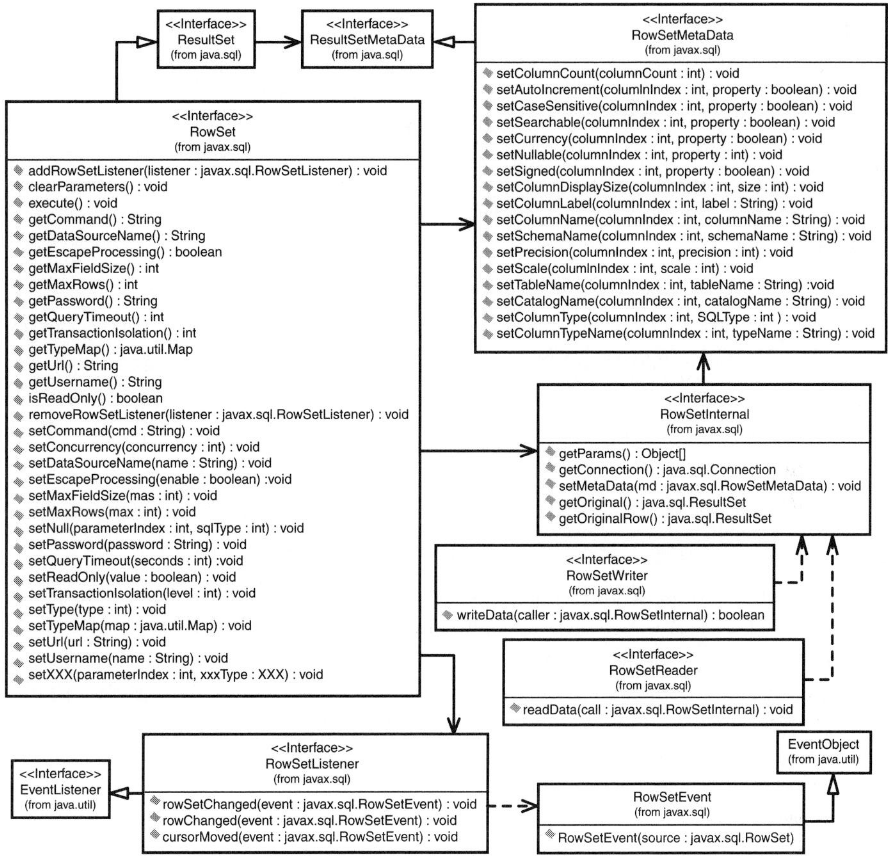

Figure 6.2 A `RowSet` and `RowSetMetaData` class diagram.

Using Row Sets

The `setCommand()` method on a `RowSet` can be set with a SQL `String` parameterized with question mark (?) input parameters. A series of `setXXX()` calls on the `RowSet` interface can then be used to set the value for each parameter according to the parameter position in the command `String` akin to the way `PreparedStatement` objects are set. For example:

```
rowSet.setCommand("SELECT * FROM CUSTOMER WHERE FIRST_NAME = ?");
rowSet.setString(1, "Roy");
rowSet.execute();
```

Scrolling forward and backward through `RowSet` objects and obtaining data from `RowSet` objects is accomplished the same way as for `ResultSet` objects. Again, the big bonus for using RowSet objects is that they can be used as a JavaBean. Different RowSet implementations may require or relax requirements for certain properties to be set. Because this will be implementation dependent, you should consult your RowSet vendor's documentation for the RowSet's precise requirements.

RowSet implementations may be provided by IDE vendors, JDBC driver vendors, or middleware vendors, or you may indeed decide to implement your own RowSet interface. Following are examples of candidate RowSet implementations:

- A Cached RowSet that can be serialized and cached inside of a JDBC client sans any cursor connectivity back to the database.
- A JDBC RowSet that maintains a connection to the database and simply serves as a JavaBeans-compliant wrapper of a ResultSet.
- A Web RowSet that provides a thin interface for Web-based clients whereby the Web RowSet communicates via HTTP to a back-end Web server for providing database access.

Managing Internal Row Set State and Behavior

The RowSetInternal interface may be implemented by a RowSet to expose some of its internal field members to another object for viewing or updating those values. Values such as the RowSet connection, the original state of the RowSet, and an array of parameters set on the RowSet may all be retrieved. Additionally, a RowSetMetaData object may also be set onto the RowSet if it implements the RowSetInternal interface.

By setting RowSetMetaData onto a RowSet, key meta-data values can be set onto the RowSet object to instruct the RowSet how to behave when retrieving and updating data. Such information as automatic column numbering, case sensitivity, column counts, column names, column types, searchability, and associated schema, catalog, and table names may all be set onto a RowSetMetaData object.

A RowSet object can call an object that implements a RowSetReader interface. The RowSetReader has one method called readData(), which takes a RowSetInternal object and uses it to populate the contents of a RowSet with new data or a data update. Similarly, a RowSet may call a RowSetWriter object's writedata() method with a RowSetInternal object in order to have the RowSetWriter write the RowSet contents to a data source. Such de-coupling of data source reader/writer capabilities can offer flexibility in delegating how data is retrieved or persisted to an underlying reader/writer.

Container-Based JDBC

Up to this point, we have seen how JDBC clients can talk directly to a database via a JDBC driver. The process of creating JDBC connections this way tends to be somewhat repetitious, however, with larger or heavily data-centric applications. These types of applications will often be architected as three-tiered applications, in which the database is one tier, the client application is another tier, and the database access code is contained within the middle tier. For this reason, many J2EE application containers provide their own database connection management facilities, which can provide performance optimizations such as connection pooling, and configuration of drivers through a standard XML-based deployment descriptor. The JDBC API contains some additional features that allow applications to take advantage of these container-provided facilities. Figure 6.3 depicts the concepts involved with clients accessing a database via container-based JDBC.

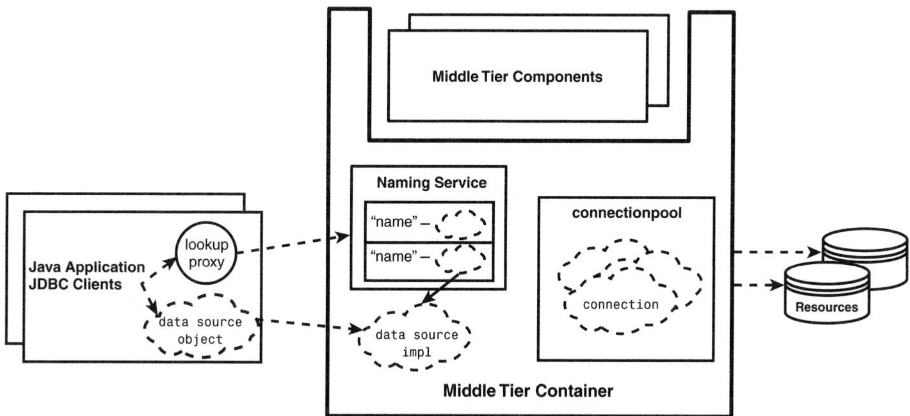

Figure 6.3 Middle-tier database access.

A middle-tier container will typically pool connections to a database for reasons of efficiency and scalability. That is, by keeping a pool of connections available, the middle tier can serve live database connections to distributed clients on demand and send the connections back to the pool when the client is finished using the connection.

An intermediate proxy to the connection that encapsulates the concept of a database handle is implemented by a data source object in the middle tier. The middle tier binds human readable names to proxy object handles of such data sources using a naming service. The JDBC client then looks up such handles to data source objects using such a naming service. After the client obtains a data source handle, a proxy to a connection can then be requested from the data source handle. Because the middle tier then doles out such a connection as just described, the JDBC client reaps the advantages of connection pooling completely transparently.

As you'll see throughout the remainder of this chapter, JDBC 3.0 provides abstractions that address all the features just mentioned and represented in Figure 6.3. Thus, the subsequent sections in this chapter discuss JDBC representations of data sources as well of connection pooling features that operate both within and outside of distributed transactions.

Data Sources

The JDBC 3.0 standard defines a means for being able to bind a name to a database reference held presumably by some server-side middle-tier entity or by some JavaBean provider. A database client can then obtain a handle to the database reference by using a simple name. This means of obtaining database references in essence replaces the need for using a `DriverManager` to register drivers and using database URLs to obtain a `Connection`. This alternative means for encapsulating database references is embodied in the `javax.sql.DataSource` interface. The `DataSource` interface is implemented by driver vendors to serve as a factory for creating and doling out JDBC connections to clients.

JNDI and Data Sources

So how does one obtain a handle to a `DataSource`? The answer lies in understanding the basic lookup features supported by the Java Naming and Directory Interface (JNDI). JNDI is a set of APIs that are part of the J2SE and J2EE used to provide a standard interface to naming and directory services. Naming services provide a mechanism for binding human-readable names to objects and resolving objects to names. Directory services are similar to naming services with the exception that more sophisticated object searching is provided. Basically, you can think of things like file systems that map filenames to and from file objects as naming services. Chapter 11, "Naming Services: JNDI," discusses naming services, and Chapter 12, "Directory Services: JNDI," discusses directory services in detail. For now, suffice it to say that JNDI provides a standard interface to access various resources within a system by looking them up by name.

JNDI clients talk to a naming or directory service that often sits physically inside of a separate process. JNDI clients obtain a handle to a naming or directory service by creating an initial context using the `javax.naming.InitialContext` class as shown in Figure 6.4.

The `InitialContext` class implements the `javax.naming.Context` interface and has methods on it to bind an object to the naming service with a name and to look up an object in the naming service given a name. `DataSource` objects are database resource handles that are registered with a naming service via JNDI. A middle-tier server often performs the registration of `DataSource` objects transparent to the JDBC client. After a handle to a `DataSource` object is retrieved from JNDI, a `DataSource.getConnection()` method is called to obtain a database connection.

> **The J2EE and JDBC 3.0**
>
> Use of JNDI is the primary means by which J2EE components obtain handles to JDBC `DataSource` objects and subsequently obtain JDBC `Connection` handles. Such a mechanism will be demonstrated throughout Part V, "Enterprise Web Enabling," and Part VI, "Enterprise Applications Enabling," when we describe how Java Servlets, JavaServer Pages, and Enterprise JavaBeans obtain JDBC 3.0 `DataSource` handles from their middle-tier container/server environments. Use of such features also best enables a middle-tier J2EE server environment to manage database connection resource pools.

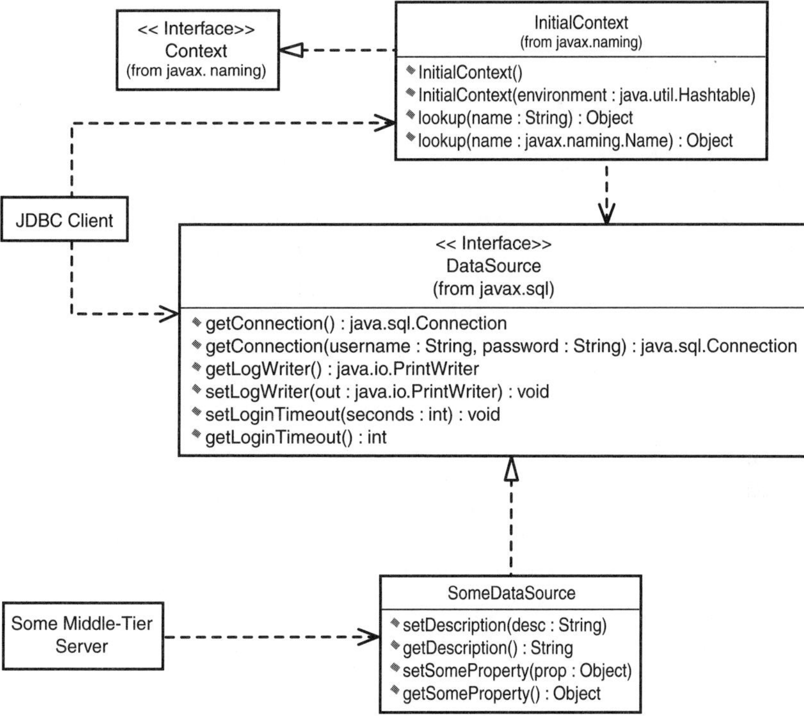

Figure 6.4 A data source class diagram.

Data Sources in the Middle Tier

There are two main differences between obtaining a connection from a `DataSource` via JNDI and using the `DriverManager`. For one, the `DataSource` is often registered with JNDI by a middle tier, and therefore any retrieved connections can be managed remotely for distributed clients versus locally, as is the case with clients that use a local `DriverManager` object. Another difference is that names used to obtain `DataSource` objects from JNDI are often registered by a middle tier, and therefore the client code is unaffected by database URL changes, as is the case with using URLs to obtain connections from a local `DriverManager` interface. Thus, if a change in the underlying means for obtaining a connection changes, use of the `DataSource` objects shields such changes from the client, which is not the case when using the `DriverManager`.

Although full-blown implementations of `DataSource` objects are most often physically located inside of a middle tier, this is not always the case nor even required. Thus code physically local to the client process can implement a `DataSource` object and manage the underlying resources. However, as will become more apparent later in this chapter, it often makes sense for a middle-tier J2EE container to implement the logic beneath a DataSource so that connection and memory resources can be managed more efficiently across multiple clients in an enterprise application scenario.

Data Sources Properties

DataSource implementations have a set of properties that are set at design-time when implemented as a JavaBean. Getters and setters for these properties should be implemented following the JavaBeans standard naming convention as described in Appendix B, "JavaBeans." Such getters and setters are typically not exposed to a JDBC client. Rather, such properties are usable by integrated development environment tools to introspect such components and allow the configuration of such properties via the tool's JavaBeans-compliant container.

Only a description property is mandatory for implementation by a DataSource JavaBean. The total set of standard property names is specified here, and DataSource vendors must adhere to this convention if implementation of such a property is provided by the JavaBean:

- String serverName: A database server name.
- String databaseName: The name of a database.
- String dataSourceName: The name of a data source used when pooling database connections.
- String description: A description of the data source.
- int portNumber: A port number for database requests.
- String networkProtocol: The protocol used by the database server.
- String user: A database username.
- String password: A database password.
- String roleName: A SQL role name.

DataSource registration is typically performed by a middle-tier or JavaBean implementation. DataSource instances are created by such middle-tier or Bean deployers, and calls to methods such as setServerName(), setDatabaseName(), and setDataSourceName() are made as such using a fictional SomeDataSource class implementation of a DataSource:

```
SomeDataSource sds = new SomeDataSource();
sds.setServerName("EASTERN_SERVER");
sds.setDatabaseName("EASTERN_US_TSHIRTS_REPOSITORY");
sds.setDescription("Eastern U.S. Data Server for TShirts Database");
sds.setPort(1521);
sds.setNetworkProtocol("TCP/IP");
```

These instances are then bound to a name server using names such as java:comp/env/jdbc/TSHIRTS/EASTERN:

```
Context initialContext = new InitialContext();
initialContext.bind("java:comp/env/jdbc/TSHIRTS/EASTERN", sds);
```

JDBC Client Use of Data Sources

After a `DataSource` is bound to a JNDI naming service instance, a JDBC client application will then look up `DataSource` object handles using associated names. The JDBC client will call `getConnection()` on the `DataSource` with or without a username and password to obtain a `Connection` handle, as illustrated in Figure 6.4, and subsequently should call `close()` on the `Connection` when finished. For example:

```
// Create a hashtable with the naming service object factory
// and the URI of the remote JNDI service
Hashtable nameServiceProperties = new Hashtable();
nameServiceProperties.put("java.naming.factory.initial",
                          "com.some.lookup.service.ClassFactory");
nameServiceProperties.put("java.naming.provider.url",
                          "protocol://remote.beeshirts.com/");

// Now, look up a handle to a DataSource object
Context ctx = new InitialContext(nameServiceProperties);
DataSource ds
       = (DataSource) ctx.lookup("java:comp/env/jdbc/TSHIRTS/EASTERN");

// get, use, and close the Connection
Connection connection = ds.getConnection("SCOTT", "TIGER");
  ...
connection.close();
```

A JDBC client can also call `setLogWriter()` and `getLogWriter()` on the `DataSource` object in order to respectively set and get a handle to a `PrintWriter` object used to log all messages associated with use of the `DataSource`. Additionally, `setLoginTimeout()` and `getLoginTimeout()` methods may be used to set and get the maximum time to wait for a login attempt to a data source when creating a `DataSource` object.

Connection Pools

Pooling of resources in general is a key feature that enterprise development projects must consider carefully. Because enterprise systems are typically designed for scalability and must often cope with many concurrent users, pools of resources that are used by user sessions are frequently implemented by middle-tier servers. The basic concept of a resource pool is to maintain a collection of "hot" resources ready to be doled out to a client upon request or need for that resource. Database connection pools are one type of important resource that can be cached in memory in the middle tier such that upon request from a client, a connection will be immediately available for use by the client (versus spending time creating and initializing a connection). When the client is done using the connection, it is returned to the pool to await allocation to another request.

The diagram in Figure 6.5 depicts the key entities and relationships involved with connection pooling. JDBC 3.0 driver vendors that implement connection pooling provide an implementation of the `javax.sql.ConnectionPoolDataSource` interface. `ConnectionPoolDataSource` has two `getPooledConnection()` methods used to return `PooledConnection` objects. `PooledConnection` objects encapsulate pooled connections to data sources.

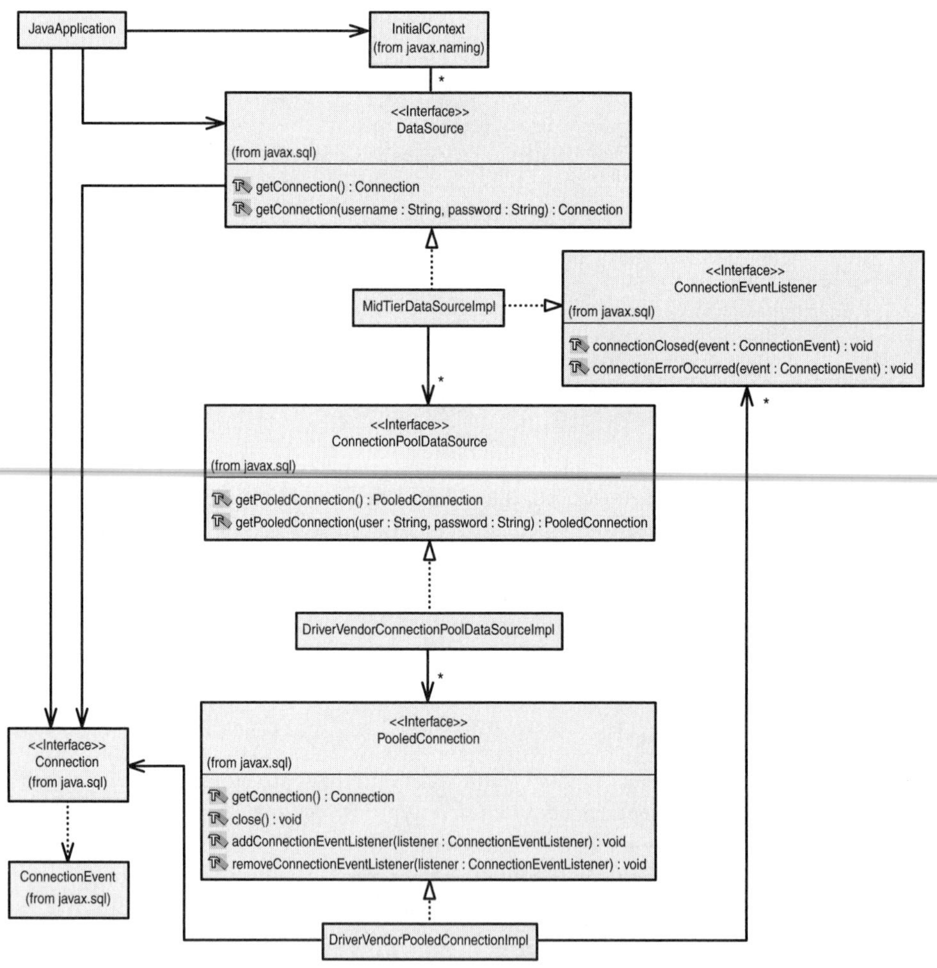

Figure 6.5 A connection pooling class diagram.

Middle-tier vendors implement DataSource objects that talk with ConnectionPoolDataSource interfaces implemented by JDBC driver vendors in order to provide handles to data sources offering pooled connection features. Middle-tier vendors maintain a pool of PooledConnection objects returned from ConnectionPoolDataSource objects. Middle-tier vendor implementations can also register a ConnectionEventListener with the PooledConnection object to be notified of connection events such as connection closing and error events encapsulated by ConnectionEvent objects.

Figure 6.6 shows the basic flow behind the scenes of connection pooling in the middle tier. Here we see the Java Application client looking up a DataSource object via JNDI and requesting a connection from the DataSource. The middle-tier remote DataSource implementation will first look within its connection pool to see whether a pooled connection is ready to hand off to the client. In this scenario we depict what occurs when a connection is not available and the data source implementation must request a new PooledConnection from a driver vendor's ConnectionPoolDataSource interface object. The middle-tier data source implementation then registers a ConnectionEventListener with the PooledConnection and subsequently obtains a reference to a new Connection object. The Connection object gets returned to the Java Application client, who then uses the connection and calls close() when it is finished. Such a call generates a ConnectionEvent instance, which gets returned to the middle-tier data source implementation registering interest in such events. Upon notification of the connection closing, the middle tier can then place the connection object back into a pool of connections.

As you can see from Figure 6.5 and Figure 6.6, connection pooling is completely transparent to middle-tier client Java applications. As described earlier, the Java application JDBC client's only visibility into such infrastructure is via the handle it obtains from performing a JNDI lookup to a DataSource object that was registered with the naming service by the middle-tier application server logic. A middle-tier implementation of the DataSource object can then interface with connection pooling logic behind the scenes using the standard JDBC APIs for connection pooling. Thus, it should be clear that the standard APIs for connection pooling aren't of direct use to the JDBC client application. Rather, the utility of such standard APIs is via the advantage of being able to more easily assemble scalable data access solutions in the middle tier using different vendor implementations for data source logic and connection pooling logic.

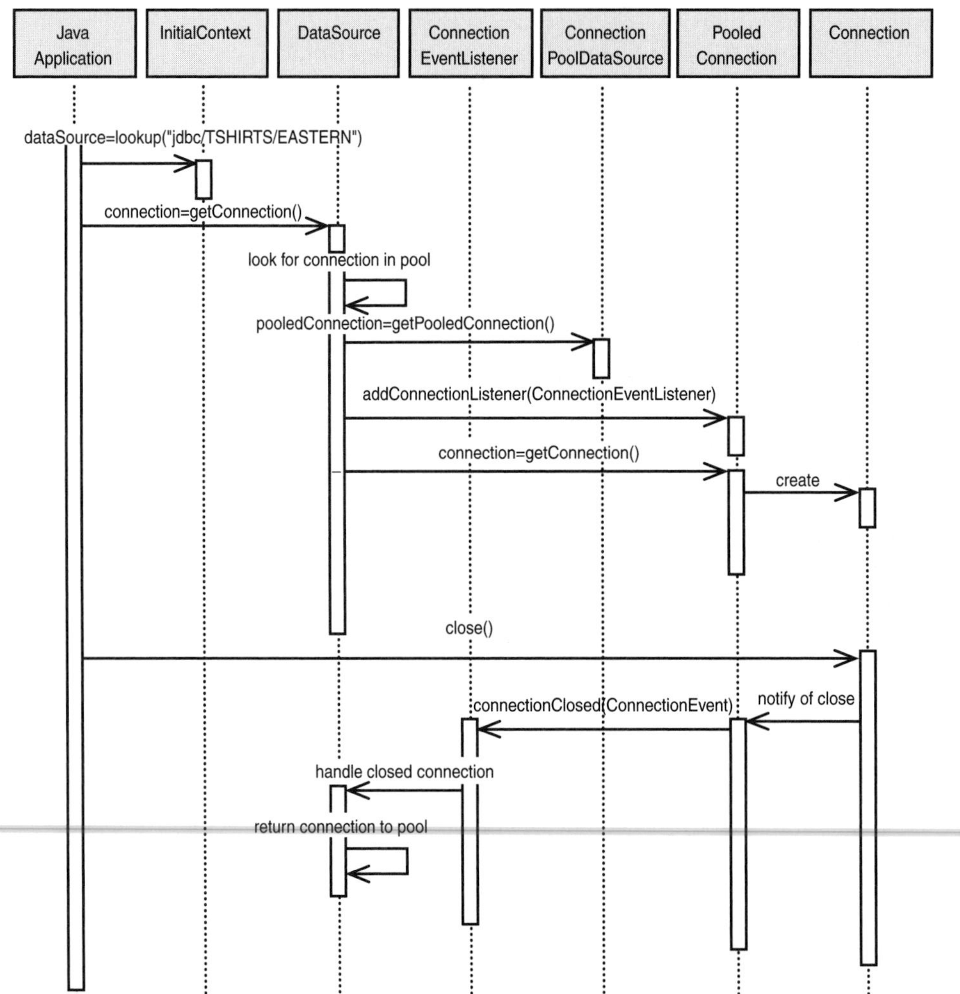

Figure 6.6 A connection pooling scenario diagram.

Distributed Transactions

In Chapter 2, "Enterprise Data," we discussed the fact that a transaction manager manages atomic transactions that can potentially span multiple resource managers (that is, DBMS servers). Such distributed transactions that can span multiple data sources and need to be treated as one atomic transaction inevitably require a centralized transaction manager to coordinate distributed commits and rollbacks. Transaction managers must also contend with issues such as concurrency and deadlock, in addition to the fact that X/Open XA standards-compliant transaction managers must guarantee that different resource managers will be assigned different branches of a transaction that compose a distributed transaction.

To facilitate a transaction manager's ease of interfacing with a heterogeneous network of resource managers, a resource adapter is often provided to present a common interface to various resource managers. The JDBC interface provides just such a resource adapter interface to DBMSs that can be used by transaction managers. The hooks needed to expose standard distributed transaction support to middle-tier database access logic are part of the JDBC 3.0 API specification.

Figure 6.7 shows some of the key entities involved in providing distributed transactions support using JDBC 3.0. This figure is very similar to Figure 6.5, which depicts the entities involved with connection pooling in general. The middle-tier vendor implements the `DataSource` interface, which now must interact with JDBC vendor-supplied `XADataSource` interfaces instead of `ConnectionPoolDataSource` interfaces. The data source implementation will also interact with an XA-compliant transaction manager via a transactions service interface. We'll talk about transaction services in more detail in Chapter 14, "Transaction Services with JTA and JTS."

`XADataSource` objects return `XAConnection` objects that extend the `PooledConnection` interface and augment the concept of a pooled connection to include participation in a distributed transaction. The middle-tier data source implementation calls `getXAResource()` on the `XAConnection` object to obtain a handle to a `javax.transaction.XAResource` object that is passed to the transaction manager. The transaction manager uses the `XAResource` object to manage distributed transactions using resources (that is, connections) managed by the associated XA-compliant resource manager. Thus, the `XAResource`, as you'll see in Chapter 23, exposes a series of methods such as `commit()` and `rollback()` used to manage distributed transaction behavior.

As with pooled connections, such standard APIs for distributed transaction management are also transparent to the Java application JDBC client. The middle tier instead interacts with such standard APIs. Thus, the middle-tier application server can assemble scalable and distributed transaction enabled data access solutions using different vendor implementations for data source logic and distributed transaction enabled connection pooling logic.

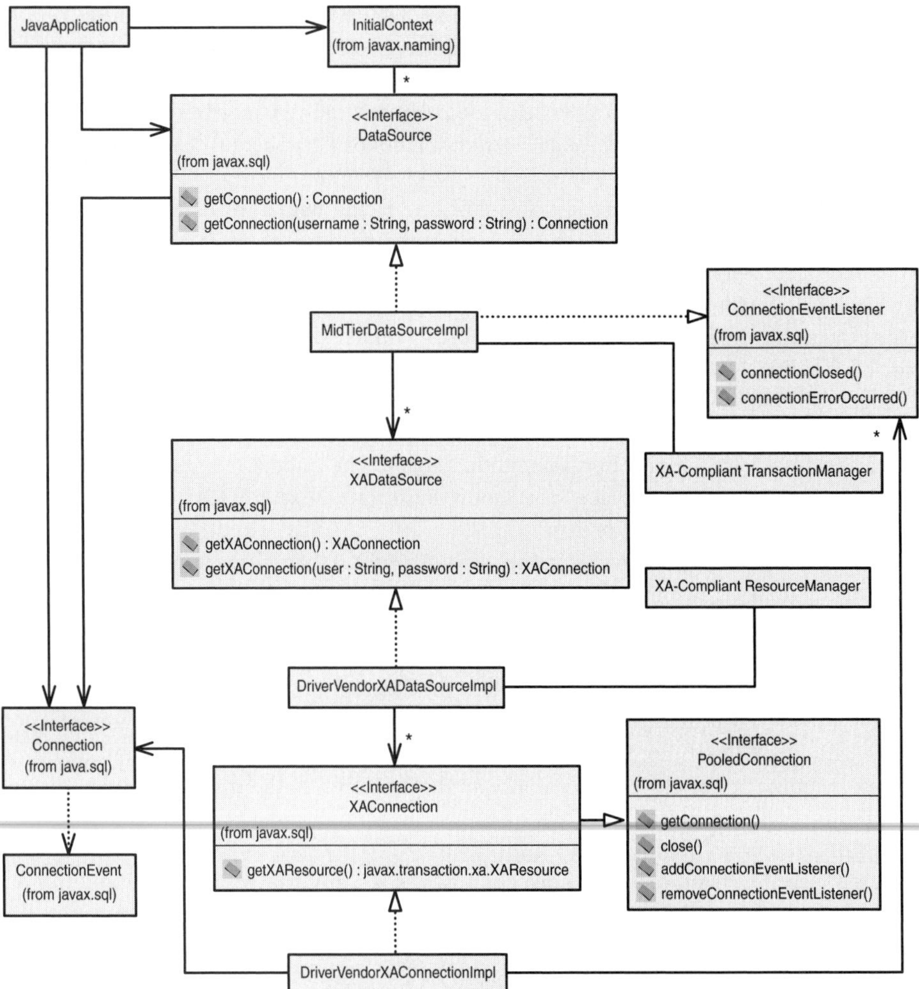

Figure 6.7 A distributed transactions class diagram.

Conclusions

JDBC has a wide range of standard APIs for use by the database applications programmer. JDBC not only offers general database access features described in the preceding chapter, but also offers finer-grained features such as the capability to scroll around JDBC result sets and make updates to the database directly from a result set for both a singular database row and a batch of database rows. JDBC applications can also capitalize on the use of SQL99 types such as BLOBs and CLOBs and map custom-defined SQL types to and from Java classes. Furthermore, the use of row sets allows one to interface with JDBC result sets during design time as a JavaBean, as well as providing a way to interact with the JDBC API. JDBC 3.0 client applications can also transparently reap the benefits of standard connection pooling and distributed transaction handling with JDBC's API extensions for the middle tier. Such APIs enable middle-tier application server vendors to assemble implementations of data sources, connection pooling, and transaction management logic from other vendors in a standard fashion.

Although many standards offer only the lowest common denominator of functionality for vendor offerings, JDBC is clearly pushing the envelope by providing extended standards for Java database connectivity. The pros of standardized database access being cross-vendor platform portable can thus be taken advantage of while being less afflicted with the cons of limited functionality often inherent in many standards. Enterprise Java applications are thus now more able to grow and scale in more sophisticated directions.

Enterprise Communications Enabling

7

Enterprise Communications

THE DISTRIBUTED ENTERPRISE SYSTEMS PROBLEM CAN involve issues such as scalability, wide-area geographical distribution, and heterogeneous platform interfacing. A better understanding of the problems you'll face in providing solutions will help you more effectively be able to partition the problem space into more discrete and solvable chunks. Having a general model against which all potential solution paradigms can be cast further enables you to more rapidly and deeply understand the pros and cons of each communications paradigm. Furthermore, activation services are fundamental enterprise communications services used to automatically activate network server objects in memory from some dormant state based on a network client's request. This chapter describes the basic concepts behind activation services and introduces the reader to the Java Activation Framework (JAF).

In this chapter, you will learn

- About the problems that affect distributed systems in general.
- About the generic logical and physical models of distributed enterprise communication solutions.
- About a general model and various kinds of network client paradigms to be examined in subsequent chapters.
- About a general model and various kinds of network server paradigms to be examined in subsequent chapters.
- The basic concept of activation services and how they generically operate.
- The basic JavaBeans Activation Framework (JAF) architecture for transforming MIME typed data to and from active objects.

Distributed Systems

A distributed system in the context of information technology is a system composed of many physically independent computing mechanisms. Whenever the need arises to make two such independently operating mechanisms talk to one another, technically speaking, you have a distributed systems problem. If you truly have only two such devices that need to talk to one another, your solution may be the quickest and dirtiest solution you can find, or perhaps it will be something somewhat proprietary in the interest of being cost-effective. However, the term *distributed system* used in the context of an enterprise system usually means connecting many more than just two independently operating devices. Thus, your solution to such a problem takes on a much different face. Your solutions will most likely have to consider economies of scale, vastly diverse computing environments, wide-area geographical distribution of computing mechanisms, and vastly diverse communications mediums (see Figure 7.1).

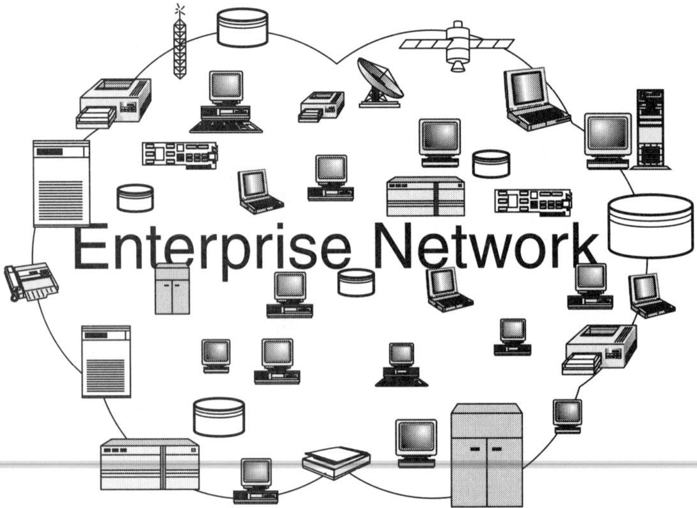

Figure 7.1 The distributed systems quagmire.

Let's compare computing to hamburgers for a moment. Mom-and-pop hamburger shops typically have to serve only a small customer base, and the decisions they make in the exchange of hamburgers for revenue may result in small inefficiencies such as using certain high-quality ingredients or perhaps using certain spices or cooking techniques to cater to the cultural region in which they run their business. For large-scale hamburger businesses, however, small inefficiencies multiplied by the thousands of businesses they may operate translate into a huge cost. Furthermore, catering a cooking style to each particular geographical region could be devastating to a large-scale hamburger business. Thus, the vastly distributed mega-hamburger businesses must agree on conventions of cooking, consider economies of scale, deal with vastly diverse customer bases, and conduct all of this business over a wide-area geographical distribution chain. Needless to say, a whole host of problems can arise.

Okay, comparing computing to hamburgers is a bit of a stretch, but the point remains valid that building a distributed system for an enterprise requires a whole different thought process than might be used to solve smaller-area distribution issues. Luckily, given that we will pursue building distributed systems using object-oriented and component-based techniques in this book, solving distributed system problems can be cast in terms that are easier to understand and that can be more modularly described. Modularity of problem description results in modularity of solution. Table 7.1 summarizes some of these distributed object system issues.

Table 7.1 **Distributed System Issues**

Distributed System Issue	Description
Reliable Transport Communications	Reliable means of communication between client and server objects
Language Dependencies	Dependencies on legacy language client and server implementations
Platform Dependencies	Dependencies on operating system and processor platforms
Client/Server Interfacing	Provide client/server interfaces for mapping requests and responses between the application and communications layers
Object Activation	Activation of server objects upon receipt of client requests
Object Name Binding and Lookup	Binding names to objects and resolving objects to names
Service Trading	Discovery, advertisement, and searching for object services using meta-data about such services
Creation and Deletion	Creation and deletion of distributed objects
Copying and Moving	Copying and moving distributed objects around a distributed system
Event Handling	Generation and notification of distributed events
Transactions	Managing a set of distributed operations as an atomic operation such that either all occur or none occurs
Concurrency	Acquiring and releasing locks to distributed resources
Persistence	Storage and retrieval of distributed objects
Security	Distributed authentication, encryption, authorization, and auditing
Usage Licensing	Acquisition, renewal, and cancellation of licenses for object usage

Distribution Mechanisms

The first step involved with attempting to solve any problem is to attempt to partition the problem into modular and individually solvable components. At the coarsest granularity of distributed enterprise communications problem partitioning, we distinguish between the application and the communications layers. In no way do we want our communications architecture to be dependent on our application code, and we would ideally prefer to have a way to keep our application code clean and free from any explicit calls to send or receive data over any communications protocol software libraries (that is, a protocol stack). Figure 7.2 depicts a layer of application/communications interface code that would ideally exist between your application code and communications code to provide just such insulation.

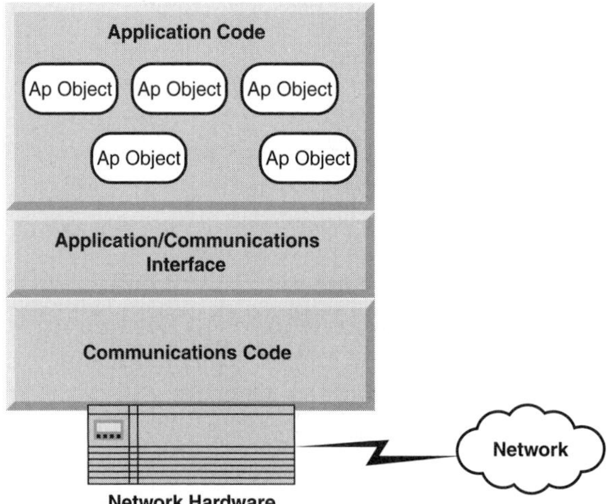

Figure 7.2 Basic distributed system layers.

Aside from the logical partitioning between application layer and communications layer as shown in Figure 7.2, the distributed systems problem can also be physically partitioned. That is, different distributed systems solutions will vary in how they physically distribute the processing load and type of processing to be performed across different distributed network elements. Figure 7.3 roughly depicts how distributed-system architectures have evolved over time. Each evolutionary stage of Figure 7.3 not only depicts a step in time of the evolutionary process, but also depicts a physical distribution architectural option that may still be employed today. The following text describes each stage in detail:

- *Dumb Terminal and Mainframe Computing:* Stage 1 depicts the basic dumb-terminal–to–mainframe relationship popular during the earliest stages of computing. A database of some sort may also be involved that maintains the corporate enterprise data.
- *Desktop Computing:* Stage 2 represents the next stage in development, in which the desktop environment becomes more powerful and computing resources can be shifted away from the mainframe to the individual workstations. Desktop platforms may now even access the database directly.
- *LAN Computing:* The birth of the LAN is depicted in Stage 3, in which standard local networking protocols begin to emerge and products that can support those protocols enter the network environment.

- *Internet Computing:* Stage 4 depicts the birth of internetworking, in which wide area networking becomes possible due to the standard interoperability offered by inter-networking protocols. Now disparate networking communities can be connected to share resources and exchange data.
- *World Wide Web Computing:* Stage 5 depicts the birth of the World Wide Web, in which Web servers assist with enabling remote Web clients to more securely interact with back-end legacy systems and databases. Clients behind the firewall and on the LAN may still communicate with such back-end systems with fewer restrictions and perhaps even communicate with an intranet Web server.
- *N-Tier Enterprise Computing:* Finally, Stage 6 depicts the N-tier architecture that has emerged today, with a middle-tier server helping to further isolate Web access from the back end to offer greater levels of security, scalability, transaction support, and a host of other centrally maintained distributed-systems management services for the enterprise.

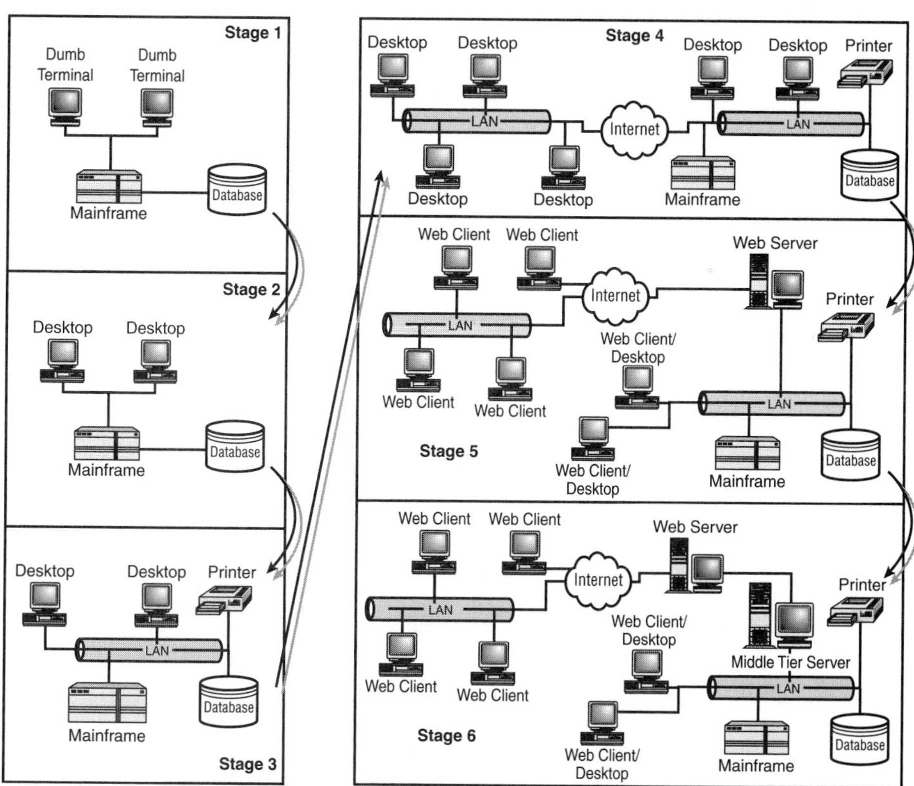

Figure 7.3 Distributed systems evolution and architectures.

Despite all the physical architecture options that can exist in a distributed system, there is still always the concept of a network client and network server (that is, there is always one client entity that desires some service from another server entity). Although it is true that such a distinction may blur in cases in which some application software may act as both network client and network server, the roles themselves still apply. The next two sections further decompose the distributed-systems problem in terms of the distributed system roles of a network client and network server. Different communications paradigms result in different architectures for both network client and server. We explore these architectures generally in this chapter and then in much more detail in Chapters 8 through 10 for the key communications paradigms utilized by enterprise Java applications.

The Network Client

Figure 7.4 depicts a generic network-client reference architecture that we use as a conceptual model to cast most other enterprise Java communication paradigms against throughout the rest of this book. The network client is composed of the network-client application code and communications code as usual. However, we will also be examining architectures that have application/communications interface layers that fit the basic structure depicted in Figure 7.4.

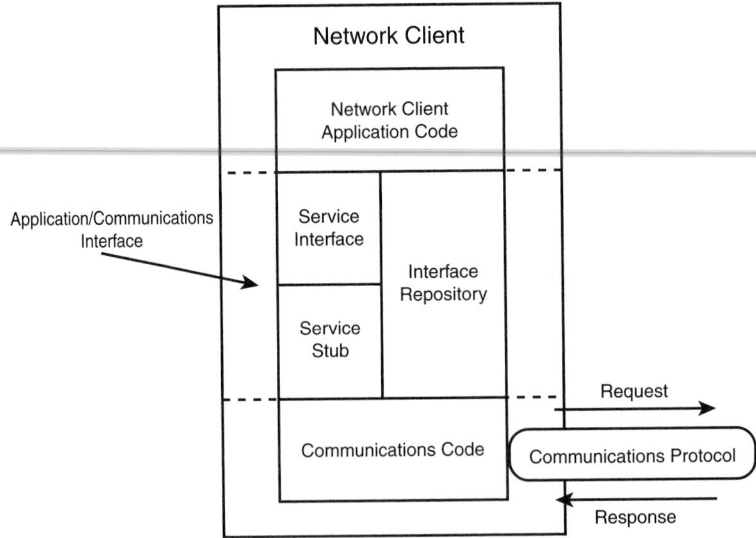

Figure 7.4 A general network client architecture.

A service interface can provide the network client with a view of a distributed network service, perhaps as it might interact with that service even if it were in the same local process (that is, location transparency). This interface is actually implemented by an underlying service stub that takes care of mapping regular Java calls into whatever message types and formats are used by the underlying distributed communications protocol code. The mapping of the language calls and parameters to the communication protocol message formats is called *marshaling* or *serialization*. The reverse process of transforming responses from messages to language types is called *unmarshaling* or *deserialization*. Note that all the communications protocols we will examine for enterprise Java-based development are hosted in some way over the popular TCP/IP protocol suite.

An interface repository may be employed to help store meta-data about service interfaces that can be accessed by the network client. Note that some paradigms may not use or need an interface repository. Rather, the stub and interface may be available at compile time for the network client to use directly.

Also note that the architecture of Figure 7.4 usually assumes a distributed object communications paradigm that can provide the necessary encapsulation and modularity of the application/communications interface. We examine the following types of network client models in this book:

- *TCP/IP clients* (Appendix D): TCP/IP-based clients either communicate directly over the TCP/IP communications protocol code or talk to a higher-level TCP/IP-based application client such as Telnet client or FTP client code. Application/communication interfaces in these paradigms are virtually non-existent or must be hand-coded.
- *HTTP clients* (Appendix E): HTTP clients create HTTP requests and process HTTP responses from HTTP servers. Such a protocol is used in Web-based communications and operates over TCP/IP. The HTTP client application here also may lack a decent application/communications interface layer. Some support for abstracting the HTTP client layer may be offered by third-party products.
- *CORBA clients* (Chapter 8): CORBA is a standard distributed object computing paradigm specified by the Object Management Group that can be used to create CORBA clients in any language. The CORBA client model has CORBA service interfaces, stubs, interface repositories, and a protocol over TCP/IP. CORBA service interfaces have a definite object-oriented flavor to them.
- *RMI clients* (Chapter 9): RMI is Java's built-in distributed object computing paradigm. RMI clients use an interface and stub to communicate over TCP/IP in either a proprietary protocol or a protocol that is compatible with the CORBA communications protocol.
- *Web Service clients* (Chapter 10): Web service clients utilize an interface and an underlying static or dynamic stub to communicate with a distributed Web service over HTTP and using XML-based requests and responses defined by a standard called SOAP.

Although we do not cover the DCOM computing paradigm in this book, it deserves some mention because it is possible to create Java-based DCOM clients. DCOM is

Microsoft's Windows-centric distributed object computing paradigm. DCOM is based on a specification by the Open Group known as the Distributed Computing Environment (DCE). DCOM clients have interfaces and stubs (although they refer to stubs as proxies). DCOM uses the DCE Remote Procedure Call (RPC) mechanism built on top of TCP/IP.

The Network Server

Figure 7.5 depicts a generic network server reference architecture that we use as a conceptual model to cast most other enterprise Java communication paradigms against throughout the rest of this book. The network server application code uses whichever communications code implements the particular communications protocol being used. Different implementations of the application/communications interface layer exist (or may not exist at all) for different communication paradigms.

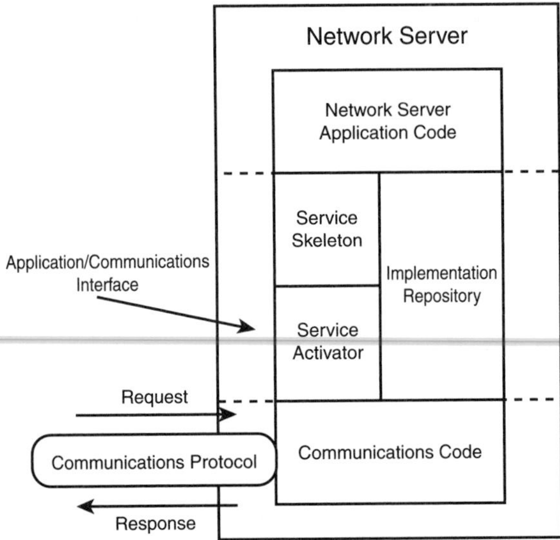

Figure 7.5 A general network server architecture.

A service activator may be used to handle requests made from network clients by bringing the requested network server into memory if it is not already active. This may involve pulling the implementation of the server from some form of implementation repository or perhaps pulling the state of the object from some sort of persistent storage. The activator then hands the request data to a service skeleton. The service skeleton acts as an intermediary on the server end to unmarshal requests from the protocol stream to actual network server application code calls. Responses from the network server are marshaled into messages that can be sent back over the wire to the network client.

Note that the architecture of Figure 7.5 also assumes a distributed object communications paradigm that can provide the necessary encapsulation and modularity of the application/communications interface, as was the case with the network client architecture. We examine the following types of network server models in this book:

- *TCP/IP servers* (Appendix D): TCP/IP-based servers listen on a TCP/IP socket for incoming client requests. Application/communication interfaces in this paradigm are virtually non-existent or must be hand-coded.
- *HTTP servers* (Appendix E): HTTP servers receive HTTP requests and generate HTTP responses. HTTP servers communicating directly with the HTTP protocol will not be offered the application insulation that an application/communications interface layer would offer. However, Java libraries such as Servlets help insulate your HTTP server applications from the HTTP protocol to a certain extent.
- *CORBA servers* (Chapter 8): CORBA servers use an object adapter (activator) and skeletons to insulate your application from the CORBA communications protocol layer. Furthermore, CORBA servers can use an implementation repository.
- *RMI servers* (Chapter 9): RMI servers are insulated from the RMI protocol using RMI skeletons. Activator functionality has recently been added to RMI, allowing for more sophisticated activation services.
- *Web Service servers* (Chapters 10, 22, and 30): Web service server implementations are invoked by a Web service runtime that unmarshals XML-based SOAP requests and marshals responses back into XML-based SOAP responses. Such SOAP messages are typically passed between client and server over HTTP. In addition to a standalone Web service runtime, a J2EE Web or EJB container may be used as a runtime within which Web services can be deployed.

It is useful to note that DCOM servers may also be implemented using Java, although we do not cover the topic in this book. DCOM servers use skeletons (referred to as stubs in DCOM lingo) and a Microsoft Windows–specific implementation registration and activation. DCOM comes built in with all modern Windows-based platforms.

Activation Services Overview

As depicted in Figure 7.6, an activation service is a component of software responsible for bringing other software from an inactive dormant state into an active in-memory state. The process of transitioning software from an inactive state to an active state is referred to as activation. Inactive software, such as a Java class file, may thus become active when it is instantiated as an object. A stored component may become active when it is allocated its own thread and brought into memory. Similarly, an entire program may be activated when it is spawned as its own process. Such examples apply mainly to transitioning software from some persistent storage mechanism into active memory. However, activation frameworks also include services that transition software into active memory from a dormant state in some other medium, such as from an I/O stream.

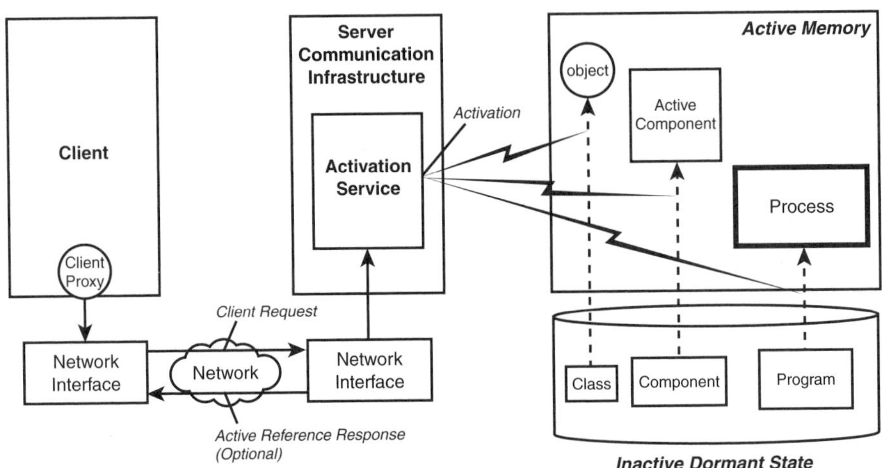

Figure 7.6 Activation services.

Given such a broad definition, as you can imagine, there are indeed many instances of activation services in computing platforms. This is due to the fact that the process of bringing code into memory from some dormant state, such as from a hard disk or floppy disk, is a fundamental aspect of everyday computing life. For example, components of an operating system that fork and execute a process are a form of activation service. Virtual machines must also provide an activation service because they operate on top of an operating-system platform and often take control of the activation of software away from the operating system directly. The Java Virtual Machine's class loader, for example, is a type of activation service.

However, most of the time when we speak of activation services with respect to distributed enterprise systems, there is also an implied client initiating the activation request from a remote network location. On the server side of HTTP request handling, Web server software brings HTML pages and possibly a set of Web client scripting instructions into memory from a file system on the Web server. Though not client request initiated per se, a MIME type handler embedded in your Web client browser may spawn an Adobe Acrobat process based on a MIME type that was associated with an HTTP response.

Perhaps most common are distributed component-based activation services that work with some server-side communications infrastructure. Component-based software has provided a model of development that has made building enterprise systems a much more economical solution than other development paradigms. Thus, it should come as no surprise that many activation service models have been implemented to handle distributed client requests on enterprise components. Such services may optionally return active references to a client proxy or may maintain the active reference on the server side. Understanding how such activation services operate helps you understand one of the most important components operating under the hood of a distributed enterprise solution. Understanding how activation works will help you make better enterprise component design decisions by enabling you to know what are both the true benefits and the limits of your component-based enterprise solution.

JavaBeans Activation Framework (JAF)

The JavaBeans Activation Framework (JAF) is a framework for building applications that can automatically activate objects that can manipulate data received via an input stream. The JAF accomplishes this task by providing support for identifying the type of data received via an input stream, identifying the types of operations that are available on the data, and automatically instantiating (that is, activating) a JavaBean component that can handle a particular operation which needs to be performed on that data. Thus the JAF is a type of activation service whose dormant inactive state of an object rests within a data input stream, as opposed to some persistent storage mechanism. The JAF is useful to applications that want to map data identified by MIME types into Java objects supporting operations on that particular data type. The JAF also enables the reverse process of streaming an object back into a byte stream from its active object state. As an auxiliary service, the JAF can provide services to map filename extensions to and from MIME types.

The JAF `javax.activation` package is a standard Java extension that can work with the J2SE. The JAF is also equipped with the J2EE platform because the J2EE JavaMail and JAX-RPC packages depend on the JAF. As an example, JavaMail depends on the JAF for handling MIME type data that is sent within e-mail messages. Aside from the underlying dependence on the JAF by JavaMail and JAX-RPC, most other J2EE applications will not have much interaction with the JAF. However, we briefly highlight the architecture of JAF here so that you can better understand it in the context of other activation services described in subsequent chapters. Furthermore, a basic understanding of JAF will help you comprehend an underlying component utilized by some of the J2EE APIs.

The basic architecture of the JAF is shown in Figure 7.7. The basic responsibilities of the core JAF components shown in Figure 7.7 are as described here:

- `DataHandler`: The `DataHandler` is the primary interface used by JAF clients to access data in different formats and to invoke conversion between an underlying byte stream and activated Java object type via a specific `DataContentHandler`. The `DataHandler` can by and large use the remaining APIs shown in Figure 7.7 transparently for the JAF client.
- `DataContentHandlerFactory`: The `DataContentHandlerFactory` takes a MIME type as a parameter and returns a specific `DataContentHandler` factory that can handle that MIME type.
- `DataContentHandler`: The `DataContentHandler` is responsible for reading data streams into objects and for writing objects to streams.

- `DataSource`: A `DataSource` offers a handle to data that has an associated object name and MIME type. Handles to input and output streams attached to an underlying data medium (for example, files and URLs) may also be obtained from the `DataSource`.
- `CommandMap`: A `CommandMap` maps MIME types to a collection of commands that can be performed on that data.
- `CommandInfo`: The `CommandInfo` encapsulates information about a particular command, including the name of the command class and the command name. The actual JavaBean object instance that can implement such a command is also returned.
- `CommandObject`: The `CommandObject` interface is implemented by JAF-aware JavaBean objects that can operate on MIME typed data.

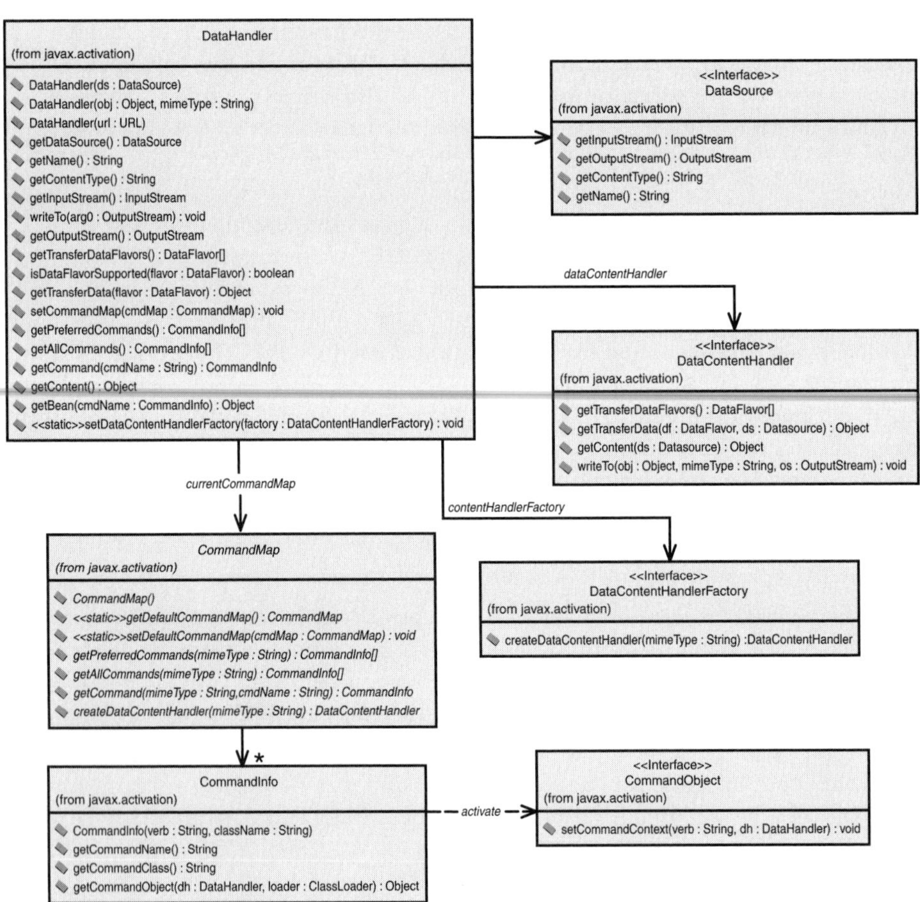

Figure 7.7 JavaBeans activation service architecture.

Conclusions

The distributed enterprise systems problem can involve issues such as scalability, wide-area geographical distribution, and heterogeneous platform interfacing. An application/communications interface layer between your application code and communications code can help make providing solutions to such problems transparent to application code. Furthermore, different physical architectures exist to support different physical distribution system needs. Finally, activation services are fundamental services implemented by many distributed communication paradigms for transforming some dormant state of a server object into active memory with a resulting object being ready to handle client requests. Many activation services perform these operations automatically for clients to handle client requests on a per-demand basis. As an example conveyed in this chapter, the JavaBeans Activation Framework provides activation of objects based on underlying MIME data streams and is utilized by other J2EE API components.

All distributed communication paradigms that we examine throughout this book operate over TCP/IP and include pure TCP/IP-based applications, HTTP-based applications, CORBA-based applications, RMI-based applications, and Web services-based applications. Each paradigm's network client and server as well as activation service approach that we examine may be referenced against the generic application/communications interface layer and distributed systems architecture model outlined in this chapter. To make it easy for you to compare and contrast such paradigms, we also implement examples using similar basic BeeShirts.com functionality, but in the context of the different distributed communication paradigms.

8

CORBA Communications

THE COMMON OBJECT REQUEST BROKER ARCHITECTURE (CORBA) is a language- and platform-neutral body of specifications for building distributed object applications. CORBA applications are built in such a way that they are largely isolated from the details of communications code. In fact, CORBA applications are so defined that, from a CORBA client perspective, the distributed nature of a CORBA server can be completely transparent. The Common Object Services Specification (CORBAservices), the Common Facilities Architecture (CORBAfacilities), and CORBA business objects are all standards built atop CORBA to provide an even richer suite of distributed communication services and frameworks. The CORBA Interface Definition Language (IDL) offers up a language-neutral mechanism for defining distributed object interfaces with standards that exist for mapping IDL to Java, as well as for mapping Java to IDL.

Building a CORBA-enabled application involves several considerations and steps. Beyond COTS product selection and scalable design considerations, you need to be cognizant of a few core CORBA server implementation issues. Creating CORBA clients is much easier, but some design options do exist. Although CORBA as an evolving standard has somewhat fallen out of favor in industry, it does represent an important underlying J2EE technology to understand because it is one of the core distributed communications paradigms used by EJB underneath the hood. CORBA understanding also can come in handy when connecting to CORBA servers from within an EJB or Java Servlet and will certainly be important if you must create a CORBA server in a standalone non-J2EE container environment. This chapter thus takes the approach of describing for you the infrastructure that is CORBA, as well as providing a basic reference for you to use when creating CORBA clients and servers.

In this chapter, you will learn:

- The concept and architecture of the OMG's Common Object Request Broker Architecture (CORBA)
- The basic structure of the Object Request Broker (ORB)

- The architecture of the General Inter-Orb Protocol (GIOP) and Internet Inter-Orb Protocol (IIOP) protocols over which CORBA clients and servers communicate
- The basic subcomponents of CORBAservices, CORBAfacilities, and CORBA business objects
- The basic structure of the CORBA Interface Definition Language (IDL), as well as the basic transformation rules for mapping IDL elements to Java elements
- How CORBA's distributed architecture can be used and how it can scale in the enterprise
- About the Java IDL and vendor-supplied CORBA packages used to build CORBA-compliant services
- How to create and compile CORBA interface definitions
- How to create CORBA servers
- How the CORBA infrastructure services are used by CORBA servers
- How to create CORBA clients
- The behavior and means by which CORBA objects can be passed around by value

CORBA Overview

Before we cast the Common Object Request Broker Architecture (CORBA) in the light of its use with Java and the J2EE, let's first attempt to understand what CORBA really is, as well as its historical context. As depicted in Figure 8.1, CORBA represents a standard model for creating objects and components whose services are to be distributable to remote clients. CORBA uses a standard communications model over which clients and servers implemented in a heterogeneous mix of languages and running on a heterogeneous mix of hardware and operating-system platforms can interact. These standard models for CORBA are described via a collection of specifications created by an organization known as the Object Management Group (OMG).

> **Note**
>
> You'll find the OMG's Web site at `www.omg.org`. All CORBA specifications, proposals for specifications, and the latest news on CORBA can be found there.

The OMG was founded in 1989 by a collection of largely hardware-oriented companies (including Sun Microsystems) with the mission of making standard and interoperable component-based software a reality. Since then, the OMG grew to include approximately 800 member organizations. The membership of the OMG ranges from large companies to smaller companies and university groups. Aside from CORBA and platform interoperability, now the OMG also oversees standards established for UML.

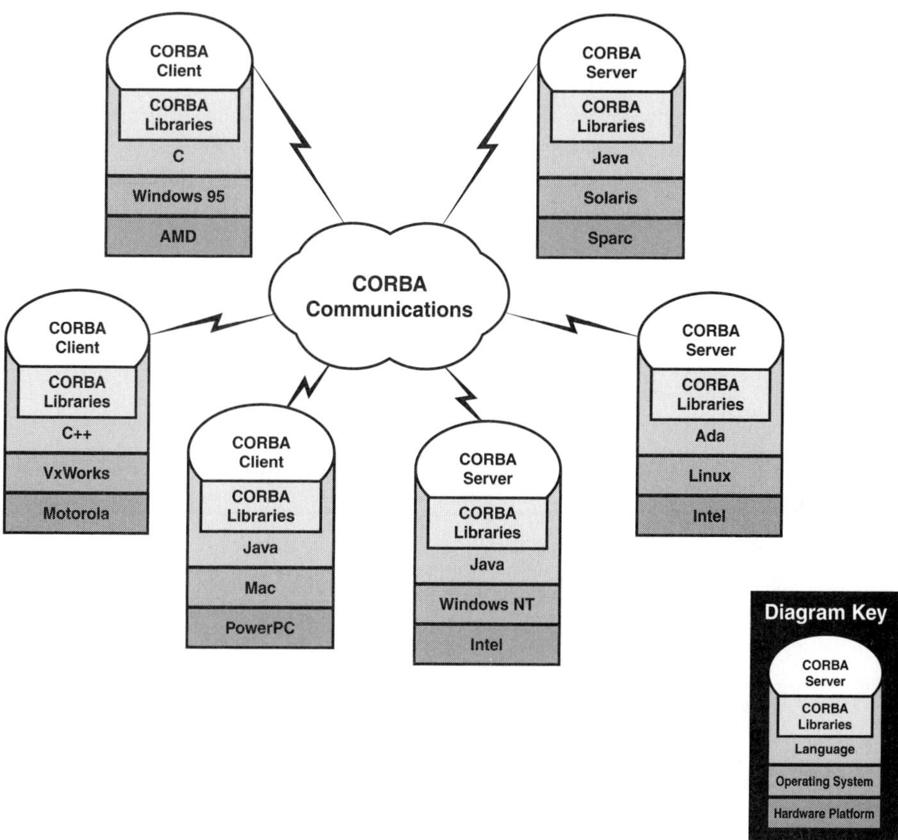

Figure 8.1 Heterogeneous CORBA communications.

The infrastructure of CORBA became one of the most widely adopted standard architectures since the CORBA 1.1 specification was published in 1991. Since that time, the CORBA 2.X series of specifications has been the standard that has enabled CORBA to become more viable for the marketplace. CORBA 2.3.1 was the specification version most fully supported by the Java 2 platform at the time of writing this book and is the standard for which we present most of our material. CORBA 3.0 was the most current final release at the time of this writing, but support of CORBA infrastructure beyond 2.3.1 has slowed.

The Object Management Architecture

Figure 8.2 depicts the Object Management Architecture (OMA). This high-level diagram provides scope and context for the CORBA specifications. At the highest level, we have application objects—perhaps created by you or purchased off the shelf—to offer business-specific services in a distributed fashion via CORBA. Application objects are specific to an application and are not governed by any CORBA specification standard. However, the application-level CORBA Domain Interfaces *are* defined in actual OMG specifications to deal with application-specific services for a particular domain such as the Telecommunications, Manufacturing, and Finance application domains. At the lowest level, specifications that deal with the Object Request Broker (ORB) define exactly how distributed clients can remotely utilize the services of distributed servers in a language- and platform-independent fashion, as well as describing the underlying communications protocol in which such service utilization occurs.

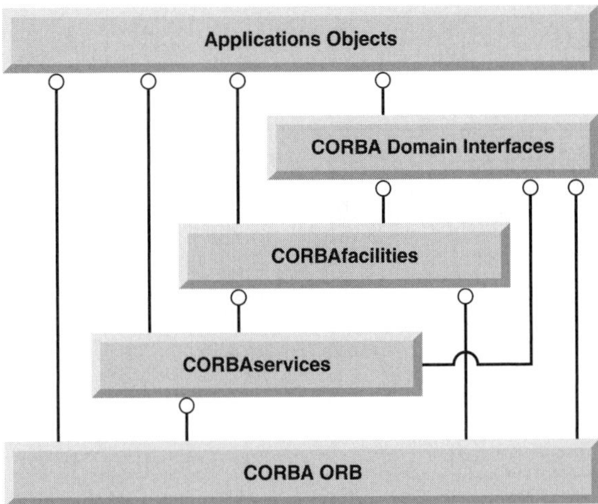

Figure 8.2 The Object Management Architecture (OMA).

Interfacing with an ORB is by far the most commonly accessed layer by CORBA application developers. Above the layer of the ORB, we have CORBAservices (aka Common Object Services) specifications to define those distributable CORBA services that CORBA-based applications commonly rely upon, such as providing human-readable object name to object reference mappings and querying for objects using some search criteria. At a higher level than CORBAservices, we have CORBAfacilities to provide frameworks for building directly useful distributed services such as printing, email, and document-management facilities. Distributable application objects may use one or more of the services provided by any one of these OMA levels.

CORBA, Java, and the J2EE

Based on this short blurb of CORBA, you can see that the OMA offers much more than distributed object communications enabling capabilities. Rather, although the ORB helps communications-enable your distributed objects, the CORBAservices, the CORBAfacilities, and the CORBA Domain Interfaces all provide higher-level services and frameworks that can be used to build distributed enterprise applications. However, although such higher-level standards exist for CORBA, their industry support over the past few years has waned significantly. As we discuss and focus on throughout this chapter, it is the ORB-level services and a few CORBAservices that have been most widely embraced. In fact, CORBA ORB-level communication protocols and a few select CORBAservices serve as the underlying distributed communications foundation for J2EE EJB-based servers.

That is, the underlying distributed object communications protocol employed by J2EE EJB is defined by CORBA. J2EE EJBs expose their services to clients using CORBA communication protocols and can also communicate with other EJB and CORBA-based server environments using CORBA communication protocols. Furthermore, a few higher-level CORBAservices, such as the CORBA naming service, CORBA transactions, and aspects of CORBA security, are embraced by the J2EE EJB standards as the means to create interoperable EJB servers. Thus, J2EE EJB is not a replacement for nor is it a competitor with CORBA. Rather, CORBA is simply a foundational technology used to implement the distributed communications paradigm required by J2EE EJB containers. It thus behooves the J2EE developer to understand the foundational concepts and technology of CORBA in order to be more capable of building J2EE EJB components that interoperate with their enterprise application clients as well as with other servers in the enterprise.

Aside from its constituting the foundation of J2EE EJB servers, CORBA is also important to the Java enterprise developer in general because of its enterprise application integration significance. For one, an enterprise developer may at times encounter legacy and auxiliary applications that are built using CORBA or that are implemented in another programming language and can easily be adapted to offer a CORBA interface. Standalone Java and J2EE applications alike can then be built to communicate with such legacy and auxiliary applications using CORBA as an interoperability standard. Also, although J2EE technologies are the centerpiece of this book, J2EE containers will not be deployable at all times for all enterprise solutions due to computing power, cost, and other practical constraints. As such, standalone Java enterprise applications may suffice and offer themselves up to the general distributed enterprise as well as to J2EE-based applications via the interoperable distributed communication standards of CORBA.

It is for all of these reasons that in this chapter we provide a basic overview of the CORBA computing model, CORBA communications infrastructure, approaches for building CORBA clients, and approaches for building CORBA servers. The next chapter discusses RMI as a strictly Java-based distributed computing platform, as well as how RMI has been adapted to incorporate the standard underlying CORBA communications protocols within RMI over IIOP (RMI/IIOP).

The ORB

The CORBA ORB is the key component of the OMA with which most CORBA developers and architects will come into contact. The reasons for this are fairly straightforward. For any technology to be useful in the practical world, it must be built from the ground up. That is, you might as well forget about building a CORBAservice unless you have an ORB to use it with. Furthermore, the robustness of any architecture greatly depends on the robustness of its lower layers. If the lower layers are unreliable, the higher-level layers will topple down or simply will not be very evolvable. Java developers using CORBA will select or have available a relatively robust and interoperable ORB software off the shelf and will spend their time either interfacing with such a product or using an ORB product transparent to them beneath the hood of a J2EE container product.

The ORB Concept

Technically speaking, the ORB is really just a set of CORBA specifications. The ORB specifications are implemented by vendors to produce what we also sometimes refer to as "an ORB." In such context, the term *ORB* actually refers to a collection of software libraries used either by CORBA clients to access distributed services or by CORBA servers to make their services distributed. The architecture of an ORB and the types of components involved with its use are shown in Figure 8.3.

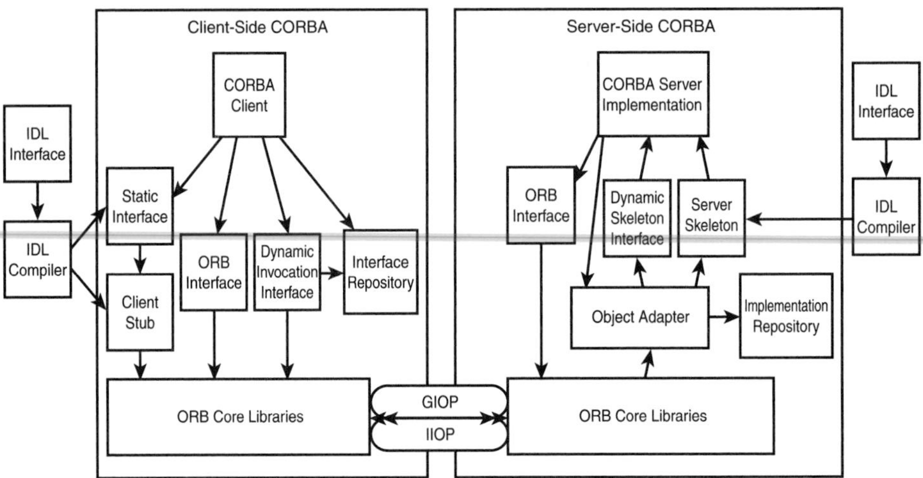

Figure 8.3 The ORB architecture.

The two most important players in distributed object communications via an ORB are the CORBA client and the CORBA server. The CORBA server is simply a distributed object offering up some of its method calls for remote access. CORBA clients are those objects that make remote method calls on CORBA servers.

Client-Side ORB Components

CORBA Interface Definition Language (IDL) interfaces are language-independent descriptions of interfaces to CORBA server objects. Think of IDL as a language used for describing the methods you want to make distributed on your CORBA server classes. Most ORB vendors or other third-party vendors provide IDL compilers that map IDL interface specifications (typically stored in IDL files) into CORBA static interfaces and CORBA client stubs. CORBA static interfaces are the language-specific analogues of the IDL interfaces from which they were mapped. The CORBA client stubs handle the transformation of calls made on the CORBA static interfaces into calls that can be made over the wire on a distributed CORBA server. Client stubs handle packing (that is, *marshaling*) method-call parameters and unpacking (that is, *unmarshaling*) method-call return values to and from CORBA communications protocol message formats. Stubs also handle identifying which method on a particular CORBA server is being invoked by packing such identifying information into the marshaled data stream to be sent to the server.

In addition to the static interfaces that can be generated from IDL, CORBA provides support for CORBA clients being able to invoke a remote method by dynamically providing information identifying the remote object and method to call, as well as providing the parameters to be used in the remote method to be invoked. This Dynamic Invocation Interface (DII) technique essentially bypasses use of any static interface definitions to directly talk with an ORB's remote method invocation mechanisms. Conceptually, you can think of DII being to CORBA programming as the Java reflection API is to Java programming.

Interface Repositories are small repositories used in some ORB implementations to hold the meta-data descriptions of CORBA server interfaces in a machine-readable version of the CORBA Interface Definition Language. Interface Repositories have a standard API callable by CORBA clients and are also used by DII implementations.

ORB Protocols

The ORB interface provides programmatic interfaces to the actual underlying ORB core. The ORB core libraries are those libraries needed on the client side for implementing the CORBA communications protocol. The higher-level CORBA communications protocol is the General Inter-ORB Protocol (GIOP), which maps messages created by stubs into message-transport formats capable of being communicated between ORB implementations. The lower-level protocol used by CORBA is called the Internet Inter-ORB Protocol (IIOP); it is a transport layer for handling how GIOP messages are communicated over TCP/IP. Although other transports besides IIOP can be used, IIOP is by far the most popular protocol used in CORBA applications today.

Server-Side ORB Components

On the server side, we have CORBA server skeletons, which are also generated by IDL compilers. Server skeletons are the server-side analogue of client stubs in that they unmarshal method parameter data into language-dependent types from the marshaled data sent over from the client. When a server skeleton method is invoked, it will unpack the marshaled data and call the appropriate server-side method with the expected parameter types. Likewise, any return data from the CORBA server implementation will be marshaled by the GIOP message data that can be sent back over the wire to the CORBA client.

The Dynamic Skeleton Interface (DSI) is basically an API your CORBA implementations can utilize, allowing your servers to avoid generating any static skeletons and instead supporting a generic interface that your server implementation object must implement. This generic interface implementation must handle determining the type of call being made and extract the parameters passed over from the client. DSI essentially requires your server implementation to handle many of the steps that a server static skeleton would provide you, but it allows your server implementation to be implemented in a flexible fashion and handle calls dynamically.

The Implementation Repository is a small repository on the server side containing a runtime description of available object implementations, as well as information on how such objects should be activated upon client request. Such activation information in the Implementation Repository is used by the Object Adapter. The Object Adapter takes requests from the ORB core communications libraries and determines how to activate (that is, bring into memory) server implementations and funnel such requests to their static or dynamic skeletons. Both the Object Adapter and the core ORB libraries have interface APIs that CORBA servers can use.

GIOP and IIOP

The General Inter-Orb Protocol (GIOP) and Internet Inter-Orb Protocol (IIOP) represent the communications layer above TCP/IP for CORBA-based applications. Both protocols are fairly simple in nature and offer the capability to build scalable CORBA servers. GIOP defines a means for mapping marshaled IDL data into a common way to represent data over the wire and a set of message formats encapsulating the request and reply semantics of distributed calls. IIOP maps GIOP message data into TCP/IP connection behavior.

GIOP Overview

GIOP maps marshaled IDL data types into binary data streams to be sent over the wire. GIOP accomplishes this using a Common Data Representation (CDR) syntax for efficiently mapping between IDL data types and binary data streams. The binary data streams are formatted in one of eight simple inter-ORB message formats. Although not discussed here, certain Environment Specific Inter-Orb Protocols (ESIOPs) serve to replace GIOP for particular communications environments and tend to use their own transport layers as well (that is, not IIOP).

Note

GIOP versions are defined according to the format *major.minor.* GIOP version 1.0 specified only seven message types, whereas GIOP versions 1.1 and 1.2 use an eighth message type.

GIOP messages also allow for object instance representations to dynamically relocate among ORBs. GIOP messages support all of CORBA's necessary functionality, as well as some fundamental CORBAservice-specific features. GIOP v1.0 and v1.1 permit only client-to-server connection establishment whereby only clients can initiate connections and send requests. GIOP v1.2 relaxes this restriction. Finally, in GIOP, multiple clients may share a connection via multiplexing.

GIOP messages sent between CORBA clients and servers contain a message header and message data. The header format simply consists of these elements:

- Four bytes of characters always of the form `GIOP`.
- Two GIOP protocol version numbers.
- A Boolean value indicating the byte order of the message (used in GIOP v1.0 messages only).
- A byte of bit flags used to indicate things such as byte ordering, as well as whether this message is fragmented into multiple subsequent messages (used in GIOP v1.1 and v1.2 messages).
- A single-byte message type identifier.
- The size of the message following the header.

These are the eight GIOP message types:

- `Request` *(type 0)*: Encapsulate CORBA server object invocations from a client to a server.
- `Reply` *(type 1)*: Encapsulate replies sent from CORBA server objects based on CORBA client requests. Exception data may be included in such messages.
- `CancelRequest` *(type 2)*: Encapsulate notifications from clients to servers that it is no longer interested in receiving a reply from a previous request.
- `LocateRequest` *(type 3)*: Encapsulate requests from a client to a server that attempt to resolve whether a server reference is valid and determine the address to which requests should be sent.
- `LocateReply` *(type 4)*: Encapsulate responses from servers to clients from `LocateRequest` messages.
- `CloseConnection` *(type 5)*: Encapsulate notifications from servers to clients about an impending connection closing.
- `MessageError` *(type 6)*: Encapsulate notifications from either server or client in the event of an erroneously received message.

- `Fragment` *(type 7)*: This message type was introduced in GIOP v1.1 and is sent following a previous message that has more fragments (that is, more messages) to send.

IIOP Overview

IIOP maps GIOP message data into TCP/IP connection behavior and input/output stream reading/writing. When a CORBA server object is to be distributed, the ORB will make information uniquely identifying that object on the network available via an Interoperable Object Reference (IOR). IORs contain the IP address and TCP port of the CORBA server object's process. CORBA servers listen on those sockets for incoming client connection requests. CORBA clients obtain IOR handles and open connections to the associated socket.

Depending on the ORB policy, the server will either accept or reject the connection requested by the client. Clients and servers then communicate GIOP messages over this connection. After a `CloseConnection` message is received, the ORB must close the TCP/IP connection.

> **Note**
>
> IIOP versions are also defined according to the format *major.minor.* IIOP v1.0 is used with GIOP v1.0, whereas IIOP v1.1 can be used with GIOP v1.0 or v1.1, and IIOP v1.2 can be used with GIOP v1.0, v1.1, or v1.2.

Interoperable Object References

An Interoperable Object Reference (IOR) is an address identifying a particular CORBA server object on a particular machine. Different transport protocols of CORBA have different IOR profiles. The standard part of an IOR and the profile of an IIOP-IOR contain such key information as this:

- Identifier of byte ordering (standard part of IOR).
- A repository ID identifying the object type (standard part of IOR).
- Two bytes designating the major and minor versions of IIOP supported (IIOP-IOR profile).
- A host or IP address string identifying where the CORBA server object resides (IIOP-IOR profile).
- A TCP port number on which the CORBA server object listens (IIOP-IOR profile).
- A sequence of bytes representing the object key to which requests are directed. This value is proprietary to an ORB implementation but is not interpreted in any way by the client (IIOP-IOR profile).
- A sequence of tagged components is also included in an IOR. Tagged components contain additional information used during object invocations (IIOP-IOR profile).

Services, Facilities, and Business Objects

CORBA provides a number of specifications for defining standard interfaces to higher-level enterprise services. Above the ORB level, a set of common services utilized by most distributed enterprise objects is defined within the CORBAservices. Above the CORBAservices level, a set of common application interfaces and standard set of interfaces for specific application markets are defined within the CORBAfacilities. Finally, CORBA also has specifications particular to certain market domains as well as a more generic business object framework. This section will briefly describe these various higher-level CORBA specifications that rest above the ORB infrastructure.

CORBA Services

The specification of the set of common CORBA object services is referred to as CORBAservices. CORBAservices are a collection of component specifications, each of which provides a service that can be used by distributed objects in general. That is, there is no application- or domain-specific nature to a CORBAservice. They represent truly modular components designed to solve one discrete and particular problem. We discuss a few of the key CORBAservices used by J2EE in more detail in the context of general distributed enterprise services in later chapters, but the following list of CORBAservices at least summarizes the distributed-system issues that each CORBAservice attempts to address:

- *Naming Service (aka `CosNaming`):* Naming is the principal mechanism for locating objects (primarily in a distributed paradigm) via a human-readable name.
- *Trading Object Service (aka `CosTrading`):* The role of a Trader Service is to let your applications discover and obtain object references based on the services they provide.
- *Relationship Service:* The Relationship Service allows for the dynamic creation of relationships between objects.
- *Life Cycle Service:* The Life Cycle Service provides services for creating, deleting, copying, and moving objects.
- *Externalization Service:* Externalization Services provide a mechanism for transforming an object into and out of an I/O stream.
- *Persistent Service:* Persistent Service provides interfaces for managing persistent objects.
- *Query Service:* The Query Service is a service for finding objects whose attributes adhere to a set of search criteria.
- *Object Collection Service:* The Object Collection Service enables one to manipulate objects in a group (that is, queues, stacks, lists, arrays, sets, trees, and bags).
- *Property Service:* The Property Service is used for dynamic association of named attributes with components.

- *Events Service:* The Events Service provides a framework for objects to dynamically register and unregister for specific events.
- *Licensing Service:* Licensing provides services for starting, stopping, and monitoring object service usage, as well as for locating license managers.
- *Time Service:* Time Services can be used to perform certain date- and time-related functions such as to obtain a commonly synchronized current time common across distributed systems, determine an ordering for events, and generate timer-based events.
- *Transaction Service:* An Object Transaction Service (OTS) lets multiple distributed objects participate in atomic transactions.
- *Concurrency Control Service:* The Concurrency Control Service manages concurrent access to a shared resource by multiple objects.
- *Security Service:* The rather-lengthy Security Service specification provides a set of services for minimizing the probability of a malicious attack on the system to be secured.

CORBAfacilities

CORBAfacilities represent higher-level and more application-specific services and frameworks used in building distributed systems than is the case with CORBAservices. CORBAfacilities can provide component services such as email, printing, and global-positioning information. CORBAfacilities are further broken down into two categories: *Horizontal Common Facilities* and *Vertical Market Facilities*.

Horizontal Common Facilities

Horizontal Common Facilities are those component service frameworks that are used by many distributed systems such as the following working specifications:

- *User Interface Common Facility:* Provide frameworks for building user interfaces with interfaces for user-interface styles, user-interface hardware, application enablers, user working-environment management, and user task management.
- *Information Management Common Facility:* Provide frameworks for building general information management systems with interfaces for modeling information, information storage and retrieval, information interchange, and information encoding and representation.
- *System Management Common Facility:* Provide frameworks for building system-administration functionality with interfaces such as policy management, quality-of-service management, instrumentation, data collection, security, and event management.
- *Task Management Common Facility:* Provide frameworks for building user task-management functionality with interfaces such as workflow management, static and mobile agents, rule management, and automation.

Vertical Market Facilities

Vertical Market Facilities are those component service frameworks that are used to achieve interoperability in specialty distributed-system markets such as the following working specifications:

- *Imagery Facility:* Provide interfaces for the exchange and access of imagery data retrieved from sensors or artificially generated.
- *International Information Superhighway (IIS) Facility:* Provide interfaces for the management of wide-area networks.
- *Manufacturing Facility:* Provide interfaces to systems used in the manufacturing of products.
- *Distributed Simulation Facility:* Provide interfaces to distributed system components used for computer simulation.
- *Oil and Gas Industry Exploration and Production Facility:* Provide interfaces to systems used in the production and exploration of natural resources such as oil and gas.
- *Accounting Facility:* Provide interfaces for accounting software used in an enterprise.
- *Application Development Facility:* Provide interfaces for systems used in the development of software applications.
- *Mapping Facility:* Provide interfaces for systems used to create geospatial maps.

CORBA Domain Interfaces and Business Objects

CORBA Domain Interfaces represent collaboration between vendors and customers of systems being used in a particular industry to create CORBA standard interfaces to such systems, allowing for interoperability between the various system implementations. CORBA Domain Interfaces have been defined already for four key industries:

- Manufacturing System Domain Interfaces
- Telecommunication System Domain Interfaces
- Financial System Domain Interfaces
- Healthcare/Medical System Domain Interfaces

Regardless of the domain-specific nature of such specifications, the OMG has created a Business Object Task Force in order to create a generic framework for creating such domain-specific objects based on a common Business Object Facility (BOF). The BOF specifies a generic business-object component from which all domain-specific business objects inherit. The BOF also specifies ways to assemble such business objects and how to mix in use of particular CORBAservices.

IDL

The Interface Definition Language (IDL) in CORBA provides a way to describe interfaces to distributed CORBA servers in a language-independent fashion. An IDL description in an IDL file may be run through an IDL compiler to generate the language-specific stubs and skeletons to be used in a distributed CORBA application. CORBA clients use the generated stubs, whereas CORBA servers make use of the CORBA skeletons. Actually, CORBA skeletons call your CORBA server implementations. Thus, in situations whereby you already have a class implemented in which you want to make its methods callable as a CORBA server object, you may then have to generate the IDL definition from the class definition manually or perhaps using a tool if it is available.

Various specifications describing mappings from IDL to particular languages exist, including mappings for Java, C++, C, Ada, Smalltalk, and COBOL. Additionally, a Java-to-IDL specification mapping also exists (to be described later).

Generic CORBA IDL File Format

IDL is not terribly foreign looking. In fact, many syntax conventions may look familiar to you. A rough general format of an IDL file is defined as shown here:

```
[#include ReferencedIDLFileName]

module ModuleName
{
   /* An IDL Comment */

   Module's Type Declarations here:
     e.g. typedef type name;
     e.g. struct StructName {StructDeclaration};
     e.g. enum EnumType {EnumValues};

   Module's Constant Declarations here:

   Module's Exception Declarations here:
     e.g., exception ExceptionName {[AttributeType name,...]};

   Module's Interface Declarations here:
     e.g., interface InterfaceName [:InheritedInterfaceName]
          {
                Interface's Type Declarations here

                Interface's Constant Declarations here

                Interface's Exception Declarations here

                Interface's Attribute Declarations here
                  e.g., [readonly] attribute AttributeType name;
```

```
                Interface's Method Declarations here
                  e.g., [ReturnType] MethodName
➥                          ([in|out|inout ParamType ParamName, ...])
➥                              [raises (ExceptionName, ...)];
          };
};
```

CORBA IDL-to-Java Mappings

Table 8.1 defines many of the key IDL entities referred to in the basic IDL file previously outlined and provides examples for how IDL maps to Java code. On the left side of the table, we present example snippets from an IDL file for the most significant types of IDL entities. On the right side of the table, we present the main elements of Java code that are generated from the example IDL. Note that the mappings in the right column reflect the most recent IDL-to-Java mappings assumed by the J2SE.

Table 8.1 **OMG IDL to Java Mappings**

	OMG IDL Entity	Java Mapping
	module	Java package
Core Constructs	`module ejava { module corba { ... }; };`	`package ejava.corba;`
	interface	Operations interface containing all defined methods of interface:
	`module ejava { module corba { interface Customer { ... }; }; };`	`public interface CustomerOperations {...}`
		And a signature interface implemented by stub and skeleton:
		`public interface Customer extends CustomerOperations, org.omg.CORBA.Object, org.omg.CORBA.portable.IDLEntity ➥{}`

Table 8.1 **Continued**

OMG IDL Entity	Java Mapping
	And helper class:
	`abstract public class CustomerHelper {...}`
	And holder class:
	`public final class CustomerHolder implements org.omg.CORBA.portable.Streamable ➥{...}`
	And stub class:
	`public class __CustomerStub extends org.omg.CORBA.portable.ObjectImpl implements ejava.corba.Customer {...}`
	And skeleton class (see "Other Constructs").
exception	Java Exception:
`exception ➥FailedToGetCustomer ➥Info { string reason; long reasonCode; };`	`public final class FailedToGetCustomerInfo extends org.omg.CORBA.UserException implements org.omg.CORBA.portable.IDLEntity { public String reason = null; public int reasonCode = (int) 0; ... }`
attribute	Get and set methods on the associated interfaces and classes:
`attribute ➥boolean hasEmail;`	`boolean hasEmail();` `void hasEmail(boolean newHasEmail);`
read-only attribute	Get method on associated interfaces and classes:
`readonly attribute boolean hasEmail;`	`boolean hasEmail();`
methods with `in` **parameters**	Java methods: `void login(String userName,`

Table 8.1 **Continued**

	OMG IDL Entity	Java Mapping
	void login(in string ➥userName, in string ➥password) raises ➥(failedToLogin);	String password) throws <Package>.failedToLogin;
	methods with out **and** inout **parameters**	Holder class for out and inout parameters and methods:
	Void getLatestOrder ➥ByCustomer(in string customerID, out Order o);	void getLatestOrderByCustomer(String customerID, <Package>.OrderHolder o);
	void addNewOrder(; ➥inout Order o)	void addNewOrder(<Package>.OrderHolder o);
	void	void
Primitive	boolean	boolean
Types	char, wchar	char
	octet	byte
	short, unsigned short	short
	long, unsigned long	int
	long long, unsigned long long	long
	float	float
	double	double
	fixed	java.math.BigDecimal
	string, wstring	java.lang.String
	FALSE	false
	TRUE	true
	const	public static final
Extended	**any**	org.omg.CORBA.Any
Constructs	**enum**	Java class version of enum:
	enum ShirtColor { RED, GREEN};	public class ShirtColor implements org.omg.CORBA.portable.IDLEntity { public static final int RED = 0; public static final int GREEN = ➥1;

Table 8.1 **Continued**

OMG IDL Entity	Java Mapping
	public static <Package>.ShirtColor from_int(int value) {...} ... }
struct	Java class with public members:

struct Order{
long orderID;
long customerID;
string
➥orderDescription;
};
	public final class Order implements
	org.omg.CORBA.portable.IDLEntity {
	public int orderID = (int) 0;
	public int customerID = (int) 0;
	public String orderDescription =
	null;
	...
	}

An array: typedef Order ➥listOfOrders[30];	Array helper: abstract public class listOfOrdersHelper{...} And Array holder: public final class listOfOrdersHolder implements org.omg.CORBA.portable.Streamable {...}
Unbounded or Bounded sequence:	Sequence helper: abstract public class ➥OrdersHelper{...}
typedef sequence<Order> Orders;	Sequence holder:
typedef sequence ➥<Order, 32> Orders;	public final class OrdersHolder implements org.omg.CORBA.portable.Streamable {...}

Table 8.1 **Continued**

	OMG IDL Entity	Java Mapping
	`union`	Java class:
	`union DataStoreUnion`	`public final class DataStoreUnion`
	`switch(DataStore){`	`implements`
	`case ORACLE:`	`org.omg.CORBA.portable.IDLEntity {`
	`➥string oracleValue;`	
	`case SYBASE:`	
	`➥string sybaseValue;`	
	`default : long ;`	`public String oracleValue()`
	`➥defaultValue`	`{...}`
	`};`	`public void oracleValue(String`
		`➥value)`
		`{...}`
		`public String sybaseValue()`
		`{...}`
		`public void sybaseValue(String`
		`➥value)`
		`{...}`
		`public int defaultValue()`
		`{...}`
		`public void defaultValue(int value)`
		`{...}`
		`...`
		`}`
		And helper:
		`abstract public class`
		`DataStoreUnionHelper{...}`
		And holder:
		`public final class`
		`DataStoreUnionHolder implements`
		`org.omg.CORBA.portable.Streamable`
		`{...}`
Other Constructs	`CORBA::ORB`	`org.omg.CORBA.ORB`
	`CORBA::Object`	`org.omg.CORBA.Object`
	`CORBA::<Type>` pseudo-objects in general	Pseudo-object definition in CORBA IDL maps to a particular type in Java such as: `org.omg.CORBA.<Type>`

Table 8.1 **Continued**

OMG IDL Entity	Java Mapping
Server implementation using inheritance (sometimes confusingly referred to as the "POA approach").	Java CORBA server implementation must extend the IDL-generated `<InterfaceName>POA` skeleton class.
Server implementation using delegation ("Tie approach").	The IDL-generated `<InterfaceName>POATie` skeleton class will delegate calls to your Java CORBA server implementation. Your Java server must implement the IDL-Generated `<InterfaceName>Operations` interface.

IDL Compilation

Compiling IDL into Java code requires the use of an IDL-to-Java compiler. An IDL-to-Java compiler utility is used with the Java IDL CORBA enterprise feature that comes equipped with the J2SE. The Java IDL IDL-to-Java compiler is a command-line utility that is used to generate Java stubs and skeletons given an IDL file. The Java IDL component IDL-to-Java tool comes packaged with the J2SE v1.4 distribution and is referred to as `idlj`.

> **Note**
>
> The J2SE v1.4 `idlj` compiler utility is located beneath the `bin` directory of your root J2SE v1.4 installation. Alternatively, a special Java class that comes with the JDK v1.4 can be used to induce an IDL-to-Java compilation and has the fully qualified class name of `com.sun.tools.corba.se.idl.toJavaPortable.Compile`. This class is located inside the JDK v1.4's `<JAVA_HOME>\lib\tools.jar` file. A complete synopsis for IDL-to-Java compilation can be found at `http://java.sun.com/j2se/1.4/docs/guide/rmi-iiop/toJavaPortableUG.html`. The basic structure for executing this special compilation class is shown here:
>
> ```
> java com.sun.tools.corba.se.idl.toJavaPortable.Compile [options] <idl
> ➥file>
> ```

To generate Java code from an `Example.idl` file, simply type the following for `idlj`:

```
idlj Example.idl
```

And similarly for the `Compile` class, we have the following:

```
java com.sun.tools.corba.se.idl.toJavaPortable.Compile Example.idl
```

To generate client-side Java bindings from an `Example.idl` file, simply type the following for `idlj`:

```
idlj -fclient Example.idl
```

Because all command options used with `idlj` can be passed to the `Compile` class when executing it as a Java application, we won't illustrate example execution for all options using `Compile`. But suffice it to say that the equivalent syntax for passing options to `Compile` is identical to that for `idlj`. For example:

```
java com.sun.tools.corba.se.idl.toJavaPortable.Compile
➥ -fclient Example.idl
```

To generate server-side Java bindings from an `Example.idl` file, simply type the following for `idlj`:

```
idlj -fserver Example.idl
```

By default, the IDL-to-Java compiler will generate server-side skeletons which will require you to implement a CORBA server that inherits from a base class in order to be CORBA-enabled (to be discussed in more detail later in this chapter). You can flag the compiler to generate skeletons that will enable your server implementation to use delegation (the "Tie" approach) versus inheritance if you so desire, by using the following for `idlj`:

```
idlj -fserverTIE Example.idl
```

IDL files can include other IDL files for definitions of types. When compiling an IDL file that includes another IDL file as reference, you may want to generate Java code for every included IDL file as follows for `idlj` using either the inheritance or tie approaches, respectively shown here:

```
idlj -fall Example.idl
idlj -fallTIE Example.idl
```

Although you can nest modules inside of modules to produce a desired package naming for your Java classes, it may be desirable to keep your IDL files fairly clean by eliminating any unnecessary outer-level modules such as this:

```
module com
{
  module BeeShirts
  {
    module Example
    {
      ...
    };
  };
};
```

You may rather prepend the package prefixes that would be generated from such module definitions and avoid adding these definitions to your IDL file by using this command for `idlj`:

```
idlj -pkgPrefix Example com.BeeShirts Example.idl
```

This will prepend the `com.BeeShirts` package prefix to a module named `Example` in your `Example.idl` file. Similarly, you can induce a translation from one package name to another as exemplified here:

```
idlj -pkgTranslate com.BeeShirts com.assuredtech.commerce Example.idl
```

As a final note, the default root output directory for such commands is the current directory. To specify a different root output directory, you simply specify the output directory as shown here:

```
idlj -td C:\MyProjects\j2ee\examples\src Example.idl
```

Java-to-IDL Mappings

In addition to mapping IDL to Java, you can map your Java code to IDL. Vendors will often provide tools to perform just such a task. Such tools provide utilities for generating CORBA stubs and skeletons and for generating actual IDL according to a set of Java-to-IDL rules. A specification that is affiliated with the CORBA 2.3.1 specification outlines a standard way to map Java classes to IDL. We will discuss this procedure in more detail in Chapter 9, "RMI Communications."

OMG standard Java-to-IDL mappings allow you to take servers defined in Java using Java's built-in distributed object communications paradigm known as RMI and convert them into CORBA-enabled servers. This paves the way for enabling your Java-based servers to be accessed by non-Java clients via the CORBA communications paradigm. This provides the benefit to Java developers of being able to create Java programs using the programming language that they are already familiar with and alleviating their having to know and understand the semantics and syntax of IDL.

CORBA Design and Development

Inherent in the specification of CORBA is its presumed application in distributed enterprise environments. Such environments mean potentially large network client bases, which means that an individual CORBA server may be required to support a large number of CORBA client requests. Designing your CORBA servers to be scalable is thus paramount to good CORBA enterprise development practices. The actual development process you follow also affects how distributable your CORBA servers will be. Development of scalable distributed object-based applications requires a different mindset than is the case with other development paradigms, such as the development of desktop applications or simple client/server interactions. This section describes which design issues affect the scalability of your CORBA servers and how the development process for building CORBA server applications generally may proceed.

Designing for Scalability

From the outset, CORBA has mainly been applied in enterprise computing environments. This is a logical expectation because building enterprise-scale applications often involves connecting heterogeneous platforms, and organizations are very sensitive to the need for building systems that can interoperate. However, the very generic nature involved with creating a CORBA server allows one to essentially make any object distributable. If you were to follow this paradigm to the extreme and indeed make every object distributed, you would also be plagued with an extremely inefficient system due to all the communications and marshaling overhead that would be involved. That is, although you may enhance the parallel processing nature of your distributed application by creating many fine-grained CORBA servers, the effects of increased communications overhead and resource utilization (for example, process and socket creation) will rapidly begin to far outweigh the benefits of parallel processing.

It thus behooves you, the enterprise developer, to follow a few simple guidelines when creating standalone CORBA applications for the enterprise:

- Create CORBA servers that act as service points that CORBA clients communicate with on a more coarse-grained basis.
- Create CORBA servers with methods that can process a large batch of similar operations and return a batch of results versus only providing finer-grained methods that must be called successively.
- Create CORBA servers that avoid offering direct getter and setter methods at the attribute layer on a distributed object.
- Create CORBA servers that act as service points to communicate with more fine-grained objects on the server side behind the wall of its service interface to the client.
- Where possible, employ a smart proxying design on the CORBA client side. Smart proxying involves a design in which your client can make getter type calls on CORBA proxy objects that retrieve data from a local cache.
- Be aware of the connection allocation policies of your ORB vendor implementation. ORBs that create a new connection for each CORBA client to CORBA server association will not scale very well. ORBs that can intelligently pool connections or use more efficient transports will offer a scalability advantage.
- Be aware of the thread allocation policies of your ORB vendor implementation. Many commercial ORBs will offer you options in terms of how threads are assigned to incoming requests. You might also consider creating your own thread pooling and request handling framework on the back end to support a scalable number of clients.

The J2EE and CORBA

CORBA application design for scalability is of particular concern when creating standalone CORBA applications. As you'll see in Part VI, "Enterprise Applications Enabling," use of J2EE containers and Enterprise JavaBeans (EJB) does not require as much developer cognizance of scalable application development techniques and principles. In that part of the book, we will also directly addresses how EJB and CORBA relate in more detail. Crafting EJBs to seem like CORBA servers to the outside world is primarily accomplished by the J2EE EJB container. EJB developers do, however, utilize CORBA APIs when the EJBs act as CORBA clients. Regardless, as we have stated throughout this book, there will indeed be instances when implementation of standalone CORBA applications is still needed to solve particular enterprise application problems.

CORBA Development Process

The steps to take in building a CORBA client and server can seem tedious at first, but at least Java-based CORBA development is easier than CORBA development in other languages. When CORBA-enabling a server, you either may have a predefined application for which you want to provide a distributed interface or may be creating a distributed server from scratch. Regardless, the same basic steps can be followed:

1. *Define your IDL interface:* You must first create an IDL file with a description of the distributed CORBA server methods to be exposed via a CORBA interface. You may also choose to define types to be passed by value between CORBA clients and servers.
2. *Compile your IDL file:* With an IDL file in hand, you can run such a file through an IDL-to-Java compiler to generate all necessary Java bindings for interfaces, stubs, skeletons, helpers, and holders. Depending on the desired server implementation method, you can generate server skeletons requiring that your server either inherit from or be delegated calls from the generated server skeletons.
3. *Implement the CORBA server:* You can then implement a CORBA server either by inheriting from a generated skeleton or by being delegated calls from a generated skeleton. If using a static skeleton is not to your liking, you can also use the Dynamic Skeleton Interface (DSI) to implement your server. After selecting how calls are mapped from either a static skeleton interface or a DSI, you can implement the functionality behind your calls if they were not already implemented, and compile your server.
4. *Implement a CORBA server registrar:* You should then typically implement a separate class that registers a CORBA server implementation with an object adapter's implementation repository. The registrar will also typically register any "frontline" server object instances with an object adapter. You may also use the CORBA Naming Service to register human-readable names to any newly created object references. Note that only initial references to certain frontline server objects need be registered with a naming service and object adapter from a server registrar. After any initial CORBA server object handles are obtained by CORBA clients, other

CORBA server objects will most typically be instantiated and registered by the CORBA servers that were initially or subsequently created.

5. *Possibly register interfaces with an Interface Repository:* You may optionally register a description of the CORBA server interfaces with an Interface Repository on the client side. However, for Java-based CORBA clients, access to a CORBA stub is usually available or perhaps remotely downloadable. If the Dynamic Invocation Interface (DII) is used, use of an Interface Repository will be needed.
6. *Implement the CORBA client:* A CORBA client can now be created using either the CORBA stubs created in a previous step or DII to make distributed calls on a CORBA server. A CORBA client must obtain a reference (IOR) to the CORBA server. It can do this by using a CORBA Naming Service, by converting an IOR in string form to a concrete IOR, or perhaps by using a vendor-specific approach. The client code can then be compiled and you are ready to begin client/server computing CORBA style.

CORBA Tools and Java IDL

Selecting the right CORBA tools to use for your enterprise application can make or break acceptance and the success of CORBA in your projects. Knowing which components of a CORBA standard you need to purchase and which ones you might pursue implementing yourself is also important. In what follows, we first describe the set of tools you'll need in order to build a CORBA-based application. We then list which major CORBA product vendors do exist and describe the Java IDL enterprise feature equipped with the J2SE v1.4.

Basic Tools and Configuration

Before you dive into developing a CORBA-based application, you'll want to pick up a few tools. Unless you're in the ORB-making business, you'll want to pick up a set of ORB libraries from a third-party vendor. You'll need to identify the target language in which you want to implement your CORBA server or from which you want to make a CORBA client. You should indeed evaluate your ORB vendor's implementation before deploying it into an enterprise application, especially in consideration of the scalability issues highlighted previously. And although you as a reader of this book will presumably be developing your CORBA-based applications in Java, you should still investigate the operating-system platform dependency of your ORB, because many commercial vendors will equip platform-specific utilities with their products.

The good news for us enterprise Java developers, however, is that we already know our target language and we already have the J2SE/J2EE's Java IDL ORB reference implementation to use during development while we take time to evaluate an actual commercial ORB implementation to plug into a deployed enterprise environment. In addition to the ORB libraries, you'll need an IDL-to-Java compiler, which usually comes packaged with a development environment from the vendor whose ORB libraries you have selected.

Although use of a CORBAservice is not necessary, your particular application's demands may warrant use of one of the services described earlier in this chapter. At the very least, use of a CORBA Naming Service will help you keep your CORBA applications more portable because without such a service, you will inevitably get locked into using a vendor-specific CORBA Naming Service analogue. CORBA Naming Services are often sold separately, however.

With the proper tools in hand, configuring the infrastructure for running CORBA applications may depend largely on the ORB implementation you've selected. In the purest scenario, you will only need to install the ORB libraries on your server and client platforms and then start a CORBA Naming Service process somewhere on your network. The remaining steps to take depend on your particular CORBA application. Particular ORB vendor implementations may also require that you kick off other processes on your network.

Although ORBs and CORBAservices have traditionally been key COTS products to purchase when building CORBA-based applications, more and more we are seeing a trend for such products to be integrated with other products. Server-side products such as Web servers, application servers, and even database servers are deploying their products with ORBs and a few CORBAservices built in. Even client-side Web browsers offer baked-in CORBA libraries that facilitate the capability to create Java applets with CORBA connectivity (aka Orblets). As more and more applications employ CORBA technology under the hood, your need for knowing the details behind creating CORBA-based applications may diminish. Rather, application servers and CORBA-based frameworks increasingly make writing distributed CORBA-based applications more transparent.

Vendor Offerings

Vendor offerings of products enabling CORBA connectivity currently tend to come in three basic flavors: (1) standalone ORB and CORBAservice products, (2) ORB and CORBAservice product suites, and (3) ORB and CORBAservice products integrated into another framework (such as a J2EE container). Although some products are free, they typically are useful only in prototype and early development environments while you select a more commercial-ready product. Of course, most commercial vendors allow you to download free evaluation copies of their software from their Web site. The vendors in the following list offer ORB and CORBAservice products for Java largely in standalone or product-suite form:

- *Iona Technologies, Inc.* (`www.iona.com`)
- *Borland Corporation* (`www.borland.com`)
- *PrismTech* (`www.prismtechnologies.com`)
- *JacORB* (`www.jacorb.org`)

Additionally, as a few key examples, the following vendors offer COTS products and server frameworks that make use of an ORB and CORBAservices:

- *Oracle* (`www.oracle.com`)
- *BEA WebLogic* (`www.beasys.com`)

Thus, as you can see, many vendors out there either have created the building blocks for building CORBA-based systems or have already begun to integrate CORBA into their server frameworks as the distributed communications enabler of choice. Apart from CORBA vendor solutions, many other more proprietary and application-specific uses of CORBA have been permeating our marketplace. Visit the OMG Web site (`www.omg.org`) to keep abreast of where CORBA is being used today.

Java IDL

Java IDL has a Java-based set of CORBA 2.3.1–compliant libraries for Java, including an IDL-to-Java compiler, CORBA Naming Service implementations (`orbd` and `tnameserv`), and a tool for managing persistent CORBA servers (`servertool`). CORBA servers built atop the Java IDL ORB can be either transient or persistent by nature. Persistent servers are dormant CORBA objects that can be stored for activation upon client request given a persistent reference to that object using the `orbd` naming service. Transient servers exist only during the lifetime of that server's processes and use the `tnameserv` naming service. Java IDL also now supports both the Basic Object Adapter (BOA) and more favored Portable Object Adapter (POA) means for object activation. Java IDL does not implement an Interface Repository, however, and as a result, Java IDL-based CORBA clients cannot use DII.

Java IDL was first available as a separately downloadable package of Java libraries that could be used with your JRE but is now included with the J2SE v1.4. The J2EE (by virtue of requiring the J2SE physical distribution) comes equipped with Java IDL for building Java-based CORBA clients and servers. Because Java IDL is packaged with the J2SE, any J2SE-based application can act as a CORBA server or client. However, use of Java IDL in commercial-grade applications is generally not recommended because it is designed to be a reference implementation with prototyping and initial development usage in mind. Hence, developers may develop their CORBA applications using Java IDL, but should seriously consider use of a commercial-grade ORB when deploying their CORBA-based applications to a production environment.

CORBA Interfaces

You should now be armed with the conceptual framework and knowledge of which tools you'll need in order to build CORBA-based applications. Now you can begin the first step in creating an actual CORBA application. Such a first step requires that you define a distributed interface to each CORBA server class via CORBA IDL. The IDL interfaces used in our example application that we will create here are shown in Listing

8.1 (Order.idl), Listing 8.2 (ClientReceiver.idl), Listing 8.3 (Customer.idl), and Listing 8.4 (QueryServer.idl).

Note

This section is the first section that begins describing an example CORBA server and client that we've created for this chapter. Because the examples can involve a significant amount of code, we take the approach in this chapter to provide snippets from such examples as they become relevant. We occasionally provide complete listings here as well for certain smaller and key source code elements. You are encouraged to examine the complete code example files for yourself as the discussion proceeds.

The CORBA IDL interfaces and all code examples used in this chapter are located as described in Appendix A, "Software Configuration," and extracted beneath the examples\src\ejava\corba directory. Four subdirectories also exist under this directory, including examples\src\ejava\corba\regular, which contains the basic CORBA example code used here. The examples\src\ejava\corba\delegation directory contains example code almost identical in nature to the basic example code with the exception that the CORBA servers use the CORBA delegation (that is, "Tie") implementation technique instead of the inheritance technique used by the core examples. The directory examples\src\ejava\corba\dynamic contains example code for DII and DSI, and the examples\src\ejava\corba\irquery directory is used to illustrate what gets inserted into an Interface Repository.

Listing 8.1 depicts an Order IDL struct and typedef for a sequence of Orders to encapsulate the minimum information needed to satisfy a simple BeeShirts.com order. Note that the Order object here could also have been appropriately defined as a valuetype if the Orbs you are using support objects by value. We illustrate just such a concept toward the end in this chapter.

Listing 8.1 **CORBA IDL Order** (Order.idl)

```
module ejava
{
  module corba
  {
    struct Order
    {
      long orderID;
      string orderDate;
      double orderValue;
    };

    typedef sequence<Order> OrdersSeq;
  };
};
```

The `ClientReceiver` interface shown in Listing 8.2 will be used to implement a CORBA server on the client side of our application that the server side will call (that is, a callback). Thus the client side's `ClientReceiver` object will simply take a sequence of `Order` objects from the server side. Such a callback mechanism simply illustrates how clients can sometimes also act as servers in CORBA interactions. A callback example will also illustrate how CORBA clients can pass references to themselves over to CORBA servers.

Listing 8.2 **CORBA IDL Client Callback (`ClientReceiver.idl`)**

```
#include "Order.idl"

module ejava
{
  module corba
  {
    interface ClientReceiver
    {
      void setResultOrders(in OrdersSeq orders);
    };
  };
};
```

The `Customer` interface of Listing 8.3 is used to distribute an interface encapsulating a BeeShirts.com customer. Note that in an actual application, you would typically want to avoid defining an interface at this low level of granularity in order to be used in scalable enterprise environments. That is, defining IDL interfaces at the attribute level in particular will mean that a distributed call will result for each client attempt to get or set an attribute value. However, for the sake of simplifying our example and seeing utility in demonstrating a CORBA anti-pattern, we will refrain from the best practices for the time being.

Listing 8.3 **CORBA IDL for a Customer (`Customer.idl`)**

```
module ejava
{
  module corba
  {
    interface Customer
    {
       attribute string firstName;
       attribute string lastName;
       attribute string address1;
       attribute string address2;
       attribute string city;
       attribute string state;
```

Listing 8.3 **Continued**

```
        attribute string zip;
        attribute string phoneNumber;
        attribute string emailAddress;
    };

    typedef sequence<string> RegisterdCustomerNames;
  };
};
```

The `QueryServer` interface of Listing 8.4 describes the primary server-side CORBA interface for our application. It is CORBAservices that operate at this level of granularity that are the most appropriate for building scalable applications. The `QueryServer` offers a very specialized set of interfaces to illustrate the CORBA-enabling concepts at work. A call to `findCustomersWhoOrderedForMoreThan()` finds customers who spend more than a certain amount of money, binds them to a lookup service, and returns a sequence of customer IDs. A method `register()` takes a `ClientReceiver` callback interface and client receiver name to register CORBA client callbacks. A method `findOrdersWhichAreFrom()` finds the orders for a given state and passes the set of associated orders to the registered `ClientReceiver` objects.

Listing 8.4 **CORBA IDL for a Query Server (`QueryServer.idl`)**

```
#include "Customer.idl"
#include "ClientReceiver.idl"

module ejava
{
  module corba
  {
    interface QueryServer
    {
      RegisterdCustomerNames
        findCustomersWhoOrderedForMoreThan(in float value);
      void findOrdersWhichAreFrom(in string state);
      void register(in string name, in ClientReceiver clientReceiver);
    };
  };
};
```

CORBA Servers and Skeletons

Whereas IDL defines the distributed interfaces available to a distributed service, a CORBA server and skeleton represent the implementation of that interface. Most of the complex design and implementation decisions associated with building a CORBA-based application are associated with server-side development. Compilation of IDL can generate CORBA skeletons that are then linked to your CORBA server implementations. The remaining discussion in this section describes how to implement CORBA servers using the CORBA skeletons generated by IDL compilation.

Compiling the IDLs and Generating Skeletons

After defining your IDL, you'll want to run the IDL through an IDL-to-Java compiler to generate the CORBA skeletons used by your CORBA server implementations. The IDL-to-Java compiler used with Java IDL is called `idlj`. Before you use `idlj`, however, you'll want to determine what type of servers you'll want to create. That is, do you want to implement your CORBA server using skeleton inheritance or delegation (aka the Tie approach)? After this decision is made, the appropriate option can be added to the command line of your `idlj` invocation to generate the appropriate skeleton types.

The `build.xml` file in the `examples\src\ejava\corba\regular` directory is used by ANT to generate stubs and skeletons for regular inheritance-based implementations using a target for each IDL file akin to this one shown here:

```
<target name="idl2java">
 <java  classname="com.sun.tools.corba.se.idl.toJavaPortable.Compile"
        fork="true">
  <arg value="-fall"/>
  <arg line="-td ${src}"/>
  <arg line="-pkgTranslate ejava.corba ejava.corba.regular"/>
  <arg file="${basedir}\ClientReceiver.idl"/>
  <classpath>
    <pathelement path="${java.class.path}"/>
  </classpath>
    ...
</target>
```

The `build.xml` file in the `examples\src\ejava\corba\delegation` directory generates stubs and skeletons for delegation-based Tie implementations using something akin to this:

```
<target name="idl2java">
 <java  classname="com.sun.tools.corba.se.idl.toJavaPortable.Compile"
        fork="true" >
  <arg value="-fallTIE"/>
  <arg line="-td ${src}"/>
  <arg line="-pkgTranslate ejava.corba ejava.corba.delegation"/>
  <arg file="${basedir}\ClientReceiver.idl"/>
  <classpath>
    <pathelement path="${java.class.path}"/>
  </classpath>
```

```
 </java>
   ...
</target>
```

The inheritance technique involves generating a skeleton from which your CORBA server implementation will inherit. The delegation technique involves generating a skeleton that will call your CORBA server, which implements a generated Java interface. The con, of course, with the inheritance approach is that your server will be unable to inherit from any other class due to Java's single-inheritance limitation.

Creating the CORBA Servers

As implied thus far, two main models exist for implementing a CORBA server. These models are the inheritance model and the delegation model. If you are using the inheritance approach, you should take note that it may be a good general idea to separate your business logic implementation from any CORBA-specific library dependencies by hand-coding the delegation of calls from your CORBA server implementation to a business logic class. This is why we illustrate such an adapter in Figure 8.4's depiction of a CORBA server built using inheritance. Note the similarity to Figure 8.5's illustration of a CORBA server built using delegation.

In both cases of building a `MyServer` implementation from the `MyServer.idl` file, a `MyServerOperations` interface is generated. However, in the case of Figure 8.4, the `MyServerPOA` abstract class needs to be inherited from your `MyServerImpl` object, which can also delegate to your business logic code. Delegation to your business logic code helps keep your logic separate from your distribution paradigm (CORBA here). Of course, in using the delegation model (that is, the Tie approach) of Figure 8.5, the `MyServerPAOTie` delegation class will be generated for you and will delegate calls to your `MyServerImpl` implementation, which now must implement the `MyServerOperations` interface.

The `CustomerImplementation`, `ClientReceiverImplementation`, and `QueryServerImplementation` classes associated with this chapter are CORBA server implementations using the inheritance model inside the `examples\src\ejava\corba\regular` directory and using the delegation model inside the `examples\src\ejava\corba\delegation` directory. Throughout the remainder of this section, we only list the inheritance-based CORBA server implementations. However, aside from what interfaces are implemented versus what classes are extended, the basic structure and implementation of the CORBA servers are the same.

> **Note**
>
> The `build.xml` file in the `examples\src\ejava\corba` directory is used by ANT to compile the server implementations for both models. A `runscript` in the `regular` and `delegation` subdirectories is generated by the ANT build process and can be used to execute each example. Pause statements are inserted into these scripts before each process that is spawned. You should wait for each process to start and initialize before allowing the next process to start.

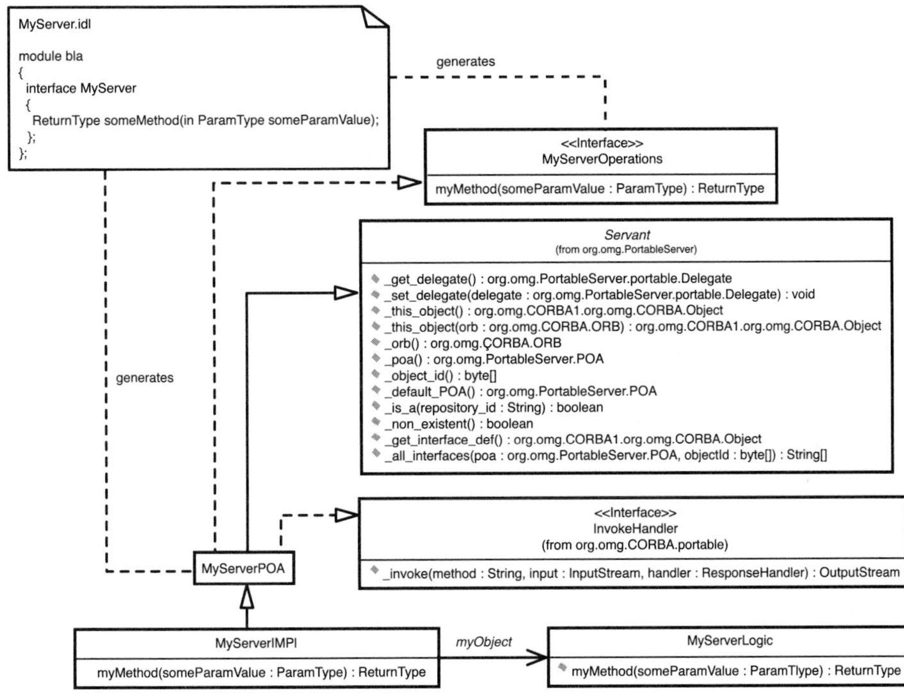

Figure 8.4 A CORBA server built using inheritance.

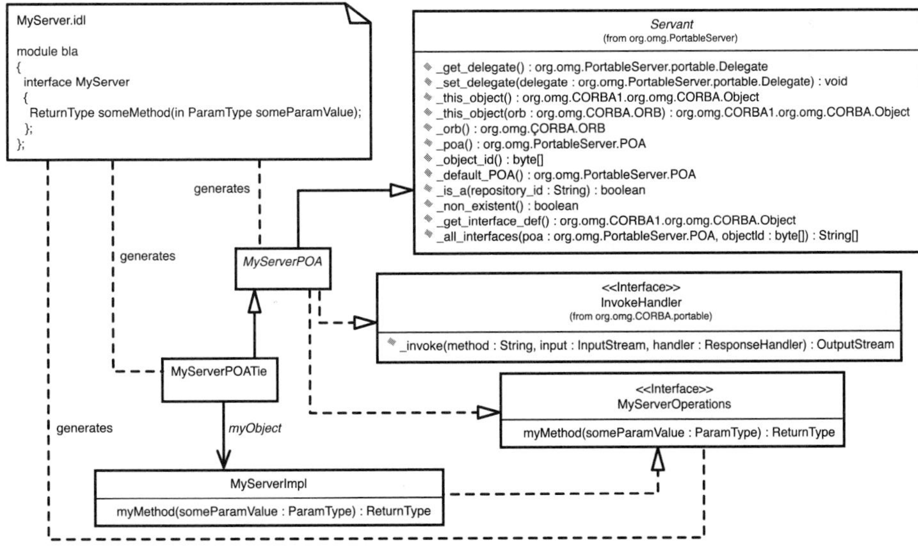

Figure 8.5 A CORBA server built using delegation.

Note that all accessor methods on the `CustomerImplementation` class needing implementation based on the attributes defined in the IDL Listing 8.3 have been implemented by this class for a distributable `Customer` object instance as illustrated in Listing 8.5.

Listing 8.5 **CORBA Server for Customer Implementation (`CustomerImplementation.java`)**

```
package ejava.corba.regular;
  ...
public class CustomerImplementation extends CustomerPOA
{
  private  String firstName;
   ...
  public String firstName(){ return firstName;}
  public void firstName(String newFirstName){ firstName = newFirstName;}
   ...
}
```

The `ClientReceiverImplementation` class implements the one remote method declared in the IDL Listing 8.2. Such a class implements a callback server implemented on the client side. The `setResultOrders()` method simply prints the list of orders received as shown in Listing 8.6.

> **CORBA Callbacks**
>
> Our CORBA callback example allows the CORBA client to pass a reference to the CORBA server such that the server can invoke a callback onto the client. We provide this example here to illustrate how CORBA applications can pass references to other CORBA servers around in a distributed fashion. As you'll discover later in this part of the book, such a feature is not available to other distributed communication paradigms such as Web services.

Listing 8.6 **CORBA Server for Client Receiver Implementation (`ClientReceiverImplementation.java`)**

```
package ejava.corba.regular;
  ...
public class ClientReceiverImplementation  extends ClientReceiverPOA
{
  public void setResultOrders (ejava.corba.Order[] orders)
  {
    System.out.println("Received :"+orders.length);
    for(int i =0; i<orders.length; i++){
      System.out.println("Received Order :"+orders[i]);
      System.out.println("Order ID:" +orders[i].orderID);
      System.out.println("Order Date:" +orders[i].orderDate);
```

Listing 8.6 **Continued**

```
            System.out.println("Order Value:" +orders[i].orderValue);
        }
    }
}
```

The `QueryServerImplementation` implements the `QueryServer` IDL interface declared in Listing 8.4. The `QueryServer` object represents the frontline interface for CORBA clients and contains most of the business logic for our example. The `QueryServerImplementation` reads Java preferences set for a database driver class, URL, username, and password. This information is used to establish a connection with the BeeShirts.com database via JDBC. As an illustration of the `QueryServerImplementation` class's skeletal structure, we have the example as shown in Listing 8.7.

Listing 8.7 **CORBA Server for Query Server Implementation (`QueryServerImplementation.java`)**

```
package ejava.corba.regular;
  ...
public class QueryServerImplementation  extends QueryServerPOA
{
   ...

  public QueryServerImplementation(){...}

  public String[] findCustomersWhoOrderedForMoreThan (float value){...}

  public void findOrdersWhichAreFrom(String state){...}

  public void register (String name,
                  ejava.corba.ClientReceiver clientReceiver){...}

  private ResultSet getResultSet(String sqlQuery, Object whereValue)
                     throws SQLException { ...}
}
```

The private `getResultSet()` method takes an SQL query for creating a prepared statement and subsequently for returning a result set. The `findCustomersWhoOrderedForMoreThan()` method retrieves the customer query from Java preferences (set as the `customer.query` property in the local `build.properties` file) and issues the query using `getResultSet()`. The results of this query are then used to create a new distributed `CustomerImplementation` object reference. We will discuss how this reference is made available to the CORBA client shortly. The `register()` method is used to register a `ClientReceiver` with the

QueryServer. The findOrdersWhichAreFrom() method retrieves an order query from Java preferences (set as the order.query property in the local build.properties file) and then issues this query for obtaining a set of related orders.

These orders are used to create a sequence of serializable Order objects and then to make a callback on the distributed CORBA client ClientReceiver references that were registered using the register() method. The Order object generated by the IDL-to-Java compilation of Listing 8.1 simply defines the data to be serialized as public field variables. Note that because the Order class implements the org.omg.CORBA.portable.IDLEntity interface, it is declared a Serializable object because IDLEntity extends the Serializable interface. A skeletal structure of the Order class is shown in Listing 8.8.

Listing 8.8 **Generated CORBA IDL Entity Object for Order Data** (Order.java)

```
package ejava.corba.regular;
...
public final class Order implements org.omg.CORBA.portable.IDLEntity
{
  public int orderID = (int)0;
  public String orderDate = null;
  public double orderValue = (double)0;

  public Order (){}
  public Order(int _orderID, String _orderDate, double orderValue){...}
}
```

DSI-Based Servers

The CORBA servers that were just implemented make use of IDL to generate skeletons to which your CORBA implementations statically relate. The Dynamic Skeleton Interface (DSI) can be implemented by your servers in order to avoid such dynamic bindings. Figure 8.6 shows how to create a DSI-based server. Your server must thus extend the org.omg.CORBA.DynamicImplementation abstract class and implement the invoke() method.

> **Note**
>
> An example is included with this chapter's code that demonstrates an implementation of such a DSI-based server. The example is contained in the examples\src\ejava\corba\dynamic directory. Note that this example would not work with Java IDL at the time of this book's writing. We have thus used the ORB included with the Borland Enterprise Application Server v5.1 downloadable from www.borland.com/products/downloads. You'll need to download and install the ORB associated with that server. Then you'll need to set the root directory of your install in the build.properties file in the examples\src\ejava\corba\dynamic directory such as visigenic.home=C:/Tools/BES. Before running ANT using the build.xml file in that directory, you also need to set the following environment variables as illustrated here:

```
SET VISIGENIC_HOME=C:\Tools\BES
SET JAVA_HOME=%VISIGENIC_HOME%\jdk
SET PATH=%JAVA_HOME%\bin;%VISIGENIC_HOME%\bin;%PATH%
```

A `run` script is generated from ANT that allows you to execute the example. Refer to Appendix A for how to configure this product and for examples in more detail.

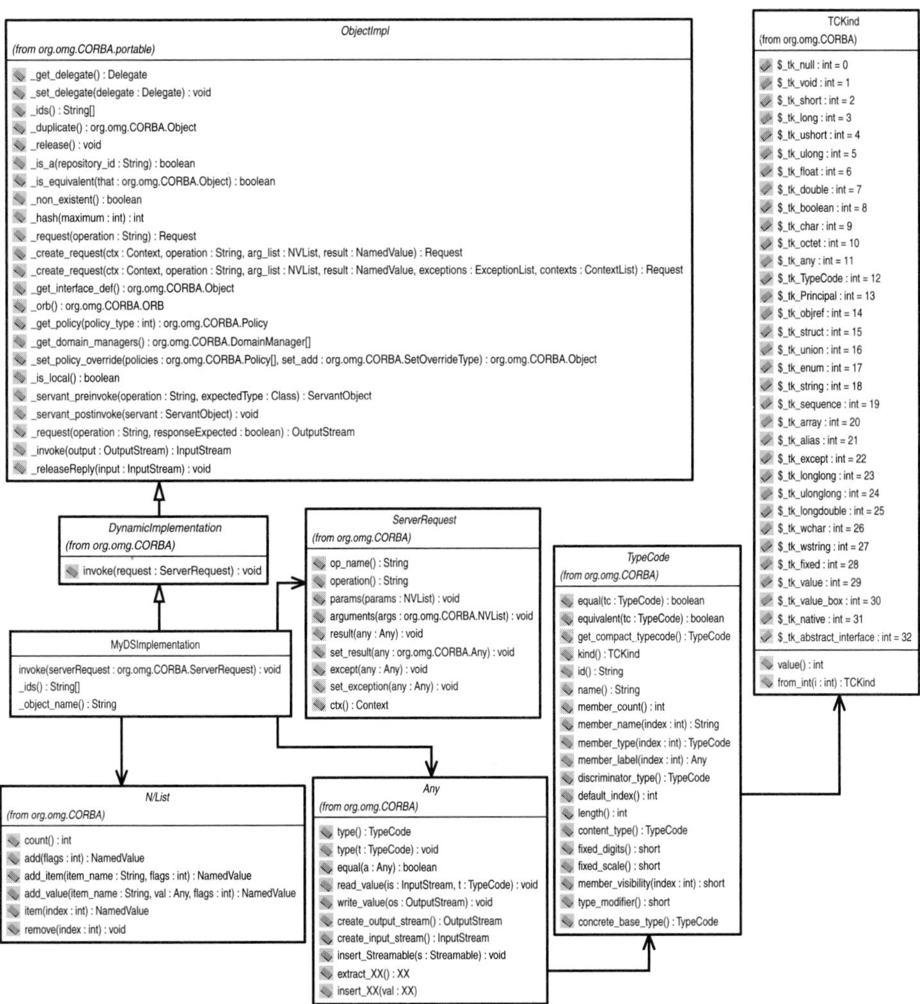

Figure 8.6 A CORBA server built using DSI.

Inside of the `invoke()` method for our example `SampleDynamic` class included with this chapter's code, the server takes an `org.omg.CORBA.ServerRequest` object as a parameter, and it uses this object to retrieve the request parameters and store the result. An `org.omg.CORBA.NVList` is used to build up a list of parameters. In our example, we use the `org.omg.CORBA.Any` object to create a parameter identified by an `org.omg.CORBA.TCKind` type and add it to the parameter list. After the parameter values are retrieved from the request object, the actual result can be generated and set onto the request object. A skeletal structure of the `SampleDynamic` class is shown in Listing 8.9.

Listing 8.9 **CORBA DSI-Based Server Sample (`SampleDynamic.java`)**

```
package ejava.corba.dynamic;
 ...
public class SampleDynamic extends DynamicImplementation
{
 ...

 public SampleDynamic(String name, POA poaRef, ORB orb){...}

 public void invoke(org.omg.CORBA.ServerRequest serverRequest)
  {
    // make sure the operation name is correct
    if(!serverRequest.operation().equals(OPERATION_NAME)) {
      throw new org.omg.CORBA.BAD_OPERATION();
    }
    // create an empty name value parameter list
    org.omg.CORBA.NVList parameters = orb.create_list(0);
    // create an any for ParameterName
    org.omg.CORBA.Any nameOfParameter = orb.create_any();
    // any's type is String
    nameOfParameter.type(
      orb.get_primitive_tc(org.omg.CORBA.TCKind.tk_string));
    // add "in" the parameter name to the parameter list
    parameters.add_value(IN_PARAMETER_NAME, nameOfParameter,
                         org.omg.CORBA.ARG_IN.value);
    // get the parameter and values from the request
    serverRequest.arguments(parameters);
    // get received value from parameter
    String receivedValue = nameOfParameter.extract_string();
    // invoke sayHello method
    String returnValue = this.sayHello(receivedValue);
    // create an any for the reply
    org.omg.CORBA.Any stringAny = orb.create_any();
    stringAny.insert_string(returnValue);
    // set the request's result
    serverRequest.set_result(stringAny);
  }
```

Listing 8.9 **Continued**

```
  String sayHello(String receivedValue)
  {
    return "You sent me :"+ receivedValue;
  }

  public String[] _ids()
  {
    return ids;
  }

  public String _object_name()
  {
    return this.objectName;
  }

  public String[] _all_interfaces(POA poa, byte[] objectId)
  {
    //Used by the ORB to obtain complete type information from
    // the servant. For this example we can return null;
    return null;
  }
}
```

ORB Infrastructure

CORBA servers rely on a certain infrastructure to be provided in order to expose their interfaces in a distributed fashion. The implementation repository encapsulates that aspect of an ORB that is cognizant of the CORBA server implementation class information. The object adapter is responsible for understanding how to activate CORBA server instances given its implementation stored in the implementation repository. An Interface Repository is used to store information about the server's interfaces such that the server can be dynamically understood by remote clients and subsequently invoked. This section looks underneath the hood a bit at such infrastructure and describes its relevance to application developers in the context of our CORBA client/server example we are evolving throughout this chapter.

Implementation Repository

After you have created a CORBA server, your server implementation must typically be registered with an implementation repository. Let's take some time here to discuss what is happening under the hood when this occurs. The implementation repository is a run-time repository of information describing the classes supported on the server side of a particular ORB. Implementation repositories are used to register and unregister object implementations on the server side as well as provide meta-data about the implementation. Other information such as current instances and object identifiers can be stored in an implementation repository. The implementation repository is mainly an idea described by CORBA specifications, and it lacked standardization in early specification versions. It is simply an assumed part of any server-side ORB needing to store object implementation information.

The implementation repository is utilized and managed by the ORB's object adapter implementation. The actual underlying storage methodology in an implementation repository is vendor specific because it depends on a vendor's object adapter implementation. Because early versions of the specification lacked sufficient definition of ORB object adapters, both object adapter and implementation repository implementations tended to contain many vendor-specific features.

Technically speaking, many implementation repositories take on more object-adapter–specific roles as well. Most often, the implementation repository can be accessed via the command line or programmatically. Common commands include the capability to register, unregister, and list implementations in the implementation repository. Java IDL also includes an implementation repository. The next subsection discusses this topic in a little more detail in the context of its integration with an object adapter and continues with the creation of our CORBA-based application.

Object Adapters

Your CORBA server objects need to be brought into memory (activated) upon a client request on those objects. The client request indeed must somehow map to a call onto the specific skeleton used by your CORBA server. Furthermore, the decision must be made as to whether a new process is to be created, a new thread is to be created, or perhaps an existing thread is to be reused for your CORBA server. The ORB's object adapter is responsible for this type of ORB functionality.

The Basic Object Adapter (BOA) was required for implementation by all CORBA 2.0–compliant ORBs, but it soon became apparent that the BOA had gaping holes in the specification. Thus, various vendor-specific features emerged. The BOA has since been deprecated, and the Portable Object Adapter (POA) specification now helps ensure that object implementations can be portable across ORBs. Because the POA now represents the de facto standard that enables activation in CORBA, we focus on the POA here.

Because CORBA is simply a set of specifications, certain implementation details regarding the CORBA activation model vary from vendor to vendor. Thus, for example, the exact model that is supported for allocating threads to active server objects is left up to the vendor implementations. The CORBA specifications naturally focus on interfaces that need to be defined to enable vendor interoperability. CORBA specifications also offer the applications that utilize them the capability to use different vendor products without, ideally, any modifications.

Although precise thread models are undefined, the POA specification does define a thread model policy identification mechanism that indicates whether a single-threaded model or ORB-controlled threading model is supported. If a POA supports only a single-threaded model, requests are managed by a single thread allocated for a servant object, and that servant object can be implemented in a thread-unaware fashion. In an ORB-controlled model of threading, the POA is responsible for creating, allocating, and destroying threads that are associated with servants. Specific thread model behavior to be expected and ways to configure an ORB-controlled thread model are vendor-specific.

Figure 8.7 depicts the CORBA activation service architecture employed by the POA via a conceptual diagram with some CORBA entities interspersed. Central to this architecture is the POA interface used to register CORBA server implementations and objects (aka servants). Depending on the servant retention policy of the POA, an active set of servants can be retained in an active object map. A servant manager can be used by the POA to activate a particular servant. A specific type of servant manager known as a servant activator will actually carry out such a task when the servants will be retained in an active object map. Another type of servant manager known as a servant locator can be used when the servant will not be retained and is used only for a single request.

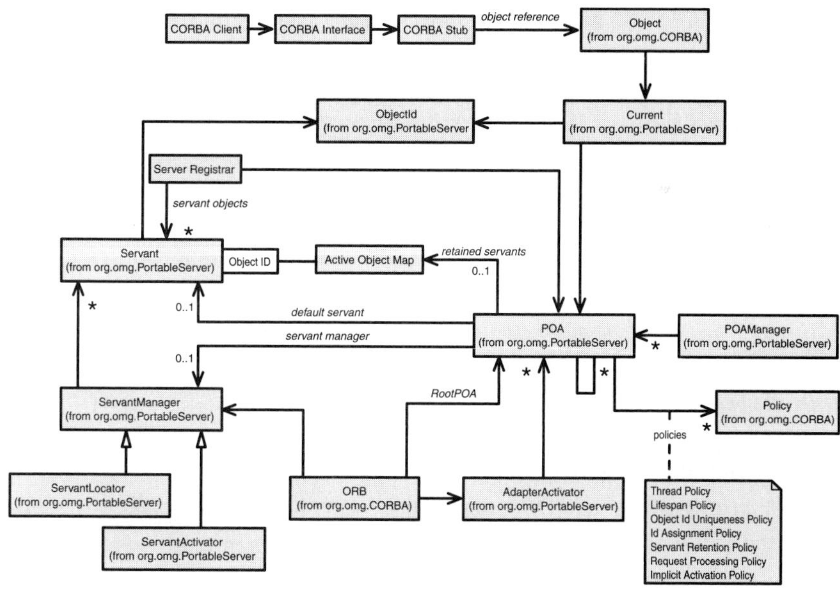

Figure 8.7 The CORBA activation service architecture.

Although object references are still held by the client, an underlying object ID is used by a POA to uniquely identify servants. A new current execution context object can be used to associate a POA and an object ID for a CORBA object.

An initial reference to a root POA can be obtained from the ORB using the `ORB.resolve_initial_references("RootPOA")` call. Adapter activators can also be associated with a POA so that ORBs can create POA instances when a particular child POA does not exist. A POA manager can be used to manage POAs in a collection and deactivate particular POAs. With a POA reference in hand, server registrars register servants with a particular POA governed by a set of POA policies. After registration of a servant with a POA, the following general sequence of steps to activate a servant that is currently inactive occurs during CORBA client requests:

1. *CORBA client attempts reference:* A CORBA client attempts to reference a remote CORBA servant object with an underlying object reference.
2. *ORB obtains POA reference:* A portable execution context is associated with the object reference. The portable current execution context associates the reference with a particular POA. The server-side ORB can use an adapter activator to instantiate an instance of the referenced POA if it does not exist.
3. *POA obtains object ID:* The server-side POA yields an object ID from the portable current execution context.
4. *POA looks for cached object instance:* The POA looks in its active object map for an active instance associated with the object ID if a retain policy is in effect for this POA.
5. *POA requests servant from servant manager:* If POA cannot find an active servant associated with the object ID, it will ask the servant manager to activate the object. This is also referred to as asking the servant manager to incarnate the object.
6. *Servant manager loads servant information:* The servant manager then must load the servant implementation and data using the object ID. The object ID can contain class location information and information indicating where initialization data can be loaded from.
7. *Servant manager instantiates servant:* The servant manager then creates an active instance of the servant object associated with the object ID.
8. *POA obtains servant handle:* The POA receives the created instance back from the servant manager and inserts the servant reference in its active object map if the servant was retrieved from the servant activator.
9. *POA invokes servant:* The POA then makes the requested call on the active object.
10. *CORBA client request satisfied:* The CORBA client is then returned any results from a distributed object invocation.

Object Adapter Examples

In the static server example, we have created a separate server registrar (`ServerRegistrar`) to register our frontline `QueryServer` object with the Java IDL ORB. After reading the server name from the Java preferences object, the

ServerRegistrar object's main() method gets a handle to an org.omg.CORBA.ORB object from a NamingCotextUtility object as shown here:

```
// read query.server.name from build.properties
String name = // read server name from Java preference

// Get orb handle
ORB    orb  = NamingContextUtility.getORB();
```

The NamingContextUtility class is simply a helper class used with many of our examples. The NamingContextUtility.getORB() method returns a handle to an ORB object as shown here:

```
 public static ORB getORB()
{
  if(orb == null) {
    String[] args = new String[0];
    initializeOrb(args);
  }
  return orb;
}

public static void initializeOrb(String[] args)
{

  if(orb == null) {
    orb = ORB.init(args, null);
  }
}
```

The main() method of the ServerRegistrar class then obtains a handle to the POA object and activates the POA manager as shown here:

```
// get reference to rootpoa & activate the POAManager
POA rootpoa =
  POAHelper.narrow(orb.resolve_initial_references("RootPOA"));
rootpoa.the_POAManager().activate();
```

The QueryServerImplementation CORBA server object is then registered with the POA as shown here:

```
// createQueryServerImplementation
QueryServerImplementation queryServerImpl =
  new QueryServerImplementation();

// get object reference from the servant
org.omg.CORBA.Object reference =
  rootpoa.servant_to_reference(queryServerImpl);
```

You will also see that the ServerRegistrar also uses the CORBA Naming Service to bind the server object to a name in the CosNaming service. We will demonstrate use of the CosNaming server toward the end of this chapter. As you'll see, the CosNaming service will allow our CORBA clients to obtain a handle to our CORBA server object in a portable fashion using the name with which it was registered on the server side into the CosNaming service.

The `ServerRegistrar` then invokes the `org.omg.CORBA.ORB.run()` call to wait for client requests until the particular server is shut down as shown here:

```
System.out.println("Waiting for clients:");
orb.run();
```

In our dynamic server example, a `main()` method in a `DynamicServer` class is used to register our `SampleDynamic` server object with the POA. An ORB handle, root POA, and POA manager are first obtained as was done for the static server examples. Subsequently, a set of server policies that define rules for managing the object such as its life cycle, request processing policy, and uniqueness are set onto the POA as shown here:

```
// Create the Dynamic Server POA with the right policies
org.omg.CORBA.Policy[] serverPolicies
  = {rootPOA.create_lifespan_policy(LifespanPolicyValue.PERSISTENT),
     rootPOA.create_request_processing_policy(
                     RequestProcessingPolicyValue.USE_DEFAULT_SERVANT),
     rootPOA.create_id_uniqueness_policy(
                     IdUniquenessPolicyValue.MULTIPLE_ID)
    };
POA dynamicPOA = rootPOA.create_POA("SampleDynamic",
                                    poaManager,
                                    serverPolicies);
```

A handle to a POA object that will handle the dynamic server is returned and used to register the `SampleDynamic` object as shown here:

```
// Create the sample servant and set onto the dynamic POA
SampleDynamic sampleServant
    = new SampleDynamic("SampleDynamic",dynamicPOA, orb);
dynamicPOA.set_servant(sampleServant);
```

Finally, the POA manager is activated and ORB run as shown here:

```
// Activate the POA Manager and run the ORB
poaManager.activate();
orb.run();
```

As a convenience, Java IDL also includes a utility new to the J2SE v1.4 called `servertool`. The `servertool` utility can be used to register, unregister, start up, and shut down CORBA servers that are persistent from the command line. Such servers must be registered with the persistent CORBA naming service `orbd` provided with Java IDL versus the transient naming service `tnameserv`. The command-line synopsis for using the `servertool` utility is provided at `http://java.sun.com/j2se/1.4.1/docs/guide/idl/servertool.html`.

Interface Repository

An Interface Repository (IR) is an online database of object interface definitions used under the hood of the client-side ORB to know how to package calls to distributed servers. The IR is thus essentially a container of runtime IDL information that describes how to interface with remote objects.

Java IDL in fact does not implement an IR and instead relies on the fact that CORBA clients will be able to generate or obtain the CORBA stubs needed to communicate with the remote server. However, IRs do come in handy when you're desiring to use things such as DII to dynamically interact with a CORBA server whose interface is unknown at compile time. DII uses the IR to understand the server's interface. Also, by providing a distributed interface to the IR itself, remote servers can actually dynamically publish their interfaces to the IR.

We have placed the discussion of IRs at this point in the chapter, because if you did not for some reason have the stubs you needed to build your CORBA clients, then you would need to be sure to register the remote interfaces with the IR to which your CORBA client desired access. An IR can be accessed via the command line, from a GUI interface, or programmatically. The Borland ORB's IR can be accessed from the command line and via a GUI interface using the `irep` command. Updates to the Visibroker IR can be made with the `idl2ir` command.

To programmatically access the IR, you'll need to use the various `org.omg.CORBA.<IDL_Entity_Name>Def` interfaces. Such an interface exists for each type of IDL entity that can exist in an IR (most of the entities listed in Table 8.1), such as `ModuleDef`, `InterfaceDef`, `StructDef`, `TypeDef`, `OperationDef`, `AttributeDef`, `ParameterDef`, `ConstantDef`, and `ExceptionDef`. Each IDL entity can inherit from a `Container` interface designating that such an IDL entity can contain other entities and from a `Contained` interface designating that such an IDL entity can be contained by other entities. Both `Container` and `Contained` types inherit from the base `IRObject` interface designating a generic IDL entity sitting inside of an Interface Repository. The IR, encapsulated by the `Repository` interface, can contain one or more `IRObjects` and itself extends the `Container` interface.

Each `IRObject` type is identifiable by a constant in the `org.omg.CORBA.DefinitionKind` class. This can be contrasted with the `TCKind` class identifying all the possible type codes that can exist but don't necessarily belong in an IR (for example, fundamental types such as `long`).

> **Note**
>
> An Interface Repository viewing example is extracted to the `examples\src\ejava\corba\irquery` directory. Note that this example would not work with Java IDL at the time of this book's writing. We have thus used the ORB included with the Borland Enterprise Application Server v5.1 as described earlier. Use the same installation process when running the dynamic server example earlier in this chapter. Refer to Appendix A for more detail on how to configure such examples. A `run` script generated by the ANT build for this example is placed into the `examples\src\ejava\corba\irquery` directory and provides a script for executing this example.

We have included an example class named `ListContentsAModule` with this chapter's code in the `examples\src\ejava\corba\irquery` directory. The `main()` method takes in the name of an IDL module from the command line, creates an instance of a `ModuleDef` interface representing that module in the IR, and passes this `ModuleDef` into the `printAModule()` call as shown here:

```
org.omg.CORBA.ORB orb = org.omg.CORBA.ORB.init(args, null);

com.inprise.vbroker.ir.Repository repository =
  com.inprise.vbroker.ir.RepositoryHelper.narrow(
    orb.resolve_initial_references("InterfaceRepository"));

org.omg.CORBA.ModuleDef moduleDefinition =
  org.omg.CORBA.ModuleDefHelper.narrow(
    repository.lookup(queryingFor));

printAModule(moduleDefinition);
```

The `printAModule()` call will first retrieve an array of the elements contained in the particular module. Depending on the type of element, some informative information will be printed. We do this only for a few key element types as exemplified here:

```
public static String getIDLName(org.omg.CORBA.IDLType idlType)
{
  org.omg.CORBA.Contained contained =
    org.omg.CORBA.ContainedHelper.narrow(idlType);
  if(contained == null){
    return idlType.type().toString();
  }else{
    return  contained.absolute_name();
  }
}

public static void printAModule(org.omg.CORBA.Container container)
{
  // get content of a module
  org.omg.CORBA.Contained[] contained =
    container.contents(org.omg.CORBA.DefinitionKind.dk_all, true);
  // For each element, run through case statement to print info
  for(int i = 0; i < contained.length; i++) {
  {
    switch(contained[i].def_kind().value())
    {
      case org.omg.CORBA.DefinitionKind._dk_Attribute:
      {
        org.omg.CORBA.AttributeDef attributeDef =
          org.omg.CORBA.AttributeDefHelper.narrow(contained[i]);
```

```
    String readonly = "";
    if( attributeDef.mode() ==
      org.omg.CORBA.AttributeMode.ATTR_READONLY ){
      readonly = "readonly \" : \"";
    }
    System.out.println(readonly + "attribute " +
      getIDLName(attributeDef.type_def()) + " " +
      attributeDef.name() + ";");
  }
    break;
      ...
  case org.omg.CORBA.DefinitionKind._dk_Interface:
  {
    org.omg.CORBA.InterfaceDef interfaceDef =
      org.omg.CORBA.InterfaceDefHelper.narrow(contained[i]);
    org.omg.CORBA.InterfaceDefPackage.FullInterfaceDescription
      interfaceDescription  =
        interfaceDef.describe_interface();
    System.out.println("Operations in :"+interfaceDef.name());
    for(int i1 = 0; i1 < interfaceDescription.operations.length;
      i1++){
      System.out.println("   " +
        interfaceDescription.operations[i1].name +";");
    }

    for(int i2 = 0; i2 < interfaceDescription.attributes.length;
      i2++){
      System.out.println("   " +
        interfaceDescription.attributes[i2].name +";");
    }
  }
    break;
      ...
  case org.omg.CORBA.DefinitionKind._dk_Operation:
  {
    System.out.println("Error : not implemented operation");
  }
    break;
     case org.omg.CORBA.DefinitionKind._dk_Module:
  {
    org.omg.CORBA.ModuleDef module =
       org.omg.CORBA.ModuleDefHelper.narrow(contained[i]);

    System.out.println("Module name :" + module.name());

    printAModule(org.omg.CORBA.ModuleDefHelper.narrow(contained[i]));
```

```
        }
        break;
          ...
      }
    }
}
```

Portable Interceptors

CORBA also defines a means for ORBs to intercept requests and responses before they are sent over the distributed communications "wire" or before they are handed off to a client or server after they are received from the "wire." Such services are appropriately named CORBA interceptors. At one point in CORBA's history, different ORB vendors had different approaches for realizing interceptors. CORBA now defines a portable interceptor approach such that ORBs provided by different implementers can be more interoperable in a distributed computing environment.

The Java IDL feature incorporated into the J2SE v1.4 in fact includes support for portable interceptors defined inside of an `org.omg.PortableInterceptor` package. To a large extent, programming CORBA interceptors is more of a systems-level task that many developers using CORBA will rarely embark upon. Although use of such interceptors is beyond the scope of this chapter and book, we list the three main types of interceptors supported by Java IDL for you here:

- `IORInterceptor`: Used to intercept an IOR to read or write information defining the services available to a particular ORB, as well as perhaps embed application security-related information.
- `ClientRequestInterceptor`: Used to intercept requests sent by a client to filter or add information before it goes to the server and to intercept responses from the server to filter information before delegated back to the client.
- `ServerRequestInterceptor`: Used to intercept requests received by a server to filter information before it is delegated to the server and to intercept responses sent back to the client to filter and add information before it is sent over the wire.

CORBA Clients and Stubs

After your CORBA servers have been registered with their server-side ORBs and perhaps registered with a CosNaming-compliant naming service, your CORBA clients can then tap their services. For your CORBA clients to use such services, you will need to obtain a CORBA stub class acting as a proxy to the remote server. This stub can be generated by the IDL description of the server. Optionally, you may be able to use DII if your ORB implementation supports an Interface Repository and a DII.

CORBA Clients and Static Stubs

The `idlj` compiler command that was used earlier with the `-fall` option also created client-side stubs. As shown by the general client-side CORBA diagram in Figure 8.8, a stub named `_MyServerStub` is generated from an IDL file with an interface named `MyServer`. The CORBA client code makes calls on the generated `MyServer` interface, which is implemented by the `_MyServerStub` class. CORBA stubs extend the `ObjectImpl` class, which in turn extends the `org.omg.CORBA.Object` class. Additionally, the IDL compiler generates a `MyServerHolder` class for passing around `inout` and `out` IDL types, as well as a `MyServerHelper` class used by the client for narrowing object references and other helper methods.

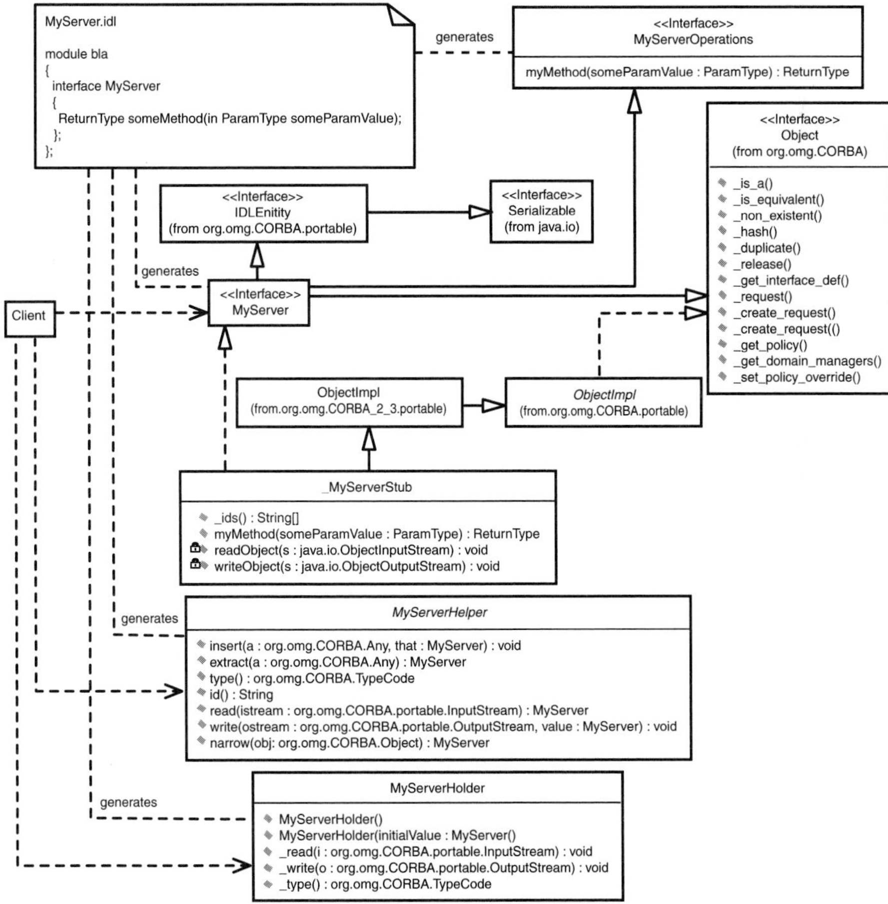

Figure 8.8 A CORBA client using static stubs.

A `Client` class included with our inheritance and delegation CORBA model examples not only demonstrates how a CORBA client can make distributed calls on a CORBA server, but also demonstrates how a CORBA client can register a distributed callback with a CORBA server.

> **Tip**
>
> Because in communications paradigms as flexible as CORBA the boundary between what is truly a server and what is truly a client becomes blurred, the term *servant* is often used to designate the merging of the traditionally distinct roles.

The `Client.main()` method first reads a Java preference that describes the name of the server to access. After obtaining a reference to a `QueryServer` (the mechanism for which is described in the next section), our `Client` creates an instance of a distributed `ClientReceiverImplementation` object and registers it with the `QueryServer` using the `register()` distributed call. The `Client` then makes the `findCustomersWhoOrderdForMoreThan()` distributed call on the `QueryServer` and displays some basic information about each returned `Customer`. When the `Client` calls `findOrdersWhichAreFrom()` on the `QueryServer`, the `QueryServerImplementation` makes a callback on the CORBA client's `ClientReceiver` object with a `ClientReceiver.setResultOrders()` call. The basic structure of the `Client.main()` method (excluding CORBA Naming service steps) is shown here:

```
// read query.server.name from build.properties
String name = // read server name from Java preference

// Get POA handle
ORB    orb  = NamingContextUtility.getORB();
POA rootpoa =
  POAHelper.narrow(orb.resolve_initial_references("RootPOA"));
  ...
QueryServer queryServer = // Lookup handle from CosNaming service

// Create client callback object
ClientReceiverImplementation clientReceiverDelegation =
  new ClientReceiverImplementation();
org.omg.CORBA.Object reference =
  rootpoa.servant_to_reference(clientReceiverImpl);
ClientReceiver clientReceiver =
  ClientReceiverHelper.narrow(reference);

// Now make remote calls...
queryServer.register("ClientReceiver", clientReceiver);
...
String[] customersNames =
```

```
        queryServer.findCustomersWhoOrderedForMoreThan(100.0f);
      ...
      queryServer.findOrdersWhichAreFrom("VA");
       ...
}
```

DII-Based Clients

As illustrated in Figure 8.9 and demonstrated in our `DynamicClient` example included with this chapter's code, your CORBA client can also use DII to communicate with a remote server. As it turns out, the `DynamicClient` DII client talks to the `SampleDynamic` DSI server we described earlier just to demonstrate both server-side and client-side dynamic communication sans any IDL. Of course, there are no limitations requiring that DII clients talk with DSI servers. DII can talk just as easily with static skeleton-based servers, and DSI servers can talk just as easily with IDL-based clients.

> **Note**
>
> The `DynamicClient` class is a simple DII example and is extracted to the `examples\src\ejava\corba\dynamic` directory. Note that this example would not work with Java IDL at the time of this book's writing. We have thus used the Borland ORB described earlier.

A DII client must first create a new `Request` object from a bound `org.omg.CORBA.Object` instance. We talk about such bindings in the next section. Thus, the first part of the `DynamicClient.main()` method must do the following:

```
// Initialize the ORB
org.omg.CORBA.Object sampleDynamic;
org.omg.CORBA.ORB    orb = org.omg.CORBA.ORB.init(args, null);

// Create Name and the manager Id
String name      = "/SampleDynamic";
byte[] managerID = name.getBytes();

// Locate SampleDynamic
sampleDynamic = ((com.inprise.vbroker.orb.ORB) orb).bind(name,
        managerID, null, null);

// Create request that will be sent to the manager
org.omg.CORBA.Request request =
  sampleDynamic._request(METHOD_NAME);
```

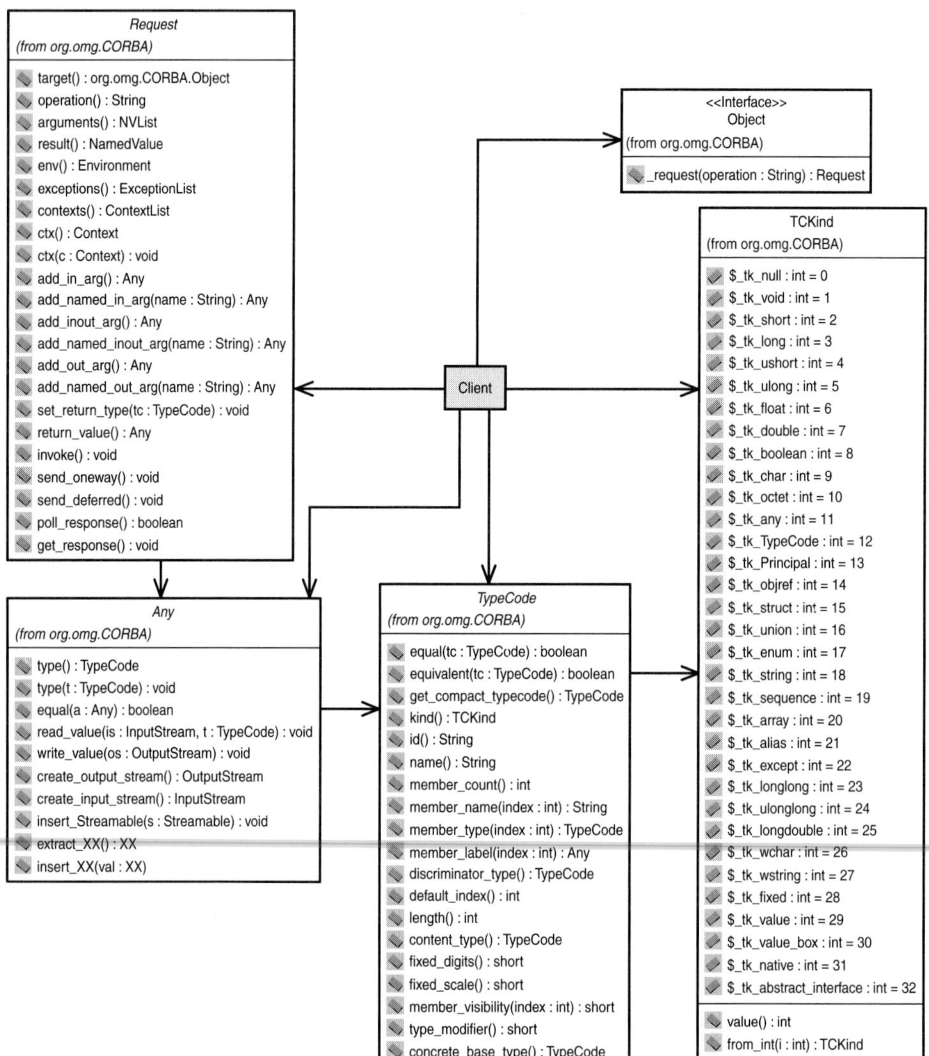

Figure 8.9 CORBA client using DII.

In DII it's key to consider the fact that after such a `Request` object is made with the name of the method to call (for example, `METHOD_NAME = "sayHello"`), a request needs to be built up in the `Request` object instance. This is accomplished by setting the return type, creating any parameter types, and setting each parameter's value directly onto the `Request` object. The request can then be invoked using `Request.invoke()`. Subsequently, the return value can be retrieved from the request stream using

`Request.return_value()`. Thus, the latter half of the `DynamicClient.main()` method must do the following:

```
request.set_return_type(
  orb.get_primitive_tc(org.omg.CORBA.TCKind.tk_string));

org.omg.CORBA.Any sendValue = request.add_in_arg();

sendValue.insert_string("Hi There");
request.invoke();

String resultValue = request.return_value().extract_string();
```

CORBA Naming

In all of our discussions thus far in this chapter, we have glossed over exactly how our clients and servers make the initial connection with one another. We've covered how to build a CORBA server, how to build a CORBA client, how to register or associate implementations on the server-side ORB, and how to register or associate interfaces on the client-side ORB. But how does a CORBA client obtain an object reference (IOR) and establish a connection with the CORBA server?

The most portable and the recommended way is to start up and use a CORBA Naming Service. The CORBA Naming Service is used on the server side by associating a human-readable name to an IOR with the CosNaming server. The CORBA Naming Service is used on the client side by using a human-readable name to obtain a handle to the CORBA server object via the IOR associated inside of the CosNaming server.

We describe the CosNaming service and naming services in general in Chapter 11, "Naming Services with JNDI," but recall that we've used a helper class throughout our examples that we created called `ejava.corba.NamingContextUtility`. The `NamingContextUtility.getNamingContext()` call simply resolves an initial reference to a CosNaming service to which your ORB can connect and narrows this reference to an `org.omg.CosNaming.NamingContext` object as shown here:

```
package ejava.corba;
  ...
public static NamingContext getNamingContext() throws Exception
{

  //get the namingContextReference and namingContext
  org.omg.CORBA.Object namingServiceReference =
    orb.resolve_initial_references("NameService");
  NamingContext namingContext =
    NamingContextHelper.narrow(namingServiceReference);

  return namingContext;
}
```

The NamingContextUtility class was used to obtain a reference to an org.omg.CORBA.ORB object as well, with relevant code shown here:

```
static ORB orb;

public static void initializeOrb(String[] args)
{
  if(orb == null) {
    orb = ORB.init(args, null);
  }
}

public static ORB getORB()
{

  if(orb == null) {
    String[] args = new String[0];

    initializeOrb(args);
  }

  return orb;
}
```

A handle to a CosNaming service will be obtained if you first have activated a CosNaming server on your network. In Java IDL, the tnameserv command can be used to start the reference implementation of a transient name server. We use the tnameserv naming service with our examples and invoke the service from within the generated run scripts before starting the CORBA server and client. We can also run the examples using the orbd command that starts a persistent CORBA naming service. The command synopsis for tnameserv can be found at http://java.sun.com/j2se/1.4.1/docs/guide/idl/tnameserv.html and the command synopsis for orbd can be found at http://java.sun.com/j2se/1.4.1/docs/guide/idl/orbd.html.

After a handle to the CosNaming server is obtained, the server-side ServerRegistrar creates an org.omg.CosNaming.NameComponent instance with a particular name String. A NameComponent array is then used as an argument to a NamingContext.rebind() call along with the CORBA server to which to register the name. For example, inside of the ServerRegistrar.main() method, we have this:

```
// create QueryServerImplementation
QueryServerImplementation queryServerImpl =
  new QueryServerImplementation();

// get object reference from the servant
org.omg.CORBA.Object reference =
```

```
  rootpoa.servant_to_reference(queryServerImpl);
QueryServer queryServer = QueryServerHelper.narrow(reference);

// Get naming context handle
NamingContext namingContext =
  NamingContextUtility.getNamingContext();

// bind the Object Reference in Naming
NameComponent namingCoponent  = new NameComponent(name, "");
NameComponent nameComponent[] = { namingCoponent };
namingContext.rebind(nameComponent, queryServer);
```

This same technique was used inside of the `CustomerImplementation` object to bind an instance of itself using a customer ID as a CORBA name `String` component as shown in its `bind()` method here:

```
public void bind(String name)
{
   ...
    NamingContext namingContext =
      NamingContextUtility.getNamingContext();

    // bind the Object Reference in Naming
    NameComponent namingComponent = new NameComponent(name, "");
    NameComponent nameComponent[] = { namingComponent };

    ORB orb = NamingContextUtility.getORB();

    // get reference to rootpoa & activate the POAManager
    POA rootpoa =
      POAHelper.narrow(orb.resolve_initial_references("RootPOA"));

    rootpoa.the_POAManager().activate();

    org.omg.CORBA.Object reference =
      rootpoa.servant_to_reference(this);
    Customer customer = CustomerHelper.narrow(reference);

    namingContext.rebind(nameComponent, customer);
   ...
}
```

On the client side, the `Client` class obtains a handle to a `NamingContext` instance via the `NamingContextUtility` helper class. The client then constructs a name for referring to the `QueryServer` in the same fashion as the `ServerRegistrar` created a name as shown here:

```
NamingContext namingContext =
  NamingContextUtility.getNamingContext();

// bind the Object Reference in Naming
NameComponent namingComponent = new NameComponent(name, "");
NameComponent nameComponent[] = { namingComponent };
```

A `NamingContext.resolve()` call made by the client using the constructed `NameComponent` array is then narrowed to a reference for the `QueryServer` object as shown here:

```
QueryServer queryServer =
  QueryServerHelper.narrow(namingContext.resolve(nameComponent));
```

With the handle to the remote `QueryServer`, the `Client.main()` method then makes a series of distributed calls to the server. One such call involves the return of an array of `String` objects that contains the names of distributed `Customer` CORBA server objects. These `String` names are then used to look up and invoke the services of the distributed `Customer` objects as shown here:

```
queryServer.register("ClientReceiver", clientReceiver);

String[] customersNames =
  queryServer.findCustomersWhoOrderedForMoreThan(100.0f);

for(int i = 0; i < customersNames.length; i++) {
  System.out.println("CustomersNames :" + customersNames[i]);

  namingComponent = new NameComponent(customersNames[i], "");
  NameComponent custNameComponent[] = { namingComponent };
  Customer customer = CustomerHelper.narrow(
                        namingContext.resolve(custNameComponent));

  System.out.println(customer.firstName());
  System.out.println(customer.lastName());
}
```

Objects by Value

Most of the distributed computing performed by CORBA-based programs involves a CORBA client invoking methods on a CORBA server sitting somewhere on the network. As discussed previously, the CORBA client by and large accomplishes this by communicating with a client-side stub that packs up the request and ships it over the wire. A server-side skeleton takes the request and calls the CORBA server, retrieves the results, and ships them back over the wire. The client-side stub then unpacks the results for the CORBA client. The client thus only communicates with a reference to the server. The actual work is performed somewhere else on the network.

Borland had originally introduced a tool that was one of the first products to introduce the idea of passing around CORBA objects by value instead of exclusively by reference. With objects by value, a CORBA object is passed by value as a method parameter. The OMG later came up with a standard CORBA objects-by-value specification that happens to be part of the CORBA 2.3.1 specification.

The inherent benefit of passing objects by value versus by reference is that distributed object reference resources need not be maintained and held by clients. For one, this frees up server resources by passing a copy of an object to a client for it to manipulate. Perhaps of most significance is that a client also does not incur the distributed communications overhead involved with invoking operations on an object passed by value as opposed to an object passed by reference. In particular, for fine-grained objects, such as an order object, a client can access its methods to get and set discrete order data elements without resulting in a distributed call for each fine-grained method invocation.

However, the CORBA objects-by-value standard, as it exists right now, is somewhat overly complicated and even has a few holes. Because CORBA is a language- and platform-independent standard, passing objects by value involves requiring distributed applications implemented in different languages and potentially on different operating systems to have a copy of the same implementation class used to reconstruct a value object on each side of the distributed communications wire. CORBA product vendors have thus been somewhat slow to implement the specification as it currently stands.

Value Types

The `valuetype` keyword is a core construct in CORBA identifying an object that is to be passed by value. The `valuetype` keyword is used inside of a module to tag such objects much in the same way that the `interface` keyword tags objects to be passed by reference. For example:

```
module ejava
{
  module corba
  {
    valuetype Order
    {
     ...
    };
  };
};
```

The identified `valuetype` can then be used as a parameter inside of a method call on a regular CORBA interface:

```
module ejava
{
  module corba
  {
    interface Customer
    {
     void setOrder(in Order myOrder);
     ...
    };
  };
};:
```

Objects by Value Behavioral Sequence

As a sample behavioral sequence involving passing objects by value, the following general sequence of events occurs between an object (`SEND`) that sends a value type (`VT`) to a receiving object (`RECEIVE`):

- `SEND` *makes a call on* `RECEIVE`*:* An object named `SEND` calls a distributed method on an object named `RECEIVE`, which takes a `valuetype` object `VT` as a parameter.
- `VT` *is marshaled on the sending side:* The ORB being used by `SEND` marshals the state of `VT` and packs this information and a Repository ID associated with the `VT` type into the GIOP message sent to the ORB used by `RECEIVE`.
- `VT` *is unmarshaled on the receiving side:* The ORB being used by `RECEIVE` unmarshals the state description sent by `SEND`'s ORB.
- *Attempt reconstitution of* `VT` *with local implementation:* The ORB being used by `RECEIVE` then uses the Repository ID associated with this type and attempts to map this ID to a locally available implementation. This step is language dependent, but a factory is generally used for this step and reconstitutes a new instance of the `VT` object on the receiving side.
- *Else, attempt reconstitution of* `VT` *with downloadable (*`CODEBASE`*) implementation:* If the implementation could not be found locally, the ORB for `RECEIVE` will attempt to load the object from a location defined in a `CODEBASE` parameter sent along in the GIOP message with the `VT` object by `SEND`'s ORB. This `CODEBASE` may refer to a downloadable implementation. This step is also language dependent.
- *Else, attempt reconstitution of* `VT` *with base class implementation:* If the implementation could not be downloaded, a base type of the `VT` object will be used if the keyword `truncatable` was used in the IDL specification for any base type used by the `VT` `valuetype`.

- *Else, throw exception:* If `VT` could not be reconstituted, the exception `NO_IMPLEMENT` is raised.
- *If* `VT` *is available, use it:* If an implementation of `VT` was available locally or was downloadable, the `RECEIVE` object can make calls onto the `VT` instance. Such calls will not be delegated to a remote server instance as is the case with passing objects by reference, but rather will be made on the local copy of the `VT` object.

Objects by Value Marshaling

Objects being passed by value can opt either to use the built-in ORB marshaling features for packing and unpacking the state of an object being passed by value or to customize how the state of an object being passed by value is packed and unpacked for over-the-wire transmission. If you want to use the built-in state marshaling, you simply use the `valuetype` keyword to identify the CORBA type as usual. Otherwise, you must prepend the keyword `custom` in front of the `valuetype` keyword to designate the desire to customize the marshaling of the state. For example:

```
module ejava
{
  module corba
  {
    custom valuetype Order
    {
      ...
    };
  };
};
```

The `org.omg.CORBA.portable.ValueBase` Java interface is mapped from the `CORBA::ValueBase` pseudo-object used to identify a CORBA value type. Two types of sub-interfaces to `ValueBase` exist: `StreamableValue` and `CustomValue`. If a value type is to use the ORB's underlying state marshaling mechanisms, the mapped Java value type will generate a class that extends the `org.omg.CORBA.portable.StreamableValue` Java interface. If you desire to customize state marshaling for your object, the `org.omg.CORBA.portable.CustomValue` Java interface is used.

On the receiving side in Java, when the ORB attempts to reconstitute an object instance with a particular implementation class, it attempts to strip off leading data in the `RepositoryID` field passed over the wire in the IIOP message and append `DefaultFactory` to the data retrieved. If the data in the middle was a valid Java class name, a factory can be reconstituted (if that factory class name is in the `CLASSPATH`). Otherwise, an exception is thrown. By declaring a method as returning a `factory` type, you can explicitly generate a factory interface to be used by the ORB on the receiving side to reconstitute an instance of the passed-by-value object implementation.

Objects by Value Code Example

As an example, let's define a type `Order` as a `valuetype` in IDL as shown in Listing 8.10.

Listing 8.10 **IDL for an Order Value Type**

```
module ejava
{
  module corba
  {
    valuetype Order
    {
      private long orderID;
      private string orderDate;
      private double orderValue;

      void setCustomerID(in string customerID);
      string getCustomerID();

      factory createOrder(in long id, in string date, in double value);
    };
  };
};
```

This IDL will generate a collection of interfaces and classes that can be used to implement pass-by-value semantics in your Java programs. For example, the `abstract class Order` implementing the `StreamableValue` interface will handle all basic state marshaling and unmarshaling functionality as shown in Listing 8.11.

Listing 8.11 **Generated Implementation for an Order Value Type**

```
package ejava.corba;

public abstract class Order implements
    org.omg.CORBA.portable.StreamableValue
{
  protected int orderID = (int)0;
  protected String orderDate = null;
  protected double orderValue = (double)0;

  private static String[] _truncatable_ids = {
    ejava.corba.OrderHelper.id ()
  };

  public String[] _truncatable_ids() {
```

Listing 8.11 **Continued**

```
    return _truncatable_ids;
  }

  public abstract void setCustomerID (String customerID);

  public abstract String getCustomerID ();

  public void _read (org.omg.CORBA.portable.InputStream istream)
  {
    this.orderID = istream.read_long ();
    this.orderDate = istream.read_string ();
    this.orderValue = istream.read_double ();
  }

  public void _write (org.omg.CORBA.portable.OutputStream ostream)
  {
    ostream.write_long (this.orderID);
    ostream.write_string (this.orderDate);
    ostream.write_double (this.orderValue);
  }

  public org.omg.CORBA.TypeCode _type ()
  {
    return ejava.corba.OrderHelper.type ();
  }
} // class Order
```

An `OrderHolder` shown in Listing 8.12 and an `Orderhelper` shown in Listing 8.13 are also generated as usual with most Java mappings.

Listing 8.12 **Generated Order Holder**

```
package ejava.corba;
public final class OrderHolder implements
    org.omg.CORBA.portable.Streamable
{
  public ejava.corba.Order value = null;

  public OrderHolder (){}
  public OrderHolder (ejava.corba.Order initialValue){...}
  public void _read (org.omg.CORBA.portable.InputStream i){...}
  public void _write (org.omg.CORBA.portable.OutputStream o){...}
  public org.omg.CORBA.TypeCode _type (){...}
}
```

Listing 8.13 **Generated Order Helper**

```
package ejava.corba;
abstract public class OrderHelper
{
  private static String  _id = "IDL:ejava/corba/Order:1.0";
  private static org.omg.CORBA.TypeCode __typeCode = null;
  private static boolean __active = false;

  public static void insert (org.omg.CORBA.Any a,
                             ejava.corba.Order that){...}
  public static ejava.corba.Order extract(org.omg.CORBA.Any a){...}
  synchronized public static org.omg.CORBA.TypeCode type (){...}
  public static String id (){...}
  public static ejava.corba.Order read (
              org.omg.CORBA.portable.InputStream istream){...}
  public static void write(org.omg.CORBA.portable.OutputStream ostream,
                           ejava.corba.Order value){...}
  public static ejava.corba.Order createOrder (
                                      org.omg.CORBA.ORB $orb, int id,
                                      String date, double value){...}
}
```

The `valuetype factory` defined within the `Order valuetype` and associated with the `createOrder()` method is used to generate and define factory objects for the `Order`. An `OrderValueFactory` interface extends the `ValueFactory` with the specific creation method defined in the interface and returning the `Order` value object as shown in Listing 8.14.

Listing 8.14 **Generated Order Value Type Factory**

```
public interface OrderValueFactory extends
    org.omg.CORBA.portable.ValueFactory
{
  Order createOrder (int id, String date, double value);
}
```

Finally, an `OrderDefaultFactory` class can provide a default implementation of the value type `factory` as depicted in Listing 8.15.

Listing 8.15 **Generated Order Default Value Type Factory**

```
public class OrderDefaultFactory implements OrderValueFactory {

  public Order createOrder (int id, String date, double value)
  {
    return new OrderImpl (id, date, value);
```

Listing 8.15 **Continued**

```
  }

  public java.io.Serializable read_value
    (org.omg.CORBA_2_3.portable.InputStream is)
  {
    return is.read_value(new OrderImpl ());
  }
}
```

Conclusions

CORBA represents a standard model for creating objects and components whose services are to be distributable to remote clients. CORBA uses a standard communications model over which clients and servers implemented in a heterogeneous mix of languages and running on a heterogeneous mix of hardware and operating-system platforms can interact. Creating a CORBA-based application involves defining an IDL interface, compiling the IDL interface to generate Java bindings, implementing a CORBA server, implementing a CORBA client, and determining how servers will register their services such that clients can obtain initial handles to them.

CORBA serves as the underlying distributed communications paradigm employed by J2EE EJB-based applications. As you'll see in chapters later in this book, container-based J2EE development using CORBA underneath the hood is significantly easier than CORBA application development in standalone environments. Nevertheless, a better understanding of CORBA provides the J2EE developer with a much better understanding of how to create EJB applications that interoperate with clients and services integrated with EJBs. Furthermore, the Java enterprise developer in general needs to have a deep understanding of CORBA to know how to better create standalone CORBA servers that integrate with legacy and auxiliary enterprise applications potentially implemented in other programming languages.

9

RMI Communications

THE JAVA REMOTE METHOD INVOCATION (RMI) framework has been Java's distributed object communications framework since Java was born. RMI was originally distributed separately from the JDK 1.0 and later was integrated with the JDK 1.1. RMI now has grown in feature richness and yet remains elegantly simple for Java developers to rapidly create distributed client/server applications. The RMI and CORBA paradigms have now also merged via the RMI/IIOP API and framework. In this chapter, you'll learn:

- The basic concepts behind and architecture of Java's Remote Method Invocation interface
- The architecture of the Java Remote Method Protocol (JRMP) as a protocol developed specifically for Java's remote object capabilities
- The architecture of RMI/IIOP, including Java to IDL mapping and the relevance of passing objects by value in RMI/IIOP
- The definition of RMI interfaces for RMI/JRMP and RMI/IIOP
- The implementation and compilation of RMI servers for RMI/JRMP and RMI/IIOP
- The registration of server objects for client lookup for both RMI/JRMP and RMI/IIOP
- The creation of RMI/JRMP and RMI/IIOP clients, including their means for looking up RMI server references
- The procedure for creating RMI objects that can be activated and brought into memory from disk upon client request
- The basics behind customizing the underlying socket transport protocol used by RMI

RMI Basics

The Remote Method Invocation platform is a Java-centric distributed object communications model in Java. By using the RMI packages and infrastructure, RMI-based Java clients can remotely invoke methods on RMI-based Java server objects. RMI is a purely distributed object communications model. Java object methods are invoked remotely versus any remote invocation of functional procedures as is the case with RMI's conceptual forerunner: Remote Procedure Calling (RPC). RMI clients transparently communicate with distributed servers by invoking methods on a client-side proxy object. The proxy serializes the method parameters passed to it and streams them to a distributed server representative. The distributed server representative then deserializes the parameters and passes them on to the appropriate distributed server object instance. Method return values go through a similar marshaling process.

RMI offers a rich set of features for the distributed enterprise communications programmer. RMI allows for client and server passing of objects as method parameters and return values either by value or by reference. If a class type used in a method parameter or return type is unknown to either the client or the server, it can be dynamically loaded. Although server objects can be explicitly constructed and bound on the server side to a lookup service, server objects can also be automatically activated upon client request without any prior server-side object instantiation. RMI also provides a means for distributed garbage collection to clean up any distributed server objects that are no longer referenced by any distributed clients. In cases in which firewalls limit port connections, RMI can tunnel through firewalls via HTTP. RMI also now allows for the complete customization of the type of underlying socket connection made between clients and servers.

Conceptually, the RMI platform provides many of the same roles that a CORBA Orb and CORBA Naming Service provide. However, RMI also has the capability to more easily pass Java objects by value and download new Java classes between clients and servers. Although the CORBA v2.3 standard has defined an Objects by Value specification for CORBA objects, it remains a rather complex and in some cases loosely defined specification. In fact, the drive to reconcile RMI and CORBA seems to have largely driven the CORBA Objects by Value specification to make CORBA interoperability possible via RMI/IIOP.

Nevertheless, transferring mobile Java objects via RMI between Java clients and Java servers is still and always will be considerably easier to implement than passing around objects by value in CORBA. RMI is also a much lighter-weight solution for Java applications. Of course, although CORBA still has language interoperability in its favor, this fact is becoming less significant as more applications are built using Java. RMI and Java are Sun-controlled platforms, whereas CORBA standard interfaces do allow for truly open distributed computing platform vendor implementations. Distributed services can be freely built atop RMI now, but use of Sun's Jini distributed communications service technology built atop RMI is not "as free" for commercial use.

RMI Architecture

The core RMI infrastructure was first shipped with the JDK 1.1 platform and is embodied by the `java.rmi.*` packages (although a beta version was available for use with the JDK 1.0). The Java 2.0 platform incorporated the RMI v1.2 distributed computing platform. RMI v1.2 added support for dynamically activatable objects, customizable sockets, distributed garbage-collection improvements, and a host of API additions. RMI v1.2 also provided a set of standard Java abstractions for supporting RMI over IIOP in the `javax.rmi.*` packages. Core RMI and RMI over IIOP are now fully incorporated with the J2SE v1.4, and are therefore the standard in J2EE v1.4 as well.

> **The J2EE and RMI**
>
> As we'll see in Part VI, "Enterprise Applications Enabling," use of J2EE containers and Enterprise JavaBeans (EJB) does not require as much detailed knowledge about how to create RMI servers as this chapter describes. J2EE EJB developers simply must be aware of a few RMI interfaces and exceptions when creating EJB components. J2EE EJB containers and deployment tools take care of creating the necessary stubs, skeletons, and resource management logic. However, creating standalone RMI servers may still be warranted in other situations you encounter in the course of enterprise development. EJB developers also utilize RMI APIs when their EJBs must act as RMI clients.

The basic RMI architecture is depicted in Figure 9.1. RMI clients talk to an object implementing a Java interface that corresponds to those remote interfaces being exposed by a particular RMI server. The interface is actually implemented by an RMI stub that takes calls from the RMI client and marshals them into serialized packets of information that can be sent over the wire. Similarly, the stubs unmarshal serialized response information from the RMI servers into Java objects that can be utilized by the RMI client. On the server side, an RMI v1.1 server was called by a server-specific RMI skeleton. RMI now uses a more generic RMI server calling mechanism, and thus no server-specific skeleton is used to call the RMI server. Regardless, an RMI skeleton of some sort unmarshals requests from the client into Java objects passed as parameters to the server's methods and marshals responses from the server into the serialized form suitable for transmission over the wire.

The RMI remote reference layer takes serialized data from RMI stubs and handles the RMI-specific communications protocol built atop a transport protocol. Duties of the remote reference layer include resolving RMI server locations, initiating connections, and activating remote servers. RMI currently supports two general reference-layer messaging protocols. JRMP is the standard RMI communications messaging protocol that has been used by RMI since its inception. CORBA's IIOP messaging protocol is now also possible with the RMI/IIOP standard extension.

The RMI transport layer is responsible for connection management and for the provision of reliable data transfer between endpoints. The more commonly used type of RMI transport layer within an enterprise is TCP. Both JRMP and IIOP operate over TCP. However, RMI v1.2 introduced the capability for customizing which type of underlying transport protocol to use, with IP still being the networking protocol. HTTP as a TCP transport may also now be used, which is more relevant for inter-enterprise communications.

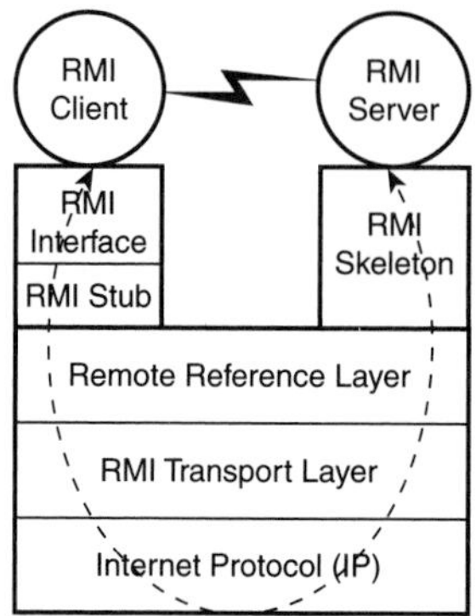

Figure 9.1 The RMI architecture.

RMI Packages and Tools

The RMI logical architecture is partitioned into several packages. We will describe the classes, interfaces, and exceptions contained in these packages as we describe how to build actual RMI applications. These are the RMI packages:

- `java.rmi` is the core package for RMI containing the Remote interface, a few key classes, and many standard exceptions.
- `java.rmi.server` is the core package for server-side RMI interfaces, classes, and interfaces.
- `java.rmi.registry` provides an interface and a class for interfacing with the RMI lookup service.
- `java.rmi.activation` provides the interfaces and classes needed to implement server objects that can be activated upon client request.
- `java.rmi.dgc` provides an interface and classes for performing distributed garbage collection.
- `javax.rmi` currently contains a class for implementing portable RMI/IIOP objects.
- `javax.rmi.CORBA` contains all CORBA-specific classes and interfaces for implementing and using RMI/IIOP objects.

In addition to the API and SPI packages that come with RMI, a set of tools is used to implement RMI applications and provide an RMI runtime infrastructure. These are the tools:

- *RMI Compiler (*`rmic`*):* This command-line utility is used to generate JRMP- and IIOP-based stub and skeleton Java class files based on a compiled RMI server implementation. This tool comes equipped with RMI in the J2SE/J2EE.
- *IDL-to-Java Compiler (*`idlj`*):* This tool is used to generate RMI/IIOP-suitable Java stubs and skeletons from an IDL definition.
- *RMI Registry (*`rmiregistry`*):* This command is used to start a process that allows one to register RMI server object references to names that can be looked up by distributed RMI clients. This tool comes equipped with RMI in the J2SE/J2EE.
- *RMI/IIOP Transient Naming Service (*`tnameserv`*):* This command is used to start a process that allows one to register RMI/IIOP server object references to names that can be looked up by distributed CORBA clients. The name and object bindings exist only for the lifetime of the server processes. This tool is equipped with the J2SE/J2EE.
- *RMI/IIOP Persistent Naming Service (*`orbd`*):* This command is used to start a process that allows one to register RMI/IIOP server object references to names that can be looked up by distributed CORBA clients. The name and object bindings persist beyond the active state of the server processes. This tool is equipped with the J2SE/J2EE.
- *RMI Activation Daemon (*`rmid`*):* This command is used to start a process that allows one to register RMI server objects that can be activated (that is, started and brought into memory) upon client request. This tool comes equipped with RMI in the J2SE/J2EE.
- *HTTP Server:* RMI can use an HTTP server for dynamically downloading Java classes to clients or servers needing to load such classes into their environments. Although any HTTP server can be used, RMI requires only minimal HTTP `GET` functionality. The COTS Web servers used with the examples in this book provide Web-serving functionality, and you can also download a minimalist Web server from Sun as described later in this chapter.

RMI Infrastructure Configuration

Before an RMI server can make its services available to RMI clients, a runtime infrastructure must be configured and brought online. We describe the details behind configuration of such infrastructures later in this chapter. However, in general these are the types of services you may need to activate to enable an RMI operational environment:

- *Configure and start HTTP servers:* You must configure and start simple HTTP servers on hosts that will serve downloadable Java code. Code that may need downloading includes any code on one side of the distributed fence (client or server) that needs to be dynamically loaded by the other side of the fence.

- *Configure and start an RMI registry:* You must configure and start an RMI registry service to which active RMI server object references are bound and from which RMI clients can look up distributed object references.
- *Configure and start an RMI/IIOP naming service:* You must configure and start an RMI/IIOP naming service (CORBA Naming) to which RMI/IIOP server object references are bound and from which IIOP clients can look up distributed object references.
- *Configure and start RMI activation daemons:* You must configure and start an RMI activation daemon on hosts that will serve activatable Java code. This step is necessary only for those RMI servers that are activatable.

RMI Development Process

Developing an RMI-based client/server application is a fairly straightforward process. Either you may already have an existing service for which you want to provide a distributed interface or you may be creating a distributed interface and a newly defined server process from scratch. Regardless, you can follow the same basic general steps for making an RMI application:

1. *Define the remote interface:* You must first define a Java interface extending the `java.rmi.Remote` interface with all the methods defined that you want to make distributed.
2. *Implement the RMI server:* You must then implement the remote interface and extend one of RMI's remote server object classes. Different remote server objects can be extended depending on the specific RMI behavior you need. These different behaviors are covered later in the chapter. You must then compile your RMI servers for use by the next step.
3. *Generate the RMI skeletons and stubs:* By using the `rmic` tool, you can generate RMI server skeletons for your compiled RMI server classes. Generation of RMI skeletons is not necessary for applications based on RMI v1.2 and above. The `rmic` tool also generates the appropriate RMI client stubs. By default, RMI v1.1- and v1.2-compliant stubs and skeletons are generated by `rmic`. Alternatively, a `-v1.1` or `-v1.2` flag can be used to specify which version of stubs and skeletons to generate.
4. *Implement an RMI server registrar:* You will then typically implement a separate class that registers an RMI server with the RMI registry, registers an activatable RMI server with the RMI activation daemon, or registers an RMI/IIOP server with the RMI/IIOP naming service. Note that only initial references to certain "front-line" server objects need be registered with a registry or naming service from a

server registrar. After any initial RMI server objects are looked up by RMI clients, subsequent RMI server objects will most typically be instantiated and registered by the RMI servers that were created initially.

5. *Implement the RMI client:* An RMI client can now be created using the RMI stubs created in a previous step. An RMI client must first look up any initial references to an RMI server object using the RMI registry or RMI/IIOP naming service. The RMI stubs that correspond to these initial RMI server references and any stubs needed for subsequently referenced RMI servers are used transparently by the client, because they make calls only on an object that happens to implement the particular RMI server interface.

JRMP

RMI is one of the more important distributed object communications paradigms employed by enterprise Java architectures. RMI and CORBA slowly reconciled as interoperable communications paradigms, but there was a time very recently when the only underlying communications messaging model available to RMI was the Java Remote Method Protocol (JRMP). JRMP is a fairly simplistic Java-proprietary wire transport protocol that operates over TCP/IP. JRMP was exclusively used by RMI in RMI v1.1 and is still used by the core RMI included with the J2SE. However, RMI is now capable of operating over either JRMP or IIOP. Nevertheless, understanding a tiny bit of the internals of JRMP helps shed light on RMI for the enterprise developer desiring to understand RMI/JRMP's true enterprise-class communications limits and capabilities.

JRMP packets sent between communications endpoints contain a message header and one or more messages. The header format is simply this:

- Four bytes of ASCII characters: `JRMI`
- A two-byte protocol version number
- A single-byte subprotocol identifier

Three subprotocol identifiers are defined to indicate the type of message data stream that follows the message header:

- `SingleOpProtocol`: Indicates that one message data packet follows.
- `StreamProtocol`: Indicates that one or more message data packets follow. The RMI client and RMI server both offer a server socket listener for incoming calls and a socket client endpoint for outgoing calls.
- `MultiplexStreamProtocol`: Indicates that one or more message data packets follow. The RMI client and RMI server multiplex incoming and outgoing messages over a single socket connection. This subprotocol is typically used when the RMI client is restricted from creating server socket listeners to handle incoming calls (for example, due to applet security restrictions).

To facilitate RMI's capability to tunnel through HTTP servers, JRMP allows for the prepending of an `HTTPPostHeader` identifier to send messages and an `HTTPResponseHeader` identifier to receive messages. Aside from these identifiers, six key message types are supported by JRMP. Three of the six JRMP message types pertain to messages that are output to an RMI protocol stream from the client's perspective:

- `Call CallData`: This form of message is used for remote method invocation calls. Call data has an object identifier used to indicate the target object of the call. An operation number is used in RMI v1.1 to identify the target operation to invoke. A hash number is used as a version identifier to verify that the stub and skeleton being used are compatible. Finally, zero or more argument values serialized according to the object serialization protocol are contained by the call data. To facilitate dynamic class loading, certain class information is embedded into the message streams.
- `Ping`: Tests to see whether a remote virtual machine is still alive.
- `DgcAck UniqueID`: This message is sent from a client to a server's distributed garbage collection to indicate that remote object references returned from a server were obtained.

The other three JRMP message types pertain to messages received by a client that are input from an RMI protocol stream:

- `ReturnData ReturnValue`: This form of message is used for returning results of remote method invocation calls. The return value has a return byte indicating whether the returned value is normal or the result of an exception. A unique ID is also sent to identify the return object used by the client when notifying the distributed garbage collector. Finally, an object serialization of the returned value or exception is sent in the return value. To facilitate dynamic class loading, certain class information is embedded into the message streams.
- `HttpReturn`: This message is sent as a result from an invocation in an HTTP call.
- `PingAck`: This message acknowledges a Ping message.

Multiplexing over a single socket connection using the `MultiplexStreamProtocol` subprotocol requires some extra JRMP logic. Five multiplexing operations are defined to accomplish multiplexing. `OPEN`, `CLOSE`, and `CLOSEACK` operations handle connection opening, closing, and close acknowledgment, respectively. `REQUEST` and `TRANSMIT` operations are used to signal when messages are being exchanged. Furthermore, because up to 65,536 virtual connections can be opened over a single concrete connection, a four-byte identifier accompanies each multiplexing operation to identify the virtual connection on which it operates. One side of the RMI client/server session can host 32,768 virtual server socket connections with identifiers in the range of 0x0000 to 0x7FFF, and the other side can host 32,768 virtual server socket connections with identifiers in the range of 0x8000 to 0xFFFF.

RMI and IIOP

RMI/IIOP is a standard Java extension incorporated as part of the J2SE and J2EE and developed jointly by both Sun and IBM. As described in Chapter 8, "CORBA Communications," CORBA represents a significant advancement for enabling the development of a standard communications framework in building enterprise software systems. With CORBA's IIOP as the standard transport wire protocol for distributed object communications, RMI's capability to communicate over IIOP enables RMI applications to interoperate with CORBA-based systems. JRMP, on the other hand, was a nonstandard protocol and could not enable communication with cross-language CORBA objects. RMI/IIOP now provides Java RMI-based communications interoperability with objects implemented in other languages. Java programmers can still make use of the simplicity of building RMI applications and then generate IDL using the new Java-to-IDL compiler also provided with RMI/IIOP.

> **RMI/IIOP Versus Java IDL**
>
> Because Java IDL and RMI/IIOP both may be utilized with the J2SE/J2EE, you may be wondering what packages to use for CORBA-enabling your Java applications. The main way to think of Java IDL is to use it as a way for your Java programs to communicate with any CORBA-compliant clients and servers. Java IDL and traditional CORBA programming will mainly be useful when you're creating Java-based CORBA clients using a predefined IDL interface or creating Java-based CORBA servers that must map to a predefined CORBA service. RMI/IIOP can be used when you want to capitalize on the relative programming simplicity of RMI to create Java-based RMI servers wanting to expose their services to CORBA clients under some minimal programming constraints. In summary, think of Java IDL when you have IDL that needs to map to distributed clients and servers (that is, from interface to code), and think of RMI/IIOP when you have Java RMI servers that need to be exposed in terms of IDL interfaces (that is, from code to interface).

Java-to-IDL Mapping

Alongside RMI's capability to operate over IIOP, the RMI compiler can map RMI directly into well-formed IDL. By providing a Java RMI-to-IDL mapping, Java developers can create RMI applications as usual and then automatically generate IDL and CORBA stubs and skeletons from Java code. To accomplish this task, some compromises have been made. The Java-to-IDL mapping allows for method overloading and for most of the Java naming conventions to be preserved in the mapping (aside from case), but not all IDL entities are supported. For example, IDL structs, unions, and inout parameters are never generated from the Java-to-IDL mapping. Furthermore, the mapping from Java to IDL does not inversely map from IDL to Java. Such compromises were made in order to make RMI/IIOP a possibility.

The various Java RMI-to-OMG IDL mappings are detailed in the CORBA v2.3 specification's Java language-to-IDL mapping (accessible from the `www.omg.org` Web site). A summary of some of the more common Java-to-IDL mappings is presented in Table 9.1.

Table 9.1 **Java RMI-to-OMG IDL Mappings**

	Java RMI Entity	**OMG IDL Mapping**
Special Cases	`java.lang.Object`	`::java::lang::Object`
	`java.lang.String`	`::CORBA::WStringValue`
	`java.lang.Class`	`::javax::rmi::CORBA::ClassDesc`
	`java.io.Serializable`	`::java::io::Serializable`
	`java.io.Externalizable`	`::java::io::Externalizable`
	`java.rmi.Remote`	`::java::rmi::Remote`
	`org.omg.CORBA.Object`	`Object`
Primitive Types	`void`	`void`
	`boolean`	`boolean`
	`char`	`wchar`
	`byte`	`octet`
	`short`	`short`
	`int`	`long`
	`long`	`long long`
	`float`	`float`
	`double`	`double`
Java Names	Java packages, such as `x.y.z`	IDL modules, such as `::x::y::z`
	Java names colliding with IDL keywords, such as oneway	Underscore added to name, such as _oneway
	Java names having leading underscores, such as `_MyClass`	`J` added before name, such as `J_MyClass`
	Java inner class names, such as `Bar` inside `Foo`	*`OuterClass_InnerClass`*, such as `Foo_Bar`
	Overloaded Java methods, s uch as `foo()` and `foo(x.y.z param)`	Method name followed by __ and fully qualified parameter types also separated by __ such as `foo__()` and `foo__x_y_z()`ˆ
	Method names colliding with variable names	Variables names get trailing underscores
RMI/IDL Interface	Methods with `set`*`XXX`*`()` and `get`*`XXX`*`()` or `is`*`XXX`*`()`	IDL read/write attribute named *XXX* with lowercase first letter and of type in `set`*`XXX`*`()`
	Methods with `get`*`XXX`*`()` and no `set`*`XXX`*`()`	IDL read attribute named *XXX* with lowercase first letter and of type returned by `get`*`XXX`*`()`
	Method parameters	IDL method in parameters
	`java.rmi.RMIException` and subclasses	CORBA system exceptions
	Other exceptions	IDL exceptions named appropriately

Table 9.1 **Continued**

	Java RMI Entity	OMG IDL Mapping
RMI/IDL Arrays	Arrays of primitive types, such as `boolean[]`	Placed in `boxedRMI` module with valuetype of primitive sequence type named `seq<arraySize>_<primitiveType>`, such as `::org::omg::boxedRMI` module with valuetype `seq1_boolean sequence<boolean>`
	Arrays of Java objects in package, such as `x.y.Z[]`	Placed in `boxedRMI ::x::y` module with valuetype of primitive sequence type named `_<primitiveType>`, such as `seq<arraySize> ::org::omg::boxedRMI::x::y` module with valuetype `seq1_Z sequence<x::y::Z>`
RMI/IDL Exceptions	Exception subclasses	Mapped to valuetypes with subclassed exceptions
	Exception names in throws clauses with or without `Exception` on the end, such as`java.io.IOException`	IDL raise clauses use any `Exception` name removed and add `Ex` to the end of the name, such as `::java::io::IOEx`

Objects by Value and RMI

Chapter 8 describes the CORBA Objects by Value specification for providing a standardized mechanism to pass CORBA objects by value, as opposed to passing objects by reference. Because the CORBA Objects by Value specification is language independent, it needs to account for the fact that types passed by value between clients and servers implemented in different languages need re-implementation in those other languages. In the case of RMI, Java clients and Java servers talking to each other do not have this problem. Irrespective of this fact, it is important to understand why RMI/IIOP depends on Objects by Value.

Java RMI allows for serializable objects to be passed as parameters to remote methods and returned from remote methods. Furthermore, Java RMI also allows for automatic downloading of Java classes between RMI clients and servers. Because pure CORBA applications could not support these features, IIOP and CORBA were extended with the Object by Value specification. The Objects by Value specification in CORBA has thus helped make RMI/IIOP a reality. So, regardless of whether Orb vendors can easily support Objects by Value in the general sense, the specification still plays an important, yet often unseen, role in reconciling the RMI and CORBA worlds. Hopefully, future versions of the CORBA standards will simplify the Objects by Value and Java-to-IDL specifications.

RMI Interfaces

With much of the conceptual framework for RMI out of the way, let's focus on building an actual RMI application now. Throughout the next few sections, we will create both an RMI/JRMP and an RMI/IIOP application side by side, not only to illustrate how RMI applications are built, but also to enable you to compare and contrast RMI/JRMP versus RMI/IIOP firsthand. Both examples are created with an RMI server registrar binding active objects for remote RMI clients to look up.

The first step in creating any RMI application (RMI/JRMP or RMI/IIOP) is to define an RMI interface. Figure 9.2 provides an overview of all RMI and application-specific entities that are involved with defining an RMI interface. We will use diagrams such as these throughout the chapter to visually summarize all the rules involved with creating RMI applications. That is, by visually examining the relations and classes in the diagram, you should be able to quickly see all the rules involved with implementing a development step to which the diagram corresponds.

Figure 9.2 summarizes the rules for defining your application-specific interface named `MyRemoteInterface`. The first thing to note is that `MyRemoteInterface` must extend the `java.rmi.Remote` interface. You can think of the `Remote` interface as a marker interface for referring to objects by reference analogous to the `Serializable` interface being a marker interface for referring to objects by value.

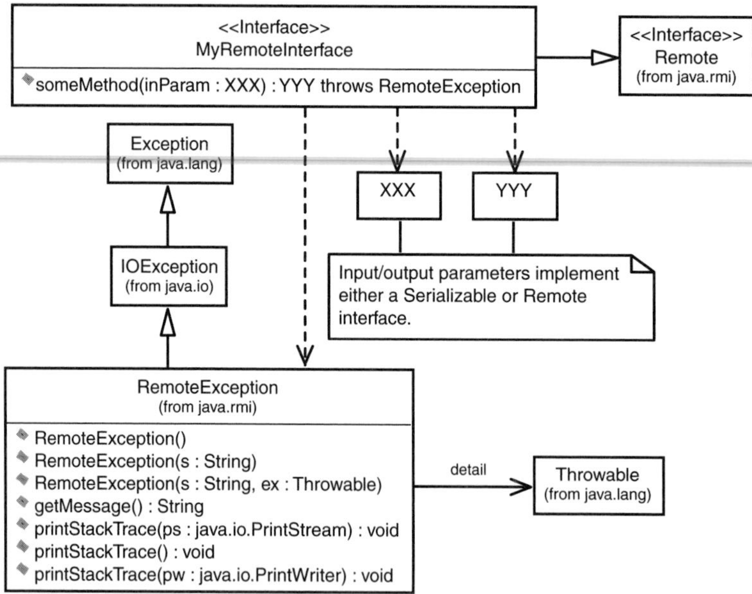

Figure 9.2 RMI interfaces.

Methods you want to distribute should be defined on your RMI interface. For example, the `someMethod()` on `MyRemoteInterface` is a remote method. Remote methods like `someMethod()` can take one or more input parameters like `XXX` and return an output parameter like `YYY`. `XXX` and `YYY` must be either serializable or remote objects. Furthermore, all remote methods must also throw the `java.rmi.RemoteException`. `RemoteException` can be constructed with a nested detail exception and is the base class for just about every other RMI-related exception. The J2SE v1.4 implementation of the `RemoteException` also preserves the server-side exception stack trace as well as client-side stack trace information associated with a `RemoteException`. Such server-side stack information may be disabled using an RMI-implementation specific property. For example, the `sun.rmi.server.suppressStackTraces` system property may be set to `true` for the RMI implementation equipped with the J2SE.

RMI Interface Definition Examples

Three RMI interfaces are defined to illustrate how to build an RMI-based application. These interfaces are the `ClientReceiver`, `Customer`, and `QueryServer` interfaces. The same interfaces are used for both the RMI/JRMP and the RMI/IIOP examples developed throughout this chapter.

> **Note**
>
> This section is the first section that begins describing an example RMI server and client that we've created for this chapter. Because the examples can involve a significant amount of code, we take the approach in this chapter to provide snippets from such examples as they become relevant. We occasionally provide complete listings here as well for certain smaller and key source code elements. You are encouraged to examine the complete code example files for yourself as the discussion proceeds.
>
> The RMI code examples used in this chapter are accessible as described in Appendix A, "Software Configuration," and extracted into the `examples\src\ejava\rmi` directory. Both RMI/JRMP and RMI/IIOP interfaces are included. All RMI/JRMP implementation classes are contained under the `examples\src\ejava\rmi\queryservicejrmp` directory. All RMI/IIOP implementation classes are contained under the `examples\src\ejava\rmi\queryserviceiiop` directory. Most RMI applications are created with the interface and implementations in the same package. We separate them into different packages here only for ease of explaining both the RMI/JRMP and the RMI/IIOP examples.

The `ejava.rmi.ClientReceiver` interface for both RMI/JRMP and RMI/IIOP is used by an RMI server to make RMI callbacks on the RMI clients. It has one simple method, `setResultOrders()`, to obtain a vector of BeeShirts.com client orders. The `ClientReceiver` interface is defined in Listing 9.1.

Listing 9.1 **The RMI Interface for RMI Client Callbacks from an RMI Server (`ClientReceiver.java`)**

```
package ejava.rmi;

import java.rmi.Remote;
import java.rmi.RemoteException;
import java.util.Vector;

public interface ClientReceiver extends Remote
{
  public void setResultOrders(Vector orders) throws RemoteException;
}
```

The `ejava.rmi.Customer` interface for both RMI/JRMP and RMI/IIOP is returned by an RMI server to conceptualize a distributed handle to a BeeShirts.com `Customer` object. It has a series of getter methods to obtain BeeShirts.com customer information. The `Customer` interface is defined in Listing 9.2.

Listing 9.2 **RMI Interface BeeShirts.com Customer Information (`Customer.java`)**

```
package ejava.rmi;

import java.rmi.Remote;
import java.rmi.RemoteException;

public interface Customer  extends Remote
{
  public String getFirstName() throws RemoteException;
  public String getLastName() throws RemoteException;
  public String getAddress1() throws RemoteException;
  public String getAddress2() throws RemoteException;
  public String getCity() throws RemoteException;
  public String getState() throws RemoteException;
  public String getZip() throws RemoteException;
  public String getPhoneNumber() throws RemoteException;
  public String getEmailAddress() throws RemoteException;
}
```

The `ejava.rmi.QueryServer` interface for both the RMI/JRMP and the RMI/IIOP examples is the main frontline interface for RMI clients to communicate with a back-end RMI server application. The `QueryServer` offers a very specific set of interfaces to illustrate some of the concepts revolving around RMI discussed thus far. The method `findCustomersWhoOrderedForMoreThan()` finds customers who spend more than a certain amount of money, binds them to a lookup service, and returns a `Vector` of customer IDs. A method `register()` takes a `ClientReceiver` callback interface and client receiver name to register RMI client callbacks. A method `findOrdersWhichAreFrom()` finds the orders for a given state and passes the set of associated orders to the registered `ClientReceiver` objects. The `QueryServer` interface is defined in Listing 9.3.

Listing 9.3 **The RMI Interface Querying the RMI Server Application (`QueryServer.java`)**

```
package ejava.rmi;

import java.rmi.Remote;
import java.rmi.RemoteException;
import java.util.Vector;

public interface QueryServer extends Remote
{
  public Vector findCustomersWhoOrderedForMoreThan(float value)
    throws RemoteException;
  public void findOrdersWhichAreFrom(String state)
    throws RemoteException;
  public void register(String name, ClientReceiver clientReceiver)
    throws RemoteException;
}
```

RMI Servers and Skeletons

With an interface properly defined, you can now create an RMI server. It is entirely possible and a common situation to already have some code you would like to turn into a distributed object. In such a case, you might create an RMI server that delegates calls to the existing code and then define those methods that should be distributed in the form of an RMI interface. Regardless of the ordering of your steps, you need to create an RMI server that implements an RMI interface. We demonstrate how to create an RMI server in this section for both regular RMI/JRMP and RMI/IIOP servers.

RMI/JRMP Servers

We are now in a position to discuss more details behind what is involved with building an RMI/JRMP server. After a description of what APIs RMI/JRMP server implementations utilize, we will demonstrate via an example of the construction of an actual server. We will then follow up that discussion with a description of how to compile such servers.

Creating the RMI/JRMP Servers

Figure 9.3 depicts some of the key classes, interfaces, and exceptions involved in building an RMI/JRMP server. The key class to focus on in this diagram is the `MyRemoteImpl` class.

`MyRemoteImpl` corresponds to your application-specific RMI server. Your RMI server must implement the RMI interface such as the `MyRemoteInterface` shown in the diagram and defined in the preceding section. It must also throw the appropriate exceptions as defined by the implemented interface. As you'll see, the RMI skeletons actually create and throw `RemoteExceptions`. Any application-specific exceptions defined for the interface of course must be thrown by the application-specific server implementation. Beyond these rules, you should also ensure that your RMI server is thread-safe.

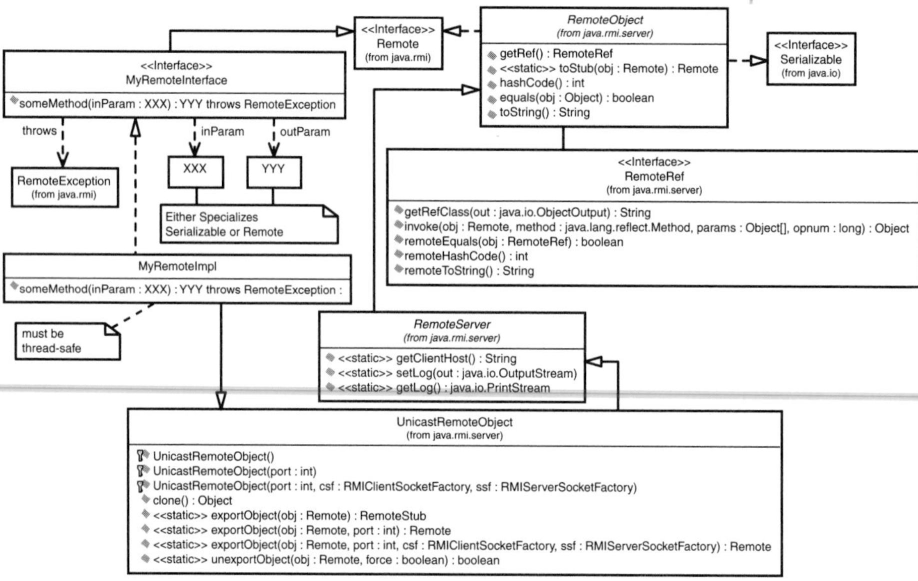

Figure 9.3 RMI/JRMP servers.

In addition to the implementation of the particular `MyRemoteInterface`, `MyRemoteImpl` needs to extend the `java.rmi.server.UnicastRemoteObject` class. The RMI/IIOP and activatable servers created later in this section and chapter extend different types of remote objects, but the `UnicastRemoteObject` class is used for RMI servers that must be pre-activated by a server process. The `UnicastRemoteObject` supports remote references of servers by clients in a point-to-point access fashion. The `UnicastRemoteObject` class itself extends from the `java.rmi.server.RemoteServer`, which in turn extends the java.rmi.server.RemoteObject class. RMI/JRMP servers may also export themselves as remote servers using one of the static exportObject() calls on the UnicastRemoteObject class and avoid subclassing from UnicastRemoteObject.

The RemoteObject class implements both the Remote and the Serializable interfaces and overrides most of the java.lang.Object methods for the purpose of making regular Java Object objects capable of remote distribution. For example, hashCode(), equals(), and toString() are all overloaded. Additionally, RemoteObject returns a remote reference to the remote object with getRef(). The java.rmi.server.RemoteRef object returned by getRef() represents a direct handle on the remote object. The RemoteServer class extends RemoteObject to provide a few server-side remote-object–specific calls such as obtaining the RMI client host name, as well as getting and setting server-side logging streams.

RMI/JRMP Server Implementation Examples

Three example RMI/JRMP server implementations are contained beneath the examples\src\ejava\rmi\queryservicejrmp directory. The three server class filenames are Customer, ClientReceiver, and QueryServer.

> **Note**
>
> The build.xml file in the examples\src\ejava\rmi directory is used by ANT to compile the server implementations for both RMI/JRMP and RMI/IIOP models. A run script in the queryservicejrmp and queryserviceiiop subdirectories is generated by the ANT build process and can be used to execute each example. Pause statements are inserted into these scripts before each process that is spawned. You should wait for each process to start and initialize before allowing the next process to start.
>
> Note that the preceding ANT build process requires that you download the source code for a small-footprint HTTP server provided by Sun called ClassFileServer from http://java.sun.com/products/jdk/rmi/class-server.zip. You should extract this zip file to a <*ROOT*>/examples/classServer directory in which <*ROOT*> is a root directory of your choice. You then must set the class file server's root source code directory as appropriate in the build.properties file equipped with this chapter's code (that is, class.file.server.src=<*ROOT*>).

Note that all getters and setters as defined in Listing 9.1 have been implemented by the CustomerImplementation class for a distributable Customer object instance as illustrated here:

```
package ejava.rmi.queryservicejrmp;
...
public class CustomerImplementation extends UnicastRemoteObject
  implements Customer {

  private String firstName;
  private String lastName;
     ...
```

```
  public CustomerImplementation() throws RemoteException{
    super();
  }

  public String getFirstName() throws RemoteException{
    return firstName;
  }

  public String getLastName() throws RemoteException{
    return lastName;
  }

  ...
}
```

The `ClientReceiverImplementation` class implements the one remote method declared in Listing 9.1. The `setResultOrders()` method simply prints the list of orders received as illustrated here:

```
package ejava.rmi.queryservicejrmp;
...

public class ClientReceiverImplementation extends UnicastRemoteObject
  implements ClientReceiver{

  public ClientReceiverImplementation() throws RemoteException{
    super();
  }

  public void setResultOrders(Vector orders) throws RemoteException{
    if(orders != null){
      System.out.println("Number of Received Orders :"+orders.size());
      for(int i=0; i<orders.size(); i++){
        System.out.println(" Values for Order :" +i);
        System.out.println((Order)orders.elementAt(i));
      }
    }
    else{
      System.out.println("Received Orders : null Results ");
    }
  }
}
```

The `QueryServerImplementation` implements the `QueryServer` interface declared in Listing 9.3. The `QueryServer` represents the frontline interface for RMI clients and contains most of the business logic for our example. As an illustration of the `QueryServerImplementation` class's skeletal structure, we have this:

```
package ejava.rmi.queryservicejrmp;
   ...
public class QueryServerImplementation extends UnicastRemoteObject
  implements QueryServer
{
  ClientReceiver clientReceiver;
  String clientReceiverName;
  Connection connection;

  public QueryServerImplementation(){...}

  public ResultSet getResultSet(String sqlQuery,  Object whereValue)
    throws SQLException{...}

  public Vector findCustomersWhoOrderedForMoreThan(float value)
    throws RemoteException{...}

  public void findOrdersWhichAreFrom(String state)
    throws RemoteException {...}

  public void register(String name, ClientReceiver clientReceiver)
    throws RemoteException {...}

  public static void main(String[] args){...}
}
```

The `QueryServerImplementation` constructor reads in Java preferences for a database driver class, URL, username, and password as defined in the `global.properties` file. This information is used to establish a connection with the BeeShirts.com database via JDBC. The `getResultSet()` method takes a SQL query for creating a prepared statement and subsequently for returning a result set. The `findCustomersWhoOrderedForMoreThan()` method retrieves the customer query from the Java preferences as set via the local `build.properties` file `customer.query` property and issues the query using `getResultSet()`. The results of this query are then used to create a new distributed `Customer` object reference. We will discuss how this reference is made available to the RMI client shortly.

The `register()` method is used to register a `ClientReceiver` with `QueryServer`. The `findOrdersWhichAreFrom()` method retrieves an order query from the Java preferences as set via the local `build.properties` file `order.query` property and then issues this query for obtaining a set of related orders. These orders are used to create a serializable `Orders` object and then for making a callback on the distributed RMI client `ClientReceiver` references that were registered using the `register()` method. The `Order` object simply defines a set of attribute getters and setters and is shown here in skeletal form:

```
package ejava.rmi;
...
public class Order implements Serializable {
  private int orderID;
  private Date orderDate;
  private double orderValue;

  public Order() {...}
  public Order(int orderID, Date orderDate, double orderValue) {...}

  public void setOrderID(int orderID) {...}
  public void setOrderDate(Date orderDate) {...}
  public void setOrderValue(double orderValue) {...}

  public int getOrderID() {...}
  public Date getOrderDate() {...}
  public double getOrderValue() {...}

  public String toString() {...}
}
```

Compiling the RMI/JRMP Servers

After you have implemented your RMI server classes, you must first compile the Java source files into Java class files. The rmic compiler is then used to generate the application-specific RMI stubs and skeletons, which are the classes that will actually implement the RMI communications. The rmic compiler takes one or more compiled RMI server class files and generates an associated set of stubs and possibly skeletons for those RMI servers; it can take a -d <directory> option indicating which directory to output generated stubs and skeletons to. The rmic compiler will generate stubs and skeletons accessible from RMI UnicastRemoteObject-based v1.1 clients and all RMI v1.2 clients. When you use the -v1.2 option, rmic will generate stubs for use only with RMI v1.2 clients. Because application-specific skeletons are not necessary with RMI v1.2, none will be generated when the -v1.2 option is used. Stubs and skeletons are generated with the same package as your RMI server. A server implementation named MyRemoteImpl generates stubs with the name MyRemoteImpl_Stub and skeletons with the name MyRemoteImpl_Skel.

The ANT build.xml script in the examples\src\ejava\rmi directory compiles stubs and skeletons for all three RMI/JRMP server class files into the examples\classes\ejava\rmi\queryservicejrmp directory using this basic ANT target form:

```
<target name="jrmprmic" depends="compile">
      <rmic base="${build}"
            includes="ejava/rmi/queryservicejrmp/*Implementation.class"
            classpath="${build}"/>
</target>
```

The command-line equivalent for one such compilation directive is as follows:

```
rmic -d <ejava_home>/examples/classes
     -classpath <ejava_home>/examples/classes
     ejava.rmi.queryservicejrmp.QueryServerImplementation
```

RMI/IIOP Servers

RMI/IIOP servers are created in a fashion that is very similar to the creation of RMI/JRMP servers. After a description of the APIs that RMI/IIOP server implementations utilize, we will demonstrate via example the construction and compilation of an actual RMI/IIOP server.

Creating the RMI/IIOP Servers

Figure 9.4 depicts the key relations and entities involved in defining an RMI/IIOP server. As can be seen, the only difference between declaring an RMI/IIOP server and declaring an RMI/JRMP server is that you extend the `javax.rmi.PortableRemoteObject` class instead of the `UnicastRemoteObject` class. Thus, the `MyRemoteImpl` for RMI/IIOP can have the same method signatures (including exception throwing) and the same method implementations. RMI/IIOP servers can also export themselves as a remote server object using the `exportObject()` method on `PortableRemoteObject` instead of subclassing `PortableRemoteObject`. In fact, using such a method can make your servers more portable between RMI/JRMP and RMI/IIOP applications.

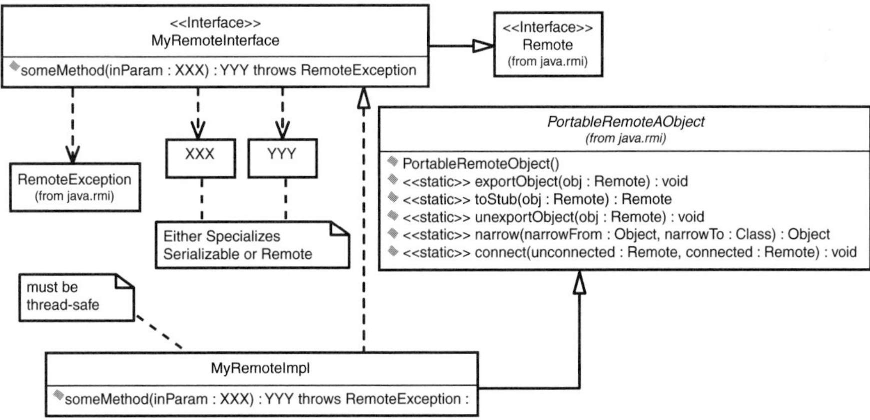

Figure 9.4 RMI/IIOP servers.

Other `PortableRemoteObject` methods also assist with the management of RMI/IIOP objects. An `unexportObject()` method is useful for making registered objects available for distributed garbage collection. The method `connect()` can be used to explicitly connect currently unconnected objects to the Orb given an object that has already been connected to the Orb. The `narrow()` method can be used to convert a general RMI/IIOP reference into a specific `java.lang.Class` type to be returned from `narrow()`. If no exceptions are thrown, the returned object can be converted into the desired type. Finally, `toStub()` returns an RMI/IIOP stub that can be used by RMI clients to talk with the RMI server. Under the hood, the `PortableRemoteObject` actually delegates calls to an object that implements the `javax.rmi.CORBA.PortableRemoteObjectDelegate` interface.

RMI/IIOP Server Implementation Examples

The RMI/IIOP server implementations for `ClientReceiver`, `Customer`, and `QueryServer` are nearly identical to the RMI/JRMP implementations. In what follows, we present only those aspects of the RMI/IIOP that differ from the RMI/JRMP servers presented earlier. The complete source-code listings for the RMI/IIOP class server implementations can be found on the book's Web site as described earlier in this chapter.

The `ejava.rmi.queryserviceiiop.ClientReceiverImplementation` class differs from its RMI/JRMP analogue only in extending the `PortableRemoteObject` as illustrated here:

```
package ejava.rmi.queryserviceiiop;

...

public class ClientReceiverImplementation
    extends PortableRemoteObject
    implements ClientReceiver
{
    ...
}
```

Similarly, the `ejava.rmi.queryserviceiiop.CustomerImplementation` differs only slightly from its RMI/JRMP counterpart. It does differ more significantly in the `bind()` method implementation, however, as you'll soon see in a subsequent section. The `CustomerImplementation` class declaration is illustrated here:

```
package ejava.rmi.queryserviceiiop;

...

public class CustomerImplementation
    extends PortableRemoteObject
    implements Customer
{
    ...
}
```

The `ejava.rmi.queryserviceiiop.QueryServerImplementation` class also differs in its base class from the RMI/JRMP class, as well as in the means for binding the server to a lookup service, as you'll see. The skeletal class declaration for `QueryServerImplementation` is shown here:

```
package ejava.rmi.queryserviceiiop;

  ...

public class QueryServerImplementation
    extends PortableRemoteObject
    implements QueryServer
{
    ...
}
```

Compiling the RMI/IIOP Servers

As with RMI/JRMP, you must also compile your RMI/IIOP classes. The same `rmic` compiler is then used to generate the RMI/IIOP stubs and skeletons as was done with RMI/JRMP. However, we now simply must pass the `-iiop` option to `rmic` when generating the stubs and skeletons.

The ANT `build.xml` script in the `examples\src\ejava\rmi` directory compiles stubs and skeletons for all three RMI/IIOP server class files into the `examples\classes\ejava\rmi\queryserviceiiop` directory using this basic ANT target form:

```
<target name="iioprmic" depends="copyfilesforclienttest">
      <rmic base="${build}"
       includes="ejava/rmi/queryserviceiiop/*Implementation.class"
       classpath="${build}"
       iiop="Yes"/>
</target>
```

The command-line equivalent for one such compilation directive is this:

```
rmic -iiop
     -d <ejava_home>/examples/classes
     -classpath <ejava_home>/examples/classes
     ejava.rmi.queryservicejrmp.QueryServerImplementation
```

IIOP skeletons (ties) are generated according to the CORBA TIE methodology for providing CORBA connectivity to your distributed objects. Thus, given some class named `MyRemoteObjectImpl`, a skeleton class will be generated with the name `_MyRemoteObjectImpl_Tie` that extends the generic `org.omg.CORBA_2_3.portable.ObjectImpl` skeleton and that implements the `javax.rmi.CORBA.Tie` interface. The `Tie` interface implemented by the skeleton class extends `org.omg.CORBA.portable.InvokeHandler` and unmarshals remote calls into regular Java calls on the MyRemoteObjectImpl object, and marshals responses as well. The rmic compiler will also generate the stubs that are utilized by the RMI client. We describe how the client uses such stubs in a subsequent section.

Alternatively, by passing the flag -poa as an option to the rmic compilation command, you can generate object implementations that use the POA approach to exposing CORBA services as described in Chapter 8. Thus you enable more portability across ORBs for your generated RMI/IIOP server implementation skeletons. In such situations, your generated _MyRemoteObjectImpl_Tie skeleton extends the org.omg.PortableServer.Servant skeleton instead of the org.omg.CORBA_2_3.portable.ObjectImpl skeleton. Recall from Figure 8.4 and Figure 8.5 that the Servant class is the base class for both POA server inheritance and delegation-based implementation styles.

RMI Registration

After you make a distributable server object, it is only natural that you would want to "distribute it." That is, you now need to make your RMI server accessible to distributed clients. Making your servers distributed involves registering remote references to your servers with a naming service. Naming services then allow clients to look up these distributed references given some name string. After a remote reference is obtained, a client may either consult the naming service again for additional remote references or perhaps be handed one directly from a server that has produced a remote reference to a new object. We discuss naming services in more detail in Chapter 11, "Naming Services with JNDI," but we step through the configuration of two different name servers in this chapter.

RMI/JRMP servers use the "RMI Registry," and RMI/IIOP servers use a "CosNaming Service." In addition to a naming service, RMI requires that you provide a means for enabling distributed JVMs to be capable of downloading new Java classes that they currently do not have loaded into memory or on their local CLASSPATH. We also discuss the use of codebases in this section for addressing dynamic and distributed class loading issues.

Registration of RMI/JRMP Servers

The diagram in Figure 9.5 contains a few important classes and interfaces for you to consider when registering an RMI/JRMP server with the RMI registry. Here we see a homegrown server registrar named MyServerRegistrar that has a handle to the MyRemoteImpl server implementation. The duty of a server registrar is to create an active instance of MyRemoteImpl and register it with the naming service. Server registrars are simple classes that take care of creating one or more server instances and registering them with a naming service. Many examples you'll see in this book implement the functionality of a server registrar inside of a main() method or other function inside the server implementation class itself. However, in production systems, you will almost always want to have one or more separate server registrar classes to register an initial set of servers to be distributed for the sake of modularity and maintainability.

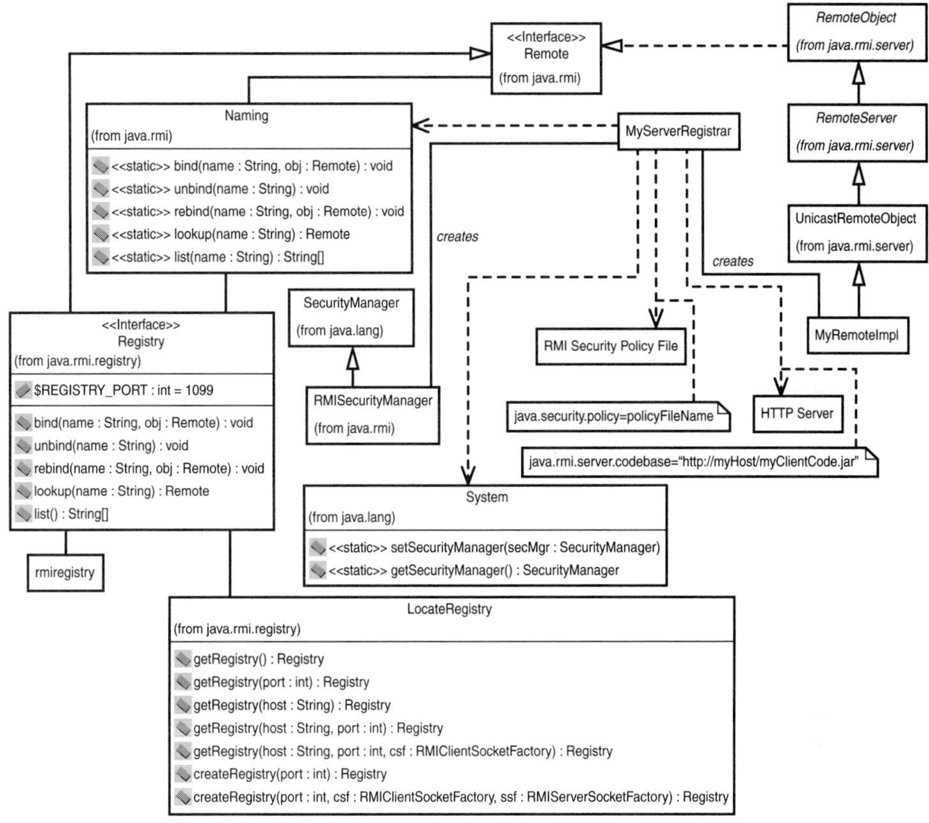

Figure 9.5 RMI/JRMP object registration.

Starting an RMI Registry

Before your Server registrar can register RMI servers, you first need to start an RMI registry process somewhere in your distributed network. The RMI registry equipped with the J2SE/J2EE can be simply invoked from the command line with this:

```
rmiregistry
```

This will cause the RMI registry to listen for incoming requests on port 1099. The RMI registry can also run on a port number specified by you on the `rmiregistry` command as shown here:

```
rmiregistry 5000
```

Configuring RMI/JRMP Security

The RMI server registrar (`MyServerRegistrar` in Figure 9.5) needs to install a security manager for the servers it will register. A default `java.rmi.RMISecurityManager` instance is created and passed into the `System.setSecurityManager()` call. We discuss Java-based security in more depth in Chapter 17, "Assurance and Security Services." Additionally, the Java security model allows for specification of security permissions in a separate properties file. Our example here uses a properties file with no restrictions for simplicity. We expand on setting Java security policy files in Chapter 17.

Figure 9.5 shows the registrar's dependence on an RMI security policy file and the fact that a server registrar is made aware of which security policy file to use with the default `RMISecurityManager`. The security policy file is designated via setting of a `java.security.policy` system property, such as in passing `-Djava.security.policy=rmi.policy` as the command-line argument when starting the RMI server registrar.

Interfacing with RMI Registries

RMI server registrars use the `java.rmi.Naming` class to interface with an RMI registry for binding remote server objects to names for distributed client access. RMI names used by `Naming` are of this general form:

```
//optionalHost:optionalPort/serverName
```

The *`optionalHost`* is the name of the host where you have started the RMI registry. This can be a remote host or perhaps `localhost` (`127.0.0.1`) if you've run the RMI registry on your local machine. If no host name is provided, the default `localhost` is used. The *`optionalPort`* is used to indicate the port number on which you've run the RMI registry. If no port is provided, the default port of 1099 is assumed. The *`serverName`* is the name you want to give for your RMI server object implementation instance.

The server registrar can use the static `Naming.bind()` or `Naming.rebind()` method to register an instantiated server object implementation with a name in the RMI registry. The difference between `bind()` and `rebind()` is that `bind()` throws an `AlreadyBoundException` if an object of that name is registered with the RMI registry, whereas `rebind()` replaces any objects already bound with that name. The `Naming` class actually uses a `java.rmi.registry.Registry` interface to an object that talks with the associated `rmiregistry` instance running. For example:

```
MyRemoteImpl myRemote = new MyRemoteImpl();
Naming.bind("//localhost/MyRemoteImplInstance", myRemote);
Naming.rebind("//localhost/MyRemoteImplInstance", myRemote);
```

The `java.rmi.registry.LocateRegistry` can be also used to obtain a direct reference to an RMI registry on the local or a remote host. The

LocateRegistry.getRegistry() methods take parameters such as a host name and port number to identify the particular RMI registry of interest. Additionally, the LocateRegistry.createRegistry() methods can also be used to create an RMI registry instance on the localhost directly from within a Java application if desired.

Dynamic RMI/JRMP Class Downloading

As most Java developers are aware, Java objects can be serialized across a network using Java's object serialization format. A standard Java network client can manipulate a serializable Java class if the Java class is already associated with the serialized object loaded into the JVM or is loadable from the client's local CLASSPATH.

Java applets also enable Java binary classes to be automatically downloaded from a Web server to a Web browser. The distributed client in this case is the Web browser making calls on a subclass of the java.applet.Applet class. From the Web browser's perspective, it is using the application-specific Applet without having any explicit reference to the application-specific class. A class loader such as an Applet class loader is then used to load classes from a "codebase." The codebase simply specifies those locations from which the class loader can download Java binary classes. Depending on the specific class-loader implementation, such locations may be specified in terms of HTTP URLs, file locations, or some other naming scheme. Of course, in the case of an Applet class loader, such codebase values specified inside of an Applet tag are typically HTTP URLs specified relative to the download location of the associated Web page.

RMI also uses such features for dynamic code downloading. RMI stubs can be dynamically downloaded to RMI clients using the same codebase infrastructure used for applet downloading. Such dynamic stub downloading alleviates the need for manually installing the proper RMI stubs inside of the RMI client. Also, any classes used by the RMI stubs can be downloaded dynamically and avoid client-side installs. Classes can be downloaded to the RMI client using a URL specified in terms of a file system (file://), via an FTP server (ftp://), or via a Web server (http://).

Although classes can be downloaded from a file system and FTP, the most common method for downloading RMI code to clients is using an HTTP server. The HTTP server for RMI class downloading needs only to implement basic HTTP GET functionality. Although any Web server will do, we utilize a very small (under 10KB above and beyond the J2SE libraries) HTTP server provided by Sun called ClassFileServer. ClassFileServer can be run using the following command:

```
java examples.classServer.ClassFileServer <port> <classpath>
```

The *<port>* specifies the port on which the HTTP server will listen for incoming requests. A default port of 2001 is assumed if no port is specified. The *<classpath>* is a CLASSPATH that tells the HTTP server where to locate Java files requested during HTTP GET requests. Such HTTP servers must be initiated to run on each machine that has RMI code to download to RMI clients.

Note

The small footprint HTTP server provided by Sun called `ClassFileServer` can be downloaded from `http://java.sun.com/products/jdk/rmi/class-server.zip`. As mentioned earlier in this chapter, you should extract this zip file to a `<ROOT>/examples/classServer` directory in which `<ROOT>` is a root directory of your choice.

To make code downloadable to RMI clients, the `java.rmi.server.codebase` system property for the JVM running the server registrar should be set equal to the base location from which all RMI client code can be downloaded to RMI clients. For example, if you have an HTTP server running on `myHost.com` and port 2001 with all downloadable code sitting in the `myClientCode` directory relative to that HTTP server, then the server codebase property might look like this:

```
-Djava.rmi.server.codebase="http://myHost.com:2001/myClientCode/" "
```

Such a property can be set for your server JVM via the command line when your server registrar is being run. When an RMI server is bound to the RMI registry, this codebase value is automatically associated with the remote server object reference. When an RMI client retrieves a reference to the remote server object, the RMI client's `CLASSPATH` will first be searched for the associated RMI stub. If the RMI stub is not found locally, the `CODEBASE` is then searched for the stub. If it's found via the `CODEBASE`, the RMI stubs and any other classes needed by the RMI client will be downloaded according to whatever protocol is specified in the `CODEBASE` (`http`, `ftp`, or file) and relative to the location specified in the server `CODEBASE` property value.

Tip

The classes to download to the RMI client should not be in the RMI registry's `CLASSPATH`. When they are absent from the RMI registry's `CLASSPATH`, the RMI registry will properly consult the `CODEBASE` property associated with the registered RMI server.

Caution

Be careful to properly define the `java.rmi.server.codebase` property. Absence of trailing forward slashes (/) in a URL (`http://host/myDir/`) or misspelled URLs can lead to hard-to-resolve `ClassNotFoundExceptions` being thrown.

When an RMI client makes a call on an RMI server method, there may be cases in which the RMI client passes a parameter to the remote method, which either implements some interface type or extends some base class specified in the remote method signature. In such a case, the RMI server itself can download the binary Java class used by the RMI client if the RMI client itself has specified a `java.rmi.server.codebase` property for its JVM process.

Example RMI/JRMP Server Registration

The `main()` method of the `QueryServerImplementation` implements the RMI server registrar functionality for registration of a `QueryServerImplementation` instance as illustrated here:

```
public static void main(String[] args)
{
  Preferences preferences =
    Preferences.userNodeForPackage(ejava.rmi.QueryServer.class);
    ...
    String name = preferences.get("QUERY_SERVER_NAME",null);

    QueryServerImplementation queryServerImpl =
             new QueryServerImplementation();

    System.setSecurityManager(new RMISecurityManager());

    String registryURL = preferences.get("REGISTRY_SERVER_URL",null);
    System.out.println("Binding :" + registryURL + name);

    Naming.rebind(registryURL + name, queryServerImpl);
    System.out.println("Bound:");
    ...
}
```

The `build.properties` file is used to set all Java preferences relevant to the particular example. Included in the preferences utilized by the `QueryServerImplementation` class are an RMI registry URL and a name for the server implementation instance set according to these two `build.properties` entries:

```
# Registry Server URL
registry.server.url=//localhost/

# Query server name
query.server.name=BeeShirtsRmiServer
```

After setting the `RMISecurityManager`, the server object instance is bound to the RMI registry using `Naming.rebind()`.

The run file generated by the ANT `build.xml` script in the `examples\src\ejava\rmi\queryservicejrmp` directory can be used to start your HTTP class download server and RMI registry. After spawning the RMI registry, the example run script spawns the `ClassFileServer` as exemplified here:

```
start %JAVA_HOME%\bin\java -classpath %CLASSPATH%
➥ examples.classServer.ClassFileServer 2001 %CODEBASE%
```

In this case the `CODEBASE` variable is set to the book's examples classes directory (that is, `<ejava_home>/examples/classes`) in order for the HTTP server to locate classes to send to the client.

The RMI server registrar for the `QueryServerImplementation` is invoked with a system security policy file and `CODEBASE` set from the `run` script as exemplified here:

```
start %JAVA_HOME%\bin\java -classpath %CLASSPATH%
➥ -Djava.security.policy=..\rmi.policy
➥ -Djava.rmi.server.codebase=http://localhost:2001/
➥ ejava.rmi.queryservicejrmp.QueryServerImplementation
```

Thus, the `QueryServerImplementation` indicates to the client that its `CODEBASE` for stubs are accessed via the HTTP server. The HTTP server then pulls classes from its `<ejava_home>/examples/classes CLASSPATH`. As you'll see later in the chapter, the client's `CLASSPATH` is set to a `<ejava_home>/examples/classes/client` and the ANT script copies a minimalist set of client classes to that directory. Thus, the client JVM will need to consult the HTTP server for retrieving stubs associated with the server's codebase.

Note that `Customer` objects are also dynamically bound to the RMI registry when the `findCustomersWhoOrderedForMoreThan()` method is called by the RMI client on the `QueryServerImplementation` object as illustrated here:

```
public Vector findCustomersWhoOrderedForMoreThan(float value)

  throws RemoteException
{
      ...
    // Issue query and create/bind Customer server for each result
    //  ...also return Vector of customer IDs
    ResultSet rs = this.getResultSet(customerQueryString,
                                     new Float(value));
      ...
    Vector customerIDs = new Vector();

    while (rs.next()) {
      String customerID = rs.getString("CUSTOMER_ID");
      String firstName = rs.getString("FIRST_NAME");
          ...
      CustomerImplementation custImpl = new CustomerImplementation();

      custImpl.setFirstName(firstName);
          ...
      String registryURL
                = preferences.get("REGISTRY_SERVER_URL",null);
      String name = registryURL + customerID;
      System.out.println(name);
      custImpl.bind(name);
      customerIDs.addElement(customerID);
    }
    return customerIDs;
   ...
}
```

The `bind()` method defined in `CustomerImplementation` calls `Naming.rebind()` with the name being passed in from the `QueryServerImplementation` `findCustomersWhoOrderedForMoreThan()` call as shown here:

```
public void bind(String customerID)
{
    ...
    Naming.rebind(customerID, this);
    ...
}
```

Registration of RMI/IIOP Servers

As with the registration of RMI/JRMP-based servers, RMI/IIOP servers can be registered using an RMI server registrar, as shown in Figure 9.6. The difference between RMI/JRMP and RMI/IIOP registration involves registration of RMI/IIOP servers with a CosNaming service versus an RMI registry. As was the case with CORBA servers created in the preceding chapter, an `Orb`, CosNaming `NamingContext`, and CosNaming `NameComponent` are all used to register an object with a CosNaming service.

Starting an RMI/IIOP Naming Service

Two CosNaming servers to use with RMI/IIOP are equipped with the J2SE. Recall from Chapter 8, "CORBA Communications," that a transient name server (`tnameserv`) and persistent naming server (`orbd`) are both available with the J2SE. The transient CosNaming server is simply started as such:

```
tnameserv
```

The `tnameserv` command starts a CosNaming service on the default port 900. To override this default port, use this:

```
tnameserv -ORBInitialPort <PortNum>
```

We use the `tnameserv` naming service with our examples and invoke the service from within the generated run scripts before starting the RMI/IIOP server and client. You can also run the examples using the `orbd` command that starts a persistent CORBA naming service. The command synopsis for `tnameserv` can be found at `http://java.sun.com/j2se/1.4.1/docs/guide/idl/tnameserv.html`, and the command synopsis for `orbd` can be found at `http://java.sun.com/j2se/1.4.1/docs/guide/idl/orbd.html`.

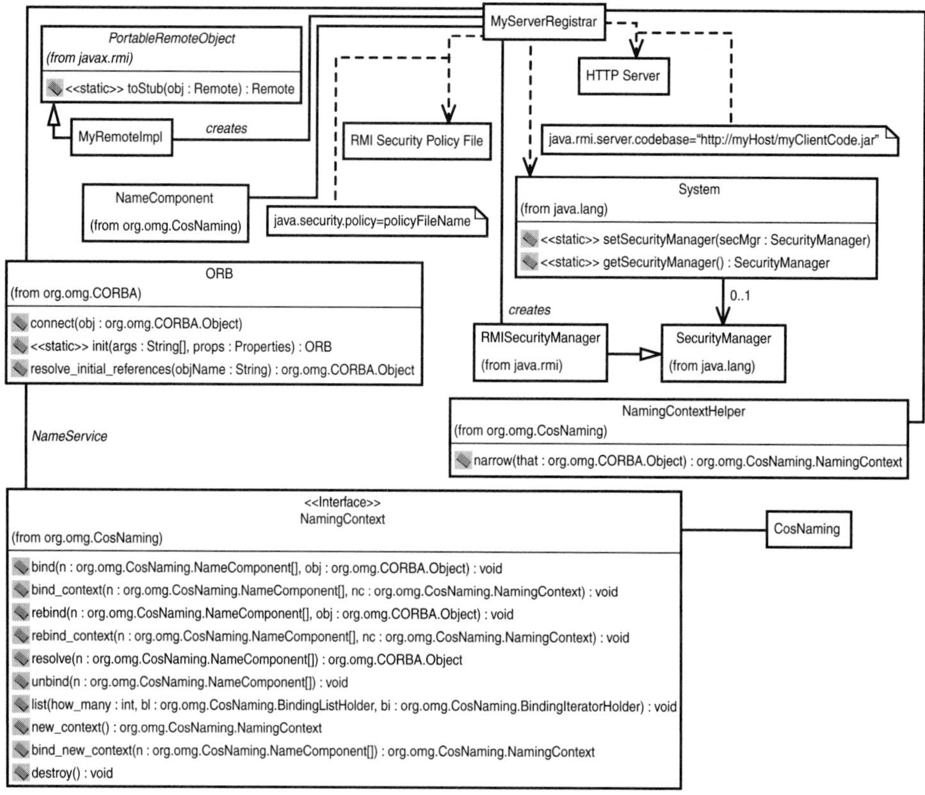

Figure 9.6 RMI/IIOP object registration.

Interfacing with RMI/IIOP Naming Services

Registering a server with CosNaming requires a few more steps than doing so using the RMI registry. Recall that the RMI registration simply involved a single call to `Naming.bind()` or `Naming.rebind()`. CosNaming registration with RMI/IIOP requires the following six general steps:

1. Obtaining an `Orb` reference:

```
ORB orb = ORB.init(args, null);
```

2. Obtaining an initial reference to a naming service:

```
org.omg.CORBA.Object namingReference =
➥ orb.resolve_initial_references("NameService");
```

3. Narrowing the naming reference:

```
cosNaming = NamingContextHelper.narrow(namingReference);
```

4. Obtaining a remote stub reference:

```
java.rmi.Remote myStub = PortableRemoteObject.toStub(myImpl);
```

5. Creating a `name` component array:

```
NameComponent path[] = {new NameComponent(name, "")};
```

6. Binding the name to the remote stub reference:

```
cosNaming.rebind(path, (org.omg.CORBA.Object) myStub);
```

Dynamic RMI/IIOP Class Downloading

Dynamic downloading of RMI stubs under RMI/IIOP is set up in the same fashion it was for RMI/JRMP. The extensions to CORBA via the Objects by Value specification include support for codebases and automatic code downloading. Thus, by running an HTTP server such as the `ClassFileServer` used for RMI/JRMP and by setting the `java.rmi.server.codebase` system property in the RMI/IIOP server process, we can dynamically download RMI/IIOP code to RMI clients on demand as was the case with RMI/JRMP.

Example RMI/IIOP Server Registration

RMI/IIOP server registration is one of the areas where RMI/JRMP and RMI/IIOP differ. The `main()` method of the `QueryServerImplementation` for RMI/IIOP implements the server registrar functionality of a `QueryServerImplementation` object as illustrated here:

```
public static void main(String[] args)
{
  Preferences preferences =
    Preferences.userNodeForPackage(ejava.rmi.QueryServer.class);

  try {
    // Get query.server.name
    String name = preferences.get("QUERY_SERVER_NAME",null);

    // Instantiate Query Server Impl
    QueryServerImplementation queryServerImpl
      = new QueryServerImplementation();

    // Set security manager
    System.setSecurityManager(new RMISecurityManager());

    // Get Name Service reference and bind server to name service
    org.omg.CORBA.ORB orb
      = org.omg.CORBA.ORB.init(args, System.getProperties());
```

```
      System.out.println("Getting Naming Reference");
      org.omg.CORBA.Object namingReference
        = orb.resolve_initial_references("NameService");

      System.out.println("Getting Context Reference and stub");
      queryServerImpl.context
        = NamingContextHelper.narrow(namingReference);
      java.rmi.Remote stub
        = PortableRemoteObject.toStub(queryServerImpl);

      NameComponent nc = new NameComponent(name, "");
      NameComponent path[] = {nc};

      System.out.println("Name Binding :"+ path);
      queryServerImpl.context.rebind(path,(org.omg.CORBA.Object) stub);

      System.out.println("Server Waiting");
    } catch (Exception ne) {
      System.out.println("Error    :" + ne);
    }
  }
```

Within the `findCustomersWhoOrderedForMoreThan()` method of `QueryServerImplementation`, a `Customer` reference (`custImpl`) is bound as illustrated here:

```
public Vector findCustomersWhoOrderedForMoreThan(float value)
  throws RemoteException
{
       ...
    // Issue query and create/bind Customer server for each result
    //  ...also return Vector of customer IDs
    ResultSet rs =
      this.getResultSet(customerQueryString,new Float(value));
      ...
    Vector customerIDs = new Vector();

    while (rs.next()) {
      String customerID = rs.getString("CUSTOMER_ID");
      String firstName = rs.getString("FIRST_NAME");
        ...
      CustomerImplementation custImpl = new CustomerImplementation();

      custImpl.setFirstName(firstName);
        ...
```

```
            String name = customerID;
            custImpl.setContext(this.context);
            custImpl.bind(name);
            customerIDs.addElement(customerID);
        }
        return customerIDs;
        ...
}
```

As another example, a `Customer` reference has its context set to a CosNaming service reference before the RMI/IIOP registration inside the `bind()` method on the `CustomerImplementation` instance is triggered:

```
public void bind(String customerID) {
      ...
    java.rmi.Remote stub = PortableRemoteObject.toStub(this);
    NameComponent nc = new NameComponent(customerID, "");
    NameComponent path[] = {nc};
    this.context.rebind(path, (org.omg.CORBA.Object) stub);
      ...
}
```

RMI Clients, Stubs, and Lookups

After active RMI servers have been registered with an RMI registry or CosNaming service, RMI clients can utilize the services provided by such servers. In this section, we cover the creation of both RMI/JRMP clients and RMI/IIOP clients. Both types of clients use a stub that delegates calls to the appropriate distributed server process. To this end, we also demonstrate how stubs can be generated and downloaded to the clients on demand.

RMI/JRMP Clients, Stubs, and Lookups

The `rmic` compiler command used to generate server-side skeletons also creates client-side stubs. As shown in Figure 9.7, a stub named `MyRemoteImpl_Stub` is generated from a server named `MyRemoteImpl`. The RMI client code makes calls on the `MyRemoteInterface`, which is implemented by the `MyRemoteImpl_Stub` class. RMI stubs extend the `RemoteStub` class, which in turn implements the `RemoteObject` class offering distributed semantics to remote object calls.

The RMI client is thus a lightweight client needing only the stub and interface for a server, plus the Java/RMI platform. Whereas regular `java.lang.Object` objects compare objects based on reference equality, the `RemoteStub` implementation class translates such types of calls into appropriate distributed object reference equality semantics transparent to the RMI client.

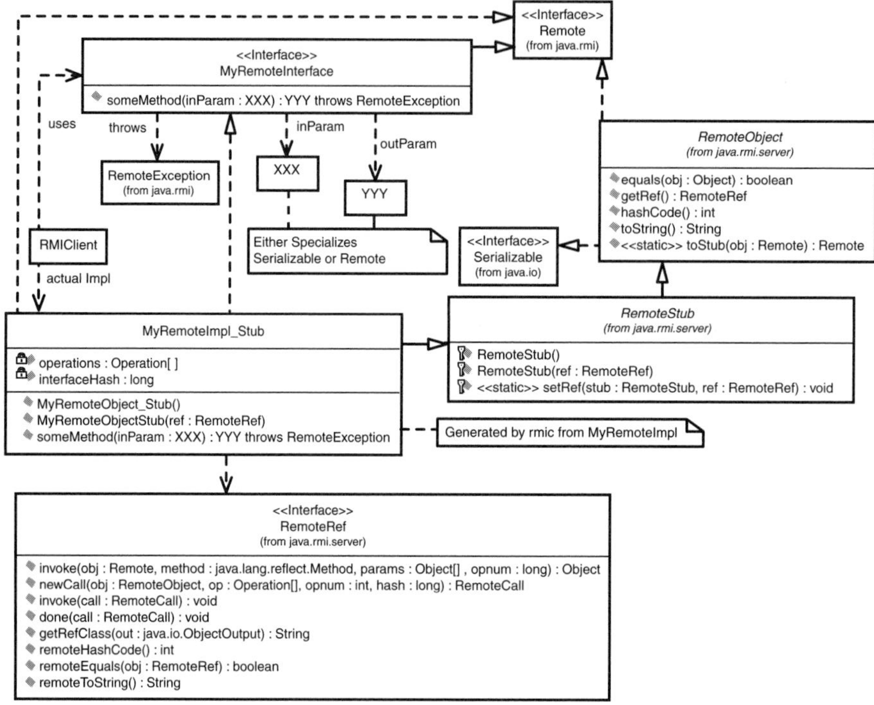

Figure 9.7 RMI/JRMP clients.

The application-specific RMI v1.1 stub uses `java.rmi.server.RemoteRef`, `java.rmi.server.RemoteCall`, and `java.rmi.server.Operation` to marshal and unmarshal calls to and from the remote object implementation. `RemoteRef` serves as a handle on the remote object. The `Operation` and `RemoteCall` constructs are not needed for RMI v1.2–style stubs and are thus deprecated. In RMI v1.1, these constructs encapsulated remote operations and calls.

The `QueryClient` equipped with this chapter's code not only demonstrates how an RMI client makes distributed calls on an RMI server but also demonstrates how an RMI client can register a distributed callback with an RMI server. The `QueryClient.main()` method first instantiates an `RMISecurityManager` to set as the system security manager using `System.setSecurityManager (new RMISecurityManager())`. After obtaining a reference to a `QueryServer` (the mechanism for which is described in the next section), our `QueryClient` makes the `findCustomersWhoOrderedForMoreThan()` distributed call on the `QueryServer`. The `QueryClient` subsequently creates an instance of a distributed `ClientReceiverImplementation` object and registers it with the `QueryServer` using the `register()` distributed call. When the `QueryClient` calls `findOrdersWhichAreFrom()` on the `QueryServer`, the

`QueryServerImplementation` makes a callback on the RMI client's `ClientReceiver` object with a `ClientReceiver.setResultOrders()` call. A skeletal structure of the `QueryClient` is shown here:

```
package ejava.rmi.queryservicejrmp;
...
public class QueryClient
{
  public void list(String rmiURL)
  {
        ...
      String[] names = Naming.list(rmiURL);
      for (int i = 0; i < names.length; i++) {
        System.out.println("Registered objects :" + names[i]);
      }
       ...
  }

  public static void main(String[] args)
  {
    Preferences preferences =
      Preferences.userNodeForPackage(ejava.rmi.QueryServer.class);
        ...
      // Get query server name
      String queryServerName =
        preferences.get("QUERY_SERVER_NAME",null);

      // Get registry name
      String registryURL =
        preferences.get("REGISTRY_SERVER_URL",null);
      String name =  registryURL + queryServerName;
      System.out.println("QueryServerName :" + name);

      // Set security manager
      if (System.getSecurityManager() == null) {
        System.setSecurityManager(new RMISecurityManager());
      }
      System.out.println("Client Looking for Server :" + name);
      System.out.println("Type Enter Key");
      System.in.read();    // to hold the screen

      // Look up QueryServer reference
      QueryServer qserver = (QueryServer) Naming.lookup(name);
      System.out.println("Client querying for customers :");
      System.out.println("Type Enter Key");
      System.in.read();
```

```
        // Query for customers and traverse results
        Vector v = qserver.findCustomersWhoOrderedForMoreThan(10.0f);

        System.out.println("Resultant Customers: " + v);

        for (int i = 0; i < v.size(); i++) {
          String cid = (String) v.elementAt(i);
          Customer c = (Customer) Naming.lookup(registryURL+cid);

          System.out.println(i + " : is " + c);
          System.out.println("FirstName :" + c.getFirstName());
          System.out.println("LastName:" + c.getLastName());
        }

        System.out.println("Server Writing Orders ");
        System.out.println("Type Enter Key");

        // Register client callback with query server
        ClientReceiverImplementation cr =
          new ClientReceiverImplementation();
        qserver.register("ClientReceiver", cr);

        // Induce callbacks to be made by requesting order info
        qserver.findOrdersWhichAreFrom("VA");
        QueryClient qc = new QueryClient();

        System.out.println("Now list all registered objects :");
        System.out.println("Type Enter Key");
        System.in.read();
        qc.list(registryURL);
          ...
  }
}
```

Distributed RMI/JRMP server objects that have been registered with a naming service are "looked up" by RMI/JRMP clients. Figure 9.5 presented the core classes and interfaces involved in RMI registration on the server side. The same constructs are used for RMI lookup on the client side. The Naming classes' static `lookup()` method is used by RMI clients to obtain a remote server object reference, given a name `String` corresponding to the name with which the server object was registered. The `list()` method can also be used to retrieve an array of distributed object name `Strings`, given a URL name `String` of a particular RMI registry.

The RMI/JRMP `QueryClient` code also demonstrates RMI/JRMP lookup. The name `//localhost/BeeShirtsRmiServer` is passed as a parameter to `Naming.lookup()`. Such a name is constructed from the `build.properties` entries:

```
# Registry Server URL
registry.server.url=//localhost/
```

```
# Query server name
query.server.name=BeeShirtsRmiServer
```

The returned `Remote` object instance is then cast to the `QueryServer` type. Similarly, `Customer` object names returned from the `QueryServer` `findCustomersWhoOrderedForMoreThan()` call are used to look up registered `Customer` object references later in the code. Such a simple means for looking up RMI objects has been one of the features of RMI that makes it attractively easy to use. Finally, one of the last steps performed by the `QueryClient` is to look up and print a list of distributed objects registered in the default RMI registry.

Finally note that the `run` script generated by the ANT build process induces the use of a different `CLASSPATH` than that of the server. This is done so that we can illustrate how the client will consult the server's codebase, which then points the client to retrieve stubs from the HTTP server.

RMI/IIOP Clients, Stubs, and Lookups

When the parameter `-iiop` was passed to the `rmic` compiler that we ran earlier in this chapter's examples, a set of client-side RMI/IIOP stubs was created. Figure 9.8 depicts the constructs involved with client-side RMI/IIOP. The `_MyRemoteImpl_Stub` class generated by the `rmic` compiler implements the `MyRemoteInterface` and extends the `javax.rmi.CORBA.Stub` class. The `Stub` class extends the OMG `ObjectImpl` class hierarchy, which implements the standard CORBA `Object` interface. The `Stub` class provides all the necessary semantics for remote object operations involved with RMI/IIOP, such as distributed versions of `equals()` and `toString()`. RMI/IIOP clients thus also remain lightweight like their RMI/JRMP counterparts.

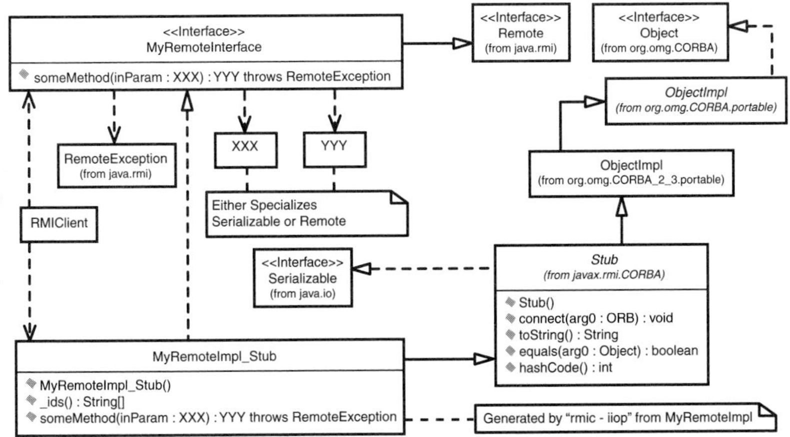

Figure 9.8 RMI/IIOP clients.

The RMI/IIOP `QueryClient` equipped with this chapter's code performs the same tasks as the RMI/JRMP Query Client. The `QueryServer` is queried and an RMI client-side callback is registered with the RMI query server. The `QueryServer` then invokes a callback on the RMI client. The only difference between the RMI/IIOP client and the RMI/JRMP client, as you'll see in the next section, is how the client interacts with the registration and lookup processes. The basic structure of the RMI/IIOP `QueryClient` is shown here:

```
package ejava.rmi.queryserviceiiop;
   ...
public class QueryClient
{
  public static void main(String[] args)
  {
    Preferences preferences =
      Preferences.userNodeForPackage(ejava.rmi.QueryServer.class);
        ...
      // Set security manager
      if (System.getSecurityManager() == null) {
        System.setSecurityManager(new RMISecurityManager());
      }

      // Get orb reference
      System.out.println("Getting initial Context");
      ORB orb = ORB.init(args, System.getProperties());

      // Get the root naming context
      org.omg.CORBA.Object objRef =
        orb.resolve_initial_references("NameService");
      NamingContext context = NamingContextHelper.narrow(objRef);

      String name = preferences.get("QUERY_SERVER_NAME",null);
      // Resolve the object reference in naming
      NameComponent nc = new NameComponent(name, "");
      NameComponent path[] = {nc};
      System.out.println("Client Looking for Server :" + name);
      System.out.println("Type Enter Key");
      System.in.read();    // to hold the screen

      // Lookup QueryServer reference
      org.omg.CORBA.Object object = context.resolve(path);
      System.out.println(object);
      QueryServer qserver =
        (QueryServer)PortableRemoteObject.narrow(object,
                               ejava.rmi.QueryServer.class);
      System.out.println("Client querying for customers :");
```

```
      System.out.println("Type Enter Key");
      System.in.read();    // to hold the screen

      // Query for customers and traverse results
      Vector v = qserver.findCustomersWhoOrderedForMoreThan(10.0f);

      System.out.println("Result Customers :" + v);

      for (int i = 0; i < v.size(); i++) {
        String cid = (String) v.elementAt(i);

        nc = new NameComponent(cid, "");
        NameComponent path1[] = {nc};

        object = context.resolve(path1);

        Customer customer = (Customer)
          PortableRemoteObject.narrow(object, Customer.class);

        System.out.println(i + " : is " + customer);
        System.out.println("FirstName :" + customer.getFirstName());
        System.out.println("LastName:" + customer.getLastName());
      }

      System.out.println("Server Writing Orders ");
      System.out.println("Type Enter Key");
      System.in.read();    // to hold the screen

      // Register client callback with query server
      ClientReceiverImplementation cr =
        new ClientReceiverImplementation();
      NameComponent nc1 = new NameComponent("ClientReceiver", "");
      NameComponent path2[] = {nc1};
      java.rmi.Remote stub = PortableRemoteObject.toStub(cr);

      context.rebind(path2, (org.omg.CORBA.Object) stub);
      qserver.register("ClientReceiver", cr);

      // Induce callbacks to be made by requesting order info
      qserver.findOrdersWhichAreFrom("VA");
      ...
  }
}
```

Distributed RMI/JRMP server objects that have been registered with a naming service are "looked up" by RMI/JRMP clients. Figure 9.6 depicts the key entities involved in both distributed CosNaming object registration and lookup in RMI/IIOP. Our

RMI/IIOP `QueryClient` goes through the same steps for obtaining an initial handle on a CosNaming service object as did the RMI/IIOP `QueryServerImplementation`. However, instead of calling `rebind()` on the CosNaming reference, the `QueryClient` calls `resolve()`, given the name of the desired server object reference. The CORBA object returned must then be narrowed via a call to `narrow()` on the `PortableRemoteObject` class.

As with the RMI/JRMP example, you should note that the `run` script generated by the ANT build process induces the use of a different `CLASSPATH` than that of the server. As previously mentioned, this is done to illustrate how the client will consult the server's codebase, which then points the client to retrieve stubs from the HTTP server.

RMI Object Activation

RMI v1.2 introduced automatic server object activation to the world of RMI. Thus, instead of activating and registering an RMI server object instance ahead of time, RMI server objects can now be activated upon RMI client request. When you make your server objects activatable, an activation daemon can activate your objects in a separate JVM process upon demand of clients.

Figure 9.9 illustrates some of the classes involved in creating and registering activatable objects. Two of the application-specific classes to focus on are `MyRemoteImpl` and `MyServerRegistrar`. `MyRemoteImpl` implements your application-specific `MyRemoteInterface` as usual, but it now extends `java.rmi.activation.Activatable` instead of `UnicastRemoteObject` or `PortableRemoteObject`. Instead of registering active objects, `MyServerRegistrar` is now responsible for creating all the information necessary to register the activatable server with the RMI activation daemon.

In addition to the RMI registry and potentially an HTTP server for dynamic class downloading, the RMI activation daemon must be started to support the use of activatable objects. You can start the RMI activation daemon simply by typing `rmid` on the command line. The RMI activation daemon will satisfy registration requests to register activatable objects on the server side and satisfy client-side requests to activate a particular RMI server object.

Creating an Activatable Server

There is nothing special to note about the `MyRemoteInterface` interface shown in Figure 9.9 and the `SampleServer` interface in Listing 9.4 that we'll be using to illustrate a simple activatable object example. The same rules for defining RMI interfaces apply for activatable as they do for the other non-activatable types of remote objects. However, `MyRemoteImpl` of Figure 9.9 and `SampleServerImplementation` of Listing 9.5 differ in two important regards. First, the servers now extend the

`Activatable` class. Second, an activatable server implementation should implement a constructor that can be used to call a constructor on the base `Activatable` object class. Classes may also opt to not extend `Activatable` and instead call one of the static `exportObject()` calls on `Activatable` with a reference to itself.

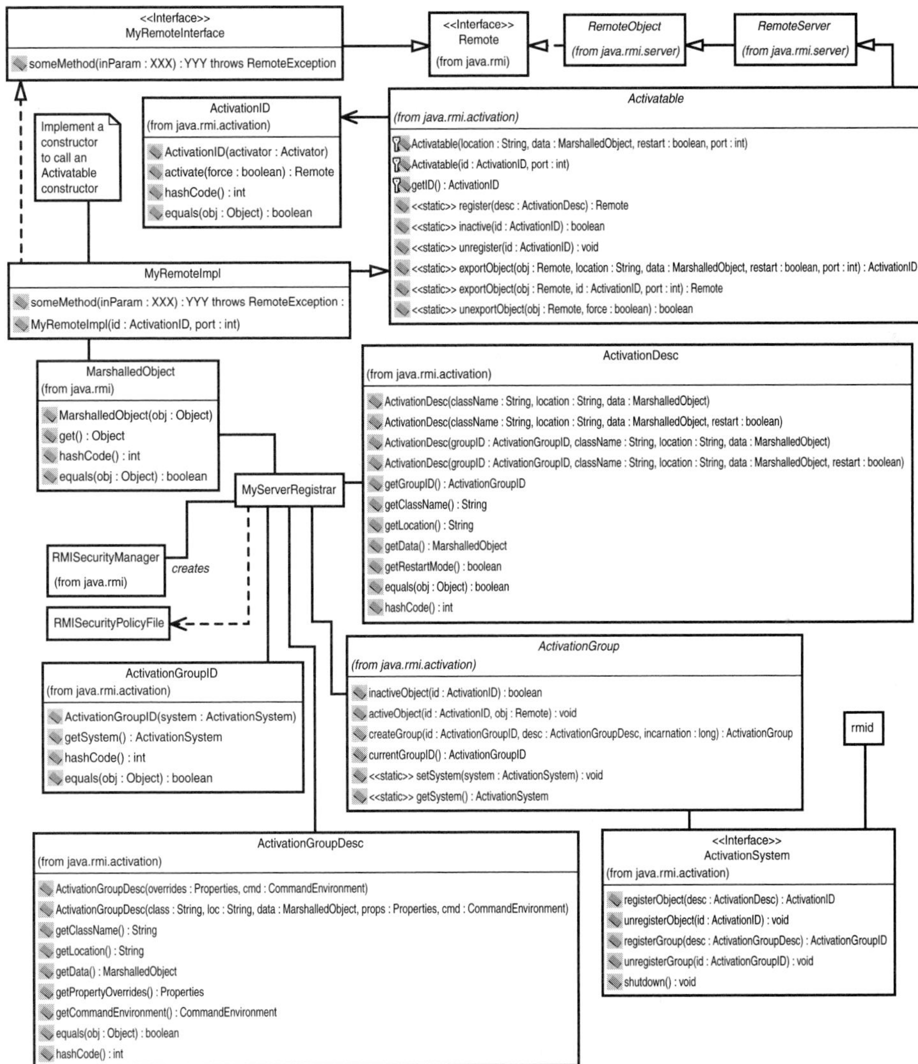

Figure 9.9 Activatable objects.

> **Note**
>
> The complete set of code examples for activatable RMI objects will be contained in the `examples\src\ejava\rmi\sampleactivatable` directory, after you have retrieved the source according to the instructions in Appendix A. The `build.properties` file in the `examples\src\ejava\rmi` directory is used to configure this example. The ANT `build.xml` script will generate a `run` script file and place it into the `sampleactivatable` directory, which can then be used to execute the example.

Listing 9.4 **The Sample Activatable Object Interface (`SampleServer.java`)**

```
package ejava.rmi.sampleactivatable;

import java.rmi.Remote;
import java.rmi.RemoteException;
import java.util.Vector;

public interface SampleServer extends Remote {
  Object[] getArrayOfObjects() throws RemoteException;
}
```

Listing 9.5 **The Sample Activatable Object Implementation (`SampleServerImplementation.java`)**

```
package ejava.rmi.sampleactivatable;

import java.rmi.RemoteException;
import java.rmi.activation.Activatable;
import java.rmi.activation.ActivationID;
import java.rmi.MarshalledObject;
import java.rmi.Remote;
import java.rmi.Naming;
import java.rmi.RMISecurityManager;

public class SampleServerImplementation extends Activatable
  implements SampleServer {
  private final int OBJECTS_TO_SEND = 10;

  public SampleServerImplementation(ActivationID activationID,
    MarshalledObject data) throws RemoteException {
    super(activationID, 0);
  }

 public Object[] getArrayOfObjects() throws RemoteException {
    // create simple test set of objects to return
```

Listing 9.5 **Continued**

```
    Object[] someObjects = new Object[OBJECTS_TO_SEND];

    for (int i = 0; i < someObjects.length; i++) {
      someObjects[i] = new Integer(i);
    }
    return someObjects;
  }
}
```

Two primary constructor forms are available to the `Activatable` object. One constructor form takes an `ActivationID` and a port on which the object takes requests (uses an anonymous port if the port number is 0). Another constructor form takes an `Activatable` class file location, a `java.rmi.MarshalledObject` instance, a `true/false` flag indicating whether the object is started with the activator daemon or on demand, and a port number. `MarshalledObject` object instances contain a marshaled byte stream of the object passed into its constructor. When `get()` is called on a `MarshalledObject`, a copy of the underlying stream is unmarshaled and returned. Constructors on your `Activatable` object are actually called by the activation system when your object is activated by the activation daemon due to a client request.

Creating an Activatable Server Registrar

`MyServerRegistrar` in Figure 9.9 represents the activatable server registrar. The server registrar for our simple example is defined in a `SampleServerConfigure` class equipped with this chapter's code. First the `SampleServerConfigure` class instantiates an `RMISecurityManager` and registers it with the JVM as was done with the non-activatable RMI registration process. After that, an activation group and activation object description are created and registered with the activation daemon as illustrated here:

```
package ejava.rmi.sampleactivatable;
...
public class SampleServerConfigure
{
  public static void main(String[] args)
  {
     Preferences preferences =
      Preferences.userNodeForPackage(ejava.rmi.QueryServer.class);

     System.setSecurityManager(new RMISecurityManager());

       ...
      // Get class name and class directory location
      String serverClassName =preferences.get("SERVER_CLASS_NAME",null);
      String location = preferences.get("LOCATION",null);
```

```
        // Initialize data to be sent to the activatable object
        MarshalledObject dataToTheObject = null;
        // for our case we will be using same jvm as rmid's
        ActivationGroupDesc.CommandEnvironment cmd = null;
        ActivationGroupID activationID =
          ActivationGroup.getSystem().registerGroup(
                   new ActivationGroupDesc(System.getProperties(), cmd));
        ActivationDesc acdesc
           = new ActivationDesc(activationID, serverClassName,
                                 location, dataToTheObject);

        // Register the activatable object
        SampleServer server = (SampleServer)Activatable.register(acdesc);

        // Now bind object to registry
        System.out.println("Registered and got the Stub :");
        String serverRegistryName
            = preferences.get("SERVER_BOUND_NAME",null);
        Naming.rebind(serverRegistryName, server);
        System.out.println("Exported Server:");
        System.exit(0);
          ...
    }
}
```

Activation groups collect groups of activatable objects and are used to notify an `ActivationMonitor` of the status of its activatable objects. As illustrated by the `SampleServerConfigure` class, an `ActivationGroupDesc` is instantiated with a properties object. An `ActivationGroupDesc` object contains all the information needed for activating an object belonging to a particular group. The `ActivationGroupDesc` is registered with the `ActivationSystem` returned from the static `getSystem()` call on `ActivationGroup` using the `ActivationSystem`'s `registerGroup()` method.

After obtaining an `ActivationGroupID` object from the `ActivationSystem.registerGroup()` method, the `ActivationGroupID` is used along with a fully qualified server class name, the location of the class, and any marshaled initialization data for the `Activatable` object to create an `ActivationDesc` object. The server class name for the `SampleServerImplementation` and location are read from the properties file associated with the example. The `ActivationDesc` object contains all the information the activation daemon needs to automatically activate a particular object. This object is passed into the static `register()` method of the `Activatable` class and returns the stub for the activatable object. Finally, the stub returned from the activation daemon registration is bound to the RMI registry.

RMI Activatable Object Client

The `SampleServerClient` equipped with this chapter's code represents the RMI client used for our activatable object example. As can be seen from the code, no special considerations need to be made on the client side. From the client's perspective, the fact that the RMI server needs to be activated is transparent to the client. Thus the following illustrative structure of the `SampleServerClient` should not be anything new to you:

```
package ejava.rmi.sampleactivatable;
...
public class SampleServerClient
{
  public static void main(String[] args)
  {
    Preferences preferences =
      Preferences.userNodeForPackage(ejava.rmi.QueryServer.class);
       ...
      if (System.getSecurityManager() == null) {
        System.setSecurityManager(new RMISecurityManager());
      }

      String serverName
            = preferences.get("REGISTRY_SERVER_URL",null)
            + preferences.get("SERVER_BOUND_NAME",null);

      System.out.println("Client Looking for Server :" + serverName);
      System.out.println("Type Enter Key");
      System.in.read();    // to hold the screen

      SampleServer server = (SampleServer) Naming.lookup(serverName);

      System.out.println("Client querying for Objects :");
      System.out.println("Type Enter Key");
      System.in.read();

      Object[] receivedObjects = server.getArrayOfObjects();

      System.out.println("Resulting Objects" );

      for (int i = 0; i < receivedObjects.length -2; i++) {
         System.out.print(((Integer) receivedObjects[i]).intValue()
                      + ":");
      }
      System.out.print(((Integer)
        receivedObjects[receivedObjects.length-1]).intValue() + "\n");
       ...
  }
}
```

Compile and Run the Example

As usual, the RMI stubs and skeletons must be generated from the RMI compiler. This is accomplished via our ANT `build.xml` script's `jrmprmic` target as before. The `run` script file generated for the activatable object examples starts the HTTP server and RMI registry also as it did with the previous examples. After starting the simple HTTP server and RMI registry, the RMI activation daemon is started with a command akin to this:

```
rmid -log . -J-Djava.security.policy=..\rmi.policy

            -J-Dsun.rmi.activation.execPolicy=none
```

The RMI activatable `SampleServerImplementation` is then registered with the RMI activation daemon by starting the RMI server registrar with a command like this:

```
java -Djava.security.policy=..\rmi.policy
     -Djava.rmi.server.codebase=http://localhost:2001/
     ejava.rmi.sampleactivatable.SampleServerConfigure
```

Finally, the RMI client is started with a command similar to the following:

```
java -Djava.security.policy=..\rmi.policy
     -Djava.rmi.server.codebase=http://localhost:2001/
     ejava.rmi.sampleactivatable.SampleServerClient
```

Custom Sockets

RMI provides the capability to replace the underlying transport protocol used by the RMI framework. Custom sockets are useful for distributed object communications using protocols that encrypt data or that must communicate via some application-specific standard. Customization of sockets in RMI is accomplished by configuring an RMI socket factory to use a different transport protocol. Not only can such sockets be customized on an object-by-object basis, but the socket factories can be downloaded to RMI clients on demand. Figure 9.10 shows the main classes and interfaces involved in customizing the underlying socket transport for RMI clients and servers.

An object that implements the `java.rmi.server.RMIClientSocketFactory` interface can be associated with RMI server objects and downloaded to RMI clients when the RMI client obtains a reference to the distributed RMI server. The `RMIClientSocketFactory` is then used to create socket connections to the RMI server for RMI calls. Thus, your custom client socket factory must simply implement the `RMIClientSocketFactory` interface and return a specialized socket from the `createSocket()` call. For example:

```
public class CustomClientSocketFactory implements
  RMIClientSocketFactory, Serializable
{
  public Socket createSocket(String host, int port)
    throws IOException
```

```
  {
    return new CustomSocket(host, port);
  }
}
```

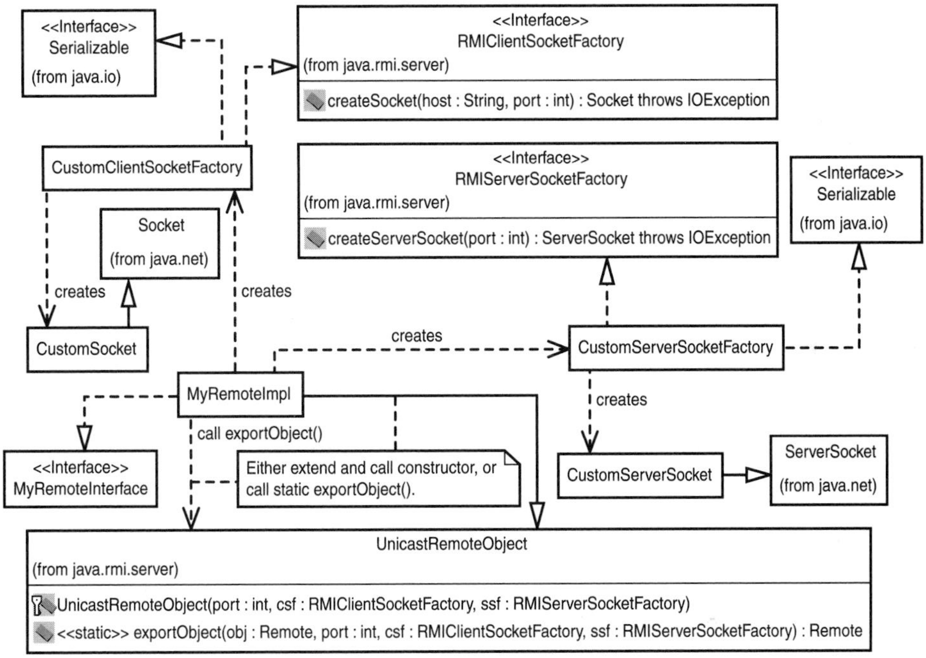

Figure 9.10 Custom sockets.

Similarly, an object that implements the `java.rmi.server.RMIServerSocketFactory` interface can be associated with RMI server objects to ensure that the correct server-side socket connection for RMI calls will be created. For example:

```
public class CustomServerSocketFactory implements
  RMIServerSocketFactory, Serializable
{
  public ServerSocket createServerSocket(int portNumber)
    throws IOException
  {
    return new CustomServerSocket(portNumber);
  }
}
```

An RMI server object is configured to utilize a specific `RMIClientSocketFactory` and `RMIServerSocketFactory` pair by passing the factories into the RMI server object's constructor or into the `exportObject()` method calls for both `UnicastRemoteObject` and `Activatable` object types. For the constructor case, we have this:

```
public class CustomSocketImpl
  extends UnicastRemoteObject
  implements CustomSocketInterface
{
  public CustomSocketImpl() throws RemoteException
  {
    // port 0 means that anonymous port is chosen
    super(0, new CustomClientSocketFactory(),
             new CustomServerSocketFactory());
  }
...
}
```

For the case in which a `UnicastRemoteObject` or an `Activatable` object is exported directly, we have this:

```
public class CustomSocketImpl
  implements CustomSocketInterface
{
  public CustomSocketImpl() throws RemoteException
  {
    UnicastRemoteObject.exportObject(this, 0,
             new CustomClientSocketFactory(),
             new CustomServerSocketFactory());
  }
...
}
```

Finally, a `java.security.policy` file must be created and set as a system property for your JVM to allow the program to create sockets.

Conclusions

RMI is a feature-rich and simple framework for providing a distributed object communications infrastructure in enterprise environments. RMI is simpler to use than CORBA but has previously been frowned upon due to its Java-centric nature. All of this changed when RMI/IIOP started to become a reality. RMI servers can now export their interfaces via IDL and offer their services to CORBA clients implemented in any language over IIOP. Furthermore, the transition between RMI/JRMP servers and RMI/IIOP servers is straightforward and differs only from a programming interface perspective in RMI/IIOP's use of the `PortableRemoteObject` and the underlying naming service.

Given RMI's direction to reconcile with CORBA and the associated language interoperability issues, RMI also offers some advantages over CORBA. Not the least of these advantages involves how practical and simple it is to exchange objects by value and entire Java classes between RMI clients and servers. In stark contrast, CORBA's Objects by Value specification is still very complicated and impractical. Although CORBA remains important as an industry standard to define interoperable services and a communications framework, as more systems are built using Java, future evolutions of RMI will always have an advantage over CORBA.

10

Web Service Communications

SENDING REMOTE REQUESTS TO SERVERS OVER the Web and receiving responses in a standard fashion using XML-based messages requires some common agreement on a standard format and protocol for such messages. The Simple Object Access Protocol (SOAP) is designed with that not-so-simple goal in mind. SOAP defines a standard for representing such requests and responses in XML. The SOAP with Attachments API for Java (SAAJ) provides the enterprise Java developer with a standard API to encapsulate such SOAP messages and their attachments. The Web Services Description Language (WSDL) provides a standard for defining the interfaces to remote Web services using XML-based interface descriptions. The Java API for WSDL (JWSDL) is an API that may be used to parse, manipulate, and generate WSDL documents. Last but not least, SOAP RPC defines the protocol for actually communicating SOAP requests and responses between Web service clients and servers. The Java API for XML-based RPC (JAX-RPC) provides the Java-based means for implementing SOAP RPC clients and servers.

In this chapter, you will learn:

- An overview description of Web services and the WS-I.
- An overview description of SOAP.
- About the SAAJ API, SOAP message formats, and how to parse and create SOAP messages using SAAJ.
- An overview of SOAP encoding conventions.
- About WSDL structure and basic JWSDL abstractions for reading, manipulating, and writing WSDL documents.
- A conceptual overview of SOAP RPC.
- About the JAX-RPC API and how to create Web service clients and servers using JAX-RPC.

Web Services and WS-I Overview

Thus far in Part III of this book, we've described CORBA and RMI as key distributed object communication paradigms. In both approaches to distributed computing, there exists the concept of a distributed client generating requests marshaled into a particular communications message format that are then sent to a server and unmarshaled from the message format into calls onto a server object. An intermediate interface definition of some sort may also be used to describe how clients can interface with such servers. As you'll see in Chapter 11, "Naming Services with JNDI," and Chapter 12, "Directory Services with JNDI," distributed communication paradigms also support a means to look up and discover handles to distributed services. In the distributed object computing world, it thus should be apparent that standards are key to delineate contracts for various aspects of a distributed communications paradigm. Such standard contracts may define the following:

- *Message Format:* A means to represent a message communicated between client and server, such as GIOP/IIOP messages in the CORBA world or JRMP or IIOP messages in the RMI world.
- *Message Transport:* An underlying communications transport protocol such as TCP/IP in both the CORBA and the RMI worlds.
- *Service RPC:* A standard way for clients to invoke remote procedure calls on servers such as the CORBA and RMI distributed object invocation protocols.
- *Interface Definition:* A standard way to describe interfaces to distributed services such as CORBA IDL or RMI interfaces.
- *Service Lookup:* A means for looking up handles to distributed services such as the CORBA naming service, CORBA trading service, RMI registries, or Jini.

In this general context of the need to standardize different aspects of a distributed communications paradigm, Web services are no different. A set of distinct standards has cropped up in industry and from organizations such as the W3C (`www.w3c.org`) and OASIS (`www.oasis-open.org`) that allow for a standard way to define how XML-based requests and responses sent over Web-based protocols can be used to implement distributed servers and clients. The Web Services Interoperability (WS-I) organization (`www.ws-i.org`) was formed to coagulate these distinct standards into cohesive profiles for Web service communications. Such cohesive profiles enable greater levels of interoperability in the Web services communication world while leveraging existing widely adopted standards.

The J2EE v1.4, in fact, requires that the WS-I Basic Profile be supported by J2EE-compliant container environments. In the WS-I Basic Profile, the following key standards are required:

- *Message Format Representation (XML v1.0):* The low-level means to represent messages in the Web services world is defined via XML as described in Chapter 3.

- *Message Format Validation (XML Schema v1.0):* The low-level means to validate and define the structure of messages in the Web services world is defined via XML Schema as described in Chapter 3.
- *Message Format (SOAP v1.1 with Attachments):* The means to represent request and response messages communicated between client and server in the Web services world is defined via the SOAP with attachments standards as described in this chapter.
- *Message Transport (HTTP v1.1):* The key underlying communications transport protocol in the Web services world is HTTP as described in Appendix E, "HTTP Communications" (see CD-ROM).
- *Service RPC (SOAP v1.1):* The standard way for Web service clients to remotely invoke Web services relies on the SOAP-RPC standards as described in this chapter.
- *Interface Definition (WSDL v1.1):* The standard way to describe interfaces to Web services is WSDL as described in this chapter.
- *Service Lookup (UDDI v2.0):* A standard means for looking up handles to Web services is defined by UDDI as described in Chapter 13 (along with ebXML registries as another standard).

Because the J2EE requires support for the WS-I Basic Profile, a set of APIs is required as part of the J2EE to encapsulate the various standards mentioned previously. These APIs are listed here as they relate to the required WS-I Basic Profile standards listed previously:

- *XML v1.0:* JAXP v1.2 allows for the manipulation of XML documents as described in Chapter 4.
- *XML Schema v1.0:* JAXP v1.2 also allows for the validation of XML documents according to XML Schema as described in Chapter 4.
- *SOAP v1.1 with Attachments:* SAAJ v1.2 encapsulates SOAP messages with attachments as described in this chapter.
- *HTTP v1.1:* HTTP used with Web services is supported under the hood of SAAJ and JAX-RPC as described in this chapter.
- *SOAP v1.1 RPC:* JAX-RPC v1.1 encapsulates SOAP-RPC as described in this chapter.
- *WSDL v1.1:* JWSDL v1.0 supports explicit WSDL document manipulation whereas JAX-RPC supports WSDL under the hood as described in this chapter.
- *UDDI v2.0:* JAXR v1.0 supports UDDI-based Web services lookup as well as ebXML registries for Web services lookup as described in Chapter 13.

Thus, as you'll begin to better understand in this chapter, Web services provide an industry-standard way to implement distributed communications using XML-based requests and responses over the Web and thus provide unparalleled support for interoperability across various distributed computing platforms and implementation languages. The J2EE platform's whole-hearted incorporation of such standards provides yet another significant hook for Java enterprise developers to integrate various inter- and intra-enterprise applications. The remainder of this chapter describes the core standards underlying Web services, as well as those J2EE APIs that allow you to program to such standards using Java.

SOAP

You've heard the term numerous times. It's a cute term, the term "SOAP." Perhaps you feel compelled to warm right up to the associated technology by virtue of the fact that it is a good "clean" word and implies good "clean" fun. Furthermore, its full name "Simple Object Access Protocol" is alluring as well. You think, *Hey, I'm an object-oriented kind of developer, I like simple stuff, I need to access objects in a distributed fashion—I might as well start using this fun SOAP thing!* But SOAP is much more and much less than what its name implies. It is not very simple, not terribly object-oriented, and not really clean either. Nevertheless, it is a technology that is important to understand, and is more easily digestible by the programmer thanks to the J2EE APIs built atop SOAP.

The SOAP specification (`http://www.w3.org/TR/SOAP`) is primarily headed by Microsoft within the standards oversight of the W3C. The SOAP specification defines the SOAP standard as consisting of three major parts:

- *SOAP Envelope:* The message structure of requests, responses, and the identification of the intended application function points.
- *SOAP Encoding:* The standard scheme for serializing SOAP messages and application-defined types inside those messages.
- *SOAP RPC Representation:* The convention for representing remote procedure calls.

Despite its name, practically speaking, SOAP is more of a standard XML-based message format for representing requests and responses to and from application functions. Thus the bottom line for us developers is that SOAP is a standard XML-based message format and protocol for distributed communications. Making an analogy to CORBA and RMI, the role of SOAP for a Web Service communications paradigm is most akin to the roles of the GIOP/IIOP, RMI/IIOP, and RMI/JRMP message protocols for their communications paradigms.

In addition to the SOAP v1.1 specification used by the J2EE v1.4 and WS-I Basic Profile, a specification known as the SOAP Messages with Attachments specification (`http://www.w3.org/TR/SOAP-attachments`) is also utilized by the J2EE v1.4. The SOAP Messages with Attachments specification defines a standard means for relating a SOAP message with a collection of attachments. Such attachments may be additional

XML files, binary images, an MS Word document, or some other body of content. Standards for defining interrelated MIME body parts are also used by this specification to represent how such attachments are associated with the SOAP message. A brief discussion of MIME and the interrelated MIME body parts standards is included as part of Appendix E.

SAAJ

Although trying to understand the SOAP message format by direct ingestion of the specifications can be tedious, it's lucky for us Java developers that the J2EE has included a standard API for encapsulating SOAP messages and their attachments. This SOAP with Attachments API for Java (SAAJ) resides in the `javax.xml.soap` package. The J2EE v1.4 requires SAAJ v1.2 as part of any EJB, Web, or Application Client container. SAAJ essentially provides an API representation of SOAP messages and its constituent elements, as well as a few helper factory classes for working with such classes.

> **Note**
>
> Throughout the sample code in this section, we assume the use of the SAAJ v1.1 or v1.2 implementation. The SAAJ x1.2 is the version that is being shipped with J2EE v1.4–compliant containers. A reference implementation of SAAJ can be downloaded from `http://java.sun.com/xml/download.html` as part of the Java XML or Web Services packs. SAAJ can also be downloaded from `http://java.sun.com/j2ee/download.html` as part of the J2EE v1.4 reference implementation. Note that the SAAJ implementation associated with the J2EE v1.4 reference implementation requires the `j2sdkee1.4/lib/j2ee.jar` file in your `CLASSPATH`. The Java XML or Web Services packs require the SAAJ API (`saaj-api.jar`) and the SAAJ reference implementation (`saaj-ri.jar`) in your `CLASSPATH`. The following libraries are also utilized by the SAAJ reference implementation bundled with the XML and Web Services packs and must be in your `CLASSPATH`: `mail.jar`, `activation.jar`, `dom4j.jar`, and `commons-logging.jar`. Appendix A, "Software Configuration," contains comprehensive information on how to locate, install, and configure software with the examples in the book.

Figure 10.1 provides a top-level overview of the SAAJ architecture. This is not a comprehensive picture of every SAAJ class or interface, but it does convey the core abstractions involved with SAAJ and thus the core concepts involved with SOAP messages. The SOAP message rests at the top of this message hierarchy as the top-level composite abstraction. Each SOAP message has attachment parts to contain the MIME-based attachments, and a SOAP part containing the actual SOAP message information (that is, the SOAP envelope) and references to the attachments. A SOAP envelope is in turn composed of a message header and a message body, each of which has one or more elements. A message body also can contain a SOAP fault that indicates errors and status information related to the SOAP message.

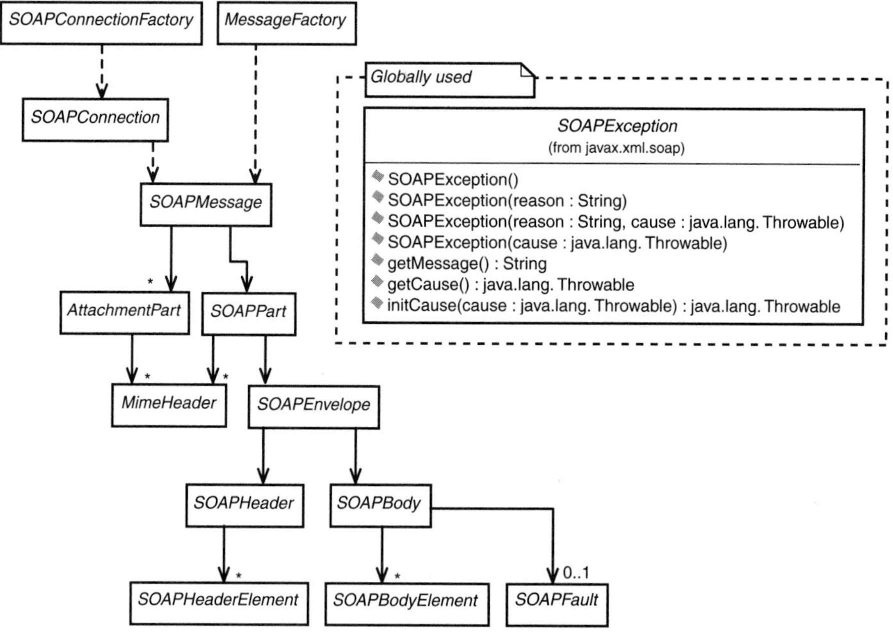

Figure 10.1 SOAP and SAAJ overview.

The `SOAPException` object is an exception thrown by various method calls throughout the SAAJ API when SOAP-related exceptions have occurred. The `SOAPException` may be composed with a reason for the exception in `String` form and nested exception in `Throwable` form. The `ejava.webservices.SOAPManager` class used in our example code associated with this section represents a base class for SOAP clients and servers containing basic SOAP management functionality. Two such functions are defined in the `printException()` methods in that class and are used to print `SOAPException` as well as other `Exception` object data as shown here:

```
public void printException(String info, Exception ex){
    System.out.println("\n" + info
                        + "\nException: " + ex.getMessage()
                        + "\nStack Trace: ");
    ex.printStackTrace();
    System.out.println("\n");
}

public void printException(Exception ex){
    printException("SOAPManager Exception...", ex);
}
```

Note

All source code associated with this section can be located as described in Appendix A and is extracted to the `examples\src\ejava\webservices` directory, whereas the code execution script templates are extracted to the `examples\config\execscripts\ejava\webservices` directory. The `build.properties` properties file in the `examples\src\ejava\webservices` directory can be configured and used with the `build.xml` ANT script used to build and run the examples. The code is compiled, preferences are set, and process execution templates are generated using the default `all` ANT target. As described in Appendix A, you must also set your database configuration properties as appropriate in the `global.properties` file in the `examples` directory. Refer to Appendix A for general database configuration instructions. You will also need to set the `j2ee.*` properties in that file to reference the J2EE reference implementation.

Because SAAJ cleanly encapsulates SOAP messages and their attachments, the approach we'll take throughout this section is to describe SOAP in the context of describing SAAJ. In this way, you will also be able to hack around with manipulating SOAP messages via our examples as you learn the concepts behind SOAP. Although the use of SAAJ is a means for describing SOAP, we should point out that SAAJ is a relatively low-level API in the J2EE world. Other APIs that we'll be discussing throughout this chapter and this book use SAAJ underneath the covers and further abstract your need to understand the details of SOAP. However, we feel that it is very important for enterprise developers to have a basic knowledge of the underpinnings of the technologies they are using and thus a basic description of SOAP and SAAJ is appropriate. Furthermore, as you encounter practical development scenarios, the use of such higher-level APIs will not always be possible, and you will need knowledge of SOAP and SAAJ as part of your bag of tricks. Thus, the remaining sections in this chapter's section on SAAJ describe more about the internals of SOAP messages and SAAJ.

SOAP Messages

The first step to start working with SAAJ and generating SOAP messages is to, well, generate a `SOAPMessage` object. Figure 10.2 illustrates the main composition of a `SOAPMessage` and the abstract `MessageFactory` class used to generate `SOAPMessage` objects. One way to use the `MessageFactory` class is to invoke the `newInstance()` static method on the class to obtain a `MessageFactory` instance. An instance of the default `MessageFactory` for the underlying SAAJ implementation is then returned. As you'll see in this and other chapters, other means for obtaining a `MessageFactory` handle are available to yield an instance while inside a J2EE container or from a particular Web Services connection type.

The `createMessage()` methods may then be used to create and return a handle to a `SOAPMessage` object. The `SOAPMessage` is the top-level representation of a SOAP message. The `AttachmentPart` of the `SOAPMessage` includes the attached content (for example, GIF files and Word documents) associated with the message. The

SOAPPart of the message contains the actual XML SOAP message information and references to the attachments. The SOAPPart thus includes a SOAPEnvelope containing the header for the message in the SOAPHeader and the body of the message in the SOAPBody. When createMessage() is invoked, the object lattice including the SOAPPart, SOAPEnvelope, SOAPHeader, and SOAPBody are all created and associated with the SOAPMessage object. When the MessageFactory object is instantiated from another source (besides the default means described previously), the factory source may prepopulate the guts of the SOAPMessage with information relevant to the underlying messaging profile.

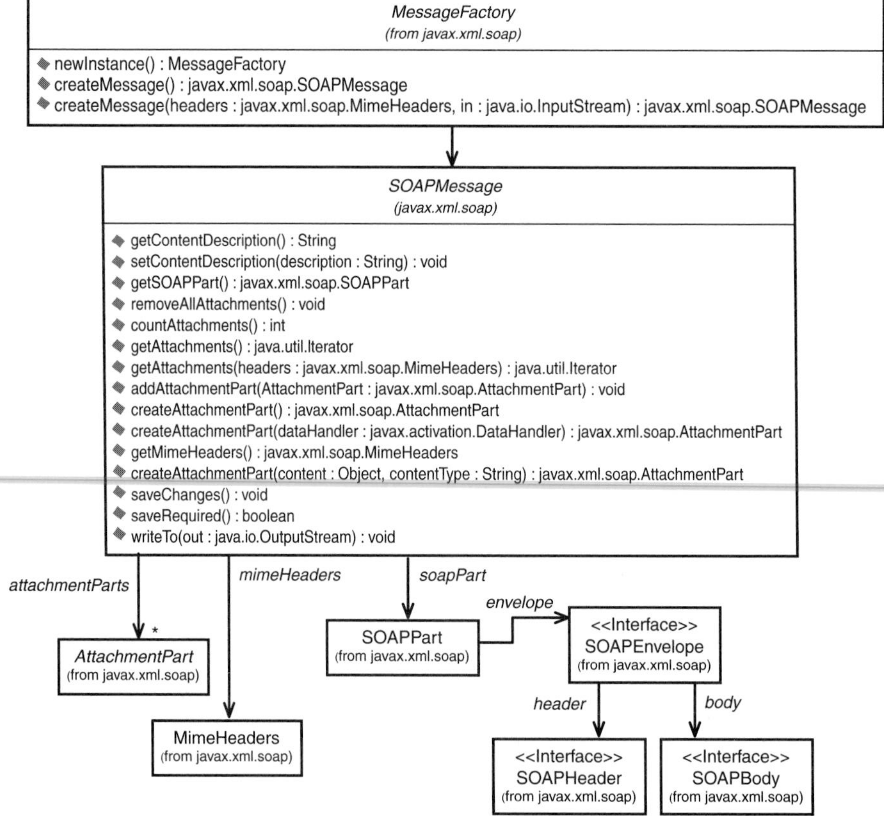

Figure 10.2 SOAP message and message factory.

The parameterless createMessage() method simply creates an empty SOAPMessage that can be used to formulate a SOAP request by a client. The createMessage (MimeHeaders, InputStream) method is used to create a SOAPMessage with an initial set of MIME headers (`MimeHeaders`) and message content (`InputStream`) which is mainly invoked when wanting to formulate a SOAP response to a SOAP request.

As an example, our base `ejava.webservices.SOAPManager` class includes a `createEmptyMessage()` method to create an empty `SOAPMessage` object as shown here:

```
public SOAPMessage createEmptyMessage(){
    MessageFactory factory = null;
    SOAPMessage message = null;

    // Create a message factory
    try{
        factory = MessageFactory.newInstance();
    }
    catch(SOAPException e1){
        printException(e1);
    }

    // Create an empty SOAP Message for our request
    try{
        message = factory.createMessage();
    }
    catch(SOAPException e1){
        printException(e1);
    }

    return message;
}
```

The `SOAPMessage` exposes interfaces that let you get, set, and remove various parts of the SOAP message. This includes the ability to get and set a description of the SOAP message content (via `getContentDescription()` and `setContentDescription()`); get a SOAP part; get and set MIME headers; and add, manipulate, remove, and create attachments. We'll review the use of such methods when we discuss the `SOAPPart`, `MimeHeaders`, and `AttachmentPart` classes shortly.

After populating the contents of a `SOAPMessage`, the message may be written to an output stream in the SOAP v1.1 with attachments format when the `SOAPMessage.writeTo(OutputStream)` method is invoked. If attachments were associated with the message, they will be written out to the stream with the SOAP part of the message; otherwise, only the SOAP envelope is written to the stream.

The `SOAPMessage.saveChanges()` method can be invoked to ensure that the contents of the `SOAPMessage` are validated and present in the message. The main purpose for this is if you desire to work with the contents of the message before sending it to a client or server. Otherwise, the underlying SOAP communications paradigm will ensure that this method is invoked before sending it over the wire. A call to `saveRequired()` can provide you with info about whether a call to `saveChanges()` needs to be made before attempting to read the content of the message.

In the following snippet taken from our `SOAPManager` example class, you can see that the `writeMessage()` example method will save changes to the `SOAPMessage`, if they are required, shortly before it writes the message to an `OutputStream`. Note also that because our examples will be sending SOAP over HTTP, we must first write an HTTP header onto the `OutputStream` via the `writeHttpHeader()` method, as we'll examine shortly. The `writeMessage()` method is shown here:

```
public void writeMessage(SOAPMessage response,
                         OutputStream outStream){
    try{
        if(response.saveRequired()){
            response.saveChanges();
         }

        writeHttpHeader(response, outStream);
        response.writeTo(outStream);
        outStream.flush();
    }
    catch(Exception e){
        printException("Trouble writing message", e);
    }
}
```

MIME Headers

MIME header information is simply a set of name-value pairs that precede attachments in order to identify and describe the content of the attachment. As we already mentioned, the SOAP v1.1 with attachments specification relies on existing MIME attachment Internet standards. Appendix E provides some background on the MIME standard if you are unfamiliar with what MIME types and headers look like. Figure 10.3 depicts the SAAJ encapsulation of MIME headers information.

The `MimeHeader` class simply contains the name and value of a MIME header with getters for that information. The `MimeHeaders` class represents a container of `MimeHeader` objects. The `MimeHeaders` class lets you add headers with the `addHeader(String name, String value)` method. Because headers with the same name are allowed, the `MimeHeaders` class allows you to add headers and replace the first existing header with the `setheader(String name, String value)` method. Removal of all headers is enabled via the `removeAllHeaders()` method, or you can remove specifically named headers via the `removeHeader(String name)` method.

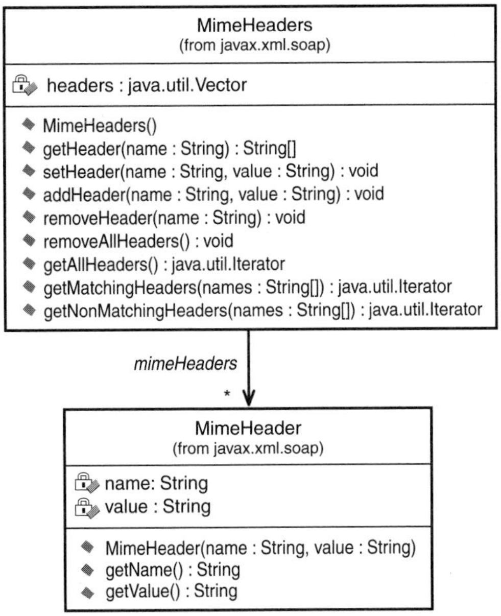

MimeHeaders
(from javax.xml.soap)

headers : java.util.Vector

MimeHeaders()
getHeader(name : String) : String[]
setHeader(name : String, value : String) : void
addHeader(name : String, value : String) : void
removeHeader(name : String) : void
removeAllHeaders() : void
getAllHeaders() : java.util.Iterator
getMatchingHeaders(names : String[]) : java.util.Iterator
getNonMatchingHeaders(names : String[]) : java.util.Iterator

mimeHeaders
*

MimeHeader
(from javax.xml.soap)

name: String
value : String

MimeHeader(name : String, value : String)
getName() : String
getValue() : String

Figure 10.3 MIME headers.

Headers may be retrieved from the `MimeHeaders` object in various ways. The `getAllHeaders()` method returns an `Iterator` of the headers, whereby the `getHeader(String name)` method returns a `String` array of headers having the associated name. The `getMatchingHeaders(String[] names)` method returns an `Iterator` of headers matching the names in the `String` array, whereas the `getNonMatchingHeaders(String [] names)` returns those headers that do not match the names in the `String` array. Finally, the `SOAPMessage` object also lets you obtain a handle to the `MimeHeaders` via the `SOAPMessage.getMimeHeaders()` method call. In summary, the `MimeHeader` and `MimeHeaders` classes are pretty straightforward and easy to use. As a trivial example, here is an example of a helper method that might be used to construct a default set of standard header information given the size of the SOAP message content:

```
public MimeHeaders createStandardHeaders(int size){
    MimeHeaders headers = new MimeHeaders();
    headers.addHeader("Content-Type", "text/xml");
    headers.addHeader("Content-Length", String.valueOf(size));
    return headers;
}
```

The `SOAPManager` class's `writeHttpHeader()` method also demonstrates how one can use the MIME header information via the classes provided by SAAJ. Recall from our earlier discussion that the `SOAPManager.writeMessage()` method invoked the

SOAPManager.writeHttpHeader() method in order to prepend HTTP header information to the SOAP message response being sent back to the client over HTTP. The writeHttpHeader() method retrieves a MimeHeaders object from the SOAPMessage and then retrieves the established MimeHeader names and values that need to be inserted into the HTTP header response. The HTTP response is then written to the OutputStream. A printMessage() method is invoked in order to print those messages that are not multipart messages with attachments (because the attachment, as we'll see, is a JPEG image that doesn't print in any meaningful way). The printMessage() and writeHttpHeader() methods are shown here:

```
public void printMessage(SOAPMessage msg)
            throws SOAPException, IOException{
    FileOutputStream fos = new FileOutputStream(FileDescriptor.out);
    DataOutputStream dos = new DataOutputStream(fos);
    msg.writeTo(dos);
    fos.flush();
}

public void writeHttpHeader(SOAPMessage msg,
                                OutputStream outStream){
    byte headerBytes[] = null;
    boolean isNotMultipart = true;
    String response = "HTTP/1.1 200 OK\n";

    try{
        // Read MimeHeaders
        MimeHeaders mhs = msg.getMimeHeaders();
        Iterator it = mhs.getAllHeaders();
        // Read each MimeHeader name and value
        // and build up response String.
        while(it.hasNext()){
            MimeHeader mh = (MimeHeader) it.next();
            String name = mh.getName();
            String value = mh.getValue();
            response += name + ": " + value +"\n";
            if(value.startsWith("multipart")){
                isNotMultipart = false;
            }
        }
        response += "\n";

        System.out.println("\n\nHTTP Header\n"+response+"\n");

        // Only print message if has no attachments.
        if(isNotMultipart){
            printMessage(msg);
        }
```

```
            // Write the HTTP header to the output stream
            headerBytes = response.getBytes("utf-8");
            outStream.write(headerBytes);
        }
        catch(Exception e){
            printException(e);
        }
    }
```

SOAP Attachments

The composition diagram for the `AttachmentPart` class is shown in Figure 10.4. An `AttachmentPart` represents an attachment to a SOAP message (for example, image file, Word document). A `SOAPMessage` can have zero or more `AttachmentPart` objects with which it is associated. An `AttachmentPart` has its content stored in an underlying `Object` whose storage and retrieval are managed by a `javax.activation.DataHandler` object. The `AttachmentPart` also has a collection of `MIMEHeader` objects that describe the attachment content using name/value MIME header pairs.

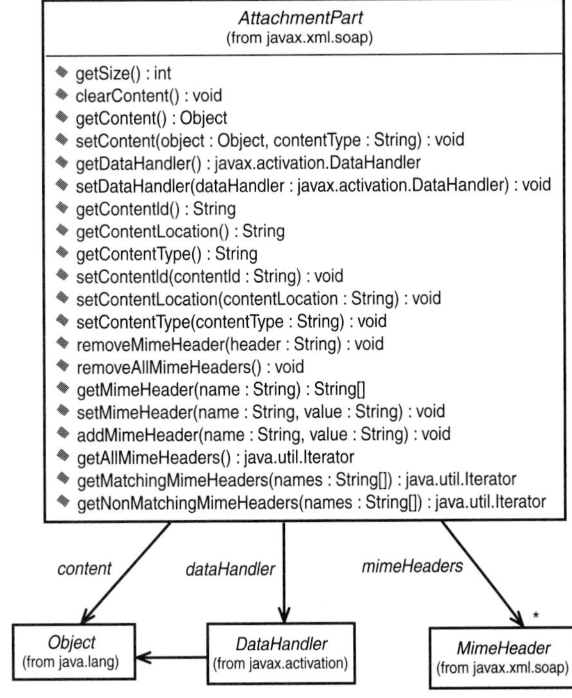

Figure 10.4 SOAP attachment part.

Note

You learned about `DataHandler` objects in Chapter 7, "Enterprise Communications." However, as a refresher, recall that `DataHandler` objects are simply JavaBeans Activation Framework objects used to access data in different formats and to invoke conversion between an underlying byte stream and an activated Java object type. For SAAJ, the conversion is from the underlying byte stream to a Java Object representation of the attachment type.

An empty `AttachmentPart` object may be created for population of content by invoking the `SOAPMessage.createAttachmentPart()` method. The `SOAPMessage.createAttachmentPart(Object, String)` method can be used to create an `AttachmentPart` with its content populated with the `Object` parameter and with its MIME type designated by the `String` parameter (for example, `text/xml`, `image/jpeg`, and `application/msword`). Alternatively, the `SOAPMessage.createAttachmentPart(DataHandler)` method can be invoked to return an `AttachmentPart` populated with the data streamed to an `Object` by the `DataHandler`.

The `AttachmentPart` object can then be associated with the `SOAPMessage` object via its `addAttachmentPart()` method. The `SOAPMessage` also enables one to remove (`removeAllAttachments()`), count (`countAttachments()`), and retrieve (`getAttachments()`) attachments from the message. The `getAttachments()` method can return an `Iterator` of `AttachmentPart` objects with all attachments using the parameterless form of `getAttachments()` or with only those attachments matching a `MimeHeaders` parameter passed into `getAttachments()`.

After you have an `AttachmentPart` object handle, you can begin populating or accessing its content. You can associate the content with the attachment using the `setContent(Object, String)` method by giving it the actual attachment `Object` and MIME type `String` name. The `DataHandler` used to stream the content can also be set onto the `AttachmentPart` object using the `setDataHandler(DataHandler)` method. Both the content `Object` and its `DataHandler` can also be retrieved from the `AttachmentPart` via the appropriately named getters. Finally, the content can be cleared from memory using the `clearContent()` method call.

Because MIME headers are associated with the attachment content, various methods exist on `AttachmentPart` to get and set such information. The MIME values for the `Content-ID`, `Content-Location`, and `Content-Type` also have appropriately named getters and setters as seen in Figure 10.4. Appropriately named methods also exist on the `AttachmentPart` that perform operations identical to those operations available on the `MimeHeaders` class described earlier and depicted in Figure 10.3. That is, operations to get, set, add, and remove MIME header information are exposed on the `AttachmentPart` class. Finally, the total size in bytes of an `AttachmentPart` can be determined via its `getSize()` method call.

Our example `SOAPManager` class includes the `insertAttachments()` method to associate `AttachmentPart` objects with a `SOAPMessage`. Our example code domain objects store domain-specific data inside `HashMap` objects for simplicity of design. Each

HashMap entry has an index as the name of a particular attachment and a String value storing the actual attachment name. In our example, the attachment name value is simply a filename on the local system from where the attachment may be retrieved. The insertAttachments() method traverses this HashMap to create and populate an AttachmentPart object as shown here:

```
public void insertAttachments(HashMap from, SOAPMessage msg){
    try{
        // Get names for the attachments from our example HashMap
        Iterator names = from.keySet().iterator();

        while(names.hasNext()){
            // Get the name of the current attachment
            String objName = (String) names.next();

            // Get the name of the attachment name from the HashMap
            // For this example, the name is simply a filename
            // where the attachment is stored on the server.
            String attachmentName = (String) from.get(objName);

            if(attachmentName != null){
                // Create a data handler for the attachment and
                //   create the attachment part with the handler
                FileDataSource fds =
                    new FileDataSource(attachmentName);
                DataHandler dh = new DataHandler(fds);
                AttachmentPart part = msg.createAttachmentPart(dh);

                // Set a MIME header type for this attachment part
                part.setMimeHeader("Content-Type", "image/jpeg");

                // Set the Content-ID as the name read from HashMap
                part.setContentId(objName);

                // Finally, add the attachment to the SOAP message
                msg.addAttachmentPart(part);
            }
        }
    }
    catch(Exception e){
        printException(e);
    }
}
```

The SOAPManager also provides a readAttachments() method, which takes a SOAPMessage as a parameter and extracts the AttachmentPart objects, their content IDs, their headers, and their content. After printing textual information about each attachment, we use a simple ImageReader class that we've created and included with this section's code to display the received image content. The readAttachments() method is shown here:

```
public void readAttachments(SOAPMessage msg)
            throws SOAPException, IOException{
    // Get an Iterator of attachments from the SOAP message
    Iterator attachments = msg.getAttachments();
    while(attachments.hasNext()){
        // Get an AttachmentPart from the Iterator
        AttachmentPart part = (AttachmentPart) attachments.next();

        // Print AttachmentPart ID and headers
        System.out.println("\nReading Attachment: "
                            + part.getContentId());
        Iterator headers = part.getAllMimeHeaders();
        while(headers.hasNext()){
            MimeHeader header = (MimeHeader) headers.next();
            System.out.println("\n  Header Name: " + header.getName());
            System.out.println("\n  Header Value: " + header.getValue());
        }

        System.out.println("\n Opening Display of Image ... ");
        ImageReader ir = null;

        // Get attachment content and pop up its display on client
        Object content = part.getContent();
        if(content instanceof InputStream){
            ir = new ImageReader((InputStream) content);
        }
        else{
            ir = new ImageReader((java.awt.Image) content);
        }
        ir.render();
    }
}
```

SOAP Elements

Before we delve any deeper into SOAPMessage, it is important to examine a few abstractions used throughout the composition of the SOAP part of a SOAP message. Figure 10.5 depicts the Node and SOAPElement super-interfaces. The Node element corresponds to an element inside a DOM-based XML document structure. The SOAPElement is a type of Node that represents a generic element in a SOAP-tree structure. It is not perfectly clear why the SAAJ API includes these two abstractions versus extending the JAXP DOM API, but suffice it to say that the roles of these two abstractions closely match the role of the org.w3c.dom.Node abstraction.

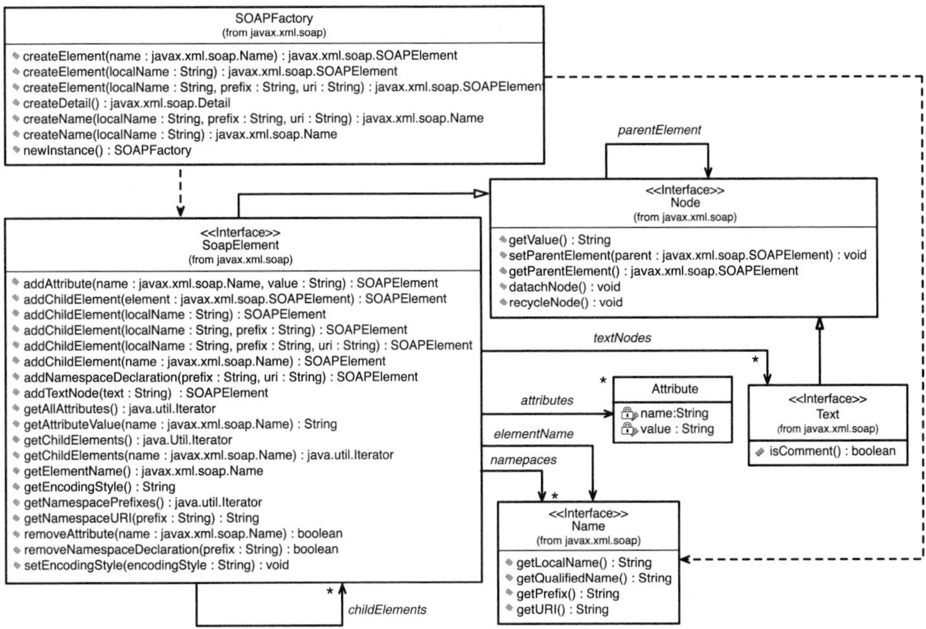

Figure 10.5 SOAP elements.

Each Node object can have a parent element. The `getParentElement()` and `setParentElement(SOAPElement)` methods return a handle to and set such parent elements, respectively. Although the cyclic dependency between the Node and the `SOAPElement` sub-interface is a slight object-oriented faux pas, it is important to note that the parent element of a node is indeed represented as a `SOAPElement` object. Some memory management of nodes can be performed using the `detachNode()` method to remove the Node from its associated DOM tree or by using the `recycleNode()` method to indicate that the node is no longer of use and can be reused by other nodes being added to memory.

If the node has purely a textual representation, the sub-interface `Text` may be used to represent the node. The parent of the text-based node can use the method `Node.getValue()` to return the `String` representation of the child node. A textual representation of a node essentially means that it may be either content that is all text-based (for example, an XML document), or perhaps a comment of some form. The `Text.isComment()` method returns a `boolean` value indicating whether the node is indeed in comment form.

A core abstraction utilized by SOAP elements is the Name interface representing a name for an element inside an XML document. XML element names consist of an XML namespace identifier, a user-defined identifier (that is, prefix), the URI defining the namespace, and the element name itself (that is, local name). Recall from Chapter 3, "XML," that we had an example similar to the following:

```
<ati:order
          xmlns:ati="http://assuredtech.com/schema"
          xmlns:beeshirts="http://beeshirts.com/b2c"
>
    ...
</ati:order>
```

Here, the namespace identifiers are xmlns, user-defined prefix examples are ati and beeshirts, URI examples are http://assuredtech.com/schema and http://beeshirts.com/b2c, the local name is order, and the fully qualified name for the element is ati:order. The element in the preceding example, of course, has two names with which it is associated and thus would be encapsulated inside two separate Name objects. The getter methods inside the Name object yield String versions of the user-defined prefix, local name, URI, and fully qualified name via the getPrefix(), getLocalName(), getURI(), and getQualifiedName() methods, respectively.

The SOAPFactory class may be used to create new Name objects. A handle to a SOAPFactory instance is first obtained by invoking the static SOAPFactory.newInstance() method. The createName() methods on SOAPFactory may then be invoked to obtain handles to Name objects initialized either with a local name String value or with a local name, prefix, and URI String value.

The SOAPElement sub-interface of Node is the base abstraction for the elements inside the SOAP part of a SOAP message. The name information for the SOAPElement can be returned via a Name object when invoking the getElementName() method. As depicted in Figure 10.5 and as illustrated previously with our ati:order example, a SOAPElement can have multiple namespaces with which it is associated. The SOAPElement object's getNamespaceURI(String) returns a String form of the URI identified by the prefix String passed in as a parameter to the method. The getNamespacePrefixes() method returns an Iterator over the collection of prefixes associated with this element. Additional namespaces can be associated with the element by invoking the addNamespaceDeclaration(String prefix, String uri) method, passing in the prefix and URI identifiers for the namespace, and returning a handle to the SOAPElement. A namespace declaration can also be removed via the removeNamespaceDeclaration(String) method passing in the namespace prefix and returning a boolean value indicating whether the operation was successful.

As with any XML element, a SOAPElement may have attributes as name/value pairs. Attributes can be added to the SOAPElement using addAttribute(Name name, String value) returning the SOAPElement object handle and removed using removeAttribute(Name name) and returning a boolean success status. Attributes may also be retrieved using the getAttribute(Name name) passing in the name of the attribute and returning the attribute String value, or via getAllAttributes(), which returns an Iterator over the collection of attribute Name names.

A SOAPElement can also have a parent element and zero or more child elements. The addChildElement() methods allow you to create and add a SOAPElement as a child to the parent SOAPElement and return a handle to the new child SOAPElement. Four addChildElement() methods exist to take name information describing the child SOAPElement in the form of a Name object; local name String; local name and prefix Strings; or local name, prefix, and URI Strings. Another addChildElement() method takes a SOAPElement object as an input parameter. The method returns the actual instance of the SOAPElement added to the current SOAPElement. The actual instance may be different from the instance passed in as an input parameter because it is at the SAAJ implementation's discretion as to how to manage the memory of the SOAPElement tree. The two getChildElements() methods are used to return an Iterator over the SOAPElement object's child SOAPElement objects for all elements using the method's parameterless form, or for the elements with the specific Name passed in as a parameter.

A new SOAPElement object can be instantiated using the createElement() methods on the SOAPFactory object. A SOAPElement can be created using SOAPFactory.createElement() by initializing the element with its name using a Name parameter, a local name String parameter, or with a local name, prefix, and URI set of String parameters. Although the SOAPElementFactory class can be used to create SOAPElement objects, it is deprecated in favor of the broader role provided by the SOAPFactory class.

Finally, a few other helper methods are offered on the SOAPElement interface. Textual-based content for the element can be added using SOAPElement.addtextNode(String text) and returning the SOAPElement handle. The encoding style of the element may also be gotten or set via the getEncodingStyle() and setEncodingStyle(String) methods, respectively. We'll talk more about SOAP encoding after this section.

In addition to reading attachment data from HashMap objects, our SOAPManager example also provides the insertElement() method for reading SOAP element data from a HashMap. Our example's domain objects in fact store element data in HashMap objects as String name and value pairs. The insertElement() method traverses such HashMap objects and extracts the name and value pairs. Each extract name is used to create a new element Name object. Each element Name is then used to crate a new child element and add it to the parent SOAPElement passed into insertElement(). Finally, the value associated with the name is used to add a text node to the newly created SOAPElement. The insertElement() method is shown here:

```
public void insertElement(HashMap from, SOAPElement to){
    try{
        // Get iterator over names of elements in the HashMap
        Iterator names = from.keySet().iterator();
        while(names.hasNext()){
            // Get the actual SOAP element name from HashMap entry
            String objName = (String) names.next();
            // get the actual SOAP element text value from entry
            String returnObject = (String) from.get(objName);
```

```
            if(returnObject != null){
                // Use the SOAPFactory to create a new Name instance
                Name element
                    = SOAPFactory.newInstance().createName(objName);
                // Create a new child element with the Name above
                SOAPElement child = to.addChildElement(element);
                // Add text information for the value of the element
                child.addTextNode(returnObject);
            }
        }
    }
    catch(Exception e){
        printException(e);
    }
}
```

SOAP Part and Envelope

Figure 10.6 depicts the composition diagram for that part of the SOAP message that actually contains the SOAP messaging data (that is, not the attachment content). There is exactly one `SOAPPart` object per `SOAPMessage` and one `SOAPEnvelope` object per `SOAPPart` object. The MIME headers for the SOAP message may also be accessed from the `SOAPPart` object as depicted in the diagram using the same `MimeHeader` method signatures as are in the `AttachmentPart` class. Although the primary MIME `Content-ID` and `Content-Location` for the SOAP part of the message have getters and setters on the `SOAPPart` class, you'll notice that the `Content-Type` cannot be set. This is because the SOAP specifications require that the `Content-Type` always be `text/xml` for SOAP messages.

The `SOAPEnvelope` class encapsulates the container for the SOAP header and SOAP body of the SOAP message. The `SOAPEnvelope` may be gotten from the `SOAPPart.getEnvelope()` method call. The content of the SOAP envelope may also be gotten as a `javax.xml.transform.Source` object via the `SOAPPart.getContent()` call. The `SOAPPart.setContent(Source)` call also allows one to set the SOAP envelope content onto the SOAP part of the message as a `Source` object.

The primary methods on the `SOAPEnvelope` class are the ones to get and set its `SOAPHeader` and `SOAPBody`. The `getHeader()` and `getBody()` methods exist, of course, to retrieve a `SOAPHeader` and `SOAPBody`. The `addHeader()` and `addBody()` methods create, add, and return a handle to a `SOAPHeader` and `SOAPBody`. These methods should be invoked only if a `SOAPHeader` or `SOAPBody` has been removed from the `SOAPEnvelope`. Because the `SOAPEnvelope` is always constructed with a default `SOAPHeader` and `SOAPBody`, you might be wondering how such elements can be removed. The answer lies in the inheritance relationships shown in Figure 10.6 with the `SOAPElement` interface. By virtue of this inheritance relationship, all the methods defined in the `SOAPElement` and `Node` interfaces shown in Figure 10.5 are provided by a `SOAPEnvelope` object. Thus, a `SOAPHeader` or `SOAPBody` may be removed from a `SOAPEnvelope` using a call to `detachNode()` on the `SOAPEnvelope` object's `SOAPHeader` or `SOAPBody`. For example:

```
SOAPEnvelope envelope = ...  // have some handle to a SOAPEnvelope
SOAPHeader header = envelope.getHeader();
SOAPBody body = envelope.getBody();
header.detachNode();
body.detatchNode();
```

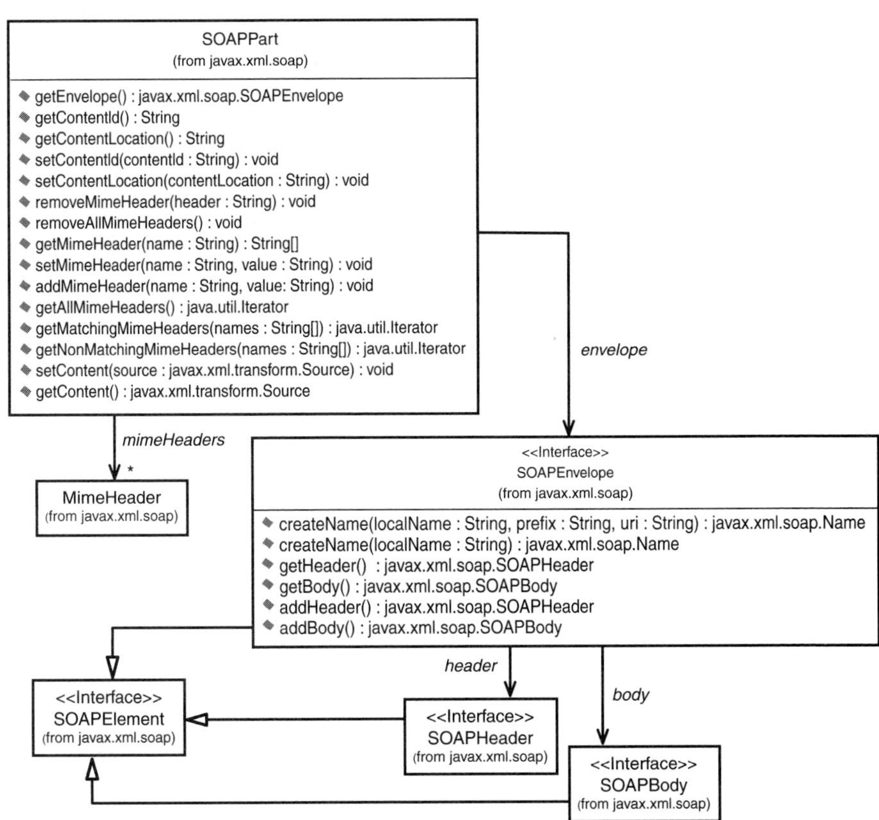

Figure 10.6 SOAP part and envelope.

Finally, the `SOAPEnvelope` also offers two `createName()` methods identical to the `SOAPFactory.createName()` methods for creating handles to new `Name` objects.

SOAP Header

The composition of a SOAP header is depicted in Figure 10.7. SOAP header elements represent that part of a SOAP message that controls how the application receiving the message should operate on the SOAP message. SOAP headers can thus convey semantics to the application such as how to interpret the associated message, security, and transactional information. SOAP header elements also may contain an attribute that defines the intended recipient of the SOAP message. There may be multiple intermediate actors (that is, message recipients) that receive the message and then must pass it along to the next actor. When no actors are specified, the intended final destination for the message becomes the default and only actor. Another attribute of a SOAP header element is the `mustUnderstand` attribute used to require that the actor reading the message process the message correctly according to the semantics of the message. If the actor cannot process the message correctly, it must fail and indicate this fact inside the message.

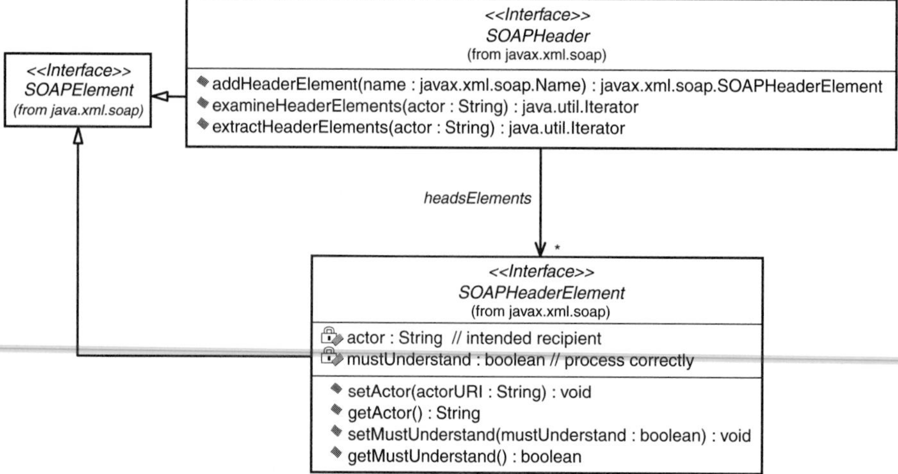

Figure 10.7 SOAP header.

The `SOAPHeader` encapsulates a SOAP header as a collection of SOAP header element entries via `SOAPHeaderElement` objects. The children of `SOAPHeader` objects must only be `SOAPHeaderElement` objects, whereas the children of `SOAPHeaderElement` objects can be `SOAPElement` objects of other types. New `SOAPElementHeader` objects can be added to `SOAPHeader` objects by passing in a `Name` for the header element into the `SOAPHeader.addHeaderElement(Name)` method, which then returns the created `SOAPHeaderElement` object.

The `SOAPHeaderElement` offers `getActor()` and `setActor(String)` methods to respectively get and set the URI `String` of an intended recipient of the SOAP message. If no actor value is set, the javax.xml.soap.SOAPConstants.URI_SOAP_ACTOR_NEXT String value (http://schemas.xmlsoap.org/soap/actor/next) becomes the default. The SOAPHeader.examineHeaderElements(String actor) method can be invoked to return an Iterator over the SOAPHeaderElement objects that have the associated actor value. The SOAPHeader.extractHeaderElements(String actor) method can also be invoked to return an Iterator over the SOAPHeaderElement objects that have the associated actor value, as well as detach those SOAPHeaderElement objects from the SOAPHeader object.

The SOAPHeaderElement also offers setMustUnderstand(boolean) and getMustUnderstand() methods to respectively set and get a boolean value indicating whether the associated actor must process the message correctly. If the message cannot be processed correctly and the mustUnderstand value is set to true, then the actor must indicate this fact in the fault information of the message to be described in the next section.

As an example, the SOAPManager class provides a createHeader() method that takes as input parameters a SOAPMessage to which a header should be attached, an actor host name, and an actor port. The createHeader() method first invokes a getHeader() method to obtain the SOAPHeader from the SOAPMessage. The createHeader() method then populates the SOAPHeader with the desired information as shown here:

```
public SOAPHeader getHeader(SOAPMessage msg){
    SOAPHeader soapHeader = null;

    try{
        SOAPPart part = msg.getSOAPPart();
        SOAPEnvelope env = part.getEnvelope();
        soapHeader = env.getHeader();
    }
    catch(Exception e){
        printException(e);
    }

    return soapHeader;
}

public SOAPHeader createHeader(SOAPMessage msg,
                               String host, String port){
    SOAPHeader headers = getHeader(msg);
    try{
        SOAPFactory soapFactory = SOAPFactory.newInstance();
        Name element = soapFactory.createName("ejava.webservices");

        SOAPHeaderElement header
            = headers.addHeaderElement(element);
```

```
        header.setMustUnderstand(true);

        header.setActor("http://" + host + ":" + port);
    }
    catch(Exception e){
        printException(e);
    }
    return headers;
}
```

SOAP Body and Fault

Figure 10.8 depicts the abstractions encapsulating a SOAP body and fault. Multiple SOAP body elements are used to contain a tree of element data associated with the SOAP message and utilized by the application reading the message. A SOAP fault represents the status and error information inside of a SOAP message. Only one SOAP fault may exist within a SOAP message and is represented as an element within the SOAP body. Within the SOAP fault, various other sub-elements are included, such as a fault code indicating the type of fault, a fault string describing the fault, a fault actor indicating who induced the fault, and application-specific body error information carried inside a set of detail entries.

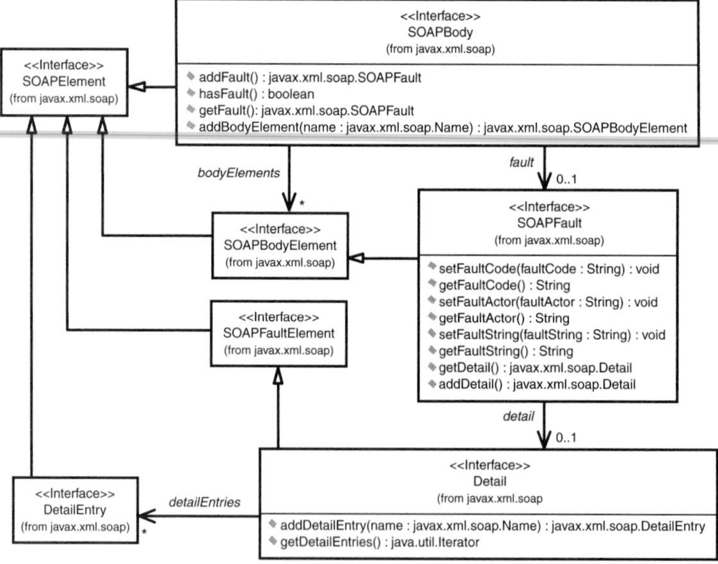

Figure 10.8 SOAP body and fault.

The SOAPBody object is a container of SOAPBodyElement objects. The SOAPBodyElement objects encapsulate those elements inside a SOAP message that contains the content data of the SOAP message. SOAPBodyElement objects can be created, added to the SOAPBody, and returned by invoking the SOAPBody.addBodyElement(Name) method with the Name for the new element. SOAPBody objects can contain only SOAPBodyElement children objects, but SOAPBodyElement objects can contain other elements in a tree of SOAP body element data.

As an example, the SOAPManager.insertBody() method is implemented to extract data from our domain-specific HashMap to create and populate an element of a SOAPBody object:

```
public void insertBody(String name, SOAPBody body, HashMap xmlData){
    try{
        SOAPFactory soapFactory = SOAPFactory.newInstance();
        Name element = soapFactory.createName(name);
        SOAPElement bodyChild = body.addBodyElement(element);
        insertElement(xmlData, bodyChild);
    }
    catch(Exception e){
        printException(e);
    }
}
```

A special helper method SOAPManager.getBody() is also provided for obtaining a handle to a SOAPBody given a SOAPMessage:

```
public SOAPBody getBody(SOAPMessage msg){
    SOAPBody soapBody = null;

    try{
        SOAPPart part = msg.getSOAPPart();
        SOAPEnvelope env = part.getEnvelope();
        soapBody = env.getBody();
    }
    catch(Exception e){
        printException(e);
    }

    return soapBody;
}
```

The SOAPFault object represents the status and error information inside of a SOAP message. If present, only one SOAPFault object may exist within a SOAPMessage and is associated with the SOAPBody. A SOAPFault may be created, added to the SOAPBody, and returned when invoking the SOAPBody.addFault() method. A SOAPFault can be gotten from a SOAPBody via SOAPBody.getFault() and its existence determined by the boolean value returned from SOAPBody.hasFault().

A `String` representation of the SOAP fault code may be gotten and set via the `getFaultCode()` and `setFaultCode(String)` methods. Fault codes are defined according to the SOAP v1.1 specification and take on a form whereby more generic codes are defined in the leftmost part of the `String` and more specific codes are defined increasingly to the rightmost part of the `String`. Subcodes are separated by the dot character (`.`). The most generic SOAP v1.1 defined fault codes are as shown here:

- `VersionMismatch`: Indicates that the SOAP message does not belong to the namespace for SOAP envelopes. The namespace thus must belong to the namespace defined by the `javax.xml.soap.SOAPConstants.URI_NS_SOAP_ENVELOPE String` (`http://schemas.xmlsoap.org/soap/envelope/`).
- `MustUnderstand`: Indicates that the SOAP message (with `mustUnderstand` flagged as on) was not capable of being processed correctly by an intended actor.
- `Client`: Indicates that class of errors associated with the SOAP client improperly forming the message. For example, the SOAP client may have not provided some required authentication information and the fault code produced might be `Client.Authentication`.
- `Server`: Indicates that class of errors associated with the SOAP server improperly being able to process the message. For example, the SOAP server may have not been able to connect to a real-time credit vetting service and the fault code produced may be `Client.PaymentAuthorization`.

The fault actor is that message recipient that induced the fault. The `getFaultActor()` and `setFaultActor(String)` methods on `SOAPFault` enable one to get and set the `String` representation of this actor's URI. A human-readable description of the fault stored in `String` form may be set or gotten from the `SOAPFault` via its `setFaultString(String)` and `getFaultString()` methods.

The `Detail` object represents application-specific error information related to the SOAP body elements when those body elements could not be successfully processed by the recipient application. The `Detail` interface extends the `SOAPFaultElement` marker interface, which indicates that the detail is an element of the SOAP fault element type. The `Detail` object may be gotten from the `SOAPFault.getDetail()` method call. A `Detail` object may be created, added to the `SOAPFault`, and returned when invoking the `SOAPFault.addDetail()` method if the `SOAPFault` object does not already contain a `SOAPDetail` object. Alternatively, the `SOAPFactory.createDetail()` method may be used to create a new `Detail` object, which then may be added to the `SOAPBody` via its inherited `SOAPElement` interfaces (see Figure 10.5).

The `Detail` object represents a collection of `DetailEntry` elements that contain the actual content of the SOAP fault detail. `DetailEntry` objects can be created, added to the `Detail` object, and returned by passing in an XML name of the detail entry element using `Detail.addDetailEntry(Name)`. The `DetailEntry` objects associated with the detail can be returned via an `Iterator` from `Detail.getDetailEntries()`.

A `SOAPManager.createBodyFault()` method on our example creates a `SOAPFault` associated with a `SOAPMessage` object's `SOAPBody`. The `SOAPFault` information is then populated with exception, failure identifier, and actor information as shown here:

```
public void createBodyFault(SOAPMessage msg, Exception exc,
                                String failureName,
                                String host, String port){
    try{
        // Get the SOAP body
        SOAPFactory factory = SOAPFactory.newInstance();
        SOAPBody body = getBody(msg);

        // Create and populate a SOAPFault
        SOAPFault fault = body.addFault();
        fault.setFaultString(exc.getMessage());
        fault.setFaultActor("http://" + host + ":" + port);
        fault.setFaultCode("MustUnderstand");

        // Create SOAP fault detail and attach to SOAPFault
        Detail detail = fault.addDetail();
        Name detailName = factory.createName(failureName,
                                "ejava.webservices.SOAPManager",
                                "http://beeshirts.com/soap");
        detail.addDetailEntry(detailName);
    }
    catch(Exception e){
        printException(e);
    }
}
```

SOAP Connections

Up until this point in the section, we have examined how SOAP messages are composed and the SAAJ APIs that can be used to compose, manipulate, and navigate SOAP messages. The `SOAPConnection` abstract class shown in Figure 10.9 represents a point-to-point connection between a SOAP client and a SOAP server. An instance of a `SOAPConnection` can be obtained by invoking the `createConnection()` method on a `SOAPConnectionFactory` object. An instance of the `SOAPConnectionFactory` can be obtained by invoking the static `SOAPConnectionFactory.newInstance()` method. SOAP connections are closed using the `SOAPConnection.close()` method call.

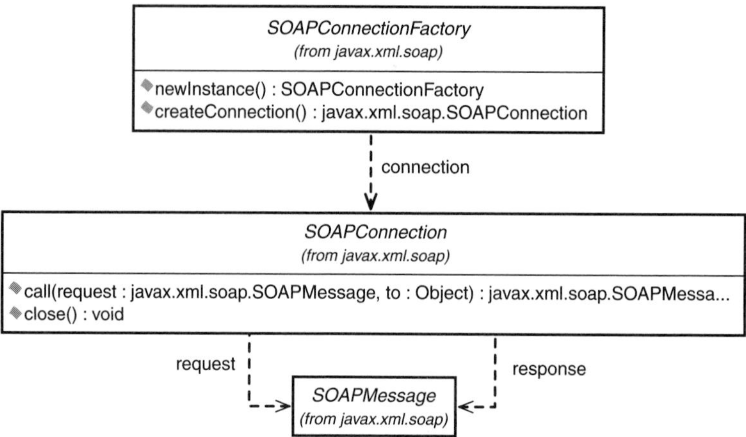

Figure 10.9 SOAP connections.

After obtaining a handle to a `SOAPConnection`, the SOAP client passes a `SOAPMessage` request as a parameter to `SOAPConnection.call(SOAPMessage, Object)`, which then blocks until the SOAP server returns a `SOAPMessage` response. In addition to the `SOAPMessage`, a URI `Object` parameter must also be passed into the `call()` method. The URI designates the endpoint of the SOAP server to where the SOAP message must be delivered. The URI may be represented as a `String` object or `java.net.URL` object (see Appendix E for a description of the URL object and URI formats).

Such a request and response paradigm provided by SAAJ is enabled only for point-to-point communication scenarios. In subsequent sections you'll see examples of higher-level SOAP message communications when we discuss JAX-RPC. As we'll also see in later chapters, a `javax.xml.messaging.URLEndpoint` object may also represent the URI passed into the `SOAPConnection.call()` method.

Our example code for this section demonstrates the use of point-to-point communication between a SOAP client and SOAP server via SAAJ. Our example `SOAPClient` class is derived from the `SOAPManager` class and is used to send requests to a SOAP server and receive responses. The `main()` method of `SOAPClient` first reads the host name and port of the server from preferences read using the `server.host` and `server.port` properties in the `build.properties` file for this section. Thereafter, the `SOAPClient` uses the `SOAPConnectionFactory` to construct a `SOAPConnection` object. The `SOAPConnection` is used via four request and response connection scenarios before the connection is closed, as shown here in the `SOAPClient.main()` method:

```
public static void main(String[] args) {
      System.out.println("This is a SOAP client.");
```

```
// Get the preferences
Preferences preferences = Preferences.userNodeForPackage(
                              ejava.webservices.SOAPClient.class);
String host = preferences.get("SERVER_HOST", "localhost");
String port = preferences.get("SERVER_PORT", "9000");

// Create a new SOAP client attached to server host and port
SOAPClient client = new SOAPClient(host, port);

try {
    // Create initial connection objects
    URL server = new URL("http://" + host + ":" + port);
    SOAPConnectionFactory connFactory
                        = SOAPConnectionFactory.newInstance();
    SOAPConnection connection = connFactory.createConnection();


    // Customer request and response
    SOAPMessage message = client.getCustomerMessage();
    System.out.println("Sending Customer Query Message....");
    client.printMessage(message);
    SOAPMessage reply = connection.call(message, server);
    System.out.println("Received Response Message....");
    client.printMessage(reply);

    // Order request and response
    message = client.getOrderMessage();
    System.out.println("Sending Order Query Message....");
    client.printMessage(message);
    reply = connection.call(message, server);
    System.out.println("Received Order Message....");
    client.printMessage(reply);

    // Send an invalid request and response
    message = client.getInvalidMessage();
    System.out.println("Sending Invalid Query Message....");
    client.printMessage(message);
    reply = connection.call(message, server);
    System.out.println("Received Invalid Message Response....");
    client.printMessage(reply);

    // Send a request generating a response w/attachment
    message = client.getCoupon();
    System.out.println("Sending Coupon Query Message....");
    client.printMessage(message);
    reply = connection.call(message, server);
```

```
            System.out.println("Received Coupon Message....");
            System.out.println("\n\nHit Ctrl-C to end application!");
            client.readAttachments(reply);

            // Close the connection
            connection.close();
        } catch(Exception e) {
            client.printException("SOAPClient Exception", e);
        }
}
```

Each request message is constructed using the simple semantics offered by the SAAJ API. An example for construction of the customer query request message is shown here and is similar for the other request message generation methods inside the `SOAPClient`:

```
public SOAPMessage getCustomerMessage(){
  // Create empty message
  SOAPMessage message = createEmptyMessage();
  try{
      SOAPPart soapPart= message.getSOAPPart();
      SOAPEnvelope envelope = soapPart.getEnvelope();
      SOAPHeader header = createHeader(message, server, port);
      SOAPBody body = getBody(message);

      Name name = envelope.createName("findCustomers",
                                      "ejava.webservices.Customer",
                                      "http://beeshirts.com/soap");
      SOAPElement e1 = body.addChildElement(name);
      SOAPElement e2 = e1.addChildElement("minimumOrder");
      SOAPElement e3 = e2.addTextNode("10");

      message.saveChanges();
  }
  catch(Exception e){
      printException(e);
  }
  return message;
}
```

Additionally, the `SOAPClient` also includes methods to generate requests for query of order information, the formulation of an invalid message to illustrate the use of `mustUnderstand` and `SOAPFault` objects, and the formulation of a request to retrieve an image attachment.

On the server side, we have the `SOAPServer` example class also extending from `SOAPManager`. The `SOAPServer.main()` method first reads in preferences and then creates a `java.net.ServerSocket` to listen for incoming requests. A new `SOAPServer` object then sets the input stream, output stream, server host, server port, client host, and client port associated with the newly created `Socket`. Subsequently, the new `SOAPServer` thread is started to handle the request. The `SOAPServer.main()` method is shown here:

```
public static void main(String[] args) {
  System.out.println("This is a SOAP Server.");

  // Get the preferences
  Preferences preferences = Preferences.userNodeForPackage(
                              ejava.webservices.SOAPServer.class);

  try {
    // Get server port
    int serverPort = preferences.getInt("SERVER_PORT", 9000);

    // Create a new socket server
    ServerSocket server = new ServerSocket(serverPort);

    /**
    * Until user exists from the server using keyboard, CTRL-C
    * or by shutting down from the server, it waits for
    * clients to connect
    */
    while (true) {
        // Wait for client to connect
        Socket client = server.accept();
        // Then create a new server handler object
        SOAPServer soaper = new SOAPServer(client);
        // Create new thread for handler object
        Thread serverThread = new Thread(soaper);
        // Start the thread (see the run method)
        serverThread.start();
    }
 }catch (Exception e) {
     System.out.println("SOAP Server Fatal Error: " + e);
     System.exit(0);
 }
}
```

Each new `SOAPServer` thread object simply induces the read and display of the request, processes the request, and then displays and writes the request:

```
public synchronized void run() {
    SOAPMessage response = null; // SOAP response

    try {
          // Parse and display request message
```

```
            String soapString = readMessage(inStream);

            // Process request and generate response
            response = process(soapString);

            // Display and send response message
            writeMessage(response, outStream);
        }
        catch (Exception e) {
            System.out.println("SOAP Server Exception: \n");
            printException(e);
        }
    }
```

The preceding `readMessage(InputStream)` method is defined inside the `SOAPManager` class to read the message data from the input stream and then construct a `String` form of the request after stripping off the transport header information.

> **Note**
>
> Note that we don't describe the `SOAPManager.readMessage()` method or other method implementations not involving example use of the SAAJ API in this section. However, you are encouraged to examine the source code for such methods if you are interested in finding out what is required to essentially create a rudimentary SOAP server using only SAAJ. Subsequent sections and chapters enable higher-level Web service processing, but we have created a basic example in the form of an overly simplified Web server to process SOAP messages over HTTP.

The `SOAPServer.process()` method takes the `String` that contains only the XML portion of the request and parses the `String` into a `HashMap` of data that is specific to a format with which our particular application handlers are designed to work, as shown here:

```
private SOAPMessage process(String soapString)
                                    throws SOAPException{
    SOAPMessage response = createEmptyMessage();
    boolean mustUnderstand = true;
    try{
        // Parse SOAP String request into HashMap
        HashMap inp = parseMessage(soapString);

        // Get mustUnderstand value
        mustUnderstand
            = ((Boolean) inp.get("mustUnderstand")).booleanValue();

        // Get the type of handler to invoke
        String classType = (String) inp.get("beeshirts:CLASS_NAME");
```

```
            // Based on request type, invoke appropriate handler
            SOAPHandler handler
                = (SOAPHandler) Class.forName(classType).newInstance();

            // Then delegate call to concrete handler instance
            HashMap outp = handler.process(inp);

            // Use HashMap response to create SOAP response
            response = createMessage(outp, host, port);
        }
        catch(Exception e){
            printException(e);
            if(mustUnderstand){
                createBodyFault(response, e, "UnsupportedHandler",
                                serverHost, serverPort);
            }
        }

            return response;
}
```

The `parseMessage()` method accomplishes the task of parsing a SOAP message `String` into a `HashMap` by using JAXP DOM parsing functionality. If during the course of parsing, a `mustUnderstand` attribute was read from the SOAP message, then a `boolean` flag is set to `true` and induces the construction of a `SOAPFault` via the `createBodyFault()` method described earlier if there was an error during the processing of the message. The particular name of the class to be invoked is read from the request's envelope name prefix (for example, `ejava.webservices.Customer`). The rest of the request data is then handed off to the particular `SOAPHandler` instance instantiated. The `Order` and `Customer` classes equipped with the code for this section are two examples of concrete `SOAPHandler` implementations. Each concrete handler reads the method name to be invoked as set in the request's envelope local name (for example, `findCustomers`). The particular method, if it exists, is then invoked with the appropriate input parameters passed as arguments. For example, the `Customer` class performs the following steps inside of its `process()` method implementation:

```
public HashMap process(HashMap inParams) throws Exception{

    HashMap result = new HashMap();
    String method = (String) inParams.get("beeshirts:METHOD_NAME");

    if(method.equals("findCustomers")){
        float f = Float.parseFloat(
            (String) inParams.get("minimumOrder"));
        Vector customers = this.findCustomers(f);
        result.put("customers", customers);
```

```
    }
    else{
        throw new Exception("Handler not found");
    }

    return result;
}
```

In our examples, the concrete `process()` methods either query the database for customer or order information, or read an image of the coupon from a file depending on the particular SOAP message received and sent to either a `Customer` or an `Order` handler instance. The `SOAPServer.process()` method then attempts to parse the returned `HashMap` result from the concrete handler into a `SOAPMessage`. The `createMessage()` method defined on the base `SOAPManager` class provides such functionality. The `createMessage()` method relies on the `createHeader()`, `insertElement()`, and `insertAttachments()` methods described earlier in this section to actually insert header, body, and attachment data into the `SOAPMessage`. Here we display only the code relevant to SAAJ:

```
public SOAPMessage createMessage(HashMap hashMessage,
                                    String host, String port){
    // Create empty SOAP Message, get Body and create Header
    SOAPMessage msg = createEmptyMessage();
    SOAPHeader header = createHeader(msg, host, port);
    SOAPBody body = getBody(msg);

    // For each element inside the return results Vector
        ...
            // Insert any attachment data into the SOAPMessage
               ...
            // Insert XML data into the SOAPBody
               ...

    // Save changes to message before proceeding
    msg.saveChanges();
        ...
    return msg;
}
```

After the `SOAPServer.process()` method returns with a `SOAPMessage` response, the `SOAPServer.run()` method invokes the `writeMessage()` method on the base `SOAPManager` class as described earlier in this section.

The `build.properties` file associated with this section can be used to define a host name and port for the SOAP server. Otherwise, a default `localhost` name (that is, your local machine) and a default `9000` port are used. The ANT script associated with this section generates a `runServer` script to execute the `SOAPServer` in a separate window, as well as a `runClient` script to execute the `SOAPClient` process in the current window. Pressing Ctrl+C in its process window can stop the `SOAPServer` process.

SOAP Encoding

Throughout the examples in this chapter thus far, we have used SAAJ to encapsulate and make the underlying details of SOAP message formats transparent. It should thus be apparent that there is an implied set of rules in which the SOAP messages are actually encoded. In fact, the `SOAPElement` abstraction exposes access to the encoding style of a SOAP element. Here, the term "SOAP encoding" essentially means those rules that should be applied when serializing the objects to be embodied inside of a SOAP message.

Although the SOAP specification defines a basic set of rules for encoding SOAP messages, it is not the default means for encoding messages. Thus, an application can define its own set of rules for encoding SOAP messages. Practically speaking, this is usually accomplished by first defining a mapping from whatever language-specific object representation paradigms are allowed into a standard XML schema. That XML schema then provides the language-independent set of encoding rules for the SOAP message and is to be used by the application when reading and writing SOAP messages. If no `encodingStyle` attribute is defined for the SOAP message or if `""` is defined as the `encodingStyle` attribute, then no assumptions can be made about the SOAP message representation.

We can in fact look to the examples in presented in this chapter to illustrate what SOAP messages actually look like. Keep in mind as well that the actual byte streams sent between client and server also included HTTP and MIME headers. Although we don't present such headers here, Appendix E provides HTTP and MIME header examples for the interested reader.

As an example of an actual SOAP request, a SOAP request message sent by our `SOAPClient` is shown here:

```
<soap-env:Envelope
         xmlns:soap-env="http://schemas.xmlsoap.org/soap/envelope/">
    <soap-env:Header>
        <ejava.webservices soap-env:mustUnderstand="1"
                      soap-env:actor="http://localhost:9000"/>
    </soap-env:Header>
    <soap-env:Body>
        <ejava.webservices.Customer:findCustomers
             xmlns:ejava.webservices.Customer="http://beeshirts.com/soap">
            <minimumOrder>
                  10
            </minimumOrder>
        </ejava.webservices.Customer:findCustomers>
    </soap-env:Body>
</soap-env:Envelope>
```

The response to such a message from the SOAPServer was composed from data retrieved from our example database and was akin to the following:

```
<soap-env:Envelope
         xmlns:soap-env="http://schemas.xmlsoap.org/soap/envelope/">
    <soap-env:Header>
        <ejava.webservices soap-env:mustUnderstand="1"
                        soap-env:actor="http://127.0.0.1:3496"/>
    </soap-env:Header>
    <soap-env:Body>
        <customers:0>
            <address2>Apt 30</address2>
            <address1>213 Frankie Five Angels Court</address1>
            <eMail>fpantangelli@example.com</eMail>
            <city>Reno</city>
            <firstName>Frank</firstName>
            <customerID>101</customerID>
            <phoneNumber>555-789-8075</phoneNumber>
            <hasAttachments>false</hasAttachments>
            <zip>12345</zip>
            <state>NV</state>
            <lastName>Pantangelli</lastName>
        </customers:0>
        <customers:1>
            <address1>785 Senator Geary St</address1>
             ...
         </customers:18>
    </soap-env:Body>
</soap-env:Envelope>
```

As another example, the SOAPClient also attempted to send an invalid example request as shown here:

```
<soap-env:Envelope
        xmlns:soap-env="http://schemas.xmlsoap.org/soap/envelope/">
    <soap-env:Header>
        <ejava.webservices soap-env:mustUnderstand="1"
                        soap-env:actor="http://localhost:9000"/>
    </soap-env:Header>
    <soap-env:Body>
        <ejava.webservices.NonExistentClass:invalidMethod
               xmlns:ejava.webservices.NonExistentClass
                            ="http://beeshirts.com/soap">
            <invalidParameter>blaBlaBla</invalidParameter>
        </ejava.webservices.NonExistentClass:invalidMethod>
    </soap-env:Body>
</soap-env:Envelope>
```

In response to the invalid example request, the `SOAPServer` threw an exception and responded with a SOAP message that also had a SOAP fault embedded into it, akin to the following:

```
<soap-env:Envelope
        xmlns:soap-env="http://schemas.xmlsoap.org/soap/envelope/">
    <soap-env:Header/>
    <soap-env:Body>
        <soap-env:Fault>
            <faultstring>ejava.webservices.NonExistentClass</faultstring>
            <faultactor>http://127.0.0.1:9000</faultactor>
            <faultcode>MustUnderstand</faultcode>
            <detail>
                <ejava.webservices.SOAPManager:UnsupportedHandler
                     xmlns:ejava.webservices.SOAPManager
                         ="http://beeshirts.com/soap"/>
            </detail>
        </soap-env:Fault>
    </soap-env:Body>
</soap-env:Envelope>
```

Whereas the SOAP messages illustrated previously are specific to our SAAJ example application, a basic set of standard rules for SOAP encoding is defined inside the SOAP v1.1 specification. The supported data types in SOAP v1.1–style encoding primarily revolve around inclusion of the built-in and enumerated XML Schema types described in Chapter 3. Compound types that contain `Struct` or `Array` types as well as built-in types are also supported.

The standard SOAP v1.1 encoding rules are identified by the URI `http://schemas.xmlsoap.org/soap/encoding/`. This URI points to a schema that defines rules for basic encoding of SOAP message elements as a subset of the basic elements defined inside XML schemas themselves. This URI is represented in SAAJ by the `javax.xml.soap.SOAPConstants.URI_NS_SOAP_ENCODING String`. This encoding rule identifier may be included as a global attribute inside the SOAP envelope to indicate the encoding style used by the SOAP message. Additional rules for encoding may also be defined inside the global attribute via identifiers separated by commas.

WSDL and JWSDL

We saw in previous chapters how enterprise communication paradigms, such as CORBA, will sometimes provide an intermediate definition of a remote interface in a fashion distinct from the actual remote interface. That is, IDL in CORBA is used to provide a description of a remote CORBA interface. It is used to define those operations that can be invoked on a remote service, including the input and output message formats. The analogous feature in the Web services world is the Web Services Description Language (WSDL).

WSDL represents a means to describe distributed Web service interfaces. Thus, the operations, their input parameters, their output parameters, and how such operations are grouped within services are all defined by WSDL documents. Each WSDL document is in the format of an XML document. Although, by virtue of its XML format, a WSDL document is human readable, the fact remains that WSDL documents are somewhat difficult to comprehend at first glance. However, WSDL documents are not necessarily meant to be created and interpreted directly by human beings anyway. The main idea behind WSDL is that WSDL documents will be interpreted by software applications in an automated format in order to determine how to communicate with a remote Web service or expose themselves as a Web service. This does not necessarily mean that your J2EE applications will magically know how to communicate with a Web service given a WSDL document. What it means is that a tool will handle the mapping from WSDL documents to either generic or concrete stubs and skeletons directly utilized by your Java code.

Such mappings from WSDL-to-Java and from Java-to-WSDL are not unlike the mappings discussed in other paradigms, such as CORBA, with respect to IDL-to-Java and Java-to-IDL mappings. The difference here is that WSDL is specific to the Web services communications paradigm and thus enables one to create Java client and server applications that can understand how to communicate with Web services implemented in other languages and on other platforms. The key to WSDL's success is in its standardization overseen by the W3C (`http://www.w3.org/TR/wsdl`).

The standard version of WSDL assumed by the WS-I Basic Profile and the Web services–related APIs within the J2EE v1.4 is WSDL v1.1. Although the J2EE v1.4 developer may not be exposed to WSDL much in the course of actual development, we think that it is important to provide you with an overview of WSDL. Indeed, in the ideal world, the J2EE tools that you use would handle the automatic generation and interpretation of WSDL documents. However, in the real world and especially when you have to debug an application wherein some cognizance of infrastructure is key, a basic working knowledge of WSDL will be invaluable. It is for this reason that we provide a basic introduction to WSDL document structure while not going into unnecessary depth on every aspect of WSDL.

JWSDL

At the time of this writing, the Java API for WSDL (JWSDL) was Java Specification Request (JSR) 110 being defined within the Java Community Process (JCP) (`www.jcp.org/en/jsr/detail?id=110`). JWSDL is an API to read, write, and manipulate WSDL documents using a Java API. Although JWSDL is not part of the J2EE v1.4, it is an interesting API to understand if you want to work directly with manipulating WSDL documents. Of course, J2EE Web services tool vendors are conceivably the folks primarily interested in working with an API like JWSDL.

However, JWSDL can also be of interest to those Java developers wanting to create their own automation-related features. Furthermore, UML diagrams are an excellent way to understand concepts and designs, and use of UML diagrams is a core approach to describing concepts and designs throughout this book. Because JWSDL represents an API encapsulating WSDL documents, UML diagrams based on JWSDL represent an excellent way to more rapidly understand the concepts behind WSDL documents themselves. This is why we provide a very basic overview of JWSDL in the text that follows. We also support such a discussion with an illustration of a WSDL example document.

The graphical nature of a UML-based description of JWSDL will help you more rapidly understand the somewhat complicated structure of WSDL documents. Conversely, the associated example WSDL document will help you reinforce the detailed understanding of what composes an actual WSDL document. Because JWSDL was not part of the J2EE at the time of this writing and because we intend to convey only a basic understanding of WSDL, we provide only a basic overview of JWSDL in the context of providing a basic overview of WSDL itself.

Top-Level WSDL Document Definitions

Figure 10.10 provides a top-level overview of the core JWSDL abstractions that define a WSDL document. We've taken the approach in this diagram to not present interface methods and rather simply present the interface names, their implied inter-relationships, and their implied attributes. Because the abstractions in Figure 10.10 are passive entity-type abstractions, the actual methods associated with such abstractions are simple getters and setters. That is, the actual getter and setter APIs deal with getting and setting information associated with the implied relationships and implied attributes shown in Figure 10.10. Thus, for example, the actual `Port` abstraction API has `getBinding()` and `setBinding()` methods associated with its implied relationship with the `Binding` abstraction. Refer to the JWSDL API for a complete listing of JWSDL methods and their signatures (`www.jcp.org/en/jsr/detail?id=110`).

The JWSDL WSDL document abstractions of Figure 10.10 can best be understood in terms of a top-down description. Such a top-down description also corresponds to a top-down description of a WSDL document. In what follows, we describe each JWSDL WSDL document abstraction and the actual WSDL document elements to which they correspond. Listing 10.1 can also be referenced throughout this discussion to map such concepts and abstractions to how they are manifested by a concrete WSDL document example (albeit a partial listing).

The `Definition` abstraction represents the top-level definition and encapsulation of a WSDL document's `definitions` element. That information which is being defined is one or more Web service definitions. A `Service` abstraction that is an aggregation of Web service ports encapsulated by the `Port` abstraction encapsulates each Web service definition. As you'll see, a port itself is ultimately an aggregation of Web service operations. The `Definition` abstraction delineates those ports (aka endpoints) that it defines by virtue of a collection of port type definitions encapsulated by the `PortType` abstraction. Listing 10.1 provides an example of the WSDL `services` sub-element of the root `definitions` element.

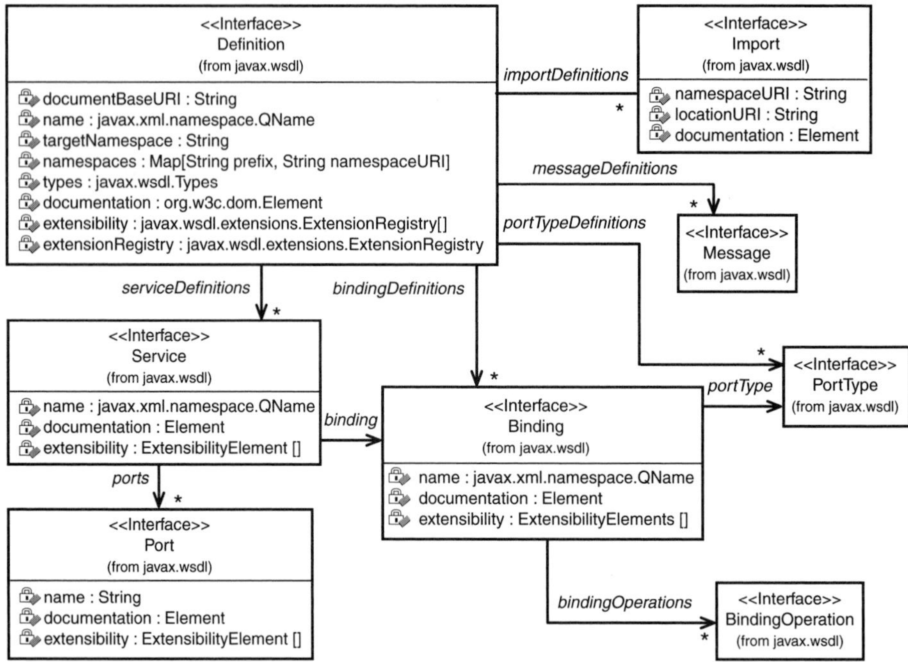

Figure 10.10 Top-level WSDL document definitions.

> **Web Service and Java Programming Concepts Analogy**
>
> Making an analogy to Java interfaces, a Web service operation corresponds conceptually to a method on a Java interface, a port or endpoint corresponds to the Java interface itself, the port type corresponds to the Java interface type, the service maps to a collection of Java interfaces somewhat akin to a Java package, and the WSDL definition defines all such services supported somewhat akin to a JavaDoc description of a set of interfaces inside various packages. Such analogies are not precise analogies, but it can help us Java developers to make some broad conceptual relationships between Web service concepts and Java programming concepts with which we are more familiar.

Listing 10.1 **WSDL Document Example (Partial Listing)**

```
<?xml version="1.0" encoding="UTF-8" ?>
<definitions xmlns="http://schemas.xmlsoap.org/wsdl/"
   xmlns:tns="http://ws.beeshirts.com/wsdl/QueryService"
   xmlns:soap="http://schemas.xmlsoap.org/wsdl/soap/"
   xmlns:xsd="http://www.w3.org/2001/XMLSchema"
   xmlns:ns2="http://ws.beeshirts.com/types/QueryService"
   name="QueryService"
   targetNamespace="http://ws.beeshirts.com/wsdl/QueryService">
```

Listing 10.1 **Continued**

```
<types>
  <schema
      xmlns="http://www.w3.org/2001/XMLSchema"
      xmlns:tns="http://ws.beeshirts.com/types/QueryService"
      xmlns:xsi="http://www.w3.org/2001/XMLSchema-instance"
      xmlns:soap-enc="http://schemas.xmlsoap.org/soap/encoding/"
      xmlns:wsdl="http://schemas.xmlsoap.org/wsdl/"
      targetNamespace="http://ws.beeshirts.com/types/QueryService">
    <import namespace="http://schemas.xmlsoap.org/soap/encoding/" />
    <complexType name="Order">
      <sequence>
        <element name="orderID" type="int" />
        <element name="orderValue" type="double" />
      </sequence>
    </complexType>
      ...
  </schema>
</types>

<message name="QueryServer_length" />
<message name="QueryServer_lengthResponse">
  <part name="result" type="xsd:int" />
</message>
<message name="QueryServer_ping" />
<message name="QueryServer_pingResponse">
  <part name="result" type="xsd:string" />
</message>
<message name="QueryServer_findOrder">
  <part name="int_1" type="xsd:int" />
</message>
<message name="QueryServer_findOrderResponse">
  <part name="result" type="ns2:Order" />
</message>
   ...

<portType name="QueryServer">
  <operation name="length" parameterOrder="">
    <input message="tns:QueryServer_length" />
    <output message="tns:QueryServer_lengthResponse" />
  </operation>
  <operation name="ping" parameterOrder="">
    <input message="tns:QueryServer_ping" />
    <output message="tns:QueryServer_pingResponse" />
  </operation>
  <operation name="findOrder" parameterOrder="int_1">
```

Listing 10.1 **Continued**

```
      <input message="tns:QueryServer_findOrder" />
      <output message="tns:QueryServer_findOrderResponse" />
    </operation>
    <operation name="lookupCustomers" parameterOrder="float_1">
      <input message="tns:QueryServer_lookupCustomers" />
      <output message="tns:QueryServer_lookupCustomersResponse" />
    </operation>
      ...
  </portType>

  <binding name="QueryServerBinding" type="tns:QueryServer">
    <operation name="length">
      <input>
        <soap:body
          encodingStyle="http://schemas.xmlsoap.org/soap/encoding/"
          use="encoded"
          namespace="http://ws.beeshirts.com/wsdl/QueryService" />
      </input>
      <output>
        <soap:body
            encodingStyle="http://schemas.xmlsoap.org/soap/encoding/"
            use="encoded"
            namespace="http://ws.beeshirts.com/wsdl/QueryService" />
      </output>
      <soap:operation soapAction="" />
    </operation>
    <operation name="ping">
      <input>
        <soap:body
          encodingStyle="http://schemas.xmlsoap.org/soap/encoding/"
          use="encoded"
          namespace="http://ws.beeshirts.com/wsdl/QueryService" />
      </input>
      <output>
        <soap:body
            encodingStyle="http://schemas.xmlsoap.org/soap/encoding/"
            use="encoded"
            namespace="http://ws.beeshirts.com/wsdl/QueryService" />
      </output>
      <soap:operation soapAction="" />
    </operation>
    <operation name="findOrder">
      <input>
        <soap:body
          encodingStyle="http://schemas.xmlsoap.org/soap/encoding/"
          use="encoded"
```

Listing 10.1 **Continued**

```
          namespace="http://ws.beeshirts.com/wsdl/QueryService" />
      </input>
      <output>
        <soap:body
            encodingStyle="http://schemas.xmlsoap.org/soap/encoding/"
            use="encoded"
            namespace="http://ws.beeshirts.com/wsdl/QueryService" />
      </output>
      <soap:operation soapAction="" />
    </operation>
      ...
    <soap:binding transport="http://schemas.xmlsoap.org/soap/http" style="rpc" />
  </binding>

  <service name="QueryService">
    <port name="QueryServerPort" binding="tns:QueryServerBinding">
      <soap:address
         xmlns:wsdl="http://schemas.xmlsoap.org/wsdl/"
         location="http://localhost:8080/jaxrpc/QueryServer" />
    </port>
  </service>
</definitions>
```

The `Definition` abstraction also defines those message types that are passed to and from Web services. Such message types are defined within the `Message` abstraction and contain the input and output parameter types associated with Web service operations. Data type information associated with such messages are separately defined within the `Definition` abstraction as a `Types` abstraction. Such WSDL data types are described using XML schema–based descriptions. Listing 10.1 also illustrates such concepts in the context of the `types` and `message` sub-elements of the `definitions` element.

Information about the underlying communications protocol for performing Web service operations is encapsulated within a `Binding` abstraction. Thus, for each port within a Web service definition, a binding indicates a port type, the operations bound to that port, and the Web service communications protocol. As can be seen in Figure 10.10 and in Listing 10.1, the association between a service and a binding is accomplished via one of its port definitions. That is, the port is defined for a service, which is in turn associated with a particular binding.

Although WSDL may be used to describe Web service endpoints independent of the message format and network transport protocols, WSDL v1.1 currently defines bindings to SOAP v1.1, HTTP, and MIME. Use of the SOAP protocol is implied via the `soap:binding` element inside of the `binding` element. The HTTP protocol is implied by virtue of specifying the `soap:binding` element's `transport` attribute value to be `http://schemas.xmlsoap.org/soap/http`.

Because the `Definition` abstraction relates to a top-level XML element, it also contains the necessary namespace information such as base URI, target namespace, and referenced namespaces. Because namespaces referenced by a WSDL document may be associated with a document location, a series of import statements represented by `Import` abstractions may also be associated with a `Definition` abstraction.

Documentation-related information inside of a WSDL `definition` element, as well as other WSDL elements, is encapsulated inside of an `org.w3c.dom.Element` object. If it is desired to embed additional information within a WSDL document, extensibility elements may be used as encapsulated by `ExtensibilityElement` abstractions. The `Definition` abstraction, as well as numerous other JWSDL abstractions, may contain a collection of `ExtensibilityElement` objects. Note also that most JWSDL elements have a name that maps to the `name` attribute of each WSDL element. Additionally, and as we'll learn in more detail later in this chapter, the `javax.xml.namespace.Qname` class is used by JWSDL abstractions to encapsulate the concept of qualified names according to the XML Schema specification.

Detailed WSDL Document Definitions

Figure 10.11 provides a more detailed look at the JWSDL abstractions that map to WSDL document definition details. Our discussion of such abstractions can also be better understood by referring to the concrete WSDL document example in Listing 10.1. Figure 10.11 illustrates those concepts involved with representing WSDL document bindings, operations, and messages, as well as their inputs and outputs.

The JWSDL `Binding` abstraction encapsulates the implied Web services protocol and is associated with the WSDL `binding` element. As previously mentioned, the `binding` element contains the `soap:binding` element identifying usage of the SOAP over HTTP protocol. The `Binding` abstraction is also associated with one or more `BindingOperation` abstractions. Each `BindingOperation` defines the protocol information associated with each operation's input (`BindingInput`), output (`BindingOutput`), and any fault information (`BindingFault`) passed over the wire. Such information, in the case of SOAP messages, includes the encoding and namespace information for the operation parameter type. Each `BindingOperation` defining the protocol for a particular operation must of course somehow be associated with an interface description about an actual operation. The WSDL document `binding` element's `operation` element `name` accomplishes this association.

Each operation interface description is contained within the `portType` element. JWSDL represents such an association by virtue of the one-to-many relationship between the `PortType` and the `Operation` abstraction. Each `Operation` may be associated with an `Input`, an `Output`, and zero or more `Fault` abstractions. Such abstractions respectively define the input message, output message, and fault message types associated with the operation.

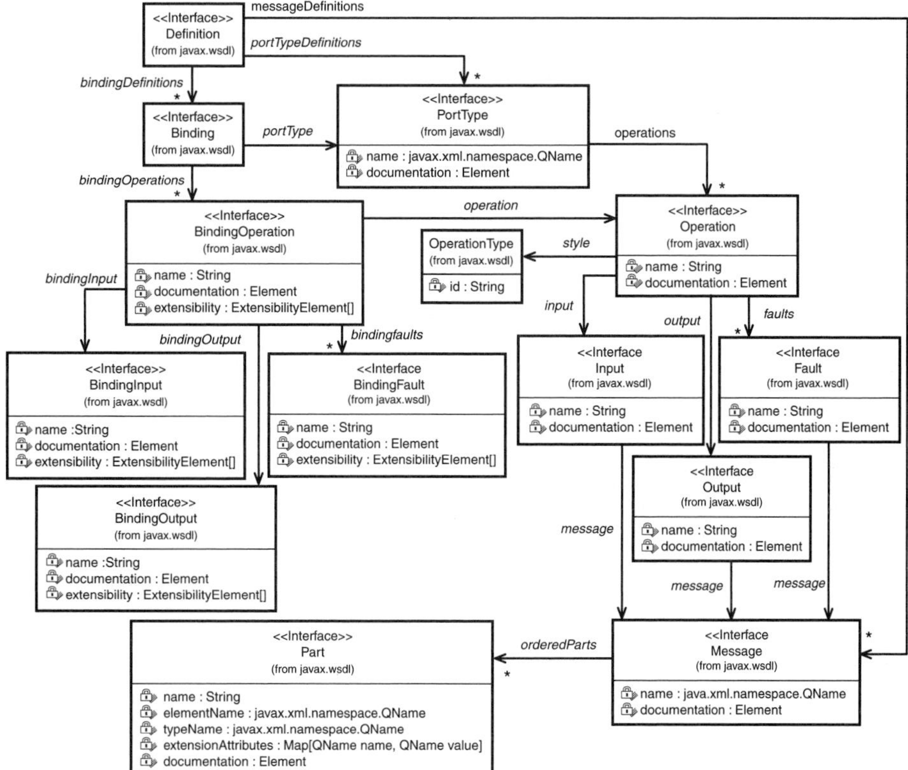

Figure 10.11 Detailed WSDL document definitions.

The definitions of such messages are encapsulated within the `Message` abstractions associated with the `Definition` abstraction. Each `Message` abstraction has an ordered collection of one or more `Part` abstractions. The `Part` abstraction simply defines one parameter within a particular message. That is, because each operation has only one input or one output message, in order to pass multiple input or output parameters to or from an operation, you need to represent such parameters as distinct parts of a message. Again, by examining Listing 10.1 in light of the design concepts captured in Figure 10.10 and Figure 10.11, the concrete mapping of such JWSDL abstractions to an actual WSDL document should reinforce and enhance your understanding of WSDL.

Manipulating WSDL Documents

Now that you have a basic understanding of WSDL document structure, you may be wondering more about how you will use such documents in practice. As we have mentioned, much of the J2EE-based Web services infrastructure that you will encounter will handle generating and reading WSDL documents. When creating a Web service, you will use such tools to generate WSDL documents that you then publish in some way such that Web service clients can understand how to interface with your Web service. When you are acting as a Web service client, the Web services runtime or auxiliary tools that you use will handle reading such WSDL documents and mapping such descriptions into interfaces and classes usable within your Java applications.

Apart from such auto-generated and interpreted manipulation of WSDL documents, JWSDL also defines a few abstractions that let you read and write WSDL documents via a Java API. Figure 10.12 provides an overview of such abstractions.

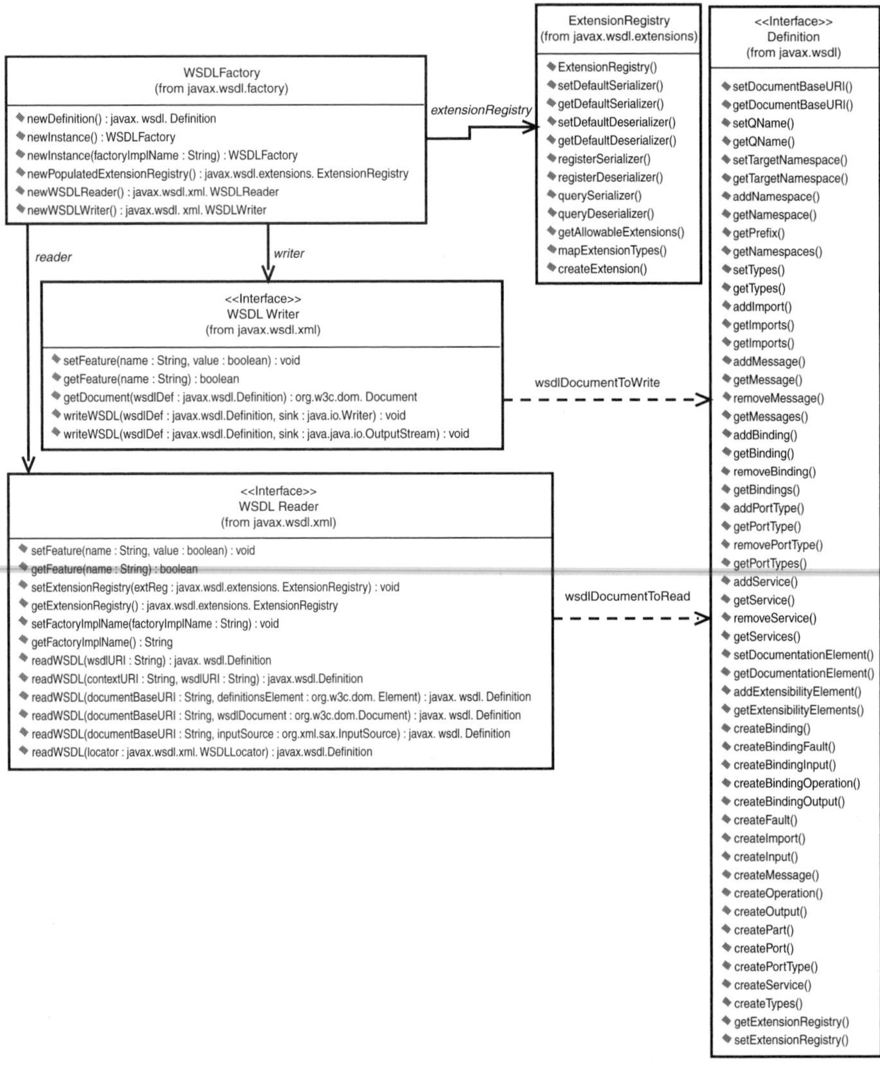

Figure 10.12 Manipulating WSDL documents.

The `WSDLFactory` class is first used to instantiate a new instance of a `WSDLFactory` object via a call to `newInstance()`. The `WSDLFactory` object may then be used to obtain a handle to a `WSDLReader` object for reading WSDL documents or to a `WSDLWriter` object for writing WSDL documents. A series of `readWSDL()` methods defined on the `WSDLReader` object may be invoked to return a handle to a `Definition` object given information about the location of the WSDL document (for example, a URI). Conversely, a series of `writeWSDL()` methods defined on the `WSDLWriter` object may be invoked to write a WSDL document to an output stream given a handle to a `Definition` object. One can create and build up the structure of a `Definition` object to write out as a WSDL document by first calling the `WSDLFactory newDefinition()` method, invoking various `Definition createXXX()` methods to create WSDL definition elements, and calling appropriate setter methods on the `Definition` abstraction and its contained JWSDL document definition abstractions.

On a final note, WSDL documents can also contain extensibility elements. Extensibility elements represent application-specific extensions to WSDL document descriptions. To read and write such elements into and from memory, a series of extension element deserializers and serializers must be defined. The `ExtensionRegistry` associated with the `WSDLFactory` object is used to manage the collection of such serializers and deserializers that perform such mappings when generating and reading WSDL documents.

SOAP RPC

A key goal for the definition of SOAP is to determine a standard format for representing how requests and responses may be exchanged between distributed clients and servers using XML. Thus, a key goal for SOAP is to define a Remote Procedure Call (RPC) mechanism. Much like CORBA has its GIOP and IIOP messaging formats, an IDL mechanism, and a protocol for sending requests and responses between CORBA clients and servers, so too do Web services need the SOAP messaging format, WSDL, as well as a protocol for sending requests and responses between Web service clients and servers (SOAP RPC). We've already described SOAP and WSDL in this chapter. Now we turn our attention to SOAP RPC. Much like CORBA embeds such RPC functionality inside of an ORB, Web services also embed such functionality into something we refer to as a SOAP RPC runtime.

Although SOAP RPC most typically takes place using SOAP over HTTP, we are not bound to the HTTP communications transport protocol for Web services. SOAP RPC requires only a URI of the target Web service, a means for identifying the remote operation and input/output parameters, and optional header information. The SOAP RPC request and response information is embedded inside of a SOAP message body. We saw an example of SOAP requests and responses earlier in this chapter. Additionally, orthogonal information about the particular request or response may be embedded into the SOAP message header. For example, transactional or security-related information may be embedded into a SOAP header.

JAX-RPC

The J2EE standard means for encapsulating SOAP RPC functionality is the Java API for XML-based RPC (JAX-RPC) standard. The JAX-RPC v1.1 standard is the standard required by J2EE v1.4. JAX-RPC defines a standard Java API to which Web service clients and servers may be written. Use of the standard JAX-RPC API allows J2EE-based applications to expose the interfaces of servers as standard Web services. Use of the JAX-RPC API also allows J2SE- and J2EE-based client applications to communicate with remote Web services. Thus, by using JAX-RPC, a Java-based Web services client can talk to a remote standard Web service implemented in any other language and on any other platform. Likewise, a Java-based Web service can expose itself to remote Web service clients implemented in any other language and on any other platform. The lingua franca is the SOAP standard that both ends of the Web services communication pipe must speak.

Associated with JAX-RPC is also the SOAP RPC runtime that we refer to as a JAX-RPC runtime. Java-based Web service clients and servers need such a runtime in order to communicate via the SOAP RPC paradigm. On the server side, such a runtime is used to receive SOAP requests from clients, deserialize such requests, look up or activate a Web service server instance, and hand off the unmarshaled request to the Java-based server object. The JAX-RPC server-side runtime also handles serializing any response from the server into a SOAP response back to the client. On the client side, a similar serialization and deserialization process occurs with requests and responses, respectively. However, the client side does not have the resource management and server activation requirements required of the server-side JAX-RPC runtime. This is why the server-side JAX-RPC runtime utilized in J2EE environments most often makes use of the resource management features employed by J2EE containers such as J2EE Web and EJB containers.

This section of this chapter describes JAX-RPC in depth. We describe how to use JAX-RPC when creating Web service clients and servers. In addition to presenting the JAX-RPC APIs, we also, of course, describe how to use such APIs in the context of example code.

> **Note**
>
> Throughout the sample code in this section, we assume the use of a JAX-RPC v1.0 or v1.1 implementation. This is the version shipped with J2EE v1.4–compliant containers. A separately bundled reference implementation can be downloaded from `http://java.sun.com/xml/download.html` as part of the Java Web Services Developer Pack.
>
> All source code associated with this chapter can be located as described in Appendix A and is extracted to the `examples\src\ejava\webservices\rpc` directory, whereas the code execution script templates are extracted to the `examples\config\execscripts\ejava\webservices\rpc` directory. The `build.properties` properties file in the source directory for this section's code can be configured and used with the `build.xml` ANT script used to build and run the examples. The code is compiled, server is deployed, preferences are set, and process execution templates are generated using the

default `all` ANT target. To rerun an application that has already been deployed, you must first run the ANT `undeploy` target. Prior to running any example, the ANT `start-tomcat` target must be run to start the JAX-RPC runtime to which the Web service server will be deployed. You can invoke the ANT `shutdown-tomcat` target to shut down the JAX-RPC runtime.

As described in Appendix A, you must also set your database configuration properties as appropriate in the `global.properties` file in the `examples` directory. Refer to Appendix A for general database configuration instructions. You will also need to set the `jwsdp.*` and `jaxrpc.*` properties in that file to reference the JAX-RPC libraries. Also unique to this chapter is the requirement that your database driver be stored inside a JAR file (for example, `classes12.jar`) and dropped into the `common\lib` directory of your Java Web Services Developer Pack installation.

Supported Types in JAX-RPC

JAX-RPC supports a limited subset of Java types that can be passed over the wire during Web service interactions. By limiting which types can be received and sent over the wire in a Web service interaction, Java-based Web service clients and servers can be guaranteed to be more interoperable with Web services implemented in other implementation languages and platforms. As a fundamental requirement, all types must of course be serializable to and from an equivalent XML document representation form. This section describes those basic types supported by JAX-RPC communications and how to create extended types supportable by JAX-RPC.

Basic Type Support

JAX-RPC provides inter-service communications support out of the box for a set of types built into Java and for custom value types. All such types are serializable by nature and design. Those basic types supported by JAX-RPC are listed here:

- *Fundamental Types:* Primitive types and their `java.lang` wrapper classes such as `boolean/Boolean`, `byte/Byte`, `short/Short`, `int/Integer`, `long/Long`, `float/Float`, and `double/Double`.
- *Standard Classes:* Standard Java classes such as `String`, `Date`, `Calendar`, `URI`, `QName`, `BigInteger`, and `BigDecimal`.
- *Exceptions:* Exceptions that extend `java.lang.Exception` but not `java.lang.Runtime` exceptions.
- *Value Types:* Types that have a default public constructor, do not implement `java.rmi.Remote`, and are related to and composed only of other JAX-RPC supported types.
- *Arrays:* Arrays of supported types such as `int[]`, `MyValueType[]`, and `String[][]`, as well as `java.lang.Object` arrays.

Note that a particular JAX-RPC runtime may also provide support for other Java collections, as well such as `ArrayList`, `LinkedList`, `Stack`, and `Vector List` objects;

HashMap, Hashtable, Properties, and TreeMap Map objects; and HashSet and TreeSet Set objects.

The example JAX-RPC code associated with this chapter uses two forms of supported types passed over the wire. The first form makes use of fundamental and standard Java types such as passing int, float, and String types over the wire between Web service client and server. The second form of type utilized is custom value types composed of fundamental and standard types. The ejava.webservices.rpc.Order and ejava.webservices.rpc.Customer classes are simple Serializable value types composed only of fundamental and standard Java types and are passed over the wire from the Web Service server side to the Web Service client in our examples.

The basic and simple structure of the Order class is illustrated here:

```
package ejava.webservices.rpc;
import java.io.Serializable;

public class Order implements Serializable{
  private int orderID;
  private double orderValue;

  public Order() {}
  public void setOrderID(int orderID) {this.orderID = orderID;}
  public int getOrderID() {return this.orderID;}
  public void setOrderValue(double orderValue) {this.orderValue =
➥orderValue;}
  public double getOrderValue() {return this.orderValue;}
}
```

The simple skeletal structure of the Customer class is illustrated here:

```
package ejava.webservices.rpc;
import java.io.Serializable;

public class Customer implements Serializable
{
  private String firstName;
  private String lastName;
       ...

  public Customer(){}
  public String getFirstName(){return firstName;}
  public String getLastName(){return lastName;}
      ...
  public void setFirstName(String newFirstName){
    firstName = newFirstName;
  }
  public void setLastName(String newLastName){
    lastName = newLastName;
```

```
    }
      ...
}
```

QNames

You'll soon discover that throughout the JAX-RPC API, a class called `javax.xml.namespace.QName` is often used. Although you may rarely use a `QName` as a supported type in passing information over the Web services wire, it is important to mention it here because subsequent abstractions throughout this chapter use the class. A `QName` object is simply a `Serialzable` object that encapsulates the concept of a qualified name according to the XML Schema specification. Thus, a `QName` will have a URI identifying an XML namespace and a local part of the qualified name.

`QName` simply wraps a local part, namespace URI, and potentially a prefix and thus has `QName(String localPart)`, `QName(String namespaceURI, String localPart)`, and `QName(String namespaceURI, String localPart, String prefix)` constructors. `QName` also has `getLocalPart()`, `getNamespaceURI()`, and `getPrefix()` getters that return a `String` form of the respective qualified name part. The `QName.toString()` method can be invoked to return a qualified name in the form {*namespaceURI*}`localPart` where the {*namespaceURI*} part will be returned only if the namespace URI value was set. Finally, the `QName` form of a {*namespaceURI*}`localPart String` can be returned using the static `Qname.valueOf(String)` method. The {*namespaceURI*} part of the `String` can be optionally set.

Extensible Type Support

JAX-RPC can also support other types of Java classes for which there is no out-of-the-box type support. Such types enable their over the Web service wire transport by utilization of pluggable "serializers" and "deserializers." Figure 10.13 depicts the class architecture associated with constructing such serializers and deserializers in JAX-RPC's `javax.xml.rpc.encoding` package. A `Serializer` is a generic interface for converting from a Java object into a corresponding XML document. A `Derserializer` is the converse of such an operation converting from an XML document into an associated Java object. A concrete implementation of a `Serializer` or `Deserializer` must be used for serializing and deserializing a concrete Java class type.

The JAX-RPC extensible type framework does not specify what particular means for Java object-XML mapping is to be used for serializing and deserializing. Thus, an underlying serialization process may use JAXP SAX, JAXP DOM, or JAXB as an example serialization/deserialization means. The marker interfaces `SerializationContext` and `DeserializationContext` are exposed by a JAX-RPC runtime to serializers and deserializers. Such context information is used to provide the serializers and deserializers with additional information they need in order to perform their duties in whatever Java object-XML specific mapping paradigm is being used.

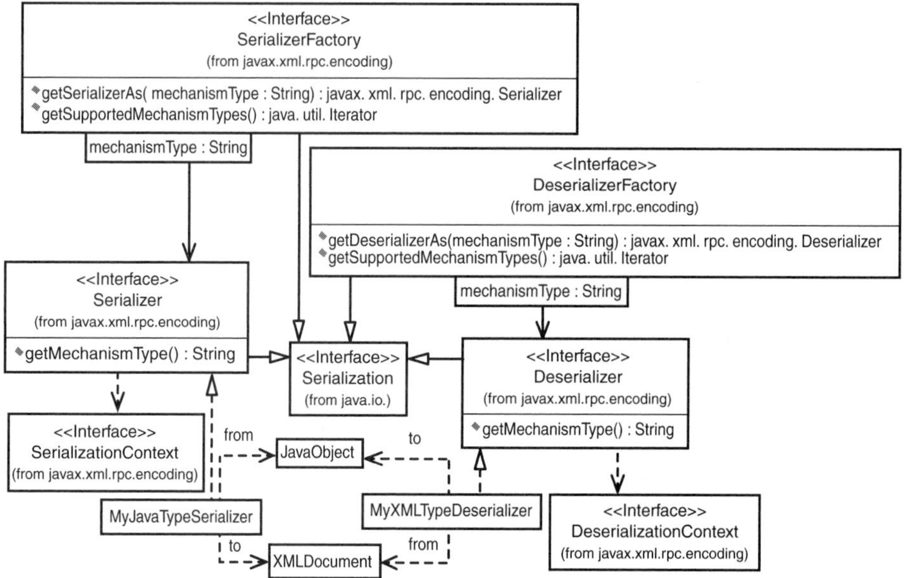

Figure 10.13 Extensible type serializers and deserializers.

The type of mechanism used by a particular serialization process must be returned from the `Serializer` and `Deserializer` `getMechanismType()` method. The only other significant requirement placed on serializers and deserializers is that they define their interfaces to satisfy the JavaBeans component contract (see Appendix B, "JavaBeans," for more detail).

The `SerializationFactory` and `DeserializationFactory` interfaces are implemented by a particular JAX-RPC runtime to create handles to serializers and deserializers, respectively. Because factories can support multiple Java object-XML mapping mechanism types, handles to serializers and deserializers are gotten from the factories using a `getSerializerAs(String)` or `getDeserializerAs(String)` method that returns the handle to a serializer or deserializer based on the desired and supported mapping type. An `Iterator` over the supported types may be retrieved invoking the `getSupportedMechanismTypes()` method on the factory objects.

Given that there may exist multiple object-XML mapping mechanism types as well as serializers and deserializers, it is natural to wonder how one obtains an initial handle to the factory mechanisms that enable one to begin such processing. Figure 10.14 depicts the core JAX-RPC abstractions used for such a task. The `TypeMapping` abstraction encapsulates the association of particular encoding styles to particular factories and serialization/deserialization mechanisms supporting such styles. The `TypeMappingRegistry` simply encapsulates the management of a collection of such `TypeMapping` objects.

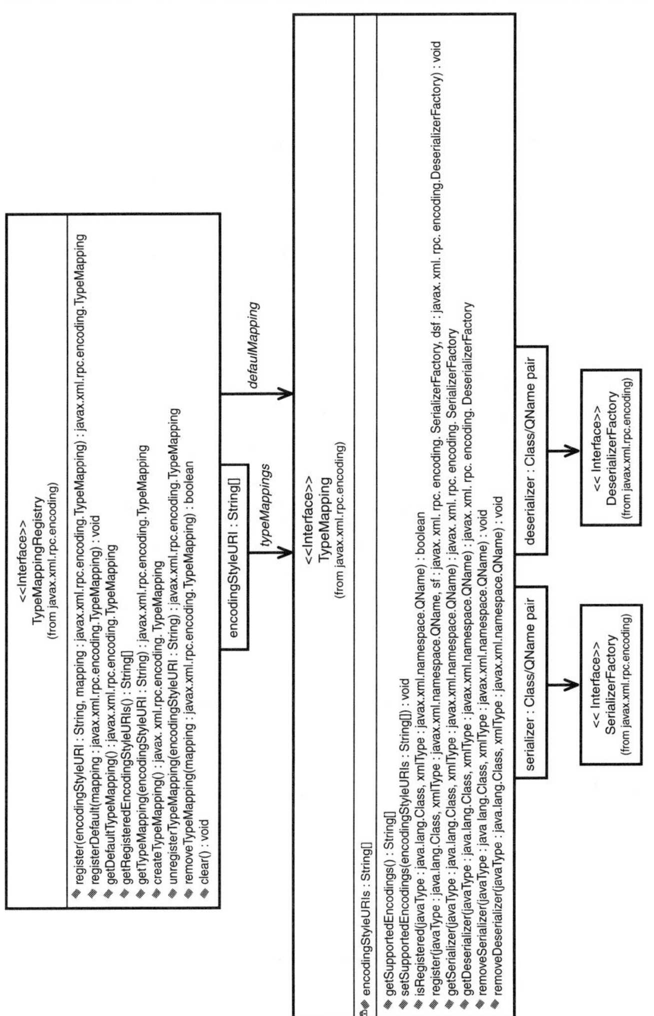

Figure 10.14 Extensible type maps and registries.

Each encoding style supported by the type mapping framework is identified by an encoding style URI. The types supported by a particular mapping can be gotten from and set onto the `TypeMapping` object using the `getSupportedEncodings()` and `setSupportedEncodings()` methods. `TypeMapping` objects are registered, gotten, cleared, and removed from a `TypeMappingRegistry` object according to encoding style URIs using appropriately named methods on the `TypeMappingRegistry` object.

Factories associated with a particular serialization process can be registered with the `TypeMapping.register()` method by specifying the class type of the serializable Java object, the qualified XML name (that is, namespace URI and local part `Qname`), and the `SerializationFactory` and `DeserializationFactory` to use to perform the mappings. Whether or not a mapping exists for a particular Java object-XML mapping can be determined via the `TypeMapping.isRegistered()` method. After the factories are registered with a `TypeMapping`, they may be retrieved or removed using appropriately named methods and given the class type and XML name for the mapping. A `javax.xml.rpc.Service.getTypeMappingRegistry()` method is used to obtain a handle to a `TypeMappingRegistry` object as associated with a particular Web service. We'll discuss how one obtains handles to a `Service` object later in this chapter.

As mentioned, JAX-RPC currently imposes no requirements on the style of extensible type serialization and deserialization process to be used by JAX-RPC runtimes. As such, JAX-RPC runtimes may implement means for serializing and deserializing extensible types in different fashions. The JAX-RPC specification does indicate that such a loosely defined requirement may be tightened in future specification versions. However, the JAX-RPC reference implementation does define a set of libraries for serializing and deserializing SOAP requests and responses. Such libraries are defined largely within the `com.sun.xml.rpc.encoding.soap` package equipped with the JAX-RPC reference implementation. Because we are able to generally utilize the basic type support features of JAX-RPC, the need to know the underlying details of how to create pluggable serializers and deserializers is beyond the scope of this chapter. Nevertheless, the intention of this brief subsection is to at least arm you with the basic concepts of how such extensibility is implemented now in JAX-RPC and make you aware of its capability and potential for more relevance in the future.

Holder Type Support

Some distributed communication paradigms require that parameters passed as input to a remote method be capable of also acting as an output parameter. For example, suppose you have the distributed operation signature `PaymentManager.makePayment(Payment)`. Now suppose that the `Payment` input parameter has payment information used for input by the `PaymentManager` and that the `PaymentManager` appends some credit vetting information to the `Payment` object. Such an input parameter thus also acts like an output parameter. You saw examples of this need in the CORBA world as well in Chapter 8, "CORBA Communications."

JAX-RPC provides support for such input/output parameters via the concept of holder objects. Holder objects can contain both input and return values when passed as an input parameter to Web service operations. The `javax.xml.rpc.holders.Holder` marker interface serves as the root interface to be implemented by all standard and custom JAX-RPC holder objects. A set of standard holder objects exists inside the `javax.xml.rpc.holders` package for all supported primitive types and their equivalent wrapper classes. Such holders define their held value as a public field and provide a default constructor and constructor taking the held value as a parameter. Thus, as an example of `float` holders for both primitive and wrapper versions of float we would have this:

```
FloatHolder fh = new FloatHolder(4.58);
FloatWrapperHolder fwh = new FloatWrapperHolder(new Float(5.75));

float f = fh.value;
Float fw = fwh.value;
```

The basic standard holders inside the `javax.xml.rpc.holders` package are `FloatHolder/FloatWrapperHolder`, `DoubleHolder/DoubleWrapperHolder`, `BigDecimalHolder`, `IntHolder/IntegerWraperHolder`, `BigIntegerHolder`, `ShortHolder/ShortWrapperHolder`, `LongHolder/LongWrapperHolder`, `BooleanHolder/BooleanWrapperHolder`, `ByteHolder/ByteWrapperHolder`, `ByteArrayHolder`, `StringHolder`, `CalendarHolder`, `ObjectHolder`, and `QNameHolder`. Custom holders can also be defined or generated and simply must implement the `Holder` interface.

Service Endpoint Interfaces

To expose a Java-based service as a Web service, you must define a service endpoint interface for that service. Figure 10.15 depicts the basic rules for defining such an interface. The interface must thus firstly extend `java.rmi.Remote`. The operations defined for the interface must throw a `RemoteException` and may also throw other application-specific supported exception types. Furthermore, the input and output parameters for such operations must be one of the valid supported JAX-RPC types defined earlier. And because Web service interface definitions currently do not support the concept of constant declarations, no public `static final` declarations can be defined on service endpoint interfaces.

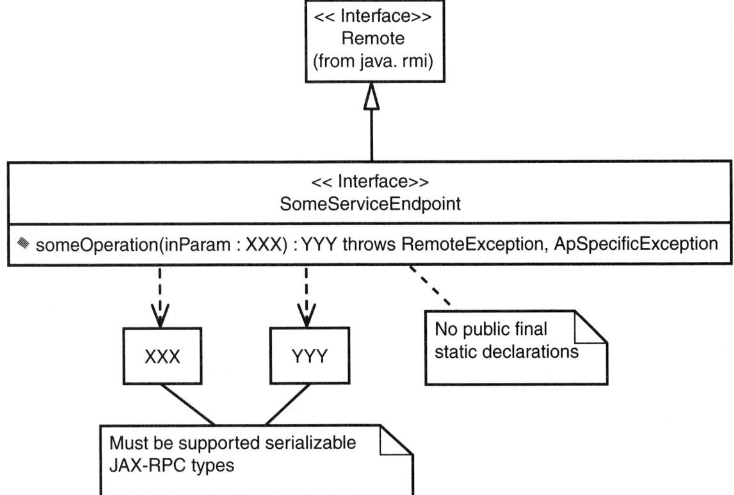

Figure 10.15 Service endpoint interface.

Listing 10.2 depicts a JAX-RPC–compliant service endpoint used with our JAX-RPC example code. Here we see a `QueryServer` interface that defines a set of operations that may be performed to ping the server to determine whether it is alive, find orders based on an order ID, and look up customers based on a minimum order value.

Listing 10.2 **JAX-RPC Service Endpoint (`QueryServer.java`)**

```
package ejava.webservices.rpc;
import java.rmi.Remote;
import java.rmi.RemoteException;

public interface QueryServer extends Remote
{
  public String ping()
          throws RemoteException;

  public Order findOrder(int orderID)
          throws RemoteException;

  public void lookupCustomers(float value)
          throws RemoteException;

  public Customer getNextCustomer()
          throws RemoteException;

  public void clearCustomers()
          throws RemoteException;

  public void resetCustomers()
          throws RemoteException;

  public int length()
          throws RemoteException;
}
```

The `ping()` and `findOrder()` methods on the `QueryServer` are simple stateless method calls that will simply return a response based on their invocation. Aside from the `ping()` and `findOrder()` methods, the remaining methods on the `QueryServer` interface seem to imply some statefulness to the nature of the service endpoint. For example, the `lookupCustomers()` method will induce the service endpoint to look up those customers whose orders are more than a specified input `float` value. Subsequently, calls to `getNextCustomer()` will return each `Customer` previously added to the service endpoint's underlying collection. As you'll see later in this chapter, indeed we may imbue our Web service endpoint with a stateful nature albeit in an underlying transport-specific fashion.

JAX-RPC Servers

When implementing a Web service server using JAX-RPC, an underlying runtime environment is needed for processing requests, finding a server-side instance to handle the request, delegating the request to the server instance, and managing the response back to the client. Such a runtime is akin to the runtime needed for RMI servers or an ORB needed for CORBA servers. As you'll see in later chapters, such a runtime is made mostly transparent to the application developer when using Java Servlets or EJBs as Web services. However, for the purposes of this chapter, we describe the construction of a Web service atop a JAX-RPC runtime without diving into the varied features and benefits of using J2EE containers. Rather, we want to illustrate and focus on the core concepts involved with creating a raw Web service atop a JAX-RPC runtime sans any focus on J2EE container features. Be aware, however, that many JAX-RPC runtimes will actually utilize a J2EE container in their implementation. We make the configuration of such containers as transparent as possible to you, the developer, in this chapter and defer such configuration discussion until later chapters when J2EE container configuration concepts are discussed in more detail.

JAX-RPC Server Application Architecture

Figure 10.16 depicts the basic set of rules and abstractions involved with constructing a Web service server (aka service endpoint). The service endpoint, for example, `MyServiceImpl`, must simply implement the service endpoint interface and provide a public default constructor. The service endpoint may also optionally implement the `javax.xml.rpc.server.ServiceLife cycle` interface, which implies that the JAX-RPC runtime will make callbacks onto the service endpoint when the instance is created and destroyed. Such are the general considerations involved with constructing a Web service endpoint. The particular JAX-RPC runtime being used will employ a particular JAX-RPC runtime delegate class to funnel requests to and receive responses from your service endpoint class. The particular JAX-RPC runtime being used will also require runtime-specific configuration files to be defined to inform the runtime of the names and properties for your service endpoint interface and implementation class.

In general and for maximum interoperability, service endpoint implementations must be designed to be stateless. That is, the JAX-RPC runtime may at its discretion utilize a particular service endpoint to handle requests from different Web service clients. Thus, no implied client conversational state may be associated with a service endpoint implementation.

If the endpoint implements the `ServiceLife cycle` interface, the service endpoint implementation must assume that `ServiceLife cycle.init()` will be called when the endpoint is instantiated. Any initialization of its parameters per an instance are performed within `init()`. A generic `Object` is passed to the endpoint instance and represents a runtime-specific context for the Web service. The endpoint instance must typecast the context object to its presumed runtime context type. The `ServiceLife cycle.destroy()` method is invoked by the JAX-RPC runtime onto the endpoint instance when it wants to retire the instance and induce the cleanup of any open resources (for example, database connections and file handles).

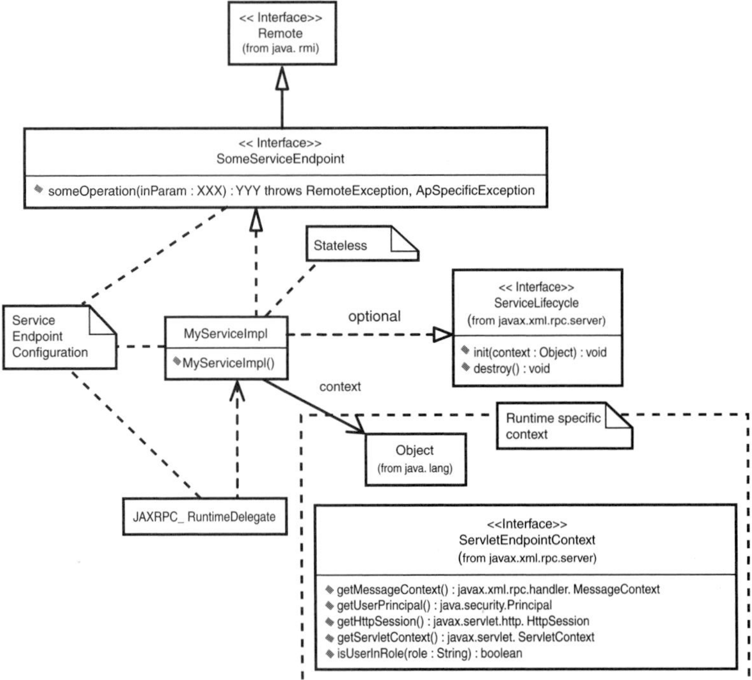

Figure 10.16 Service endpoint.

A `javax.xml.rpc.server.ServletEndpointContext` interface is defined as a standard runtime context type used inside Java Servlet Web containers. Figure 10.16 illustrates this interface and the getters it provides to obtain a handle to a Servlet context object, authenticated username accessing the service, and any HTTP Web session information. The `ServletEndpointContext` interface also provides an `isUserInRole()` method that may be invoked to determine if the authenticated user accessing this service belongs to a particular security role represented as a `String`. The Servlet endpoint context can also be used to obtain a handle to a `MessageContext` object for accessing lower-level Web service message information.

In the JAX-RPC example code for this chapter, the `ejava.webservices.rpc.QueryServerImpl` class serves as our Web service endpoint implementation with its partial implementation shown here:

```
package ejava.webservices.rpc;
  ...
public class QueryServerImpl implements QueryServer, ServiceLife cycle
{
   private Connection connection = null;

   public static String ORDER_QUERY
```

```
  = "SELECT ORDERS.order_id, ORDERS.order_date, ITEM.total_price "
  + "FROM TSHIRTS.ORDERS, TSHIRTS.ITEM, TSHIRTS.CUSTOMER WHERE "
  + "ORDERS.order_id = ITEM.order_id_fk  AND ORDERS.CUSTOMER_ID_FK "
  + "= CUSTOMER.CUSTOMER_ID AND ORDERS.order_id = ?";

public QueryServerImpl(){
}

public void init(Object context){
       ...
    // Get connection properties from preferences
    Preferences preferences =
            Preferences.userNodeForPackage(
               ejava.webservices.rpc.QueryServer.class);
    String driverClass = preferences.get("DRIVER_CLASS", "");
    String dbURL    = preferences.get("DATABASE_URL","");
    String userName = preferences.get("USER_NAME","");
    String password = preferences.get("PASSWORD","");

    // Get JDBC connection based on preferences information
    Class.forName(driverClass);
    if(userName == null || password == null ||
       userName.length() == 0|| password.length() == 0) {
      connection = DriverManager.getConnection(dbURL);
    } else {
      connection =
         DriverManager.getConnection(dbURL, userName,password);
    }
     ...
}

protected void setConnection(Connection conn){
  connection = conn;
}

protected Connection getConnection(){
  return connection;
}

public void destroy(){
     ...
  // Close the JDBC connection
  connection.close();
     ...
}

protected ResultSet getResultSet(String sqlQuery, Object whereValue)
```

```
        throws SQLException{
      // Get a result set based on a prepared statement
      PreparedStatement preparedStatement =
            connection.prepareStatement(sqlQuery);
      preparedStatement.setObject(1, whereValue);
      ResultSet rs = preparedStatement.executeQuery();
      return rs;
   }

   public String ping(){
     // Return the hello world PING info
     return "QueryService is alive! \n";
   }

   public Order findOrder(int orderID){
      Order order = new Order();
          ...
      // Issue order query and return order to client
      ResultSet rs = getResultSet(ORDER_QUERY,
                                      new Integer(orderID));
      rs.next();

      orderID = rs.getInt("ORDER_ID");
      double orderValue = rs.getDouble("TOTAL_PRICE");
      order.setOrderID(orderID);
      order.setOrderValue(orderValue);
        ...
      return order;
   }
   ...
}
```

The preceding snippet from the `QueryServerImpl` example class illustrates how our Web service implements the `ServiceLife cycle` as well as the `QueryServer` interface. By virtue of implementing the `QueryServer` interface, the `ping()` and `findOrder()` methods must be implemented. The `ping()` method simply returns a `String` indicating that the server is alive. The `findOrder()` method takes the order ID, uses JDBC to retrieve the order information, and returns such information inside of an `Order` value object. By virtue of implementing the `ServiceLife cycle` interface, the `init()` and `destroy()` methods are used to create and destroy the JDBC connection associated with the service implementation appropriately.

JAX-RPC Stateful and Stateless Servers

As stated, in general, Web services are designed to be stateless. That is, a Web service object receives a request, generates a response, and then can service another client's request later. No guarantee is made for state to be preserved per client. However, Web services can be designed to be stateful albeit with some drawbacks. At the time of this writing, stateful Web services were generally accomplished in a way that utilizes features of the underlying communications transport, such as HTTP.

That is, session-related information may be embedded into the HTTP headers. A Web services client runtime then makes sure that such information is embedded into the HTTP request, and the Web services server runtime makes sure that such information is read from the HTTP request and associated with the state maintained on the server side for that particular client session. This functionality thus necessarily implies that the particular JAX-RPC runtime implementations being used make use of the session-related features available to the HTTP communications transport. This also thus implies less interoperability. Future standards may define standard SOAP headers to contain session information for greater interoperability when utilizing stateful Web services.

As an example, note that our `QueryServerImpl` example class also is implemented to assume stateful behavior as illustrated in the snippets shown here:

```
package ejava.webservices.rpc;
  ...
public class QueryServerImpl implements QueryServer, ServiceLife cycle
{
   private ServletEndpointContext ctx = null;
   private static final String CUSTOMERS = "CUSTOMERS";
   private static final String INDEX = "INDEX";
   private static final String LENGTH = "LENGTH";
     ...
   public static String CUSTOMER_QUERY
     = "SELECT C.* FROM TSHIRTS.CUSTOMER  C, TSHIRTS.ORDERS  O, "
     + "TSHIRTS.ITEM  I WHERE C.CUSTOMER_ID = O.CUSTOMER_ID_FK AND"
     + " O.ORDER_ID = I.ORDER_ID_FK  AND I.TOTAL_PRICE > ?";
      ...

   public void init(Object context){
          ...
       // Get the service context (runtime specific)
       setContext(context);
         ...
   }

   protected void setContext(Object context){
      // Get the service context (runtime specific)
      ctx = (ServletEndpointContext) context;
   }

   protected ServletEndpointContext getContext(){
      return ctx;
   }
```

```
...

public void lookupCustomers(float value){
   Vector customers = new Vector();

   // Issue query and create/bind Customer for each result
   //  ...also return Vector of customer IDs
        ...
      ResultSet rs = this.getResultSet(CUSTOMER_QUERY,
                                    new Float(value));

      int length = 0;
      while (rs.next()) {
        String customerID = rs.getString("CUSTOMER_ID");
        String firstName = rs.getString("FIRST_NAME");
        String lastName = rs.getString("LAST_NAME");
        String address1 = rs.getString("ADDRESS_1");
        String address2 = rs.getString("ADDRESS_2");
        String city = rs.getString("CITY");
        String state = rs.getString("STATE");
        String phoneNumber = rs.getString("PHONE");
        String eMail = rs.getString("EMAIL");
        String zip = rs.getString("ZIP_CODE");
        Customer custImpl = new Customer();

        custImpl.setFirstName(firstName);
        custImpl.setLastName(lastName);
        custImpl.setAddress1(address1);
        custImpl.setAddress2(address2);
        custImpl.setCity(city);
        custImpl.setState(state);
        custImpl.setZip(zip);
        custImpl.setEmailAddress(eMail);
        custImpl.setPhoneNumber(phoneNumber);

        customers.addElement(custImpl);
        length++;
      }

      ctx.getHttpSession().setAttribute(CUSTOMERS, customers);
      ctx.getHttpSession().setAttribute(INDEX, new Integer(0));
      ctx.getHttpSession().setAttribute(LENGTH, new Integer(length));
        ...
 }

public Customer getNextCustomer(){
```

```
    Object customers = ctx.getHttpSession().getAttribute(CUSTOMERS);
    if(customers == null){
      return new Customer();
    }

    int index =
       ((Integer) ctx.getHttpSession().getAttribute(INDEX)).intValue();
    ctx.getHttpSession().setAttribute(INDEX, new Integer(index + 1));

    return ((Customer) ((Vector) customers).get(index));
  }

  public void clearCustomers(){
    ctx.getHttpSession().setAttribute(CUSTOMERS, null);
    ctx.getHttpSession().setAttribute(INDEX, new Integer(0));
    ctx.getHttpSession().setAttribute(LENGTH, new Integer(0));
  }

  public void resetCustomers(){
     ctx.getHttpSession().setAttribute(INDEX, new Integer(0));
  }

  public int length(){
    Integer lengthInteger
       = (Integer) ctx.getHttpSession().getAttribute(LENGTH);
    return lengthInteger.intValue();
  }

  protected void handleException(Exception e){
    System.out.println("\n QUERY SERVER EXCEPTION:\n" +e.getMessage());
  }
}
```

The first thing to note in the preceding example is that the `QueryServerImpl` stores a handle to a `ServletEndpointContext` object as a private attribute. This value is set using the object passed into the `init()` method. The `ServletEndpointContext` object can be used to obtain a handle to an HTTP session object that manages storing HTTP session-related information. Thus, in our example implementation, we bind ourselves to an HTTP transport protocol.

The `lookupCustomers()` method uses JDBC to look up customer information, creates a `Vector` of `Customer` objects, and stores this `Vector` inside of the HTTP session object. Because this is a stateful Web service example, subsequent calls to `getNextCustomer()` on the `QueryServerImpl` pull a `Customer` from the HTTP session, increment an index, and return the `Customer` object to the Web service client. Methods also exist to clear the stored customer information, reset the index, and return the length of the customer vector stored by the stateful Web service.

JAX-RPC Server Deployment

As we've stated previously, it is not our intention in this chapter to describe in detail the internal configuration of a particular JAX-RPC runtime. One key reason for this is that future chapters on J2EE Web components and EJB describe the preferred way for deploying Web services inside of J2EE containers, and we defer descriptions of J2EE container configuration until we discuss J2EE Web components and EJBs. Another key reason is that JAX-RPC runtime configuration can vary from vendor offering to vendor offering. A third key reason is that a main goal of this chapter is to focus on the core concepts and APIs behind Web service communications in the context of the other core Java enterprise communication paradigms (CORBA and RMI). We thus want to abstract away the details of the JAX-RPC runtime much like the details of a CORBA ORB and RMI runtime have been abstracted.

> **Web Services with J2EE Components**
>
> Rest assured that we will describe how to configure Web services inside of a J2EE container in due time. Because this book describes J2EE technologies from the ground up, we first thoroughly describe JAX-RPC as an API and runtime in this chapter. After we've had the chance later in this book to describe J2EE Web components, EJBs, and their J2EE-compliant deployment descriptors, we will subsequently describe how to deploy such components as Web services. Chapter 22, "Web Services with Web Components," and Chapter 30, "Web Services with EJB," in fact heavily build on the examples in this chapter to describe how Web services can be deployed inside of J2EE containers in a standard fashion.

Although such abstraction helps focus attention on what is involved with creating Web service endpoint implementation and client code, there can be significant overhead in configuring your particular JAX-RPC runtime for use. The configuration of the Java Web Service Developer's Pack JAX-RPC runtime on the server side used with our examples is largely accomplished via two XML files. The `jaxrpc-ri.xml` file included with our examples is used to configure the bulk of the server-side Web services. Among other information contained in this file, the service endpoint name, service endpoint interface class name, service endpoint implementation class name, and mapping of the Web service URL to the service endpoint name are defined as illustrated here:

```
<?xml version="1.0" encoding="UTF-8"?>

<webServices
    xmlns="http://java.sun.com/xml/ns/jax-rpc/ri/dd"
    version="1.0"
    targetNamespaceBase="http://ws.beeshirts.com/wsdl"
    typeNamespaceBase="http://ws.beeshirts.com/types"
    urlPatternBase="/ws">

    <endpoint
        name="QueryService"
        interface="ejava.webservices.rpc.QueryServer"
```

```
        implementation="ejava.webservices.rpc.QueryServerImpl">
           ...
   </endpoint>

    <endpointMapping
        endpointName="QueryService"
        urlPattern="/QueryServer"/>

</webServices>
```

One or more `<endpoint>` elements may be defined inside of the `<webServices>` element because one or more service endpoints may compose a Web service. Of course, an `<endpointMapping>` element must also be defined for each service endpoint.

As a final note on server-side configuration files, because the JAX-RPC runtime reference implementation we use operates inside of a J2EE Web container, a special J2EE `web.xml` file is also used to configure the J2EE Web container.

Our ANT script also abstracts away the packaging and deployment of the Web service. The JAX-RPC reference implementation utilizes a running Apache Tomcat server with a J2EE Web container and JAX-RPC runtime. As such, the compiled code for the Web service implementation and configuration files are packaged inside of a JAR file for deployment inside of the Apache Tomcat server. A special `wsdeploy` tool specific to the JAX-RPC runtime implementation is invoked to create a deployable Web service. The invocation of the `wsdeploy` tool also induces the creation of a WSDL file based on the associated Web service interface. After a deployable Web service and WSDL file are generated, the Web service is deployed into the running Apache Tomcat environment by use of a special `DeployTask` class included with the JAX-RPC reference implementation.

After the Web service is deployed, the WSDL file may be viewed with our example using the URL `http://localhost:8080/jaxrpc/QueryServer?WSDL` in your Web browser (assuming you have not altered the URL information inside of the `build.properties` file). You can retrieve the status of the server after it has been deployed by entering the URL `http://localhost:8080/jaxrpc/QueryServer` in your Web browser.

If the default example JAX-RPC values do not suit you, the server environment and deployment information may be additionally configured via the following `build.properties` entries:

```
# Username and password established for your
#   Apache Tomcat installation
username=tomcat
password=tomcat

# Web Service Deployment information including
#    URL, Context,and deployable JAR file path
url=http://localhost:8080/manager
context.path=jaxrpc
war.path=${ejava.home}/examples/src/ejava/webservices/rpc/jaxrpc-ws.war
```

JAX-RPC Clients

JAX-RPC was designed with the idea that both standalone J2SE applications and J2EE components can act as Web service clients using JAX-RPC. Much like a JAX-RPC server is supposed to have no dependency on the particular platform or language employed by the Web service client application, so too is the JAX-RPC client not supposed to require any knowledge of the particular platform or language employed by the Web service server. This section describes how to implement a Java-based Web service client using JAX-RPC. Although we employ a standalone J2SE-based environment for this example, similar means can be used to create Web service clients using J2EE Web and EJB components.

Web Service Lookup

Before a JAX-RPC client can obtain a handle to a Web service interface, it obviously needs a means for looking up such handles. This may be accomplished in one of two ways as depicted in Figure 10.17. In the first means, a `javax.xml.rpc.Servicefactory` object is used to create a handle to a Web service object. In the second means, a lookup is performed via JNDI. In both cases, an in-process representation of the Web service is returned via some implementation or extension of the `javax.xml.rpc.Service` interface.

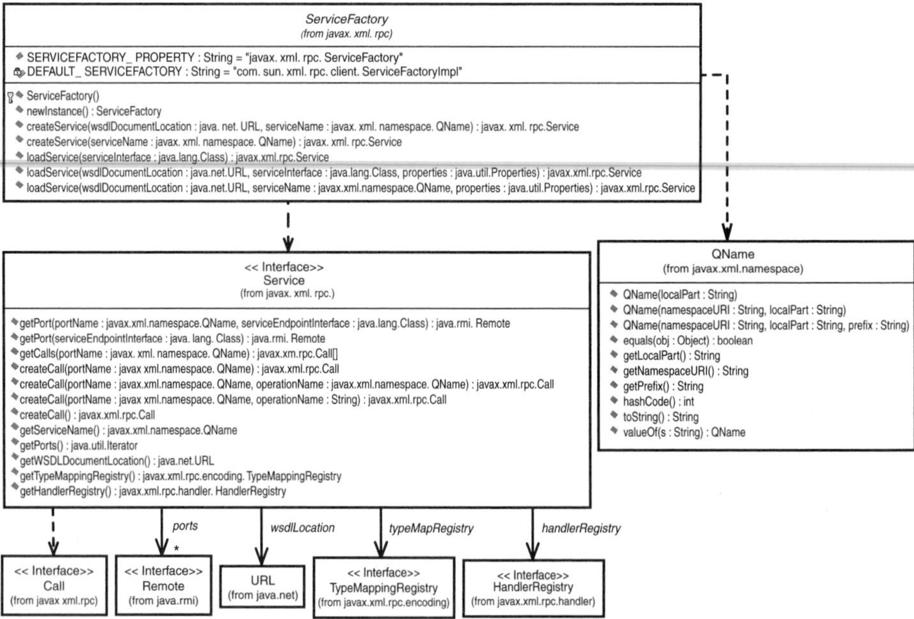

Figure 10.17 JAX-RPC Web service lookup.

A handle to a `ServiceFactory` is obtained by calling the static `newInstance()` method on the class. The system property `SERVICEFACTORY_PROPERTY` may be used to define the fully qualified class name of the factory implementation to instantiate. A handle to a `Service` object may then be returned using one of the `createService()` methods. The `QName` of the service and URL of the WSDL document that defines the remote Web service may be passed as parameters to `createService()` in order to identify the `Service` object to instantiate.

As an example, the Web services client, `QueryClient`, equipped with the JAX-RPC code for this chapter obtains a `Service` object handle in the following fashion:

```
public Service getOrderServiceProxy(){
    Service service = null;
        ...
    QName qname = new QName(prefs.get("SERVICE_NAMESPACE", ""),
                  prefs.get("SERVICE_LOCALNAME", ""));
    URL url = new URL(prefs.get("SERVICE_URL", ""));

    ServiceFactory sf = ServiceFactory.newInstance();
    service = sf.createService(url, qname);
       ...
    return service;
}
```

The associated preferences are read in from the `build.properties` file with the default values shown here:

```
service.namespace=http://ws.beeshirts.com/wsdl/QueryService
service.localname=QueryService
service.url=http://localhost:8080/jaxrpc/QueryServer?WSDL
```

Alternatively, JNDI may be used to obtain references to Web service handles. We'll learn more about JNDI in Chapter 11, "Naming Services with JNDI"; however, the basic use of JNDI to look up services is rather straightforward and is briefly described here. When operating inside a J2EE container, a Web services client often instantiates a default JNDI context object and uses a reference name for the `Service`. The reference name for the `Service` is then bound to the actual remote name of the service inside of the container. For example:

```
Context ctx = new InitialContext();
Service service
  = (Service) ctx.lookup("java:comp/env/SomeService");
```

Alternatively, a remote JNDI service may be accessed from a standalone J2SE environment by passing in initial connection information to the JNDI context as illustrated here:

```
// Create a hashtable with the naming service object factory
// and the URI of the remote JNDI service
Hashtable nameServiceProperties = new Hashtable();
nameServiceProperties.put("java.naming.factory.initial",
                          "com.some.web.lookup.service.ClassFactory");
nameServiceProperties.put("java.naming.provider.url",
                          "http://webservices.beeshirts.com/");

// Now, look up a handle to a Service object
Context ctx = new InitialContext(nameServiceProperties);
Service service
  = (Service) ctx.lookup("java:comp/env/SomeService");
```

Finally, a series of `loadService()` methods defined on the `ServiceFactory` object may be used to load a `Service` instance into memory given a generated service interface. The `loadService(Class)` method loads the `Service` instance associated with the given generated `Class` type if available via the class loader. The `loadService(URL, Class, Properties)` method may be used to identify a URL for the WSDL document of the service interface along with a set of interface-specific `Properties` that can be used to help locate the service interface. Alternatively, the `loadService(URL, QName, Properties)` method can be used to identify the interface via a `QName` instead of a `Class` type.

JAX-RPC Dynamic Proxy Clients

In the preceding section we saw that the `Service` abstraction encapsulates a handle for the client to a remote Web service. Let's now examine the `Service` interface in a bit more detail, see how it can be used by a JAX-RPC client to obtain handles to remote Web service endpoint interfaces, and begin Web service communications. Figure 10.18 depicts in more detail the `Service` interface used by dynamic proxy clients. The `Service` interface actually acts as the primary and base interface for constructing three types of Web service client handles. We will examine the means for constructing a dynamic proxy to a Web service in this section.

A minimal amount of meta-data about the Web service can be retrieved from the `Service` interface. Notice from the figure that the `Service.getServiceName()` method can be used to return the `QName` of the particular Web service. The URL for the WSDL document associated with the service can be retrieved via a call to the `Service.getWSDLDocumentLocation()` method.

The dynamic proxy Web services client, however, focuses its attention on the `getPort()` methods. The client invokes `Service.getPort()` with a `java.lang.Class` object for the desired service endpoint interface and possibly a `QName` of the service endpoint interface's port name. The `Service.getPorts()` method can be used to obtain an `Iterator` over the `Qname` objects for the ports part of this `Service`.

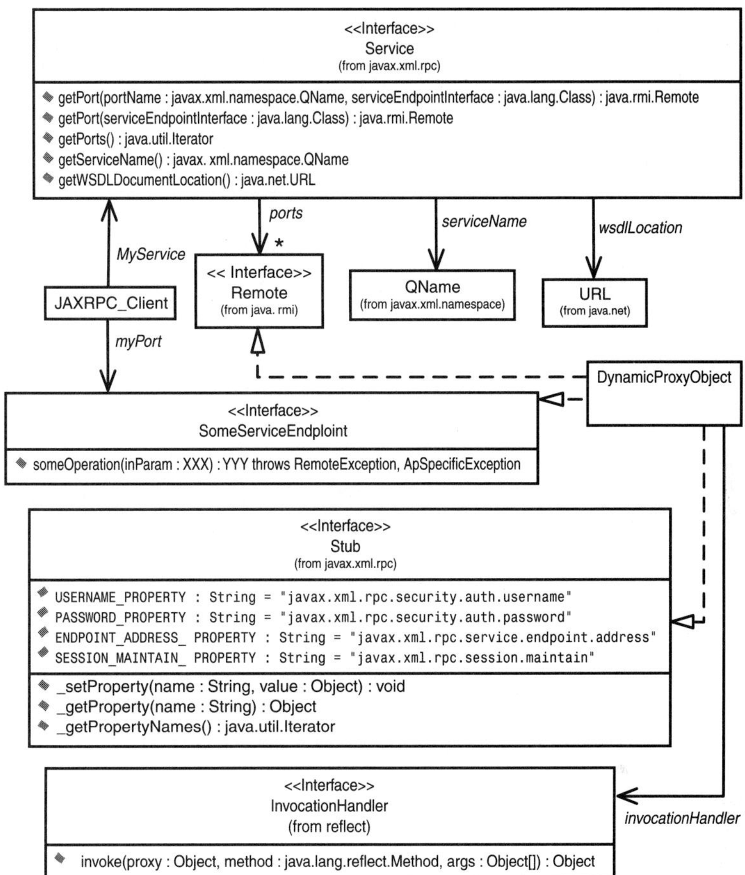

Figure 10.18 JAX-RPC dynamic proxy clients.

The `Remote` object returned from the `getPort()` methods may be a dynamic proxy object created using the `java.lang.reflect.Proxy` class. In such a case, the dynamic proxy implements the methods of the service endpoint interface at runtime. Underneath the hood, the proxy instance implements the `java.lang.reflect.InvocationHandler` interface that performs the actual processing of the method invocation on the proxy instance. The `invoke()` method of the `InvocationHandler` returns a resultant `Object` output parameter and takes as input the proxy instance upon which the method was invoked, a reflective description of the method invoked, and an array of input parameter objects. For example, transparent to your Web service client, the client-side JAX-RPC runtime may perform the following illustrative steps to create a dynamic proxy for `SomeServiceEndpoint` interface:

```
// Create an invocation handler to deal with requests and responses
InvocationHandler handler = new JAXRPCRuntimeInvocationHandler(...);
// Create a reflective set of methods and attach to handler
Method [] serviceMethods = SomeServiceEndpoint.class.getMethods();
handler.addMethods(serviceMethods);
// Create and return the dynamic proxy instance that implements
//    the service endpoint and the remote interface
Object proxy
  = Proxy.newProxyInstance(
      SomeServiceEndpoint.class.getClassLoader(),
      new Class[] {SomeServiceEndpoint.class, Remote.class, Stub.class},
      handler
                         );
```

Then, as calls are made by the client onto the dynamic proxy object, the invocation handler deals with the actual management tasks needed to delegate the call across the wire to the Web service. Again, all such operations occur transparently to the Web service client. Rather, from the Web services client perspective, the client simply deals with the concrete service endpoint interface. For example, the `QueryClient` returns a handle to the dynamic proxy port as shown here:

```
public QueryServer getOrderPortProxy(Service service){
    QueryServer port = null;
      ...
    QName qname = new QName(prefs.get("PORT_NAMESPACE", ""),
                  prefs.get("PORT_LOCALNAME", ""));
    port = (QueryServer) service.getPort(qname, QueryServer.class);
      ...
    return port;
}
```

The associated preferences are defined in the `build.properties` file as shown here:

```
port.namespace=http://ws.beeshirts.com/wsdl/QueryService
port.localname=QueryServerPort
```

The client may then invoke any business-specific methods on the port as illustrated here in the `QueryClient` example to invoke the `findOrder()` Web service operation:

```
public Order getOrder(QueryServer queryServer){
    Order order = null;
    int orderID = prefs.getInt("OPERATION_PARAMVALUE_ORDER", 1005);
      ...
    order = queryServer.findOrder(orderID);
      ...
    return order;
}
```

The associated preference value used in this example is defined in the `build.properties` file as shown here:

```
operation.paramValue.order=1002
```

Notice from Figure 10.18 that the dynamic proxy will also implement the JAX-RPC `Stub` interface serving as the base interface for JAX-RPC stubs. The `Stub` interface provides a means for getting and setting configuration properties associated with a stub as a set of name and value pairs. A set of optional standard properties defined for stubs has a set of associated `public static String` names defined on the `Stub` interface. Such properties include a means for specifying a username and password, the target address for the service endpoint, and a `Boolean` value indicating whether a session should be maintained for the particular service endpoint.

JAX-RPC Static Clients

Figure 10.19 depicts the abstractions involved with generating static JAX-RPC clients. In such situations, an application-specific `Service` class and service endpoint stub are generated. A concrete `Service` object, for example, `SomeService`, provides type-safe methods to obtain handles to the concrete service endpoint ports of interest. A concrete stub, for example, `SomeServiceEndpoint_Stub`, is also generated that implements the base `Stub` and service endpoint interfaces. Such concrete stubs are akin to the stubs generated and used beneath the hood by CORBA and RMI clients.

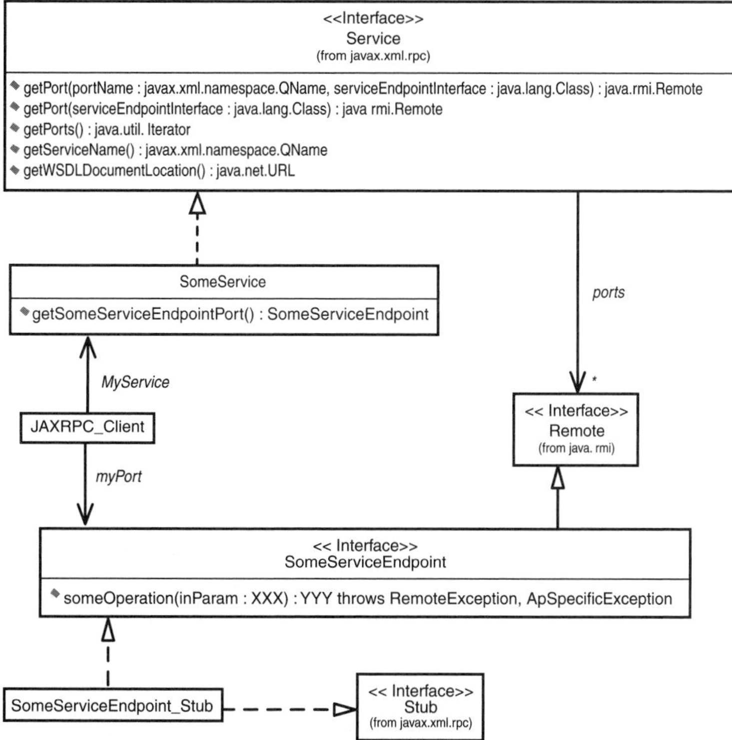

Figure 10.19 JAX-RPC static clients.

As an example, a concrete service and use of a static stub are illustrated here:

```
// Lookup Service handle as described earlier...using JNDI example here.
SomeService myService
    = (SomeService) ctx.lookup("java:comp/env/SomeService");
SomeServiceEndpoint myPort
    = (SomeServiceEndpoint) myService.getSomeServiceEndpointPort();
Order order = myPort.findOrder(orderID);
```

Although Web service clients can utilize JNDI to obtain a handle to a concrete `Service` object, a directory server or JNDI container service may not always be available to a standalone J2SE Web service client. In such situations, a JAX-RPC runtime-specific means for obtaining a concrete `Service` handle may be employed. As an example, our `QueryClient` defines a method to obtain a concrete `Service` handle using the JAX-RPC reference implementation's means for doing so as follows:

```
public QueryService getOrderServiceStatic() {
       // Return the static QueryService in runtime-specific fashion.
       return (QueryService)(new QueryService_Impl());
}
```

In this situation, we use the `QueryService_Impl` class generated by the JAX-RPC runtime to obtain the concrete `Service` handle of the type `QueryService`. The `QueryClient` obtains a handle to the static `QueryServer` stub by virtue of the following method that invokes a concrete method name defined on the `QueryService` object:

```
public QueryServer getOrderPortStatic(QueryService queryService) {
       // Return the QueryServer static stub
       return queryService.getQueryServerPort();
}
```

JAX-RPC Dynamic Invocation Clients

Figure 10.20 depicts the abstractions involved with creating JAX-RPC Dynamic Invocation Interface (DII) clients. Such clients have no type-specific handles to the Web service. Rather, a generic `Call` interface is used to configure and induce the dynamic invocation of a remote Web service. Such a DII technique is similar to the use of the Java reflection APIs and the DII interface techniques available in CORBA.

The `Service` interface provides a means for obtaining handles to `Call` objects for DII. The `createCall()` methods may be invoked to create handles to `Call` objects initialized to varying degrees. The parameterless `createCall()` method creates a `Call` object with no specific target information. The `QName` for a port may be provided to the other `createCall()` methods when creating `Call` objects. A `String` or `QName` form of an operation name within a port may also be provided to the `createCall()` methods. The `getCalls()` method can also be used to retrieve a preconfigured set of `Call` objects for each operation associated with a particular port name.

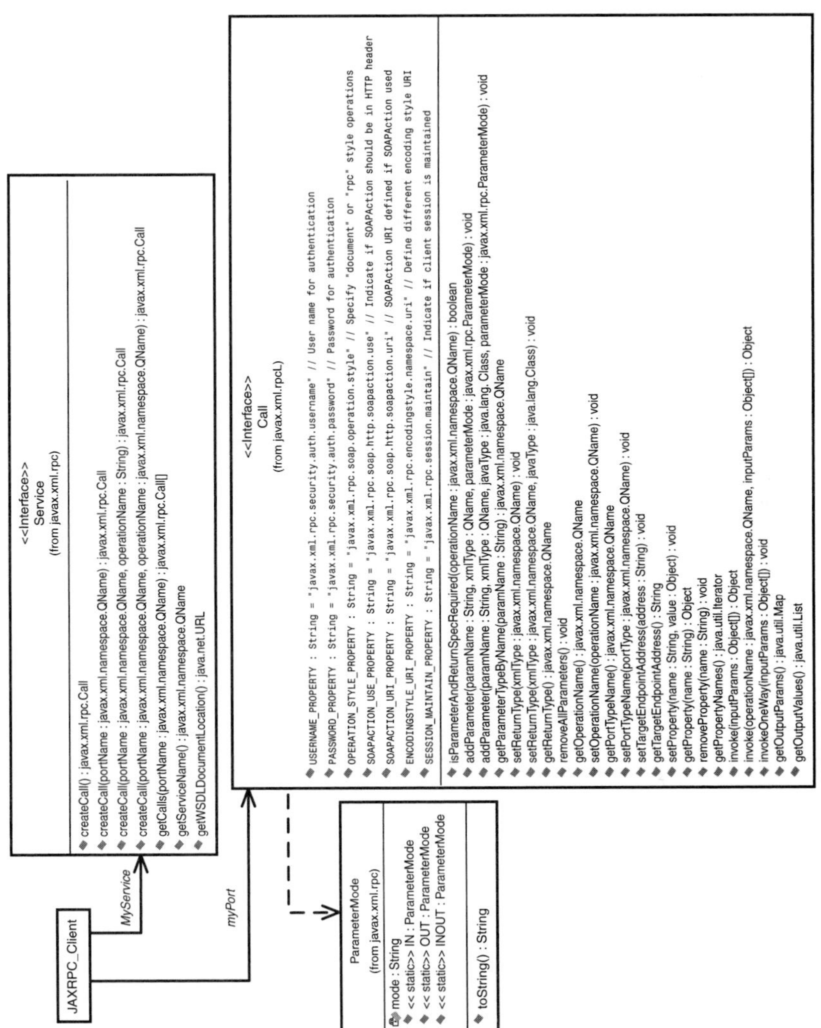

Figure 10.20 JAX-RPC DII clients.

After a handle to a `Call` object is retrieved, it may be configured (if it is not preconfigured) with initial DII data. A configured `Call` object may then be invoked to induce the operation request and response. If the port type name and operation name have not yet been specified for the `Call` object, you can call `setPortTypeName()` and `setOperationName()`. Getters for the port type name and operation name also exist on the `Call` interface. Additionally, the target URI for the invocation may be specified and gotten via the `setTargetEndpointAddress()` and `getTargetEndpointAddress()` methods, respectively.

After a port and operation have been identified, you may now add any input and output parameter information to the `Call` object. You can call `isParameterAndReturnSpecRequired()` first given the operation name to determine whether the input and return type information should be defined before an `invoke()` operation is called. If such information is required, you can call one of the `addParameter()` methods. The `addParameter()` methods require a `String` name of the particular parameter, the XML type `QName` for the parameter, and the parameter mode. The parameter mode is defined as an input-only parameter (`ParameterMode.IN`), an output-only parameter (`ParameterMode.OUT`), or an input and output parameter (`ParameterMode.INOUT`). Additionally, one of the `addParameter()` methods also allows you to define the return class type when defining an `OUT` or `INOUT` parameter. Similarly, the single return type from an operation can be defined using the `setReturnType()` methods. The XML type name for any parameter can be gotten using either the `getParameterTypeByName()` method or the `getReturnTypeName()` method. As a measure for cleanup or starting anew, any parameters (except for the return type) set on a `Call` object can be cleared by invoking the `removeAllParameters()` method.

A set of meta-data related to an operation may also be specified and retrieved. Properties are simply a set of name/value pairs and are set, gotten, and removed via an appropriately named set of methods on the `Call` interface shown in Figure 10.20. Optional standard property names are defined for the `Call` interface as well and are defined as shown in Figure 10.20.

As an example of creating a `Call` object handle, our `QueryClient` example first obtains a `Service` handle as shown here:

```
public Service getOrderServiceDII(){
    Service service = null;
       ...
    QName qname = new QName(prefs.get("SERVICE_LOCALNAME", ""));

    ServiceFactory sf = ServiceFactory.newInstance();
    service = sf.createService(qname);
       ...
    return service;
}
```

The preference used previously is defined in `build.properties`:

```
service.localname=QueryService
```

Using the returned `Service` handle, a `Call` object for our `QueryClient` example is constructed given the `Service` object handle as illustrated here to create and configure a dynamic call for the Web service `ping()` operation:

```
public Call getOrderPortDII(Service service){
    Call call = null;
      ...
    QName port = new QName(prefs.get("PORT_LOCALNAME_DII", ""));
    call = service.createCall(port);
    call.setTargetEndpointAddress(prefs.get("SERVICE_URL_DII", ""));

    call.setProperty(ENCODING_NAMESPACE, ENCODING_URI);
    call.setProperty(Call.SOAPACTION_USE_PROPERTY, new Boolean(true));
    call.setProperty(Call.SOAPACTION_URI_PROPERTY, "");

    QName stringParamType
            = new QName(SCHEMA_NAMESPACE,
                        prefs.get("OPERATION_OUTPARAM_ORDER", ""));
    call.setReturnType(stringParamType);


    QName operation = new QName(prefs.get("OPERATION_NAMESPACE", ""),
                                prefs.get("OPERATION_LOCALNAME", ""));
    call.setOperationName(operation);
      ...
    return call;
}
```

At this point, the following static attributes of `QueryClient` are utilized:

```
public static final String ENCODING_NAMESPACE
    = "javax.xml.rpc.encodingstyle.namespace.uri";
public static final String ENCODING_URI
    = "http://schemas.xmlsoap.org/soap/encoding/";
public static final String SCHEMA_NAMESPACE
    = "http://www.w3.org/2001/XMLSchema";
```

And the following preferences defined inside `build.properties` are utilized:

```
service.url.dii=http://localhost:8080/jaxrpc/QueryServer
port.localname.dii=QueryServer
operation.namespace=http://ws.beeshirts.com/wsdl/QueryService
operation.localname=ping
operation.outParam.order=string
```

After a `Call` object is configured, it may now be invoked. In all invocation cases, an `Object` array of parameter values must be defined and passed into one of the invocation methods. The `invoke()` methods may be used to send a request and block for a response. One of the `invoke()` methods lets you define the intended operation name on-the-fly if it had not already been configured for this `Call` object. The `invokeOneWay()` method lets you invoke a Web service without blocking and waiting for a response. After an invocation is made, a `Map` of name/value pairs for the output parameters or a `List` of the output parameter values may be retrieved respectively via the `getOutputParams()` and `getOutputValues()` calls.

As a simple example, our `QueryClient` example uses DII to invoke the `ping()` method on the Web service using the `Call` object previously constructed as shown here:

```
public String getPingResponse(Call pingServiceCall){
    String pingResponse = null;
        ...
    Object[] inParam = { };
    pingResponse = (String) pingServiceCall.invoke(inParam);
     ...
    return pingResponse;
}
```

JAX-RPC Stateful Clients

Recall that our Web service `QueryServer` example also assumed the use of a stateful client/server interaction for looking up and retrieving customer information. To accomplish this on the client side, the JAX-RPC client must indicate that it will maintain a stateful session with the server by setting a special property onto the JAX-RPC client-side stub. The following method accomplishes this inside of our `QueryClient` example:

```
public void createStatefulSession(QueryServer server){
      Stub stub = (Stub) server;
      stub._setProperty(Stub.SESSION_MAINTAIN_PROPERTY,
                        new Boolean(true));
}
```

Upon invocation of this method, the `QueryClient` and `QueryServer` then maintain a stateful session in which session-related information is embedded in the underlying HTTP header information. The `QueryClient` may then invoke customer lookup and retrieval operations on the `QueryServer` that require dedicated state to be maintained for the client on the server side.

JAX-RPC Client Execution

As you've seen, the snippets presented thus far for our `QueryClient` example indicate that the `QueryClient` demonstrates static, dynamic proxy, DII, and stateful client behaviors. The `main()` method of `QueryClient` invokes all the behaviors and methods previously described (with the exception of the handler chain example to be described shortly). The `QueryClient main()` method is shown here:

```
public static void main(String[] args) {
        ...
      // Construct a new query client and read preferences
      QueryClient client = new QueryClient();
      Preferences prefs = Preferences.userNodeForPackage(
                              ejava.webservices.rpc.QueryClient.class);


      // Demonstrate invoking a DII client interface for pinging
      //    the remote service
```

```
Service queryServiceDII = client.getOrderServiceDII();
client.addHandlerChain(queryServiceDII);
Call pingServiceCall = client.getOrderPortDII(queryServiceDII);
String pingResponse = client.getPingResponse(pingServiceCall);
System.out.println("<QueryServer.ping() - DII>:\n"
                   + pingResponse + "\n");

// Demonstrate invoking a static client interface for finding
//    order information
QueryService queryServiceStatic = client.getOrderServiceStatic();
QueryServer queryServerStatic
                 = client.getOrderPortStatic(queryServiceStatic);
Order order1 = client.getOrder(queryServerStatic);
System.out.println("<QueryServer.findOrder() - STATIC>\n");
System.out.println("  <Order>: { "
                      + order1.getOrderID() + ", "
                      + order1.getOrderValue() + " }\n");

// Demonstrate invoking a proxy client interface for finding
//      order information (if serialization w/proxies supported)
if(prefs.getBoolean("PROXY_SUPPORT", false)){
       Service orderService = client.getOrderServiceProxy();
       QueryServer orderPort
                       = client.getOrderPortProxy(orderService);
       Order order2 = client.getOrder(orderPort);
       System.out.println("<QueryServer.findOrder() - PROXY>\n");
       System.out.println("  <Order>: { "
                          + order2.getOrderID() + ", "
                          + order2.getOrderValue() + " }\n");
}

// Demonstrate session-based Web servicing over HTTP
//     (if supported)
if(prefs.getBoolean("SESSION_SUPPORT", false)){
   client.createStatefulSession(queryServerStatic);
   Iterator customers = client.getCustomers(queryServerStatic);

   System.out.println("<QueryServer.lookupCustomers()"
                      + "  - SESSION>\n");
   while(customers.hasNext()){
         Customer customer = (Customer) customers.next();
         System.out.println("  <Customer>: { "
            + customer.getFirstName() + ", "
            + customer.getLastName() + ", "
            + customer.getAddress1() + ", "
            + customer.getAddress2() + ", "
            + customer.getCity() + ", "
            + customer.getState() + ", "
```

```
                        + customer.getZip() + ", "
                        + customer.getPhoneNumber() + ", "
                        + customer.getEmailAddress() + " }\n");
                }
        }
        ...
}
```

A JAX-RPC runtime is also utilized on the client side by the `QueryClient` example. However, the JAX-RPC runtime on the client side is run inside of a standalone J2SE environment. Nevertheless, the JAX-RPC reference implementation requires use of a special XML-based configuration file to be packaged along with the Web services client source code. This JAX-RPC runtime-specific `config.xml` file generally focuses on defining the location of the Web service to which the Web service client will communicate. As an example, the `config.xml` file used with our `QueryClient` example needs to know from where the `QueryServer` Web services' WSDL information may be retrieved. The `QueryClient`'s JAX-RPC runtime then uses such information to know how to serialize and deserialize information to and from the remote Web service. The main structure of the Web service client's `config.xml` file used with our example is illustrated here:

```
<?xml version="1.0" encoding="UTF-8"?>

<configuration xmlns="http://java.sun.com/xml/ns/jax-rpc/ri/config">
  <wsdl
   location="http://localhost:8080/jaxrpc/QueryServer?WSDL"
   packageName="ejava.webservices.rpc">
        ...
  </wsdl>
</configuration>
```

JAX-RPC Message Handlers

Thus far we have examined how JAX-RPC servers and clients are created to handle Web service requests and responses. There may be times, however, when you will want to filter a request or response before it is handed off or received back from a JAX-RPC server or client. You may want to add or filter some information in the message header or body before it is read or sent out over the wire. JAX-RPC provides a set of standard abstractions known as message handlers to accomplish this task. Message handlers are conceptually similar to interceptors in the CORBA world or, as you'll see, filters in the Java Servlet world. This section describes message handlers and how to use them.

Message Handler Implementations

Figure 10.21 depicts the basic architecture of message handlers and how to create them using `javax.xml.rpc.handler` package abstractions. At the root of the hierarchy is the `Handler` interface. The `Handler` interface is implemented by concrete message handlers to provide message-handling functionality. A message handler may intercept and manipulate requests, responses, and faults.

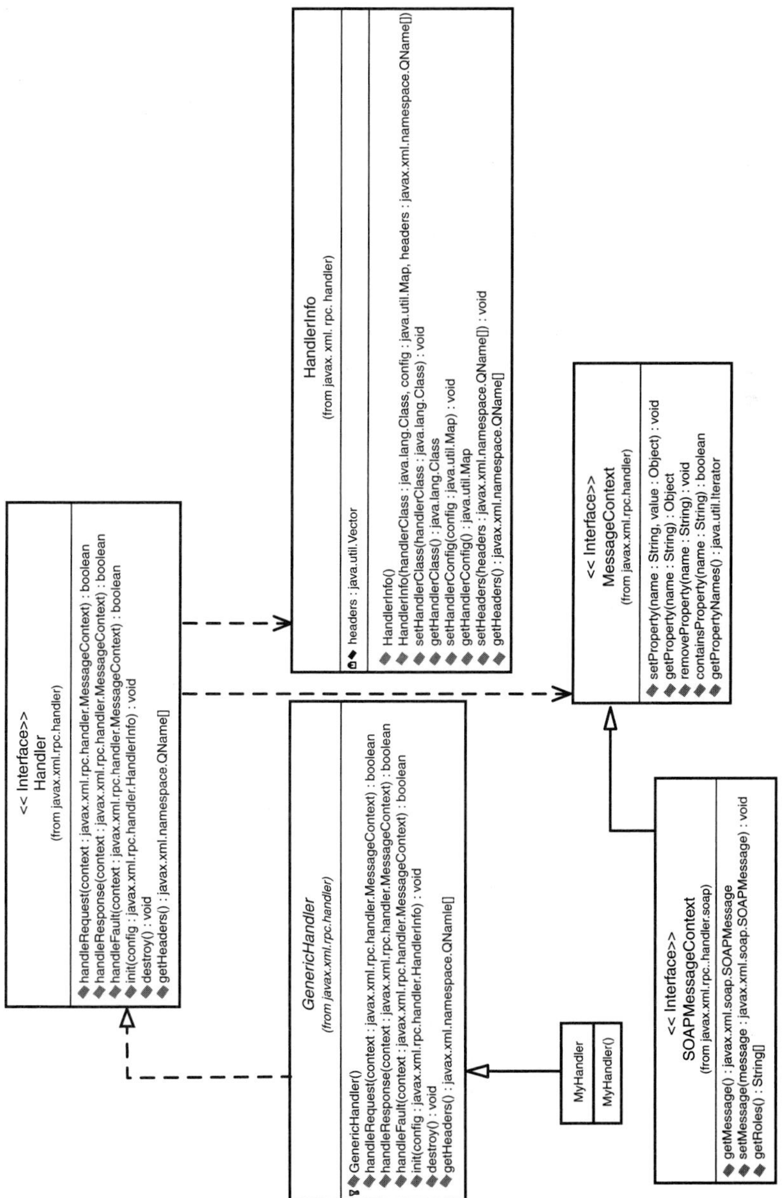

Figure 10.21 JAX-RPC message handlers.

The Handler.init() and Handler.destroy() methods are invoked by the JAX-RPC runtime when a particular Handler instance is created or destroyed. These callbacks enable the Handler to initialize and clean up resources as necessary. Note, however, that handler instances are assumed to be stateless and thus not bound to a particular client session. The Handler.init() method is initialized with HandlerInfo data generated by the JAX-RPC runtime. HandlerInfo can be used to get and set the handler Class object, a Map of handler configuration name/value pairs, and the header XML names processed by the Handler. This QName array of header names that may be processed by a Handler can also be retrieved from Handler.getHeaders().

The handleRequest(), handleResponse(), and handleFault() methods are called by the JAX-RPC runtime when a request, response, or message fault is received and intercepted by this handler. The Handler implementation receives a MessageContext object containing the view that the handler has into the runtime and message intercepted. A handler implementation returns true from these methods to indicate that processing of any additional handler interceptions should continue. If the handler returns false, this flags the JAX-RPC runtime to process messages in the following manner depending on the handle*XXX*() method invoked:

- handleRequest(): Additional handleRequest() interceptions are not performed. The request is not delivered to the target service endpoint. The runtime begins invoking the handleResponse() methods in reverse order from which handleRequest() methods were invoked at that point.
- handleResponse(): Additional handleResponse() interceptions are not performed.
- handleFault(): Additional handleFault() interceptions are not performed.

A MessageContext object is what the JAX-RPC runtime passes to the handler implementation of the handle*XXX*() methods. The base MessageContext interface simply has a set of name/value pairs of properties about a particular message that was intercepted. Such properties can be gotten, set, and removed, and their existence can be determined.

The sub-interface javax.xml.rpc.soap.SOAPMessageContext provides a means for accessing SOAP messages when SOAP is the underlying message format and paradigm employed (that is, most of the time). A SOAPMessage may be gotten from the context or set into the context. The SOAPMessage abstraction is simply the SAAJ representation of a SOAP message as described earlier in this chapter. Additionally, the SOAPMessageContext allows you to obtain an array of String-based URIs that represent those SOAP actor roles that are associated with a particular sequence of handler interceptions.

Implementing a Handler is rather straightforward. Generally, you will want to extend the GenericHandler helper class that provides a default implementation for the Handler interface. As such, you can focus on implementing the particular Handler callback methods of interest to your specific Handler.

In our JAX-RPC example associated with this chapter, we use the `SecurityHandler` class as a base class for implementing a Web service message handler. The base `SecurityHandler` class simply extends the JAX-RPC `GenericHandler` class and provides a base minimal implementation for initialization of our handler example. Specifically, awareness of a special application-specific SOAP security header element is defined within the `SecurityHandler` example class as shown here:

```
package ejava.webservices.rpc;
   ...

public class SecurityHandler extends GenericHandler{

  protected QName securityHeader = new QName("","");

  public static final String USERNAME = "username";
  public static final String PASSWORD = "password";
  public static final String NAMESPACE = "headerNamespace";
  public static final String NAME = "headerName";
  public static final String PREFIX = "headerPrefix";

  public void init(HandlerInfo config){
    // Read the security header name
    System.out.println("  -- SECURITY HANDLER INIT --");
    Map configMap = config.getHandlerConfig();
    securityHeader = new QName(
                           (String) configMap.get(NAMESPACE),
                           (String) configMap.get(NAME));
  }

  public QName[] getHeaders(){
    // Return the header names
    QName[] headers = {securityHeader};
    return headers;
  }

   public void printSOAPInfo (SOAPElement element) {
         // Helper method to print out SOAP element info
     ...
  }
}
```

On the Web service client side, we define the `LoginHandler` class to extend the base `SecurityHandler` class. The `LoginHandler` also defines a `handleRequest()` method that constructs a SOAP header with a username and password inserted into the header element as shown here:

```
package ejava.webservices.rpc;
 ...
public class LoginHandler extends SecurityHandler {

  public LoginHandler(){}

  public void init(HandlerInfo config){
    // Read parent security header name
    super.init(config);
  }

  public boolean handleRequest(MessageContext ctx){
    // Handle the request by appending the username/password
    //    into the SOAP header as read from preferences
    boolean status = false;
    try{
      System.out.println("  -- HANDLE REQUEST ON CLIENT --");

      // Get client username and password from JVM properties
      String username = System.getProperty("USERNAME", "");
      String password = System.getProperty("PASSWORD", "");


      // Get SOAP Message Context and Envelope
      SOAPMessageContext soapCtx = (SOAPMessageContext) ctx;
      SOAPMessage message = soapCtx.getMessage();
      SOAPPart part = message.getSOAPPart();
      SOAPEnvelope envelope = part.getEnvelope();

      // Get/add SOAP header
      SOAPHeader header = envelope.getHeader();
      if(header == null){
        header = envelope.addHeader();
      }

      // Add SOAP header element security info
      SOAPElement securityElement
        = header.addChildElement(NAME, PREFIX, NAMESPACE);
      securityElement.addChildElement(USERNAME).addTextNode(username);
      securityElement.addChildElement(PASSWORD).addTextNode(password);

      status = true;
    }
    catch(Exception e){
       System.out.println("LoginHandler error: "
                          + e.getMessage());
    }
```

```
    return status;
  }
}
```

The username and password for the `QueryClient` are read in from JVM system properties. In our example, the ANT build process will generate a `runClient` script that passes in a username and password similar to the following:

```
java  -DUSERNAME=sysop -DPASSWORD=btgllyra
➥ ejava.webservices.rpc.QueryClient
```

The `runClient.sh.tmpl` (for Unix) or `runClient.bat.tmpl` (for Windows) script templates beneath the `examples\config\execscripts\ejava\webservices\rpc` directory can be modified to experiment with use of a different username or password to demonstrate an invalid login attempt.

On the Web service server side, we define the `AdminHandler` class that extends our base `SecurityHandler` and checks to see whether the username and password passed from the client are valid. If the username and password read from the SOAP header are valid, the `handleRequest()` method returns `true` and allows processing to continue. Otherwise, the `handleRequest()` method returns `false` and all further Web service client requests are denied. The `AdminHandler` reads the valid username and password, against which the client given username and password are tested, from the `HandlerInfo` configuration map passed into the handler's `init()` method by the JAX-RPC runtime. You'll see how such configuration information is conveyed to the JAX-RPC runtime in the next section. The `AdminHandler` structure is illustrated here:

```
package ejava.webservices.rpc;
  ...
public class AdminHandler extends SecurityHandler {

  protected String username = "";
  protected String password = "";

  public AdminHandler(){}

  public void init(HandlerInfo config){
    // Read parent security header and the admin username
    //   and password from the runtime configuration
    super.init(config);
    java.util.Map configMap = config.getHandlerConfig();
    username = (String) configMap.get(USERNAME);
    password = (String) configMap.get(PASSWORD);
  }

  public boolean handleRequest(MessageContext ctx){
    // Handle the request by checking the username/password
    boolean status = false;
```

```
String givenUsername = "";
String givenPassword = "";
try{
  System.out.println("  -- HANDLE REQUEST ON SERVER --");

  // Get SOAP Message Context and Envelope
  SOAPMessageContext soapCtx = (SOAPMessageContext) ctx;
  SOAPMessage message = soapCtx.getMessage();
  SOAPPart part = message.getSOAPPart();
  SOAPEnvelope envelope = part.getEnvelope();

  // Get SOAP header
  SOAPHeader header = envelope.getHeader();

  // Print what is received as part of the header
  //    (look in Apache's catalina.log file)
  super.printSOAPInfo(header);

  // Get SOAP Header security info
  SOAPHeaderElement theHeader
    = (SOAPHeaderElement) header.getChildElements().next();
  Name securityHeaderName
    = SOAPFactory.newInstance().createName(NAME, PREFIX, NAMESPACE);
  Name usernameName
    = SOAPFactory.newInstance().createName(USERNAME);
  givenUsername
    = (String)((SOAPElement)
    theHeader.getChildElements(usernameName).next()).getValue();
  Name passwordName
    = SOAPFactory.newInstance().createName(PASSWORD);
  givenPassword
    = (String)((SOAPElement)
      theHeader.getChildElements(passwordName).next()).getValue();

 // Compare the username/password given by the client
 //   to the admin username/password read by the init() method
 if(givenUsername.equals(username) &&
      givenPassword.equals(password)){
    status = true;
  }
  else{
    status = false;
  }
}
catch(Exception e){
 e.printStackTrace();
}
```

```
        return status;
    }
}
```

Message Handler Chains and Registration

As implied in our discussion thus far, there may exist more than one `Handler` that gets invoked upon interception of a message. Such an ordered list of `Handler` objects is contained within a `HandlerChain` as shown in Figure 10.22. JAX-RPC runtimes thus group `Handler` objects into a `HandlerChain`. One `HandlerChain` is established per service endpoint port. The `handleXXX()` methods are actually called on the `HandlerChain`, which then delegates the calls to the `Handler` objects. As a default, the order in which handlers are invoked is in the order in which they were registered with the `HandlerChain`. However, a JAX-RPC runtime may provide additional control over how the handlers are invoked within a chain.

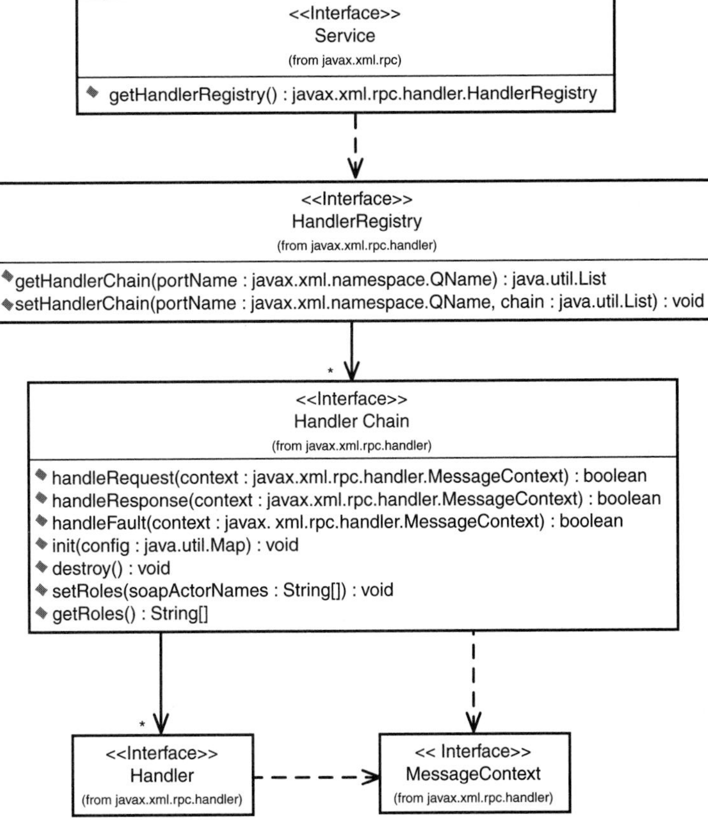

Figure 10.22 JAX-RPC message handler chains and registry.

The life cycle of a `HandlerChain` is rather straightforward. When a `HandlerChain` is created, the JAX-RPC runtime will call its `init()` method passing in a `Map` of configuration name/value pairs. The `HandlerChain.destroy()` method is invoked by the runtime when the chain is retired from memory. The `HandlerChain.setRoles()` method is invoked by the runtime to associate a set of SOAP actor roles for the handler chain. Such information indicates those roles adopted by the handler chain when processing messages. The `getRoles()` method can be invoked to obtain a handle to these roles.

`HandlerChain` objects are managed by a `HandlerRegistry`. Because `HandlerChain` objects are associated with a service endpoint port, the registration and lookup of `HandlerChain` objects is relative to an XML port `QName`. The `List` object returned from the `getHandlerChain()` and used by the `setHandlerChain()` methods is a list of `HandlerInfo` objects that describe meta-data about each `Handler` inside the `HandlerChain` object. Although handles to `HandlerRegistry` objects may be obtained by some vendor-specific or J2EE container-specific means, the `Service` object may also be used to obtain a handle to such a `HandlerRegistry` object.

As an example, our `QueryClient` DII example induces the invocation of an `addHandlerChain()` method that adds header information for the `LoginHandler` to the local JAX-RPC runtime's handler registry handler chain as illustrated here:

```
public void addHandlerChain(Service service){
    // Get handler chain
    QName port = new QName(prefs.get("PORT_LOCALNAME_DII", ""));
    javax.xml.rpc.handler.HandlerRegistry handlerRegistry
       = service.getHandlerRegistry();
    java.util.List handlerChain
       = handlerRegistry.getHandlerChain(port);

    // Create handler header info
    java.util.HashMap map = new java.util.HashMap();
    map.put("headerNamespace",
             "http://ws.beeshirts.com/wsdl/QueryService");
    map.put("headerName","Security");
    map.put("headerPrefix","beeshirts");
    javax.xml.rpc.handler.HandlerInfo handlerInfo =
    new javax.xml.rpc.handler.HandlerInfo(LoginHandler.class,map,null);

    // Add handler header info to the handler chain
    handlerChain.add(handlerInfo);
}
```

Handlers may also be associated with a JAX-RPC runtime using configuration files. The actual registration of handlers by the JAX-RPC runtime using configuration files may vary among JAX-RPC runtime implementations. As you'll see in Chapter 22 and Chapter 30, J2EE containers with JAX-RPC runtimes enforce a standard way to define JAX-RPC handlers inside of J2EE deployment descriptors.

In this chapter's example use of the JAX-RPC reference implementation, the server-side registration of the `AdminHandler` is accomplished by configuring the `jaxrpc-ri.xml` file properly. Specifically, each handler class name to be utilized must be associated with the Web service endpoint. Additionally, any property values to be read into the handler must also be defined. Thus, in our `AdminHandler` example, the valid username and password must be defined as handler properties in the `jaxrpc-ri.xml` file as illustrated here:

```
<?xml version="1.0" encoding="UTF-8"?>

<webServices...>
    <endpoint
        name="QueryService"
        interface="ejava.webservices.rpc.QueryServer"
        implementation="ejava.webservices.rpc.QueryServerImpl">
       <handlerChains>
         <chain runAt="server" >
            <handler className="ejava.webservices.rpc.AdminHandler">
               <property name="headerNamespace"
                    value="http://ws.beeshirts.com/wsdl/QueryService"/>
               <property name="headerName" value="Security"/>
               <property name="headerPrefix" value="beeshirts"/>
               <property name="username" value="sysop"/>
               <property name="password" value="btgllyra"/>
            </handler>
         </chain>
      </handlerChains>
   </endpoint>
       ...
</webServices>
```

On the client side, our client process is associated with the `config.xml` file when using the JAX-RPC reference implementation. The `LoginHandler` class and its properties are similarly defined on the client side inside the `config.xml` file as illustrated here:

```
<?xml version="1.0" encoding="UTF-8"?>

<configuration xmlns="http://java.sun.com/xml/ns/jax-rpc/ri/config">
  <wsdl
   location="http://localhost:8080/jaxrpc/QueryServer?WSDL"
   packageName="ejava.webservices.rpc">
   <handlerChains>
         <chain runAt="client">
         <handler className="ejava.webservices.rpc.LoginHandler">
               <property name="headerNamespace"
                    value="http://ws.beeshirts.com/wsdl/QueryService"/>
               <property name="headerName" value="Security"/>
```

```
                <property name="headerPrefix" value="beeshirts"/>
            </handler>
        </chain>
    </handlerChains>
  </wsdl>
</configuration>
```

Conclusions

Throughout this chapter we have examined various WS-I Basic Profile–related standards required by the J2EE specification and encapsulated by J2EE APIs. The SOAP with Attachments API for Java (SAAJ) provides a means for encapsulating Simple Object Access Protocol (SOAP) messages and their attachments. Although SAAJ provides a basic API for SOAP and is simple to use for SOAP clients, we have also seen how the use of SAAJ alone offers little to be desired when creating SOAP servers. Nevertheless, the enterprise developer with an understanding of SAAJ has at his disposal another tool to add to his bag of tricks for easily creating SOAP clients and for traversing raw SOAP messages. We then saw how WSDL documents are defined and used to describe the interfaces of a Web service in a language- and platform-independent fashion. JAX-RPC was subsequently described as the de facto means within Java for creating Web service clients and servers. Although the JAX-RPC runtime can involve vendor-specific configuration, as you'll see in future chapters, such configuration can be eased when creating Web service clients and servers inside of J2EE container environments.

IV

Common Enterprise Services

11

Naming Services with JNDI

A NAMING SERVICE IS THE PRINCIPAL mechanism used in distributed and nondistributed systems for referring to objects from within your applications via a name identifying that object. The term *name* used here typically means a name that is human readable or at least easily converted into a human-readable `String` format. A file system uses filenames when doling out references associated with file media to programs requesting access to those files. Similarly, CORBA clients can use object names to obtain handles to CORBA objects, which reference objects that may be sitting in some remote system process. These name-to-object associations are referred to as *name bindings*. A name binding is always defined relative to a naming context. Here, a naming context encapsulates a domain of names in which each name binding in that naming context is unique.

This chapter describes the basic concepts and programmatic interfaces available for accessing naming services in Java-based enterprise systems. The distributed computing paradigms described in Part III, "Enterprise Communications Enabling," all use a naming service to either explicitly or implicitly bind object references to names and resolve names to objects. This chapter explores naming services in more detail from a general perspective, as well as specific and common implementations of naming services. The Java Naming and Directory Interface (JNDI) component of the J2SE and J2EE is described and exemplified as the primary means for hooking into naming systems from enterprise Java applications.

In this chapter, you will learn:

- Naming service–related concepts such as compound and composite names, name bindings, naming contexts, and the common roles of a name service.
- The architecture, API components, and use of Java's framework for commonly accessing various naming services via the Java Naming and Directory Interface.
- Why a file system is a naming service and how to use JNDI to access your file system.
- The architecture of a CORBA Naming Service (CosNaming) and the access of a CosNaming Service via JNDI.

- How to access the RMI Registry via JNDI.
- How to use JNDI with RMI/IIOP.
- How to use JNDI to access the Microsoft Windows Registry.

Naming Services in a Nutshell

Naming services provide a way for you to write code that refers to objects in a system using human-readable names. Names very often have a string form enabling you to write code that is more readable, as well as providing you with a simple way to obtain an initial handle to an object. Handles, names, and the context in which names are scoped are all fundamental concepts relevant to an understanding of naming systems. Before we explore the different types of naming systems and a standard way to interface with such systems, we'll first explore the general concepts involved in naming systems in this section. When you're armed with this knowledge, understanding each naming system will most often simply be a matter of translating service-specific terminology into the terms of our basic naming service concepts. Such conceptual framework will also aid in understanding the standard naming service interfaces provided by the Java Naming and Directory Interface service infrastructure.

Handles

An object in a system corresponds to an instance in memory or some range of addresses relating to some discrete collection of functions or data. "Handles" to such objects are often referred to as *references* or *pointers*. Such handles can be associated with objects residing in a process local to your current execution environment or with distributed objects on an entirely different machine. However, these handles are often not human readable, frequently are numeric by nature, perhaps have some embedded communications protocol-specific information, sometimes are platform-dependent, and usually are dependent on the current execution environment. That is, a handle to an object instance `hallwayPrinter` of some class `NetworkPrinter` may have some 32-bit reference value at time t_1 on machine A and an entirely different value at time t_2 on some machine B.

Names

Object handles referring to some logical entity can take on different values over time and across different process spaces but still refer to the same logical entity from your program's perspective. Variable or object instance names in traditional nondistributed programs are one way to refer to the same logical entity even though the underlying object reference may perhaps vary in value over time and in different execution scenarios of the code. Variable and object instance names are meaningful only to the compiled code in your current execution environment, however. For example, given the object instance name `hallwayPrinter` from

```
NetworkPrinter hallwayPrinter = new NetworkPrinter();
```

the `hallwayPrinter` name is meaningful only to your current execution environment's compiled program and is completely meaningless to a process running somewhere else on the network. Given the need to access such an object from distributed processes, it would be nice to simply refer to this object as a "hallwayPrinter" in code. That is precisely what naming services allow you to do.

A name is simply a logical and generally human-readable value for referring to an object in both distributed and nondistributed systems. Here are some examples of what a name can be:

- A filename string referring to a file object reference.
- An Internet host-name string referring to a machine on the Internet.
- An object service name referring to a CORBA server object on a remote machine.

Each name is expressed in a syntax understandable by the naming system for which it is relevant (for example, the file system, the Internet, a CORBA Naming Service). Each naming system has its own naming convention syntax for which valid names are expressed. Thus, for example, a Windows file-naming system requires absolute filenames to be expressed in terms of a root drive and semicolon with directory names separated by backslashes (\) and ending with a filename and extension (for example, `C:\MyDir\myFile.txt`). Each name-to-object association is typically referred to as a name binding.

Naming Contexts and Systems

Names always have some meaning in a specific context. For example, the name "Leesburg" designates a U.S. city in the states of Virginia, New Jersey, Florida, Georgia, Alabama, Indiana, and Ohio. The fully qualified name of "Leesburg, Virginia, USA" pinpoints the name "Leesburg" to the context of "Virginia, USA."

The same need for referring to names within some context also applies to computer systems. Thus, as illustrated in Figure 11.1, the name `index.html` on your computer hosting a Web server refers to a specific file on your filesystem residing in the directory `C:\public_html`. In addition, this same filename in your Web server's directory `C:\public_html\sales` refers to an entirely different file object. The name `index.html` has to be put in context to determine what specific file object is being referenced. Any files that are to be uniquely referenced relative to your local file system's root context have names such as `C:\public_html\index.html` and `C:\public_html\sales\index.html`. Such filename-to-file-object mapping is provided by your machine's file-naming system.

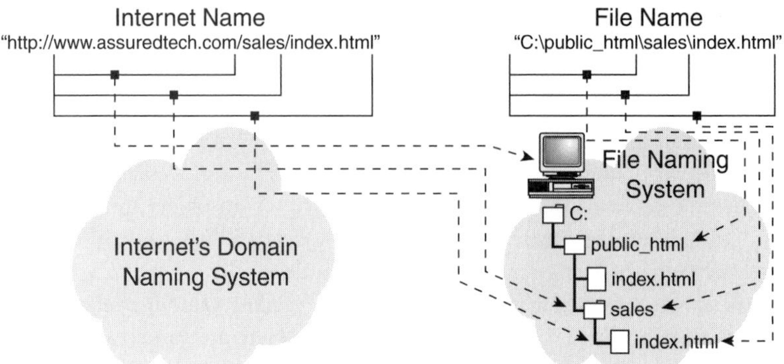

Figure 11.1 Naming systems.

Other computers wanting to read such HTML files served up by your Web server via the Internet need an entirely new naming system and a different context. For example, suppose your company has reserved the name `assuredtech.com` as your corporate domain name, and you establish a machine within your corporate domain named www to be your Web server. Let us further assume that you've configured your Web server such that the root context for all incoming HTTP requests is your machine's `C:\public_html` directory. Remote systems connected to the Internet use the Internet's domain name system to first retrieve access to your machine's Web server with the first part of a name like `www.assuredtech.com`. Such requests are directed to the root context for your Web server (that is, `C:\public_html` from your local file system's point of view). Thus, a request for a page named `http://www.assuredtech.com/sales/index.html` will be used by the domain name system and your Web server to retrieve the appropriate file object relative to your Web server's root context. Your Web server's root context is actually a subcontext of the Internet domain name system's root context.

Each context thus holds a set of name-to-object bindings in which the object may be an actual system resource (for example, file object) or perhaps another context (that is, a subcontext). Each context will have its own standard for naming the objects and subcontexts to which it binds names. A naming system serves to provide a standard for managing a set of contexts with the same naming convention and with similar means for binding names to objects and resolving objects to names.

There are many systems, such as the Domain Name System (DNS) and the Lightweight Directory Access Protocol (LDAP), that provide the name binding and resolving functionality of naming services. We will defer discussion of such services until the next chapter, where they're covered in the context of directory services. As you'll see, such services can go beyond providing pure naming-service functionality and provide support for more sophisticated retrieval of object handles via more complex lookups using characteristics and properties of such objects. In this chapter, we stick with the pure OMG approach for classifying naming services as those services providing pure name-to-object associations, much like a telephone White Pages. Services such as DNS, LDAP, NIS, and NDS may indeed provide such services, but their sophisticated services for retrieval and advertisement by object characteristics render them more like a telephone Yellow Pages service. The OMG has distinguished between these two service types via specification of a CORBA Naming Service and CORBA Trading Service.

JNDI Naming Services

The Java Naming and Directory Interface (JNDI) provides a standard Java interface-to-naming system that can be used with various types of underlying naming systems. JNDI can also be used to name and reference objects that lie outside of a particular naming system. Furthermore, JNDI also provides interfaces for encapsulating and handling events that can be generated from a naming service. This section first describes the architecture of JNDI and then follows that discussion with a description of the interfaces used to name objects and resolve object references from names in a naming system. The means for referencing objects outside of the naming system and for handling naming-system events are also described. Finally, we describe a generic sample program that can be used with various actual underlying naming services.

JNDI Architecture

As depicted in Figure 11.2, JNDI is a fundamental component of the J2SE, providing a standard way to interface with many naming services and directory services. JNDI provides a Java API for commonly interfacing with any naming or directory service for which there exists an adapter to map JNDI API calls to the specific calls provided by the particular naming or directory service provider. After a few simple initialization parameters are set that tell the JNDI API to which service to delegate calls, all calls to the JNDI API are properly delegated to the particular service via the adapter. This adapter is referred to as a *Service Provider Interface (SPI)*. SPIs are provided by Sun Microsystems for some of the more popular services, by the vendors of those services wanting to provide their users a JNDI interface, or by third parties that have implemented an SPI.

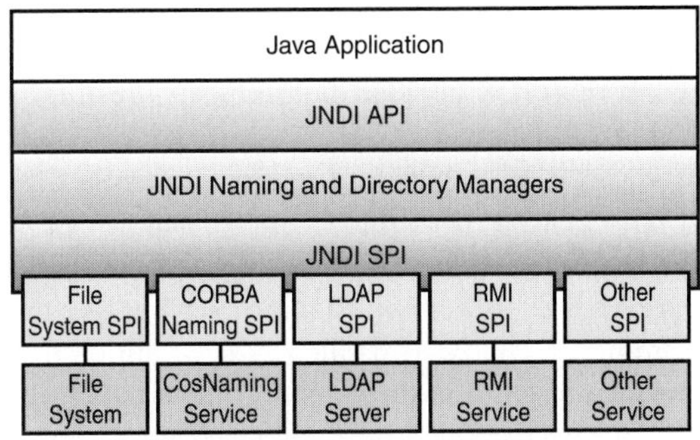

Figure 11.2 A JNDI architectural overview.

The JNDI class libraries are included as a core component of the J2SE. As of the writing of this book, the latest version of JNDI available is version 1.2 associated with the J2SE v1.4. You will also need an SPI for the naming system used in your Java application. The J2SE v1.4 comes equipped with SPIs for RMI, CORBA naming, LDAP, and DNS out of the box. The Java Web site also offers a collection of SPIs for some of the more popular naming systems at `http://java.sun.com/products/jndi/serviceproviders.html`. Vendor-specific SPI implementations will also typically be shipped with the vendor's product and may even include the specific JNDI class library version for which it has been certified for use. Of course, the availability of the underlying naming service is specific to each type of naming system. The file-naming system, for example, is a given for most environments, but a naming service for CORBA will typically be purchased off the shelf or packaged as part of an overall vendor-specific product offering.

The JNDI class libraries are partitioned into the following packages:

- `javax.naming`: Contains all the core JNDI API classes and interfaces used by Java applications needing access to various naming services.
- `javax.naming.directory`: Contains the JNDI API classes for performing more sophisticated directory-service functionality extending the basic naming-service functionality.
- `javax.naming.event`: Contains the JNDI API classes and interfaces for providing event notification services for naming and directory systems.
- `javax.naming.ldap`: Contains the JNDI API classes and interfaces for specific support of the more advanced management features of the LDAPv3 standard when using the LDAP SPI.
- `javax.naming.spi`: Contains the JNDI SPI classes and interfaces for implementers of SPIs to map standard JNDI API calls to a particular naming or directory service.

This chapter on naming services and the next chapter on directory services make use of the JNDI APIs for naming services and directory services. The JNDI SPI classes and interfaces are transparent to the API programmer and are of specific interest to those programmers creating SPIs for specific naming or directory services. Thus, the JNDI SPI package is not covered in this book because the needs for the enterprise applications programmer are of primary concern.

The goal of describing the JNDI APIs for naming services in this chapter is met by first describing JNDI with general API usage examples that can be flexibly configured to work with different JNDI SPIs. We then use this general JNDI API sample framework in the specialized context of a few of the more significant types of naming services. Specifically, the file-naming system, RMI naming system, and CORBA naming system are all described in this chapter with illustrations and use of the JNDI APIs where appropriate. An auxiliary means for interfacing with each associated naming system is also mentioned. Finally, a means by which Windows applications name and look up objects is covered in more detail.

Naming Objects

Before a naming service can be utilized, JNDI clients need to obtain handles to an initial JNDI context. Names can then be bound to objects, and objects can be looked up relative to such a context using standard JNDI interfaces. Names have a syntax that can be described using regular Java `String` objects or using some of the interfaces provided by JNDI to encapsulate names. Various other JNDI operations such as listing the contents of a particular naming context can also be performed using JNDI. This subsection describes JNDI contexts, name binding and lookup, name formatting and encapsulation, and context listing using JNDI.

JNDI Contexts

The JNDI client API user will first be required to create a reference to an initial context of the naming service of interest. When this happens, the client establishes a connection with the service given a set of properties describing the specific naming or directory service provider library to use, the URL of the naming or directory service process, and optionally a username and user credentials. Other properties may also be set whose names are defined as static public attributes in the `javax.naming.Context` interface, as shown in Figure 11.3. A `javax.naming.InitialContext` class implementing the `Context` interface can be used to create an actual handle to a particular naming service. The constructor for `InitialContext` can take a `HashTable` argument, which can be populated with name-value pairs that will be used during initialization of the context. The valid key names are defined as `static public` members of the `Context` interface. These valid `static public` properties are listed here in Table 11.1.

Table 11.1 **Context Properties**

Context Property	Description
`INITIAL_CONTEXT_FACTORY`	Fully qualified package and classname of class used to create a JNDI context.
`PROVIDER_URL`	URL specifying the protocol, host, and port on which the naming or directory service is running, that is, *`<protocol>://<host>:<port>`*.
`SECURITY_PRINCIPAL`	Principal name (for example, username) to be checked by the naming or directory service if authentication for use is required.
`SECURITY_CREDENTIALS`	Principal's credentials (for example, a password) to be checked by the naming or directory service if authentication for use is required.
`OBJECT_FACTORIES`	Colon-separated list of object context factories to use during invocation of naming and directory service operations.
`STATE_FACTORIES`	Colon-separated list of state factories used to get an object's state given a reference to the object.

Table 11.1 **Continued**

`URL_PKG_PREFIXES`	Colon-separated list of package prefixes to use when loading context factories.
`DNS_URL`	URL defining the DNS host to use for looking up addresses associated with JNDI URLs.
`AUTHORITATIVE`	Value of `true` indicates that service access offers the most authoritative source.
`BATCHSIZE`	Specifies batch size of data returned from service protocol.
`REFERRAL`	Value of `follow` causes naming service to follow a service referral, `ignore` causes service referrals to be ignored, and `throw` causes a `javax.naming.ReferralException` to be thrown.
`SECURITY_PROTOCOL`	Specifies security protocol to use (for example, `SSL`).
`SECURITY_AUTHENTICATION`	Specifies security level to use such as `none`, `simple`, or `strong`.
`LANGUAGE`	Colon-separated list of human languages to use for this naming service scheme using tags as defined by RFC 1766.
`APPLET`	Specifies applet to use by initial context for finding additional properties.

The J2EE and JNDI

The JNDI v1.2 API is required to be equipped with the J2SE v1.4. J2EE v1.4 containers assume the use of J2SE v1.4. The means by which J2EE components obtain handles to J2EE-managed `InitialContext` objects is simplified in J2EE environments, as compared with the approach described in this section. J2EE components can then use this `InitialContext` object to access configurable environment information, obtain references to Enterprise JavaBeans, and obtain references to resource connection factories (for example, factories for JDBC, URL, and messaging service connections). Initial context creation and use of the JNDI API in the more generalized sense described within this chapter, however, will still be useful in many different Java enterprise application scenarios.

Out of all properties defined in Table 11.1, the first two properties (`INITIAL_CONTEXT_FACTORY` and `PROVIDER_URL`) will probably be the most commonly used properties in your programs. The `SECURITY_PRINCIPAL` and `SECURITY_CREDENTIALS` properties are also sometimes used. If any property is left undefined, a default value is usually assumed, which is typically fine for many situations encountered. The creation of an `InitialContext` is therefore typically straightforward:

```
Properties properties = new Properties();
properties.setProperty("INITIAL_CONTEXT_FACTORY",
      "com.sun.jndi.fscontext.RefFSContextFactory");
properties.setProperty("PROVIDER_URL", "file:C:\\public_html");
Context  context = new InitialContext(properties);
```

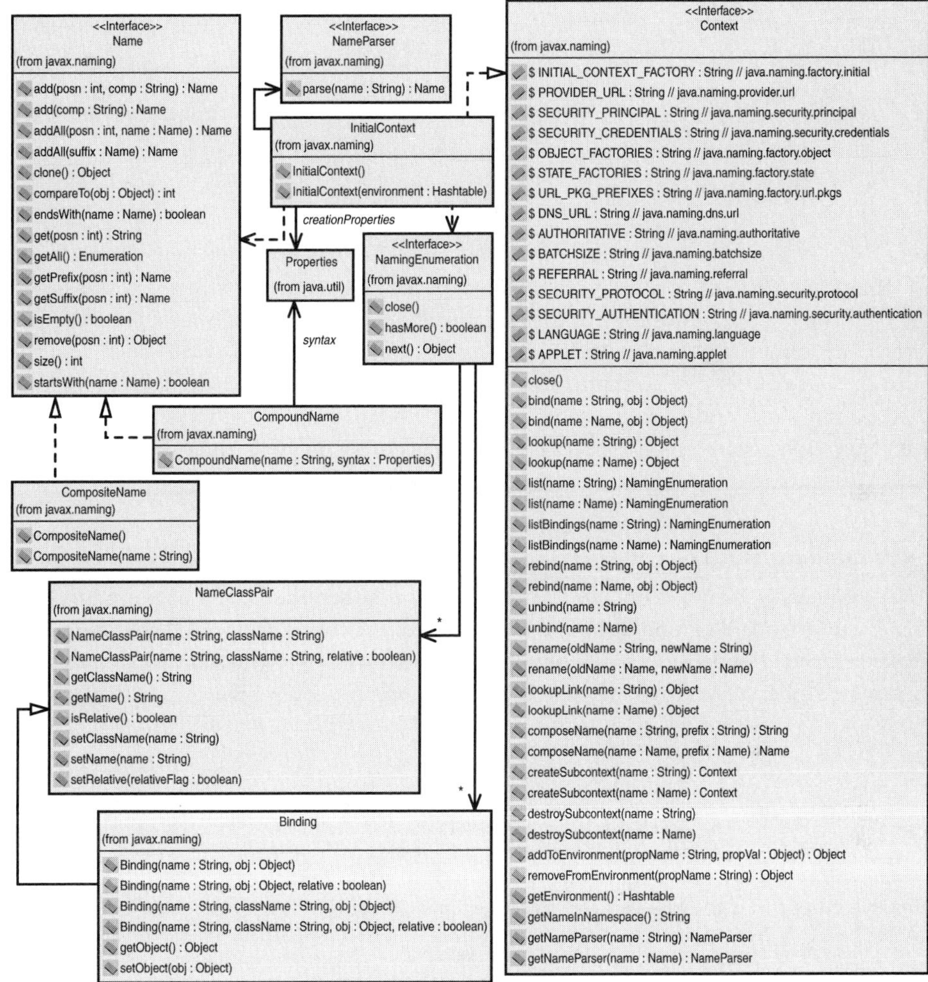

Figure 11.3 Core JNDI naming entities.

In general, it is a good idea to close a context when you are done using it to ensure graceful resource cleanup. When attempting to close a context from within a block that can throw an exception, you may want to surround the context closing within a `finally` block to ensure that it is called:

```
try{
  ...
}
catch(...){
  ...
```

```
}
finally{
  try{
    context.close();
  }
  catch(NamingException ex){
    ...
  }
}
```

JNDI also supports the concept of subcontexts, which can be useful when you want to perform naming operations relative to some already existing context. Subcontexts can be created and removed using the `InitialContext` `createSubcontext()` and `destroySubcontext()` methods, respectively. Subcontexts can be looked up by using the `lookup()` method, with the subcontext name defined according to whatever naming convention is employed to separate components of the name, such as this:

```
Context salesBrochureContext = context.lookup("sales\\brochures");
```

JNDI Binding and Lookup

After a context reference is obtained, an object from the server side can be bound to the context in a standard fashion using the `bind()` and `rebind()` methods. The difference between `bind()` and `rebind()` is simply that `rebind()` overwrites any existing bindings, whereas `bind()` throws an exception. As an example of a rebind call, we have this:

```
String eProducts = "eProducts.html";
Brochure eProductBrochure = new Brochure();
 ...
salesBrochureContext.rebind(eProducts, eProductBrochure);
```

From the client side, a lookup of a particular object yields a reference to that object which is simply cast to the object of the appropriate type:

```
String eProductsName = "sales\\brochures\\eProducts.html";
Brochure brochure = (Brochure) context.lookup(eProductsName);
```

One thing that is important to remember is that the actual class file of the class you are looking up (`Brochure` in this case) needs to be available on the class path on both the server and the client.

JNDI Names

Binding objects to names and looking up objects by a given name can be accomplished using a `String` form of a name, as well as using a class implementing the `javax.naming.Name` interface. A `Name` is composed of a sequence of name components. `Name` objects provide a more type-safe means to manipulate names according to the syntax convention of the particular naming system with which the name is associated. One can add and remove name components as well as accomplish other helper operations on names given a `Name` interface implementation.

One such implementation of the Name interface is the CompoundName class. CompoundName is typically used for names that are confined within a single hierarchical naming system. Thus, the CompoundName can be viewed as a more type-safe way to manipulate regular names in a particular naming system. The syntax convention of the particular naming system for a compound name is established via a set of properties that can be passed into the CompoundName constructor. These are the valid properties that can be passed into the CompoundName constructor:

- jndi.syntax.direction: Parsing direction such as left_to_right, right_to_left, or flat. The default is flat, which means the namespace has no hierarchical structure.
- jndi.syntax.separator: Separator to use between name components (for example, / or .). This is not required if jndi.syntax.direction is flat.
- jndi.syntax.ignorecase: Name components are case-insensitive if true. The default is false, which means that myJNDIName and MyJndiName are treated as different names.
- jndi.syntax.escape: Escape string for overriding separators, quotes, and escape characters (for example, \). If the escape character appears before any special character, that special character is treated as its literal value.
- jndi.syntax.beginquote: Beginning of quote delimiter. Usually either ' or ".
- jndi.syntax.endquote: Ending of quote delimiter. If not specified, it uses the value of jndi.syntax.endquote.
- jndi.syntax.beginquote2: Alternative begin quote.
- jndi.syntax.endquote2: Alternative end quote.
- jndi.syntax.separator.typeval: Name-value separators (for example, = as in mfg=Dodge).
- jndi.syntax.separator.ava: Specifies the separator for attribute-value-assertions (for example, , as in mfg=Dodge,make=Raider,color=red).
- jndi.syntax.trimblanks: Leading and trailing whitespace of a name is trimmed if true. If false or not present, blanks are considered significant.

For example, the following String may be parsed into a compound name using the CompoundName class:

```
String name = "PrinterPublicGroup.Printer19";
CompoundName cName = new CompoundName(name, rmiNamingProperties);
```

The javax.naming.CompositeName class also implements the Name interface. It provides a method of uniformly joining name components that may span one or more naming systems. Each name component of a CompositeName belonging to a particular naming system may itself be parsed into a hierarchical name for that naming system using the CompoundName class. CompositeName objects represented as Strings are parsed from left to right and with name components separated by forward slashes (/). Escape characters (\), single quotes ('), and double quotes (") can also be used in

CompositeNames.

Each separate component of a CompositeName can be added, removed, and accessed individually, with the add(), remove(), and get() methods, respectively. The add() method returns a reference to the updated Name object, making it easy to chain operations. The toString() method returns the full String representation of the name, as described previously. For example, the statement

```
new CompositeName().add("my").add("JNDI").add("name").toString()
```

would return the string my/JNDI/name.

JNDI Context Listings

The contents of a JNDI naming service may also be listed using the list() and listBinding() methods defined by the Context interface and implemented by InitialContext. The list() method requires a name parameter identifying the particular context level at which to search for name service bindings. The list() method returns a javax.naming.NamingEnumeration of javax.naming.NameClassPair objects in which each NameClassPair represents an object name and its classname of an object bound at the desired context level. For example (exception handling excluded):

```
NamingEnumeration namesList = context.list(someContextName);
 ...
while(namesList.hasMore()){
  NameClassPair pair = (NameClassPair) namesList.next();
  String objectName = pair.getName();
  String className = pair.getClassName();
  ...
}
```

In addition to returning the object name and its associated classname, the listBindings() method call on a context returns the actual bound object as well. Given the particular context level to list, the listBindings() method returns a NamingEnumeration of javax.naming.Binding objects that extend NameClassPair objects with the capability to store and retrieve the object bound at the listed context level. For example, to retrieve each name, classname, and bound object from a NamingEnumeration returned from a listBindings() call, we would use this:

```
NamingEnumeration namesList = context.listBindings(someContextName);
 ...
while(namesList.hasMore()){
  Binding binding = (Binding) namesList.next();
  String objectName = binding.getName();
  String className = binding.getClassName();
  MyObject obj = (MyObject) binding.getObject();
  ...
}
```

Referenceable Objects

Aside from binding and looking up object references in a naming system using names via JNDI, JNDI also provides support for binding and looking up references to objects that sit somewhere outside of the naming system. A *referenceable object*, in JNDI lingo, is an object with a reference that can be stored in a JNDI service with information telling JNDI how to associate lookups for that object to the object itself. For an object to be referenceable, it must implement the `Referenceable` interface. The set of classes and interfaces provided by JNDI to support such an infrastructure is shown in Figure 11.4.

Referenceable objects can be useful when an object not belonging to any particular naming system needs to be bound to a naming service for ease of lookup. Referenceable objects are also useful when an object from one naming system needs to be bound to an entirely different naming system. For example, the driver class for a networked printer might be available only on a remote machine. If the name "NetworkPrinter" were added to a JNDI naming service, it would be unable to bind that name to the actual driver itself. But if the driver implemented the `Referenceable` interface, the naming service could bind to the `Reference` object returned by a call to `getReference()`. The `Reference` object would contain the information needed to access the actual driver class.

A referenceable object is first created by implementing the `javax.naming.Referenceable` interface. The `Referenceable` interface has one method called `getReference()`, which returns a handle to a `javax.naming.Reference` object. The `Reference` object corresponds to a reference to an object located somewhere outside of the naming system (that is, not bound to the naming service).

`Reference` objects contain sequences of `javax.naming.RefAddr` objects. `RefAddr` objects represent communications addresses having both a type and a value. The type of address is retrieved from the `RefAddr.getType()` method. The particular address value can be retrieved via the `getContent()` abstract method that is defined specifically by each subclass of the abstract `RefAddr` class. The `javax.naming.BinaryRefAddr` class is a specific type of `RefAddr` encapsulating binary communications addresses expressible in terms of byte arrays such as a serialized object handle or network card address. The `javax.naming.StringRefAddr` subclass of `RefAddr` can be used to encapsulate communications address strings such as URLs and host names.

As a special type of `Reference`, a `javax.naming.LinkRef` provides a reference corresponding to a link that can be followed to a particular object. The content of the `LinkRef` object is a link name that can be resolved to other links. The `Context.lookupLink()` methods can be used to look up an object following any links to get to that object.

Reference objects also contain information useful to JNDI object factories for creating instances of referenced objects such as the referenced object classname, as well as the classname and the URL of the object's specific class factory. Your application-specific referenceable object (such as `MyReferenceableObject` in Figure 11.4) implements the

`Referenceable` interface with an implementation of the `getReference()` method. `getReference()` creates a `Reference` object using such objects as an application-specific object factory (for example, `MyReferenceableObjectFactory` in Figure 11.4), the type of object, and the content of the object. The `MyReferenceableObjectFactory` can then be used by the JNDI service to reconstruct the state of a `MyReferenceableObject` after calling `getContent()` on the `Reference` object.

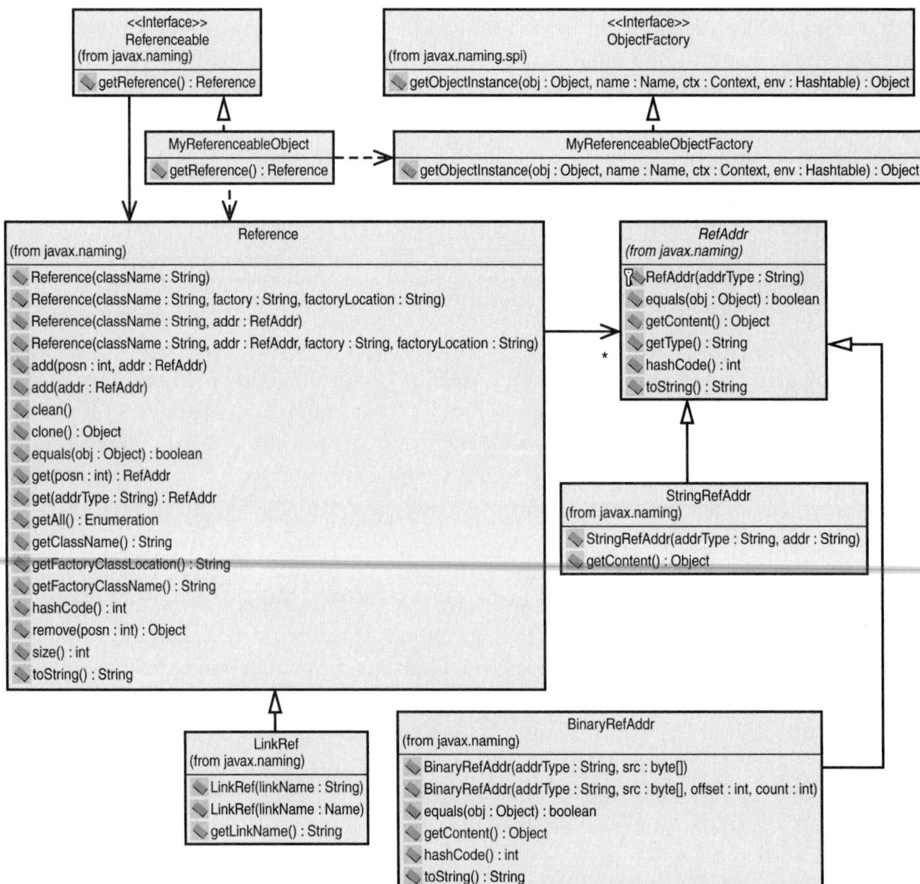

Figure 11.4 Referenceable objects.

For example, some `com.beeshirts.customer.Customer` class that you've defined may implement the `getReference()` method as shown here:

```
public javax.naming.Reference getReference()
      throws NamingException
{
```

```
  String className = "com.beeshirts.customer.Customer";
  String factoryName = "com.beeshirts.customer.CustomerFactory";
  String contents = this.getAsString(); // Get state as a String

  javax.naming.StringRefAddr refAddr
      = new javax.naming.StringRefAddr("Customer", contents);

  return new javax.naming.Reference(className, refAddr,
                                    factoryName, null);
}
```

After binding the Customer referenceable object, the naming service can reconstruct the object during a lookup by consulting the com.beeshirts.customer.CustomerFactory object factory implementing the getObjectInstance() method like this (excluding error handling):

```
public Object getObjectInstance(Object obj, Name objName,
                                Context objContext, Hashtable objEnv)
                                throws Exception
{
  javax.naming.Reference reference = (javax.naming.Reference) obj;
  javax.naming.StringRefAddr refAddr
        = (javax.naming.StringRefAddr) reference.get("Customer");

  String contents = (String) refAddr.getContent();

  Customer customer= new Customer();
  customer.setAsString(contents); // Reconstructs state from a String

  return customer;
}
```

Naming Events

JNDI also provides an infrastructure for encapsulating and handling naming and directory service events. Naming and directory services can generate naming-related events such as the renaming of an object, the removal or addition of an object from or to the naming service, and the state change of an object registered with the naming service. Distributed naming and directory service clients may be interested in such events, and the JNDI infrastructure now provides a standard means for interfacing with such features. Of course, support for such features is completely dependent on the underlying SPI implementation. Figure 11.5 depicts the core entities defined for the event-handling infrastructure for naming services.

The javax.naming.event.NamingEvent class represents an event that can be generated from a naming service when one of its registered objects changes. NamingEvent objects extend the standard java.util.EventObject; they have a type and contain an event source, SPI-specific change information, and a reference to binding information both before and after the event. The source of an event is a context implementing the `javax.naming.event.EventContext` interface. An `EventContext` is simply a type of `Context` that allows for the addition and removal of listeners interested in naming events. A special `javax.naming.event.NamingExceptionEvent` event object can also be generated in the event of a failure during the generation of a normal naming event for notifying naming listeners. When objects of an identified target and scope generate a naming event, any `javax.naming.event.NamingListener` that has registered to receive such an event will be contacted:

```
EventContext eventContext = // Construct an event context
NamespaceChangeListener customerManager = // Construct a listener
eventContext.addNamingListener("AllisonPerrone",
                               EventContext.OBJECT_SCOPE, customerManager);
```

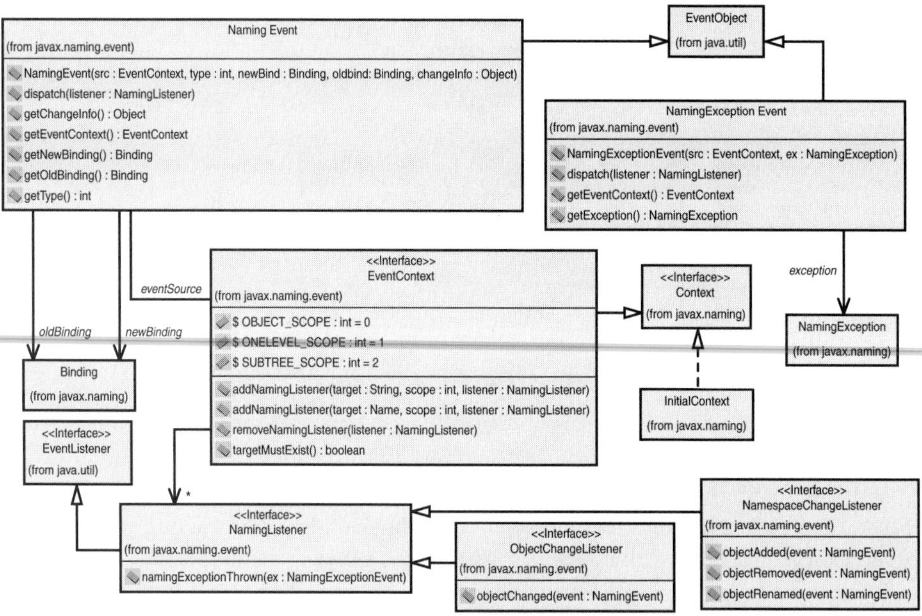

Figure 11.5 JNDI naming service events.

Either the `javax.naming.event.ObjectChangeListener` or the `javax.naming.event.NamespaceChangeListener` sub-interfaces of `NamingListener` typically is implemented to handle generated naming events. The `ObjectChangeListener` interface is implemented to handle events associated with an object's state change (`NamingEvent.OBJECT_CHANGED`), such as attribute addition, deletion, or modification, as well as the replacement of an object in the naming system. The old and new bindings of an object may be examined to determine the specific type of change. The `NamespaceChangeListener` interface is implemented by those objects wanting to handle the addition (`NamingEvent.OBJECT_ADDED`), removal (`NamingEvent.OBJECT_REMOVED`), or renaming (`NamingEvent.OBJECT_RENAMED`) of objects registered with the naming service. As an example of a naming event listener, the following skeleton structure implements methods for handling both object change and namespace change naming events:

```
import javax.naming.event.NamespaceChangeListener;
import javax.naming.event.ObjectChangeListener;
import javax.naming.event.NamingEvent;
import javax.naming.event.NamingExceptionEvent;

public class SampleNamingListener
  implements NamespaceChangeListener, ObjectChangeListener
{
  public void objectAdded(NamingEvent namingEvent)
  {
      // Handle object addition
  }

  public void objectRemoved(NamingEvent namingEvent)
  {
     // Handle object removal
  }

  public void objectRenamed(NamingEvent namingEvent)
  {
    // Handle object renaming
  }

  public void objectChanged(NamingEvent namingEvent)
  {
    // Handle object attribute changing
  }

  public void namingExceptionThrown(NamingExceptionEvent
                                     namingExceptionEvent)
  {
    // Handle naming exception
  }
}
```

JNDI Examples

This section introduces how to use JNDI in your enterprise applications as a generic naming service interface. To highlight the generic nature of JNDI, we develop a set of base examples whose code does not change at all between use, with a few important

SPIs introduced in later sections. In fact, the only things that will differ from one example to another are a set of properties stored in a properties file and the underlying SPI and naming service to use.

> **Note**
>
> The complete set of code examples for all code listed in this chapter is available by following the directions given in Appendix A, "Software Configuration." The examples for this chapter will then be found in the `examples\src\ejava\jndi\naming` directory.

The `SampleLookupExample` class in Listing 11.1 demonstrates how JNDI clients can generically look up distributed object references given a prebound object name. By passing in an object name to the example from the command line, the `main()` method will serve as the main driver to illustrate a lookup. After some initial error checking, the `main()` method uses a set of properties read in from a `jndi.properties` file to construct a `SampleLookupExample` instance. After the construction of a `SampleLookupExample` object, the `lookupBoundObject()` method is called to perform the actual lookup given the object name passed in from the command line.

The `lookupBoundObject()` method first calls `getInitialContext()` to retrieve a handle to an `InitialContext` object constructed using the properties read in during the `SampleLookupExample` constructor call. As you'll see in subsequent sections, these properties will vary per SPI example. The `String` name passed into the `lookupBoundObject()` method call is then used as a parameter to a `Context.lookup()` call, and the associated object reference is returned.

> **Note**
>
> You will be able to experiment with the generic JNDI examples given in Listings 11.1 through 11.3 only when you run these examples with a specific SPI to be described in subsequent sections.

Listing 11.1 **A Generic JNDI Lookup Example (`SampleLookupExample.java`)**

```
package ejava.jndi.naming;

import javax.naming.Context;
import javax.naming.InitialContext;
import javax.naming.NamingException;
import java.util.Hashtable;
import java.util.Properties;
import java.io.FileInputStream;
import java.io.IOException;

/**
 * This example looks up an object for a given name.
 */
public class SampleLookupExample
```

Listing 11.1 **Continued**

```
{
  private Context context;
  private Properties contextProperties = new Properties();

  public SampleLookupExample()
  {
    super();
  }

  /**
   * Constructor
   * Naming Client which is initialized with a jndi.properties file.
   */
  public SampleLookupExample(String propertiesFileName)
    throws IOException
  {
    // Open a file input stream for the associated properties
    // fileName.
    FileInputStream propertiesFileStream =
      new FileInputStream(propertiesFileName);

    // Now load the file input stream into the JNDI environment
    // properties. This of course assumes that the file input stream is
    // in a valid Properties format.
    contextProperties.load(propertiesFileStream);
  }

  public SampleLookupExample(Properties contextProperties)
  {
    this.contextProperties = contextProperties;
  }

  /**
   * Method to create initial context
   */
  public Context getInitialContext()
    throws NamingException
  {

    // Create initial context if it is not already created
    if (context == null) {
      // Read in a set of default parameters.
      context = new InitialContext(contextProperties);
    }
    return context;
```

Listing 11.1 **Continued**

```
  }

  /**
   * Look up the object associated with the name
   * @param name to look up
   * @return object matched with name
   */
  public java.lang.Object lookupBoundObject(String name)
    throws NamingException
  {
    java.lang.Object boundObject = null;

    // Retrieve initial context from our NamingInterface class
    if(context == null){
      getInitialContext();
    }


    // Now look up the bound object with this name
    try {
      boundObject = context.lookup(name);
    } catch (NamingException namingException) {
      System.out.println("Error : " + namingException);
      namingException.printStackTrace();
      return null;
    }
    System.out.println(" Name is : " + name +
"     Bound Object is : "+ boundObject);

    return boundObject;
  }

  /**
   * Returns the context properties
   */
  public Properties getContextProperties()
  {
    return contextProperties;
  }

  /**
   * Main Test Driver:
   *        java ejava.jndi.naming.SampleLookupExample <ObjectNameToLookup>
   * @param args command line argument
```

Listing 11.1 **Continued**

```
   */
  public static void main(String[] args)
    throws Exception
  {
    if (args.length != 1) {
      System.out .println("Run example as: java "
         + "ejava.jndi.naming.SampleLookupExample <ObjectNameToLookup>");
      System.exit(0);
    }
    // Set name of properties file to use in initializing the simple
    // lookup.
    String propertiesFileName = "jndi.Properties";
    // Set name of properties file to use in initializing the
    // simple lookup.
    // Instantiate an instance of this NamingClient
    SampleLookupExample sampleLookupExample = null;
    sampleLookupExample = new SampleLookupExample(propertiesFileName);
    // Demonstrate lookup of a bound object name
    String name = args[0];
    System.out.println("Going to Lookup " + name);
    sampleLookupExample.lookupBoundObject(name);
  }
}
```

The `SampleListAndSearchExample` class of Listing 11.2 extends the `SampleLookupExample` class by demonstrating how one can generically list the names and the bindings of a naming context. The `main()` example driver method also assumes that a name is passed in from the command line as with the `SampleLookupExample`. This target name will be used as the context name whose contents should be listed. The `jndi.properties` file is used to load a set of properties from within a `SampleListAndSearchExample` constructor. The `listNames()` and `listNamesAndBindings()` methods are then called to demonstrate the listing of a context and the listing of a context's bound objects, respectively. By constructing a `CompoundName` using a set of syntax properties read from the properties file, we also demonstrate the `listNames()` and `listNamesAndBindings()` calls that take a `Name` object.

Listing 11.2 **A Generic JNDI List and Search Example (`SampleListAndSearchExample.java`)**

```
package ejava.jndi.naming;

import javax.naming.Context;
import javax.naming.InitialContext;
import javax.naming.NamingException;
```

Listing 11.1 **Continued**

```
import javax.naming.NamingEnumeration;
import javax.naming.CompoundName;
import javax.naming.CompositeName;
import javax.naming.Binding;
import javax.naming.Name;
import javax.naming.InvalidNameException;
import java.util.Properties;
import java.io.FileInputStream;
import java.io.IOException;
import java.util.StringTokenizer;

/**
 * This class lists and searches the given object in a naming or
 * directory service
 */
public class SampleListAndSearchExample extends SampleLookupExample
{

  /**
   * This constructor simply uses the super class constructor
   */
  public SampleListAndSearchExample(String propertiesFile)
   throws IOException
  {
    super(propertiesFile);
  }

  /**
   * List names in a given target
   * @param target to look up
   */
  public void listNames(String target)
  {
    Context context;

    try {
      //get the initial context
      context = super.getInitialContext();

      NamingEnumeration namesList = context.list(target);

      if (namesList == null) {
        System.out.println(target + " contains no names ");
      } else {
        while (namesList.hasMore()) {
```

Listing 11.1 **Continued**

```
          //print the names in the context
          System.out.println(namesList.next());
        }
      }
    } catch (NamingException namingException) {
      System.out.println("Error : " + namingException);
    }
  }

  /**
   * list Names in a given target Name
   * @param target to look up
   */
  public void listNames(Name target)
  {
    Context context;

    try {
      //get the initial context
      context = super.getInitialContext();

      NamingEnumeration namesList = context.list(target);

      if (namesList == null) {
        System.out.println(target + "contains no names ");
      } else {
        while (namesList.hasMore()) {
          //print the names in the context
          System.out.println(namesList.next());
        }
      }
    } catch (NamingException namingException) {
      System.out.println("Error : " + namingException);
    }
  }

  /**
   *List bindings for the given target Name
   * @param target to look up
   */
  public void listNamesAndBindings(Name target)
  {
    Context context;

    try {
```

Listing 11.1 **Continued**

```
      //get the initial context
      context = super.getInitialContext();

      NamingEnumeration namesList = context.listBindings(target);

      if (namesList == null) {
        System.out.println(target + "contains no names ");
      } else {
        while (namesList.hasMore()) {
          Binding binding = (Binding) namesList.next();

          //print the names of classes and objects in the context
          System.out.println("Name is : " + binding.getName()
            + " Binding is : " + binding.getObject()+ " ");
        }
      }
    } catch (NamingException namingException) {
      System.out.println("Error :" + namingException);
    }
  }

  /**
   * list Bindings for the given target
   * @param target to look up
   */
  public void listNamesAndBindings(String target) {
    Context context;

    try {
      // get the initial context
      context = super.getInitialContext();

      NamingEnumeration namesList = context.listBindings(target);

      if (namesList == null) {
        System.out.println(target + " contains empty names ");
      } else {
        while (namesList.hasMore()) {
          Binding binding = (Binding) namesList.next();
          System.out.println("Name is : " + binding.getName()
             + " Binding is : " + binding.getObject() + " ");
        }
      }
    } catch (NamingException namingException) {
      System.out.println("Error :" + namingException);
```

Listing 11.1 **Continued**

```
    }
  }

  /**
   *main method to test the SampleListAndSearchExample class
   */
  public static void main(String[] args) {

    // Ensure that a filename to look up is passed as a parameter.
    if (args.length != 1) {
      System.out.println("Run example as: java "
      + "ejava.jndi.naming.SimpleListAndSearchExample"
      + " <TargetObjectName>");
      System.exit(0);
    }

    // Set name of properties file to use in initializing the lookup.
    String propertiesFileName = "jndi.Properties";
    SampleListAndSearchExample sampleListAndSearchExample = null;

    // Instantiate an instance of this NamingClient
    try {
      sampleListAndSearchExample =
        new SampleListAndSearchExample(propertiesFileName);
    } catch (IOException ioException) {
      System.out.println("Error :" + ioException);
      System.exit(0);
    }


    // e.g., for file system Naming Provider the target bookp
    String target = args[0];

    System.out.println(
      "Listing Names using listNames(String target) method");
    sampleListAndSearchExample.listNames(target);
    System.out.println(
      "Listing Names and Bindings using listNamesAndBindings " +
        " (String target) method");
    sampleListAndSearchExample.listNamesAndBindings(target);

    try {
      String str = target;
      Properties prop
        = sampleListAndSearchExample.getContextProperties();
```

Listing 11.1 **Continued**

```
        // construct a Compound Name using the Compound Name
        // properties in the properties file.
        CompoundName compoundName = new CompoundName(str, prop);

        // Search the Name Repository using the CompoundName
        System.out.println("Listing Names using "
           +"listNames(Name target) method: Here target is CompoundName");
        sampleListAndSearchExample.listNames(compoundName);

        // Search the Name Repository Names and
        //     Binding Object using CompoundName
        System.out.println("Listing Names and Bindings"
           + " using listNamesAndBindings(Name target) method: Here"
           + " target is CompoundName");
        sampleListAndSearchExample.listNamesAndBindings(compoundName);

        // CompositeName is hierarchical name space, the atomic parts
        // of the CompositeName may be CompoundName.
        String strName1 = compoundName.toString();
        CompositeName compositeName = new CompositeName(strName1);

        // Search the Name Repository using the CompoundName
        System.out.println("Listing Names using listNames(Name target)"
           + " method: Here target is CompositeName");
        sampleListAndSearchExample.listNames(compositeName);
        System.out.println("Listing Names and Bindings using"
           + " listNamesAndBindings(Name target) method: Here"
           + " target is CompoundName");

        // Search the Name Repository Names and Binding Object using
        //CompoundName
        sampleListAndSearchExample.listNamesAndBindings(compositeName);
      } catch (InvalidNameException invalidNameException) {
        System.out.println("Error :" + invalidNameException);
        System.exit(0);
      }
   }
 }
```

The `SampleBindingExample` of Listing 11.3 extends the `SampleListAndSearchExample` class and demonstrates how JNDI objects can be bound, renamed, and deleted within a context. The `main()` method uses a set of properties read in from a `jndi.properties` file to construct a `SampleBindingExample` instance. The target object name passed in from the command line is then used to call lookupBoundObject() on the SampleBindingExample's base SampleLookupExample class. After renaming the target name to a new object name via a call to renameAnObject() on the SampleBindingExample object, the object is bound to its original target name with a call to bindNewObject(). At this point the object is bound to both the target name and the newObjectName. A call to deleteAnObject() with the newObjectName then deletes that particular named object instance.

Listing 11.3 **A Generic JNDI Binding Example (SampleBindingExample.java)**

```
package ejava.jndi.naming;

import javax.naming.Context;
import javax.naming.InitialContext;
import javax.naming.NamingException;
import javax.naming.NamingEnumeration;
import javax.naming.CompoundName;
import javax.naming.CompositeName;
import javax.naming.Binding;
import javax.naming.Name;
import java.util.Properties;
import java.io.FileInputStream;
import java.io.IOException;
import java.io.File;

/**
 * This class implements the deletion and renaming of the objects in
 * the context
 *
 */
public class SampleBindingExample extends SampleListAndSearchExample
{

  /**
   * Constructor
   *
* @param propertiesFile
   *
   * @see
   */
  public SampleBindingExample(String propertiesFile)
    throws IOException
  {
    super(propertiesFile);
  }
```

Listing 11.3 **Continued**

```
/**
 * fsContext provider will not delete directory.
 * Some of the providers may not support delete method at all.
 * LADP provider deletes corresponding name and object from directory
 * @param target to delete
 */
public void deleteAnObject(String target)
  throws NamingException
{
  Context context;

  context = super.getInitialContext();
  // unbinds the named object from the given namespace.
  context.unbind(target);

  // This method is called to check that it removed the name.
  super.listNames("");
}

/**
 * This method deletes an object from naming service
 * @param target to delete
 */
public void deleteAnObject(Name target)
  throws NamingException
{
  Context context;

  context = super.getInitialContext();
  // unbinds the named object from the given namespace.
  context.unbind(target);

  // This method is called to check that it removed the name.
  super.listNames("");
}

/**
 * This method renames any target ObjectName
 * @param target to rename
 */
public void renameAnObject(String target, String newName)
  throws NamingException
{
  Context context;
```

Listing 11.3 **Continued**

```
    context = super.getInitialContext();

    context.rename(target, newName);

    // This method is called to check that it removed the name.
    super.listNames("");
  }

  /**
   * This method renames any target ObjectName
   * @param target to rename
   */
  public void renameAnObject(Name target,  Name newName)
    throws NamingException
  {
    Context context;

    context = super.getInitialContext();

    context.rename(target, newName);
  }

  /**
   * Bind a new Object for the existing name
   * @param target to bind
   */
  public void bindNewObject(String target, Object newObject)
    throws NamingException
  {
    Context context;

    context = super.getInitialContext();

    context.rebind(target, newObject);
  }

  /**
   * Bind a new Object for the existing Name
   * @param target to bind
   */
  public void bindNewObject(Name target, Object newObject)
    throws NamingException
  {
    Context context;
```

Listing 11.3 **Continued**

```
    context = super.getInitialContext();

    context.rebind(target, newObject);
  }

  /**
   * Main method to test the SampleBindingExample class
   */
  public static void main(String args[])
  {

    // Ensure that a name to look up is passed as a parameter.
    if (args.length != 1) {
      System.out.println("Run example as: "
          + "java ejava.jndi.naming.SampleBindingExample "
          + "<targetObject>");
      System.exit(0);
    }

    // Set name of properties file to use in initializing the lookup.
    String propertiesFileName = "jndi.Properties";
    String target = args[0];

    try {
      SampleBindingExample simpleBindingExample =
        new SampleBindingExample(propertiesFileName);
      // to test the delete object construct CompoundName like in
      // SimpleListAndSearchExample and
      // call deleteAnObject.
      String newObjectName = "newObject1";
      Object obj = simpleBindingExample.lookupBoundObject(target);

      // Renaming can be done only for the object not the subcontext.
      // file system Service provider does not know how to rename the
      // directory. It knows how to rename file only.
      simpleBindingExample.renameAnObject(target, newObjectName);
      simpleBindingExample.bindNewObject(target, obj);

      // To delete an object always give a complete
      //    Name or Composite Name
      simpleBindingExample.deleteAnObject(newObjectName);
    } catch (IOException ioException) {
      System.out.println("Error opening jndi.properties file :"
          + ioException);
```

Listing 11.3 **Continued**

```
      System.exit(0);
    } catch (NamingException namingException) {
      System.out.println("Error  :" + namingException);
      System.exit(0);
    }
  }
 }
```

Naming Files

The file-naming system is the most basic and common naming system that computer users encounter. In a file-naming system, filenames correspond to the names of the naming service, file-system directories correspond to the contexts that make up names, and the file objects and descriptors correspond to the handles of the system resource of interest. Different file systems will have different naming syntax conventions. Thus, whereas Windows-based file systems use the backslash (\) to separate context-space (that is, directories) and components of a name, UNIX-based systems use the forward slash (/). Similarly, Windows-based systems ignore differences between upper- and lowercase, whereas UNIX-based systems are case-sensitive.

File-System Interfaces

Before JNDI, the most common and obvious way to interact with a file system was to use the classes available in the `java.io` package, as shown in Figure 11.6. The `File` class encapsulates an interface to a file system's files and directory paths. Operations such as file renaming and deleting, as well as directory listing, can be achieved via the `File` class. The `FileInputStream` and `FileOutputStream` classes can be used to create new files, as well as populate such files with data or reading files. The `FileReader` and `FileWriter` classes can also be used to read and write character files.

JNDI File SPI

A file-system SPI exists for use with the JNDI API. Many developers may still elect to use the core Java support for file manipulation via use of the file streaming and reader/writer APIs provided in the `java.io` package. In fact, the JNDI file SPI provided by Sun actually heavily depends on the `java.io.File` class. However, use of a JNDI file-system SPI has its advantages by providing classes and interfaces for making file management more implementation independent across different file-system types (depending on your underlying SPI implementation), as well as providing a standard interface to the file system that can be used even in a composite naming scheme.

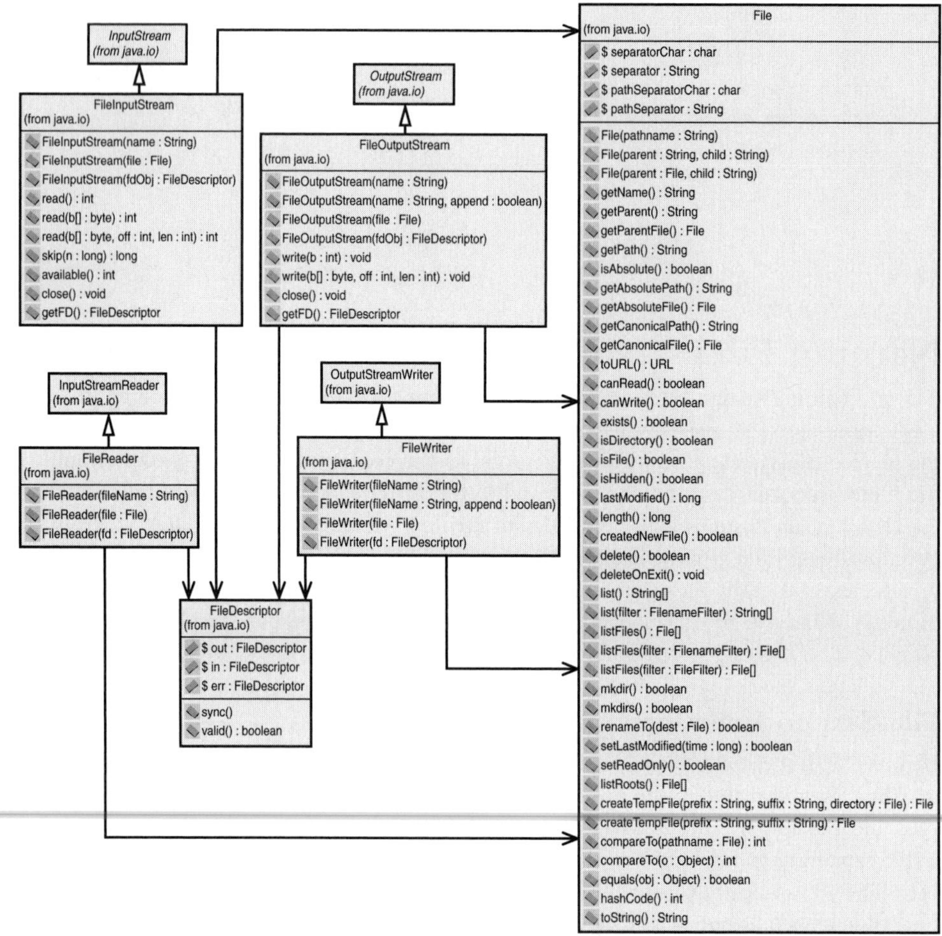

Figure 11.6 Traditional Java file-system interfaces.

> **Note**
>
> A file-system JNDI SPI provided by Sun is available for download from `http://java.sun.com/products/jndi/serviceproviders.html`. Download and extract the SPI to a directory of your choice. After installing the SPI on your local machine, be sure to modify the `fs.context.root.dir` property found in the `build.properties` file to point to this directory location. The `build.properties` file is contained in the `examples\src\ejava\jndi\naming` directory.

Depending on the set of properties passed into the constructor of an `InitialContext` class or on those set via the system properties, a file-system SPI can be configured to function with your particular file system. Because the Sun file SPI uses the `java.io.File` object, it can be used with whatever platform to which your JRE has been ported. The Sun file SPI can be used with a local file system, as well as a networked file system. The Novell corporation also offers a file SPI for the NetWare file system.

> **Note**
>
> By running the `ANT` command, the `build.xml` file associated with this chapter's code will generate a `runfscontext` script under the `examples\src\ejava\jndi\naming` directory to demonstrate use of the file-system JNDI SPI. The `jndifsContext.properties` file can be configured to establish a set of particular file-SPI-specific properties. The `java.naming.provider.url` property of the `jndifsContext.properties` file should be set to the base directory of where the examples are located, for example, `file:/c:/j2eebook`.

The `runfscontext` script copies the file-SPI–specific `jndifsContext.properties` file to the `jndi.properties` filename read by the generic examples in Listings 11.1 through 11.3. After that, the `SampleLookupExample`, `SampleListAndSearchExample`, and `SampleBindingExample` programs are all run to illustrate use of the generic JNDI API with a file system. You will need to change the value of `jndi.naming.provider.url` in the `jndifsContext.properties` file to point to the directory where this book's examples are installed on your system. Feel free to experiment with establishing your own JNDI properties (shown in Figure 11.3 and described in Table 11.1). These are the properties of interest in the `jndifsContext.properties` file:

```
# Sun file system SPI context factory
java.naming.factory.initial=com.sun.jndi.fscontext.RefFSContextFactory

# File system root context used with the example
java.naming.provider.url=file:/c:/Projects/Books/j2ee2nded

# File system naming syntax properties
jndi.syntax.direction=left_to_right
jndi.syntax.separator="\"
```

CORBA Naming

The OMG's CORBA Naming Service (also called Object Naming Service and CosNaming) presents the primary and standard way for mapping between names and objects on a CORBA ORB. The Object Naming Service was proposed by the OMG as a means to provide a standard interface to various underlying naming services. The idea was that the Object Naming Service standard would serve as the language-independent and standard way to wrap existing name servers for connectivity from various clients. As you are now aware, this goal for providing a standard way to interface with naming services is also the goal of JNDI but only in the context of Java clients. Although the JNDI

API has some similarities to the Java mapping of the CORBA Naming Service API, it is not identical. It is conceivable that you could encounter a situation in which your Java client will use JNDI with a CORBA SPI that maps calls to a CORBA name server. The server in turn actually maps CORBA Naming calls to a naming service that could have been directly communicated with from your Java application or at least via another Java SPI. Alas, these multiple layers of interface mapping are the price that must be paid for flexibility and maintainability.

CosNaming IDL

Names in CORBA are sequences of name components. A name with a single component is referred to as a *simple name*, whereas a name with more components is called a *compound name*. Name components are defined by an ID and a kind. The "kind" attribute of a name simply serves to classify names for use by application software. Each ID is unique within a particular naming context. Naming contexts in CORBA contain a list of names that are all unique to that context in which each binding has a binding type indicating whether the name is bound to either a CORBA object or another naming context. Even though a logical name can be bound to a naming context, naming contexts do not need to be associated with logical names. Operations on naming contexts include binding and rebinding names to objects, resolving objects given a name, unbinding objects, creating subcontexts, and listing names associated with the context. The CosNaming module shown in Listing 11.4 defines the CORBA Naming Service IDL interfaces.

Listing 11.4 **The CosNaming IDL**

```
module CosNaming
{
  typedef string Istring;

  struct NameComponent {
    Istring id;
    Istring kind;
  };

  typedef sequence <NameComponent> Name;

  enum BindingType {nobject, ncontext};

  struct Binding {
    Name binding_name;
    BindingType binding_type;
  };

  typedef sequence <Binding> BindingList;
```

Listing 11.4 **Continued**

```
interface BindingIterator;

interface NamingContext {
  enum NotFoundReason { missing_node, not_context, not_object};

  exception NotFound {
    NotFoundReason why;
    Name rest_of_name;
  };
  exception CannotProceed {
    NamingContext cxt;
    Name rest_of_name;
  };
  exception InvalidName{};
  exception AlreadyBound {};
  exception NotEmpty{};

  void bind(in Name n, in Object obj)
    raises(NotFound, CannotProceed, InvalidName, AlreadyBound);
  void rebind(in Name n, in Object obj)
    raises(NotFound, CannotProceed, InvalidName);
  void bind_context(in Name n, in NamingContext nc)
    raises(NotFound, CannotProceed, InvalidName, AlreadyBound);
  void rebind_context(in Name n, in NamingContext nc)
    raises(NotFound, CannotProceed, InvalidName);
  Object resolve (in Name n)
    raises(NotFound, CannotProceed, InvalidName);
  void unbind(in Name n)
    raises(NotFound, CannotProceed, InvalidName);
  NamingContext new_context();
  NamingContext bind_new_context(in Name n)
    raises(NotFound, AlreadyBound, CannotProceed, InvalidName);
  void destroy( )
    raises(NotEmpty);
  void list (in unsigned long how_many,
             out BindingList bl, out BindingIterator bi);
};

interface BindingIterator {
  boolean next_one(out Binding b);
  boolean next_n(in unsigned long how_many, out BindingList bl);
  void destroy();
};
 };
```

Because naming is such a fundamental part of manipulating objects, the CORBA Naming Service specification also provides for the efficient representation of names with a names library pseudo-IDL (PIDL) specification as shown in Listing 11.5. The names library is implemented in the CORBA client's native language. These client-side libraries provide the client with a lightweight means for manipulating names in which the names actually refer to CORBA pseudo-objects. Although these pseudo-object references cannot be passed between CORBA entities, the names library does provide a means for converting between library names and values usable by the CosNaming module's naming context.

Listing 11.5 **A CORBA Names Library PIDL**

```
// PIDL
interface LNameComponent {
  exception NotSet{};
  string get_id() raises(NotSet);
  void set_id(in string i);
  string get_kind() raises(NotSet);
  void set_kind(in string k);
  void destroy();
};

// PIDL
interface LName {
  exception NoComponent{};
  exception OverFlow{};
  exception InvalidName{};
  LName insert_component(in unsigned long i, in LNameComponent n)
    raises(NoComponent, OverFlow);
  LNameComponent get_component(in unsigned long i)
    raises(NoComponent);
  LNameComponent delete_component(in unsigned long i)
    raises(NoComponent);
  unsigned long num_components();
  boolean equal(in LName ln);
  boolean less_than(in LName ln);
  Name to_idl_form() raises(InvalidName);
  void from_idl_form(in Name n);
  void destroy();
};

// C and C++
LName create_lname();
LNameComponent create_lname_component();
```

CosNaming Service Implementations

The CORBA name service used in Chapter 8, "CORBA Communications," and Chapter 9, "RMI Communications," was the transient name service that comes equipped with Java IDL and RMI/IIOP. The command `tnameserv` is used to start the CosNaming-compliant name service on a particular machine on the default port 900. The command-line flag `-ORBInitialPort <PortNum>` may also be used to run the name service on a different port number. From within your CORBA client and server applications, a handle to the name service can be retrieved using the `org.omg.CORBA.ORB.resolve_initial_references()` method. If the name service is run on a new port number other than the default, naming-service clients must set the `org.omg.CORBA.InitialPort` property associated with the ORB object.

The term *transient* is used in referring to the `tnameserv` naming service to highlight the fact that all name/object binding information is lost whenever the naming service terminates. Other naming-service options do exist, however. Java IDL also includes a persistent CORBA naming service referred to as `orbd`. Most commercial CORBA vendors also provide Java-based, CosNaming-compliant naming services.

CORBA Naming Interfaces

Figure 11.7 presents the key programmatic interfaces to a CosNaming service. Only key components are shown; the helpers and holders associated with the various interfaces are not shown to simplify the diagram.

By narrowing an initial reference to the `NameService` returned from the ORB, we can obtain a handle to a `NamingContext` interface like this:

```
ORB orb = ORB.init(args,null);
org.omg.CORBA.Object namingRef =
    orb.resolve_initial_references("NameService");
NamingContext namingContext = NamingContextHelper.narrow(namingRef);
```

A CORBA server can then be registered from the server side by first creating a `NameComponent` array (that is, a CORBA name) and calling `bind()` or `rebind()` on the `NamingContext` reference as shown here:

```
MyMessageImpl server = new MyMessageImpl();
NameComponent nameComponent = new NameComponent("SampleServer", "");
NameComponent nameComponent1 = new NameComponent("SampleServer2", "");
NameComponent path[] = { nameComponent , nameComponent1 };
namingContext.rebind(path, server);
```

A CORBA client obtains an initial reference to a naming service in the same fashion as a CORBA server. The CORBA client can then use the naming context to look up (that is, "resolve" in CORBA lingo) the object reference given the CORBA name as shown here:

```
NameComponent nameComponent = new NameComponent("SampleServer", "");
NameComponent nameComponent1 = new NameComponent("SampleServer2", "");
NameComponent path[] = { nameComponent , nameComponent1 };
MyMessage obj = MyMessageHelper.narrow(namingContext.resolve(path));
```

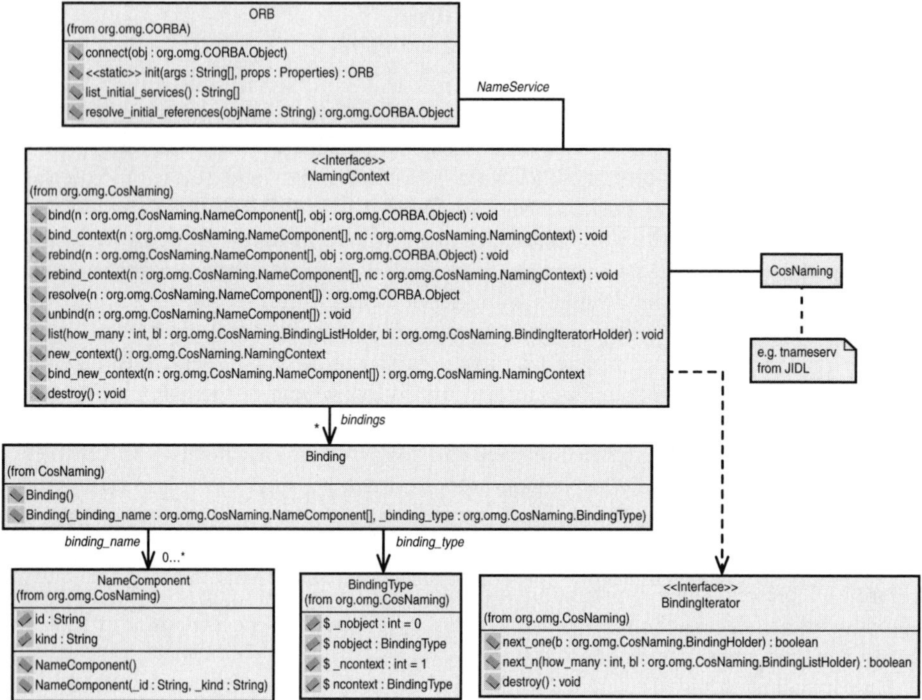

Figure 11.7 Traditional CosNaming service interfaces.

JNDI CosNaming SPI

A CosNaming JNDI SPI exists as part of the J2SE v1.4. When you interface with the CosNaming service directly, you need to understand a host of CosNaming-specific APIs. By using JNDI with a CosNaming SPI, you are provided with a standard way (as a Java developer) to interact with a host of naming-service interfaces, and thus it is not necessary to learn all of the semantics specific to CosNaming. However, as mentioned, JNDI with a CosNaming SPI adds an extra layer of processing into the mix. Furthermore, when an SPI is used, there exists additional risk associated with requiring proper JNDI SPI-to-CosNaming mapping by your vendor above and beyond that already required of the CosNaming vendor's mapping from the CORBA interface standard to the actual underlying naming service implementation.

> **Note**
>
> Updated CosNaming JNDI SPIs provided by Sun are available for download from `http://java.sun.com/products/jndi/serviceproviders.html` and can be used with the J2SE v1.4 platform.

Note

Under the `examples\src\ejava\jndi\naming` directory, a `runcosnamingcontext` script file is generated by the ANT build process and is used to demonstrate use of the CosNaming JNDI SPI. The `jndiCosNamingContext.properties` file is used to establish a set of CosNaming SPI-specific properties. `Sample.idl` and `SampleCosNamingServer` classes are also used to illustrate JNDI CosNaming SPI usage.

The `Sample.idl` file in Listing 11.6 exports a simple "Hello-World" sample method embedded inside of a `Message` interface. The `SampleCosNamingServer` of Listing 11.7 implements this interface and also registers the server with a CosNaming server via JNDI. The generated `runcosnamingcontext` script copies the `jndiCosNamingContext.properties` file over to the `jndi.properties` filename used by both the `SampleCosNamingServer` of Listing 11.7 and the generic JNDI examples of Listings 11.1 through 11.3.

After a `Message` server is bound to two different names from within the `SampleCosNamingServer.bindWithDifferentNames()` method, the `SampleLookupExample`, `SampleListAndSearchExample`, and `SampleBindingExample` programs are all run to illustrate usage of the generic JNDI API with a CosNaming system. These are the properties of interest in the `jndiCosNamingContext.properties` file that comes with the book:

```
# Sun CosNaming system SPI context factory
java.naming.factory.initial=com.sun.jndi.cosnaming.CNCtxFactory

# CosNaming system root context
java.naming.provider.url=iiop://localhost/

# CompoundName properties
jndi.syntax.separator="."
jndi.syntax.escape = "\"
jndi.syntax.beginquote =""","'"
jndi.syntax.endquote=""","'"
jndi.syntax.reservednames: ".:", "..."
jndi.syntax.codeset= ISOLatin1
jndi.syntax.locale = US_EN

# These properties are used by the SampleCosNamingServer
SIMPLE_NAME1=SampleServer
SIMPLE_NAME2=SampleServer2
COMPOUND_NAME1=Samples.SampleServer6
COMPOUND_NAME2=Samples.Servers.SampleServer5
```

Listing 11.6 **A Sample Message IDL (`Sample.idl`)**

```
module ejava
{
  module jndi
  {
    module naming
    {
      module sample
      {
        interface Message
        {
          string sayHi(in string value);
        };
      };
    };
  };
 };
```

Listing 11.7 **A Sample CosNaming Server (`SampleCosNamingServer.java`)**

```
package ejava.jndi.naming;

import java.util.Properties;
import java.io.FileInputStream;
import java.io.IOException;
import org.omg.CORBA.ORB;
import org.omg.PortableServer.POA;
import org.omg.PortableServer.POAHelper;
import javax.naming.NamingException;
import javax.naming.Context;
import javax.naming.InitialContext;
import ejava.jndi.naming.sample.MessagePOA;
import ejava.jndi.naming.sample.MessageHelper;
import ejava.jndi.naming.sample.Message;

/**
 * CosNaming Server class implementation
 */
public class SampleCosNamingServer extends MessagePOA
{

  /**
   * Constructor
   */
  public SampleCosNamingServer()
```

Listing 11.7 **Continued**

```
{
  super();
}

/**
 * Implementation of Sample Interface only method
 * @param s input string
 * @return string to return after manipulation
 */
public String sayHi(String s)
{
  return "You Sent :" + s;
}

/**
 * This method binds the object with different names
 * @param context to get names to bind
 */
public static void bindWithDifferentNames(Context context,
 Message message)
 throws NamingException
{
  Properties prop = (Properties) context.getEnvironment();
  String namingServerURL =
    (String) prop.get("java.naming.provider.url");

  String simpleName1 = (String) prop.get("SIMPLE_NAME1");
  String simpleName2 = (String) prop.get("SIMPLE_NAME2");
  // binding this object with different Names
  context.bind(namingServerURL + simpleName1, message);
  System.out.println("Bound As :" + namingServerURL + simpleName1);
  context.bind(namingServerURL + simpleName2, message);
  System.out.println("Bound As :" + namingServerURL + simpleName2);
}

/**
 * Main method to test the functionality of the server
 */
public static void main(String[] args) {
  if (args.length == 0) {
    System.out.println(" You should provide properties file :" +
        "java ejava.jndi.naming.SampleCosNamingServer jndi.properties");
    System.exit(0);
  }
```

Listing 11.7 **Continued**

```
  String propertiesFileName = args[0];

  try {
    FileInputStream fin = new FileInputStream(propertiesFileName);
    Properties properties = new Properties();
    properties.load(fin);

    ORB    orb  = ORB.init(args, null);

    // get reference to rootpoa & activate the POAManager
    POA rootpoa =
      POAHelper.narrow(orb.resolve_initial_references("RootPOA"));

    rootpoa.the_POAManager().activate();

    // createQueryServerImplementation
    SampleCosNamingServer serverObjectImpl =
      new SampleCosNamingServer();

    // get object reference from the servant
    org.omg.CORBA.Object reference =
      rootpoa.servant_to_reference(serverObjectImpl);
    Message message = MessageHelper.narrow(reference);

    Context context = new InitialContext(properties);
    serverObjectImpl.bindWithDifferentNames(context,message);
    System.out.println("Bound : Waiting for clients...");

    orb.run();
  } catch (NamingException namingException) {
    System.out.println(" Failed to Bind :" + namingException);
    namingException.printStackTrace();
    System.exit(0);
  } catch (IOException ioException) {
    System.out.println(" Failed to open properties file :"
                       + ioException);
    System.exit(0);
  }
  catch (Exception exception) {
    exception.printStackTrace();
    System.exit(0);
  }
 }
}
```

RMI Naming

As with any well-thought-out distributed computing paradigm, RMI also has a means to bind objects to names and look up object references via a name. As we saw in Chapter 9, both RMI/JRMP and RMI/IIOP had distinct ways to communicate with a naming service. Of course, RMI/IIOP used the CosNaming service interfaces as shown in Figure 9.6. RMI/JRMP used the built-in RMI Registry interfaces as shown in Figure 9.5.

RMI Naming System Interfaces

Chapter 9 demonstrates how to utilize a naming service for both RMI/JRMP and RMI/IIOP. The RMI Registry provides a simple mechanism for interfacing with a naming service, but it is dependent on RMI/JRMP, which is a Java-centric means for distributing objects. RMI/IIOP uses a CosNaming server, and thus one can both create RMI/IIOP clients to communicate with CORBA servers implemented in another language and implement RMI/IIOP servers that can offer their services to a language-independent community of CORBA clients. The CosNaming service running under such a scenario can conceivably be any service that implements the CORBA Naming Service interface and supports the special ORB extensions required of RMI/IIOP.

JNDI RMI SPI

An RMI Registry JNDI SPI that works with RMI/JRMP is packaged with the J2SE v1.4. RMI/IIOP-based applications thus can use a CosNaming JNDI SPI. Because our sample RMI/IIOP applications use the `tnameserv` CosNaming service provided with RMI/IIOP, our RMI/IIOP applications also require use of the CosNaming SPI provided by Sun to work with the `tnameserv` CosNaming service.

Note

Updates to the RMI/JRMP registry JNDI SPI provided by Sun are available for download from `http://java.sun.com/products/jndi/serviceproviders.html`.

Note

Under the `examples\src\ejava\jndi\naming` directory, two sets of files are generated and exist to illustrate use of RMI with JNDI. A `runrmicontext` script file is generated, and a `jndirmiContext.properties` file, a `Sample.java` RMI interface, and a `SampleJRMPServerUsingNamingContext.java` RMI/JRMP server and registrar exist to illustrate use of the JNDI RMI Registry SPI with the RMI Registry. A `runrmiiiopcontext` script file is generated, and a `jndirmiiiopContext.properties` file, the same `Sample.java` RMI interface, and a `SampleRMIIIOPServer.java` RMI/IIOP server and registrar exist to illustrate use of the JNDI CosNaming SPI with the `tnameserv` CosNaming server.

The `Sample.java` RMI interface in Listing 11.8 exports a simple "Hello-World" example RMI method implemented by both the RMI/JRMP server (`SampleJRMPServerUsingNamingContext`) of Listing 11.9 and the RMI/IIOP server (`SampleRMIIIOPServer`) of Listing 11.10. The generated `runrmicontext` script copies the `jndirmiContext.properties` file over to the `jndi.properties` file used by the `SampleJRMPServerUsingNamingContext` program and by the generic JNDI examples of Listings 11.1 through 11.3. Similarly, the generated `runrmiiiop-context` script file copies the `jndirmiiiopContext.properties` file over to the `jndi.properties` file used by the `SampleRMIIIOPServer` program, as well as by the generic JNDI examples of Listings 11.1 through 11.3.

Listing 11.8 **A Sample RMI Interface (`Sample.java`)**

```
package ejava.jndi.naming;
import java.rmi.Remote;
import java.rmi.RemoteException;

public interface Sample extends Remote
{
  String sayHi(String s)
    throws RemoteException;
  }
```

After reading in a set of properties from the property file, the `SampleJRMPServerUsingNamingContext.main()` method creates an instance of a `SampleJRMPServerUsingNamingContext` object, creates an `InitialContext` with the set of read properties, and then calls the `bindWithDifferentNames()` method. The `bindWithDifferentNames()` method binds a reference to the RMI/JRMP server to the initial context using a host of different names read from the property file. In addition to two simple names, the server is also bound to two compound names.

Listing 11.9 **A Sample RMI/JRMP Server (`SampleJRMPServerUsingNamingContext.java`)**

```
package ejava.jndi.naming;

import java.rmi.server.UnicastRemoteObject;
import java.rmi.Naming;
import java.rmi.NotBoundException;
import java.rmi.RemoteException;
import java.util.Hashtable;
import java.util.Properties;
import java.net.MalformedURLException;
import java.rmi.AlreadyBoundException;
import java.io.FileInputStream;
import java.io.IOException;
```

Listing 11.9 **Continued**

```
import javax.naming.Context;
import javax.naming.InitialContext;
import javax.naming.NamingException;
import java.rmi.RMISecurityManager;

/**
 * JRMP server using naming context class implementation
 */
public class SampleJRMPServerUsingNamingContext
  extends UnicastRemoteObject implements Sample
{

  /**
   * Constructor
   *
   */
  public SampleJRMPServerUsingNamingContext()
    throws RemoteException
  {
    super();
  }

  /**
   * Implementation of Sample Interface only method
   * @param s input string
   * @return string to return after manipulation
   */
  public String sayHi(String s)
    throws RemoteException
  {
    return "You Sent:" + s;
  }

  /**
   * This method binds the object with different names
   * @param context to get names to bind
   */
  public void bindWithDifferentNames(Context context)
   throws   NamingException,
            MalformedURLException,
            AlreadyBoundException
  {
    Properties properties = (Properties) context.getEnvironment();
    String namingServerURL =
      (String) properties.get("java.naming.provider.url");
```

Listing 11.9 **Continued**

```
    String simpleName1 = (String) properties.get("SIMPLE_NAME1");
    String simpleName2 = (String) properties.get("SIMPLE_NAME2");

    // binding this object with different Names
    context.bind(namingServerURL + simpleName1, this);
    System.out.println("Bound As :" + namingServerURL + simpleName1);
    context.bind(namingServerURL + simpleName2, this);
    System.out.println("Bound As :" + namingServerURL + simpleName2);

    String compoundName1 = (String) properties.get("COMPOUND_NAME1");
    String compoundName2 = (String) properties.get("COMPOUND_NAME2");

    context.bind(compoundName1, this);
    System.out.println("Bound as :" + compoundName1);
    context.bind(compoundName2, this);
    System.out.println("Bound as :" + compoundName2);
  }

  /**
   * Main method to test the SampleJRMPServerUsingNamingContext
   * class functionality
   */
  public static void main(String[] args)
  {
    if (args.length == 0) {
      System.out.println("Usage : java -Djava.security.policy"
      + "=rmi.policy ejava.jndi.naming.SampleJRMPServerUsingNamingContext"
      + " jndi.namingrmiContext.Properties");
      System.exit(0);
    }

    String propertiesFileName = args[0];

    try {
      FileInputStream fin = new FileInputStream(propertiesFileName);
      Properties properties = new Properties();

      properties.load(fin);

      if (System.getSecurityManager() == null) {
        System.setSecurityManager(new RMISecurityManager());
      }

      SampleJRMPServerUsingNamingContext serverObject =
        new SampleJRMPServerUsingNamingContext();
```

Listing 11.9 **Continued**

```
      Context namingContext = new InitialContext(properties);

      serverObject.bindWithDifferentNames(namingContext);
      System.out.println("Bound : Waiting for clients...");
    }
    catch (IOException ioException) {
      System.out.println("Failed to open properties :" + ioException);
      System.exit(0);
    }
    catch (AlreadyBoundException alreadyBoundException) {
      System.out.println("Already Bound :" + alreadyBoundException);
      System.exit(0);
    }
    catch (NamingException namingException) {
      System.out.println(" Naming Error: " + namingException);
      namingException.printStackTrace();
      System.exit(0);
    }
  }
 }
```

The `SampleRMIIIOPServer` class is very similar to the `SampleJRMPServerUsingNamingContext` class. After reading in a set of properties from the property file, the `SampleRMIIIOPServer.main()` method creates an `InitialContext` with the set of read properties, creates an instance of a `SampleRMIIIOPServer` object, and then calls the `bindWithDifferentNames()` method. The `bindWithDifferentNames()` method binds a reference to the RMI/IIOP server to the initial context using two simple names read from the property file.

Listing 11.10 **A Sample RMI/IIOP Server (`SampleRMIIIOPServer.java`)**

```
package ejava.jndi.naming;

import javax.rmi.PortableRemoteObject;
import javax.naming.NamingException;
import javax.naming.InitialContext;
import java.rmi.Naming;
import java.rmi.NotBoundException;
import java.rmi.RemoteException;
import java.util.Hashtable;
import java.util.Properties;
import java.net.MalformedURLException;
import java.rmi.AlreadyBoundException;
```

Listing 11.10 **Continued**

```
import java.io.FileInputStream;
import java.io.IOException;
import java.rmi.RMISecurityManager;
import javax.naming.Context;
import javax.naming.NameNotFoundException;

/**
 * RMIIIOP Server class implementation
 */
public class SampleRMIIIOPServer extends PortableRemoteObject
  implements Sample
{

  /**
   * Constructor
   */
  public SampleRMIIIOPServer()
      throws RemoteException
  {
    super();
  }

  /**
   * Implementation of Sample Interface only method
   * @param s input string
   * @return string to return after manipulation
   */
  public String sayHi(String s)
    throws RemoteException
  {
    return "You Sent:" + s;
  }

  /**
   * This method binds the object with different names
   * @param context to get names to bind
   */
  public void bindWithDifferentNames(Context context)
          throws NamingException
  {
    Properties prop = (Properties) context.getEnvironment();
    String namingServerURL =
      (String) prop.get("java.naming.provider.url");
    String simpleName1 = (String) prop.get("SIMPLE_NAME1");
    String simpleName2 = (String) prop.get("SIMPLE_NAME2");

    // binding this object with different Names
```

Listing 11.10 **Continued**

```
    context.bind(namingServerURL + simpleName1, this);
    System.out.println("Bound As :" + namingServerURL + simpleName1);
    context.bind(namingServerURL + simpleName2, this);
    System.out.println("Bound As :" + namingServerURL + simpleName2);
  }

  /**
   * Main method to test the functionality
   */
  public static void main(String[] args) {
    if (args.length == 0) {
      System.out.println("Usage : java -Djava.security.policy"
       + "=rmi.policy ejava.jndi.naming.SampleRMIIIOPServer "
       + "jndi.Properties");
      System.exit(0);
    }

    String propertiesFileName = args[0];

    try {
      FileInputStream fin = new FileInputStream(propertiesFileName);
      Properties properties = new Properties();

      properties.load(fin);

      if (System.getSecurityManager() == null) {
        System.setSecurityManager(new RMISecurityManager());
      }

      Context namingContext =
        new InitialContext((Hashtable) properties);
      SampleRMIIIOPServer serverObject = new SampleRMIIIOPServer();

      serverObject.bindWithDifferentNames(namingContext);
      System.out.println("Bound : Waiting for clients...");
    }
    catch (IOException ioException) {
      System.out.println("Failed to open properties :" + ioException);
      System.exit(0);
    }
    catch (NamingException namingException) {
      System.out.println("Failed to bind :" + namingException);
      System.exit(0);
    }
  }
 }
```

Running the execution scripts for either the RMI/JRMP or the RMI/IIOP examples will register a server instance to two different names with their respective naming services (RMI Registry or CosNaming Service) using the appropriate JNDI SPI. After a server is bound to two different names, the `SampleLookupExample`, `SampleListAndSearchExample`, and `SampleBindingExample` programs are all run to illustrate use of the generic JNDI API with either the RMI Registry or the CosNaming system.

The following are the RMI Registry JNDI SPI properties of interest in the `jndirmiContext.properties` file:

```
# Sun RMI Registry system SPI context factory
java.naming.factory.initial=
➥com.sun.jndi.rmi.registry.RegistryContextFactory

# RMI Registry system root context
java.naming.provider.url=rmi://localhost:1099/

# CompoundName properties
jndi.syntax.separator="."
jndi.syntax.escape = "\"
jndi.syntax.beginquote =""","'"
jndi.syntax.endquote=""","'"
jndi.syntax.reservednames: ".:", "..."
jndi.syntax.codeset= ISOLatin1
jndi.syntax.locale = US_EN

# These properties are used by the SampleJRMPServerUsingNamingContext
SIMPLE_NAME1=SampleServer
SIMPLE_NAME2=SampleServer2
COMPOUND_NAME1=Samples.SampleServer6
COMPOUND_NAME2=Samples.Servers.SampleServer5
```

The following are the RMI/IIOP CosNaming JNDI SPI properties of interest in the `jndirmiiiopContext.properties` file:

```
# Sun CosNaming system SPI context factory
java.naming.factory.initial=com.sun.jndi.cosnaming.CNCtxFactory

# CosNaming system root context
java.naming.provider.url=iiop://localhost/

# CompoundName properties
jndi.syntax.separator="."
jndi.syntax.escape = "\"
jndi.syntax.beginquote =""","'"
jndi.syntax.endquote=""","'"
jndi.syntax.reservednames: ".:", "..."
```

```
jndi.syntax.codeset= ISOLatin1
jndi.syntax.locale = US_EN

# These properties are used by the SampleRMIIIOPServer
SIMPLE_NAME1=SampleServer
SIMPLE_NAME2=SampleServer2
COMPOUND_NAME1=Samples.SampleServer6
COMPOUND_NAME2=Samples.Servers.SampleServer5
```

Windows Registry Naming

The Microsoft Windows Registry acts as a repository for storing information about hardware, software, and users. A Windows Registry can be accessed local to the machine and certain information can also be accessed remotely. The information stored in a Windows Registry takes the form of a naming service with a hierarchical tree of information. Each leaf binding in the tree has a name, a type, and a value. For example, the name "`J2EE_HOME`" may be of a string type (`REG_SZ`) and have the value "`C:\J2sdkee1.4`" indicating where you have located the home directory for a J2EE v1.4 reference implementation.

Contexts in the Windows Registry parlance are referred to as "keys." Thus, a naming service context concept maps to a Windows Registry key concept. The most commonly used groups of information in a Windows Registry are those defined beneath the keys `HKEY_LOCAL_MACHINE` and `HKEY_CURRENT_USER`. The `HKEY_LOCAL_MACHINE` context contains that information used to store system information such as information about hardware, security profiles, software applications, and device drivers. Information specific to a particular user is stored beneath the `HKEY_CURRENT_USER` context with information such as a user's environment variables, application configuration, and preferences.

As an example, the `JAVA_HOME` information for a particular user's environment may be stored at `HKEY_CURRENT_USER\\Environment\\JAVA_HOME`. As another example, first note that we have used the Java preferences API in examples throughout this book. User preferences for the examples run for Chapter 5, "Core JDBC," were stored at `HKEY_CURRENT_USER\\software\\JavaSoft\\Prefs\\ejava\\jdbc\\core`. Under that context you can find all the bindings for preferences set, such as `DATABASE_URL` and `DRIVER_CLASS`.

A Windows Registry JNDI SPI is provided by a company called Cogent Logic Corporation and may be downloaded from `http://cogentlogic.com/cocoon/CogentLogicCorporation/JNDI.xml`. The JNDI SPI from Cogent can be used from Java applications to access a Windows Registry locally or remotely. To use Cogent Logic's SPI you'll need to define a set of JNDI properties such as this:

```
java.naming.factory.initial
➥=com.cogentlogic.jndi.winreg.WinregInitContextFactory
java.naming.provider.url= winreg://localhost/HKEY_CURRENT_USER
```

```
# To access another computer's registry, you'll need the computer's
#   Windows network name such as...
#java.naming.provider.url
➥=winreg://COMPUTER_NAME/HKEY_CURRENT_USER
# To access another computer's registry, you'll also need a username
#   and password such as...
#java.naming.security.principal=username
#java.naming.security.credentials=password
```

With the preceding context parameters passed as properties to an `InitialContext` object, you can then use JNDI as usual to look up and bind information in a Windows Registry. As an example, to look up a user's `JAVA_HOME` environment value, you might have this:

```
String javaHome
  = (String) initialContext.lookup("\\Environment\\JAVA_HOME");
```

As a final example, to look up the preferences set from running Chapter 5's examples, you might do the following:

```
Context context = (Context)
   initialContext.lookup("software\\JavaSoft\\Prefs\\ejava\\jdbc\\core");
String databaseDriverClass = (String) context.lookup("DRIVER_CLASS");
String databaseURL = (String) context.lookup("DATABASE_URL");
```

Conclusions

Naming services fulfill a basic distributed enterprise communications need for mapping between names in a context and object references. Given an object reference, a server can bind this object to a name in a naming service, and given that name, a client can look up the object reference in the naming service. JNDI is a core component of the J2SE that provides a standard interface for Java applications to access naming services. JNDI naming-service providers exist for file systems, RMI applications, and CORBA programs. Mapping Microsoft Windows Registry names to Registry entries is also possible via a third-party JNDI naming-service provider. Beyond mere mapping between names and objects, characteristics about such objects can also be associated with an extended form of naming system known as a directory or trading system. The next chapter describes how naming systems are extended to offer more sophisticated forms of object registration by object attributes and look up by object attributes.

12

Directory Services with JNDI

THIS CHAPTER DESCRIBES THE CONCEPT AND application of directory services and a special extension to directory services called trading services. Directory services provide a mechanism for looking up objects in different naming contexts given a set of object attributes. Similarly, trading services provide a framework for objects to identify themselves in a distributed system, provide facilities for looking up and discovering other services, and provide services to remote objects. Example use of directory services with JNDI, the CORBA Trading Service, and Jini as a trading service are illustrated in this chapter. We also present a brief description of Microsoft's Active Directory Service implementation.

In this chapter, you will learn:

- The basic concepts used to describe what a directory service and a trading service are.
- The architecture and use of JNDI as a standard directory service API.
- A description of the Lightweight Directory Access Protocol (LDAP) and how it is used with JNDI.
- An overview of the Directory Service Markup Language (DSML) and how it is used with JNDI.
- An overview of the Domain Name System (DNS) and how it can be used with JNDI.
- An overview of the Network Information System (NIS) and Novell Directory Service (NDS) directory services and how they can be used with JNDI.
- An overview of the Microsoft Active Directory Service.
- A description of the CORBA Trading Service and how to use it for basic object service trading.
- A description of Jini and how to use it for object service trading in a dynamic discovery-based network.

Directory and Trading Services Overview

A directory service can be viewed as a type of naming service augmented with the capability to perform more sophisticated searches for objects. Directory service searching can be based on attributes of that object with search filter criteria and search controls. Directory services also enable modification of object attributes. You can think of naming services as a sort of telephone White Pages approach to associating names with objects, whereas directory services provide a telephone Yellow Pages approach by associating attributes with the object of interest. For example, if you want to find someone's phone number, you can look it up by their name in the White Pages. But if you want to find a list of restaurants that sell pizza and deliver, you might look in the Yellow Pages under "Restaurants/Pizza/Delivery."

Akin to naming services, directory services typically have a hierarchical structure in which a directory object has a context in some directory structure. Thus, each context will contain zero or more subcontexts and zero or more named directory objects. The directory object corresponds to some enterprise resource such as a file, a printer, or a person. This directory object itself is manifested in a directory service as a collection of attributes describing this object and perhaps even contains an object reference or some serialized object. An attribute of a directory object has an identifier and one or more values. A directory object in a directory service tree can be retrieved by its name or via use of a set of search criteria expressed as a function of the directory object's name and attributes.

For example, a directory service search for a particular user may first involve formulating a query given a particular last name and geographical location such as city, state, and country. The search result from this query may yield one or more directory objects matching this criterion, each with a collection of attributes. Example attributes in this resultant collection for a particular user may include an attribute with a `lastName` ID and associated last name value, as well as an attribute with a `reference` ID and an associated distributed object reference value. The fact that an attribute can have only one ID but one or more values is typically used in scenarios in which those values are synonymous, such as a `firstName` attribute ID being associated with the values `Robert`, `Rob`, or `Bob`.

Directory services are used in many distributed enterprise applications in which a set of distributed objects or information useful to other distributed objects may be registered, unregistered, and queried based on a set of descriptive attributes. LDAP directories of security certificates, NDS printing and network services, and NIS system information are all sample uses of directory services. When directory services are used to add, delete, modify, and search for attributes of directory objects, they bear a striking resemblance to database services. However, directory services are by and large used in more of a retrieval-only fashion versus updates and typically lack the transaction semantics and large-scale data warehouse support that commercial databases offer.

Directory services also are similar to trading services. The OMG's CORBA Trading Service provides a means for CORBA servers to register their services with an independent trader process along with a set of descriptive attributes. A CORBA client consults the trader for a suitable CORBA server using some search criteria over the set of attributes provided by the CORBA servers offering their services. The CORBA client may then invoke the services of these CORBA servers. Thus, the CORBA Trading Service is sort of a sophisticated directory service in which the directory objects contain attributes and service type information on distributed objects, as well as handles to the distributed objects themselves.

Sun's Jini technology is also essentially a trading service in which descriptive information about remote processes or devices is registered with a lookup service. Jini clients can then search for such services using a service template description and obtain a set of matching service items from such a search. Proxy objects returned from these searches can represent handles to remote processes or devices. Jini also adds a mechanism for Jini services and clients to dynamically discover Jini lookup services used for trading.

JNDI Directory Services

In addition to a standard naming service interface, JNDI offers a Java-based interface to directory services. Thus, the same standardization advantages offered to Java applications for interfacing with naming services also exist for interfacing with directory services. Using the extended directory service API capabilities available through JNDI, Java clients can perform more complicated object and attribute lookups based on certain object properties than was the case with pure naming service interfacing. Furthermore, because the JNDI directory service API inherits all the JNDI naming service APIs, directory service clients inherit naming service functionality as well.

Directory Contexts

In the JNDI naming service client API described in the preceding chapter, the user obtained a handle to a `javax.naming.InitialContext` object. For JNDI directory services, the client API user obtains a handle to a `javax.naming.directory.InitialDirContext` object. As shown in Figure 12.1, the `InitialDirContext` class inherits from the `InitialContext` class and implements the extended set of directory service interface operations from the `javax.naming.directory.DirContext` interface. As you'll soon see, use of the `InitialDirContext` class will enable API clients to be able to bind object attributes to names, search for objects based on such attributes as well as more sophisticated search control criteria, and modify attributes. Note that we have shown operation signatures in Figure 12.1 so that we could fit all relevant classes and interfaces into one diagram.

A handle to an `InitialDirContext` can be obtained in the same fashion as was done with obtaining a handle to an `InitialContext`. However, now you will have a handle to an object implementing the `DirContext` interface versus the pure `Context` interface as shown here:

```
Properties properties = new Properties();
// Set properties in some fashion
DirContext dirContext = new InitialDirContext(properties);
```

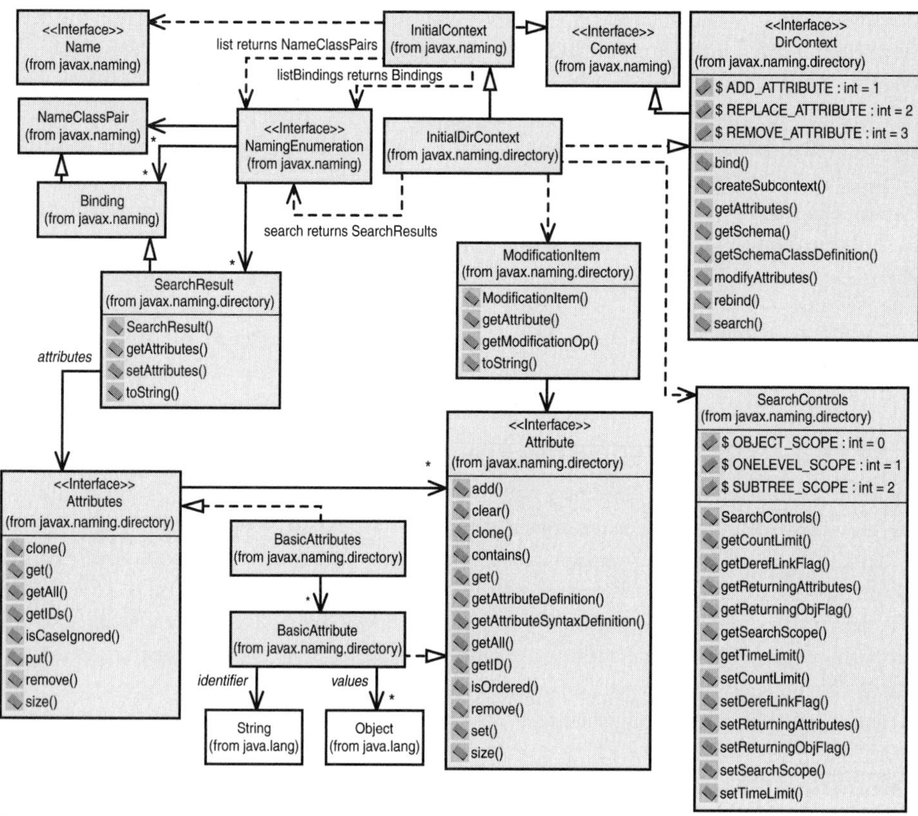

Figure 12.1 Core JNDI directory entities.

Directory Object Attributes

After you obtain a handle to a directory context, you can bind objects to the directory service or perhaps create special subcontexts identifiable with attributes. In either case, you will need to create one or more attributes that get associated with such objects or subcontexts. The `javax.naming.directory.BasicAttribute` class that implements the `javax.naming.directory.Attribute` interface represents an encapsulation of a basic attribute about an object in the directory service. Each `BasicAttribute` has a `String` name identifier and can have zero or more `Object` attribute values. The `javax.naming.directory.Attributes` interface and the `javax.naming.directory.BasicAttributes` class, which implements that interface, encapsulate a basic collection of `Attribute` instances. A directory object can be described using one or more attributes encapsulated by such an `Attributes` collection construct.

Creating attributes and collections of attributes is rather straightforward. For example, to create an attribute with a name, name-value pair, or name and set of values, we have the following examples:

```
BasicAttribute at1 = new BasicAttribute("name"); // Name only
BasicAttribute at2 = new BasicAttribute("building", "A"); // Name/value
BasicAttribute at3 = new BasicAttribute("floor", "5");
BasicAttribute at4 = new BasicAttribute("room", "506");
BasicAttribute at5 = new BasicAttribute("IP", "209.207.135.133");
BasicAttribute at6 = new BasicAttribute("Port"); // Name only
at6.add("8020"); // Add a port value to attribute at6
at6.add("8021"); // Add another valid port value to attribute at6
```

To add such attributes to an attribute collection as well as a few extra attributes, we can create a `BasicAttributes` instance and add attributes to it as shown here:

```
Attributes bindAttrs = new BasicAttributes(true);
bindAttrs.put(at1);
bindAttrs.put(at2);
bindAttrs.put(at3);
bindAttrs.put(at4);
bindAttrs.put(at5);
bindAttrs.put(at6);
bindAttrs.put("color", "yes");
bindAttrs.put("maxSize", "C");
```

As shown in Figure 12.1, other fairly intuitive operations also exist on objects implementing the `Attribute` and `Attributes` interfaces. In addition to adding new attributes, the `Attributes` interface allows one to remove an attribute, retrieve its contents, determine its size, and clone its contents. The `Attribute` interface implements methods to clear all of its values, get one or more of its values, remove its values, get its identifier, and determine the status of its size and contents.

Directory Schemas

The `Attribute` interface also offers two not-so-intuitive operations that return a `DirContext` object. The `getAttributeSyntaxDefinition()` and `getAttributeDefinition()` methods return a syntactical definition and schema definition of an attribute, respectively, both in the form of a `DirContext` object. The exact structure of such definitions will be directory service specific. You will similarly notice `getSchemaClassDefinition()` and `getSchema()` methods on the `DirContext` class itself. The `getSchema()` method returns the schema of the associated named object, and the `getSchemaClassDefinition()` method returns a collection of schema objects for the associated named object. The exact structure of the returned `DirContext` objects from these operations is also directory service specific.

Schemas describe the structure of an object or attribute and can be useful for dynamically querying and manipulating the directory service structure based on schema information. Although such dynamic directory service interfacing can be useful, you should be aware that because the returned DirContext values describing these schemas are directory service specific, you will most likely compromise some aspects of the standardized directory-access nature of your applications.

Directory Object Binding

Binding a name and object to the directory service with a collection of attributes is performed via either a bind() or a rebind() call to the DirContext. The only difference between bind() and rebind() is that bind() can throw a NameAlreadyBoundException if an object of that name is already bound to the directory service, whereas rebind() simply overwrites the original binding. However, both calls may throw an InvalidAttributesException if an attribute that is required to be bound with the name is missing. For example, we might have the following bind to a Printers subcontext for a particular directory service:

```
Attributes bindAttrs = // Attributes as set earlier
Printer printerObj = // Example Serializable printer object
DirContext printerContext = (DirContext) dirContext.lookup("Printers");
printerContext.bind("Printer.AI.HP550", printerObj, bindAttrs);
```

Basic Directory Searches

Searching for objects in a directory context can be accomplished in various ways through the JNDI directory service API using one of the search() methods on the DirContext class. As a first example, to search the directory-tree context for objects that have a certain set of attributes, we can simply create a set of attributes that should be matched and do the following:

```
BasicAttribute atr1 = new BasicAttribute("building", "A");
BasicAttribute atr2 = new BasicAttribute("floor", "5");
Attributes where = new BasicAttributes(true);
where.put(atr1);
where.put(atr2);

NamingEnumeration enum = dirContext.search("Printers", where);
```

As you'll see shortly, the NamingEnumeration object contains the results of your search.

If you are interested only in retrieving certain attribute values from the search() command, you can filter down the result list with an additional String array of attribute names. Such a filtering capability is similar to the SELECT clause in a SQL statement. For example:

```
BasicAttribute atr1 = new BasicAttribute("building", "A");
BasicAttribute atr2 = new BasicAttribute("floor", "5");
Attributes where = new BasicAttributes(true);
where.put(atr1);
```

```
where.put(atr2);
String select[] = {"IP", "Port"};

NamingEnumeration enum = dirContext.search("Printers", where, select);
```

Directory Search Results

Note that if you already know the name of the directory object, you can retrieve its set of attributes directly using this:

```
Attributes attributes = printerContext.getAttributes("Printer.AI.HP550");
```

The `search()` method will yield a `NamingEnumeration` object containing a set of `javax.naming.directory.SearchResult` objects, each of which matches the criteria submitted to the `search()` method. The `SearchResult` class extends the `javax.naming.Binding` class described in the preceding chapter. Thus, not only can the bound object name and object be retrieved (by virtue of inheriting from the `Binding` class), but the entire set of `Attributes` associated with that object also can now be obtained from the `SearchResult` instance. For example, the following `while` loop would examine each `SearchResult` object returned via such a `NamingEnumeration` and would print each contained `Attribute` identifier `String` and set of attribute values:

```
while (enum != null && enum.hasMore()) {

  SearchResult sr = (SearchResult) enum.next();
  System.out.println(" Result Name :" + sr.getName() );
  Attributes attrs = sr.getAttributes();

  if(attrs == null) {
    System.out.println(" No Attributes :");
  }
  else {
    for(NamingEnumeration ne = attrs.getAll();ne.hasMoreElements(); ){
      Attribute attribute = (Attribute)ne.next();
      String id = attribute.getID();

      for (Enumeration vals = attribute.getAll();
                       vals.hasMoreElements();){
        System.out.println(id + ": " + vals.nextElement());
      }
    }
  }
  System.out.println();
}
```

Directory Searches Using Search Controls and Filters

A `javax.naming.directory.SearchControls` object can be passed into a few of the `search()` methods to further refine the scope and set of results returned from a search. A `SearchControls` object can be constructed with a set of control parameters or can be constructed with no parameters, indicating that the default search controls should be used. For each search-control parameter type that can be passed into the non-default `SearchControls` constructor, there also exists a getter and setter on the `SearchControls` class. Table 12.1 shows each search-control parameter type and its Java type, a description of the parameter, the associated getter/setter, and the default value if no value is set. If a `null` `SearchControls` object or a `SearchControls` object created with the default constructor is passed into the `search()` method, the default search control values are used.

Table 12.1 **Directory Search Controls**

Search Control	Description	Getter and Setter	Default
Search Scope (`int`)	If set to `ONELEVEL_SCOPE`, then search one level of the context. If set to `SUBTREE_SCOPE`, then search entire context subtree. If set to `OBJECT_SCOPE`, then search named object only.	`getSearchScope` `setSearchScope`	One level scope
Result Count Limit (`long`)	Maximum number of entries to return in a result.	`getCountLimit` `setCountLimit`	Max count limit
Search Time Limit (`int`)	Maximum time to spend searching (in milliseconds).	`getTimeLimit` `setTimeLimit`	Max time limit
Result Attributes (`String []`)	Specifies array of attributes to return from a search.	`getReturningAttributes` `setReturningAttributes`	Return all attributes
Return Object Flag (`boolean`)	Indicates whether the bound object should be returned.	`getReturningObjFlag` `setReturningObjFlag`	`False`
Dereference Flag (`boolean`)	Indicates whether dereferencing of links should occur.	`getDerefLinkFlag` `setDerefLinkFlag`	`False`

Whenever a `SearchControls` object is passed to a `search()` method on the `DirContext`, a filter expression `String` must also be passed as an argument. The exact syntax of the filter expression becomes more apparent when cast in the light of a specific directory service SPI, but suffice it to say for now that the search filter `String` (as defined by RFC 2254 found at `ftp://ftp.isi.edu/in-notes/rfc2254.txt`) may contain a series of name-value pairs as well as search criteria expressible in something similar in role to a SQL WHERE clause. Each search expression of the filter String is typically enclosed in parentheses and uses the search filter symbols listed in Table 12.2.

Table 12.2 **Directory Search Filter Symbols**

Symbol	Description
=	Equality of attributes
~=	Approximate equality of attributes
<=	Attribute is less than or equal to value
>=	Attribute is greater than or equal to value
!	Negation of an associated expression evaluation
&	The logical AND of two associated expressions
|	The logical OR of two associated expressions
*	A wildcard value used in expressing values
\	An escape character used inside values expressions

As an example, we might construct a String filter like this:

```
String filter = "(&(building=A)(floor=*))" ;
```

And then we might create and use a set of SearchControls like this:

```
SearchControls searchControls = new SearchControls();
String[] resultAttributes = {"name", "building", "floor", "room"};
searchControls.setReturningAttributes(resultAttributes);
searchControls.setCountLimit(2);
NamingEnumeration searchResults =
    dirContext.search("Printers", filter, searchControls);
```

The filter String argument may also be constructed such that variables in the filter String are expressed in the form of {i}, in which i is an array index number. The array for which this value is an index refers to an Object[] array parameter passed to the search() method along with the SearchControls object and filter String. For example:

```
String filter = "(&(building={0})(floor={1}))" ;
Object [] filterArgs = {"A", "5"};
SearchControls searchControls = new SearchControls();
NamingEnumeration searchResults =
    dirContext.search("Printers", filter, filterArgs, searchControls);
```

Directory Object Attribute Modification

There are two primary ways to add, replace, and remove attributes associated with an already-bound directory object. The first way involves calling modifyAttributes() on the DirContext with a modification operation type and set of attributes to be modified according to this modification operation type. The second way involves creating an array of Serializable ModificationItem objects, each of which is composed of a modification operation type and attribute. In this way another modifyAttributes() method can be called with this array of ModificationItem objects to perform a batch update with a different modification operation per attribute. The modification operation types that can be performed are defined by DirContext.ADD_ATTRIBUTE to add an attribute, DirContext.REPLACE_ATTRIBUTE to replace the attribute, and DirContext.REMOVE_ATTRIBUTE to remove the attribute.

As an example of modifying an attribute collection using the same modification operation, we have this:

```
Attributes attrs = new BasicAttributes(true);
attrs.put("floor","4");
attrs.put("room","404");

printerContext.modifyAttributes("Printer.AI.HP550",
                                DirContext.REPLACE_ATTRIBUTE, attrs);
```

As an example of performing a batch of modification updates using ModificationItem objects, we have this:

```
ModificationItem mod1 = new ModificationItem(
                              DirContext.REPLACE_ATTRIBUTE,
                              new BasicAttribute("room", "408"));
ModificationItem mod2 = new ModificationItem(
                               DirContext.REMOVE_ATTRIBUTE,
                               new BasicAttribute("color"));
ModificationItem mod3 = new ModificationItem(
                               DirContext.ADD_ATTRIBUTE,
                               new BasicAttribute("status", "online"));

ModificationItem modItems[] = {mod1, mod2, mod3};

printerContext.modifyAttributes("Printer.AI.HP550", modItems);
```

Directory Events

The JNDI naming event infrastructure described in Chapter 11, "Naming Services with JNDI," is also extended for directory service events. Figure 12.2 depicts this fact via the addition of a javax.naming.event.EventDirContext interface that extends the naming service–specific EventContext interface. Two new general types of the addNamingListener() method have been added to the EventDirContext. The first general form takes a SearchControls object and search filter String, as was the case with the directory search() methods, except that now the search filter and controls are used to identify those object attributes at the associated named directory object whose events must be directed toward the associated NamingListener. Similarly, the second general form of the addNamingListener() method also takes an Object[] array of filter arguments to be used in conjunction with the search filter String to identify indexed directory service objects, as was also the case with the directory `search()` methods.

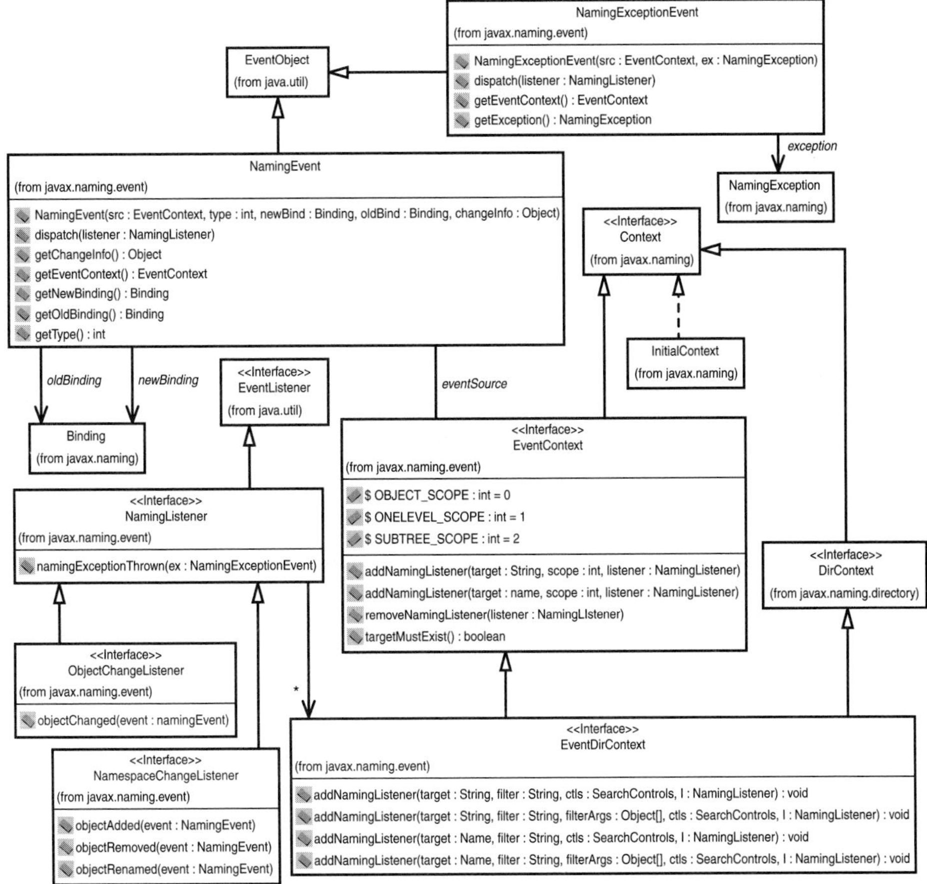

Figure 12.2 JNDI directory service events.

Thus, if we wanted to create a printer event listener that implemented the `ObjectChangeListener` interface and add it to our directory service that implemented the `EventDirContext`, we might have something like this:

```
SearchControls searchControls= new SearchControls();
searchControls.setSearchScope( SearchControls.SUBTREE_SCOPE );

EventDirContext eventContext = // Construct a directory event context
ObjectChangeListener printerEventManager = // Construct a listener
eventContext.addNamingListener("Printer.AI.HP550", "(status=*)",
                               searchControls, printerEventManager);
```

LDAP

The Lightweight Directory Access Protocol (LDAP) is implemented by servers that store user, organizational, file, and network resource information in the form of a directory service. LDAP is a lighter-weight version of the X.500's Directory Access Protocol (DAP) standard and offers efficiencies by being tailored for information retrieval versus updates and by operating over the TCP/IP protocol. Due to its lightweight and open-standards nature, LDAP is becoming a very popular directory-service alternative.

A fully defined name of a directory object in an LDAP directory structure, including its context, is referred to as a *distinguished name (DN)*. Each component of a distinguished name is referred to as a relative distinguished name (RDN). Each RDN represents a directory-service entry and has one or more attributes. Each attribute of an RDN is described by a type and a value. Multiple attributes within an RDN are separated by a plus sign (+). For example, each RDN may be expressed in the following terms:

```
rdnComponent1=value1 + rdnComponent2=value2 + ... + rdnComponentN=valueN
```

RDNs within a DN are separated by commas (`,`) or semicolons (`;`) and typically proceed from right to left in terms of highest-level context to lower-level context. Thus, a root context of an LDAP system will be positioned in the rightmost portion of a DN, and each subcontext is separated by commas or semicolons. For example, a DN may be generally expressed in these terms:

```
rdnN, ..., rdn2, rdn1
```

The LDAP context structure is typically described in a hierarchical, treelike format following a top-down geographical and organizational description. That is, the LDAP root context is typically followed by a country subcontext, followed by an organizational subcontext, which in turn is followed by an individual/resource subcontext (that is, people or computing resource). Because of this geographical and organizational hierarchical convention, a set of standard RDN component type names have been defined as shown in Table 12.3.

Table 12.3 **LDAP Standard RDN Type Names**

RDN Type	Description
`C`	Country name
`ST`	State or province name
`L`	Locality or city name
`STREET`	Street address
`O`	Organization name
`OU`	Organizational unit name
`CN`	Common name

As an example of an LDAP DN defined using such conventions, we might have this:

```
CN=Paul J. Perrone, OU=Consulting, O=Assured Technologies,
➥L=Leesburg, ST=Virginia, C=US
```

In addition to providing a standard naming model, the Internet Engineering Task Force (IETF) standards body also defines a standard API for interfacing with an LDAP server. The LDAP API supports most of the basic directory service functionality, including the following:

- Bind (connect/authenticate) to an LDAP directory server.
- Unbind (disconnect) from an LDAP directory server session.
- Add a new directory object entry.
- Delete a directory object entry.
- Modify a directory object entry.
- Rename a directory object entry.
- Search for directory object entries.
- Compare an entry with particular attribute values to determine whether it contains those values.

Although version 2 of the LDAP standard defined much of what is in current use today with respect to LDAP implementations, the LDAP v3 standard has defined several enhancements that make LDAP more generic for use. LDAP v3–style conventions define generic approaches for submitting LDAP requests, retrieving responses, and setting behavior controls.

LDAP Interfaces

The IETF has defined a standard Java API for performing LDAP v2 and LDAP v3 operations. The LDAP Java API defines a set of Java-based interfaces to LDAP enabling you to build Java applications that can communicate with LDAP servers and invoke some of the basic directory service functionality outlined earlier for LDAP. More information on the most current Java API standard is available at `www.ietf.org/html.charters/ldapext-charter.html`. Although the IETF has defined a standard Java API to LDAP, the Mozilla Organization provides the source code and SDK for the Netscape Directory Service implementation of the IETF Java LDAP standard API. More information on the Mozilla Organization's release of the LDAP SDK is available at `www.mozilla.org/directory`, and specific Java API binding information is available at `www.mozilla.org/directory/javasdk.html`. It should be noted that although the Mozilla Organization does implement a very clean and freely downloadable Java LDAP API, many package suffixes for such constructs follow Netscape Directory SDK suffixes, such as `netscape.ldap`, `netscape.ldap.util`, and `netscape.ldap.controls`.

The core class utilized by the LDAP Java API and implemented by the Mozilla Organization's distribution is the `LDAPConnection` class. An `LDAPConnection` object can be used to perform all the basic operations available to an LDAP client, including binding to and unbinding from LDAP connections, and searching for LDAP entries, as well as adding, deleting, modifying, comparing, and renaming LDAP entries. Additionally, these are the other core classes and interfaces that compose the LDAP Java API and that are implemented by the Mozilla Organization distribution:

- `LDAPv2`: An interface summarizing all the basic operations available in LDAP v2.
- `LDAPv3`: An interface extending the `LDAPv2` interface and providing additional LDAP v3–type operations.
- `LDAPConstraints`: A class encapsulating a set of generic operation constraints such as operation time limits and maximum number of server hops.
- `LDAPSearchConstraints`: A subclass of `LDAPConstraints` encapsulating a set of search preferences.
- `LDAPControl`: A class encapsulating LDAP v3 information that can be used to control a particular LDAP operation.
- `LDAPEntry`: A class encapsulating an LDAP entry.
- `LDAPAttribute`: A class encapsulating the name and values of an attribute in an LDAP entry.
- `LDAPAttributeSet`: A class encapsulating a collection of LDAP attributes.
- `LDAPMessage`: A base class for LDAP requests and responses.
- `LDAPResponse`: An LDAP response from an LDAP operation.
- `LDAPSearchResult`: An LDAP result from an LDAP search operation.
- `LDAPSearchResults`: A collection of LDAP results from an LDAP search operation.
- `LDAPModification`: A class describing the changes to be made to an LDAP entry.
- `LDAPModificationSet`: A collection of LDAP modifications.
- `LDAPExtendedOperation`: An LDAP v3–style extended operation.
- `LDAPExtendedResponse`: An LDAP v3–style response to an extended operation.

As a simple example illustrating the use of such an API, the following snippet demonstrates how you might use the `LDAPConnection` class to go about connecting to a particular LDAP server host on a particular port, authenticating yourself to that LDAP server, and then issuing a search operation using a filter and set of `LDAPSearchConstraints`:

```
LDAPConnection client = new LDAPConnection();

String ldapHost = "ldap.myserver.com";
```

```
int    ldapPort = 389;
client.connect( ldapHost, ldapPort );

int ldapVersion = 3;
String bindDN = "cn=Joe L. Dapp";
String password = "ldappwd";
client.authenticate( ldapVersion, bindDN, password );

LDAPSearchConstraints constraints = client.getSearchConstraints();
constraints.setMaxResults( 100 );
constraints.setTimeLimit( 1000 );
LDAPSearchResults results =
    client.search("ou=People", 0, "(&(sn=Carter)(givenname=*))",
                  null, null, constraints );
```

JNDI LDAP SPI

Although the Java LDAP API is a standard and tends to offer you support for the latest and greatest in LDAP API features, there also exists a JNDI SPI available for use with LDAP. Not only is there a JNDI SPI for LDAP, but there also exists a special JNDI `javax.directory.ldap` package for supporting some of the more sophisticated LDAP v3 features. The LDAP JNDI SPI is incorporated as part of the J2SE v1.4 and updates to the SPI are freely downloadable from the Sun Web site at `http://java.sun.com/products/jndi/serviceproviders.html`.

> **Note**
>
> The complete set of code examples for all the examples listed in this chapter are available as described in Appendix A, "Software Configuration." The example code will then be found in the `examples\src\ejava\jndi\directory` directory. General software download, build, and configuration instructions are also given in Appendix A.

To illustrate the use of the JNDI directory service interface, we will first demonstrate various basic directory service operations with the LDAP SPI and an LDAP directory service. We use the iPlanet Directory Server as our LDAP server. If you are interested in running our examples, consult Appendix A for details on installing and configuring such a server. Regardless of what LDAP server you decide to use, the LDAP SPI will make use of some basic property types that we store in a `jndildapContext.properties` file equipped with this chapter's example code:

```
# Sun's JNDI LDAP SPI Context Factory:
java.naming.factory.initial= com.sun.jndi.ldap.LdapCtxFactory

# LDAP Server URL
java.naming.provider.url=ldap://localhost:389/dc=gcti,dc=com
# Example LDAP Authentication Information
```

```
java.naming.security.authentication=simple
java.naming.security.credentials=admin
java.naming.security.principal=uid=admin,ou=administrators,
➥ou=topologymanagement,o=netscaperoot
```

> **Note**
>
> Under the `examples\src\ejava\jndi\directory` directory, a `runldap` script file is generated from the ANT build script and can be run to demonstrate use of the LDAP JNDI SPI. The `jndildapContext.properties` file is used to establish a set of JNDI LDAP SPI–specific properties. Finally, a `SampleSearchExample` class and a `SampleNamingListener` class are used to illustrate JNDI LDAP SPI usage. Of course, an LDAP directory server must also be running at the URL defined by the `java.naming.provider.url` property specified in the `jndildapContext.properties` file. You will have had to configure the LDAP directory server with a set of initial data as described in Appendix A.

Listing 12.1 presents a basic demonstration of using the JNDI SPI directory service functionality with an LDAP SPI. To use this example, you must first configure and copy the `jndildapContext.properties` file to a `jndi.Properties` file in the directory in which you'll execute the example. Running the generated `runldap` script will actually copy this file for you. The `SampleSearchExample.main()` method reads property information from the `jndi.Properties` file and instantiates an instance of the `SampleSearchExample` JNDI LDAP SPI test driver class. The `main()` method then executes eight different sample driver methods on the `SampleSearchExample` object. Each driver method creates a connection to the LDAP server via the `getInitialContext()` method, which passes the read-in properties to an `InitialDirContext` constructor. Subsequently, the following eight methods illustrate different uses of the JNDI directory service API:

- `addAnEventListenerTotheContext()`: Simply demonstrates how to add a `NamingListener` (defined in Listing 12.2) to an `EventDirContext` given a particular LDAP name, filter, and `SearchControls`.
- `getEveryAttributeUsingSearch()`: Creates two `BasicAttribute` objects that are added to a `BasicAttributes` object and used to search a directory service context. The `NamingEnumeration` of `SearchResult` objects returning every attribute per entry is then traversed and displayed.
- `getSelectedAttributesUsingSearch()`: Performs the same basic search as the last `getEveryAttributeUsingSearch()` call but filters out which attributes per entry are returned in the `SearchResult` objects.
- `searchUsingFilterUsingSearch(filter)`: Searches the directory service context by creating a set of `SearchControls` and using a filter `String` passed into the method. The `NamingEnumerations` of `SearchResult` objects are traversed and displayed.

- `getEveryAttributeUsingGetAttributes()`: Retrieves the set of `Attributes` associated with a particular directory object name and prints its contents.
- `addANewAttribute()`: Demonstrates how to add an attribute by adding `Attribute` objects to an `Attributes` object and then calling `modifyAttributes()` with the `Attributes` object to add on the directory service context.
- `removeAttributes()`: Demonstrates how to remove an attribute by creating a `ModificationItem` array with a `BasicAttribute` element and then calling `modifyAttributes()` with the `ModificationItem` containing the attribute to remove.
- `replaceAttributes()`: Demonstrates how to replace an attribute by creating a `ModificationItem` array with two `BasicAttribute` elements and then calling `modifyAttributes()` with the `ModificationItem` containing the attributes to replace.

Listing 12.1 **Sample LDAP Search (`SampleSearchExample.java`)**

```
package ejava.jndi.directory;

// imports excluded from text
...

public class SampleSearchExample
{
  DirContext context = null;
  Properties properties = new Properties();

  public SampleSearchExample(Properties properties)
  {
    super();
    this.properties = properties;
  }

  public SampleSearchExample(String propertiesFileName)
    throws IOException
  {
    // Open a file input stream for the associated properties
    // fileName.
    FileInputStream propertiesFileStream =
      new FileInputStream(propertiesFileName);
    // Now load the file input stream into the JNDI environment
    // properties.
    // This of course assumes that the file input stream is in a valid
```

Listing 12.1 **Continued**

```
    // Properties format.
    properties.load(propertiesFileStream);
  }

  public DirContext getInitialContext()
    throws NamingException
  {
    // Create initial context if it is not already created
    if (context == null) {
      System.out.println("Properties :" + properties);
        // Read in a set of default parameters.
      context = new InitialDirContext(properties);
      System.out.println("Context is :" + context);
    }
    return context;
  }

  public static void printSearchResults(Attributes attrs)
    throws NamingException
  {
      if(attrs == null) {
        System.out.println(" No Attributes :");
      }
      else {
        for(NamingEnumeration ne = attrs.getAll();
          ne.hasMoreElements(); ){
          Attribute attribute = (Attribute)ne.next();
          String id = attribute.getID();
          for (Enumeration vals = attribute.getAll();
            vals.hasMoreElements();){
            System.out.println(id + ": " + vals.nextElement());
          }
        }
      }
  }

  public static void printSearchResults(NamingEnumeration enum)
    throws NamingException
  {
    while (enum != null && enum.hasMore()) {
      SearchResult sr = (SearchResult)enum.next();
      System.out.println(" Result Name :" + sr.getName() );
      Attributes attrs = sr.getAttributes();
      if(attrs == null) {
```

Listing 12.1 **Continued**

```
        System.out.println(" No Attributes :");
      }
      else {
        for(NamingEnumeration ne = attrs.getAll();
          ne.hasMoreElements(); ){

          Attribute attribute = (Attribute)ne.next();
          String id = attribute.getID();
          for (Enumeration vals = attribute.getAll();
            vals.hasMoreElements();){
            System.out.println(id + ": " + vals.nextElement());
          }
        }
      }
       System.out.println();
    }
  }

  public void searchUsingFilterUsingSearch(String filter)
  {
    try{
      DirContext context = getInitialContext();
      SearchControls searchControls = new SearchControls();
      String[] resultAttributes = {"cn", "sn", "telephonenumber" };
      searchControls.setReturningAttributes(resultAttributes);
      // set the number of results
     searchControls.setCountLimit(10);

      // Search for objects with those matching attributes
      NamingEnumeration searchResults
        = context.search("ou=People ", filter,
          searchControls);
      SampleSearchExample.printSearchResults(searchResults);
    }
    catch(NamingException namingException){
      namingException.printStackTrace();
    }
}
  public void addANewAttribute()
  {
    try{
      DirContext context = getInitialContext();
      Attribute objclasses = new BasicAttribute("objectclass");
      objclasses.add("top");
      objclasses.add("person");
```

Listing 12.1 **Continued**

```
      objclasses.add("organizationalPerson");
      objclasses.add("inetOrgPerson");
      Attribute cn = new BasicAttribute("cn", "John Doe");
      Attribute sn = new BasicAttribute("sn", "Doe");
      Attribute telephonenumber = new BasicAttribute("telephonenumber",
        "777777777");
      Attribute givenNames = new BasicAttribute("givenname", "John");
      //Specify the dn we are adding
      String dn = "uid=jdoe, ou=People";
      Attributes organization = new BasicAttributes();
      organization.put(objclasses);
      organization.put(cn);
      organization.put(sn);
      organization.put(telephonenumber);
      organization.put(givenNames);
      context.createSubcontext(dn, organization);
    }
    catch(NamingException namingException){
      namingException.printStackTrace();
    }
  }

  public void replaceAttributes()
  {
    try{
      DirContext context = getInitialContext();
      ModificationItem modificationItems[] = new ModificationItem[2];
      modificationItems[0] = new ModificationItem(
        DirContext.REPLACE_ATTRIBUTE,
        new BasicAttribute("sn", "Carter") );
      modificationItems[1] = new ModificationItem(
        DirContext.REPLACE_ATTRIBUTE,
        new BasicAttribute("telephonenumber", "111111111111") );

      context.modifyAttributes("uid=scarter, ou=People ",
        modificationItems);

      String filter = "(&(sn=Carter)(mail=*))";
      searchUsingFilterUsingSearch(filter);
    }
    catch(NamingException namingException){
      namingException.printStackTrace();
    }
  }
```

Listing 12.1 **Continued**

```
public void removeAttributes()
{
  try{
    DirContext context = getInitialContext();
    ModificationItem modificationItems[] = new ModificationItem[1];

    modificationItems[0] = new ModificationItem(
      DirContext.REMOVE_ATTRIBUTE,
      new BasicAttribute("telephonenumber") );

    context.modifyAttributes("uid=jdoe, ou=People ",
      modificationItems);

    String filter = "(&(sn=Doe)(givenname=*))";
    searchUsingFilterUsingSearch(filter);
  }
   catch(NamingException namingException){
    namingException.printStackTrace();
  }
}

public void getSelectedAttributesUsingGetAttributes()
{
  try{
    DirContext context = getInitialContext();
    // search for the object with attribute value uid is scarter
    // and has the attribute givenname
    String resultAttributes[] = {"uid", "givenname",
                          "sn", "telephonenumber"};
    // ignore name case
    // Search for objects with those matching attributes
    Attributes searchResults
      = context.getAttributes("uid=scarter,ou=People ",
      resultAttributes);
    SampleSearchExample.printSearchResults(searchResults);
  }
  catch(NamingException namingException){
    namingException.printStackTrace();
  }
}

public void getEveryAttributeUsingGetAttributes()
{
  try{
```

Listing 12.1 **Continued**

```
      DirContext context = getInitialContext();
      // search for the object with attribute value uid is scarter
        // ignore name case, Search for objects with those matching attributes

      Attributes searchResults
        = context.getAttributes("uid=scarter, ou=People");
      SampleSearchExample.printSearchResults(searchResults);
    }
    catch(NamingException namingException){
      namingException.printStackTrace();
    }
  }

  public void getEveryAttributeUsingSearch()
  {
    try{
      DirContext context = getInitialContext();
      // search for the object with attribute value uid is scarter
      // and has the attribute givenname
      BasicAttribute atr1 = new BasicAttribute("uid", "scarter");
      BasicAttribute atr2 = new BasicAttribute("givenname");
      Attributes matchAttrs = new BasicAttributes(true);
      matchAttrs.put(atr1);
      matchAttrs.put(atr2);
      // ignore name case
      // Search for objects with those matching attributes
      NamingEnumeration searchResults
        = context.search("ou=People", matchAttrs);
      SampleSearchExample.printSearchResults(searchResults);
    }
    catch(NamingException namingException){
      namingException.printStackTrace();
    }
  }

  public void getSelectedAttributesUsingSearch()
  {
    try{
      DirContext context = getInitialContext();
      // search for the object with attribute value uid is scarter
      // and has the attribute givenname
      BasicAttribute atr1 = new BasicAttribute("uid", "scarter");
      BasicAttribute atr2 = new BasicAttribute("givenname");
      Attributes matchAttrs = new BasicAttributes(true);
      matchAttrs.put(atr1);
```

Listing 12.1 **Continued**

```
      matchAttrs.put(atr2);

      String resultAttributes[] = {"uid",
                                   "givenname",
                                   "sn",
                                   "telephonenumber"
                                   };
      // ignore name case
      // Search for objects with those matching attributes
      NamingEnumeration searchResults
        = context.search("ou=People", matchAttrs,
        resultAttributes);
      SampleSearchExample.printSearchResults(searchResults);
    }
     catch(NamingException namingException){
      namingException.printStackTrace();
    }
  }

  public void addAnEventListenerTotheContext(){
    try{
      DirContext context = getInitialContext();
      SearchControls searchControls= new SearchControls();
      searchControls.setSearchScope( SearchControls.SUBTREE_SCOPE );
      EventDirContext eventContext =
        (EventDirContext)context.lookup("");
      eventContext.addNamingListener("ou=People,uid=scarter",
        "(objectclass=*)", searchControls, new SampleNamingListener());
    }
    catch(NamingException namingException){
      namingException.printStackTrace();
    }
  }

  public static void main(String[] args)
  {
    // get System properties
    Properties p = System.getProperties();
    // Set name of properties file to use in initializing the simple
    // lookup.
    String propertiesFileName = "jndi.Properties";

    SampleSearchExample sampleSearchExample = null;
    try {
      // Instantiate an instance of this NamingClient
```

Listing 12.1 **Continued**

```
        sampleSearchExample =
          new SampleSearchExample(propertiesFileName);
    } catch (IOException ioException) {
      System.out.println("Error :" + ioException);
      System.exit(0);
    }

    sampleSearchExample.addAnEventListenerTotheContext();
    sampleSearchExample.getEveryAttributeUsingSearch();
    sampleSearchExample.getSelectedAttributesUsingSearch();

    // Ask for objects with attribute sn == Carter and which have
    // the "mail" attribute.
    String filter = "(&(sn=Carter)(mail=*))" ;
    sampleSearchExample.searchUsingFilterUsingSearch(filter);

    sampleSearchExample.getEveryAttributeUsingGetAttributes();

    sampleSearchExample.addANewAttribute();
    sampleSearchExample.removeAttributes();
    sampleSearchExample.replaceAttributes();
  }
}
```

Listing 12.2 **Sample Directory Service Event Listener (`SampleNamingListener.java`)**

```
package ejava.jndi.directory;
// imports excluded from text
...

public class SampleNamingListener  implements NamespaceChangeListener,
  ObjectChangeListener
{
  public void objectAdded(NamingEvent namingEvent)
  {
    System.out.println(" Object Added :");
    System.out.println("Change information :"
                      + namingEvent.getChangeInfo());
    System.out.println("New binding :"+ namingEvent.getNewBinding());
  }

  public void objectRemoved(NamingEvent namingEvent)
  {
    System.out.println(" Object Removed :");
```

Listing 12.2 **Continued**

```
    System.out.println("Old binding :"+ namingEvent.getOldBinding());
  }

  public void objectRenamed(NamingEvent namingEvent)
  {
    System.out.println(" Object Renamed :");
    System.out.println("Old binding :"+ namingEvent.getOldBinding());
    System.out.println("New binding :"+ namingEvent.getNewBinding());
  }

  public void objectChanged(NamingEvent namingEvent)
  {
    System.out.println(" Object Changed :");
    System.out.println("Change information :"
                       + namingEvent.getChangeInfo());
    System.out.println("Old binding :"+ namingEvent.getOldBinding());
    System.out.println("New binding :"+ namingEvent.getNewBinding());
  }

  public void namingExceptionThrown(NamingExceptionEvent
                                namingExceptionEvent)
  {
   System.out.println(" NamingException Event :");
   NamingException namingException = namingExceptionEvent.getException();
   System.out.println(" Exception :"+ namingException);
  }
}
```

The preceding examples illustrate interacting with a directory service at a known URL. However, new to the JNDI LDAP SPI provided with the J2SE, multiple URLs or URLs without host names or ports may be provided to the JNDI LDAP SPI. In the case of multiple URLs, the `java.naming.provider.url` property is set with a space-separated list of URLs, each of which includes the host name, port, and distinguished name. The JNDI LDAP SPI will then consult each URL in sequence until it finds a service for which a connection can be established. In the case of URLs with no host name or port being provided, the URL only defines a distinguished name such as `ldap:///dc=gcti,dc=com`. In such a scenario, the LDAP service provider will attempt to dynamically locate the directory service using information provided to it by the Domain Name System's (DNS) resource records. We discuss DNS and DNS resource records later in this chapter.

JNDI LDAP V3 API Extensions

The `javax.naming.ldap` package contains a set of JNDI API classes and interfaces that support some of the LDAP v3 extended set of operations and controls. Figure 12.3

depicts the classes and interfaces composing the `javax.naming.ldap` package. The `LDAPContext` interface extends the basic directory service operations supported by the `DirContext` interface with additional LDAP v3–style operations. The concrete `InitialLdapContext` class implements the `LDAPContext` interface and is the primary class used to invoke LDAP v3–style functionality.

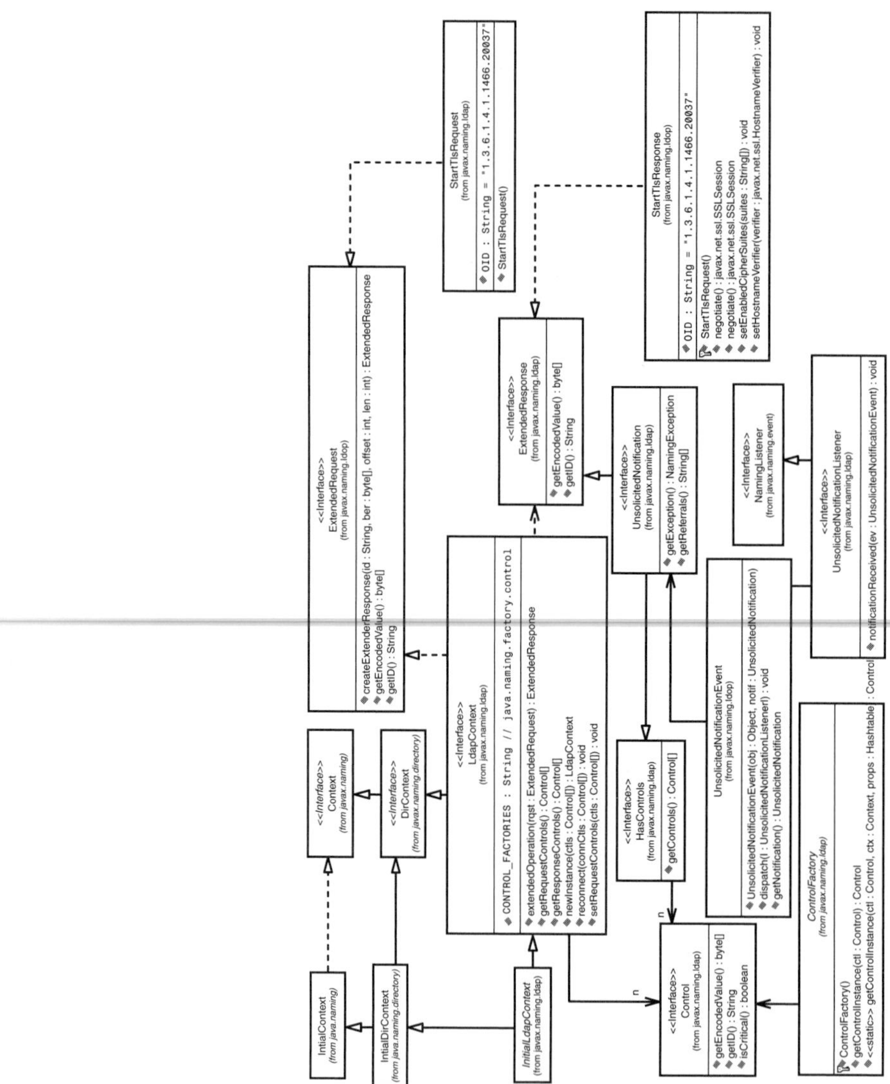

Figure 12.3 JNDI LDAP v3 extensions.

The `extendedOperation()` method on the `LDAPContext` is used to issue LDAP v3–style `ExtendedRequest` objects and receive LDAP v3–style `ExtendedResponse` objects. A service provider implements these interfaces for particular extended operations, and the API user then uses such concrete classes to interact with the `LDAPContext`. An `ExtendedRequest` service provider implementation uses the generic nature of LDAP v3 to create a generic request object consisting of a sequence of name-value pairs that are to be sent to the LDAP v3 server. Similarly, the `ExtendedResponse` service provider implementation returns a generic response object consisting of a sequence of name-value pairs received from the LDAP v3 server.

Service provider objects that implement the `Control` interface encapsulate generically defined controls used to affect the extended request and response behavior of the LDAP v3 server. These are referred to as request controls and response controls, respectively. For example, a `limit` request control may be used to limit the number of results returned from an LDAP search. Or a `change-notify` response control may be returned by the server, to notify clients of changes to the directory.

Such `Control` objects can be set onto the `LDAPContext` itself. They can also be returned from an `UnsolicitedNotification` object received from the LDAP server for unsolicited extended responses by virtue of the fact that the `UnsolicitedNotification` interface extends the `HasControls` interface. When an event is generated due to an `UnsolicitedNotification`, an `UnsolicitedNotificationEvent` object is created and can be dispatched to an object implementing the `UnsolicitedNotificationListener` interface.

New to the J2SE v1.4 is the JNDI LDAP SPI's support for standard LDAP security requirements. LDAP security requirements revolve around providing support for the Transport Layer Security (TLS) protocol, which extends the Secure Socket Layer (SSL) protocol's support for encrypted communications with better provisions made for authentication via SSL. The `StartTlsRequest` class implements the `ExtendedRequest` interface and embodies support for sending a request in a secure fashion to an LDAP server over an existing connection. After invoking the `InitialLdapContext.extendedOperation()` method with a `StartTlsRequest` object, a `StartTlsResponse` object is returned. The `StartTlsResponse` object may then be used to induce an SSL session with the LDAP server by invoking the `StartTlsResponse.negotiate()` method. The `InitialLdapContext` object may then be used to perform confidential requests and responses with the LDAP server.

JNDI LDAP Connection Pooling

Also new to the JNDI LDAP SPI in J2SE v1.4 is the concept of connection pooling. When an LDAP client indicates that it wants to use connection pooling, it informs the LDAP SPI service provider that connections to an LDAP server are to be pooled and doled out to the client on a request-by-request basis. That is, the LDAP service provider will create and manage a collection of LDAP connections in a pool. When the client issues a request, one of the connections in the pool will be used and then returned to the pool after the response is satisfied. Because connections are not associated per client, care should be taken to not use connection pooling when a stateful LDAP session is assumed, such as when using a secure TLS SSL LDAP connection.

To specify that connection pooling should be used, the JNDI LDAP client simply sets the `com.sun.jndi.connect.pool` property to `true` inside the `Hashtable` used when constructing an `InitialDirContext` object. For example:

```
Properties props = new Properties();
props.setProperty(Context.PROVIDER_URL,
                  "ldap://localhost:389/dc=gcti,dc=com");
props.setProperty(Context.INITIAL_CONTEXT_FACTORY,
                  "com.sun.jndi.ldap.LdapCtxFactory");
props.setProperty("com.sun.jndi.ldap.connect.pool", "true");
DirContext context = new InitialDirContext(props);
```

DSML

XML and Web services have come along as the de facto standards for representing data and communicating in a distributed fashion via XML-based requests and responses. It should thus come as no surprise that there is a standard not only for representing data in a directory service using XML but also for representing directory service requests and responses using XML. This standard is referred to as the Directory Services Markup Language (DSML) standard.

DSML may thus be used to represent the structure of a directory service's data using an XML-based format. Such a format enables interoperability among directory servers for exporting and importing information. Directory servers may also expose their services to clients using DSML and Web services protocols. Thus, a directory service client may issue DSML SOAP/HTTP requests to a directory service and receive a DSML SOAP/HTTP response. The particular type of directory service implementation is thus shielded to the client. Because SOAP/HTTP is used as the protocol over which DSML requests and responses are sent, the directory services and client can communicate in the lingo of a Web services paradigm.

Because XML and Web services are wholly supported by Java as described throughout this book, it should also come as no surprise that JNDI now offers an SPI for DSML. DSML is spearheaded by the OASIS standards body (`www.oasis-open.org/committees/dsml`) and was on version 2 at the time of this book's writing. Throughout the remainder of this section, we describe a bit more the structure of a DSML document and how JNDI can be used to communicate with a directory server via DSML.

DSML Document Structure

DSML is a data representation format whose structure is largely transparent to the Java developer. Rather, a Java developer instead focuses on using higher-level APIs that can issue DSML requests and receive DSML responses underneath the hood. The fact that a directory server uses DSML and SOAP/HTTP for such communication exchanges matters to the developer only in terms of the interoperability it provides. Nevertheless, it helps to get a sense of what DSML looks like in order to better appreciate its usage and benefits.

To get a sense for the structure of DSML documents, we will present a few examples of DSML documents here in the context of associated JNDI calls. Thus, for example, a JNDI API call to search based on particular attribute values, such as

```
BasicAttribute atr1 = new BasicAttribute("building", "A");
BasicAttribute atr2 = new BasicAttribute("floor", "5");
Attributes where = new BasicAttributes(true);
where.put(atr1);
where.put(atr2);
NamingEnumeration enum = dirContext.search("Printers", where);
```

may have an associated DSML request snippet of the following form:

```
<dsml:searchRequest requestID="1" dn="ou=Printers" scope="singleLevel"
   derefAliases="derefAlways">
   <dsml:filter>
      <dsml:and>
         <dsml:equalityMatch name="building">
            <dsml:value>A</dsml:value>
         </dsml:equalityMatch>
         <dsml:equalityMatch name="floor">
            <dsml:value>5</dsml:value>
         </dsml:equalityMatch>
      </dsml:and>
   </dsml:filter>
</dsml:searchRequest>
```

Such a DSML request is actually embedded inside of a more general batch request that may contain not only search requests but also modify requests and other types of requests as illustrated here:

```
<dsml:batchRequest
   xmlns="urn:oasis:names:tc:DSML:2:0:core"
   xmlns:dsml="urn:oasis:names:tc:DSML:2:0:core"
   xmlns:xsd="http://www.w3.org/2001/XMLSchema"
   xmlns:xsi="http://www.w3.org/2001/XMLSchema-instance">
  <dsml:searchRequest>...</dsml:searchRequest>
  <dsml:modifyRequest>...</dsml:modifyRequest>
</dsml:batchRequest>
```

DSML requests may also encapsulate search filters. For example, a JNDI search filter request of the form

```
BasicAttribute atr1 = new BasicAttribute("building", "A");
BasicAttribute atr2 = new BasicAttribute("floor", "5");
```

```
Attributes where = new BasicAttributes(true);
where.put(atr1);
where.put(atr2);
String select[] = {"IP", "Port"};
NamingEnumeration enum = dirContext.search("Printers", where, select);
```

may manifest itself as a DSML search request of the following form:

```
<dsml:searchRequest requestID="1" dn="ou=Printers" scope="singleLevel"
   derefAliases="derefAlways">
   <dsml:filter>
      <dsml:and>
         <dsml:equalityMatch name="building">
            <dsml:value>A</dsml:value>
         </dsml:equalityMatch>
         <dsml:equalityMatch name="floor">
            <dsml:value>5</dsml:value>
         </dsml:equalityMatch>
      </dsml:and>
   </dsml:filter>
   <dsml:attributes>
      <dsml:attribute name="IP"/>
      <dsml:attribute name="Port"/>
   </dsml:attributes>
</dsml:searchRequest>
```

Search controls are also another type of directory service request that can be handled by DSML requests. Thus, a JNDI-based request using the search control

```
String filter = "(&(building=A)(floor=*))" ;
SearchControls searchControls = new SearchControls();
String[] resultAttributes = {"name", "building", "floor", "room"};
searchControls.setReturningAttributes(resultAttributes);
NamingEnumeration searchResults =
    dirContext.search("Printers", filter, searchControls);
```

could be performed in DSML as shown here:

```
<dsml:searchRequest requestID="1" dn="ou=Printers" scope="singleLevel"
   derefAliases="derefAlways">
   <dsml:filter>
      <dsml:and>
         <dsml:equalityMatch name="building">
            <dsml:value>A</dsml:value>
         </dsml:equalityMatch>
         <dsml:present name="floor"/>
      </dsml:and>
   </dsml:filter>
   <dsml:attributes>
      <dsml:attribute name="name"/>
      <dsml:attribute name="building"/>
```

```
      <dsml:attribute name="floor"/>
      <dsml:attribute name="room"/>
   </dsml:attributes>
</dsml:searchRequest>
```

As mentioned, modification requests are also possible with DSML. Thus, a modification to a directory service using JNDI may look like

```
Attributes attrs = new BasicAttributes(true);
attrs.put("floor","4");
attrs.put("room","404");
printerContext.modifyAttributes("Printers",
                                DirContext.REPLACE_ATTRIBUTE, attrs);
```

with an associated DSML request looking like this:

```
<dsml:modifyRequest requestID="1" dn="ou=Printers">
   <dsml:modification name="floor" operation="replace">
      <dsml:value>4</dsml:value>
   </dsml:modification>
   <dsml:modification name="room" operation="replace">
      <dsml:value>404</dsml:value>
   </dsml:modification>
</dsml:modifyRequest>
```

And as mentioned earlier, because all DSML requests are formulated as batch requests, a batch of modification requests implemented via JNDI, such as

```
ModificationItem mod1 = new ModificationItem(
                              DirContext.REPLACE_ATTRIBUTE,
                              new BasicAttribute("room", "408"));
ModificationItem mod2 = new ModificationItem(
                               DirContext.REMOVE_ATTRIBUTE,
                               new BasicAttribute("color"));
ModificationItem mod3 = new ModificationItem(
                               DirContext.ADD_ATTRIBUTE,
                               new BasicAttribute("status", "online"));

ModificationItem modItems[] = {mod1, mod2, mod3};
printerContext.modifyAttributes("Printers", modItems);
```

manifests itself as a DSML request similar to the following:

```
<dsml:batchRequest
   xmlns="urn:oasis:names:tc:DSML:2:0:core"
   xmlns:dsml="urn:oasis:names:tc:DSML:2:0:core"
   xmlns:xsd="http://www.w3.org/2001/XMLSchema"
   xmlns:xsi="http://www.w3.org/2001/XMLSchema-instance">
   <dsml:modifyRequest requestID="1" dn="ou=Printers">
      <dsml:modification name="room" operation="replace">
         <dsml:value>408</dsml:value>
```

```
      </dsml:modification>
      <dsml:modification name="color" operation="remove"/>
      <dsml:modification name="status" operation="add">
         <dsml:value>online</dsml:value>
      </dsml:modification>
   </dsml:modifyRequest>
</dsml:batchRequest>
```

And as a skeletal example of a DSML batch response resulting from a DSML search query, we might have this:

```
<?xml version="1.0" encoding="UTF-8" ?>
<dsml:batchResponse
                 xmlns="urn:oasis:names:tc:DSML:2:0:core"
                 xmlns:dsml="urn:oasis:names:tc:DSML:2:0:core"
                 xmlns:xsd="http://www.w3.org/2001/XMLSchema"
                 xmlns:xsi="http://www.w3.org/2001/XMLSchema-instance">
    <dsml:searchResponse>
       <dsml:searchResultEntry dn="uid=admin,ou=people,dc=gcti,dc=com">
          <dsml:attr name="uid">
             <dsml:value>admin</dsml:value>
          </dsml:attr>
          <dsml:attr name="ou">
             <dsml:value>People</dsml:value>
          </dsml:attr>
             ...
       </dsml:searchResultEntry>
    </dsml:searchResponse>
          ...
</dsml:batchResponse>
```

JNDI DSML SPI

Now that we have a basic understanding of what a DSML document looks like, let's look at some examples using JNDI to manipulate DSML documents and to communicate with a directory server via DSML and SOAP/HTTP. At the time of this writing, a JNDI SPI for DSML v1.0 existed but was already becoming outdated by the new JNDI SPI for DSML v2.0. DSML v2.0 is the version of DSML that specified support for passing DSML documents around via a SOAP/HTTP Web services paradigm.

> **Note**
>
> A set of basic examples for using JNDI with DSML is provided beneath the `examples\src\ejava\jndi\directory\dsml` directory. All such examples are created with DSML v2.0 in mind. However, at the time of this writing, support for DSML v2.0 by the directory servers on the market and by the JNDI DSML v2.0 SPI was limited. The latest JNDI DSML v2.0 SPI is downloadable from `http://java.sun.com/products/jndi/serviceproviders.html`.

> Note also that some of the examples here were based on an early access version of the JNDI DSML v2 SPI, that SPI's documentation, and the SPI's examples provided with that SPI's distribution.
>
> For each example, a different `runXXX` script is generated from the ANT build and deposited into the `examples\src\ejava\jndi\directory\dsml` directory. A `jndiXXX.properties` file in that same directory is copied to a `jndi.properties` file used by the examples when each example's script is executed. You'll want to modify each `jndiXXX.properties` file as appropriate before executing each example.

As a first example, the `GenerateDSMLRequest` class equipped with this chapter's code builds up a DSML request and writes the results to a file for your convenience. Typically, such a request would be imported or somehow delivered to a DSML-compliant directory server to satisfy the request. There is nothing really new about this example aside from the fact that it lets you see for yourself what DSML requests look like. Inside of the `GenerateDSMLRequest.main()` method, a series of calls to a JNDI directory service context is induced. A special DSML request SPI factory and a pseudo-URL of the directory storage mechanism (here it is a file) are defined as follows in the `jndidsmlrequest.properties` file:

```
# JNDI DSML SPI Factory for DSML requests
java.naming.factory.initial
➥=com.sun.jndi.dsmlv2.request.DsmlRequestCtxFactory
# Test file to output a sample DSML request
java.naming.provider.url=file:dsmlRequest.xml
```

Thus, when `GenerateDSMLRequest` constructs a new `InitialDirContext` object and conducts a series of operations on that context, a collection of DSML requests are discreetly being batched inside of the context object. The request is then written in memory using the `generateDSMLRequestAsAMemoryObject()` method, which uses a Sun JNDI DSML SPI proprietary class called `BatchRequest` as shown here:

```
private void generateDSMLRequestAsAMemoryObject()
{
  // Generate BatchRequest Object
  Element batchRequest =
       BatchRequest.toDomFromContext(context);
  // Generate Request as SOAP Envelope
  Element soapEnvelope =
       BatchRequest.toDomSoapEnvelopeFromContext(context);
}
```

Finally, when the `InitialDirContext` object is closed, the DSML request is written to the `dsmlRequest.xml` file. After running the example, check out the file and see for yourself what a DSML request document looks like. We also provide a `dsmlRequestGenerated.xml` file with the example code illustrating what the output should look like.

The `SearchUsingUrl` example demonstrates use of the JNDI DSML SPI to read directory service entries at a specified URL and return the information as a DSML document in the form of a DSML response. The crux of the `SearchUsingUrl` example is shown here:

```
// Context From where Search Starts
String rootContextUrl =
  (String)properties.get("java.naming.provider.url");
// Set the protocol Property
String protocol =
  (String)properties.get("java.protocol.handler.pkgs");
System.setProperty("java.protocol.handler.pkgs",protocol);

// Create URL object with URL Provider
URL connectingURL = new URL(rootContextUrl);
// Open Connection to the URL
URLConnection urlConnection = connectingURL.openConnection();
// Read the Result into BufferedReader
BufferedReader readResult = new BufferedReader(
        new InputStreamReader(urlConnection.getInputStream()));
String currentResultLine = null;
// Print the contents of BufferedReader on to Console.
while((currentResultLine = readResult.readLine()) != null){
    System.out.println(currentResultLine);
}
```

The preceding example uses a JNDI DSML v2 SPI factory and iPlanet LDAP directory service URL read from a copied form of the `jndildapurlreader.properties` file set like so:

```
java.protocol.handler.pkgs=com.sun.jndi.dsmlv2.protocol
java.naming.provider.url=ldap://localhost:389/ou=people,dc=gcti,dc=com
```

After the `runurlsample` file is executed, a `dsmlResponse.xml` file is generated with the directory service query response formatted as a DSML response document. We also provide a `dsmlResponseURL.xml` file with the example code illustrating what the output should look like. And by the way, you indeed need to be running the iPlanet LDAP directory server as described earlier in this chapter for this example to work.

The `GenerateDSMLResponse` class illustrates use of a special JNDI DSML SPI for generating DSML responses via queries executed over a DSML data source. In our example case, we simply use the DSML data source generated from the `SearchUsingUrl` example. In this example, the DSML response SPI, the URL of the `dsmlResponse.xml` file, and a context search string are defined inside of the `jndidsmlresponse.properties` file as shown here:

```
java.naming.factory.initial=
➥com.sun.jndi.dsmlv2.response.DsmlResponseCtxFactory
java.naming.provider.url=file:dsmlResponse.xml
NAME_OF_CONTEXT_TO_SEARCH=ou=people,dc=gcti,dc=com
```

The GenerateDSMLResponse class makes use of the JNDI API as usual whereby an InitialDirContext is created using the dsmlResponse.xml file as the URL and JNDI operations are performed. The dsmlResponse.xml file is then modified when the closeContext() method is invoked to print and close the context as shown here:

```
public void closeContext(){
    System.out.println("DSML Context:\n"
                       + context.toString());
    try{
        context.close();
    }
    catch(Exception ex){
        ex.printStackTrace();
    }
}
```

Note that we also provide a dsmlResponseGenerated.xml file with the example code illustrating what the output should look like.

Finally, the SampleSOAPToDSMLServer.java example searches a directory service that exposes itself via SOAP/HTTP and to DSML requests and prints the results of the search. Standard JNDI API calls are made as usual. The difference, however, lies in what properties are passed into the construction of an InitialDirContext object. Two key JNDI properties to be set in the jndisoapdsmlcontext.properties file for the DSML SOAP/HTTP SPI example are properties for the DSML SOAP/HTTP context factory and the URL for the DSML SOAP/HTTP-compliant directory server as shown here:

```
java.naming.factory.initial=com.sun.jndi.dsmlv2.soap.DsmlSoapCtxFactory
java.naming.provider.url=http://localhost:8080/dsml
```

Thus, as you can see, the JNDI DSML 2.0 SPI offers you numerous ways to interface with DSML document data and to DSML-compliant directory servers. You can generate and import DSML document data files directly or talk to a DSML-compliant directory server via SOAP/HTTP with embedded DSML requests and responses. By using the JNDI DSML 2.0 SPI with servers that are DSML and SOAP/HTTP compliant, you can maximize interoperability with your enterprise Java applications that need to tap the services of directory servers.

DNS

In this section we introduce the Domain Name System (DNS), and describe how both simple DNS name lookups and more sophisticated DNS name management functionality can be performed with Java and JNDI. An understanding of DNS is important for any enterprise Java developer. Fortunately, the level of support for DNS via Java with JNDI now goes beyond the previously limited means offered by earlier version of the J2SE. Before, Java developers were limited to performing only simple lookups. But now that a JNDI SPI for DNS has been implemented, you only have to be aware of the same JNDI API that you've already familiarized yourself with for directory services.

The Domain Name System

The DNS provides a translation of the hierarchically defined machine host names that we are all familiar with (for example, www.assuredtech.com) to and from IP addresses (for example, 66.95.40.122). DNS names have a syntax convention and map to IP addresses that are logical addresses of network devices or hosts. As discussed in Appendix D, "TCP/IP Communications," these IP addresses are used by network routing elements to determine how to deliver IP-based messages to a host machine. When human-readable and structured names are used, the task of the developer is simplified and less dependent on a prior knowledge of the internals of routing tables and machine configurations.

The names in DNS adhere to the syntax convention of case-insensitive name components separated by dots (.). Parsing of the names occurs from right to left with the rightmost name component corresponding to a top-level domain context. Many organizations use the set of top-level domain names presented in Table 12.4.

Table 12.4 **Top-Level DNS Names**

Name	Description
com	Commercial entities
edu	Four-year collegiate educational institutions
net	Network access providers and administrators
gov	U.S. federal government organizations
mil	U.S. military organizations
org	Miscellaneous and nonprofit organizations
int	International organizations

Additionally, a country code can also serve as a top-level domain name, such as the code US for United States–based organizations. Names are then created according to this standard format:

```
<Entity Name>.<Locality>.<State Code>.US
```

For example:

```
AssuredTech.Leesburg.VA.US
```

However, few commercial U.S. organizations adhere to this standard; they utilize the top-level domain names of Table 12.4. U.S. state- and city-level organizations to a certain extent do use the US country code and their state code for such things as K–12 schools (K12), community colleges (CC), state government organizations (STATE), and libraries (LIB). Country codes are used by many organizations outside of the U.S., such as co.uk for corporations in the United Kingdom and ac.uk for United Kingdom academic institutions.

A subdomain is prepended to a top-level domain name with a dot as a separator to formulate a "registered" domain name. Thus, assuredtech.com is a registered domain with `assuredtech` as the subdomain and `com` as the top-level domain. Regionally designated authority to grant "registered" domain names is provided by Internet Resource Registries such as with Verisign, Inc., or Register.com.

An organization that has registered a domain name with an Internet Resource Registry can then define various subdomains for the registered domain name within their own network. These subdomains can be organized in any way according to the organization's liking, such as `sales.myCorp.com` and `products.myCorp.com`. Host names for machines within these subdomains can then be assigned. Thus, `joeSalesman.sales.myCorp.com` and `elPresidente.myCorp.com` may be valid, fully qualified domain names adhering to the following format:

```
<Hostname>.<Optional One or More Dot-Separated Subdomains>.
➥<Registered Domain Name>
```

Sometimes, the individual name components between the "dots" of a domain name are also referred to as "labels."

A DNS server can run DNS software offered by various COTS packages on various platforms. A popular implementation for Unix systems is the Berkley Internet Name Domain (BIND) package, which has also been ported to Windows platforms (`www.isc.org/bind.html`). When establishing a domain name, the Internet Resource Registry of the U.S. (Network Solutions, Inc., at `www.networksolutions.com`) requires that primary and secondary IP addresses be designated for a primary and backup DNS server. The designated DNS servers must then be configured to map host names and IP addresses for hosts and subdomains within the domain. Each host machine in the domain must be configured to know the IP addresses of the local DNS servers.

When a TCP/IP request is made with a host name, the TCP/IP protocol consults the DNS server with which it has been configured to look up the IP address with the associated host name. If a DNS server cannot resolve a host name to an IP address, it forwards the request to another DNS server. If none of the DNS servers can resolve the host name, a root DNS server is finally consulted that uses the top-level domain name to consult master DNS servers for a top-level domain. These master DNS servers map the full domain name to an IP address or return the fact that they could not resolve the host name.

This whole DNS lookup process may seem as though it would be very time-consuming. However, each DNS server is typically configured with a cache in which each cache entry has a "time to live" parameter associated with it for refreshing a new host name to IP address mapping (typically refreshed every one to two days). Each DNS server also has a timeout value associated with it and returns the fact that it could not resolve the name even though it is possible that it could have been given enough time. A subsequent request may indeed return a resolved IP address because the DNS server may have had more time to reply and make use of more information in its cache. When surfing the Net, you might observe this behavior from time to time when you see that a Web page request proves unfruitful one instance but then proves fruitful with a new request shortly thereafter.

As you can see, the DNS is a hierarchical structure beginning with a top-level DNS name such as "com" or "gov." Each subsequent subdomain helps flesh out the tree of the DNS. Each subdomain or label in the DNS tree is sometimes referred to as a "node." In the parlance of a naming or directory service, these nodes are akin to contexts. Thus, the root context of DNS may contain "com" and "gov" as subcontexts (that is, nodes). The "com" context may then contain "assuredtech" and "beeshirts" as subcontexts. The "assuredtech" context may contain "www" as a subcontext, and so on.

Although you might think that the DNS could be represented as a simple naming service whereby each node may map to an IP address, the fact is that each node may also be associated with attributes about a particular DNS name. Such a name-to-resource and attribute mapping leads one to consider the DNS more as a directory service.

Each node in the DNS is associated with a "resource record." A resource record is simply a collection of attributes associated with a domain name and IP address. A resource record typically consists of these components:

- Owner Name: The fully qualified domain name, an alias name, or a subdomain to which a parent domain name (aka "zone") will be appended.
- TTL: The Time To Live indicating the number of seconds until a cached DNS entry is refreshed.
- Record Class: Indicates the scheme used to define records. Almost all systems use "Internet" (`IN`) as a scheme. "Hesiod" (`HS`) and "Chaos" (`CH`) are other record schemes but are rarely used.
- Record Type: Indicates the type of record defined by this node and as defined in more detail in the following text.
- Record Data: Contains the actual values for the record and is a function of the Record Type.
- Comments: An optional component provides a placeholder to define textual descriptions about the resource record.

As mentioned previously, each resource record will have a record type and values. A list of common DNS record types, their textual monikers, and numeric identifiers are defined here:

- Address Record (`A` = 1): The record data contains an IP address associated with the domain name for this resource record.
- Canonical Name Record (`CNAME` = 5): The record data contains the domain name, and the owner name contains an alias for that domain name.
- Name Server Record (`NS` = 2): Declares a name server that is responsible for handling requests to a particular zone.
- Start Of Authority Record (`SOA` = 6): Indicates that the name server responsible for the current zone is the authoritative server knowing how to map all names within the zone.

- Pointer Record (`PTR` = 12): Designates a reverse mapping of IP addresses to canonical names. The name of the record is the reverse order of the IP address prefixed to `IN-ADDR.ARPA` (for example, `122.40.95.64.IN-ADDR.ARPA`).
- Mail Exchange Record (`MX` = 15): Designates a mail server for a domain name. The mail exchange record with the lowest number serves as the primary mail server with others as backups.
- Text Record (`TXT` = 16): The record data can contain up to 255 characters of informational text.
- Host Information Record (`HINFO` = 13): The record data contains information about the host such as the operating system and platform type.
- Service Record (`SRV`): Contains information about available services from the host whereby each service is named according to its service name, protocol used, and domain name with which it is associated. The priority of the service to be executed, weighting of its scalability, service port, and host name are all associated with SRV records.
- Naming Authority Pointer Record (`NAPTR`): Defines a URI rewriting rule in the form of a regular expression. Thus, a URI submitted to the name server in one form may invoke this rewriting rule and re-issue the query in the resulting rewritten form.

Thus, viewing DNS as a directory service, we can see that DNS nodes map to directory service contexts, and DNS components and resource records map to directory service attributes. A name issued to DNS is typically in the form of a domain name, and the IP address is typically the handle response value. In what follows, we will apply these concepts to see how core Java can perform basic DNS name and IP address mappings and how JNDI can provide a more complete view of a DNS tree.

Java-Based DNS Interfacing

A simple way to interact with the DNS via Java is by use of the `java.net.InetAddress` class to look up an IP address given a host name. Three primary static methods defined on `InetAddress` can be used to return `InetAddress` object instances:

- `InetAddress getByName(String hostName)` returns a handle to an `InetAddress` object given an IP address in the form *`X.X.X.X`* (for example, `66.95.40.122`) or a machine name `String` (for example, `www.assuredtech.com`).
- `InetAddress[] getAllByName(String hostName)` returns a handle to an array of all known `InetAddress` objects for a particular `hostName` defined as in the `getByName()` call.
- `InetAddress getLocalHost()` returns a handle to an `InetAddress` object for your local host machine.

After an `InetAddress` object is returned, the following calls can be used to obtain host naming and IP address information for use by your applications:

- `String getHostName()` returns a `String` defining the host name associated with this IP address by performing a DNS lookup.
- `String getHostAddress()` returns a `String` containing the IP address in the form *X.X.X.X*.
- `byte[] getAddress()` returns a byte array of the IP address in network order with `byte[0]` as the most significant byte.

Thus, the `InetAddress.getHostName()` call is where the DNS lookup really transpires. All three static `InetAddress` methods and the `getHostName()` method map to native calls from your Java platform implementation to your specific machine's DNS client libraries. The configuration of which DNS servers to contact via your DNS client machine is platform-specific. On Windows NT, for example, DNS is configured from the Network icon accessible from the Control Panel. DNS configuration is then configured from within the Network Control Panel, Protocols tab, TCP/IP Properties, and DNS tab.

JNDI DNS SPI

A JNDI SPI exists for DNS and is included with the J2SE v1.4. Newer versions of the SPI may also be downloaded from the JavaSoft Web site at `www.javasoft.com/products/jndi/serviceproviders.html`. Because we illustrated use of the JNDI Directory Service API capabilities in more depth for the LDAP SPI earlier in this chapter, we don't go into a detailed explanation of JNDI DNS use here. However, we do highlight some salient points, provide snippets, and provide an example for how to use the JNDI DNS SPI here.

To begin with, the DNS SPI factory and a URL for a DNS server must be defined when using the JNDI DNS SPI. A pseudo-URL is defined in the form `dns://`*`HostName`*`:`*`Port/Domain`* to indicate a DNS server to which you want to connect. A default host name of `localhost`, default port of `53`, and default domain of `.` are used if they are not specified. The properties for such values may thus be constructed as exemplified here:

```
Properties props = new Properties();
props.setProperty(Context.PROVIDER_URL,
                 "dns://dns.beeshirts.com:53/beeshirts.com");
props.setProperty(Context.INITIAL_CONTEXT_FACTORY,
                 "com.sun.jndi.dns.DnsContextFactory");
DirContext ctx = new InitialDirContext(props);
Attributes a1 = ctx .getAttributes("www", new String[] {"A"});
Attributes a2 = ctx .getAttributes("b2c", new String[] {"CNAME"});
Attributes a3 = ctx .getAttributes("b2b", new String[] {"A", "SRV"});
Attributes a4 = ctx .getAttributes("mail", new String[] {"MX", "SRV"});
```

Thus, in the preceding snippet, we use JNDI to connect to a DNS server named `dns.beeshirts.com` and retrieve any DNS resource records as attributes associated with host names in the `beeshirts.com` domain.

> **Note**
>
> Under the `examples\src\ejava\jndi\directory` directory, three files exist to illustrate use of DNS with JNDI. In this directory, a `rundnscontext` file is generated from the ANT build, and a `jndiDNSContext.properties` file and a `SampleDNSExample.java` file are provided to illustrate use of the JNDI DNS SPI with a DNS service. Note that you will need to have access to a DNS server to run this example. The generated `rundnscontext` script copies the `jndiDNSContext.properties` file to the `jndi.Properties` filename looked for by the `SampleDNSExample`.

The `SampleDNSExample.java` file in the `examples\src\ejava\jndi\directory` directory reads a target DNS lookup name of interest from the JNDI properties file. Then it simply instantiates an instance of the `SampleDNSExample` and calls a method that lists the contents of the DNS server, given the target lookup name. Two key JNDI properties to be set in the `jndiDNSContext.properties` file for the DNS SPI example are the DNS context factory and the DNS server URL properties:

```
#  Factory Context property for DNS
java.naming.factory.initial=com.sun.jndi.dns.DnsContextFactory

# DNS Server URL
java.naming.provider.url=dns://localhost:53/.
```

Additionally, an example target name to look up must be specified in the `jndiDNSContext.properties` file:

```
# Use this entry to enter an example target name
dns.target.name=foo
```

Although JNDI can be used to communicate with DNS servers, not all methods available on the `DirContext` interface and `InitialDirContext` object are usable by the DNS SPI. The only methods in fact currently usable are these:

```
lookup()
lookupLink()
list()
listBindings()
getAttributes()
composeName()
getNameInNamespace()
getNameParser()
addToEnvironment()
getEnvironment()
removeFromEnvironment()
close()
```

NIS as a Directory Service

The Network Information System (NIS) is a directory service (formerly referred to as the Yellow Pages, or YP) developed by Sun Microsystems in the 1980s and widely used in Unix-based platforms. NIS was designed to allow for the centralized administration of resources shared by a network of machines. Machines in an NIS network share an NIS domain and speak to an NIS domain server to look up and update network information (for example, passwords). NIS also allows clients access to files and other system resources available over a local area network. NIS+ is a later version of NIS providing enhancements to security and other services.

JNDI NIS SPI

A JNDI SPI exists for NIS and is downloadable from the JavaSoft Web site at `www.javasoft.com/products/jndi/serviceproviders.html`. Because we illustrated use of the JNDI Directory Service API capabilities in more depth for the LDAP SPI in this chapter, and because use of the NIS SPI requires NIS server access, we won't go into a detailed explanation of sample NIS use here. However, a simple NIS lookup example is available under the `examples\src\ejava\jndi\directory` directory.

> **Note**
>
> Under the `examples\src\ejava\jndi\directory` directory, three files exist to illustrate use of NIS with JNDI. In this directory, a `runniscontext` script is generated by the ANT build, and a `jndiNISContext.properties` file and a `SampleNISExample.java` file are provided to illustrate use of the JNDI NIS SPI with a remote NIS service. Note that you will need to have NIS running on your network somewhere to run this example and have access to that service from your client program. The `runniscontext` file copies the `jndiNISContext.properties` file to the `jndi.properties` filename looked for by the `SampleNISExample`. Note also that the `build.properties` file must have its `nis.context.root.dir` property set to the root directory of your JNDI NIS SPI install for the example to work.

The `SampleNISExample.java` file in the `examples\src\ejava\jndi\directory` directory reads a target NIS lookup name of interest from the JNDI properties file. Then it simply instantiates an instance of the `SampleNISExample` and calls a method that lists the contents of the NIS server given the target lookup name. Two key JNDI properties to be set in the `jndiNISContext.properties` file for the NIS SPI example are the NIS context factory and the NIS server URL properties:

```
#  Factory Context property for NIS
java.naming.factory.initial=com.sun.jndi.nis.NISCtxFactory

# NIS Server URL
java.naming.provider.url=nis://sampleYPServer/tracking.tshirts.com
```

Additionally, an example target name to look up must be specified in the `jndiNISContext.properties` file:

```
# Use this entry to enter an example target name
nis.target.name=user
```

NDS as a Directory Service

The Novell Directory Service (NDS) is a popular directory service for managing enterprise network resources and network user information. NDS's multiplatform support and its easy-to-use GUI administration toolkit have made it fairly popular with network administrators. NDS servers allow NDS clients to obtain access to such resources as networks, file servers, print servers, and database servers from a centrally managed location. Using NDS, administrators can enable access, limit access, and disable access to such resources by users in an easily configurable fashion.

JNDI NDS SPI

Novell currently offers a JNDI SPI for Java applications to interface with the NDS at `http://developer.novell.com/ndk/download.htm`. As with the DNS and NIS SPI, we provide only a very basic illustration of its use in this chapter because the LDAP section covered the JNDI directory service API in more depth and because use of the NDS SPI requires access to an NDS server. However, we will highlight some key points for NDS access via the NDS SPI here with a more complete example contained under the `examples\src\ejava\jndi\directory` directory.

> **Note**
>
> Under the `examples\src\ejava\jndi\directory` directory, three files exist to illustrate use of NDS with JNDI. In that directory, a `runndscontext` script is generated by the ANT build, and a `jndiNDSContext.properties` file and a `SampleSearchExampleNDS.java` file are provided to illustrate use of the JNDI NDS SPI with a remote NDS server. Note that you will need to have NDS running on your network somewhere to run this example and have access to that service from your client program. The `runndscontext` script copies the `jndiNDSContext.properties` file to the `jndi.Properties` filename looked for by the `SampleSearchExampleNDS`. You will need the `jncpv2.dll` NDS client DLL in your path for Windows environments. Note also that the `build.properties` file must have its `nds.context.root.dir` property set to the `lib` directory beneath the root directory of your JNDI NIS SPI install for the example to work.

The first thing to note about configuring a Java-based JNDI NDS client, such as the `SampleSearchExampleNDS` Java client, is that you will need to configure a few key properties such as the NDS context factory, the URL of your NDS server, and a distinguished name identifying the root context of your NDS server. For example:

```
#  NDS Factory Context property
java.naming.factory.initial=
➥com.novell.service.nds.naming.NdsInitialContextFactory

# NDS Server URL with format of...
#            nds://<treeName>/[fullyDistinguishedName]
java.naming.provider.url=nds://BeeShirtsTree/

# NDS Distinguished Name
NDS_ENTRY_DN=tshirts
```

After connecting to an `InitialDirContext` object using such properties, you can search for a set of basic NDS attributes perhaps by listing the `GivenName`, `Surname`, `PhoneNumber`, `Description`, and `EMail Address` of the NDS server contents using something along these lines:

```
DirContext context = new InitialDirContext(properties);
String entryDN = (String) properties.get("NDS_ENTRY_DN");

BasicAttribute atr1 = new BasicAttribute("Description");
BasicAttribute atr2 = new BasicAttribute("EMail Address");
Attributes matchAttrs = new BasicAttributes(true);
matchAttrs.put(atr1);
matchAttrs.put(atr2);

String resultAttributes[] = {"GivenName", "Surname", "PhoneNumber",
                             "Description","EMail Address"};
NamingEnumeration searchResults
      = context.search(entryDN, matchAttrs, resultAttributes);
```

Finally, you might also search for NDS entries using a set of `SearchControls` as shown here:

```
DirContext context = new InitialDirContext(properties);
String entryDN = (String) properties.get("NDS_ENTRY_DN");
String filter = "(&(surname=Carter)(givenname=*))" ;

SearchControls searchControls = new SearchControls();
String[] resultAttributes = {"GivenName", "Surname", "PhoneNumber"};
searchControls.setReturningAttributes(resultAttributes);
searchControls.setCountLimit(2);

NamingEnumeration searchResults
      = context.search(entryDN, filter, searchControls);
```

Microsoft Active Directory Services

The Microsoft Active Directory Service (ADS) is a directory service that comes preinstalled with the Windows 2000 operating system. The ADS maintains user, security, and network resource information used on a Windows 2000 network. Administration of Windows networks and network resources is all managed by an ADS running on a Windows 2000 server. ADS also provides a GUI interface for managing user information, managing network resources such as printers, and managing distributed applications. ADS employs a DNS naming hierarchy, and ADS servers act as domain controllers for a network.

ADS stores elements in its structure as ADS objects. Each object is defined by a set of attributes and is also uniquely identified by a globally unique identifier (GUID) assigned by the ADS server. Each object also has a schema defining its structure in an LDAP-compatible fashion. ADS objects can assume different name formats as well, including LDAP-style distinguished names, GUIDs, security principal names, secure identifiers, and user login names. ADS objects are published to an ADS server to expose their information to a Windows network domain. ADS servers can be organized in various federated domain configurations.

.NET components can use the ADS by storing their activation and connection information in the ADS. Updates to such information can then be propagated and made available to interested .NET clients on the Windows network. Standard ADS connection information interfaces exist for .NET applications, as well as for RPC and Winsock applications. .NET servers publish connection information using a .NET-specific class storage mechanism inside the ADS.

In addition to a direct LDAPv2- and LDAPv3-compliant C API to the ADS, the Active Directory Service Interface (ADSI) provides a means for exposing application programming interfaces to ADS objects as .NET objects. Behind the scenes of the ADSI, a Service Provider Interface (SPI) also offers a .NET interface to various types of concrete directory service implementations. ADSI SPIs currently exist for connectivity to LDAP, NDS, Novell NetWare 3.x, Windows NT/2000, and Microsoft Internet Information Service Web Server metabases. Thus, whereas ADS represents a concrete implementation of a directory service, the ADSI offers an interface to it as well as potentially other concrete directory service implementations. ADSI interfaces are offered in Java, C++, C, and Visual Basic. Microsoft also has defined a DSML v2.0–compliant interface to ADS. Thus, a Java-based JNDI client can conceivably talk to a Microsoft ADS instance when the JNDI client uses a JNDI DSML v2.0 SPI.

CORBA as a Trading Service

The directory services we have examined thus far all provide a service in which names and attributes information can be registered with a directory server potentially in some hierarchically organized structure. Directory service clients can then list, look up, and search for such attribute information as well as bound objects using a set of search criteria. The CORBA Trading Service (also called CosTrading) is a CORBAservice that is very similar in concept to a directory service. However, the CORBA Trading Service implies more than just support for registering descriptive attributes about an object and support for searching for such objects using some intelligent search criteria. Rather, the CORBA Trading Service also provides support for registering type and interface information about a particular object, as well as support for allowing other federations of trading services to pool their registered objects such that they are available to any clients of the federation. Although such functionality is not necessarily precluded from being used with a directory service, the CORBA Trading Service provides explicitly defined interfaces for such support.

In CORBA Trading Service lingo, a *service exporter* is a CORBA service that exports a service offer to the trading service, which includes either a reference to the distributed service being offered or proxy information that can be used to obtain the service object reference during requested use of the service. The exporter also registers some attribute information about the service being offered. A *service importer* is a trading service client that can look up references or proxies to a service of interest based on a search expression akin to a SQL query or an LDAP query. The service client then has the handle it needs to the CORBA service of interest and can make distributed calls on that object in the typical fashion of CORBA remote invocation. Furthermore, given the federated capabilities offered by the CosTrading interfaces, a particular CORBA Trading Service may be able to satisfy a service client's request by returning a handle to a service that was registered with another trading service which is part of the current trading service's federation.

CORBA Trading Service Components

At the highest level of detail, one of five major trading service components can be supported by a particular trading service implementation. An `org.omg.CosTrading.TraderComponents` base interface provides hooks for which to obtain handles to these five major trading service components, as shown in Figure 12.4. A call to `ORB.resolve_initial_references("TradingService")` will return a handle to a `TraderComponents` object. This can then be used to obtain handles to any of the five major components of a trading service, shown as sub-interfaces of the `TraderComponents` interface in Figure 12.4. If any particular component is not implemented, the `XXX_if()` call on `TraderComponents` will return a null value.

The `org.omg.CosTrading.Lookup` interface is used to query the trading service for desired service matches. Because it is a core component of the trading service, it may even be the object that is returned from the `ORB.resolve_initial_references()` call. The `org.omg.CosTrading.Register` interface is used by service exporters to export their services, as well as modify and withdraw their services. The org.omg.CosTrading.Proxy interface is used to export delayed references to services by service exporters such that the reference to the service will be determined only on a per-demand basis from service clients. The org.omg.CosTrading.Link interface is used to add and remove trading services from a trading service federation. Finally, the org.omg.CosTrading.Admin interface can be used to set various trading service properties and obtain more detailed information about the current registered services.

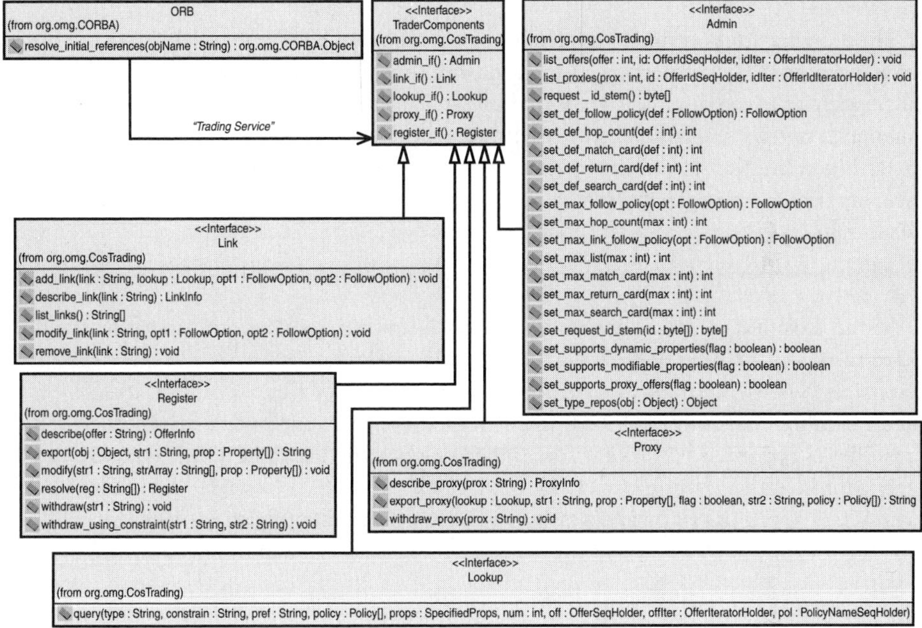

Figure 12.4 CORBA Trading Service components.

The goal of this section is to merely illustrate how one can use the CORBA Trading Service to perform basic object registration and discovery in the context of the other directory and trading services presented in this chapter. Therefore, we do not go into the details behind federating traders via the Link interface, deferring references via the Proxy interface, or managing the trading service via the Admin interface. Rather, we aim to describe the basic and most common use of the CORBA Trading Service via a description and illustration of the Lookup and Register interfaces from a service exporter and service importer point of view.

Service Exporting

Figure 12.5 depicts the primary components involved with exporting a service to a CORBA Trading Service. The MyExporter class in the diagram represents your home-grown class that is responsible for exporting one or more `MyCORBAService` objects also of your own creation. After obtaining a reference to a default `TraderComponents` object such as a `Lookup` object, you can use such an object to obtain references to other supported trading service interfaces such as the `Register` interface using the `TraderComponents.register_if()` call inherited by the `Lookup` interface. However, before you export your objects to the trading service, you should define the interfaces supported by your `MyCORBAService` objects with the trading service.

To describe your service interfaces, you must obtain a handle to an `org.omg.CosTradingRepos.ServiceTypeRepository` object via a call to the `type_repos()` method also supported by your initial reference to either the `Lookup` or the `Register` interface objects. The `type_repos()` interface and a set of interfaces used to determine the level of support for certain operation types are inherited by the `Lookup` and `Register` interfaces from the `org.omg.CosTrading.SupportAttributes` interface. The `ServiceTypeRepository` then offers you a set of interfaces available for adding, describing, listing, removing, and managing various service type interfaces registered with the trading service.

As an example, to add a service type to the `ServiceTypeRepository`, you would need to supply an array of `org.omg.CosTradingRepos.ServiceTypeRepositoryPackage.PropStruct` objects to the `ServiceTypeRepository.add_type()` method. Each `PropStruct` object would need to be populated with the name of the attribute, the mode in which the attribute may be gotten or set using `org.omg.CosTradingRepos.ServiceTypeRepositoryPackage.PropertyMode` identifiers, and the `CORBA::TypeCode` identifying the type of object. After building up an array of `PropStruct` objects describing each attribute of an interface, this `PropStruct` array is then used along with a `String` identifying the name for the new type, an identifier `String` describing the interface, and an array of `String` objects used to indicated any base type names of this type.

After a service type is registered describing the type of objects that will be exported to the trading service, your service exporter can export the object service instances themselves. You accomplished this by calling `export()` on the `Register` interface with the object instances you want to export (that is, your `MyCORBAService` objects), the service type name registered with the `ServiceTypeRepository` with which the object is associated, and an array of `org.omg.CosTradingRepos.ServiceTypeRepositoryPackage.Property` objects. Each `Property` object simply defines a set of name-value pairs describing particular attributes about the object. Note that each attribute name in the `Property` object will typically correspond to a property name associated with this type of object via one of the `PropStruct` objects created and registered with the `ServiceTypeRepository` for this service type.

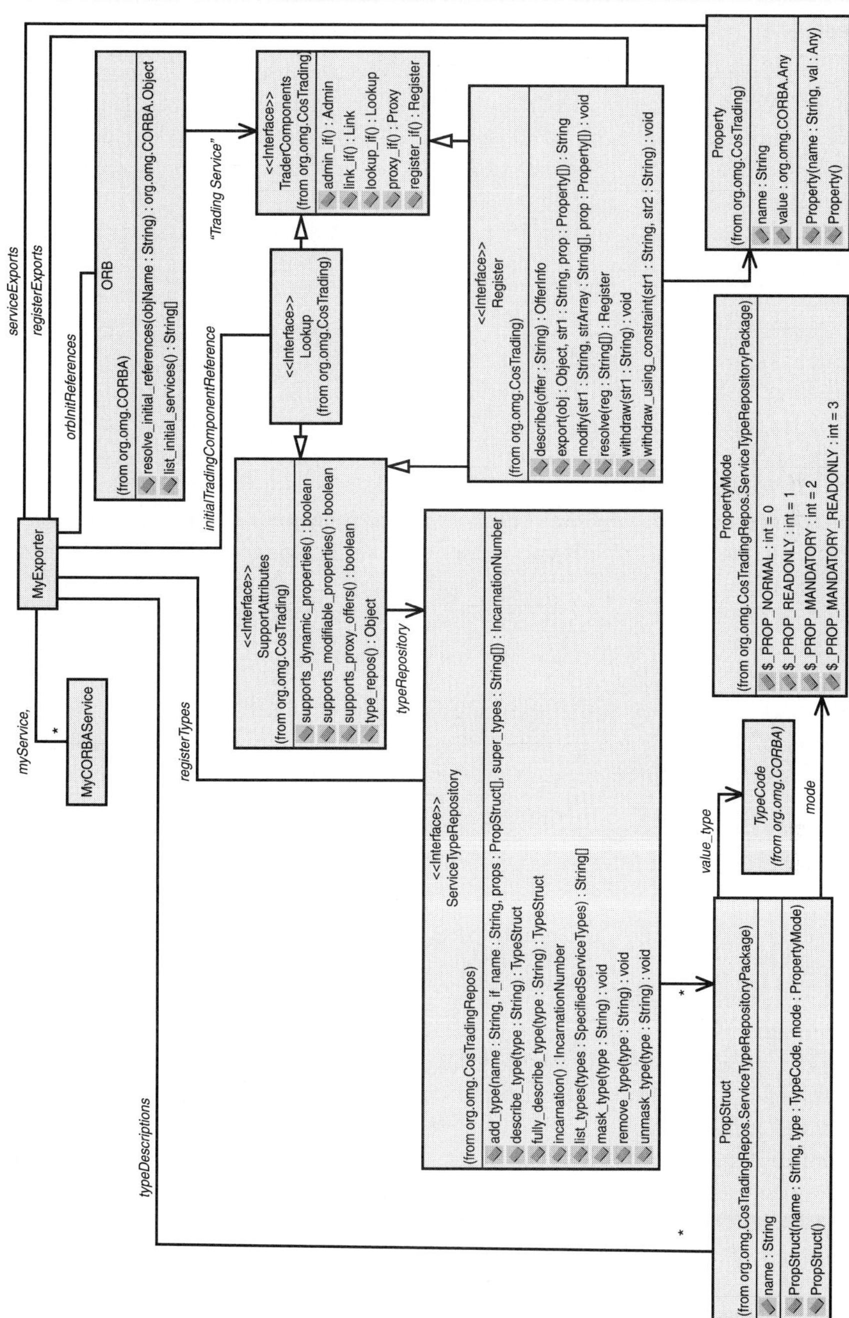

Figure 12.5 CORBA Trading Service exporting.

Service Importing

Figure 12.6 depicts the primary components involved with the client import of a service from a CORBA Trading Service. The MyImporter client obtains a handle to the Lookup interface in the same fashion, as does an exporter. However, the client does not need to obtain a Register interface handle. The client may need to obtain a handle to a ServiceTypeRepository object, however.

The client can list all the service types in a ServiceTypeRepository by calling list_types() with a given org.omg.CosTradingRepos.ServiceTypeRepositoryPackage.SpecifiedServiceTypes instance. The all_dummy() method on the SpecifiedServiceTypes instance can be called with no parameter indicating that all service types should be listed or called with a number designating the fact that only those service types registered because a particular export incarnation number should be listed. Furthermore, given a particular service type name String, a describe_type() call on the ServiceTypeRepository object can be made to return a org.omg.CosTradingRepos.ServiceTypeRepositoryPackage.TypeStruct instance that describes the particular type requested. The TypeStruct object contains the interface name String of the type, a String array of super type names, the PropStruct array describing the registered type, the incarnation number associated with the type when it was added, and a boolean type indicating whether the type is deprecated.

Of course, the primary operation of interest to an importer is the query() method on the Lookup interface. It unfortunately also happens to have a rather complex operation signature, which is perhaps one of the key reasons why the CORBA Trading Service has been a difficult standard to adopt in practice. A type name parameter to a query method specifies the desired type to be retrieved. In addition to a type name parameter, a constraint String, a preferences String, an array of policies, a specification of desired properties, and a number indicating how many results should be returned are used as input to the query() method. Additionally, three CORBA holders to contain output values are also passed into the query() method, including a holder of a returned offer sequence, an offer iterator, and a sequence of policy limits that were applied to the requested query.

A constraint String captures search criteria specified in a standard trading service constraint language. Different constraint languages (such as SQL) implemented by your particular trading service implementation can be designated between << >> in the beginning of the String.

Similarly, a preference String is also passed to the query() method, which can be used to designate the order in which results are returned from the query. If no preference is supplied, the order in which service matches are found is returned.

An array of org.omg.CosTrading.Policy values is passed into the query() method to specify name-value pairs in which each name defines a particular policy that should be followed by the trading service when returning results.

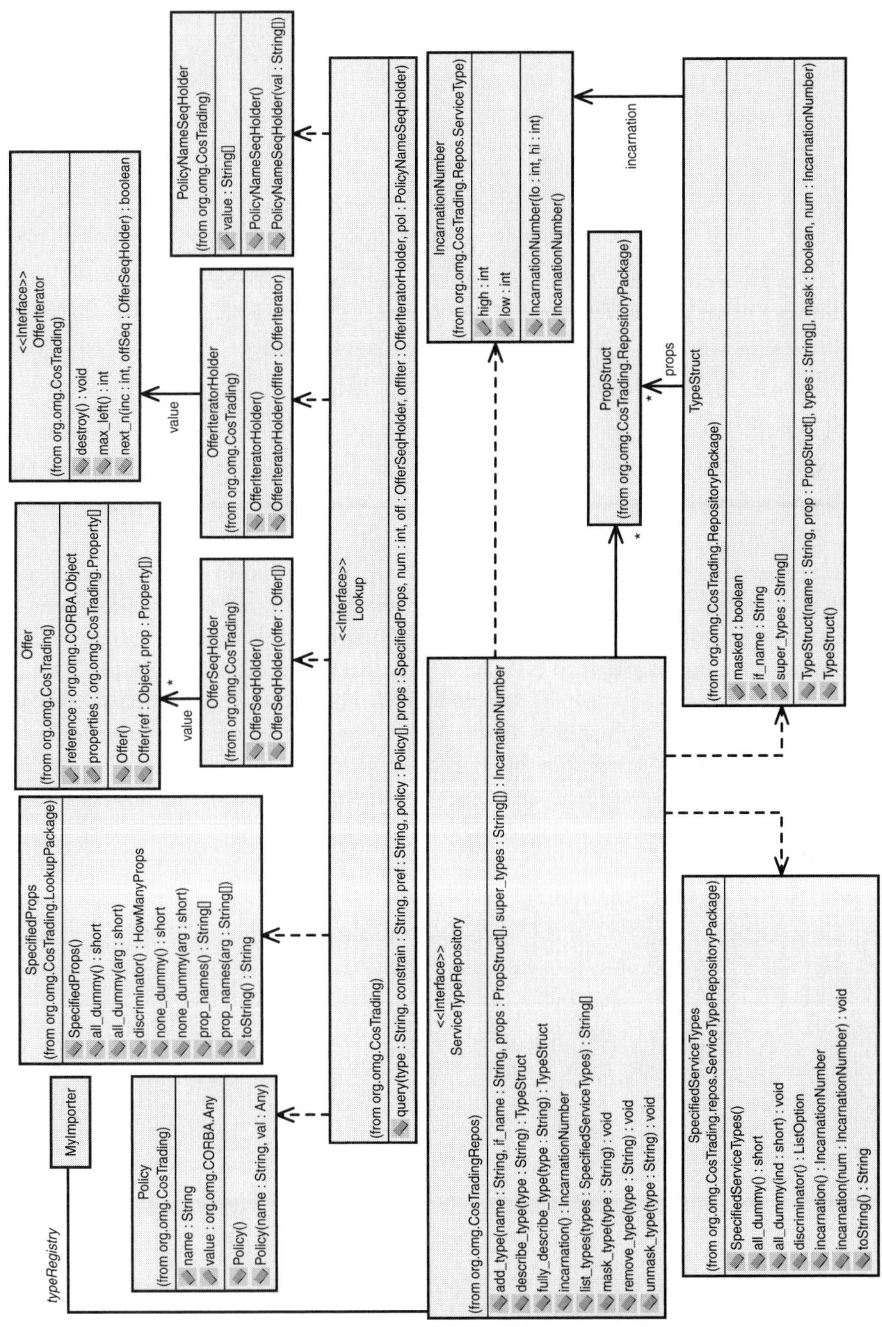

Figure 12.6 CORBA Trading Service importing.

An `org.omg.CosTrading.LookupPackage.SpecifiedProps` object can be used to specify that all properties (`all_dummy()`) or a selected set of property names (`prop_names()`) are to be returned from the query. The integer input into the `query()` statement designates how many results to return.

> **Tip**
>
> All of these input values to the `query()` command make issuing a query to the `Lookup` service rather complicated. To make it easier to understand how to use such parameters, it may help to compare a few of the individual parameters to elements of a SQL statement, which may be more familiar to you. For example:
>
> - The constraint `String` may be viewed as similar in role to the `WHERE` portion of a SQL statement.
> - The preferences `String` is similar in role to a SQL `ORDER_BY` clause.
> - The service name itself is akin in role to specifying a SQL `FROM` clause.
> - The specified properties may be viewed as similar in role to a SQL `SELECT` statement.
>
> Although role similarities exist, of course all querying is done in the context of a type-safe object-oriented paradigm, and there are indeed still differences between the two querying paradigms.

The values returned in the `org.omg.CosTrading.OfferSeqHolder` object are in an array of `org.omg.CosTrading.Offer` objects. Each `Offer` object contains a reference to the associated CORBA service (the `MyCORBAService` objects in Figure 12.5) and an array of `Property` objects associated with this service. The `org.omg.CosTrading.OfferIteratorHolder` contains a returned `org.omg.CosTrading.OfferIterator` object, which may be used to traverse the list of offered objects. Finally, if any limits were applied by the trading service during the query, an `org.omg.CosTrading.PolicyNameSeqHolder` object will contain an array of policy name `Strings` indicating those policies that were applied.

CORBA Trading Example

We have developed a basic CORBA Trader export and import example that is provided with the code associated with this chapter. Although we don't explicitly list the example here, we will describe the example's basic structure. The example illustrates how to export a collection of CORBA objects to a trading service from a server-side object and how to look up and import these services from the client side. A few simple classes are used to illustrate the concepts and mechanisms involved in using the CORBA Trading Service. Because of the complexity involved with many of the CORBA services such as the CORBA Trading Service, finding a suitable mix of COTS that can be used with Java is difficult.

> **Note**
>
> Under the `examples\src\ejava\jndi\directory\tradingExample` directory, six files exist to illustrate use of the CORBA Trading Service: `Customer.idl`, `CustomerImpl.java`, `CustomerServer.java`, `CustomerTradingClient.java`, `CustomerInfo.txt`, and

runtrading.bat. The generated runtrading script can be used to execute the example. Two properties must be set in this example's build.properties file. A Borland Enterprise Server property must be set to the root installation directory of your Borland Enterprise Server installation (see Appendix A). An OpenFusion property must be set to the root directory of an OpenFusion CORBA Services product installation (see Appendix A).

The Customer.idl file is the sample IDL file that we use with the example. We've purposely kept the IDL interface straightforward so that we can focus on the salient features of using a CORBA Trading Service. The IDL interface simply exposes a few read-only attributes of a customer, which, when run through an IDL-to-Java compiler, produce the CORBA skeleton utilized by our customer implementation class contained in the CustomerImpl.java file. The CustomerImpl class thus simply implements all the attribute retrieval methods exposed by the IDL, as well as a collection of attribute setter methods used by the server-side code.

The CustomerServer class in the CustomerServer.java file serves as our trading service exporter of Customer CORBA objects. When the CustomerServer is run from the command line, its main() method first initializes itself with the ORB and resolves an initial reference to the CORBA Trading Service. The default reference is narrowed to a Lookup object reference, and we subsequently obtain a handle to a Register object using the register_if() call inherited by the Lookup object. A call to the addServiceTypesToTradingService() method from main() registers the type information about a Customer with the trading service's service type repository. A call to registerCustomerObjects() from main() then exports a collection of Customer CORBA objects with the trading service register. After all objects have been exported, the main() method waits for client requests with the server blocking input from the standard user input stream.

The addServiceTypesToTradingService() method first obtains a handle to the ServiceTypeRepository from the lookup service's inherited type_repos() method. A PropStruct object is then filled out with a single customer ID attribute name, mode, and type. After a PropStruct object is created, it is passed in as an array along with a service type name, an interface name, and super type information (none to provide here) to the add_type() method on the ServiceTypeRepository. Note that we could have passed more attribute type information to the service type repository, but we use only one attribute here to keep the example simple.

The registerCustomerObjects() method first calls the getAllCustomers() method to obtain a Hashtable of Customer object references. The getAllCustomers() method accomplishes this task by reading and parsing the list of customers present in the CustomerInfo.txt file provided with this example. The first line of CustomerInfo.txt is ignored, but each subsequent line contains customer information and is used to instantiate and initialize a new Customer CORBA object reference. Each Customer object is added to the Hashtable using its customer ID as a reference. The CustomerInfo.txt file looks something like this:

```
CUSTOMER_ID, FIRSTNAME, LASTNAME, STREET, CITY, STATE, ZIP, EMAIL
120, Ghosh, Anup, 244 Demon Trail, Fairfax, VA, 12345,
➥snupy@dooleys.com
121, Kirkitelos, Paul, 33A Pauly Shorr Apartments, Los Angeles, CA,
➥12346, pk@doinitforyou.com
122, Hoekstra, Geoff, 88 Bewtsilla Avenue, Austin, TX, 12347,
➥gp@jackrabbitsnap.com
123, Woosely, Mike, Van Down By the Lake, Baltimore, MD, 12348,
➥mlw2d@crigglers.com
124, Kretsinger, Stein, 87 Zinimba St, Charlottesville, CA, 34759,
➥sz@digmole.com
125, Stauffer, Andy, 432 Chauseutte Lane, Boston, MA, 29876, andy@tb.com
126, Szadja, Doug, 332 S. Finktur Ave, Richmond, VA, 12536,
➥dz@litifo.com
127, Hubbard, Tom, 231 Bigguns Rd, San Francisco, CA, 34567,
➥hubbs@herve.com
128, Choi, Charles, 2 Errehhuhh Ave, San Francisco, CA, 34567,
➥cc@heeheehee.com
129, Ebert, Jeff, 43 Depends Blvd, Half Moon Bay, CA, 34759,
➥gg@angryman.com
130, Wasmley, Jim, 2 Snappiak Drive, Cocoa Beach, FL, 26942,
➥fredo@burglars.com
```

After the `Hashtable` of `Customer` objects is returned, the `registerCustomerObjects()` method cycles through the collection of returned customers and creates a `Property` element containing `customer_id` as the `Property` name and the actual customer ID value as the `Property` value. The `Property` (in the form of an array) along with the service type name and the `Customer` object reference are then exported to the `Register` object.

The `CustomerTradingClient.java` file contains the code for a CORBA Trading Service importer. When the `CustomerTradingClient` is executed from the command line, it too must go through the initial sequence of ORB initialization and obtaining handles to trading service `Lookup` and `Register` object interfaces. Subsequently, a `listAllServiceTypes()` is called to list all the available services in the trading service. The schema of the `Customer` type is then displayed with the `describeAType()` method. One or more `Customer` objects with an ID greater than 123 is then queried for and accessed within the `queryAndDisplayCustomers()` method. Finally, the service type is removed from the service type repository. All actions actually demonstrate basic interaction with the trading service apart from simply importing a service.

The `listAllServiceTypes()` method in the `CustomerTradingClient` example uses an instance of the `SpecifiedServiceTypes` interface to list all types in the service type repository with a call to `ServiceTypeRepository.list_types()` method. Each returned type is then output to standard output. The `describeAType()` method on `CustomerTradingClient` calls `describe_type()` on the

ServiceTypeRepository and displays the contents of the returned TypeStruct describing the particular type.

The queryAndDisplayCustomers() method in CustomerTradingClient first creates a Policy and SpecifiedProps object. The SpecifiedProps object is initialized to indicate no properties to specify. After the output Holder classes are created, the query() method on Lookup is called. The content of the Offer returned from the query() method is then accessed to obtain a handle to the Customer object. The contents of the returned Customer object are then accessed and displayed.

Finally, as a simple illustration of how to use the trading service, a call to ServiceTypeRepository.remove_type() removes the particular service type interface that was registered with the trading service.

Jini as a Trading Service

Jini is a collection of Java APIs and components that at one point was heavily marketed and touted by Sun as the next-generation technology for building distributed systems. Jini is a lightweight layer of Java code that rests atop the Java 2 platform. Thus, Jini can run on top of the J2SE and J2EE, as well as the J2ME. Jini depends on Java's Remote Method Invocation (RMI) distributed communications infrastructure. Jini and RMI together offer a set of APIs and infrastructure for building distributed services that can dynamically register traits about themselves and register their availability to the Jini community such that Jini network clients can dynamically discover and use those services.

The most significant types of distributed Jini-based services that Sun had in mind were those services offered by embedded devices on a network. Thus, with proper Jini-enabling, devices such as printers, phones, PDAs, pagers, and storage devices can all offer their services to a dynamic network in a Jini-standard fashion. Jini clients such as other embedded devices, PCs, and enterprise servers can plug into this dynamic network and immediately obtain access to the Jini services made available to the enterprise network community.

Because Jini sits atop the Java RMI infrastructure and provides auxiliary distributed object communications services, the analogy can be made between Jini and RMI to that of a few CORBAservices and the CORBA ORB. As you'll soon see, Jini offers a programming model to provide distributed event, transaction, and leasing services that have overlapping logical role analogies to the CORBA Events, Transactions, and Licensing Services, respectively. The core functionality of Jini, however, revolves around its dynamic discovery, lookup, and network community joining behavior. The lookup behavior is analogous to the roles that would be played by a CORBA Trading Service in a CORBA distributed object community. Although there exists a clear overlap in terms of roles between the Jini paradigm and the CORBA paradigm, there are a few distinct design differences. CORBA is language independent and Jini is defined in terms of the Java language. Furthermore, although object passing-by-value semantics are part of the CORBA specification, the Java platform makes mobile objects much easier to implement precisely because of its language and Java platform dependence.

Jini Component Architecture

The basic logical and physical component architecture of Jini and Jini's architectural context are shown in Figure 12.7. The logical architecture depicted in the left half of the diagram shows Jini's dependence on the Java 2 platform and how Jini services are built atop the Jini platform. The right half of the diagram shows the physical architecture components (that is, Java packages) used by Jini and the development kits with which these components are distributed. Arrows are used to demonstrate how each physical component roughly relates to the logical architecture components.

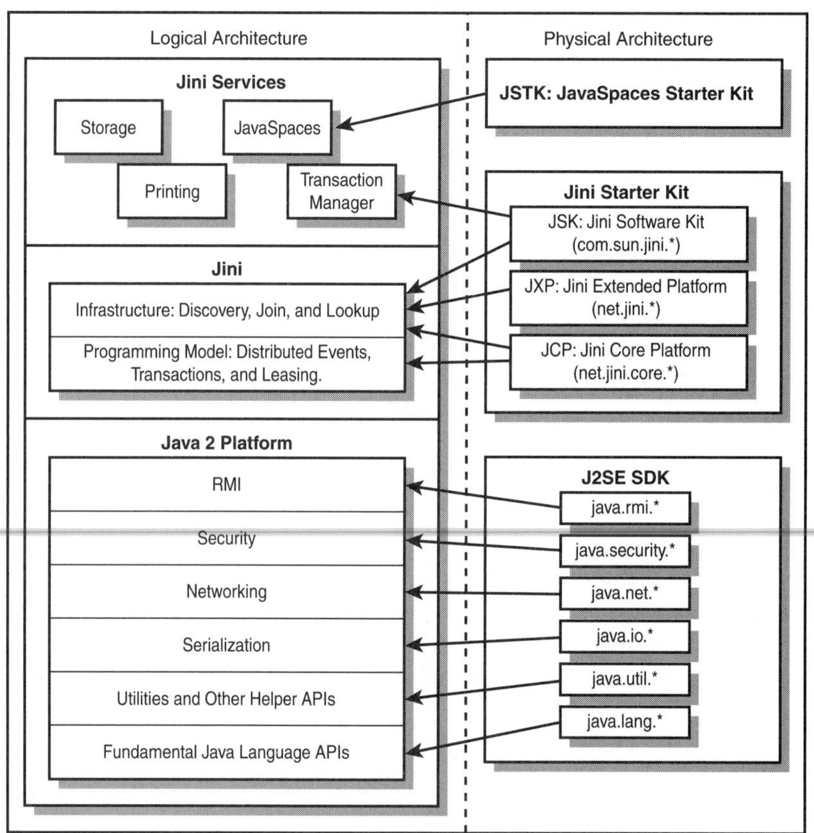

Figure 12.7 Jini component architecture.

Jini depends on many of the new security and distributed communication mechanisms in the Java 2 platform. RMI and its support for activatable objects are one key feature used by Jini. The Java 2 security model provides a set of fine-grained access-control mechanisms on which both RMI and Jini depend. Finally, Java's basic networking, object serialization, utility, and core language components all are also utilized by the Jini platform.

Jini itself is partitioned into three collections of Java packages, all of which are currently distributed by Sun with the Jini Starter Kit. These are the package collections:

- The Jini Core Platform (JCP) distribution contains those Java packages below `net.jini.core` that encapsulate the core Jini specification standard classes and interfaces.
- The Jini Extended Platform (JXP) distribution contains packages below `net.jini` aside from `net.jini.core.*` that encapsulate the Jini specification standard classes and interfaces to provide additional Jini functionality and utilities.
- The Jini Software Kit (JSK) contains packages below `com.sun.jini` offered by Sun as a specific implementation of the key services defined in the JCP and JXP specifications.

Jini Programming Model

The Jini programming model is composed of three major distributed service APIs for distributed events, distributed leasing, and distributed transactions. The distributed event programming model offers a set of interfaces that extend the JavaBeans event model to provide a means for remote objects to be notified of asynchronously generated events from other distributed objects.

The distributed leasing model provides a set of interfaces that can be used to require distributed objects to obtain a lease for use of a particular distributed resource. Leases have a timeout associated with them before which they must be either renewed or cancelled by the holder. If the lease is not renewed or cancelled, access to the distributed resource expires, and the resource is released from the holder. Leasing is used by higher-level Jini services to clean up resources no longer in use by potentially failed distributed objects.

Finally, the distributed transactions programming model is used to provide services for coordinating distributed operations that either all must occur atomically (commit) or none must occur at all (rollback).

Jini Infrastructure

The Jini infrastructure represents the quintessential layer of Jini utilized by distributed objects to first discover a community of Jini services, join a Jini community, and look up a particular Jini service. Objects first must locate a Jini community using a discovery protocol. The discovery process may involve simply finding local Jini communities via a multicast request, receiving notification from newly formed communities via multicast announcements, or simply binding to a known Jini lookup service. Each Jini community may have a group name and is composed of one or more Jini lookup services belonging to that group.

Jini services join those Jini communities that they have discovered and have an interest in joining. When a Jini service joins a Jini community's lookup service, it provides a service item to the lookup service. These service items contain a collection of meta-data attribute information describing the Jini service, as well as a service proxy object. The service proxy object is simply a serializable Java object that is downloaded to clients of the Jini service. Operations invoked on the service proxy object may actually be handled by the proxy object itself or marshaled as requests to a remote back-end device proxy and unmarshal any responses (for example, service proxy as an RMI client).

Lookup services are used by Jini clients to locate Jini services. The clients first fill out a service template describing the service of interest. The service template can be filled out with a service identifier, a set of base Java class types, and a set of service meta-data attributes. A lookup call using this service template is invoked on the lookup service, which subsequently returns a set of service matches containing one or more service items that matched the service template. With a set of matching service items in hand, the client can then extract the service proxy item of interest and begin distributed computing with that object.

Jini Tools and Configuration

Jini services are created using the Jini infrastructure and programming model. The Jini lookup service is really itself a Jini service; it is provided with the JSK distribution and is referred to with the codename "reggie." The JSK also contains a transaction management service with a codename "mahalo." Finally, Sun also provides a Jini service called JavaSpaces, codename "outrigger," as a product that can be used to store and retrieve Java objects in a distributed network.

> **Note**
>
> Building Jini-enabled systems requires a couple of tools that are freely downloadable from the Sun Web site. However, we should note that use of Jini in commercial applications still did incur licensing fees payable to Sun at the time of this book's writing (`www.sun.com/jini/licensing/licenses.html`).

After installing a Java 2 platform such as the J2SE, you'll need to download the Jini System Software Starter Kit from Sun at `http://developer.java.sun.com/developer/products/jini`. The Jini System Software Starter Kit contains the distribution packages for the JCP, JXP, JSK, and other tools you'll need in order to get started.

Developing Jini services involves setting up a runtime infrastructure on which Jini communities depend, as well as creating the actual Jini service. Setting up a runtime environment for Jini involves the following basic tasks:

- *Configure HTTP Servers:* Configure and start simple HTTP servers on hosts that will serve downloadable Java code. Automatic downloading of code between clients and servers is a feature actually provided by the underlying RMI libraries.

Code that may need downloading includes the core Jini components and any Jini service code. The HTTP servers need only support simple `GET` operation functionality, and the Jini starter kit itself comes equipped with a very slender server.

- *Configure RMI Activation Daemons:* Configure and start an RMI activation daemon on hosts that will serve activatable Java code. This is yet another artifact of the underlying RMI toolkit; the RMI activation daemon is used to allow RMI activatable server objects to be activated (that is, started and brought into memory) on an as-needed basis from RMI client requests. Activatable objects include the Jini lookup service, the Jini transaction manager, and any Jini services.
- *Configure and Start a Lookup Service:* The RMI registry may be used as a lookup service. However, the Jini lookup service provides a much richer set of features that enable it to perform Jini infrastructure services. Because the Jini infrastructure is the key feature of Jini, the Jini lookup service is recommended rather than the RMI registry. The Jini lookup service must have an RMI activation running on the same host machine it is running. The RMI activation daemon activates the Jini lookup service and needs to know which system resources the lookup service is allowed to access. Thus, the Jini lookup service must be started with an associated security policy file (a Java 2 security feature) telling the activation daemon which system resources the lookup may access and how it may access them. You can also pass in a list of group names designating to which Jini clusters the lookup service belongs. Finally, the Jini lookup service must be started with a codebase parameter indicating via a URL the location of RMI client class files needed for using the lookup service. Thus, this URL points to a machine where you've typically run a Web server to serve up the subset of Jini lookup service code needed by lookup clients.
- *Configure Optional Transaction Manager:* You can also optionally configure and start a Jini transaction manager service that comes packaged with the JSK.

Jini Class Architecture and Development Process

Using Jini technology requires that you build both a server side and a client side, as is the case with all distributed object communication development paradigms. Our server side in this case involves building the Jini service implementation, a Jini service proxy to that service, and any connectivity needed to a back-end device or process. The Jini client simply must look up and utilize such a service.

Figure 12.8 illustrates the core class architecture behind a Jini service, and Figure 12.9 illustrates the core class architecture behind a Jini client. Although many other classes and interfaces exist throughout the many Jini packages, we have presented only those class and interfaces that will most commonly be used by enterprise developers looking to Jini-enable their enterprises and take advantage of the trading service features of Jini. We also present only those constructs that we will use to describe the basic development process involved in building a Jini-based application and that we will use in an example included with the code associated with this chapter.

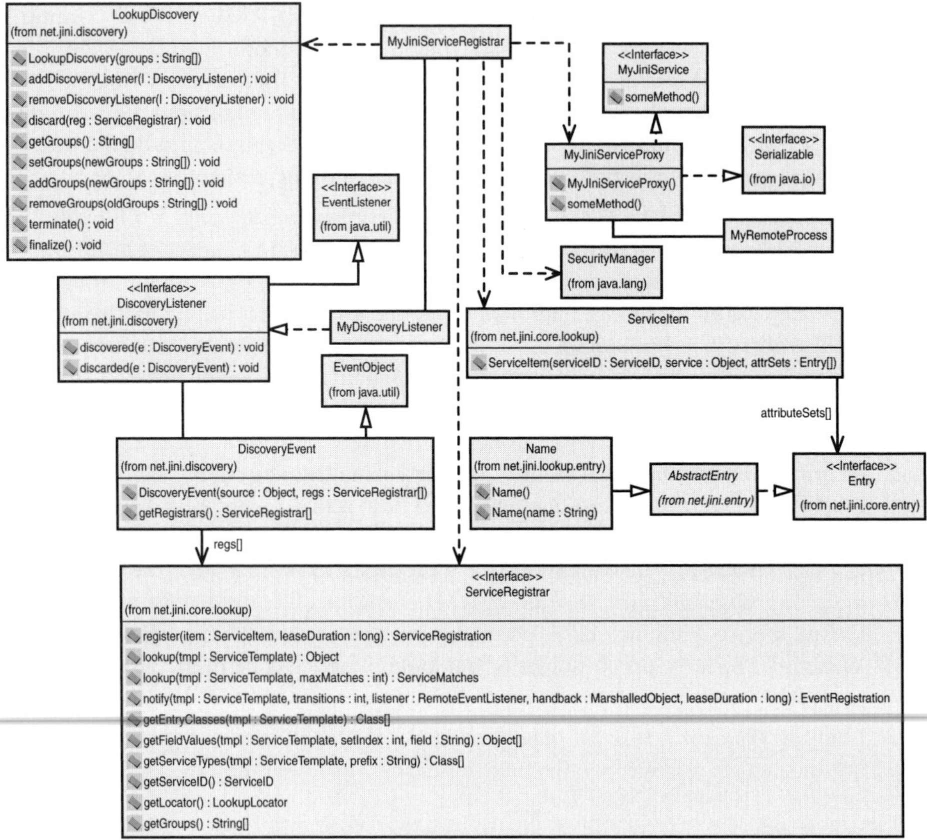

Figure 12.8 The Jini service architecture.

Each class and interface of Figure 12.8 is described here in the context of how it is used to build a Jini-enabled service. Creating a Jini service can be a straightforward process. The basic tasks (with entities from Figure 12.8 in parentheses) for creating a Jini service are as shown here:

- *Define Jini Service Interface:* Define a Jini service interface (`MyJiniService`) with all distributable method signatures defined.
- *Implement Jini Service Proxy:* Implement a Jini service proxy class (`MyJiniServiceProxy`) that implements the `Serializable` interface, implements the Jini service interface, and implements a default no-argument constructor (for serializability). Note that the service proxy is what gets downloaded to the Jini

client machine. The proxy can talk with any back-end process (`MyRemoteProcess`) using any communications technique or protocol whose interface can be downloaded to the client machine. Thus, for example, the proxy can act as a basic TCP/IP, RMI, or CORBA client to a corresponding back-end process.

- *Implement Remote Process Interface:* If the remote process interface (`MyRemoteProcess`) that can be called by your Jini service proxy does not already exist, you will need to create it during this step. The remote process may be an interface to a piece of hardware such as a printer or PDA, or it can be an interface to just about any other enterprise resource.
- *Implement the Jini Service Registrar:* A Jini service registrar (`MyJiniServiceRegistrar`) should be implemented to create the Jini service proxy and register the proxy with any discovered lookup services.

Because the implementation of the Jini Service Registrar is a somewhat more-involved process, we further expand on the tasks involved with Jini Service Registrar implementation here:

- *Create Jini Service Proxy:* Create an instance of a service proxy object (`MyJiniServiceProxy`).
- *Create a Jini Service Item Description:* Create a service item (`net.jini.core.lookup.ServiceItem`) that contains a reference to the service proxy object and a description of the Jini service's attributes (`net.jini.core.entry.Entry` array of `net.jini.lookup.entry.Name` objects).
- *Establish a Security Manager:* The registrar should also create a Security Manager (`SecurityManager`) instance to enable use of Java 2 application security features.
- *Discover a Lookup Service:* Implement a discovery process to locate one or more lookup services on the network by using multicast requests (using `net.jini.discovery.LookupDiscovery`, `net.jini.discovery.DiscoveryListener`, and `net.jini.discovery.DiscoveryEvent`), relying on multicast announcements (using the same classes as with multicast requests), or directly connecting to a lookup service (using `net.jini.core.discovery.LookupLocator`). Using multicast requests, the registrar will add (call `LookupDiscovery.addDiscoveryListener()`) with a listener representative (`MyDiscoveryListener`) that implements a discovery listener interface (`DiscoveryListener`).
- *Select a Lookup Service:* Implement the selection of one or more discovered lookup services to join. Note that when a discovery event (`DiscoveryEvent`) is received from the discovery infrastructure by an object (`MyDiscoveryListener`) that implements the discovery listener interface, that listener object can filter which

callbacks should be made onto the registrar for the discovered lookup service. The list of Jini lookup services (`net.jini.core.lookup.ServiceRegistrar`) that were discovered can then be retrieved from the discovery event passed to the discovery listener (`DiscoveryEvent.getRegistrars()`).

- *Join a Lookup Service:* Implement the joining process by registering the service item (`ServiceItem`) with the lookup service of interest (`ServiceRegistrar.register()`).
- *Provide Additional Services:* Optionally use a richer set of Jini services such as distributed event, leasing, and transaction services.

Jini clients that want to utilize the published Jini services are even simpler to create. Figure 12.9 presents the basic classes and interfaces used to build a Jini client.

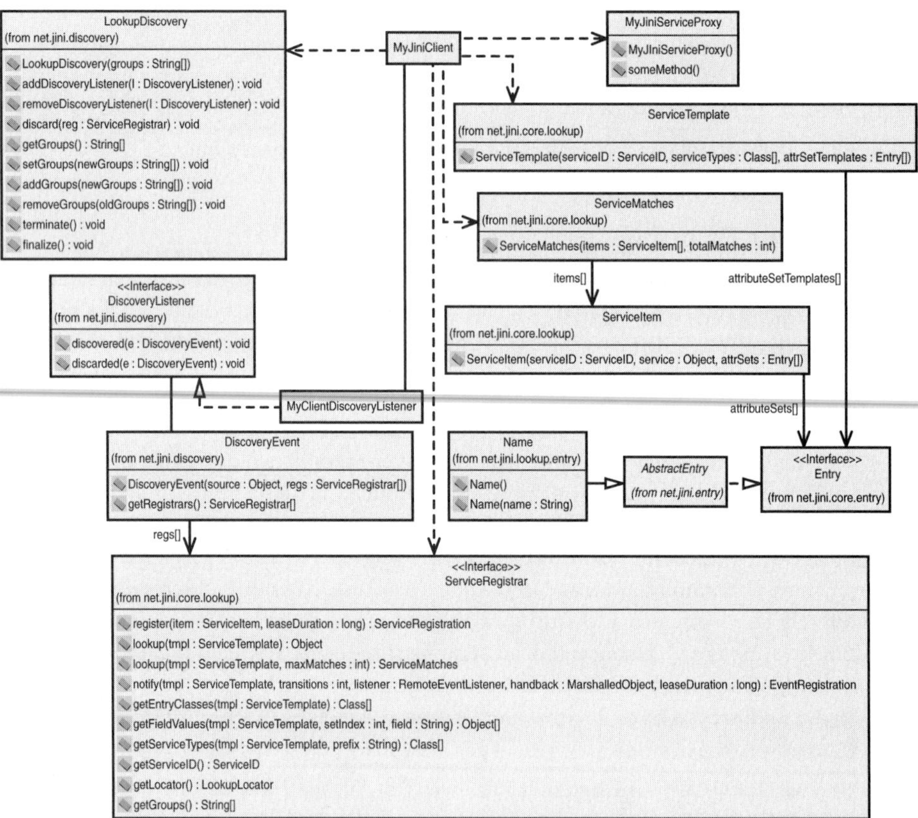

Figure 12.9 The Jini client architecture.

The basic steps for creating a Jini client are shown here (with entities from Figure 12.9 in parentheses):

- *Discover a Lookup Service:* Implement the discovery process to locate a lookup service as was the case with the service registrar. Uses discovery listener (`MyClientDiscoveryListener`) as before to obtain a list of discovered lookup services (`ServiceRegistrar`).
- *Create a Jini Service Template:* Implement the creation and initialization of a service template (`net.jini.core.lookup.ServiceTemplate`) defining how items in a lookup service should be matched with the desired items designated by the template.
- *Look Up a Jini Service:* Implement the lookup of a Jini service using the service template (`net.jini.core.lookup.ServiceRegistrar.lookup()`).
- *Handle Jini Service Lookup Matches:* Implement the handling of service matches (`net.jini.core.lookup.ServiceMatches`) from a lookup to obtain a reference to the service proxy object.
- *Use the Jini Service:* Implement usage of the service proxy object that represents the client interface to the Jini service.

Jini Service Example

We have developed a basic Jini service example, which is provided with this chapter's code. As with the CORBA Trading Service example, we also don't explicitly list the example here in the interest of conserving space and because it is slightly beyond the scope of this book. However, we encourage you to examine the sample code, and we describe the example's basic structure here. The Jini example illustrates how a Jini service registrar can discover lookup services in its community and then register a Jini service with a discovered lookup service. The example also shows how a Jini client can discover a lookup service and then look up a reference to registered Jini services.

> **Note**
>
> Under the `examples\src\ejava\jndi\directory\jiniexample` directory, a set of files exists to illustrate creation of a Jini service: `Customer.java`, `CustomerServiceProxy.java`, `CustomerActivatableInterface.java`, `CustomerActivatable.java`, `CustomerServiceRemote.java`, `CustomerDiscoveryListener.java`, `CustomerJINIClient.java`, `ClientDiscoveryListener.java`, `CustomerInfo.txt`, and `rmi.policy`, as well as a `runjiniexample` script generated by the ANT build. As described earlier in the chapter, you will also need to download the Jini SDK to run this example. This example assumes that you've installed the Jini SDK in a root directory identified by a `jini.home` property inside this example's `build.properties` file.

The Customer.java file contains a Customer interface defining getter methods for customer information and is implemented by the CustomerServiceProxy Jini proxy in the CustomerServiceProxy.java file. The CustomerServiceProxy is serializable so that it can be downloaded to a Jini client. The proxy acts as an RMI client to an RMI server existing somewhere else on a network. The CustomerServiceProxy is instantiated with a reference to that RMI server.

The CustomerActivatableInterface.java file contains the CustomerActivatableInterface RMI interface to the CustomerActivatable activatable RMI server object in the CustomerActivatable.java file. The CustomerActivatable server implements the needed semantics for supporting activatable RMI servers, including the implementation of a constructor that takes activation and marshaled object information used during the reconstruction of the object from a non-active state. CustomerActivatable stores all customer information in an underlying java.util.Hashtable and implements getters and setters for all customer attributes.

The CustomerServiceRemote class in the CustomerServiceRemote.java file implements the Jini service registrar functionality. When started from the command line, the CustomerServiceRemote.main() method will first create a security manager instance and then call a static registerCustomers() method on itself to perform all discovery, joining, and registration steps. The static registerCustomers() method first retrieves a collection of customer information returned as a Vector of Hashtable objects returned from the CustomerServiceRemote.getAllCustomers() call. After a CustomerServiceRemote object is instantiated, each Hashtable of customer information is then passed as a parameter in a call to registerACustomerService() on the CustomerServiceRemote object. The getAllCustomers() creates the Vector of Hashtable objects from a parsed list of customer information read from a CustomerInfo.txt file assumed to be in the current working directory.

When CustomerServiceRemote.registerACustomerService() is called with a Hashtable of customer information, a Name is constructed using a customer's ID, which is then in turn used to create a single-element array of Entry objects. A ServiceItem is then constructed with the Entry array, and a reference to a CustomerServiceProxy object is returned from the CustomerServiceRemote.getProxy() call. The getProxy() call creates and registers an activatable RMI server (note that this is a regular RMI registration process and not a Jini registration process). The RMI server handle is then used in the construction of a CustomerServiceProxy object. Subsequently, inside of the CustomerServiceRemote.registerACustomerService() method, a handle to a LookupDiscovery object is constructed indicating no preference for a particular discovery process group. The LookupDiscovery object is then used to add a CustomerDiscoveryListener object implemented in the CustomerDiscoveryListener.java file. The CustomerDiscoveryListener object is constructed with a handle to the CustomerServiceRemote object and the ServiceItem object created by the CustomerServiceRemote object.

The CustomerDiscoveryListener is called by the Jini discovery process (encapsulated by LookupDiscovery) whenever it discovers a lookup service in the available community. The discovered() method implementation will make a callback onto the CustomerServiceRemote.registerWithLookupService() method when it is invoked by the discovery process for each discovered lookup service represented by a ServiceRegistrar object. The registerWithLookupService() method will then register the ServiceItem with the lookup service for a requested MAX_LEASING_TIME.

On the client side, we have the CustomerJINIClient.java file implementing the Jini client functionality. The CustomerJINIClient.main() method also creates a security manager instance and then creates an instance of a CustomerJINIClient object before blocking for user input from the standard input stream. The CustomerJINIClient constructor first creates a ServiceTemplate object with a specified array of Customer class types to look for. This ServiceTemplate is stored in a private variable. The client discovery process that follows then invokes a newly created LookupDiscovery object to add a ClientDiscoveryListener instance. The ClientDiscoveryListener class is contained in the ClientDiscoveryListener.java file.

When the Jini discovery process discovers a lookup service in the client's community, it then calls lookForThisService() on the CustomerJINIClient for each instance of a ServiceRegistrar (that is, lookup service) that is discovered. When lookForThisService() is called, the ServiceRegistrar is used to look up any customers that match the criteria stipulated in the ServiceTemplate created earlier with an additional constraint of returning only MAX_MATCHES number of matches in the ServiceMatches object. For each item that has a match, the CustomerServiceProxy object is accessed to invoke the various getter methods defined on its Customer interface. The proxy in turn makes such calls to the remote RMI server.

Conclusions

Directory services represent key components of many enterprise systems for storing enterprise resource–related information. Directory service clients can search a directory service using a user-friendly querying methodology. LDAP, DSML, NIS, NDS, and DNS all represent common directory service standards with a large amount of industry support. JNDI offers a standard Java-based interface to directory services that can be used with directory services supporting standards such as LDAP, DSML, NIS, NDS, and DNS. Additional APIs specific to more advanced LDAP v3 features are also part of the JNDI API. The Microsoft ADS provides a directory service implementation and standard interface for .NET-based applications and now offers greater interoperability with other platforms via its support for DSML.

The CORBA Trading Service adds to the directory service concept by providing support for associating distributed CORBA object references to the type of object attribute information that would be found in a directory service. The CORBA Trading Service is unfortunately a somewhat-complicated framework to use. Jini is a type of trading service that adds support for dynamically discovering lookup services on a network by both servers and clients. Although Jini has a simpler API, configuring the runtime infrastructure required for Jini can be somewhat tedious.

Regardless, it should be apparent after reading this chapter and the preceding chapter that support for interfacing to naming, directory, and trading services via Java is far-reaching. A wide variety of options are available to the Java enterprise developer. In the next chapter, we will continue this line of discussion by describing how Web Services are registered with a directory service and the means available from within Java to communicate with such Web Service directory services.

13

Web Services Lookup with JAXR

THE PRECEDING TWO CHAPTERS EXAMINED JNDI and the means to look up handles to objects based on names and possibly some descriptive information about such objects. Among other uses, JNDI service features are used to look up handles to CORBA and RMI objects. As you saw in those chapters, other types of directory and trading services are also available to look up handles to distributed objects. Not unlike other distributed communication paradigms, Web services also need a lookup service so that clients can locate them and begin communicating with them. Such functionality is accomplished via Web service registries (aka XML registries). This chapter explores such registries and how the Java API for XML Registries (JAXR) exposes access to such services.

In this chapter, you will learn:

- An overview of Web service registry concepts and standards.
- A top-level understanding of Web service registry features and support offered by JAXR.
- The information model used by JAXR to represent passive object data stored inside of Web service registries.
- The means by which JAXR clients establish connections with Web service registries.
- The basic interfaces provided by JAXR to allow a client to communicate with a Web service registry.
- The interfaces provided by JAXR allowing a client to look up and retrieve information from a Web service registry.
- The interfaces provided by JAXR allowing a client to create, update, and delete information in a Web service registry.

Web Services Registries Overview

The basic role and functionality of Web service registries are not unlike the various naming, directory, and trading service roles and functionalities that we have examined thus far. What is different, however, is that Web service registries often store much more meta-data and have very specific meta-data requirements used by Web service clients to refer to Web services. Furthermore, given the very nature of Web service communications, Web service registries are often used in a much more dynamic and asynchronous fashion than are naming and directory services.

Web service registry standards have been defined with e-business in mind. That is, Web service registry standards assume that the primary use of such registries is in the exchange of Web service–related information between organizations to facilitate discovery, identification, and utilization of business services. Although Web service registries arguably can have a broader and less restricted scope of usage, the design concepts embodied in Web service registries clearly reflect such a business-to-business and inter-enterprise usage consideration. This may be contrasted with directory services, which, though they may be used in an inter-enterprise fashion, embody design concepts that reflect their usage inside of an enterprise.

Much like naming and directory services contain meta-data about distributed object services that may be referenced, Web service registries contain meta-data about Web services that may be referenced. The actual content stored behind the wall of a Web service registry is sometimes referred to as a repository item. Such repository items relate to that content needed for Web service communications such as XML schema documents, WSDL documents, or DTDs. A registry object inside of the Web service registry itself refers to the meta-data used to reference or describe a repository item. Such registry objects are uniquely referenceable within and external to the registry by virtue of having a universally unique identifier (UUID).

A Web service registry provider has a distinct set of processes that may be accessed in a distributed fashion to expose access to Web service registry objects and repository items. Naturally, a registry must have some registry operator who is responsible for maintaining and operating the registry processes. Content may be published, updated, and deleted in a registry via a set of services exposed by the registry referred to as life-cycle management services. The user performing such operations with a registry is often referred to as the content submitter and belongs to a submitting organization (SO). Content inside of a registry may be looked up and retrieved by other users via a set of services exposed by the registry referred to as query management services.

For Web service registries to be useful to a broad base of organizations accessing such services, there must of course be standards defining the communications protocol with Web service registries. Two primary standards exist in this regard:

- *OASIS ebXML Registry Services* (`www.oasis-open.org/committees/regrep`): Standards headed by the Organization for the Advancement of Structured Information Standards (OASIS) to define standard means for XML-based registry and repository communications designed for general and business-to-business registry functionality.

- *Universal Description, Discovery, and Integration (UDDI) services* (`www.uddi.org`): Standards now also integrated with OASIS but started out separate from OASIS. Defines a means for robust and dynamic XML-based registry communications, as well as a rich meta-data model for representing registry information. UDDI v2.0 is required for support by the WS-I Basic Profile.

JAXR Overview

With a fundamental Web services feature such as Web service registries, Java enterprise applications wanting to communicate in the Web services world need some way to access these registries. The Java API for XML Registries provides a standard API for Java enterprise applications. In fact, the JAXR v1.0 API as well as a JAXR registry provider are required as part of the J2EE v1.4.

Figure 13.1 provides an architectural overview of JAXR. A JAXR provider implements the JAXR API to provide a concrete mapping of standard JAXR API calls to a specific Web service registry type. A JAXR client uses the JAXR API to tap the resources of such services in a standard fashion. JAXR clients use the JAXR API to establish connections with a registry service. JAXR clients then use the registry service to communicate with the registry's life cycle or query management services. JAXR clients interact with JAXR abstractions that encapsulate registry objects to read and manipulate the meta-data in a registry. JAXR provides an entire hierarchy and set of abstractions that encapsulate registry objects and other objects in a registry by virtue of an information model. The JAXR information model abstractions are contained within the `javax.xml.registry.infomodel` package, and the JAXR abstractions encapsulating action-oriented services with an XML-based registry are contained within the `javax.xml.registry` package.

As we explore the JAXR API in more depth throughout this chapter, you should be aware that not all JAXR providers will provide, nor are they required to provide, support for every method and abstraction defined by the JAXR API. Two distinct support levels are in fact delineated that indicate such requirements:

- *Level 0 Profile:* This profile level is associated with those methods and abstractions that provide basic Web service registry functionality. This level is required to be supported by all J2EE v1.4 JAXR providers. This level is also required to be supported by JAXR providers offering UDDI service support. Because the WS-I Basic Profile requires UDDI v2.0 support, the J2EE v1.4 also requires support for UDDI v2.0 by JAXR.
- *Level 1 Profile:* This profile level is associated with those methods and abstractions above and beyond the level 0 profile providing more advanced and often more generic Web service registry functionality. This level is optionally required to be implemented by JAXR providers. However, this level is required to be supported by JAXR providers offering ebXML Registry Service support.

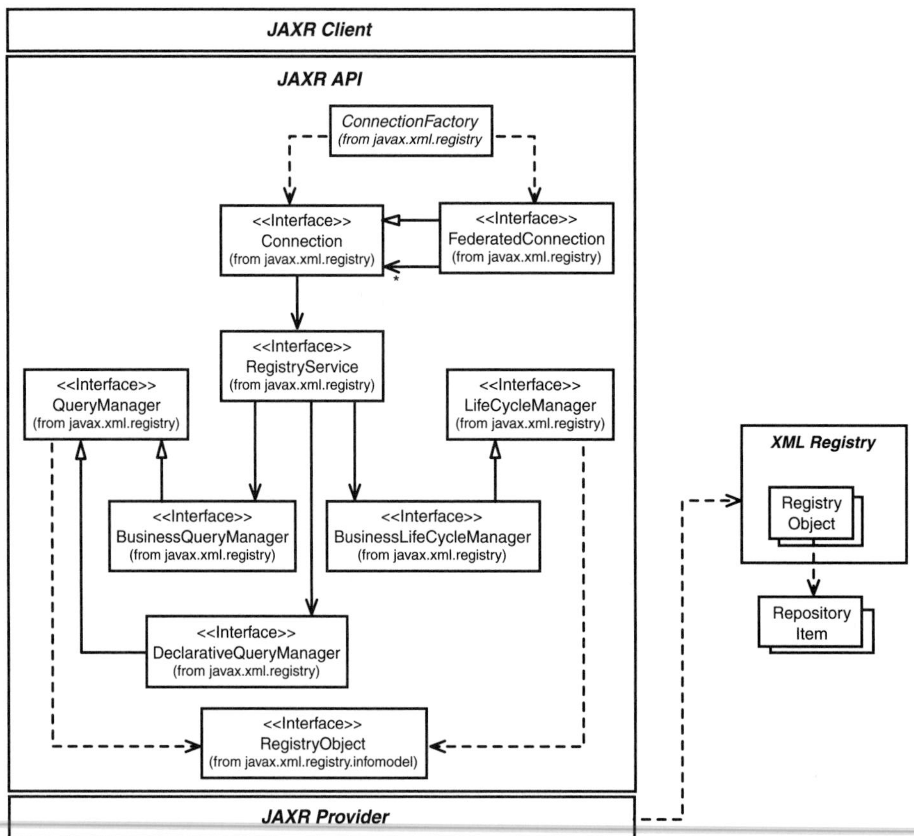

Figure 13.1 JAXR architecture overview.

JAXR Information Model

The JAXR information model APIs provide a set of interfaces used to encapsulate data that can be stored within a Web service registry. By this nature, such interfaces correspond to those abstractions representing passive entities of data. Such data is operated on and utilized by the various registry services. Because the JAXR information model abstractions encapsulate such registry data, their interfaces are rather simple accessor type methods. This section describes the JAXR information model APIs.

Extensible Objects

Figure 13.2 depicts the basic architecture of the JAXR information model's base `ExtensibleObject` type. An `ExtensibleObject` represents a generic object having a set of attributes that can be set and gotten with arbitrary object types. These generic attributes of an `ExtensibleObject` are represented as slots. A `Slot` object represents such an attribute and has a name, type name, and collection of values.

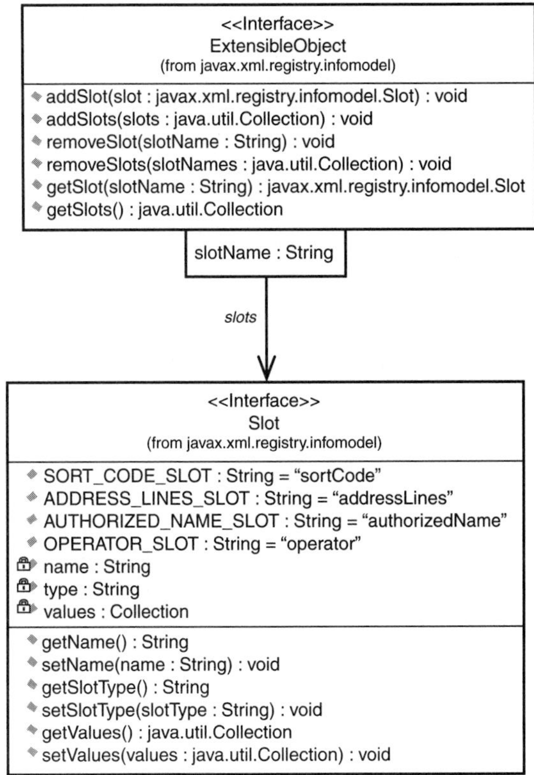

Figure 13.2 JAXR extensible objects.

Slots can be added, removed, or retrieved from an `ExtensibleObject`. Each `Slot` object associated with an `ExtensibleObject` has a unique name in the form of a `String` by which it may be referenced. The `Slot` interface also defines a set of predefined slot names as constants that may be used with JAXR UDDI providers.

Registry Objects

Figure 13.3 depicts a `RegistryObject` abstraction representing an object stored inside of a Web services registry. Such an object serves to encapsulate much of the basic functionality embodied by the different objects that can reside inside of a Web service registry. The `RegistryObject` inherits the generic attribute getter and setter behavior of the `ExtensibleObject` interface. The `RegistryObject` embellishes this generic functionality by providing a means to add, remove, get, and set various concrete types of registry objects that can be stored inside of a Web service registry. A `RegistryObject` has a UUID stored in the form of a `Key` object that is associated with the `RegistryObject`.

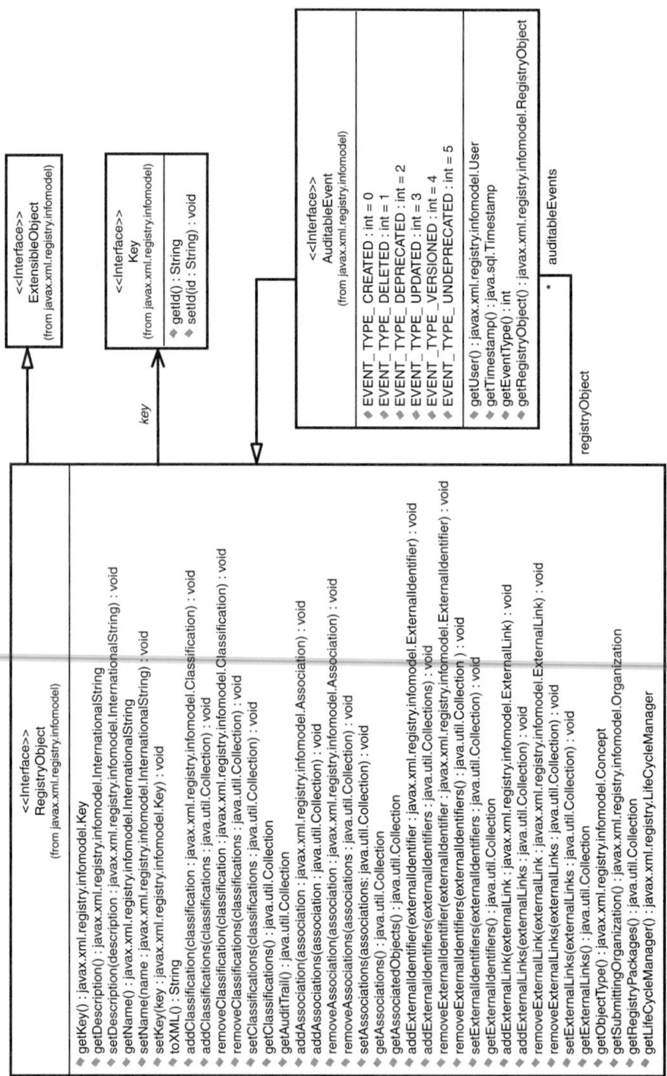

Figure 13.3 JAXR registry objects.

When a user accesses a registry, events associated with access of a particular registry object may be logged. The `AuditableEvent` object encapsulates such events. The `AuditableEvent` object can be used to obtain the user information associated with the user inducing such an event, the time of the event, and the type of event. The type of event is represented via a series of constants defined on the `AuditableEvent` interface. Such event types include indication of an event on a registry object associated with its creation, deletion, deprecation (that is, soon to be deleted), undeprecation (that is, reversal of deprecation), updating, or versioning.

International Strings

Given the international nature of Web services, a universal means to represent registry object names must be provided. A registry object uses a special string type that can be used in an International fashion to represent the registry object's name and a description of the object. Such a string is encapsulated by an `InternationalString` object as depicted in Figure 13.4. An `InternationalString` contains a collection of strings according to different international locales as stored in a collection of `LocalizedString` objects. The `InternationalString` provides a means for `LocalizedString` values to be set, gotten, added, and removed from its underlying collection. A standard Java `Locale`, the canonical name for the localized string's character set, and the actual localized value of the `String` can all be gotten and set via a `LocalizedString` handle.

Registry Entries

Figure 13.5 depicts abstractions that relate to Web service registry entries. A `RegistryEntry` is a type of `RegistryObject` providing additional meta-data above and beyond a `RegistryObject` indicating the life-cycle status, level of change expected (that is, stability), and time at which the stability level becomes dynamic for a registry object. A series of constants defined on the `RegistryEntry` can be used to identify a stability or status level.

A `RegistryEntry` is a type of `Versionable` object. This simply means that the entry can have a version associated with it indicating that it is one iteration of a single object (akin to versions of Java class). The version of the object is identifiable by its major, minor, and user-defined version numbers.

A `RegistryPackage` is a type of `RegistryEntry` that encapsulates a set of registry objects having some logical grouping. Likewise, a `RegistryObject` can also reference a collection of registry packages of which it is a part.

An `ExtrinsicObject` is another type of `RegistryEntry` embodying some repository content whose type is not inherently understood by the registry. As such, a MIME type is used to describe the data and a `DataHandler` object is used to access the repository content. The opaqueness of such content to the registry operator (that is, readability) may also be set or gotten via the `ExtrinsicObject` interface.

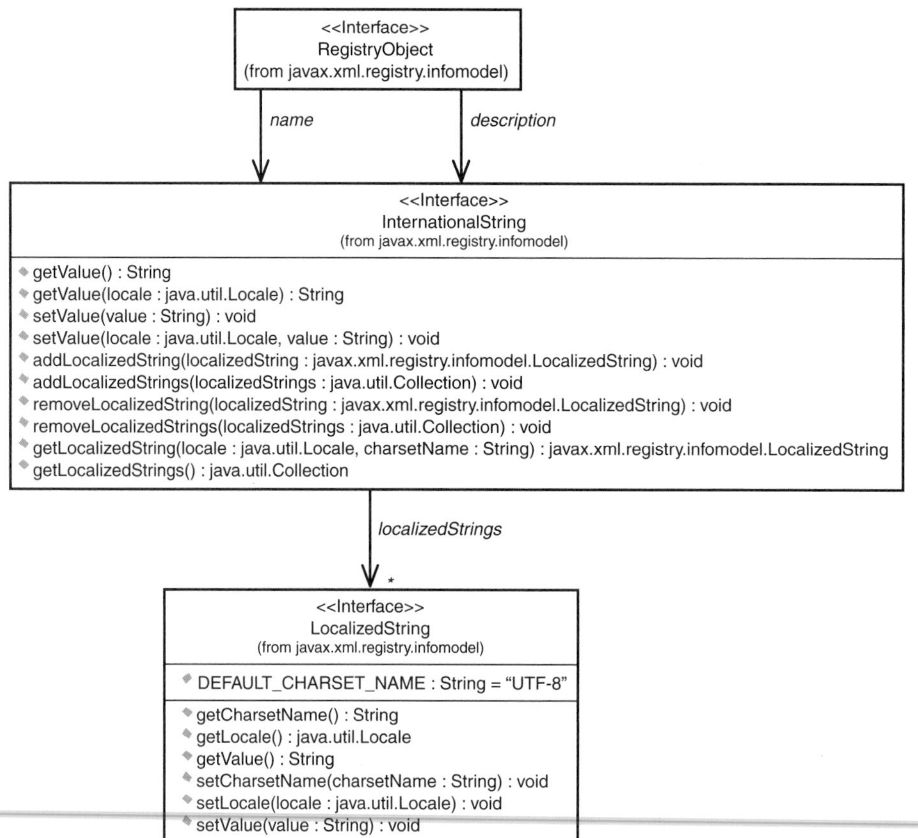

Figure 13.4 JAXR international strings.

External Links

An `ExternalLink`, as depicted in Figure 13.6, embodies a URI that links to information existing external to the Web service registry. The collection of registry objects about which the link provides external linking information may be gotten from the `ExternalLink` object. By virtue of the fact that an `ExternalLink` extends a `URIValidator`, the validation of a URI when it is set may be established and determined via inherited `URIValidator` methods.

Users, Addresses, Phone Numbers, and Email

Thus far, we've examined some very abstract representations of registry objects. Before exploring how such registry objects are structured and related inside of a registry using even more abstract JAXR types, we switch gears here to describe some of the more tangible registry object abstractions provided by JAXR.

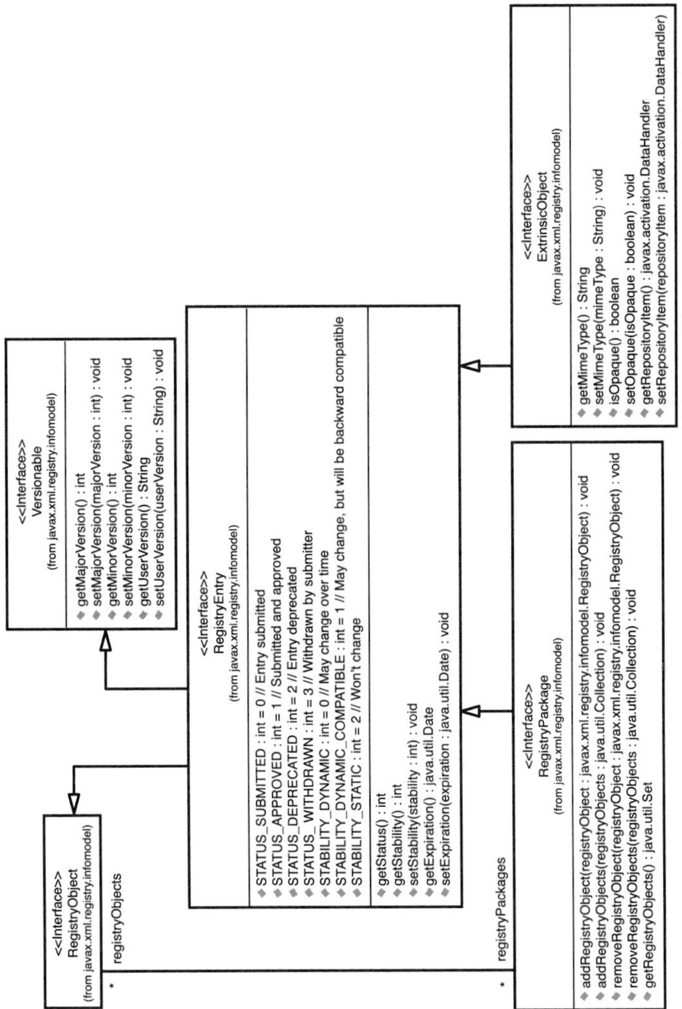

Figure 13.5 JAXR registry entries.

For starters, Figure 13.7 illustrates a concrete `User` registry object abstraction encapsulating meta-data about a registry user. A `User` has a name encapsulated by a `PersonName` object, a collection of postal addresses represented by `PostalAddress` objects, a collection of phone numbers represented by `TelephoneNumber` objects, and a collection of email addresses represented by `EmailAddress` objects. As you can see from the figure, in addition to other commonly required data, users and telephone numbers can also have URLs mapping to Web site addresses for the user or a telephone dialing service, respectively. Many of the objects in the figure also have a type `String` that identifies what specific type of object they are representing (for example, a "shipping" or "billing" type of `PostalAddress`).

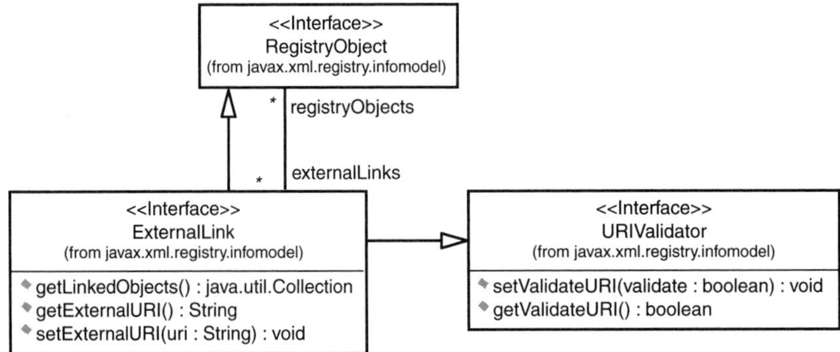

Figure 13.6 JAXR external links.

Organizations

As can be seen in Figure 13.7, a `User` is also associated with an `Organization` object. An `Organization` type of `RegistryObject`, as shown in Figure 13.8, represents an organization interacting with a registry (for example, a submitting organization). As represented in the diagram, an `Organization` can have a parent `Organization` and children `Organization` objects. Additionally, an `Organization` has a primary contact and set of users represented by `User` objects, a set of telephone numbers represented by `TelephoneNumber` objects, and a set of addresses represented by `PostalAddress` objects. Of paramount interest is the fact that organizations have a set of Web services offered. The `Service` object described next represents a Web service offered by the organization.

Services

Figure 13.9 depicts the abstractions related to encapsulating a Web service registry entry. A `Service` registry entry has a providing organization and a collection of Web service bindings. Web service binding information provides technical detail on how to access a particular Web service interface and is represented by a `ServiceBinding` object. A service binding typically indicates a next target service binding to reference in the event of a redirection and also provides a collection of specification links. Specification links are used to provide the link between a Web service binding and one of its interface specifications (for example, WSDL or CORBA IDL). Specification links are represented as `SpecificationLink` objects and contain a description of the specification, information on how to use the specification, and of course a reference to the actual interface specification stored as a `RegistryObject`.

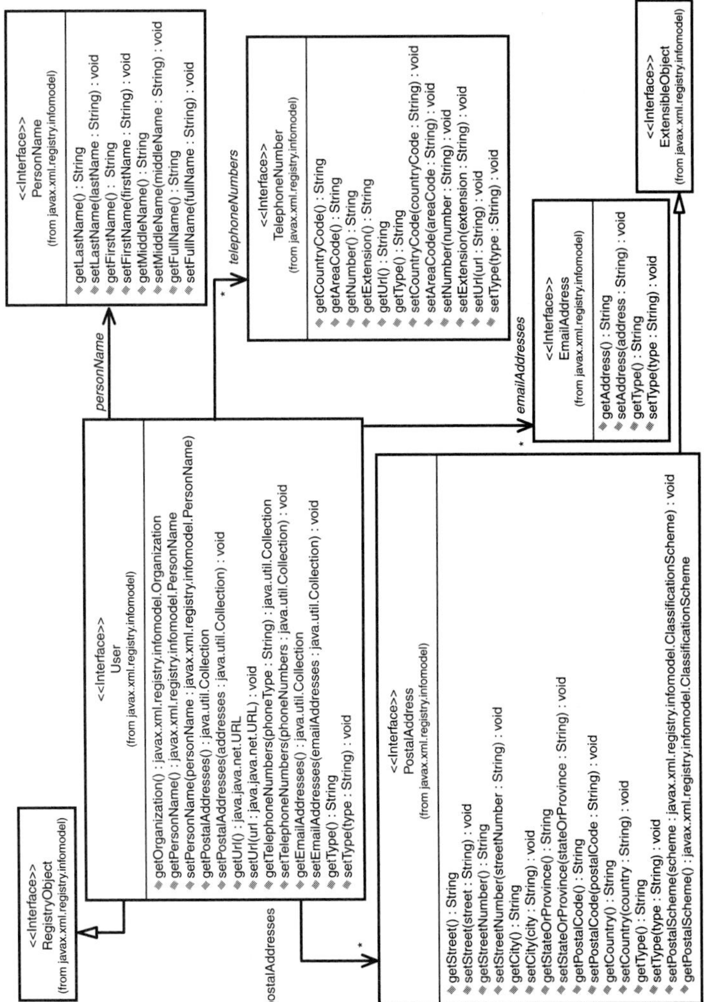

Figure 13.7 JAXR users, addresses, phone numbers, and email.

Classifications and Concepts

A registry object may be classified in different manners. That is, a registry object may be classified in ways such that it may be looked up by JAXR clients according to different schemes. If the registry objects and their relationships that are part of the classification are stored internal to a service provider, this is referred to as internal classification. If the registry objects and their relationships are stored external to a service provider, this is referred to as external classification. The advantage of internal classification is that registry object lookup is of course more efficient than if such information is stored external to the service. The advantage of external classification is that references to registry objects and their relationships are managed across external and different service providers and thus information consistency and distributed maintenance of such information are simplified.

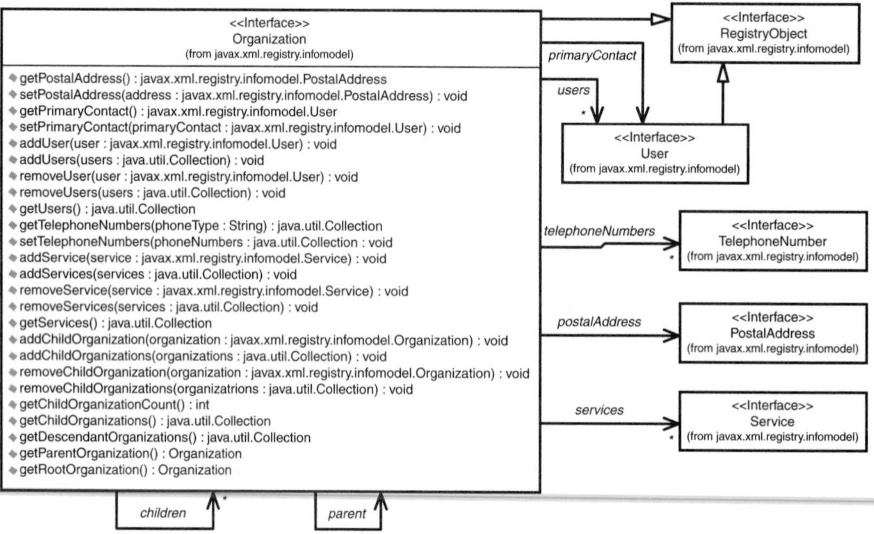

Figure 13.8 JAXR organizations.

The `Classification` abstraction depicted in Figure 13.10 encapsulates a classification of a `RegistryObject` via JAXR. A `Classification` has a `ClassificationScheme` that identifies the particular approach or model used to classify registry objects. If internal classification is used, a `Concept` object can be used to represent some idea or entity within a particular classification scheme taxonomy. Otherwise, a reference in `String` form to some registry object must be used to reference it external to the registry provider.

As an analogy, suppose you have a classification scheme defined according to some government boundaries. The root of this classification taxonomy would be a classification scheme indicating this fact. The next level may be registry values associated with the USA, UK, Italy, Ireland, India, Germany, Russia, and so on. The next level within the USA may be New Jersey, Virginia, New York, and so on. Each nation and state in this example corresponds to a registry value wherein the classification scheme is defined according to government boundaries.

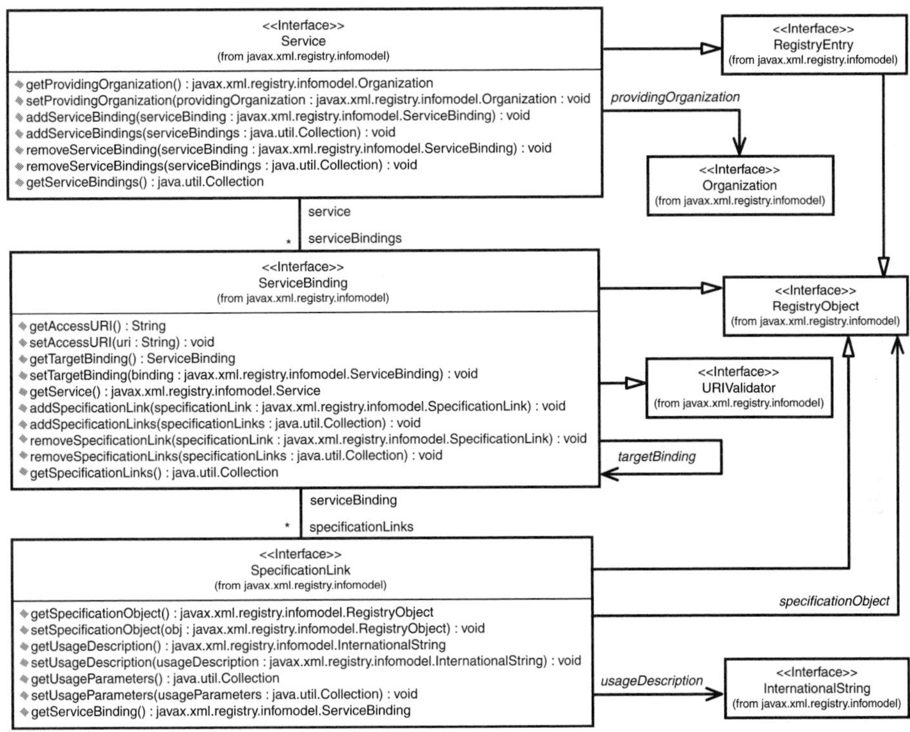

Figure 13.9 JAXR services.

If such a scheme and associated registry objects were all stored internally in a Web services registry, the registry objects would correspond to JAXR `Concept` objects. Because concepts are part of a taxonomy, a `Concept` object can have zero or more children `Concept` objects associated with it and a parent `Concept`. Methods exist on the `Concept` interface to add, remove, and get such children concepts. A `getChildrenConcepts()` method returns the `Concept` object's immediate children, whereas the `getDescendentConcepts()` method returns all the `Concept` object's descendent children. If a `Concept` is a child of another concept, it may call `getParentConcept()` to obtain its parent concept. If a `Concept` has either another `Concept` or a `ClassificationScheme` as a parent, the `Concept` object's `getParent()` method can be used to return such objects (because the `ClassificationScheme` and `Concept` both ultimately extend the `RegistryObject`). The actual value of the concept (for example, "Virginia") can be gotten and set on the `Concept` object as a `String` value.

For a particular `Concept`, its path name is represented akin to a directory structure name. That is, a root classification scheme ID is identified with each subconcept leading up to the concept in question. The `Concept` object's `getPath()` method returns this path value. This path is represented according to a path syntax with a government ID as the classification scheme, USA as a child concept, and then Virginia as a child of the USA concept as exemplified here: `/Government-id/USA/Virginia`.

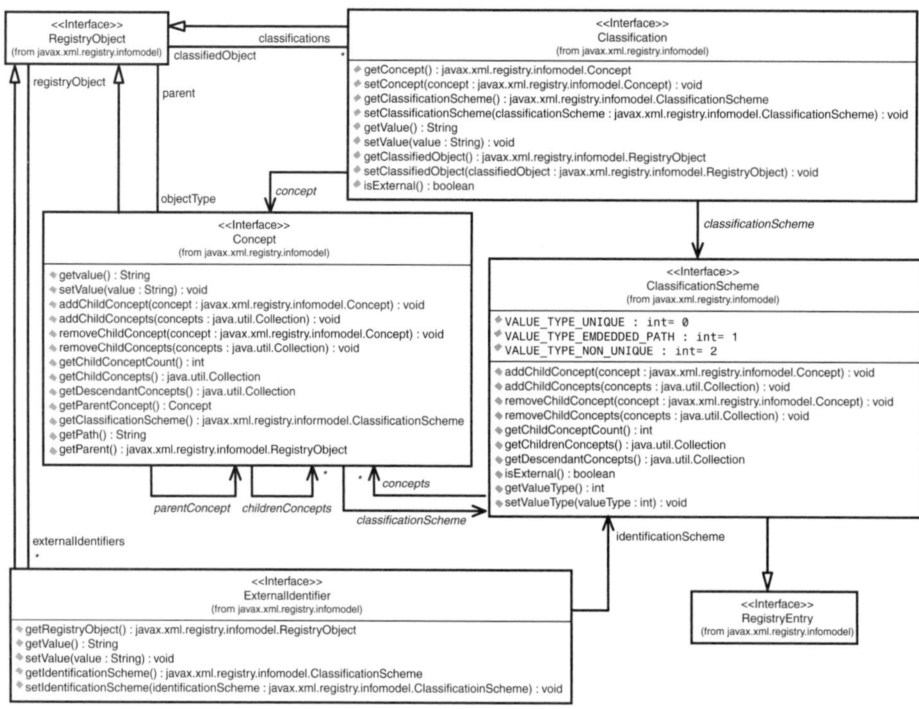

Figure 13.10 JAXR classifications and concepts.

Because a classification scheme serves as the root node of a taxonomy of concept value types, the `ClassificationScheme` object also has methods on it that allow for the adding, removing, and getting of child `Concept` objects. Additionally, the uniqueness of the values inside of a `ClassificationScheme` may also be gotten and set in accordance to a set of constants defined on the `ClassificationScheme` interface. Such concepts in a classification scheme may be categorized as unique throughout the scheme (`VALUE_TYPE_UNIQUE`), as non-unique throughout the scheme but unique as siblings of the same parent (`VALUE_TYPE_NON-UNIQUE`), or as embedding the full path name of the `Concept` in their value (`VALUE_TYPE_EMBEDDED_PATH`).

When internal classification is being used, a `Concept` registry object must be explicitly associated with a `Classification` via invoking `setConcept()` on its `Classification` objects that relate to internal classifications. When external classification is being used, a `String` value identifying the classification is set on the `Classification` object to indicate the relationship with an associated external concept registry object. An explicit call to `setClassificationScheme()` on the `Classification` object must also be made for external classification schemes.

An `ExternalIdentifier` may be used to refer to a classification scheme for a registry object that is defined external to the registry. That is, common identification schemes, such as Social Security numbers, may be encapsulated by an `ExternalIdentifier` object and associated with a registry object. The identification scheme itself is represented on the `ExternalIdentifier` as a `ClassificationScheme` object, whereas the value of the scheme is set as a `String` on the `ExternalIdentifier`.

Associations

A registry object may be associated with other registry objects via associations. An association between two `RegistryObject` objects is encapsulated by the `Association` abstraction as depicted in Figure 13.11. The `Association` object holds a reference to the source and the target `RegistryObject` involved with the association. A `Concept` object is used to identify the type of association according to one of the following standard association types: `RelatedTo`, `HasChild`, `HasMember`, `HasParent`, `ExternallyLinks`, `Contains`, `EquivalentTo`, `Extends`, `Implements`, `InstanceOf`, `Supercedes`, `Uses`, `Replaces`, `ResponsibleFor`, and `SubmitterOf`.

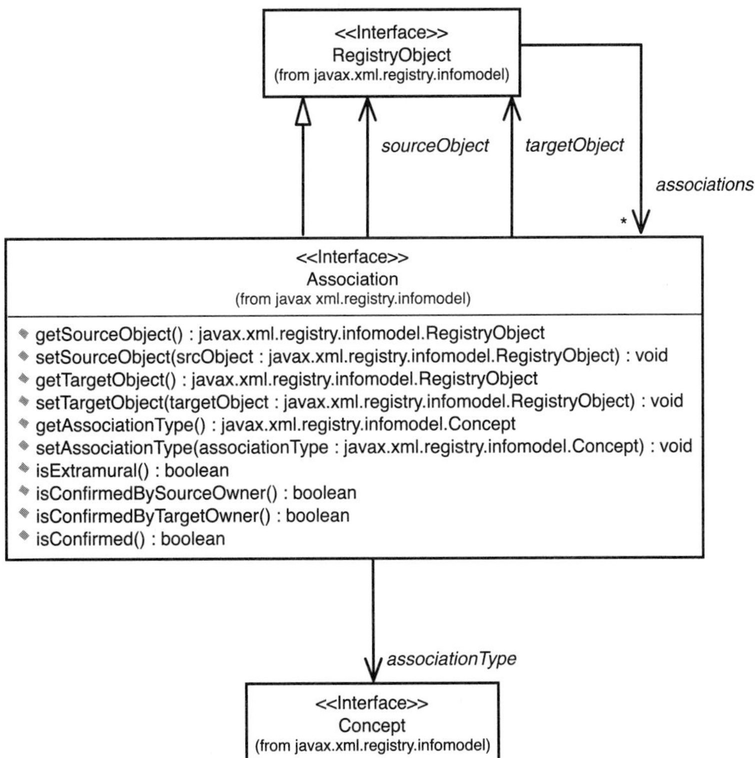

Figure 13.11 JAXR associations.

When an association between two registry objects is created by the same registry user, this is referred to as an intramural association. An extramural association is one in which either or both registry objects that take part in the association are owned by a user different from the user creating the association. When an extramural association between two registry objects is being made, the users may require some confirmation that such associations are allowed. As you can see in Figure 13.11, the `Association` interface exposes methods that allow one to determine whether the association is extramural or intramural and for determining whether either or both users involved with an extramural association have confirmed the association.

JAXR Connections

Now that we've looked at the various JAXR APIs corresponding to information stored in a Web service registry, let's turn our attention to how we access such information using JAXR. To begin with, a JAXR client must establish a connection with a Web services registry. The `ConnectionFactory`, shown in Figure 13.12, provides a way for JAXR clients to create handles to JAXR connections. The `ConnectionFactory` may then be used to obtain handles to a connection or federation of connections.

A handle to a `ConnectionFactory` object itself may be obtained in one of two ways. For one, a JAXR client may use JNDI to look up a handle to a `ConnectionFactory` object if such objects have been registered with a JNDI service. Components operating inside of J2EE containers can use this approach to look up `ConnectionFactory` object handles based on some logical JNDI name akin to the following:

```
Context ctx = new InitialContext();
ConnectionFactory cf
  = (ConnectionFactory) ctx.lookup("java:comp/env/SomeFactory");
```

Alternatively, a remote JNDI service may be accessed from a standalone J2SE environment by passing in initial connection information to the JNDI context as illustrated here:

```
// Create a hashtable with the naming service object factory
// and the URI of the remote JNDI service
Hashtable nameServiceProperties = new Hashtable();
nameServiceProperties.put("java.naming.factory.initial",
                          "com.some.web.lookup.service.ClassFactory");
nameServiceProperties.put("java.naming.provider.url",
                          "http://webservices.beeshirts.com/");

Context ctx = new InitialContext(nameServiceProperties);
ConnectionFactory cf
  = (ConnectionFactory) ctx.lookup("java:comp/env/SomeFactory");
```

The other approach is to create a handle to a default `ConnectionFactory` instance implemented by the JAXR provider by invoking the `static newInstance()` method on `ConnectionFactory`. You can override the default `ConnectionFactory` returned by defining the Java system property `javax.xml.registry.ConnectionFactoryClass` for the JVM.

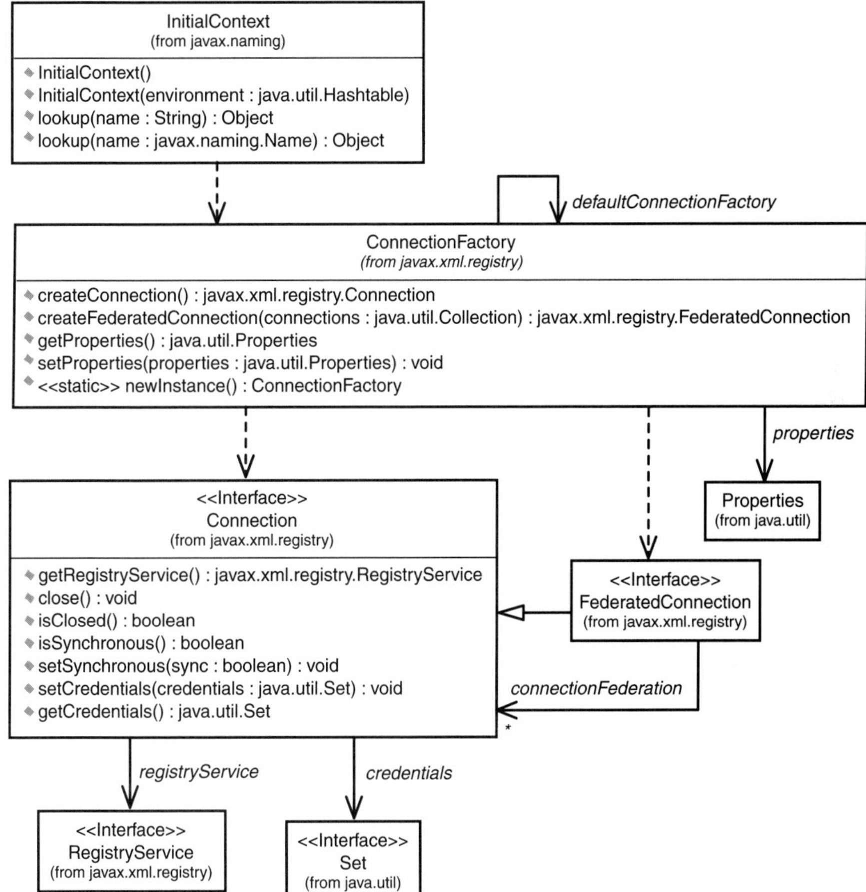

Figure 13.12 JAXR registry connections.

Before you use the `ConnectionFactory` to create a `Connection` object handle, you can configure the nature of the connection returned by setting configuration properties onto the `ConnectionFactory` object. Such properties are stored in a `java.util.Properties` object and can be vendor-specific or refer to a set of standard JAXR properties. These are the standard JAXR properties:

- `javax.xml.registry.queryManagerURL`: A URL to a Web service registry's query manager service.
- `javax.xml.registry.lifeCycleManagerURL`: A URL to a Web service registry's life-cycle manager service (default is `queryManagerURL`).

- `javax.xml.registry.semanticEquivalences`: A `String` that indicates those registry object concepts that are equivalent in meaning. The `String` is defined such that the UUIDs for a pair of semantically equivalent concepts are separated by commas, each pair is separated by a pipe symbol (|), and it allows for a line continuance character (\) to be used as part of the `String`. For example:

```
javax.xml.registry.semanticEquivalences = \
urn:uuid:12345678-90ab-cdef-0123-010101010101, \
urn:uuid:12345678-90ab-cdef-0123-020202020202 | \
urn:uuid:12345678-90ab-cdef-0123-030303030303, \
urn:uuid:12345678-90ab-cdef-0123-040404040404
```

- `javax.xml.registry.security.authenticationMethod`: A `String` that indicates the type of authentication to be provided with the registry with potential values such as basic HTTP authentication (`HTTP_BASIC`), certificate-based authentication (`CLIENT_CERTIFICATE`), UDDI token-based authentication (`UDDI_GET_AUTHTOKEN`), or Microsoft Passport authentication (`MS_PASSPORT`).
- `javax.xml.registry.uddi.maxRows`: An integer indicating the maximum number of rows returned from a UDDI query.
- `javax.xml.registry.postalAddressScheme`: A `String` for a UUID that indicates a postal address classification scheme to be used. When you're setting a postal address classification scheme, the semantic equivalent between your JAXR provider's default postal address scheme concepts and the postal address scheme concepts to use must also be defined using the `javax.xml.registry.semanticEquivalences` property.

The JAXR client sets any such standard properties as well as any JAXR provider-specific properties using the `ConnectionFactory` object's `setProperties()` method.

> **Note**
>
> Before you can run any JAXR client code, you must of course identify a JAXR registry service to which you will connect. Although many JAXR registry services to which you may connect allow you to perform read-only queries, you will likely need permission from a registry service to update the registry. A few third-party UDDI registry services exist to which you may connect. The URLs for obtaining permission to update an IBM test registry are `http://uddi.ibm.com/testregistry/registry.html` and, for a Microsoft registry, `http://uddi.microsoft.com`.
>
> For the `JAXRClient` example included with this chapter, we use a registry service that you can start up on your own machine. This Web service registry service is started when you start Tomcat included with the Web Service Developer's Pack. The example code and scripts associated with this chapter can be located as described in Appendix A, "Software Configuration," and extracted to an `examples/src/ejava/jaxr` directory. The ANT `build.xml` file in that directory has a `start-tomcat` and `shutdown-tomcat` target to start and shut down Tomcat, respectively. A set of configuration properties must also be set in a local `build.properties` file. Refer to Appendix A for more information on configuration and installing the software associated with this chapter.

After setting properties onto the `ConnectionFactory`, the client then induces the `ConnectionFactory` to create a connection using its `createConnection()` method. The `JAXRClient` included with this chapter's examples performs such operations inside of its `getConnection()` method as shown here:

```
public Connection getConnection(){
    Connection conn = null;
      ...
      // Get a connection factory
      ConnectionFactory cf = ConnectionFactory.newInstance();

      // Set connection factory properties
      Properties cfProps = new Properties();
      cfProps.setProperty(QUERY_URL_PROPNAME, queryManagerURL);
      cfProps.setProperty(LIFECYCLE_URL_PROPNAME, lifeCycleManagerURL);
      cf.setProperties(cfProps);

      // Create the connection
      conn = cf.createConnection();
      ...
    return conn;
}
```

The constants referenced in the preceding text are defined as shown here:

```
public static String QUERY_URL_PROPNAME
    = "javax.xml.registry.queryManager";
public static String LIFECYCLE_URL_PROPNAME
    = "javax.xml.registry.lifeCycleManagerURL";
```

The `queryManagerURL` and `lifeCycleManagerURL` strings are read in from `Preferences` inside the `JAXRClient`. For our example, both URL preferences are set as configured by the chapter code's `build.properties` file. Both URLs are set to the URL of a locally running Tomcat registry server with the value `http://localhost:8080/RegistryServer`.

After a `Connection` is created, a few discrete operations may be performed on the connection. Whether the JAXR client communicates with the registry service in a synchronous or asynchronous fashion can be set and determined via `Connection` methods. Additionally, a `Set` of `java.lang.Object` credential objects used to authenticate the client with the registry service can be set and gotten from the connection. Finally, when a `Connection` is finished with, it should be closed via its `close()` method.

As mentioned, a JAXR client will likely have to authenticate itself with a registry if it intends to modify the registry's contents. Our example `JAXRClient` authenticates itself with the Tomcat registry server by setting a set of `java.net.PasswordAuthentication` type credentials onto the `Connection` as illustrated here:

```
public void authenticate(Connection conn){
        ...
      // Create a java.net.PasswordAuthentication object
      //    with the registry username and password
      PasswordAuthentication credential
        = new PasswordAuthentication(registryUsername,
                                     registryPassword);
      // Create a credentials Set
      Set credentials = new HashSet();
      credentials.add(credential);
      // Set credentials onto JAXR connection
      conn.setCredentials(credentials);
        ...
}
```

On a final note about connections, JAXR also supports the capability for a client to connect to a federation of registry connections. Such a feature allows a client to use a `FederatedConnection` object, as shown in Figure 13.12, that represents a logical grouping of `Connection` objects. When the client invokes services on a `FederationConnection`, connections in the federation may service the request in a distributed fashion. The client induces the creation of a `FederationConnection` by invoking the `createFederatedConnection()` method on the `ConnectionFactory` object with a `Collection` of `Connection` objects to be federated.

JAXR Registry Service

After a client obtains a `Connection` handle, it obtains a handle to a `RegistryService` object, as shown in Figure 13.13. The `RegistryService` object represents the front-line interface to a Web service registry. The `RegistryService` object is used to obtain handles to the registry's query and lifecycle services. The `RegistryService` also indicates the capability level version number and JAXR specification version supported by the underlying JAXR provider and registry service and as encapsulated by a `CapabilityProfile` object. As an example, the `JAXRClient` returns the `CapabilityProfile` for a JAXR provider as shown here:

```
public CapabilityProfile getCapabilityProfile(Connection conn){
    CapabilityProfile cp = null;
      ...
    RegistryService rs = conn.getRegistryService();
    cp = rs.getCapabilityProfile();
      ...
    return cp;
}
```

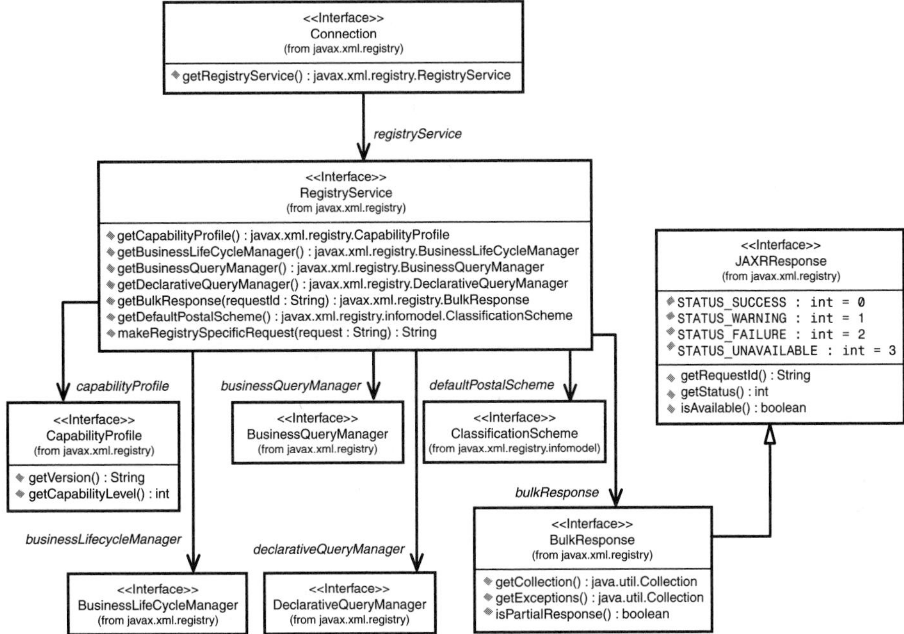

Figure 13.13 JAXR registry service.

Whether or not certain code is executed is then made a function of the JAXR provider's capability level, as exemplified here in the `JAXRClient main()` method:

```
JAXRClient jaxr = ...
Connection conn = ...
   ...
CapabilityProfile cp = jaxr.getCapabilityProfile(conn);
if(cp.getCapabilityLevel() == 1){
   ...
}
```

Given some `String` identifier for a previous asynchronous request made, the `RegistryService.getBulkResponse()` method can be used to obtain the response from such a request. The `BulkResponse` object encapsulates a collection of results from a request. The base class `JAXRResponse` encapsulates a general response from a JAXR registry service request and contains an associated request ID; an indication of whether the response is actually available to retrieve; and a status value mapping to a constant indicating whether the response failed, was a success, is currently unavailable to retrieve, or was a success but with warnings.

The `BulkResponse` object extends the `JAXRResponse`. The `BulkResponse getCollection()` method retrieves a `Collection` of the response objects and blocks until all response objects are returned. If all the response objects could not be returned due to a large result set, the `isPartialResponse()` method on the `BulkResponse` object will return `true`. If the registry has indicated any errors in processing, the `BulkResponse` `getExceptions()` method will return a `Collection` of `RegistryException` objects indicating such errors.

As an example, the `JAXRClient` method named `processBulkResponse()` demonstrates a generic method used to traverse a `BulkResponse` and print its contents as shown here:

```
public void processBulkResponse(BulkResponse response){
      ...
      // Get info from the bulk response
      String id = response.getRequestId();
      int status = response.getStatus();
      boolean available = response.isAvailable();
      Collection objCollection = response.getCollection();
      Collection exCollection = response.getExceptions();
      boolean partial = response.isPartialResponse();

      // Display the info
      System.out.println("    Response with ID " + id
                        + " has status " + status
                        + " and isAvailable as " + available
                        + " and isPartialResponse as " + partial);

      // If the response collection is not null, print it out
      if(objCollection != null){
        Iterator objects = objCollection.iterator();
        System.out.println("  - Contents of response...");
        while(objects.hasNext()){
          Object obj = objects.next();
          System.out.println("    -- Response object of type "
                              + obj.getClass().getName());

          processBusinessObject(obj);
        }
      }

      // If the exception collection is not null, print it out
      if(exCollection != null){
        Iterator exceptions = exCollection.iterator();
        System.out.println("- Exceptions in response...");
        while(exceptions.hasNext()){
          Object obj = exceptions.next();
          if(obj instanceof Exception){
            Exception ex = (Exception) obj;
```

```
            System.out.println("-- Exception is " + ex.getMessage());
          }
        }
      }
      ...
}
```

The `processBuinessObject()` method previously referenced simply examines the returned object's type and prints some information for our examples depending on that object's type, as shown here:

```
public void processBusinessObject(Object obj){
      ...
      if(obj instanceof Organization){ // Print Organization info
        Organization org = (Organization) obj;

        String key = org.getKey().getId();
        String name = org.getName().getValue();
        String desc = org.getDescription().getValue();

        System.out.println("       Organization with ID " + key
                          + " and with name " + name
                          + " and description " + desc);

        Iterator users = org.getUsers().iterator();
        while(users.hasNext()){
          User user = (User) users.next();
          System.out.println("        User name = "
                          + user.getPersonName().getFullName());
        }
      }
      else if(obj instanceof Key){ // Print out a Key
        Key key = (Key) obj;
        System.out.println("       Key with ID " + key.getId());
      }
      ...
}
```

Finally, the `RegistryService` also provides a way to induce registry-specific requests not yet encapsulated by JAXR abstractions and methods. The `RegistryService makeRegistrySpecificRequest()` method takes a XML registry-specific request in `String` form and returns an XML registry-specific response in `String` form.

JAXR Query Managers

One of the most common and basic uses of a Web service registry is to query for information via its query management service. Figure 13.14 depicts the JAXR abstractions for such functionality. The JAXR client uses such abstractions to formulate registry queries and retrieve resultant registry objects.

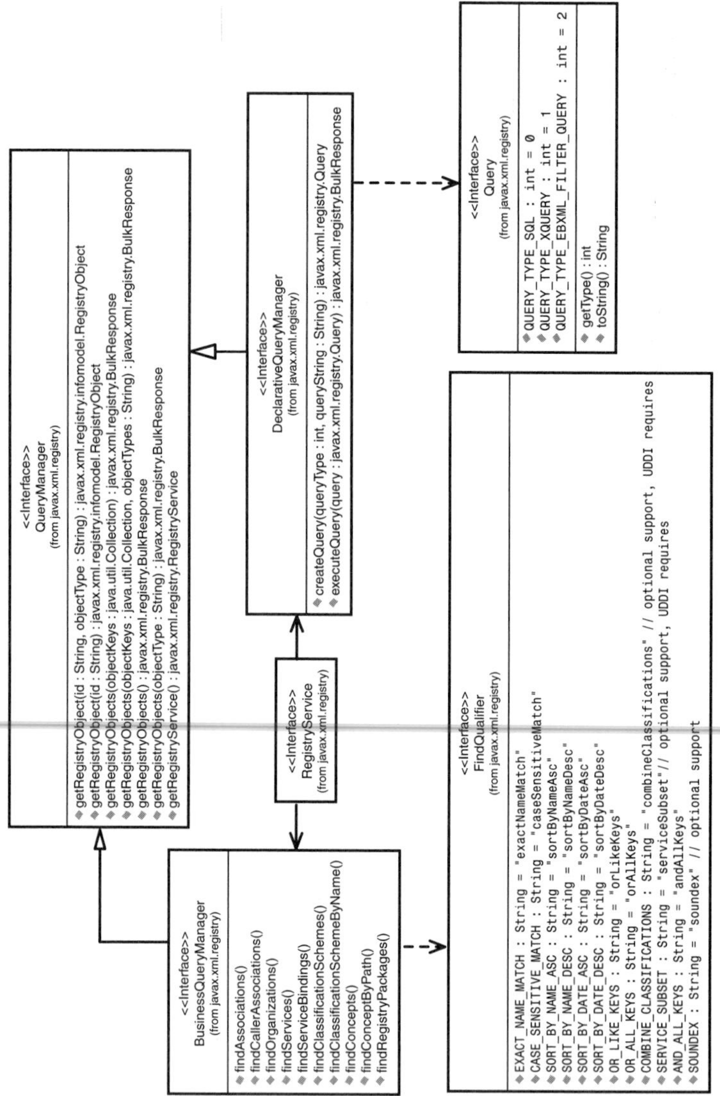

Figure 13.14 JAXR query managers.

The JAXR client obtains handles to such query management services via the `RegistryService` object's `getBusinessQueryManager()` and getDeclarativeQueryManager() methods, as exemplified by these two JAXRClient methods:

```
public BusinessQueryManager getBusinessQueryManager(Connection conn){
    BusinessQueryManager queryMgr = null;
      ...
    RegistryService rs = conn.getRegistryService();
    queryMgr = rs.getBusinessQueryManager();
      ...
    return queryMgr;
}

public DeclarativeQueryManager
  getDeclarativeQueryManager(Connection conn){
    DeclarativeQueryManager queryMgr = null;
      ...
    RegistryService rs = conn.getRegistryService();
    queryMgr = rs.getDeclarativeQueryManager();
      ...
    return queryMgr;
}
```

Base Query Manager

The base QueryManager abstraction shown in Figure 13.14 provides basic support for retrieving bulk responses of RegistryObject objects using identifiers and keys for such objects via the following methods:

- getRegistryObject(String): Get a RegistryObject based on its UUID.
- getRegistryObject(String, String): Get a RegistryObject based on its UUID and registry object type whereby the registry object type value is one of the constant String values defined on the LifeCycleManager interface to be shown later in Figure 13.15.
- getRegistryObjects(): Get a bulk response of RegistryObject objects that are owned by the registry user inducing the lookup.
- getRegistryObjects(Collection): Get a bulk response of RegistryObject objects that are associated with a Collection of Key objects.
- getRegistryObjects(Collection, String): Get a bulk response of RegistryObject objects that are associated with a Collection of Key objects and that are of a particular registry object type.
- getRegistryObjects(Collection, String): Get a bulk response of RegistryObject objects that are of a particular registry object type.

As an example, the JAXRClient lookupObjectsByKey() method induces the lookup of Organization objects given a Collection of Key objects associated with such Organization objects as shown here:

```
public BulkResponse lookupObjectsByKey(QueryManager qm,
                                       Collection keys){
  BulkResponse resp = null;
      ...
  // Lookup Organization objects with keys
  resp = qm.getRegistryObjects(keys,LifeCycleManager.ORGANIZATION);
      ...
  return resp;
}
```

Note

Some of the methods defined on the base QueryManager require capability level 1 compliance. The Java Web Service Developer's Pack JAXR provider implementation was only level 0 compliant at the time of this writing. Thus, for example, use of the getRegistryObjects(Collection) method with the Java Web Service Developer's Pack in the previous example code would throw a javax.xml.registry.UnsupportedCapabilityException, whereas the getRegistryObjects(Collection, String) method does not.

Declarative Query Manager

One extension of the QueryManager is the DeclarativeQueryManager, which provides a way to query for registry objects in a declarative query language (for example, SQL) fashion. A declarative query must first be created using the createQuery() method as shown in Figure 13.14. The createQuery() method takes a query type and associated query String value. The query type is defined by one of the Query abstraction's constants indicating whether a SQL query (QUERY_TYPE_SQL), W3C XQuery (QUERY_TYPE_XQUERY), or OASIS ebXML Registry XML Filter Query (QUERY_TYPE_EBXML_FILTER_QUERY) is used. The associated String passed into createQuery() is formulated according to whatever query type is used. The createQuery() method then returns a Query object representing such a query, which is then passed by the client to the executeQuery() method to generate a resulting bulk response of RegistryObject objects.

As an example, the JAXRClient lookupDeclaratively() method demonstrates the lookup of information based on a SQL statement issued to the registry:

```
public BulkResponse lookupDeclaratively(DeclarativeQueryManager dqm){
    BulkResponse resp = null;
      ...
    Query query = dqm.createQuery(Query.QUERY_TYPE_SQL, queryString);
    resp = dqm.executeQuery(query);
```

```
        ...
    return resp;
}
```

Business Query Manager

The BusinessQueryManager extends the base QueryManager to define a set of find*XXX*() type methods that look up registry objects using concrete registry information model types. The operation signatures of these various find*XXX*() methods are too lengthy to display in Figure 13.14, but we describe each method in more detail in the text that follows.

It is important to first understand that various String constants defined on the FindQualifier abstraction are used as parameters by almost all the find*XXX*() methods. These various constants affect the behavior of the find*XXX*() methods. Furthermore, not all input parameters to a method must be supplied. If an input parameter is not to be used during a lookup, a null value may be used in its place. The find*XXX*() type method names, their functionality, their input parameters, and their output parameters are defined here:

- findAssociations(): Finds a BulkResponse of Association objects matching input parameters ordered this way: (1) Collection of FindQualifier String objects; (2) source registry UUID String; (3) target registry object UUID String; and (4) Collection of association type String objects.
- findCallerAssociations(): Finds a BulkResponse of Association objects owned by the invoking registry user matching input parameters ordered this way: (1) Collection of FindQualifier String objects; (2) Boolean value indicating whether the object must have been confirmed by the caller; (3) Boolean value indicating whether the object must have been confirmed by the other party; and (4) Collection of association type String objects.
- findClassificationSchemeByName(): Finds a ClassificationScheme object matching input parameters ordered this way: (1) Collection of FindQualifier String objects and (2) a SQL LIKE style String indicating the classification scheme name pattern to match.
- findClassificationSchemes(): Finds a BulkResponse of ClassificationScheme objects matching input parameters ordered this way: (1) Collection of FindQualifier String objects; (2) a SQL LIKE style String indicating the classification scheme name pattern to match; (3) Collection of Classification objects that classify the registry object; and (4) Collection of ExternalLink objects that link from the registry object.
- findConceptByPath(): Finds a Concept object matching the following input parameter (1) a String identifying the canonical path name for the concept.

- `findConcepts()`: Finds a `BulkResponse` of `Concept` objects matching input parameters ordered this way: (1) `Collection` of `FindQualifier String` objects; (2) a SQL `LIKE` style `String` or `LocalizedString` indicating the concept name pattern to match; (3) `Collection` of `Classification` objects that classify the registry object; (4) `Collection` of `ExternalIdentifier` objects that externally identify the registry object; and (5) `Collection` of `ExternalLink` objects that link from the registry object.
- `findOrganizations()`: Finds a `BulkResponse` of `Organization` objects matching input parameters ordered this way: (1) `Collection` of `FindQualifier String` objects; (2) a SQL `LIKE` style `String` or `LocalizedString` indicating the organization name pattern to match; (3) `Collection` of `Classification` objects that classify the registry object; (4) `Collection` of `RegistryObject` objects that represent a service technical specification; (5) `Collection` of `ExternalIdentifier` objects that externally identify the registry object; and (6) `Collection` of `ExternalLink` objects that link from the registry object.
- `findRegistryPackages()`: Finds a `BulkResponse` of `RegistryPackage` objects matching input parameters ordered this way: (1) `Collection` of `FindQualifier String` objects; (2) a SQL `LIKE` style `String` or `LocalizedString` indicating the registry package name pattern to match; (3) `Collection` of `Classification` objects that classify the registry object; and (4) `Collection` of `ExternalLink` objects that link from the registry object.
- `findServiceBindings()`: Finds a `BulkResponse` of `ServiceBinding` objects matching input parameters ordered this way: (1) a `Key` object identifying a `Service`;(2) `Collection` of `FindQualifier String` objects; (3) `Collection` of `Classification` objects that classify the registry object; and (4) `Collection` of `RegistryObject` objects that represent a service technical specification.
- `findServices()`: Finds a `BulkResponse` of `Service` objects matching input parameters ordered this way: (1) a `Key` object identifying an `Organization`; (2) `Collection` of `FindQualifier String` objects; (3) `Collection` of `Classification` objects that classify the registry object; and (4) `Collection` of `RegistryObject` objects that represent a service technical specification.

As an example, the `JAXRClient lookupObject()` method looks up a `Collection` of `Organization` objects given a name pattern `String` read in from the `build.properties` file. The `lookupObject()` method is depicted here:

```
public BulkResponse lookupObject(BusinessQueryManager bqm){
    BulkResponse resp = null;
      ...
    // Create find qualifiers
    Collection quals = new ArrayList();
```

```
    quals.add(FindQualifier.SORT_BY_NAME_ASC);
    // Create a name pattern
    Collection names = new ArrayList();
    names.add(namePattern);
    // Now induce the finder method query
    resp
      = bqm.findOrganizations(quals, names, null, null, null, null);
      ...
  return resp;
}
```

The name pattern `String` read in from the `build.properties` file can be configured in any way you desire. However, the default setting in the `build.properties` file indicates the lookup of organizations with the `String` "`BeeShirts`" in its name:

```
namePattern=BeeShirts
```

In addition to being invoked from within the `JAXRClient main()` method, this `lookupObject()` method is also used by the `JAXRClient lookupKeys()` method. The `lookupKeys()` method simply traverses the `BulkResponse` returned from `lookupObject()` and plucks out a `Collection` of `Key` objects associated with each object returned as shown here:

```
public Collection lookupKeys(BusinessQueryManager bqm){
    Collection keys = new ArrayList();
      ...
    // First look up the object
    BulkResponse resp = lookupObject(bqm);
    // Iterate through the response collection
    Collection objCollection = resp.getCollection();
    Iterator objects = objCollection.iterator();
    while(objects.hasNext()){
      // Add the organization key to the collection
      Organization org = (Organization) objects.next();
      keys.add(org.getKey());
    }
      ...
    return keys;
}
```

JAXR Life-Cycle Managers

In addition to querying for registry object data, a JAXR client may also want to create, delete, update, deprecate, and undeprecate registry objects. This is accomplished via a registry's life-cycle manager service. JAXR provides a set of interfaces that expose such functionality to the JAXR client. However, because these operations involve altering objects in a Web service registry, JAXR clients must often obtain appropriate permissions and hence such clients must authenticate themselves with the service. Earlier in this chapter, you saw how the `JAXRClient` accomplished this via its `authenticate()` method.

The JAXR client obtains a handle to such query life-cycle management services via the `RegistryService` object's `getBusinessLifeCycleManager()` method, as exemplified here via the `JAXRClient getBusinessLifeCycleManager()` method:

```
public BusinessLifeCycleManager
        getBusinessLifeCycleManager(Connection conn){
    BusinessLifeCycleManager lifecycleMgr = null;
     ...
    RegistryService rs = conn.getRegistryService();
    lifecycleMgr = rs.getBusinessLifeCycleManager();
     ...
    return lifecycleMgr;
}
```

Base Life-Cycle Manager

Figure 13.15 depicts the base `LifeCycleManager` abstraction provided by JAXR. In addition to the various `static` constants used for identifying registry object types, a series of methods that modify a registry in some way are defined. Such methods provide a way to create, delete, update, deprecate, and undeprecate objects.

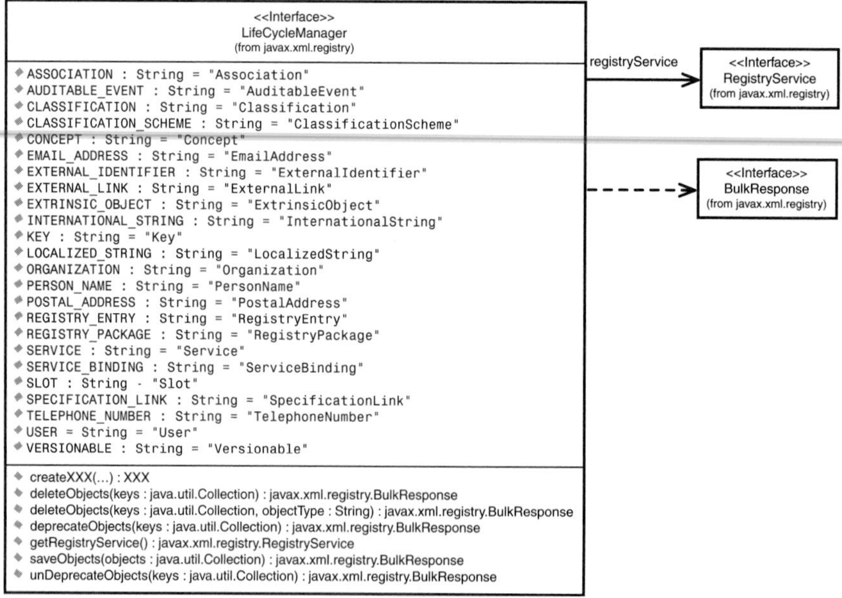

Figure 13.15 JAXR base life-cycle manager.

Because there are a very large number of methods defined on the `LifeCycleManager` interface that can be used to create objects, we cannot depict them all in the diagram. The basic format of such methods is `create`*`XXX`*`(...)`, given an arbitrary set of input parameters, and where *`XXX`* refers to some information model object type, the manager will return an object of *`XXX`* type. The `LifeCycleManager` supports the following `create`*`XXX`*`(...)` type methods:

- `createAssociation()`: Create an `Association` given a target object as a `RegistryObject` and an association type as a `Concept`.
- `createClassification()`: Create a `Classification` given (a) a scheme as a `ClassificationScheme` object, `InternationalString` name, and `String` value; (b) a scheme as a `ClassificationScheme` object, `String` name, and `String` value; or (c) a specified `Concept` object.
- `createClassificationScheme()`: Create a `ClassificationScheme` given (a) an `InternationalString` name and `InternationalString` description; (b) a `String` name and `String` description; or (c) a specified `Concept` object.
- `createConcept()`: Create a `Concept` given either (a) a parent `RegistryObject`, an `InternationalString` name, and a `String` value; or (b) a parent `RegistryObject`, a `String` name, and a `String` value.
- `createEmailAddress()`: Create an `EmailAddress` given either (a) an email address `String`; or (b) an email address `String` and email type `String`.
- `createExternalIdentifier()`: Create an `ExternalIdentifier` given either (a) an identification scheme as a `ClassificationScheme`, an `InternationalString` name, and a `String` value; or (b) an identification scheme as a `ClassificationScheme`; a `String` name, and a `String` value.
- `createExternalLink()`:Create an `ExternalLink` given either (a) an external URI `String` and `InternationalString` description; or (b) an external URI `String` and `String` description.
- `createExtrinsicObject()`: Create an `ExtrinsicObject` given a `DataHandler` repository item reference.
- `createInternationalString()`: Create an `InternationalString` given (a) a parameterless method resulting in an empty instance; (b) a `Locale` and `String` value; or (c) a `String` value.
- `createKey()`: Create a `Key` given a `String` identifier.
- `createLocalizedString()`: Create a `LocalizedString` given either (a) a `Locale` and `String` value; or (b) a `Locale`, `String` value, and character set name as a `String`.
- `createObject()`: Create an information model object returned as a `java.lang.Object` given a `String` as defined by one of the `LifeCycleManager` constant values.

- createOrganization(): Create an Organization given either (a) an InternationalString name; or (b) a String name.
- createPersonName(): Create a PersonName given either (a) a full name String; or (b) a separate first name, middle name, and last name String.
- createPostalAddress(): Create a PostalAddress given separate String objects for the street number, street, city, state or province, country, postal code, and address type.
- createRegistryPackage(): Create a RegistryPackage given either (a) an InternationalString name; or (b) a String name.
- createService(): Create a Service given either (a) an InternationalString name; or (b) a String name.
- createServiceBinding(): Create an empty ServiceBinding with no input parameters.
- createSlot(): Create a Slot given either (a) a String name, a Collection of values, and a slot type as a String; or (b) a String name, a String value, and a slot type as a String.
- createSpecificationLink(): Create an empty SpecificationLink with no input parameters.
- createTelephoneNumber(): Create an empty TelephoneNumber with no input parameters.
- createUser(): Create an empty User with no input parameters.

As an example, the JAXRClient defines a createOrganization() method that is used to construct an Organization object and some of its elements. The data for such elements are read from local variables of the JAXRClient. Such local variables are set in the JAXRClient via preferences whose corresponding values are defined inside of the local build.properties file. The JAXRClient createOrganization() method is shown here:

```
public Organization createOrganization(BusinessLifeCycleManager lcm){
    Organization org = null;
    try{
      // Organization
      org = lcm.createOrganization(orgName);

      // Organization description
      InternationalString od
        = lcm.createInternationalString(orgDescription);
      org.setDescription(od);

      // User1 Info (is a primary user too)
      User u1 = lcm.createUser();
```

```
// Person name for user1
PersonName pn1 = lcm.createPersonName(user1Name);
u1.setPersonName(pn1);
u1.setType(user1Type);
// Phone for user1
TelephoneNumber tn1 = lcm.createTelephoneNumber();
tn1.setNumber(phone1);
Collection tns1 = new ArrayList();
tns1.add(tn1);
u1.setTelephoneNumbers(tns1);
// Email for user1
EmailAddress e1 = lcm.createEmailAddress(email1);
Collection es1 = new ArrayList();
es1.add(e1);
u1.setEmailAddresses(es1);

// User2 Info (is a primary user too)
User u2 = lcm.createUser();
// Person name for user2
PersonName pn2 = lcm.createPersonName(user2Name);
u2.setPersonName(pn2);
u2.setType(user2Type);
// Phone for user2
TelephoneNumber tn2 = lcm.createTelephoneNumber();
tn2.setNumber(phone2);
Collection tns2 = new ArrayList();
tns2.add(tn2);
u2.setTelephoneNumbers(tns2);
// Email for user2
EmailAddress e2 = lcm.createEmailAddress(email2);
Collection es2 = new ArrayList();
es2.add(e2);
u2.setEmailAddresses(es2);

// Add users and primary contact to the organization
org.setPrimaryContact(u1);
org.addUser(u1);
org.addUser(u2);

// Service
Service s = lcm.createService(serviceName);
InternationalString sd
  = lcm.createInternationalString(serviceDescription);
s.setDescription(sd);

// Service bindings
```

```
            ServiceBinding b = lcm.createServiceBinding();
            InternationalString sbd
              = lcm.createInternationalString(serviceBindingDescription);
            b.setDescription(sbd);
            b.setValidateURI(false); // don't validate link since phony
            b.setAccessURI(serviceBindingURI);
            Collection sbs = new ArrayList();
            sbs.add(b);

            // Add service binding to the service
            s.addServiceBindings(sbs);

            // Add service to the organization
            Collection ss = new ArrayList();
            ss.add(s);
            org.addServices(ss);
          }catch(JAXRException e){
            handleException(e);
          }
          return org;
    }
```

The `saveObjects()` method can be generically used to save a `Collection` of information model objects. Thus, such a method acts as an update method whereby if you've create some object and have added information to it, the `saveObjects()` method can be used to reflect such changes in the registry. If the object doesn't exist in the registry, it will be created. The `BulkResponse` from such a method returns the keys for those objects successfully saved. Any `SaveException` that was generated during this operation may also be returned in the response.

In addition to these various ways to create information model objects, a more generic means for deleting objects is provided by the `deleteObjects()` methods requiring that a `Collection` of keys for the objects be input. Another form of the `deleteObjects()` method can be used to specify what type of object should be deleted. The `BulkResponse` from this method contains the keys for those objects deleted and any `DeleteException` that may have been thrown during processing.

Finally, when a JAXR client wants to mark an object such that it is on notice to be deleted soon, the `deprecateObjects()` method is used with a `Collection` of keys for those objects to be deleted. Contrarily, the `unDeprecateObjects()` method may be used to mark those objects as no longer deprecated. The `BulkResponse` from each operation returns the keys associated with those objects for which the operation was successful. A `JAXRException` may also be returned if there was an error in processing.

Business Life-Cycle Manager

The `BusinessLifeCycleManager` abstraction, depicted in Figure 13.16, extends the base `LifeCycleManager` to provide business-specific methods for saving and deleting certain registry objects. The various `saveXXX(...)` methods take a `Collection` of registry objects of some *XXX* type and save them or create them in the registry if they don't exist. Similarly, a series of `deleteXXX(...)` methods attempt to delete registry objects of some *XXX* type and associated with keys input as a `Collection` to the method. Both methods return a `BulkResponse` having keys associated with those objects for which the operation was successful. Finally, the `BusinessLifeCycleManager` also defines a `confirmAssociation()` method, which is used to induce the confirmation of an extramural association by the invoking user. The `unConfirmAssociation()` reverses this operation.

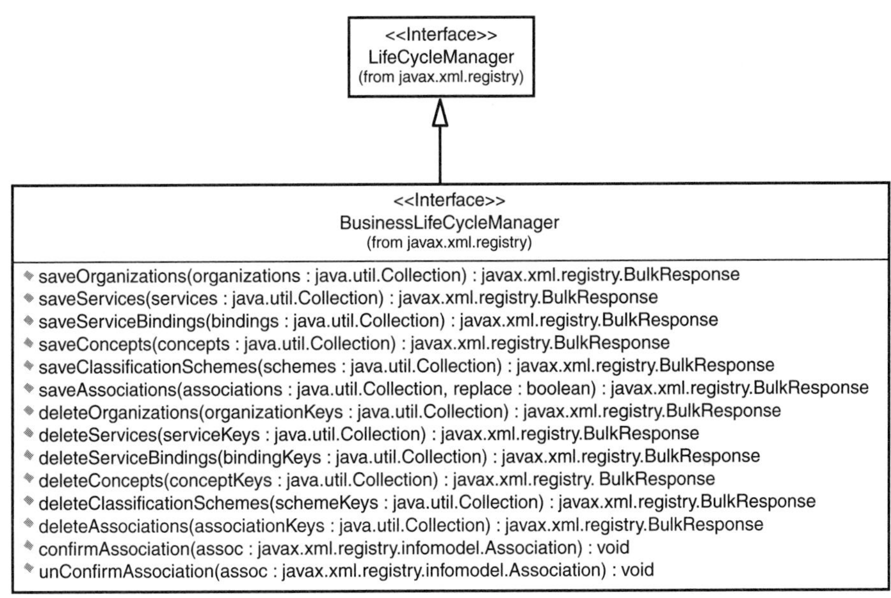

Figure 13.16 JAXR business life-cycle manager.

As an example, the `JAXRClient` defines a `createObject()` method that uses a `BusinessLifeCycleManager` object to create an `Organization` object using the `createOrganization()` defined earlier and then saves the `Organization` (via a collection) to the registry like this:

```
public BulkResponse createObject(BusinessLifeCycleManager lcm){
    BulkResponse resp = null;
        ...
    // Create Organization object from configurable info
    Organization organization = createOrganization(lcm);

    // Create Collection of Organization objects
```

```
    Collection organizations = new ArrayList();
    organizations.add(organization);

    // Save Organization updates to the registry
    resp = lcm.saveOrganizations(organizations);
      ...
    return resp;
}
```

The reverse of such a procedure occurs from within the `deleteObject()` method in the `JAXRClient`. That is, the `deleteObject()` method deletes an `Organization` given a `Collection` of `Key` objects containing the `Key` for that `Organization` as shown here:

```
public BulkResponse deleteObject(BusinessLifeCycleManager lcm,
                                 Collection keys){
    BulkResponse resp = null;
      ...
    // Delete the organizations associated with the keys
    resp = lcm.deleteOrganizations(keys);
      ...
    return resp;
}
```

Note

The various example methods described throughout this chapter were taken from the `JAXRClient` class associated with this chapter's code. The `main()` method of that class invokes the functionality of such methods by first creating an object, looking it up, deleting it, and then attempting to look it up again. We encourage you to look at that code and modify the `build.properties` file to suit your environment and modify the example data that you want to enter and browse in a Web services registry.

Conclusions

Web service registries provide a means for Web services to publish their handle information to a central repository such that Web service clients can look up such handles and thus tap their services. The ebXML Registry Services and UDDI specifications define standard protocols for such registry services. JAXR provides a standard J2EE API for Java clients to use when interacting with Web service registries. JAXR clients can traverse the rather complicated hierarchy of registry objects as well as look up, create, delete, and update registry information using JAXR.

14

Transaction Services with JTA and JTS

WE INTRODUCED THE TOPIC OF TRANSACTIONS in Chapter 2, "Enterprise Data," within the context of database management systems. Chapter 2 discussed the basic concept of transactions, the ACID principles for transactions, and standards for distributed transaction processing. Chapter 6, "Advanced JDBC," built on this conceptual database transaction groundwork with specific application to JDBC. Updateable result set change visibility and transaction isolation levels can be managed using the JDBC API. Furthermore, middle-tier transaction management interfaces support distributed transactions via the JDBC specification. The transaction material of Chapters 2 and 6 just scratched the surface of concepts and which interfaces are exposed for interacting with transactions in the context of databases. And to a certain extent, given the broad range of issues and discussion that could surround the topic of transactions, this chapter is only able to scratch a little bit more off of the transactions topical surface.

In this chapter, we describe more than the mere application of transactions to databases. We explore those services used to manage transactions in a distributed enterprise system. Distributed objects need to coordinate and define boundaries for access to shared resources. Transaction services provide such support. This chapter expands on the transaction problem and generic transaction service architecture, the CORBA Object Transaction Service (OTS), the Java Transaction API (JTA), and the Java Transaction Service (JTS). As you'll see, the JTS is a Java mapping of the OTS. Finally, we also touch on the latest developments in industry and with Java as it regards transactional Web services.

The JTA and OTS/JTS are all core underlying components that can be utilized by J2EE-based servers. The J2EE specification, in fact, requires that certain APIs defined by the JTA be incorporated into J2EE-compliant servers. Although the J2EE's declarative model for using transactions simplifies application programming, much of the literature and declarative programming conventions describing transaction usage with the J2EE is described in the context of JTA and OTS/JTS constructs and concepts. A basic understanding of the underlying transactions framework will help you make better decisions as an enterprise developer to determine what the best model for declaring transactions is for your components, as well as perhaps being useful for creating standalone distributed enterprise applications.

In this chapter, you will learn:

- The concept of transactions and the problems encountered by distributed objects with transaction management.
- How transaction services solve the problems encountered by distributed objects with transactions.
- The CORBA Object Transaction Service as a standard distributed transaction service solution.
- The Java Transaction API for specifying local Java interfaces between a transaction manager and the various distributed entities involved in a transaction.
- The JTA high-level transaction manager interface for allowing an application server to control the boundaries of an application under control of an application server.
- The JTA high-level application interface that allows a transaction-savvy application to delineate transaction boundaries.
- The JTA mapping of the X/Open XA standard protocol that enables a resource manager to take part in a transaction controlled by an external transaction manager.
- The Java Transaction Service for implementation of the OTS via a Java mapping, as well as the implementation of a Transaction Manager supporting the JTA specification.
- The latest developments with Web service transaction standards and the Java APIs, such as JAXTX, that are being created to encapsulate such standards.

Transactions

Recall from Chapter 2 in the discussion of transactions that we covered ACID principles. ACID stands for Atomicity, Consistency, Isolation, and Durability. Guaranteeing that your enterprise system adheres to the ACID principles is an important first step in understanding the need for transactions

Atomicity for a collection of operations can be very important for enterprise applications. For example, as illustrated in Figure 14.1, our BeeShirts.com application may desire to place a customer's order with a particular T-shirt supplier. The customer's order and associated credit-card information may then be used to charge the customer's account. If for some reason the order cannot be placed (for example, an item is out of stock), we would not want to charge the customer's account. Likewise, if for some reason the customer's account could not be charged (for example, the customer exceeded his maximum credit), we would not want to place the order with the supplier. Some means for treating these individual operations as an atomic and inseparable operation need to be provided. In enterprise applications, much more complicated requirements for atomicity can exist when many individual operations can have such a codependence.

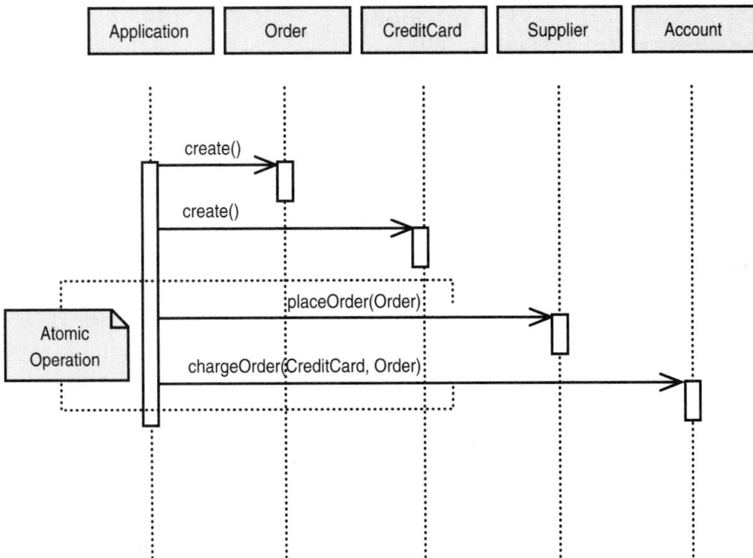

Figure 14.1 Transaction atomicity.

Consistency of system state is also important for enterprise applications. As shown in Figure 14.2, the placement of an order without the charging of an order can lead to the display of inconsistent information. It could be particularly troublesome to a customer visiting your e-commerce site if she sees that her account has been charged for an order that does not exist. Similarly, it could be particularly troublesome to the e-commerce storefront owner to discover that an order has been placed with one of his suppliers but that a customer was never charged. Thus, consistency of system state is a key requirement for your applications. This involves making sure that state embedded in different distributed objects and database elements is consistent.

The isolation of dependent operation changes to the system should be restricted to the application inducing the operations. Figure 14.3 illustrates the case in which an application `Bar` does not see the effect of a placed order by an application `Foo` until the changes can be committed by `Foo`. Isolation of change is thus important to present a consistent and accurate view of the system to other applications. Applications like `Bar` can then see changes only when they are committed.

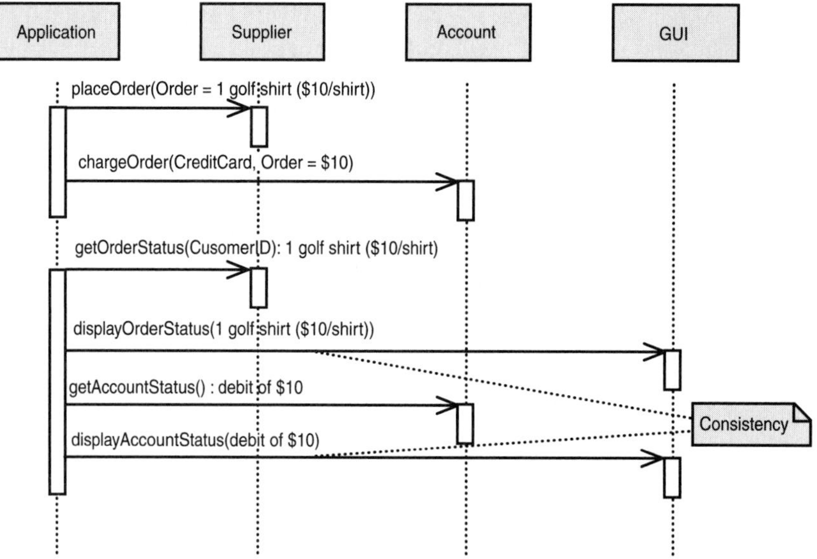

Figure 14.2 Transaction consistency.

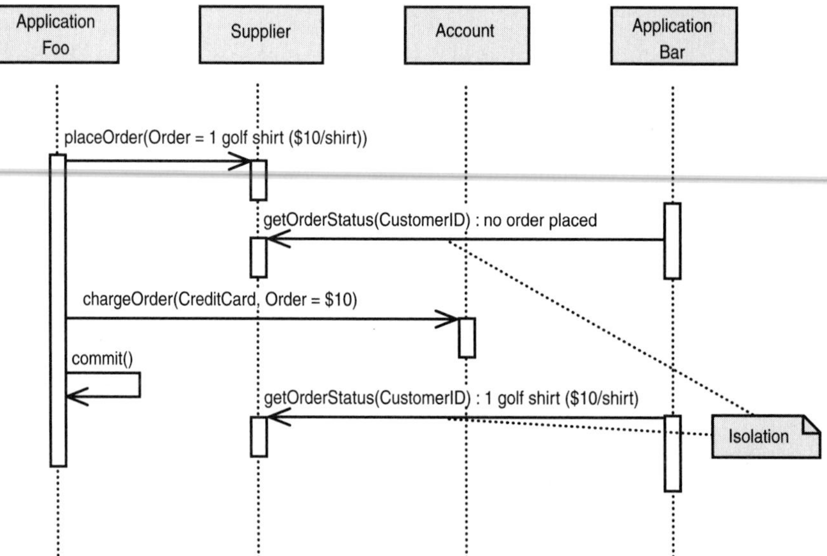

Figure 14.3 Transaction isolation.

Finally, Figure 14.4 depicts the need for ensuring durability or dependability of system state changes. If a failure occurs during the processing of operations before a change can even be committed or rolled back, a certain level of assurance must be provided that the system will still remain in a stable state when it comes back online. Durability of a system ensures that the system still behaves appropriately even in the event of system failure during the processing of inseparable operations.

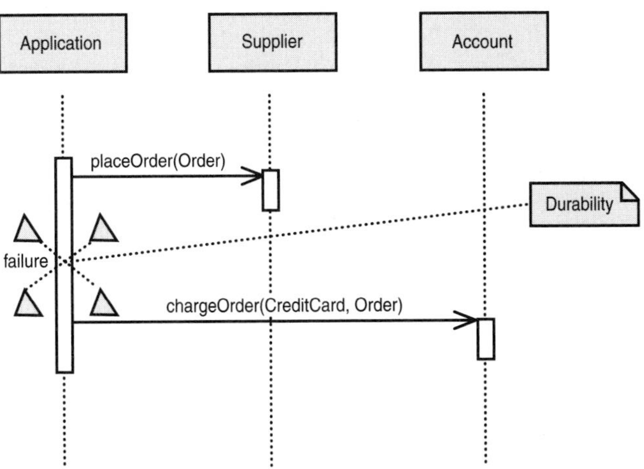

Figure 14.4 Transaction durability.

A transaction, as depicted in Figure 14.5, is a sequence of processing steps that either must all take place or must have no individual step take place at all. We can commit the transaction and make it permanent when all steps occur as an inseparable operation. When no steps are allowed to occur because one or more steps failed, we say that the transaction must be rolled back to the original system state. By building your enterprise systems with transactions, you can guarantee that your system follows the ACID principles.

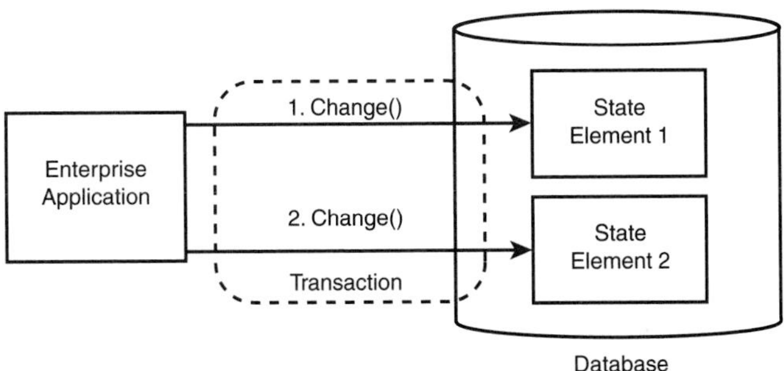

Figure 14.5 Transactions.

Distributed transactions are particularly important for enterprise applications. Transactions may need to encapsulate operations that affect the state of the system where the elements making up the state reside in multiple distributed system locations as illustrated in Figure 14.6. Such a distributed system state may rest in a database or perhaps within another enterprise resource such as a distributed communications server.

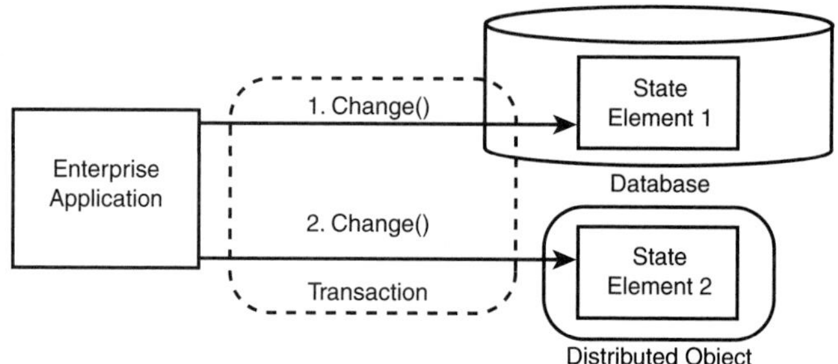

Figure 14.6 Distributed transaction state.

Transactions may also need to encapsulate operations invoked by different distributed applications as illustrated in Figure 14.7.

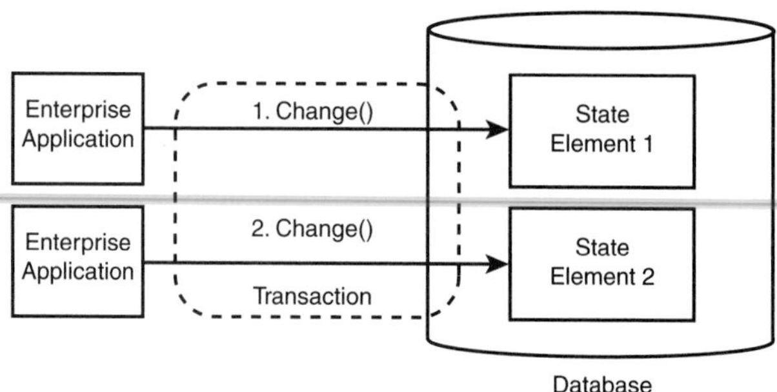

Figure 14.7 Distributed transaction applications.

Transaction Services Overview

Guaranteeing that your enterprise applications employ transactions and adhere to ACID principles can require a lot of hand-coding overhead. It is true that you could conceivably identify every scenario in your system in which a collection of operations must occur within a transaction and subsequently write code to commit or rollback depending on the outcome of processing. For a few simple transactional scenarios, this may be a reasonable approach. However, for even moderately more complex applications, the number of transaction scenarios and number of operations per transaction scenario add a significant burden to your set of programming tasks and keep you from focusing on application logic.

Furthermore, the large-scale distribution of both application and state in an enterprise system mandates a need for sophisticated distributed transaction management services. The heterogeneity of platforms on which these applications run can further complicate matters as you strive to implement a standard distributed transaction processing methodology. As we saw in Chapter 2, standards such as the X/Open Distributed Transaction Processing Model (as shown in Figure 2.2) provide a common framework within which transactions may operate in a heterogeneous distributed environment. The standard propagation of transaction context information between distributed applications enables a standard mechanism within which distributed transaction applications may operate.

Transaction services are middleware services that facilitate the provision of transaction semantics and ACID principle behavior for your enterprise applications. Transaction services provide an API for programmers to use that enables them to encapsulate which operations should be contained within a transaction. J2EE relies on an underlying transaction service infrastructure with an exposed programmatic interface and also provides a means to declaratively define transactional semantics for enterprise components using separate descriptor files, as you'll see later in this book.

Transaction Attributes

Declarative programming of transactions involves defining transaction attributes for components or their individual operations. The container then manages transactional processing for the component by using an underlying transaction service. J2EE enables the declaration of transactional attributes for application components such as Enterprise JavaBeans (EJB). These are the latest standard transaction attribute classifications defined by the J2EE, with older EJB standard style analogues shown in parentheses:

- `Required` (`TX_REQUIRED`): The component is required to operate inside of a transaction. If the calling client provides a transaction context within which the component operation is invoked, that transaction context is used. Otherwise, the container environment will provide a new transaction context within which the operation runs and will then attempt to commit the transaction when the operation completes.
- `RequiresNew` (`TX_REQUIRES_NEW`): The container creates a new transaction when the component is invoked and attempts to commit the transaction when the operation completes. Any transactions that were propagated by the calling client will be suspended and then resumed when the operation completes.
- `NotSupported` (`TX_NOT_SUPPORTED`): The container will not support the operation of a component within a transaction context. Any transaction context that was propagated by the calling client will be suspended and then resumed when the operation completes.
- `Never` (some `TX_BEAN_MANAGED` similarities): The container requires that the client does not propagate a transaction context for use with the invoked

component operation. Otherwise, an exception will be thrown. In such cases, the component may manage its own transaction programmatically.

- `Supports` (`TX_SUPPORTS`): The container itself will not create any new transaction context within which the component may operate. However, any transaction context that was propagated by the calling context can be used with the called component. That is, the operation of the component will process within the context of the propagated transaction.
- `Mandatory` (`TX_MANDATORY`): The container requires that the client propagate a transaction context for use with the invoked component operation. Otherwise, an exception will be thrown.

Transaction Isolation Levels

Transaction services also allow for the specification of isolation levels. The isolation level defines how and when changes made to data within a transaction are visible to other applications accessing that data. Isolation levels range from rigidly restricting visibility of changes to not limiting visibility of changes at all. We defined and introduced the concept of isolation levels in Chapter 6 in the context of JDBC updates to databases. However, because isolation levels can also apply to concurrent transactions involving general back-end enterprise information systems (EISs) and messaging services, we redefine transaction isolation levels here to incorporate the broader definition of transactions:

- `TRANSACTION_NONE`: Transactions are not supported at all when identified by this isolation level.
- `TRANSACTION_READ_UNCOMMITTED`: This level allows other transactions to see state changes made by this transaction before a commit has been issued.
- `TRANSACTION_READ_COMMITTED`: This level does not allow other transactions to see state changes made by this transaction until a commit has been issued (that is, does not allow "dirty reads"). Also sometimes referred to as `ReadCommitted`.
- `TRANSACTION_REPEATABLE_READ`: In addition to `TRANSACTION_READ_COMMITTED` level support, this level also does not allow a transaction to read data more than once and observe different data values because some other transaction made state changes to that data in the meantime (that is, does not allow "nonrepeatable reads" or "dirty reads"). Also sometimes referred to as `RepeatableRead`.
- `TRANSACTION_SERIALIZABLE`: In addition to `TRANSACTION_REPEATABLE_READ` level support, this level does not allow a transaction to read a collection of data more than once and as constrained by a particular predicate condition. It also does not allow a transaction to observe newly added data because some other transaction added data satisfying the same predicate condition in the meantime (that is, does not allow "phantom reads," "nonrepeatable reads," or "dirty reads"). Also sometimes referred to as `Serializable`.

Transaction Models

Transaction services can also support different models for encapsulating operations in a transaction. Simple transactions need to simply define the beginning of a transaction at some stage of processing and then conclude with either committing or aborting (that is, rolling back) the transaction. More complicated models of transaction processing also exist, however. The primary models for transaction processing are illustrated in Figures 14.8 through 14.10.

The flat transaction model depicted in Figure 14.8 relies on simple begin, commit, and abort functionality of a transaction service. A transaction context is created by a transaction service and encapsulates all operations until the transaction is committed or aborted.

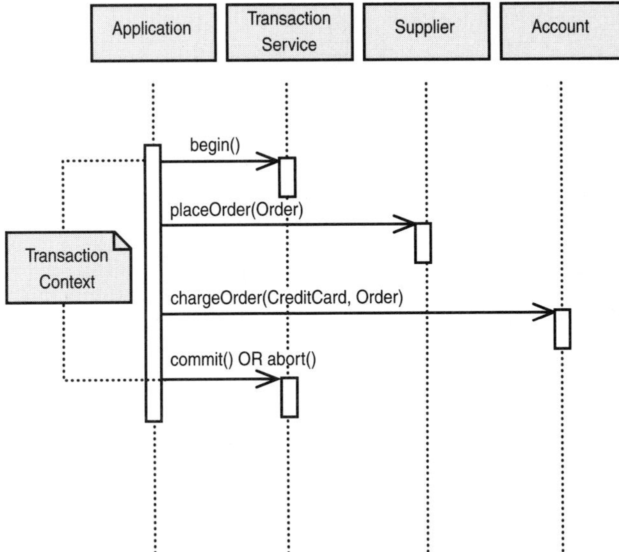

Figure 14.8 The flat transaction model.

The chained transaction model depicted in Figure 14.9 allows for one to persistently save a portion of the work accomplished up until a certain point. Rollback to the beginning of the chained transaction is allowed if the chained transaction follows the "saga model."

The nested transaction model depicted in Figure 14.10 allows transactions to be nested within other transactions. A nested subtransaction can be committed or aborted individually. Thus, complex transactions can be decomposed into more manageable subtransactions. Subtransactions can commit or rollback without requiring the entire transaction to commit or rollback.

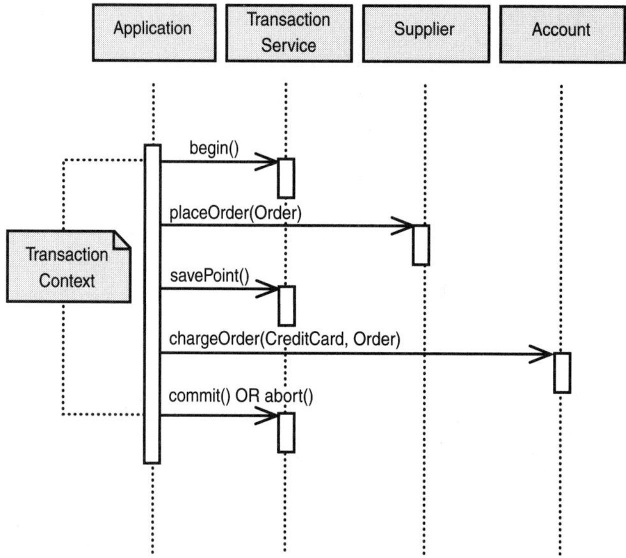

Figure 14.9 The chained transaction model.

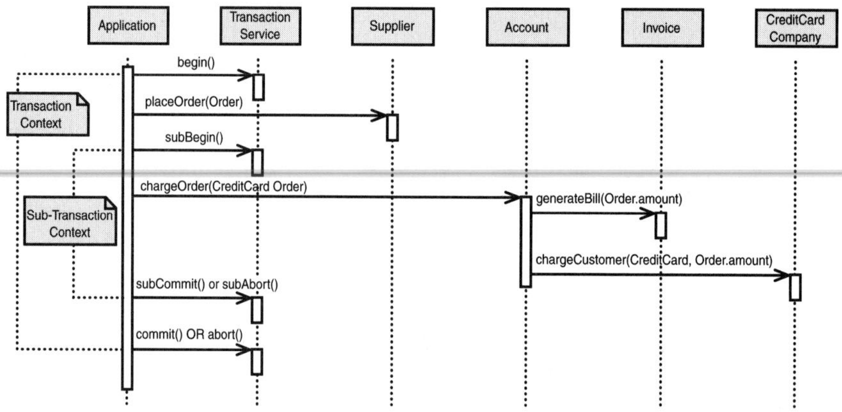

Figure 14.10 The nested transaction model.

X/Open Distributed Transaction Processing Standard

Chapter 2 described the standard X/Open Distributed Transaction Processing (DTP) model utilized by the Java transactions architecture for providing a standard distributed transaction processing framework (see Figure 2.2). An X/Open resource manager (RM) is used to describe a management process for any shared resource but is most often used to mean a DBMS. The X/Open transaction manager (TM) is the module responsible for coordinating transactions among the various distributed entities. A TX interface between application programs and TMs enables applications to initiate the begin, commit, and rollback of transactions, as well as to obtain the status of transactions. RMs participate in distributed transactions by implementing a transaction resource interface (XA) to communicate information needed by TMs for coordinating transactions.

TMs are often configured to manage a particular domain of distributed RMs and applications. Communication resource managers (CRMs) provide a standard means for connecting distributed transaction managers to propagate transaction information between different transaction domains for more widely distributed transactions. The standard interface between TMs and CRMs is defined by an XA+ interface, whereas communication resource manager to application program interfaces are defined by three interfaces known as TxRPC, XATMI, and CPI-C.

Two-Phase Commit Protocol

A TM can guarantee that all steps in a distributed transaction are atomically completed using information from the distributed RMs. A TM accomplishes this using a two-phase commit protocol. The two-phase commit protocol helps guarantee ACID principles by ensuring that all RMs commit to transaction completion or rollback to an original state in the event of a failure. These are the two-phase commit protocol steps:

- *Phase One—Commit Preparation:* A prepare for commit message is first sent to each resource manager (for example, DBMS) with updated data involved in a transaction. Each resource manager then persists a description of the updates it has made within the context of the current transaction. Resource managers can also opt to abort the transaction at this stage, and then the whole transaction can be aborted by the transaction manager.
- *Phase Two—Actual Commit:* If the transaction was not aborted, the transaction manager will send a commit message to all resource managers involved in the transaction. The resource managers will then commit their updates.

Object Transaction Service

The CORBAservice known as the Object Transaction Service (`http://www.omg.org/cgi-bin/doc?formal/00-06-28`) defines interfaces to implement transactional behavior for distributed CORBA objects. Distributed CORBA objects can participate in transaction via an ORB and the OTS. The OTS supports both flat and nested transactions. Because OTS relies on the X/Open DTP standard, non–CORBA-based applications can also interoperate with OTS. OTS is defined primarily in the `org::omg::CosTransactions` module, but an auxiliary `org::omg::CosTSPortability` module also defines two interfaces defined for portable transaction context propagation.

OTS currently represents perhaps the only CORBAservice that has been wholeheartedly adopted by the J2EE distributed computing services paradigm. As you'll see later in the chapter, the Java Transaction Service (JTS) is simply a Java mapping of the OTS. At the time of this writing, the OTS and JTS were not required by J2EE vendors to be implemented as a means for providing transactional interoperability between J2EE servers. However, the J2EE specifications do recommend that J2EE vendors support OTS and JTS for more greater interoperability and suggest that such support may be mandatory in a future specification.

Core OTS Types

As with other CORBA specifications, the OTS depends on a set of fundamental types. Two IDL `enum` types and three IDL `struct` types define the most important types defined in the `CosTransactions` IDL module. The Java mapping for these types is depicted in Figure 14.11. The five types of interest are listed here:

- `Status`: `Status` is an IDL `enum` that identifies the various states of a transaction.
- `Vote`: `Vote` is an IDL `enum` that identifies the responses from resource managers after the commit preparation phase (Phase One) of a two-phase commit protocol.
- `otid_t`: `otid_t` is an IDL `struct` that is a transaction identifier. It is based on the X/Open notion of a transaction ID referred to as XID.
- `TransIdentity`: `TransIdentity` is an IDL `struct` that encapsulates a handle to a transaction. A `TransIdentity` has an `otid_t` transaction identifier as well as a handle to its transaction coordinator and terminator.
- `PropagationContext`: `PropagationContext` is an IDL `struct` that encapsulates transaction context information to be propagated between distributed entities involved in a transaction. A transaction timeout and current transaction identity are part of the context. A sequence of parent transaction identities in a nested transaction can also be included. Implementation-specific data can also be added to a propagation context.

OTS Interfaces

The primary OTS interfaces involved in encapsulating access to transactional objects, resources, and their coordination are shown in Figure 14.12. A transaction coordinator manages communication with transactional objects and resources that participate in transactions. Each interface of Figure 14.12 is described here:

- `TransactionalObject`: This marker interface is implemented by those objects that want to participate in a transaction. An ORB will automatically propagate the transaction context of a client thread when a method on a `TransactionalObject` implementation is invoked.
- `Synchronization`: The `Synchronization` interface is used to notify `TransactionalObject` instances before a commit is prepared (that is, `before_completion()`) and after a commit or rollback operation is performed (that is, `after_completion()`) during a two-phase commit protocol.
- `Resource`: The `Resource` interface is implemented by resources that participate in a two-phase commit protocol.

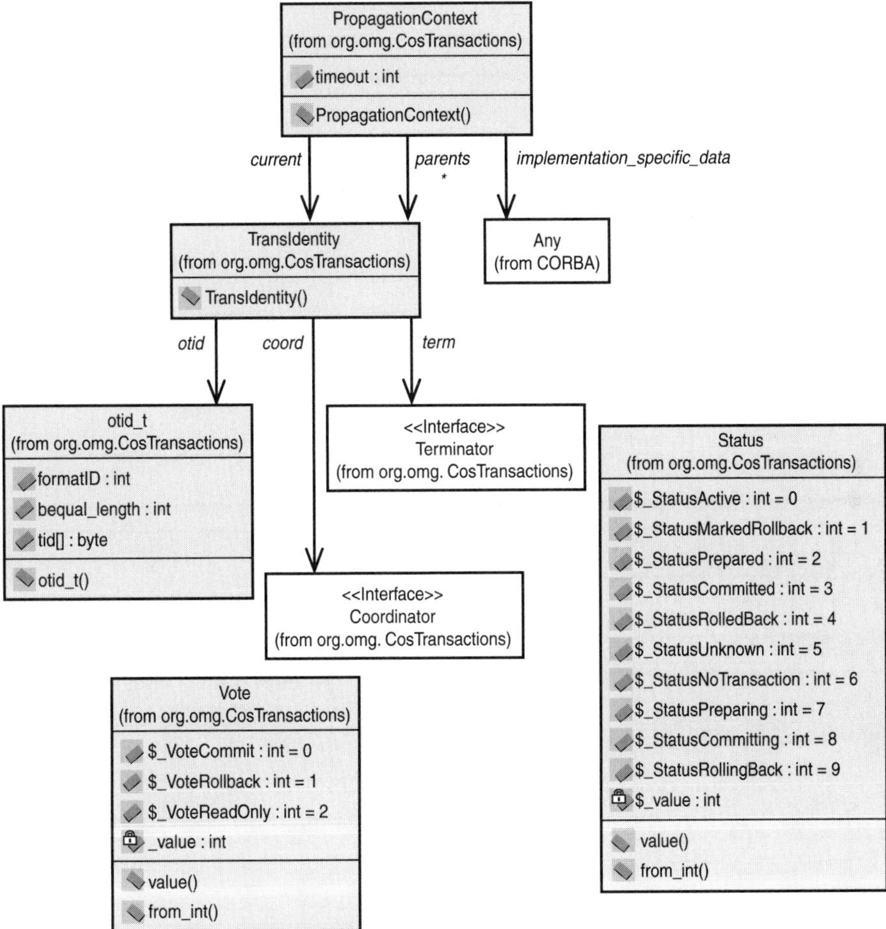

Figure 14.11 Basic OTS types.

- `SubtransactionAwareResource`: This sub-interface of the `Resource` interface is implemented by resources that participate in a two-phase commit protocol that employs a nested transaction model.
- `Coordinator`: The `Coordinator` interface can be used to create transactions and manage their behavior, obtain transaction status and information, compare transactions, register resources and synchronization objects, and create subtransactions in a nested transaction.
- `RecoveryCoordinator`: When a `Resource` is registered with the `Coordinator`, a `RecoveryCoordinator` handle is returned to enable the handling of certain recovery scenarios. The resource can ask the coordinator to replay the transaction completion sequence if it did not receive a transaction completion request within a certain transaction timeout.

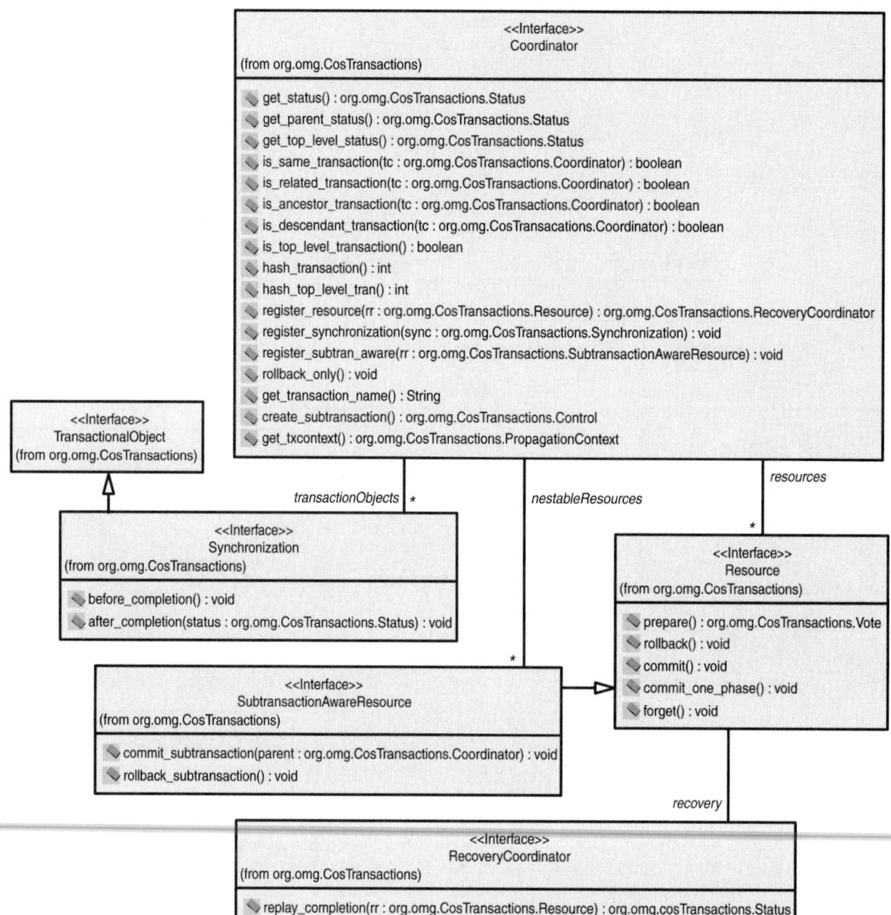

Figure 14.12 OTS coordination, resource, and transactional object interfaces.

Figure 14.13 depicts those OTS interfaces used to create and manage transactions. We have already described the `Coordinator` interface, but the interfaces that rely on the `Coordinator` interface are also shown here. APIs such as the `Current` interface can be utilized by application programs to manage transactions at a higher level. The transaction management interfaces depicted in Figure 14.13 are described here:

- `Terminator`: A `Terminator` interface is used to commit or rollback a transaction. Thus, although a transaction may have been created by another application, this interface provides a mechanism to terminate the transaction from another application.
- `Control`: The `Control` interface provides a handle to manage a transaction context that can be propagated between applications. Can return a handle to a transaction coordinator or terminator to accomplish these tasks.

- `Current`: `Current` is a frontline IDL interface for applications to use when creating transactions. `Current` provides operations to begin, commit, rollback, suspend, and resume transactions. The status of a transaction can also be obtained from the `Current` object. The current transaction context can be obtained from the initial ORB references.
- `TransactionFactory`: A transaction can also be created with a `TransactionFactory`. Operations exist to create a new transaction with a particular timeout value and to re-create an existing transaction given a propagation context.

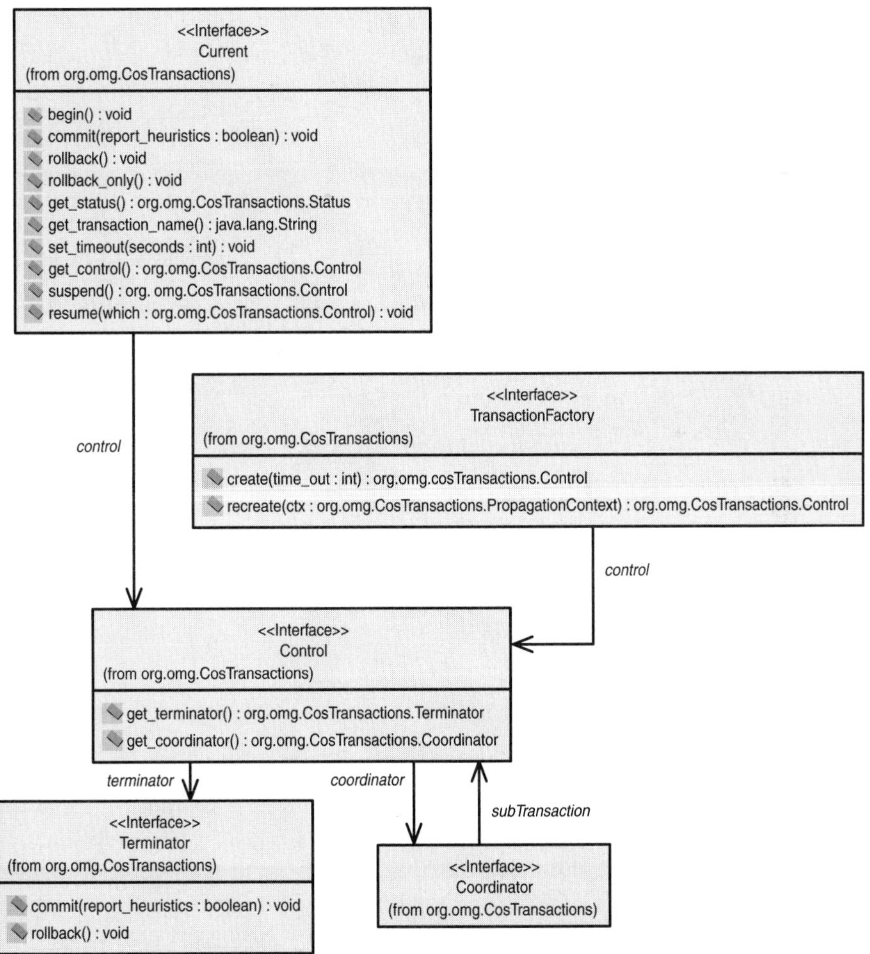

Figure 14.13 OTS transaction creation and management interfaces.

Java Transaction API

The Java Transaction Architecture (JTA) specifies standard interfaces for Java-based applications and application servers to interact with transactions, transaction managers, and resource managers (`http://java.sun.com/products/jta/`). The JTA model follows the basic X/Open DTP model described earlier in this chapter and in Chapter 2, as depicted in Figure 2.2. The main components of the JTA architecture are shown in Figure 14.14. The JTA components in this diagram are defined in both the `javax.transaction` and the `javax.transaction.xa` packages. Three main interface groupings of the JTA are also shown, including JTA transaction management, JTA application interfacing, and JTA XA resource management. The relation to the Java Transaction Service (JTS) is also shown in this diagram.

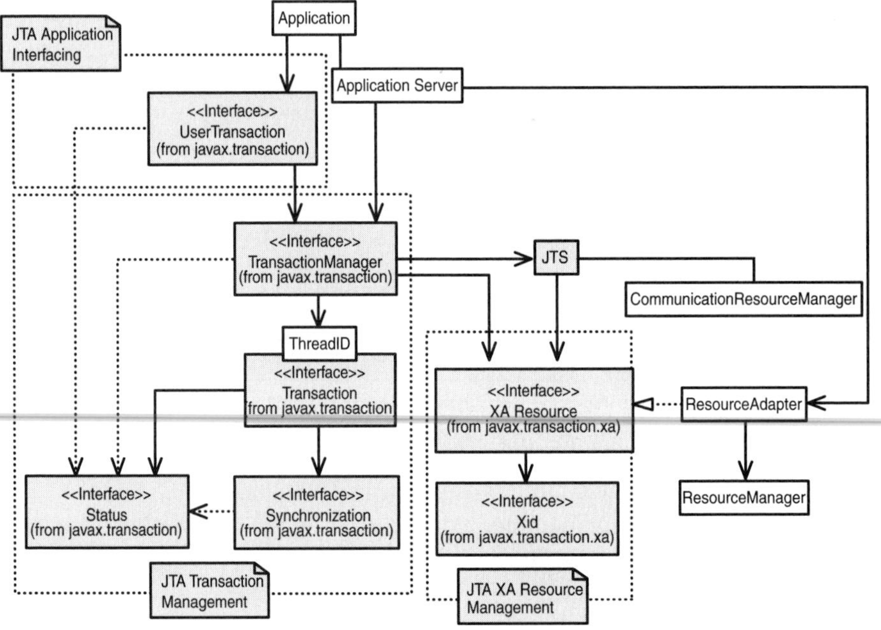

Figure 14.14 The JTA architecture.

JTA transaction management provides a set of interfaces utilized by an application server to manage the beginning and completion of transactions. Transaction synchronization and propagation services are also provided under the domain of transaction management. The JTA `Transaction`, `TransactionManager`, `Synchronization`, and `Status` interfaces all belong to the realm of JTA transaction management. An application server will typically implement a container environment within which enterprise application components can run and utilize the services of transaction management.

An application server environment such as J2EE can provide a declarative model for applications to utilize transaction management services. JTA application interfacing also provides a programmatic interface to transaction management for use by applications. An application uses the `UserTransaction` interface for this very purpose.

The X/Open XA resource management interface provides a standard means for transaction managers to interact with resources (for example, a DBMS) involved in a distributed transaction. A resource adapter, such as JDBC, implements the `XAResource` interface that is also used by an application server environment.

Finally, the Java mapping of OTS known as the JTS provides a lower-level interface to a distributed transaction service. A JTS implementation will propagate transaction context to other transaction managers via standard X/Open communications resource manager interfaces.

The JTA interfaces are required as a part of the J2EE and thus JTA application interfaces must be implemented by J2EE server products. No specific protocol for transaction propagation interoperability across J2EE servers has been defined. However, the J2EE v1.4 standards indicate that a future version of the J2EE specification will require OTS-based interfaces and therefore require standard protocol interoperability via IIOP.

JTA Transaction Manager Interface

The JTA supports a standard interface to transaction management services. An application server accesses these services primarily through the `TransactionManager` and `Transaction` interfaces. Figure 14.15 depicts these interfaces and two other key JTA interfaces utilized by an application server to interact with an underlying transaction manager.

The `Status` interface defines a set of static constants that indicate the state of a transaction. The `Synchronization` interface is provided to enable notification before a commit is prepared (that is, `beforeCompletion()`) and after a commit or rollback operation is performed (that is, `afterCompletion()`). A call to `Transaction.registerSynchronization()` can register a `Synchronization` object with a transaction associated with a current thread so that the `beforeCompletion()` and `afterCompletion()` calls can be made by a transaction manager.

The `Transaction` interface, as the name implies, encapsulates a transaction. A `Transaction` is created by a transaction manager and enables operations to be invoked on a transaction that is associated with a target transactional object. A `Transaction` object can be told to commit or rollback by invoking the methods `commit()` or `rollback()`, respectively. A `Transaction` object can also be told to only enable rollbacks (that is, and no commits) to be performed on a transaction using the `setRollbackOnly()` call. The constant `Status` of a transaction can be obtained via a call to `Transaction.getStatus()`. You'll learn more about the `enlistResource()` and `delistResource()` methods in a subsequent section.

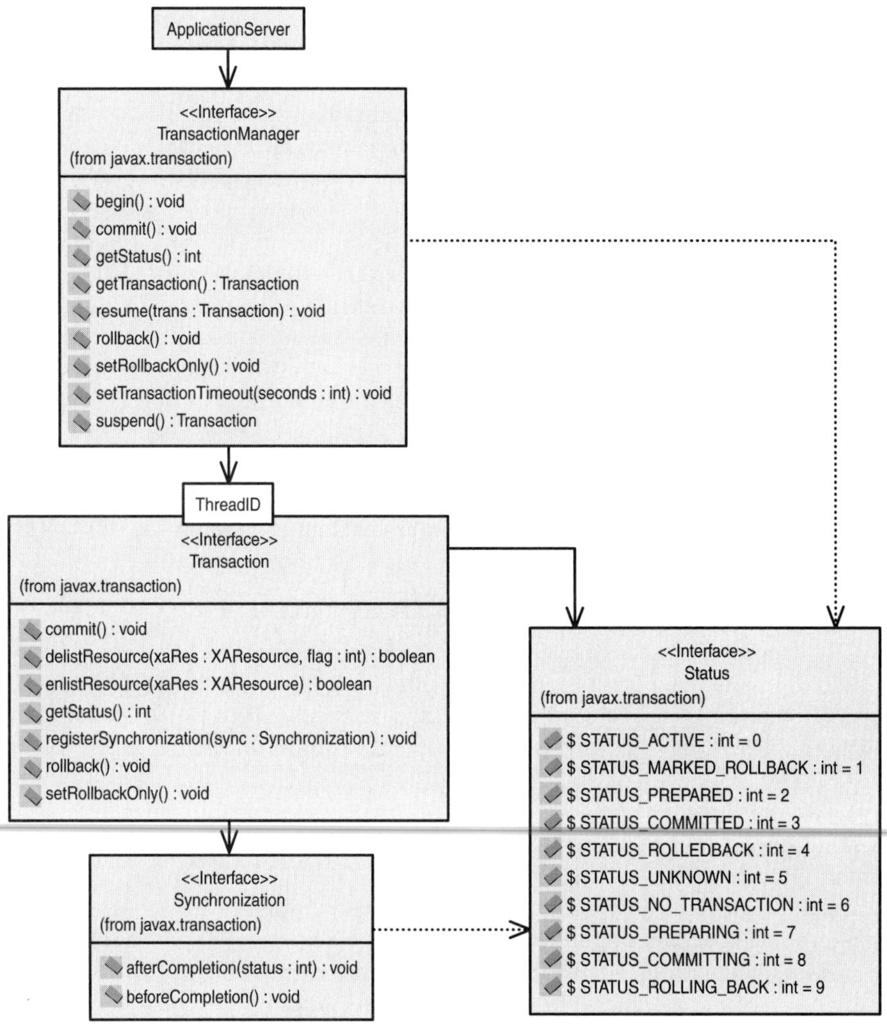

Figure 14.15 JTA transaction management.

The `TransactionManager` interface is used by an application server to manage transactions for a user application. The `TransactionManager` associates transactions with threads. The methods `begin()`, `commit()`, and `rollback()` on a `TransactionManager` are called by an application server to begin, commit, and rollback transactions for a current thread, respectively. The `TransactionManager` also supports a `setRollbackOnly()` method to designate the fact that only a rollback will be supported for the current thread's transaction. A `setTransactionTimeout()` method also defines a timeout for a transaction in terms of seconds, and a `getStatus()` method returns the static constant `Status` of the current thread's transaction.

A handle to the current thread's transaction can be obtained by calling `TransactionManager.getTransaction()`. By calling `TransactionManager.suspend()`, you can suspend the current transaction and also obtain a handle to the `Transaction` object. The `TransactionManager.resume()` method can resume the current transaction.

JTA Application Interface

The JTA application interface consists of the `javax.transaction.UserTransaction` Java interface, which is of most importance to an enterprise Java application developer. `UserTransaction` is used by an application to control transaction boundaries. Figure 14.16 depicts this interface and the relation between it, an application, and the underlying JTA transaction management architecture.

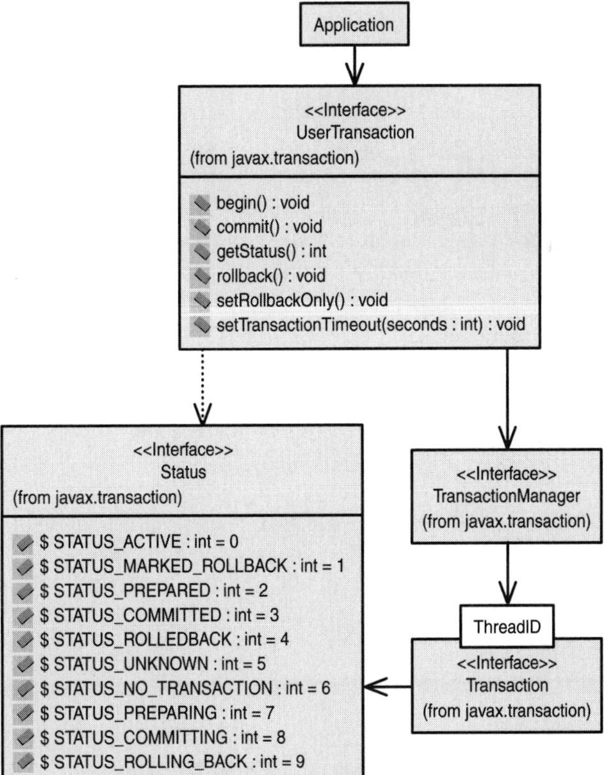

Figure 14.16 JTA user application interfacing.

The UserTransaction.begin() method can be called by an application to begin a transaction that gets associated with the current thread in which the application is running. An underlying transaction manager actually handles the thread to transaction association. A NotSupportedException will be thrown by the begin() call if the current thread is already associated with a transaction and there is no capability to nest the transaction.

The UserTransaction.commit() method terminates the transaction associated with the current thread. The UserTransaction.rollback() method induces an abort of the current transaction associated with the current thread. With a call to UserTransaction.setRollbackOnly(), the transaction associated with the current thread can only be aborted.

A timeout associated with the transaction can be set by calling UserTransaction.setTransactionTimeout() with an int value in seconds. Finally, the constant Status of a transaction can be yielded from the UserTransaction.getStatus() call.

J2EE application server components (that is, Enterprise JavaBeans) by and large can rely on the declarative and container-managed transaction semantics, but they also utilize the UserTransaction interface if it is desired to have the component programmatically manage its own transactions. Java Web components (that is, Java Servlets and JavaServer Pages) can also utilize the UserTransaction interface to demarcate transactions. Java Web components may look to using the UserTransaction interface directly when there is not an Enterprise JavaBeans tier involved with managing transactions or if the business logic for a particular set of transactional related actions are embedded directly within the Java Web components themselves. A handle to a UserTransaction may be gotten from a JNDI lookup or directly from the container environment in the case of Enterprise JavaBeans.

For example, you might retrieve the UserTransaction via JNDI using this:

```
UserTransaction trans

    = (UserTransaction) jndiContext.lookup("java:comp/UserTransaction");
```

Or an EJB may obtain the UserTransaction directly from the container context using this:

```
UserTransaction trans = containerContext.getUserTransaction();
```

The transaction can then be demarcated programmatically using this:

```
trans.begin();

// Do some work...

// rollback if there is an issue...
trans.rollback();

// commit if all was ok...
trans.commit();
```

JTA and X/Open XA

The XA interface defined by the X/Open group (`www.opengroup.org`) specifies the interface to distributed resource managers as accessed by distributed transaction managers in the X/Open standard DTP model. The JTA encapsulates this interface using the `XAResource` and `Xid` interfaces depicted in Figure 14.17. The `XAResource` interface is utilized by a transaction manager to manage distributed transactions among resources.

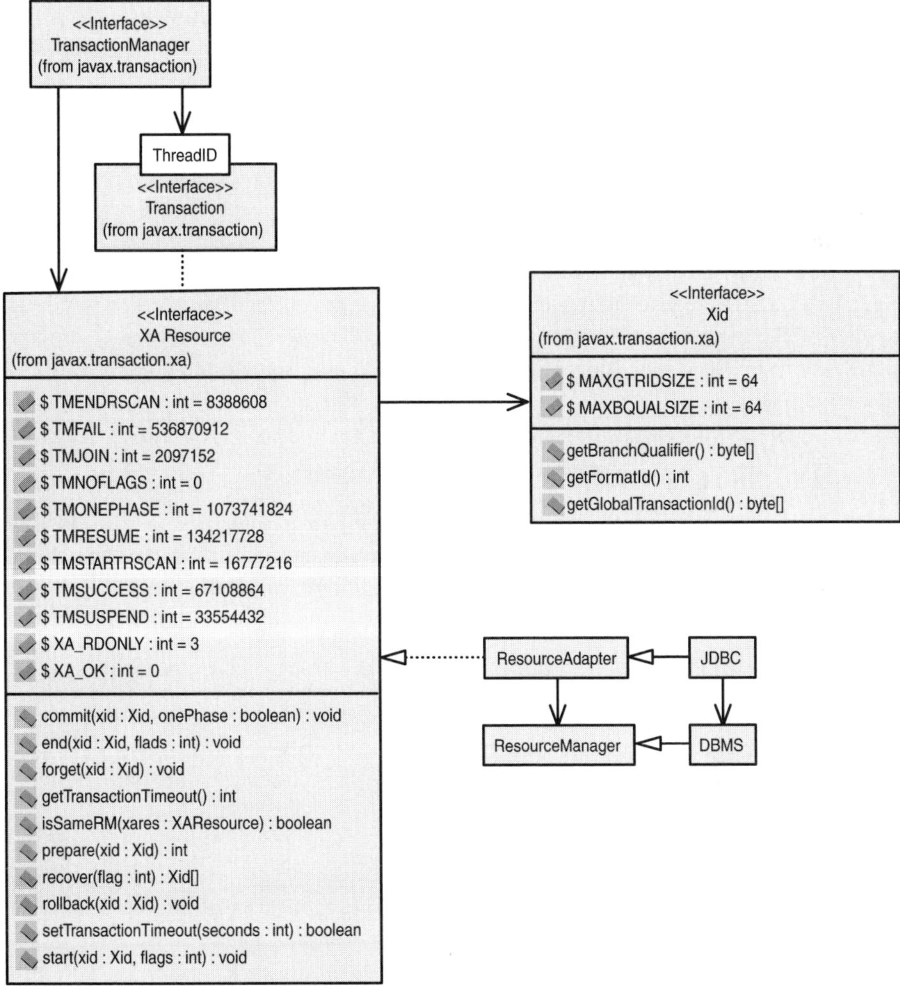

Figure 14.17 JTA resource management interfaces.

The Xid interface is an identifier for a distributed transaction specified in X/Open standard parlance. The standard X/Open format identifier, global transaction identifier bytes, and branch identifier bytes may all be retrieved from the Xid interface. Additionally, two static constants define characteristics of a transaction.

The XAResource interface is a Java mapping of the standard X/Open interface between a transaction manager and a resource manager. A resource manager's resource adapter must implement the XAResource interface to enable a resource to participate in a distributed transaction. A sample resource manager is a DBMS and a sample resource adapter is the JDBC interface to a DBMS. A transaction manager obtains an XAResource handle for every resource that participates in a distributed transaction.

The XAResource.start() method is used to associate a distributed transaction with a resource. In addition to the Xid, one of the XAResource static constant flags TMJOIN, TMRESUME, or TMNOFLAGS is used to, respectively, indicate whether the caller is joining an existing transaction, the caller is resuming a suspended transaction, or no flags are to be set. The XAResource.end() method is called to disassociate the resource from the transaction. In addition to an Xid, the end() call uses a flag TMSUSPEND, TMRESUME, TMFAIL, or TMSUCCESS to, respectively, indicate whether the transaction is suspended, is resumed, is to be rolled back, or is to be committed. The XAResource also provides methods to commit, prepare for a commit, rollback, recover, and forget about distributed transactions. The transaction timeout can also be set and retrieved from the XAResource.

Java Transaction Service

Figure 14.18 presents the system context in which the JTS architecture operates. JTS (http://java.sun.com/products/jts/) is a Java mapping of the OTS. Therefore, the JTS API is by and large defined by the org.omg.CosTransactions and org.omg.CosTSPortability packages. Java-based applications and Java-based application servers access transaction management functionality via the JTA interfaces. The JTA interacts with a transaction management implementation via JTS. Similarly, the JTS can access resources via the JTA XA interfaces or can access OTS-enabled non-XA resources. JTS implementations can interoperate via CORBA OTS interfaces. JTS supports a flat transaction model. JTS can support, but is not required to support, a nested transaction model.

There is no specified mechanism for an OTS-based transaction manager and an ORB to locate one another. The javax.jts.TransactionService interface is provided to facilitate a transaction manager and an ORB being able to locate one another, and is the only non-OTS standard interface defined by JTS.

The TransactionService.identifyORB() method is called by an ORB during initialization to let a transaction manager be aware of the ORB identity and attributes. The TSIdentification interface defined as an extension to the standard CORBA framework by the OTS is used by a JTS implementation to register Sender and

Receiver objects with an ORB. Sender objects are registered with an ORB during initialization so that the ORB can issue a callback on the transaction service during the propagation of a transaction context from the transaction service. Receiver callback objects are also registered with the ORB to receive propagated transaction contexts. A Sender can also receive context propagation replies, and a Receiver can send propagation replies.

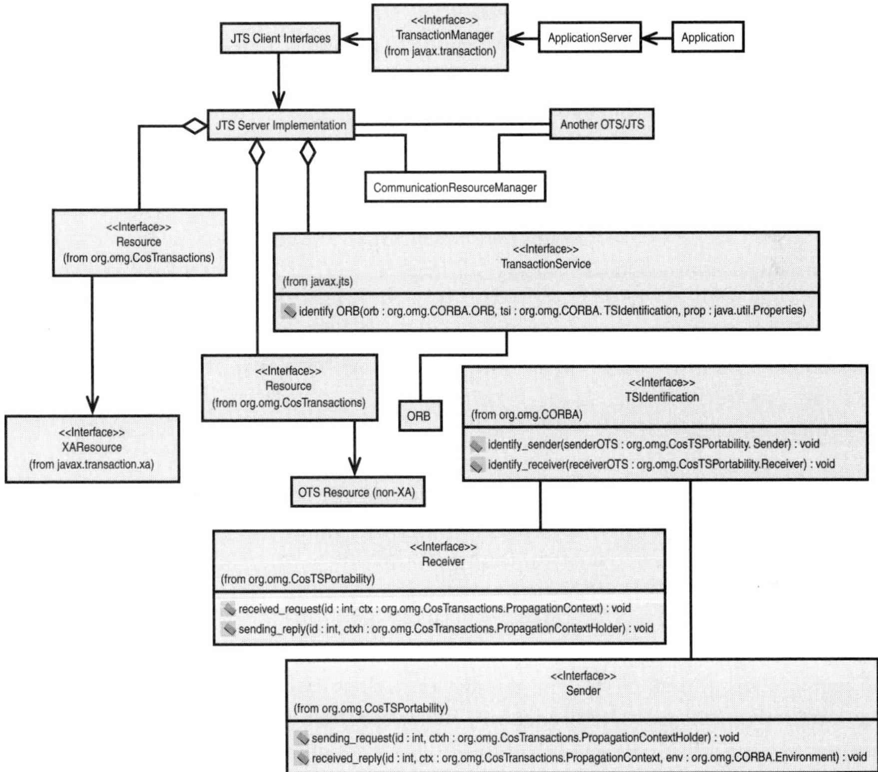

Figure 14.18 The JTS system context.

Web Services Transactions

In a Web services environment, many remote Web services communicate in a loosely coupled and widely distributed environment. Although use of OTS is the current recommended means by the J2EE standards for enhancing the interoperability of transaction context propagation, OTS and its dependence on IIOP are catered more for closely coupled albeit distributed environments. Furthermore, the strict adherence to ACID principles by mechanisms such as OTS do not map well to all Web service communication scenarios. Because of these reasons, a new set of standards needs to be crafted for the broader transaction interoperability needs of Web services.

The bad news is that at the time of this writing, there was no widely adopted standard means for incorporating transaction context into Web service communications. However, standards bodies such as the W3C and OASIS were working toward defining such a standard. Their aim is to ensure that the needs of Web services are met to enable loosely coupled transactional behavior as well as both strict and relaxed requirements for adhering to ACID principles. The good news is that there is a Java Specification Request (JSR) that is actively working on the incorporation of such standards into Java-based Web services when such standards become final.

The XML Transactioning API for Java (JAXTX), `www.jcp.org/en/jsr/detail?id=156`, is being created to define a standard Java API for creating, parsing, and exchanging transactional information in a Web services communication paradigm. Thus, JAXTX largely focuses on defining how standard transaction context information can be read from and written to SOAP message headers. The JAXTX specification members are closely in tune with the W3C and OASIS standards bodies that are defining the general way for encapsulating transactional information inside of SOAP message headers. When such standard bodies converge on a solution, the intention is that JAXTX will incorporate such standards.

Additionally, another JSR called is being created and intended to be utilized by JAXTX to further broaden the scope for how transactions are managed in loosely coupled distributed environments. The J2EE Activity Service for Extended Transactions, `http://jcp.org/en/jsr/detail?id=9`, is being created to provide Java support for the OMG's Activity Service standard (`http://cgi.omg.org/cgi-bin/doc?orbos/2000-06-19`), which is an extension to the OTS. Such a standard and associated Java API will provide support for allowing long-running business transactions to be implemented more efficiently. That is, if a transaction spans a long amount of time and perhaps crosses multiple system boundaries, such as can be the case for Web services, then a more efficient means is needed to decompose the transaction into shorter running transactions. This is accomplished to prevent the locking up of all involved resources for the entire duration of the long-running transaction.

So stay tuned to the Web sites mentioned previously and keep an eye out for when a standard means for Web service transaction context propagation is defined and for when the Java APIs implementing such standards become available.

Conclusions

The need for transaction semantic support in distributed enterprise applications very frequently arises in the context of managing transactions that involve DBMS resources. There is a distinct and standard model for providing transaction service support to Java enterprise applications. The transaction services model available to Java enterprise applications revolves around the standard CORBA OTS and X/Open DTP models. The OTS is a CORBAservice for transactions, and the JTS is the Java mapping of this standard model. The JTA defines standard interfaces with the OTS/JTS, between applications and the transaction service, between transaction managers and application servers, and between transaction managers and X/Open XA–compliant resource managers. Finally, a set of standards and associated Java APIs are now brewing to enable interoperability in the Web services world.

Transaction services in Java are thus one of the J2EE components perhaps most in sync with other industry-standard transaction models. Because transaction services are one of the core components of a middle-ware architecture, many vendors will be able to better support the J2EE standard. Furthermore, interoperability with other DTP frameworks is better enabled. As you'll discover later in the book, interfacing with such transaction services is tremendously simplified for the application programmer when the J2EE declarative model for component transaction specification is used.

15

Messaging Services with JMS and JAXM

PASSING MESSAGES BETWEEN APPLICATIONS IN A distributed system is a very common service for an enterprise information system. In an abstract sense, this is precisely what happens when one makes a distributed object call using such communication models as CORBA, RMI, and Web services using JAX-RPC. Messaging services can be distinguished from these remote procedure–oriented communication models by the added layer of abstraction that is provided above a communications paradigm to uncouple the connection between distributed message sender and receiver. Rather, an intermediate service exists between a message producer and a message consumer that handles the delivery of messages from producer to consumer. Furthermore, producers do not block on messages they deliver. Rather, messages are sent asynchronously by the producer. This chapter describes the core concepts behind messaging services as well as the primary means for tapping such services within Java and J2EE. We describe and provide examples for use of the Java Message Service (JMS) API serving as the standard and a generic API for sending and receiving asynchronous messages in the J2EE world. We also describe and provide code snippets for use of the Java API for XML Messaging (JAXM) serving as a non-J2EE but nonetheless Java standard for XML- and SOAP-based messaging.

In this chapter, you will learn:

- The basic concepts behind messaging services and variations in message service models
- The ideas behind Message-Oriented Middleware (MOM) as a more traditional means for exchanging messages between MOM-aware applications
- The basic concepts behind JMS
- The core and generic JMS API
- The JMS API and examples specific to the point-to-point messaging domain model via queues

- The JMS API and examples specific to the publish-subscribe messaging domain model via topics
- The use of the generic JMS API and examples for messaging without coding to any specific messaging domain model
- The JAXM API for performing XML- and SOAP-based messaging

Messaging Overview

A messaging service is software that provides support for passing messages between distributed applications in a reliable, asynchronous, loosely coupled, language-independent, platform-independent, and often configurable fashion.

Messaging services accomplish this task by encapsulating messages that are sent between a sender and a receiver and providing a software layer that sits between distributed messaging clients. A messaging service also provides an interface for messaging clients to use that isolates the underlying message service implementation such that heterogeneous clients can communicate using a programmer-friendly interface. Such an infrastructure can also be viewed as an event notification type service in which messages are events and the delivery of these messages between messaging clients acts as sort of an event notification mechanism. Event notification types of messaging systems, however, are typically designed to handle lighter-weight messages than are Message-Oriented Middleware applications that are developed for more general-purpose message passing. In this section, we explore the various facets of messaging services utilized by enterprise systems.

Message Service Locality

Figure 15.1 and Figure 15.2 depict two types of messaging service implementations. Figure 15.1 shows the most common type of messaging service implementation, in which some middleware software implements the functionality of a messaging service to receive asynchronously generated messages from a message producer and route them to a message consumer. A messaging client utilizes the services of the centralized messaging service in a transparent fashion via a messaging client interface. Figure 15.2 depicts a messaging service implementation in which the messaging software is embedded directly into a thick messaging client.

Most of our discussions here assume the use of messaging middleware. Messaging middleware enhances the reliability and availability of a messaging service by virtue of a focus on the use of centrally managed persistent and redundant mechanisms in the middleware. Messaging middleware also alleviates the need for clients to manage connections to multiple messaging service endpoint locations by allowing a connection between a messaging client and a messaging service middleware server.

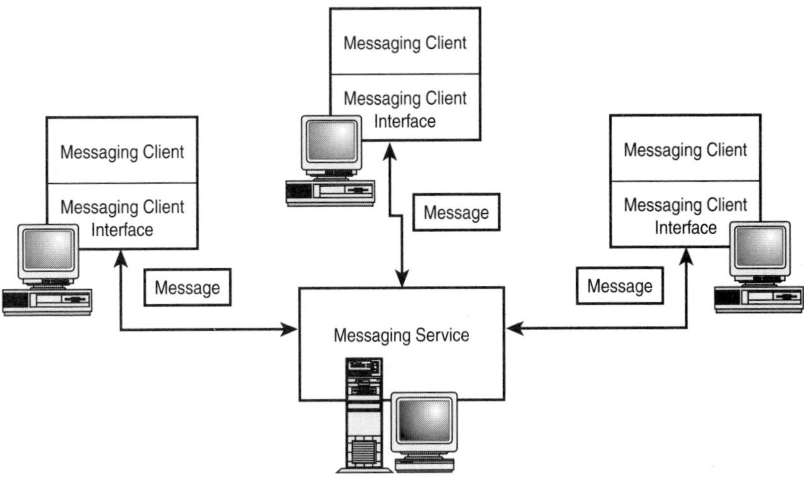

Figure 15.1 Messaging middleware.

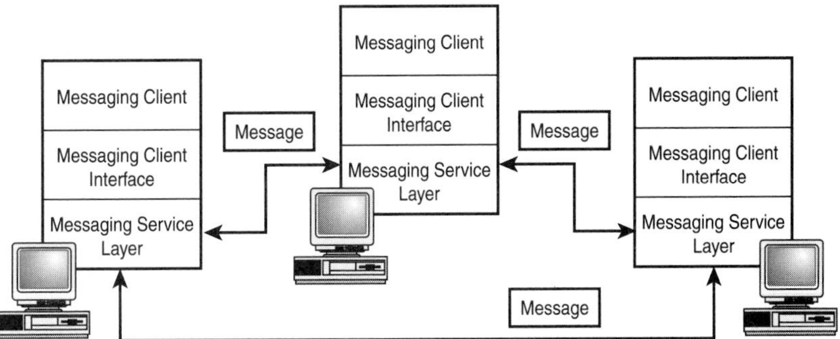

Figure 15.2 Messaging thick client software.

Point-to-Point Messaging

Figure 15.3 depicts one type of messaging service used for point-to-point communication between a message producer and a message consumer. A message producer sends a message to a particular consumer identified by some name (for example, "Foo"). This name actually corresponds to some queue in the message service used to store the message until it can deliver the message to the consumer associated with that queue. The queue may be persistent to help guarantee the delivery of a message even in the event of a message service failure. That is, a persistent queue can be read by a backup message service instance and used to deliver messages to a message consumer even if the primary message service fails.

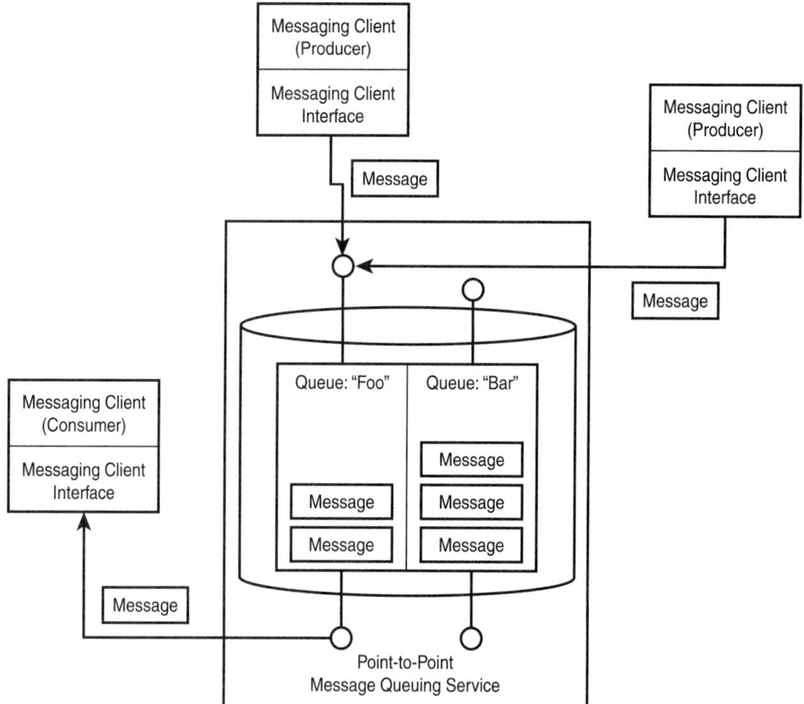

Figure 15.3 The point-to-point message queuing service.

Publish-Subscribe Messaging

Figure 15.4 depicts another popular model of messaging known as a publish-subscribe messaging service. With publish-subscribe, a message publisher publishes a message to a particular topic. Multiple subscribers can register to receive messages that have been published to a particular topic. Topics can be hierarchically arranged and can further enable the publication of messages and subscriptions to receive messages within a particular topic context. For example, we might subscribe to receive only those messages published specifically to the "Stocks" topic, or subscribe to receive all of those messages published to the "Stocks" topic and its subtopics, such as "OTC."

Push and Pull Messaging Models

Messaging services can also be distinguished according to their implementation of a message push or message pull model. A push model of messaging is the most typical style, in which a message producer sends a message to a messaging service, which pushes the message to the message consumer as shown in Figure 15.5. A pull model of messaging involves a consumer asking a message service to receive a message, at which point the message service pulls the message from the message producer as shown in Figure 15.6.

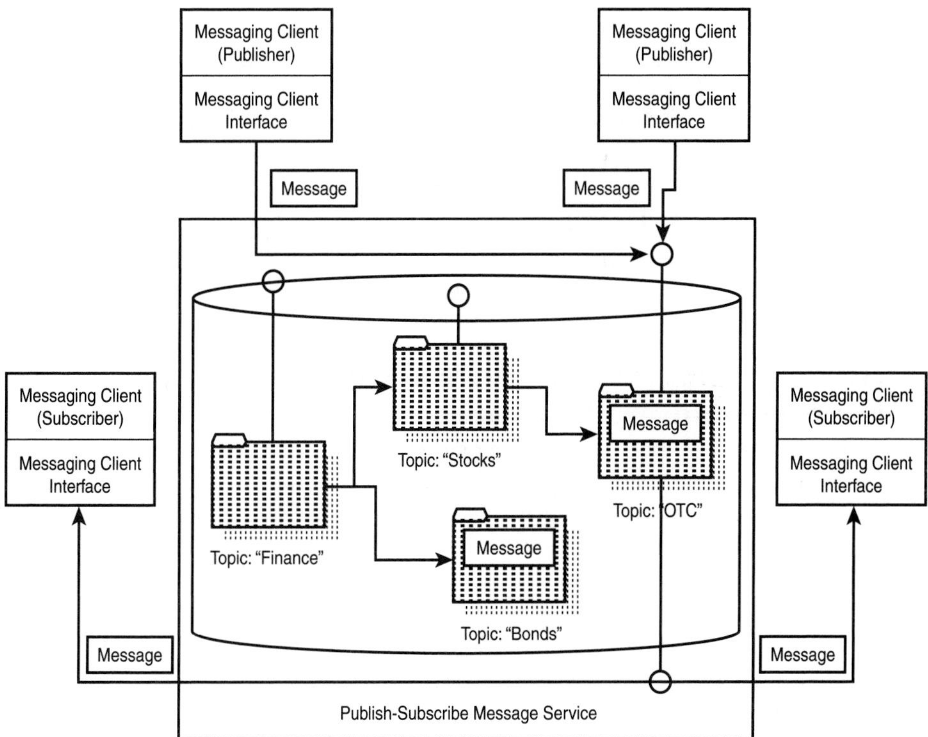

Figure 15.4 The publish-subscribe messaging service.

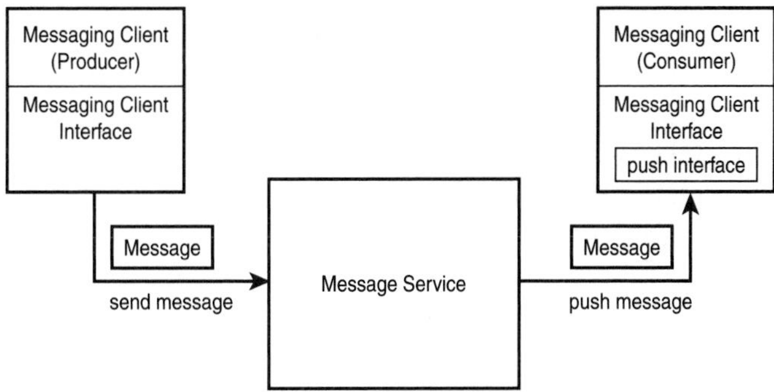

Figure 15.5 The messaging push model.

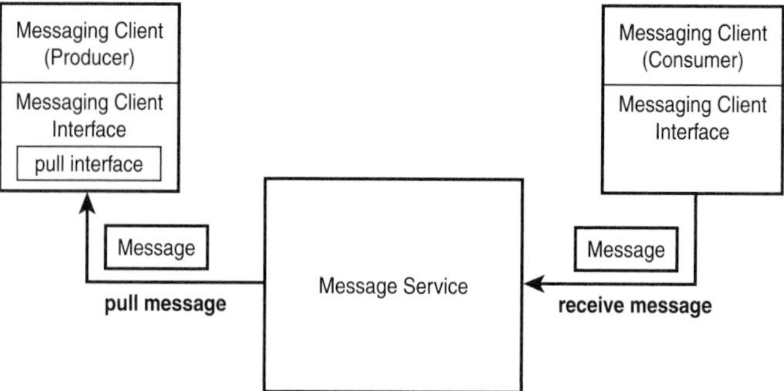

Figure 15.6 The messaging pull model.

Message Filtering, Synchronicity, and Quality

In the event that a message consumer desires to receive only certain messages based on some function of the message attributes, a message filtering scheme may be employed. Message filtering involves distinguishing between which messages should be delivered and which messages should not be delivered to a message consumer as a function of some filtering criteria. The filtering criteria are described in some language (for example, SQL) and can refer to attributes and values of a message. Thus, for example, you may subscribe to messages from a "Stocks" topic but filter out those messages whose "StockSymbol" attribute does not match the stock symbols in your stock portfolio.

Although various models of messaging exist, all messaging services share a common attribute of asynchronicity. Messages are sent by message producers to message consumers and do not require that the message producer block processing until the message is received. Typical remote method invocation protocols, however, such as RMI and CORBA, by default implement calls such that the distributed client does block until the call completes (that is, synchronous calls). Asynchronous calls thus offer a certain level of time-independence for the message producers and consumers.

As we've already alluded, a message service can also provide a certain level of assurance associated with message delivery. Reliability and availability of message delivery provide a Quality of Service (QoS) that can often be specified at various levels. Mission-critical messages must have a higher QoS than lower priority messages. Many messaging services will provide a means to designate the QoS at the connection, message-type, and individual-message level.

Email Messaging

Of the various types of messaging services that exist, the delivery and reception of email messages is perhaps one of the most familiar and widely used types of messaging. An email server queues messages that have been sent to specific email addresses such that the email messages can be later retrieved by an email user. Email client software contains a transport mechanism for sending mail to a mail server. The mail server places such email in a message store such that it can be downloaded by email client software later. Email messaging thus typically serves as a point-to-point type of messaging service that uses a pull model of messaging. We discuss a few of the more popular types of email messaging service standards in the next chapter when we discuss the use of the JavaMail service.

MOM

The terms *Message-Oriented Middleware* (*MOM*) and *messaging service* are nearly synonymous. MOM is simply an implementation of a messaging service albeit in a fashion that is standard for a particular type of MOM system. A MOM API defines how distributed applications should utilize an underlying MOM message channel or queue for communicating messages to one another. Messages are passed between applications via MOM in a way that does not block the sender of that message. That is, the sender can send a message and allow the MOM to ensure that it gets to the intended receiver without waiting for a response from the receiver.

MOM implementations can implement one or more types of messaging models. For example, one MOM implementation may employ simple point-to-point or push and pull models of messaging. Another MOM implementation may implement a more sophisticated publish-and-subscribe model and perhaps provide a server to manage message queuing in a centralized fashion and using redundant middleware server processes for enhanced reliability and availability.

MOM has historically been so popular that various organizations have been created and have gotten involved in providing standardization of MOM approaches. The Message-Oriented Middleware Association (MOMA) is a consortium of vendors, users, and interested parties that promote interoperability between MOM products. The Business Quality Messaging (BQM) organization focuses on providing standardization of MOM products for business-critical and highly reliable distributed and Internet-based commercial applications.

Although the efforts of such organizations help standardize MOM, MOM is not the only thing needed for enterprise applications. Other enterprise services and infrastructure such as standard communications, naming, transactions, and application-enabling frameworks are all key ingredients for building distributed enterprise applications. The Object Management Group (OMG) provides standards for MOM-based applications in the context of its CORBA model for building enterprise applications. OMG MOM-like functionality comes in the form of numerous specifications such as the CORBA Event Service, CORBA Notification Service, and CORBA Messaging. Because MOM is such a core part of an enterprise application, the Java Message Service provides a standard MOM API for Java-based applications usable in a J2EE context. Though not traditionally labeled as MOM, email messaging has also been standardized on the Internet via various email protocols, and the JavaMail service provides a Java interface to such a system. Finally, the Java API for XML Messaging service defines a standard Java API for encapsulating asynchronous messaging via Web services.

MOM vendors abound and the MOMA standard has helped drive standard interfaces to such products. Companies such as PeerLogic, Inc., provide their PIPES Platform product for dynamic applications that want to communicate with other applications on a network using reliable messaging protocols. Veri-Q Inc. provides its VCOM product for reliable and secure messaging that can be developed using Java interfaces. IBM's MQSeries product is a popular messaging system for building platform-independent MOM systems. The Microsoft Message Queue Server (MSMQ) is a Microsoft platform-specific messaging solution integrated with the Windows NT platform.

As an example of MOM messaging using the IBM MQSeries product, a number of classes and interfaces can be used from the `com.ibm.mq` package libraries to perform basic message queuing. Message queuing first involves connecting to a middleware messaging server:

```
// Set up MQ environment hostname and channel (default port 1414)
MQEnvironment.hostname = "suppliers.BeeShirts.com";
MQEnvironment.channel  = "ServerChannel";

// Create a connection to the queue manager using MQ environment
MQQueueManager mqQueueManager = new MQQueueManager("SupplierManager");
```

We then open a specific queue on the message queue server:

```
// Set up the options on the queue we wish to open...
int openOptions = MQC.MQOO_INPUT_AS_Q_DEF | MQC.MQOO_OUTPUT ;

// Now specify the queue that we wish to open, and the open options...
MQQueue systemDefaultLocalQueue =
    mqQueueManager.accessQueue("SYSTEM.DEFAULT.LOCAL.QUEUE",
                               openOptions, null, null, null);
```

A particular message to send is also encapsulated using MOM APIs:

```
// Define a simple MQ message, and initialize it in UTF format...
MQMessage helloWorld = new MQMessage();
helloWorld.writeUTF("Hello World!");

// specify the message options as default
MQPutMessageOptions putMessageOptions = new MQPutMessageOptions();
```

The particular message is then added to the queue:

```
// put the message on the queue
systemDefaultLocalQueue.put(helloWorld,putMessageOptions);
```

On the message consumer side, we connect to a message queue in a fashion similar to the message producer. We then retrieve the message from the queue:

```
// First define an MQ message buffer to receive the message into...
MQMessage receivedMessage = new MQMessage();

// Set the get message options using default options...
MQGetMessageOptions getMessageOptions = new MQGetMessageOptions();
```

```
// Get the message off the queue with a max size of 1024...
systemDefaultLocalQueue.get(receivedMessage, getMessageOptions, 1024);

// Display the UTF message text
System.out.println("The message is: " + receivedMessage.readUTF());
```

On both sides of a message queuing application, the queue and connection to the centralized queue manager should be closed:

```
// Close the queue
systemDefaultLocalQueue.close();
// Disconnect from the queue manager
mqQueueManager.disconnect();
```

As you can see, use of MOM APIs for messaging can be rather straightforward with the help of MOM objects to provide a high-level interface to messaging. As you'll see in the next section, the Java Message Service also provides a means for interfacing with messaging systems and thus implements a standard Java-based interface to MOM.

Java Message Service (JMS) Overview

The Java Message Service (JMS) is a Java API that defines how messaging clients can interface with underlying messaging service providers in a standard fashion. JMS also provides an interface that underlying messaging service providers implement to provide JMS services to clients. Thus, JMS follows the familiar model of providing both an application programmer interface and a service-provider interface to implement standard services akin to the model followed by JDBC, JNDI, and many other Java enterprise component interfaces.

The J2EE v1.4 specification requires that the JMS v1.1 API and an underlying service provider be included with a J2EE implementation. JMS defines interfaces with transaction semantics that may be dependent on the Java Transaction Architecture and Java Transaction Service if transactions are supported. JMS also defines interfaces in which initial factory objects used to create JMS connections are retrieved from a naming service via JNDI.

JMS provides both a point-to-point and a publish-subscribe model of messaging. Such messaging models are also referred to as "messaging domains" within the JMS specification. Point-to-point messaging is accomplished by the implementation of message queues to which a producer writes a message to be received by a consumer. Publish-subscribe messaging is accomplished by the implementation of a hierarchy of topical nodes to which producers publish messages and to which consumers can subscribe.

JMS provides a core abstract messaging architecture that is extended by both the point-to-point message queuing model and the publish-subscribe model. In this chapter, we cover the core JMS architecture, basic point-to-point message queuing model, and basic publish-subscribe model. New to JMS v1.1 is the unification of messaging domains such that the core JMS API can be used to send and receive messages in either a point-to-point or a publish-subscribe fashion. Thus, in JMS v1.1, one may either use the generic JMS APIs to send and receive messages or utilize the concrete point-to-point and publish-subscribe JMS APIs that subclass the generic JMS API.

JMS Core Architecture

The core architecture behind JMS is depicted in Figure 15.7. Here we see that JNDI is used to create an initial context to a JMS connection factory that is then used to create connections to JMS-based service providers. Given a JMS connection, a particular session context can be retrieved to create message producers and message consumers. Messages sent from a producer to a consumer are associated with a particular endpoint destination. At the consumer end of a messaging session, filtering of messages can be achieved using a message selector `String`.

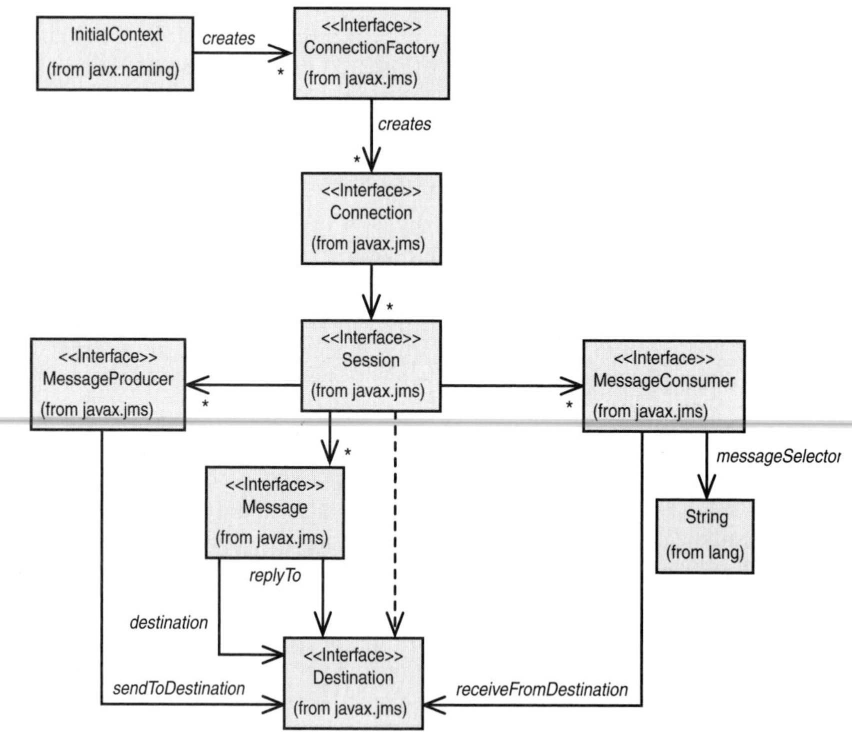

Figure 15.7 The JMS core architecture.

JMS Connections

Figure 15.8 depicts the detailed architecture behind JMS connections. JMS connections represent a connection between a JMS client and a JMS service provider's messaging server. The JMS connection-related interfaces shown here are base interfaces that are further extended for the two messaging domain models of JMS. JMS v1.1 also allows a JMS client to use the base interfaces directly in a more domain-independent fashion.

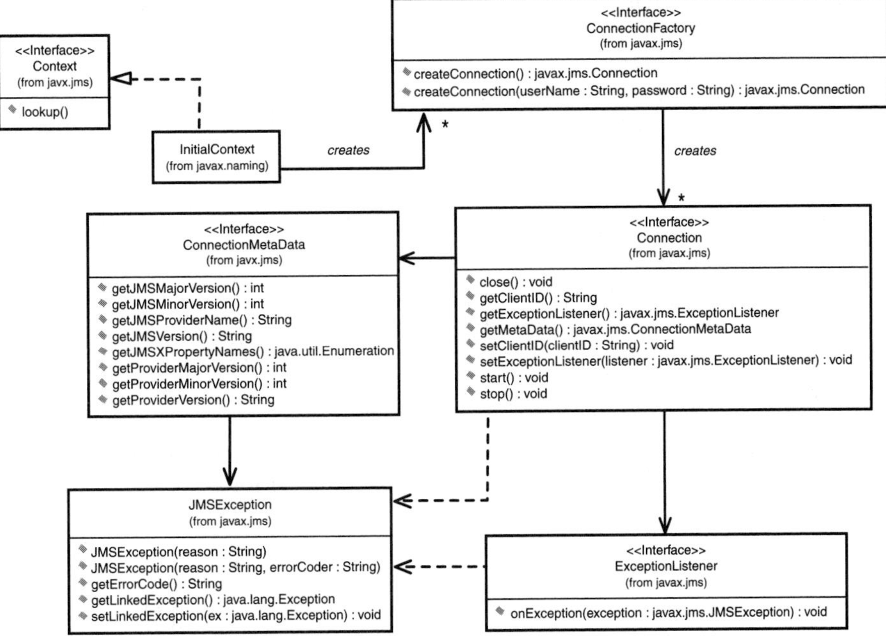

Figure 15.8 JMS connections.

A `ConnectionFactory` interface is used to create a connection to a particular JMS service provider's message service. JNDI is used to look up a handle to an initial `ConnectionFactory` object managed by a JMS service provider. Sub-interfaces of `ConnectionFactory` and objects that implement the `ConnectionFactory` interface provide methods for returning specific `Connection` object instances. New to JMS v1.1, a JMS client can also use a base `ConnectionFactory` object directly to create handles to generic `Connection` objects that ultimately may encapsulate connections to either point-to-point or publish-subscribe messaging models. The `ConnectionFactory.createConnection()` method can be used to create handles to `Connection` objects either by using a default user identity or by passing in a username and password explicitly.

The J2EE and JMS

J2EE components can obtain handles to JMS connection factory objects via JNDI and subsequently obtain JMS `Connection` handles. Such a mechanism will be demonstrated in Part VI, "Enterprise Applications Enabling," when we describe how Enterprise JavaBeans obtain JMS connection factory handles from their middle-tier container/server environments.

A `Connection` interface encapsulates a JMS client's connection with a JMS service-provider instance. When a connection is created, it is in a "stopped" mode. That is, the consumers associated with the connection do not receive messages until `Connection.start()` is called. `Connection.stop()` can be used to return the connection to stopped mode. The `Connection.close()` method is called when the JMS client is finished with the connection and wants to clean up resources.

It should be noted that the `JMSException` class is an exception that is thrown by nearly every JMS API method call. It is also the root class for all other JMS exceptions. A `JMSException` can have a JMS service provider–specific error code `String` associated with it. A `JMSException` can also return its link to a lower-level exception that was responsible for the higher-level messaging exception.

A JMS client can be notified of asynchronously occurring exceptions that are associated with the connection. The JMS client can register an object implementing the `ExceptionListener` interface with the connection by calling the `Connection.setExceptionListener()` method. The `ExceptionListener` implements the single `onException()` method to be notified of the `JMSException` occurring on the connection. As with any listener, the exception listener must be sure to provide an `onException()` implementation that can handle multiple client threads attempting to notify the listener. The listener may be retrieved by a call to `Connection.getExceptionListener()`.

A JMS service provider–specific client ID associated with a connection can be retrieved with `Connection.getClientID()` and set with `Connection.setClientID()`. Typically, the client ID will be associated with a connection by the JMS service provider when creating the connection using the `ConnectionFactory`. If the JMS client attempts to set the client ID using `setClientID()`, an `IllegalStateException` will be thrown in the event that the ID set by the client is not permitted by the JMS service provider. If the client does attempt to set a client ID, it will be set immediately upon connection creation before any further actions are taken.

Meta-data about the connection can also be returned from the `Connection` object using the `getMetaData()` call. The `ConnectionMetaData` object that is returned can return the named version, major version numbers, and minor version numbers for both the JMS API and the service-provider code being used. Additionally, an enumeration of JMS properties associated with the connection can be returned from the `ConnectionMetaData` object.

JMS Sessions

Figure 15.9 depicts the core relations involved in JMS sessions. A JMS session is associated with a connection and represents a context within which messages are created. A session may be used to define a transaction within whose boundaries may exist a set of messages being sent and received within the transaction. Thus, all such messages may be contained within an atomic transaction.

The `Session` interface encapsulates the context within which JMS messages are created and received. The `Session` interface also extends the `java.lang.Runnable` interface, signifying that each session runs in the context of a single thread. The `Connection.createSession()` method can be used to create a handle to a `Session` object. A `boolean` parameter to the method value indicates whether the session is transactional. As we will discuss shortly, the mode for acknowledging received messages may also be specified when creating a `Session` object. Objects implementing sub-interfaces of the `Connection` interface may also be used to create object instances implementing sub-interfaces of the `Session` interface. The `Session.close()` method is used to close a session resource when the JMS client is finished with its use.

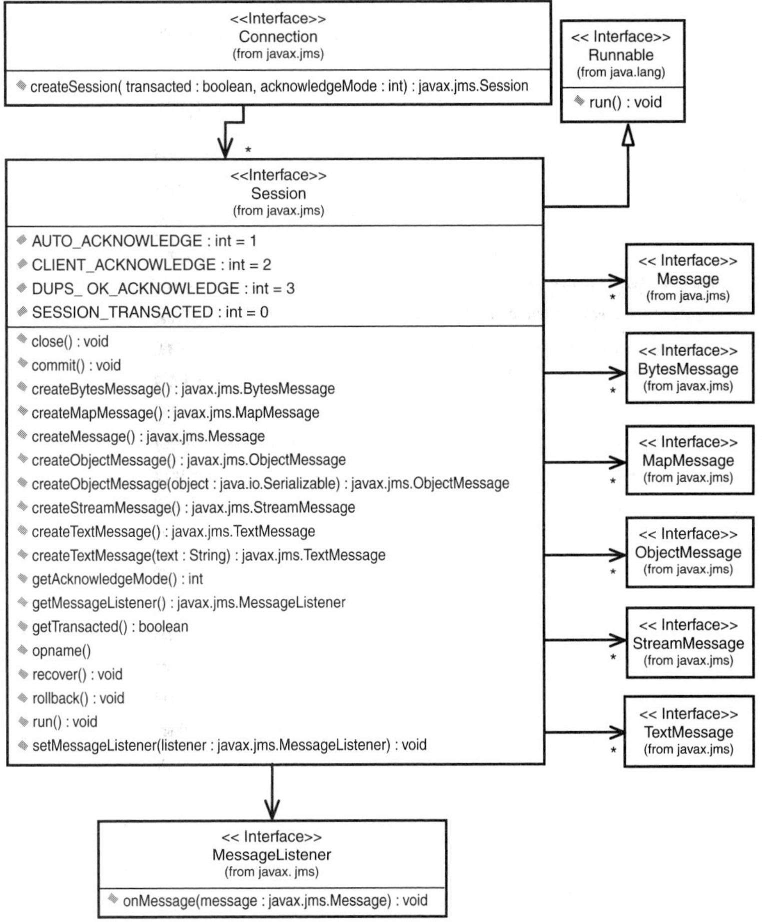

Figure 15.9 JMS sessions.

A set of `create`*`XXX`*`Message()` methods on the `Session` interface are used to create instances of messages that are to be associated with a session. Messages that are created using the same `Session` object are optionally stored in the same session context until they are committed for delivery using the `Session.commit()` method if the particular `Session` object instance is transaction-sensitive. If `Session.rollback()` is called, the messages created within the context of this session are not sent. Such commit and rollback semantics ensure either that messages created within the same session context are all sent or that none is sent. The `Session.getTransacted()` method can be called to determine whether a session is transaction-aware via the return of a `boolean` value.

`Session` objects that are not transaction-aware require an acknowledgment that a message was received. Such messages are then marked as sent and will not be redelivered. Messages in transaction-aware sessions are delivered when they are sent and do not wait for a commit or rollback command to be issued on the session. Optionally, a `Session.recover()` method may be called to stop the current delivery of messages and restart the message delivery process for all messages that have yet to be acknowledged as delivered. Three `static public` constants designate the mode in which messages are sent:

- `AUTO_ACKNOWLEDGE`: The session automatically acknowledges that a message was received by the client.
- `CLIENT_ACKNOWLEDGE`: The session requires that the client explicitly acknowledge that it has received a message.
- `DUPS_OK_ACKNOWLEDGE`: The session acknowledges that a message was received by a client, but the overhead that it assumes to ensure that duplicate messages were not delivered is relaxed. Thus, duplicate messages may be sent to the client in the event of some failure.

If the session is instead transactional, the `Session.SESSION_TRANSACTED` constant value is instead associated with the acknowledgment mode.

Listeners attached to sessions may also be used to enable more asynchronous callback behavior. A `MessageListener` interface implementation can be associated with a `Session` object to enable such behavior. The `MessageListener` implements an `onMessage()` method that takes a `Message` object as a parameter for any message that is received by this `Session` object. The `Session` object's `setMessageListener()` and `getMessageListener()` set and get the `MessageListener`, respectively.

JMS Session Pools

JMS also provides a set of standard abstractions that JMS messaging servers implement in order to manage a pool of JMS sessions. Figure 15.10 depicts such abstractions and relevant methods on other JMS classes. Here, a connection is used to create a handle to an object that encapsulates a consumer of messages. Such a consumer is associated with a pool of JMS sessions on the messaging server.

A `ServerSession` object is a wrapper object used by messaging server environments to wrap a handle to a JMS `Session` object. The `ServerSession.getSession()` method is used to retrieve the handle to the wrapped `Session` object. A `start()` method on the `ServerSession` object is used to ultimately induce the invocation of the `Session` object's `run()` method to start the thread associated with the session. A `ServerSessionPool` object encapsulates a managed collection of `ServerSession` objects in a messaging server's pool of such objects. The `ServerSessionPool.getServerSession()` returns a handle to one such `ServerSession` object from its pool.

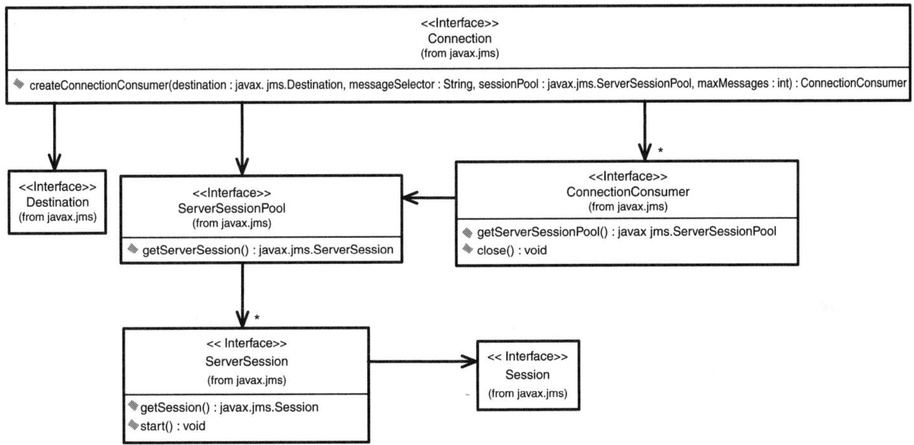

Figure 15.10 JMS session pools.

The `ConnectionConsumer` interface encapsulates a consumer of messages associated with a particular connection. A `ConnectionConsumer` is associated with a particular destination point to which messages are delivered and as encapsulated by the `Destination` marker interface. Concrete implementations of such a `Destination` interface represent endpoints for the particular messaging domain model being used. A `ConnectionConsumer` is also associated with a `String`-representation of a message selector which signals that only those messages with a particular message property are to be processed by the `ConnectionConsumer` or indicates a null/empty-string if all messages are to be processed. A `ConnectionConsumer` also has a maximum bound for those messages that may be handled at one time by a `ServerSession`. Finally, an underlying `ServerSessionPool` is also associated with a `ConnectionConsumer`.

The `Connection.createConnectionConsumer()` method initializes and constructs a `ConnectionConsumer` given those attributes just described for a `ConnectionConsumer`, including the destination point, message filter, server session pool, and maximum number of messages processed. After a `ConnectionConsumer` handle is created, the pool of sessions associated with the `ConnectionConsumer` may be gotten by invoking its `getServerSessionPool()` method. The `close()` method should be invoked by clients when use of the `ConnectionConsumer` is no longer needed by the client to ensure that resources allocated outside of the current JVM process are released and closed.

JMS Transactional Connections and Sessions

The JMS API also defines a set of interfaces depicted in Figure 15.11 that may optionally be implemented by JMS-based messaging servers to provide transactional functionality for JMS connections and sessions. Because JMS clients are discouraged from being coded to talk directly to these interfaces, we only briefly discuss their relevance here. JMS clients in fact should use whatever transactional mechanisms (often declarative) are defined for the messaging environment in which they operate.

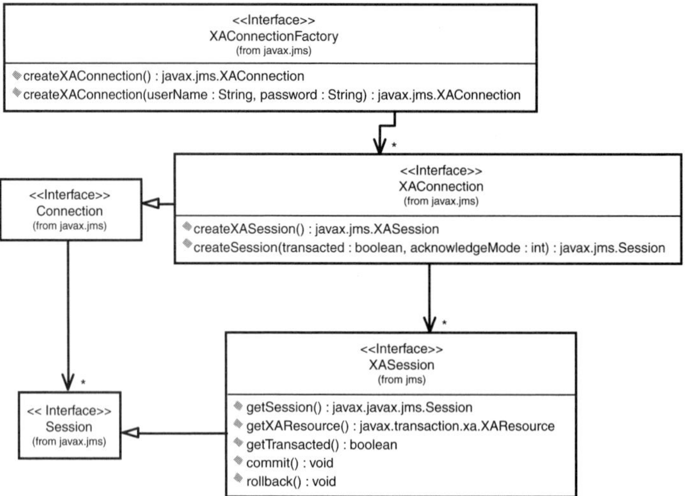

Figure 15.11 JMS XA-compliant connections and sessions.

Similar to the `ConnectionFactory`, the `XAConnectionFactory` is used to create a handle to an `XAConnection` object as opposed to a plain `Connection` object. The `XAConnection` object subclasses the `Connection` object to indicate that transactional support is implied by the particular JMS connection. Thus, messages sent and received as part of a session via such a connection are imbued with the basic JTA behavior and ACID principles as discussed in Chapter 14, "Transaction Services with JTA and JTS." The `XAConnection` object, in fact, is used to create handles to `XASession` objects that subclass JMS `Session` objects. A JTA `XAResource` may be gotten from the `XASession` object and exposes other transactional management behavior.

JMS Generic Messages

Figure 15.12 depicts the core interfaces and conceptual relations of the base JMS `Message` type. The `Message` interface is the root interface for all messages that flow through a JMS-based messaging system. The `Destination` interface is a marker interface used to represent an endpoint of message delivery. Because `Message` objects may have relationships to a destination and reply-to location, conceptual relationships with a `Destination` interface are shown in the diagram. Similarly, because a delivery mode for a message also exists, a conceptual relationship to a `DeliveryMode` interface is also shown.

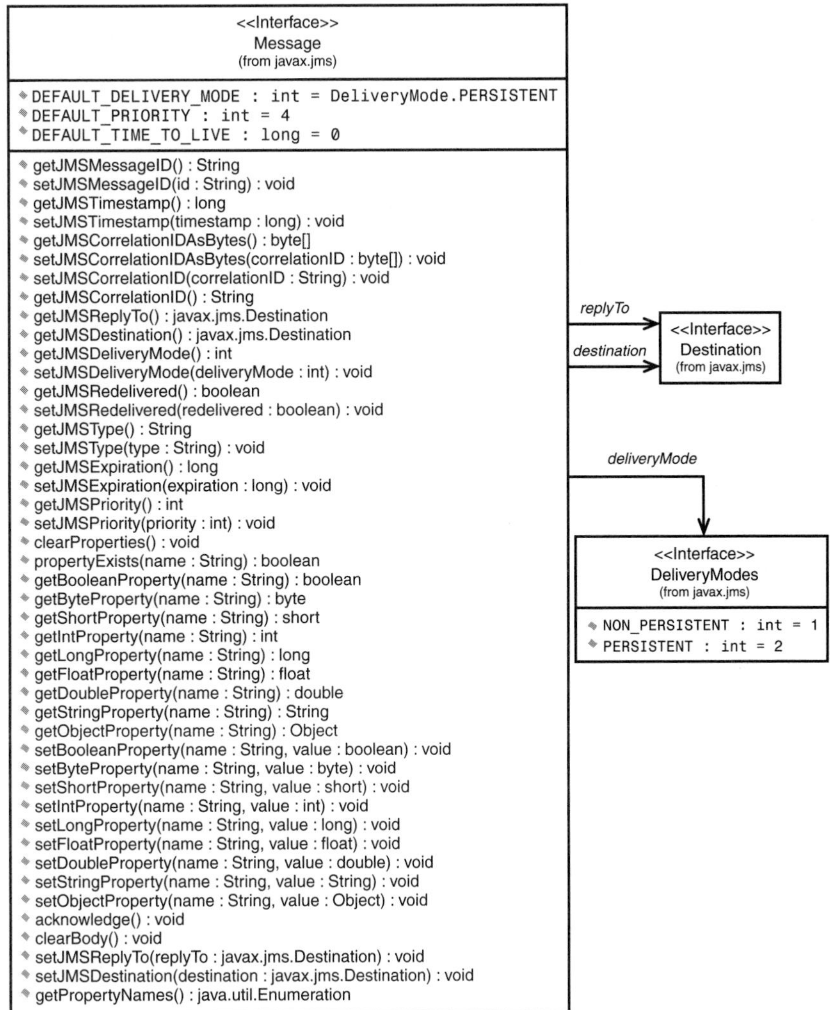

Figure 15.12 The JMS base message type.

These are the major elements of a message encapsulated by the `Message` interface:

- *Header:* The header is a collection of control information items used for routing and identification of messages.
- *Body:* The actual data content of the message.
- *Properties:* Optional application-specific properties of a message used to support an extensible set of message types.

Header information can be gotten or set using a standard getter and setter syntax of `getXXX()` and `setXXX()`, where *XXX* is the name of a header property. Standard header properties defined as getters and setters on the `Message` interface are listed here:

- `JMSMessageID`: Unique ID associated with the message and beginning with the prefix `ID:`.
- `JMSTimestamp`: The time at which a message was sent.
- `JMSCorrelationID`: An identifier that can be used to link one message to another.
- `JMSCorrelationIDAsBytes`: A correlation identifier as an array of bytes.
- `JMSReplyTo`: A destination location to which a reply to this message should be sent.
- `JMSDestination`: A destination location to which a message is being sent.
- `JMSDeliveryMode`: The delivery mode of the message supported by the message service provider defined by `DeliveryMode.PERSISTENT` if the message is to be stored persistently during messaging, or by `DeliveryMode.NON_PERSISTENT` if the message is to be cached in memory during messaging.
- `JMSRedelivered`: Indicates whether the message was sent in a previous transmission but has not yet been acknowledged.
- `JMSType`: The type of message.
- `JMSExpiration`: The time at which the message is to be considered expired. A default value of `0` indicates no expiration.
- `JMSPriority`: The priority of a message with `0` as the lowest priority and `9` as the highest priority.

Provider-specific properties of a message can also be gotten and set onto a message using a host of `getXXXProperty()` and `setXXXProperty()` methods, respectively, where *XXX* specifies the property type. Each property has a name identified by a `String` and a value of its specific type. The existence of a named property can be tested using `Message.propertyExists(String)`. The `Message.getPropertyNames()` method returns an `Enumeration` of property names defined for this message. Property types supported are `boolean`, `byte`, `short`, `int`, `long`, `float`, `double`, and `String`.

This is the generic form of getter:

```
XXX getXXXProperty(String name) throws JMSException;
```

The `getObjectProperty()` method is the only exception to this rule. It allows retrieval of the types `Boolean`, `Byte`, `Short`, `Integer`, `Long`, `Float`, `Double`, and `String`.

This is the generic form of setter:

```
void setXXXProperty(String name, XXX value) throws JMSException;
```

The setObjectProperty() method is the only exception to this rule. It allows setting of the types Boolean, Byte, Short, Integer, Long, Float, Double, and String.

Property values are set before a message is sent and are in read-only mode when received by a client. A value written as a byte, short, int, or long can be read as a value of its own type or higher precision in the same type family. Thus, a short, for example, can be read as a short, an int, or a long. Values written as a float can be read as a float or double. All values can be read as a String, and String objects can possibly be read as another value of a particular type if they can be parsed into that type.

All properties can be removed from a message using the Message.clearProperties() method. When clearProperties() is called, the properties are no longer in read-only mode. If a client attempts to read a property when it is read-only, a MessageNotWriteableException is thrown.

Properties whose names begin with the JMS_<provider_name> prefix are reserved for the JMS service provider's defined properties. Properties whose names begin with the JMSX prefix are reserved for standard JMS properties. The properties JMSXGroupID and JMSXGroupSeq are required, but the remaining properties defined with the JMSX prefix are optional. The names of supported JMSX properties can be gotten from a call to ConnectionMetaData.getJMSXPropertyNames(). These are the standard JMSX properties:

- JMSXGroupID: Identifier for a group of messages
- JMSXGroupSeq: Message sequence number for a message in a message group
- JMSXUserID: User ID of the message sender
- JMSXAppID: Identifier of the application that sent the message
- JMSXProducerTXID: Identifier of the transaction that sent the message
- JMSXConsumerTXID: Identifier of the transaction that received the message
- JMSXDeliveryCount: Number of attempted deliveries of this message
- JMSXRcvTimestamp: Time at which the message was sent to the consumer by the JMS service provider
- JMSXState: Identifier for the state of a message in a service provider's message repository: waiting = 1, ready = 2, expired = 3, and retained = 4

On a final note about generic JMS messages, sometimes it is important for a JMS client to know whether a message is received by its intended recipient. By calling Message.acknowledge(), a client can acknowledge that the associated message and all previous messages associated with a session were received. The last message in a group of messages that is acknowledged designates that all previous messages were received in that group.

JMS Specialized Messages

The generic JMS message interface just described offers a lot of generic functionality that any message inside of a messaging system may expose. However, the JMS API also defines five additional types of messages that extend the `Message` interface and that correspond to five types of message body data, as shown in Figure 15.13. Byte data is encapsulated by the `BytesMessage`, a `Serializable` object is encapsulated by the `ObjectMessage`, a `String` message is encapsulated by the `TextMessage`, key and value pairs are encapsulated by the `MapMessage`, and I/O streams are encapsulated by the `StreamMessage`. Individual methods on the message sub-interfaces define getters and setters for the type-specific data body, but a generic `clearBody()` method to clear the data body of a message and place it in write-only mode exists on the base `Message` interface.

These are the various message body specialization types:

- `BytesMessage`: Interface encapsulates a message whose body is a collection of bytes. Various `read`*`XXX`*`()` and `write`*`XXX`*`()` methods defined in the `BytesMessage` interface are used to read and write specific types from and to the underlying byte stream, respectively. A `BytesMessage.reset()` call resets the pointer to the underlying byte stream and renders the object in read-only mode. Additionally, a `getBodyLength()` method may be used to retrieve the number of bytes associated with the message.
- `StreamMessage`: Interface encapsulates a message whose body is an underlying I/O stream of information. Various `read`*`XXX`*`()` and `write`*`XXX`*`()` methods also exist on the `StreamMessage` interface to read and write specific types from and to the underlying stream, respectively. A `StreamMessage.reset()` call resets the pointer to the underlying stream and renders the object in read-only mode.
- `MapMessage`: Interface encapsulates a message whose body is an underlying collection of key and value pairs. A collection of `get`*`XXX`*`(String)` methods returns a typed value from the `MapMessage` given a particular `String` name. A collection of `set`*`XXX`*`(String, `*`XXX`*`)` methods sets a typed value into the `MapMessage` with a particular `String` name. The `getMapNames()` method returns an `Enumeration` of `String` key names associated with the `MapMessage`. The `itemExists(String)` method returns a `boolean` value indicating whether a particular `String` named value exists in the `MapMessage`.
- `ObjectMessage`: Interface encapsulates a message whose body is an underlying `Serializable` object. Has `getObject()` and `setObject()` methods.
- `TextMessage`: Interface encapsulates a message whose body is an underlying `String` value. Has `getText()` and `setText()` methods.

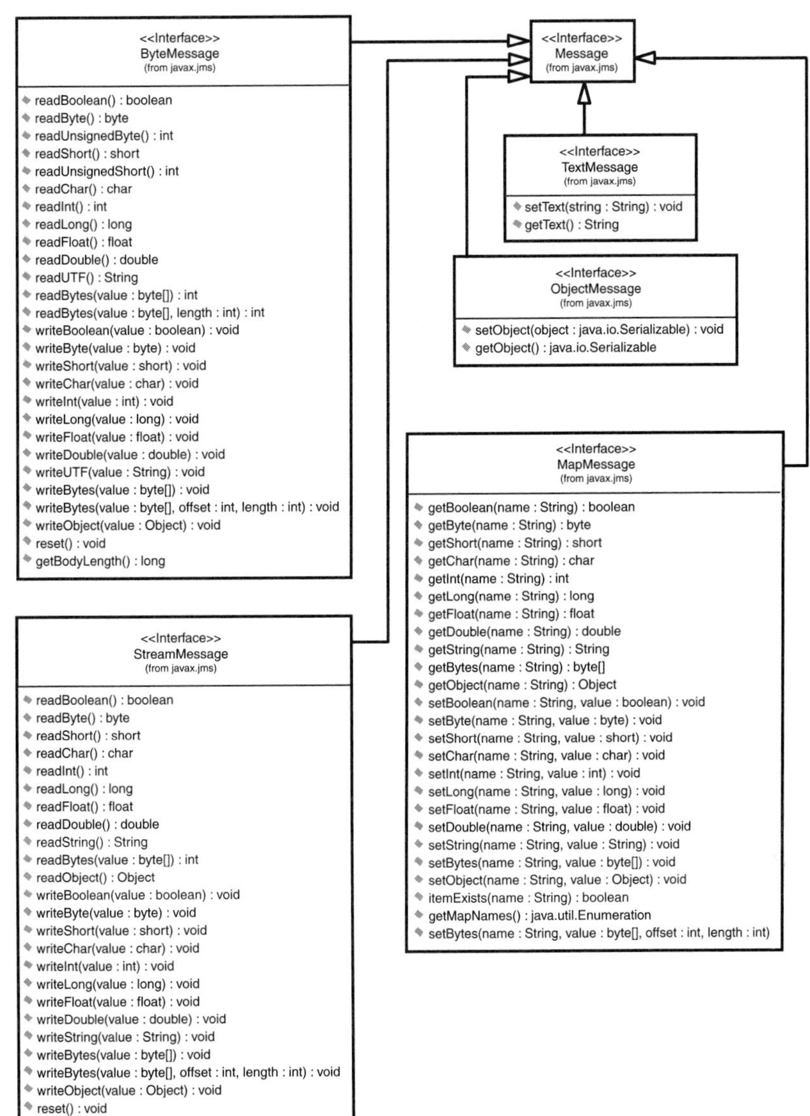

Figure 15.13 The JMS message body specialization types.

Message Producers, Consumers, and Selectors

With all of this talk about JMS connections, sessions, and messages, you might be wondering when we'll finally get to the point of actually being able to send and receive these messages within such sessions and over such connections. Indeed, there are a lot of abstractions within JMS to enable the sending and receiving of messages. Although such abstractions are many, it does illustrate the well-thought-out object-oriented nature of the JMS API. Nevertheless, we have come to the point in our discussion where it becomes more apparent how messages are sent and received via JMS as described in this section.

JMS provides base encapsulations for message producers and consumers as shown in Figure 15.14. Message producers generate messages in a session context that are to be received by message consumers. Message consumers can filter which messages they receive using a message selector.

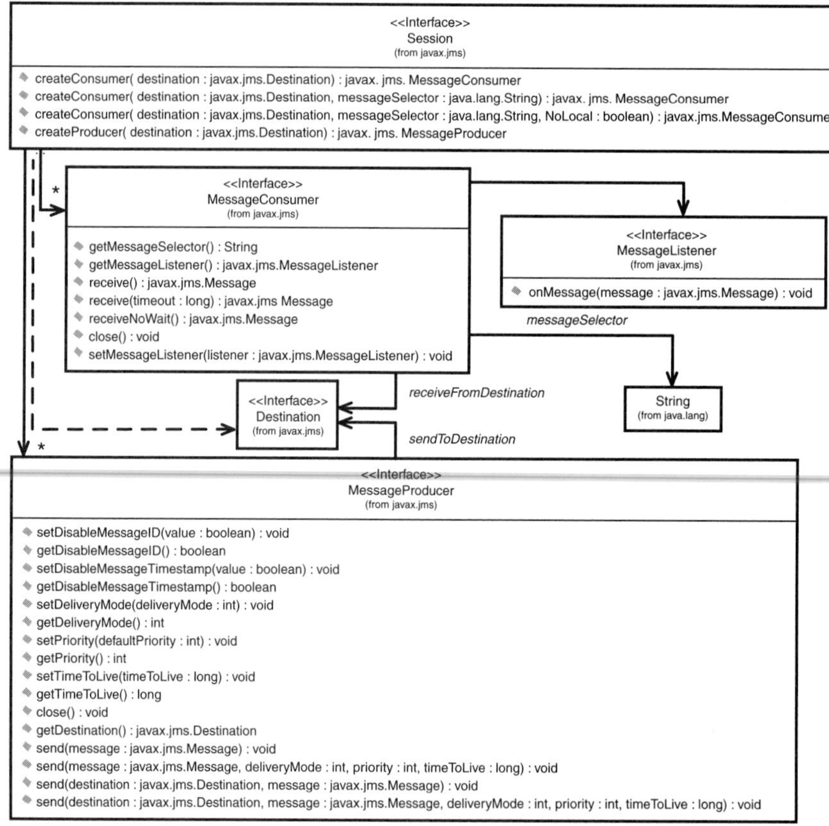

Figure 15.14 JMS message producers, consumers, and selectors.

The `MessageProducer` interface is the base interface for producers of messages. `MessageProducer` objects are created by passing a `Destination` for a message as an argument to a message producer creation method on a `Session` object. When utilizing the unified domain model of JMS v1.1, the method `Session.createProducer()` can be used to create a handle to a `MessageProducer` object. As you'll soon see, sub-interfaces of the `Session` interface that are specific to a particular messaging domain model also provide more concrete methods for returning messaging domain-specific message producer object handles. Methods on the `MessageProducer` interface permit the setting and getting of a producer's default delivery mode, the associated message priority, and the time (in milliseconds) for which a message in the message system has to live. Setters also exist for disabling message ID and timestamps along with getters of these values. Finally, because the producer itself represents a destination point, its own `Destination` may be gotten using the `getDestination()` method.

Of course, of primary importance when using a `MessageProducer` is to actually produce (that is, send) a message to a particular destination point. A series of `MessageProducer.send()` methods permit such behavior. If the destination is associated with a `Message` object, the `MessageProducer` object's `send(Message)` and `send(Message, int, int, long)` methods may be invoked to send that message to its intended destination. If default values for the `Message` object are undesirable, the message's priority number, time to live in milliseconds, and `DeliveryMode` setting may be submitted as parameters to the `send()` method. Alternatively, a `Destination` point may be explicitly identified by using the `MessageProducer` object's `send(Destination, Message)` or `send(Destination, Message, int, int, long)` methods.

The `MessageConsumer` interface is the base interface for consumers of messages. `MessageConsumer` objects are created using the unified domain model by invoking one of the `createConsumer()` methods on the `Session` object. Sub-interfaces of the `Session` object may also be used to create handles to domain-specific messaging model consumers, as we'll see later in this chapter. Regardless of the consumer creation method used, a `Destination` object must be passed as an input parameter to a message consumer creation method. The `Destination` object identifies that destination point with which the message consumer is associated to receive messages.

A `MessageConsumer` may also be created using a particular message selector `String` parameter passed into two of the `Session.createConsumer()` methods. Message selectors define a filter that is used to determine which messages should be routed to a message consumer. For example, a particular message consumer may be interested only in receiving messages from a system administrator with a `JMSXUserID` property of `admin` (for example, `String exampleSelector = "JMSXUserID = admin"`). A message selector `String` is expressed in a subset of SQL92 syntax and can refer only to header and property information in a message. A selector is expressed using the following types of expression elements:

- *Literal:* A `String` in single quotes, a numeral, and `boolean` identifiers.
- *Identifier:* A sequence of letters and digits beginning with a letter that refers to a header name or property name in a message.
- *Whitespace:* A space, a tab, a form feed, or an end of line.

- *Expression:* Conditional, arithmetic, and Boolean expressions.
- *Brackets:* The `()` brackets group elements.
- *Operators:* Logical operators `NOT`, `AND`, `OR`. Comparison operators `=`, `>`, `>=`, `<`, `<=`, `<>`. Arithmetic operators unary `+`, unary `-`, `*`, `/`, `+`, `-`.
- `BETWEEN`*:* Use of `BETWEEN` operator to specify a range using *`expression`* `[NOT] BETWEEN` *`expression`* `and` *`expression`*.
- `IN`*:* Use of `IN` to specify inclusion in a set using *`identifier`* `[NOT] IN (`*`literal`*`,` *`literal`*`, ...)`.
- `LIKE`*:* Use of `LIKE` to specify similarity in a pattern using *`identifier`* `[NOT] LIKE` *`pattern`*.
- `IS`*:* Use of `IS` for identifier `IS [NOT] NULL`.

The `MessageConsumer.getMessageSelector()` call returns the `String` object defining a message selector for that `MessageConsumer`.

Notice that one form of the `Session.createConsumer()` method also enables one to provide a Boolean input parameter named `NoLocal`. This parameter enables one to specify whether a consumer sharing the same connection as the producer of a message should consume those messages sent to the consumer's destination point by that producer. By default, this value is `false`, indicating that a consumer will receive messages sent by a producer even if they share the same connection.

The `MessageConsumer` also allows a `MessageListener` to be registered with it to independently receive messages for the `MessageConsumer`. The `MessageConsumer.close()` method is used to close the resources used to implement the message consumer by the service provider. Various methods on the `MessageConsumer` are defined to receive messages from a destination. The `MessageConsumer.receive()` method blocks until a particular message is received for use by the consumer or until the `MessageConsumer` is closed. The `MessageConsumer.receive(long)` method can be used to specify a timeout in milliseconds for which the message consumer should wait to receive a message. `MessageConsumer.receiveNoWait()` can be called to receive a message only if it is immediately available and without blocking.

Extending the BeeShirts.com Example Data Model

Before we introduce concrete examples in the subsequent sections illustrating how JMS can be used in an enterprise application, we need to extend our BeeShirts.com model beyond what has been introduced thus far in the book. Figure 15.15 depicts our addition of a `SUPPLIER` table to persist data related to a BeeShirts.com business-to-business (B2B) partner that supplies particular T-shirts retailed by BeeShirts.com. The BeeShirts.com server software sends asynchronous messages to a JMS server that handles distributing these messages to the appropriate supplier. A `SUPPLIER` table contains contact information for a supplier. To support the relationship between a supplier and a requested T-shirt item, the `TSHIRT` table is also augmented with a foreign key to reference the particular `SUPPLIER`.

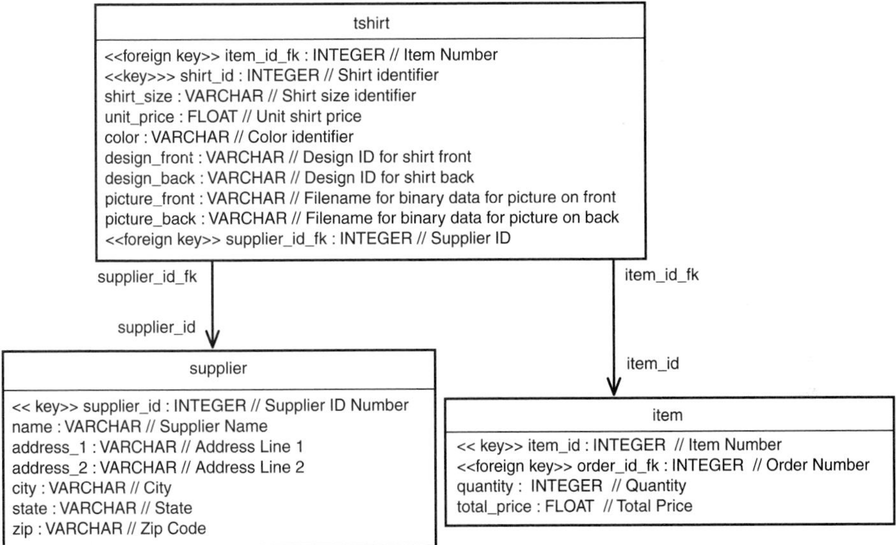

Figure 15.15 The BeeShirts.com supplier, T-shirt, and items data model.

> **Note**
>
> The complete data model can be found in Appendix A, "Software Configuration," but here we only introduce an augmentation to the model above and beyond what has already been introduced. Appendix A also contains scripts for configuring the database to support the schema assumed by this book, as well as for configuring the database with some sample data.
>
> Recall that the `TSHIRT` table first presented in Figure 6.1 of Chapter 6, "Advanced JDBC," was defined with a `PICTURE_FRONT` and `PICTURE_BACK` column that assumed SQL `BLOB` types. We defined the `TSHIRT` table in that way and in a separate database schema namespace to illustrate advanced SQL type access via JDBC 3.0. Figure 15.15 depicts the `TSHIRT` table representation as it is used throughout all other chapters except Chapter 6. Here, the `TSHIRT` table's `PICTURE_FRONT` and `PICTURE_BACK` columns assume SQL `VARCHAR` types.

JMS Point-to-Point Queue Model

Figure 15.16 depicts the basic JMS architecture elements that support point-to-point message queuing. The message queuing architecture is really an extension of the core JMS architecture with features that specifically focus on message queuing behavior.

Connection factories, connections, sessions, message producers, message consumers, and endpoint destinations are all extended with point-to-point message queuing model interfaces. Thus, by understanding the core JMS architecture presented earlier, you can most rapidly understand the specific point-to-point message queuing specializations presented here. As we'll also illustrate later in this chapter, new to JMS v1.1, the more generic JMS architecture may also be used to implement point-to-point messaging sans much consideration for the messaging domain-specific APIs illustrated in Figure 15.16.

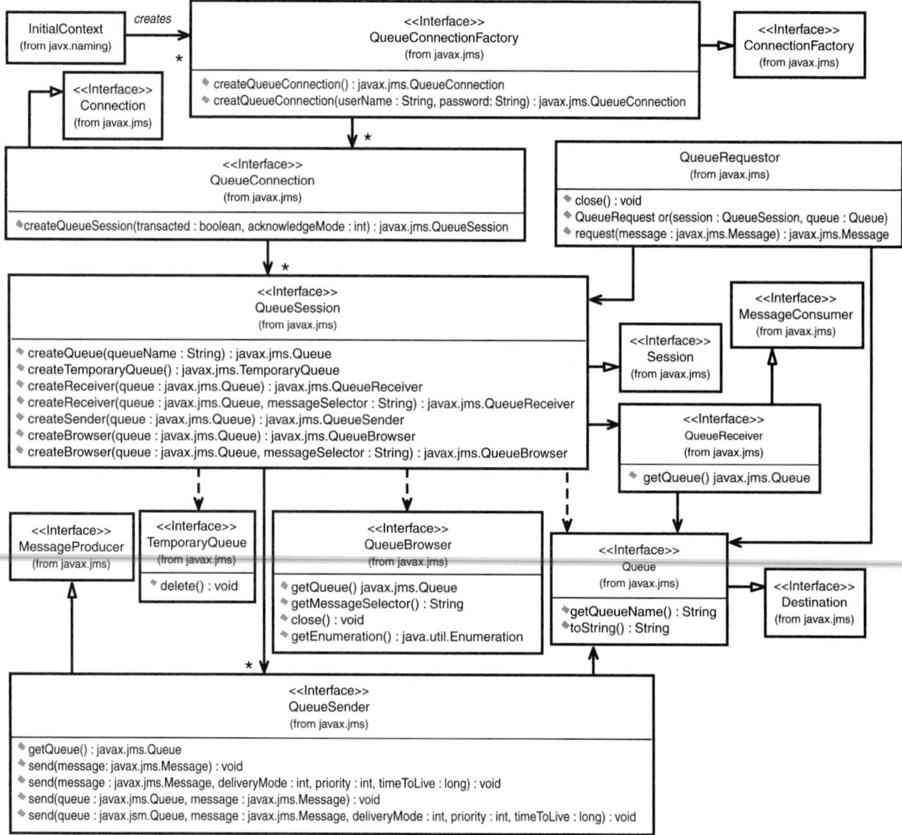

Figure 15.16 JMS point-to-point message queuing.

JMS clients may use JNDI to obtain an initial reference to a named `QueueConnectionFactory` object. One of the `QueueConnectionFactory.createQueueConnection()` methods is used to create an instance of a `QueueConnection` object. The `createQueueConnection()` method can be called with a username and password or by using the parameterless version of the method with a default user identity assumed.

The `QueueConnection` interface is a type of `Connection` interface that represents a connection to a JMS point-to-point messaging queue service. The `createConnectionConsumer()` method is not used by regular JMS clients and is primarily used by a messaging server to manage queue service connections. The `createQueueSession()` method is called by JMS clients to create a `QueueSession` instance. Whether or not transactions are to be implemented by the `QueueSession` object is designated by a `boolean` parameter to `createQueueSession()`. Also, the acknowledgment mode is specified in the call to `createQueueSession()` using one of the static session identifiers, such as `Session.AUTO_ACKNOWLEDGE`, `Session.CLIENT_ACKNOWLEDGE`, or `Session.DUPS_OK_ACKNOWLEDGE`. The `QueueSession` interface extended from the `Session` interface implements various message queuing–specific entity creation methods.

`QueueSession.createQueue()` creates an instance of a `Queue` object given a provider-specific name for that queue. Most service-provider implementations will provide other means for creating named queues, but this interface can be used by JMS clients for creating queues. The `Queue` interface encapsulates an interface to a queue destination using JMS's point-to-point messaging queue model and has a `getQueueName()` method to return the queue name. The `QueueSession.createTemporaryQueue()` method creates a `TemporaryQueue` object. The `TemporaryQueue` is deleted when its `QueueConnection` is closed.

The `QueueSession.createBrowser()` methods create an instance of a `QueueBrowser` object associated with a particular message queue. The `QueueBrowser` can be used to passively observe the live contents of a particular message queue without modifying the queue contents. If the `QueueBrowser` was created with a message selector, only those messages identified in the message selector expression will be viewable. The `getEnumeration()` method returns the list of messages associated with the queue and perhaps refined by the message selector.

The `QueueSession.createSender()` method creates a `QueueSender` message producer that is used to send messages to a `Queue`. Messages can be sent to a `Queue` using the various `QueueSender.send()` methods. Variations of these methods enable the delivery of messages to the `QueueSender` object's associated `Queue` or to a newly specified `Queue` object passed to the `send()` method. Delivery modes, priorities, and time to live for a message can also be specified during calls to `QueueSender.send()`. Messages to send to a `Queue` can be created using the various message-creation methods defined on the `Session` interface from which `QueueSession` extends.

The `QueueSession.createReceiver()` methods create a `QueueReceiver` message consumer used to receive messages from a `Queue`. A variation of the `createReceiver()` method also permits the specification of a message selector to filter out which messages are received by the `QueueReceiver`. Above and beyond the built-in message consuming methods provided by the `QueueReceiver` interface's base `MessageConsumer` interface, a `QueueReceiver.getQueue()` method returns a handle to the associated `Queue`.

A `QueueRequestor` helper class can also be used to simplify use of the JMS queue model for request and reply behavior. A `QueueRequestor` object is first created with a handle to a `QueueSession` and `Queue` object. The request method may then be used to send a `Message` to a queue destination and wait for a response in the form of a `Message`. To release and close any open distributed resources associated with the `QueueRequestor` and the underlying `QueueSession`, the JMS client invokes the `close()` method on the `QueueRequestor`.

Finally, as depicted in Figure 15.17, a set of interfaces exists to encapsulate transactional support for point-to-point message queuing. As mentioned before, the JMS client should not be coded to talk directly to such interfaces. Rather, the messaging server will use such interfaces to imbue a point-to-point message queue connection factory, connection, and session with JTA XA-compliant transaction management functionality. The interfaces in Figure 15.17 simply extend the interfaces presented in Figure 15.11 and provide method signatures specific to the message queue domain model.

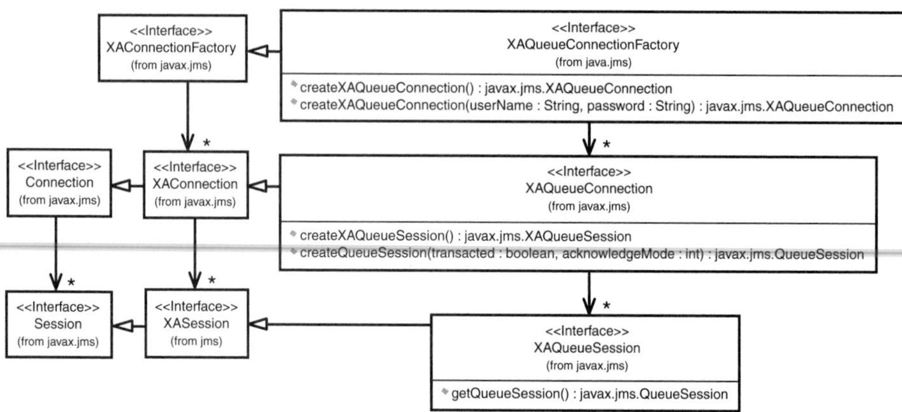

Figure 15.17 JMS transactional point-to-point message queuing.

Point-to-Point Message Queuing Example

We present a brief example here to illustrate the use of JMS point-to-point message queuing. Our example implements a `QueueSupplier` that would typically sit on the server side of BeeShirts.com. It submits `OrderRequest` objects to `Queue` objects managed by a JMS service provider that correspond to T-shirt suppliers. A T-shirt supplier implements a `QueueConsumer` that plucks `OrderRequest` objects from the `Queue`.

> **Note**
>
> The sample code strewn throughout this section leaves out some exception handling and other non-essential features in the interest of simplifying the description. The complete set of code examples for this JMS message queue example can be located as described in Appendix A. The JMS code for this chapter is extracted to an `examples\src\ejava\jms` directory. The `QueueSupplier.java` and `QueueConsumer.java` files implement this example, and an `OrderRequest.java` and `OrderManager.java` class are also used. After running the ANT script for this chapter's code, the generated `runqueue-supplier` and `runqueue-consumer` script files can be used for executing the example. The local `build.properties` file is used to configure the example for use with the chapter's ANT script.
>
> This example may be run with a WebLogic server JMS implementation or a J2EE reference implementation of JMS. As a basic summary, you must first configure the `global.properties` `j2ee.dir` and `j2ee.lib` properties to respectively point to the root directory of your J2EE JMS server and J2EE JMS libraries. You must also uncomment or set the appropriate set of JNDI and JMS connection properties as defined in the chapter's local `build.properties` file. When using WebLogic, you'll also need to configure a special XML file to identify the appropriate JMS destination point names and types. Likewise, when using the J2EE reference implementation, you need to run a special tool or configure a file to indicate the JMS destination point names and types that will be used. Refer to Appendix A for detailed configuration instructions.

Order Request

An `OrderRequest` class implements a `Serializable` object encapsulating a BeeShirts.com T-shirt order request message. The `OrderRequest` has a size, the design of the T-shirt front, the design of the T-shirt back, a T-shirt color, and an order quantity. Aside from a set of public `OrderRequest` attributes, an `OrderRequest.toString()` prints the order request contents:

```
package ejava.jms;
import java.io.Serializable;

public class OrderRequest implements Serializable
{
  public String size;
  public String designFront;
  public String designBack;
  public String color;
  public int    howMany;

  public String toString()
  {
    return "Size :"+ size + " Design Front :" + designFront
      + " Design Back :" +  designBack + " Color :" +color
      +" How Many : "+howMany;
  }
}
```

Order Manager

We won't list the details behind the OrderManager JDBC helper class here because its single getNewOrders() method is a rather long method that has nothing to do with demonstrating JMS. The getNewOrders() method implementation can be found in the source code example directory associated with this chapter. After reading a set of database connection properties from Java preferences and as configured by the build.properties file, it creates a JDBC connection. A list of distinct BeeShirts.com suppliers is then queried from the database. For each distinct supplier, the T-shirt supply information is queried for that supplier, and the number of T-shirts of the desired kind available from that supplier is retrieved. If the number of available shirts is less than a maximum value, an OrderRequest object is created with a queue name associated with that supplier. The queue name serves as a key to the Hashtable for each OrderRequest entry, and the Hashtable is returned from the getNewOrders() method call.

Queue Supplier

The QueueSupplier.main() method obtains a Hashtable of new BeeShirts.com order requests using the OrderManager.getNewOrders() call. For each queue name in the Hashtable of orders, a queue is created and an order request is sent within the createAQueueAndSendOrder() method. The QueueSupplier.main() method is shown here:

```
public static void main(String[] args)
{
    ...
    // Get new orders from database using order manager class
    Hashtable newOrders = OrderManager.getNewOrders();
    Enumeration keys = newOrders.keys();
    // For each order, get order request and send to consumer
    while(keys.hasMoreElements()){
      String queueName = (String)keys.nextElement();
      OrderRequest orderRequest =
        (OrderRequest)newOrders.get(queueName);
      createAQueueAndSendOrder(queueName,orderRequest);
    }
  // exception handling excluded here...
}
```

The createAQueueAndSendOrder() method called from main() first creates an InitialContext reference with a call to getInitialContext(). A new QueueSupplier instance is then created given the context reference and queue name. The QueueSupplier.send() then sends the order request message. The QueueSupplier.close() and Context.close() methods close up resources before returning. The createAQueueAndSendOrder() method is shown here:

```
private static void createAQueueAndSendOrder(
  String queueName, OrderRequest orderRequest)
{
    ...
    InitialContext context = getInitialContext();
    QueueSupplier queueSupplier =
      new QueueSupplier(context, queueName);
    queueSupplier.send(orderRequest);
    queueSupplier.close();
    context.close();

   // Exception handling here...
}
```

The `getInitialContext()` method simply creates and returns a JNDI `InitialContext` reference using the Java preferences set during the ANT build process. The Java preferences are configured using the `build.properties` file and specify a JNDI SPI with a `JNDI_FACTORY` property set (for example, `weblogic.jndi.WLInitialContextFactory`) and a `JNDI_PROVIDER_URL` set to the IP address and port on which the application server's naming service is running (for example, `t3://localhost:7001/`). After the context is retrieved, the `QueueSupplier.context` variable is set. The `getInitialContext()` method is shown here:

```
private static InitialContext getInitialContext()
     throws NamingException
{
  System.out.println(" Getting Initial Context :");
 // Connect to naming Service
  Preferences preferences =
    Preferences.userNodeForPackage(OrderManager.class);
  Hashtable env = new Hashtable();
  String jndiFactory = preferences.get("JNDI_FACTORY", null);
  String providerURL  = preferences.get("JNDI_PROVIDER_URL", null);
  env.put(Context.INITIAL_CONTEXT_FACTORY, jndiFactory);
  env.put(Context.PROVIDER_URL, providerURL);
  return new InitialContext(env);
}
```

The `QueueSupplier` constructor is where all messaging queue initialization is performed on the supplier side. A reference to a JMS `QueueConnectionFactory` is first looked up from the JNDI context using the `JMS_FACTORY_FOR_QUEUE` preference value (for example with WebLogic, `javax.jms.QueueConnectionFactory`). A `QueueConnection` and `QueueSession` are then created. The `Queue` is created and bound to JNDI if it cannot be looked up using JNDI. Finally, a `QueueSender` is created. The `QueueConnectionFactory`, `QueueConnection`, `QueueSession`, `Queue`, and `QueueSender` objects are all saved as private variables in this `QueueSupplier` class. The `QueueSupplier` constructor is shown here:

```
public QueueSupplier( Context context,
  String queueName)
  throws NamingException, JMSException
{
  Preferences preferences =
    Preferences.userNodeForPackage(OrderManager.class);
  String jmsFactoryName =
       preferences.get("JMS_FACTORY_FOR_QUEUE",null);
  // Create Queue Connection Factory
  queueConnectionFactory = (QueueConnectionFactory)
    context.lookup(jmsFactoryName);
  // Create Queue Connection to The Factory
  queueConnection = queueConnectionFactory.createQueueConnection();
  // Create Session to the Connection
  queueSession = queueConnection.createQueueSession(false,
    Session.AUTO_ACKNOWLEDGE);
  try {
    // if queue already created
    queue = (Queue) context.lookup(queueName);
  } catch (NamingException namingException) {
    // if needed to create new Queue
    queue = queueSession.createQueue(queueName);
    // bind the queue with a name
    context.bind(queueName, queue);
  }
  // Create Receiver
  queueSender = queueSession.createSender(queue);
}
```

The `QueueSupplier.send()` method sends an object to a JMS queue. In our sample case, the object is always the `OrderRequest` object called from the `createAQueueAndSendOrder()` method. To illustrate two types of message sending, if the object passed to `send()` was a `String`, we create a `TextMessage` and send it using our `QueueSender`. Otherwise, we create an `ObjectMessage` with the object and send it using our `QueueSender`:

```
public void send(Object newMessage)
     throws JMSException
{
  if(newMessage instanceof String){
    TextMessage sendingMessage = queueSession.createTextMessage();
    queueConnection.start();
    sendingMessage.setText((String)newMessage);
    queueSender.send(sendingMessage);
  }else {
    ObjectMessage sendingMessage = queueSession.createObjectMessage();
    queueConnection.start();
```

```
    sendingMessage.setObject((Serializable)newMessage);
    queueSender.send(sendingMessage);
  }
}
```

Finally, our `QueueSupplier.close()` method simply cleans up `QueueSender`, `QueueSession`, and `QueueConnection` resources:

```
public void close()
     throws JMSException
{
  queueSender.close();
  queueSession.close();
  queueConnection.close();
}
```

Queue Consumer

Our sample `QueueConsumer` represents a T-shirt vendor that the BeeShirts.com application, represented by the `QueueSupplier`, talks to. The `QueueConsumer` has a queue named `PureShirts` that the `QueueSupplier` uses to place an order request with the T-shirt vendor. The `QueueConsumer.main()` method first creates a JNDI context via a call to `getInitialContext()`. The `QueueConsumer` is then constructed with the JNDI context as a parameter. The `QueueConsumer` then receives messages until the user exits the program and the `QueueConsumer.quitFromReceiving` flag is set. Finally, `QueueConsumer.close` resources are cleaned up, along with the JNDI context. The `QueueConsumer.main()` method is shown here:

```
public static void main(String[] args)
     throws Exception
{
    // Exception handling excluded...

    // Create initial context and queue consumer
    InitialContext context = getInitialContext();
    QueueConsumer queueConsumer = new QueueConsumer(context);
    System.out.println(" Queue Client is ready to receive Message");
    // Wait for messages to receive, until user quits from program.
    synchronized(queueConsumer) {
      while (! queueConsumer.quitFromReceiving) {
        try {
          queueConsumer.wait();
        }
        catch (InterruptedException interruptedException){
          System.out.println(" Error :"+ interruptedException);
          interruptedException.printStackTrace();
        }
      }
```

```
    }
    queueConsumer.close();
    context.close();
    System.exit(0);

   // Exception handling excluded...
}
```

The `getInitialContext()` method used to obtain a handle to the initial JNDI context for `QueueConsumer` is identical to the `getInitialContext()` method for the `QueueSupplier`. The `QueueConsumer` constructor looks up the `QueueConnectionFactory`, creates a `QueueConnection`, creates a `QueueSession`, and looks up or creates a `Queue` in a fashion also similar to the `QueueSupplier`. The `QUEUE_NAME` property is retrieved from a Java preference and is configured with the `build.properties` file. In our example, the `QUEUE_NAME` is initially set to `PureShirts`. The `QueueConsumer` then creates a `QueueReceiver` and registers itself as a `MessageListener` with the `QueueReceiver`. The `QueueConnection` is then initialized to start receiving messages. The `QueueConsumer` constructor initialization is shown here:

```
public QueueConsumer(Context context)
  throws NamingException, JMSException
{
  Preferences preferences =
    Preferences.userNodeForPackage(OrderManager.class);
  String jmsFactoryName =
       preferences.get("JMS_FACTORY_FOR_QUEUE",null);
  // Create Queue Connection Factory
  queueConnectionFactory = (QueueConnectionFactory)
    context.lookup(jmsFactoryName);
  // Create Queue Connection to The Factory
  queueConnection = queueConnectionFactory.createQueueConnection();
  // Create Session to the Connection
  queueSession = queueConnection.createQueueSession(false,
    Session.AUTO_ACKNOWLEDGE);
  String queueName = preferences.get("QUEUE_NAME",null);
  try {
    queue = (Queue) context.lookup(queueName);
  } catch (NamingException namingException) {
    // if not created, create new queue
    queue = queueSession.createQueue(queueName);
    // bind the queue with a name
    context.bind(queueName, queue);
  }
  // Create Receiver
  queueReceiver = queueSession.createReceiver(queue);
  // Register QueueConsumer as Message Listener
  queueReceiver.setMessageListener(this);
```

```
    // Start Receiving Message
    queueConnection.start();
}
```

Because the `QueueConsumer` is a message listener by virtue of implementing `MessageListener`, it must implement the `onMessage(Message)` method. The `QueueConsumer.onMessage()` is called when the JMS service provider receives an `OrderRequest` from the `QueueSupplier`. The `onMessage()` method will first display information from the received `Message` header and then display the message body information, depending on whether it is a `TextMessage` or an `ObjectMessage`. After it receives a message, we induce an exit from the program by setting the `QueueConsumer.quitFromReceiving` flag to `true`. The `onMessage()` implementation is shown here:

```
public void onMessage(Message message)
{
  try {
    // print information about the message
    System.out.println(message.getJMSMessageID());
    System.out.println("MessageID :" + message.getJMSMessageID() +
                       " for " + message.getJMSDestination());
    System.out.print("Message Expires        ");
    if (message.getJMSExpiration() > 0) {
        System.out.println( new Date( message.getJMSExpiration()));
    }
    else{
        System.out.println("never  Expires ");
    }
    System.out.println("Priority :" + message.getJMSPriority());
    System.out.println("Mode    : " + (
      message.getJMSDeliveryMode() == DeliveryMode.PERSISTENT ?
      "PERSISTENT" : "NON_PERSISTENT"));
    System.out.println("Reply to :       " + message.getJMSReplyTo());
    System.out.println("Message type :  " + message.getJMSType());
    if (message instanceof TextMessage) {
      String receivedMessage = ((TextMessage)message).getText();
      System.out.println("Received Message :" + receivedMessage);

    } else if(message instanceof ObjectMessage){
      String receivedMessage = message.toString();
      System.out.println("Received Message :" + receivedMessage);
    }
    quitFromReceiving = true;
  }
  catch (JMSException jmsException) {
    jmsException.printStackTrace();
  }
}
```

Finally, all `QueueReceiver`, `QueueSession`, and `QueueConnection` resources are closed:

```
public void close()
     throws JMSException
{
  this.queueReceiver.close();
  this.queueSession.close();
  this.queueConnection.close();
}
```

JMS Publish-Subscribe Model

Figure 15.18 depicts the basic JMS architecture elements that support publish-subscribe messaging. The publish-subscribe messaging architecture is also an extension of the core JMS architecture with features specialized to suit a publish-subscribe messaging model. Connection factories, connections, sessions, message producers, message consumers, and endpoint destinations are all extended with publish-subscribe message model interfaces. As we'll also illustrate later in this chapter, new to JMS v1.1, the more generic JMS architecture may also be used to implement publish-subscribe messaging sans much consideration for the messaging domain–specific APIs illustrated in Figure 15.18.

JMS clients use JNDI to obtain an initial reference to a named `TopicConnectionFactory` object. The `TopicConnectionFactory.createTopicConnection()` methods are used to create an instance of a `TopicConnection` object. The `createTopicConnection()` method can be called with a username and password or by using the parameterless version of the method with a default user identity assumed.

The `TopicConnection` interface is a type of `Connection` interface that represents a connection to a JMS publish-subscribe messaging service. The `createConnectionConsumer()` and `createDurableConnectionConsumer()` methods are not used by regular JMS clients and are primarily used by a messaging server to manage publish-subscribe message service connections. The `createTopicSession()` method is called by JMS clients to create a `TopicSession` instance. Session transactions and acknowledgment mode are also established during the creation of a `TopicSession`.

`TopicSession.createTopic()` creates an instance of a `Topic` object given a provider-specific name for a topic. As with creating queues using `QueueSession`, the creation of named topics is something that will be provided using other means by most service-provider implementations. The `Topic` interface encapsulates a topic destination to which publishers publish messages and from which subscribers subscribe to receive messages. Different service providers will implement a hierarchy of topic names differently, but a `Topic.getTopicName()` can be used to obtain the `String` representation of the topic. The `TopicSession.createTemporaryTopic()` method creates a `TemporaryTopic` object. The `TemporaryTopic` is deleted when its `TopicConnection` is closed.

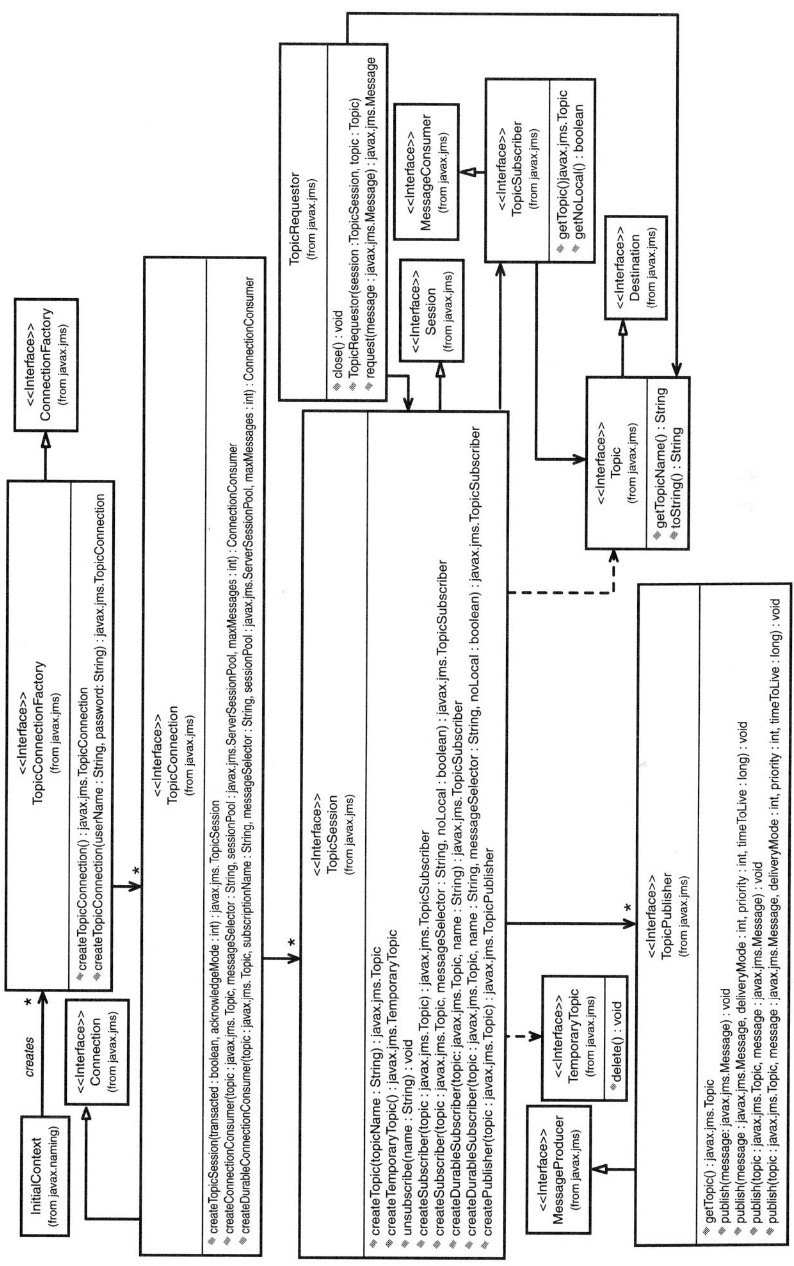

Figure 15.18 JMS publish-subscribe messaging.

The `TopicSession.createPublisher()` method creates a `TopicPublisher` message producer that is used to publish messages to a particular `Topic`. Messages can be published to a `Topic` using the various `TopicPublisher.publish()` methods. Variations of these methods enable the publishing of messages to a `TopicPublisher` object's associated `Topic` or to a newly specified `Topic` object passed to the `publish()` method. Delivery modes, priorities, and time to live for a message can also be specified during calls to `TopicPublisher.publish()`. Messages to publish to a `Topic` can be created using the various message-creation methods defined on the `Session` interface from which `TopicSession` extends.

Two types of `TopicSubscriber` creation methods exist on `TopicSession`. The `TopicSession.createSubscriber()` methods create nondurable `TopicSubscriber` instances. Nondurable `TopicSubscribers` are those subscribers who receive notification only of published messages to which they have subscribed while the subscriber is active. Durable subscribers are those who can receive messages later even after they were temporarily unavailable; they can be created using the `TopicSession.createDurableSubscriber()` calls. Durable subscribers have a name associated with the published messages stored for their deferred notification. Versions of `TopicSession.createSubscriber()` and `TopicSession.createDurableSubscriber()` exist to also enable use of message selector filters and a `boolean noLocal` flag indicating that messages published by their own connection should be ignored.

A `TopicRequestor` helper class can also be used to simplify the use of the JMS publish-subscribe model for request and reply behavior. A `TopicRequestor` object is first created with a handle to a `TopicSession` and `Topic` object. The request method may then be used to publish a `Message` to a topic destination and wait for a response in the form of a `Message`. To release and close any open distributed resources associated with the `TopicRequestor` and the underlying `TopicSession`, the JMS client invokes the `close()` method on the `TopicRequestor`.

Finally, as depicted in Figure 15.19, a set of interfaces exists to encapsulate transactional support for publish-subscribe messaging. As mentioned before, the JMS client should not be coded to talk directly to such interfaces. Rather, the messaging server will use such interfaces to imbue a publish-subscribe message connection factory, connection, and session with JTA XA-compliant transaction management functionality. The interfaces in Figure 15.19 simply extend the interfaces presented in Figure 15.11 and provide method signatures specific to the publish-subscribe message domain model.

Publish-Subscribe Example

We present a brief example here to illustrate the use of JMS publish-subscribe messaging. Our example implements a `TopicSupplier` implemented on the BeeShirts.com server side to publish `OrderRequest` objects to a `TshirtsSupplier` topic name. A `TopicConsumer` mimics a sample T-shirts vendor's `TopicSubscriber` which subscribes to receive `OrderRequest` messages.

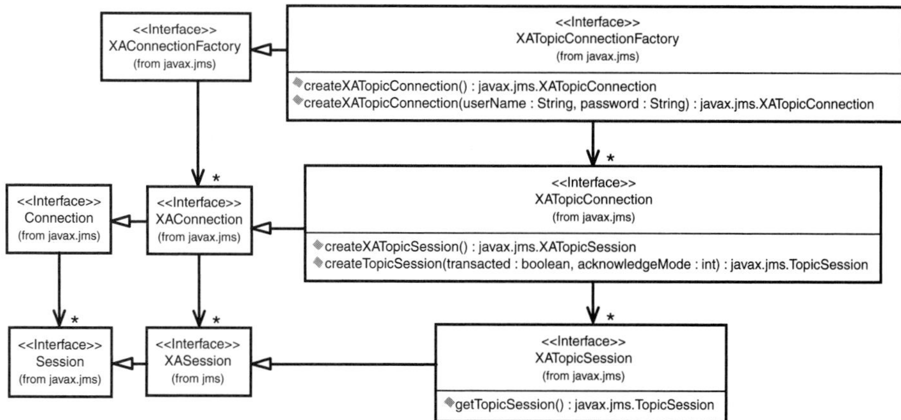

Figure 15.19 JMS transactional publish-subscribe messaging.

> **Note**
>
> The sample code strewn throughout this section leaves out some exception handling and other non-essential features in the interest of simplifying the description. The complete set of code examples for this JMS message queue example can be located as described in Appendix A. The JMS code for this chapter is extracted to an `examples\src\ejava\jms` directory. The `TopicSupplier.java` and `TopicConsumer.java` files implement this example, and `OrderRequest.java` and `OrderManager.java` classes are also used. After running the ANT script for this chapter's code, the generated `runtopic-supplier` and `runtopic-consumer` script files can be used for executing the example. The local `build.properties` file is used to configure the example for use with the chapter's ANT script. This example may be run with a WebLogic server JMS implementation or a J2EE reference implementation of JMS. Refer to Appendix A for detailed configuration instructions.

Topic Supplier

The `TopicSupplier.main()` method retrieves the `Hashtable` of orders from the `OrderManager.getNewOrders()` call. For each key name in the `Hashtable`, a call to `createATopicAndPublishOrder()` is made with an extracted `OrderRequest`:

```
public static void main(String[] args)
     throws Exception
{
      ...
    // Get The Orders if any
    Hashtable newOrders = OrderManager.getNewOrders();
    Enumeration keys = newOrders.keys();
    // For each order, create order request and publish it
    while(keys.hasMoreElements()){
```

```
        String  key = (String)keys.nextElement();
        OrderRequest orderRequest =
          (OrderRequest)newOrders.get(key);
        createATopicAndPublishOrder(orderRequest);
    }

    // Exception handling excluded here...
}
```

The `TopicSupplier.createATopicAndPublishOrder()` method obtains a JNDI context via a call to `getInitialContext()` in the same fashion as was performed by the `QueueSupplier` and `QueueConsumer`. Subsequently, a `TopicSupplier` instance is created and a call to `send()` on that instance is made to publish a message to a topic. Finally, the `TopicSupplier.close()` and `Context.close()` methods are called to clean up resources. The `createATopicAndPublishOrder()` method is shown here:

```
public static void createATopicAndPublishOrder(
   OrderRequest orderRequest)
{
    ...
    InitialContext context = getInitialContext();
    TopicSupplier topicSupplier =
      new TopicSupplier( context);
    topicSupplier.send(orderRequest);
    topicSupplier.close();
    context.close();
   // Exception handling excluded...
}
```

Inside the `TopicSupplier` constructor, a `TopicConnectionFactory` is looked up from the JNDI context with a Java preference named `JMS_FACTORY_FOR_TOPIC` mapping to a value of `javax.jms.TopicConnectionFactory`. The `TopicConnectionFactory` is then used to create a `TopicConnection`, which in turn is used to create a `TopicSession`. A `Topic` is then created and bound to JNDI if it cannot be looked up using JNDI. The topic name used is `TshirtsSuppliers` read from the Java preference named `TOPIC_NAME`. Finally, a `TopicPublisher` is created. The `TopicConnectionFactory`, `TopicConnection`, `TopicSession`, `Topic`, and `TopicSender` objects are all saved as private variables in this `TopicSupplier` class. The `TopicSupplier` constructor is shown here:

```
public TopicSupplier(Context context)
  throws NamingException, JMSException
{
  Preferences preferences =
    Preferences.userNodeForPackage(OrderManager.class);

  String jmsFactoryName =
```

```
      preferences.get("JMS_FACTORY_FOR_TOPIC",null);
  // get TopicFactory
  topicConnectionFactory = (TopicConnectionFactory)
    context.lookup(jmsFactoryName);
  // Get TopicConnection
  topicConnection = topicConnectionFactory.createTopicConnection();
  // Get Session for the Connection
  topicSession =
      topicConnection.createTopicSession(false,
        Session.AUTO_ACKNOWLEDGE);
  String topicName = preferences.get("TOPIC_NAME",null);
  try {
    // determine if topic by this name already exists
    topic = (Topic) context.lookup(topicName);
  } catch (NamingException namingException) {
    // if not there, create new topic
    topic = topicSession.createTopic(topicName);
    // bind the topic with a name
    context.bind(topicName, topic);
  }
  topicPublisher = topicSession.createPublisher(topic);
}
```

The `TopicSupplier.send()` method publishes an object to a JMS topic. In our sample case, the object is always the `OrderRequest` object called from the `createATopicAndPublishOrder()` method. The published `ObjectMessage` is published using the created `TopicPublisher`, which publishes messages to the `TshirtsSuppliers` topic name:

```
public void send(Object newMessage)
     throws JMSException
{
  if(newMessage instanceof String){
    TextMessage sendingMessage = topicSession.createTextMessage();
    topicConnection.start();  // start Sending
    sendingMessage.setText((String)newMessage); // set the Text message
    topicPublisher.publish(sendingMessage); // send Message
  }else {
    ObjectMessage sendingMessage = topicSession.createObjectMessage();
    topicConnection.start();    // start Sending
    sendingMessage.
         setObject((Serializable)newMessage); // set Object Message
    topicPublisher.publish(sendingMessage); // send message
  }
}
```

Finally, the `TopicSupplier.close()` method closes its `TopicPublisher`, `TopicSession`, and `TopicConnection` resources:

```
public void close()
     throws JMSException
{
  topicPublisher.close();
  topicSession.close();
  topicConnection.close();
}
```

Topic Consumer

The sample `TopicConsumer` represents a T-shirt vendor that subscribes to receive orders from the `TshirtsSuppliers` topic. The `TopicConsumer.main()` method first creates a JNDI context with a call to `getInitialContext()`. The `TopicConsumer` is then constructed with the JNDI context as an input parameter. The `TopicConsumer` receives messages until the user exits the program and the `TopicConsumer.quitFromReceiving` flag is set. Finally, `TopicConsumer.close()` ensures that all resources are cleaned up along with the JNDI context. The `TopicConsumer.main()` method is shown here:

```
public static void main(String[] args)
      throws Exception
 {
      ...
     // Create context and topic consumer
     InitialContext context = getInitialContext();
     TopicConsumer topicConsumer =
        new TopicConsumer( context);
     System.out.println(" Topic Client is ready to receive Message");
     // Wait for messages to be received, until user quits from program.
     synchronized(topicConsumer) {
       while (! topicConsumer.quitFromReceiving) {
         try {
           topicConsumer.wait();
         }
         catch (InterruptedException interruptedException){

           System.out.println(" Error :"+ interruptedException);
           interruptedException.printStackTrace();
         }
       }
     }
     topicConsumer.close();
     context.close();
     System.exit(0);

     // Exception handling here...
 }
```

The getInitialContext() method to obtain a handle to the initial JNDI context for a TopicConsumer is identical to the getInitialContext() method for the QueueSupplier. The TopicConsumer constructor also looks up the TopicConnectionFactory, creates a TopicConnection, creates a TopicSession, and looks up or creates a Topic in a fashion similar to the TopicSupplier. That is, the Java preference named TOPIC_NAME as configured via the build.properties file is set to TshirtsSuppliers. The TopicConsumer then creates a TopicSubscriber and registers itself as a MessageListener with the TopicSubscriber. The TopicConnection is then initialized to start receiving published messages. The TopicConsumer constructor initialization is shown here:

```
public TopicConsumer(Context context)
  throws NamingException, JMSException
{
  Preferences preferences =
    Preferences.userNodeForPackage(OrderManager.class);
  String jmsFactoryName =
      preferences.get("JMS_FACTORY_FOR_TOPIC",null);

  // Create Queue Connection Factory
  topicConnectionFactory = (TopicConnectionFactory)
    context.lookup(jmsFactoryName);
  // Create Queue Connection to The Factory
  topicConnection = topicConnectionFactory.createTopicConnection();
  // Create Session to the Connection
  topicSession = topicConnection.createTopicSession(false,
    Session.AUTO_ACKNOWLEDGE);
  String topicName = preferences.get("TOPIC_NAME",null);

  try {
    topic = (Topic) context.lookup(topicName);
  } catch (NamingException namingException) {
    // create topic, if not created
    topic = topicSession.createTopic(topicName);
    // bind the topic with a name
    context.bind(topicName, topic);
  }
  // Create Receiver
  topicSubscriber = topicSession.createSubscriber(topic);
  // Register TopicClient as Message Listener
  topicSubscriber.setMessageListener(this);
  // Start Receiving Message
  topicConnection.start();
}
```

Because the TopicConsumer is a message listener implementing a MessageListener, it must implement the onMessage(Message) method. The

`TopicConsumer.onMessage()` is called when the JMS service provider receives an `OrderRequest` published by the `TopicSupplier`. The `onMessage()` method will first display information from the published `Message` header and then display the message body information depending on whether it is a `TextMessage` or an `ObjectMessage`. After it receives a message, we induce an exit from the program by setting the `TopicConsumer.quitFromReceiving` flag to `true`. The `onMessage()` implementation is shown here:

```
public void onMessage(Message message)
{
  try {
    // print information about the message
    System.out.println(message.getJMSMessageID());
    System.out.println("MessageID :" + message.getJMSMessageID() +
                         " for " + message.getJMSDestination());
    System.out.print("Message Expires        ");
    if (message.getJMSExpiration() > 0) {
        System.out.println( new Date( message.getJMSExpiration()));
    }
    else{
        System.out.println("never  Exprires ");
    }
    System.out.println("Priority :" + message.getJMSPriority());
    System.out.println("Mode   : " + (
      message.getJMSDeliveryMode() == DeliveryMode.PERSISTENT ?
      "PERSISTENT" : "NON_PERSISTENT"));
    System.out.println("Reply to :      " + message.getJMSReplyTo());
    System.out.println("Message type :  " + message.getJMSType());

    if (message instanceof TextMessage) {

      String receivedMessage = ((TextMessage)message).getText();
      System.out.println("Received Message :" + receivedMessage);
    } else if(message instanceof ObjectMessage){

      String receivedMessage = message.toString();
      System.out.println("Received Message :" + receivedMessage);
    }

    quitFromReceiving = true;
    notifyAll(); // notify to main Thread to leave from the program
  } catch (JMSException jmsException) {
    jmsException.printStackTrace();
  }
}
```

Finally, all TopicReceiver, TopicSession, and TopicConnection resources are closed:

```
public void close()
     throws JMSException
{
  topicSubscriber.close();
  this.topicSession.close();
  this.topicConnection.close();
}
```

Publish-Subscribe Example with Temporary Topics and Selectors

As another example within the domain of publish-subscribe messaging, we provide an example that now illustrates how a topic supplier can use a temporary topic to publish a request and then receive a response on that topic from the topic consumer. We also illustrate use of a message selector with the example snippets shown here. Aside from such differences in the examples to illustrate a few more JMS API features, the topic supplier and topic consumer code examples in this section are identical to the previous examples.

> **Note**
>
> The code snippets throughout this section leave out a significant amount of code because it is similar to the previous publish-subscribe example and in order to focus on the new JMS features not demonstrated in the previous example. The complete set of code examples for this JMS message queue example can be found as described in Appendix A. The JMS code for this chapter is extracted to an `examples\src\ejava\jms` directory. The `TopicRequestSupplier.java` and `TopicReplyConsumer.java` files implement this example, and an `OrderRequest.java` and `OrderManager.java` class are also used. After running the ANT script for this chapter's code, the generated `runtopic-request-supplier` and `runtopic-reply-consumer` script files can be used for executing the example. The local `build.properties` file is used to configure the example for use with the chapter's ANT script. This example may be run with a WebLogic server JMS implementation or a J2EE reference implementation of JMS. Refer to Appendix A for detailed configuration instructions.

Topic Request Supplier

The TopicRequestSupplier example code is by and large identical to the TopicSupplier example described earlier. It does differ, however, by virtue of its send() method. The createATopicAndPublishOrder() method ultimately invokes the send() method when it wants to publish a message to a topic. The send() method in this example instead creates a TemporaryTopic to which a message is published as illustrated here:

```
public void send(Object newMessage)
     throws JMSException
{
  System.out.println(" Sending :"+newMessage);
```

```
  if(newMessage instanceof String){
    TextMessage sendingMessage = topicSession.createTextMessage();
    topicConnection.start();  // start Sending
    sendingMessage.setText((String)newMessage); // set the Text message
    System.out.println("Creating Temp Topic1:");
    Topic tempTopic = topicSession.createTemporaryTopic();
    System.out.println("Temp Topic:1"+tempTopic);
    sendingMessage.setJMSReplyTo(tempTopic);
    topicPublisher.publish(sendingMessage); // send Message
  }else {
    ObjectMessage sendingMessage = topicSession.createObjectMessage();
    topicConnection.start();   // start Sending
    sendingMessage.setObject((OrderRequest)newMessage); // set Object Message
    System.out.println("Creating Temp Topic:");
    Topic tempTopic = topicSession.createTemporaryTopic();
    System.out.println("Temp Topic:"+tempTopic);
    sendingMessage.setJMSReplyTo(tempTopic);
    topicPublisher.publish(sendingMessage); // send message
    readReply(tempTopic);
  }
}
```

After publishing an `ObjectMessage` to a `TemporaryTopic`, the `send()` method invokes a `readReply()` method given the `TemporaryTopic`. The `readReply()` method uses a message selector to synchronously read responses that were published back to the `TemporaryTopic` as illustrated here:

```
public void readReply(Topic tempTopic)
  throws JMSException
{
    String messageSelect = "DeliveryDays < 5 AND Region like 'Eastern' ";
    TopicSubscriber topicSubscriber =
       topicSession.createSubscriber(tempTopic,messageSelect,false);
    Message replyMessage = topicSubscriber.receive();
    System.out.println("Received Reply message is :"+replyMessage);
}
```

Topic Reply Consumer

The `TopicReplyConsumer` example code is nearly identical to the `TopicConsumer` example described earlier. It does differ, however, by virtue of its `onMessage()` method. The `onMessage()` method is invoked asynchronously when a message is available on the topic in which the consumer is interested. The `onMessage()` method in this example calls a `sendReply()` method as shown here:

```
public void onMessage(Message message)
{
  try {
    if(message instanceof ObjectMessage){
```

```
        String receivedMessage = message.toString();
        System.out.println("Received Message :" + receivedMessage);
        ObjectMessage objectMessage = (ObjectMessage)message;
        OrderRequest orderRequest =
            (OrderRequest)objectMessage.getObject();
        if(orderRequest.howMany >5){
          System.out.println("Sending reply ");
          sendReply(message);
        }
      }
      quitFromReceiving = true;
      //notifyAll(); // notify to main Thread to leave from the program
    } catch (JMSException jmsException) {
      jmsException.printStackTrace();
    }
}
```

The `sendReply()` method then publishes a response message back to the topic for the topic request supplier as illustrated here:

```
private void  sendReply(Message message)
  throws JMSException
{
  System.out.println("Received Request:");
  if(message.getJMSReplyTo() == null){
    System.out.println("Nothing to reply......");
    return;
  }
  Topic replyTopic = (Topic)message.getJMSReplyTo();
  System.out.println("Replied on :"+replyTopic);
  TopicPublisher  topicPublisher =
      topicSession.createPublisher(replyTopic);
  TextMessage textMessage =
      topicSession.createTextMessage(
       " We can deliver these shirts in 3 days"+
       " at your eastern location");
  textMessage.setStringProperty("Reagion","Eastern");
  textMessage.setIntProperty("DeliveryDays",3);
  topicPublisher.publish(textMessage);
  textMessage =
      topicSession.createTextMessage(
       " We can deliver these shirts in 3 Days"+
       " at your western location");
  textMessage.setStringProperty("Reagion","Western");
  textMessage.setIntProperty("DeliveryDays",3);
}
```

JMS Unified Messaging Domain Model

Throughout this chapter, we have mentioned the fact that the core JMS API abstractions can now be used to support both the point-to-point queuing and publish-subscribe messaging models. Indeed, this unified messaging domain model is a feature new to JMS v1.1 and thus part of J2EE v1.4. In fact, the JMS v1.1 specification indicates that one should generally code JMS applications using this new unified model. The specification even hints that the JMS APIs that are specific to point-to-point queuing and publish-subscribe messaging may be deprecated in a future JMS specification version. Regardless, the domain-specific JMS APIs will still be used for some time because many legacy JMS-based applications already exist and because many developers may still prefer the domain-specific model to the unified model.

We discuss the unified model in this section. In reality, you have already been introduced to this model by virtue of the fact that we've already examined core JMS architecture earlier in this chapter and we've also discussed the types of domain-specific destinations and two models that the unified messaging model can support. Figure 15.20, in fact, depicts the main abstractions involved with the unified domain model, and as you can see, the APIs involved in this diagram have already been introduced. Now let's discuss how they are used for unified domain messaging.

As depicted in Figure 15.20, a generic `ConnectionFactory` is looked up using JNDI and then the `ConnectionFactory` is used to create a `Connection`, which in turn is used to create a `Session` handle as before. The JMS v1.1 `Session` interface now offers a host of methods that enable one to create `QueueBrowser`, `TopicSubscriber`, `Queue`, `TemporaryQueue`, `Topic`, and `TemporaryTopic` objects. You've already seen all of these method signatures on the domain-specific `QueueSession` or `TopicSession` interfaces described earlier and depicted in Figure 15.16 and Figure 15.18. The JMS v1.1 `Session` interface also now offers methods that allow one to create generic `MessageConsumer` and `MessageProducer` object handles that actually may implement domain-specific message consumer and message producer functionality, respectively. These methods are simply more generic forms of methods previously defined for the `QueueSession` and `TopicSession` interfaces also as depicted in Figure 15.16 and Figure 15.18.

In fact, using the generic methods on the core JMS APIs, you don't even have to code your JMS application to have any specific knowledge of queues or topics. This is because after you have a handle to a generic `Session` object, you can use JNDI to look up a handle to a `Destination` object given a name for the destination. You can then use the generic `createProducer()` and `createConsumer()` methods on the `Session` interface to create handles to generic `MessageProducer` and `MessageConsumer` objects, respectively. Such object handles can then also be used to generically send and receive JMS messages, respectively.

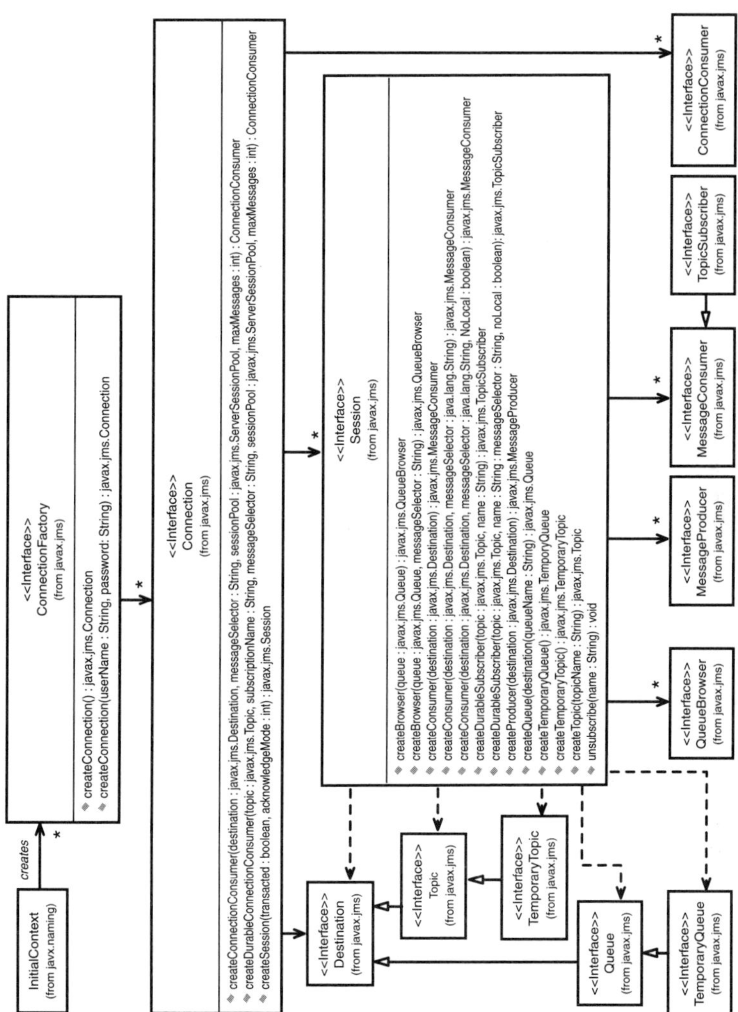

Figure 15.20 JMS unified domain messaging.

Unified Domain Messaging Example

We present an example here to illustrate the use of JMS domain-independent messaging. Our example manifests itself in two classes. A `UnifySupplier` class implements a generic message producer that publishes a message to a topic. The message published to the topic may then be read by the `TopicConsumer` class as described before. A `UnifyConsumer` class implements a generic message consumer that reads a message from a queue that is sent using the `QueueSupplier` class described earlier.

> **Note**
>
> The sample code snippets in this section are extracted from the `UnifyConsumer` and `UnifySupplier` example classes associated with this chapter's code. The complete set of code examples for this JMS message queue example can be found as described in Appendix A. The JMS code for this chapter is extracted to an `examples\src\ejava\jms` directory. The `UnifySupplier.java` and `UnifyConsumer.java` files implement these two examples, and `OrderRequest.java` and `OrderManager.java` classes are also used. After the ANT script for this chapter's code is run, the generated `rununify-supplier` and `rununify-consumer` script files can be used for executing the example. You should run the `rununify-supplier` script along with the `runtopic-consumer` script to demonstrate the `UnifySupplier` working with the `TopicConsumer` class. You should run the `runqueue-supplier` script along with the `rununify-consumer` script to illustrate the `QueueSupplier` working with the `UnifyConsumer` class. The local `build.properties` file is used to configure the example for use with the chapter's ANT script. Refer to Appendix A for detailed configuration instructions.

Unify Supplier

There is nothing tremendously special about the `UnifySupplier` class aside from the fact that it uses generic JMS API calls. The `UnifySupplier` constructor simply looks up a generic `ConnectionFactory`, creates a generic `Connection`, creates a generic `Session`, looks up a generic `Destination` (manifested as a topic), and then creates a generic `MessageProducer` as shown here:

```
public UnifySupplier(Context context)
  throws NamingException, JMSException
{
  Preferences preferences =
    Preferences.userNodeForPackage(OrderManager.class);

  String jmsFactoryName =
      preferences.get("JMS_FACTORY_FOR_TOPIC",null);
  // get ConnectionFactory
  connectionFactory = (ConnectionFactory)
    context.lookup(jmsFactoryName);
  // Get TopicConnection
  connection = connectionFactory.createConnection();
  // Get Session for the Connection
  session =
      connection.createSession(false,
        Session.AUTO_ACKNOWLEDGE);
  String topicName = preferences.get("TOPIC_NAME",null);
    // determine if topic by this name already exists
  destination = (Destination) context.lookup(topicName);

  producer = session.createProducer(destination);
}
```

When it comes time to send the message, the generic MessageProducer is used to send a JMS message as usual and as illustrated here:

```
public void send(Object newMessage)
     throws JMSException
{
  System.out.println(" Sending :"+newMessage);
  if(newMessage instanceof String){
    TextMessage sendingMessage = session.createTextMessage();
    connection.start();  // start Sending
    sendingMessage.setText((String)newMessage); // set the Text message
    producer.send(sendingMessage); // send Message
  }else {
    ObjectMessage sendingMessage = session.createObjectMessage();
    connection.start();   // start Sending
    sendingMessage.setObject((OrderRequest)newMessage); // set Object Message
    producer.send(sendingMessage); // send message
  }
}
```

The TopicConsumer class can be executed as usual to receive the message published by the UnifySupplier class.

Unify Consumer

There is also nothing tremendously special about the UnifyConsumer class aside from the fact that it also uses generic JMS API calls. The UnifyConsumer constructor simply looks up a generic ConnectionFactory, creates a generic Connection, creates a generic Session, looks up a generic Destination (manifested as a queue), creates a generic MessageConsumer, sets itself as a MessageListener on the MessageConsumer, and then starts receiving messages on the connection as shown here:

```
public UnifyConsumer( Context context)
  throws NamingException, JMSException
{
  Preferences preferences =
    Preferences.userNodeForPackage(OrderManager.class);
  String jmsFactoryName =
      preferences.get("JMS_FACTORY_FOR_QUEUE",null);
  // Create Queue Connection Factory
  connectionFactory = (ConnectionFactory)
    context.lookup(jmsFactoryName);
  // Create Queue Connection to The Factory
  connection = connectionFactory.createConnection();
  // Create Session to the Connection
  session = connection.createSession(false,
    Session.AUTO_ACKNOWLEDGE);
```

```
    String queueName = preferences.get("QUEUE_NAME",null);
    destination = (Destination) context.lookup(queueName);

    // Create Receiver
    messageConsumer = session.createConsumer(destination);
    // Register QueueConsumer as Message Listener
    messageConsumer.setMessageListener(this);
    // Start Receiving Message
    connection.start();
}
```

The `UnifyConsumer.onMessage()` method then receives and processes JMS messages as they are received from the queue after they are sent to the queue by the `QueueSupplier` class.

JAXM

The Java API for XML Messaging (JAXM) defines a standard way to send and receive XML-based messages in an asynchronous fashion. JAXM provides a means to send and receive XML-based messages in a synchronous fashion as well. However, it is JAXM's asynchronous XML-based messaging behavior that is of most interest because it was not supported by any other enterprise Java API at the time of this writing. Although JAXM is designed to support any XML-based messaging protocol, JAXM v1.1 requires and relies heavily upon SOAP v1.1. Furthermore, HTTP is also the underlying transport protocol of choice, although you are not explicitly bound to such a protocol via use of JAXM.

JAXM is implemented according to the API-provider model that is common to most J2EE APIs. That is, a standard API is exposed to the developer, and an underlying implementation supports different messaging provider approaches. A particular messaging providers implements a particular messaging profile. A messaging profile simply defines a convention for what data is communicated within a particular messaging format. In the case of SOAP messages, a messaging profile defines conventions for what information is inserted into SOAP headers and SOAP bodies.

One popular messaging profile is defined by the ebXML Message Service specification (`www.oasis-open.org/committees/ebxml-msg`). Such a specification defines a convention for information to be embedded into SOAP messages that are used in electronic business transactions. Additionally, the specification also defines standards for security, reliable messaging, error handling, message delivery, and message statusing. As an example, the ebXML messaging profile defines a standard set of SOAP header elements for identifying the "parties" involved in sending and receiving a message, such as from whom a message is sent and to whom the message is to be delivered.

Additionally, another special messaging profile has been defined, known as the SOAP Routing Protocol (SOAP-RP). SOAP-RP was defined as a protocol for embedding information into SOAP messages to allow for asynchronous and synchronous messaging.

Information is embedded into SOAP headers to indicate the intended receiver, intermediaries, and originating sender. Thus, SOAP-RP's primary focus is in defining the path over which a SOAP message should travel independent of the underlying transport protocol such as HTTP, TCP, and UDP.

The JAXM v1.1 reference implementation, in fact, supports the ebXML and SOAP-RP messaging profiles. JAXM v1.1 is not included as part of the J2EE v1.4. There was a point in time when JAXM was clearly going to be included with the J2EE v1.4, but sometime in late 2002, the decision was made to not include JAXM. The primary reason for this decision seems to be that a few vendors participating in defining the J2EE v1.4 thought that JAXM would be too confusing to developers and is perhaps redundant with other APIs inside the J2EE. In fact, one thought is that much of the synchronous messaging functionality of JAXM can be accomplished effectively with SAAJ and JAX-RPC. Another thought is that the asynchronous messaging functionality of JAXM could potentially be accomplished by using JMS with an underlying XML- and SOAP-based messaging format and profile. Although such overlap in functionality may seem to exist, the converse argument is that the transactional nature of Web services and SOAP-based messaging is different than the transactional nature of MOM-based messaging and thus requires a distinct API. Nevertheless, most agree that XML-based and SOAP-based messaging was in its early stages and had an unknown level of industry acceptance, and thus it was too early to commit the J2EE to support such functionality via incorporation of JAXM.

The J2EE and JAXM

As discussed, JAXM is not part of J2EE v1.4. Furthermore, it was not clear at the time of this writing how popular XML-based messaging would be. As such, the fate of JAXM was unknown at the time of this writing. It is for that reason that we take a conservative approach to describing JAXM in this chapter. Our intention is to simply describe the API and provide example code snippets to illustrate how it may be used. In such a way, you are at least armed as a developer with the knowledge of how to begin using JAXM and of where to turn should XML-based messaging and JAXM increase in importance.

Because of JAXM's lack of incorporation into the J2EE, there is also no standard way to use and configure JAXM inside of a J2EE container. There are, however, general agreed-upon ways in which a JAXM runtime could be used inside of a J2EE container. A JAXM runtime is generally needed on the message producer side when communicating with a messaging provider. That is, the producer needs a messaging provider to handle the asynchronous delivery of a SOAP message to the intended consumer. A JAXM runtime is needed on the consumer side to handle the asynchronous reception and delegation of a SOAP message to the intended receiver object. When used inside of a J2EE container, a Java servlet container or EJB container can be used in conjunction with a JAXM runtime to enable a servlet or an EJB to both produce and send SOAP messages, as well as to act as listeners for asynchronous SOAP messages.

JAXM Architecture Overview

All JAXM-specific API abstractions are contained within the `javax.xml.messaging` package. JAXM relies upon the API packages defined within SAAJ as well. The JAXM API may be best understood by realizing that it provides APIs for both message producing and consuming functionality and APIs that implement both synchronous and asynchronous messaging. Such categorization in the context of the JAXM API is depicted in Figure 15.21.

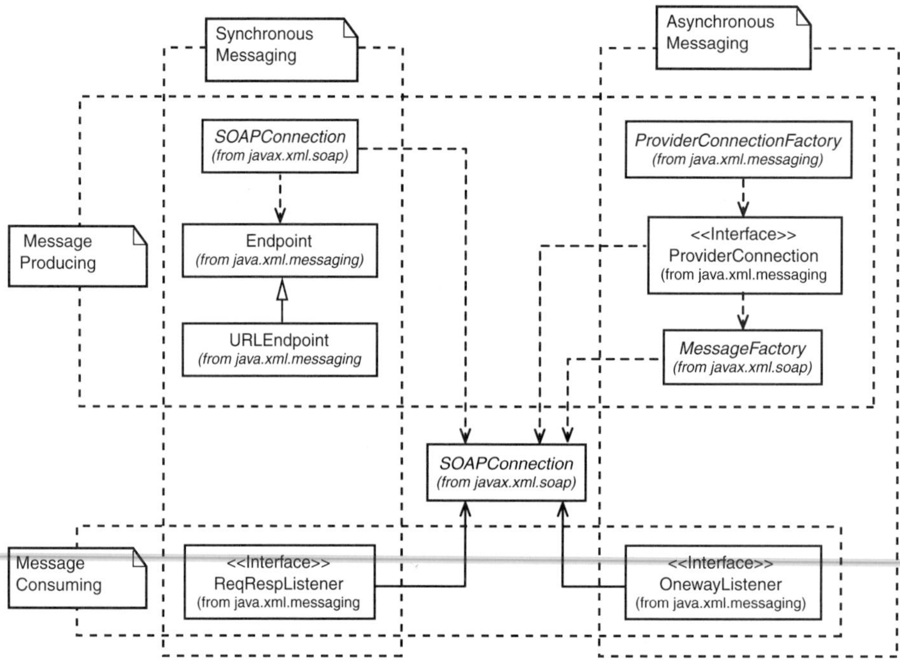

Figure 15.21 JAXM architecture overview.

On the left side of Figure 15.21, we see the abstractions involved with synchronous SOAP messaging. The producer-related abstractions are at the top of the diagram, whereas the consumer-related abstractions are at the bottom. A SOAP connection (from SAAJ) uses endpoints defined by the JAXM API to produce a SOAP message in a synchronous point-to-point fashion. A JAXM request and response listener may be implemented on the consumer side to receive and respond to SOAP messages in a synchronous fashion.

On the right side of Figure 15.21, we see the abstractions involved with asynchronous SOAP messaging. This is clearly the most important usage and feature of JAXM. At the top of the diagram on the right side, a JAXM messaging provider is used to create and produce a SOAP message that is then sent over the provider connection in an asynchronous fashion. In the lower-right part of the diagram, we see that a JAXM one-way listener handles consuming SOAP messages in an asynchronous fashion. In what follows, we examine the JAXM API in detail and discuss how it can be used to produce and consume SOAP messages in both a synchronous and an asynchronous fashion.

JAXM Endpoints

An endpoint represents a physical location at which a message is to be received. Programmatically, some logical address mechanism is needed to identify this physical location. Such addressing information may be contained within a message header or may be external to the message. JAXM provides the `Endpoint` class shown in Figure 15.22 for identifying such information as a URI external to a message header.

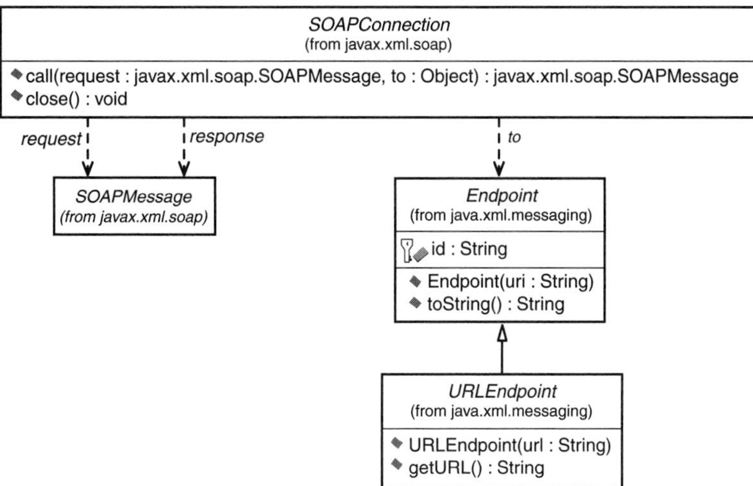

Figure 15.22 JAXM endpoints.

An `Endpoint` object may be passed as a parameter to a SAAJ `SOAPConnection` object's `call()` method. Such an invocation is made when making a synchronous point-to-point call as discussed in Chapter 10, "Web Service Communications." The `SOAPMessage` passed into the `call()` method thus does not have any implied destination information baked into the SOAP header. This is why the destination information may be specified within an `Endpoint` object and passed. The `URLEndpoint` class may also be used as a specialized form of `Endpoint` with location address information stored as a URL.

JAXM Messaging Providers

Although synchronous messaging may be performed using JAXM endpoint abstractions, it is likely that you would use pure SAAJ and JAX-RPC for most synchronous Web service communication situations. JAXM's main advantage is in its asynchronous messaging capabilities offered by an underlying messaging provider. Figure 15.23 depicts the most useful aspect of JAXM in terms of its encapsulation of messaging providers and using them to send messages asynchronously.

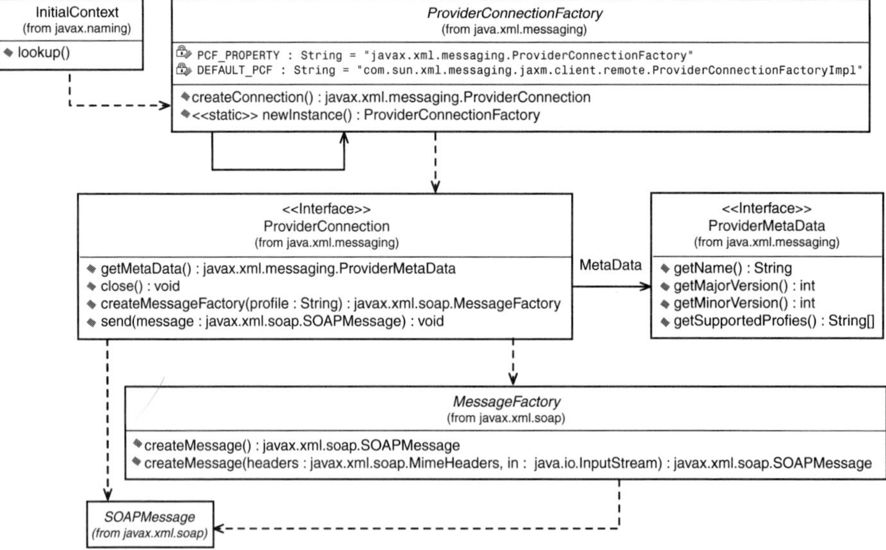

Figure 15.23 JAXM messaging providers.

A handle to a `ProviderConnectionFactory` must first be obtained in some fashion. Inside of a J2EE container, one might use JNDI to look up a handle to a `ProviderConnectionFactory` as such:

```
InitialContext ctx = new InitialContext();
ProviderConnectionFactory cf
  = (ProviderConnectionFactory) ctx.lookup("SomeProvider");
```

Otherwise, the default `ProviderConnectionFactory` may be gotten by invoking the static `newInstance()` method as shown here:

```
ProviderConnectionFactory cf = ProviderConnectionFactory.newInstance();
```

Subsequently, a handle to a `ProviderConnection` may be gotten from the `ProviderConnectionFactory` by invoking the `createConnection()` method. When the `ProviderConnection` object is instantiated, it can use whatever messaging provider profiles are allowed by the underlying JAXM implementation. The JAXM reference implementation can support both the SOAP-RP and the ebXML profiles. A particular JAXM runtime implementation may even allow the specification of which underlying provider profiles can be used via configuration files. Here's an example of obtaining a `ProviderConnection` handle:

```
ProviderConnection conn = cf.createConnection();
```

The `ProviderConnection` object is consulted to obtain a SAAJ `MessageFactory` object via the `createMessageFactory()` method. A String name of the particular messaging profile to be used (for example, `ebxml`) is passed to this method, which returns a `MessageFactory` object that can be used to create `SOAPMessage` objects adhering to the particular messaging profile. The SAAJ `MessageFactory` and `SOAPMessage` are manipulated as described in Chapter 10. As an example, the `MessageFactory` may be constructed like this:

```
MessageFactory mf = conn.createMessageFactory("ebxml");
```

The `SOAPMessage` may then be cast to the class type of the specific message profile implementation provided by your JAXM implementation. In the case of the JAXM reference implementation, a `com.sun.xml.messaging.jaxm.ebxml.EbXMLMessageImpl` class is used for an ebXML profile, and a `com.sun.xml.messaging.jaxm.soaprp.SOAPRPMessageImpl` class is used for a SOAP-RP profile, both of which ultimately extend the `SOAPMessage` class. Here's an example:

```
// Possibly cast SOAPMessage to specific message
// profile class such as:
//   com.sun.xml.messaging.jaxm.ebxml.EbXMLMessageImpl
//   com.sun.xml.messaging.jaxm.soaprp.SOAPRPMessageImpl
EbXMLMessageImpl msgProf = (EbXMLMessageImpl) msg;
```

After a `SOAPMessage` is created and possibly cast to a specific message profile type, the content of the message may be populated. You might use the methods on the `SOAPMessage` directly to populate the message as shown here:

```
// Add information to SOAPMessage using SAAJ API
SOAPPart soapPart= msg.getSOAPPart();
SOAPEnvelope envelope = soapPart.getEnvelope();
SOAPBody body = envelope.getBody();
Name name = envelope.createName(...);
SOAPElement e1 = body.addChildElement(name);
SOAPElement e2 = e1.addChildElement("state");
SOAPElement e3 = e2.addTextNode("VA");
```

You might also use the methods defined on the message profile `SOAPMessage` subtype as illustrated here for the JAXM reference implementation's ebXML profile:

```
// Add information using profile-specific API
Party producer = new Party("http://vendors.beeshirts.com");
Party consumer = new Party("http://orders.wowweeshirts.com");
msgProf.setSender(producer);
msgProf.setReceiver(consumer);
```

The message then may be sent in an asynchronous fashion by invoking the `send()` method on the `ProviderConnection` object. The `send()` method returns immediately after invocation and does not block as the message provider handles the asynchronous delivery of the SOAP message. The `close()` method can also be invoked on the `ProviderConnection` in order to inform the underlying messaging provider implementation to clean up any resources associated with the connection. Thus, the invocation on the `ProviderConnection` and cleanup is as simple as this:

```
conn.send(msg);
conn.close();
```

The `ProviderConnection` object's `getMetaData()` method may also be invoked to obtain a handle to a `ProviderMetaData` object that provides information about the underlying messaging provider's profiles and support. The name of the provider, major version number, and minor version number may be obtained via appropriately named `ProviderMetaData` methods depicted in Figure 15.23. The `getSupportedProfiles()` method returns an array of `String` objects that identify those messaging profiles supported by the messaging provider implementation. Here's an example:

```
ProviderMetaData providerInfo = conn.getMetaData();
String[] msgProfiles = providerInfo.getSupportedProfiles();
for(int i=0; i < msgProfiles.length; ++i){
  if(msgProfiles[i].equals("ebxml")){
    System.out.println("ebXML is supported");
  }
  else{
    System.out.println(msgProfiles[i] + " is supported");
  }
}
```

JAXM Messaging Services

The JAXM abstractions examined thus far describe how JAXM can be used on the producer side of the SOAP messaging paradigm. That is, a JAXM endpoint and SAAJ connection abstractions may be used to send synchronous SOAP messages, and the JAXM messaging provider abstractions may be used to send asynchronous SOAP messages. On the server side, a JAXM runtime may also be used to handle such messages. Figure 15.24 depicts such JAXM-based messaging service implementations.

A synchronous SOAP messaging service implementation implements a special `ReqRespListener` interface that takes a `SOAPMessage` as a request and produces a `SOAPMessage` response. The implementation thus implies a synchronous message handling consumer paradigm whereby the producer is assumed to block until the `SOAPMessage` response can be generated and delivered back to the producer.

An asynchronous SOAP messaging service implementation implements the `OnewayListener` interface. This implementation takes a `SOAPMessage` as input and then simply goes off to do some unit of work. The implementation may or may not produce a response of some sort to the producer. If a response of some sort is generated, it is delivered to the producer as if the producer is now a consumer and the message service implementation is itself a message producer. That is, the producer of the SOAP message to the service implementation does not block and simply receives a response at some later time. Of course, some means for correlating the asynchronous response with the original request will be provided in some messaging profile–specific fashion.

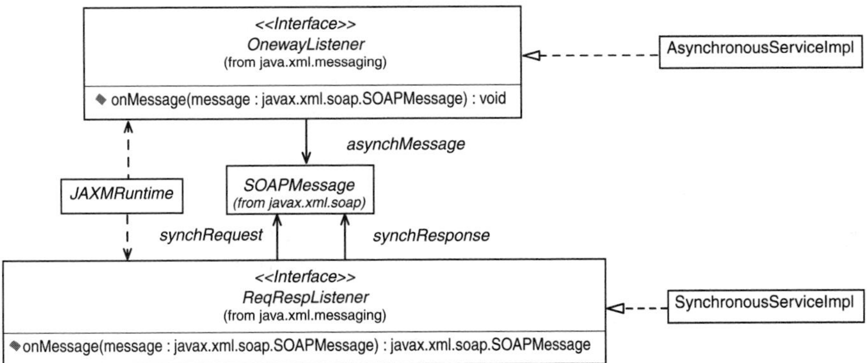

Figure 15.24 JAXM messaging services.

JAXM Service Deployment

As depicted in Figure 15.24, a JAXM runtime handles determining how to delegate the SOAP message to an appropriate JAXM messaging service instance. The JAXM messaging service implementation instance is most likely implemented as a stateless object. However, it is conceivable that a particular messaging profile can embed the concept of a session identifier into a message such that a stateful message service can be implemented by the JAXM runtime.

In the context of a J2EE environment, a Java servlet or EJB container is the most appropriate implementation of a JAXM runtime. In the case of a servlet container with a JAXM runtime extension, the servlet container handles delegating requests to a Java servlet component. A special `JAXMServlet` helper class is provided by the JAXM API that can be used to receive SOAP/HTTP messages. In the case of an EJB container with a JAXM runtime extension, the EJB container handles delegating requests to an EJB component.

Although such support may be provided by J2EE containers, the J2EE v1.4 specification does not require JAXM support. The EJB v2.1 specification, which is included by reference in the J2EE v1.4 standard, does very briefly indicate a way that message-driven asynchronous EJBs can designate that they will receive SOAP messages via JAXM. We discuss such implementation possibilities as appropriate in later chapters of the book.

Nevertheless, because J2EE v1.4 does not require JAXM support, there is a gaping standards hole in how JAXM services can be implemented and deployed inside of J2EE containers. That is, there is no standard way to deploy JAXM services inside J2EE containers, and there is also no standard deployment descriptor mechanism specifying how JAXM services and providers are configured inside of a J2EE container. Thus, vendors that have decided to implement JAXM functionality do so in a nonstandard fashion. Furthermore, the fate of JAXM is also questionable because more than a few J2EE vendors have considered the JAXM API to be too confusing to developers and too redundant with the JMS API. As such, the JAXM API may go the way of being deprecated in the future, integrated with the JMS API, maintained as a separate API and integrated into the J2EE, or forever remain a separated API external to the J2EE.

Conclusions

We have explored the fundamental concepts involved with messaging services and examples in the context of JMS- and JAXM-based messaging services in this chapter. Messaging services provide a means for message producers to send messages to message consumers in an asynchronous and time-independent fashion. Message consumers can also pull messages from a messaging service at their convenience, receive messages directly queued to them from a messaging service, or receive messages to which they've subscribed based on a topic name. Messaging services provide all of this functionality in a manner that enhances the underlying reliability and availability of applications that tap their services.

Although various MOM implementations can be used for messaging in Java applications, JMS provides a standard Java-based messaging API and SPI framework that can be used to tap into different messaging implementations. Furthermore, JMS is part of the J2EE standard suite of enterprise components. JMS offers a core and generic API that may be used to send and receive messages in a generic fashion independent of any particular messaging domain model. JMS also has APIs that are derived from the core and generic JMS API to provide domain-specific messaging behavior for point-to-point messaging via message queues and publish-subscribe messaging via message topics. JMS is clearly the most generic and standard way to infuse MOM functionality into your J2EE applications. Alternatively for XML-based messaging, an enterprise Java developer may use the JAXM API albeit in a non–J2EE-compliant fashion.

16

JavaMail

THE VARIOUS MESSAGING SERVICES DESCRIBED so far in this book have a generic enterprise application nature. Email messaging systems also have a very important albeit application-specific role in the enterprise. JavaMail provides a way to interact with an email messaging system. Using JavaMail, enterprise applications can both send and receive email messages via the Internet. The JavaMail v1.3 API is included with the J2EE v1.4. In addition, as part of the J2EE specification, a mail server is required to support the JavaMail API. In this chapter, we will briefly cover the basic concepts involved in understanding email messaging systems. We will also describe the JavaMail API, and then delve into a specific JavaMail API example.

In this chapter, you will learn:

- The general concepts surrounding email messaging systems
- An overview of the JavaMail API architecture
- The generic JavaMail message architecture
- The Internet-specific MIME-based JavaMail message architecture
- The JavaMail architecture for encapsulating events and receiving notification of events
- The means for establishing and managing email sessions with an email server
- The means for receiving, storing, and managing email messages in a message store and folders
- The means for sending email via a message transport
- A concrete example for using JavaMail to send and receive email messages

Email Messaging Systems

Although email messaging systems can have various underlying protocol implementations, by far the most popular implementations are those defined by the Internet protocol suite. Email is typically sent from an email client using a standard Internet transport protocol. Email is then stored in a repository and later retrieved by email clients with the help of another standard Internet protocol.

Email Messages

An email message has a header and a body. Email headers are text-based name/value pairs identifying characteristics of a message, such as the sender email address, destination email address(es), subject information, and sent date. Most email addresses adhere to the format `UserName@HostName.DomainName`, such as `pperrone@babbage.assuredtech.com`. If a specific host name for a mail server is excluded, DNS attributes associated with the domain name by the DNS can be referenced to determine the specific mail server name to which the email message should be delivered.

The body of a mail message is defined by the Multipurpose Internet Mail Extensions (MIME) standard. MIME message bodies have multiple parts to them that can assume different multimedia forms, including text, audio, images, and file attachments. MIME has a set of standard headers defined for it that includes content encoding format for any binary data and content type fields such as those defined in Table E.1 of Appendix E, "HTTP Communications." In addition to the types defined in Appendix E, a `multipart` MIME type can be defined to identify the fact that multiple parts of a message are embedded into the message itself. The body of such a multipart message then contains one or more body parts, each with its own content type.

The multipart MIME type can be associated with various subtypes. The `mixed` subtype indicates that the body parts are independent and packaged in a particular sequence. An `alternative` subtype designates that the body parts represent alternative versions of one another, with the last body part being the most desirable form. A `digest` subtype changes the value of a body part from one type to a type that is more readable. The `parallel` subtype designates that the order of the body parts is irrelevant.

SMTP

The Simple Mail Transfer Protocol (SMTP) is a protocol that operates above TCP/IP and is used as a messaging transport for sending and receiving email messages. SMTP servers listen on a default port of 25. SMTP clients communicate with SMTP servers using a simple set of text-based commands. After establishing a connection, SMTP clients first issue a command to identify their email address in order to receive responses. The SMTP client then issues a command to identify the destination address. If the SMTP server accepts the sender and receiver identification commands, it acknowledges each command with an `OK` response. Another command sent by the client then signifies the beginning of the email message body, which is terminated with a period (`.`) on a line by itself. The SMTP server will then deliver the message to its destination.

SMTP is purely an email transport protocol. This means that there is no storage or queuing mechanism associated with SMTP itself. This is why SMTP is often used in conjunction with another messaging service that provides queuing of the email sent to a receiver by a sender for later retrieval by the receiver. The POP and IMAP protocols both provide such support.

POP

Post Office Protocol Version 3 (POP3) describes a standard mechanism for queuing mail messages for later retrieval by receivers. POP3 servers also operate over TCP/IP and listen on a default port of 110. After an initial handshake between a client and a server, a sequence of text-based commands can be exchanged. POP3 clients authenticate themselves with a POP3 server using a password-based authentication method with a username and password. Authentication in POP3 occurs over an unencrypted session. A series of commands from the POP3 client may then be issued to the POP3 server, such as the request of status for the client's mailbox queue, requests for listing mailbox queue contents, and requests to retrieve the actual messages.

POP represents a store-and-forward type of messaging service that forwards email to the POP client on request and deletes it from the POP server queue. Many hosts are set up to let you use SMTP to send mail and POP3 to receive email messages.

IMAP

The Internet Message Access Protocol (IMAP) is an email message queuing service that represents an improvement over POP's store-and-forward limitations. IMAP also uses a text-based command syntax over TCP/IP with IMAP servers typically listening on the default port 143. IMAP servers enable IMAP clients to download header information for an email and do not impose the requirements for downloading entire messages from the server to client as does POP. Folders of email messages can also be remotely maintained and managed on the IMAP server. IMAP servers provide a queuing mechanism to receive messages and must also be used in conjunction with SMTP's capability to send messages.

JavaMail Architecture Overview

The top-level architecture of the JavaMail v1.3 system is depicted in Figure 16.1. Sessions with a mail server are encapsulated by the `Session` object. A `Session` object can be used to obtain a handle to a message `Store` service (for example, POP or IMAP server) and a message `Transport` service (for example, SMTP server). The `Store` and `Transport` services both extend a generic `Service` object. A mail `Store` can store messages in one or more mail `Folder` objects. A hierarchy of `SearchTerm` objects can be used to search for messages in a folder using sophisticated search criteria based on email message attributes.

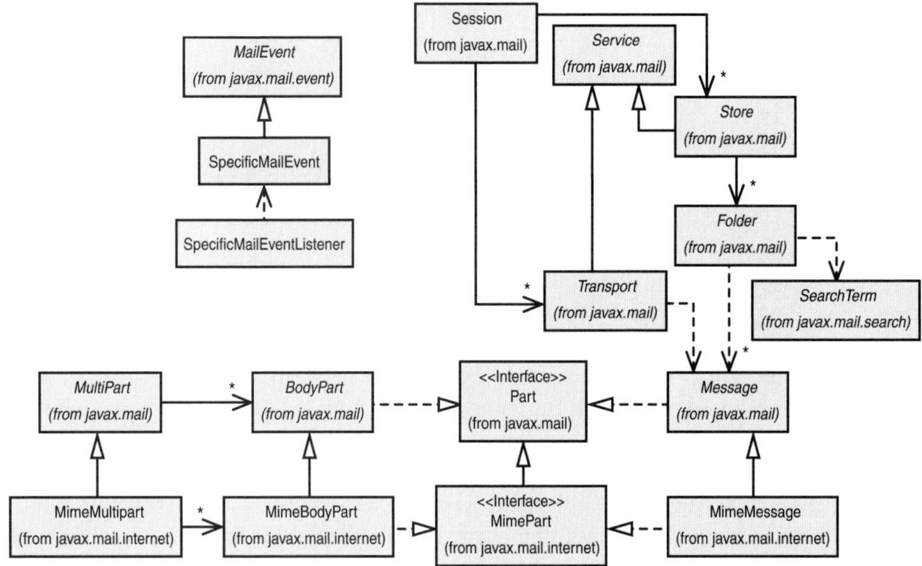

Figure 16.1 The JavaMail architecture.

Email messages are encapsulated by the `Message` object and by using a concrete `MimeMessage` object to encapsulate email messages on the Internet. `Multipart` objects encapsulate messages with multiple `BodyPart` elements. Concrete `MimeMultipart` and `MimeBodyPart` message implementations also exist. The `Part/MimePart` interfaces define a set of common operations implemented by both `BodyPart/MimeBodyPart` and `Message/MimeMessage` objects.

JavaMail also defines an event model for mail-system event handling. Mail-system events are implemented as specific mail event objects. Specific mail event listeners are also defined for each mail event type.

All of this mail-system interface functionality is implemented across four packages provided with JavaMail v1.3 associated with the J2EE v1.4:

- `javax.mail`: Defines the basic JavaMail utilities and mail message system abstractions.
- `javax.mail.internet`: Defines a concrete implementation of the JavaMail abstractions for an Internet mail system using MIME messages.
- `javax.mail.event`: Defines mail-system events and listeners.
- `javax.mail.search`: Defines a hierarchy of search items used to express search criteria when searching for messages in mail folders.

Generic Email Parts and Messages

The JavaMail API defines a set of generic abstractions that encapsulate the concepts of email message parts and email messages as a whole. Figure 16.2 depicts the basic architecture of an email messaging part forming the top-level abstraction for such a generic email message hierarchy. The `Part` interface defines a set of operations that can be performed on a mail message part. Objects that implement a part have data content that can be returned as a Java object using the `Part.getContent()` call, as a message-specific stream using the `Part.getInputStream()` call, and as a `javax.activation.DataHandler` object using the `Part.getDataHandler()` call. The `DataHandler` class is utilized from the JAF (discussed in Chapter 7, "Enterprise Communications"), and it allows access to data in different formats, discovers how to manipulate data, and can solicit data manipulation help from content handlers. Various getters and setters for common attributes of a message part are also defined on the `Part` interface. Message headers that are associated with a part can be retrieved and set on the `Part` interface. A name/value pair field of a header is represented by the `Header` class.

Figure 16.3 represents the abstract JavaMail message architecture. The abstract `Message` class encapsulates an email message. A `Message` implements the `Part` interface and defines additional attributes above and beyond what the `Part` interface defines. Attributes specific to an email message have setters and getters and include a subject, sent date, and received date. Various endpoint address attributes are also associated with a `Message` and include message "from" addresses, recipient addresses, and "reply-to" addresses. Each address is encapsulated by the `Address` object, which defines an address type and value for the address. When a `Message` object is retrieved by an application from a message store, not all of its attribute values will be populated. Attributes of a message are often retrieved as an application requests them from the `Message` interface.

The `Message` class also has an inner class called `RecipientType`. The `RecipientType` class is used to identify those recipients allowed for a particular message. Recipient types include primary recipients ("`TO`"), carbon copy recipients ("`CC`"), and blind carbon copy recipients ("`BCC`"). The `Message.RecipientType` inner class is used as an enumerated type when invoking the `getRecipients()` and `addRecipient()` methods on the `Message` class (for example, `message.getRecipients(Message.RecipientType.TO)`).

`Message` objects also have flags associated with them that indicate the state of the message in a message store. The `Flags` class encapsulates this state of a message. User-defined flags can be added and removed as `String` objects to a `Flags` object. A set of system-defined flags can also be identified using the `Flag` class, which is an inner class to the `Flags` class. The system flags that describe a message's state as defined by the `Flags.Flag` inner class are listed here:

- `ANSWERED`: Message has been answered.
- `DELETED`: Message has been deleted.
- `DRAFT`: Message is a working draft.
- `FLAGGED`: Message has been flagged with no particular meaning associated with the flag.

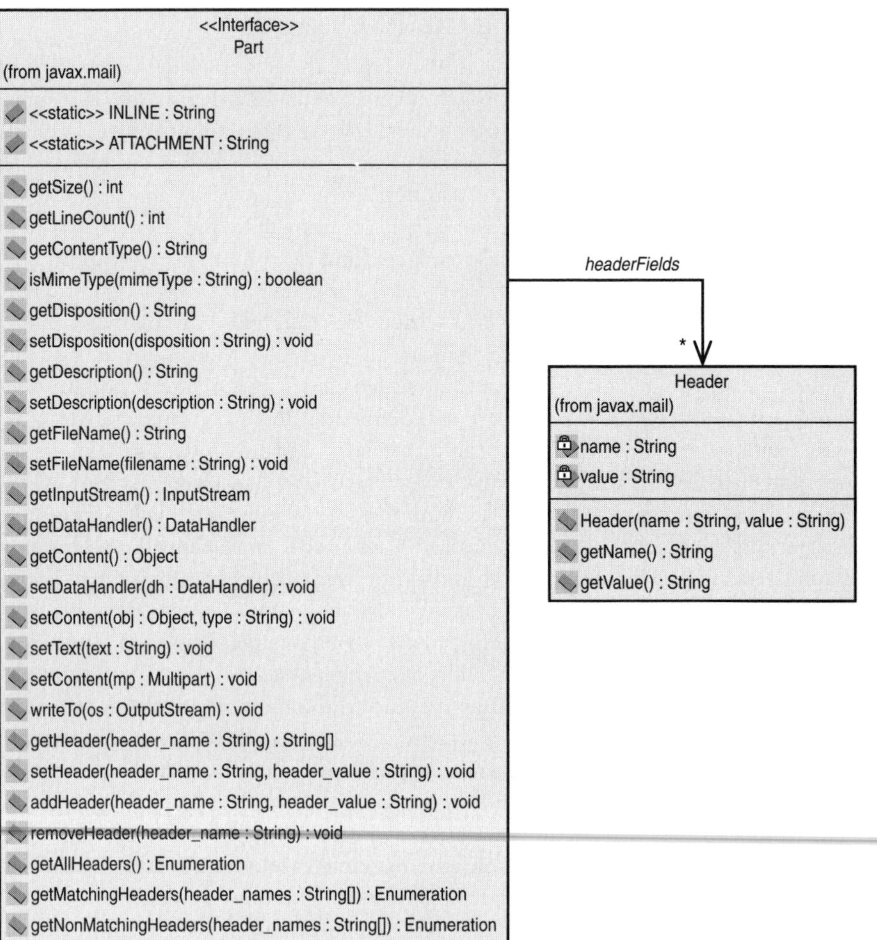

Figure 16.2 JavaMail parts.

- `RECENT`: Message is recent.
- `SEEN`: Message has been examined.
- `USER`: Message can have user-defined flags associated with it.

Multipart message abstractions are also defined by the JavaMail API, as shown in Figure 16.4. The `Multipart` abstract class contains multiple parts of a message. Each message part that belongs to a `Multipart` message is encapsulated by the abstract `BodyPart` class, which implements the `Part` interface. Aside from methods to add, remove, and retrieve `BodyPart` elements from a multipart message, the `Multipart` class can also return the MIME content type via the `getContentType()` method.

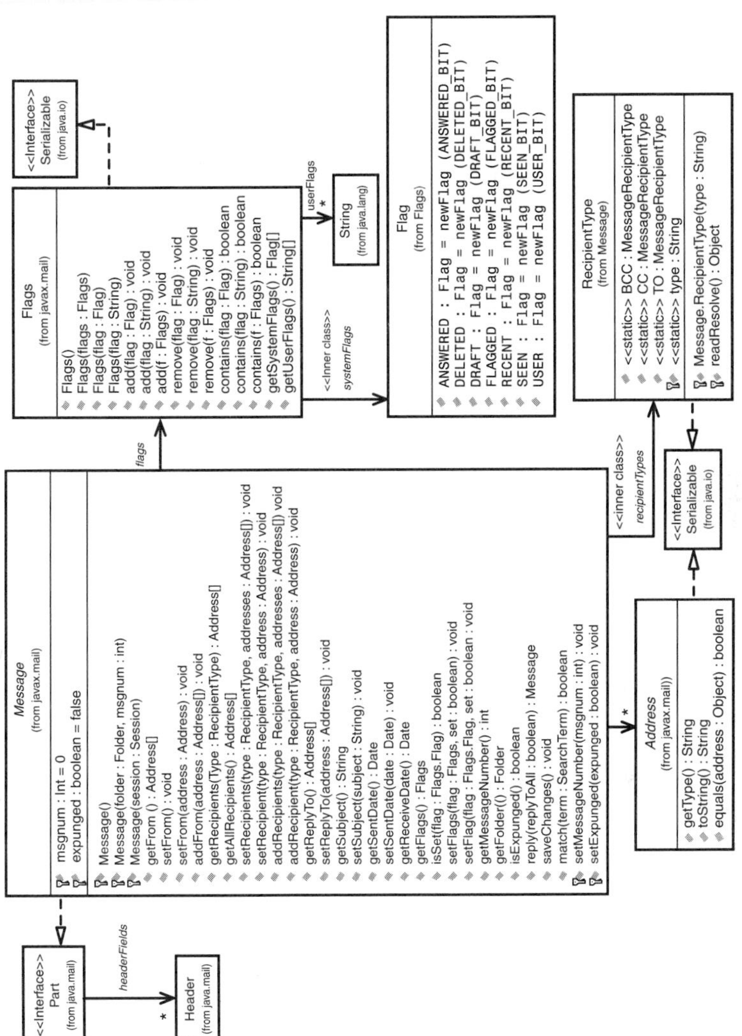

Figure 16.3 JavaMail messages.

The protected `Multipart.setMultipartDataSource()` method is set by concrete subclasses of a `Multipart` message to establish the data source of body-part data for the `Multipart` object. The `MultipartDataSource` interface is implemented by classes as a means to separate data-source location and protocol from the simple matter of reading `BodyPart` elements for the `Multipart` message. The `MessageAware` interface may also be implemented by a data source to return a context for the message. A `MessageContext` class encapsulates this message context by returning a handle to the part and message containing the message content, as well as the mail session in which the message is being manipulated.

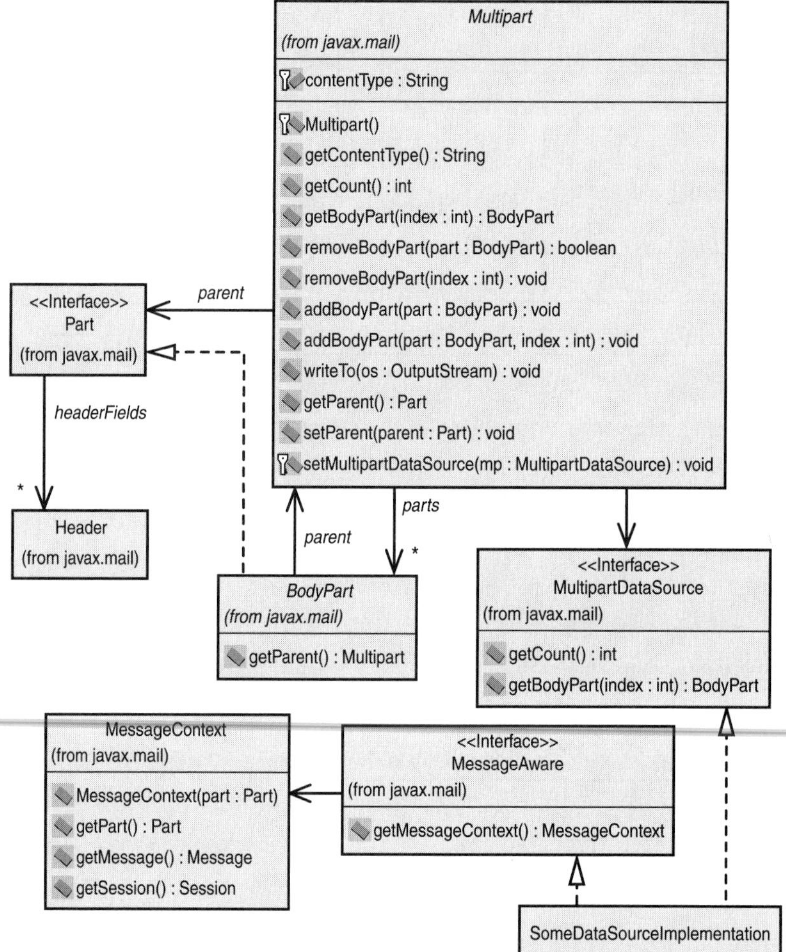

Figure 16.4 JavaMail multipart messages and data sources.

MIME Parts and Messages

In addition to the generic email part and message abstractions defined by the JavaMail API, a set of concrete abstractions specific to email messaging using MIME parts is also defined. The `MimePart` interface shown in Figure 16.5 extends the `Part` interface with additional semantics provided to work with parts of a MIME message. Individual header lines, the MIME content ID, MIME encoding, the MIME MD5 message digest, and MIME content language tags can all be retrieved from a `MimePart` object. Additionally, lines to the header, content language tags, and content text can also be set on a `MimePart` object.

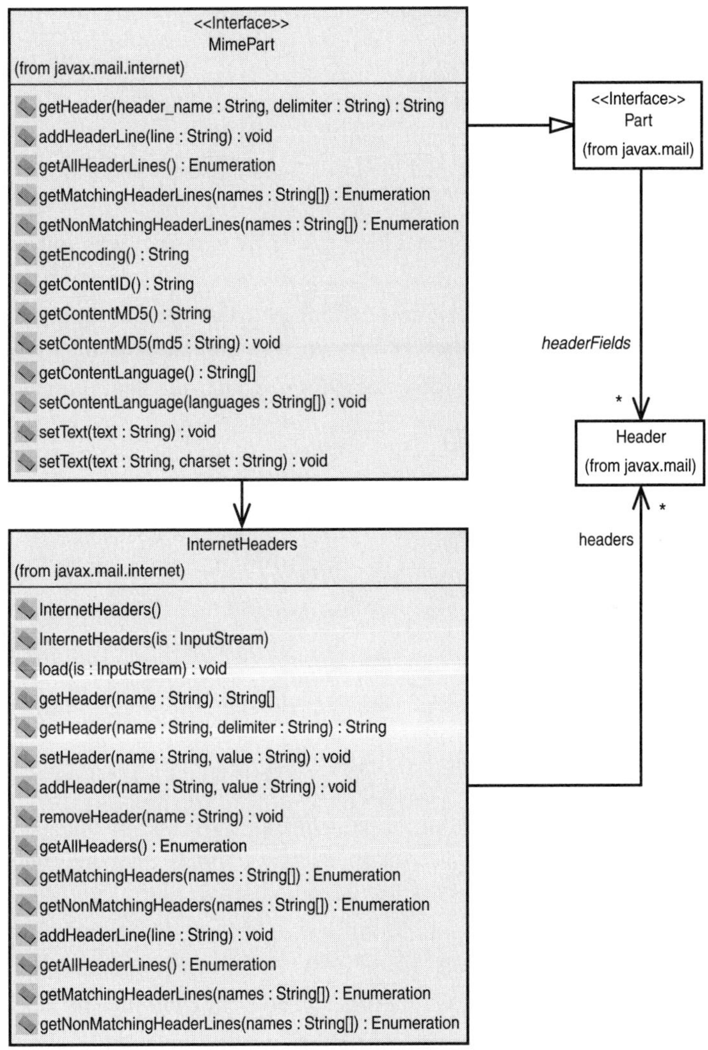

Figure 16.5 JavaMail MIME parts.

`MimePart` objects are associated with `InternetHeaders`. The `InternetHeaders` class represents a collection of individual `Header` fields and provides much of the helper functionality needed by objects that implement `MimePart` interfaces. The `InternetHeaders` class reads `Header` field information from an underlying `InputStream`. The `InternetHeaders` object, mainly used by service providers, transparently provides functionality to the API user via the `MimePart` objects that utilize it.

The `MimeMessage` class shown in Figure 16.6 implements a concrete MIME-style email message by extending the abstract `Message` class and implementing the `MimePart` interface. A `MimeMessage` may be created with an associated mail `Session` object and then have its attributes populated. A `MimeMessage` may also be constructed and initialized with the contents of another `MimeMessage` object.

Various other attributes of a `MimeMessage` may also be set, retrieved, and possibly removed based on appropriately named methods. Such `MimeMessage` attributes are listed here:

- `Recipients`: Multiple recipient addresses to which a message is sent may be added, set, and retrieved.
- `From Addresses`: Multiple addresses from which an email is sent may be added, set, and retrieved. A local address is used when no from address is specified.
- `Reply To Addresses`: Multiple addresses to which an email is replied may be added, set, and retrieved.
- `Sender Address`: The sender address indicating from whom an email was sent may be set as a sender field in the MIME message.
- `Subject`: The subject of the message may be set and retrieved.
- `Sent Date`: The date a message was sent may be set and retrieved.
- `Received Date`: The date a message was received may be retrieved.
- `Headers`: Message header names and values may be added, set, retrieved, and removed.
- `Content`: The message content as an object and the content's data handler may be retrieved and set. MIME type content that is "plain/text" may also be set as a text string for convenience.
- `Content Fields`: The content ID, content language, content MD5, content type, content description, content disposition, content transfer encoding, and content filename field information may be retrieved and set.
- `Content Line Count`: The line count for the message's content may be retrieved.
- `Content Size`: The size of the message's content in bytes may be retrieved.
- `Message ID`: The message's message ID field may be retrieved.

Two Internet-specific types of addresses provide concrete implementations of the abstract `Address` class, as shown in Figure 16.6. The `InternetAddress` class provides a means for encapsulating a user's Internet email address in RFC-822 format. Information such as the user's email address, the personal name, and any individual address from a group email address may be set and retrieved on the `InternetAddress` object. The `NewsAddress` provides a means to encapsulate an Internet newsgroup address including the newsgroup name and host name.

Figure 16.6 JavaMail MIME messages.

The `MimeMultipart` class shown in Figure 16.7 provides a concrete implementation of the abstract `Multipart` class for MIME multipart data. The `MimeMultipart` object's data source may be a `MimePartDataSource` object that implements a particular data source using a `MimePart` object. The `MimeBodyPart` class provides a concrete implementation of an abstract `BodyPart` class for MIME type messages and implements the `MimePart` interface. `MimeBodyPart` objects are contained inside of `MimeMultipart` object messages.

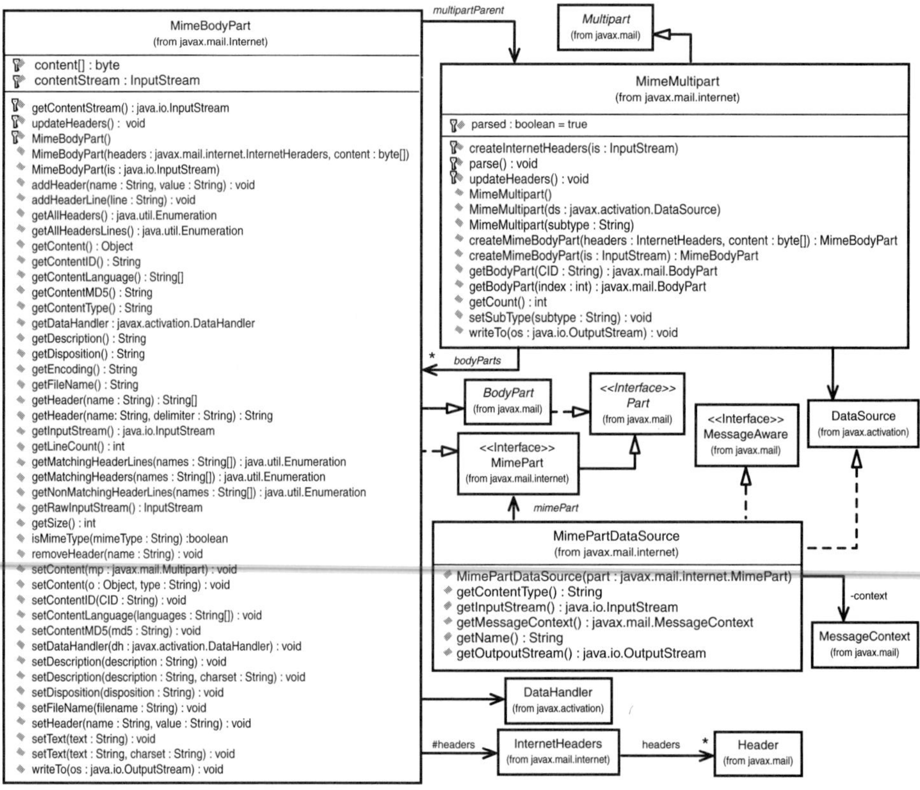

Figure 16.7 JavaMail multipart MIME messages and MIME data sources.

The `MimeBodyPart` class also provides a host of getter and setter type methods to manage various attributes associated with a MIME body part akin to getters and setters defined for the `MimeMessage` class shown in Figure 16.6. Such commonality of attributes should come as no surprise because both the `MimeBodyPart` and `MimeMessage` classes represent abstract MIME parts. Accordingly, both the `MimeBodyPart` and `MimeMessage` classes implement the `MimePart` interface.

There is also a set of helper classes and interfaces that can be used when working closely with MIME-based data. Although most JavaMail API users will not use these helper classes, it is at least useful to point them out in case you ever do need to parse low-level MIME-based data. The MIME-based helper classes and interfaces are listed here for your reference:

- `ParameterList`: Encapsulates a collection of MIME attribute name/value pairs.
- `ContentDisposition`: Encapsulates a MIME `ContentDisposition` value with parsing functionality as well as getters and setters for content disposition string values, parameters, and parameter lists.
- `ContentType`: Encapsulates a MIME `ContentType` value with parsing functionality as well as getters and setters for the content base type string values, primary type string values, subtype string values, parameters, and parameter lists.
- `HeaderTokenizer`: Encapsulates a means to parse and tokenize headers in a MIME message. Also includes an inner class named `HeaderTokenizer.Token` that defines constant names for MIME token types such as an atom, a comment, end of input, and a quoted string.
- `MailDateFormat`: Extends the `java.text.SimpleDateFormat` class and encapsulates a means for parsing and representing a time and date inside of a MIME message.
- `MimeUtility`: Encapsulates a means to parse, decode, and encode data inside of MIME messages.
- `SharedInputStream`: Defines an interface for representing email data that is shared by concurrent readers.

JavaMail Event Architecture

Figure 16.8 depicts the event architecture utilized by the JavaMail APIs. The JavaMail event model follows the basic Java event model architecture with events specializing in the `EventObject` class and event listeners extending the `EventListener` class. A base `MailEvent` class encapsulates a general event occurring somewhere in the mail system. Event listener interfaces that have more than one method defined have an associated event listener adapter class defined. Event listener adapters provide a set of empty method implementations as a convenience, so developers extending a listener need only implement the methods they want to override.

The various event/listener combinations defined for JavaMail events are shown here:

- *Connection Event Model:* Manages mail session connection opening, closing, and disconnect events.
- *Folder Event Model:* Manages mail folder creation, deletion, and renaming events.
- *Store Event Model:* Manages mail message notification events.

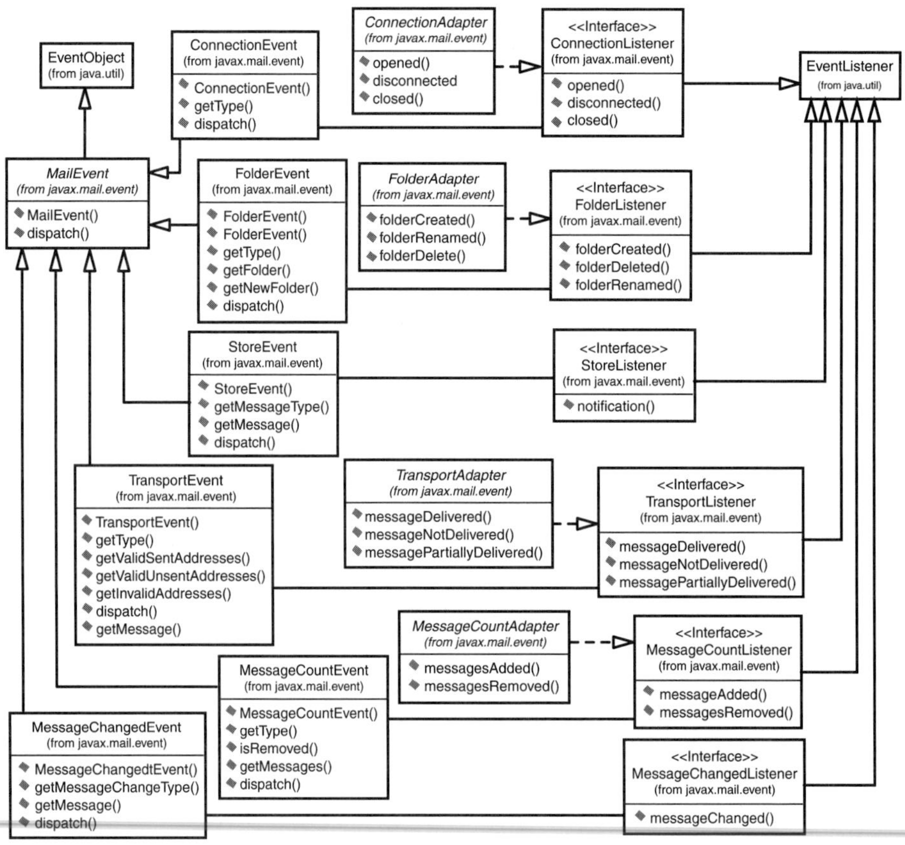

Figure 16.8 JavaMail events.

- *Transport Event Model:* Manages mail communication delivery, nondelivery, and partial-delivery events.
- *Message Count Event Model:* Manages message folder addition and deletion events.
- *Message Changed Event Model:* Manages message content change events.

Creating Mail Sessions

Before a JavaMail client can interact with an email messaging system, it must establish a mail session with a mail server. The entities involved in establishing a JavaMail session are depicted in Figure 16.9. The `Session` class encapsulates a session with a mail server. We display only a subset of the total methods on the `Session` class of Figure 16.9 to focus attention on the interfaces relevant to this section. Additional methods on the `Session` class are covered in subsequent sections.

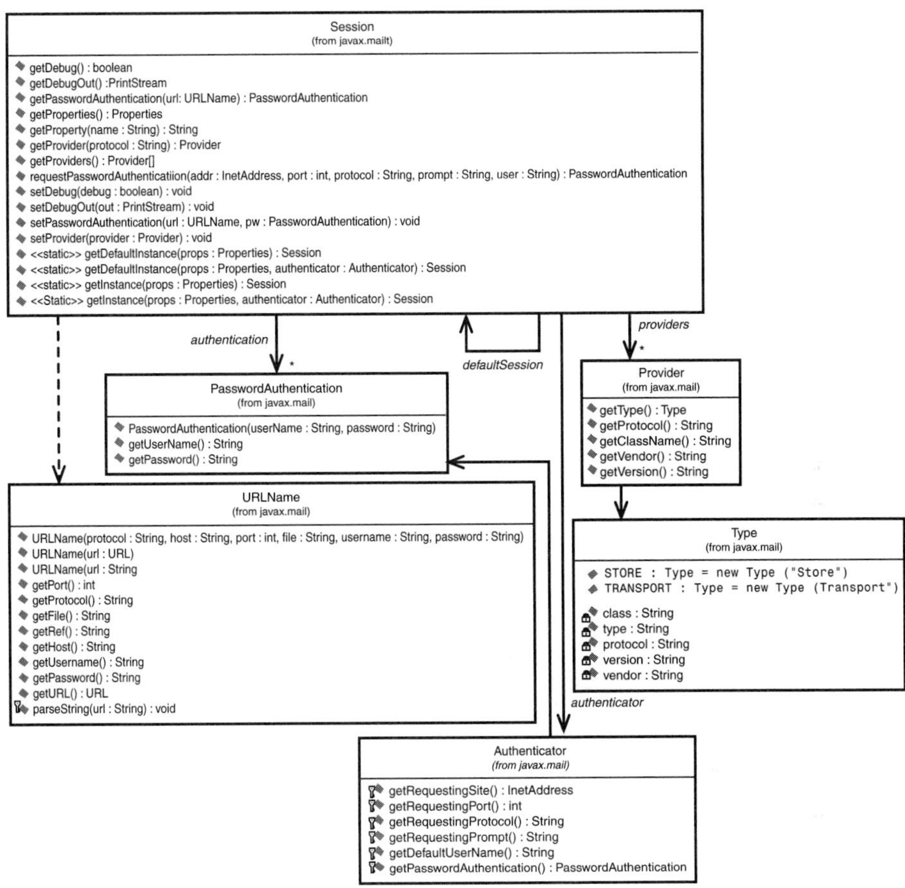

Figure 16.9 JavaMail sessions.

A handle to a `Session` is obtainable from a JNDI context if an application environment, such as the J2EE, has been used to register such objects. Four static methods on the `Session` class can also be used to obtain a `Session` instance. The `getDefaultInstance()` methods are used to return an instance of a mail session that can be shared by other applications running on the same platform. The `getInstance()` methods can be used to create a mail session that is unique and not shared with other applications. Both methods take a `Properties` object as an argument that can have values set with a set of standard property elements. When created, `Session.getProperty()` can return an individual property given a name, and `Session.getProperties()` can return the entire `Properties` collection associated with the session. These are the various session property element types and their descriptions:

- `mail.store.protocol`: Protocol for accessing message store.
- `mail.transport.protocol`: Default protocol for email message transport communications.
- `mail.host`: Default mail server. The `localhost` is the default otherwise.
- `mail.user`: Default user for connecting to mail server. The `user.name` system property is the default.
- `mail.protocol.host`: Protocol-specific mail server host. The `mail.host` system property is the default.
- `mail.protocol.user`: Protocol-specific default username for connecting to the mail server. The `mail.user` system property is the default.
- `mail.from`: Address of sender. The current *`userName@hostName`* is the default.
- `mail.debug`: Initial debug mode. The default is `false`.
- `mime.address.strict`: Indicates whether strict RFC 822–based syntactical processing of email addresses should be followed. The default is `true`.

The J2EE and JavaMail

J2EE components can obtain handles to JavaMail `Session` objects via JNDI. Such a mechanism will be demonstrated in Chapter 29, "EJB Integration and Management," when we describe how Enterprise JavaBeans obtain JavaMail session object handles from their middle-tier container/server environments.

The creation of a `Session` object may also involve the use of an optional `Authenticator` parameter. The abstract `Authenticator` class is extended by service provider implementations that know how to authenticate a user with a mail server. If a `null Authenticator` is used to create a `Session` object using the `Session.getDefaultInstance()` method, and the default instance has already been created, then the `Authenticator` object must match the instance used to create the original session. The `Authenticator` is primarily utilized by the mail messaging service environment as a callback to request user authentication information.

The `PasswordAuthentication` class is used to encapsulate a username and password, which can be set onto the `Session` object using `setPasswordAuthentication(URLName, PasswordAuthentication)` for later use in the session or by other applications. The `URLName` encapsulates the data elements of a URL that, in this case, is used to associate a mail server URL with the password authentication information.

The `Session` class's `getProvider()` and `setProvider()` methods allow a `Provider` object to be retrieved and set, respectively. The `Provider` object encapsulates a handle to an underlying mail service provider implementation. Providers are typically configured in standard files named `javamail.providers` and `javamail.default.providers`. Such files are searched for in the `java.home\lib` directory first and then referenced in the `META-INF` directory of a JAR file in the `CLASSPATH`.

Default files are always referenced after other files have been referenced. Values for providers correspond to the private attributes defined in the package private `Provider.Type` class, as shown earlier in Figure 16.9.

Message Stores and Folders

Figure 16.10 depicts the basic architecture of JavaMail message stores and their relation to generic JavaMail services. The `Service` class is an abstract class encapsulating common mail messaging service functionality. `Service` instances are created by `Session` objects and have a `URLName` associated with them. `Service` objects can be connected to and disconnected from TCP/IP sockets. Connection listeners can also be added to and removed from `Service` objects to be notified of connection events.

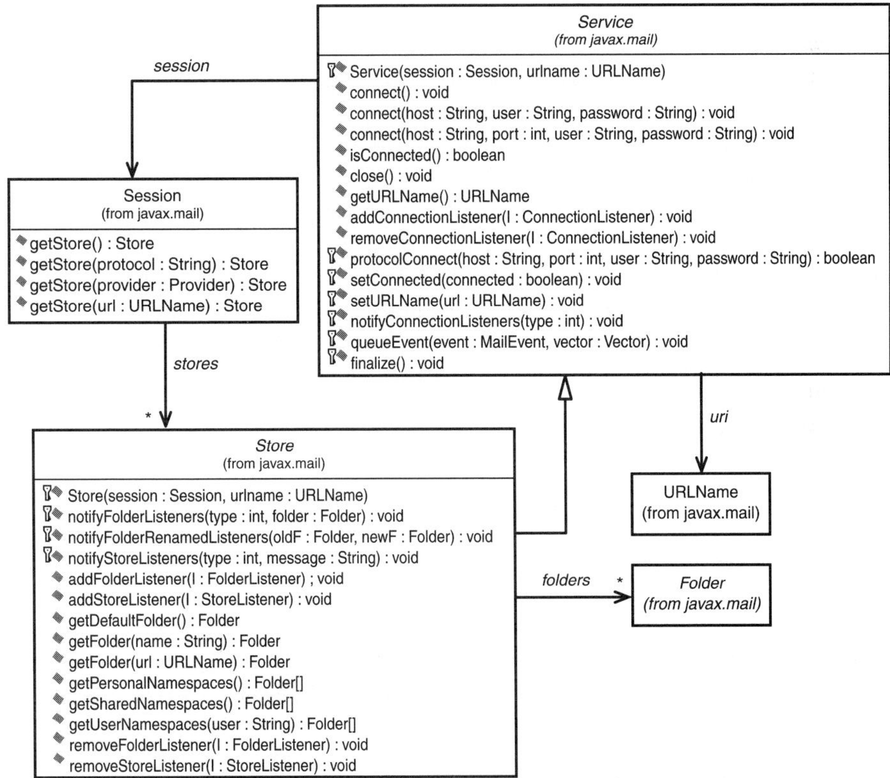

Figure 16.10 The JavaMail message store service.

The `Store` class encapsulates access to a message store. A `Store` object contains one or more folders, represented by the `Folder` class, that hold mail messages. The `Store.getDefaultFolder()` method returns a `Folder` corresponding to the default root folder of the message store. Two `Store.getFolder()` methods also allow a folder to be retrieved using either a `String` form of the folder name or a `URLName`. Store listeners and folder listeners can also be added to and removed from `Store` objects such that clients can be notified of store and folder events.

Folders grouped by different namespaces inside of a message store may also be retrieved. Such grouping according to namespaces is a distinction made by IMAP message stores. The `getPersonalNamespaces()` method returns those folders associated with the current authenticated user's namespace. The `getUserNamespaces(String)` method returns those folders associated with the given `user`. The `namespaces` will be returned only if that user's namespace grants permission to the currently authenticated user. The `getSharedNamespaces()` method returns those folders that have no specific user namespace and that are shared by multiple users.

The `Session` object defines various `getStore()` methods that enable you to retrieve a handle to a `Store`. The `Session.getStore()` method returns a `Store` object defined in the `mail.store.protocol` property. Other versions of the `Session.getStore()` methods also return `Store` objects associated with a `String` name, a `URLName`, and a `Provider` specification.

The `Folder` class, shown in Figure 16.11, encapsulates mail folders in a message store. The contents of a folder can include messages as well as other folders. There are many methods on the `Folder` class. We don't delve into all of these methods here, but we do provide you with a good idea of how each method is generally used.

Folder names are implementation-dependent, and folder elements are arranged in a hierarchical fashion. The folder elements are delimited by an implementation-specific character, specified by `Folder.getSeparator()`. The folder name `INBOX` is reserved to mean the primary folder in which mail messages are received.

Because a `Folder` object is returned from folder retrieval methods regardless of whether the folder exists in the mail store, the `Folder.exists()` method can be used to determine whether the folder does indeed exist. When a `Folder` object is retrieved, it is initially closed. The `Folder.open()` method opens the folder for access. Folders can also be closed, deleted, renamed, and tested for their current state using various intuitively named methods on the `Folder` object. The `Session.getFolder()` can be used to return a closed mail `Folder` object given the folder `URLName`.

The name of the `Folder` can be retrieved in various forms using methods such as `getName()`, `getFullName()`, and `getURLName()`. The containing message store and any parent folder of the `Folder` object can be obtained with calls to `getStore()` and `getParent()`, respectively. A `Folder` object also supports interfaces for notifying listeners of folder events, connection events, message count events, and message change events.

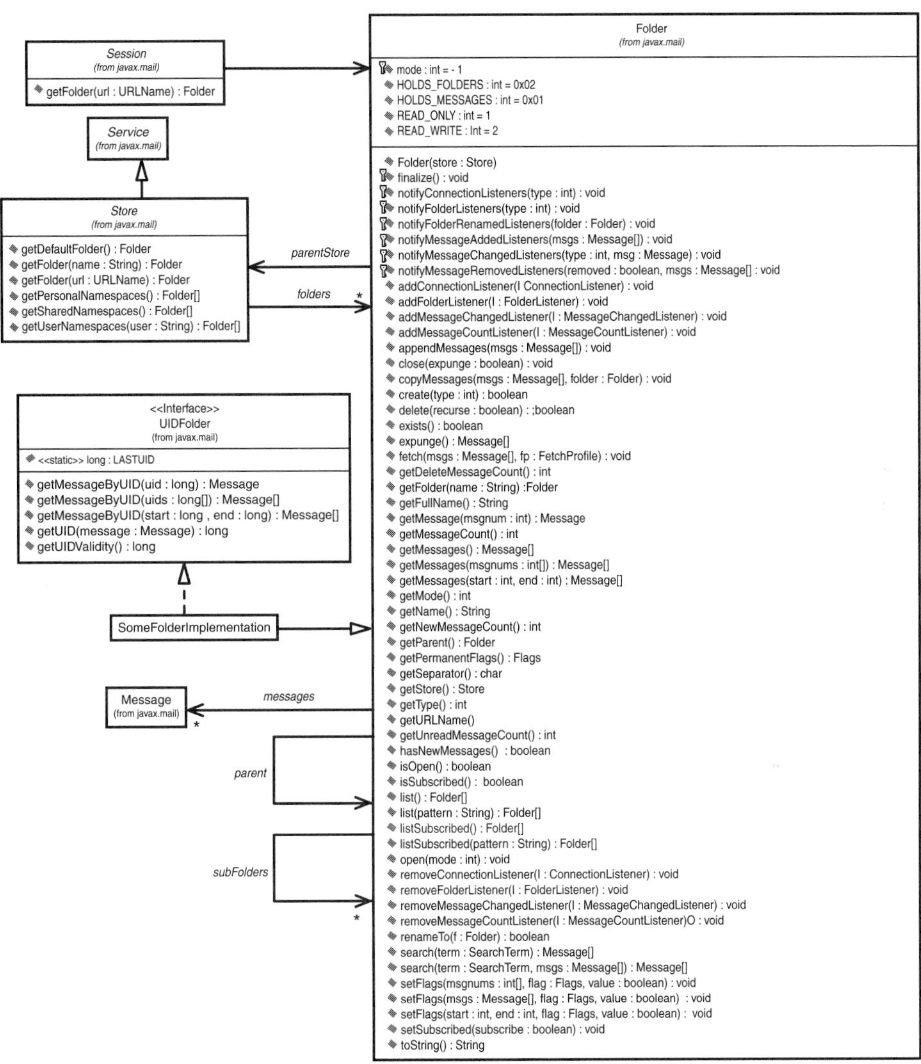

Figure 16.11 JavaMail folders.

The capability of a `Folder` to contain folders and messages is indicated by the `Folder.getType()` method returning a static bit field set with the `HOLDS_FOLDERS` and/or `HOLDS_MESSAGES` bits. The `getMode()` method returns the mode of the folder such as the `READ_ONLY` or `READ_WRITE` constants. The flags that are supported by a folder can be returned from the `getPermanentFlags()` method call.

Various methods exist to manage the messages in the folders as well. The total number of messages, new messages, deleted messages, and unread messages can be obtained via the getMessageCount(), getNewMessageCount(), getDeletedMessageCount(), and getUnreadMessageCount() methods, respectively. An individual message can be retrieved with the getMessage() call, whereas groups of messages can be obtained with the getMessages() call. Messages can be appended to the folder with the appendMessages() method and can be copied to a folder with the copyMessages() method. Messages that have been marked for deletion are removed when the expunge() method is called. Flags on messages are set with the various setFlags() method variations.

The UIDFolder interface can also be implemented by those concrete folder implementations that offer the capability to retrieve messages given a unique ID (UID) for a message. Each UID is a long type and is assigned to each message in a folder. The UIDs are assigned in an ascending sequence. The getUIDValidity() method is used to obtain a folder UID that can be used to verify that any cached UIDs from a previous session are not stale.

You'll note that a series of methods exists on the Folder object to list its contents. The Folder.list() method simply returns the Folder objects contained by the Folder. The Folder.list(String) method returns the Folder objects contained by the Folder that match the String parameter name pattern. The % wildcard character matches any character except hierarchy separators, and the * wildcard character matches any character. The listSubscribed() methods can similarly be used to return a list of subscribed Folder objects contained by the current Folder object.

Sometimes email client applications only want to pre-fetch a subset of attributes about email messages on a mail server before fetching the entire email. The Folder.fetch() method allows applications to designate those attributes to acquire during pre-fetch of email information from a mail folder. A FetchProfile object is used to designate such attributes using the item's header name in String form or via a constant inside of the FetchProfile.Item inner class.

Messages within a folder can also be searched for a given pattern. Both Folder.search() methods take a serializable SearchTerm parameter describing the criteria that should be used to return a set of matching Message objects. A version of the search() method also takes a set of Message objects to be used as the messages to be searched. Figure 16.12 shows the hierarchy of classes that can be used to formulate a search expression with each class element described here:

- `SearchTerm`: Base search term used to describe search criteria in a search expression.
- `AndTerm`: Logical `AND` operator used in a `SearchTerm`.
- `OrTerm`: Logical `OR` operator used in a `SearchTerm`.
- `NotTerm`: Logical `NEGATION` operator used in a `SearchTerm`.
- `FlagTerm`: Comparison operator for message flags.
- `ComparisonTerm`: Generic comparison operator.
- `DateTerm`: Base comparison operator for dates.
- `ReceivedDateTerm`: Comparison for the message received dates.
- `SentDateTerm`: Comparison for the message sent dates.
- `IntegerComparisonTerm`: Base comparison using integers.
- `MessageNumberTerm`: Comparison for message numbers.
- `SizeTerm`: Comparison for message size.
- `AddressTerm`: Base comparison for message addresses.
- `FromTerm`: Comparison for from addresses.
- `RecipientTerm`: Comparison for recipient addresses.
- `StringTerm`: Base comparison using `String` objects.
- `AddressStringTerm`: Comparison for message addresses expressed as `String` objects.
- `FromStringTerm`: Comparison for message from addresses expressed as `String` objects.
- `RecipientStringTerm`: Comparison for message recipient addresses expressed as `String` objects.
- `BodyTerm`: Comparison for message body elements.
- `HeaderTerm`: Comparison for message header elements.
- `MessageIDTerm`: Comparison for message ID elements.
- `SubjectTerm`: Comparison for message subject elements.

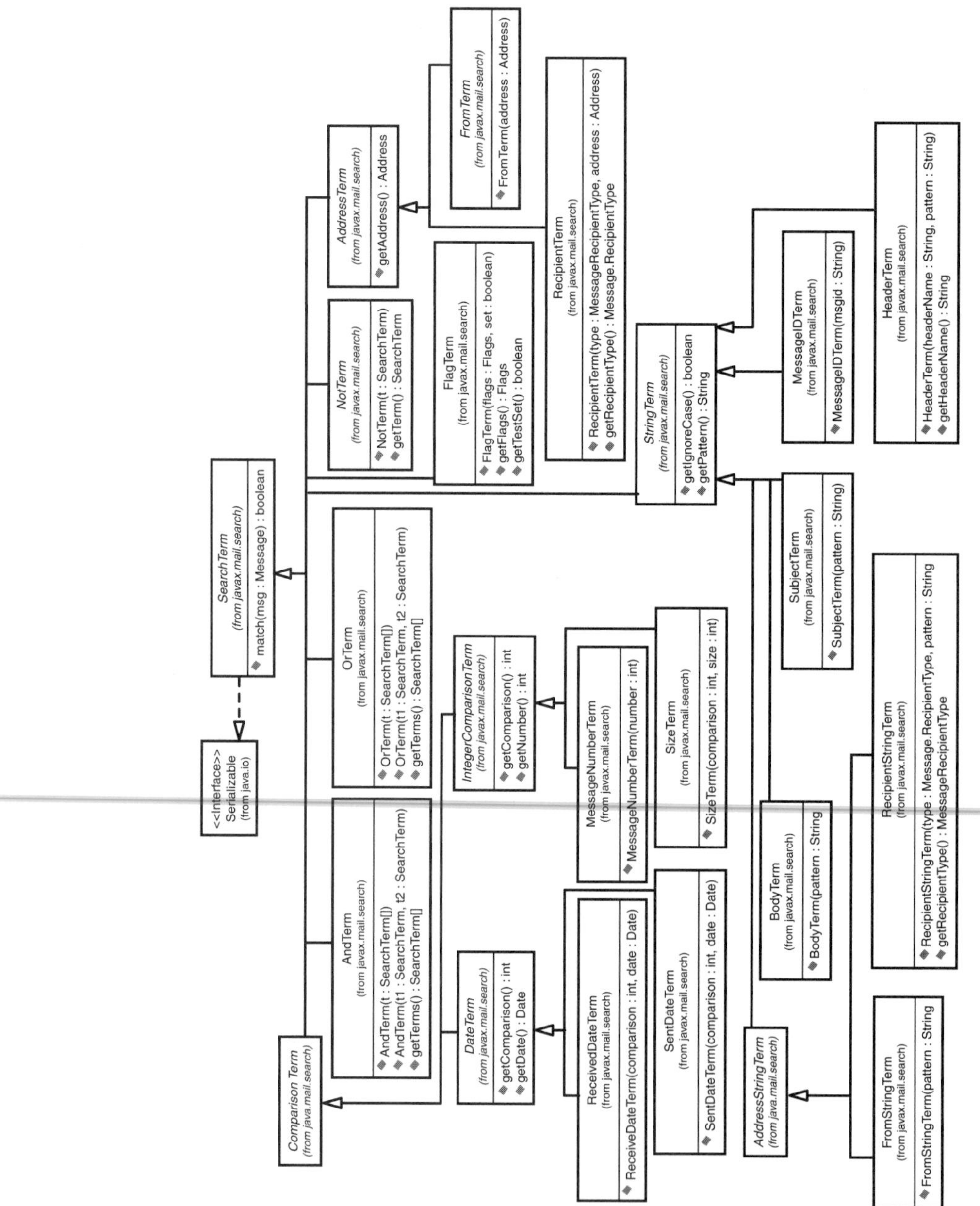

Figure 16.12 JavaMail folder search terms.

Message Transports

Figure 16.13 depicts the architecture used to send messages using JavaMail transport services. The abstract `Transport` class is implemented by service providers to provide message transport functionality. The `Transport` class extends the `Service` class and provides `send()` and `sendMessage()` methods for sending messages to specific email addresses (if not specified inside the `Message` itself). Additionally, methods on the `Transport` class are also defined to enable the notification of listeners of events that take place with the `Transport` object.

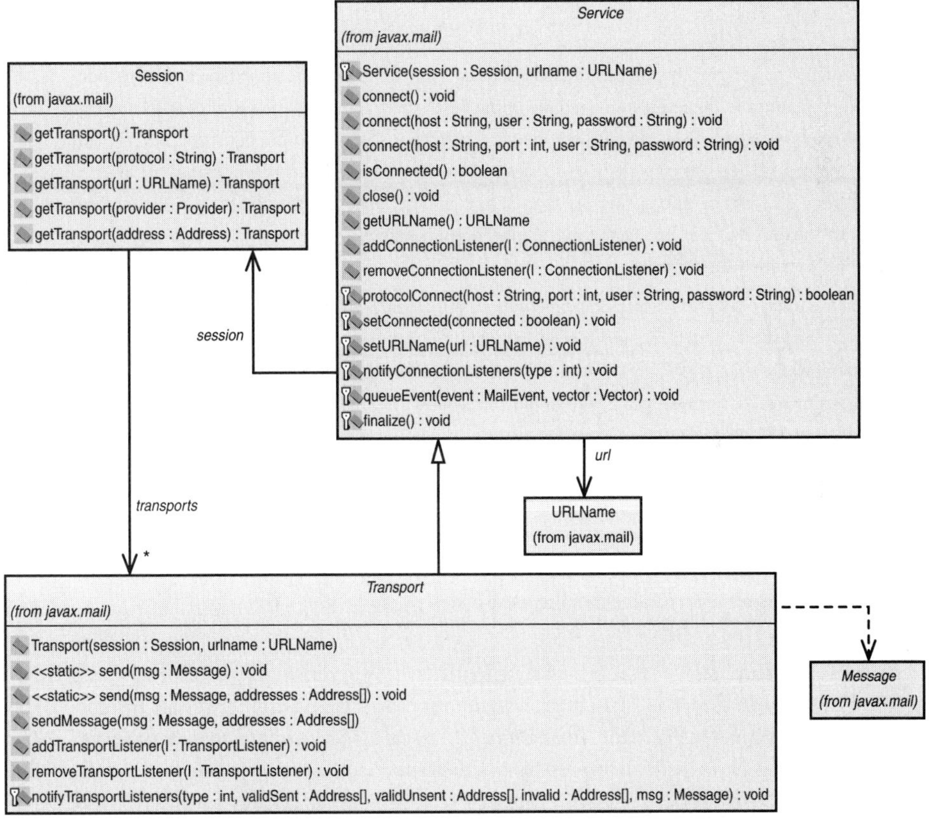

Figure 16.13 The JavaMail message transport service.

The `Session` object defines several `getTransport()` methods that enable you to retrieve a handle to a `Transport` object. The parameterless `Transport.getStore()` method returns a `Transport` object defined by the `mail.transport.protocol` property. Other versions of the `Session.getTransport()` methods also return

Transport objects associated with a String name, a URLName, and a Provider specification.

JavaMail Example

Now that we've examined the JavaMail architecture and infrastructure, we're ready to look at a JavaMail example. We've created a MailClient class to demonstrate the capability to connect to a mail server, read messages from a message store, send a message via a mail transport, and search for messages in the message store. As you'll see, all of this work is accomplished rather easily with the JavaMail API.

Note

The sample code strewn throughout this section leaves out some exception handling and other non-essential features in the interest of simplifying the description. The complete set of code examples for this JavaMail example can be located as described in Appendix A, "Software Configuration," and are associated with the examples\src\ejava\javamail directory. The MailClient.java file implements this example. A build.properties file is used to configure properties specific to your environment and is used by the ANT build.xml script as described in Appendix A. The generated runmail script can be used for executing the example.

If you are using a J2EE v1.4 server implementation, you already will have the necessary JavaMail classes installed and configured. If not, you'll need to modify the build.properties file to point to the root directory where your JavaMail v1.3 installation is located. You'll also need to modify the build.properties file to point to the JAR file for the Java Activation Framework that is used by JavaMail. The JavaMail v1.3 standard extension is available from http://java.sun.com/products/javamail/ and the Java Activation Framework v1.0 is available from http://java.sun.com/products/javabeans/glasgow/jaf.html.

In either case, you will need to modify the values of smtp.host and pop3.host to point to SMTP and POP3 servers that you have access to. The properties mail.username and mail.password should also be changed to your mail account's username and password.

The MailClient.main() method first loads Java preferences as set after running the ANT build script. The MailClient.main() method then instantiates an instance of a MailClient object, calls connectToMailServer() to connect to a mail server, calls readMessages() to read messages from the server, calls sendAMessage() with a set of message data properties to send a message to a user, and searches for email messages that match address "from" and "subject" strings. The main() method with exceptions excluded for simplicity is shown here:

```
public static void main(String[] args)
{


    Preferences preferences =
      Preferences.userNodeForPackage(
```

```
        ejava.javamail.MailClient.class);

    // Create new MailClient
    MailClient mailClient = new MailClient();

    // Connect to mail server
    mailClient.connectToMailServer();

    // Read messages from server
    mailClient.readMessages();

    // Send a message to the server with property data
    mailClient.sendAMessage();

    String from = preferences.get("MESSAGE_FROM","");
    String subject = preferences.get("MESSAGE_SUBJECT","");
    // Search for e-mail with matching from and subject fields
    mailClient.searchFrom(from,subject);

    // Exception handling code left out of listing here...
}
```

Various private attributes are defined for the `MailClient` class as shown here:

```
// SMTP host name
private String  SMTPHost;
// Message store host name
private String  MessageStoreHost;
// Message Store Server port  -1 is for default Port
private int MessageStorePort  = -1;
// E-mail Username
private String  userName;
// E-mail user password
private String  password;

// we read the messsges only from inbox.
private final String  INBOX = "INBOX";
// read messages from message store server
private final String  MSG_STORE_MAIL="pop3";
// read messages from smtp mail.
private final String  SMTP_MAIL="smtp";
// mail Header types
private final String MAIL_HEADER = "X-Mailer";

// Mail session handle
private Session mailSession;
// Mail message store handle
private Store   mailStore;
// Mail folder handle
```

```
private Folder  mailFolder;
```

The `MailClient` constructor called by `main()` reads Java preferences and uses such preferences to establish a few of the private `MailClient` attributes as shown here:

```
public MailClient()
{
  // Read properties from properties object
  Preferences preferences =
    Preferences.userNodeForPackage(MailClient.class);
  SMTPHost = preferences.get("SMTPHOST","");
  MessageStoreHost = preferences.get("STOREHOST","");
  userName = preferences.get("USERNAME","");
  password = preferences.get("PASSWORD","");
  MessageStorePort = preferences.getInt("STOREPORT",-1);
      ...
}
```

The `connectToMailServer()` method called by `main()` first retrieves a non-authenticated SMTP session handle. A message store handle of the type defined in the `MSG_STORE_MAIL` private attribute is then retrieved from the `Session` object. Finally, a connection to a message store is created given the message store host name, host port, username, and password information read in from the Java preferences and set as attributes onto the `MailClient` object. The `connectToMailServer()` method is shown here:

```
  public void connectToMailServer()
        throws NoSuchProviderException,
     AuthenticationFailedException , MessagingException
{
  // Retrieve session object with the mail.smtp.host property
  Properties sessionProperties = new Properties();
  sessionProperties.put("mail.smtp.host", this.SMTPHost);
  mailSession = Session.getDefaultInstance(sessionProperties, null);

  // Get a message store that implements the protocol specified
  mailStore = mailSession.getStore(this.MSG_STORE_MAIL);

  // Connects to message store host/port with username and password
  mailStore.connect(MessageStoreHost, MessageStorePort,
                    userName, password);
          ...
}
```

At various instances throughout our program, we want to print the contents of a message. The `MailClient.printMessage()` method demonstrates how to do this by first reading the contents of a `Message` object and then printing each element to standard output as shown here:

```
public void printMessage( Message  message)
  throws MessagingException
{
  // Get various data elements from message
  if(message != null){
   // Get various data elements from message
   String subject = message.getSubject();
   Date sentDate = message.getSentDate();
   int messageSize    = message.getSize();
   String[] headers = message.getHeader(this.MAIL_HEADER);
   Address[] mailFrom = message.getFrom();
   Address[] allRecipients = message.getAllRecipients();
   InputStreamReader inputStream = null;
   char[] buf = new char[messageSize];
   String contents = "";
   try{
     inputStream =
        new InputStreamReader(message.getInputStream());
     int len = 0;
     do
     {
        len = inputStream.read(buf, 0, messageSize);
        if (len > 0)
           contents += new String(buf);
     }
     while (len != -1);
   }
   catch(IOException ioException){
    System.out.println("Error: " +ioException);
    return;
   }

   // Print out various elements that were read from message
   System.out.println("Message Subject :"+subject);
   System.out.println("Message Date: "+sentDate);
   System.out.println("messageSize :"+messageSize);
   System.out.println("Headers :");
   for(int i = 0; headers != null && (i<headers.length); i++){
    System.out.print(headers[i]);
   }
   System.out.println("From :");
   for(int i = 0; i < mailFrom.length; i++){
    System.out.print("Address :" +mailFrom[i].toString());
   }
   System.out.println();
   System.out.println("Contents :");
```

```
    System.out.println(contents);
    System.out.println("\nEnd Of Contents");
  }
}
```

A private `MailClient.createFolder()` method is used in subsequent code to create a handle to the `INBOX` mail folder in the message store, and then it stores this handle in a private `mailFolder` attribute. We attempt to retrieve the `INBOX` folder as shown here:

```
private void createFolder() throws MessagingException
{
  // Get INBOX folder
  mailFolder = mailStore.getFolder(INBOX);
  if(mailFolder == null){
     throw new NullPointerException("Unable to get Inbox folder");
  }
}
```

After the mail folder handle is obtained, we can open the folder and retrieve a count of the number of available messages using a private `MailClient.openFolder()` method as defined here:

```
private int openFolder() throws MessagingException
{
  // Open folder for read-only access
  mailFolder.open(Folder.READ_ONLY);
  // Get number of inbox messages
  int numberOfMessagesInInbox = mailFolder.getMessageCount();

  if(numberOfMessagesInInbox == 0){
    System.out.println("No Messages");
    mailFolder.close(true);
  }

  return numberOfMessagesInInbox;
}
```

The `readMessages()` method called from `main()` first creates a folder and then opens the folder using the `createFolder()` and `openFolder()` methods. A vector of `Message` objects is then retrieved from the mail folder. Each message not yet seen is then printed using the `printMessage()` method, and read messages are marked for deletion. The `readMessages()` folder is shown here:

```
  public void readMessages() throws MessagingException
  {
    createFolder();
    if( openFolder() == 0 ) return; // Return if no messages

    // Retrieve the messages
    Message[]  newMessages = mailFolder.getMessages();
```

```
    // Print each message that hasn't been seen
    for (int i = 0; i < newMessages.length; i++)
    {
      if (!newMessages[i].isSet(Flags.Flag.SEEN)){
        printMessage(newMessages[i]);
        // Mark message to delete
        newMessages[i].setFlag(Flags.Flag.DELETED, true);
      }
    }

    // close folder and store
    this.mailFolder.close(true);
}
```

The `sendAMessage()` method called from `main()` takes a collection of message elements and uses them to create a message that it sends. A `MimeMessage` is first created using the SMTP session object. The various elements of a message are then set before the message object is sent over the messaging transport. The `sendAMessage()` method is shown here:

```
public void sendAMessage( String from,
  String messageTo, String messageCCTo,
  String subject , String body)
  throws Exception
{
   Preferences preferences =
       Preferences.userNodeForPackage(MailClient.class);
    // Read from, to, cc, subject, and body elements from preferences
   String from = preferences.get("MESSAGE_FROM","");
   String messageTo = preferences.get("MESSAGE_TO","");
   String messageCCTo = preferences.get("MESSAGE_CC","");
   String subject = preferences.get("MESSAGE_SUBJECT","");
   String body = preferences.get("MESSAGE_BODY","");
   String attachment1 = preferences.get("ATTACH_PART1","");
   String attachment2 = preferences.get("ATTACH_PART2","");

   // construct a message using SMTP session
   MimeMessage message = new MimeMessage(mailSession);
   boolean parseStrict = false;
   // set who message is from
   message.setFrom(InternetAddress.parse(from, parseStrict)[0]);
   // set recipients of message
   message.setRecipients(Message.RecipientType.TO,
              InternetAddress.parse(messageTo, parseStrict));
   if(messageCCTo.trim().length() != 0){
    message.setRecipients(Message.RecipientType.CC,
              InternetAddress.parse(messageCCTo, parseStrict));
```

```
    }
    // set subject
    message.setSubject(subject);
    // set header
    String mailer = "sendMessage";
    message.setHeader("X-Mailer", mailer);
    // set date
    message.setSentDate(new Date());
    // Body Part Section
    MimeBodyPart mimeBodyPart = new MimeBodyPart();
    mimeBodyPart.setText(body);
    // Another Body Part
    MimeBodyPart mimeBodyPartAnother = new MimeBodyPart();
    mimeBodyPartAnother.setText(attachment1);
    // Another Body Part
    MimeBodyPart mimeBodyPartAnother1 = new MimeBodyPart();
    mimeBodyPartAnother1.setText(attachment2);
    MimeMultipart multiPart = new MimeMultipart();
    multiPart.addBodyPart(mimeBodyPart);
    multiPart.addBodyPart(mimeBodyPartAnother);
    multiPart.addBodyPart(mimeBodyPartAnother1);

    // set body
    message.setContent(multiPart);
    // send message
    Transport.send(message);
    System.out.println("\nMail was sent successfully.");
}
```

The `searchFrom()` method called from `main()` first creates a folder using the `createFolder()` method and then opens a folder using the `openFolder()` method. The `searchFrom()` method then creates and combines a set of search items for a message subject, a message sender address, and the current date. The mail folder is then searched using the newly created search-term criteria. Each message that matches the criteria is then returned. The `searchFrom()` method is shown here:

```
public void  searchFrom(String fromAddress, String subject)
  throws MessagingException
{
  createFolder();
  if( openFolder() == 0 ) return; // Return if no messages

  // Create a new subject term
  SearchTerm searchTerm = new SubjectTerm(subject);
  // Create a new 'from' term
  FromStringTerm fromStringTerm = new FromStringTerm(fromAddress);
```

```
  // Combine from and search term
  searchTerm = new OrTerm(searchTerm, fromStringTerm);
  // Create a new date term (today's)
  ReceivedDateTerm receivedDateTerm =
    new ReceivedDateTerm(ComparisonTerm.EQ, new Date());
  // Combine date term
  searchTerm = new OrTerm(searchTerm,receivedDateTerm);
  // Induce search for messages
  Message[]  newMessages = mailFolder.search(searchTerm);
  if(newMessages == null || newMessages.length == 0){
    System.out.println(" no message matches search Criteria");
  }
  // Print each found message
  for (int i = 0; i < newMessages.length; i++)
  {
    if (!newMessages[i].isSet(Flags.Flag.SEEN)){
      printMessage(newMessages[i]);
    }
  }

  // Close folder and store
  this.mailFolder.close(true);
  this.mailStore.close();
}
```

To run the `MailClient` example, you can use the `runmail` script generated by the ANT script associated with the example. The `build.properties` file has entries for each property used for the example. The various properties used for the example are shown here and should be customized for your own mail server configuration and desired message data:

```
# SMTP Host, your mail smtp server
smtp.host=smtp.beeshirts.com
# POP3 Host, your mail pop3 server
pop3.host=pop.beeshirts.com
# POP3 port for POP3 Server, default port is 110
pop3.store.port=110

# Username on mail server
mail.username=username
# Password on mail server
mail.password=password

# Message FROM
message.from=test@beeshirts.com
# Message TO
message.to=test@beeshirts.com
```

```
# Message CC
message.cc=test@beeshirts.com

# Message Subject
message.subject=Test
# Messasge Body
message.body=Greetings
# Attachment1
message.attach.part1=Attachment1
# Attachment2
message.attach.part2=Attachment2
```

Conclusions

JavaMail is a large but robust API that lets you send and receive email messages from within your J2EE enterprise applications. In one sense, JavaMail is just another asynchronous messaging paradigm. However, it has been specifically customized to deal with those lightweight messages known as email and with those lightweight messaging servers known as SMTP, POP, and IMAP email servers. Although the JavaMail API is rather large, it is also a fairly simple and easy-to-understand API that facilitates incorporation of basic email functionality into enterprise applications. JavaMail is also extensive enough to permit you to layer in more sophisticated email functionality as your enterprise application email needs grow.

17

Assurance and Security Services

ASSURANCE DEALS WITH ENHANCING THE SECURITY, RELIABILITY, availability, maintainability, and perhaps safety of your enterprise system. Out of all assurance facets, enterprise security represents perhaps the most important and widely needed assurance requirement. Java, in fact, employs a comprehensive security model relied upon for building secure distributed enterprise Java applications in general. Java security provides a collection of APIs and tools for infusing security into your Java applications. Additionally, one of the CORBA components that relates to assurance is the CORBA Security Service and is leveraged by a few J2EE server offerings. This chapter presents those underlying concepts and technologies that form the infrastructure of assurance and security when building J2EE applications.

In this chapter, you will learn:

- The concepts of assurance for security, reliability, availability, safety, and maintainability.
- The basic model for providing security for enterprise applications.
- An overview of the Java security model as provided by the Java 2 platform.
- About the APIs available to the Java security programmer.
- An overview of the CORBA Security Service.

Assurance Services

Your first encounter with a particular enterprise development effort will typically involve being introduced to what the project aims to provide in the way of information technology functionality for the enterprise. Subsequently, you'll begin to unravel the requirements and features being targeted for deployment into the enterprise. More often than not, you will focus on the functional and behavioral requirements that must be incorporated by the project. This is largely because, by its very definition, enterprise development aims to infuse information technology into the corporation and put it to work by providing some business advantage to the corporation. Such business advantages may include enhancing the productivity of its employees, enhancing the productivity of product or service output, increasing revenue received from customers, or minimizing the cost of its operations.

With such fundamental business-critical issues at hand, issues of software assurance can sometimes be overlooked. That is, you might engage in a development process that perhaps sacrifices the quantity or even presence of coding documentation and thus are left with difficult-to-maintain code. Or perhaps in the rush to deploy your new online e-commerce Web site, you didn't carefully examine your overall approach to providing a secure solution. Maybe you've even elected to use a particular technology for your online Web-based storefront because you were familiar with the technology or it was free. And then perhaps you soon became painfully aware that when more than five customers log on to your Web site, your server solution crashes, rendering your store completely unavailable. Providing assurance for your enterprise means solving these types of problems and more.

In general, providing assurance for your enterprise solutions means providing a secure, reliable, available, maintainable, and perhaps safe solution. All such marks of assurance correspond to providing high levels of satisfaction for their related probabilistic counterparts:

- *Security:* The likelihood that your system will operate in a secure and security-breach–free fashion. High assurance here means providing a secure system.
- *Reliability:* The likelihood that your system will operate correctly and as intended. High assurance here means providing a reliable system.
- *Availability:* The likelihood that your system will be operational and offering service. Scalability of your system to support growth in usage is one aspect of availability. High assurance here thus means providing an available and scalable system.
- *Maintainability:* The likelihood that your system will be capable of being maintained, upgraded, and extended for future growth. High assurance here means providing a maintainable system.
- *Safety:* The likelihood that your system will operate in a safe and accident-free manner. Here, considerations for safety include reducing likelihood of physical harm to people, machinery, the environment, or other physical world entities to which damage may be induced. High assurance here means providing a safe system.

Assurance Problems

Various techniques can be used for identifying assurance issues. However, with the use of previous project assurance data, system and product technical data, and perhaps some outside assurance mentoring, a practical solution for many corporations is to simply direct the technical engineering staff to identify potential assurance problems via the generation of technical memos. Depending on the size of the project, one or more project members on a part-time basis can help collect this data into a centralized repository and help coordinate the timely flow of the remaining assurance process steps. An identified assurance problem should be expressed in terms of one or more causes that lead to one or more possible effects. Following are assurance problems needing identification by the technical staff:

- *Security Problems:* Security holes, weaknesses, and potential threats.
- *Reliability Problems:* Potential failure modes, potential bottlenecks, and code-usage assumptions.
- *Availability Problems:* Potential single points of failure, denial of service possibilities, scalability concerns, and code-usage assumptions.
- *Maintainability Problems:* Difficult-to-maintain designs, code dependencies, code modules lacking encapsulation, software configuration, processing distribution, and extensibility to future demands.
- *Safety Problems:* Hazardous scenarios, safety-critical code modules, and fail-safe components.

To best identify particular assurance problems, it is usually beneficial to at least have some concept in mind for how problems of that type may occur. As an enterprise developer, you are usually in an excellent position to provide such insight because you know how your particular systems are built and are perhaps used to hearing how they have also failed on occasion via bug or defect reports. Nevertheless, in general, the assurance error model classification adapted from some earlier work by one of the authors (Paul Perrone) is presented here. In most cases the errors may occur throughout various aspects of the system, such as during communication of data and applications, during the storage of data and applications, or perhaps while such data and applications are being used. Of course, in an object-oriented system, the distinction between data and applications blurs because an object can encapsulate both data and application code. Nevertheless, we distinguish between data and application in the general error model presented here:

- *Corrupted Data Errors:* Data can be corrupted (for example, during communication, while in storage, or even while being used).
- *Corrupted Application Errors:* Your application might be corrupted to perform certain operations incorrectly (for example, during mobile code communication, while in storage, or even while being used).
- *Incorrect Data Reference Errors:* Your application might be corrupted to reference the wrong data.
- *Incorrect Application Reference Errors:* Your application might be corrupted to execute the wrong set of operations.
- *Delayed Data Delivery Errors:* Data may be delayed for delivery during communications or during an attempt to access results.

- *Delayed Application Processing Errors:* Your application may be experiencing processing delays.
- *A Priori Data Creation Errors:* Data enters your system corrupted to begin with.
- *A Priori Application Creation Errors:* Applications enter your system corrupted to begin with.

Security Services

In the preceding section, we provided an overview of the general assurance problems that relate to security. Figure 17.1 depicts the basic security model that results from such problems and assurance-provisioning mechanisms. At the top of the diagram we have a resource provider offering some security-critical data or application resources. Such resources are security-critical because a malicious being, such as the hacker depicted at the bottom of the diagram, can corrupt, reference (that is, access), replace, delay access to, or deny access to such resources. A security service provider, depicted on the left side of the diagram, attempts to protect such resources from attack by providing protection services such as integrity, confidentiality, authorization and access, identity, authenticity, availability, nonrepudiation, and auditing protection services. Such services attempt to thwart the best efforts of a hacker from accomplishing their goals. The right side of the diagram shows the beneficiary of such security services, which include the following:

- *Integrity Verification:* The beneficiary has some verification that the data or application is accurate.
- *Confidentiality Preservation:* The beneficiary has some assurance that confidentiality of the data or application has been preserved.
- *Authorization/Access Permission:* Properly authorized permission to access some security-critical data, application, or other resource has been provided.
- *Identity Verification:* The beneficiary has some verification that the identity associated with the data or application source is who they say they are.
- *Authenticity Permission:* Properly authenticated permission to access some data, application, or other resource has been provided.
- *Availability of Service:* The beneficiary has access to the data, application, or other resource when he or she expects to have access.
- *Nonrepudiation Evidence:* The beneficiary has some evidence regarding from whom the data or application comes or has some evidence that an intended receiver actually received data sent.
- *Auditing Evidence:* The beneficiary has some evidence of security-critical operations that take place in the system.

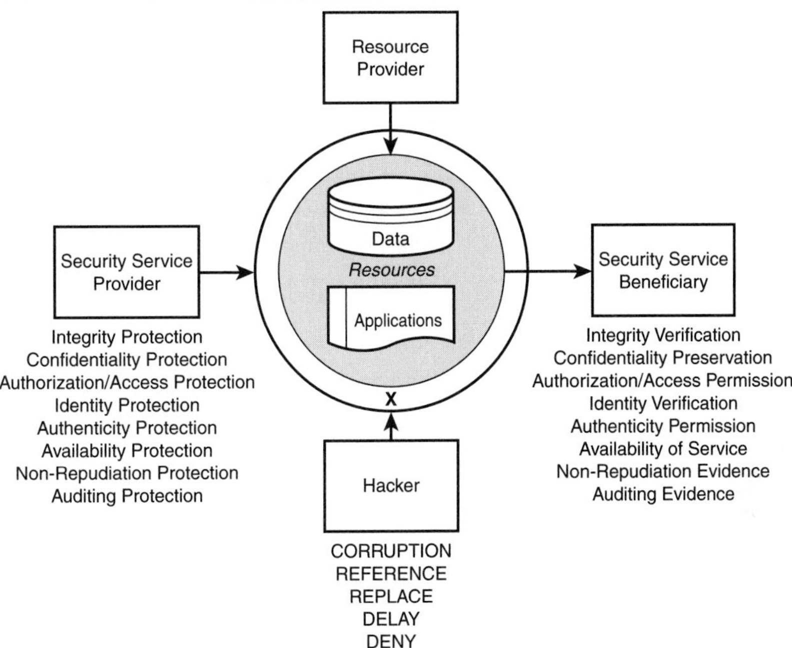

Figure 17.1 The basic security model.

Cryptography

Cryptography not only provides integrity and confidentiality protection, but also is a key technology used by other security service components such as identity, authenticity, and nonrepudiation protection mechanisms. Because cryptography is such a fundamental component of a security solution, some people mistakenly think that providing a secure solution means to provide a solution using cryptography alone. This, as you have just seen in the preceding section, is not the case.

Classes of Cryptography

So what is cryptography, you ask? Cryptography is the basic science behind the process of taking some data or perhaps some code and running it through a cryptographic engine to generate some cryptographic material. Sometimes the process of generating cryptographic material is referred to in general as cryptographic processing because it takes a stream of input data and generates a stream of bits that may represent some scrambled form (also called cipher text) of the original input data (also called clear text) or perhaps may represent some token (also called message digest) generated uniquely for a particular input sequence. Different classes of cryptographic engines exist, and different algorithms that implement these different engine classes have varying characteristics such as performance, security, licensing cost, and strength or quality of protection (QOP).

As shown in Figure 17.2, if the output of the cryptographic engine represents some uniquely generated message digest, such a message digest can be used and sent to a receiver along with the data over which it was generated. The receiver can then run the received data through an identical cryptographic engine and generate its own message digest. If the received message digest matches the newly generated message digest, the received data can be presumed to be accurate, and integrity is thus provided. The associated cryptographic engine is said to implement a message digest algorithm.

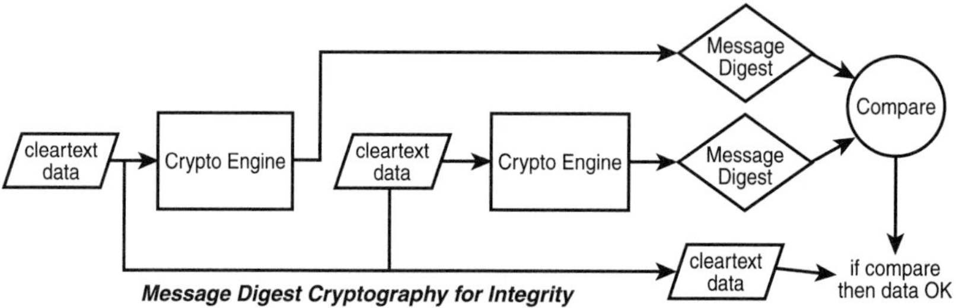

Figure 17.2 A message digest crypto for integrity.

If the output of the cryptographic engine represents some cipher text data, we can send such information over a communications network or perhaps store it somewhere and be assured that confidentiality of the data is preserved. A reverse process can then run the data through another cryptographic engine and convert the cipher text data into its clear-text original form. Only cryptographic engines that have some secret key and know the algorithm to run can perform the reverse cryptographic process. The cipher text creation process in this context is referred to as encryption, and the cipher text conversion to clear text is referred to as decryption. Very often, however, the entire process is simply referred to as encryption.

As you'll see, two general categories of key encryption algorithms can be used to perform the encryption process: symmetric key encryption and asymmetric key encryption. With symmetric key encryption, both encryption and decryption occur using the same secret key. As shown in Figure 17.3, secret symmetric keys can be used to maintain confidentiality only if no one else obtains access to the secret key. With asymmetric encryption, the two ends use keys with different values. One end uses a private key that must be kept secret and must not be given to anyone else. The other end uses a public key that can be freely distributed.

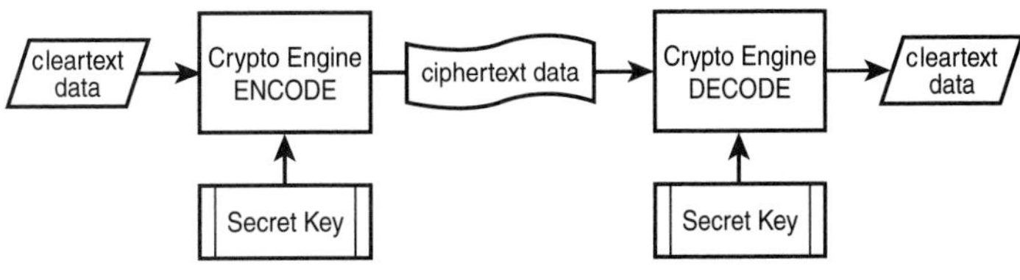

Figure 17.3 Symmetric key crypto for confidentiality.

If a private key is used to encrypt some data as shown in Figure 17.4, a public key must be used to decrypt the data. In such a scenario, because the public key is freely distributed, no confidentiality is maintained. Rather, the data encrypted with the private key can be guaranteed to be signed by the holder of that key because no one else is supposed to have access to that key. Thus, identity is provided in such a scenario. Furthermore, because a piece of data is encrypted with your private key, it is possible to implement certain nonrepudiation algorithms under such circumstances in which receivers may be able to prove that a particular data item was sent by you.

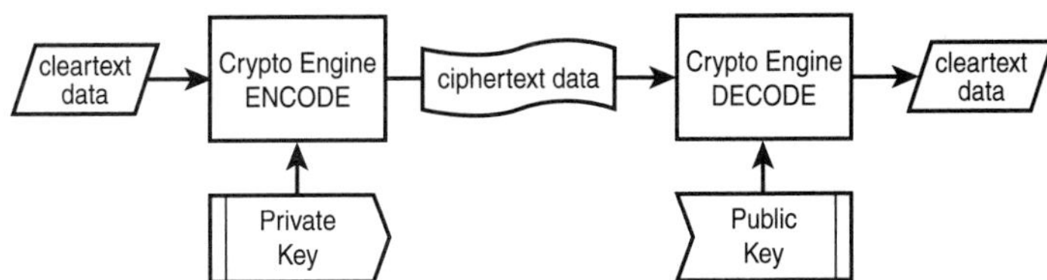

Figure 17.4 Asymmetric key crypto for identity and nonrepudiation.

Figure 17.5 illustrates the fact that if a public key is used to encrypt some data, a private key must be used to decrypt the data. Thus, confidentiality can be provided because only the holder of the private key can decrypt the data.

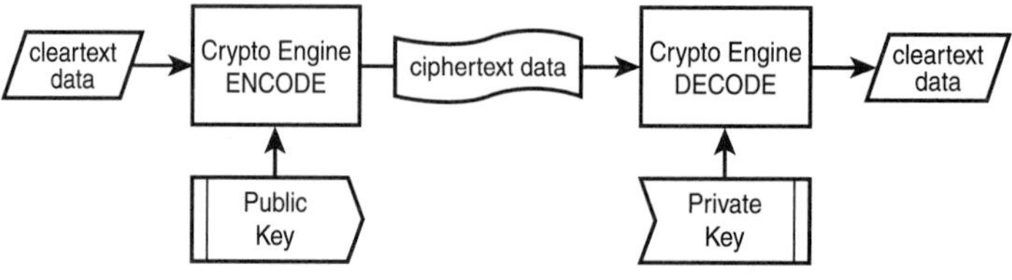

Figure 17.5 Asymmetric key crypto for confidentiality.

Message Digests

A message digest algorithm is a one-way function that generates a unique set of output bits based on a sequence of input bits. Different sequences of input bits generate a unique pattern of output bits within some probabilistic measure. Message digest algorithms come in various flavors:

- *MD2:* Message Digest #2 is a slow but very secure message digest algorithm producing 128-bit digest values.
- *MD4:* Message Digest #4 is faster but fairly insecure and also generates a 128-bit digest value.
- *MD5:* Message Digest #5 is a more secure version of MD4 and MD2 but with speed advantages and also produces a 128-bit digest value.
- *SHA:* The Secure Hash Algorithm produces a 160-bit digest value.
- *SHA-1:* Secure Hash Algorithm 1 is a modification of SHA, overcoming a minor security flaw with SHA.
- *MAC:* The Message Authentication Code uses a secret key along with a message digest algorithm to create message digests.

Symmetric Keys

Symmetric key (also called secret key) algorithms typically require less processing time than asymmetric key algorithms and can lead to very strong encryption possibilities. The main drawback with symmetric keys is that both sides of the encrypted stream need to have the same key. This presents a problem in terms of sharing keys and poses a greater risk that someone could obtain your secret key. In practice, secret keys are usually first exchanged using an asymmetric key algorithm. Such key agreement or key exchange algorithms enable one to use a more powerful and secure asymmetric key algorithm to confidentially exchange a secret key and then use the secret key throughout the remainder of an encrypted communications session. These are some of the most common symmetric key algorithms:

- *DES:* The Data Encryption Standard uses a 56-bit secret key that is strong but possible to crack.

- *Triple-DES:* Triple DES strengthens DES by performing the DES algorithm three times with three different DES keys.
- *RC2 and RC4:* These can be used with up to 2,048-bit keys and provide for a very secure algorithm.
- *RC5:* This uses a configurable key size.

Asymmetric Keys

As shown in Figure 17.4 and Figure 17.5, asymmetric keys can be used for providing identity, confidentiality, and to a certain extent nonrepudiation. Asymmetric key algorithms (also called public key algorithms) are generally more computationally intensive than symmetric and message digest algorithms. However, because asymmetric keys permit one to hold a private key that does not need to be distributed to other participants in an encryption session, the security of asymmetric keys is hard to compromise. Public keys can be freely distributed to those members of a community who want either to encrypt data using your public key and send you confidential messages or to verify the fact that an encrypted message supposedly sent from you was indeed sent from you. When you encrypt data using your private key, the generated cipher text data is sometimes referred to as a signature, because only the identity of the private key holder could have created such a pattern of bits. Following are some of the most common asymmetric key algorithms:

- *DSA:* The Digital Signature Algorithm uses keys of any length but is commonly restricted to keys between 512 bits and 1,024 bits via the Digital Signature Standard (DSS).
- *RSA:* The Rivest Shamir Adleman algorithm uses keys that can vary in length.
- *Diffie-Hellman:* The Diffie-Hellman algorithm is used as a key exchange algorithm in which a secret key is generated and securely exchanged so that both parties can participate in a particular encrypted session.

Authentication and Nonrepudiation

In security systems, the term *principal* is used to mean an individual, an organization, or some other sender or receiver of messages. Identity protection in secure systems provides a way to uniquely identify a principal. Principal identification is a fundamental security operation utilized by many other security-protection mechanisms. For example, in determining whether access to a particular resource is allowed, the identity of the principal desiring access must be determined. Such principal identification itself must be performed in a secure manner. That is, we just can't have someone saying that he is of a particular identity. He could then identify himself as a principal with more system privileges than he actually has and obtain access to certain parts of a system to which he should not have access. Thus the assignment of principal identity itself in a system is a security-critical operation.

Authentication represents the means by which principals securely identify themselves to a system. To accomplish this task, they usually must interact with some principal authenticator process or login module that takes certain secret information that only a particular principal would know or perhaps be able to generate. With such information in hand, the authenticator will determine whether a principal should be granted access to the system and perhaps (depending on the authentication technique) return a set of credentials defining the rights ascribed to that principal. Such credentials may be valid only for a particular session or perhaps for use within a certain security context. The security context in which valid credentials are defined may be a function of whatever thread or process from which the principal (or proxy for that principal) is acting.

Optionally, principals may allow other intermediate objects to delegate their credentials to calls on other objects on their behalf. Thus, object A making a call on object B may authenticate itself with object B first, and then object B might call object C and delegate the credentials of object A to object C. As a more explicit example of where delegation can be useful, consider a BeeShirts.com CORBA client that interfaces with a CORBA-based query server providing a common interface to many back-end database-related constructs such as customer, order, and credit-card objects. Now suppose that the CORBA client makes a call on the CORBA query server and its credentials get passed to the server (this assumes that the client already was authenticated and given credentials). Now the server will make calls to the database-related constructs such as a credit-card object, and it needs certain credential information before it satisfies the query server's request. Delegation would allow the query server to pass the credentials of the CORBA client onto the credit-card object so that the operation can be performed on behalf of the CORBA client. This may be important, because perhaps certain client identities (for example, an administrator) may be allowed access to certain credit-card data to which other identities (for example, a customer) may not have access. Without delegation, the credit-card object would see all calls as being made by the identity of the query server. Thus, credit-card data access control will not be as fine-grained.

Authentication Types

Various techniques for securely allowing principals to identify themselves and authenticate themselves with a system have evolved over the years, including these:

- Password-based identity and authentication
- Physical token–based identity and authentication
- Biometrics-based identity and authentication
- Certificate-based identity and authentication

Perhaps the most common and familiar form of authentication is password-based authentication. With password-based authentication, a principal ID (for example, a user ID) and password are entered into the system and passed to a principal authenticator, who determines whether the associated password matches its stored version of that particular principal's password. Password-based identification is very easy to implement and is thus very common. However, a password is similar to a secret key in that both of the ends of a secure session must have a copy of the secret value (that is, the key or password). The password must also be transmitted from the principal's location to the principal authenticator's location, which may expose itself to being stolen by a hacker if the path between principal and principal authenticator does not provide confidentiality protection.

Kerberos is a particular type of password-based authentication system in which a user password is known to a dedicated Kerberos-based server process. Because both the Kerberos-based server and the principal know the password, they can encrypt and decrypt messages sent between them using the password as a secret symmetric key.

Physical token–based authentication techniques offer a powerful but more costly and thus less common authentication solution. Physical token–based authentication techniques typically involve using a physical item such as an automatic teller machine (ATM) card as principal identification. Smart cards are ATM-like cards with embedded miniprocessors on them that can be used to provide a more configurable means of physical token identity.

Biometrics-based authentication solutions are even less common than physical token–based solutions, but they can provide a very powerful and difficult-to-crack identity and authenticity solution. Biometrics involves using some physical aspect of a person (for example, fingerprint or retinal characteristics of an eye) to identify that person. Needless to say, a hacker would be hard-pressed to mimic such identity unless, of course, the hacker could hijack someone's finger or eye. All such security is, however, predicated on the fact that the digital representation of this biometric information cannot be stolen. After such information is obtained, a hacker may be able to use it to bypass the security of a biometrics-based solution. This is problematic, because new fingers and eyes are not easily adapted for users, whereas a new password or physical token can be easily created.

Certificate-based authentication is another type of authentication technique that has grown in popularity over recent years. A certificate is simply a block of data containing information used to identify a principal. Information in the certificate includes the principal's public key, information about the principal, dates during which the certificate is valid, information about the issuer of a certificate, and a signature generated by the certificate issuer.

As previously mentioned, a signature can be generated using a private key over some block of data to produce another block of data known as the signature. The generator of this signature using the private key is referred to as the signer. This signature can then be decrypted only using the public key of the signer, thus providing assurance of the identity of the signer.

Certificates come in handy when you're sending your public key to other entities so that they can identify information that you send to them which was encrypted with your private key. Certificates also facilitate other entities being able to send information to you that only you can decrypt with your private key. Without a certificate, hackers could send some other entity a public key that they say is yours but that is really not, and then sign messages to that entity (for example, an e-commerce Web site) with a private key corresponding to the public key that they falsely claim is yours.

Different certificate implementations have evolved with different formats, but the X.509 v3 certificate standard represents one of the more popular certificate types. The X.509 standard can be used to sign certificates using various signature algorithms. X.509 certificates contain version and serial-number information, information identifying the signature algorithm and its parameters, the CA identity and signature, the dates of validity, and the principal identity and public key.

The Public Key Cryptography Standards (PKCS) define a binary format that can be used for storing certificates. PKCS itself is defined using formats identified by a number, such as PKCS #1 and PKCS #2. PKCS #7, for example, defines the cryptographic message syntax, and PKCS #8 defines the private key information syntax. Certificates are also sometimes stored using the Privacy Enhanced Mail (PEM) ASCII format.

A certificate is signed by a third party known as a Certificate Authority (CA) such that if that CA says that the associated public key in the certificate is yours, then the receiving entity can be assured that the public key is indeed yours and not one from some hacker. Of course, the same problem exists for initially providing a public key associated with the CA to a receiving entity. Such a problem can be made simpler, however, by using a common CA (such as Verisign) whose public key has been given to a community of users in a secure fashion. This one-time secure provision of a CA's public key used to verify certificates from multiple principals is certainly simpler than attempting to securely provide a public key for each principal in the community. Tools such as Web browsers also often come preconfigured with the certificates of many common and trusted CAs.

Furthermore, certificates can be chained such that you might send your certificate to some receiving entity in which your certificate was signed by CA-bar and CA-bar's certificate, which was signed by CA-foo. If the receiving entity trusts CA-bar's signature, it can trust your public key. Otherwise, it can consult the CA-bar certificate that was chained with yours and determine whether it trusts CA-foo's signature. If it trusts CA-foo, it can trust CA-bar's signature and therefore can trust your public key. The moral of this story, however, is that there always must be a trusted foo-like signer somewhere in the certificate chain for the receiving entity to trust your public key.

Certificates are typically requested from a certificate server at the site of a CA. A certificate signing request (CSR) is sent to the CA's certificate server by you along with some other information used to identify yourself as required by the CA. Very often the CA's certificate server will provide a Web-based interface for submitting CSRs. The CA staff will then process your CSR and generate a public and private key pair for you if they grant your request. They will most likely send you a public key via email but should require that you retrieve your private key from them via some secure means such as through a secure Web connection download.

CAs also can maintain a certificate revocation list (CRL) that manages the list of certificates that have been revoked before their validity dates have expired. Entities may consult such CRLs periodically to be able to determine whether your certificate is still valid.

After you obtain your own private key and as you build up a collection of public keys and certificates from other principals, you'll need to store this information somewhere. Because your private key represents security-critical data, the storage mechanism should itself be secured. A key store represents a mechanism for storing private keys, public keys, and certificates. Web browsers and Web servers that support certificates come equipped with secured key stores. Furthermore, the Java 2 platform has a proprietary secured key store with which it comes equipped, referred to as the Java Key Store (JKS).

Nonrepudiation

Nonrepudiation (NR) provides a way to prove that certain principals sent or received a particular message. NR tokens providing this evidence are generated and verified according to the following two general ways that NR is used:

- Generation and verification of an NR token for a message sent by a principal. Thus, the principal cannot deny sending a particular message.
- Generation and verification of an NR token for a message received by a principal. Thus, the principal cannot deny receiving a particular message.

When another principal obtains an NR token generated according to one of the preceding two scenarios, he essentially has evidence that the particular action occurred. Such evidence can be presented to some arbitrator or NR authority later in the event of a dispute over whether such actions occurred. NR involves the use of asymmetric keys to generate the NR tokens used as proof of principal identity.

Secure Socket Layer (SSL)

The Secure Socket Layer (SSL) is a communications protocol layer created by the Netscape Communications Corporation that rests atop the TCP/IP protocol stack. SSL provides secure services over TCP/IP, such as confidentiality through data encryption, integrity via a MAC algorithm, and optional authenticity and nonrepudiation of both a socket client and a socket server. While operating over TCP/IP, SSL can also operate under other TCP/IP-based protocols such as HTTP and IIOP. Thus, SSL can be viewed as a layer that operates between TCP/IP and higher-level communications protocols such as HTTP and IIOP to provide a secure communications solution.

SSL v1 was never publicly used, but SSL v2 was introduced by Netscape with version 1 of Netscape Navigator. SSL v3 currently represents the most current SSL standard in wide use. The Transport Layer Security (TLS) protocol developed by the Internet Engineering Task Force (IETF) extends the SSL v3 protocol with enhancements to the authentication aspects of the SSL algorithm. The Wireless Transport Layer Security (WTLS) protocol, as its name implies, is a version of TLS used in wireless communications.

The basic SSL v3 algorithm is described here:

1. An SSL Client connects to an SSL Server.
2. The SSL Client sends a client hello message to the SSL Server containing the SSL version, any crypto methods supported by the client, and a random byte stream.
3. The SSL Server sends a server hello message to the SSL Client containing the SSL version, the selected crypto method, a session ID, and a random byte stream.
4. The SSL Server sends a server X.509 certificate to the SSL Client.
5. (Optional Client Authentication) The SSL Server sends a certificate request to the SSL Client.
6. The SSL Client authenticates the SSL Server using the server certificate by checking the validity date on the certificate, determining whether the signing CA is trusted, verifying the signature, and possibly determining whether the domain name of the server certificate matches the domain name of the server.
7. The SSL Client generates a premaster secret key and encrypts it with the server public key.
8. The SSL Client sends the encrypted premaster secret key to the SSL Server.
9. (Optional Client Authentication) The SSL Client sends a client X.509 certificate and another signed piece of data to the SSL Server.
10. (Optional Client Authentication) The SSL Server authenticates the SSL Client using the client certificate by checking the validity date on the certificate, determining whether the signing CA is trusted, and verifying the signature.
11. The SSL Client and SSL Server both then use the premaster secret to generate a master secret.
12. The SSL Client and SSL Server both independently generate a secret session key from the master key.
13. The SSL Client and SSL Server exchange change cipher specification messages indicating that any subsequent messages should be encrypted using the secret session key.
14. The SSL Client and SSL Server exchange a handshake-finished message encrypted with the session key indicating that the SSL session can now begin.

Access Control

In this book we use the terms *access control* and *authorization* interchangeably. Having access control protection means providing a means for limiting access by principals to valued resources based on their identity. Their identity may also be associated with security attributes such as a set of classification levels, privileges, permissions, or roles that can be used to provide more fine-grained access control decision making. Access control comes in many flavors, including discretionary, role-based, mandatory, and firewall types of access control. We briefly present these various forms of access control here.

Discretionary Access Control

Although some principal Foo may have access to your file system, principal Bar may not. Such a Boolean decision-making process can be alleviated by using permissions. That is, perhaps giving specific permission to principal Bar for read-only access and full access to principal Foo more closely models the access control protection you desire. Because principals can also identify a particular group, such permissions and privileges as previously described can be used to establish access control for groups of individuals. Such access control based on principal (that is, individual or group) identity is sometimes referred to as discretionary access control. Discretionary access control mechanisms typically maintain a list of principals and their associated permissions in an access control list (ACL). ACLs can be stored in a file or database and help make the administration of access control a fairly simple task.

Role-Based Access Control

A particular system-usage role can be associated with a collection of users. For example, an administrative role may be assigned to one or more system administrators responsible for maintaining your enterprise server. Roles are mapped to a particular principal or to a particular user group. When roles are mapped to a principal, the principal name involved with a particular role-sensitive operation is compared with the principal name extracted from the role to determine whether the operation is permitted to proceed. When roles are mapped to a group, a group associated with a principal involved with a particular role-sensitive operation is compared with the group extracted from the role to determine whether the operation is permitted to proceed. Such role-based access control requires that a list of roles be maintained and that mappings from role to user or user group be established.

Mandatory Access Control

Apart from using some explicit permission or privilege per individual or group, other certain access-control techniques are based on a classification level that a principal assumes. A classification level specifies the level of trust associated with that principal (for example, Top Secret, Confidential, Unclassified). Classification levels specified for principals have an implicit level of trust in which higher classification levels (for example, Top Secret) signify a higher level of trust than lower classification levels (for example, Unclassified). A classification level is also associated with a valued resource designating the minimum classification level needed by a principal to access that resource. If the principal's classification level is higher than or equal to the valued resource's classification level, the user can obtain access to the resource. This type of access control is sometimes referred to as mandatory access control. Mandatory access control techniques alleviate the need for maintaining ACLs because the access decision logic is built into the classification scheme. Rather, only a hierarchy of classification levels needs to be defined.

Firewall Access Control

A firewall is a mechanism by which access to particular TCP/IP ports on some network of computers is restricted based on the location of the incoming connection request. If the request is made from outside of the network, access may be restricted, but if it is made from within the network, access may be granted. Firewalls can also limit requests made from within its protected network to IP addresses outside of the network. Sometimes, however, such outgoing requests are routed around the firewall restrictions using a proxy server. Proxy servers used with firewall restrictions limit access to outgoing IP addresses in a more fine-grained fashion.

Domains

Access control can also be defined per some domain of protection. That is, various host machines or processes that all have the same access control policy may be grouped into a security domain (also called a realm or security policy domain). Thus, a set of permissions may be granted for one domain and another set of permissions may be granted for another domain. A security domain may also refer to a location where mobile code comes from (that is, a codebase). Thus, by specifying a set of permissions for a particular domain, you might actually be specifying a set of permissions to be granted to mobile code coming from a particular URL. These permissions dictate what access to valued resources is permitted for such mobile code running on your local machine. Such is the case with the Java security model.

Code in a domain may trust other code in the same domain to invoke certain operations on one another that would not be permitted for code that sits outside of the domain. The domain is thus termed a *trusted domain*. Trusted domains are also sometimes referred to as *trusted computing bases*. Thus, for example, you may not require an encrypted SSL session for database access from within a trusted domain but may require it for code that wants to access the database from outside the trusted domain.

Domains can also be partitioned into subdomains in which one or more subdomains are contained within an enclosing domain. The permissions applied to the outer domain may thus be inherited by the subdomains. Subdomains may further restrict which permissions apply to themselves, but they cannot generally specify permissions that are less restrictive than the enclosing domain.

Domains can also be federated. Federations of domains grant access to each other's resources at the domain level. For example, a domain named `sales.mysite.com` may grant one set of permissions to a domain named `accounting.mysite.com` but grant another set of more restrictive permissions to a domain named `partner.othersite.com`.

As a final note, when a particular security mechanism is used across multiple security domains, that security mechanism itself forms a domain of security. To distinguish this domain from security policy domains, the term *security technology domain* is used.

Auditing

Auditing involves logging security-critical operations that occur within a security domain. Auditing of such operations may be useful in trying to track down the sequence of events that led to a hack or perhaps in determining the identity of the hacker. Auditing is usually performed during authentication (logins), logouts, trusted resource access (for example, file access), and any modification of the security properties of a system.

This is the typical information logged during a security audit:

- Audit event type
- Timestamp of the event
- Identity of the principal initiating the event
- Identification of the target resource
- Permission being requested on the target resource
- Location from which the resource request is made

Because audit logs are used to provide evidence with respect to security-critical operations, the audit process and log itself tend to be security-critical. Thus they too must be protected in some way from hackers corrupting, denying, or perhaps replacing log information. Audit logs are thus often maintained behind a trusted computing base and possibly encrypted for added confidentiality.

Policies and Administration

Whereas a security solution selects a set of security mechanisms to use in a security domain, the security policy represents the particular state in which these mechanisms are configured. If the particular security approach has provided security mechanisms that are not very configurable, the range of security policies you can define for such mechanisms will obviously be limited.

For example, suppose that a particular access control protection solution you have defined in software has hard-coded method signatures on some access control class for each type of permission being requested. Thus, for a particular permission request, you'll need to add a call from code to make such a request. Although this solution provides an access control solution, a solution that enables you to define such permission in a file would be more configurable and enable you to define more manageable security policies. Such is a key difference between Java 1.1 security and Java 1.2/2.0 security.

Both security administration APIs and GUIs to manage such policies are sometimes provided to make the administration of security for a domain more manageable. Security administration tasks and associated policies that are commonly provided relate to the security-protection mechanisms previously mentioned and include the following:

- Administration of the quality of protection (QOP) for cryptographic functions employed by a security domain.
- Administration of which principals can be authenticated with a domain.

- Administration of certificates, private keys, and public keys in a key store.
- Administration of issuing certificates if you are a CA.
- Administration of CRLs if you are a CA.
- Administration of which individuals belong to which groups.
- Administration of permissions associated with particular principals.
- Administration of classification levels associated with particular principals and resources.
- Administration of other domain permissions and privileges.
- Administration of which security-critical operations need to be audited.
- Generation of audit log reports.
- Generation of reports on the state of security in the system.

Java Security Model and Infrastructure

One of the original ways in which Java was promoted for use by developers was for creating Java applets. Java applets enable code to be downloaded directly into a Web browser. This technology was one of the first that turned the Web browser into a framework that could support the execution of applications downloaded over the Web. Such a framework made many promises in terms of providing a new paradigm for computing starkly contrasted with the traditional way of desktop computing. With desktop computing, your applications were loaded and executed by you on your machine. Whenever updates to the application software were needed, you had to obtain such distributions from such sources as CDs and disks and load the updates yourself. Java applets promised a new paradigm in which mobile code would be downloaded dynamically to your Web browser and automatically updated whenever you revisited the Web site from which the code was downloaded.

However, network performance has helped curb such grand visions by limiting the size of Java applets that users consider reasonable to download and therefore limiting the complexity of applications downloaded. Furthermore, the performance of JVM implementations equipped with Web browsers has also hampered the proliferation of Java applets on the Internet. Nevertheless, because Java applets brought mobile code into the limelight, Sun wisely considered security early in developing the Java APIs. After all, if you are now downloading mobile Java code from some remote Web site onto your local machine, how much access to your local machine would you want to relinquish to such code? Many traditional desktop applications require access to your local file system, but do you really want a Java applet downloaded from some malicious Web site to have access to your file system?

Thus, security was a key consideration for Java from day one. Enterprise applications can benefit from these security features as well. Although early models for Java security addressed Java applet issues, Java applications can now take advantage of the more sophisticated security model available in the Java 2 platform for enhancing the security of your distributed enterprise services.

The evolution of the Java security model introduced with each major Java version release is depicted in Figures 17.6 through 17.8. The Java version 1.0 platform provided a very limited security model known as the "sandbox" model, as shown in Figure 17.6. In the sandbox model, only local code had access to all the valuable resources (for example, files, new network connections) that are exposed and accessed by the Java Virtual Machine (JVM). Code downloaded from remote sources such as applets would have access only to a limited number of resources. Thus, file-system access and the capability to create new connections would be limited for remote code. This was a primary concern for JVM implementations equipped with Web browsers.

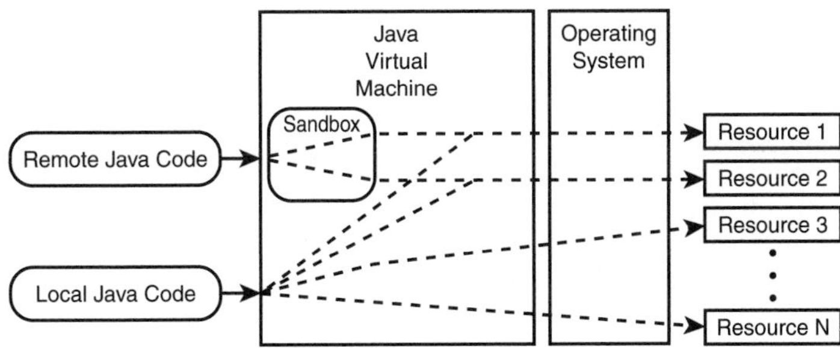

Figure 17.6 The Java 1.0 sandbox security model.

The Java 1.0 security model was somewhat too restrictive, however. The vision for providing downloadable applications over the Web was being stifled by the fact that such applications could not perform key operations such as file access or create new network connections. If Web-browser vendors treated remote code like local code, the path would have been opened for malicious code to corrupt the local machine. Such an all-or-none model was replaced in Java 1.1 when a trusted security model was employed, as depicted in Figure 17.7.

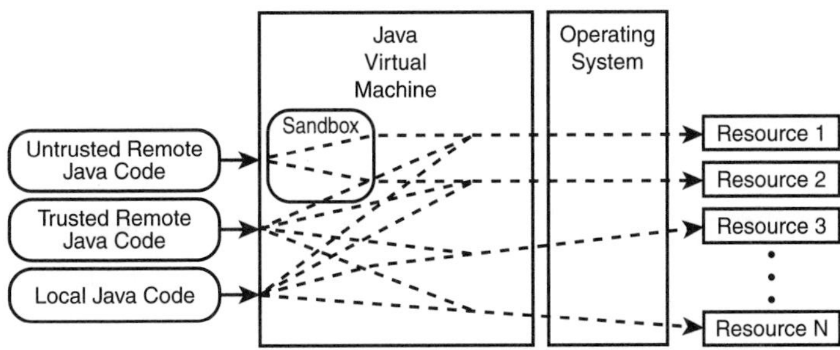

Figure 17.7 The Java 1.1 trusted code security model.

With the trusted code model, you could optionally designate whether code "signed" by certain providers would be allowed to have the full resource access it desired. Thus, you might actually trust that some Java code from Microsoft would be able to run inside of your browser with full access to your system resources much like you trust Microsoft when you install one of its many products on your system. Code or applet signing permits a company like Microsoft to sign its applet in such a way that you can verify that this code indeed came from this company. Thus, the signed applet would be granted access to all of your system resources, whereas untrusted code could still be confined to the sandbox.

The Java 2 platform (sometimes historically called Java 1.2) really has paved the way for application security with a finer-grained security model, as depicted in Figure 17.8. Now local and remote code alike can be confined to utilize only particular domains of resources according to configurable policies. Thus, some Java code Foo may be limited to access resources confined by one domain, whereas some other Java code Bar may have access to a set of resources confined by some other domain. Domains of access and configurable security policies make the Java 2 platform much more flexible. Furthermore, relieving us from the distinction between remote and local code allows for better support of the more widely applicable enterprise application security problems instead of simply focusing on mobile code and Java applet security problems.

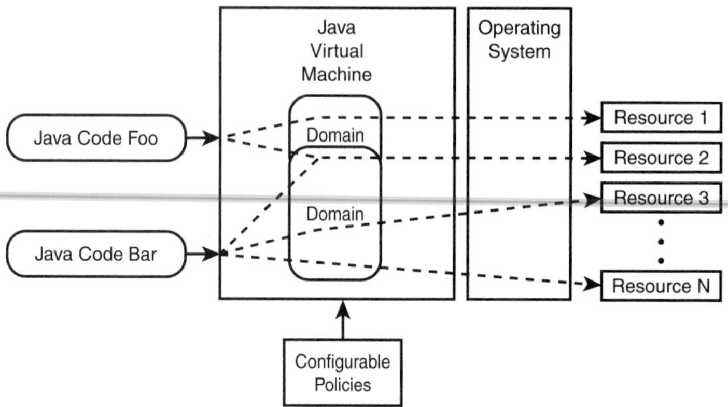

Figure 17.8 Java 2 configurable and fine-grained access security model.

Java Security Architecture

Figure 17.9 depicts the primary components that compose the standard set of APIs and mechanisms used to provide security for Java 2–based applications. In the lower half of the diagram are the core Java 2 security architecture and Java Cryptography Architecture (JCA), which together compose the Java 2 security platform that comes with the Java 2 platform. In the upper half of the diagram are the standard Java security extensions now included with the Java 2 platform and dependent on different aspects of that platform. Although many COTS packages external to the components shown here are available, the components in Figure 17.9 represent what Sun designates as those components that provide a standard interface. Various service-provider implementations of different aspects of these components that adhere to the interface standards defined by the Java security extension components are indeed available.

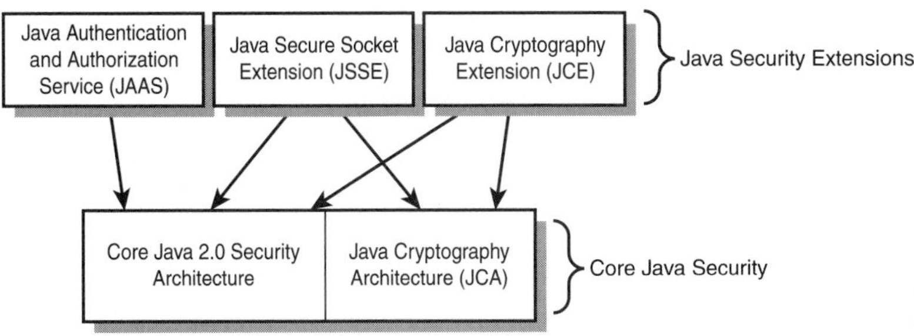

Figure 17.9 Java security architecture standard components.

Core Java 2 Security Architecture

The core Java 2 security architecture in context of the rest of the Java 2 platform, operating system, resources, and Java code running atop the Java 2 platform is shown in Figure 17.10. The pieces of this architecture that form the core of Java Security are the byte code verifier, class loader, security manager, access controller, permissions, policies, and protection domains. The byte code verifier verifies that the byte codes being loaded from Java application code external to the Java platform adhere to the syntax of the Java language specification. The class loader is then responsible for actual translation of byte codes into Java class constructs that can be manipulated by the Java runtime environment. In the process of loading classes, different class loaders may employ different policies to determine whether certain classes should even be loaded into the runtime environment. The class loader and the Java 2 platform classes themselves help limit access to valued resources by intercepting calls made to Java platform API and delegating decisions as to whether such calls can be made to the security manager. Java 1.0 and 1.1 made exclusive use of a security manager for such decision making, whereas Java 2 applications can use the access controller for more flexible and configurable access control decision making. Finally, execution of code would not be possible without the beloved runtime execution engine.

Access control is the most significant addition to the Java 2 security platform, helping extend the security model to allow configurable and fine-grained access control. Java 2 permissions encapsulate configurable and extendable ways to designate access limitations and allowances that may be associated with valued resources. Java 2 policies provide the mechanisms needed to actually associate such permissions with valued resources in a configurable fashion. Finally, means for encapsulating domains of access control are also provided with the core Java 2 security model.

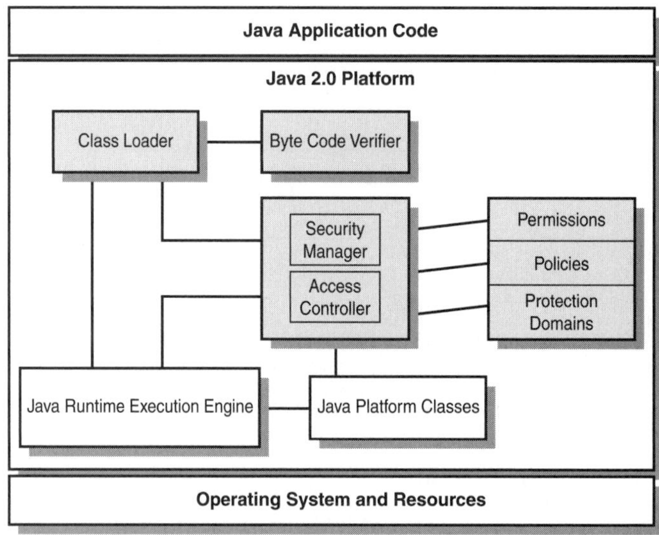

Figure 17.10 The core Java security architecture.

The `java.security` package contains the classes and interfaces that define the core Java security architecture. The `java.security.acl` package also contained access control classes and interfaces that were core to the Java 1.1 security architecture, but they have been superseded as of Java 2 by newer access control constructs. Finally, other security-related classes are embedded throughout the entire collection of Java platform packages. Along the way in this chapter and the next, we highlight which classes play a role in supporting the core Java security architecture.

Java Cryptography Architecture

The Java Cryptography Architecture (historically referred to as the JCA) provides an infrastructure for performing basic cryptographic functionality with the Java platform. The scope of cryptographic functionality includes protecting data against corruption for the sake of data integrity using basic cryptographic functions and algorithms. Cryptographic signature generation algorithms used for identifying sources of data and code are also built into the JCA. Because keys and certificates are a core part of identifying data and code sources, APIs are also built into the JCA for handling such features.

Although the JCA is part of the built-in Java security packages as are the core Java 2 security architecture features, we distinguish the JCA from such core APIs largely due to the JCA's underlying service provider interface. That is, different cryptographic implementations can be plugged into the JCA framework, whereas Java applications can still adhere to the same basic JCA interfaces. Sun does equip a default set of cryptographic functions with the JCA, however.

Java Cryptography Extension

The terms *encryption* and *cryptography* are sometimes used interchangeably. However, Sun adheres to the definition of *cryptography* that designates the provision of the basic data integrity and source identity functions supported by the JCA. *Encryption* is used to mean those functions used to encrypt blocks of data for the added sake of confidentiality until the data can be subsequently decrypted by the intended receiver. The Java Cryptography Extension (JCE) is now provided as part of the J2SE for these auxiliary encryption purposes.

Java Secure Socket Extension

Because SSL happens to be one of the more commonly used encryption-based protocols for integrity and confidentiality, Sun also now includes the Java Secure Socket Extension (JSSE) in the J2SE. The JSSE provides a standard interface along with an underlying reference implementation for building Java applications with SSL. Different commercial-grade underlying SSL implementations can be used with the JSSE and still provide the same interface to the applications developer. The JSSE is also more generically defined to provide a standard interface to support other secure socket protocols such as the Transport Layer Security (TLS) and Wireless Transport Layer Security (WTLS) protocols.

Java Authentication and Authorization Service

The Java Authentication and Authorization Service (JAAS) now included with the J2SE was developed to provide a standard way for limiting access to resources based on an authenticated user identity. Thus, standard APIs for login and logout are provided in which a standard interface for passing around secure user credentials and context makes it possible to swap in and out different underlying authentication model implementations. Thus, whether you use Kerberos or Smart Cards, the same API is provided.

Byte Code Verifier

Before the class loader bothers to register a class that it loads with the Java runtime environment, it passes the loaded Java class byte codes to the byte code verifier (also called the class file verifier). The byte code verifier then analyzes the byte code stream for the Java class and verifies that this byte stream adheres to the Java language rules defined for classes. The byte code verifier accomplishes this task in two phases. In phase one of byte code verification, the internals of the Java class byte stream itself are analyzed. In phase two, verifications of references to other classes from this class are made.

Phase two verification occurs when the classes to which a class refers are actually referenced at runtime. Not only will the references be verified for correctness, but the relationship rules involving that reference also will be verified. For example, a referenced method on another class will be checked to see whether that method is visible (that is, public, package, protected, or private) to the current class.

Class Loader

The class loader is one of the key components of a JVM responsible for managing the loading of Java class byte codes into the Java runtime environment. The class loader is responsible for the following:

- Loading Java class byte codes from an input stream (for example, file or network).
- Inducing the byte code verifier to verify these byte codes.
- Inducing the security manager and access controller to verify access to resources.
- Handing the classes off to the Java runtime execution engine.

The class loader component is actually composed of one or more individual class loaders. A primordial class loader is baked into the JVM and is responsible for loading the core Java platform classes. Other class loaders can be implemented by adhering to a standard class loader interface. However, such class loaders are subject to more stringent security verifications than is the primordial class loader. Different class loader implementations are provided to enable different ways to load classes from different input streams and using different policies.

Class Loader Architecture and Security

Figure 17.11 depicts the basic class loader architecture assumed by the Java security model. As a generic rule enforced by the standard class loader interface framework, when asked to load a class from an input stream, a class loader first checks its cached collection of classes to determine whether the class is already loaded. If it is loaded, the class loader can return the class without further processing. The security manager and access controller can then be consulted to determine whether access to the particular class is allowed. The primordial class loader is then consulted first to determine whether it can load the class. In Java 2, the primordial class loader loads core Java platform classes, whereas the Java 1.1 primordial class loader also loads classes from the `CLASSPATH`. In Java 2, auxiliary class loaders are consulted to load classes from the `CLASSPATH` as well as remote classes.

If the class is not loaded by the primordial class loader, the class is then read from the input stream. The actual type of input stream used depends on the type of class loader. An input stream connected to a local file medium location or to a network medium location requires a class loader that can read classes from such mediums. The bytes read from the input stream are then fed through the byte code verification process. If successful byte code verification is performed, a `java.lang.Class` object is created that is used to describe the class for the virtual machine. Before the class is created, the security manager is conferred with again to determine whether creation of such a class is permitted. Finally, if the class is loaded, the class is then cached with its collection of other loaded classes.

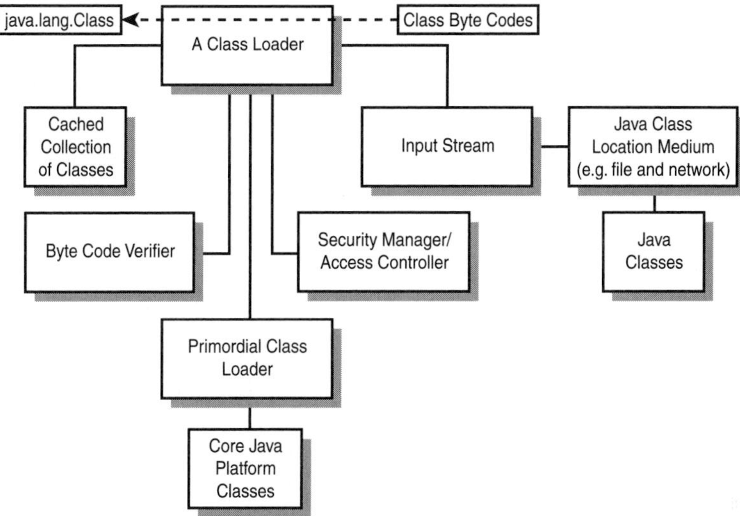

Figure 17.11 The class loader architecture.

When a class loaded by the class loader refers to another class, the same basic process for finding the referenced class is followed. Thus, you can see that a particular class loader will consult only the primordial class loader, its own cached collection of classes, and its associated input stream for a class to load. Different class loader instances within the same virtual machine thus do not consult one another to load classes. This separation of class loaders results in a separation of name spaces such that different implementations of classes with the same fully qualified name may live in different class loaders. This provides a security advantage in that a malicious class loader cannot corrupt the classes used by another class loader in the same virtual machine by purposely loading a malicious class into that class loader's name space.

Class Loader Interfaces

In addition to the primordial class loader that is part of the Java platform, other common and predefined class loaders also exist. Perhaps one of the first common class loader types to be implemented was the applet class loaders. Applet class loaders were implemented by Web browser vendors to provide support for loading classes, which form the code of an applet, from the network via HTTP from within a Web browser. Applet class loaders typically determine where to load these classes from based on a `CODEBASE` tag that accompanies an applet tag in an HTML file.

Although no standard API for an applet class loader exists, Figure 17.12 shows the standard base class loader class and three standard class loader implementations that come equipped with the Java platform. These standard class loader types are briefly described here:

- `java.lang.ClassLoader`: Represents the base class loader from which other class loaders should be extended. Core interfaces exist on the `ClassLoader` for loading classes, defining classes, finding classes, obtaining resource handles, and accessing class libraries. The `loadClass()` method is the most important method on the `ClassLoader` responsible for performing the actual load of a class.
- `java.security.SecureClassLoader`: The `SecureClassLoader` was introduced in Java 2 as a base class that offers the capability to associate classes with permissions and a code source. A code source identifies the URL and certificate associated with a class.
- `java.net.URLClassLoader`: This class loader was also introduced in Java 2 to load classes from a list of URLs. The URLs can be either jar files or directories.
- `java.rmi.server.RMIClassLoader`: Existing since Java 1.1, the `RMIClassLoader` is used by RMI applications during marshaling and unmarshaling of classes passed as parameters or return values. The `RMIClassLoader` loads classes from the network using a list of URLs.

The `URLClassLoader` class may offer all you need in a class loader that can load classes from the network via HTTP or from the file system. However, you may indeed encounter a situation in which you need to implement your own class loader. For example, you may desire to load classes from a database or perhaps via some other protocol besides HTTP. In such a situation, you should still subclass `ClassLoader`, `SecureClassLoader`, or `URLClassLoader`. You'll then want to overload a few of the protected methods of the class you are extending.

Whereas Java 1.1 style class loader implementations often overrode the protected `ClassLoader.loadClass(String, boolean)` method, Java 2 style class loader implementations are encouraged to override the protected `ClassLoader.findClass(String)` method. This is because most of the generic class loading logic can still be utilized by leaving the `loadClass()` method as is. The `loadClass()` method calls the `findClass()` method after preliminary calls are made, such as determining whether the class is already loaded and checking with the primordial class loader. The `findClass()` method can thus be specialized to look for the class on the specialized input stream that your class loader implementation desires to search for classes matching the fully qualified classname as an input parameter. If you have a block of data you've read from your input stream, you can then run this class through the byte code verifier, as well as create an instance of a `Class` object by calling the `defineClass()` method. For example:

```
public MyClassLoader extends ClassLoader
{
  protected Class findClass(String className){
    byte[] buffer = getMyData(className);
    Class returnClass = defineClass(className, buffer, 0, buffer.length);
    return returnClass;
  }
```

```
  private byte[] getMyData(String className){
    // This arbitrarily named method contains the logic
    // needed to retrieve the named class from the input stream
    // associated with your class loader implementation. Thus, this
    // method may read some data from a TCP/IP socket, for example,
    // given the name of a class and then return the bytes (byte codes)
    // associated with the read Java class.
  }
  ...
  // Implement other methods as needed
  ...
}
```

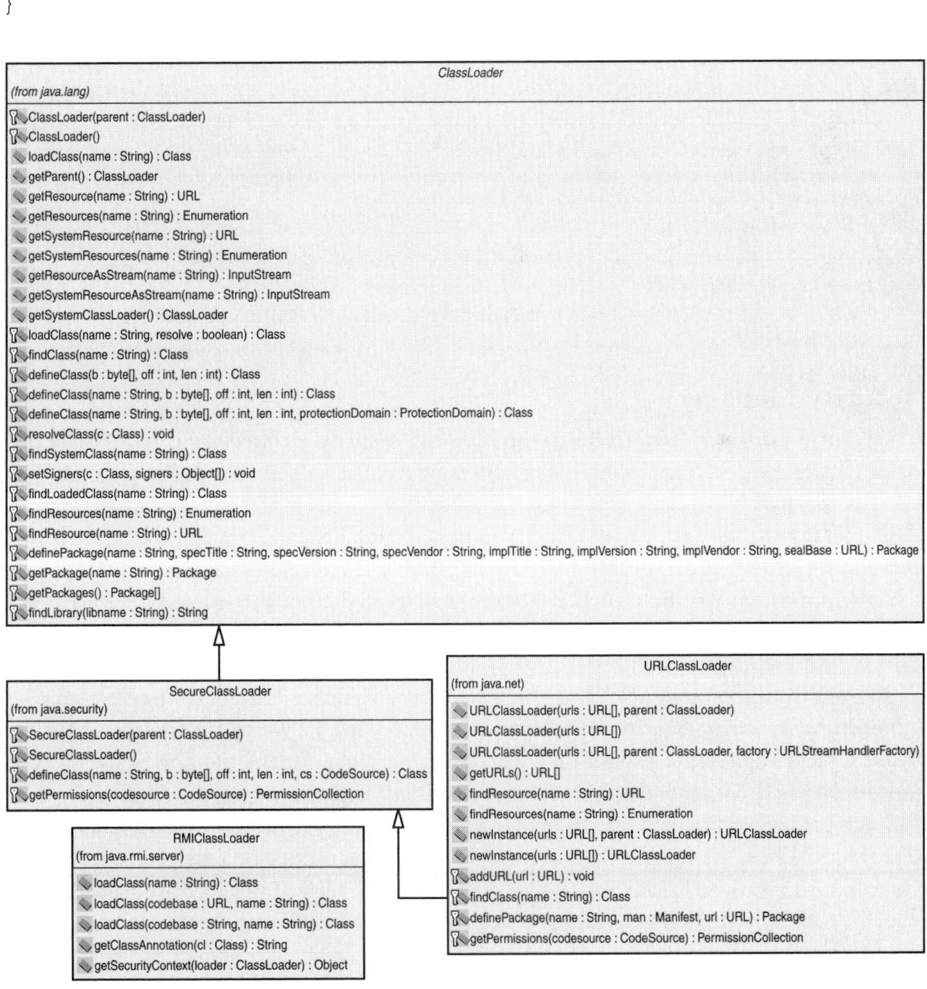

Figure 17.12 Standard class loader APIs.

An explicit request to load a class using your custom class loader can be accomplished using the static `forName(String, boolean, ClassLoader)` method on `java.lang.Class`. The `String` parameter specifies the fully qualified classname to load, the `boolean` flag indicates whether the class should be initialized, and the `ClassLoader` parameter designates the class loader to use. Thus, you might explicitly load a class using your custom class loader and instantiate an instance of the class given the following call:

```
MyClassLoader myClassLoader = new MyClassLoader();
Class myQueryServerClass = Class.forName("com.beeshirts.QueryServer",
                                         true, myClassLoader);
QueryServer myQueryServer
               = (QueryServer) myQueryServerClass.newInstance();
```

Every reference to unloaded classes from the `myQueryServer` object can then use the class loader with which it was loaded. Of course, you can also call `loadClass()` on an instance of your custom class loader and use it to load the class initially, as shown here:

```
MyClassLoader myClassLoader = new MyClassLoader();
Class myQueryServerClass
             = myClassLoader.loadClass("com.beeshirts.QueryServer");
QueryServer myQueryServer
             = (QueryServer) myQueryServerClass.newInstance();
```

Security Manager

The security manager component of the core Java security architecture is responsible for determining whether certain requests to access particular valued resources are to be allowed. To make this decision, the security manager considers the source (that is, Java class) making the request. Because access to many valued resources must first pass through the core Java classes from a Java class making the request, the core Java classes take the opportunity to first ask the security manager whether the request is allowed. If access is denied, a `java.lang.SecurityException` is thrown. If access is permitted, the call will proceed as normal.

Each JVM process instance allows only one security manager instance to exist (that is, a singleton). After the security manager is instantiated, the JVM can be configured such that the security manager cannot be replaced. It thus exists for the lifetime of the JVM process. Many JVMs embedded in Web browsers will instantiate a security manager instance before the first Java applet is ever loaded and not permit the security manager to be replaced. Thus, the security manager in Web browsers cannot be replaced by a malicious Java applet. A malicious Java applet could, after all, replace the security manager with its own security manager instance that relaxes restrictions on which valued resources can be accessed.

Although Java applets run in a JVM process that has already instantiated a security manager, regular Java applications you create don't have the benefit of this fact. In Java 1.1, creating your own security manager was a tad tedious. Java 2 makes creating your own security manager for a Java application much simpler and makes it easily configurable. This is because a default and configurable security manager that is rich enough in flexible feature support for many applications can be used with Java 2 applications. Thus, as you'll see, use of a security manager to protect access to valued resources can also be provided for Java applications in the enterprise.

Use of the default security manager can be specified from the command line during startup of your Java applications. The `java.security.manager` property can be passed to the JVM as a system property specifying use of the default security manager in the following fashions:

```
java -Djava.security.manager MyApplication
java -Djava.security.manager=default MyApplication
```

Security Manager Interfaces

The `java.lang.SecurityManager` class encapsulates the key interface to the security manager instantiated in a Java process. The `java.lang.System.getSecurityManager()` method returns a handle to the currently instantiated `SecurityManager` object. If no security manager is instantiated, a null value is returned. The `java.lang.System.setSecurityManager()` call takes a `SecurityManager` input parameter and first checks to see whether the existing security manager is allowed to be replaced by the calling class. If the security manager does not exist or if the class is allowed to replace the existing security manager, the operation proceeds and returns. Otherwise, a `SecurityException` is thrown.

The `SecurityManager` class is mainly populated with public `check`*`XXX`*`()` style methods. Each `check`*`XXX`*`()` method is defined to check whether access is allowed for a particular valued resource. If access is not allowed, the `check`*`XXX`*`()` methods will throw `SecurityException` objects. Most of these methods are left over from the Java 1.0 and 1.1 versions of the `SecurityManager`. Java 2 has introduced the `checkPermission(Permission)` and `checkPermission(Permission, Object)` methods, which are more generic forms of the other `check`*`XXX`*`()` methods. In fact, each `check`*`XXX`*`()` method now calls a generic `checkPermission()` method under the hood of Sun's Java 2 platform implementation. The `checkPermission()` method in turn calls the `java.security.AccessController` class.

The `AccessController` was added in Java 2 to provide the fine-grained and configurable access control functionality that is central to the new security model. Although the `SecurityManager` is still maintained for backward compatibility with existing applications and to serve as a primary security management interface, the `AccessController` really subsumes the responsibility for algorithmic access checking that was once the province of the `SecurityManager`. We describe the `AccessController` in more detail later in this chapter.

Java Cryptography Architecture

The Java Cryptography Architecture (JCA) equipped with the Java platform was first introduced with Java 1.1. The JCA provides basic cryptographic functions used for the following primary purposes:

- To protect data communicated or stored for integrity.
- To identify a principal associated with data that has been communicated or retrieved from storage.
- To provide support for generating keys and certificates used to identify data sources.
- To provide a framework for plugging different cryptographic algorithms from different service providers.

Note

Be cognizant of the context for use of the acronym *JCA*. It is also sometimes used to refer to the J2EE Connector Architecture (described in Chapter 29, "EJB Integration and Management").

You should not assume too much by the word *cryptography* in JCA. The JCA is not really useful for encrypting data communicated or stored for decryption by an intended receiver. Such cryptographic functionality used to provide confidentiality is possible with the JCE. Furthermore, although SSL represents one of the more popular crypto-related protocols in the Internet era, it is not packaged with the JCA. Rather, SSL interface support is provided separately inside of the JSSE package.

The Architecture of JCA

The JCA is composed of various classes and interfaces that implement basic cryptographic functionality. These are the Java 2 platform packages which contain classes and interfaces that make up the JCA:

- `java.security`: The set of core classes and interfaces for the JCA plug-and-play service provider framework and cryptographic operation APIs. Note that this package also contains core Java security architecture classes and interfaces.
- `java.security.cert`: A set of certificate management classes and interfaces.
- `java.security.interfaces`: A set of interfaces used to encapsulate and manage DSA and RSA public and private keys.
- `java.security.spec`: A set of classes and interfaces used to describe public and private key algorithm and parameter specifications.

Figure 17.13 depicts the top-level architecture of the JCA with a mixture of actual Java classes and conceptual classes (that is, not real code-based classes, but simply representative of concepts). At the top of the diagram, we have the `java.security.Security` class mainly responsible for managing a collection of Cryptographic Service Providers (CSPs). A CSP represents a service provider that implements one or more cryptographic functions that adhere to the cryptographic interfaces defined in the JCA. Information about each CSP is encapsulated by the `java.security.Provider` abstract class. CSPs (shown as `SomeCSPImpl` in Figure 17.13) extend the `Provider` abstract class with specific implementations of methods on the `Provider` class.

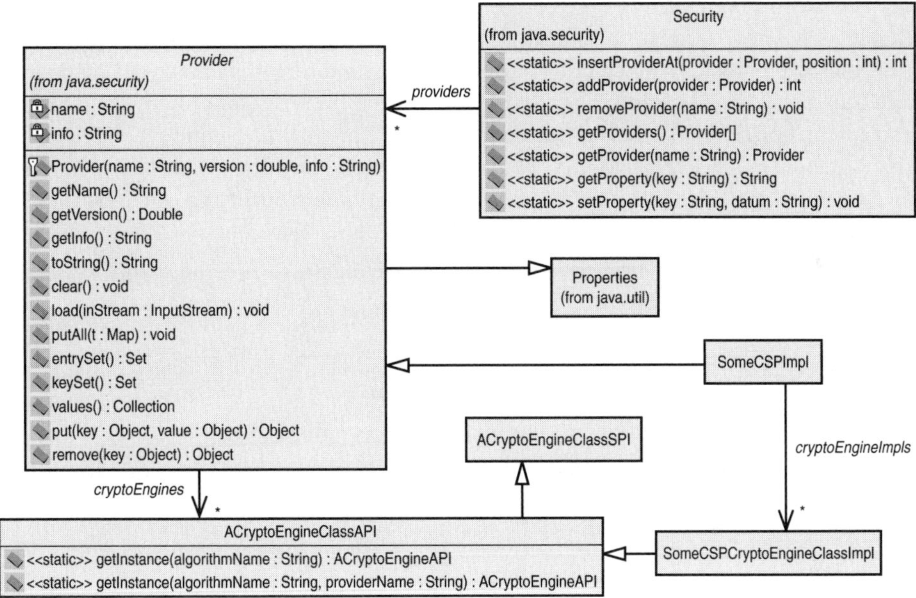

Figure 17.13 The top-level architecture of JCA.

Each CSP will implement one or more cryptographic engines. A cryptographic engine represents a particular cryptographic algorithm and set of parameters to that algorithm which perform some cryptographic functionality. For example, the MD5 message digest algorithm described earlier in this chapter is a particular algorithm and set of parameters used to generate an encrypted stream of data based on another stream of data. MD5 belongs to a general class of cryptographic engines referred to as a message digest cryptographic engine.

The various cryptographic engines (for example, `SomeCSPCryptoEngineImpl`) supplied by a CSP implement some standard cryptographic service provider interface (for example, `ACryptoEngineClassSPI`) provided by the JCA. Each service provider interface is extended by a cryptographic engine API (for example, `ACryptoEngineClassAPI`) used by the applications programmer. Each cryptographic engine API provides a static `getInstance(String)` method that takes the name of a particular algorithm name related to that engine class and returns a concrete instance of the requested cryptographic engine using that algorithm if it exists. Otherwise, a `java.security.NoSuchAlgorithmException` exception is thrown. A static `getInstance(String, String)` method on each cryptographic engine API specifies a particular CSP to use.

Cryptographic Engines

The `java.security.MessageDigest` abstract class is an example of a cryptographic engine API, whereas the `java.security.MessageDigestSpi` abstract class represents the cryptographic service provider interface that must be implemented. The protected methods of `MessageDigestSpi` will be visible and relevant only to the CSP's implementation. The JCA defines various standard cryptographic engine types. These cryptographic engine APIs and their helper classes rest at the core of how the JCA is used by enterprise application developers. The primary functionality provided by each core cryptographic engine type provided by the JCA is described here:

- `MessageDigest`: Creates and verifies message digests.
- `Signature`: Creates and verifies digital signatures.
- `KeyPairGenerator`: Generates public and private key pairs.
- `KeyFactory`: Converts between secure keys and key specifications.
- `KeyStore`: Modifies information in a secure key storage repository.
- `CertificateFactory`: Generates certificates and certificate revocation lists.
- `AlgorithmParameters`: Encodes crypto algorithm parameters.
- `AlgorithmParameterGenerator`: Creates crypto algorithm parameters.
- `SecureRandom`: Creates random numbers.

Cryptographic Service Providers

The JCA shipped with the Java platform comes equipped with a default CSP implemented by Sun. The `String` name used with the JCA APIs to designate this default provider is `SUN`. The default Sun CSP implementation provides support for the following cryptographic engine and algorithm combinations:

- MD5 message digest algorithm
- SHA-1 message digest algorithm
- DSA for signatures
- DSA key pair generator
- DSA algorithm parameters
- DSA algorithm parameter generator
- DSA key factory
- JKS key store (JKS involves a proprietary algorithm)

- X.509 certificate factory
- SHA1PRNG pseudo-random number generator algorithm (an IEEE standard)

You can install a CSP for use with your Java runtime environment by simply placing a JAR or ZIP file with the classes that implement the JCA CSP interfaces somewhere on your `CLASSPATH`. You will then need to configure the `java.security` file under the root directory of your Java installation in the `<JavaRootInstall>\lib\security\` directory. In that file, you need to add the fully qualified classnames of your CSPs that extend the `Provider` class. The order of preference specifies which CSP to use in the event that an algorithm selected for use is implemented by another CSP. For example, the following `java.security` file entries specify that Sun's default CSP is preferred before Sun's RSA JCA CSP implementation:

```
# List of providers in order from most to least preferred CSP
security.provider.1=sun.security.provider.Sun
security.provider.2=com.sun.rsajca.Provider
```

CSPs can also be added and removed programmatically from within your JVM process. Only trusted applications can perform such operations, however. A trusted application here refers to an application running without a security manager installed or an application that has been granted permission to add and remove CSPs. Adding and removing CSPs with the `Security` class is rather straightforward, assuming that your application has the proper permissions:

```
// Install SunJCE CSP by first creating a Provider instance
Provider providerSunJce = new com.sun.crypto.provider.SunJCE();
// Then add provider using Security class and obtain preference number
int providerPreferenceJCE = Security.addProvider(providerSunJce);

// Or set the preference number yourself increasing preference numbers
// of any providers already installed at that preference level
Provider providerATI = new com.assuredtech.security.JCAProvider();
int providerPreferenceATI = Security.insertProviderAt(providerATI, 1);

// A provider can be removed dynamically using Security class
// For example, to remove default Sun CSP
Security.removeProvider("SUN");
```

Java Security Programming

We've just taken a look at the Java security model and underlying infrastructure in depth in the preceding section. Now it is time to take a look at how a developer can begin to programmatically tap the features offered by the Java security model. Specifically, the Java programmer is enabled a high degree of controllability over authorization, principal identification, integrity, confidentiality, and authentication. This section explores the most important facets of such Java security programming.

Permissions

As part of the new Java 2 security model for providing fine-grained and configurable access control, a hierarchy of extendable permissions APIs has been added to the Java platform. Permission objects encapsulate the concept of a permission to access some valued resource. Permissions have names referring to a target resource for which a permission is to be granted or denied. Permissions also have a series of actions which scope the set of operations that may be performed on that target resource. Permissions are classified according to types using subclasses from base permission types in the Java API. Thus, for example, a file permission extends the concept of an abstract permission such that the target name represents one or more filenames or directories and the action list represents actions that may be performed on targets, such as "read" or "write." These Java 2 permission objects replace the permission-related constructs in the `java.security.acl` package.

Permissions Architecture

Figure 17.14 shows the basic architecture of Java 2 permissions. At the root of the permissions architecture is the `java.security.Permission` abstract class, which conceptualizes a permission to access some valued resource. A `Permission` object has a target name of a valued resource (for example, a filename) that is retrieved via the `getName()` method. A `Permission` object can also return a `String` defining the set of actions that are desired to be performed on the target resource. The actions' `String` is typically a comma-separated list of actions related to a target. For example, actions such as "read, write" might be the set of actions related to a particular target filename. The `implies(Permission)` method on the `Permission` class is used to indicate whether the permission actions associated with the `Permission` object passed in as a parameter are implied by or granted by the current `Permission` object's permission actions. The `checkGuard()` method on the `Permission` object is implemented by virtue of the fact that the `Permission` object implements the `java.security.Guard` interface. The `Guard` interface is described later in this chapter.

Subclasses of `Permission` can also implement the `newPermissionCollection()` method to return an object that extends the `java.security.PermissionCollection` abstract class. The `PermissionCollection` object is used to encapsulate a collection of one or more `Permission` objects and includes methods to add permissions and return the list of permissions it contains. Adding permissions to a `PermissionCollection` object is allowed only if it is not read-only. Read-only access can be set with the `setReadOnly()` method and tested with the `isReadOnly()` method. For certain subclasses of `Permission`, it may be necessary to store them as a homogeneous collection of permissions so that a call to `implies()` on the `PermissionCollection` object can make sense for that particular permission type. Whereas the `PermissionCollection` represents a collection of `Permission` objects of the same type, the `java.security.Permissions` class encapsulates a collection of heterogeneous permissions. The `Permissions` class accomplishes this by storing permissions of the same type into their own separate `PermissionCollection` objects.

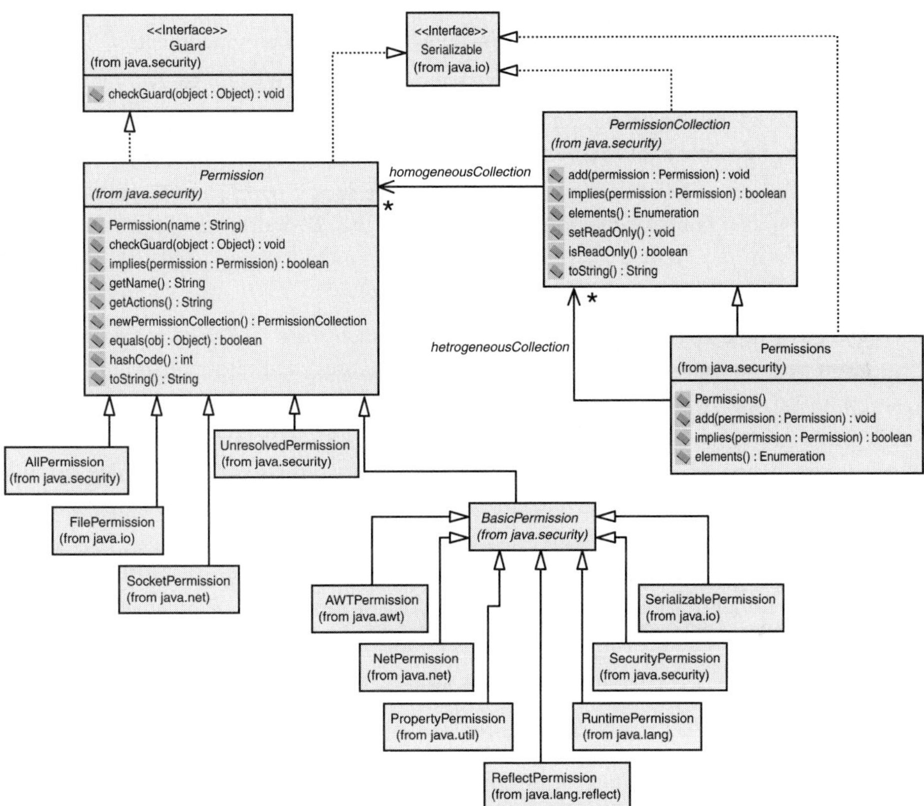

Figure 17.14 The Java 2 permissions architecture.

Permission Types

The `Permission` class contains several subclasses included with the standard J2SE API, most of which are shown in Figure 17.14. In the interest of conserving space, we've left the operation signatures of such classes out of the diagram. However, all the classes simply overload methods defined on the base `Permission` class. Although each class does define its own constructors, most classes have two constructors of the form *`Constructor`*`(String name)` taking a permission name parameter or *`Constructor`*`(String name, String actions)` taking a permission name and action `String`.

As a simple example, to specify the permission to read a particular file, you might programmatically use the `FilePermission` class as shown:

```
FilePermission fp
                = new FilePermission("C:\\temp\\sampleFile.txt","read");
```

A brief description of how each permission subclass is used is provided here:

- `java.security.AllPermission`: Used to grant permission to every resource.
- `java.io.FilePermission`: Used to give file access permissions such as to read files, read directory information, write files, execute files, and delete files.
- `java.net.SocketPermission`: Used to give socket permissions such as to accept socket connections from particular domains, IP addresses, and ports.
- `java.security.UnresolvedPermission`: Used to indicate that a permission has yet to be assigned.
- `java.security.BasicPermission`: An abstract base class used to indicate that you do or do not have permissions to access an associated resource and define a standard format for specifying permissions.
- `java.awt.AWTPermission`: Used to give access to user interface resources such as permission to access the system clipboard, access the system event queue, listen to AWT events, and show windows without warning banners.
- `java.net.NetPermission`: Used to give networking permissions such as to get a password from a registered system authenticator, to register authenticators for getting authentication information, and to designate a stream handler when creating URLs.
- `java.util.PropertyPermission`: Used to give permission to get and set properties.
- `java.lang.reflect.ReflectPermission`: Used to give permission for performing Java reflection operations such as to access methods and fields in a class for public, default package, protected, and private elements on reflected objects.
- `java.lang.RuntimePermission`: Used to give various Java runtime permissions such as to create a new class loader, get the current class loader, change security managers, exit from a JVM, set different socket factories, change standard I/O streams, change the state of a thread, stop a thread, modify the thread group, read from and write to a file descriptor, load dynamic shared libraries, start a print job, access declared members, define classes in a package, and access classes in a package.
- `java.security.SecurityPermission`: Used to give security management permissions such as to get and set security policies, set a new signed key pair, get a private key, add a new certificate, get/set/delete a security identity, get and set a security property, change system scope, and add or remove a security provider.

- `java.io.SerializablePermission`: Used to give certain Java serialization permissions such as to implement subclasses of object input and output streams for serialization and to substitute objects during serialization.

Custom Permission Types

Although the standard permission types already encapsulate permissions for most of the predefined valued resources with which a JVM can interact, the creation of application-specific permissions may be necessary from time to time. Customization is accomplished simply by extending one of the permission types. Typically, you will want to extend either the `Permission` class or the `BasicPermission` class. If you are extending the `Permission` class, implementing the `implies()`, `equals()`, `getActions()`, and `hashCode()` methods will be your primary concern, as well as implementing any permission-specific constructors. If you are extending the `BasicPermission` class, you can rely on the default implementation of methods that `BasicPermission` provides or provide implementation for such methods yourself. You will want to implement both constructor forms defined in the `BasicPermission` class, however, for taking a name and name/actions pair as parameters even if you do not make use of actions. For example:

```
public class BeeShirtsPermission extends BasicPermission
{
  public BeeShirtsPermission(String name){...}
  public BeeShirtsPermission(String name, String actions){...}
  // Will rely on BasicPermission default method implementations
}
```

Security Policies

Although permissions to access valued resources from a JVM are encapsulated by the Java API hierarchy for permissions, the management of such permissions in a configurable fashion is encapsulated by the Java 2 security policy infrastructure. Security policies provide a programmer-friendly way to configure which permissions are granted to which resources. Although a minimalist API exists to encapsulate security policy configuration, a default policy management framework is provided with the Java 2 platform to enable the configuration of security policies for a Java application without any additional tools. Such a default security policy management framework provides a mechanism for you to define security policies using a simple ASCII policy file format. Furthermore, a GUI-based policy tool utility can also be used to manipulate the security policy file.

As you'll see shortly, a policy file can be used to define which permissions are granted to certain domains of protection. A domain of protection is defined by a URL indicating where the code to be subject to a particular set of security policies comes from. A domain of protection can also be defined by one or more identities that define whom the code comes from.

Security Policy File Format

In the default implementation of security policy management with the Java 2 platform, a security policy is defined in an ASCII text file. A security policy file defines an optional key-store entry, and one or more permissions grant entries of the following general form:

```
[keystore "keystore_URL", "keystore_type";]

grant [SignedBy "list of names"]
      [, CodeBase "URL"]
      [, Principal ["principal_class_name"] "principal_name"
       , Principal ...]
{
   permission permission_class_name [ "name" ] [, "actions"]
                                     [, SignedBy "list of names"];
   permission ...
};
```

Keywords used in the policy file, designated by boldface words in the preceding lines, are case-insensitive. Each policy file entry specified for a security domain begins with the `grant` keyword and contains one or more permission definitions for the particular domain of protection. Each permission entry begins with the `permission` keyword and is followed by the fully qualified permission classname. Permission target names and a comma-separated list of actions also follow a permission designation. The `SignedBy` field following the permission is optionally provided with a comma-separated list of alias names that indicate who must have signed the Java code for the permissions class. As you'll see in a later section, Java code may be signed such that you can securely verify that such code is from the intended supplier. The `keystore` entry designates which URL and type of storage mechanism to consult for signed classes.

Each grant entry delimiting a domain of protection can also contain a `SignedBy` field designating the fact that code being executed in the JVM associated with the grant entry must be signed by the named signers. A `CodeBase` field may also be associated with a grant entry to relate a set of permissions with a resource location from where the code is loaded. A code base URL that ends with / indicates all Java class files in a particular directory. A code base URL that ends with /* indicates all Java class files and JAR files in a particular directory. A code base URL that ends with /- indicates all Java class files and JAR files in a particular directory and its subdirectories.

> **Subject-Based Access Control and JAAS**
>
> As reflected in the general policy file format previously discussed and new to the J2SE v1.4 is also the concept of subject-based access control. Subject-based access control involves specifying one or more principals that may be associated with a particular permission grouping. Hence, only principals identified by such entries are allowed the associated permissions. Subject-based access control is associated with the integration of the Java Authentication and Authorization Service (JAAS) with the J2SE v1.4. We discuss JAAS later in this chapter and in much more detail in Chapter 28, "EJB Assurance Services."

Custom permission types and each of the standard Java permission types can be defined in a security policy file of the previously mentioned format. As an example (excluding concern for permissions code security), the following security policy file entries represent valid grant permission entries using a few of the standard Java permission types:

```
grant
{
 permission java.io.FilePermission "C:\\temp\\sampleFile.txt", "read";
 permission java.io.FilePermission "C:\\temp", "read";
 permission java.io.FilePermission "C:\\temp\\*", "read";
 permission java.io.FilePermission "<<ALL_FILES>>", "read";
 permission java.io.FilePermission "C:\\temp\\test.exe ",
                                  "read, write, delete, execute";
};

grant CodeBase http://code.beeshirts.com/-"
{
 permission java.net.SocketPermission "www.beeshirts.com", "accept";
 permission java.util.PropertyPermission "java.*", "read, write";
 permission java.lang.RuntimePermission "setSecurityManager";
};
```

Referencing Properties in Policy Files

You'll notice that in the preceding policy file example, a system-dependent file separator (\\) was used in the policy file definitions. Usage of such constructs makes your policy file system-dependent. You might consider it desirable to use the standard Java `file.separator` system property instead to refer to such a construct in order to keep your security policy file system-independent. You can refer to such properties and others defined for your currently running JVM process using a simple convention in your security policy file. The convention simply requires that you encapsulate properties between two curly braces preceded by a dollar sign as shown here:

```
${aProperty}
```

The JVM will expand such a property when it reads the security policy file. For example, the standard `user.home` and `file.separator` Java system properties can be referenced in your security policy file to grant file read permissions to all files from a user's home directory as shown here:

```
grant
{
 permission java.io.FilePermission "${user.home}${file.separator}* ",
                                          "read";
}
```

Using Security Policy Files

Now that you know how to define policies in a security policy file, you may be wondering where to create such files and how to make your Java applications use the policies defined in such files.

A default system security file is defined relative to the root directory of your Java install and is contained in `[JAVA_HOME]\lib\security\java.security`. That file contains two entries created during the installation of your Java environment that indicate where a default Java system security policy file and user-specific security policy file are installed:

```
policy.url.1=file:${java.home}/lib/security/java.policy
policy.url.2=file:${user.home}/.java.policy
```

The system security policy file is referenced first. If it is not present, the user security policy file is referenced. If neither file is present, a most-restrictive security policy is assumed akin to the Java 1.0 sandbox model. Additional policies can be referenced in the `java.security` file using incremental `policy.url.X` indices (that is, `policy.url.3` and so on). These index numbers specify the search order for which the JVM should attempt to load security policy files. As soon as a file is located, the search stops and that policy file is used.

If you want to define a policy file to be read from your own application-specific location, you can pass in the `-Djava.security.policy` system property to the command line when starting your Java application. Such a property is used to define the location of your own security policy file as exemplified here:

```
java -Djava.security.policy=beeshirts/beeshirts.policy
➥ -Djava.security.manager com.beeshirts.MySecureServer
```

Note that the `-Djava.security.manager` property designates that the default system security manager should be used as opposed to an application installing its own security manager. As a final note, if you desire to disable the capability for applications to define their own policy files, a `policy.allowSystemProperty` property in the `java.security` file can override the default value of `true` by setting the property to `false`.

Security Policy Tool

The Java 2 environment also comes equipped with a GUI-based tool for editing security policy files if hand-editing ASCII files is not to your liking. The `policytool` program is located under the root directory of your Java installation in `[JAVA_HOME]\bin\policytool`. Figure 17.15 shows what the `policytool` looks like after you have selected an entry of a particular policy file for editing. You can also create and save new policy files. When the policy file is open, you can add, remove, and edit individual permissions with an easy-to-understand GUI. As you can see from Figure 17.15, editing principals associated with these permissions can also be accomplished with the `policytool`.

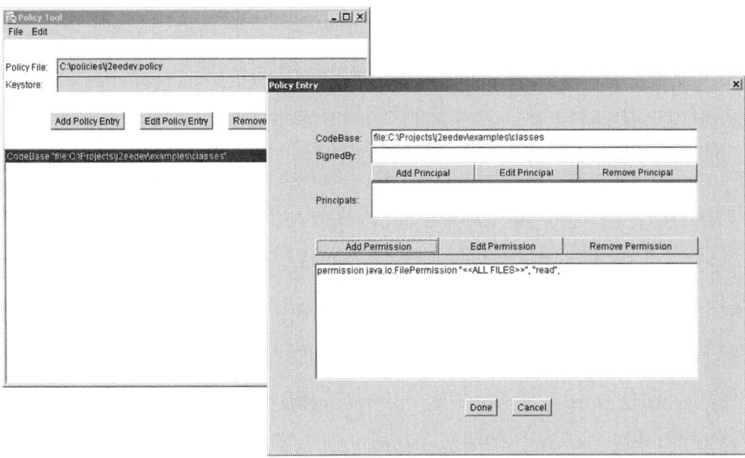

Figure 17.15 Viewing an entry with the Java security policy tool.

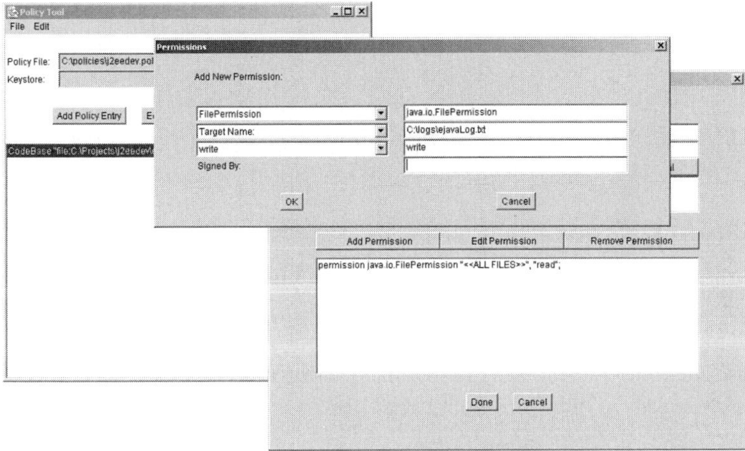

Figure 17.16 Adding permissions with the Java security policy tool.

Adding permissions is particularly simple, as shown in Figure 17.16. Here we see that drop-down lists of permission types, candidate names, and candidate actions can simplify adding permissions to an entry.

Security Policy APIs

A minimalist API does exist for encapsulating security policies. The `java.security.Policy` abstract class implements a static `getPolicy()` method returning a handle to the current installed policy, and the static `setPolicy()` method allows one to set a new system-wide security policy. The `getPolicy()` method can be invoked if the SecurityPermission getPolicy allows it to be, and the setPolicy() method can be invoked if the SecurityPermission setPolicy allows it to be.

When you're setting a new security policy, the new policy must extend the Policy class and implement the getPermissions() and refresh() methods. One form of the getPermissions() method takes a java.security.CodeSource object defining the code base URL and signed by certificates (to be discussed later) and returns the defined permissions allowed for such a code source as a PermissionCollection object. Another form of the getPermissions() method may be used that takes a javax.security.auth.Subject (from JAAS) and CodeSource object to be associated with those permissions granted to such principals and location and returns the defined permissions allowed as a PermissionCollection object. The refresh() method simply must refresh the policy information from the underlying policy storage mechanism associated with the newly defined Policy implementation.

Alternatively, the default policy implementation to use with your JVM instance can be specified with a policy.provider property in the java.security file:

```
policy.provider=com.assuredtech.security.GenericPolicy
```

As a final note, if a new policy object is not set using Policy.setPolicy() or if the policy.provider property is set, the default security policy provided by Sun is used. Sun's implementation of the default security policy that extends the Policy class and reads policy information from the previously mentioned policy files is contained in the class sun.security.provider.PolicyFile.

Java Access Control

Access control in Java 2 is managed by an access controller construct. As we mentioned earlier, the SecurityManager interfaces of Java 1.1 are still maintained for backward compatibility, but all check*XXX*() methods defined on the SecurityManager now delegate to the new java.security.AccessController class. The SecurityManager implements such delegation by calling the generic checkPermission(Permission) methods now defined on the SecurityManager for every check*XXX*() previously defined. The SecurityManager.checkPermission() method can then delegate calls to the AccessController.checkPermission() method. For example, for an implementation of the SecurityManager.checkRead(String fileName) method, we might have this:

```
checkPermission( new FilePermission(fileName, "read") );
```

And the corresponding SecurityManager.checkPermission(Permission permission) method might look like this:

```
java.security.AccessController.checkPermission( permission );
```

Thus, whereas permissions and policies help encapsulate and configure access levels to valued resources, the access control mechanisms in Java provide the infrastructure between Java code making calls to valued resources and the actual implemented access control for such resources. That is, Java access control provides the mechanisms in the Java security architecture that uses permissions and policies to actually allow or disallow access to valued resources.

Access Control Architecture

Figure 17.17 presents the architecture of access control in Java 2. At the top of this architecture is the `SecurityManager` revealing only the two `checkPermission()` methods new in Java 2 that simply delegate calls to `AccessController` and the `AccessControlContext` classes. The `AccessController` represents a decision maker for determining access allowance or denial (`checkPermission()`), a manager for designating which code should run as privileged (`doPrivileged()`), and a way to obtain a handle to the current access control context for use in other contexts (`getContext()`). The `AccessControlContext` class encapsulates the context pertinent to access control such as a particular stack state of execution. Thus, contexts can obtain handles to `AccessControlContext` objects from other contexts to determine whether access is permitted in that context.

An `AccessControlContext` can have one or more `ProtectionDomain` objects. Each `ProtectionDomain` object encapsulates the permissions granted to a particular code base. A `ProtectionDomain` can thus be viewed as one grant entry in a policy file in which the entry has one or more permissions, a potential code base, and a potential set of code-signing alias names. A `ProtectionDomain` object stores such permissions in a `PermissionCollection` object and the code base in a `CodeSource` object. A `ProtectionDomain` object may also be constructed and associated with a `ClassLoader` and set of `Principal` objects for subject-based access control.

The `CodeSource` object encapsulates the `CodeBase` location in a URL and the `SignedBy` entries in an array of `Certificate` objects. Thus, code from the same code source and signed by the same signers belongs to the same protection domain. Thus, when `checkPermission()` is called on an `AccessControlContext` object, it checks the permissions associated with the collection of `ProtectionDomain` objects associated with its context.

The `doPrivileged()` methods on the `AccessContoller` can be used to perform certain actions as a privileged caller. Access control decisions will short-circuit permission checking if the calling code action was called from a `doPrivileged()` call assuming that the calling domain was allowed to execute such operations. Normal use of the `doPrivileged()` operation uses the `PrivilegedAction` interface to mark privileged operations that do not throw exceptions:

```
AccessController.doPrivileged( new PrivilegedAction()
  {
    public Object run()
```

```
    {
      // some privileged action
      // perhaps return some value or return null
    }
  }
);
```

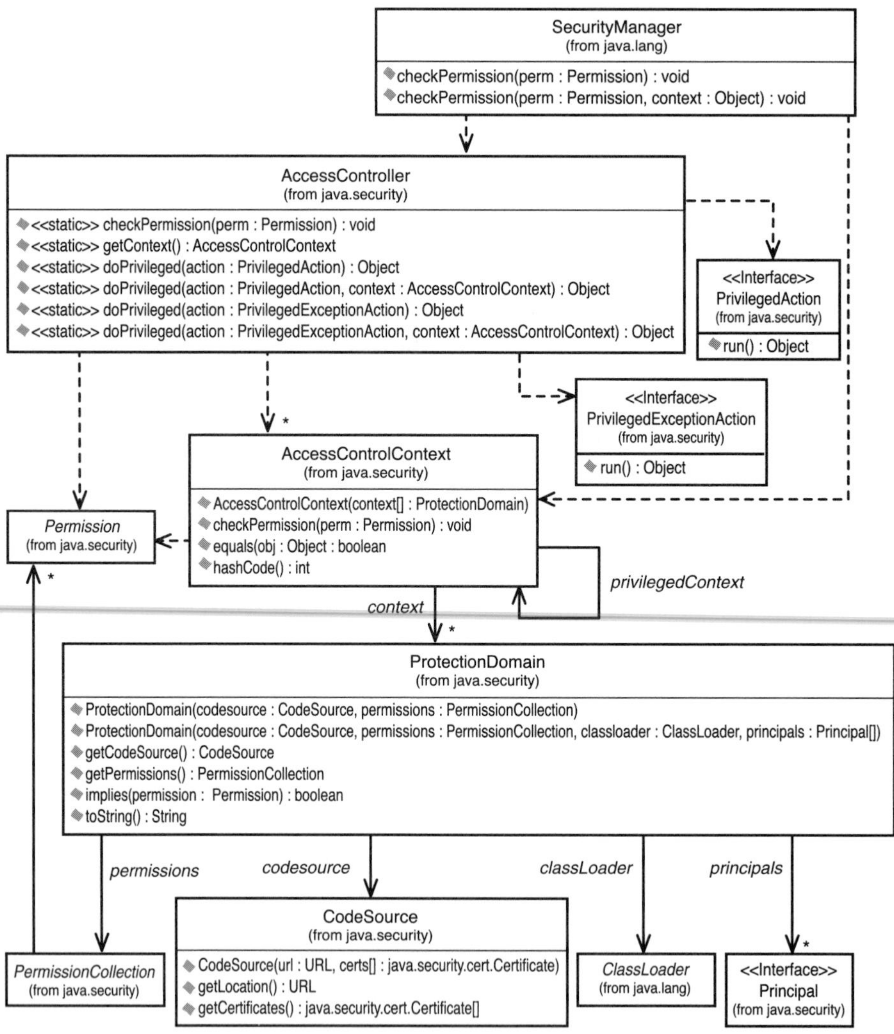

Figure 17.17 The Java 2 access control architecture.

If your privileged operation does throw an exception, you will want to use the `PrivilegedExceptionAction` interface as shown here:

```
AccessController.doPrivileged( new PrivilegedExceptionAction()
  {
    public Object run() throws SomeException
    {
      // some privileged action that throws some exception
      // perhaps return some value or return null
    }
  }
);
```

Both forms of the `doPrivileged()` method also take an `AccessControlContext` object as a second argument to designate a particular context to use for restricting privileges.

Because the `getContext()` method exists on `AccessController`, a current `AccessControlContext` can be retrieved and used later to check the permissions associated with one context from another context by calling `checkPermission()` on that `AccessControlContext`. The `SecurityManager` also has a `checkPermission(Permission, Object)` method, which takes an `AccessControlContext` object as an argument and performs the same check. For example:

```
// Store AccessControlContext for use in another context
AccessControlContext acc = AccessController.getContext();
 ...
 // Change context
 ...
FilePermission myPermission = new FilePermission("MyFile.txt", "read");
// Call check permission on context directly...
acc.checkPermission(myPermission);
// ...or call check permission on security manager, which does
//    same thing as above method call...
(System.getSecurityManager()).checkPermission(myPermission, acc);
```

Guarded Objects

When resource access needs to be provided to an object in a different thread, a `java.security.GuardedObject` can be used to protect access to that resource as depicted in Figure 17.18. The sender in this case creates a `GuardedObject` with the `Object` encapsulating an interface to that resource and another object that implements the `java.security.Guard` interface. An object that implements the `Guard` interface is responsible for taking the resource object as a parameter to a `checkGuard()` call, and it throws a `SecurityException` if access is not allowed. After a `GuardedObject` is constructed, a receiver in another thread will have to first call `getObject()` on the

GuardedObject to obtain access to the resource object. The GuardedObject then calls checkGuard() on the Guard implementation. Because the java.lang.Permission class implements the Guard interface, it can be used in situations as shown here:

```
// Create the guarded object in one thread
Socket sock = new Socket("myHost.com", 8000);
SocketPermission perm
  = new SocketPermission "myHost.com:8000", "connect,accept");
GuardedObject gObject  = new GuardedObject(sock, perm);
  . . .
// Now need to use gObject from another thread
// This will throw exception if this thread is not allowed access
Socket mySock = (Socket) gObject.getObject();
```

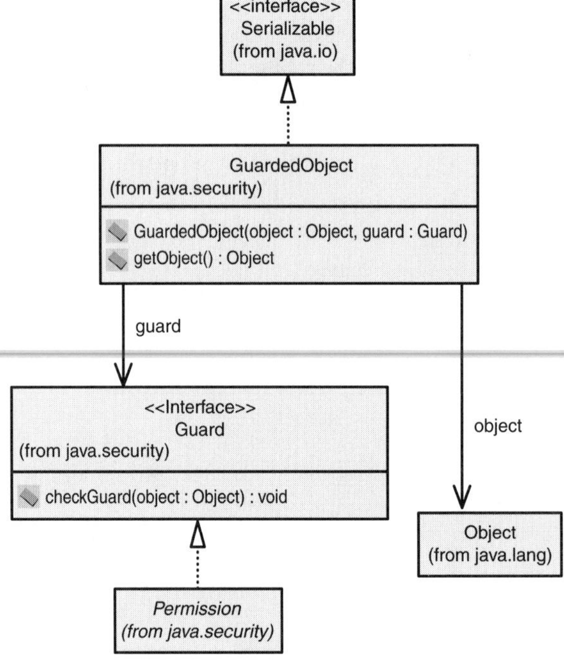

Figure 17.18 Guarded objects.

Fine-Grained and Configurable Access Control Example

Given the fine-grained and flexible configuration of permissions via a security policy file and an understanding of how the access controller can provide security for your applications, the following snippet illustrates how simple making a Java application utilizing such features can be:

```
public class CheckPermissions
{
  public static void main(String[] args)
  {
    // check whether the application has permission to read
    // properties.

    String operatingSystem = (String)System.getProperty("os.name");
    String javaVersion = (String)System.getProperty("java.version");
    try{
      String javaDirectory = (String)System.getProperty("java.home");
      String userHomeDir = (String)System.getProperty("user.home");
      String myFile = (String)System.getProperty("myFile");
      FileInputStream fin = new FileInputStream(myFile);
    }
    catch(FileNotFoundException fne){
      System.out.println("File not found Exception "+fne);
      System.exit(0);
    }
    catch(AccessControlException ace){
      System.out.println("Security Access Control Exception "+ace);
      System.exit(0);
    }
  }
}
```

The example first attempts to read a number of system properties and subsequently creates a file input stream associated with a file read in from the `myFile` system property. Files and the `java.home` and `os.home` system properties all represent valued resources that can be protected by default Java security permissions. With no security manager (the default), such an example will run fine because no security checks are performed. You simply specify an arbitrary file for which to check read permissions using the `myFile` system property. As an example, we might run the preceding code without a security manager as follows:

```
java -DmyFile=CreditCards.txt CheckPermissions
```

If you run the example by loading a security manager, the program will throw a runtime `AccessControlException` when the system property `java.home` is attempted to be read. `AccessControlException` objects will also be thrown for attempted access to `os.home` and when an attempt is made to read the file. This is because the default security manager and security policies that come equipped with a JDK distribution restrict access to such system properties. Thus, an exception will be thrown when the example is run with this:

```
java -Djava.security.manager -DmyFile=CreditCards.txt CheckPermissions
```

Now suppose that you have a security policy file as shown here named `checkPermissionsPolicy`:

```
grant{
 permission java.util.PropertyPermission  "java.home" , "read";
 permission java.util.PropertyPermission  "user.home" , "read";
 permission java.util.PropertyPermission  "myFile", "read";
 permission java.io.FilePermission "${myFile}", "read";};
};
```

If you now use such a security policy file, all desired permissions will be granted and the program can be run successfully. Thus your command to run the example utilizing the security policy file may look like this:

```
java -Djava.security.manager
➥ -Djava.security.policy=checkPermissionsPolicy
➥ -DmyFile=CreditCards.txt
➥ CheckPermissions
```

Principal Identification

By using Java security policy files, we saw that access control decisions could sometimes be based on the identity of the principal that signed code needed permission to run in a JVM. The JCA provides a means by which the identity of principals can be encapsulated and managed. Certificate, key store, and CRL interfaces in the Java 2 platform provide one means by which principal identity can be encapsulated, stored, and managed. To support such interfaces, interfaces for public and private keys also need to be supported. Thus, a core set of interfaces related to asymmetric keys is also provided by the JCA.

Although many of the JDK 1.1–related security identity entities have been deprecated, the `java.security.Principal` interface first introduced in JDK 1.1 is still being maintained. The `Principal` interface represents the concept of a principal such as a person or an organization. Aside from defining a `getName()` method that returns a `String` name form of the principal, methods for requiring `equals()`, `hashCode()`, and `toString()` semantics are also defined on the `Principal` interface.

Keys

Figure 17.19 depicts the basic and core architecture behind keys and how they are created using the JCA. The `java.security.Key` interface defines three methods corresponding to three aspects of a key. The `getAlgorithm()` method returns a `String` name of the algorithm used to encode a key (for example, `DSA` or `RSA`). The `getFormat()` method returns a `String` name of the particular format in which the key was encoded (for example, `X.509` and `PKCS#8`). The `getEncoded()` method returns a `byte` array containing the key in its encoded format. The `java.security.PublicKey` interface extends the `Key` interface to represent public keys, whereas the `java.security.PrivateKey` interface extends the `Key` interface to represent private keys. A `java.security.KeyPair` class that can be constructed with both a `PublicKey` and a `PrivateKey` simply offers a way to group the two keys as a pair.

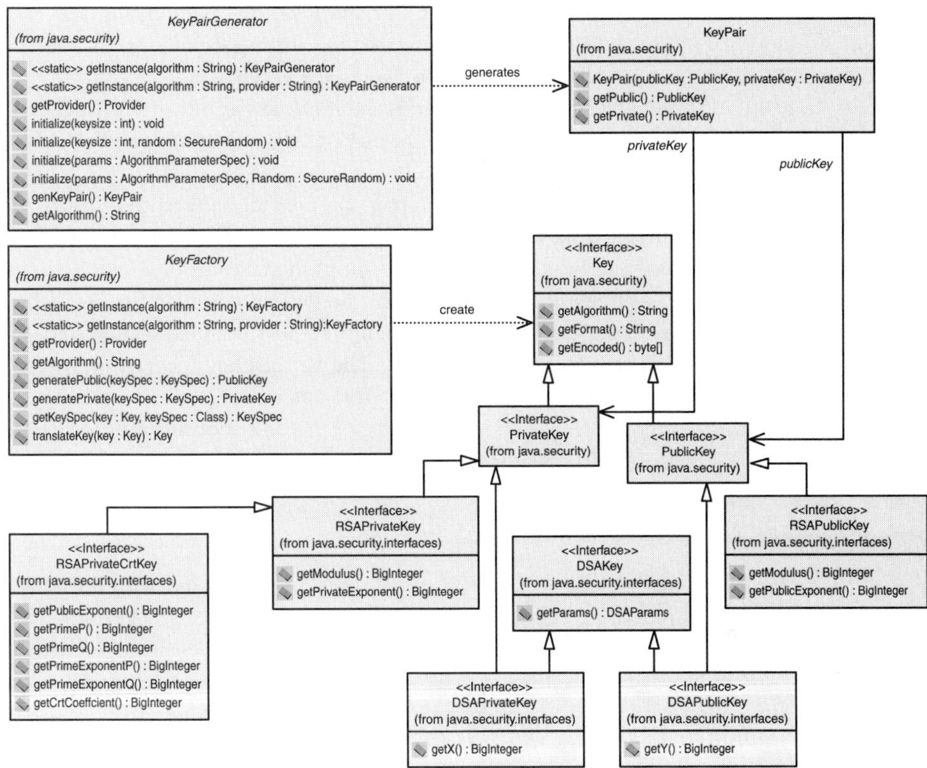

Figure 17.19 The JCA keys architecture.

The `java.security.KeyPairGenerator` class can be used to generate pairs of public and private keys. Because the `KeyPairGenerator` is a cryptographic engine, it provides two `static getInstance()` methods that support the creation of a particular cryptographic engine instance. The `getInstance(String)` method takes the name of a particular algorithm and returns an instance in accordance to the provider preference order mentioned earlier in this chapter. The `getInstance(String, String)` method takes the name of a provider as well, to specify exactly which provider's implementation to use.

After obtaining a `KeyPairGenerator` object, you can initialize the engine to generate keys according to a particular strength. Key strength can be specified as an integer defining the bit length of the key and also by the designation of other algorithmic parameters encapsulated by classes that implement the java.security.spec.AlgorithmParameterSpec interface. Finally, the KeyPairGenerator.getKeyPair() method returns the randomly generated KeyPair object containing the public and private keys of interest.

The JCA provides standard interfaces for DSA and RSA keys in the java.security.interfaces package. A DSAPublicKey and RSAPublicKey interface both extend the PublicKey interfaces with additional algorithm-specific operations. Similarly, a DSAPrivateKey and RSAPrivateKey interface extend the PrivateKey interface. An RSAPrivateCrtKey interface extends the RSAPrivateKey with additional RSA algorithmic constraints. Finally, the DSAPublicKey and DSAPrivateKey interfaces extend a common DSAKey interface.

The java.security.KeyFactory cryptographic engine can be used to translate keys between different compatible key types. That is, for example, a DSA key can be translated into an X.509 key and vice versa. This is accomplished by use of a java.security.spec.KeySpec implementation of the desired key type from which to translate. Then a KeyFactory can be created with a particular compatible key algorithm to which you want to translate the existing key. The various key specifications supported by the JCA out of the box are defined in the java.security.cert package and include EncodedKeySpec, PKCS8EncodedKeySpec, X509EncodedKeySpec, DSAPublicKeySpec, DSAPrivateKeySpec, RSAPublicKeySpec, RSAPrivateKeySpec, and RSAPrivateCrtKeySpec.

Certificates

Figure 17.20 depicts the basic architecture of security certificates provided with the JCA. Fundamental to this architecture is the new java.security.cert.Certificate abstract class, which encapsulates an interface to a certificate associating a principal with a public key. Core interfaces on the Certificate class include the getEncoded() interface returning a byte array of the certificate in its encoded form. The verify(PublicKey) interface can be used to verify that a certificate was signed by the private key associated with the given public key. If the certificate was not signed by such a private key, the verify() method throws a java.security.InvalidKeyException.

A few common certificate revocation list (CRL) operations are encapsulated by the java.security.cert.CRL abstract class. Specific CRL implementations subclass this abstract CRL class.

The java.security.cert.CertificateFactory class is a JCA cryptographic engine that can generate both certificates and CRLs. The type of Certificate and CRL implementation depends on the type of CertificateFactory created during a call to getInstance() (for example, X.509). A single Certificate or Collection of Certificate objects can be created with an InputStream using either the generateCertificate() or the generateCertificates() method, respectively. Similarly, a single CRL or Collection of CRL objects can be created with an InputStream using either the generateCRL() or the generateCRLs() method, respectively. In both cases, the InputStream contains the certificate- or CRL-specific data that will be used to instantiate `Certificate` or `CRL` objects of that associated type.

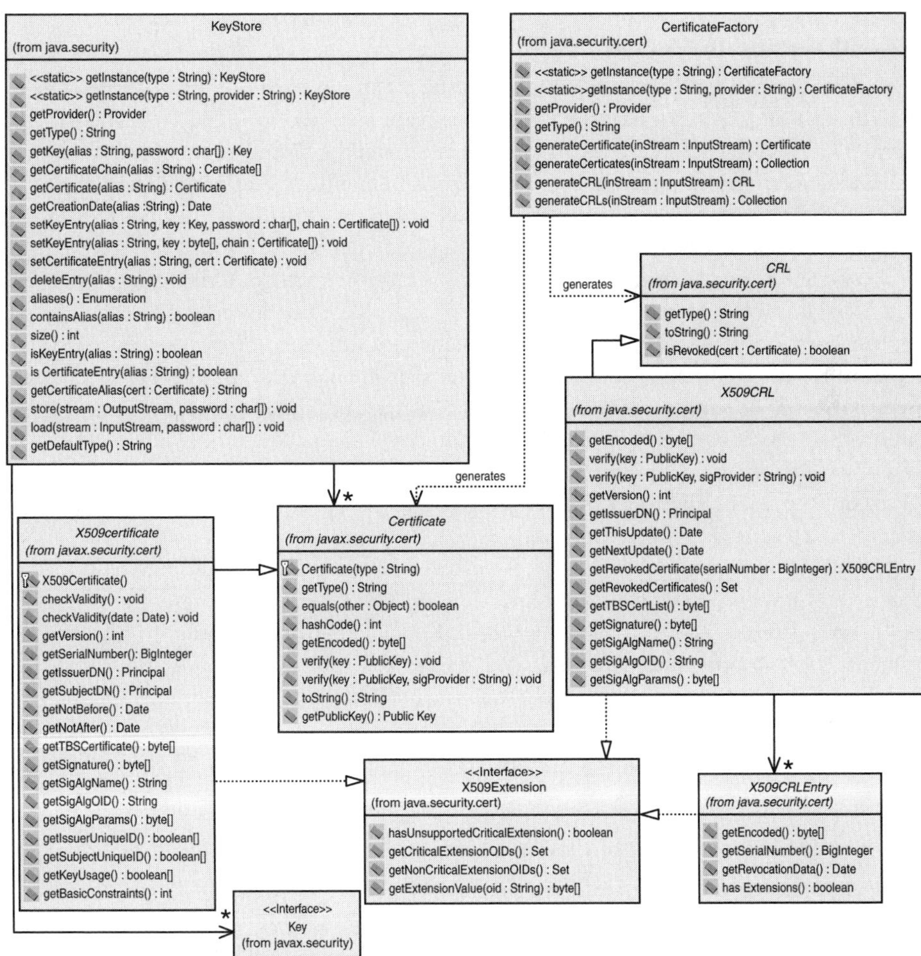

Figure 17.20 The JCA certificates architecture.

The JCA also provides a set of standard interfaces and classes for interacting with X.509-based certificates and CRLs. The `java.security.cert.X509Extension` defines a few methods for retrieving specific attributes common to X.509-related entities. The `java.security.cert.X509Certificate` abstract class encapsulates a standard interface to X.509 certificates. The `X509Certificate` extends the basic `Certificate` class to implement a number of certificate attribute retrieval methods for X.509-specific certificates. The `java.security.cert.X509CRL` class extends the `CRL` class to offer specific operations and attribute retrieval of X.509 CRLs. Finally, the `java.security.cert.X509CRLEntry` class encapsulates an interface to a revoked X.509 certificate.

Key and Certificate Storage

The `java.security.KeyStore` class encapsulates an interface to a stored collection of certificates and keys. Because the `KeyStore` is a cryptographic engine, a particular provider's algorithm specific to a particular certificate and key storage implementation must be generated from one of the `getInstance()` methods. Sun provides a default proprietary key store with the Java platform referred to as `JKS`.

Private key entries stored in a `KeyStore` can be obtained only with a valid key-store alias name and password using the `KeyStore.getKey()` method. Certificate entries in a `KeyStore` can be obtained with just the key-store alias name because the `Certificate` contains only the public key. Each certificate and private-key entry in the key store has its own unique alias name. Before an in-memory `KeyStore` object can be used to manage key and certificate information, it must be loaded from an `InputStream` with a password using the `KeyStore.load()` method. Thus, the key-store format stored in a file using Sun's proprietary key store can be loaded using a `FileInputStream`. The `KeyStore` object also provides a variety of other methods useful for managing key-store entities.

The Java 2 platform supplies a default file-based key-storage mechanism and a tool to manage this store from the command line. This `keytool` command-line utility partially replaces the `javakey` utility equipped with JDK 1.1. The `keytool` utility can be used to manage X.509 certificates and associated private keys. Some of the operations that the `keytool` utility supports are specified via command-line options as listed here:

- `genkey`: Generate a public and private key pair and store it in the key store along with a self-signed certificate.
- `selfcert`: Generate a self-signed certificate to store in the key store.
- `import`: Import X.509 or PKCS#7 certificates from a file into the key store.
- `export`: Export certificates from the key store to a file.
- `printcert`: Print the contents of a certificate store in a separate file.
- `list`: List the contents of the key store.
- `certreq`: Generate a certificate signing request in PKCS#10 format.
- `keyclone`: Clone an entry in the key store.
- `delete`: Delete an entry from the key store.
- `storepasswd`: Change the password used to access the key store.
- `keypasswd`: Change the password used to access a particular private key in the key store.
- `identitydb`: Read in JDK 1.1–style identity information.

Protecting Objects

When sending data and objects from point A to point B across a network or when storing data and objects to some medium and later retrieving them, some security issues arise that the JCA is designed to address:

- How can we be certain as receivers of this data or object that the information has not been corrupted in some fashion?
- How can we be certain as receivers of this data or object that it is from an intended or trusted source?

Message digests in the Java security API address the first issue, and signatures and signed objects in the Java security API address the second issue. In this section, we discuss how to use message digests, signatures, and signed objects to solve these particular security issues.

Message Digests

Java provides built-in support for creating and verifying message digests. When you have some data you want to protect from corruption while it's being sent to a receiver or being stored for later retrieval, you can use a few JCA APIs to create a message digest that can be sent or stored with the data. A retriever of that data can then use the JCA APIs to create their own message digest that is compared with the retrieved message digest. If the newly generated message digest and retrieved digest are equal, the message can be assumed to be uncorrupted. Of course, the probability of there being an undetectable corruption is a function of both the message digest algorithm and its parameters.

Figure 17.21 depicts the primary message digest–related classes you will interface with as a developer. The `static getInstance()` methods on the `java.security.MessageDigest` class can be used to return an instance of a particular `MessageDigest` implementation. The `MessageDigest.getInstance(String)` method takes the name of a particular algorithm (for example, `MD5` or `SHA-1`) and returns an instance associated with the provider which implements that algorithm according to the provider preference order. The `MessageDigest.getInstance (String, String)` method takes the name of a provider as well (for example, `SUN`) to specify exactly which provider's implementation to use. For example:

```
String ALGORITHM_USED = "SHA-1";
MessageDigest messageDigestAlgorithm = null;
try{
   // JDK1.2 comes with two algorithms for message digest,
   // they are SHA-1 and MD5
   // We are using SHA-1.
   messageDigestAlgorithm =
     MessageDigest.getInstance(ALGORITHM_USED);
 }catch(NoSuchAlgorithmException noae){
   System.out.println("Error :"+noae);
```

```
    noae.printStackTrace();
    System.exit(0);
  }
```

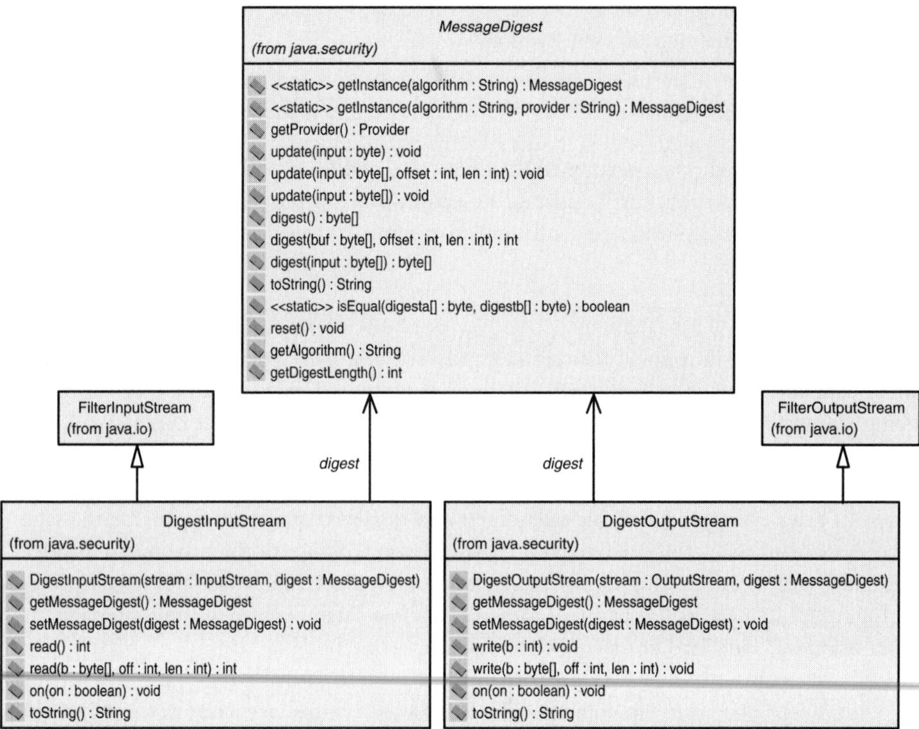

Figure 17.21 The message digest class.

The `MessageDigest.update()` methods take the data byte(s) to be protected as a parameter. The `update()` methods can be called as many times as needed. The message digest algorithm will simply continue to compress the data it receives into an underlying digest. The accumulated digest can then be retrieved using the `MessageDigest.digest()` method. The `MessageDigest.digest()` method can also be called with a set of data bytes that are to be accumulated in generating the digest before the digest is returned. Such calls are useful if you want to pass in the data to be compressed and receive the digest all in one operation. For example:

```
// Message to send or store
String message = "12345678901234:12/2001:SamMellone";

byte[] messageInBytes = message.getBytes();
byte[] digestValue = null;
```

```
if(messageDigestAlgorithm != null){
  // make sure it is empty
  messageDigestAlgorithm.reset();
  // update the message to digest
  messageDigestAlgorithm.update(messageInBytes);
  // get digest Value from MessageDigest
  digestValue = messageDigestAlgorithm.digest();
}
```

After the data has been stored or sent to some location, a retriever or receiver of that data can use the same `update()` and `digest()` calls to generate a new message digest over the data. The `MessageDigest.isEqual()` method can then be used to compare the contents of the retrieved/received digest with the newly generated digest. If no corruption was detected, the `isEqual()` call returns `true`. Otherwise, a `false` value is returned.

```
// Read message that was sent or stored. If all was OK, the below
// message should be = "12345678901234:12/2001:SamMellone"
String message = // received message

// Read received digest as well that comes with message
byte[] receivedDigest = // received message digest

byte[] messageInBytes = message.getBytes();
byte[] digestValue = null;
if(messageDigestAlgorithm!= null){
  messageDigestAlgorithm.reset();
  messageDigestAlgorithm.update(messageInBytes);
  digestValue = messageDigestAlgorithm.digest();
  boolean trueIfEqual
    = messageDigestAlgorithm.isEqual(digestValue , receivedDigest);
}
```

Also shown in Figure 17.21 are `java.security.DigestInputStream` and `java.security.DigestOutputStream` classes. These classes can be used to facilitate how the data to be compressed is input and output from the message digest algorithm. Thus, manipulating data to be compressed as bytes can be avoided. The `DigestOutputStream(OutputStream, MessageDigest)` constructor is called with a target output stream and a `MessageDigest` object. If you construct an output stream with the `DigestOutputStream` object, then whenever `write()` calls are made to that output stream, the `MessageDigest` object's `update()` method is called. Compression of calls to the `MessageDigest` object can be turned on and off with the `DigestOutputStream.on(boolean)` call. After the stream is completely written, the computed digest can be retrieved from the `MessageDigest` as usual via the `MessageDigest.digest()` call.

The reverse process occurs with the `DigestInputStream` object. It is constructed with an `InputStream` and `MessageDigest` object. If you then construct another input stream with the DigestInputStream as a parameter and invoke read calls on the input stream, this will result in update() calls being made to the MessageDigest as well. The on() method on DigestInputStream can also be used here to dictate whether the data being read should be compressed. Finally, the MessageDigest.digest() and MessageDigest.isEqual() methods can be used to obtain and verify the digest, respectively.

Signatures

Although using message digests helps protect data against corruption and therefore helps provide data integrity, it may be desirable to know from whom your data is coming. That is, the principal identity of the message sender may need to be securely provided to a receiver such that the receiver can be certain the data is from a trusted sender. For example, as an e-commerce vendor, you may be interested in knowing that the credit-card information being sent to you from a particular customer is actually from that customer. Much like a customer signs a receipt acknowledging a credit-card purchase in real life, a digital signature may be desirable to identify the signer of a credit-card purchase over the Internet. Otherwise, someone else could simply use your stolen credit-card information and make purchases from an e-commerce vendor over the Internet with no proof of identity provided. Figure 17.22 presents the interface to the Signature object used for creating and verifying signatures.

Because the Signature class is a cryptographic engine, it has the standard getInstance() static methods used to create instances of a particular provider's signature engine objects. As an example using the default Sun JCA provider, we have the following:

```
String ALGORITHM_NAME = "DSA";
Signature signature = null;
 try{
   // JDK comes with algorithm DSA
   signature = Signature.getInstance(ALGORITHM_NAME);
 }catch(NoSuchAlgorithmException noae)
 {
   System.out.println("Error :"+noae);
   noae.printStackTrace();
 }
```

Making a signature on the sender's side is then a matter of initializing the signature-creation process by calling initSign() on the Signature object with the sender's PrivateKey. You can optionally tweak the randomness of this initial seeding process as well by using a form of the initSign() that takes a random value. Calls to update() on the signature can be performed with the message bytes that are to be signed. Then a call to sign() on the signature actually generates the byte stream containing the signature. As an example, here we first generate a random public and private key pair so that we can use the private key to later sign the message:

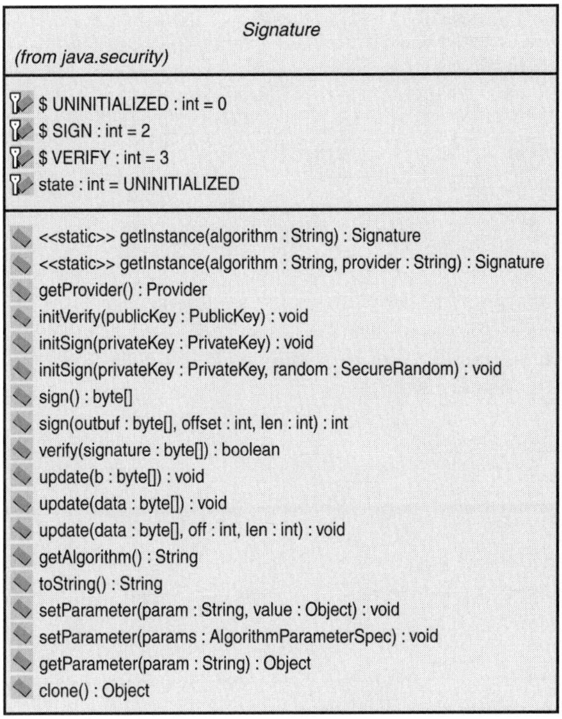

Signature
(from java.security)

$ UNINITIALIZED : int = 0
$ SIGN : int = 2
$ VERIFY : int = 3
state : int = UNINITIALIZED

<<static>> getInstance(algorithm : String) : Signature
<<static>> getInstance(algorithm : String, provider : String) : Signature
getProvider() : Provider
initVerify(publicKey : PublicKey) : void
initSign(privateKey : PrivateKey) : void
initSign(privateKey : PrivateKey, random : SecureRandom) : void
sign() : byte[]
sign(outbuf : byte[], offset : int, len : int) : int
verify(signature : byte[]) : boolean
update(b : byte[]) : void
update(data : byte[]) : void
update(data : byte[], off : int, len : int) : void
getAlgorithm() : String
toString() : String
setParameter(param : String, value : Object) : void
setParameter(params : AlgorithmParameterSpec) : void
getParameter(param : String) : Object
clone() : Object

Figure 17.22 The signature class.

```
String ALGORITHM_NAME = "DSA";
KeyPairGenerator keyPairGenerator = null;
try{
  // JDK comes with algorithm DSA
  keyPairGenerator = KeyPairGenerator.getInstance(ALGORITHM_NAME);
}catch(NoSuchAlgorithmException noae)
{
  System.out.println("Error :"+noae);
  noae.printStackTrace();
}

//initialize keypairGenerator with a given Strength
int KEY_PAIR_STRENGTH = 512;
keyPairGenerator.initialize(KEY_PAIR_STRENGTH);
// Generate KeyPair
KeyPair keyPair = kPairGenerator.generateKeyPair();
// get private key from KeyPair
PrivateKey privateKey = keyPair.getPrivate();
PublicKey sendersPublicKey = keyPair.getPublic();
```

The private key can then be used to sign a message as shown here:

```
// Message to send or store
String message = "12345678901234:12/2001:SamMellone";

byte[] messageInBytes = message.getBytes();
byte[] digestValue = null;

try{
    // initialize signature with private Key
    signature.initSign(privateKey);
    // update message to the signature
    signature.update(messageInBytes);
    digestValue = signature.sign();
 }
 catch(InvalidKeyException invE){
  System.out.println(" Error :"+invE);
  invE.printStackTrace();
 }
 catch(SignatureException se){
  System.out.println(" Error :"+se );
  se.printStackTrace();
 }
```

The receiver of the message will need the `PublicKey` of the sender to be able to verify that the message came from a sender that the receiver trusts. This can be accomplished by packing the public key in a certificate that the receiver can import into its local key store. After the receiver has a `PublicKey`, it can then call `initVerify()` on a `Signature` object with the `PublicKey` as a parameter. The receiver can then call `update()` on the `Signature` object as usual with the message bytes it receives. The receiver must finally call `verify()` on the `Signature` object with the received message signature that it receives from the sender to verify whether the message was sent from that sender. For example:

```
// Read message that was sent or stored. If all was OK, the below
// message should be = "12345678901234:12/2001:SamMellone"
String message = // received message
// Read received signature as well that comes with message
byte[] receivedDigest = // received message signature

byte[] messageInBytes = message.getBytes();
byte[] digestValue = null;
if(signature != null){
 try{
  // initialize verification
  signature.initVerify(sendersPublicKey);
  signature.update(messageInBytes);
  boolean trueIfVerified = signature.verify(receivedDigest);
```

```
}
catch(InvalidKeyException inve)
{
 System.out.println("Error :"+inve);
 inve.printStackTrace();
}
catch(SignatureException se){
 System.out.println(" Error :"+se );
 se.printStackTrace();
}
```

Signed Objects

A signed object in Java 2 lingo refers to a simple way to sign entire objects using a private key, serializing that object, and then sending it to a receiver. The receiver can then verify that the object is from the intended sender by using the sender's public key. Figure 17.23 depicts the interface for the `java.security.SignedObject` class. The constructor of a `SignedObject` must be called with a `Serializable` object to be signed with a `PrivateKey` using a particular `Signature` engine object also passed into the constructor. This `SignedObject` is created on the sending side as shown here:

```
CreditCard creditCard = // create some Serializable object
PrivateKey privateKey = // sender's private key
Signature signature = // create new signature
SignedObject signedObject = null;
try{
    // Create a signed object using a privateKey
    signedObject =
      new SignedObject(creditCard, privateKey, signature);
 }
 catch(InvalidKeyException invE){
  System.out.println(" Error :"+invE);
  invE.printStackTrace();
 }
 catch(SignatureException se){
  System.out.println(" Error :"+se );
  se.printStackTrace();
 }
```

Because the `SignedObject` and its payload are `Serializable`, it can be communicated to a receiver using any of various serialization techniques. After the `SignedObject` is reconstructed on the receiver side, the `verify()` method on the `SignedObject` can be called to determine whether a trusted sender has signed the object. The receiver passes in the `PublicKey` of the presumed sender and a `Signature` engine object in order for verification to occur. The object to be accessed can be retrieved using the `SignedObject.getObject()` method. As an example on the receiving side, we then have this:

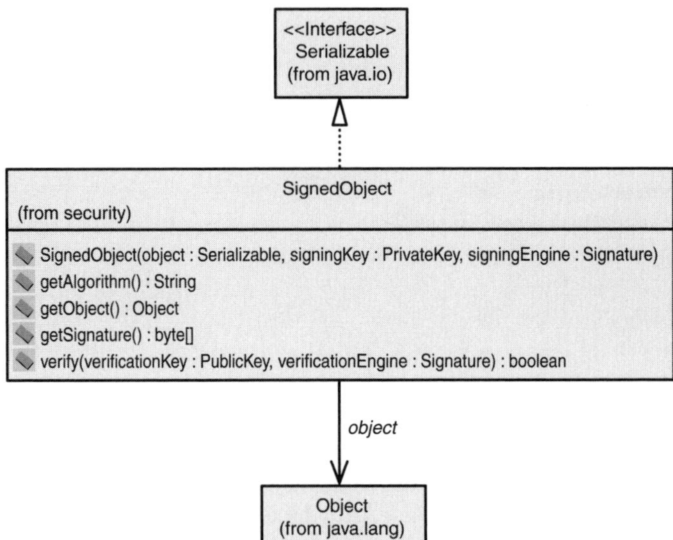

Figure 17.23 The signed object class.

```
PublicKey sendersPublicKey = // sender's public key
Signature signature = // create new signature
SignedObject signedObject = // a received signed object
try{
    boolean isTrueIfVerified =
       signedObject.verify(sendersPublicKey, signature);
    if(isTrueIfVerified){
      CreditCard creditCard =
           (CreditCard) signedObject.getObject();
      // now rest assured knowing that you can use signed credit card
    }
 }
 catch(InvalidKeyException inve)
 {
  System.out.println("Error :"+inve);
  inve.printStackTrace();
 }
 catch(SignatureException se){
  System.out.println(" Error :"+se );
  se.printStackTrace();
 }
}
```

Signing Code

Signatures and signed objects in Java are used for much more than signing data and discrete objects. Signing an entire program can be effected using the code-signing support built into Java. Code signing in Java once almost exclusively meant applet code signing. In Java 1.1, signed applet code could be executed within a Web browser if the signer of that code was recognized as a trusted source. If the trusted source was verified, the Web browser let the applet code access valued resources that lay outside of the original sandbox restrictions. Mismatching between applet signing tools equipped with the JDK and applet signing tools equipped with Web-browser vendors such as Netscape did cause some signed-code compatibility problems, however.

What we as enterprise developers are concerned with here is how to sign Java application code. Such a need may arise if you simply want to verify that an entire application you receive for use in your enterprise has been signed by a trusted source. You may also want to download a jar file of component code from a Web site for use in your application and desire to subject it to the same identity source verification process. Furthermore, with the mobile capabilities inherent with Java code, you may also want to subject code that is automatically loaded by your applications during runtime to some sort of identity check. This section describes how to sign code and verify signed code that you use in your Java enterprise applications.

The JAR Signer Tool

As an enterprise developer, you have no doubt used the `jar` utility to create JAR files before. After you create a JAR file, you can sign this file with your own principal identification keys using a utility called `jarsigner`. The Java 2 `jarsigner` utility replaces one aspect of the `javakey` tool used in JDK 1.1. The `jarsigner` utility is a command-line utility that can be used to both generate signed JAR files and verify signed JAR files. These are the command-line options available for use with the `jarsigner` utility:

- `keystore`: Specifies the key-store URL.
- `storetype`: Designates the key-store type.
- `storepass`: Designates the key-store password.
- `keypass`: Designates a private key password.
- `sigfile`: Designates the filename base to use when generating signature files.
- `signedjar`: Designates the name of the signed JAR file.
- `verify`: Indicates that the named JAR file is to be verified as opposed to signed.
- `certs`: Designates that certificate information should be included with the verification process.
- `verbose`: Indicates that extra information should be displayed during operations.
- `internalsf`: Indicates that a DSA file should not include a copy of signature file information.
- `sectionsonly`: Indicates that a signature file should not include a manifest.

Code Signing Process

These are the general steps involved with a principal signing code to associate an identify with that code:

1. Compile the code to be signed into class files.
2. Create a JAR file from class files.
3. Sign the JAR file.
4. Export a public key certificate.

On the receiving end, a Java application that wants to accept code only from a trusted source that has signed the code must carry out these steps:

1. Import the certificate as a trusted certificate.
2. Create a policy file indicating that such a principal should be trusted for certain permissions.
3. Load the trusted code with your Java application. (Access will be determined by the policy file.)

Code Signing Example

As a simple example of signing code, suppose we have a hypothetical example application that simply writes some information to a log file. Then suppose we have some policy file, named `codeSignPolicy`, that designates which permissions are actually allowed for a particular code signer. Suppose also that the `codeSignPolicy` designates the keystore URL that our application consults for code signer information. The key store at the specified location thus must be loaded with the appropriate code signer information. Because our hypothetical example application need only write to a log file, it needs the appropriate file write permission for that file, as illustrated here:

```
keystore "file:/C:/Documents/keys/myKeyStore";
grant signedBy "BShirts"
 {
  permission java.io.FilePermission "C:\\temp\\bshirts.log", "write";
};
```

The actual steps to take in signing such code are summarized here:

1. Compile the code:

   ```
   javac SomeLogger.java
   ```

2. Generate the jar file:

   ```
   jar -cvf Code.jar SomeLogger.class
   ```

3. Generate the certificate:

   ```
   keytool -genkey -alias codeSign
   ➥ -keystore bshirtsStore -keypass bshirtsp
   ➥ -dname "cn=bshirts" -storepass 524316
   ```

4. Sign the jar file:

```
jarsigner -keystore bshirtsStore
➥ -storepass 524316 -keypass bshirtsp
➥ -signedjar SignedCode.jar Code.jar codeSign
```

5. Export the certificate for use by the receiver:

```
keytool -export -keystore bshirtsStore
➥ -storepass 524316 -alias codeSign -file BShirts.cer
```

The user of such code would typically perform the following steps on his own target application environment. However, for this example, we demonstrate the steps to take in granting trusted access to the signed code on the Java application side assuming the same machine, directory, and files for simplicity in illustration:

1. Import the certificate:

```
keytool -import -alias BShirts -file BShirts.cer
➥ -keystore myKeyStore -storepass ij#kgl
```

2. The Java application can then be run using the signed JAR file with permissions granted through an associated security policy file:

```
java -Djava.security.manager
➥ -Djava.security.policy=codeSignPolicy
➥ SomeLogger
➥ C:\\temp\\bshirts.log
```

Java Cryptography Extension (JCE)

The JCE is provided with the J2SE v1.4 for providing functions used to encrypt blocks of data for the sake of confidentiality until it can be subsequently decrypted by the intended receiver. Such functionality can be contrasted with the cryptography support offered by the JCA. The JCA primarily provides support for protecting data for integrity via message digests and provides a means for principal identification of data, objects, and code using signatures, keys, and certificates. Recall that the data, objects, or code itself was never encrypted. This is where the JCE steps in. Thus, whereas the JCA relies on an asymmetric public and private key infrastructure for secure identity (of principals), the JCE relies on a symmetric key infrastructure for secure confidentiality. In fact, the JCE symmetric key infrastructure class has many analogues to JCA asymmetric key infrastructure classes.

Encryption is an extremely important security function to provide, but Sun previously decided to not include encryption with the Java platform so that U.S. export restriction on encryption technology didn't hamper global use of the Java platform. Of course, other third-party Java-based encryption products came into being to fill this market gap. To provide a standard interface to such encryption technologies, the JCE uses a service-provider architecture similar to the JCA that provides a standard API to encryption functionality, but it allows for the use of different underlying encryption library providers.

The following packages compose the JCE architecture:

- `javax.crypto`: The set of core classes and interfaces for the JCE plug-and-play service provider framework and cryptographic operation APIs.
- `javax.crypto.interfaces`: A set of interfaces used to encapsulate and manage Diffie-Hellman keys.
- `javax.crypto.spec`: A set of classes used to key algorithm and parameter specifications.

Figure 17.24 depicts the core architecture for the JCE. Note that we are not showing overloaded methods or method signatures in this diagram in order to keep the discussion brief. At the top of the diagram, there are five new cryptographic engine classes, each with the standard static `getInstance()` methods. Below that are a `SecretKey` designating a symmetric key, a `SealedObject`, Diffie-Hellman key interfaces, and helper classes for working with ciphers. The following list describes the role of each major API class or interface in the JCE architecture:

- `Cipher`: A cryptographic engine that provides the basic interface for encrypting and decrypting blocks of data bytes.
- `NullCipher`: A subclass of `Cipher` that provides a basic interface that does not encrypt or decrypt data (that is, cipher text and clear text are equal).
- `CipherInputStream`: An input stream class used to read cipher data from a decrypting `Cipher` object and enable chaining of an input stream with another input stream.
- `CipherOutputStream`: An output stream class used to write cipher data to an encrypting `Cipher` object and enable chaining of an output stream with another output stream.
- `SecretKey`: A marker interface for secret symmetric keys.
- `KeyAgreement`: A cryptographic engine that provides an interface for implementing a key exchange algorithm in which keys are first exchanged and a secret key is eventually created.
- `KeyGenerator`: A cryptographic engine that implements a symmetric key generator. Its asymmetric key generator analogue is the `KeyPairGenerator`.
- `SecretKeyFactory`: A cryptographic engine that can be used to translate keys between different compatible secret key types. Its asymmetric key generator analogue is the `KeyFactory`.
- `Mac`: A cryptographic engine that implements a Message Authentication Code algorithm for checking message integrity using secret symmetric keys.
- `SealedObject`: A class for protecting the confidentiality of an object using symmetric keys. Its asymmetric analogue is the `SignedObject`.
- `DHKey`, `DHPublicKey`, and `DHPrivateKey`: Base, public key, and private key interfaces for Diffie-Hellman keys, respectively.

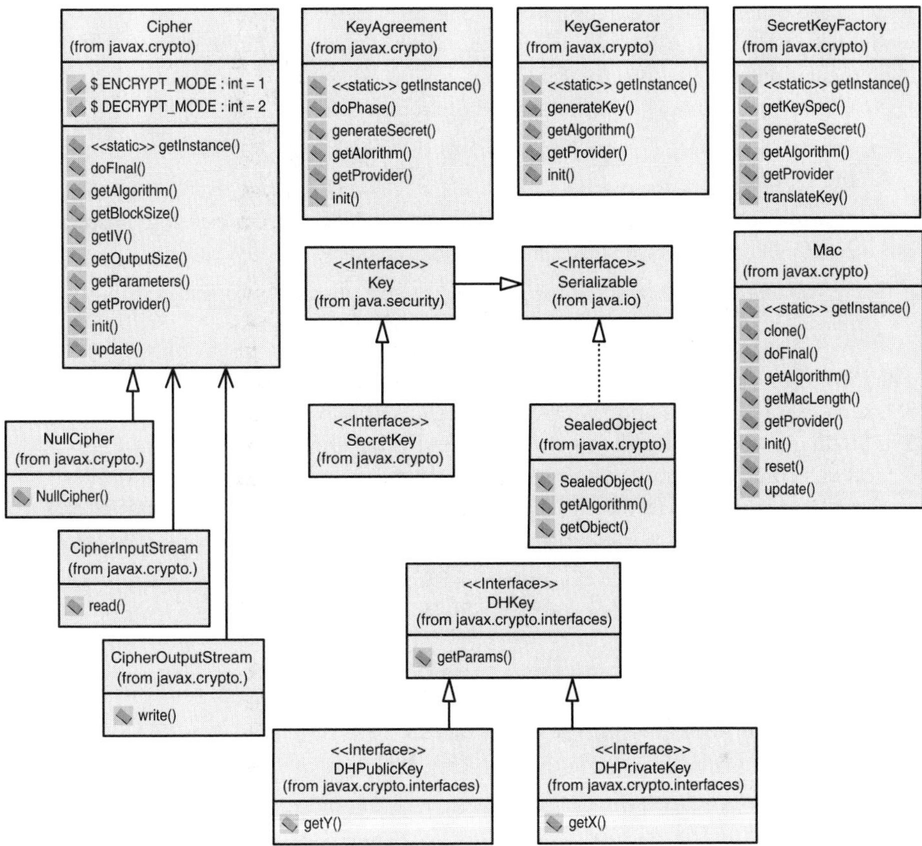

Figure 17.24 The JCE architecture.

Java Secure Socket Extension (JSSE)

Earlier in this chapter we described a few of the more popular secure socket protocols. The JSSE included with the J2SE v1.4 provides a standard API to secure socket protocols such as Secure Socket Layer (SSL). The JSSE also supports an API to the Transport Layer Security (TLS) and Wireless Transport Layer Security (WTLS) secure socket protocols. These are the specific protocol versions that are supported:

- SSL version 2 and 3
- TLS version 1
- WTLS version 1

As with the other security extensions, the JSSE architecture follows the same adapter model of providing an API and a service provider interface for different underlying implementations to plug into the JSSE.

The following packages compose the JSSE architecture:

- `javax.net.ssl`: This package contains the set of core classes and interfaces for the JSSE APIs.
- `javax.net`: This package is not specific to the JSSE but is needed to support basic socket and server socket factory functionality.
- `javax.security.cert`: This package is also not specific to the JSSE but is needed to support basic certificate management functionality.

The JSSE class architecture is primarily useful for its encapsulation of SSL socket and SSL server socket objects and factories. SSL session handles can also be useful. Finally, SSL binding and handshake event and listener APIs are also provided. Figure 17.25 depicts this core architecture of the JSSE. Note that we are not showing overloaded methods or method signatures in this diagram in order to keep the discussion brief. The following list describes the role of each major API class or interface in the JSSE architecture:

- `SSLSocket`: A socket that supports SSL, TLS, and WTLS secure socket protocols.
- `SocketFactory`: A factory for `Socket` objects.
- `SSLSocketFactory`: A factory for `SSLSocket` objects.
- `SSLServerSocket`: A server socket that supports SSL, TLS, and WTLS secure socket protocols.
- `ServerSocketFactory`: A factory for `ServerSocket` objects.
- `SSLServerSocketFactory`: A factory for `SSLServerSocket` objects.
- `SSLSession`: An interface to an object encapsulating an SSL session.
- `SSLSessionContext`: An interface to an object encapsulating a collection of SSL sessions identified with a session ID.
- `SSLBindingEvent`: An event class encapsulating SSL session binding and unbinding events.
- `SSLBindingListener`: A listener interface implemented by objects wanting to be made aware of SSL session binding and unbinding events.
- `HandshakeCompletedEvent`: An event class encapsulating the fact that an SSL handshake has completed.
- `HandshakeCompletedListener`: A listener interface implemented by objects wanting to be made aware of SSL handshake completion events.

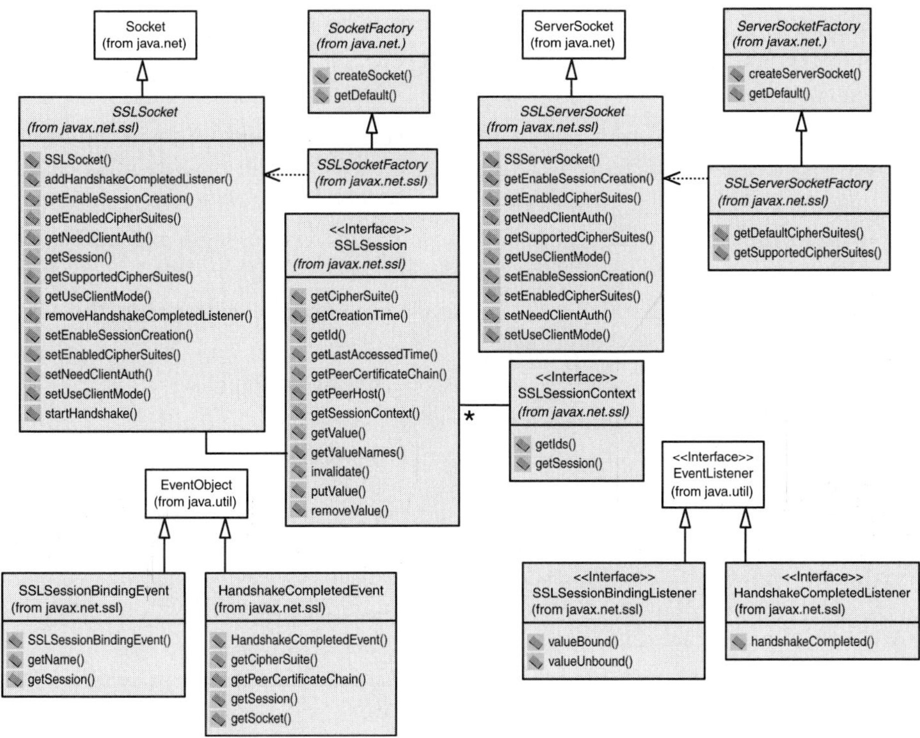

Figure 17.25 The JSSE architecture.

Java Authentication and Authorization Service (JAAS)

The JAAS, now included with the J2SE v1.4, was developed to provide a standard way for limiting access to resources based on an authenticated user identity. JAAS APIs for login and logout also provide a standard technique for authenticating users and passing around secure context and credential information. Different underlying authentication and authorization models can be plugged into the JAAS service provider interface model while enabling API users to have a stable and standard interface. Although we only briefly highlight the architecture of JAAS here, Chapter 28 discusses JAAS in much more detail and in the context of its J2EE use with Enterprise JavaBeans (EJB).

The following packages compose the JAAS architecture:

- `javax.security.auth`: Contains base classes and interfaces for authentication and authorization.
- `javax.security.auth.callback`: Contains a framework of classes and interfaces defining a contract between an application and a security service that enable the security service to pass certain authentication information to the application.
- `javax.security.auth.login`: Contains classes used for login to a security domain.
- `javax.security.auth.spi`: Currently contains one interface that is implemented by JAAS service providers.
- `javax.security.auth.kerberos`: Contains classes used to encapsulate Kerberos-based authentication via JAAS.
- `javax.security.auth.x500`: Contains classes used to encapsulate X.500 certificate-based authentication with JAAS.

Figure 17.26 depicts the core architecture of the JAAS. Note that we are not showing overloaded methods or method signatures in this diagram in order to keep the discussion brief. The following list describes the role of each major API class or interface in the JAAS architecture depicted in Figure 17.26:

- `Subject`: Represents an individual or organization with multiple principal identities and therefore public and private credentials.
- `LoginContext`: Provides a basic API for subjects to log in and log out.
- `LoginModule`: Defines an interface to be implemented by service providers that support JAAS.
- `Configuration`: Encapsulates an entity used to configure an application with particular login modules.
- `AuthPermission`: Encapsulates permissions used during authentication.
- `CallbackHandler`: Defines an interface to be implemented by applications if they want to allow the authentication service to pass it information.
- `Callback`: Specifies a marker interface implemented by objects that are passed to a `CallbackHandler` implementation. A `Callback` object contains data to be given to an application.

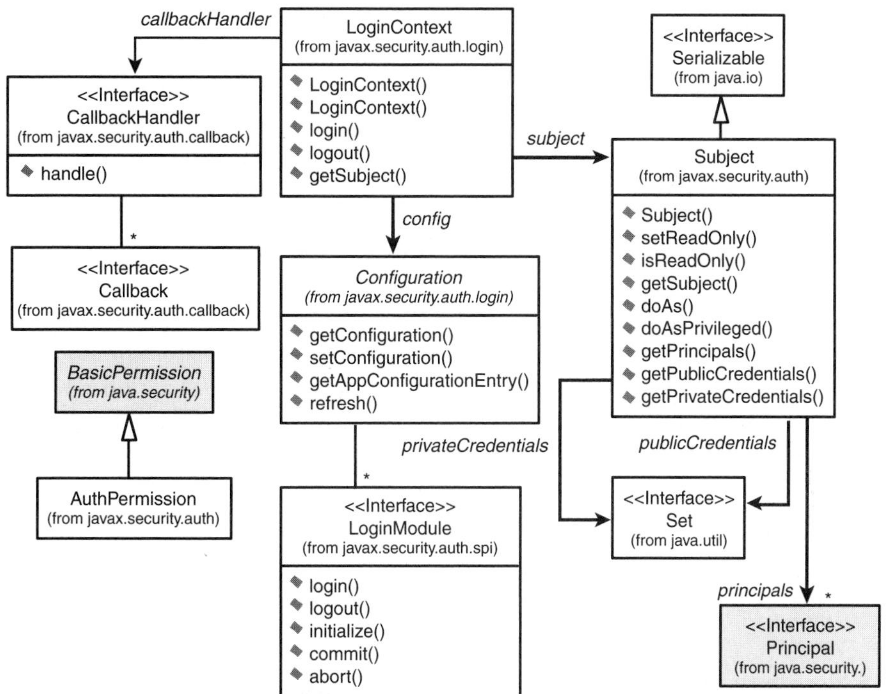

Figure 17.26 The JAAS architecture.

CORBA Security

For J2EE servers to be interoperable with other J2EE servers, the CORBA standards may be employed. In terms of interoperability at a security level, CORBA security interoperability standards may be employed. Additionally, pure Java-based CORBA servers and clients may leverage more extensive use of CORBA security standards. CORBA security defines standard interfaces to services that operate on top of and to a certain extent are part of an ORB that provides security protection for your CORBA objects. CORBA security in general provides security protection for identity, authenticity, nonrepudiation, authorization, auditing, integrity, and confidentiality.

In this section we briefly highlight CORBA security features as defined in the CORBA Security Service Specification (CSSS) and CORBA security interoperability requirements as defined in the OMG's Common Secure Interoperability v2 (CSIv2) specification. Interoperable J2EE EJB applications support Conformance Level 0 of the CSIv2, as discussed in this section.

CORBA Security Architecture

Many of the security features defined in the CSSS actually map closely to IDL modules and therefore to packages in the Java binding for CORBA Security. For example, the following CORBA Security IDL modules and how they map to associated Java packages (listed next in the form of *`IDL_Module`* ~ *`Java_Package`*) are of primary interest to those seeking to understand the CORBA Security model:

- `org::omg::Security` ~ `org.omg.Security`: Contains core and common CORBA Security types as needed by various security packages.
- `org::omg::SecurityLevel1` ~ `org.omg.SecurityLevel1`: Contains an interface defined for minimal CORBA Security support for application interfacing as needed CORBA applications that are largely security unaware.
- `org::omg::SecurityLevel2` ~ `org.omg.SecurityLevel2`: Contains the large majority of interfaces relevant to CORBA Security Service application interfacing as needed CORBA applications that are security aware.
- `org::omg::NRService` ~ `org.omg.NRService`: Contains the interfaces used for nonrepudiation application interfacing.
- `org::omg::SecurityReplaceable` ~ `org.omg.SecurityReplaceable`: Contains the interfaces for enhancing vendor interoperability used for pluggable service-provider interfacing.
- `org::omg::SecurityAdmin` ~ `org.omg.SecurityAdmin`: Contains system administration and security policy–related interfaces used for administrative interfacing.

The core interfaces depicted in Figure 17.27 scope the CORBA Security architecture. Security features supported by the architecture of Figure 17.27 include these:

- Support for authenticating a client proxy with a CORBA Security domain using a principal authenticator (`PrincipalAuthenticator`) and obtaining credentials (`Credentials`) for that object.
- Support for transparent transmission of credentials from a current secure execution context (`Current`) via a security context (`SecurityContext`) over the wire from client-side secure invocation (`SecClientSecureInvocation` and `Vault`) to server-side secure invocation (`SecTargetSecureInvocation`) with delegation of credentials as an option.
- Support for access control decision making (`AccessDecision`) based on the required rights (`RequiredRights`) for authorized access.
- Support for nonrepudiation of messages sent or received from a principal by generating tokens and verifying evidence associated with that principal's credentials (`NRCredentials`).
- Support for determining whether certain events should be audited (`AuditDecision`) and then potentially logging the event to an audit log (`AuditChannel`).

- Support for configuring cryptographic quality of protection levels (`QOPPolicy`) according to integrity and confidentiality.
- Support for the configuration of various security policy types (`Policy` sub-interfaces).

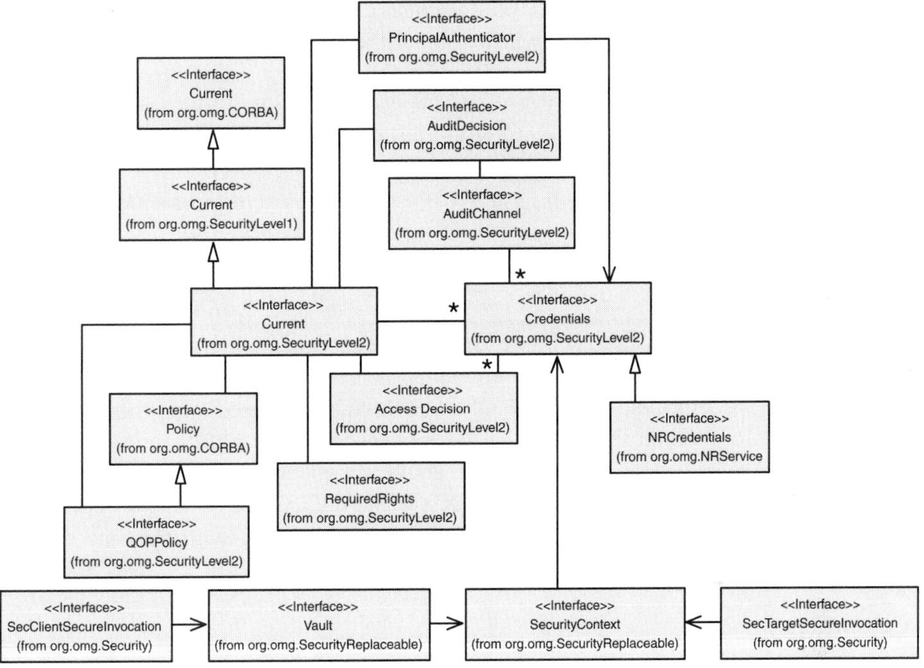

Figure 17.27 CORBA Security architecture.

Authentication

A principal authenticator represents a frontline interface for CORBA clients to use when authenticating themselves with the CORBA Security Service. After authenticating themselves, clients are given a set of credentials that are stored along with their current security context. When the client makes a remote invocation on a CORBA server, its security context is passed along with the marshaled call parameters to the server-side ORB. The target server's Security Service can use this information to determine whether the client should be allowed to make the call and optionally allow the server object to obtain access to the client's credential information that was passed along with the security context.

Interoperable J2EE servers are required to support CSIv2 Conformance Level 0's authentication requirements. At this level, identity information is passed by the client either at the transport level (via SSL/TLS) or inside of IIOP messages. At a minimum, password-based authentication must be supported such that a username and password are transferred by the client via SSL/TLS or IIOP messages to an authentication service.

Delegation

CORBA Security supports three modes of operation for delegation of credentials during security-sensitive object invocations. Recall from an earlier section in this chapter that delegation pertains to issues regarding how some Object A's credentials propagate during a call to some Object C by some Object B when Object A first calls Object B. With a "No Delegation" mode of CORBA Security, the client's identity is not delegated, and thus an Object A's credentials would not propagate to Object C in this example. With a "Simple Delegation" mode, Object A's credentials would get propagated to Object C. With "Composite Delegation," both Object B's and Object A's credentials propagate to Object C.

Authorization

Authorization in CORBA follows a role-based access control model in which ACLs are maintained that describe which rights are required for particular operations, which roles are assigned to which principal identities, and which rights get associated with which roles. For particular calls on the server side, a target invocation may use the received client credential information and information about the operation being invoked to consult a CORBA Security access decision-making object for a yes or no answer regarding whether the operation is to be permitted. The required rights for such operations can also be determined a priori using the CORBA Security Service.

Auditing

Auditing of security-critical operations under the CORBA Security Service requires one to make an audit decision to first determine whether an audit is needed based on a particular audit event. If an audit is needed, the audit event data, the invoking principal's credentials, and the time are all written to an audit channel.

Nonrepudiation

CORBA Security also provides a set of interfaces for performing nonrepudiation (NR) of operation invocations. The generation of an NR token associated with received data from some principal can be used later to prove that the principal sent such data. This is accomplished using evidence that can be used later in case of a dispute. NR can also be used to prove that some principal received data as well.

Encryption

CORBA objects are understood to need cryptographic support for both integrity and confidentiality. Integrity protection would mean use of something like message digests, whereas confidentiality protection would include the use of key-based encryption. A quality of protection (QOP) level can be set for both requests and responses, indicating whether any protection, integrity protection, confidentiality protection, or both integrity and confidentiality protection are assumed. The underlying interfacing that takes place for providing a requested QOP is transparent to the API developer.

Various underlying protocols that operate below the CORBA Security Service layer (for example, SSL) are by and large utilized transparently to the applications developer. Various common security interface protocols supported by the CSSS are SSL, Kerberos, SPKM, ECMA, and DCE-IOP (Distributed Computing Environment Inter-ORB Protocol). However, specifications for use of such secure protocols in the CSSS are defined at the ORB-to-ORB level to ensure interoperability between ORBs supporting such protocols. Thus an ORB from vendor A using SSL could theoretically talk to an ORB from vendor B using SSL.

The level of ORB-to-ORB interoperability is defined according to a CSIv2 conformance level. CSIv2 Conformance Level 0 defines an interoperable secure identity-passing scheme with no delegation allowed. CSIv2 Conformance Level 1 allows delegation of identity for the principal that initiated an operation. CSIv2 Conformance Level 2 signifies that the ORB supports all Security Service functionality, and thus all the information that can be passed along with a security context such as privileges is also communicated between ORBs. Interoperable J2EE servers support CSIv2 Conformance Level 0. The particular encryption-related requirements at this level include support of SSL v3.0 and TLS v1.0 transport level security, as well as their associated mandatory cipher-suites.

Security Policies and Administration

The CSSS security domain is defined according to which security policy governs that domain. Security policies for the various protection mechanisms of CORBA Security can be defined using a standard set of CORBA Security policy interfaces that inherit from a base `org::omg::CORBA::Policy` interface.

Support for administration of security policies in a domain can take advantage of the base class inheritance from the `org::omg::CORBA::Policy` interface. Thus, any generic interface defined for administering the `Policy` interface can apply to the CORBA Security policies. The problem is that standard support for even generic policy administration is lacking. The `org::omg::CORBA::DomainManager` interface can be used to retrieve security policies for access of their information, but it offers little use beyond that. It seems that support for any significant policy administration interfaces was deferred to the CORBA facilities layer.

Conclusions

In this chapter we saw how assurance deals with enhancing the security, reliability, availability, maintainability, and perhaps safety enterprise systems. Security protection in an enterprise comes in the form of integrity verification, confidentiality preservation, authorization, identity verification, authenticity permission, availability of service, nonrepudiation evidence, and auditing evidence. The Java security architecture provides a standards-based interface for Java developers to create secure Java applications. Because security is an involved problem with many facets of protection that must be provided, we saw that the Java security architecture is proportionately involved. Yet given the security protection built into the platform, Java provides a relatively simple API to these protection mechanisms. We also saw how CORBA Security is a rather comprehensive security standard addressing most of the problems encountered in building secure applications. However, largely transparent to the J2EE developer, J2EE leverages use of the CORBA Security standards only by virtue of enabling interoperability between J2EE servers. Such concepts and technologies form the underlying infrastructure that any J2EE developer should be aware of in order to better construct high-assurance enterprise applications.

V

Enterprise Web Enabling

18

Web Development and Services

ALMOST ALL MODERN ENTERPRISE APPLICATION DEVELOPMENT tasks involve exposing the services of such applications via the Web. Thus, it is imperative to understand how to develop Web-based applications and to understand the platforms atop which they run. This chapter introduces the two primary computing platforms used to Web-enable an enterprise: Web browsers and Web servers. Understanding the basic architecture of Web browsers and Web servers, as well as understanding the common problems and solutions encountered with their use, is fundamental to understanding how to Web-enable an enterprise using J2EE Web technologies. Furthermore, this chapter introduces the basic techniques involved with developing Web applications atop such platforms.

In this chapter, you will learn:

- The basic services and restrictions of Web clients
- The basic services and restrictions of Web servers
- The use of Web Services within Web servers and browsers
- The basic approaches for developing Web applications running inside of Web server and browser environments

Web Clients

A Web client is any application that sends and receives information from an HTTP server. The most common type of Web client is a Web browser. A browser is an application whose primary role is to transform GUI requests into HTTP requests and to transform HTTP responses into GUI display content. HTTP requests are, of course, sent to Web servers, and HTTP responses are received from Web servers. Requests for Web content are cast in the form of URLs that identify remote resource media accessible via the Internet. Web responses are often in the form of documents, more commonly known as Web pages, with multimedia and HTML-based presentation content such as text, static and animated images, hyperlinks, GUI components, audio clips, and video clips.

Additionally, referenced documents of various types managed by external handlers, Java applets, and executable browser script language commands (for example, JavaScript) can be returned in an HTTP Web response.

Because HTTP is the standard protocol for the World Wide Web (WWW), Web browsers become the GUI windows to the WWW. However, current Web browser GUI component types, the bandwidth for most HTTP connections, and the nature of HTTP itself constrain the GUI designs of current Web browser–based document content. Some Web browsers may take advantage of more sophisticated GUI component interactions, but often at the cost of standards compliance or additional bandwidth consumption. It is for these reasons that the state of the art for most Web browser Web pages tends to be limited to supporting a set of core multimedia features for use over the Internet and limited Web page presentation features with the bulk of presentation built with HTML.

Web Browser Architecture

Figure 18.1 presents a basic conceptual architecture for Web browsers to provide a glimpse into their underlying structure. At the heart of a Web browser is a main controller process. This process manages the local content cache, handles HTTP requests and responses, configures the browser, and drives the basic presentation of Web page content. Request handlers map GUI-based requests into HTTP network requests, and response handlers map HTTP responses into GUI-based events and display requested content. Each request and response drives the I/O of HTTP data to and from a network interface. The HTTP protocol is used for unsecured connections, and HTTPS is used for HTTP with SSL-based connections.

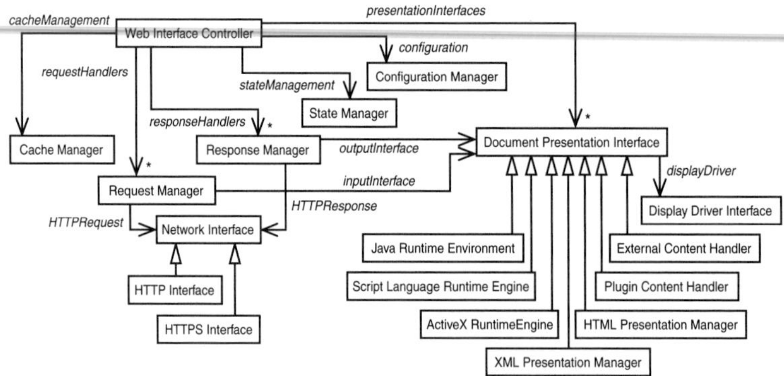

Figure 18.1 Web browser architecture.

A cache manager is often employed within Web browser architectures to store previously requested data in an effort to avoid making unnecessary network requests. A state manager may also be employed to provide some management of session information using cookies or to facilitate some other form of session tracking. Furthermore, a configuration manager may be used to configure the properties and behavior of a Web browser.

A document presentation interface is used to drive the actual display of GUI-based browser content. Web browsers typically support one or more of the following types of document presentation interfaces:

- *HTML Presentation Manager:* All Web browsers have some form of HTML-based presentation manager to output HTML display content and receive user inputs via HTML entities such as input forms and hyperlinks.
- *XML Presentation Manager:* Many Web browser implementations now also support parsing of XML documents.
- *Java Runtime Environment:* A Java runtime environment may be embedded into a Web browser to execute Java applets, as well as to invoke the services of downloaded JavaBean components.
- *ActiveX Runtime Engine:* A Microsoft ActiveX runtime engine is embedded into Microsoft browsers to execute downloaded ActiveX/COM components.
- *Scripting Language Runtime Engine:* One or more runtime scripting language engines may also be used to execute scripting commands that were embedded into HTML pages (for example, JavaScript).
- *External Content Handler:* External content handlers may be used to dynamically execute the content of retrieved URL information in an application that runs in a process external to the Web browser (for example, an unzip utility that opens compressed archive files).
- *Plug-In Content Handler:* Alternatively, certain content handlers can execute the content of retrieved URL information directly integrated within a Web browser window via a content handler plug-in. These plug-ins are browser-specific extensions that need to be loaded by the browser beforehand.

Web Browser Implementations

Various Web browser implementations exist, but the Netscape Navigator (NN) and Microsoft Internet Explorer (IE) Web browser products are by far the most popular. NN runs on various platforms, whereas IE is targeted for Microsoft platforms. Both browsers support the latest and greatest in HTML presentation standards, as well as various extensions to HTML. Both browser implementations also support a JavaScript scripting language runtime environment and a Java applet execution environment. Despite the presence of standards, NN and IE do differ in feature support. Thus, it is often a challenge for developers of Web page content to determine the lowest common denominator of support across both NN and IE. However, by designing to such a lowest common denominator, you can help ensure a maximal level of Web client base support.

Web Servers

A Web server is a server-side application whose primary role is to handle or delegate HTTP requests and to generate or route HTTP responses. Web servers come in various flavors and can support various needs. The most simplistic form of Web server may simply receive `GET` or `POST` requests, read a local file based on a requested URL, and stream the file data back to the Web client. Higher-end enterprise-class Web servers support concurrent requests from a scalable number of clients, implement some form of secure access control, and support various APIs for extending the functionality of a Web server to dynamically generate Web documents in an application-specific fashion. This section briefly describes a generic architecture for Web servers and highlights those commercial Web server implementations currently pervading the marketplace.

Web Server Architecture

Figure 18.2 presents a basic conceptual architecture of a Web server. The Web server controller serves to represent the main process controller context in which a Web server runs. A Web server controller typically manages a pool of threads that are used to handle requests from clients as they are received. A Web handler thread is allocated to manage a particular client request and response. Each request and response passes through a network interface. The HTTP protocol is used for unsecured connections, and HTTPS is used for HTTP with SSL-based connections.

A Web server controller may also maintain session management information between successive requests from a client such that statefulness for the otherwise stateless HTTP protocol may be implemented. Caches of response information may also be maintained by a Web server such that successive instances of the same request may be used to rapidly generate a cached response. The behavior of the Web server will often be manageable through some means of configuring the server environment. Management of the Web server environment may also include the specification of ACLs limiting access to server-side resources for particular Web users. Furthermore, most Web server environments will also provide some mechanism for logging Web server requests and responses.

Interfaces that can generate Web-based documents according to HTTP requests are central to a Web server architecture. Web servers typically support one or more of the following types of document-serving interfaces:

- *File Request Handler:* Most Web servers have file request handlers that map a URL to a file (for example, an HTML file) local to the Web server that is to be read and sent back to the client in an HTTP response stream.
- *CGI Engine:* The Common Gateway Interface (CGI) provides a standard interface mechanism for spawning external processes implemented in any language to handle HTTP requests and generate HTTP responses.
- *ISAPI:* The Internet Server Application Program Interface (ISAPI) defines an interface for calling Microsoft platform DLLs to handle HTTP requests and generate HTTP responses.

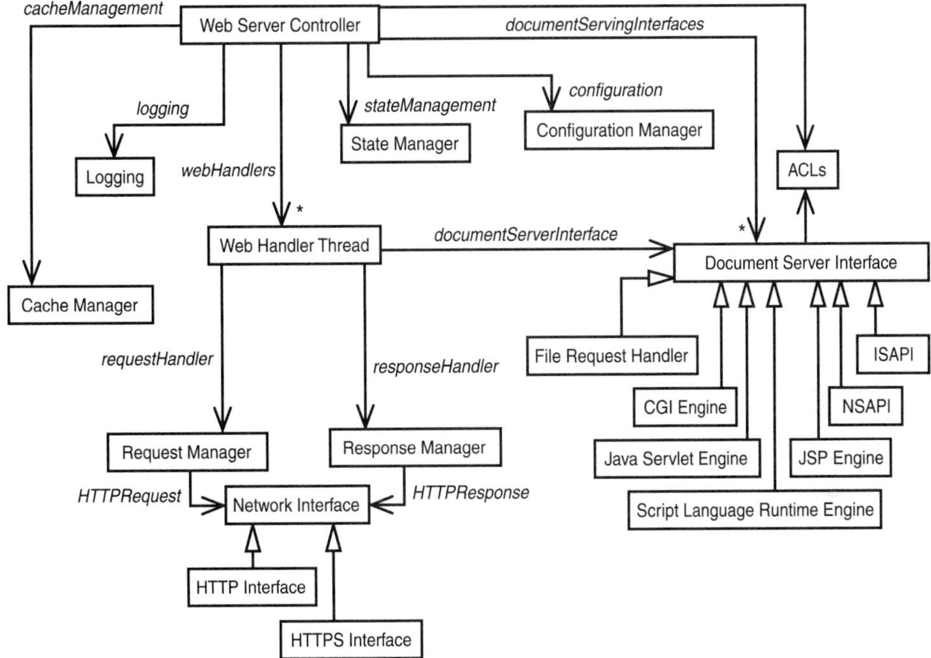

Figure 18.2 Web server architecture.

- *NSAPI:* The Netscape Server Application Programming Interface (NSAPI) defines an interface for calling binary libraries to handle HTTP requests and generate HTTP responses.
- *Script Language Runtime Engine:* Script language runtime engines allow scripting language commands, such as JavaScript and VBScript, stored in HTML files to be executed within the Web server's process space. Such commands are used to generate dynamic HTML content to be sent back to the requesting client.
- *Java Servlet Engine:* Java Servlet engines allow Java code adhering to a particular interface to be executed within the Web server's process space to handle HTTP requests and generate HTTP responses.
- *JSP Engine:* JavaServer Pages (JSP) engines are used to compile special Java scripting language commands into executable Java Servlet content, which is then executed within a Web server's process space to handle HTTP requests and generate HTTP responses.

Web Server Implementations

Web server implementations can be extremely simplistic in nature or support various sophisticated enterprise-class features. Web servers may be started from the command line and be configured from a simple text file, or they may come equipped with a nifty GUI interface for starting, stopping, creating, deleting, and configuring server instances. We've already seen an example of a simple Web server implementation such as the one used in Chapter 9, "RMI Communications," for dynamic RMI code downloading. However, more sophisticated Web servers are needed for commercial and enterprise-class applications.

The Microsoft Internet Information Server (IIS) is used on server-side Microsoft platforms as the Microsoft platform-specific solution for Web serving. IIS is tightly integrated with Windows NT and Windows 2000 platforms and can be used with Microsoft's other enterprise solutions. IIS provides document serving interfaces such as file serving, CGI, ISAPI, and the Active Server Pages (ASP) scripting environment.

The Java Web Server is a Web server implemented completely in Java and thus offers a platform-independent Web server solution. The Java Web Server provides document serving interfaces for file serving, CGI, and Java Servlets.

The BEA WebLogic Server is an enterprise-class Web server and is also largely built on top of the Java platform. Web servers that come equipped with BEA WebLogic Server follow the J2EE model and offer an environment for both Java Servlets and JSPs. In addition to file serving and CGI support, the BEA WebLogic Server also supports basic NSAPI and ISAPI document serving interfaces.

The Apache Web Server is a freeware server and has been developed according to the open source shareware model of development. Apache operates on UNIX and Windows platforms and is actually used in many enterprise-class Web serving applications. The Apache Web Server not only includes basic file serving and CGI support, but has also been extended for use with various scripting languages and Java Servlets. In fact, the Apache Tomcat server is the J2EE reference implementation for Web serving using J2EE Web components.

Many other Web server implementations exist beyond the core products mentioned here. The J2EE enables you to create Web server–based applications with Java Servlet and JSP technology that is independent of the underlying Web server vendor implementation. J2EE-compliant Web server implementation vendors are required to provide J2EE-compliant container environments within which Java Servlet and JSP components run. These container environments are standardized versions of the previously mentioned document serving engines for such technologies. Many of the Web server implementations mentioned here either have already implemented or have begun to implement J2EE-compliant container environments. Even if a particular Web server vendor's J2EE Web environment is not up to snuff, many vendor implementations make it easy for you to plug in third-party Web container environments.

Web Services

As discussed, Web clients and servers have always communicated via HTTP. As we saw in Part III, "Enterprise Communications Enabling," a few key higher-level protocols have been defined that represent a more meaningful way for communications to occur between enterprise application client and server. One such higher-level protocol was detailed in Chapter 10, "Web Service Communications." Web Services involve XML-based requests (that is, SOAP requests) adhering to a particular format sent from Web services client to Web services server and then similar XML-based responses (that is, SOAP responses) being sent back from server to client.

Most often such SOAP requests and responses are sent over HTTP. However, other transport protocols may be used for Web servicing. Nevertheless, because SOAP over HTTP is the most popular means for implementing Web services, most Web server platforms have already been or are being tooled to support Web service communications. In the context of Figure 18.2 presented earlier, a special Web service engine may be provided as another type of document server interface. That is, the Web service engine needs to provide support for parsing SOAP requests out of an HTTP request stream, translating the SOAP request into an information format usable by a Web service endpoint (that is, deserialization or unmarshaling), and then handing that information off to the Web service endpoint. Similarly, the Web service engine also needs to provide support for receiving the response information from the Web services endpoint, translating that information into a SOAP response (that is, serialization or marshaling), and packing the SOAP response inside of an HTTP response back to the client.

Not many Web browsers supported communicating via Web services at the time of this writing. However, it is conceivable that such implementations are forthcoming. The advantage is that such Web browsers would be able to open the doors for the richer and higher-level communications offered by Web service communications. In terms of how such support may be provided inside of Web browsers, we can take a look at Figure 18.1, presented earlier. In the context of such an architecture, a new Web browser document presentation interface type would be needed for Web service presentation. Thus, such a Web service presentation manager would handle the generation of SOAP requests to a server and be able to handle information embedded into SOAP responses from a server. Essentially, although some Web browsers can already handle communications and presentation via XML, a SOAP style of communication would enable the Web browser to focus on a particular XML format and open the gateway for greater interoperability in the world of Web services.

Web Development

Thus far in this chapter, we have examined the basic architecture and model for Web clients and servers. Such clients and servers represent the platforms to which Web developers write Web-based applications. That is, on the server side, Web developers must write applications that run and operate inside of a Web server environment. Thus, the services as well as restrictions inherent in such Web server platforms must be taken into consideration when writing server-side Web applications. On the client side, Web developers must create presentation content to be served by a Web server such that it can take advantage of the services as well as limit itself to the restrictions imposed by Web browsers. The remainder of this chapter defines those development approaches that a

Web developer may take in creating applications that operate atop such Web server and client platforms. We'll first take a brief look at more traditional models of Web development as a short historical backdrop for introducing the J2EE-based Web development paradigms that are the focus of this part of the book.

CGI Programming

The Common Gateway Interface (CGI) defines a standard interface contract between a Web server and a Web-enabled application. This interface allows Web servers to delegate the responsibility for generating HTTP responses to independent CGI-capable applications. Such applications can thus be used to dynamically generate HTTP responses. This may be contrasted with a Web server's typical support for reading statically defined HTML files and sending back their contents in an HTTP response stream.

Whenever an HTTP request is made and references a URL that refers to a CGI application, the Web server spawns the application, passing it inputs via environment variables, as well as through standard input. Results from the CGI application can then be returned via standard output to the Web server. If the CGI application supports generation of HTTP response header information, the Web server can then simply send the entire response back to the Web browser without further processing. Otherwise, the Web server may need to prepend HTTP response header information to the CGI application's generated HTTP response body.

The basic flow of a CGI request via a Web server works as shown here:

- A Web browser sends an HTTP request formulated from some URL. For example, the URL `http://www.bla.com/cgi-bin/customerQuery.cgi?customer=heilmann` may get transformed into an HTTP request with the HTTP request header line `POST /cgi-bin/ customerQuery.cgi?customer=heilmann HTTP/1.0`.
- A Web server receives an HTTP request with a resource ID specifying the path to a resource, the resource name, and possibly a set of parameters to pass to this resource.
- If the Web server supports CGI, it must be configured either to recognize that the path refers to a directory where CGI programs are stored (for example, `cgi-bin`) or to recognize that the resource name ends with an appropriate extension (for example, `cgi`).
- The Web server will set certain environment variables derived from the HTTP request used by the CGI program. It will then spawn the CGI program identified by the pathname and resource name as a separate process, passing it the parameters also sent over to the Web server via the HTTP request.
- The spawned CGI program uses the environment variables and parameters passed to it to do whatever job it is supposed to do (for example, database query or remote printing).

- By virtue of being a CGI program, the program either must format the results in the form of an HTML page for the response body or must return the response headers and alleviate the Web server from this duty (that is, it is a nonparsed CGI program).
- The CGI program returns the results to the Web server via a standard output stream.
- The Web server then returns the results to the Web client by either first prepending the header values or sending the results back without further modification (if the CGI program is of the nonparsed persuasion).

Such a scenario can also be described at a higher level above pure HTTP communications in terms of a user's interaction with HTML GUI components embedded inside of a Web browser (see Appendix F, "HTML"). An HTML form captures input data entered into Web-based `INPUT` components with a `METHOD` of either `GET` or `POST` and an `ACTION` designating a target CGI application URL (for example, `http://www.beeshirts.com/cgi-bin/contact`). A `SUBMIT` type of `INPUT` component packages data into an HTTP request to be sent to a CGI application referenced in the target URL. At this point, the same basic flow of CGI behavior previously described applies.

Each request to a CGI application spawns a new process, and there is no direct means for persisting state across application invocations. CGI programmers have to hand-code such mechanisms themselves. One programmatic approach for preserving state is to embed some session identifier information into an HTML `HIDDEN INPUT` field and use this identifier to refer to a client's sessions state that is stored on the server side in some persistent store. More state information can also be embedded into a `HIDDEN` field and referenced, but there is a practical limit on how much information you would want to be stored in such fields because it would have to be transmitted in every HTTP request and response.

When a Web client begins a Web-based interaction session with a Web server, a session ID can be generated on the server side and stored inside of an HTML form's `INPUT` tag whose type is `HIDDEN` (for example, `<INPUT TYPE="HIDDEN" NAME="SessionID" VALUE="id8245">`). The server side can also persist such client session ID information in a database, a file, or perhaps a separate running process. When the HTML form submits an HTTP request to the Web server, the `HIDDEN INPUT` field data associated with this form and containing the session ID can be sent to the Web server. A CGI application can use this session ID to look up other client session information persisted in the database, file, or separate process. As long as the session ID is always generated on the server side and stored in a `HIDDEN INPUT` field and always sent back to the Web server via an HTML form `GET` or `POST`, the Web client session can be tracked.

> **Note**
>
> The value of the "SessionID" attribute above ("id8245") was chosen for brevity, but real session ids should be much more sophisticated. They should encode enough information to uniquely identify the user across an entire application that might run on multiple servers simultaneously. In addition, they should somehow encode the user's IP address or some other characteristic to prevent another browser from "spoofing," or pretending to be another user by hand-crafting their own session ID.

As we alluded, session IDs are not the only way in which state can be embedded into a CGI-based interaction. Depending on the amount of state needed for the application, only the state used for subsequent transactions needs to be embedded into a HIDDEN INPUT field. If this state is minimal, it may always be stored in a HIDDEN INPUT field, sent to the Web client in HTTP responses, and then sent back to the Web server in HTTP requests. The need to persistently store session information in a back-end database, file, or separate process may thus be alleviated.

Scripting Languages

Scripting languages provide another popular solution for programming both client-side and server-side Web behavior. Figure 18.3 shows how scripting languages can be used for Web enabling on both the client and the server side. Scripting language code that is embedded into HTML documents that are sent to a Web browser are processed by client-side script runtime engines that can interpret scripts embedded within special <SCRIPT> and </SCRIPT> HTML tags. Scripting language code is also supported by most Web servers, often by the provision of server-side runtime engines that process scripts embedded into HTML documents before they are sent to the Web browser. Server-side script processing involves interpreting script language code embedded within special server script HTML tags and dynamically generating content that is output to an HTML document stream before it is sent to a Web browser. Server-side scripting languages are also used in CGI application development.

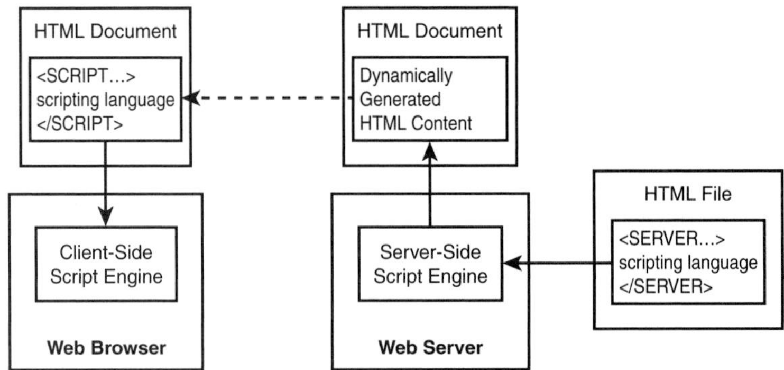

Figure 18.3 Scripting languages on the Web.

Scripting language Web solutions on the client side are good for performing data and input validation and for displaying basic messages. On the server side, however, pure scripting solutions to Web enabling have scalability, maintainability, and performance problems when used for anything besides dynamic Web presentation logic. Because scripting languages are not OO by nature, the lack of inheritance and encapsulation leads to limitations for true enterprise class usage when they're used to implement business and interface logic. However, scripting languages are often employed in development scenarios in which the language is already known or can be easily understood due to the language's inherent simplicity. A few of the more common client- or server-side scripting language solutions for Web enabling are JavaScript, VBScript, and Perl.

Active Server Pages

Active Server Pages (ASP) is Microsoft's answer to Web-enabling applications using a server-side scripting language technique. ASP requires use of Microsoft's Internet Information Server Web server to process server-side ASP files upon a Web request and to dynamically generate Web response content. IIS uses a special Windows platform–specific dynamic link library (`ASP.DLL`) to process ASP files. ASP files having the `.asp` extension contain special ASP commands that are processed by the IIS Web server to generate dynamic content.

ASPs can be created using server-side scripting languages such as VBScript and JScript, although VBScript is by far the most popular language used in ASP implementations. ASPs are HTML files that contain embedded scripting language code in which the first line in an ASP identifies the language. ASP commands embedded in the HTML document are encapsulated by `<%` and `%>` tags. Inside of such tags, ASP employs special proprietary Microsoft objects for writing to a client output stream. ASP code can not only utilize such objects directly, but also utilize other objects to access databases and other system resources using standard scripting language syntax.

ASPs thus provide the same advantages as other scripting language–based server-side Web programming paradigms in the context of a Microsoft Web server platform-specific architecture. Because the `ASP.DLL` is needed to transform HTML pages sprinkled with server-side ASP commands into dynamic HTML response content, ASPs rely on a server-side Microsoft platform. Some COTS products do exist to transform ASPs into an intermediate format usable on other platforms. However, the added overhead required by such a process is typically necessary only if an existing legacy of ASPs have been developed in the first place on a Windows platform and then need to be run on another platform such as UNIX.

Java-Based Web Programming

We have described a few non–Java-based Web-enabling techniques thus far in this section so that you as a developer tasked with Web-enabling your enterprise can best understand the alternative technologies that are available and sometimes used in the enterprise. You can then better trade off the advantages and disadvantages of these other technologies with the recommended J2EE-based Web-enabling techniques of Java Servlets and JavaServer Pages (JSPs) to be described in this book. Not only are Java Servlets and JSPs part of the J2EE and therefore germane to this book's topical discussion, but they also represent the most optimal option for Web-enabling most enterprise systems. Servlets and JSPs offer advantages of platform independence, rapid application development, performance, and the capability to use a familiar Java paradigm that other Web-enabling technologies cannot offer.

J2EE Servlets provide a way to allow Web servers to hand off Web requests to Java-based code by starting such code as a separate thread, handing request data to the servlet, and then receiving response data. Servlets have numerous advantages over CGI-based applications in that servlet requests are handled by a separate thread inside of a running JVM process as opposed to having a separate process for each request. Servlets can also easily maintain state between requests and provide built-in APIs to session management facilities. Servlets also share data among multiple servlet instances as an added advantage over CGI.

Although many server-side scripting language approaches to Web enabling support stateful sessions and threaded processing, servlets offer the rich OO API of Java that scripting languages inherently do not support. Thus, the maintainability and reusability of code across enterprise Java applications can be provided by virtue of a Java Servlet–based approach to Web enabling. Servlets also running on top of J2EE also offer platform and COTS server independence that no other non-Java scripting-based Web-enabling technology can provide. We describe servlets in much more detail in Chapter 19, "Java Servlets."

JSP is a Java-based scripting language approach for Web enabling. JSPs are server-side HTML documents with embedded JSP commands as is the case with ASP. JSPs are converted into Java Servlets as they are processed by a J2EE-based Web server. Although JSPs may initially seem like an undesirable Web programming solution given the disadvantages of other scripting language–based solutions, JSP technology in J2EE servers focuses on the use of JSP as a strictly presentation-layer description of Web-page content. All the enterprise-critical business and interface logic rests in either a servlet or an Enterprise JavaBean. Thus, the maintainability and reuse pertinent to business and interface logic can rest inside more OO-based constructs, and JSPs can be used to describe the Web screen presentation in a fashion more familiar to Web page development personnel. JSPs also offer an advantage of platform and COTS Web server independence not offered by other scripting-based Web-enabling solutions. We describe JSPs in more detail in Chapter 20, "JavaServer Pages (JSP)," and in Chapter 21, "JSP Tags."

Web Services Programming

Because Web Services are playing an increasingly large role in Web development paradigms, it behooves us to learn an efficient means for programming Web service applications. We've already gotten a glimpse of such programming methods in Chapter 10,

"Web Service Communications." In that chapter we explored J2EE-based APIs for Web services development using SAAJ and JAX-RPC. The good news for us J2EE developers is that Web services programming for constructing scalable Web applications can be even simpler when utilizing J2EE containers. In fact, the primary J2EE approach for developing Web services relies on the use of a J2EE container and existing J2EE application development techniques.

Chapter 22, "Web Services with Web Components," describes how one can leverage use of a J2EE Web container to construct and deploy Web services in a relatively simple fashion. As we'll see, the J2EE v1.4 Web container now in fact contains a Web services runtime engine along with a Java Servlet and JSP engine. Chapter 30, "Web Services with EJB," describes a technique for exposing the functionality of EJBs directly as Web services. We'll soon learn that creating Web services using J2EE containers can be a relatively simple task not involving much more knowledge than you'll already be equipped with by learning how to create and deploy Java Servlets, JSPs, and EJBs inside of J2EE container environments.

Conclusions

Web browsers and Web servers are the platforms used to Web-enable an enterprise. Enterprise users utilize Web browsers to submit Web requests from Web servers and receive Web document responses that are to be displayed within the client-side Web browser environment. Additionally, the use of a scalable, secure, and highly available Web server is paramount to effective enterprise Web-enabling. This chapter briefly explored the architecture of Web browsers and Web servers such that a Web developer can understand what services and restrictions are offered by such platforms. We also explored how Web Services technology is and will continue to be incorporated into such Web server and browser architectures. Finally, we examined the various means by which Web applications may be developed to operate atop such platforms and introduced the J2EE-based technologies used for Web development. Subsequent chapters in this part of the book describe such J2EE-based Web development technologies.

19

Java Servlets

Java Servlets provide one of the core means for Web-enabling enterprises using Java technology. Custom J2EE-compliant Java Servlet components are built by application developers to handle business-specific requests and generate responses via HTTP and the Web. Stateful HTTP behavior can also be provided using a simple collection of Java Servlet APIs. J2EE-based Web containers make it easy to configure, deploy, and build robust Web applications using Java Servlets. This chapter describes how to build Web-enabled Java enterprise systems using Java Servlets as part of a J2EE Web solution. Our discussion centers around a description of the rich Java Servlet API abstractions and sample usage of these APIs in the context of BeeShirts.com—an example e-commerce storefront. We also describe how to configure and deploy this application in the context of a J2EE Web server environment.

In this chapter, you will learn:

- The architecture of J2EE-based Java Servlet Web component and container frameworks.
- The generic Servlet API framework.
- The HTTP Servlet API framework.
- The HTTP Servlet request and request-dispatch model.
- The HTTP Servlet response model.
- Servlet HTTP session and cookie management.
- The Java Servlet request and response filtering abstraction.
- Web application configuration and deployment using the deployment descriptor.
- Utilization of Web container service management of resources, security, transactions, and availability.

Servlet Architecture

The Java Servlet API provides a standard interface that allows developers to handle requests from client applications, and generate appropriate responses to those requests. As such, they provide a fundamental building block for server-side application development. The Java Servlet API defines a generic request and response framework, but they are most commonly used for handling HTTP requests and generating HTTP responses via the Web. J2EE 1.4 has adopted version 2.4 of the Java Servlet API. This section explores the logical, physical, and dynamic architecture of such J2EE-compliant Java Servlets.

Servlet Logical and Physical Architecture

Figure 19.1 depicts the Java Servlet architecture assumed by J2EE-based Web applications and v2.4 of the Java Servlet Specification. As the diagram shows, HTTP requests and responses are built atop generic servlet requests and responses. A custom Java Servlet is built by an enterprise Web applications developer to specialize an HTTP servlet abstraction, which in turn specializes a generic servlet framework. Abstractions for managing data associated with the same user across multiple requests from that user are also possible via HTTP session management and cookies. Additionally, special servlet filters may be used to intercept and transform requests and responses before and after a Java servlet interacts with such requests and responses.

At the heart of the diagram is the J2EE-compliant Java Servlet container. The container, which is typically supplied by a third-party vendor, implements many of the core services needed to deploy enterprise applications. These services may include many of the topics we've already covered in this book, such as a JNDI registry, JDBC connection pools, and JMS messaging, as well as other J2EE technologies such as Enterprise JavaBeans, which we will introduce in Part VI of the book, "Enterprise Applications Enabling." In fact, this component/container model of application deployment has many advantages, in terms of the portability and scalability of the applications that can be developed.

There are several J2EE-compliant servlet containers available off-the-shelf today. Tomcat, from the Apache Group, is an open-source solution that is quite popular with developers. The development effort of the Tomcat server has typically been more focused on standards compliance than performance, and has actually been chosen by Sun to be the reference implementation of the Java Servlet and JSP specifications. It is available from `http://jakarta.apache.org/tomcat/index.html`. Several commercial Servlet containers are available as well, such as WebLogic from BEA (`www.bea.com`) and WebSphere from IBM (`www.ibm.com`). These commercial products tend to focus on performance and reliability enhancements, and administrative and management tools. However, they all provide a consistent implementation of the Servlet API, and can all be configured using the J2EE standard deployment descriptors that are discussed in this chapter.

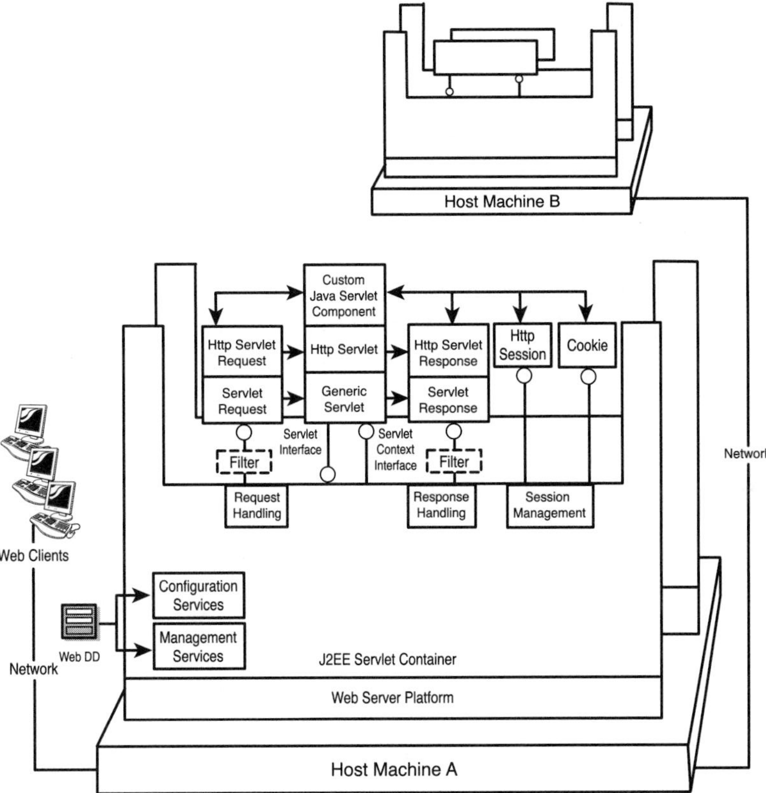

Figure 19.1 The Java Servlet architecture.

Servlet Life Cycle

Understanding the life cycle of a servlet is useful in understanding the dynamic behavior of the Java Servlet architecture. The basic life cycle of a Java Servlet in the context of a concrete HTTP request and response handling scenario is as given here:

1. The container loads a Java `Servlet` class either when the servlet's services are requested by a Web client or when the Web server is started.
2. The container also either creates a `Servlet` object instance based on a client request or creates multiple instances of a `Servlet` object and adds these instances to a servlet instance pool.
3. The container calls a servlet's initialization method, `HttpServlet.init()`, upon servlet instantiation.

4. The container constructs an `HttpServletRequest` and `HttpServletResponse` object to encapsulate a particular HTTP request received from a Web client and the response to be generated by the servlet.
5. The container passes the `HttpServletRequest` and `HttpServletResponse` objects to the `HttpServlet.service()` method. A custom Java Servlet then has access to such HTTP request and response interfaces.
6. The custom Java Servlet reads HTTP request data from the `HttpServletRequest` object, accesses any state information from an `HttpSession` or `Cookie` object, performs any application-specific processing, and generates HTTP response data using the `HttpServletResponse` object.
7. When the Web server and container shuts down, the `HttpServlet.destroy()` method is called to close any open resources.

Servlet Interfaces

The classes and interfaces defined in the `javax.servlet` package encapsulate an abstract framework for building components that receive requests and generate responses (that is, servlets). Abstractions for these servlets, requests, and responses are all encapsulated within this package. Additionally, an interface to the servlet's container context is also defined within this package. This section describes the base exceptions and basic component and container abstractions that form the servlet framework. Although the material presented in this section is necessarily abstract, we do illustrate how to utilize some of the interfaces defined in this section via sample code snippets toward the end of the section.

Base Servlet Framework Abstractions

Figure 19.2 shows the core entities involved in defining the base Java Servlet interface framework contained within the `javax.servlet` package. These entities define the basic abstract framework from which all concrete Java Servlet request and response paradigms (that is, HTTP communications) are extended. Base servlet and servlet configuration interfaces are implemented by a generic servlet class that represents an abstract view of a Java Servlet component. Servlets operate inside of a servlet container context that controls the life cycle of a servlet and provides a servlet with configuration and management services. We only display the method signatures for those base servlet entities used to encapsulate servlet components and containers in Figure 19.2 and defer a detailed discussion of requests and responses until a later section.

Base `Servlet` Interface

The `javax.servlet.Servlet` interface is the base interface for all Java Servlets. The `Servlet.init()` method is called once by a servlet component's container when the servlet is instantiated. When the servlet container is ready to take the servlet out of service, the container calls the `Servlet.destroy()` method, giving the servlet an opportunity to clean up any resources before it becomes dormant. The `init()` method takes a `javax.servlet.ServletConfig` object as a parameter that contains initialization information from the container environment. The `Servlet.getServletConfig()` method may subsequently be used to return a handle to the `ServletConfig` object. Additional information about a servlet, such as author and version information, may also be obtained from a `Servlet` instance using the `getServletInfo()` method.

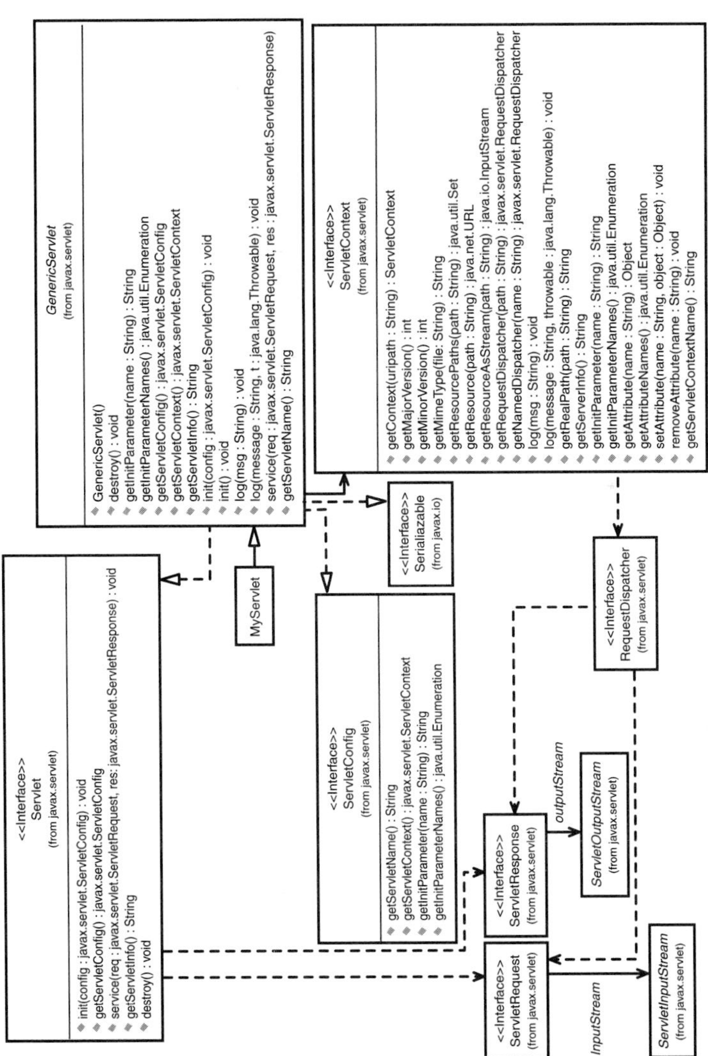

Figure 19.2 Base servlet interfaces.

The `Servlet.service()` method is called by a servlet's container to handle requests and generate responses during regular operational usage of the servlet. A `javax.servlet.ServletRequest` object is passed to the `service()` method containing all servlet request information to be read from an input stream. A `javax.servlet.ServletResponse` object is also passed to a `service()` method and is used to generate response information from within the servlet by way of writing information to an output stream.

It is important to note that to serve multiple client requests concurrently, a servlet container may allow more than one thread to call a `Servlet` object instance's `service()` at the same time. For this reason, the implementer of a particular `Servlet` must provide for the thread safety of the servlet.

`ServletConfig` Interface

The `ServletConfig` interface is implemented by servlets that want to receive initialization information from the servlet container environment. Named initialization parameter value strings can be retrieved from the `ServletConfig.getInitParameter()` method by passing in the name of the parameter. The entire `Enumeration` of initialization parameter `String` names can be retrieved from the `ServletConfig.getInitParameterNames()` method. Any name for a servlet can also be retrieved from the `ServletConfig.getServletName()` method. Finally, a handle to the servlet's context can be retrieved from the `ServletConfig.getServletContext()` method.

`GenericServlet` Class

The abstract `javax.servlet.GenericServlet` class provides a default implementation for much of the `Servlet` and `ServletConfig` interfaces that it implements. The `GenericServlet` class also defines a convenience `init()` method definition and defines two `log()` methods used to write log messages and exception information to an underlying servlet log destination. Concrete subclasses of `GenericServlet` define specific request and response handling mechanisms (for example, HTTP request and response handling). Most application developers will actually extend subclasses of the `GenericServlet` class (for example, `HttpServlet`), but service providers are required only to define an implementation for the abstract `GenericServlet.service()` method.

`ServletContext` Interface

The `javax.servlet.ServletContext` interface provides a handle to a servlet's container context. There is one `ServletContext` instance per servlet application per JVM instance. In the case of an `HttpServlet`, the servlet context is specified relative to a root context for a particular URL. Thus, a particular root context of `http://www.beeshirts.com/customers` may serve as the root context for a particular servlet context that will receive any requests sent to the `/customers` context on the www.beeshirts.com host machine. The ServletContext.getContext() method may be used to obtain a handle to another ServletContext object on the same Web server by passing in the absolute pathname of a server's document root beginning with a slash (/). A null value may be returned from the getContext() call if permission to the other ServletContext is not allowed. We talk about RequestDispatcher objects later in the chapter, but for now suffice it to say that the ServletContext also serves as the entry point from which Web requests can be dispatched to other servlets within the same servlet context via its getRequestDispatcher() and getNamedDispatcher() calls.

Resources and underlying system pathnames can be retrieved from the container environment given a pathname relative to the servlet's context. The real path of a particular path relative to a servlet's context can be obtained from the ServletContext.getRealPath() method. By passing in a virtual path to this method, the real path associated with the underlying operating-system environment can be returned in String form. A URL to a particular resource may be made available to a servlet by calling ServletContext.getResource() with a path relative to a servlet's context. A resource may also be retrieved in the form of an InputStream object via a call to the ServletContext.getResourceAsStream() with a path relative to the servlet's context.

Various product information about a servlet's container environment may also be obtained through ServletContext calls. The ServletContext.getServerInfo() method returns a String of servlet container and server information of the format *ServerName/VersionNumber (OptionalInformation)*. The major and minor version of the container's supported Java Servlet API may also be obtained from calls to getMajorVersion() and getMinorVersion() on a ServletContext object.

Configuration information about the container environment is obtained in various ways from ServletContext. MIME type mappings that have been configured for a particular Web server environment will be used to return the appropriate MIME type/subtype String from a call to ServletContext.getMimeType() given a particular filename. Configuration parameter values for a container environment can be returned from the ServletContext.getInitParameter() method given a named configuration parameter. The names of all container-wide parameters can also be returned from a call to Servlet.Context.getInitParameterNames() in the form of an Enumeration of String names.

In addition to configuration parameters, a collection of named java.lang.Object types can be associated with a container environment as attributes of the ServletContext environment. These attributes can be shared by other servlets in the context and can be declared, retrieved, or removed using the ServletContext object's setAttribute(), getAttribute(), and removeAttribute() methods, respectively. An Enumeration of String names for all attributes can also be retrieved via the getAttributeNames() call.

The `ServletContext.log()` methods are used to write log messages and exception information to an underlying servlet log destination (usually a flat text file). This presumes that the servlet container environment will allow for some way to specify the name and type of log to generate.

Servlet Framework Examples

The servlet framework APIs presented thus far are not typically used alone to build fully functional Java Servlets. Rather, the HTTP extensions presented in the next section provide the means for building Web-based servlets. Nevertheless, an `ejava.servlets.ServletsHelper` class that we equip with our sample software for this chapter does demonstrate some basic usage of the servlet framework abstractions presented thus far. The `ServletHelper` class will be used by HTTP servlet sample code presented in subsequent sections to provide some common utilities for the sample servlets.

> **Note**
>
> See Appendix A, "Software Configuration," for details on retrieving the example code for this chapter. Full listings of the code for this chapter will be extracted to the `examples\src\ejava\servlets` directory. Only relevant snippets are shown here. In addition, a Servlet v2.4–compliant application server is required to run the sample code. Instructions on building and deploying the samples on several of the most popular application servers are also given in Appendix A.

The `printServletContextInformation()` method defined on the `ServletHelper` class demonstrates use of a few `javax.servlet.ServletContext` methods. The `printServletContextInformation()` simply retrieves and logs a set of attributes, parameters, version information, path information, and resource information as shown here:

```
public static void printServletContextInformation(
  ServletContext servletContext) throws ServletException
{
  // Get attribute names from servlet context
  Enumeration attributes = servletContext.getAttributeNames();
  // For each attribute, print name and value to log
  while(attributes.hasMoreElements()){
    String attributeName = (String)attributes.nextElement();
    Object attribute = servletContext.getAttribute(attributeName);
    servletContext.log("Attribute :" +attributeName +
      " Attribute :" + attribute);
  }
```

```
  // Get parameter names from context
  Enumeration parameters = servletContext.getInitParameterNames();
  // For each parameter, print name and value to log
  while(parameters.hasMoreElements()){
    String parameterName = (String)parameters.nextElement();
    Object parameterValue = servletContext.getAttribute(parameterName);
    servletContext.log("Parameter :" +parameterName +
      " Parameter Value :" + parameterValue);
  }

  // Get and log real path
  String servletPath = servletContext.getRealPath("/");
  servletContext.log("Servlet Path :"+servletPath);
  // Get and log server info
  String serverInformation = servletContext.getServerInfo();
  servletContext.log("Server Information  :"+serverInformation);
  // Log major and minor version of API
  servletContext.log("Major Version :"
      + servletContext.getMajorVersion());
  servletContext.log("Minor Version :"
      + servletContext.getMinorVersion());

  // Get and log resource info
  try{
    java.net.URL resource = servletContext.getResource("/");
    servletContext.log("Resource : " +resource);
  }
  catch(MalformedURLException malformedURLException){
    servletContext.log(" Error :" +malformedURLException);
  }
}
```

The `printServletConfigInformation()` method defined in the `ServletHelper` class demonstrates use of a few `javax.servlet.ServletConfig` methods. The `printServletConfigInformation()` retrieves a `ServletContext` object from a `ServletConfig` object, retrieves and prints `ServletConfig` parameters, and calls the `printServletContextInformation()` method as shown here:

```
public static void printServletConfigInformation(
  ServletConfig servletConfig) throws ServletException
{
  // Retrieve servlet context and log message
  ServletContext servletContext = servletConfig.getServletContext();
  servletContext.log("Servlet Initial Parameters Names:");
  // Retrieve parameter names from ServletConfig
```

```
  Enumeration enumeration = servletConfig.getInitParameterNames();
  // For each parameter, log the name and value
  while(enumeration.hasMoreElements()){
    String parameterName = (String)enumeration.nextElement();
    String value = servletConfig.getInitParameter(parameterName);
    servletContext.log("Parameter :" +parameterName +
      " Parameter Value :"+value);
  }

  // Now print the ServletContext information
  servletContext.log("Servlet Context information :");
  printServletContextInformation(servletConfig.getServletContext());
}
```

Events and Listeners

A relatively new addition to the Servlet API is the concept of events and listeners. Much like other event/listener systems, their purpose here is to provide a callback facility to allow a servlet container to notify an application of important events. Specifically, an application can now receive notification on the initialization and destruction of its `ServletContext`, or if an attribute of the `ServletContext` is added, removed, or changed. The same can also be said for the `ServletRequest`. Figure 19.3 illustrates the event and listener classes.

To provide notification of the initialization and destruction of a `ServletContext` or a `ServletRequest`, the API defines the interfaces `ServletContextListener` and `ServletRequestListener`, respectively. The `ServletContextListener` defines two methods, `contextInitialized()` and `contextDestroyed()`, each of which takes a single argument of type `ServletContextEvent`. The `ServletContextEvent` object contains a handle to the `ServletContext` it refers to, and is accessed through the `getServletContext()` method. Similarly, the `ServletRequestListener` has the methods `requestInitialized()` and `requestDestroyed()`, each of which takes an argument of type `ServletRequestEvent`.

Along those same lines, the `ServletContextAttributeListener` and `ServletRequestAttributeListener` interfaces provide notification of an attribute being added, removed, or changed inside a `ServletContext` or `ServletRequest`. Each defines the methods `attributeAdded()`, `attributeRemoved()`, and `attributeReplaced()`, which take an argument of type `ServletContextAttributeEvent` or `ServletRequestAttributeEvent`. Each of these event objects has two methods, `getName()` and `getValue()`, which retrieve the name and value of the affected attribute.

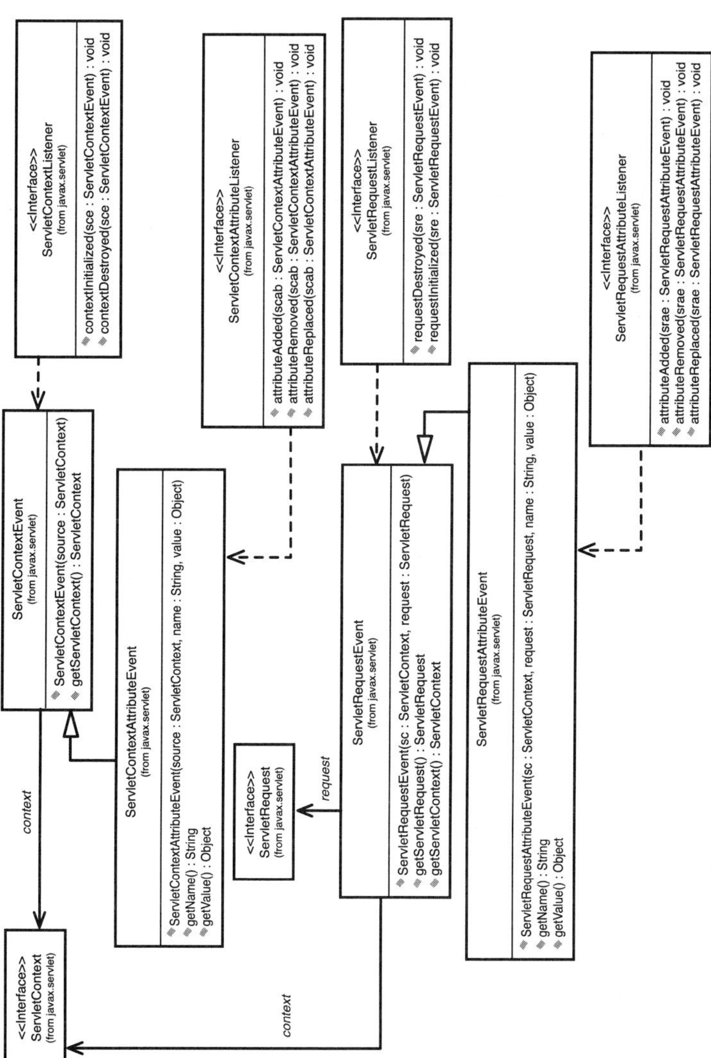

Figure 19.3 Servlet event/listener interfaces.

Applications that want to receive notification of these events will need to have a class that implements the appropriate listener interface(s) for the events they want to handle, and register that class in the application's deployment descriptor. Deployment descriptors are covered in more detail later in the chapter, but suffice it to say now that this step is necessary to make the servlet container aware that the application has requested notification of these events. In the following example, the class simply outputs a message whenever an attribute is added, removed, or changed in the `ServletContext`:

```
package ejava.servlets;

import javax.servlet.ServletContextAttributeEvent;
import javax.servlet.ServletContextAttributeListener;

/**
 *  This class implements the ServletRequestAttributeListener
 *  interface.  It simply writes a log message whenever an
 *  attribute is added, changed, or removed from a ServletContext.
 */
public class ServletContextAuditor
                implements ServletContextAttributeListener
{

    public ServletContextAuditor()
    {
    }

    public void attributeAdded(ServletContextAttributeEvent scab)
    {
       String message = "Added attribute name=" + scab.getName();
       message += " value=" + scab.getValue() + " to context.";

       scab.getServletContext().log(message);
    }

    public void attributeRemoved(ServletContextAttributeEvent scab)
    {
        String message = "Removed attribute name=" + scab.getName();
        message += " value=" + scab.getValue() + " from  context.";

        scab.getServletContext().log(message);
    }

    public void attributeReplaced(ServletContextAttributeEvent scab)
    {
        String message = "Replaced attribute name=" + scab.getName();
        message += " value=" + scab.getValue() + " in  context.";

        scab.getServletContext().log(message);
    }
}
```

Servlet HTTP Interfaces

The `javax.servlet.http` package defines a concrete extension of the basic servlet framework for HTTP-based servlets. HTTP-based servlets are, of course, used in Web-based scenarios in which HTTP requests flow into Web servers, which in turn generate HTTP responses. This section describes the basic HTTP servlet component type and the means by which application-specific components extend the HTTP servlet. We then present the basic structure of a sample BeeShirts.com e-commerce storefront based on HTTP servlets.

Base HTTP Servlet Framework Abstractions

Figure 19.4 presents the collection of core interfaces and classes in the `javax.servlet.http` package. The entities in this package extend the abstract entities in the `javax.servlet` package to provide a concrete framework for handling HTTP requests and generating HTTP responses. Note that we only display the method signatures for the base HTTP servlet component type class in Figure 19.4. We defer a detailed discussion of HTTP servlet requests, responses, stateful sessions, and event handling until later sections in this chapter.

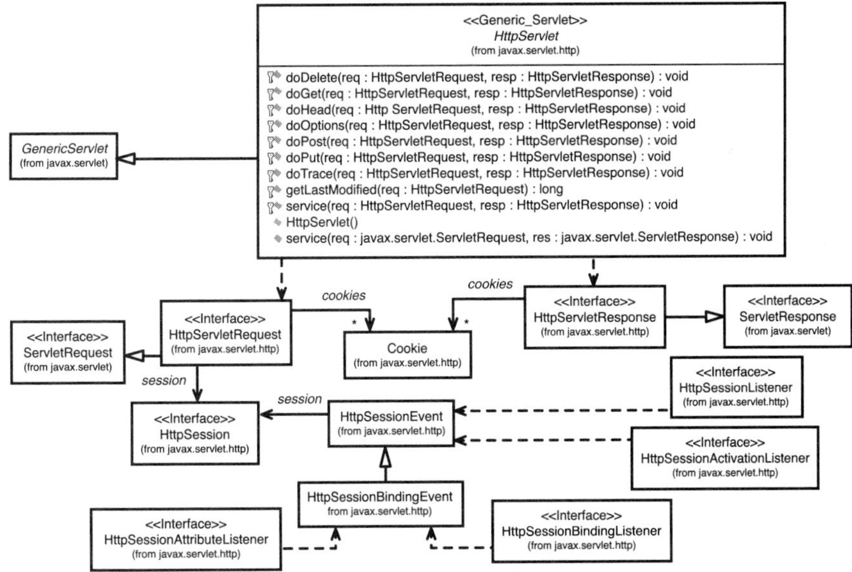

Figure 19.4 Base HTTP servlet interfaces.

The `javax.servlet.http.HttpServlet` abstract class specializes the `GenericServlet` class to specifically deal with HTTP requests and responses. HTTP requests and responses are encapsulated by the javax.servlet.http.HttpServletRequest and javax.servlet.http.HttpServletResponse interfaces, respectively.

Browser-based cookies, which can maintain state information over multiple HTTP requests, are encapsulated by the javax.servlet.http.Cookie class. A richer set of session state information can be managed on the server side through the javax.servlet.http.HttpSession interface.

Several listener interfaces are available to provide an application notification of events related to the HttpSession. Classes that implement the javax.servlet.http.HttpSessionListener interface can receive notification when sessions are created and destroyed, and implementations of the javax.servlet.http.HttpSessionActivationListener interface are notified when the container activates or passivates a session. Classes that implement the HttpSessionAttributeListener are notified when attributes are added, changed, or removed from the session, and the HttpSessionBindingListener interface allows an implementing class to receive notification when it is being bound or unbound from a session.

HttpServlet **Class**

The HttpServlet class is extended by application-specific servlet classes to handle HTTP requests and generate HTTP responses. Application-specific classes override one or more of the HttpServlet methods, as well as its base GenericServlet class methods. The init(), destroy(), and getServletInfo() methods inherited from the GenericServlet class are the most common types of methods implemented by application-specific classes. We also show a custom MySingleThreadedHttpServlet class in Figure 19.3 that extends the HttpServlet class and implements the SingleThreadModel to clue the container into allowing only a single thread to access the servlet object at one instant. Otherwise, a servlet such as MyMultiThreadedHttpServlet simply extends the HttpServlet class.

An HTTP request can come in one of many varieties defined by the request method field of an HTTP request. The request method is an identifier for the type of HTTP request being made. One of the do*XXX*() methods defined on HttpServlet is called by a servlet container environment on HttpServlet instances when the container receives an associated HTTP request method type. Each do*XXX*() method receives an HttpServletRequest and HttpServletResponse as input parameters used to handle HTTP requests and generate HTTP responses. One of the following HttpServlet method types is invoked under the specified HTTP request method scenarios:

- doGet(): Called when an HTTP GET request is received by the Web server. GET requests are used to retrieve the contents of specific resources, such as HTML pages, from a Web server.
- doPost(): Called when an HTTP POST request is received by the Web server. POST requests are also used to retrieve data from a Web server, but can also be used to send information to the Web server. As an example, POST requests can contain data posted by an HTML INPUT FORM.

- `doPut()`: Called when an HTTP `PUT` request is received by the Web server. `PUT` requests are used to upload data to a Web server.
- `doDelete()`: Called when an HTTP `DELETE` request is received by the Web server. `DELETE` requests are used to delete data from a Web server. This method is very rarely used in practice, due to the obvious risks of allowing users to delete resources from a server.
- `doHead()`: Called when an HTTP `HEAD` request is received by the Web server. `HEAD` requests are similar to `GET` requests, except that they retrieve only the HTTP header from an HTTP response.
- `doOptions()`: Called when HTTP `OPTIONS` request method types are received by the Web server. `OPTIONS` requests are used to retrieve the configuration options supported by a Web server.
- `doTrace()`: Called when HTTP `TRACE` request method types are received by the Web server. `TRACE` requests are used to ask the Web server to return the HTTP header information sent by the client for debugging purposes.

Of the seven methods defined previously, typically there is a need for application-specific overriding of only the `doGet()`, `doPost()`, `doPut()`, and `doDelete()` methods.

Recall that the `service(ServletRequest, ServletResponse)` method defined on the parent `GenericServlet` class is used to handle general requests from the servlet container context environment and generate responses for the environment. The `HttpServlet.service(HttpServletRequest, HttpServletResponse)` method is called by the `HttpServlet.service(ServletRequest, ServletResponse)` method to specifically handle HTTP requests and generate responses, and there is generally no reason to override either form of method. The `service(HttpServletRequest, HttpServletResponse)` form of method is implemented by the Servlet API to dispatch specific requests to one of the `do`*`XXX`*`()` method types depending on the received HTTP request method types.

The `HttpServlet.getLastModified()` method is called by servlet containers to determine the last time at which the state of a servlet was modified. Containers may use this information to aid in enabling Web browser and Web server caches to operate more efficiently by being able to determine whether they need to issue a request to a servlet or whether they can rely on a previously cached response. Given a particular `HttpServletRequest`, the time in milliseconds since midnight January 1, 1970, is returned to indicate the last time of change. Unknown state change times result in a negative return value.

BeeShirts.com Java HTTP Servlet Examples

The `HttpServlet` class serves as the base class from which we can build Web-enabled Java Servlets. We have in fact developed a Web-enabled BeeShirts.com e-commerce storefront using Java Servlets. Figure 19.5 provides a logical diagram of the various

HTTP servlet and HTML pages used to service requests and generate responses for this sample code.

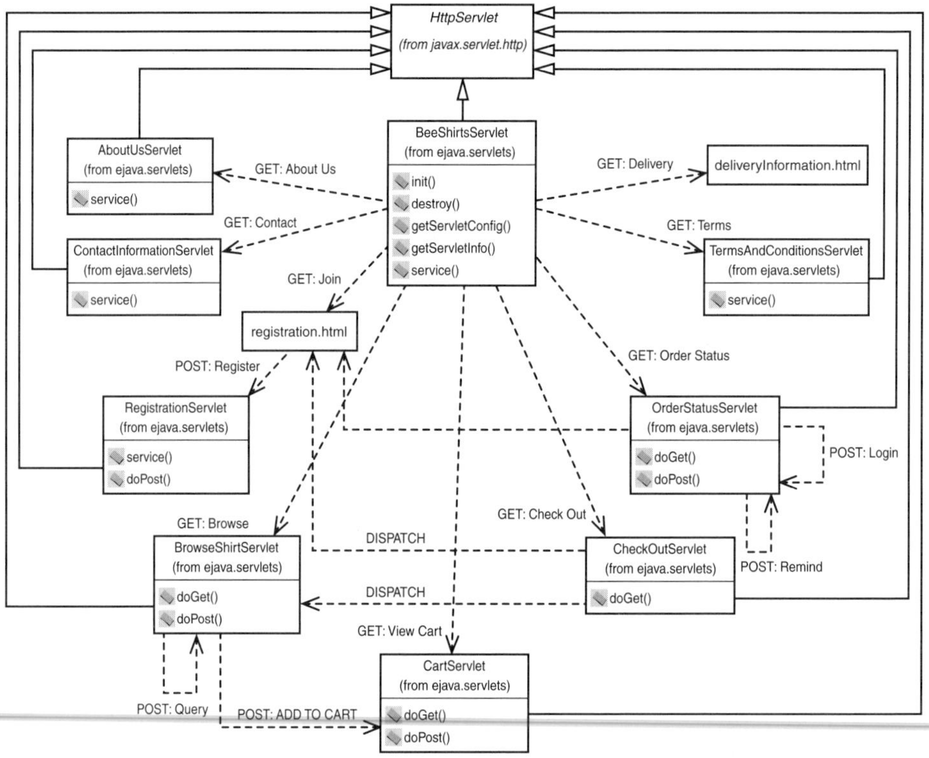

Figure 19.5 BeeShirts.com Java Servlets and HTML.

All the classes shown in Figure 19.5 extend the `javax.servlet.http.HttpServlet` class and override one or more of the `HttpServlet` methods. The various servlets also define a few private application-specific methods not shown in the diagram. The `BeeShirtsServlet` class serves as the root servlet for the BeeShirts.com e-commerce storefront. Lines drawn between the `BeeShirtsServlet` and other servlets and HTML pages are followed when requests are made from one resource to another. The lines are labeled with the type of HTTP request made and the HTML button label that induced the request.

As you can see with the main `BeeShirtsServlet` of Figure 19.6, the basic BeeShirts.com screens are divided into three sections. For all servlets, the top portion of the screen displays the BeeShirts.com logo, and the left side of the screen displays the main set of button controls. The center page area changes for each servlet requested.

Figure 19.7 shows some of the problem domain entities used by the BeeShirts.com Java Servlets. The classes shown in Figure 19.7 actually correspond to entities that map from persisted elements of our BeeShirts.com database. We saw how entities such as `Order` and `Customer` could be mapped from a database via JDBC in previous chapters. We will demonstrate how such mapping can occur in the context of Enterprise JavaBean entity beans in Chapter 26, "Entity EJB." However, for simplicity in this chapter, we simply implement the entities shown in Figure 19.7 as classes that we load with dummy data and data received from Web browser interaction. Most of the BeeShirts.com entities displayed in Figure 19.7 also contain a few helper methods to extract the contents of the objects in the form of HTML tables for use with these examples.

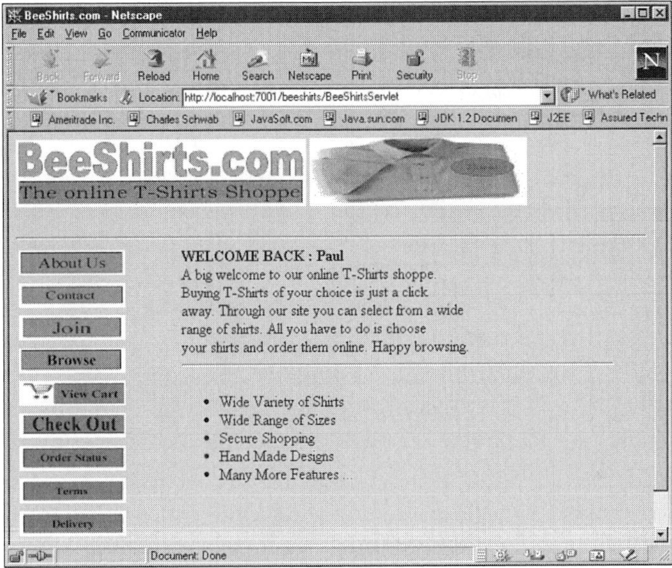

Figure 19.6 The BeeShirts.com root screen.

Now that you've gotten a taste for the basic structure of the BeeShirts.com storefront, let's examine the main elements of BeeShirts.com business logic as implemented with Java Servlets. The BeeShirts.com servlets and two HTML files shown in Figure 19.5 are described here:

- `BeeShirtsServlet`: Handles the initial BeeShirts.com site requests as the root servlet that generates the starting page as shown in Figure 19.6. This servlet also creates a session object for the user and checks to see whether the user has a cookie. If the user has a cookie, this servlet displays a personalized `WELCOME BACK` message.
- `AboutUsServlet`: Handles the HTTP request generated from clicking the About Us button and displays some simple BeeShirts.com information.

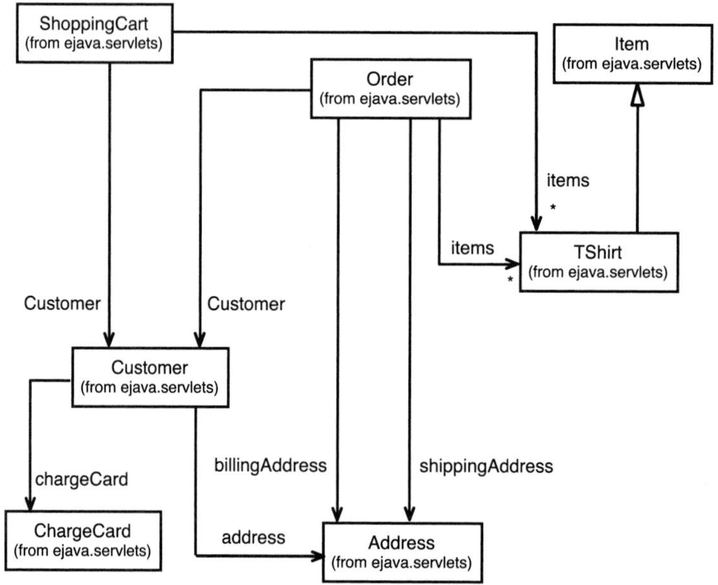

Figure 19.7 BeeShirts.com entities.

- `ContactInformationServlet`: Handles the HTTP request generated from clicking the Contact button and displays some simple contact information.
- `registration.html`: Contains a static HTML page referenced from the Join button that displays a registration form and Register button. Performs some minimal field validation functions via JavaScript. It posts data to the `RegistrationServlet`.
- `RegistrationServlet`: Handles the HTTP `POST` generated by clicking the Request button from the `registration.html` page. This servlet creates a `Customer` object and associates this object with an HTTP session. It also generates a personalized cookie to be sent back to the customer's Web browser. The registration information is also displayed.
- `BrowseShirtsServlet`: Handles the HTTP `GET` generated from clicking the Browse button and allows a user to query for the T-shirts he might be interested in purchasing. After selecting some query criteria, this servlet submits an HTTP `POST` to itself with form data after the user has selected some T-shirt search criterion. The posted query data is used to display search results. The user is given the option to add a shirt to his shopping cart.
- `CartServlet`: Handles the HTTP `POST` from the `BrowseShirtsServlet` Add to Cart button. It first creates a `ShoppingCart` object in the HTTP session if it was not created yet and subsequently adds the posted T-shirt data to the `ShoppingCart` object. It also handles the HTTP `GET` request from the View Cart

button and displays the items, if any, from the ShoppingCart stored in the session.

- CheckOutServlet: Handles the HTTP GET request generated from clicking the Check Out button. If a Customer object is not associated with the session, the user is redirected to the registration.html page. If the cart is empty, the user is redirected to the BrowseShirtsServlet. Otherwise, the servlet simply displays what is in the current shopping cart.
- OrderStatusServlet: Handles the HTTP GET generated from clicking the Order Status button. The generated response then provides fields for accepting a username and password, as well as displaying Login and Remind buttons. When the Login button is pressed, the user information is posted to the servlet itself. The HTTP POST then stimulates the display of a dummy order status. For this chapter's example, we require the entry of a sam@sam.com email address and sam password value to retrieve dummy order status data because we defer illustrating database connectivity until a subsequent chapter. If the user enters invalid login information five times in a row, the user is directed to registration.html. If the user clicks the Remind button, the user is told that she will be emailed her password information. Clicking the Remind button also results in the HTTP POST to OrderStatusServlet.
- TermsAndConditionsServlet: Handles the HTTP request generated from a click of the Terms button and displays some simple order terms-and-conditions information.
- deliveryinformation.html: Contains a static HTML page referenced from the Delivery button and displays some canned delivery information.

The BeeShirtsServlet class defines methods for init(), destroy(), getServletConfig(), and getServletInfo(). The init() method is used to receive and store a private ServletConfig object. The basic structure of the BeeShirtsServlet, excluding request and response handling code, is shown here:

```
public class BeeShirtsServlet extends  HttpServlet
{
  private ServletConfig servletConfig;
  public static final String  SERVLET_NAME = "/BeeShirtsServlet";


/**
  * This is the first method the Web Server calls and it is called once.
  */
  public void init (ServletConfig config)
    throws ServletException
  {
    servletConfig = config;
  }
```

```
/**
  * This is the last method WebServer calls and it is called only once.
  */
  public void destroy()
  {
  }

/**
  * return the Configuration information about the Servlet
  */
  public ServletConfig getServletConfig()
  {
    return servletConfig;
  }

/**
  * Return Servlet Information
  */
  public String getServletInfo()
  {
    return "BeeShirts.com Welcome page Servlet";
  }

  // ...more code to display here in subsequent sections...

}
```

Request Processing

Handling requests is one of the primary responsibilities of servlets. To facilitate this, the servlet container encapsulates requests for application-specific servlets and enables manipulation of requests in a programmer-friendly fashion. HTTP requests have many elements that can be sent from a client to a server. Request parameters, attributes, header values, and body data all have programmatic interfaces defined via Java Servlet request handling abstractions (see Appendix E, "HTTP Communications," for a discussion on the HTTP protocol). Abstractions also exist to encapsulate the forwarding of requests from one servlet to another Web resource. This section describes these various request processing abstractions and demonstrates how such processing is implemented via snippets from our BeeShirts.com example.

Request Handling Abstractions

Figure 19.8 depicts many of the major API elements and method signatures related to handling servlet and HTTP requests. Servlet container environments create and pass servlet request objects to `Servlet` objects in the abstract servlet framework model and pass HTTP servlet request objects to an `HttpServlet` in the more concrete HTTP paradigm. An abstraction for a servlet request exists at the basic servlet framework level that is extended by a more concrete HTTP servlet request. Access to the input stream for data sent from the client via a request body is encapsulated at the abstract servlet framework level.

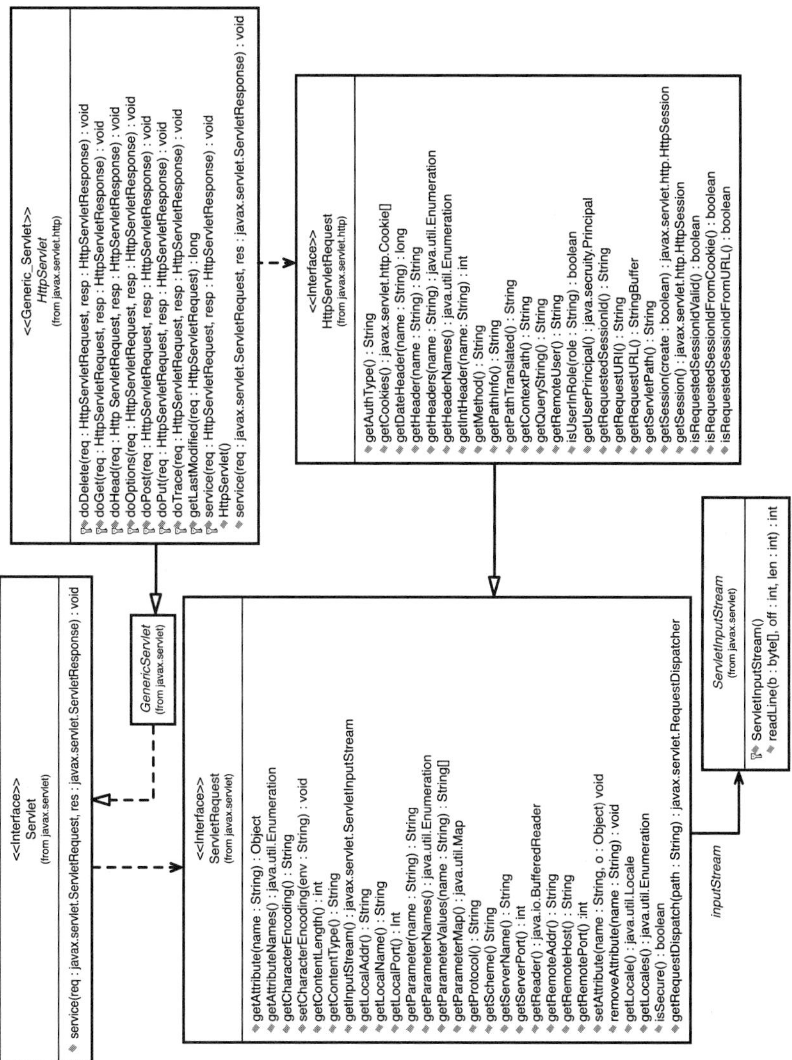

Figure 19.8 Handling HTTP servlet requests.

`ServletRequest` Interface

The `javax.servlet.ServletRequest` interface encapsulates a generic request sent to a Java Servlet. When a request is received by the underlying container environment from a distributed client, the servlet container creates a `ServletRequest` object to encapsulate the data sent in the request. The `ServletRequest` is then passed as a parameter to the target servlet's `service()` method. `ServletRequest` objects contain request parameter data, attributes, and an associated input stream from which request data is read.

As a first step in understanding the type of request received, a servlet can issue inquisitive calls on a `ServletRequest` object. The `getProtocol()` method is used to retrieve the name and version of the protocol used to deliver the request (for example, "HTTP/1.1"). The `getScheme()` method can be used to retrieve the name of the scheme used in the request (for example, "http" or "ftp"). The fact that the channel over which the request was made is secure can be determined via the `isSecure()` call. Additionally, the encoding format of the request is yielded from the `getCharacterEncoding()` call, and the MIME type/subtype of the request body is returned from the `getContentType()` call. The locale preference information of the client as retrieved from the request is determined from either the `getLocale()` method or the `getLocales()` method in the form of an `Enumeration` of `Locale` objects in decreasing order of preference.

Certain socket-level information about the request can also be determined from `ServletRequest`. The `getRemoteAddr()` call returns the IP address of the client, and the `getRemoteHost()` returns the host name of the client if it can be determined via DNS. The `getRemotePort()` method returns the TCP/IP source port of the client making the request. Server-side socket information can also be determined from the request with the `getServerName()` and `getServerPort()` methods returning the server name and port number to which the request was sent, respectively. Similarly, the `getLocalAddr()`, `getLocalName()`, and `getLocalPort()` methods can be used to determine the IP address, name, and port of the server that actually received and processed the request.

Parameters of requests are `String` values that can be identified by a `String` name. HTTP request parameters are sent in a request query string or via form post data. The first parameter value of a named type can be returned from the `getParameter()` call, whereas zero or more `String` values of a named type can be retrieved from the `getParameterValues()` call. An `Enumeration` of `String` names for all parameters in a request is obtained via the `getParameterNames()` method call.

Whereas parameters consist of data sent by a client to the server on the HTTP query string, attributes of a request are often added to a `ServletRequest` object by a servlet container environment. An attribute can be any `Object` value that has a `String` name. Attributes can also be set onto a `ServletRequest` using the `setAttribute()` method call. Attribute values are retrieved from the `ServletRequest` via the `getAttribute()` call. Attributes are removed from the `ServletRequest` using the removeAttribute() call. Finally, the names of all attributes can be retrieved using the getAttributeNames() call to return an Enumeration of String names.

The request body contains data from which application-specific information can be read and used by the servlet. The number of bytes in the request body data stream can be obtained via the getContentLength() call. The getBufferedReader() call can be made to retrieve a handle to a BufferedReader I/O stream form of the data. Alternatively, the getInputStream() call can be made to retrieve a handle to a special ServletInputStream helper object that is used to read data from the input stream as lines of binary data. Either the getInputStream() or the getBufferedReader() method may be called during a particular request service call, but not both.

ServletInputStream **Class**

The abstract javax.servlet.ServletInputStream class extends the java.io.InputStream class and provides the readLine() method definition as a means for reading bytes of information from a request body one line at a time. A handle to an instance of this class is returned through the getInputStream() method. A byte array into which data should be read, a beginning offset into that array, and a number of bytes to read are all passed as parameters to the readLine() method. When protocols such as HTTP are used, data from the HTTP request body can be retrieved via the ServletInputStream. The BufferedReader returned from the getReader() call can also be used to read such request body data.

HttpServletRequest **Interface**

The javax.servlet.http.HttpServletRequest interface extends the ServletRequest interface to specifically encapsulate HTTP requests. The servlet container creates an HttpServletRequest object when an HTTP request is received and passes this object to the public service() method call. The HttpServlet object then ultimately calls an appropriate do*XXX*() method. The exact do*XXX*() method to be called is driven by the HTTP request method type received, which may also be determined from the getMethod() call.

Specific HTTP request header information can also be read from the HttpServletRequest object. The getHeaderNames() method will return an Enumeration of String names for the various HTTP request headers received. The getHeader() method retrieves the String value of a header given the header name. Certain header values that can be converted to an int value can also be retrieved using the getIntHeader() method given the header name. Headers that correspond to dates can be retrieved in terms of milliseconds since January 1, 1970, GMT, using the getDateHeader() method.

Various portions of information from the target URI path of the requested resource can be retrieved using the HttpServletRequest object. The getRequestURI() method is used to return the entire requested URI field extracted from the HTTP request data excluding any URI query parameter data. The getContextPath() method can be used to retrieve that part of the request URI that corresponds only to the context of an HTTP request. The `getServletPath()` method is used to return only that portion of the requested URI used to identify the servlet to be called relative to the root servlet context. The `getQueryString()` method returns any data contained within the query parameter `String` portion of a requested URI. Finally, the `getPathTranslated()` method is used to retrieve any data between the servlet pathname and the query `String` within the requested URI. For example, given a request of `http://www.beeshirts.com/myApp/BeeShirtsServlet/saleitems/shirts?size=XL`, the following values would be returned:

- `getRequestURI()` returns `myApp/BeeShirtsServlet/saleitems/shirts`.
- `getContextPath()` returns `myApp`.
- `getServletPath()` returns `BeeShirtsServlet`.
- `getPathTranslated()` returns `saleitems/shirts`.
- `getQueryString()` returns `size=XL`.

Certain security-related information associated with an HTTP request can be extracted from the `HttpServletRequest` when needed. Methods such as `getAuthType()`, `getRemoteUser()`, `getUserPrincipal()`, and `isUserInRole()` can all be used in the context of providing secure servlet access to be discussed later in this chapter. We also defer discussion until a later section of various servlet session and cookie management facilities that can be tapped from `HttpServletRequest` object methods.

Servlet Request Dispatching Abstractions

Figure 19.9 depicts the basic entities involved in dispatching requests received by one servlet to another resource (for example, another servlet). This may involve forwarding a servlet request using a special request dispatcher object. It may also involve the inclusion of output from another resource within the output of the initial target resource.

`RequestDispatcher` Interface

The `javax.servlet.RequestDispatcher` interface is used to encapsulate an object that is used to dispatch requests from a client to another server resource such as a servlet or JavaServer Page. As you'll see in a later section, servlets and JSP Web components can be named using deployment descriptor properties. A request dispatcher associated with these named components can be obtained using the `ServletContext.getNamedDispatcher()` method.

`RequestDispatcher` objects can also be created from `ServletContext.getRequestDispatcher()` method calls by passing in a URL pathname (beginning with /) for a resource relative to the root servlet context. The returned `RequestDispatcher` object can then be used as a handle to forward a `ServletRequest` object to the associated resource URL path. A call to `ServletContext.getContext()` can be used to obtain a `ServletContext` object for another servlet context environment. The returned `ServletContext` can then be used to obtain a `RequestDispatcher` object for forwarding requests to resources in that foreign context. Alternatively, the `ServletRequest.getRequestDispatcher()` method may also be used to obtain a `RequestDispatcher` object.

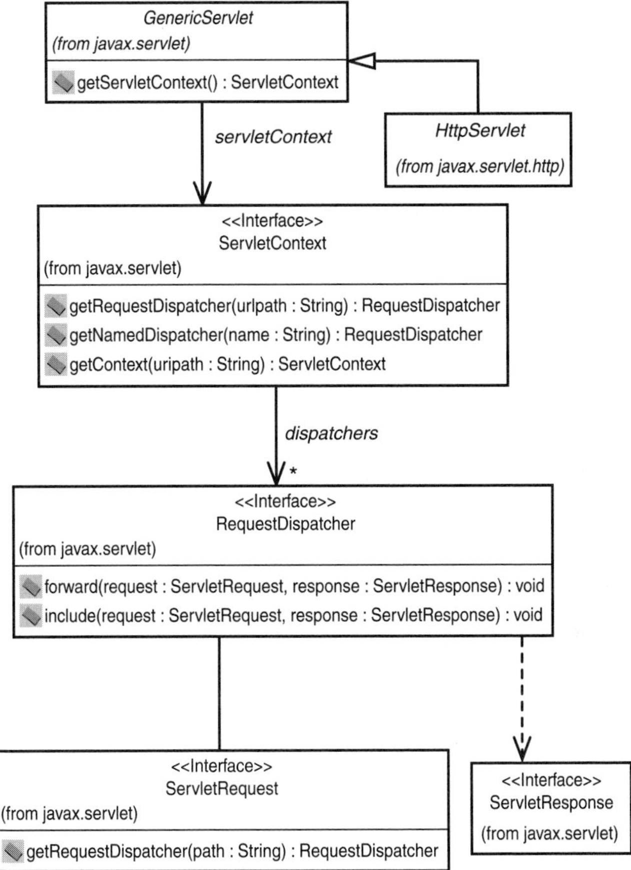

Figure 19.9 Forwarding HTTP servlet requests.

After a `RequestDispatcher` handle is obtained, one of two methods on the `RequestDispatcher` may be called. The `RequestDispatcher.forward()` method is used to forward a servlet request to another resource. Thus, the initial servlet may process the servlet request in some way first before it redirects the request to another URL. Although the request may be preprocessed in some way, no output to the servlet response stream may be performed before the request is forwarded. Alternatively, the `RequestDispatcher.include()` method is used to include the contents of a targeted resource with the output of the current servlet.

Request Handling Examples

The `service()` method of the `BeeShirtsServlet` is the initial point of entry into our BeeShirts.com e-commerce servlet storefront. When the `BeeShirtsServlet` deployed to a particular Web server is referenced from within the URL of a Web browser, the `service()` method receives an `HttpServletRequest` from the servlet container environment. The `BeeShirtsServlet.service()` method first extracts some server information from the HTTP request as shown here:

```
public void service (HttpServletRequest servletRequest,
  HttpServletResponse servletResponse)
  throws ServletException, IOException
{
  // Extract server information from HTTP request
  String serverInfo = ServletsHelper.getServerInfo(servletRequest);

// ...more code to be described in later sections...

}
```

The static `ServletsHelper.getServerInfo()` method simply extracts info from the `HttpServletRequest` and returns a concatenated form of the server host name, server port, and context path:

```
public static String getServerInfo(HttpServletRequest servletRequest)
{
  String serverHost = servletRequest.getServerName();
  int serverPort = servletRequest.getServerPort();
  String context = servletRequest.getContextPath();

  return serverHost +":"+serverPort + context;
}
```

As exemplified in the `doGet()` request handling method of the `CheckOutServlet`, we also need to redirect the user to another servlet from within the `CheckOutServlet` on occasion. The `CheckOutServlet.doGet()` method first retrieves `Customer` information from the HTTP session and then invokes a special `redirectRegistrationScreen()` method if no `Customer` information was stored in the session. Subsequently, if no `ShoppingCart` information is stored in the session object, a special `redirectBrowseScreen()` method is invoked. Otherwise, the current user's shopping-cart information is displayed. The `doGet()` method is defined this way:

```
public void doGet(HttpServletRequest servletRequest,
 HttpServletResponse servletResponse)
 throws ServletException, IOException
{
// Get stored customer session information
  Customer customer = getCustomerFromSession(servletRequest);
```

```
  // If no stored customer info, redirect to registration screen
  if(customer == null){
    redirectRegistrationScreen(servletRequest, servletResponse);
  }

  // Get stored shopping-cart information
  ShoppingCart cart = getShoppingCartFromSession(servletRequest);

  // If no stored cart info, redirect to browse screen
  if(cart == null){
    redirectBrowseScreen(servletRequest, servletResponse);
  }
  else{ // Else display the cart info and request card info
     displayTheCartAndTakeUserCardInformation(servletRequest,
                                              servletResponse, cart);
  }
}
```

The `CheckOutServlet.redirectRegistrationScreen()` method first obtains a `RequestDispatcher` object associated with the `registration.html` page. The `RegistrationServlet.REGISTRATION_HTML` constant is used to identify the `/registration.html` page. The request and response parameters are then submitted to the `RequestDispatcher.forward()` method to be redirected as shown here:

```
private void redirectRegistrationScreen(
  HttpServletRequest servletRequest,
  HttpServletResponse servletResponse)
    throws ServletException, IOException
{
  // First retrieve servlet context handle
   ServletContext ctx = getServletContext();
   // Obtain dispatcher handle to registration.html
   RequestDispatcher dispatcher =
      ctx.getRequestDispatcher(RegistrationServlet.REGISTRATION_HTML);
   // Forward to registration.html
   if(dispatcher != null){
     dispatcher.forward(servletRequest, servletResponse);
   }
}
```

Similarly, the `CheckOutServlet.redirectBrowseScreen()` method is used to create a `RequestDispatcher` object associated with the `BrowseShirtsServlet`, and the Web request is redirected to that servlet, as shown here:

```
private void redirectBrowseScreen(HttpServletRequest servletRequest,
  HttpServletResponse servletResponse)
    throws ServletException, IOException
{
```

```
    RequestDispatcher dispatcher
       = getServletContext().getRequestDispatcher(
                                   BrowseShirtsServlet.SERVLET_NAME);
    if(dispatcher != null){
      dispatcher.forward(servletRequest, servletResponse);
    }
}
```

We encourage you to examine all the HTTP request handling semantics defined for the BeeShirts.com storefront code downloaded from the Web site. For the most part, requests to BeeShirts.com servlets serve as triggers to stimulate the servlet to generate a response. Data sent within the request is used minimally. The `ServletsHelper.getServerInfo()` method and retrieval of session information represent the most frequent uses of `HttpServletRequest` objects. However, there are a few more sample uses of request information by the BeeShirts.com servlets. These nontrivial usage scenarios are described here:

- `RegistrationServlet`: The `RegistrationServlet.doPost()` method receives information posted from the Register button inside the `registration.html` page. The `registration.html` page posts user registration form data from a collection of `INPUT TEXT` fields. The `RegistrationServlet.doPost()` method calls the private `RegistrationServlet.registerNewCustomer()` method to extract this form data by using `HttpServletRequest.getParameterValues()` calls using a set of `String` name constants as shown here:

```
String firstName =
  (String)servletRequest.getParameterValues(Customer.FIRST_NAME)[0];
String lastName =
  (String)servletRequest.getParameterValues(Customer.LAST_NAME)[0];
    ...
String state =
  (String)servletRequest.getParameterValues(Address.STATE)[0];
String zip_code =
  (String)servletRequest.getParameterValues(Address.ZIP_CODE)[0];
```

- `BrowseShirtsServlet`: Recall that the `BrowseShirtsServlet doGet()` method displays a query form for users to submit an HTTP `POST` to the `BrowseShirtsServlet` with shirt size and color query criteria. The servlet's `doPost()` method must retrieve this information from the received `HttpServletRequest` like this:

```
String queriedSize = servletRequest.getParameter(SHIRT_SIZE);
String queriedColor = servletRequest.getParameter(SHIRT_COLOR);
```

- `CartServlet`: A `POST` from the `BrowseShirtsServlet` induced by the Add to Cart buttons associated with each shirt passes along a `Tshirt` ID and quantity to the `CartServlet.doPost()` method. The `CartServlet.doPost()` method extracts this information and uses it to locate `Tshirt` objects from within an HTTP session and add them to the user's `ShoppingCart`. The retrieval of the `POST` data is rather straightforward:

```
// Get shirt ID from POST
String selectedShirtIDString =
  servletRequest.getParameterValues(TShirt.SHIRT_ID)[0];
// Get number of shirts from POST
String numberSelectedString =
 servletRequest.getParameterValues(TShirt.ORDERED_FIELD)[0];
```

- `OrderStatusServlet`: A `POST` to `OrderStatusServlet.doPost()` is sent from within the `OrderStatusServlet.doGet()` method response. The `POST` results from a user clicking a Login or Remind button. The extraction of the relevant data from the `HttpServletRequest` object for either post from within the `doPost()` method is shown here:

```
// Check whether the user is asking to remind him/her
// This occurs when Remind button is pressed
String[] remindValues  =
  servletRequest.getParameterValues(EMAIL_LOOKUP_FIELD_NAME);

if(handleRemindRequest(remindValues,
                       servletRequest, servletResponse)){
  return;
}

// Otherwise user hit Login button
// Get email and password info
String emailAddress =
  servletRequest.getParameterValues(EMAIL_FIELD_NAME)[0];
String password =
  servletRequest.getParameterValues(PASSWORD_FIELD_NAME)[0];
```

Response Generation

We saw in the preceding section how the Servlet API encapsulates HTTP requests to allow for convenient processing. However, that is really only half of the picture. At some point, a servlet must ultimately generate a response. The Java Servlet framework offers a set of servlet response abstractions that are used for this purpose. Responses to Web clients contain response headers and contain response body data that can be buffered in various ways depending on your specific application. We describe the Java Servlet response abstractions in this section, as well as illustrate some basic examples for usage of these abstractions in the context of our sample BeeShirts.com e-commerce storefront.

Response Handling Abstractions

Figure 19.10 depicts the basic set of abstractions involved in encapsulating servlet responses. A basic protocol-independent servlet response abstraction is used to encapsulate a set of basic response operations to a client. An output stream for sending data in such a response body is provided as its own abstraction. A concrete HTTP-specific extension of the servlet response abstraction is also provided. The HTTP servlet response abstraction provides many operations specific to the HTTP response protocol and also defines a collection of response type constants.

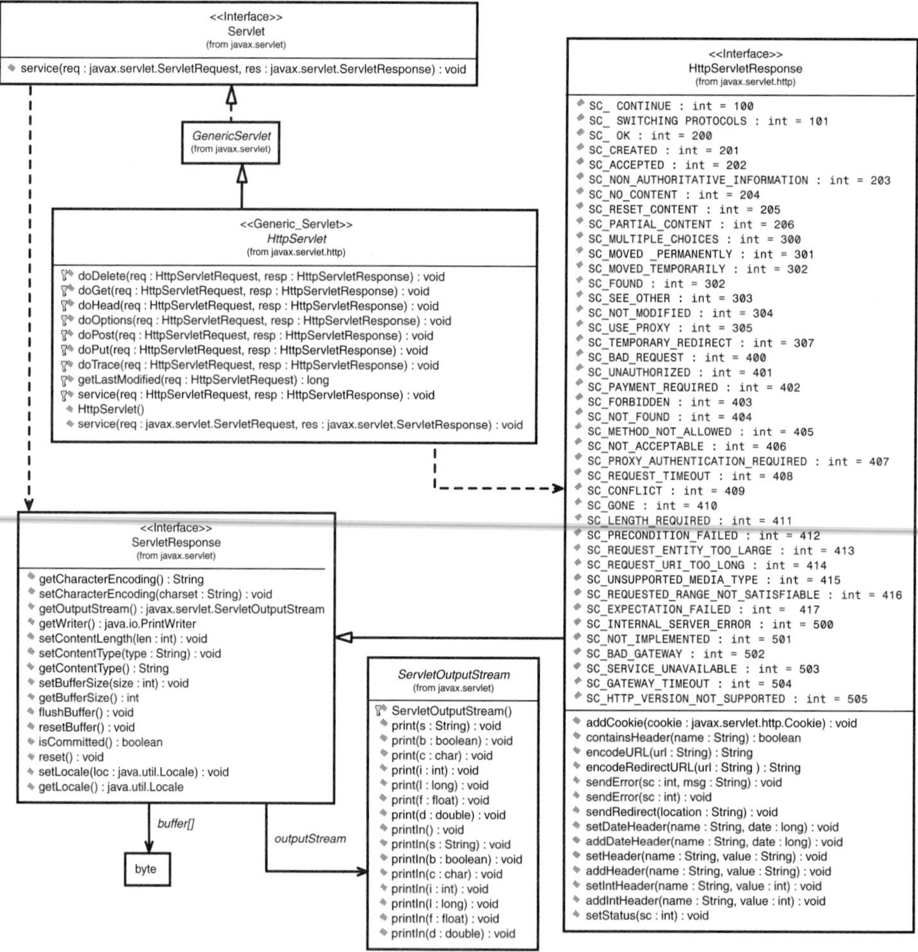

Figure 19.10 Generating HTTP servlet responses.

`ServletResponse` Interface

The `javax.servlet.ServletResponse` interface encapsulates an object used to send responses from a servlet to a client. The actual creation of a `ServletResponse` object is performed by the servlet container and passed as a parameter to the `Servlet.service()` method. `ServletResponse` objects have various base interfaces defined that allow one to obtain a handle to a response body data stream, configure the format of a response, and tune the performance of a response.

The `getOutputStream()` method is used to obtain a handle to a `ServletOutputStream` object used to write binary data to an HTTP response body. Alternatively, the `getWriter()` method can be used to obtain a handle to a `PrintWriter` object for writing character text data to a response body. Either the `PrintWriter` or the `ServletOutputStream` object can be used to write response data, but not both. The particular format of character data can be established by first calling `setContentType()` with the MIME type/subtype and character encoding format to be used (for example, `text/html; charset=ISO-8859-1`). The `getCharacterEncoding()` method can be used to retrieve the value of the `charset` to send the response (for example, `ISO-8859-4`). The `Locale` of the `ServletResponse` can be read and set using the `getLocale()` and `setLocale()` methods, respectively.

The size of a response body is important to consider when trading off performance and memory utilized on the server and client. The desired buffer size to be used for the response body can be set using the `setBufferSize()` method. The buffer size actually allocated can be retrieved using the `getBufferSize()` method. By establishing the buffer size for servlet responses, applications can better manage server performance and memory resource utilization trade-offs. Furthermore, smaller buffer sizes allow servlet clients to receive response data sooner. Any buffer-size setting must occur before the writing of content to an output stream. Additionally, any servlet header field for specifying content length (for example, `Content-Length` for HTTP responses) can also be set using the `setContentLength()` method.

The data from a response buffer can be flushed to the client with a call to `flushBuffer()`. Such a call commits all header and status information as well. The status of whether such a commit has taken place is determined from a call to `isCommitted()`. If a response has yet to be committed, a call to `reset()` will clear all response data, headers, and status information written from the response buffer.

`ServletOutputStream` Class

The abstract `javax.servlet.ServletOutputStream` class extends the `OutputStream` class to encapsulate an interface to a servlet output stream. A collection of `print()` and `println()` methods is defined on the `ServletOutputStream` class to facilitate writing information to a servlet response body stream. The `print()` methods write information to the servlet output stream with no carriage-return line feed added. The `println()` methods write information to the servlet output stream with a carriage-return line feed added. Various fundamental Java types and Java `String` objects can be written to the output stream using `print()` and `println()`. The parameterless `println()` method simply writes a carriage-return line feed to the stream.

`HttpServletResponse` Interface

The `javax.servlet.http.HttpServletResponse` interface extends the basic `ServletResponse` interface with specific HTTP response semantics. An HTTP servlet container creates an `HttpServletResponse` object and passes it along with an `HttpServletRequest` to the `service()` method. The application-specific `HttpServlet` then uses the `HttpServletResponse` to create the HTTP response information to be sent back to the HTTP client. The `sendRedirect()` method can also be used to send a redirect response to an HTTP client that redirects the client to request information from another specified URL `String`. Although absolute URLs can be passed to the `sendRedirect()` method, the servlet container environment will convert any URLs specified in relative form to an absolute URL.

The `HttpServletReponse` exposes a collection of methods specifically meant to deal with HTTP response header writing. The `setHeader()` method is used to write a particular header value to be associated with a header name. The `addHeader()` method is used to add multiple values that are to be associated with a particular header name. Similarly, the `setDateHeader()` and `addDateHeader()` methods can be used to write date values associated with a named header, and the `setIntHeader()` and `addIntHeader()` methods can be used to write `int` values to a header. The `containsHeader()` returns a `boolean` value indicating whether a particular named header exists in the response stream.

The `setStatus()` method is used to write status information into the HTTP response header if no error has occurred. Otherwise, the `setError()` methods are used to set error messages in the HTTP response header. In both cases, an HTTP response code is used as encapsulated by one of the `static public final int` attribute values in the `HttpServletResponse` interface, as shown in Figure 19.10. Referencing RFC 1945, these status codes may be broadly classified as informational (100–199), successes (200–299), redirection (300–399), client request errors (400–499), and server-side errors (500–599) (see Appendix E for more information about HTTP response codes).

Response Handling Examples

As previously mentioned, the `BeeShirtsServlet.service()` method is the initial point of entry into our BeeShirts.com e-commerce servlet storefront. After extraction of a `String` of server information from the `HttpServletRequest`, the `service()` method manages the writing of response data back to the client via the `HttpServletResponse` object. This response consists of the construction of some initial document response type and header data, the writing of the response body, and the closing of the document response tags and stream as shown here:

```
public void service (HttpServletRequest servletRequest,
  HttpServletResponse servletResponse)
  throws ServletException, IOException
{
  // Extract server information from HTTP request
  String serverInfo = ServletsHelper.getServerInfo(servletRequest);

  String sessionCookie = // session management shown in later section

  // Create initial document type and headers
  PrintWriter printWriter =
    ServletsHelper.createInitialDocumentResponse(servletResponse);

  // Write the body of the page to the stream
  writePageBody(printWriter, serverInfo, sessionCookie);

  // Close with BODY and HTML closing tags
  ServletsHelper.createClosingDocumentResponse(printWriter);
}
```

The common means by which the initial document response is created is encapsulated within the BeeShirts.com `ServletsHelper.createInitialDocumentResponse()` method. This method sets the common context type for the document (that is, `text/html`), obtains a handle to a `PrintWriter`, and writes the common initial document `DOCTYPE`, `HTML`, `HEAD`, `TITLE`, and `BODY` tags as shown here:

```
public static PrintWriter createInitialDocumentResponse(
      HttpServletResponse servletResponse)
  throws IOException
{
  // Set common text/html content type for all of our documents
  servletResponse.setContentType(CONTENT_TYPE);
  // Retrieve the PrintWriter handle
  PrintWriter printWriter = servletResponse.getWriter();
  // Print common DOCTYPE, HTML begin tag, HEAD, and TITLE tags
  printWriter.println(
    "<!DOCTYPE HTML PUBLIC \"-//W3C//DTD HTML 4.0 Transitional//EN\">"
    + "\n <HTML> \n <HEAD> \n <TITLE> "
    + "\n BeeShirts.com </TITLE>\n </HEAD>\n");
  // Print common BODY begin tags
  printWriter.println( "<BODY ALINK=\"#FFCC66\"  BGCOLOR=\"#ffcc66\" "+
    " LINK=\"#FFFFFF\" VLINK=\"#FFFFFF\"> " );

  return printWriter;
}
```

Similarly, the `ServletsHelper.createClosingDocumentResponse()` method can be used to close the `PrintWriter` stream after closing `BODY` and `HTML` tags are written as shown here:

```
public static void createClosingDocumentResponse(
  PrintWriter printWriter)
{
  printWriter.println(" </BODY> ");
  printWriter.println( "</HTML>" );
  printWriter.close();
}
```

The `writePageBody()` method implements some of the custom layout and page body logic specific to this root servlet. The `writePageBody()` first invokes the `ServletsHelper.writePageTopArea()` method to write the top area of the Web page common to all BeeShirts.com servlets, which consists of the BeeShirts.com logo. The lower half of the screen is then partitioned into two areas, with the left side corresponding to the common selection of buttons as created by the `ServletsHelper.writePageLeftArea()` method. The center page area is then written by the custom `BeeShirtsServlet.writePageCenterArea()` method. The `writePageBody()` method is shown here:

```
private void writePageBody(PrintWriter printWriter,
  String serverInfo, String cookieValue)
{
  // Write common top portion of page
  ServletsHelper.writePageTopArea(printWriter);

  // Partition lower page portion into one row of two TABLE columns
  printWriter.println("<TABLE BORDER=0 COLS=2 WIDTH=\"100%\" >");
  printWriter.println(" <TR> ");

  // Write the common left-hand portion of the page
  ServletsHelper.writePageLeftArea(printWriter, serverInfo);

  // Write this servlet's specific center of the page info
  writePageCenterArea(printWriter, cookieValue);

  // Close with TABLE end tags
  printWriter.println("</TR>");
  printWriter.println("</TABLE> <br> ");
}
```

The `BeeShirtsServlet.writePageCenterArea()` method generates the welcome page body of our root servlet as shown here:

```
private void writePageCenterArea(PrintWriter printWriter,
  String cookieValue)
{
```

```
  // Write the body of the page
  printWriter.println("<TD  > ");
  // If the cookie session value is valid, then user has visited
  // the site before, so display a welcome message...
  if(cookieValue != null){
    printWriter.println("   <STRONG> WELCOME BACK : "
                        + cookieValue +"</STRONG> <BR>");
  }
  String msg = "";
  try{
    // Get initial context and look up welcome message via JNDI
    // Note: WelcomeMessge is configured in the
    // deployment descriptor, web.xml
    InitialContext ctx = new InitialContext();
    msg = (String) ctx.lookup("java:comp/env/WelcomeMessage");
  }
  catch(NamingException namingException){
    namingException.printStackTrace();
  }
  // Print the root screen promo and welcome...
  printWriter.println(msg + "</TD>");
}
```

We also encourage you to examine all the HTTP response handling semantics defined for the BeeShirts.com storefront sample code provided. Almost all the responses from the BeeShirts.com servlets manage display of the top and left portions of the BeeShirts.com screens with custom development for the center area of the screen. In between HTTP request handling and HTTP response generation, some session management takes place, as we describe in the next section. However, in general, BeeShirts.com servlet response generation follows the same basic pattern. In summary, the basic response generation scenarios are as shown here:

- `BeeShirtsServlet`: When a `GET` or `POST` request is made, this servlet generates the display of a welcome message and a welcome-back message to users with cookies wherein most of the presentation display is generated within the `writePageCenterArea()` method.
- `AboutUsServlet`: When a `GET` request is made, this servlet generates the display of some information about the BeeShirts.com Web site with most of the presentation display generated within the `writePageCenterArea()` method.
- `ContactInformationServlet`: When a `GET` request is made, this servlet generates the display of some contact information at BeeShirts.com with most of the presentation display generated within the `writePageCenterArea()` method.
- `registration.html`: When a `GET` request is made, this static HTML page generates a form with `INPUT TEXT` fields for entering user registration information. Also generates some minimal JavaScript data field validation code.

- `RegistrationServlet`: When a `POST` request is made, this servlet creates a `Customer` object from the `POST` data sent from `registration.html` and adds this info to the session via the `registerNewCustomer()` method and also creates a personalized cookie for the user. The success or failure status of the attempted registration is then generated with most of the presentation display generated from within the `writePageCenterArea()` method.
- `BrowseShirtsServlet`: When a `GET` request is made, an HTML `FORM` used to query for T-shirts is generated with most of the presentation encapsulated within the `writePageCenterAreaForForm()` method. When a `POST` request is made, the result of the `T-Shirt` query is generated with most of the presentation encapsulated within the `writePageCenterAreaResults()` method.
- `CartServlet`: When a `GET` request is made, the contents of the current `ShoppingCart` object are generated via the `displayItemsInTheCart()` method, or a message indicating that the cart is empty is generated via the `displayNoItemsInTheCart()` method. When a `POST` message is received to add a T-shirt to the `ShoppingCart`, the `displayAddedOrFailedToAdd()` method is called to generate most of the presentation response for such a scenario.
- `CheckOutServlet`: When a `GET` request is received, the user may be redirected to the `registration.html` page or `BrowseShirtsServlet` as described in the preceding section. However, if neither redirection scenario occurs, the user and cart information is generated via the `displayTheCartAndTakeUserCardInformation()` method.
- `OrderStatusServlet`: When the `GET` request is received, an HTML `INPUT FORM` is generated via the `writePageBodyForLoginForm()` and `writePageCenterAreaForLoginForm()` methods. The form provides a means for accepting login information sent via a Login button and for requesting a password information reminder sent via a Remind button. When an HTTP `POST` is received, the `handleRemindRequest()` determines whether the user clicked the Remind button and will call the `writeEmailReminderPage()` method to generate a message indicating that the user's password will be mailed to him. If the Login button was clicked and incorrect login data was sent by the `POST` method, the user will be told he has erred via the `informUserThatLoginFailed()` method and will be presented with another login form. If the Login button was clicked and the user attempted to log in more than five times, the `askTheUserToRegister()` method will redirect the user to the `registration.html` page.

In the interest of simplicity, we eliminate any database connectivity in this example. For this reason, a single user email and password are predefined. `OrderStatusServlet` requires that the user enter `sam@sam.com` for an email address and `sam` as the password to log in. A set of predefined order data is then generated via the `constructOrderForThisCustomer()` method and displayed with the `showUserOrders()` method.

- `TermsAndConditionsServlet`: When a `GET` request is made, this servlet generates the display of some terms and conditions about BeeShirts.com purchases with most of the presentation display generated within the `writePageCenterArea()` method.
- `deliveryinformation.html`: When a `GET` request is made, this static HTML page generates the display of some dummy delivery information.

Session Management

HTTP is a stateless communication paradigm. However, most Web applications try to exhibit "stateful" behavior, by remembering a user's name, which items they have placed in their cart, and so on. To achieve this effect over a purely stateless protocol would require the client to either (a) send all state information along with every request, or (b) provide another means to identify the client to the server. Obviously, scenario (a) could get unmanageable very quickly with a complicated application. But fortunately, browser cookies and server-side URL rewriting enable scenario (b) to be possible.

The Servlet API leverages this capability to provide an abstraction of a stateful session, with the `javax.servlet.http.HttpSession` interface. After a session is created, the API developer can bind objects to an HTTP session during the handling of one HTTP request and retrieve these objects during a subsequent request from the same user. The servlet container environment shields the programmer from the need to know the details behind the underlying implementation of session management.

Apart from satisfying the need to store and retrieve objects related to the same Web client user session, cookies, as a particular session management implementation type, also satisfy another need. Cookies are sometimes used to store information on the client side for an extended period beyond a single user session for later retrieval by the server side. For example, an e-commerce storefront may induce your Web browser to store some information about you on your client machine such that a visit to that site later will result in the site being able to recognize you individually. This permits the site to be able to customize the Web presentation of the storefront to your interests (as well as perhaps permit certain violations of your privacy). The Java Servlet framework thus also offers an abstraction for manipulating cookies explicitly to facilitate such functionality on the server side. This section describes cookie and HTTP session abstractions, as well as presenting some sample uses of these abstractions within the context of our BeeShirts.com storefront.

Session Management Abstractions

Figure 19.11 presents the abstractions provided by the Java Servlet API for managing Web-based sessions within the context of HTTP servlets. At the core of this framework lies an HTTP session abstraction for manipulating session information across multiple requests from the same user. An abstraction for manipulating cookies is also provided.

Finally, a means for listening to and generating events related to session is also provided, as illustrated in Figure 19.12.

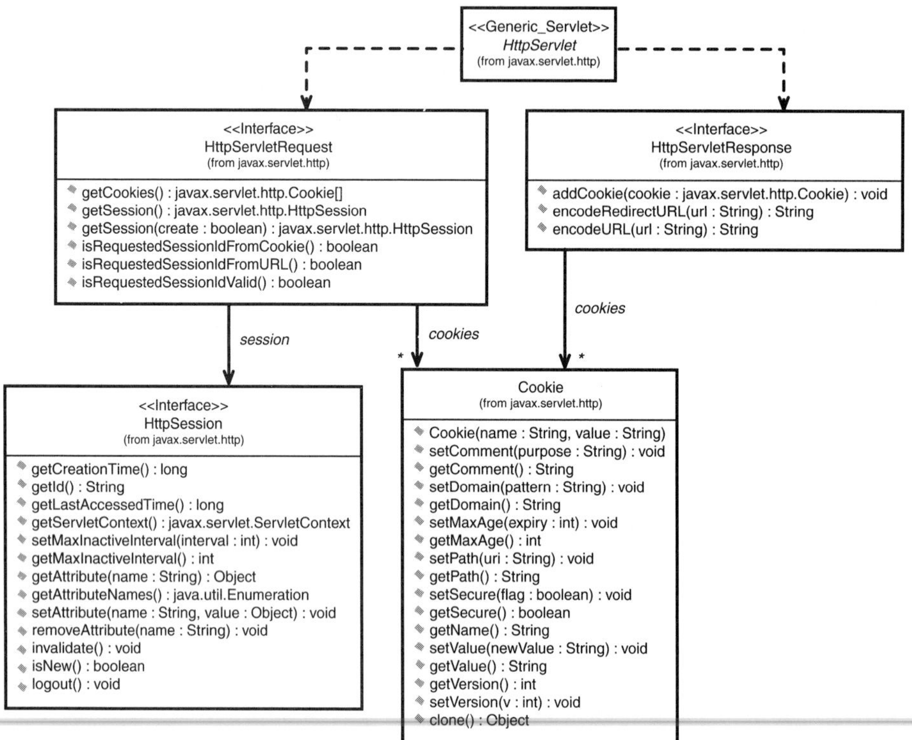

Figure 19.11 HTTP session management.

`HttpSession` Interface

The `javax.servlet.http.HttpSession` interface encapsulates the concept of an HTTP session associated with a particular Web client's access of a Web server over multiple requests within some scope of time. Because the `HttpSession` is associated with a particular Web client user, information associated with the user can be maintained by associating the information with an `HttpSession` object. The servlet container environment may actually implement the management of sessions underneath the hood using one of the HTTP session management techniques discussed in Appendix E. However, the servlet applications developer will still have the same consistent and easy-to-use interface to manage session information via the `HttpSession` object.

The `getSession()` method returns the current `HttpSession` object associated with the request and creates one if none yet exists. Optionally, the `getSession(boolean)` method may be used to do the same thing, but it will return a null value if a false value was used as a method parameter and if no session yet exists. The HttpSession.isNew() method indicates whether the client is aware of an HTTP session. The isNew() method returns true if the client is not yet session-aware.

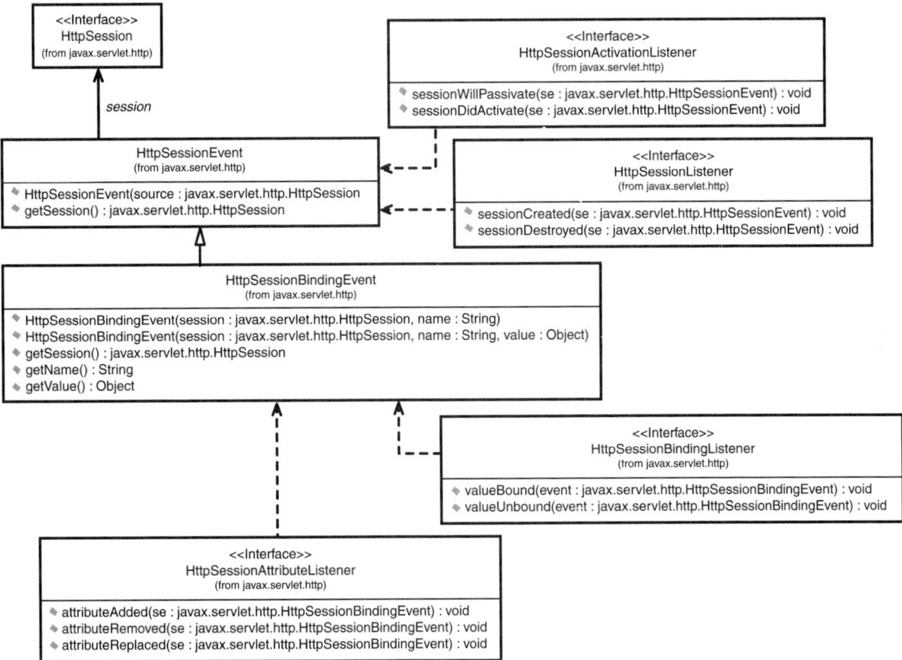

Figure 19.12 HTTP session events and listeners.

The HttpServletRequest object can also be used to determine the nature of session management. A call to isRequestedSessionIdFromCookie() indicates whether the received session ID came from a cookie, whereas the isRequestedSessionIdFromURL() method indicates whether the received session ID came from a rewritten URL. The isRequestedSessionIdValid() method indicates whether the current request received an ID that could be associated with a valid session. The servlet container implementation-dependent session ID value may be returned from a call to HttpSession.getId().

When URL rewriting is being used for session management, it is important to properly embed session ID information into URLs that are sent back to the Web client. The HttpServletResponse.encodeURL() method takes a URL String parameter and encodes a session ID into the String. If the Web client supports cookies or session management is disabled, the returned String is unchanged. URLs created by a servlet should use this method just in case a particular Web client does not support cookies for session management. Similarly, before using the sendRedirect() method, the encodeRedirectURL() should be used to create a URL that can modify the URL to send with session ID information.

The maximum inactive interval for which a session is to be maintained by a servlet container environment can be managed via the HttpSession object. The setMaxInactiveInterval() method is used to designate the number of seconds between requests that must pass before a servlet container will render a session invalid. A negative number passed to setMaxInactiveInterval() is used to designate that no time limit should be set. The getMaxInactiveInterval() method may be used to retrieve this value. Of course, a session may be invalidated beforehand with a call to invalidate(). Any objects that were associated with a session are unbound when the session becomes invalid.

Two methods on the HttpSession object are used to determine certain statistical timing information related to a user's session. The time when the session was created is returned from getCreationTime(), whereas the time that has passed since the Web client last accessed the server can be determined from getLastAccessedTime(). Both times are expressed in terms of milliseconds since January 1, 1970, GMT.

HttpSession objects have named attribute values associated with them. The attribute names are in String form and the attribute values assume a general Object form. An Enumeration of all attribute name String objects can be retrieved via a call to the getAttributeNames() method. Attributes can furthermore be read, set, and removed using the getAttribute(), setAttribute(), and removeAttribute() methods, respectively.

HttpSessionEvent **and Listeners**

The javax.servlet.http.HttpSessionEvent object encapsulates a notification message about changes to a session object within a Web application. This object is passed to an object implementing the HttpSessionListener interface, through the sessionCreated() and sessionDestroyed() methods, which provide notification that a particular session has been created or destroyed by the container. The HttpSessionActivationListener interface also receives notifications through the sessionDidActivate() and sessionDidPassivate() methods. These methods are called by the container when a session has been serialized to persistent storage, and when a session has been reactivated from persistent storage. Applications wanting to receive these notifications will implement these interfaces and register the implementations in the deployment descriptor, web.xml.

HttpSessionBindingEvent **and Listeners**

The javax.servlet.http.HttpSessionBindingEvent class is used to create an event which indicates that a particular attribute has been bound to or unbound from a session. The HttpSession object to which the object was bound and the name of the attribute object are both associated with an HttpSessionBindingEvent object. The javax.servlet.http.HttpSessionBindingListener interface is implemented by those objects wanting to be notified of HttpSessionBindingEvent instances. The valueBound() and valueUnbound() methods are used to listen for both session binding and unbinding events, respectively. To receive HttpSessionBindingEvents, an application will derive a class from HttpSessionBindingListener and register it in the deployment descriptor.

After a session has been created, an application can be notified of changes in state of that session. The javax.servlet.http.HttpSessionAttributeListener interface provides the attributeAdded(), attributeChanged(), and attributeRemoved() callback methods. These methods all take an HttpSessionBindingEvent argument, which contains the affected session object, plus the name and value of the attribute being operated on. An application will provide its own implementation of this interface and register it within the deployment descriptor to process these notifications.

Cookie Class

The javax.servlet.http.Cookie class encapsulates a Web cookie used to store information sent between Web browsers and servers inside of HTTP requests and responses. Although many modern browsers support cookies, some limitations may be imposed by your browser on what it can support. The Cookie class supports both v0 of the Netscape cookie specification and the v1 RFC2109 cookie specification. Because some browsers may support only v0 of the cookie specification, the default for this class is the v0 version. The version supported by a cookie (0 or 1) can be determined and set via the Cookie.getVersion() method. A browser is expected to be capable of handling 20 cookies from each Web server and a minimum of 300 cookies total. Browsers may limit the size of a cookie to 4KB per cookie.

Cookies can be constructed with both a name and a value. The name of the cookie can also subsequently be read via the getName() method. The value can also be set and read using setValue() and getValue(). The cookie name can be composed only of ASCII alphanumeric characters.

The Cookie class also provides support for getting and setting various other security, comment, and lifetime expiration data. A comment that describes the purpose of the cookie can be set or read using the setComment() and getComment() methods. Comments are not supported for v0-style cookies. The security of the cookie can be specified using the setSecure() method and determined from the getSecure() method. Cookie security simply indicates whether the cookie is to be transmitted over a secure protocol. The getMaxAge() and setMaxAge() methods are used to read and set the maximum number of seconds for the cookie's validity. A negative age number indicates that the cookie will be deleted when the Web client browser exits. Zero seconds implies that the cookie should be deleted immediately.

After a Cookie object is first created on the server side, it should be added to an HttpServletResponse object using the HttpServletResponse.addCookie() method. Multiple cookies can be added to an HttpServletResponse object. The Cookie objects that have been sent back from the Web client during subsequent requests can be retrieved from the HttpServletRequest.getCookies() method call. The URL path to which the Web client should return a cookie can be specified via the `setPath()` method. All server resources in or below the path of the specified return path can use the cookie for session management. The `getPath()` method returns this path value. Similarly, the domain within which the cookie is visible can be specified and read via the `setDomain()` and `getDomain()` methods, respectively. The domain name format begins with a dot and defines that domain within which the cookie is visible (for example, `.beeshirts.com`).

Session Management Examples

Our BeeShirts.com application uses both `HttpSession` and `Cookie` objects for state management over HTTP. The `registration.html` page sends a `POST` request to the `RegistrationServlet` where the creation of a cookie is first induced. The `doPost()` method first calls the `registerNewCustomer()` method to create a `Customer` object that is added to the user's `HttpSession` as shown here:

```
private String registerNewCustomer(HttpServletRequest servletRequest)
  throws ServletException
{
  // Exclude code here to extract following data from servletRequest:
    // firstName, lastName, middleName, password, phone, eMail,
    // address_1, address_2, city, state, zip_code

  ...

  // Create an Address object from POST data
  Address address = new Address(address_1, address_2, city,
                               state,zip_code);
  // Create a Customer object from Address object and POST data
  Customer customer = new Customer(firstName, lastName, middleName,
                                  address, phone, eMail, password);
  // Get session and add Customer object to session
  HttpSession session  = servletRequest.getSession();
  session.setAttribute(Customer.CUSTOMER_OBJECT, customer);

  // Return user's first name
  return firstName;
}
```

The `RegistrationServlet.doPost()` method retrieves the user's first name from the `registerNewCustomer()` method and creates a `Cookie` with the standard name of `BEESHIRTS` and the user's first name as the cookie value. After setting the maximum age of the cookie to six months, the cookie is added to the `HttpServletResponse` to be sent back to the client as shown here:

```
public void doPost(HttpServletRequest servletRequest,
  HttpServletResponse servletResponse)
```

```
  throws ServletException, IOException
{
    ...
    // Create Customer object in session from POST data
    String firstName = registerNewCustomer(servletRequest);
    // Get session object and the cookie name value
    HttpSession session = servletRequest.getSession(false);
    String cookieValue
        = (String)session.getAttribute(ServletsHelper.COOKIE_NAME);
    // If no cookie, then add user's first name to cookie
    if(cookieValue == null){
      // create Cookie for this customer
      // ServletsHelper.COOKIE_NAME equals "BEESHIRTS"
      Cookie cookie = new Cookie(ServletsHelper.COOKIE_NAME, firstName);
      cookie.setMaxAge(SIX_MONTHS_IN_SECONDS);
      servletResponse.addCookie(cookie);
    }
  ...
}
```

Our BeeShirts.com `BeeShirtsServlet` front page uses the `HttpServletRequest` object to obtain cookie information from the Web client. The `BeeShirtsServlet.service()` method calls a `BeeShirtsServlet.manageSession()` method to extract a value for a cookie like this:

```
public void service (HttpServletRequest servletRequest,
  HttpServletResponse servletResponse)
  throws ServletException, IOException
{
   ...
  // Extract session information
  String sessionCookie = manageSession(servletRequest);
  ...
}
```

The `BeeShirtsServlet.manageSession()` method first extracts or creates an `HttpSession` object, as well as retrieving any cookies received from the `HttpServletRequest`. The `ServletsHelper.getOurCookieValue()` method is then called to search the array of `Cookie` objects for the standard `BEESHIRTS` cookie value. If the returned cookie value is not `null`, the cookie value is then added to the `HttpSession` object. The cookie value or `null` value is then returned from the `manageSession()` method as shown here:

```
private String manageSession(HttpServletRequest servletRequest)
{
  // Create a Session each time the user comes to this site.
  HttpSession session =  servletRequest.getSession(true);
```

```
    // Get any cookies from servlet request
    Cookie[]  cookies = servletRequest.getCookies();

    // Retrieve value for standard BEESHIRTS cookie if present,
    // otherwise will return a null value.
    String cookieValue = ServletsHelper.getOurCookieValue(cookies);
    System.out.println("Cookie Value :" +cookieValue);
    // If cookie value is present, then add this to the HttpSession
    if(cookieValue != null){
       session.setAttribute(ServletsHelper.COOKIE_NAME, cookieValue);
    }

    // Return cookie value if present...or null if not present
    return cookieValue;
  }
```

The cookie value returned from the `manageSession()` method is ultimately used by the `BeeShirtsServlet.writePageCenterArea()` method to display a personalized welcome-back message to the user as shown here:

```
private void writePageCenterArea(PrintWriter printWriter,
  String cookieValue)
{
  ...
  if(cookieValue != null){
    printWriter.println("   <STRONG> WELCOME BACK : " +
         cookieValue +"</STRONG> <BR>");
  }
  ...
}
```

We encourage you to examine all the session management handling semantics defined for the BeeShirts.com storefront sample code on the Web site. Information stored in a session includes customer information, order information, shopping-cart information, current T-shirt search query results, and number of failed login attempts. The cookie previously described also is used to store a personalized username for subsequent logins. These are the basic session management scenarios employed by the examples:

- `BeeShirtsServlet`: Saves the user's `Cookie` value if present to the `HttpSession` via the `manageSession()` method called from `service()`.
- `RegistrationServlet`: Retrieves the user's `Cookie` value from the `HttpSession` inside of `doPost()` to determine whether a new `Cookie` should be created. Saves a `Customer` object to the `HttpSession` via the `registerNewCustomer()` method called from `doPost()`. Also extracts this `Customer` object later from the `HttpSession` to print customer information from within the `writePageCenterArea()` method.

- `BrowseShirtsServlet`: Saves a `Vector` of `TShirt` objects created from a browse query result to the `HttpSession` from within the `writePageCenterAreaResults()` method called from `doPost()`.
- `CartServlet`: Retrieves the user's current `ShoppingCart` and `Vector` of `TShirt` objects from the `HttpSession` via the `doPost()` method. Each `TShirt` selected to be added to the shopping cart is added to the `ShoppingCart` object, and the updated `ShoppingCart` object is added to the `HttpSession` object from within the `doPost()` method. The `doGet()` method retrieves the `ShoppingCart` object from the `HttpSession` object to display its contents.
- `CheckOutServlet`: The `doGet()` method induces the retrieval of both `Customer` and `ShoppingCart` information from the `HttpSession` object to effect a customer checkout.
- `OrderStatusServlet`: The `doPost()` method induces the retrieval and update of an integer value from the `HttpSession` object that is used to indicate the number of attempted failed logins. A canned object of `Customer` information is also added to the `HttpSession` from within the `constructDefaultUserInformation()` method during an attempted login. The `constructOrderForThisCustomer()` method also uses the `HttpSession` object to retrieve the `Customer` information and also saves `Order` information to the `HttpSession`. The display of user order information retrieved from the `showUserOrders()` method accesses this stored `Order` object from the `HttpSession`.

Servlet Request and Response Filters

An important addition to the Servlet API is the concept of filters. In much the same way that a photographer can add a series of filters to modify what his camera sees, Servlet filters provide a flexible, modular way for pre- and post-processing requests and responses. For example, a reporting servlet can filter out credit-card numbers that might appear in a certain data view. A document retrieval servlet could present a document in HTML or PostScript format, and additionally compress that data as it was being returned to the user. Servlet filters provide a standard mechanism for implementing these types of behaviors. Furthermore, the reuse of filters is encouraged through filter chaining, which allows the output of one filter to be passed to the input of another.

Filters are added to a Web application by adding a `<filter>` element and a `<filter-mapping>` element to the J2EE Web deployment descriptor, `web.xml`. We cover such deployment in greater detail shortly in this chapter, but suffice it to say for now that the `<filter>` element captures the registration of a particular class as a filter, as shown here:

```
<filter>
   <filter-name>CustomerAuditFilter</filter-name>
```

```
    <filter-class>ejava.servlets.CustomerAuditFilter</filter-class>
</filter>
```

And the <filter-mapping> element binds that filter to a specific resource, which can be either a servlet or a URL pattern:

```
<filter-mapping>
    <filter-name>CustomerAuditFilter/filter-name>
    <servlet-name>BeeShirtsServlet</servlet-name>
</filter-mapping>
<filter-mapping>
    <filter-name>CustomerAuditFilter</filter-name>
    <url-pattern>/*</url-pattern>
</filter-mapping>
```

Filtering is provided through the `Filter` interface as illustrated in Figure 19.13. As with the listeners discussed before, a developer who wants to use filters in an application needs to create a class that implements this interface. It provides an `init()` method, which takes a `FilterConfig` argument, which the application server will call to pass in initialization information when the filter is created. There is also a `destroy()` method that allows the filter to perform any cleanup before the server destroys it. But the vast majority of the filtering work is done through the `doFilter()` method.

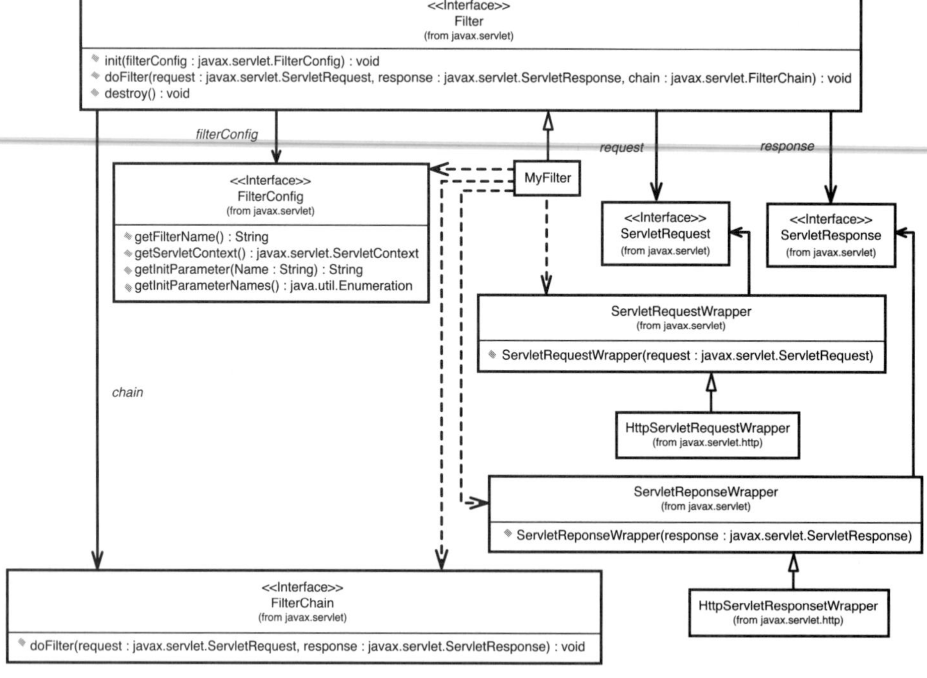

Figure 19.13 Servlet filters.

The `doFilter()` method is called by the server when a request comes in that matches one of the filter-mappings defined in the deployment descriptor. The arguments to this method are a `ServletRequest`, a `ServletResponse`, and a `FilterChain` object. When called, the `doFilter()` method will perform one or more of the following operations:

- Wrap the incoming request object in a class derived from `ServletRequestWrapper` (or an `HttpServletRequestWrapper` extending the `ServletRequestWrapper` in the case of HTTP servlets). This allows the request to be modified before further processing, while retaining access to the original request.
- Wrap the response object in a class that extends `ServletResponseWrapper` (or an `HttpServletResponseWrapper` extending the `ServletResponseWrapper` in the case of HTTP servlets).
- Call the `doFilter()` method on the incoming `FilterChain` object, passing in either the original request and response, or their wrapped counterparts. This allows the next filter in the chain to continue processing.
- Terminate any further processing by not invoking the `chain.doFilter()` method. In this case, the filter is responsible for filling out the response, typically by sending character data to the `PrintWriter` returned by `response.getWriter()`.

In the following example, we have implemented a simple filter, which adds some simple user tracking to our BeeShirts.com site. It looks in the request's `HttpSession` object for an attribute of type `Customer`. The filter prints the user's name and the URI that he requested to the servlet's log file.

```
package ejava.servlets;

import java.io.IOException;


import javax.servlet.Filter;
import javax.servlet.FilterChain;
import javax.servlet.FilterConfig;
import javax.servlet.ServletContext;
import javax.servlet.ServletException;
import javax.servlet.ServletRequest;
import javax.servlet.ServletResponse;
import javax.servlet.http.HttpServletRequest;
import javax.servlet.http.HttpSession;

/**
 *  Finds a Customer object in the HttpSession.
 *  Prints request string along with customer name
```

```
 *  out to a log file, to audit customer trail
 *  through the site.
 */
public class CustomerAuditFilter implements Filter
{

    private FilterConfig filterConfig = null;

    public CustomerAuditFilter()
    {
    }

    /**
     * Initialize the filter
     *
     * @param filterConfig The filter configuration object
     */
    public void init(FilterConfig filterConfig) throws ServletException
    {
        this.filterConfig = filterConfig;
    }

    /**
     *  Clean up when filter exits
     */
    public void destroy()
    {
        filterConfig = null;
    }


    /**
     * The container invokes this method for every filter in the
     * chain, in the order they were specified in the deployment
     * descriptor.
     * The filter has the choice of returning a response here, thus
     * ending the chain, or else it must call
     * chain.doFilter(request, response) to continue processing.
     */
    public void doFilter(ServletRequest request,
                         ServletResponse response,
                         FilterChain chain)
         throws IOException, ServletException
    {
        if (filterConfig == null)
            return;
```

```
        // Render the HTTP servlet request properties
        if (request instanceof HttpServletRequest)
        {
            HttpServletRequest httpReq = (HttpServletRequest)request;
            HttpSession sess = httpReq.getSession();
            Customer customer =
               (Customer)sess.getAttribute(Customer.CUSTOMER_OBJECT);
            if (customer != null)
               logCustomerRequest(customer, httpReq);
        }

        // pass the request on
        chain.doFilter(request, response);
    }


    /**
     * Outputs message to the log file.
     */
    private void logCustomerRequest(Customer customer,
                                    HttpServletRequest request)
    {
        ServletContext ctx = filterConfig.getServletContext();

        String requestURI = request.getRequestURI();
        String customerName = customer.getFirstName() + " " +
                              customer.getLastName();

        ctx.log("User " + customerName + " requested " + requestURI);
    }
}
```

Java Servlet Deployment

In the previous sections, we have covered the development aspects of Java Servlets by understanding the role they play in enterprise software systems and how the API addresses those needs. But that represents only half of the story. Another important design goal of J2EE, and Servlets in particular, is portability of configuration and deployment. That is to say that any J2EE-compliant code should be able not only to run on any J2EE-compliant application server but also to utilize standard configuration files used to deploy such applications. J2EE provides this capability through the use of deployment descriptors. Deployment descriptors provide standard information to the container about the desired configuration of the servlet, and additionally allow an application server vendor to provide custom deployment and performance tuning options.

Web Application Deployment Procedures

> **Note**
>
> Although we focus on the deployment of our J2EE-based Java Servlet application in this section, you will see in upcoming chapters that deployment of JSP and EJB applications follow a very similar pattern. This similarity is what allows more complex applications to be built and deployed using smaller J2EE application components.

The process for deploying J2EE applications involves establishing environment variables, configuring server properties, compiling Java code, creating XML-based deployment descriptors, packaging archive files, and deploying archives to a J2EE server environment. J2EE Web applications may be deployed as distinct standalone application modules or as part of a larger J2EE application composed of multiple modules. The procedure for deploying J2EE-based Web applications assumes the following general steps (with optional J2EE application deployment steps indicated):

1. *Set J2EE Server Environment Variables:* Environment variables must often be set for running a J2EE server environment and will vary per vendor implementation and operating-system platform.
2. *Configure J2EE Server Properties:* Configuration properties for most J2EE server implementations can be set to suit your particular network and operating environment.
3. *Compile J2EE Web Application Code:* All J2EE Web component code must be compiled using a standard Java compiler.
4. *Create a J2EE Web Application Deployment Descriptor:* An XML-based deployment descriptor (that is, `web.xml`) is created according to a standard Web application XML schema. Many products create this file for you from a GUI-based configuration tool.
5. *Package J2EE Web Application Code:* The Web deployment descriptor, all compiled J2EE servlet classes, all HTML files, all image files, and all other Web resources need to be packaged into a Web application archive file with a `.war` extension. J2EE-based products may supply command-line or GUI-based utilities, or both, for this purpose.
6. *Start the J2EE Server:* The J2EE-compliant server must generally be started or already be started at this stage. The exact mechanism for starting a server is often vendor dependent but can be as simple as invoking a single startup command from the command line.
7. *(Optional) Create a J2EE Application Deployment Descriptor:* A J2EE application deployment descriptor (that is, `application.xml`) may also be created to collect one or more Web, EJB, and application client modules into a cohesive J2EE application. Many products will create this file for you automatically or via a GUI-based configuration tool.

8. *(Optional) Package J2EE Application Code:* The application deployment descriptor, Web applications, EJB applications, and application clients may be associated with an enterprise archive (EAR) file with a `.ear` extension. Many products also create this archive for you automatically or via GUI-based development tools.
9. *Deploy the J2EE Web Application Code:* Finally, the standalone Web application module `.war` file or integrated J2EE application `.ear` file is deployed to the J2EE server environment for access by enterprise application clients. This step also is often automated via GUI tools.

In the next section, we will take a closer look at some of the steps just listed, including the proper packaging of a J2EE Web application, and configuring the Web application deployment descriptor (`web.xml`).

Web Application Package Structure

A J2EE Web application may be composed of Java Servlet classes, JavaServer Page components, auxiliary Java classes and class libraries, HTML files, image and other multimedia files, client-side Java code, and meta-information used to describe the Web application. In the interests of simplicity and portability, all the files that compose a Web application must be arranged according to a specific directory structure. All of these files are collected into a Web application archive (WAR) file, which is simply a JAR file having a `.war` extension and embodying a standard directory structure. Table 19.1 illustrates this directory structure.

Table 19.1 **Web Application Standard Directory Structure**

Directory Name	Description
/*rootContext*	Top-level directory. Serves as the document root for all HTML, JSP, image, multimedia, or other files that are to be served to the client.
/*rootContext*/WEB-INF	Contains special information needed by the application server. This directory contains the deployment descriptor, `web.xml`.
/*rootContext*/WEB-INF/classes	Contains required Java classes to implement the servlets contained within this Web application.
/*rootContext*/WEB-INF/lib	Contains JAR files that contain class libraries required by this Web application.

The *rootContext* directory serves as the context path for the application. For example, if we called the *rootContext* directory `beeshirtsApp`, the `BeeShirtsServlet` would be available at `/beeshirtsApp/BeeShirtsServlet`.

When deploying a Web application to an application server, typically it is sufficient to copy the entire *rootContext* directory to a specific location where the application server knows to look for it. This is sometimes referred to as "exploded format."

Alternatively, the contents of the directory can be archived to a file *rootContext*.war, which is known as a WAR (Web archive) file. The WAR file is the same as a JAR file, but with a .war extension. To continue the preceding example, we could make a file called beeshirtsApp.war that would be copied to the application server for deployment.

Web Application Deployment Descriptor

The web.xml deployment descriptor for J2EE 1.4 is an XML file that conforms to an XML schema, which is defined at http://java.sun.com/xml/ns/j2ee/web-app_2_4.xsd. To support legacy applications, this schema is backward-compatible with earlier DTD specifications, so deployment descriptors written for earlier versions will work in a J2EE 1.4 container. The new schema does extend the earlier capabilities, though. Rather than show the full XML schema here, we will work with a sample web.xml file and discuss the key elements contained therein.

Web-App Element

The root element for the deployment descriptor is <web-app>, which must be declared like this:

```
<web-app xmlns="http://java.sun.com/xml/ns/j2ee"
  xmlns:xsi="http://www.w3.org/2001/XMLSchema-instance"
  xsi:schemaLocation="http://java.sun.com/xml/ns/j2ee web-app_2_4.xsd"
  version="2.4">
```

This declares that the document adheres to the XML schema document and is compliant with the Servlet v2.4 specification. There are several sub-elements that are used to add resources, such as servlets, filters, and EJBs to a Web application, and several additional elements that can be used to override and customize the container's default behavior.

Servlet Context and Session Elements

The deployment descriptor provides some global configuration options for the Web application context it defines. Initialization parameters that are provided to the ServletContext implementation at startup are defined by the <context-param> element as name-value pairs. For example:

```
<web-app>
  ...
  <context-param>
    <param-name>StoreName</param-name>
    <param-value>BeeShirts Site 105</param-value>
    <description>Defines the actual name of this site.</description>
  </context-param>
  ...
  <context-param>
    ...
```

```
  </context-param>
  ...
</web-app>
```

In this example, a servlet wanting to use this value would make a call like this:

```
String storeName = getServletContext().getInitParameter("StoreName");
```

The session is also configurable, through the `<session-config>` element. Currently, the only configurable property is the "timeout," the amount of time it takes for the container to consider a session to be expired. That time, expressed in minutes, is configured like so:

```
<session-config>
  <session-timeout>30</session-timeout>
</session-config>
```

Welcome Files

A welcome file is the name of the default file returned when a request URL maps to a directory path. The most commonly accepted standard among Web servers is `index.html`, but the deployment descriptor allows this to be configured through the `<welcome-file-list>` element. This contains an ordered list of files to be returned when a specific resource is not requested. For example,

```
<welcome-file-list>
   <welcome-file>index.jsp</welcome-file>
   <welcome-file>home.html</welcome-file>
</welcome-file-list>
```

would cause a request of `http://beeshirts.com/myApp` to return `myApp/index.jsp` if no default servlet was defined to handle the request, or `myApp/home.html` if `index.jsp` was also not present.

Servlet Elements

To register and configure a servlet with an application server, the deployment descriptor uses several elements. The first of these is the `<servlet>` element, which contains two sub-elements, `<servlet-name>` and `<servlet-class>`. The servlet name is an arbitrary name given to the servlet that is used as a handle to refer to this servlet elsewhere in the deployment descriptor. The servlet class is the full class name of the specific implementation of the `GenericServlet` (usually `HttpServlet`, more specifically) interface that implements this servlet. For example, for our BeeShirts.com application, we have this:

```
<servlet>
   <servlet-name>BeeShirts </servlet-name>
   <servlet-class>ejava.servlets.BeeShirtsServlet</servlet-class>
</servlet>
```

The <servlet> element can also contain one or more <init-param> elements, which can be used to pass initialization parameters to a servlet on startup. Each <init-param> element contains a name-value pair, plus a description that can be useful for deployment descriptor editing tools. For example:

```
<servlet>
  <servlet-name>BrowseShirts </servlet-name>
  <servlet-class>ejava.servlets.BrowseShirtsServlet</servlet-class>
     <init-param>
       <param-name>numberOfShirts</param-name>
       <param-value>8</param-value>
       <description>Number Of Shirts to Read </description>
     </init-param>
     <init-param>
       <param-name>shirt_0 </param-name>
       <param-value>0,XL,White,11.5,123,145,shirtOne.jpg</param-value>
       <description>First Shirt Information </description>
     </init-param>
     …
</servlet>
```

These parameters are available to the servlet at runtime by calling the `ServletConfig.getInitParameterNames()` and/or `ServletConfig.getInitParameter()` methods.

After a servlet is declared, the <servlet-mapping> element is used to bind that servlet to incoming requests. It contains a <servlet-name> element, which maps to the <servlet-name> defined in the <servlet> element, and a <url-pattern> element, which specifies the URL pattern to match against. In our example,

```
<servlet-mapping>
    <servlet-name>BeeShirts</servlet-name>
    <url-pattern>/BeeShirtsServlet</url-pattern>/
</servlet-mapping>
```

maps the URL `/BeeShirtsServlet` to the BeeShirts servlet.

URL Mapping

J2EE defines several rules for how URL-pattern strings are to be interpreted by the container. These rules allow for a wide variety of configuration situations. The rules are applied in the following order, with the first successful match selecting the servlet with no further searching:

1. An exact match always takes highest precedence.
2. A path mapping, which is defined by a string that begins with a /, and ends with /*, where * is a wildcard character. The longest path-prefix that matches the request path is the one selected.

3. A filename extension that matches an extension mapping. Extension mappings are declared by `*.ext`, where `ext` is the file extension.
4. The "default" servlet for the application is chosen if none of the above finds a successful match. The default servlet is specified simply with the / character.
5. If no default servlet is defined, the container attempts to match the request to one of its implicit mappings. Implicit mappings depend on the specific application server vendor. Typically, however, there will be an implicit mapping to handle JSP files with a `.jsp` extension, and another mapping to handle HTML and other types that simply returns the contents of the named file.

Table 19.2 and Table 19.3 illustrate how the container handles URL mapping.

Table 19.2 **Example Servlet Mappings**

`<url-pattern>`	`<servlet-name>`
`/shopping/cart/*`	`cartServ`
`/login`	`loginServ`
`*.prod`	`productServ`

Table 19.3 **Servlet Handling of Incoming Requests**

Incoming Request	`<servlet-name>`
`/shopping/cart/index.jsp`	`cartServ`
`/login`	`loginServ`
`/login/index.html`	handled by container
`/shopping/cart/item.prod`	`cartServ`
`/homepage.prod`	`productServ`

Filter Elements

Filters are configured in a similar fashion to servlets, with a few small differences. The `<filter>` element is used to declare a filter, which contains sub-elements `<filter-name>`, `<filter-class>`, and `<init-param>`, and performs an equivalent role to the `<servlet>` element described previously.

The `<filter-mapping>` element is used to bind a filter to a particular Web resource. It contains a `<filter-name>` sub-element, which refers it to a filter declared in a `<filter>` element, and a `<url-pattern>` sub-element, which obeys the same rules forth in the preceding "URL Mapping" section. In the following example, all incoming URLs will be passed through the `CustomerAuditFilter`:

```
<filter>
   <filter-name>CustomerAuditFilter</filter-name>
   <filter-class>ejava.servlets.CustomerAuditFilter</filter-class>
```

```
</filter>

<filter-mapping>
   <filter-name>CustomerAuditFilter</filter-name>
   <url-pattern>/*</url-pattern>
</filter-mapping>
```

In addition, a filter can be mapped directly to a servlet through a `<servlet-name>` element specified within the `<filter-mapping>` section. Finally, one or more `<dispatcher>` elements can be declared, each of which can be one of the following values:

- `REQUEST`: Filter is applied only when the request comes directly from the client.
- `FORWARD`: Filter is applied only when the request is the result of a `RequestDispatcher.forward()` call.
- `INCLUDE`: Filter is applied only when the request is the result of a `RequestDispatcher.include()` call.
- `ERROR`: Filter is applied only when the request is the result of the error page mechanism.

So, continuing with our previous example,

```
<filter-mapping>
   <filter-name>CustomerAuditFilter</filter-name>
   <servlet-name>CheckOutServlet</servlet-name>
   <dispatcher>REQUEST</dispatcher>
</filter-mapping>
```

will invoke the `CustomerAuditFilter` only if the client directly requests a resource that maps to the `CheckOutServlet`.

MIME Type Mappings

The deployment descriptor provides a means for the developer to specify MIME content types based on file extension with the `<mime-mapping>` element. These mappings will override the container's built-in mappings within the scope of the Web application, or define additional ones. For example,

```
<mime-mapping>
   <extension>zip</extension>
   <mime-type>application/x-compressed-zip</mime-type>
</mime-mapping>
```

will add the header `Content-Type:application/x-compressed-zip` to the response of any request that ends with a `.zip` extension.

Servlet Application Configuration Elements

Access to parameters of a servlet environment can return only `String` value parameters. A more generic means to access Java objects managed from within a servlet container environment is provided via JNDI lookup services through the J2EE container. Using the `<env-entry>` element, the deployment descriptor can add values into the container's JNDI registry. For example,

```
<env-entry>
   <description>Sales Tax for Virgina</description>
   <env-entry-name>salesTaxVA</env-entry-name>
   <env-entry-type>java.lang.Float</env-entry-type>
   <env-entry-value>4.50</env-entry-value>
</env-entry>
```

adds an entry into the JNDI registry at `java:comp/env/salesTaxVA` of type `java.lang.Float`, and initializes it to the value `4.50`. Within a servlet, this value can be retrieved in the following fashion:

```
Context ctx = new InitialContext();
// exception handling omitted
Float vaTax = (Float)ctx.lookup("salesTaxVA");
```

It is also important to note that not all Java object types are permitted within an `<env-entry-type>` declaration. The only permissible values are `java.lang.String`, `java.lang.Character`, `java.lang.Byte`, `java.lang.Short`, `java.lang.Integer`, `java.lang.Long`, `java.lang.Boolean`, `java.lang.Double`, and `java.lang.Float`.

For more information on JNDI lookups, see Chapter 11, "Naming Services with JNDI."

Servlet Service Management

J2EE servlet containers provide various services that can be tapped by Java Servlet component implementations. These management services provide for an efficient, scalable, configurable, and dependably assured computing environment. To provide such management services, J2EE servlet containers often restrict what a servlet component can do by use of Java security restrictions, such as providing read/write-only file permissions, connect-only socket permissions (that is, cannot create server sockets), and read-only system property permissions. Servlet containers can thus effectively provide service management for thread pooling, servlet activation and instance pooling, transactions, security, availability, EJB object naming, and resource interface object naming. Although we have explored many of these services in a broader API context in previous chapters, we explore their specific application here to use with servlets inside of J2EE Web container environments.

Servlet Resource Management

When a Web application is deployed within the context of a fully J2EE-compliant container, all the additional services that the container provides are available for the Web application to use. Such resources can include JDBC data sources, JavaMail sessions, JMS connections, and Enterprise JavaBeans. These services are made available to the application through a JNDI lookup of a logical name, in similar fashion to the `<env-entry>` element described previously.

Although it is often the case that J2EE containers will automatically provide such configured resources to all deployed Web applications, the Web application deployment descriptor does allow resources to be declared explicitly. This permits an application server vendor to provide a fully Servlet v2.4–compliant Web application server, along with whatever subset of additional J2EE features they deem appropriate.

Because these resources can often be configured independent of a Web application, their configuration syntax is defined in the global J2EE v1.4 XML Schema, which can be found at `http://java.sun.com/xml/ns/j2ee/j2ee_1_4.xsd`. Also, most of these topics are covered in greater detail elsewhere in this book, so we will provide only a brief synopsis of each here.

`<resource-ref>` Element

The `<resource-env-ref>` element defines a reference to an instance of a resource manager connection factory class, such as a `javax.sql.DataSource`, which serves as a factory for `javax.sql.Connection` instances. For example:

```
<resource-ref>
   <res-ref-name>jdbc/BeeShirtsDataSource</res-ref-name>
   <res-type>javax.sql.DataSource</res-type>
   <res-auth>Container</res-auth>
   <res-sharing-scope>Shareable</res-sharing-scope>
</resource-ref>
```

The `<res-auth>` element can have a value of either `Container` or `Application`. If it is set to `Container`, the container is responsible for performing authentication when a client accesses the resource. If it is `Application`, the application must implement the authentication.

The `<res-sharing-scope>` element can have a value of either `Shareable` or `Unshareable`, indicating the shareability of the connections acquired from this resource manager.

`<resource-env-ref>` Element

The `<resource-env-ref>` element defines a reference to an instance of a container-administered object, such as a JMS queue. It simply consists of a JNDI name and a type. For example:

```
<resource-env-ref>
   <resource-env-ref-name>jms/MessagingQueue</resource-env-ref-name>
   <resource-env-ref-type>javax.jms.Queue</resource-env-ref-type>
</resource-env-ref>
```

`<message-destination-ref>` Element

The `<message-destination-ref>` element declares a JMS message destination for use within the Web application. For details on configuring JMS messaging, see Chapter 15, "Messaging Services with JMS and JAXM."

`<ejb-ref>` and `<ejb-local-ref>` Elements

The `<ejb-ref>` and `<ejb-local-ref>` elements are used to declare Enterprise JavaBeans to be used within the Web application. The `<ejb-local-ref>` element declares an EJB that runs in the same JVM as the Web application, that is, is "local." The `<ejb-ref>` element refers to an EJB that can be deployed within the same JVM or a remote JVM. EJBs and EJB deployment are covered in much greater detail in Part VI, "Enterprise Applications Enabling."

Servlet Security

The Java Servlet framework is integrated with many Java 2 security features and also augments the Java 2 security framework to provide an easy way to provide secure servlets. Servlet security deals with identity and authentication, authorization, integrity, and confidentiality. In particular, the J2EE Java Servlet framework provides a means to declaratively define security attributes in a Web application XML deployment descriptor that is used to configure the online operational security aspects of the associated servlets. Alternatively, certain features of the security framework are also exposed to servlets via APIs that enable more elaborate programmatic security provisioning by servlet application developers.

Servlet Authentication

The `<login-config>` element defined within the `<web-app>` element of the Web application XML deployment descriptor is used to define the particular authentication configuration used by a Web application. The `<auth-method>` sub-element of `<login-config>` defines the type of authentication used. Authentication of principals that access servlets is accomplished in one of four ways, including basic, digest-based, forms-based, and SSL client certificate–based authentication. These four authentication types, with their associated `<auth-method>` element value in parentheses, are defined here:

- *Basic Authentication* (`BASIC`): A Web server asks the Web client to authenticate the user within a particular domain identified by a string sent to the client. The `<realm-name>` sub-element of `<login-config>` defines this domain name string. The Web client responds with a username and password solicited from the Web user.
- *Digest-Based Authentication* (`DIGEST`): Although a username and password are used to authenticate a user as with basic authentication, an added layer of security is provided by encoding the password using a simple cryptographic algorithm.

- *Forms-Based Authentication* (FORM): Standard HTML forms for login and failed login can be defined using a forms-based authentication scheme within the <form-login-config> sub-element of <login-config>. When a user attempts to log in, standard field names of j_username and j_password are posted to a specified Web server URL using a standard action named j_security_check. As a sample snippet, the form within the referenced login HTML page may be defined as shown here:

```
<form method="POST" action="j_security_check">
  <input type="text" name="j_username">
  <input type="password" name="j_password">
</form>
```

- *SSL Client Certificate–Based Authentication* (CLIENT-CERT): Client authentication via SSL using client certificates is perhaps the most secure means for authentication. Because this form of authentication requires SSL over HTTP, this form of authentication is sometimes referred to as HTTPS-based client authentication.

Certain authentication-related information associated with an HTTP request can be extracted from the HttpServletRequest when needed. The getAuthType() method can be used to identify any secure authentication scheme used to protect access to the servlet (for example, BASIC, DIGEST, or null for "none"). The user identity name that was authenticated and associated with an HTTP servlet request (optionally null if no authentication) is obtained via a call to getRemoteUser(). Finally, a handle to an authenticated user in java.security.Principal form can be obtained from a call to getUserPrincipal().

Secure Servlet Communications

When a servlet request is sent to a Web server using a secure protocol, the ServletRequest.isSecure() method call can be used to return a boolean value indicating this fact. When SSL is used with HTTP, an array of javax.security.cert.X509Certificate objects is returned from a call to ServletRequest.getAttribute() using the attribute name javax.servlet.request.X509Certificate. The security of a cookie can also be specified using the Cookie.setSecure(boolean) method and determined from the Cookie.getSecure() method. Cookie security simply indicates whether the cookie is to be transmitted over a secure protocol.

Servlet Authorization

After a user has been identified using one of the previously defined authentication mechanisms, the authorization to servlet resources identified by URLs can be determined. Servlet authorization is based on a role-based access control technique. Security roles are mapped to principals or groups. When a request is made by a particular principal on a resource with an associated security role, the principal name or group to which the principal belongs is compared with the principal name or group associated with the required role to determine whether access to the resource is allowed.

A collection of security roles valid for a particular J2EE servlet environment can be defined within the XML deployment descriptor's `<security-role>` sub-element of the `<web-app>` element. The `<security-role>` simply defines a set of valid role names and optional descriptions in this way:

```
<web-app>
  <security-role>
    <description>Sytem Administration Role</description>
    <role-name>admin</role-name>
  </security-role>
  ...
</web-app>
```

Access to a particular servlet can then be restricted to access by users of a defined role using the `<security-role-ref>` sub-element of a `<servlet>` element. A `<role-name>` element defines a security role assumed by the application, and a `<role-link>` element refers to one of the servlet container-managed `<security-role>` element's `<role-name>` values as illustrated here:

```
<web-app>
  <servlet>
    <servlet-name>UserAccountManagement</servlet-name>
      ...
    <security-role-ref>
      <role-name>SystemAdmin</role-name>
      <role-link>admin</role-link>
    </security-role-ref>
  </servlet>
  ...
</web-app>
```

The role of a user associated with a particular HTTP servlet request can be determined via a call to the `HttpServletRequest.isUserInRole(String)` method with a role name parameter designating the security role defined within a Web deployment descriptor.

More sophisticated Web resource authorization can be specified with the `<security-constraint>` sub-element of `<web-app>`. A collection of Web resources can be specified and associated for access only by principals belonging to certain associated roles. Furthermore, the secure nature of the communications link over which access occurs can also be defined. As an example for limiting access to detailed user information stored on a Web server, we might have this:

```
<web-app>
    ...
  <security-constraint>
```

```
      <web-resource-collection>
        <web-resource-name>UserInfo</web-resource-name>
        <description>URL for all detailed user information</description>
        <url-pattern>/users/*</url-pattern>
        <http-method>POST</http-method>
      </web-resource-collection>
      <auth-constraint>
        <description>Only allow system administrator access</description>
        <role-name>admin</role-name>
      </auth-constraint>
      <user-data-constraint>
        <description>Require SSL session to get user info</description>
        <transport-guarantee>CONFIDENTIAL</transport-guarantee>
      </user-data-constraint>
    </security-constraint>
      ...
</web-app>
```

Servlet Transactions

Servlets can begin, commit, and rollback transactions using the `javax.transaction.UserTransaction` interface as described in Chapter 14, "Transaction Services with JTA and JTS." Using such an interface, servlets can access multiple shared resources and EJBs within the context of a single atomic transaction. A handle to a `UserTransaction` object is obtainable using JNDI with a lookup via the name of `java:comp/UserTransaction`. A servlet transaction may be begun only within a `service()` method thread, and the transaction must be committed or rolled back before returning from the `service()` method. Otherwise, the servlet container will abort the transaction. Thus, we might have access to and demarcation of a transaction as shown here:

```
public void service (HttpServletRequest servletRequest,
    HttpServletResponse servletResponse) throws ServletException
{
  try{
    InitialContext ctx = new InitialContext();
    UserTransaction transaction
      = (UserTransaction) ctx.lookup("java:comp/UserTransaction");

    transaction.begin();

    // Do some work involving shared resources...

    if( // Everything is OK? )
      transaction.commit();
    else
```

```
        transaction.rollback();
    }
    catch(...){
      // Handle exceptions
    }
}
```

Transaction context information must be propagated from process to process in a standard fashion for distributed transactions to be possible. A J2EE servlet container environment primarily concerns itself with such matters. However, the following rules may be assumed by Web component developers for transaction propagation in J2EE environments:

- *Servlet to EJB:* The transaction context of a JTA transaction must be propagated from a servlet to an EJB when both operate inside of a J2EE container environment.
- *Servlet to Data Resource:* A servlet's access to a resource (that is, DBMS via JDBC) can be managed within the context of a JTA transaction as long as the servlet did not create its own thread and instead has relied on the creation of the thread by the J2EE container.
- *Servlet to Web Server Resource:* Servlets are required to propagate transaction context to other Web resources only when requests are dispatched via a `RequestDispatcher`.
- *Web Client to Servlet:* Servlets are not required to handle a transaction context propagated by their Web clients.

JDBC connection resources are perhaps the most common type of resource that servlet developers encounter and must take into consideration when dealing with transactional environments. Servlet component developers should be particularly sensitive to the following rules related to JDBC connection handling:

- *Inter-Thread Sharing:* JDBC connections should not be shared between threads.
- *Class Attribute Storage:* JDBC connections should not be stored in `static` servlet class attributes.
- *Single Threaded Storage:* JDBC connections can be stored in servlet class instance attribute fields if the servlet implements the `SingleThreadModel`.
- *Multithreaded Storage:* JDBC connections should not be stored in servlet class instance attribute fields if the servlet does not implement the `SingleThreadModel`.

Servlet Availability

Web-enabling an enterprise opens the gateway to an enterprise system for access by a large Internet or intranet community. Although access to resources can be restricted to authorized users via security mechanisms, the demand for service by Web clients placed on a Web server can be significantly large for most Web-enabled enterprise applications. Thus, availability of service for Web-enabled applications built using servlets must be considered from the outset of design. Multiple Web client requests must not bring your Web-enabled enterprise interface to its knees. Furthermore, the scalability of Web client usage will need to be considered by any enterprise system that wants to expand its Web client base.

Fortunately for the Java Servlet developer, the management of such availability can be kept transparent to the developer and managed by a particular Java Servlet container and server implementation environment. Most Web servers and servlet container implementers support scalability and availability in part by providing efficient techniques for thread pooling and servlet instance pooling. As a client request is received by the server, the server framework handles the efficient allocation of system memory and thread resources to the request transparently to the servlet application developer. Transaction management services also provide a certain degree of availability by managing distributed access to shared distributed resources in a fashion that permits for the atomicity, consistency, isolation, and durability of operations.

More sophisticated means for providing highly available Web-enabled applications may also be provided by vendors that implement load-balancing, clustering, and failover techniques. Load-balancing and clustering basically involve the management of multiple JVM processes within the same machine or across different distributed machines to spread the load of client requests. In the event of a particular process or machine's failure, a failover technique may be employed to distribute client requests to another redundant JVM process or machine. Such features are relatively simple for stateless servlets, but the storage of `HttpSession` information in stateful Web applications makes such redundancy management more difficult. Vendors thus may have to guarantee the capability to persist `HttpSession` information or provide the capability to serialize and deserialize `HttpSession` information across different JVM processes.

J2EE servlet container environments that support distributable servlets can deploy instances of servlets to different JVM processes on the same machine or on other networked host machines in a standard fashion. A container environment can be viewed as a distributed environment domain that contains and manages multiple distributed JVM processes. An optional `<distributable>` element placed within the `<web-app>` element of a Web application's XML deployment descriptor designates the capability to run the Web application inside of a distributable servlet environment. By specifying that a Web application can operate in a distributable fashion, we are telling the servlet container environment that the Web application adheres to a few behavioral constraints to facilitate distribution. Web containers can then implement features of clustering and failover that would otherwise not be possible for nondistributable servlets.

The restrictions that must be adhered to by the servlets mainly revolve around the type of objects that are stored in an `HttpSession` object. Only `java.io.Serializable`, `javax.ejb.EJBObject`, `javax.ejb.EJBHome`, `javax.transaction.UserTransaction`, and `javax.naming.Context` objects may be stored in an `HttpSession` by a distributable servlet. Otherwise, an `IllegalArgumentException` may be thrown by the container when an attempted `HttpSession` storage operation is performed. By restricting such object types to being added to a servlet `HttpSession` object, the servlet container can guarantee the mobility of servlet session object state during failover or clustering.

Conclusions

We have covered the gamut of development topics that concern the Web-enabling of enterprise applications using Java Servlets. The J2EE Java Servlet architecture provides a component-container model that can result in a significant amount of simplified HTTP communications paradigm and management service abstraction for the servlet developer. The Servlet API provides a powerful set of tools to develop meaningful applications that are easily Web-enabled. The API provides high-level abstractions for important concepts such as requests, responses, stateful session tracking, and filtering, to name a few. We have also explored the use of a J2EE server environment for the deployment of Java Servlet Web components. Deploying and configuring Java Servlets is simplified and standardized with the J2EE. J2EE servers also provide many management services, such as security and availability, that can be configurably managed from within the context of XML deployment descriptors. In the next chapter, we will introduce JavaServer Pages, which are essentially servlets, but can be written using a markup-style language to ease the sometimes-cumbersome task of presentation logic programming.

20

JavaServer Pages (JSP)

JavaServer Pages (JSPs) can be thought of as a cross between HTML and Java. They serve the purpose of enhancing HTML's static behavior with server-side Java, while still retaining the easily readable markup language style. As such, they can provide a powerful tool for Web-enabling an enterprise that may be more familiar to Web developers. JSP developers can use a simplified scripting language–based syntax for embedding HTML into JSPs, for directing how JSPs are translated into Java Servlets, for embedding Java into JSPs, and for accessing standard objects and actions provided by JSP containers. The configuration and deployment of JSPs also has a simplified XML-based deployment descriptor approach akin to the approach provided for Java Servlets.

In this chapter, you will learn:

- The architecture and concepts behind the use of JavaServer Pages.
- The basic language of JSPs and the basic structure of JSP documents.
- The standard built-in objects and APIs exposed for access by JSPs.
- The standard scripting language elements used to dynamically add content to JSPs.

JSP Overview

JavaServer Page technology provides a means for specifying special scripting language commands inline with formatted text, which the server will process to generate a response to a client. As is the case with Java Servlets, JSPs use HTTP as the default request/response communications paradigm and thus make JSPs ideal as a Web-enabling technology. HTML, XML, and other template data can be defined in a JSP and are sent directly to a Web client without any additional processing on the server side. However, JSP scripting language commands inserted into the same page are processed by the server before a requested page is delivered back to a Web client.

JSP is often attractive to a Web-enabling enterprise developer because regular template data can be used directly within a JSP, the JSP scripting command language has a simple XML-like syntax, and Java code can be used within the page. JSP is also defined in a generic enough fashion that future versions of the specification will be able to support other embedded languages besides Java. However, the most recent JSP v2.0 standard requires use of only Java as the embedded scripting language. JSP v2.0 is required by the J2EE v1.4 and also depends on the Java Servlet v2.4 standard described in Chapter 19, "Java Servlets."

JSP Architecture

Figure 20.1 depicts the basic architecture of a JSP environment. The first thing to note is that JSP extends and depends on the Java Servlet API and implementation. Although JSPs are written by application developers, they are ultimately converted to Java Servlets. An implementation class of the JSP is actually an underlying servlet representation of the JSP. However, additional semantics are imposed on the implementation to satisfy the expected interface contract between the JSP container and the JSP implementation class. This allows developers to create JSP components using elements that are more suited for presentation-side logic, such as HTML markup, XML, JSP command syntax, and an embedded scripting language. At the same time, all the benefits provided to the Java Servlet component by its container environment are also provided to the JSP component. Because JSPs and Java Servlets are both generically viewed as Web components from a J2EE container's perspective, they share the same mechanisms for configuration and service management.

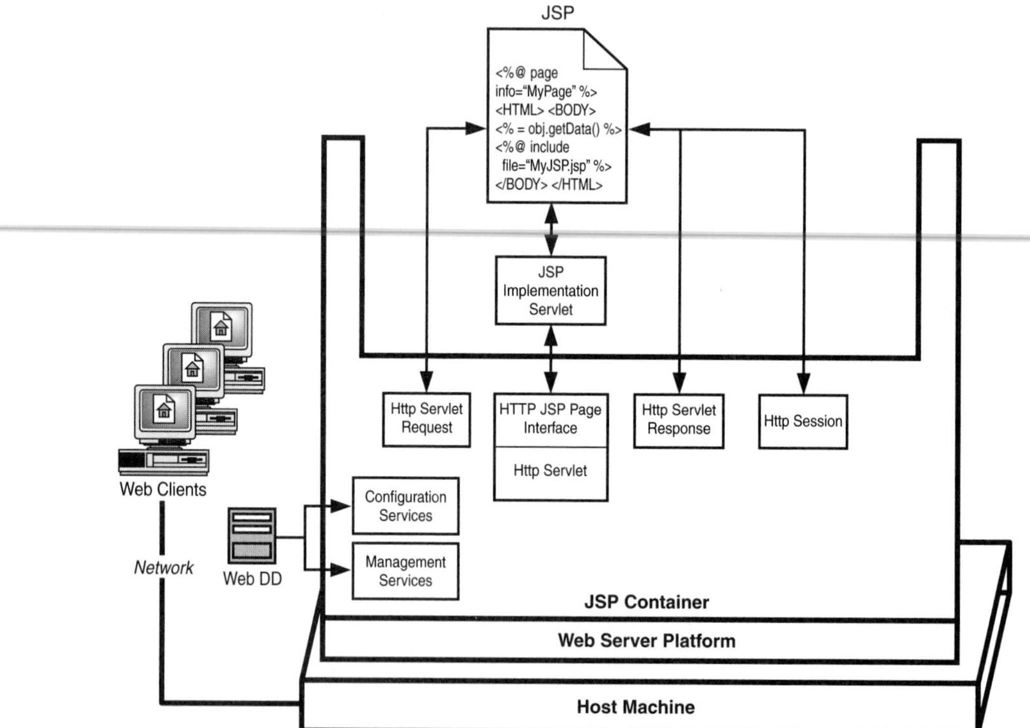

Figure 20.1 The JSP architecture.

JSPs can also refer to request, response, and session management objects created by a container directly from the JSP. As you'll see in later sections, such objects can be used to perform request handling, response handling, and session management from within a JSP using the same APIs for such objects as were used with Java Servlets. JSPs thus reap all the benefits provided by Java Servlets and Web container environments, but they have the added advantage of being simpler and more natural to program for Web-enabling enterprise developers.

Phases of a JSP

Figure 20.2 depicts the various transformations a JSP must go through before it can process requests online. A developer first creates a JSP using JSP syntax and the collection of request, response, and session management abstractions provided by the JSP API and programming model. A translation tool, sometimes referred to as a JSP compiler, is then used to transform the JSP into Java Servlet implementation source code, which in turn is compiled into a Java Servlet implementation class file by a Java compiler tool. This translation and compilation process may be performed offline before or during deployment, or it may be performed online by the JSP container upon request of a particular JSP. The specific approach depends on a developer's preference and the specific JSP vendor tools provided. Finally, the compiled Java Servlet implementation class is activated by the JSP container in the same manner that a Java Servlet is activated. The activated JSP representative object is then capable of processing actual requests, responses, and session actions.

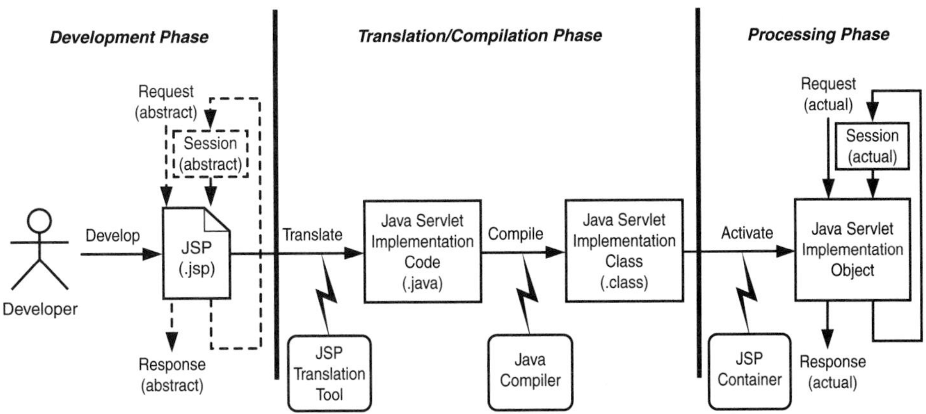

Figure 20.2 The phases of a JSP.

BeeShirts.com JSP Examples

For illustration purposes, we have created a JSP version of the Java Servlet–based BeeShirts.com e-commerce storefront that was presented in Chapter 19. Figure 20.3

does, however, provide you with a logical diagram of the various JSPs used to service requests and generate responses for this sample code. These JSPs essentially provide the same functionality as the code from Chapter 19. We also utilize the images and BeeShirts.com entity classes (`Customer`, `Item`, and so on) developed in Chapter 19.

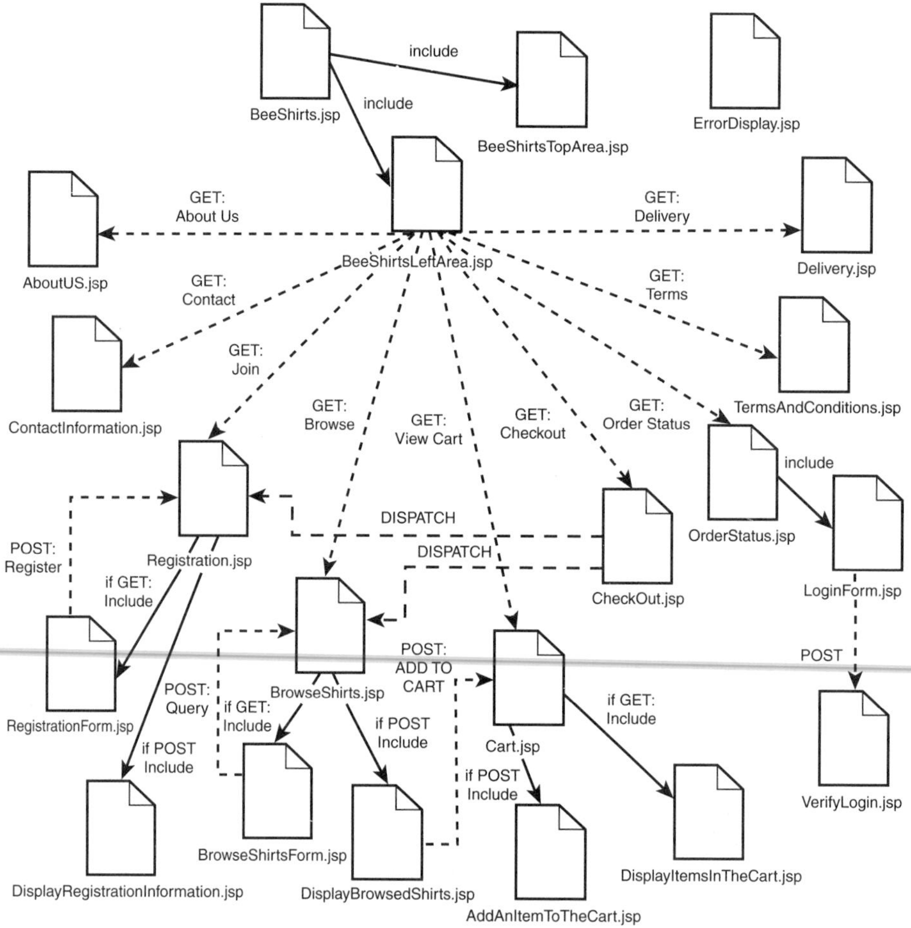

Figure 20.3 BeeShirts.com JSPs.

> **Note**
>
> The example code for this chapter may be located according to Appendix A, "Software Configuration," and is extracted beneath the `examples\src\ejava\jsp` root directory. This code also depends on some of the code from Chapter 19 stored beneath the `examples\src\ejava\servlets` directory. See

> Appendix A for detailed instructions on how to install and run the example code contained in this chapter. In addition, a Servlet v2.4–compliant application server is required to run the sample code. Instructions on building and deploying the samples on several of the most popular application servers are also given in Appendix A.

The BeeShirts.com JSPs shown in Figure 20.3 and the Chapter 19 Java Servlet classes and HTML pages to which they relate are briefly defined here:

- `ErrorDisplay`: Is a global JSP to provide a standard page for displaying JSP errors as they occur. JSPs experiencing errors automatically are routed to this page.
- `BeeShirts`: Provides the root JSP that generates the BeeShirts.com starting page akin to the `BeeShirtsServlet` of Chapter 19.
- `BeeShirtsTopArea`: Is a special JSP to display the top logo portion of the BeeShirts.com Web page. This JSP is included by all the root page JSPs.
- `BeeShirtsLeftArea`: Is a special JSP to display the left portion of the BeeShirts.com Web page displaying the BeeShirts.com button options. This JSP is included by all the root page JSPs.
- `AboutUs`: Handles the request generated by clicking the About Us button and displays some simple BeeShirts.com information akin to the `AboutUsServlet` of Chapter 19.
- `ContactInformation`: Handles the request generated from clicking the Contact button and displays some simple contact information akin to the `ContactInformationServlet` of Chapter 19.
- `Registration`: Is referenced from the Join button and handles display of registration form or registration information. Will execute an included `RegistrationForm` JSP if a `GET` request is received and will execute an included `DisplayRegistrationInformation` JSP if a `POST` is received.
- `RegistrationForm`: Displays a registration form and submits a `POST` to the current `Registration` JSP when the Register button is clicked akin to the `registration.html` file of Chapter 19.
- `DisplayRegistrationInformation`: Displays the results of a user registration akin to the `RegistrationServlet` of Chapter 19.
- `BrowseShirts`: Is referenced from the Browse button and handles display of a browsing query form or display of browse result information. Will execute an included `BrowseShirtsForm` JSP if a `GET` request is received and will execute an included `DisplayBrowsedShirts` JSP if a `POST` is received.
- `BrowseShirtsForm`: Creates a display that allows a user to query for the T-shirts they might be interested in purchasing akin to the `BrowseShirtsServlet` of Chapter 19. Submits a `POST` to `BrowseShirts` when a Query button is clicked.
- `DisplayBrowsedShirts`: Displays search results from a browse query akin to the `BrowseShirtsServlet` of Chapter 19. Submits a `POST` to `Cart` when an Add to Cart button is clicked.

- `Cart`: Is referenced from the View Cart button and handles display of current shopping-cart contents or display of a status message when an item is added to the cart. Will execute an included `DisplayItemsInTheCart` JSP if a `GET` request is received and will execute an included `AddAnItemToTheCart` JSP if a `POST` is received.
- `DisplayItemsInTheCart`: Handles the `GET` to display the current contents of the shopping cart akin to the `CartServlet` of Chapter 19.
- `AddAnItemToTheCart`: Handles the `POST` from the `DisplayBrowsedShirts` JSP Add to Cart button to add a `TShirt` item to the shopping cart akin to the `CartServlet` of Chapter 19.
- `CheckOut`: Handles the `GET` request generated from the Check Out button and dispatches requests appropriately akin to the `CheckOutServlet` of Chapter 19.
- `OrderStatus`: Handles the `GET` request generated from clicking the Order Status button and includes the `LoginForm` JSP.
- `LoginForm`: Displays an order status login form akin to the `OrderStatusServlet` of Chapter 19. Whenever the Login or Remind button is clicked, a `POST` is sent to the `VerifyLogin` JSP.
- `VerifyLogin`: Handles the `POST` from either a Login or a Remind button being clicked akin to the `OrderStatusServlet` of Chapter 19.
- `TermsAndConditions`: Handles the request generated from clicking the Terms button and displays some simple terms and conditions information akin to the `TermsAndConditionsServlet` of Chapter 19.
- `Delivery`: Handles the request generated from the Delivery button and displays some canned delivery information akin to the `deliveryinformation.html` page of Chapter 19.

JSP Language Basics

JSPs contain a mixture of template data (for example, HTML and XML) interspersed with JSP elements. JSP elements are defined within begin and end tags and are the portions of a JSP that are translated and compiled by a JSP compiler into Java Servlets. These JSP elements are the portions of a JSP that represent the commands that are interpreted by JSP containers to service requests from clients. The template data, on the other hand, represents the commands that are ultimately interpreted by clients and therefore simply pass unaffected through the JSP compiler and container processing infrastructure.

These are the basic components used to compose a JSP:

- *Template Data:* Content such as HTML and XML that is embedded directly inside of a JSP as static presentation content.
- *Directives:* JSP elements that are interpreted at translation time and used to tell a JSP compiler to include other files in the compilation of a JSP, define attributes

about the JSP page being translated, and define any libraries of custom elements used in the JSP.

- *Scripting Elements:* JSP elements used to define any variable and method declarations, expressions to be evaluated, and blocks of commands known as scriptlets all in terms of the host language supported by the JSP container (for example, Java).
- *Action Elements:* JSP elements that are commands having a purely taglike look to them but are implemented by the host language transparently to the JSP programmer. A set of *standard actions* is used to do such things as forward requests to other resources or look up and create JavaBean objects for use within a JSP. You can also create and define your own *custom actions* via JSP's tag extension support.

Within certain JSP scripting and action elements, the JSP developer can also access Java objects from directly within the JSP. The invocations that occur on such objects look similar to invocations on any Java object as part of any Java program. As you'll see, the main difference is in how handles to such objects are obtained from within the particular JSP element.

JSP Standard and XML-Based Elements

JSP elements can be interpreted by the JSP container. Elements should not be confused with tags. JSP elements represent a unit of interpretable JSP syntax with a start and end tag. JSP tags, on the other hand, simply represent a small piece of markup code that may be used inside of a JSP element and do not necessarily have start and end tags.

JSP elements have a syntax similar to XML elements and have start and end tags, have case-sensitive element names, can be empty elements, have optional attribute values, and have an optional element body. Although JSP element syntax is identical to XML in some cases, it is only similar to XML in other cases. The JSP specification does define a convention for expressing JSPs as XML documents, known as JSP documents. However, it is not recommended that such a convention be used for hand-authoring of JSPs. Rather, due to the sometimes-awkward syntax that must result from expressing JSPs via XML, the JSP document specification is primarily intended for use by JSP development tools. Although we do make mention of JSP documents at a few points in this chapter, an in-depth discussion is beyond the scope of this book.

Tags

Although we sometimes think of tags as discrete snippets of markup that define parts of a JSP or an HTML page, the term *tags* as it relates to custom tag extensions is actually an important part of the JSP specification with a very specific meaning. Custom tags relate to custom actions that can be defined by developers using a special set of JSP tag extension Java classes and interfaces. These custom actions are implemented by custom Java-based tag handler classes that handle any custom tags inserted into a JSP. A collection of these tag handlers is referred to as a tag library, which can be referenced and utilized by

JSPs using a special tag library directive. Furthermore, an XML-based tag library descriptor file can also be used to configure a particular tag library. We have much more to say about custom tags and actions in the next chapter.

Comments

Comments in JSP pages can be used to document JSP source code or used to embed information to be sent to the client. Comments that are to be ignored during processing and used to document JSP source code are included between `<%--` and `--%>` characters. Comments specific to the type of scripting language being used with the JSP may also be used within scripting elements. Thus, for Java-based JSP scripting, we would place documentation comments between `<% /**` and `**/ %>` characters. For example:

```
<%-- JSP documentation comment --%>

<% /** Java-specific JSP documentation comment **/ %>
```

Comments that are to be sent to the client response stream are defined within `<!--` and `-->` characters. Such comments can also have data dynamically generated within them between `<%=` and `%>` characters that are inserted between client comment boundaries. For example:

```
<!-- Comment that gets sent to JSP client -->

<!-- Client comment with a dynamic expression: <%= a + b %> -->
```

Special Character Handling

Characters that are used as part of regular JSP language syntax may occasionally need to be inserted inside of quoted expressions and comments. Single quotes (`'`), double quotes (`"`), and backslashes (`\`) can all be escaped when they're prepended with a backslash. The `<%` and `%>` character sequences can be escaped via a backslash inserted in between their characters. For example, we can escape all such characters as shown here:

```
<MyElement attribute1=" \'escaped single quotes\' "
           attribute2=" \"escaped double quotes\" "
           attribute3=" \\escaped backslashes\\ "
           attribute4=" <\%escaped literals %\> "   />
```

JSP Objects

A few abstractions have been added to the Java Servlet API framework to support JSP. Many of these core new abstractions are contained within the `javax.servlet.jsp` package. The abstract classes and interfaces contained within this package are implemented by the JSP container environment and encapsulate post-translation JSP implementation objects. JSP programmers use many of these APIs via implicit object handles provided by the container and from within JSP scripting elements, as described in subsequent sections. We simply provide the API and definitions here and defer examples for how to tap their services from within JSPs to sections that follow.

JSP Context

The abstract `javax.servlet.jsp.JspContext` class, shown in Figure 20.4, encapsulates that context information of a JSP that is not specific to Web serving. That is, it simply represents a very abstract container of name and value attribute pairs for a managed server object, a means for accessing the output stream for that object, and the general set of container services offered to that object. The abstract `javax.servlet.jsp.PageContext` class, also shown in Figure 20.4, encapsulates the context of a JSP with specific consideration for use in Web serving. JSP developers will most often interface with an object representation of the `PageContext` object that inherits all the methods provided by the `JspContext` class and defines some new methods.

Such context objects' primary role is to manage access to named objects belonging to particular scopes of visibility from within JSPs. Although the creation and initialization of a `PageContext` is usually transparent to the JSP programmer, as you'll see in subsequent sections, a JSP programmer will be able to obtain a handle to a `PageContext` representative from within a JSP and therefore make use of its many varied APIs. In the remainder of this section, we focus on the primary interfaces offered by these classes that are of most interest to the JSP developer.

The `PageContext.initialize()` method is called such that the `PageContext` can be used by a JSP implementation class during request servicing. Much of the information passed to the `initialize()` method is taken directly from the page directive attributes for a particular JSP. This information includes a handle to the JSP implementation class servlet, a request object, a response object, the URL of an error page, a `boolean` indicator for whether a session is needed, the buffer size, and a buffer overflow auto flush indicator. The `PageContext.release()` method is also called to subsequently release such resources.

A series of methods can subsequently be called from within a JSP to obtain handles to and utilize many of the JSP implementation objects managed by the JSP container, such as the request object, the response object, the session object, the page implementation servlet object, an output response `JSPWriter` object, any propagated exception object, the servlet configuration object, and a servlet context object. The `PageContext.handlePageException()` method is used to pass an uncaught exception from a JSP to the `PageContext`, which handles forwarding the exception to any specified error page URL for the JSP or to a default error handler. A `PageContext` object's `forward()` and `include()` methods are also used to dispatch requests to other URLs.

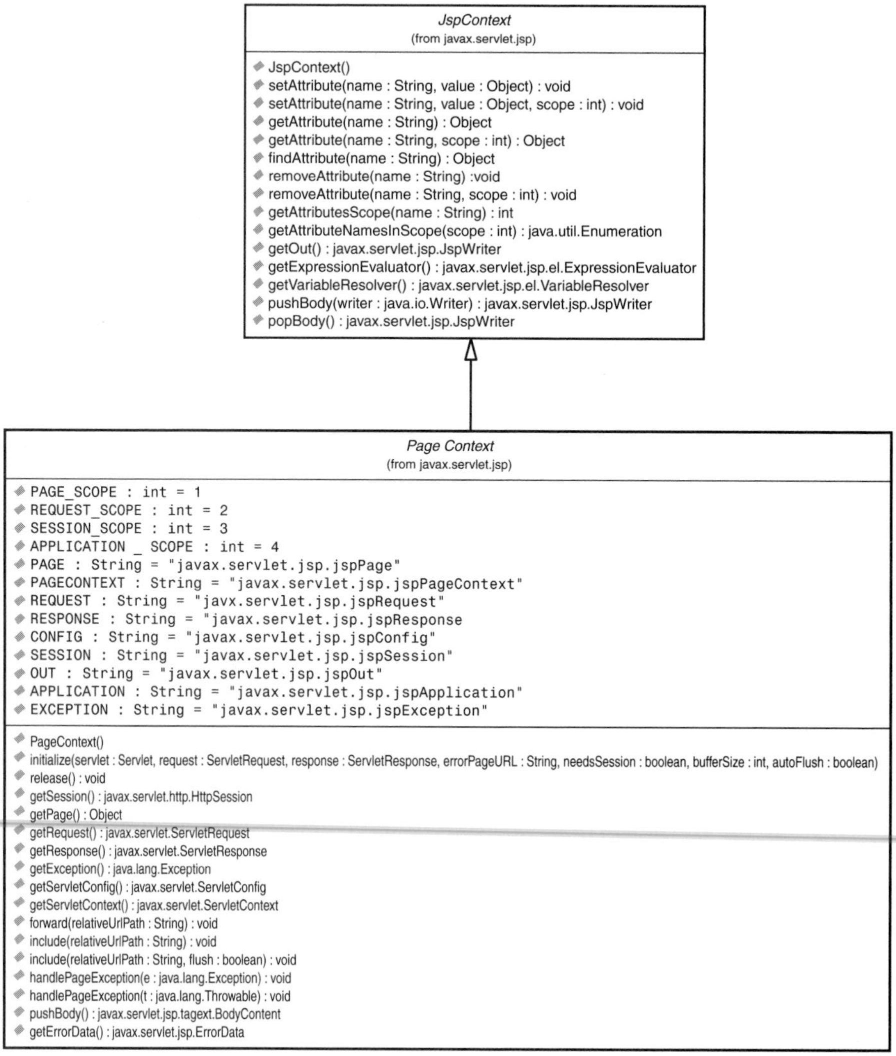

JspContext
(from javax.servlet.jsp)

- JspContext()
- setAttribute(name : String, value : Object) : void
- setAttribute(name : String, value : Object, scope : int) : void
- getAttribute(name : String) : Object
- getAttribute(name : String, scope : int) : Object
- findAttribute(name : String) : Object
- removeAttribute(name : String) :void
- removeAttribute(name : String, scope : int) : void
- getAttributesScope(name : String) : int
- getAttributeNamesInScope(scope : int) : java.util.Enumeration
- getOut() : javax.servlet.jsp.JspWriter
- getExpressionEvaluator() : javax.servlet.jsp.el.ExpressionEvaluator
- getVariableResolver() : javax.servlet.jsp.el.VariableResolver
- pushBody(writer : java.io.Writer) : javax.servlet.jsp.JspWriter
- popBody() : javax.servlet.jsp.JspWriter

Page Context
(from javax.servlet.jsp)

- PAGE_SCOPE : int = 1
- REQUEST_SCOPE : int = 2
- SESSION_SCOPE : int = 3
- APPLICATION _ SCOPE : int = 4
- PAGE : String = "javax.servlet.jsp.jspPage"
- PAGECONTEXT : String = "javax.servlet.jsp.jspPageContext"
- REQUEST : String = "javx.servlet.jsp.jspRequest"
- RESPONSE : String = "javax.servlet.jsp.jspResponse
- CONFIG : String = "javax.servlet.jsp.jspConfig"
- SESSION : String = "javax.servlet.jsp.jspSession"
- OUT : String = "javax.servlet.jsp.jspOut"
- APPLICATION : String = "javax.servlet.jsp.jspApplication"
- EXCEPTION : String = "javax.servlet.jsp.jspException"

- PageContext()
- initialize(servlet : Servlet, request : ServletRequest, response : ServletResponse, errorPageURL : String, needsSession : boolean, bufferSize : int, autoFlush : boolean)
- release() : void
- getSession() : javax.servlet.http.HttpSession
- getPage() : Object
- getRequest() : javax.servlet.ServletRequest
- getResponse() : javax.servlet.ServletResponse
- getException() : java.lang.Exception
- getServletConfig() : javax.servlet.ServletConfig
- getServletContext() : javax.servlet.ServletContext
- forward(relativeUrlPath : String) : void
- include(relativeUrlPath : String) : void
- include(relativeUrlPath : String, flush : boolean) : void
- handlePageException(e : java.lang.Exception) : void
- handlePageException(t : java.lang.Throwable) : void
- pushBody() : javax.servlet.jsp.tagext.BodyContent
- getErrorData() : javax.servlet.jsp.ErrorData

Figure 20.4 JSP context.

The main function of a `PageContext` object is to manage access to objects that are referenceable from JSPs. The scope of each object is particularly important for considering object access and defines the scope within which an object reference is valid. The four valid types of object scope are identified by static constant `int` values in the `PageContext` object and are listed here:

- PAGE_SCOPE: Such objects are accessible only in the page in which they were instantiated. The lifetime of the object ends when the response is generated. Any such objects created with page scope are stored in the PageContext object. A named object is retrieved from PageContext.getAttribute().
- REQUEST_SCOPE: The request associated with the page in which an object was created may be handled by other pages as well. Request objects are accessible from such pages that are handling the same request. The lifetime of the object ends when the request is processed. Any such objects created with request scope are stored in a request object of a subtype form of javax.servlet.ServletRequest. A named object is retrieved from ServletRequest.getAttribute().
- SESSION_SCOPE: The session associated with the page in which an object was created may be associated with other pages as well. Session objects are accessible from such pages that are associated with the same user session. The lifetime of the object ends when the session terminates. Any such objects created with session scope are stored in a session object of the javax.servlet.http.HttpSession type. A named object is retrieved from HttpSession.getAttribute().
- APPLICATION_SCOPE: Such objects are accessible in the Web application in which they were instantiated. The lifetime of the object ends when the application's ServletContext is destroyed. Any such objects created with application scope are stored in an application object of the javax.servlet.ServletContext type. A named object is retrieved from ServletContext.getAttribute().

Each object is also associated with a case-sensitive String name that is used to uniquely identify an object within a translation unit. For example, a set of core implicit objects of JSP to which handles can be obtained all have static String names defined on the PageContext class. Each implicit object has a particular type defined as shown here in parentheses along with the static String implicit object ID name:

- REQUEST (javax.servlet.ServletRequest subclass): A request to a JSP valid only within the scope of a JSP request. For HTTP, this object maps to an object of the javax.servlet.http.HttpServletRequest type.
- RESPONSE (javax.servlet.ServletResponse subclass): A response from a JSP valid within the scope of the JSP page. For HTTP, this object maps to an object of the javax.servlet.http.HttpServletResponse type.
- OUT (javax.servlet.jsp.JspWriter): An object that writes data to the output response stream and is valid within the scope of the JSP page.
- SESSION (javax.servlet.http.HttpSession): A session for a JSP client using HTTP that is valid only within the scope of JSPs processing requests within the same session.

- PAGECONTEXT (javax.servlet.jsp.PageContext): The page context of a JSP that is valid within the scope of the JSP page.
- PAGE (java.lang.Object): A handle to the JSP's implementation class object that is valid for the scope of the JSP page. When Java is the scripting language, the this object name may also be used to refer to this object.
- CONFIG (javax.servlet.ServletConfig): A handle to JSP's configuration handler that is valid for the scope of the JSP page.
- APPLICATION (javax.servlet.ServletContext): A handle to the servlet context for the JSP's implementation object that is valid for the scope of the Web application.
- EXCEPTION (java.lang.Throwable): An exception that was not caught by a JSP and propagated into the JSP container environment and is valid only within the scope of a JSP error page.

Getter, setter, and finder methods on the base JspContext object are the methods used to manage access to such objects according to different object scopes. The getAttribute() methods can be used to obtain a handle to a named object either in a default page scope if no scope is specified or in another scope if a constant int value identifying that scope is specified. Additionally, the scope of a particular named object can be retrieved from the getAttributeScope() method, and an Enumeration of String names for each attribute in a specified scope can be retrieved from a call to getAttributeNamesInScope(). The findAttribute() method can also be used to search for a named attribute in the order of page, request, session, and then application scope. Finally, the setAttribute() methods and removeAttribute() methods have method forms that can respectively set or remove named objects either in a default page scope or from a specified object scope.

JSP Context Services

Figure 20.5 depicts some of the additional services provided by the JSP context abstractions. Among its more arcane services, the JSP context enables you to obtain a handle to an ExpressionEvaluator object that permits one to parse and evaluate certain JSP expressions defined according to the JSP Expression Language discussed later in this chapter. The JSP context also enables you to obtain a handle to a VariableResolver object that permits you to specify how variables defined using the JSP Expression Language are resolved by the JSP container.

The abstract javax.servlet.jsp.JspWriter class is associated with a PrintWriter of a ServletResponse and is very similar in functionality. The JspWriter delegates print() and println() calls directly to the PrintWriter object if buffering for the page is deactivated. If page buffering is activated, the JspWriter will otherwise manage buffering before it delegates calls to the PrintWriter and handle correct throwing of exceptions. The JspContext enables you to obtain a handle to the JspWriter object, as well as pushing and popping a

JspWriter object onto and off a page scope stack. Similarly, the PageContext may be used to push and pop a special BodyContext type of JspWriter used to encapsulate that information evaluated inside the body of a JSP tag. Such concepts are discussed in more depth in the next chapter.

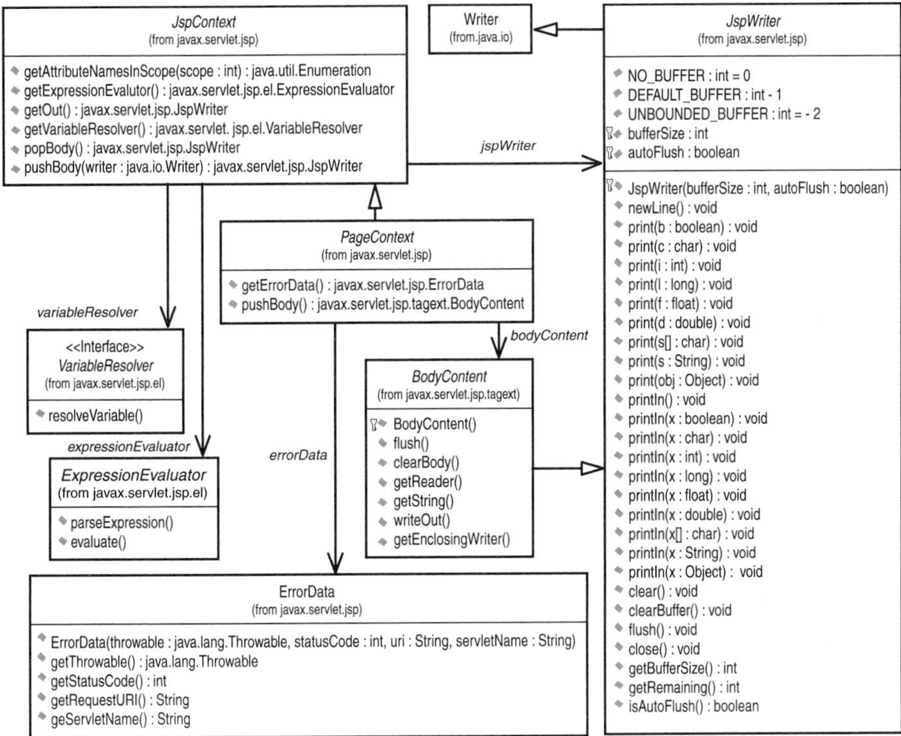

Figure 20.5 Additional JSP context services.

Finally, the page context may also be used to obtain a handle to an ErrorData object. Such an object encapsulates that information describing an error inside of an error-related page. Thus, for example, when in the context of displaying an error page to an end user, information such as the requesting URL, the name of the servlet that was requested, any error status code, and the associated exception may be obtain via an ErrorData object.

Implicit Objects

Many of the APIs presented in the preceding sections can be utilized from within a JSP page in the form of objects created by a JSP container. In fact, JSP containers create and expose such objects, as well as objects encapsulating many of the Java Servlet APIs such as request, response, and session objects. JSPs can use this standard suite of objects from within JSP scripting elements by referring to them with a standard object name. This section describes these standard implicit objects and describes the scope within a JSP in which they are valid.

Implicit objects are handles to objects created by the JSP container for use within JSPs. Implicit objects thus do not have to be declared or created by JSP developers, but rather can be assumed to exist from certain vantage points of execution within a JSP. These vantage points define the scope in which such implicit objects are usable by JSPs. Although each implicit object has its own JSP object name, each object also has an implicit type that maps to a particular class or interface after JSP-to-servlet translation. The class or interface to which the implicit object is mapped indicates those methods that can be invoked on the implicit object. All objects relate to a `String` ID name stored by the `PageContext` object that defines their scope and additional semantics as defined in an earlier section. The standard set of implicit JSP objects, their `PageContext` ID name, and their target translation type or super-type definition are defined in Table 20.1.

Table 20.1 **Implicit Objects, Their Names, and Their Types**

Object Name	`PageContext` ID	Type/Super-Type
`request`	`REQUEST`	`javax.servlet.ServletRequest`
`response`	`RESPONSE`	`javax.servlet.ServletResponse`
`out`	`OUT`	`javax.servlet.jsp.JspWriter`
`session`	`SESSION`	`javax.servlet.http.HttpSession`
`pageContext`	`PAGECONTEXT`	`javax.servlet.jsp.PageContext`
`page`	`PAGE`	`java.lang.Object`
`config`	`CONFIG`	`javax.servlet.ServletConfig`
`application`	`APPLICATION`	`javax.servlet.ServletContext`
`exception`	`EXCEPTION`	`javax.lang.Throwable`

Object Scope

The scope in which an object (such as an implicit object) is valid is defined in one of four ways. The way in which an object scope is defined directly relates to the valid types of object scope identified by `static` constant `int` values on the `PageContext` object, as described earlier. Each type of object scope indicates which type of implicit object is used to store an object in that scope. Table 20.2 reiterates each object scope type identified from a `PageContext` constant and the implicit object used to store objects in that scope.

Table 20.2 **Object Scope and Implicit Object Storage**

`PageContext` **Scope**	**Implicit Object Storage**
`PAGE_SCOPE`	`pageContext`
`REQUEST_SCOPE`	`request`
`SESSION_SCOPE`	`session`
`APPLICATION_SCOPE`	`application`

Scripting Elements

Scripting elements provide a convenient way for JSP pages to perform calculations or other actions to dynamically alter the content of the page. There are four basic types of scripting elements: declarations, scriptlets, expressions, and EL language expressions.

Declarations

Declarations are essentially the same as Java variable or method declarations. An object declared in a declaration block is available to all other scripting elements on that page. Declarations are defined within the `<%!` and `%>` character sequences. For example:

```
<%! Integer count = new Integer(0);  %>
```

Scriptlets

Scriptlets are segments of Java code embedded directly within a JSP page. A scriptlet is defined by placing code between the `<%` and `%>` character sequences. For example:

```
<%
   String firstName = pageContext.findAttribute("FIRST_NAME");
%>
```

A scriptlet can access any variable declared in a declaration block, and define new ones. Oftentimes, several scriptlets will appear on the same page. The code within these scriptlets is processed by the JSP sequentially, so it is possible to intersperse JSP markup code within an arbitrary Java statement. One situation in which this commonly occurs is within conditionals. For example:

```
<%
   ShoppingCart cart = session.getAttribute("SHOPPING_CART");
   if (cart.isEmpty())
   {
%>
Your cart is empty.<p>
<%
   }
%>
```

Expressions

Expressions provide a more convenient method to evaluate a Java expression and insert the result directly into the JSP output stream. Expressions that are to be evaluated in this fashion are placed between the <%= and %> character sequences. For example:

```
There are <%= cart.getNumItems() %> items in your cart.<br>
Total cost is $<%= cart.getTotal() %>
```

It is important to note that any expression contained within an expression block, as just shown, will be automatically cast to a `java.lang.String` by the JSP container. It will throw a translation-time error if it is known at translation time that such a casting operation will not be possible. Otherwise, a `ClassCastException` will be thrown at request time if the conversion fails.

EL Language Expressions

The JSP v2.0 specification has added a new expression language capable of performing scripting operations, called the JSP Expression Language, or simply EL. The motivation for EL was to provide a simpler, syntactically cleaner scripting language that would still be flexible enough to handle most common scripting tasks. It bears a resemblance to both ECMAScript and XPath. It has support for arithmetic and logical operators, user-defined functions, and a set of implicit objects.

EL expressions are of the form `${`*`expression`*`}`. For example:

```
Elapsed time is ${endTime - startTime} seconds
```

EL expressions can appear in the body of a JSP page, as in the preceding example, or as the value of a tag attribute, as shown here:

```
<jsp:include page="${pageName}" />
```

EL Implicit Objects

EL contains several implicit objects, which can be handy for writing expressions. They are similar in nature to the implicit objects defined on the JSP page itself, listed earlier. These are the EL implicit objects:

- `pageContext`: Contains the `PageContext` object.
- `pageScope`: A `java.util.Map` containing all the attribute-value pairs with page-level scope.
- `requestScope`: A `Map` containing all the attributes in the request scope.
- `sessionScope`: A `Map` of all the attributes contained in the session.
- `applicationScope`: A `Map` of all the attributes in the application scope.
- `param`: A `Map` of the parameter name-value pairs passed on the query string.
- `paramValues`: A `Map` that maps parameter names to a `String[]` of all the values defined for each parameter.

- `header`: A `Map` of request header names to their values.
- `headerValues`: A `Map` of request header names to a `String[]` of all the values defined for each header.
- `cookie`: A `Map` of cookie names to their corresponding `Cookie` objects.
- `initParam`: A `Map` of the servlet context initialization parameter name-value pairs.

Operators

EL contains a rich set of arithmetic, relational, and object access operators. The arithmetic operators `+`, `-`, `*`, `/`, and `%` work the same as in Java and most other languages. The keywords `div` and `mod` are synonyms for `/` and `%`, respectively. The relational operators also follow Java convention: `==`, `!=`, `<`, `>`, `<=`, and `>=` are available. The keywords `eq`, `ne`, `lt`, `gt`, `le`, and `ge` are synonymous with those operators and can be useful, particularly due to the special treatment of the `<` and `>` characters in JSP. Also, the logical operators `&&`, `||`, `!`, and their synonyms `and`, `or`, and `not` are defined. Finally, the prefix operator `empty` used before a variable returns a Boolean value of `true` if that variable is `null`, or is a string or collection of zero length.

Attributes of an object and elements of a collection can be accessed with the `.` and `[]` operators almost interchangeably, using a syntax similar to ECMAScript and XPath. For example,

```
${sessionScope.cart}
```

is equivalent to

```
${sessionScope["cart"]}
```

Functions

EL also provides the capability to call user-defined functions. The syntax for calling an EL function is of the following form:

```
${prefix:fname(arg1,..argN)}
```

For example:

```
Total Price is: ${beeshirts:moneyFormat(item_price)}
```

EL Functions are implemented in a Java class and are declared `public static` access. The method is then made accessible through the tag library descriptor, which is covered in the next chapter.

JSP Directives

As stated earlier in this chapter, JavaServer Pages provide a convenient way to add dynamic behavior to what ordinarily would be static HTML. JSP allows special commands to be embedded inline with formatted HTML code, which can be processed by the application server before returning a response. In this section, we introduce some of those special commands. JSP directives contain special processing instructions for the JSP container and are evaluated at page-compilation time. As the name suggests, JSP directives direct a JSP compiler in how it should translate and compile JSPs into Java Servlet implementation classes. Directives define data for ultimate use by a JSP container and do not directly affect the output of information to the client response stream. Directives are thus independent of any particular request to be processed. Directives are defined according to this general form:

```
<%@ DirectiveTypeName attribute1="value1" attribute2="value2" ... %>
```

Here, the *DirectiveTypeName* corresponds to the specific type of directives defined for the JSP v2.0 specification: `include`, `page`, and `taglib`. Each directive type has its own set of valid attributes that further define how the particular directive should be processed. Directives also have a special format for JSP documents that follows this form:

```
<jsp:directive.DirectiveTypeName attribute1="value1"
➥ attribute2="value2" ... />
```

`include` Directive

The `include` directive is used to insert a file into a JSP as the JSP is being translated into its implementation class. Files that can be included into a JSP may be a text file, an HTML file, or perhaps another JSP file. A JSP and its static include files are sometimes collectively referred to as a translation unit because they are all in the translation of JSPs. The `include` directive takes the form

```
<%@ include file="relativeURL" %>
```

where *relativeURL* refers to a file location relative to the location of the current JSP. For example:

```
<%-- Begins with '/', absolute URL rooted at application context --%>
<%@ include file="/sales/SalesTemplate.html" %>

<%-- Relative to current JSP file --%>
<%@ include file="CommonTopArea.jsp" %>
```

`page` Directive

One or more `page` directives are used to define information about a JSP file and any of its statically included files. JSP containers use `page` directives to determine the nature and characteristics of a JSP. A `page` directive has various standard attributes that can be defined only once in the JSP file and its static include files. The `import` attribute, however, can be defined more than once in the JSP translation unit. The valid `page` directive attributes are listed here:

- `language`: Specifies the type of scripting language that is used inside of the JSP. The only defined, required, and default value for this attribute in JSP v2.0 is `java` to indicate that Java-based language scripts will be used within the JSP.
- `extends`: Specifies a fully qualified class name of a superclass from which this JSP's implementation class is extended. This attribute should be used with caution and requires that the servlet superclass implement `service()`, `init()`, and `destroy()` methods appropriately for JSP processing as described later in this chapter.
- `import`: Specifies a comma-separated list of classes and packages used by the JSP. For Java-based scripting languages, this list is akin to Java `import` statements. The default and implicitly defined value is `java.lang.*, javax.servlet.*, javax.servlet.jsp.*, javax.servlet.http.*`.
- `session`: Specifies a value of `true` (the default) or `false` indicating whether this JSP participates in an HTTP session. If this value is `true`, the implicit scripting variable `session` is available and contains a reference to an instance of `javax.servlet.http.HttpSession` which represents the current session.
- `buffer`: Specifies the minimum buffer size to be allocated for containing output stream response data. If none is specified, all data is output directly to an underlying `ServletResponse PrintWriter`. Otherwise, a value of the form *n*`kb` designates that *n* kilobytes are to be used for buffering. The default is `8kb`.
- `autoFlush`: Specifies a value of `true` or `false` (the default is `true`) indicating whether the buffer should automatically be flushed when full. Otherwise, a buffer overflow exception will be thrown when the value is set to `false` and the buffer overflows.
- `isThreadSafe`: Specifies a value of `true` or `false` (the default is `true`) indicating whether the JSP is thread-safe. A value of `false` will induce the JSP container to dispatch client requests to JSPs one at a time by making the implementation class implement the `javax.servlet.SingleThreadModel` interface. A value of `true` will allow multiple requests to be dispatched to the JSP at a time, and the JSP therefore must provide thread safety.
- `info`: Specifies a string of information describing the JSP that relates to a call from `Servlet.getServletInfo()`.
- `errorPage`: Specifies a URL for a JSP that handles any `Throwable` exception objects that were uncaught by the current JSP page.
- `isErrorPage`: Specifies a value of `true` or `false` (the default is `false`) indicating whether the current JSP is the target of another JSP's `errorPage` attribute. If it is `true`, the implicit scripting variable `exception` is available and is set to the `Throwable` object that contains the error in question.
- `pageEncoding`: Specifies a character encoding for the JSP page. Must be an IANA standard name of a character encoding. The default is `ISO-8859-1`.

- `contentType`: Specifies a MIME type for the response of the JSP page and a character encoding for the JSP page and its response. Takes the form of either `MIMETYPE` or `MIMETYPE;charset=CHARSET`. The default MIME type is `text/html`, and the default charset is set to the value of `pageEncoding`, if present, or otherwise `ISO-8859-1`; for example, `text/html;charset=ISO-8859-1`.
- `isELIgnored`: Specifies whether Expression Language (EL) expressions that appear on this page are ignored by the container (`true`) or evaluated by the container (`false`). The default is `false` for a Servlet v2.4–compliant container, `true` otherwise.

Here are some examples of `page` directives:

```
<%-- Importing classes --%>
<%@ page import="java.util.Date, java.util.Enumeration" %>

<%-- Specify JSP page information and an error page --%>
<%@ page info="This JSP contains the BeeShirts.com root page"
        errorPage="ErrorDisplay.jsp" %>

<%-- Setting minimum buffer size and autoflushing --%>
<%@ page buffer="20kb" autoFlush="true" %>

<%-- Specify an output response type --%>
<%@ page contentType="text/plain;charset=UTF-8" %>
```

`taglib` Directive

JSP technology gives developers the ability to define special tags that can be used to extend the capabilities of a JSP page. These special tags are defined in a *tag library*. The `taglib` directive instructs the JSP compiler to include the given tag library into the current translation unit. The `taglib` directive essentially associates a prefix ID with a tag library location that is used by the JSP compiler. A `prefix` attribute is used to define the tag prefix ID that the JSP compiler should use to identify which tags in the JSP belong to an external library. The tag IDs `jsp`, `jspx`, `java`, `javax`, `servlet`, `sun`, and `sunw` are all reserved tag prefix IDs. A `uri` attribute is used to identify the location of the tag library as identified with the `prefix` attribute when parsing the JSP. Alternatively, the `tagdir` attribute can be used to specify a tag library installed in the standard `/WEB-INF/tags` directory tree. For example:

```
<%---  taglib directive using uri attribute --%>
<%@ taglib uri="http://www.beeshirts.com/tags" prefix="beeshirts" %>

<%---  taglib directive using tagdir attribute --%>
<%@ taglib tagdir="/WEB-INF/tags/ecommerce" prefix="beeshirts" %>
```

Thus, a tag library located at `http://www.beeshirts.com/tags` will be referenced whenever tags with the prefix of `beeshirts` are encountered in a JSP. The JSP document version of a `taglib` differs somewhat from the standard, in that a root `<jsp:root>` element of the JSP document is augmented with an `xmlns:` namespace definition attribute identifying the tag library like this:

```
<jsp:root ... xmlns:beeshirts="http://www.beeshirts.com/tags" ... >
   ...
</jsp:root>
```

Tag libraries are covered in much greater detail in Chapter 21, "JSP Tags."

JSP Examples

With an understanding of directives, scripting elements, and implicit objects, you are now armed with the knowledge you need in order to comprehend most of the BeeShirts.com JSPs. Listing 20.1, in fact, is a cohesive snapshot of code that composes the BeeShirts front-page JSP. You'll notice a healthy sprinkling of template data mixed with JSP code. The JSP code is processed on the server side and generates HTML, which, along with the predefined template data, is the HTML that is interpreted by the client-side Web browser.

Listing 20.1 **BeeShirts.com Home Page JSP (`BeeShirts.jsp`)**

```
<%@ page info="BeeShirts Page" import=
    "javax.naming.InitialContext, javax.naming.NamingException,
     ejava.jsp.JSPHelper"
%>

<HTML>
<HEAD>
  <TITLE>
    BeeShirts.com
  </TITLE>
</HEAD>
<BODY ALINK="#FFCC66"  BGCOLOR="#ffcc66" >
<%-- Add Error page to display Error --%>
<%@ page errorPage="ErrorDisplay.jsp" %>

<%-- Get the server information --%>
<% String serverInfo = JSPHelper.getServerInfo(request); %>

<%-- Display the Top and Left part of JSP --%>
<TABLE BORDER=0 COLS=2 WIDTH=\"100%\" >
 <TR>
   <%@ include file="BeeShirtsTopArea.jsp" %>
 </TR>
```

```
 <TR>
   <%@ include file="BeeShirtsLeftArea.jsp" %>

<%-- Create session object and obtain cookie value --%>
<%
  // Create a session each time the user comes to this site.
  boolean createNew = true;
  session =  request.getSession(createNew);
  // Check if it is the first time visiting and if has cookie
  Cookie[]  cookies = request.getCookies();
  String cookieValue = JSPHelper.getOurCookieValue(cookies);
  if(cookieValue != null){
     session.setAttribute(JSPHelper.COOKIE_NAME, cookieValue);
  }
%>
  <TD  VALIGN=TOP>
<%-- Print welcome message --%>
<%
  // If have cookie, then print welcome back message
  if(cookieValue != null){
     out.println("   <STRONG> WELCOME BACK : "
                  + cookieValue +"</STRONG> <BR>");
  }
  try{
    JSPHelper.initialContext = new InitialContext();
    String welcomeMessage =
      (String)JSPHelper.initialContext.
        lookup(JSPHelper.WELCOME_MESSAGE_ENV);
    // Print the root screen promo and welcome...
    out.println(welcomeMessage);
  }
  catch(NamingException namingException){
    namingException.printStackTrace();
  }
%>
  </TD>
</TR>
</TABLE>
</BODY>
</HTML>
```

After a page directive and some preliminary HTML, the BeeShirts JSP first makes a call to the `static` `getServerInfo()` method on a `JSPHelper` class used as a utility class with our examples. The `static` `JSPHelper.getServerInfo()` method simply extracts the server host name, server port, and context path from the request object and returns a formatted `String` of this information as shown here:

```
public static String getServerInfo(HttpServletRequest request)
{
  String serverHost = request.getServerName();
  int serverPort = request.getServerPort();
  String context = request.getContextPath();
  String protocol = "HTTP://";
  String serverInfo = protocol+serverHost+":"+serverPort+context;
  return serverInfo;
}
```

The returned `serverInfo String` from the `JSPHelper.getServerInfo()` method to the `BeeShirts` JSP is not actually used within the `BeeShirts.jsp` file, but it is in fact used by the included `BeeShirtsTopArea.jsp` and `BeeShirtsLeftArea.jsp` files. Because they are part of the same translation unit, they can refer to objects defined within parent JSPs such as the `BeeShirts` JSP.

The BeeShirts JSP then demonstrates how the `request` object can be used just like calls to an `HttpServletRequest` object, but now the call occurs within a JSP scriptlet. A handle to an `HttpSession` object is created and used to retrieve any `Cookie` values associated with the session. Recall from the preceding chapter that this same type of functionality was embedded within the `BeeShirtsServlet` class to extract the first name of a user stored in a `Cookie` if the user had previously visited the site. Any extracted cookie value is then used to display a personalized `WELCOME BACK` message.

Also recall from the preceding chapter that the `RegistrationServlet` added the personalized cookie to the response stream during registration of a user. This functionality is now embedded in the `DisplayRegistrationInformation` JSP. That portion of the `DisplayRegistrationInformation` JSP that creates a `Cookie` named `BEESHIRTS` with the value of the customer's first name is shown here:

```
<%-- Declare an easier-to-read reference to six months' time --%>
<%!
  private final int SIX_MONTHS_IN_SECONDS =  60*60*24*183;
%>

<%-- customer and address objects created above in this JSP --%>
<%
   // Set address onto customer object now
   customer.setAddress(address);

   // Get any cookie value named "BEESHIRTS" from chapter 32's
   // JSPHelper static constant COOKIE_NAME
   String cookieValue
       = (String)session.getAttribute(JSPHelper.COOKIE_NAME);

   // If no cookie, then add user's first name to cookie
   if(cookieValue == null){
     // create Cookie for this customer
```

```
        Cookie cookie = new Cookie(JSPHelper.COOKIE_NAME,
                                   customer.getFirstName());
        // Set maximum age of cookie
        cookie.setMaxAge(SIX_MONTHS_IN_SECONDS);
        // Now add the cookie to the response stream
        response.addCookie(cookie);
      }
      // Output the customer info to the HTML page as a table
      out.println(customer.getCustomerAsHTMLTable());
%>
```

After the BeeShirts JSP retrieves and prints any WELCOME BACK message stored in the cookie, note that it uses Web component environment settings as was the case with this JSP's servlet counterpart. The BeeShirts JSP creates a handle to an InitialContext object, which is then used to look up a named welcome message String object. The JSPHelper.WELCOME_MESSAGE_ENV constant maps to the java:comp/env/WelcomeMessage value in our example, which refers to an <env-entry> element in our web.xml deployment descriptor as shown here:

```
<env-entry>
  <description>
    Customizable description for the Application
  </description>
  <env-entry-name>WelcomeMessage</env-entry-name>
  <env-entry-value> A big welcome to our online T-Shirts shoppe.
       ...
  </env-entry-value>
  <env-entry-type>java.lang.String</env-entry-type>
</env-entry>
```

Finally, the BeeShirts JSP uses the out object to print any specialized WELCOME BACK message, as well as the message looked up from the JNDI java:comp/env/WelcomeMessage named environment entry.

As a final example of implicit object usage with exception handling, our ErrorDisplay.jsp standard error handler JSP, shown in Listing 20.2, uses the exception object to print the contents of the received exception, as well as a stack trace for the exception. Although exceptions are a rather ugly thing to display on a Web page, for our development purposes they can be very informational. We thus print such exception information in the ErrorDisplay JSP.

Listing 20.2 **BeeShirts.com Standard Error Page JSP** (ErrorDisplay.jsp)

```
<%@ page isErrorPage="true" import="java.io.*" %>

<HTML>
<HEAD>
  <TITLE>
```

```
    BeeShirts.com Error Display Page
  </TITLE>
</HEAD>
<BODY ALINK="#FFCC66"  BGCOLOR="#ffcc66" >

<TABLE BORDER=0 COLS=2 WIDTH=\"100%\" >
 <TR>
  <TD  VALIGN=TOP>
   Error occurred in accessed page :
   <%=exception%>
   and exception occurred in :
   <%exception.printStackTrace(new PrintWriter(out)); %>
  </TD>
</TR>
</TABLE>
</BODY>
</HTML>
```

Standard Actions

JSP standard actions define a set of operations that are to be performed as directed by a JSP using scripting language tags. JSP actions, in fact, are defined within JSPs using XML syntax and thus have no need to define a special XML-based representation. And unlike directives, which are processed at translation time, actions are processed at request time, which allows for dynamic behavior. Actions have a begin tag and an end tag, along with an action name to identify the specific type of action to be performed. Actions also can have a collection of name/value attribute pairs defined within the action. An optional body between the begin and end tags may contain other actions or parameters defined in terms of names and values. Using these standard actions, you can do the following:

- Obtain server-side JavaBean reference identifiers.
- Set properties on a server-side JavaBean.
- Get properties from a server-side JavaBean.
- Forward requests to other resources.
- Include responses from other resources.
- Embed applet and JavaBean tags into a page.

`<jsp:useBean>` Action

The standard `<jsp:useBean>` action element is used to associate a JavaBean object instance within a specified scope to an identifier. The identifier can then be used as an object reference to the newly retrieved object for subsequent method calls on the object. The `<jsp:useBean>` action first attempts to locate an object based on the value of an object identifier name, the type name, and the scope in which the object should be located. If it cannot find the specified object, a new object of a specified type will be created.

The `<jsp:useBean>` element has the following general form:

```
<jsp:useBean id="identifierName" scope="page|request|application|session"
          [   class="className"
            | type="typeName"
            | class="className" type="typeName"
            | beanName="beanName|<%= expression %>" type="typeName" ] />
```

Or if a body is to be associated with the action, we have this:

```
<jsp:useBean id="identifierName" scope="page|request|application|session"
          [   class="className"
            | type="typeName"
            | class="className" type="typeName"
            | beanName="beanName|<%= expression %>" type="typeName" ] >
    body
    ...
</jsp:useBean>
```

The `id` and `scope` attributes are individually specified, but the `class`, `type`, and `beanName` attributes must be defined according to one of the four combinations shown previously. The `jsp:useBean` attributes are defined here:

- `id`: A case-sensitive name value that is used to uniquely identify an object within a translation unit (that is, a JSP and its statically included pages). Is also synonymous with the name of the scripting variable that was declared with this object reference.
- `scope`: Specifies the scope in which the object defined by the `id` attribute can be found. The valid object scope values are of the type `page`, `request`, `session`, and `application`, as described in an earlier section. The `page` object scope is the default value.
- `class`: A case-sensitive fully qualified class name for the class of the object. If the object cannot be located, this class name will be used to instantiate an instance of the class with a public and parameterless constructor for the class.
- `beanName`: A case-sensitive fully qualified class name for location and possible instantiation of a JavaBean using the `java.beans.Beans.instantiate()` method. If the JavaBean is serialized, this name can be used to read a serialized form of the JavaBean with a class loader.
- `type`: A case-sensitive fully qualified name of the class, super-class of, or interface implemented by the class of the object. Allows for the distinct use of a special type with the object. If it's used with no `class` or `beanName` attribute, no object is newly instantiated.

If the object could not be located within the page context of the JSP, it may need to be instantiated by the container. If it has been instantiated instead of located, other elements within the body of the `<jsp:useBean>` element will be processed to initialize the object. Mainly, the `<jsp:setProperty>` action defined next is used in this context.

As an example of associating an object from a session scope to an identifier used to manage some system user information, we have the following sample cases:

```
<%-- Create object from class --%>
<jsp:useBean id="user"
             class="com.assuredtech.security.identity.User"
             scope="session" />

<%-- Create object from class in terms of other type --%>
<jsp:useBean id="user"
             class="com.assuredtech.security.identity.User"
             type="com.assuredtech.security.identity.Principal"
             scope="session" />

<%-- Create object from JavaBean name --%>
<jsp:useBean id="user"
             beanName="com.assuredtech.security.beans.User.ser"
             scope="session" />
```

`<jsp:setProperty>` Action

The standard `<jsp:setProperty>` action element is used to set the value of properties in a JavaBean object. A `<jsp:setProperty>` element has a name attribute that refers to the identifier of an object located or instantiated via a `<jsp:useBean>` action. Attributes are also defined that describe a mapping from named JSP request parameters to named JavaBean properties whose values are to be set.

The `<jsp:setProperty>` action element has the following general form:

```
<jsp:setProperty name="JavaBeanNameID"
    [  property="*"
     | property="JavaBeanPropertyName"
     | property="JavaBeanPropertyName"
         param="requestParameterName"
     | property="JavaBeanPropertyName"
         value="JavaBeanPropertyValue|<%= expression %>"] />
```

The `name` attribute is required, and the valid combinations of `property` attributes with `param` and `value` attributes are indicated in the preceding text. JavaBean properties that have types of `String`, `boolean/Boolean`, `byte/Byte`, `char/Character`, `int/Integer`, `long/Long`, `double/Double`, `float/Float`, `short/Short` or indexed arrays of these types can all be set using this action. The attributes of the `<jsp:setProperty>` element are as shown here:

- name: Contains the name of a JavaBean instance that has previously been defined within the id value of a <jsp:useBean> action element or some other element.
- property: Defined with a value that describes how named request parameter values can be used to set associated JavaBean property values. The property="*" form can be used to indicate that any named request parameters received by the current JSP are to be set into matching JavaBean properties that share the same name. The property="*propertyName*" form can be used to specifically designate the name of the JavaBean property that should be set.
- param: Contains the name of a request parameter to be used with a named property attribute value if the name of the JavaBean property differs from the name of the request parameter.
- value: Contains a value that will be used to directly set a JavaBean property named by the property attribute. The value can be a String form of the JavaBean property type or an expression to be evaluated.

For example, suppose we have already defined a user id from a <jsp:useBean> action as illustrated in the preceding example. We can populate the property values of this JavaBean from request information in one of the following ways:

```
<%--
     Populate with userName and password request info.
     Thus, the userName and password request parameters will be set
     onto the userName and password JavaBean properties.
--%>
<jsp:setProperty name="user" property="userName" />
<jsp:setProperty name="user" property="password" />

<%--
     Populate using different names from request object.
     Thus, the user and pwd request parameters will be passed
     into the userName and password JavaBean properties.
--%>
<jsp:setProperty name="user" property="userName" param="user"/>
<jsp:setProperty name="user" property="password" param="pwd"/>

<%--
    Populate with specific values.
    Thus, the userName and password JavaBean properties will
    be set with the specific tjefferson and UVA1819 values.
--%>
<jsp:setProperty name="user" property="userName" value="tjefferson"/>
<jsp:setProperty name="user" property="password" value="UVA1819"/>

<%--
    Populate with all request values that match.
```

```
    Thus, all of the request parameter values that match the JavaBean
    properties will be set onto those JavaBean properties.
--%>
<jsp:setProperty name="user" property="*" />
```

`<jsp:getProperty>` Action

The standard `<jsp:getProperty>` action element is used to retrieve the value of a named JavaBean property for display in a JSP. A `name` attribute identifies the JavaBean `id`, which needs to be previously established in the JSP by a `<jsp:useBean>` action. A `property` attribute refers to the name of the property on the JavaBean.

The `<jsp:getProperty>` action element has the following general form:

```
<jsp:getProperty name="JavaBeanNameID" property="JavaBeanPropertyName"/>
```

For example, using the same `user id` from a `<jsp:useBean>` action previously established, we have this:

```
<HTML>
  <BODY>
    Welcome back <jsp:getProperty name="user" property="userName" /> !
  </BODY>
</HTML>
```

`<jsp:include>` Action

The standard `<jsp:include>` action element is used to include the output response from another resource into the output from the current JSP. If the other resource is a static file, the content is simply included with the current output response. If the other resource generates a dynamic response, the request dispatched to that resource is used to generate the dynamic response, which is included in the current JSP's output response. The `<jsp:include>` name is used as the XML element name and can be used to define either an empty element or an element with start and end tags. If start and end tags are used, the element can be defined with one or more `<jsp:param>` sub-elements used to add parameters to the dispatched request object for use by resources that generate dynamic content. The URL of the resource to which the request will be dispatched is defined via the `page` attribute within the `<jsp:include>` element. There is also an optional `flush` attribute that specifies whether the response buffer is flushed prior to performing the inclusion. The default is `false`.

The general form of this action can be in either of these two forms:

```
<jsp:include page="targetURL|<%= expression %>" flush="true"/>


<jsp:include page="targetURL|<%= expression %>" flush="true">
  <jsp:param name="param1" value="param1Value|<%= expression %>" />
  <jsp:param name="param2" value="param2Value|<%= expression %>" />
```

```
    ...
</jsp:include>
```

For example:

```
<jsp:include page="<%= copyrightPage.getPageName() %>" />
```

<jsp:forward> Action

The standard `<jsp:forward>` action element is used to dispatch a request to another resource in the same Web application context, such as an HTML file, a JSP, or a servlet. The `jsp:forward` name is used as an XML element name and can be used to define either an empty element or an element with start and end tags. If start and end tags are used, the element can be defined with one or more `<jsp:param>` sub-elements used to add parameters to the forwarded request object. The relative URL of the resource to which the request will be dispatched is defined by the `page` attribute within the `<jsp:forward>` element. The `page` attribute can be defined in terms of a string or an expression that evaluates to a string and is described in terms of a URL relative to the JSP Web application context (if it begins with a `/`) or relative to the JSP file.

The general form of this action can be in either of these two forms:

```
<jsp:forward page="targetURL|<%= expression %>" />
```

```
<jsp:forward page="targetURL|<%= expression %>">
  <jsp:param name="param1" value="param1Value|<%= expression %>" />
  <jsp:param name="param2" value="param2Value|<%= expression %>" />
    ...
</jsp:forward>
```

For example:

```
<jsp:forward page="/OrderStatus" />
```

```
<jsp:forward page="/CustomerService/Feedback">
  <jsp:param name="user" value="pperrone" />
  <jsp:param name="email" value="pperrone@assuredtech.com" />
  <jsp:param name="message" value="Help Me!" />
</jsp:forward>
```

<jsp:param> Action

The `<jsp:param>` sub-element is used to define name-value pairs that have meaning specific to an enclosing action element. This element may be used only within a `<jsp:include>`, a `<jsp:forward>`, or the `<jsp:params>` sub-element of `<jsp:plugin>` (described below). Names and values are defined as case-sensitive attributes of the `<jsp:param>` element. The value attribute can be either a string value or an expression evaluating to a string value. The <jsp:param> sub-element has the following general form:

```
<jsp:param name="paramName" value="paramValue|<%= expression %>" />
```

See the previous example for usage of the <jsp:param> element.

<jsp:plugin> Action

The standard <jsp:plugin> action element is used to embed a JavaBean or Java applet within a JSP response page. When the JSP response is received by the Web client browser, the browser is directed to utilize the Java Plug-in technology in order to activate and display the JavaBean or Java applet. The <jsp:plugin> element handles the correct formatting and insertion of either OBJECT tags or EMBED tags as appropriate, depending on the Web client's particular browser requirements. The attributes defined within the <jsp:plugin> element either are derived from or directly map to attributes defined within the standard HTML APPLET and OBJECT tags. Furthermore, two sub-elements of the <jsp:plugin> element are used to define JavaBean or Java applet parameters and alternative text displays. The first, <jsp:params>, contains a set of nested <jsp:param> elements that define the parameters to be passed to the plug-in. The other, <jsp:fallback>, is used to define content to be used by the Web client if it is unable to load or run the plug-in for some reason.

The <jsp:plugin> action element has the following general form:

```
<jsp:plugin
    type="bean|applet"
    code="componentClassName"
    codebase="codebaseURL"
    [ archive="commaSeparatedListOfJARs" ]
    [ name="componentInstanceName" ]
    [ width="widthInPixels" ]
    [ height="heightInPixels" ]
    [ align="bottom|top|middle|left|right" ]
    [ hspace="spaceLeftAndRightInPixels" ]
    [ vspace="spaceAboveAndBelowInPixels" ]
    [ jreversion="majorAndMinorVersionOfJRE" ]
    [ nspluginurl="NetscapeNavigatorPluginURL" ]
    [ iepluginurl="InternetExplorerPluginURL" ]
    [ mayscript="true|false" ]
>

        [ <jsp:params>
          [ <jsp:param name="parameterName"
                       value="parameterValue|<%= expression %>" />
            <jsp:param name="parameterName"
                       value="parameterValue|<%= expression %>" />
                ...
```

```
            ]
            </jsp:params>
        ]

        [ <jsp:fallback>
              Alternative message if failed to load
          </jsp:fallback>
        ]

</jsp:plugin>
```

The code, codebase, archive, name, width, height, align, hspace, vspace, and mayscript attributes of the jsp:plugin element all directly map to attributes of the HTML OBJECT tag. Additionally, the remaining attributes of a jsp:plugin element are defined here:

- type: Indicates whether the component is a JavaBean or Java applet.
- jreversion: Defines the version number of the JRE that this component requires to run. The value of 1.2 is the default and refers to the JRE v1.2.
- nspluginurl: Defines the URL from where the Netscape Navigator JRE plug-in can be downloaded. The default is dependent on the particular implementation of JSP.
- iepluginurl: Defines the URL from where the Internet Explorer JRE plug-in can be downloaded. The default is dependent on the particular implementation of JSP.

The body for the <jsp:plugin> action element can also define a <jsp:params> element that contains one or more <jsp:param> elements. Each <jsp:param> element then defines the name and value of parameters used to initialize the Java applet or JavaBean. This is, of course, akin to the PARAM tags within an APPLET tag. Finally, the <jsp:fallback> element within the <jsp:plugin> element can be used to display an alternative text message if the Java applet or JavaBean cannot be loaded in the Web client's browser. This is similar to the ALT attribute of an APPLET tag or to any text added within the body of an APPLET tag.

For example:

```
<jsp:plugin
    type="applet" code="com.beeshirts.MyApplet.class" codebase="."
    archive="MyApplet.jar" name="MyGloriousApplet" jreversion="1.2"
    width="400" height="300" align="middle" vspace="10" hspace="10"
    nspluginurl="http://java.sun.com/products/plugin/1.2/
➥plugin-install.html"
    iepluginurl=" http://java.sun.com/products/plugin/1.2.2/
➥jinstall-1_2_2-win.cab#Version=1,2,2,0"
>
  <jsp:params>
```

```
    <jsp:param name="sample_value" value="123" />
  </jsp:params>
  <jsp:fallback>
    Cannot load Java Applet.
  </jsp:fallback>
</jsp:plugin>
```

`<jsp:attribute>` Action

The `<jsp:attribute>` element is used to define the value of an attribute for either a standard or a custom tag action. It may only appear as a sub-element of another action. The name attribute indicates the name of the attribute being defined, and the body contains the value of the attribute. The optional `trim` attribute can be used to indicate whether leading or trailing whitespace in the body should be discarded during translation time. The default is `true`. For an example of usage, look at the description of the `<jsp:element>` that follows.

`<jsp:body>` Action

The `<jsp:body>` action is a sub-element used to explicitly declare the body of a standard or custom action. Its use is required if a `<jsp:attribute>` sub-element is present, and a non-empty body needs to be declared. The `<jsp:body>` element accepts no attributes. See the examples for the `<jsp:element>` in the following text for a usage example.

`<jsp:element>` Action

The `<jsp:element>` action can be used to insert a dynamically generated XML element into the current page output. The body of this standard action can be empty, in which case an empty XML element will be created. If the body is present, it will form the body of the new element. Any attributes of the resulting XML element must be declared using `<jsp:attribute>` sub-elements, and if so, the body must be defined explicitly with a `<jsp:body>` sub-element. The `<jsp:element>` action has one mandatory attribute, name, which defines the name of the resulting XML element.

For example,

```
<jsp:element name="user">
  <jsp:attribute name="username">${user.name}</jsp:attribute>
  <jsp:body>${user.info}</jsp:body>
</jsp:element>
```

creates a simple XML element, `<user>`, which has a `username` attribute and a body containing some information about that user.

As another example,

```
<jsp:element name="date">${currentDate}</jsp:element>
```

creates a `<date>` element whose body contains the date stored in the variable `currentDate`.

Finally,

```
<jsp:element name="${element.name}"/>
```

illustrates creating an empty XML element whose name is the value of `element.name`.

`<jsp:text>` Action

The `<jsp:text>` action is used to enclose template data inside a tag. The standard action simply sends the body contents of the tag to the `out` object. The action has no attributes, and may not contain any sub-elements. The enclosed text may contain expressions. For example:

```
<jsp:text>
   Welcome back, ${user.name}
</jsp:text>
```

Although this tag can be used on JSP pages, its primary usefulness is in the context of JSP documents, where all elements must conform to strict XML syntax.

`<jsp:output>` Action

The `<jsp:output>` action is legal only within the context of a JSP document. Its purpose is to set certain properties of the output of a JSP document. In JSP v2.0, the only property that `<jsp:output>` can modify is whether an XML declaration is to be generated at the beginning of the output document. The tag's body must be empty, and it defines one optional attribute, `omit-xml-declaration`, whose value can be one of `true`, `false`, `yes`, or `no`. If the JSP document contains a `<jsp:root>` element, the default value is `yes`; otherwise, it is `no`.

Other Standard Actions

A few other standard actions that are part of JSP v2.0 should be mentioned here, although we will not cover them in detail. These are actions that are used only in JSP documents, or are used only in Tag Files, which we will discuss in the next chapter.

To completely describe a JSP page as an XML document, there are four additional standard actions besides the ones just described. They are `<jsp:root>`, `<jsp:declaration>`, `<jsp:scriptlet>`, and `<jsp:expression>`. The `<jsp:root>` element can appear only as the root element of a JSP document, and its purpose is to indicate to the processor that the document is in XML format, and is not a regular JSP page. Its one required attribute is `version`, which contains the JSP version number of the document ("2.0"). Any namespaces used in the document should also be declared with `xmlns` attributes in this element. The `<jsp:declaration>`, `<jsp:scriptlet>`, and `<jsp:expression>` actions serve to represent JSP declarations, scriptlets, and expressions within the XML document.

Two additional actions, `<jsp:invoke>` and `<jsp:doBody>`, are valid only within the context of Tag Files. Tag Files are new with the JSP v2.0 specification, and we will defer further discussion of these elements until Chapter 21.

Standard Action Examples

The `CheckOut` JSP provides a good example of a JSP making effective use of the `<jsp:forward>` standard action. As Listing 20.3 demonstrates, the `CheckOut` JSP first attempts to retrieve a `Customer` object from the session. If no `Customer` object is retrieved, the client is redirected to the `Registration` JSP. Subsequently, a `ShoppingCart` object is looked up in the session object. If no `ShoppingCart` is present, the client is redirected to the `BrowseShirts` JSP; otherwise, it's redirected to the `Cart` JSP.

Listing 20.3 **Check Out JSP (`CheckOut.jsp`)**

```
<%@ page info="BeeShirts.com Browse Shirts Page"
  import=" ejava.jsp.JSPHelper,
           ejava.servlets.Customer,
           ejava.servlets.ShoppingCart,
           java.util.Vector "  %>
<HTML>
<HEAD>
  <TITLE>
    BeeShirts.com
  </TITLE>
</HEAD>

<BODY ALINK="#FFCC66"  BGCOLOR="#ffcc66" >

<%
  // Get stored customer session information
   Customer customer = (Customer)session.getAttribute("customer");


   // If no stored customer info, redirect to Registration JSP
   if(customer == null){
%>
    <jsp:forward page="<%=JSPHelper.REGISTRATION_PAGE%>" />
<%
   }

   // Get stored shopping cart information
   ShoppingCart cart =
     (ShoppingCart)session.
```

```
        getAttribute(ShoppingCart.SHOPPING_CART_OBJECT);

   // If no stored cart info, redirect to BrowseShirts JSP
   if(cart == null){
%>
     <jsp:forward page="<%=JSPHelper.BROWSE_SHIRTS_PAGE%>" />
<%
   }
   else{ // Else redirect to Cart JSP
%>
     <jsp:forward page="<%=JSPHelper.CART_PAGE%>" />
<%
   }
%>
```

As another example, recall from our earlier illustration of standard JSP objects that the `DisplayRegistrationInformation` JSP used `Customer` and `Address` objects to set a cookie value into the client response object. The means by which the `DisplayRegistrationInformation` JSP retrieved these `Customer` and `Address` object references was via `<jsp:useBean>` actions. Because the `Customer` and `Address` objects are JavaBeans, we can also set properties onto these values. We set request parameters received from the `POST` created by the `RegistrationForm` JSP onto the `Customer` and `Address` properties as shown here:

```
<%-- Get handle to a Customer JavaBean --%>
<jsp:useBean id="customer"
  class="ejava.servlets.Customer"
  scope="session" >
  <jsp:setProperty name="customer" property="firstName"  />
  <jsp:setProperty name="customer" property="lastName"  />
  <jsp:setProperty name="customer" property="middleName"  />
  <jsp:setProperty name="customer" property="email"  />
  <jsp:setProperty name="customer" property="phone"  />
  <jsp:setProperty name="customer" property="password"  />
</jsp:useBean>

<%-- Get handle to an Address JavaBean --%>
<jsp:useBean id="address"
  class="ejava.servlets.Address"
  scope="session" >
  <jsp:setProperty name="address" property="address_1"  />
  <jsp:setProperty name="address" property="address_2"  />
  <jsp:setProperty name="address" property="city"  />
  <jsp:setProperty name="address" property="state"  />
  <jsp:setProperty name="address" property="zipCode"  />
</jsp:useBean>
```

JSP Configuration and Deployment

As we stated in the beginning of the chapter, JSPs are essentially text markup pages that will get translated into Java Servlets, which will then be deployed to the container. With JSP, most of the deployment work is done by the translator and container, so it is often the case that simple JSP applications will require no manual editing of the deployment descriptor. However, there are a few additional elements defined in the web.xml to customize JSP applications.

<jsp-config> Element

Most of the configuration options for JSP are contained within the <jsp-config> element. More specifically, most of the configuration is specified by one of its two sub-elements, <jsp-property-group> and <taglib>.

The <taglib> element is used to map a canonical name for a custom tag library to its location. The sub-element <taglib-uri> contains a URI that acts as the canonical name for the library, and the sub-element <taglib-location> specifies the path to the library, relative to the root of the application context. Tag libraries are covered more thoroughly in the next chapter.

The <jsp-property-group> element contains sub-elements that can configure various properties of a JSP or a group of JSPs. Table 20.3 lists the sub-elements with a brief description of their function:

Table 20.3 <jsp-property-group> **Sub-elements**

Element	Description
<url-pattern>	Specifies a pattern to match against all incoming URLs. All settings contained in this property group will be applied to JSPs matching the given URL pattern.
<el-ignored>	Is identical to the isELIgnored attribute of the page directive.
<page-encoding>	Is identical to the pageEncoding attribute of the page directive.
<scripting-invalid>	Disables all scripting elements on the group of JSP pages if set to true. The default is false.
<is-xml>	Indicates that the group of pages are JSP documents, written with XML syntax instead of the more typical JSP syntax. The default is false.
<include-prelude>	Specifies the path to a resource that will be included (as if by an include directive) at the beginning of each JSP page in this group.
<include-coda>	Is similar to <include-prelude>, but includes the resource at the end of the page.

The following snippet illustrates usage of the <jsp-config> element within a deployment descriptor:

```
<jsp-config>
   <jsp-property-group>
      <url-pattern>/beeshirts/*</url-pattern>
      <el-ignored>false</el-ignored>
      <include-prelude>/include/header.jsp</include-prelude>
      <include-coda>/include/footer.jsp</include-coda>
   </jsp-property-group>
   <jsp-property-group>
      <url-pattern>/beeshirts/checkout/*</url-pattern>
      <scripting-invalid>true</scripting-invalid>
   </jsp-property-group>
</jsp-config>
```

`<jsp-file>` Element

The `<jsp-file>` element contains the full path to a JSP file that is to be included as part of the Web application. This element is very rarely needed, because the JSP container will generate this information implicitly from the files that it finds in its Web application context. As an example:

```
<jsp-file>/include/header.jsp</jsp-file>
```

JSP Application Organization and Deployment

As we have said, JSPs are a part of the J2EE Web application standard, and they follow all the standard conventions. They can be configured using the standard `web.xml` deployment descriptor, as you have just seen. As for the files themselves, they are simply placed at the root level of the Web application context, or in any subdirectory, excluding the `WEB-INF` directory, which is reserved for meta-information. This collection of files, along with the `WEB-INF` directory, can then be bundled into a WAR file and deployed to any J2EE-compliant application server.

When the Web application is deployed to the application server, several things happen. Although the specific details of deploying an application will vary from server to server, the fundamental principles are the same. When the server starts up, it will first find the deployed Web application, whether it is deployed in its "exploded" directory format or as a WAR file. It will typically register an application context corresponding to the name of that directory or WAR file. So if our application was bundled into a file called `beeshirts.WAR`, the application context would be `/beeshirts`.

After the application server has started up and the application has deployed, nothing really happens until a page is actually requested. At this point, the requested JSP, and any included JSPs, will be translated by the server's JSP compiler into Java source code files, which will then in turn be compiled by `javac` into the servlet classes that will actually service the request. This has some practical considerations worth noting. The first is that there is typically a substantial performance hit the first time a page is accessed. The second is that translation-time errors on a page are not discovered until the page is requested. To address these issues, some application server vendors and other third parties will supply tools that allow JSPs to be precompiled.

After the JSPs are compiled and running, they do not need to be compiled again unless a JSP file is changed. Different application servers handle this situation in different ways. Some require the server to be stopped and restarted. Others, and certainly most of the more common commercial servers, will automatically detect changes and recompile as needed. This feature also has its merits and disadvantages. It can be a convenient time-saving feature during development and testing of an application. In a high-availability production environment, however, there is an inherent risk, because it cannot be told with 100% certainty that the new file will work with the currently running files until a user actually requests that page and forces it to be recompiled. Thus, many people believe that a Web application should consist of all its elements and dependencies, and should always be deployed all together. This is one of the motivating design factors behind the application context model and the WAR file format.

Conclusions

JavaServer Pages (JSPs) provide a Web programmer–friendly means to Web-enable enterprise applications. JSPs enable direct embedding of HTML template data into server-side Web documents and use of a syntax that is more familiar to Web-oriented developers and to developers who may be less familiar with enterprise-class Java programming. The use of actions, tags, and implicit objects from directly within the JSP provides the Web developer with a more familiar script-based programming environment. However, arbitrarily complex Java code can also be inserted into JSPs as a scripting language and thus provides added benefit to those developers who know Java and want to mix its more powerful syntax with the simplicity of creating JSPs. And as you will see in the next chapter, the functionality of JSP tags can be greatly extended through the use of custom tags.

21

JSP Tags

In the preceding chapter, you saw how a few standard JSP actions can be used to make writing JSPs an easier task and more natural to developers used to writing scripting language–based Web-enabling code. JSP actions encapsulate a set of operations that are implemented behind the scenes in Java code. Such actions can then be used to provide a simple set of scripting tags and attributes describing an action to be performed. JSP also defines a mechanism for extending the capability of JSP actions by providing a mechanism to create your own custom actions and tags. This chapter describes such JSP tag extension mechanisms and how to use them for extending the functionality available to JSP-based applications.

In this chapter, you will learn:

- The core class architecture of JSP tag extensions.
- The life cycle of a custom tag object inside of a JSP container.
- The basic approach to implementing custom tags.
- The abstractions behind obtaining meta-data information about JSP tags and tag libraries.
- A simpler approach to implementing JSP custom tags and use of JSP fragments.
- The structure and nature of JSP tag files.
- Methods for providing custom JSP tag library validation.
- The packaging and deployment of custom tags into Tag Libraries.

Tag Extension Architecture

JSP actions defined in terms of a begin tag, attributes, an optional body, and an end tag can be implemented using a set of special Java classes and interfaces. A set of custom classes that extend these abstractions is then inserted into a class archive referred to as a tag library. Such libraries can be configured at deployment time and referenced from within JSPs using `taglib` directives. The custom classes are referred to as tag handlers and are simple nonvisible JavaBean components that implement a special tag handling interface contract. A JSP container can create or locate tag handler objects whenever an associated action is defined in the JSP. The JSP 2.0 specification, which is part of J2EE v1.4, defines a set of tag extension abstractions and how they are used with tag libraries, tag library descriptor files, and `taglib` directives to extend the functionality available to JSP-based applications.

A few core abstractions from the `javax.servlet.jsp.tagext` package are used to create custom tag extensions. To create a custom tag handler, you must implement the `Tag`, `IterationTag`, or `BodyTag` interface. There is also a `SimpleTag` interface, which is discussed later in the chapter. The API also provides two default implementation classes, `TagSupport` and `BodyTagSupport`, which serve as convenient base classes for custom tag implementations. Figure 21.1 and Figure 21.2 depict these key tag extension abstractions and how they relate to custom tag handlers.

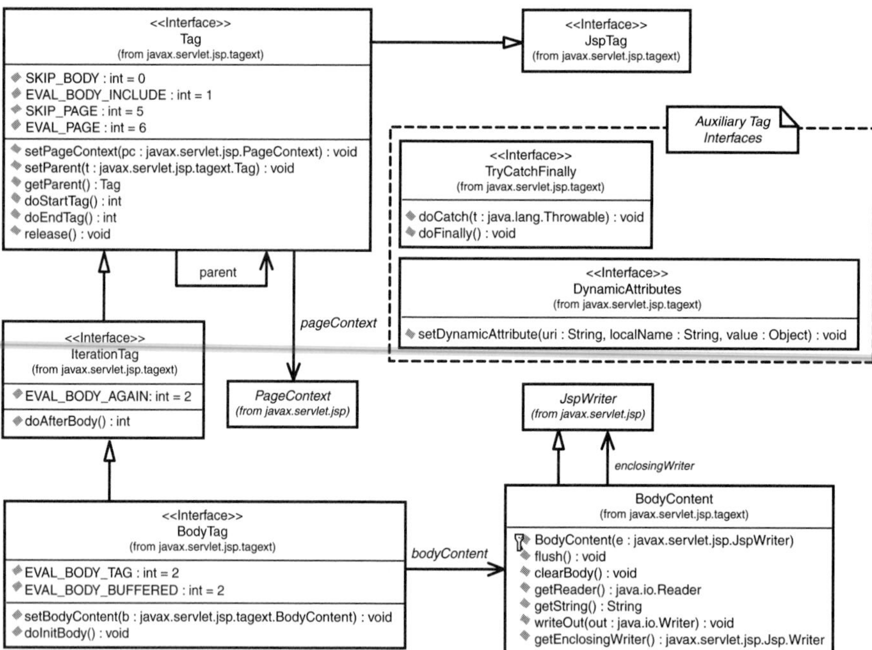

Figure 21.1 JSP custom tag extension interfaces.

The `Tag` interface defines a set of basic operations called by the container to manage a custom action defined within a JSP. A container will first set a `PageContext` object and any parent tags onto the `Tag` implementation when the container encounters an associated custom tag in the JSP. Any attributes of the custom action are then set through JavaBean methods implemented by the tag handler. The container then calls doStartTag() when it wants the tag handler to begin processing an action. A call to doEndTag() occurs when the container processes the end tag in the JSP. The TagSupport class is a utility class with some helper methods that can also be directly extended by a custom tag handler instead of implementing the Tag interface.

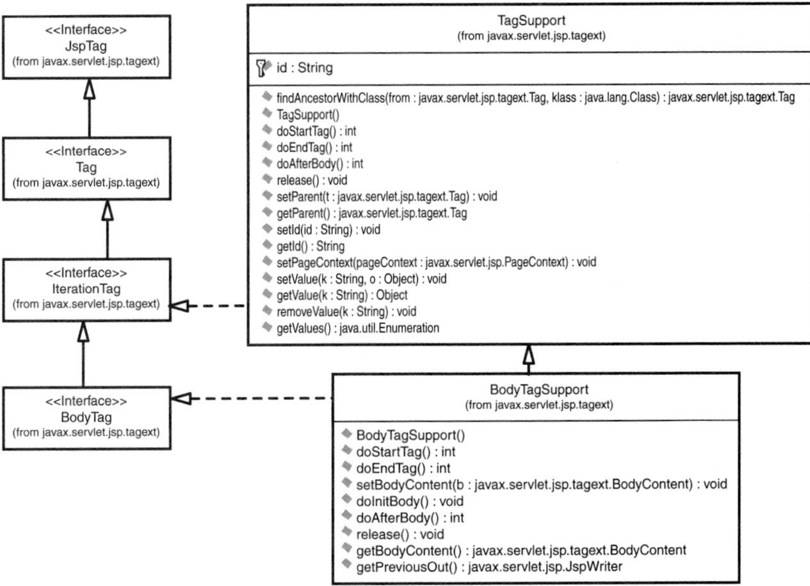

Figure 21.2 JSP custom tag extension classes.

The BodyTag interface is used when a custom action wants to process and/or modify the body contents of the tag. The tag is started by a call to doStartTag(). If doStartTag() returns the value EVAL_BODY_BUFFERED, the container calls the setBodyContent() method with a handle to a BodyContent object. The BodyContent object can be used to read the body data that has been output to an output stream by the container. The doInitBody() method is then called by the container to ask the tag handler to begin evaluating the body that is output to the output stream. The container then calls doAfterBody() as parts of the body are evaluated. The BodyTagSupport class is a utility class that implements the BodyTag interface and can also be extended by custom body tag handlers.

Tag Life Cycle

Although there are several variations of custom tags, they are all processed in the same general manner by the container. When the JSP container encounters a tag, it does the following:

- Invokes the zero-argument constructor on the Tag implementation.
- Sets the `pageContext` implicit variable, and calls bean setters for all tag attributes.
- Calls the `doStartTag()` method, which can return one of several values.
- If `EVAL_BODY_BUFFERED` is returned, the `setBodyContent()` method will be called, immediately followed by `doInitBody()`. This method is where the tag should initialize any scripting variables or otherwise preprocess the body of the tag. The body is then evaluated, and `doAfterBody()` is called. The body will be reevaluated each time `doAfterBody()` returns `EVAL_BODY_AGAIN`, which implements an iterative tag.
- If `EVAL_BODY_INCLUDE` is returned, the body is evaluated and passed directly through to the current `out` object, and then `doAfterBody()` is called. For an iterative tag, this method can return the value `EVAL_BODY_AGAIN`, which will cause the body evaluation process to repeat.
- When `SKIP_BODY` is returned by either `doAfterBody()` or `doStartTag()`, the `doEndTag()` method is called. At this time any data that has not yet been sent will be written to the `pageContext`'s `JspWriter` for display.
- When the container frees the tag from memory, the `release()` method is called to give the implementation a chance to do any cleanup.

Custom Tag Implementations

As discussed, the `javax.servlet.jsp.tagext` package provides default implementation classes for the `IterationTag` and `BodyTag` interfaces, in `TagSupport` and `BodyTagSupport`, respectively. Most custom tag implementations will extend one of these classes, overriding the default methods where needed.

The `TagSupport` class provides the most basic tag features. It is typically used to implement empty-body tags that simply perform some action, or tags that may contain a body but do not want to modify the contents of the body. However, because `TagSupport` does implement `IterationTag`, a non-empty body can be repeatedly processed as long as `doAfterBody()` returns `EVAL_BODY_AGAIN`. The base class implementation returns `SKIP_BODY`.

> **Note**
>
> See Appendix A, "Software Configuration," on this book's CD, for details on locating and installing the example code for this chapter. All the example code for this chapter is extracted to the `examples/src/ejava/jsp` and `examples/src/ejava/jsp/tagext` directories. In addition, a JSP v2.0-compliant Web application server is required to run the sample code. Instructions on building and deploying the samples on several of the most popular application servers are also given in Appendix A.

The `BodyTagSupport` class extends `TagSupport` and implements `BodyTag`, and serves as the base class for tag implementations that want to modify the contents of the tag body. Listing 21.1 shows an implementation of a custom tag that performs an iterative task, and adds scripting variables to the body of the tag.

Listing 21.1 **Custom Tag Implementation (`CartItemsTag.java`)**

```
package ejava.jsp.tagext;

import ejava.servlets.Item;
import ejava.servlets.ShoppingCart;
import ejava.servlets.TShirt;

import java.io.IOException;
import java.util.Vector;

import javax.servlet.jsp.JspException;
import javax.servlet.jsp.tagext.BodyTagSupport;
import javax.servlet.jsp.tagext.IterationTag;

public class CartItemsTag extends BodyTagSupport
{
    private int count;
    private ShoppingCart cart;
    private Vector items;

    public CartItemsTag()
    {
    }

    /**
     *  Called by the container when the start tag is processed, but
     *  before any body contents have been read
     */
    public int doStartTag() throws JspException
    {
        // returning EVAL_BODY_BUFFERED will cause
        // doInitBody() to be invoked before the first
        // pass through the body of the tag
        return BodyTagSupport.EVAL_BODY_BUFFERED;
    }

    /**
     *  Called when the closing tag is read
     */
    public int doEndTag() throws JspException
    {
        return BodyTagSupport.EVAL_PAGE;
    }
```

Listing 21.1 **Continued**

```
    /**
     *  Initializes the values that will be dynamically
     *  inserted into the body of the tag
     */
    public void doInitBody() throws JspException
    {
       count = 0;
       cart = (ShoppingCart)pageContext.findAttribute
            (ShoppingCart.SHOPPING_CART_OBJECT);
       items = cart.getItems();

        // initialize scripting variables for display on page
        setScriptingVariables();
    }

    /**
     *  Called after each successive processing of the body contents
     */
    public int doAfterBody() throws JspException
    {

        // then increment counter
        count++;

        // and decide to continue iterating or not
        if (count < items.size())
        {
            setScriptingVariables();
            return BodyTagSupport.EVAL_BODY_AGAIN;
        }
        else
        {
           // after all iterations are complete, send the whole thing
           try
            {
                System.out.println(bodyContent.getString());
                bodyContent.writeOut(bodyContent.getEnclosingWriter());
            }
            catch (IOException e)
            {
            }
            // and continue on with the rest of the page
            return BodyTagSupport.SKIP_BODY;
        }
    }
```

Listing 21.1 **Continued**

```
    private void setScriptingVariables()
    {
        if (count >= items.size())
            return;

        TShirt shirt = (TShirt)items.get(count);

        pageContext.setAttribute("item_id",
                                 new Integer(shirt.getItemID()));
        pageContext.setAttribute("item_quantity",
                                 new Integer(shirt.getQuantity()));
        pageContext.setAttribute("item_price",
                                 new Float(shirt.getTotalPrice()));
        pageContext.setAttribute("item_unit_price",
                                 new Float(shirt.getUnitPrice()));
        pageContext.setAttribute("item_size", shirt.getSize());
        pageContext.setAttribute("item_color", shirt.getColor());
        pageContext.setAttribute("item_design_front",
                                 shirt.getDesignFront());
        pageContext.setAttribute("item_design_back",
                                 shirt.getDesignBack());
        pageContext.setAttribute("item_front_image",
                                 shirt.getPictureFrontFileName());
        pageContext.setAttribute("item_back_image",
                                 shirt.getPictureBackFileName());

    }

    /**
     *  Called when this tag exits to free any resources
     */
    public void release()
    {
        cart = null;
        items = null;
    }
}
```

Listing 21.1 illustrates the workings of the custom tag API. As described earlier, the container will first call `doStartTag()` on this object, followed immediately by `doInitBody()`, because `EVAL_BODY_BUFFERED` was returned. The implementation prepares itself to process the tag, which in this case will display all the items in a shopping cart. It then sets the scripting variables to their initial values for the first pass through the tag body.

After each pass through the body, `doAfterBody()` is called, and the scripting variables are set to their next values, if there are any more elements in the list left to process. Returning `EVAL_BODY_AGAIN` displays the next element, and `SKIP_BODY` is returned when processing is finished. Finally, `doEndTag()` is called and the rest of the JSP page is processed.

`TryCatchFinally` Interface

Custom tags, like all other software components, sometimes will cause, and will need to deal with, unexpected conditions or exceptions. Although many of the exceptions that a custom tag implementation could generate can be caught and handled by the tag itself, there remains a wide variety of exceptions that can be thrown inside the container-generated Java code that makes up the actual page implementation. JSP v2.0 provides the `TryCatchFinally` interface to give custom tags the opportunity to handle unexpected exceptions without needing to supply any details about the underlying implementation classes.

The `TryCatchFinally` interface defines two methods: `doCatch()` and `doFinally()`. If a `Throwable` occurs during the tag's body evaluation, or inside the `doStartTag()`, `doEndTag()`, `doAfterBody()`, or `doInitBody()` methods of a custom tag, the container will trap the `Throwable` error and pass it back to the tag as the argument to `doCatch()`. At this time, the implementing tag can deal with the condition, or rethrow the same or another `Throwable`.

The `doFinally()` method is called from within the `finally` block of the calling page's `try-catch-finally` block. Under ordinary circumstances, `doFinally()` will be called after `doEndTag()`. If an exception has occurred, it will be called after `doCatch()` has been called. The custom tag implementation should perform all necessary cleanup and resource deallocation within this method.

Dynamic Attributes

Another feature of custom tags is the capability to accept dynamic attributes. Dynamic attributes are tag attributes whose names are determined only at runtime. This allows greater flexibility when using the tag on a JSP page, because the attribute names can be generated through a `<jsp:attribute>` tag on the page. Of course, the trade-off is greater risk, because there is less that can be validated during translation.

Tags that are willing to accept dynamic attributes need to implement the `DynamicAttributes` interface. It contains one method, `setDynamicAttribute()`, which takes as arguments a URI corresponding to the namespace the attribute belongs to (or `null` if the default), the local name of the attribute, and finally an `Object` representing the value of the attribute. In addition, the tag library descriptor must indicate that this tag accepts dynamic attributes (tag library descriptors are covered later in the chapter). The container will call this method once for each attribute in a tag invocation that has not been explicitly declared in the TLD. It is then the responsibility of the tag implementation to manage the names and values of its dynamic attributes.

Listing 21.2 shows a simple custom tag that illustrates the use of the `TryCatchFinally` and the `DynamicAttributes` interfaces. The tag prints the names and values of the attributes that get passed to it, and also contains simple implementations of the `doCatch()` and `doFinally()` methods.

Listing 21.2 **Tag Supporting** `DynamicAttributes` **and** `TryCatchFinally` **(**`DynAttribExampleTag.java`**)**

```
public class DynAttribExampleTag extends TagSupport
            implements DynamicAttributes, TryCatchFinally
{

    private HashMap attributeMap;

    public DynAttribExampleTag()
    {
        attributeMap = new HashMap();
    }

    /**
     * implementation of DynamicAttributes interface
     */
    public void setDynamicAttribute(String uri,
                                    String localName,
                                    Object value)
    {
        attributeMap.put(localName, value);
    }

    /**
     * implementation of TryCatchFinally
     */
    public void doCatch(Throwable t) throws Throwable
    {
        System.out.println(t.toString());
    }

    public void doFinally()
    {
        // perform any cleanup necessary,
        // such as open JDBC connections, file handles, etc.
        // is always called when tag exits
        System.out.println("doFinally called");
    }

    /**
     *  Called by the container when the start tag is processed
```

Listing 21.2 **Continued**

```
     */
    public int doStartTag() throws JspException
    {
        Iterator it = attributeMap.keySet().iterator();

        while (it.hasNext())
        {
            String name = (String)it.next();
            String value = (String)attributeMap.get(name);
            try
            {
                pageContext.getOut().println("Attribute name = "
                                              + name + "<br>");
                pageContext.getOut().println("Attribute value = "
                                              + value + "<br>");
            }
            catch (Exception e)
            {
                throw new JspException(e);
            }
        }

        return TagSupport.SKIP_BODY;
    }
}
```

A typical invocation of this tag might look like the following (taken from the example file `DemoDynamicAttribute.jsp`):

```
<%! String attValue = "Optional"; %>
...
    <beeshirts:dyn_attrib>
       <jsp:attribute name="attrib-one" trim="true">
          Dynamic
       </jsp:attribute>
       <jsp:attribute name="attrib-two" trim="true">
          <%= attValue %>
       </jsp:attribute>
    </beeshirts:dyn_attrib>
```

Tag Meta-Data Information Abstractions

In addition to the core custom tag extension abstractions described thus far, a collection of abstractions is also defined to describe meta information about libraries used to collect implementation classes. Figure 21.3 and Figure 21.4 depict these abstractions and their relations.

The `TagExtraInfo` class is extended by a custom tag implementation to provide additional information about a custom tag library. A `TagExtraInfo` object can use `TagData` (name/value attribute pairs) to retrieve `VariableInfo` to describe any scripting variables created or modified by a tag. Information related to a particular custom tag is extracted from the `TagInfo` class. Attributes associated with that tag can then be extracted from a collection of associated `TagAttributeInfo` objects. Additionally, variable information for a tag can also be extracted via a collection of `TagVariableInfo` objects. A `TagLibraryInfo` object can be used to provide more information about the tag library itself, including information about any functions defined via the `FunctionInfo` class and information about tag files inside of the tag library via the `TagFileInfo` class. Finally, the `TagExtraInfo` class provides the capability to perform custom validation by overloading the `validate()` method, which returns an array of `ValidationMessage` objects. We will look at validation more closely later in the chapter, in the section "JSP and Tag Validation."

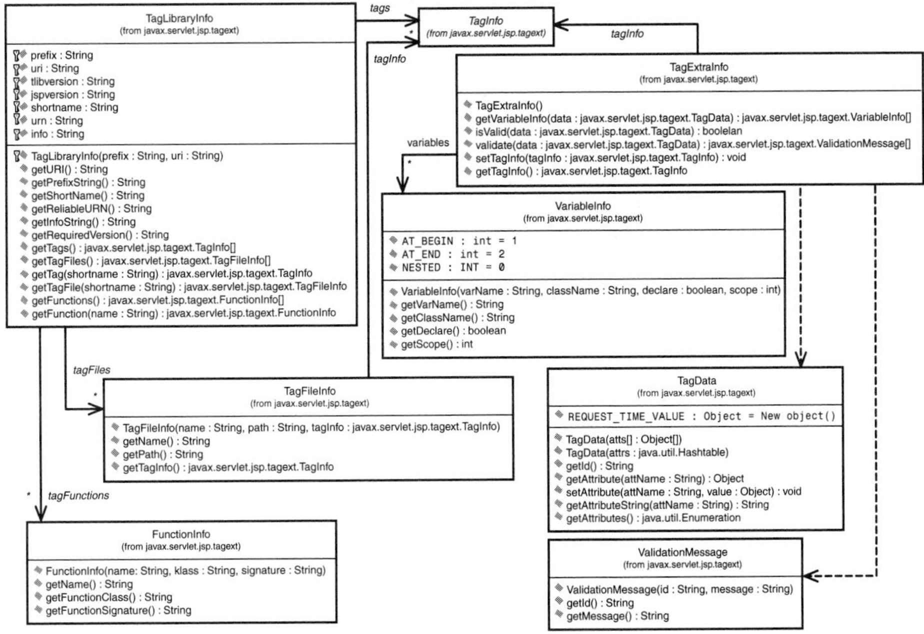

Figure 21.3 JSP custom tag library info abstractions.

As you saw in an earlier example, it is possible for custom tags to introduce new scripting variables into the JSP environment, which can be used to pass data from the tag handler up to a calling JSP page. But to do this, specific information about the variables being introduced needs to be provided to the container at translation time. This is done by extending the `javax.servlet.jsp.tagext.TagExtraInfo` class. This implementation class is then associated with its corresponding tag handler in the TLD file.

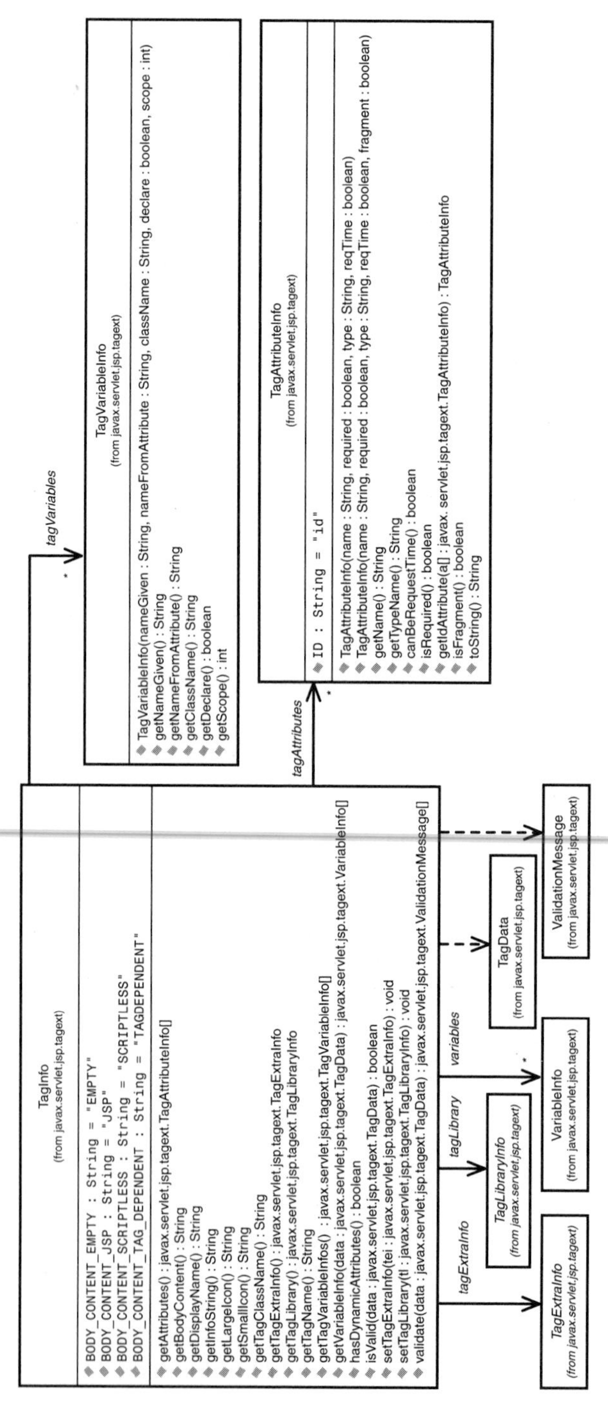

Figure 21.4 JSP custom tag info abstractions.

To add scripting variables through a tag, it is necessary to overload the `getVariableInfo()` method, which is called by the container at translation time. The `getVariableInfo()` method returns an array of `javax.servlet.jsp.tagext.VariableInfo` objects. Each `VariableInfo` object declares a single scripting variable by specifying the variable's name, its class, a `Boolean` value indicating whether this is a new variable, and an `int` value specifying the variable's scope. The scope can be one of the following values:

- `VariableInfo.AT_BEGIN`: Variable's scope starts at the beginning of the tag, and continues to the end of the tag's scope.
- `VariableInfo.AT_END`: Scope starts after the end of the tag, and continues to the end of the tag's scope.
- `VariableInfo.NESTED`: Variable is scoped only between the beginning and the end of the tag.

Listing 21.3 shows a sample `TagExtraInfo` implementation class that defines the scripting variables used in conjunction with the custom tag implementation of Listing 21.1.

Listing 21.3 `TagExtraInfo` **Implementation** (`CartItemsTagExtraInfo.java`)

```
package ejava.jsp.tagext;

import javax.servlet.jsp.tagext.TagData;
import javax.servlet.jsp.tagext.TagExtraInfo;
import javax.servlet.jsp.tagext.VariableInfo;

public class CartItemsTagExtraInfo extends TagExtraInfo
{
  public VariableInfo[] getVariableInfo(TagData tagData)
  {
    VariableInfo[] varInfo = {
      new VariableInfo("item_id", "java.lang.Integer", true,
                       VariableInfo.NESTED),
      new VariableInfo("item_quantity", "java.lang.Integer", true,
                       VariableInfo.NESTED),
      new VariableInfo("item_price", "java.lang.Float", true,
                       VariableInfo.NESTED),
      new VariableInfo("item_size", "java.lang.String", true,
                       VariableInfo.NESTED),
      new VariableInfo("item_color", "java.lang.String", true,
                       VariableInfo.NESTED),
      new VariableInfo("item_design_front", "java.lang.String", true,
                       VariableInfo.NESTED),
      new VariableInfo("item_design_back", "java.lang.String", true,
                       VariableInfo.NESTED),
```

Listing 21.3 **Continued**

```
        new VariableInfo("item_front_image", "java.lang.String", true,
                         VariableInfo.NESTED),
        new VariableInfo("item_back_image", "java.lang.String", true,
                         VariableInfo.NESTED),
        new VariableInfo("item_unit_price", "java.lang.Float", true,
                         VariableInfo.NESTED)
      };

      return varInfo;
    }
}
```

The code in the preceding two listings together make up a custom tag implementation. Before the tag can be used on a JSP page, it must be declared as part of a tag library. Because we defer the discussion of creating tag libraries until later in the chapter, let us for now assume that the custom tag implementation in the preceding example was given the name `cart_items` in a tag library called `taglib`. A JSP that wanted to use that tag would first place a `taglib` directive at the top of the page:

```
<%@ taglib uri="taglib" prefix="beeshirts" %>
```

And then it could use the tag as shown here:

```
<TABLE BORDER=0 CELLSPACING=0 CELLPADDING=0 BGCOLOR='#FFCC66'>
    <TR><TD><STRONG> Your Cart Contains : <STRONG></TD></TR>
    <TR></TR>
    <TR><TD VALIGN=TOP>

      <beeshirts:cart_items>

          <TABLE BORDER=0 CELLSPACING=0 CELLPADDING=0
                 BGCOLOR='#FFCC66'>
             <TR>
               <TD>Item ID: </TD>
               <TD> <%= item_id %></TD>
             </TR>
             <TR>
               <TD>Quantity: </TD>
               <TD><%= item_quantity %> </TD>
             </TR>
...

            <TR>
               <TD>SHIRT: </TD>
               <TD> <IMG SRC=<%= item_back_image %> > </TD>
             </TR>
```

```
            </TABLE>
        </beeshirts:cart_items>

    </TD></TR>
  </TABLE>
```

Simple Tags and JSP Fragments

Up to this point, we have described what has come to be known as the "classic" Tag Handler API. It is called as such for several reasons, primarily because it was the API included with previous versions of JSP. It also provides the most thorough and complete picture of how the JSP container implements custom tags behind the scenes, and thus offers the most sophisticated customization options. However, many applications do not require this level of detail, which is the motivation behind two new additions, the "simple" Tag Handler API, and Tag Files.

A Simple Tag, as depicted in Figure 21.5, is defined by the `javax.servlet.jsp.tagext.SimpleTag` interface. This interface simplifies the tag life cycle by providing a method, `doTag()`, that is called once and only once by the container for each invocation of the tag. The method returns `void`, so there is no need to worry about returning different values to the container to perform certain actions, as with iteration and body tags. As with the `IterationTag` and `BodyTag` interfaces described earlier, though, the API provides an implementation class, `javax.servlet.jsp.tagext.SimpleTagSupport`, which developers should use as the base class of their simple tags.

The `SimpleTag` interface reduces the number of options the developer has in deciding when and how the tag handler is invoked, how the body of the tag may be processed, and how data can be returned to the page and how that data is scoped. To provide the rich set of functionality of classic tags with the more concise syntax of the `SimpleTag` interface, JSP v2.0 introduced another concept known as JSP fragments. Simply put, a JSP fragment is just that: a specific segment of JSP code that can invoked any number of times by a tag handler.

JSP fragments are defined by the `javax.servlet.jsp.tagext.JspFragment` interface. This interface has one method, `invoke()`, which takes as an argument the output `Writer` object. When a `SimpleTag` is invoked by the container, the body of the tag is turned into a `JspFragment` and passed to the tag handler through the `setJspBody()` method. This object can be accessed by the `getJspBody()` method. Listing 21.4 shows an example of a `SimpleTag` implementation of a tag. This particular tag is designed to emulate the standard HTML hyperlink tag (`<a href=...></a>`), but with the option of specifying a "secure" attribute to indicate whether the link is to be served secure or nonsecure. Note that in the `doTag()` method, text is written directly to the `JspWriter` object, and the body contents are invoked as a `JspFragment`.

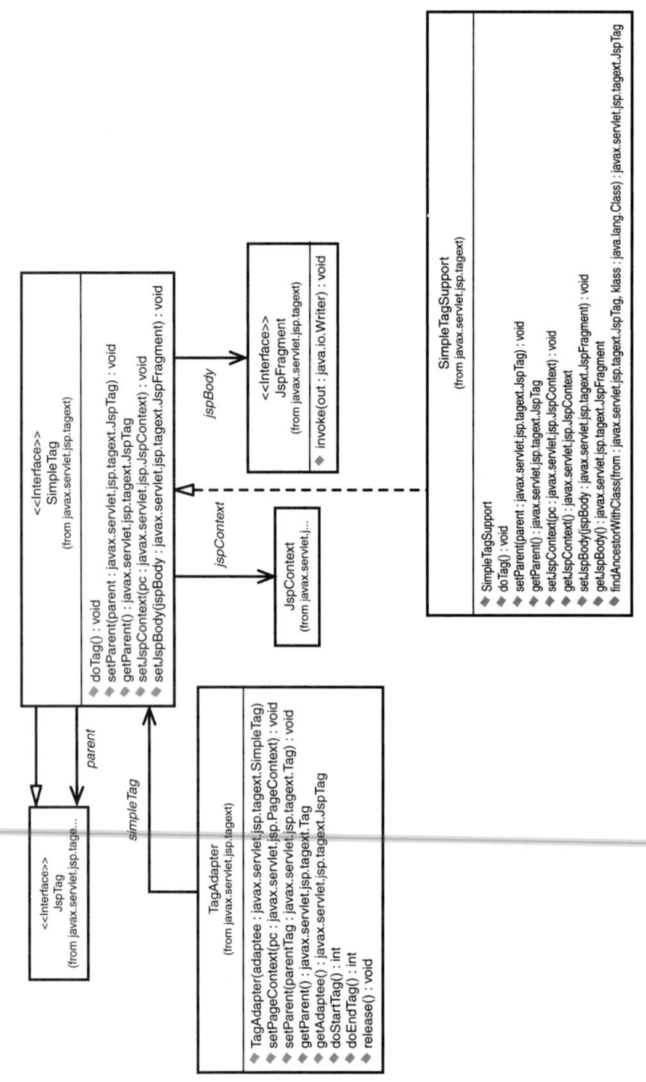

Figure 21.5 JSP simple tag abstractions.

Listing 21.4 **Class Illustrating** `SimpleTag` **API (**`SecureHrefTag.java`**)**

```
package ejava.jsp.tagext;

import java.io.IOException;
import java.util.HashMap;
```

Listing 21.4 **Continued**

```
import javax.servlet.jsp.JspException;
import javax.servlet.jsp.JspWriter;
import javax.servlet.jsp.PageContext;
import javax.servlet.jsp.tagext.SimpleTagSupport;
import javax.servlet.http.HttpServletRequest;

/**
 *  Tag designed to emulate a standard HTML <a href=...> tag
 *  but takes an additional attribute "secure", which will
 *  rebuild the URL starting with "https://hostname" instead
 *  of the normal relative URL
 */
public class SecureHrefTag extends SimpleTagSupport
{
    private String href;
    private Boolean secure;

    public SecureHrefTag()
    {
        secure = new Boolean(false);
    }

    public void doTag() throws JspException, IOException
    {
        HttpServletRequest request =
          (HttpServletRequest)jspContext.findAttribute(
                                          PageContext.REQUEST);
        String newHref;
        if (secure.booleanValue())
        {
            // change http to https
            newHref = "https://" + request.getServerName() + href;
        }
        else
           newHref = href;

        JspWriter out = getJspContext().getOut();
        // start the <a href tag
        out.write("<a href='" + newHref + "'>");
        // write out the body
        getJspBody().invoke(out);
        // close the tag
        out.write("</a>");     }

    public void setHref(String href)
```

Listing 21.4 **Continued**

```
    {
        this.href = href;
    }

    public void setSecure(Boolean secure)
    {
        this.secure = secure;
    }
}
```

Assuming that this tag was called `secure_href` in our example tag library, a JSP page could use the tag like this:

```
<beeshirts:secure_href secure="${linkIsSecure}" href="${pageURI}">
    Click here to go to the page
</beeshirts:secure_href>
```

Tag Files

Tag files are a means of writing custom tag implementations using pure JSP syntax. Instead of writing custom Java implementation code and declaring that code in a TLD file, ordinary JSP markup can be placed in a file with a `.tag` extension, deployed to the `WEB-INF/tags` directory, and the JSP container will automatically create a custom tag that conforms to the `SimpleTag` interface described previously. The tag can then be referenced from a JSP in the usual manner. Listing 21.5 shows a very simple tag file.

Listing 21.5 **Basic Tag File Example (`copyright.tag`)**

```
<%--
    Very basic tag file that displays Copyright information on a page
--%>
<p align='CENTER'>Copyright &copy Beeshirts.com 2003</p>
```

This tag is available on a JSP page in the following fashion:

```
<%@ taglib prefix="tagfile" tagdir="/WEB-INF/tags" %>
...
<tagfile:copyright />
```

Note the use of the `tagdir` attribute in the `taglib` directive as opposed to the `uri` attribute.

Tag File Directives

Although a tag file is written in JSP syntax, it is a distinct entity that is treated differently than a JSP page. As such, there are certain directives that are available only in tag files, and some that are forbidden in tag files. Specifically, tag files support all the JSP directives except for `page`. In addition, it supports the directives `tag`, `attribute`, and `variable`.

The `tag` directive is similar in purpose to the `page` directive but applies only to tag files. It contains the attributes listed in Table 21.1, all of which are optional.

Table 21.1 **Optional Attributes of `tag` Directive**

Name	Description
`display-name`	A short name to be displayed by authoring tools.
`body-content`	One of the following: `empty`, `tagdependent`, or `scriptless`. `Tagdependent` implies that the body contents are of a specific nature and the tag will know how to process them, such as an embedded SQL query. `Scriptless`, which means containing only JSP markup and EL expressions, is the default.
`dynamic-attributes`	A `true` indicates that the tag supports attributes with dynamic names. The default is `false`.
`small-icon`	A path to an image file to be displayed by tools.
`large-icon`	Similar to `small-icon`.
`description`	A human-readable message describing the tag.
`example`	A string showing an example usage of the tag.
`language`	Identical to the `language` attribute of the `page` directive.
`import`	Identical to the `import` attribute of the `page` directive.
`pageEncoding`	Identical to the `pageEncoding` attribute of the `page` directive.
`isELIgnored`	Identical to the `isELIgnored` attribute of the `page` directive.

The `attribute` directive is used to declare attributes of the tag action. It is analogous to the `<attribute>` element of the tag library descriptor, as you will see in the next section. It has one required attribute, `name`, which is the name of the attribute. In addition, it has the optional attributes shown in Table 21.2.

Table 21.2 **Optional Attributes of `attribute` Directive**

Name	Description
`required`	Whether or not this attribute is required by the tag. The default is `false`.
`fragment`	If `true`, the attribute is treated as a JSP fragment that will be processed by the tag handler. Otherwise, the container treats it as an ordinary attribute.
`rtexprvalue`	If `true`, allows the attribute's value to be determined by a runtime expression. The default is `false`.
`type`	The class type of the attribute. The default is `java.lang.String`.
`description`	A text description of the attribute.

The variable directive's purpose is to define the semantics of any variables introduced by the tag handler back to the calling page, similar to a VariableInfo definition within a TagExtraInfo implementation. It is analogous to the <variable> element of the tag library descriptor, which is covered in the next section. The directive has the attributes shown in Table 21.3.

Table 21.3 **Optional Attributes of** variable **Directive**

Name	Description
name-given	The name of the variable that will be defined in the calling page. One of either name-given or name-from-attribute is required.
name-from-attribute	Defines an attribute whose value at the start of the tag invocation will specify the name of the variable.
alias	Defines an attribute with local scope that will hold the value of the variable. This is required when name-from-attribute is specified.
variable-class	The class name of the variable. The default is java.lang.String.
declare	Whether the variable is declared in the calling page. Defaults to true.
scope	The scope of the variable: AT_BEGIN, AT_END, or NESTED. NESTED is the default.
description	A description of the variable.

Tag Files and Fragments

As with simple tags, tag files have the capability to process their body contents or JSP fragments. Two standard JSP actions are provided to facilitate this, <jsp:doBody> and <jsp:invoke>. Unlike other standard actions, these may be used only from within a tag file.

The <jsp:invoke> action has one required attribute, fragment, which contains the name of the JSP fragment to be invoked. JSP fragments are named within the body of the tag by the <jsp:attribute> action. Parameter values can be introduced directly into the namespace of the tag file itself, and will be picked up by the JSP fragment when it is processed. A convenient way to set variables using JSP syntax is with the <set> action, which is part of the Java Standard Tag Library (see the sidebar).

Java Standard Tag Library (JSTL)

The Java Standard Tag Library (JSTL) is a collection of commonly used actions that are considered a standard extension to JSP. It provides programming language features such as conditional branching and looping, plus convenient tags for doing XML processing and SQL queries. The current version of JSTL, 1.0, is available for download at http://java.sun.com/jstl.

Listing 21.6 shows a tag file that invokes JSP fragments defined within the tag.

Listing 21.6 **Tag File Invoking Fragments (`contactInfo.tag`)**

```
<%@ taglib prefix="c" uri="http://java.sun.com/jstl/core" %>

<%--
   Inserts contact information into page
--%>

<%@ attribute name="displayInfo" fragment="true" %>
<%@ variable name-given="full-name" %>
<%@ variable name-given="email" %>

<table>
  <tr>
    <td>
      <c:set var="full-name" value="Johnny Mott"/>
      <c:set var="email" value="johnny@beeshirts.com"/>
      <jsp:invoke fragment="displayInfo"/>
    </td>
    <td>
      <c:set var="full-name" value="Joey Sack"/>
      <c:set var="email" value="joey@beeshirts.com"/>
      <jsp:invoke fragment="displayInfo"/>
    </td>
  </tr>
</table
```

The following code snippet shows how the preceding tag might be used on a JSP page:

```
<table>
  <tr><td>This site maintained by</td></tr>
   <tagfile:contactInfo>
     <jsp:attribute name="displayInfo">
        <b>Name: </b>${full-name}<br>
        <b>Email: </b>${email}<br>
     </jsp:attribute>
   </tagfile:contactInfo>
  </td></tr>
</table>
```

The `<jsp:doBody>` action behaves similarly to the `<jsp:invoke>` action, but operates on the entire body content rather than a named JSP fragment.

Both <jsp:invoke> and <jsp:doBody> also support the following optional attributes:

- var: Contains the name of a scoped attribute that will receive the java.lang.String object that results from this invocation. Cannot be specified if varReader is specified.
- varReader: Like var, but stores the result of the invocation in a java.io.Reader object. Cannot be specified if var is also specified.
- scope: The scope where the var or varReader attribute is stored. Valid values are page, request, session, or application. The default is page.

JSP and Tag Validation

The JSP v2.0 API contains several provisions for performing translation-time validation of JSP pages and tag libraries. The more translation-time validation that can be done on a page or tag, the less risk there is of runtime errors. Validation can also assist development, allowing page authors to quickly verify usage and syntax without needing to run their application. Figure 21.6 shows a class diagram of some of the more prominent classes used in JSP validation.

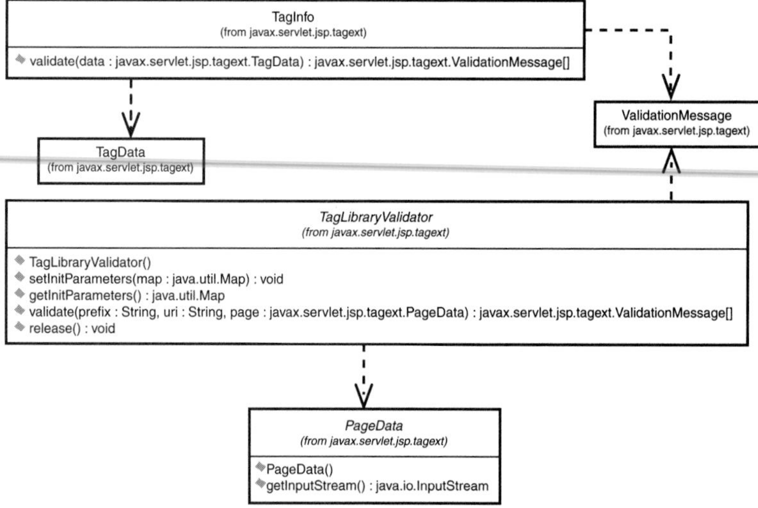

Figure 21.6 JSP page validation abstractions.

The TagLibraryValidator class is used at translation time to validate a tag library's usage on a given JSP page. Developers who want to provide custom validation of their tag library will subclass this class, and reference the derived class in the <validator>

element of the TLD (described later in the chapter). Typically, the `validate()` method will be overloaded to implement the custom validation service.

To perform validation, the translator must first generate the XML view of the JSP page. Then, for each `taglib` directive on the page, `validate()` is invoked on that library's `TagLibraryValidator`. The arguments to validate are the `taglib` directive's `prefix` and `uri` attributes, passed as `Strings`, and a `PageData` object, which contains a handle to the XML view of the page. The XML page view can be read by invoking the `getInputStream()` method of `PageData`. This data can be passed through a JAXP XML schema validator, for example, or through any other type of validation. The `validate()` method returns an array of `ValidationMessage` objects, each of which contains a message corresponding to a single validation error discovered during the validation process. A return value of `null` or a zero-length array signals that validation was successful.

When the XML view of a JSP page is generated, the container assigns each element a unique ID attribute using the `<jsp:id>` tag. This ID can provide useful information that the validator can use to track and report validation errors.

The following example shown in Listing 21.7 depicts a class that does some very simple tag library validation. For a page with a given `taglib` directive, it scans the contents of that page for any invocations of tags defined in that library. If none exists, it will throw a validation error.

Listing 21.7 **Tag Library Validation (`BasicTagLibraryValidator.java`)**

```
public class BasicTagLibraryValidator extends TagLibraryValidator
{

    public BasicTagLibraryValidator()
    {
    }

    public ValidationMessage[] validate(String prefix,
                                        String uri,
                                        PageData page)
    {
        // simple validation checks prefix declared in taglib
        // directive, searches content of page to see if it
        // is used on page anywhere.  Returns error message if
        // taglib declared but no tags used on the page.
        InputStream is = page.getInputStream();
        InputStreamReader isr = new InputStreamReader(is);
        BufferedReader br = new BufferedReader(isr);
        StringBuffer buf = new StringBuffer();
        String line = null;

        try
```

Listing 21.7 **Continued**

```
        {
            line  = br.readLine();
            while (line != null)
            {
                buf.append(line);
                line = br.readLine();
            }

            System.out.println("validating tag lib");

            String pageString = buf.toString();
            // now find an actual tag reference on the page
            if (pageString.indexOf("<" + prefix + ":") == -1)
            {
                ValidationMessage[] msgs = new ValidationMessage[1];
                String errMsg = "No tags from the " +  prefix +
                    "library are used on this page.";

                msgs[0] = new ValidationMessage(null, errMsg);
                return msgs;
            }
            else
            {
                return null;
            }
        }
        catch (Exception e)
        {
            // handle exception here
        }

        return null;
    }
}
```

If this example were to be coupled with an XML validating parser, for example, much more useful validation could be performed. For instance, it could verify that the names of all the tags matched all of those defined within the tag library. In addition, more useful error information could be generated, such as the `id` of the element that caused the error.

Just as the `TagLibraryValidator` is used to validate a tag library's use on a page, further translation-time validation can be performed on each tag's attributes. The `TagExtraInfo` class described earlier also implements a `validate()` method, which gets called by the container once for each invocation of a tag on a JSP page. It takes a

TagData object as an argument, which provides access to the names and translation-time values of all the attributes used for that invocation of the tag. The getAttribute(String name) method of TagData returns the value of the named attribute as an Object, or the constant value TagData.REQUEST_TIME_VALUE if the attribute has been declared as accepting runtime expressions, and thus cannot be evaluated at translation time.

Tag Libraries

Just as with servlets, using JSP tags is a two-step process. First, the tag handlers are implemented, using the methods described previously. Second, they are configured for deployment with an XML deployment descriptor. In the case of JSP tags, several tags can be included in a single descriptor, making up a tag library. The XML descriptor is called a Tag Library Descriptor, or TLD file. This descriptor conforms to a standard XML schema, which is defined at http://java.sun.com/xml/ns/j2ee/web-jsptaglibrary_2_0.xsd.

As was previously stated, a tag library is a collection of custom tag handler implementation classes. A tag library can be packaged as a standalone JAR file or incorporated directly into a Web application. In the case of a standalone JAR file, the TLD file must reside in the META-INF directory or one of its subdirectories, with the rest of the JAR containing the implementation classes. This JAR file should then be placed in the WEB-INF/lib directory of the Web application that uses the library. To include a tag library directly within a Web application, the TLD file must be in the WEB-INF directory or a subdirectory, while the implementation classes are contained in WEB-INF/classes.

The root element of the TLD file is the <taglib> element. It consists primarily of sub-elements that define tags (<tag>), tag files (<tag-file>), and EL functions (<function>). It also contains the following elements:

- <description>: Contains text describing the use of the tag library.
- <display-name>: A name for this tag library that can be used by editing tools.
- <icon>: An optional icon representing this tag library that can be displayed by tools.
- <tlib-version>: The version of this tag library.
- <short-name>: A default name that can be used by authoring tools, for automatically creating the prefix value in a taglib directive.
- <uri>: A URI that identifies this tag library, specified relative to the WEB-INF directory of the application. Referenced in the uri attribute of the taglib directive.
- <validator>: Contains a <validator-class> sub-element that defines the name of a class that extends javax.servlet.jsp.tagext.TagLibraryValidator, which performs customized translation-time validation of the JSP pages that reference this tag library.

- <listener>: Contains a <listener-class> sub-element that defines the name of a class which specifies an event listener.
- <taglib-extension>: Extensions that can provide tools with additional information about this tag library. Contains one or more <extension-element> sub-elements, and a boolean attribute mustUnderstand, which indicates whether the container will need to know how to process this extension in order to use the tag library. Right now, only ignorable (mustUnderstand=false) extensions are supported in tag libraries.

The <tag> Element

Custom tags are defined in the TLD with the <tag> element. It supports the sub-elements <description>, <display-name>, and <icon>, which behave similarly to those defined within the <taglib> element discussed previously. It also contains the following elements:

- <name>: The action name for this tag, which will be used in the JSP to invoke this tag. This value must be unique across all <tag> elements within a TLD.
- <tag-class>: The class implementing the tag handler.
- <tei-class>: A class that extends TagExtraInfo, used to provide information about scripting variables that the tag adds to the page.
- <body-content>: Gives information about the body contents of the tag. Legal values are JSP, empty, scriptless, and tagdependent.
- <dynamic-attributes>: A boolean value indicating whether the tag supports attributes with dynamic names. If true, the tag handler must implement the javax.servlet.jsp.tagext.DynamicAttributes interface. The default is false.
- <example>: Shows an example usage of this tag.
- <tag-extension>: Provides the capability to add extensions to this tag, to be used by development tools. Has the same structure as <taglib-extension> described previously. Right now, only ignorable tag extensions are supported.

The <tag> element supports two additional sub-elements, <variable> and <attribute>, each of which has its own set of sub-elements.

The <variable> Element

The <variable> element is used to define scripting variables that will be introduced by the tag. It is meant as an alternative to the <tei-class> element, and it does not require an implementation of TagExtraInfo. In fact, it is a translation-time error for a <tag> element to have both a <variable> and a <tei-class> element declared.

The `<variable>` element works in an analogous fashion to the `TagExtraInfo` class, by using the following sub-elements:

- `<description>`: A text description of this variable.
- `<name-given>`: The name of the variable.
- `<name-from-attribute>`: The name of an attribute whose value will specify the name of the variable. Either this or `<name-given>` must be specified.
- `<variable-class>`: The class name of this variable. Defaults to `java.lang.String`.
- `<declare>`: Whether this is a new variable being declared. `True` is the default.
- `<scope>`: The scope of the variable. Can be `AT_BEGIN`, `AT_END`, or `NESTED` (the default).
- `<fragment>`: The JSP fragment to which this variable is scoped. Cannot be defined if `<scope>` is defined.

The `<attribute>` Element

The `<attribute>` element is used to define the attributes that the tag action can accept. This information is needed by the JSP translator to generate the appropriate code. The following sub-elements are defined:

- `<description>`: A text description of this attribute.
- `<name>`: The name of the attribute.
- `<required>`: A Boolean indicating whether the attribute is required or optional.
- `<rtexprvalue>`: A Boolean indicating whether the attribute's value can contain a runtime evaluated expression.
- `<type>`: The class name of this attribute. This is always `java.lang.String` when `<rtexprvalue>` is `false`.
- `<fragment>`: Boolean indicating whether this attribute's value contains a JSP fragment.

The `<tag-file>` Element

It is often not necessary to declare tag files in the deployment descriptor, because the JSP translator will find them and automatically generate their TLD files, if they follow convention and reside in the `WEB-INF/tags` directory. Nonetheless, the `<tag-file>` element provides a means to explicitly notify the container of a tag file. It contains two elements: `<name>`, which defines the action name for the tag, and `<path>`, which supplies the path to the tag file, relative to the Web application context or, in the case of a standalone deployment, relative to the JAR file.

The <function> Element

The <function> element enables components of the tag library to be made available to the EL processor as functions. It can contain the following sub-elements:

- <description>: Contains text describing the use of this function.
- <display-name>: A name for this function that can be used by editing tools.
- <icon>: An optional icon representing this function that can be displayed by tools.
- <name>: The name of this function. Must be unique across all <function> elements in this TLD.
- <function-class>: The name of the Java class that implements this function.
- <function-signature>: The Java language signature of the method that implements this function.
- <example>: Contains example usage of the function.

Listing 21.8 shows the TLD file used for all the examples in this and the preceding chapter.

Listing 21.8 **Tag Library Descriptor (taglib.tld)**

```
<?xml version="1.0" encoding="UTF-8" ?>

<taglib xmlns="http://java.sun.com/xml/ns/j2ee"
    xmlns:xsi="http://www.w3.org/2001/XMLSchema-instance"
    xsi:schemaLocation=
        "http://java.sun.com/xml/ns/j2ee web-jsptaglibrary_2_0.xsd"
    version="2.0">

  <tlib-version>1.0</tlib-version>
  <jsp-version>1.2</jsp-version>
  <short-name>simple</short-name>
  <uri>/taglib</uri>
  <description>
      A simple tag library for the examples
  </description>

  <validator>
     <validator-class>
        ejava.jsp.tagext.BasicTagLibraryValidator
     </validator-class>
  </validator>

  <tag>
    <name>cart_items</name>
    <tag-class>ejava.jsp.tagext.CartItemsTag</tag-class>
    <description> Display shopping cart items</description>
```

Listing 21.8 **Continued**

```
    <tei-class>ejava.jsp.tagext.CartItemsTagExtraInfo</tei-class>
  </tag>

  <tag>
    <name>secure_href</name>
    <tag-class>ejava.jsp.tagext.SecureHrefTag</tag-class>
    <description> Rewrites hyperlinks if secure</description>
    <body-content>scriptless</body-content>
    <attribute>
        <name>href</name>
        <required>true</required>
        <rtexprvalue>true</rtexprvalue>
        <type>java.lang.String</type>
    </attribute>
    <attribute>
        <name>secure</name>
        <required>false</required>
        <rtexprvalue>true</rtexprvalue>
        <type>java.lang.Boolean</type>
    </attribute>
  </tag>

  <tag>
    <name>dyn_attrib</name>
    <tag-class>ejava.jsp.tagext.DynAttribExampleTag</tag-class>
    <description> Demonstrate dynamic attributes</description>
    <dynamic-attributes>true</dynamic-attributes>
  </tag>

  <function>
    <description>Converts number to money format string</description>
    <name>moneyFormat</name>
    <function-class>ejava.jsp.tagext.ELFunctions</function-class>
    <function-signature>
       java.lang.String moneyFormat(java.lang.Float )
    </function-signature>
  </function>

</taglib>
```

Conclusions

JSP custom tags provide a functionally rich method for extending the capabilities of JSP pages. Tags are a modular solution that can be reused repeatedly on a single page or a collection of pages. Their modularity is further extended by the use of tag libraries, whereby many Web applications can share a common tag library. New features of the JSP specification, such as tag files and JSP fragments, greatly simplify the development of custom tag functionality, with little sacrifice in flexibility. However, a full Java API still exists for the more sophisticated implementations.

22

Web Services with Web Components

CHAPTERS 19 THROUGH 21 DESCRIBED HOW TO construct J2EE Web components that operate inside of a J2EE Web container to reap the advantages of standard HTTP-based resource management and deployment services. Chapter 10, "Web Service Communications," described Web service communications as a means to construct interoperable applications communicating via SOAP and HTTP. This chapter represents a fusing of J2EE Web component and Web services technologies. That is, J2EE v1.4 defines a means for J2EE Web components to be deployed and exposed as Web services.

In this chapter, you will learn:

- An overview of how J2EE Web components can expose themselves as Web services.
- How J2EE Web components are implemented as Web services.
- How to configure J2EE Web component deployment descriptors to be Web service ready.
- How to configure J2EE Web components as Web services.
- How to configure type mappings between Java types and WSDL types for Web service deployment.
- How to configure J2EE Web components to reference other Web services.
- How to package and deploy J2EE Web components as Web services.

Web Components as Web Services Overview

As the introduction to this chapter implies, there is a lot of configuration work to be done when deploying a J2EE Web component as a Web service. In fact, the most significant amount of work involved with deploying an existing Web component as a Web service is in the configuration of the deployment descriptors associated with that component. It is for this reason that the bulk of this chapter focuses on a description of and examples for configuring Web components to be deployed as Web services.

We already examined how J2EE Web components operate inside of a J2EE Web container in Chapters 19 through 21. Chapter 10 described how to construct JAX-RPC Web service clients and service implementations. J2EE v1.4 now requires that compliant Web containers include a JAX-RPC runtime to allow Web components to be exposed as Web services. Specifically, a J2EE v1.4 Web container (that is, Java Servlet v2.4 and JSP v2.0 compliant) must provide a JAX-RPC v1.1 runtime environment. The implication of this fact means that the Web container must perform the following general sequence of events when handling Web service requests:

1. *Receive Request:* Listen for incoming SOAP/HTTP requests on a predefined port or at the URL defined inside of the deployed Web service's WSDL file.
2. *Identify Endpoint Type:* Map the SOAP message's target information into an intended Web service endpoint implementation class type according to J2EE deployment descriptor information.
3. *Unmarshal Request:* Unmarshal and deserialize the SOAP request message into Java type representations according to the JAX-RPC standards for such type mapping.
4. *Delegate Request:* Delegate the resulting Java type input parameters to a J2EE Web component instance of the appropriate type.
5. *Receive Response:* Receive any Java type response parameters from the J2EE Web component.
6. *Marshal Response:* Marshal and serialize any Java response object to a SOAP response message according to the JAX-RPC standards for such type mapping.
7. *Deliver Response:* Pack the SOAP message into an HTTP response and deliver back to the client.

The remainder of this chapter describes how to construct the Web components operating inside of such a container environment, as well as how to configure and deploy such components as Web services.

Web Service Web Component Implementations

Because you've made it to this point in the book, you'll find the implementation of a Web component that exposes itself as a Web service inside of a J2EE Web container to be rather straightforward. To a large extent, we covered how this is done in Chapter 10. Figure 10.16 from that chapter in fact serves to model the same requirements imposed on a J2EE Web component that is implemented as a Web service. We won't rehash all the rules and requirements here in detail, but it is important to recall the most basic rules for constructing a service endpoint implementation class:

- Must be a public, final, and non-abstract class.
- Must have a parameterless constructor.

- Must not define a `finalize()` method.
- Must implement the method signatures defined by the service endpoint interface. Although it technically does not have to indicate that it is implementing the service endpoint interface, it is a good idea from a design perspective to do so.
- Must be implemented as a stateless component for maximum interoperability.
- May optionally implement the `javax.xml.rpc.server.ServiceLifecycle` interface.
- May obtain a handle to a `javax.xml.rpc.server.ServletEndpointContext` interface as its context inside of a J2EE Web container.

Because such a service implementation instance operates inside of a J2EE Web container, it may use the `ServletEndpointContext` to obtain a handle to a few key Java servlet abstractions described in Chapter 19, "Java Servlets." For one, a `ServletContext` object handle can be obtained so that you can perform all the various operations allowed to Servlets and JSPs for interacting with its Web container. A handle to an `HttpSession` object may also be obtained for getting and setting information associated with a Web session if stateful processing is assumed by the Web service client (described in Chapter 10).

One difference between standard JAX-RPC services and J2EE Web components implemented as Web services is that J2EE Web component-based services do not support custom JAX-RPC serializers and deserializers. The main reason is that JAX-RPC custom serializers and deserializers are not portable across containers and thus are not mandated for use inside standard J2EE Web containers.

Handlers for Web Components

Web services implemented inside of J2EE Web containers can also use JAX-RPC handlers as described in Chapter 10. Here, such handlers act in a manner not unlike Java servlet filters. That is, handlers can be created to preprocess SOAP requests before they are unmarshaled and make their way to the service implementation component. Handlers can also be created to post-process responses after the response from the service implementation component is marshaled into a SOAP response.

J2EE containers, however, will also perform some processing on a message before handing it off to a JAX-RPC handler. For example, security checking will be done by the container before handing off a request to a handler. As such, the handler in fact cannot process security information used by the container in a portable manner. Furthermore, if a handler modifies the security information embedded into a SOAP header in any way that affects the security of the application, the container is required to generate a SOAP fault back to the client indicating this event.

A service endpoint implementation component can use a `ServletEndpointContext` object to obtain a handle to the component's JAX-RPC `javax.xml.rpc.handler.MessageContext` object. In the case of SOAP/HTTP, this context is a `javax.xml.rpc.handler.soap.SOAPMessageContext` type. Recall from Chapter 10 that such a context can be used to access the message context and SOAP messages shared with any handlers.

Web Service Web Component Example

The `ejava.webservices.rpc.QueryServerImpl` class described in Chapter 10 serves as the basis for this chapter's example because that class was essentially a Web service implementation as a Web component. The only modifications we make here, now that certain J2EE container features have been described, is to make use of obtaining a handle to a database connection via JNDI per the J2EE Web container standard fashion for obtaining such connections.

> **Note**
>
> The example code in this chapter makes significant use of the code provided for Chapter 10 and extracted beneath the `examples\src\ejava\webservices\rpc` directory. Additional code elements for this chapter are located as described on this book's CD in Appendix A, "Software Configuration," and extracted to the `example\src\ejava\j2eeweb\webservices` directory.

The `ejava.j2eeweb.webservices.WebQueryServerImpl` class extends the `QueryServerImpl` class and overrides the `init()` method to perform such database connection establishment as shown in Listing 22.1.

Listing 22.1 **Web Services Web Component Example (`WebQueryServerImpl.java`)**

```
package ejava.j2eeweb.webservices;
   ...
public class WebQueryServerImpl
   extends  ejava.webservices.rpc.QueryServerImpl
{
   private String connectionPoolName =
      "java:comp/env/jdbc/ejavaPool";

   public WebQueryServerImpl(){
      super();
   }

   public void init(Object context){
     try {
       // Set super class context
       super.setContext(context);

       // Get database connection from JNDI and set onto super class
       InitialContext ic = new InitialContext();
       DataSource ds = (DataSource)ic.lookup(connectionPoolName);
```

Listing 22.1 **Continued**

```
            super.setConnection(ds.getConnection());
            ic.close();
        } catch (Exception ex) {
            System.err.println("Fatal Exception :" + ex);
            ex.printStackTrace();
        }
    }

    public void destroy(){
        super.destroy();
    }
}
```

Web Service Web Component Clients

Clients to such Web services are implemented as any client to any Web service would be implemented. The Web service client has no need to understand how the Web service is implemented nor does it need to know that the Web service is implemented using J2EE Web components. The Web service client simply communicates with the Web service using SOAP/HTTP and is provided interoperability with the service by virtue of the SOAP protocol and messaging format as well as the underlying HTTP transport protocol. Hence for our example code associated with this chapter, we simply use the `ejava.webservices.rpc.QueryClient` class described in Chapter 10.

Web Component Deployment Configuration (web.xml)

As discussed, the primary new concepts to consider when building a Web service using J2EE Web components are the deployment mechanisms. That is, a series of Web service deployment descriptor files are used when building a Web service that informs the J2EE Web container how it should deploy the service implementation bean to handle SOAP requests. This section and sections that follow describe these mechanisms in more detail.

There are no Web service implementation–related properties that really need establishment inside of the standard `web.xml` deployment descriptor. However, when deploying a Web service implemented as a J2EE Web component service implementation bean, the `web.xml` file must identify this deployment as a Java servlet via the `<servlet-class>` element described in Chapter 19. Furthermore, a single `<servlet-mapping>` element may also be defined for a Java servlet that exposes itself as a Web service. Such a `<servlet-mapping>` must have a `<url-pattern>` that is an exact matching URL for the Web service. As an example for our `WebQueryServerImpl`, we have the `web.xml` file shown in Listing 22.2.

Listing 22.2 **J2EE Web Component Deployment Descriptor** (`web.xml`)

```
<?xml version="1.0" encoding="ISO-8859-1"?>

<web-app xmlns="http://java.sun.com/xml/ns/j2ee"
  xmlns:xsi="http://www.w3.org/2001/XMLSchema-instance"
  xsi:schemaLocation="http://java.sun.com/xml/ns/j2ee web-app_2_4.xsd"
  version="2.4">

  <display-name>QueryWebService</display-name>

  <servlet>
     <servlet-name>QueryServletImpl</servlet-name>
     <servlet-class>
        ejava.j2eeweb.webservices.WebQueryServerImpl
     </servlet-class>
     <load-on-startup>0</load-on-startup>
  </servlet>

  <servlet-mapping>
     <servlet-name>QueryServletImpl</servlet-name>
     <url-pattern>/QueryServer</url-pattern>
  </servlet-mapping>

  <session-config>
     <session-timeout>60</session-timeout>
  </session-config>

  <resource-ref>
     <res-ref-name>jdbc/ejavaPool</res-ref-name>
     <res-type>javax.sql.DataSource</res-type>
     <res-auth>Container</res-auth>
  </resource-ref>
</web-app>
```

Listing 22.2 demonstrates the fact that our `WebQueryServerImpl` service implementation class is to be deployed by the container as a Java servlet Web component with the servlet name `QueryServletImpl` and that the `QueryServer` URL pattern maps to instances of this Web services Web component. Note also that the `WebQueryServerImpl` class is configured with a `<resource-ref>` element for fetching a JDBC connection.

Web Services Web Component Deployment Configuration (`webservices.xml`)

A new standard deployment descriptor is used to define those deployment and configuration characteristics associated with a Web service deployed using J2EE components.

This deployment descriptor is defined inside of a webservices.xml file. For J2EE Web components deployed as Web services, this file must always accompany the web.xml file used to deploy those Web components into a J2EE Web container. Thus, the web.xml file informs the J2EE Web container how to deploy and configure J2EE Web components, whereas the webservices.xml file informs the container how to deploy and configure such services to interact with a JAX-RPC runtime, enabling them to function as Web services.

The XML schema that defines this standard webservices.xml deployment descriptor is located at www.ibm.com/webservices/xsd/j2ee_web_services_1_1.xsd. This XML schema also references common J2EE elements defined via the XML schema at http://java.sun.com/xml/ns/j2ee/j2ee_1_4.xsd.

The required top-level header of the webservices.xml file is illustrated here:

```
<?xml version="1.0" encoding="ISO-8859-1"?>
<webservices xmlns="http://java.sun.com/xml/ns/j2ee"
  xmlns:xsi="http://www.w3.org/2001/XMLSchema-instance"
  xsi:schemaLocation="http://java.sun.com/xml/ns/j2ee
  http://www.ibm.com/webservices/xsd/j2ee_web_services_1_1.xsd"
  version="1.1">
```

Web Services Deployment (<webservices>)

The <webservices> element defines the top-level structure of a webservices.xml file with these elements:

- <webservices>: Top-level element in the webservices.xml file used to identify those J2EE components deployed as Web services via the sub-elements that follow.
- <description>: Generally used to describe its containing element (zero or more).
- <display-name>: Generally used as a name for display by tools (zero or more).
- <icon>: Contains an optional <small-icon> sub-element defining the name for a small 16×16-pixel GIF or JPG file, and an optional <large-icon> sub-element defining the name for a large 32×32-pixel GIF or JPG file (zero or more).
- <webservice-description>: Defines the deployment and configuration properties of a single Web service (one or more).

Individual Web Service Deployment (<webservice-description>)

As you can see, each individual Web service is deployed as a separate unit defined by an individual <webservice-description> element within the <webservices> element. Each <webservice-description> element is in turn composed of elements such as these:

- <webservice-description>: Defines the deployment and configuration properties of a single Web service via the sub-elements that follow.
- <description>: Generally used to describe its containing element (optional).
- <display-name>: Generally used as a name for display by tools (optional).
- <icon>: Contains an optional <small-icon> sub-element defining the name for a small 16×16-pixel GIF or JPG file, and an optional <large-icon> sub-element defining the name for a large 32×32-pixel GIF or JPG file (optional).
- <webservice-description-name>: Logical name for this Web service unique to this deployment descriptor.
- <wsdl-file>: Relative path name for the WSDL file located within the module's archive file (for example, WAR or EJB JAR file).
- <jaxrpc-mapping-file>: Relative path name for the file located within the module that defines a mapping between Java types utilized by the Web service J2EE component and WSDL types defined in the WSDL file associated with this Web service.
- <port-component>: Defines the deployment and configuration for a port component associated with this Web service (one or more).

Web Service Port Component Deployment (<port-component>)

The <webservice-description> element defines those standard elements common across the various port components that compose the Web service such as its WSDL file and type mappings between Java types and WSDL types. Each port component is in turn defined as shown here:

- <port-component>: Defines the deployment and configuration for a port component via the sub-elements that follow.
- <description>: Generally used to describe its containing element (optional).
- <display-name>: Generally used as a name for display by tools (optional).
- <icon>: Contains an optional <small-icon> sub-element defining the name for a small 16×16-pixel GIF or JPG file, and an optional <large-icon> sub-element defining the name for a large 32×32-pixel GIF or JPG file (optional).
- <port-component-name>: Logical name for this port component unique to this deployment descriptor.
- <wsdl-port>: Contains a <namespaceURI> element and <localpart> element to define the namespace URI and local part of the associated WSDL port component's QName.

- <service-endpoint-interface>: Fully qualified class name of the service endpoint interface associated with this port component.
- <service-impl-bean>: Contains a single <servlet-link> sub-element that references a <servlet-name> element value as defined in the web.xml file associated with this WAR module.
- <handler>: Defines that information needed to configure and associate a handler with a Web service J2EE component (zero or more).

Web Service Handler Deployment (<handler>)

Each <port-component> is associated with a Java service implementation bean and service endpoint interface. A set of handlers may also be associated with each service endpoint via <handler> elements defined this way:

- <handler>: Defines that information needed to configure and associate a handler with a Web service J2EE component via the sub-elements that follow.
- Description group: A collection of optional description-related elements including <description>, <display-name>, and <icon> (optional).
- <handler-name>: Logical name for this handler unique to this J2EE module.
- <handler-class>: Fully qualified class name of the associated handler class implementation.
- <init-param>: Contains <description>, <param-name>, and <param-value> sub-elements, which respectively describe, identify via a logical name, and ascribe a value used inside of the Map object associated with a handler's initial HandlerInfo configuration (zero or more).
- <soap-header>: Defines a QName of a SOAP header that the handler will process and as associated with the handler's HandlerInfo configuration object (zero or more).
- <soap-role>: Defines a SOAP actor role name that the handler will assume (zero or more).

Web Service Deployment Example

Listing 22.3 provides an example webservices.xml deployment descriptor used to deploy our WebQueryServerImpl class. A single Web service is deployed within the <webservice-description> element. A single port component is also defined and associated with the QueryServletImpl logical name defined in the web.xml file as our example <servlet-name> and identified in the webservices.xml file via the <service-impl-bean> element's <servlet-link> element value.

Listing 22.3 **J2EE Web Services Web Component Deployment Descriptor (`webservices.xml`)**

```
<?xml version="1.0" encoding="ISO-8859-1"?>

<webservices xmlns="http://java.sun.com/xml/ns/j2ee"
  xmlns:xsi="http://www.w3.org/2001/XMLSchema-instance"
  xsi:schemaLocation="http://java.sun.com/xml/ns/j2ee
  http://www.ibm.com/webservices/xsd/j2ee_web_services_1_1.xsd"
  version="1.1">

<webservices>
  <description>Web Component Exposed as a Web Service</description>

  <webservice-description>
    <webservice-description-name>
        QueryServiceWebService
    </webservice-description-name>

    <wsdl-file>QueryService.wsdl</wsdl-file>
    <jaxrpc-mapping-file>java-wsdl-mapping.xml</jaxrpc-mapping-file>

    <port-component>
      <port-component-name>QueryServerPort</port-component-name>
      <wsdl-port>
        <namespaceURI>http://ws.beeshirts.com/wsdl</namespaceURI>
        <localpart>QueryServerPort</localpart>
      </wsdl-port>
      <service-endpoint-interface>
          ejava.webservices.rpc.QueryServer
      </service-endpoint-interface>
      <service-impl-bean>
        <servlet-link>QueryServletImpl</servlet-link>
      </service-impl-bean>

      <handler>
          <description> User security handler example </description>
          <handler-name>AdminHandler</handler-name>
          <handler-class>
              ejava.webservices.rpc.AdminHandler
          </handler-class>

          <init-param>
              <param-name>username</param-name>
              <param-value>sysop</param-value>
          </init-param>
          <init-param>
```

Listing 22.3 **Continued**

```
                <param-name>password</param-name>
                <param-value>btgllyra</param-value>
            </init-param>
            <init-param>
                <param-name>headerNamespace</param-name>
                <param-value>
                     http://ws.beeshirts.com/wsdl/QueryService
                 </param-value>
            </init-param>
            <init-param>
                <param-name>headerName</param-name>
                <param-value>Security</param-value>
            </init-param>
            <init-param>
                <param-name>headerPrefix</param-name>
                <param-value>beeshirts</param-value>
            </init-param>
        </handler>
      </port-component>
  </webservice-description>
</webservices>
```

Note that the AdminHandler for this Web service is defined in the webservices.xml file. Here we see that a series of <init-param> values are defined and used by the AdminHandler class and its base SecurityHandler class as presented in Chapter 10. As another way to configure the headers for this handler, you could also modify the SecurityHandler class to utilize <soap-header> elements that identify the security header used by the example.

Web Services Type Mapping Deployment Configuration (java-wsdl-mapping.xml)

Thus far, we've seen how the web.xml deployment descriptor informs the J2EE Web container that a J2EE Web component is to be deployed and how the webservices.xml deployment descriptor informs the container that the Web component is to act as a Web service. Recall also that each <webservice-description> element defined in the webservices.xml file contained a <jaxrpc-mapping-file> element. This element identifies a file within the deployed module that defines a mapping between Java types utilized by the Web service Web component and WSDL types defined in the WSDL file associated with the Web service. Such type mapping is generally contained in a java-wsdl-mapping.xml file and defined by the XML schema http://www.ibm.com/webservices/xsd/j2ee_jaxrpc_mapping_1_1.xsd.

Such a schema is referenced at the top of the java-wsdl-mapping.xml file as shown here:

```
<?xml version="1.0" encoding="UTF-8"?>
<java-wsdl-mapping xmlns="http://java.sun.com/xml/ns/j2ee"
      xmlns:xsi="http://www.w3.org/2001/XMLSchema-instance"
      xsi:schemaLocation="http://java.sun.com/xml/ns/j2ee
      http://www.ibm.com/webservices/xsd/j2ee_jaxrpc_mapping_1_1.xsd"
      version="1.1">
```

Java to WSDL Mapping (<java-wsdl-mapping>)

Generally speaking, this mapping deployment descriptor can contain a minimal amount of information provided by the developer to allow for the mapping of Java types to and from WSDL types by the container. However, we provide an overview of the entire file in this section. The top-level elements for this mapping file are defined here:

- <java-wsdl-mapping>: Defines a mapping between Java types and types used in a WSDL file with the sub-elements that follow.
- <package-mapping>: Indicates those mappings between a Java package name and a WSDL XML namespace (one or more).
- <java-xml-type-mapping>: Defines a mapping between a Java class and an associated WSDL type (zero or more).
- <exception-mapping>: Defines a mapping between a Java exception type and an associated WSDL message (zero or more).
- <service-interface-mapping>: Defines a mapping between a Java type for a Web service and a WSDL type (optional). The <service-interface-mapping> element and the <service-endpoint-interface-mapping> element may be paired together zero or more times.
- <service-endpoint-interface-mapping>: Defines a mapping between the Java service endpoint interface type and the associated WSDL port and binding (one or more). The <service-interface-mapping> element and the <service-endpoint-interface-mapping> element may be paired together zero or more times.

Java Package Mapping (<package-mapping>)

Perhaps the most fundamental of these mappings is the package mapping that defines the mapping between a Java package name and WSDL XML namespace in this way:

- <package-mapping>: Indicates a mapping between a Java package name and a WSDL XML namespace with the sub-elements that follow.
- <package-type>: Fully qualified Java package name.
- <namespaceURI>: URI type to which the Java package name is mapped.

As a simple example, the `java-wsdl-mapping.xml` file included with this chapter's example in fact only needs to define this most critical element as shown here:

```
<package-mapping>
    <package-type>ejava.webservices.rpc</package-type>
    <namespaceURI>http://ws.beeshirts.com/wsdl</namespaceURI>
</package-mapping>
```

Java Class Mapping (`<java-xml-type-mapping>`)

The mapping between a Java class type and a WSDL type is accomplished via the following:

- `<java-xml-type-mapping>`: Defines a mapping between a Java class and an associated WSDL type with the sub-elements that follow.
- `<class-type>`: Fully qualified Java class name.
- `<root-type-qname>`: QName type associated with a WSDL document.
- `<qname-scope>`: Scopes the reference of a QName with the WSDL type to which it applies: `simpleType`, `complexType`, or `element`.
- `<variable-mapping>`: Defines a mapping between a Java variable and a corresponding WSDL element (zero or more).

Java Class Variable Mapping (`<variable-mapping>`)

The mapping between a variable on the Java class and a WSDL element is accomplished via the following:

- `<variable-mapping>`: Defines a mapping between a Java variable and a corresponding WSDL element with the sub-elements that follow.
- `<java-variable-name>`: The name of a data member on a Java class or property on a JavaBean.
- `<data-member/>`: Empty element used to indicate that the Java variable is a data member versus a JavaBean property if present (optional).
- `<xml-element-name>`: The name attribute value of the WSDL element corresponding to this Java variable.

Java Exception Mapping (`<exception-mapping>`)

The mapping between a Java exception type and a WSDL type is accomplished via the following:

- `<exception-mapping>`: Defines a mapping between a Java exception type and an associated WSDL message with the sub-elements that follow.
- `<exception-type>`: Fully qualified class name of the exception.

- `<wsdl-message>`: QName for a WSDL message mapped to and from this exception.
- `<constructor-parameter-order>`: Contains a collection of one or more `<element-name>` sub-elements that contain the names of the parameters associated with the exception's constructor (optional).

Java Service Interface Mapping (`<service-interface-mapping>`)

The mapping between a Java type for a Web service and a WSDL type is accomplished via the following:

- `<service-interface-mapping>`: Defines a mapping between a Java type for a Web service and a WSDL type via the following sub-elements.
- `<service-interface>`: Fully qualified class name of the Java type for the Web service either as `javax.xml.rpc.Service` for a static service or the generated interface.
- `<wsdl-service-name>`: QName type for the associated WSDL service name.
- `<port-mapping>`: Defines a mapping between a WSDL port name attribute in a `<port-name>` element and a Java name used to generate the service interface's `get`*`XXX`*`()` method to get the port in a `<java-port-name>` element (zero or more).

Java Service Endpoint Interface Mapping (`<service-endpoint-interface-mapping>`)

The mapping between a Java type for a Web service endpoint interface and WSDL port is accomplished via the following:

- `<service-endpoint-interface-mapping>`: Defines a mapping between the Java service endpoint interface type and the associated WSDL port and binding with the sub-elements that follow.
- `<service-endpoint-interface>`: Fully qualified Java class type for the service endpoint interface.
- `<wsdl-port-type>`: QName for the WSDL port type associated with the service endpoint.
- `<wsdl-binding>`: QName for the WSDL binding element associated with the service endpoint.
- `<service-endpoint-method-mapping>`: Defines a mapping between Java methods and WSDL operations (zero or more).

Java Service Endpoint Method Mapping (<service-endpoint-method-mapping>)

The mapping between Java methods for a Web service endpoint interface and WSDL port operations is accomplished via the following:

- <service-endpoint-method-mapping>: Defines a mapping between Java methods and WSDL operations with the sub-elements that follow.
- <java-method-name> Name of a Java method on the service endpoint interface.
- <wsdl-operation>: Name of the WSDL operation associated with the Java method.
- <wrapped-element/>: Empty element used to indicate that the WSDL message wraps an element type with the element name matching the operation name (optional).
- <method-param-parts-mapping>: Defines the mapping of Java input parameters to WSDL operation input messages (zero or more).
- <wsdl-return-value-mapping>: Defines the mapping of a Java output parameter to a WSDL operation output message (optional).

Java Service Endpoint Method Input Parameter Mapping (<method-param-parts-mapping>)

The mapping between Java method input parameters for a Web service endpoint interface method and WSDL port operation input messages is accomplished via the following:

- <method-param-parts-mapping>: Defines the mapping of Java input parameters to WSDL operation input messages with the sub-elements that follow.
- <param-position>: A non-negative integer indicating the position of the parameter.
- <param-type>: Fully qualified class name of the Java input parameter type.
- <wsdl-message-mapping>: Identifies a WSDL message associated with the Java input parameter.

Java Service Endpoint Method Parameter WSDL Message Mapping (<wsdl-message-mapping>)

The specification for the WSDL message to which a Java input parameter is mapped is accomplished via the following:

- <wsdl-message-mapping>: Identifies a WSDL message associated with the Java input parameter with the sub-elements that follow.
- <wsdl-message>: A QName for the WSDL message type.

- <wsdl-message-part-name>: A string name for the WSDL message part name.
- <parameter-mode>: Defines the input/output nature of the message as IN, OUT, or INOUT.
- <soap-header/>: Indicates whether the parameter is mapped to a SOAP header (optional).

Java Service Endpoint Method Output Parameter Mapping (<wsdl-return-value-mapping>)

The mapping between a Java method output parameter for a Web service endpoint interface method and WSDL port operation output message is accomplished via the following:

- <wsdl-return-value-mapping>: Defines the mapping of a Java output parameter to a WSDL operation output message with the sub-elements that follow.
- <method-return-value>: Fully qualified class name of the Java output parameter type.
- <wsdl-message>: QName for the WSDL message type associated with this output parameter.
- <wsdl-message-part-name>: String used to indicate a WSDL message part name (optional).

Web Services Web Component References

Up until this point in the chapter, we've discussed how to define deployment descriptor information such that a J2EE Web component may be deployed as a Web service. However, what if a J2EE Web component, or any J2EE component for that matter, wants to communicate with a Java-based Web service? If a J2EE Web component or other J2EE component wants to tap the services of a Web service, it must define a reference to that service from within its deployment descriptor. This is accomplished using the <service-ref> element as defined via the Web services client XML schema located at www.ibm.com/webservices/xsd/j2ee_web_services_client_1_1.xsd. This <service-ref> element is included as part of a jndiEnvironmentRefsGroup schema grouping defined as part of a common group used by other J2EE v1.4–compliant applications via the schema http://java.sun.com/xml/ns/j2ee/j2ee_1_4.xsd.

The <service-ref> element is defined inside of the web.xml file relatively positioned as illustrated here:

```
<web-app>
   ...
  <env-entry> ... </env-entry>
  <ejb-ref> ... </ejb-ref>
```

```
  <ejb-local-ref> ... </ejb-local-ref>
  <service-ref> ... </service-ref>
  <resource-ref> ... </resource-ref>
   ...
</web-app>
```

Web Service Reference (<service-ref>)

Zero or more of such <service-ref> elements can be defined within the <web-app> element. A <service-ref> element can contain the following sub-elements:

- Description group: A collection of optional description-related elements, including <description>, <display-name>, and <icon> (optional).
- <service-ref-name>: Logical name for a reference to a Web service with the name usually beginning with the string `service/`.
- <service-interface>: Fully qualified class name for the Web service client interface: `javax.xml.rpc.Service` or a generated interface name.
- <wsdl-file>: URI of the service's WSDL file relative to the module in which this component is contained (optional).
- <jaxrpc-mapping-file>: Location of a Java-WSDL mapping file relative to the module in which this component is contained (optional).
- <service-qname>: QName for the Web service being referenced in an associated WSDL file (optional).
- <port-component-ref>: Contains a <service-endpoint-interface> with the fully qualified class name of a service endpoint and a <port-component-link> containing a value as defined inside of a `webservices.xml` file's <port-component-name> element (zero or more). The port component name may be in the same module archive file (for example, WAR or EJB JAR file) or in another module file that is in the same J2EE enterprise application (for example, EAR file). The relative path name of the module's archive file followed by a # character may be prepended to the `port-component-name` to explicitly indicate which Web service in which module archive file is referenced.
- <handler>: Defines that information needed to configure and associate a client-side handler with a port component client interface akin to the format used to describe server-side handlers for the `webservices.xml` file (zero or more).

As a simple example, if another J2EE Web component wanted to reference our example Web service, we might have the following in the `web.xml` deployment descriptor as a <service-ref> element:

```
<service-ref>
  <description> Reference to a Web service </description>
  <service-ref>service/QueryService</service-ref>
  <service-interface>javax.xml.rpc.Service</service-interface>
```

```
  <wsdl-file>QueryService.wsdl</wsdl-file>
  <jaxrpc-mapping-file>java-wsdl-mapping.xml</jaxrpc-mapping-file>
  <service-qname>QueryService</service-qname>
  <port-component-ref>
    <service-endpoint-interface>
      ejava.webservices.rpc.QueryServer
    </service-endpoint-interface>
    <port-component-link>QueryServerPort</port-component-link>
  </port-component-ref>
</service-ref>
```

The J2EE Web component referencing this Web service may then do so using JNDI to look up the Web service handle as exemplified here:

```
String serviceName = "java:comp/env/service/QueryService";
InitialContext ctx = new InitialContext();
Service webService = (Service) ctx.lookup(serviceName);
```

Web Services Web Component Deployment

This last section completes the J2EE Web component as a Web service deployment picture by describing the remaining steps needed for deployment. Primarily, in addition to the standard deployment descriptors described, a set of vendor-specific deployment descriptors must also be generated. The various compiled classes and deployment descriptors are then packaged inside of a WAR module file. Finally, the WAR file is deployed into a J2EE Web container with a JAX-RPC runtime.

Vendor-Specific Deployment Configuration

The standard deployment descriptors described thus far in this chapter enable you to specify the bulk of deployment configuration parameters involved with deploying a J2EE Web component as a Web service. In addition to such standard deployment descriptors, vendor container implementations will also require other deployment descriptors to complete the deployment configuration process. Primarily, vendor-specific deployment descriptors are needed to map from any defined logical values in the standard deployment descriptors to physical process-related values associated with the vendor's server.

Such vendor-specific as well as standard deployment descriptor files are often generated by either command-line or GUI tools. However, it may behoove you to be moderately cognizant of such deployment descriptors specific to your vendor's deployment environment in order to better understand the runtime deployment behavior associated with your J2EE applications.

> **Note**
>
> The example in this chapter is deployable to J2EE v1.4–compliant environments supporting Web services with J2EE Web components. The J2EE v1.4 reference implementation is of course one such environment. Appendix A provides more detailed information on how to configure and deploy the example in this chapter.

Appendix A also provides a link to a Web site to which additional supported configuration profiles will be posted as more vendors begin to support J2EE v1.4–compliant Web services.

The J2EE reference implementation uses a `sun-j2ee-ri.xml` file to configure J2EE Web component information such as mapping the JDBC connection pool logical name to a physical JNDI name. The `config.xml` and `config-client.xml` files included with this chapter's examples are also needed and respectively associated with configuring the JAX-RPC runtime on the server-side and client side.

Web Service Web Component Packaging

Chapter 19 described how to package and deploy Java servlets using WAR files. The same packaging rules apply here but include the packaging of Web service deployment descriptors and additional Web service–related classes. Some additional rules must be considered when packaging a J2EE Web component as a Web service. For one, the `webservices.xml` file must be packaged beneath the `WEB-INF` directory of the WAR file. Furthermore, the JAX-RPC type-mapping file (for example, `java-wsdl-mapping.xml`) must be located and named according to the `<jaxrpc-mapping-file>` element contained beneath a `<webservice-description>` element defined in the `webservices.xml` file.

After placing the files in their appropriate directory structure, the WSDL file and any Web service skeletons may be generated using a vendor's compilation tool. A WAR file for the J2EE Web components implemented as Web services may then be constructed as described in Chapter 19. A J2EE enterprise application file may also be constructed to cohesively combine one or more WAR files as well as other J2EE module archive files into the same enterprise application (to be described in Chapter 23, "Enterprise Application Services"). Finally, a vendor-specific deployment tool is then used to deploy the J2EE Web application to a running J2EE Web container/server process.

Note

Different J2EE vendor implementations provide different types of tools for generating Web service skeletons and WSDL files, as well as for deploying J2EE applications. The J2EE reference implementation uses a program called `ws-compile` to generate WSDL files from Java-based Web services and any skeletons to implement such service. The J2EE reference implementation uses a program called `deploy-tool` to deploy J2EE applications.

Appendix A describes the configuration instructions associated with deploying the example for this chapter. Appendix A also provides a link to a Web site that may be referenced for additional J2EE v1.4–compliant Web service configuration instructions as they become available.

Conclusions

J2EE Web components may be deployed as Web services using J2EE v1.4–compliant Web containers. The implementation of such components follows the model described in Chapter 10 for creating Web service implementation classes. Standard `web.xml` deployment descriptors are configured and used to deploy the component as J2EE Web components. Standard `webservices.xml` and `java-wsdl-mapping.xml` deployment descriptors are used to configure the component to expose itself as a Web service and enable the container to map between Java and WSDL types. As seen throughout this chapter, much of the work involved with deploying a J2EE Web component as a Web service involves specifying the configuration of such deployment descriptors. Although vendors may provide you with tools that allow you to automatically generate such deployment descriptors, it behooves the enterprise class developer to understand such file formats to better ensure portability across J2EE Web server implementations, as well as to tune such files for your particular deployment needs.

VI

Enterprise Applications Enabling

23

Enterprise Application Services

ENTERPRISE APPLICATION PLATFORMS PROVIDE OFF-THE-SHELF and standard reference architectures for building enterprise applications. Enterprise platforms provide enterprise applications with distributed accessibility, common distributed services, data-enabling services, Web-enabling services, and connectivity to legacy applications. This chapter initially covers the basic evolution of enterprise application platforms and the most basic architecture of such platforms for enabling scalable and dependable access to enterprise applications. This chapter then gives more specific details behind how such services are provided to enterprise application components and who fulfills what roles in these application server architectures. Throughout our discussions, we specifically focus on and introduce the notion of Enterprise JavaBeans (EJBs) and discuss how EJB application servers help application-enable an enterprise.

In this chapter, you will learn:

- The basic context of an enterprise application platform and its role in the enterprise, as well as the various manifestations and evolutions of such platforms.
- The pros and cons of building enterprise applications in a standalone runtime environment.
- The architecture and pros and cons of building enterprise applications using an application server and EJBs.
- The partitioning of knowledge among architecture providers and the roles they assume when application servers are used.
- The basic approach for building enterprise application components to operate within an application server with a specific discussion of EJB component implementations.
- The basic approach for building enterprise application client interfaces to enterprise application components with a specific discussion of EJB client interfaces.
- The basic approach for implementing enterprise application clients including EJB standalone and J2EE application clients.

- The features provided by application servers for configuring and deploying applications with a specific discussion of XML-based EJB deployment descriptors.
- The basic underlying approaches by application servers for providing management services to enterprise application components.

Enterprise Application Platforms

As we've already discussed throughout the book, enterprise applications have particular needs that make rapidly building them a complicated proposition at times. We've discussed numerous methods for effectively building enterprise applications such as object-oriented and component-based development paradigms. We've also described many techniques and technologies for communications-enabling, providing common standard COTS services, providing systems assurance, and Web-enabling an enterprise system. Enterprise platforms can encapsulate all such development paradigms, techniques, technologies, and services inside of an integrated framework for building enterprise applications. Such frameworks often follow the component-container model of development advocated throughout this book.

Figure 23.1 depicts a high-level overview of an enterprise application framework and its context. At the center of the diagram is the framework itself with a set of services that it provides for use by enterprise application components. Interface contracts from component to framework and from framework to component often exist to provide well-defined responsibility boundaries. From an enterprise application client's perspective, they are able to tap the application-specific functionality of the enterprise application component with all the distribution, usability, scalability, assurance, and accessibility benefits enabled by the enterprise application framework. Such services are often provided transparent to the enterprise application component or are encapsulated by framework APIs. Enterprise application frameworks also often offer seamless connectivity to external enterprise systems and resources such as DBMSs. Finally, many frameworks provide a means to easily configure and deploy enterprise applications, as well as sometimes provide an integrated environment for developing enterprise application components.

TP Monitor Platforms

Transaction Processing (TP) monitors were one of the first types of enterprise platforms having significant commercial success whose services could be relied on and utilized by enterprise applications. The enterprise applications involved here are transaction-processing applications that have requirements to operate within the context of a transaction. TP monitors are operating environments that manage the transactional behavior of transaction-processing applications. TP monitors handle the creation, termination, and management of the transactional contexts for the transaction-processing application. Because effective transaction management involves the management of database connections, network resources, and operating-system resources, a TP monitor can offload a significant amount of coding effort that would otherwise need to be developed by applications programmers. Furthermore, because transaction-processing applications have enterprise class client request scalability requirements, TP monitors are designed to manage the scalability and availability of applications as well.

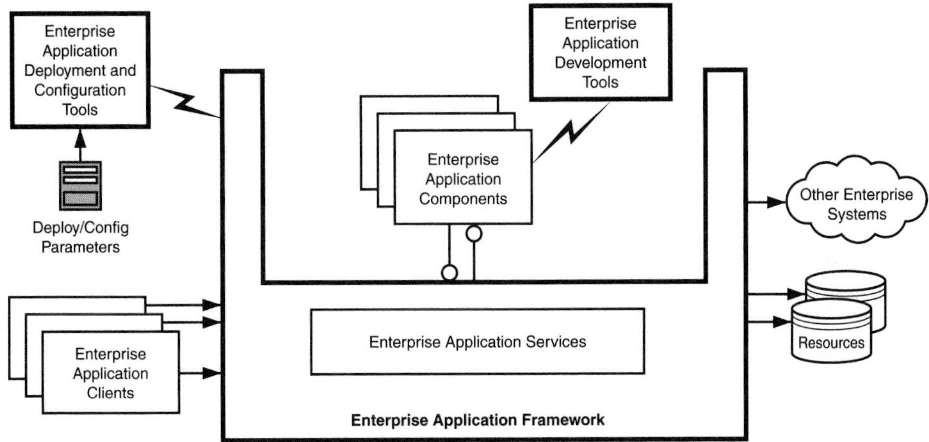

Figure 23.1 The enterprise application framework architecture.

TP monitors are middle-tier servers that sit between a distributed transaction application client and resources (for example, DBMSs), as depicted in Figure 23.2. TP monitors provide the following services to transaction-processing applications that run inside of their environment:

- *Naming Service Support:* TP monitors often manage the mapping of a client's request of a named application service to the actual reference for that application running in the TP monitor's domain.
- *Connection Handling:* Client connections are multiplexed by a TP monitor process connection handler. The connection handler helps manage the utilization of network resources and funnels client requests to transaction processing applications.
- *Resource Handling:* A TP monitor can also be configured to use information embedded in a particular client request to an application and determine which resource (for example, DBMS) should be used to satisfy the request. Furthermore, standard interfaces to resources, such as the X/Open XA interface, can provide access to a heterogeneous variety of resources.
- *Availability Assurance:* TP monitors can provide for a more scalable client request base via load balancing across redundant servers. TP monitors can also often support fail-over to redundant processes in the event of a failure.

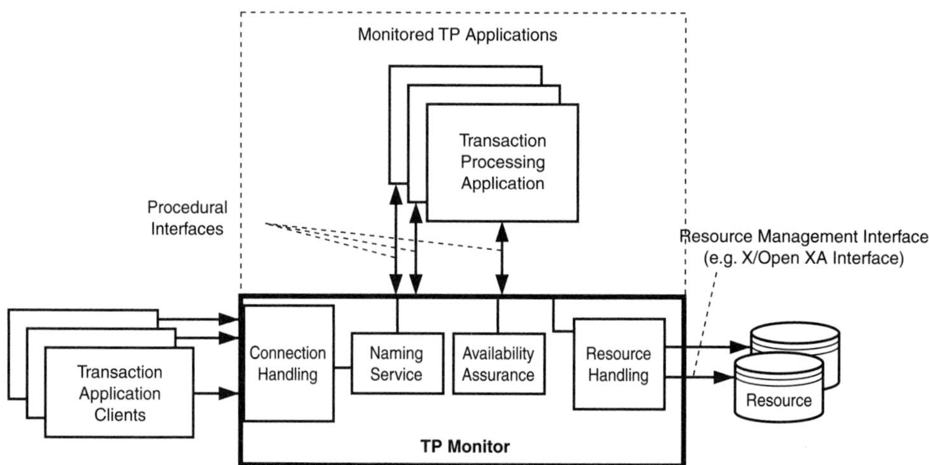

Figure 23.2 The transaction-processing monitor architecture.

TP monitors were popular precursors to the application frameworks that we utilize in this book. Many TP monitors adopt the X/Open DTP standard. TP monitors thus function as transaction managers with additional services needed to build scalable enterprise-class transaction processing applications. However, the need to build enterprise class applications with more general needs aside from pure transaction processing alone has given rise to new terminology and to more generic application frameworks. Furthermore, the need for standards that support object- and component-based application models also has driven the evolution of TP monitors. You'll learn about a few of the more significant evolutions from TP monitoring models to more generic and standard application platforms throughout the remainder of this chapter.

OTMs

The popularity of TP monitor products has been indicative of the general need for assistance by organizations that want to build enterprise systems more rapidly and more robustly than was previously possible. However, the modern heterogeneous enterprise has also placed a higher premium on standard interoperability, as well as on use of object-oriented and component-based system development paradigms. The largely proprietary and remote procedure-oriented nature of the older TP monitors fell short in these regards. This has been the reason for the introduction of the Object Transaction Monitor (OTM) into the marketplace.

OTMs, as depicted in Figure 23.3, offer various features and services that make them an attractive solution for modern enterprise systems development. For one, OTMs extend the TP monitor concept to define and interact with object-oriented interfaces. OTMs are also constructed according to the component-container model of development and therefore provide TP monitor services to component-based enterprise applications. Thus, transaction services, connection handling services, naming services, resource management, and availability services can all be provided to components built on top of OTM frameworks. Because OTMs follow the component-container model, they also quite naturally augment the TP monitor suite of general services to provide a form of component activation service.

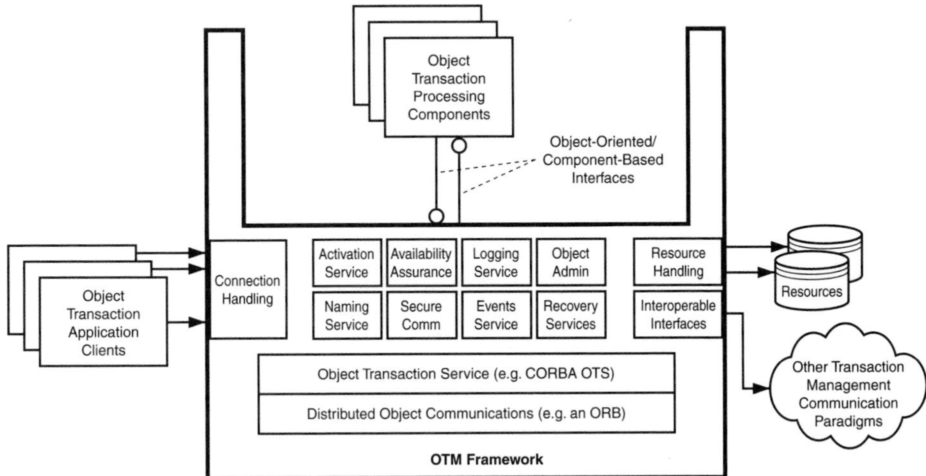

Figure 23.3 The Object Transaction Monitor architecture.

As another general rule, OTMs are also built on top of a distributed object computing paradigm such as CORBA. In fact, most popular OTM implementations are built on top of an ORB and also utilize CORBA Object Transaction Services. The core OTM products in the marketplace have also beefed up their product offerings with additional features and services for applications. These services include asynchronous event messaging services, secure communication services, logging services, distributed object administration services, recovery and fault-tolerance services, and interoperability interfaces with other transaction monitoring and communication paradigms. Thus, as OTM products have matured, they have also grown in the scope of their enterprise application applicability.

Generic Application Frameworks

As more services are added to an OTM framework, any pure transaction processing application focus of the framework becomes blurred. Rather, the framework begins to serve as a more generic framework for building a more general class of enterprise applications. These more generic application frameworks have consequently assumed a new marketing term and have now become what we refer to as *application servers*. Although we have highlighted the evolutionary path of such application servers from TP monitors and OTMs, vendors from other market focuses have also beefed up their product offerings with application server–oriented features. Database vendors, such as Oracle and Sybase, have particularly been aggressive with building auxiliary application services atop their existing database management service frameworks. Web server vendors, such as Netscape (whose products are now owned by Sun), also evolved their Web-serving product suites to support more generic enterprise application serving capabilities. Of course, as perhaps the only example of a vendor who has attempted to grow an enterprise application framework out of an operating system, Microsoft has also defined an enterprise application service framework that is dependent on and integrated with the Microsoft Windows operating system.

Figure 23.4 depicts a generic architecture for such a convergence of enterprise application service provisioning. Although not all application server products contain all the services depicted in this diagram, most of the core services provided by any particular product have a representative set of services in the diagram. With such a generic set of enterprise application services provided by an enterprise application framework, enterprise application components can be more rapidly built and allow a developer to focus on the business logic of an application rather than on common application infrastructure services. Some enterprise application service products will also provide tools to facilitate the development, deployment, and configuration of enterprise applications within the enterprise application framework.

Many of the services depicted in Figure 23.4 have already been described in this book. However, the enterprise application framework provides a means to offer access and utilization of such services to enterprise application components in a fashion that simplifies enterprise application development. We have already seen an example of this with the enterprise Web-enabling interfaces described in the context of J2EE Java Servlets and JSPs in Part V, "Enterprise Web Enabling." This part of the book begins to focus on the general enterprise application–enabling aspects of an enterprise system as provided by an enterprise application framework. In fact, we typically distinguish between products that provide Web-enabling services and products that provide more general enterprise application–enabling services because Web-enabling solutions can require less in the way of service support than can more generic enterprise application–enabling solutions.

Although we indeed have covered many of the services shown in Figure 23.4 throughout this book, a few new terms should jump out at you. For one, object persistence services within a data connectivity service suite of tools can help map application objects into relational database models. Enterprise application integration services may also be provided to enable connectivity to legacy and auxiliary enterprise applications from enterprise application components built atop the enterprise application framework. A set of management services for managing enterprise applications such as network and system administration, logging, and debugging services may also be provided within a framework. Furthermore, a set of configuration and deployment services is almost always provided to facilitate the configuration and deployment of enterprise application components that operate inside of the enterprise application framework environment. Generic enterprise application frameworks thus provide a platform for creating enterprise applications and allow enterprise application developers to focus on implementation of enterprise business logic and rules.

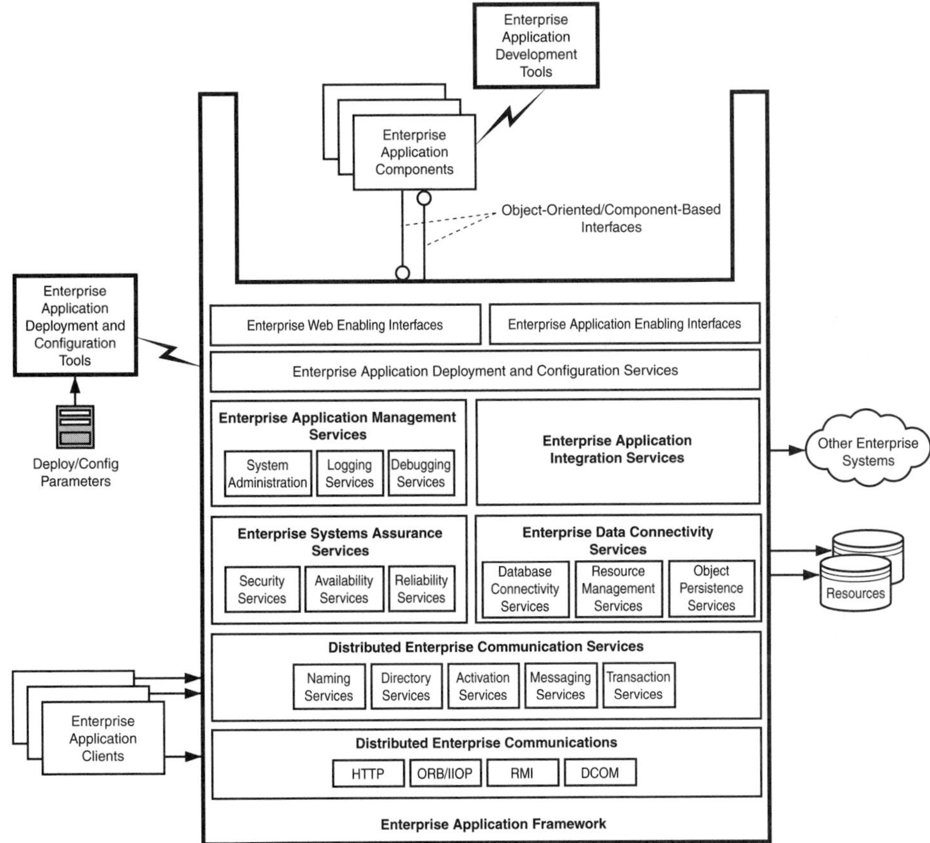

Figure 23.4 The generic application server framework architecture.

Standard Java-Based Generic Application Framework

As many vendor-specific enterprise application framework solutions began to enter the market, the threat of many divergent camps of enterprise application development solution provisioning was heightened. Enterprise application components developed for one framework would be able to operate only inside the confines of that framework vendor's product suite. Even though CORBA technologies for vendor interoperability were being used inside of the framework, there was no assurance that components which were developed for one vendor product would also work inside of another product. Sun

Microsystems began to address this threat with the introduction of the Enterprise JavaBeans (EJB) 1.0 specification in 1998.

The EJB specification defined a Java-based standard interface contract that exists between enterprise application components and enterprise application service framework products. Thus, EJBs implemented for one vendor's enterprise application service framework product solution could run atop another vendor's enterprise application service framework product solution. The interfaces remain fixed, but the underlying service provisioning implementations naturally vary from vendor to vendor. Sun later extended this concept to the more pervasive J2EE specification. Figure 23.5 depicts the standard server-side enterprise application serving architecture defined by the J2EE specification. Java Servlets, JSPs, and EJBs can all be developed to utilize the Java enterprise APIs shown in Figure 23.5, which provide standard interfaces to many of the services of an application server framework.

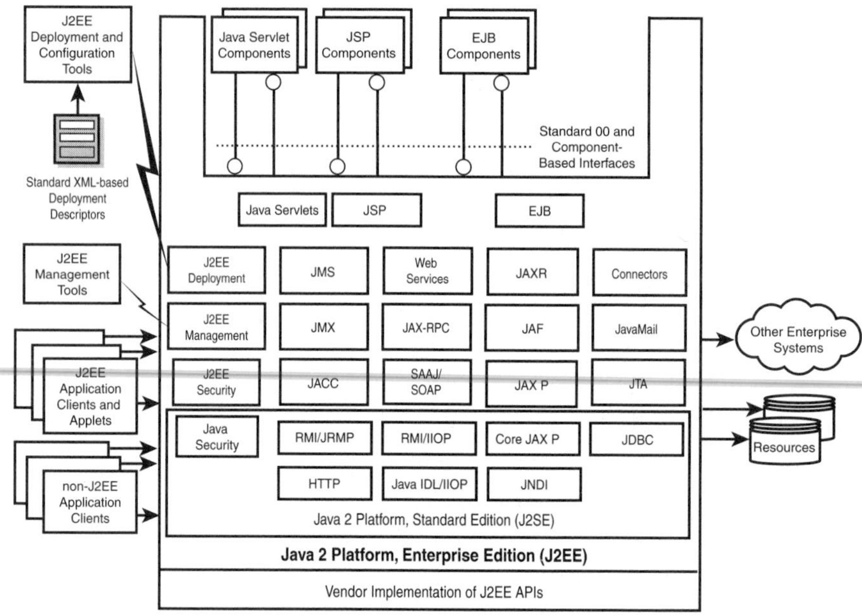

Figure 23.5 The J2EE standard application server framework architecture.

Because the J2EE incorporates the J2SE into its architecture, J2EE vendors can also implement application service products that are operating-system and hardware-platform independent. However, some vendors may still indeed opt to take advantage of certain platform-specific optimization features within their application service implementations. Within the confines of the standard APIs, vendors in fact will primarily differentiate their product offerings based on levels of system assurance and performance. Vendors are also currently able to differentiate their products in terms of offering sophisticated development and deployment tools and tools that integrate J2EE-based applications with other enterprise systems, resources, and clients. Perhaps most significant is the fact that vendors currently and will most likely continue to define value-added functionality via APIs that lie outside of the standards. It is thus up to the applications developer to provide adapter logic for such APIs to fully enable migration between platform implementations. Nevertheless, the level of platform interoperability achievable through even the current set of J2EE specifications has never before been possible.

In addition to standard application service API specifications, the J2EE specification has also defined a standard format for describing how applications should be deployed via XML-based deployment descriptors. Additionally, standard means for building Java-based application clients and Java applets to connect with J2EE server-side applications are also defined. The effort to provide standard interfaces for enterprise application components has thus come a long way in a relatively short time. Standards have already begun to spill over into other areas of application development that lie outside of pure server-component standardization. Only time will tell how fully vendors will embrace all of these standards. We suspect that as the scope of J2EE standardization grows, levels of compliance will be and should be established to provide a compromise for some vendors to allow their products to shine, as well as to lower the barrier of entry for newcomers.

CORBA Components

As Sun was defining a pure Java-based standard for creating enterprise applications via EJBs, the OMG was also hard at work to define a CORBA-based enterprise application framework. The CORBAcomponents specification defines language-independent standards for building enterprise components using existing and extended CORBA technology standards according to a new model of development referred to as the CORBA components model. Because of the popularity of EJBs, the CORBA components model also defines an explicit mapping to the EJB model and allows for the deployment of EJB components to CORBA components-based frameworks. The CORBA components model, however, is touted to be extendable to other application server interface models as well and is certainly language independent.

Figure 23.6 illustrates the architecture of the CORBA components model and the new interface models that have emerged as a result. Interfaces to CORBA components from a client perspective are still defined according to CORBA IDL. CORBA component interfaces are associated with facets or views of the component's overall interface as well. CORBA components can be defined to connect to other CORBA enterprise objects via an interface syntax for the component known as receptacles. Component attributes, sources of events from components, and events that a component consumes can also be defined for a component and enable the container to manage configuration and event handling services for components. Additionally, a means for defining local interfaces to the container from the component and interfaces to components from containers is specified. As a final note on interface models, the Component Implementation

Definition Language (CIDL) provides a means to describe the structure and state of component implementations that play a significant role for containers to provide object persistence services.

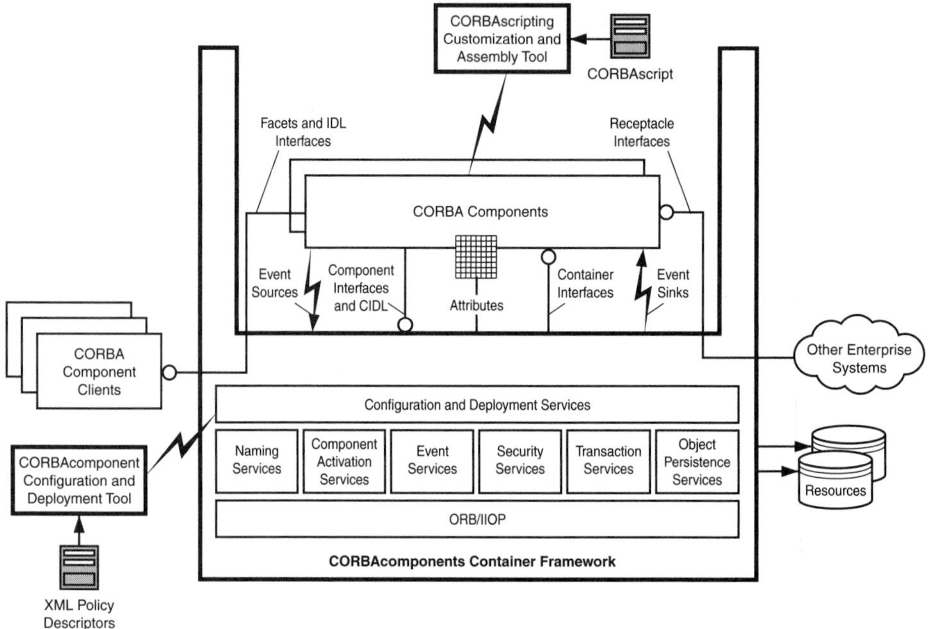

Figure 23.6 The CORBAcomponents framework architecture.

Configuration and deployment is also a concern for CORBAcomponents, and a standard means for configuring and deploying components via XML-based descriptors is specified in the CORBA Components specification. Such an approach and supporting tools simplify the capability for CORBAcomponents to use CORBAservices that are otherwise very difficult for application developers to use out of the box. Although XML descriptors can be used to describe how to configure and deploy a particular application, a complement to CORBA Components, known as the CORBA Component Scripting specification, is also utilized to provide a more elaborate means for customizing the business logic and assembly of components using easy-to-use scripting languages. All of these features make CORBAcomponents an interesting standard to monitor and watch for further development and signs of industry acceptance. Although CORBAcomponents has shown some promise with its effort to define compatibility with the EJB model of development, only time will tell how compatible the technologies will remain in the future.

Microsoft's Generic .NET Application Framework

As you are probably aware and as should come as no surprise to you, Microsoft also has defined its own enterprise application framework architecture that is tightly integrated with the Microsoft software and services. Although some people frown on such high levels of dependency and tight coupling, others argue that such a high level of integration and platform-dependent solutions have produced a more cohesive enterprise architecture for more immediate use by industry. Figure 23.7 depicts the .NET architecture of Microsoft.

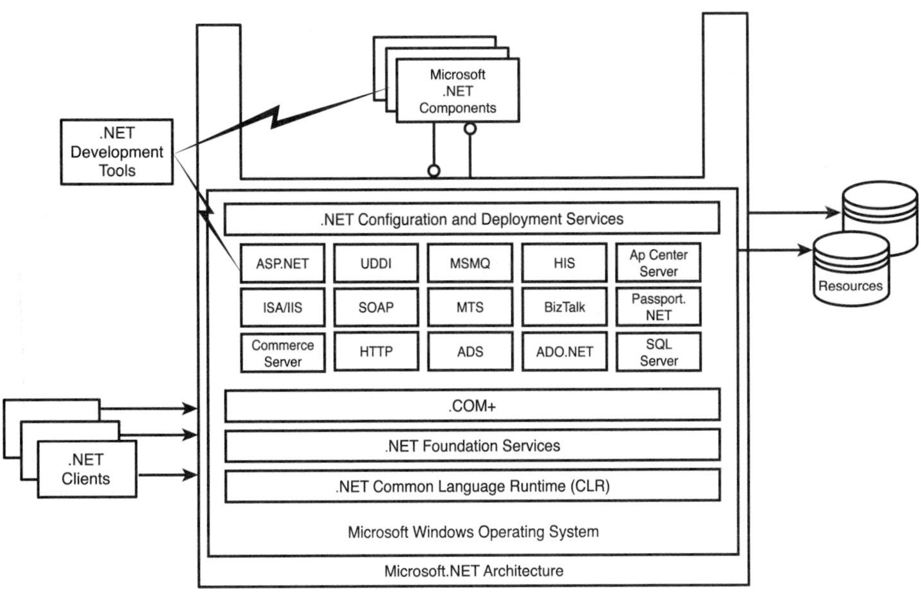

Figure 23.7 Microsoft .NET architecture.

At the center of the Microsoft .NET architecture is the Common Language Runtime (CLR) engine. Microsoft has adopted the Java concept of creating a runtime engine atop of which an intermediate byte code language interfaces. The CLR is thus akin to the Java Runtime Engine (JRE), and the Microsoft Intermediate Language (MSIL) is akin to the Java bytecodes that run atop the JRE. Thus, .NET development tools (such as Microsoft's Visual Studio) are used to compile source code into MSIL, which is then run inside a CLR. Although the CLR is theoretically portable to other operating systems, it is currently interwoven with the Microsoft Windows operating system platform. It was uncertain at the time of this writing whether the CLR was being ported to other operating systems, whether there were any licensing issues with such porting, and whether such porting was even technically feasible. Suffice it to say, however, that the CLR is optimized and designed with the Microsoft Windows operating system in mind.

A key .NET concept is to allow various languages to be compiled into MSIL and thus offer the developer a choice of programming language when working with .NET. However, such languages must adhere to the Common Type System (CTS) in order to enable compilation into MSIL and become code manageable by the CLR. For many languages targeted to .NET, this means that either certain features common to those languages cannot be used and/or additional features must be added to that language. As an example, to compile Visual Basic (VB) code to run atop a .NET CLR, a variation of VB must be utilized that supports certain object-oriented features. Thus, although VB programmers do not have to learn a new syntax for running code atop the .NET CLR, they must learn a new programming paradigm that may be arguably more or less difficult than learning a new syntax. Microsoft has also introduced a new programming language called C# (pronounced "see-sharp"), which is optimized to run atop the CLR and is syntactically very similar to the Java language.

Even more programming restrictions must be considered if you want your code to interoperate with code implemented in other languages. The Common Language Specification (CLS) specifies a set of features that must be supported by a language in order to interoperate with other languages. Regardless, .NET greatly simplifies assembly and deployment of .NET-based code by providing a set of configuration and deployment services to ensure that all the right libraries for a particular application are properly assembled.

.NET also includes a wide range of foundation services. The foundation services include a set of common system services that have roles strikingly similar to the roles of many of the core J2SE APIs. For example, .NET system services include APIs offering services such as base language types, collections, basic database access, I/O streams, TCP/IP networking, HTTP, reflection, distributed object access, authorization, and fundamental UI widgets. Sitting logically above the Windows operating system, CLR, and the foundation services, COM+ is also provided to support a more sophisticated container-component model of development for COM-based applications that can also take advantage of new .NET features. Additional foundational services include SOAP, UDDI, Microsoft Message Queue Server (MSMQ), Microsoft Transaction Server (MTS), Active Directory Service (ADS), Active Server Pages presentation services (ASP.NET), and Active Data Objects data access services (ADO.NET).

Unlike the J2SE and J2EE standards, the .NET architecture also includes various Microsoft tools, software, and servers. On the development tools front, the Microsoft Visual Studio toolset is used to build .NET applications and components. .NET also aggregates various Microsoft tools, software, servers and services such as Windows 2000, SQL Server (database server), Host Integration Server (HIS for mainframe EAI), application center server (cluster management), Internet Information Server (IIS for Web serving), Internet Security and Acceleration Server (ISA Web serving and firewall), BizTalk Server (EAI server), Commerce Server (e-commerce engine), and Passport.NET services (authentication service). The .NET architecture also assumes that software will be installed on various embedded and mobile devices that enable such devices to interoperate with the .NET world. Finally, .NET also includes the various Microsoft end user software utilities that have been historically offered via the desktop (for example, Word and Excel) and that now have evolved to be integrated with the .NET architecture.

In summary, the .NET architecture is Microsoft's view of how computing in any environment and throughout the world should occur. This view includes how enterprise, desktop, and embedded platforms should operate and those Microsoft products they should utilize. .NET is under the control of Microsoft and is thus more of a proprietary standard than a global enterprise standard. .NET is also more of a monolithic and relatively closed architecture than a layered, modular, and open architecture. Nevertheless, .NET is an important architecture to which any enterprise developer should pay attention due to Microsoft's significant market presence. Developers should pay special attention to how to integrate with applications developed atop .NET. Luckily for the readers of this book, the primary and most significant means for such integration will be performed via Web Services, and thus the Java-based Web Service APIs and technologies described throughout this book are specifically relevant to integration with .NET-based services.

Application-Specific Platforms

Instead of supplying general platforms and frameworks for building enterprise applications, a few companies have earned their revenue by supplying more application-specific frameworks to use in enterprise application environments. Such frameworks are designed to facilitate one or more specific business activities of an enterprise and perhaps even within a specific application domain. Some of these application-specific frameworks build on existing generic enterprise application platforms, although others are built on proprietary platforms. The key advantage to using such platforms is that they are often more rapidly deployed when the abstract application model for which they've been built closely matches the actual enterprise application to which it is applied. The key disadvantage to using such platforms is the lack of extensibility and interoperability of such products.

The OMG has partially addressed the issue of application-specific interoperability within its suite of higher-level CORBA specifications. CORBAfacilities are specifications defined at a higher level than the CORBA ORB and CORBAservices specifications. CORBAfacilities defined at the vertical market level define standard interfaces to specific types of applications such that vendors who implement those specifications can provide a standards-based interface to an application-specific framework. Similarly, CORBA Domain Interfaces define standard interfaces to systems from certain industrial domains, such as manufacturing.

Enterprise Resource Planning (ERP) software systems are nonstandardized application-specific frameworks that have been very popular with enterprise IT departments in the past. ERP software platforms, such as those by PeopleSoft, SAP, BAAN, and J.D. Edwards, are used to manage some specific aspect of a business such as parts purchasing, product planning, inventory management, order tracking, supply management, customer service, finance, quality management, and human resources. ERPs are often supplied with client software, server software, and a database connectivity solution all tightly integrated with one another. Although ERP software is catered to a specific business activity, customization of that business activity for a specific enterprise is often possible via some form of scripting and database configuration. Although ERPs have seen some success in industry due to the near-term benefits from their application, a lack of extensibility and interoperability of certain ERP products can lead to a stagnant and isolated enterprise systems solution.

Product Data Management (PDM) systems are another application-specific type of enterprise system mainly catering to the manufacturing domain and used to manage engineering design information as it evolves from initial concept to production and maintenance. Engineering information managed by PDM systems includes product part information, specifications, schematics, and so on. PDM system frameworks typically provide a generic set of business modeling libraries that can be customized for a particular PDM application. PDM systems include data persistence services, data classification and relationship management services, and software services for managing the flow of data and the tracking of operations performed on data.

Even Sun and some Java Community Process specifications have ventured into the application-specific framework business and standards process with a collection of Java-based application-specific frameworks. As an example, the Java Telephony API (JTAPI) framework is used to provide a standard Java-based means for supporting telephony networks across a range of platforms.

Application-specific frameworks are very attractive to IT departments and to enterprise organizations that want to rapidly deploy a specific type of business enterprise application. However, organizations need to be wary of whether the abstract model for which the application-specific framework has been built can be customized well enough to sufficiently model the enterprise's actual business process. More often than not, such application-specific frameworks require extensive consulting time to assist with the customization and help with redefining the organization's business process to fit into the new model provided by the framework. Enterprises also need to be aware of the underlying architecture on which the application-specific framework has been built. Application-specific frameworks built atop CORBA and the J2EE may have a greater chance for extensibility and interoperability than those products built atop proprietary underpinnings.

Enterprise Application Management

Thus far, this chapter has described many of the enterprise application frameworks of the past, present, and imminent future. This book in general focuses on the specific Java-based enterprise application technologies and frameworks you can use to build enterprise systems. Although a detailed discussion of how these applications can be managed in a distributed enterprise network at runtime is beyond the scope of this book, it is nonetheless an important consideration and something that warrants some mention here. Enterprise application management deals with the management of enterprise applications across a heterogeneous distributed network for applications that range from scalable distributed applications to embedded enterprise applications. The management of such applications is greatly facilitated when they can be configured, monitored, shut down, restarted, and updated from a remote administration location.

Although many standard network management frameworks exist, Sun and a few key industry leaders have developed a Java-based standard via the Java Community Process that is now partially incorporated within J2EE. The Java Management Extension (JMX) specification defines a framework, a set of APIs, and services for managing distributed network services. An instrumentation-level standard defines a means for making any Java-based object resource capable of being managed by the JMX framework. An agent-level standard defines a means for building distributed agent containers of instrumented Java-based object resources. Agents provide services to such resources and communicate with distributed network management servers defined at a management-level standard. Finally, JMX also defines APIs to enable the use of existing network management standards.

Enterprise application management thus may require some instrumentation considerations when you're building your enterprise applications so that they can be managed by a distributed network management framework such as JMX. Some enterprise-class J2EE environments indeed provide a means to manage Java Servlets, JSPs, and EJBs via a user-friendly GUI-based management interface. However, effective use of such services may require nonstandard instrumentation of your J2EE components. To address this issue, J2EE v1.4 now includes the J2EE Management API that offers a standard interface to vendor-supplied tools that need to monitor and manage J2EE applications. The J2EE Management API inside the J2EE v1.4 requires partial support for v1.1 of the JMX API now but will likely require broader JMX support in a future J2EE specification.

Standalone Enterprise Applications

Throughout this book, we have described the technologies that can be used to build Java enterprise applications. Direct use of these technologies without any augmented server environment typically requires an application architecture as depicted in Figure 23.8. Here we see a "standalone" enterprise application utilizing the APIs offered by a database connectivity solution (for example, JDBC), a distributed enterprise communications paradigm (for example, CORBA, RMI), a set of distributed communications services (for example, JNDI, JMS, JTS), and an enterprise security assurance solution (for example, Java Security). Of course, all of our sample applications of these services built in this book use a Java runtime environment.

Some of the sample Java enterprise applications we have built using these services have run in a standalone fashion without the use of any container environment or enterprise application framework. These applications are just the plain old Java applications with which you are probably most familiar, and they operate using a J2SE type of environment along with separately packaged standard Java extension APIs and implementations. Such standalone applications were often, in fact, the only option available to enterprise programmers using Java before the birth of application server environments.

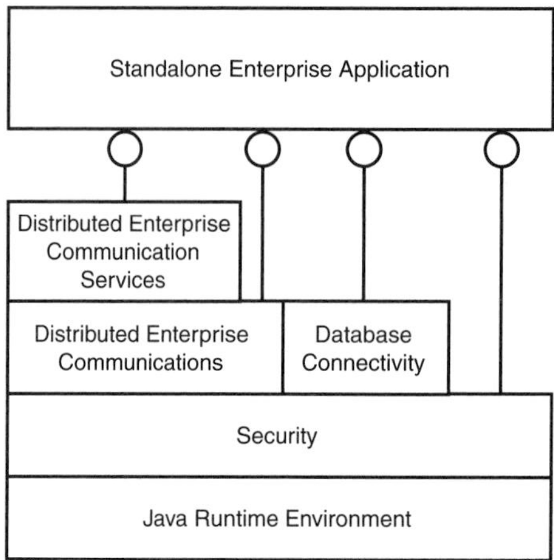

Figure 23.8 Standalone enterprise applications.

Standalone enterprise applications, however, can require a lot of coding effort to make them fully functional in a multiuser, heterogeneous, distributed, secure, and scalable enterprise environment. Recall from Part III, "Enterprise Communications Enabling," that use of the communications-enabling technologies often requires the need to understand a special interface language, requires thread-safety design considerations, and requires an understanding of how to create scalable server implementations. Also recall from Part II, "Enterprise Data Enabling," that use of JDBC requires careful consideration of which drivers to use and how to create connection resources. The preceding section introduced some of the concepts for why application server frameworks, such as J2EE EJB frameworks, help alleviate some of these concerns, but the remainder of this chapter further explains how such application server frameworks accomplish this task. Furthermore, we pursue this discussion in the context of EJB application servers.

Application Server–Based Enterprise Applications

Thus far in this chapter we have described the various types of enterprise application frameworks that have evolved over the years and the types of services they provide for enterprise application developers. These application services essentially provide all the services shown under the standalone enterprise application depicted in Figure 23.8 and help alleviate some of the infrastructure coding that would otherwise be embedded within the standalone enterprise application. Figure 23.9 depicts another view of an application server architecture, including the primary elements that compose a functioning enterprise application serving environment. Specific relationships to J2EE and EJB concepts are also indicated in the diagram. These are the primary application server elements:

- *Enterprise Application Development Tools:* Enterprise application development tools represent those software utilities used to design, implement, build, and deploy enterprise applications. Some development tools come equipped or are integrated with application servers. The J2EE Deployment API, in fact, specifies a standard interface contract between tools and containers for deploying J2EE-compliant applications.
- *Enterprise Application Component:* The enterprise application component encapsulates the business logic and data of an enterprise application. Enterprise application components are written in a fashion that frees them from directly managing lower-level infrastructure services. The Enterprise JavaBean is the enterprise application component for J2EE-based environments.
- *Enterprise Application Module:* The enterprise application module contains one or more enterprise application components to form an individual enterprise service. Enterprise application modules also contain a module deployment descriptor for defining the configuration and deployment properties of the module. Such entities correspond to EJB modules packaged into JAR files in the J2EE environment, along with XML-based EJB application module deployment descriptors.
- *Enterprise Application:* The enterprise application represents a cohesive collection of enterprise application modules. In the J2EE world, other types of modules can be assembled into an enterprise application, such as Web application modules, dependent class and resource library modules, and external resource adapter modules. An enterprise application deployment descriptor contains any enterprise application assembly information. J2EE enterprise applications are composed of one or more EJB, Web, dependent class library, and external resource adapter modules represented by EJB JAR, WAR, utility JAR, and RAR files packaged into an EAR file along with an XML-based J2EE application deployment descriptor.
- *Enterprise Application Container:* The enterprise application container provides the runtime environment in which enterprise applications operate. They also provide the interfaces and glue logic between enterprise application components and the services provided by an underlying application server implementation. To provide a means to deploy enterprise applications, containers also implement configuration and deployment services. Finally, containers also sometimes offer tools to enable the runtime deployment and management of enterprise applications. With J2EE v1.4 containers, such as servlet, JSP, and EJB containers, the new J2EE Deployment and J2EE Management specifications address such needs in a standard fashion. J2EE standards also exist for the set of Java enterprise APIs that need to be provided and for the means by which applications are deployed and configured using XML-based deployment descriptors.
- *Enterprise Application Server:* An enterprise application server provides systems infrastructure functionality such as enterprise communication services (for example, ORBs), transaction management services, security, and other services contained in an integrated server environment. In a J2EE environment, the application server

provides the implementation of J2EE-based services and APIs. Although there are now a few core standard interfaces defined between a J2EE container and an application server, many times in the trade literature and even in this book, the terms *application server* and *container* are used to mean both the container and the server.

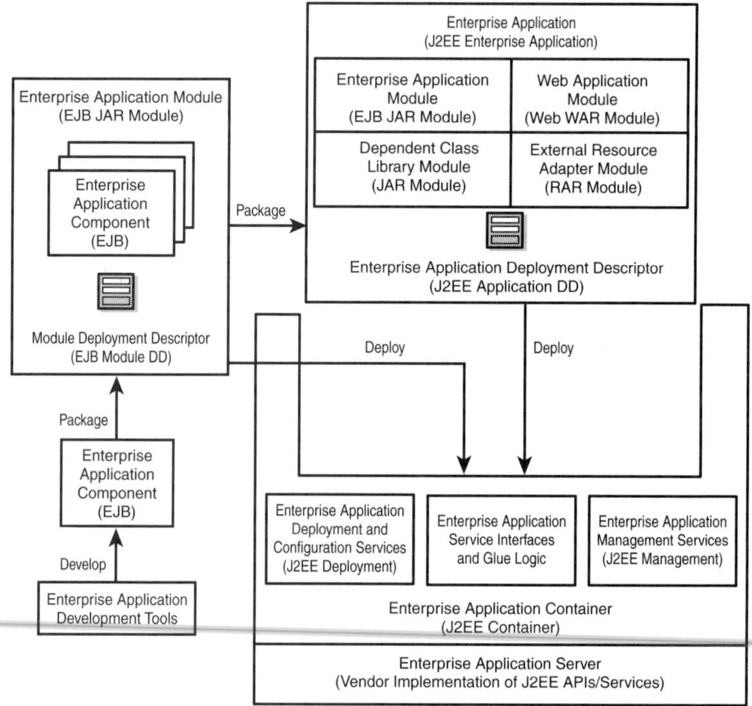

Figure 23.9 Primary application server architecture elements.

Application server frameworks do not negate the need for understanding the technologies described earlier in this book. For one, as you'll see, application server environments provide a means for configuring many of the services that we have described thus far and shield the developer from understanding all aspects of the Java enterprise APIs, but they do not completely negate the need to understand these APIs. Many application server frameworks, such as EJB, still at least require the developer to have an understanding of a subset of the APIs. Application servers often manage how associated objects are created, deleted, and allocated but still expose the main parts of an API for enterprise applications to utilize those services.

Moreover, use of an application server at every distributed location within an enterprise where some application service must be provided will be impractical in certain scenarios. Application servers can have a significant monetary cost associated with them and can require a powerful enough underlying platform that enterprise engineers will almost always opt for the use of standalone enterprise applications in many scenarios. Furthermore, certain enterprise applications may not have the assurance demands that usually warrant use of application servers. This is an especially important consideration when the organization has time and human resource limitations. However, application servers are the hubs and engines of the enterprise with assurance needs, whereas standalone applications become more suited for minimally scalable or perhaps embedded types of applications distributed throughout an enterprise.

Although one might argue on more theoretical grounds that standalone applications fall into the high-end desktop realm of J2SE applications or even the more embedded realm of J2ME applications, we contend based on practical experiences that such applications are still an integral part of building enterprise systems. Such standalone enterprise applications still have a need to use the various enterprise technologies described in this book and often require distributed communications, JNDI services, trading services, JMS services, transaction management services, security services, and database connectivity. The truly enterprise-class architect and developer will thus always need to understand and be able to employ the full suite of Java enterprise technologies for building Java enterprise applications in both standalone and application server–based environments such as the J2EE.

Application Server Architecture Provider Roles

Given the basic enterprise application server architecture elements defined in the preceding section, we can better understand who plays what role in providing such an architecture within an enterprise system. Figure 23.10 depicts the primary role-players involved in providing the enterprise application server architecture elements defined in Figure 23.9. Some of the roles indicated in this diagram may actually be provided by software tools as opposed to actual people, or may perhaps be a combination of both people and tools. Furthermore, one or more roles may actually be implemented by one person/tool, or one or more people/tools may in fact implement one or more of the roles. However, defining such roles does provide a more natural encapsulation of which person/tool contains what engineering knowledge and how they provide that knowledge to an enterprise application server architecture. These primary application server architecture provider roles are listed here:

- *Enterprise Application Container Provider:* The enterprise application container provider supplies the enterprise application runtime environment, service interfaces and glue logic, deployment and configuration services, and management services. The roles of container and application service provider are often the same. The J2EE specification defines this role as the "Product Provider."
- *Enterprise Application Server Provider:* The enterprise application server provider is the provider of systems infrastructure functionality contained within an application server implementation. In a J2EE environment, the application server provider

provides the underlying implementation of J2EE-based services and APIs. Although the roles of container and application service provider are often the same, it can also be the case that a Service Provider Interface (SPI) built into the J2EE specifications enables container/server providers to select implementations of particular enterprise application services from other vendors. The J2EE specification defines the role of general application server provider as "Product Provider" and the role of specific underlying discrete service provisioning as "System Component Provider."

- *Enterprise Application Tools Provider:* The enterprise application tools provider provides tools that are used in the development of enterprise applications. The J2EE specification defines this role as "Tools Provider."
- *Enterprise Application Component Developer:* The enterprise application component developer primarily represents a domain expert skilled in understanding the business logic and data needs of an enterprise application. Their main duty is to create enterprise application components and combine them into a cohesive module along with any deployment descriptor information on the structure and dependencies of the components. With respect to EJB and the J2EE specifications, this role is also referred to as the "Application Component Provider" or "Bean Provider." EJB providers create EJBs and package them into EJB JAR modules along with XML-based EJB application module deployment descriptors.
- *Enterprise Application Assembler:* The enterprise application assembler composes one or more enterprise application modules into a cohesive enterprise application. The application assembler also defines any application assembly deployment descriptor properties, as well as perhaps adding or altering the module-level deployment descriptors to provide assembly configuration information. In the J2EE world, this "Application Assembler" may involve collecting one or more modules into a cohesive enterprise application. Thus, WAR, EJB JAR, dependent JAR, and RAR files may be packaged into an EAR file along with an XML-based J2EE application deployment descriptor.
- *Enterprise Application Deployer:* The enterprise application deployer takes an assembled enterprise application and deploys this application to the enterprise application container/server environment. Deployers are knowledgeable of the specific container/server and operating environment to which an application will be deployed. An enterprise application deployer may need to modify or add to existing module or application-layer deployment descriptor properties to accomplish this task before they deploy the enterprise application into the container/server environment. Although standard deployment descriptors exist for the J2EE, deployers often define additional vendor-specific deployment properties or extensions to the standard descriptors in order to support configuration of container/server-specific environment properties. Furthermore, deployers will also generate the appropriate stubs, skeletons, and implementation classes needed by a

container to support use of the enterprise application components. The J2EE specification refers to this role simply as the "Deployer."

- *Enterprise Application System Administrator:* The enterprise application system administrator monitors and manages the runtime communications, database, security, and computing resources of an enterprise application operating within the enterprise application container/server environment. The J2EE Management specification defines a minimalist set of system administration interfaces and services for J2EE application environments. The J2EE specification refers to this role as the "System Administrator."

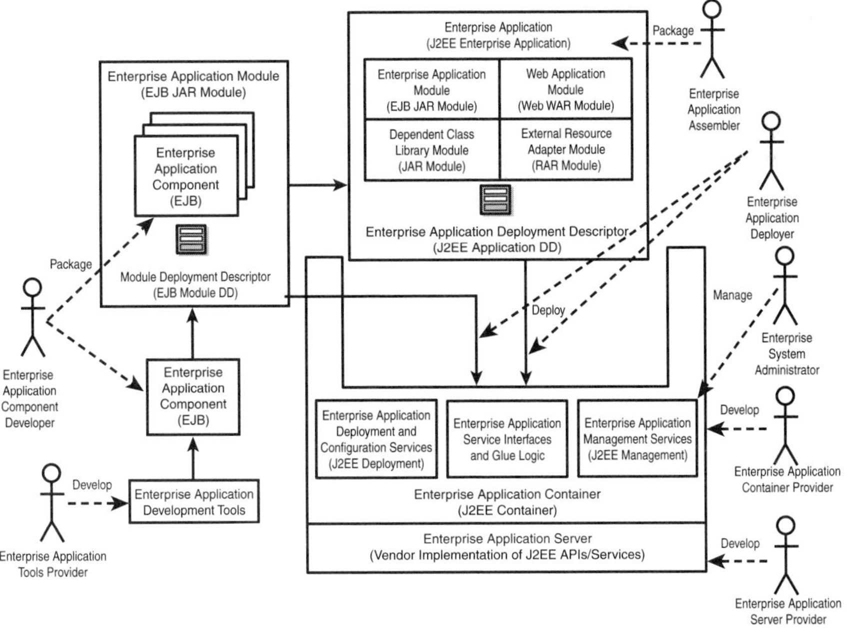

Figure 23.10 Application server element providers.

Application Server Components

One of the most attractive features of an application server is the capability it provides for enterprise software developers to be able to focus on developing the business logic and data for an enterprise application. Business logic and data are encapsulated within the enterprise application components that get plugged into an application server environment. For the J2EE, these enterprise application components are implemented as Enterprise JavaBeans. Thus, enterprise developers focus on defining the application logic and data within the component, and the application server handles how distributed clients access such components in a scalable and secure fashion. Application servers also implement much of the infrastructure logic that components use to access other enterprise systems and enterprise database resources.

Very often, application servers define an interface contract to which enterprise application components must adhere if they want to enable the application container/server environment to be able to manage the life cycle of that component. Life cycle management of components includes instance creation, instance destruction, state management, and perhaps database connectivity management.

EJB containers, in fact, require an interface contract that must be honored for a particular type of EJB component. EJB components indicate their capability to operate inside of an EJB container by implementing a particular interface type. Various methods defined on the EJB support this interface contract and enable the EJB to operate inside of a J2EE EJB container. Thus, by implementing a few simple methods and providing its own business logic, the EJB component becomes a first-class citizen of a J2EE enterprise application environment and can be managed by the EJB container.

Application Server Client Interfaces

Enterprise application components are written to provide some type of service to enterprise application clients. Thus, application server environments must define some way for clients to tap the services of these components. The mechanism by which application servers offer these services is via some distributed application service interface. These are the basic client interface problems that application servers must solve:

- *Distributed Business-Specific Interfaces:* The application service interface needs to expose only the business-specific operations defined on a component that have been defined to be distributable.
- *Distributed Business-Specific Naming and Life cycle Management:* The application service interface must provide a means for clients to look up, create, and destroy component instances and references.
- *Interface Definition Language:* The application service interface must utilize some language for defining interfaces usable by clients.
- *Interface Communications Protocol:* The application service interface must utilize some underlying communications protocol usable by clients.

To satisfy these needs, J2EE application service frameworks define standards for creating client interfaces to EJB components. These corresponding standards include the following:

- *EJB Component Interfaces:* EJB component interfaces define the business-specific operations to be exposed by an EJB to its clients. These operations may be exposed as remote interfaces for distributed access or as local interfaces for in-process access by clients.

- *EJB Home Interfaces and JNDI:* EJB home interfaces define business-specific and standard means for creating and destroying EJB components, as well as for looking up certain EJB component instances. JNDI is also used to obtain initial EJB home interface handles. The EJB home interfaces may be remote interfaces for distributed access or local interfaces for in-process access by clients.
- *Java and IDL:* Because EJB used in a distributed fashion depends on RMI, Java-based EJB client interfaces can be defined. Additionally, CORBA IDL EJB client interfaces can also be defined via a CORBA-to-EJB mapping.
- *IIOP:* The standard protocol over which EJB clients remotely communicate with EJB application server environments is IIOP. RMI/IIOP and a CORBA-to-EJB mapping both support this capability. The underlying protocol, however, is transparent to both the EJB client and the component developer.

Application Server Client Implementations

Application server clients may use the aforementioned interfaces to speak with enterprise application components operating inside of an application server either in a standalone fashion or perhaps inside of a container environment. Standalone clients provide their own runtime environment and communicate with the application server tier using a distributed communications paradigm such as CORBA or RMI. Standalone application clients are also responsible for ensuring that they have communications and service libraries installed on their machine that are compatible with the application server's communications and service libraries. Some application server environments may also provide a container environment in which their clients can operate that helps guarantee that the client and server have compatible communications and service libraries, as well as providing a hook for more sophisticated client/server communications.

The same two general approaches apply to clients of J2EE v1.4 EJB v2.1. EJB v2.1 clients operating in a standalone fashion include regular Java-based clients perhaps operating on top of a J2SE v1.4–based platform with the correct Java libraries needed for communications with the EJB v2.1 server. Standalone EJB clients may also be CORBA clients talking with an EJB server that supports a pure EJB-CORBA mapping. EJB clients can also operate inside of a standard J2EE container environment. Such clients may be other EJBs, Java Servlets, JSPs, or J2EE application clients.

J2EE Application Clients

J2EE application clients may be viewed simply as J2SE-based Java applications along with support for a minimal set of container environment requirements. J2EE application clients essentially require a J2SE runtime environment complete with Java IDL, JNDI, RMI-IIOP, JAXP, and JDBC. J2EE application clients additionally require that their container provide the standard Java enterprise EJB client-related, JMS, JavaMail, JAF, JAX-RPC, SAAJ, JAXR, Web services extensions, J2EE Management, and JMX libraries.

Additionally, J2EE application clients have a minimalist standard XML-based deployment descriptor for configuring their operating environment.

The APIs and deployment descriptor entries available to a J2EE application client may be viewed as a subset of those available to EJBs acting as clients to other J2EE services. That is, an EJB that acts as a client to another EJB or perhaps to a Web service uses the same APIs that a J2EE application client would use in such scenarios. Chapters 24 through 28 describe EJB-based applications in much greater detail and also present an example J2EE application client implemented as an EJB client.

Enterprise Application Configuration and Deployment

Application server configuration and deployment involves establishing a set of properties that define how your enterprise applications should behave and interact at runtime. The establishment of these properties may be performed manually via setting of a text-based configuration file, or it may be performed via use of some GUI-based configuration and deployment tool. J2EE-based configuration, as you have already seen in Part V, "Enterprise Web Enabling," involves defining standard element values in an XML-based deployment descriptor file. Many J2EE vendor products also define GUI-based mechanisms for setting these deployment descriptors.

In the case of EJB server-side configuration and deployment, a standard XML-based deployment descriptor is employed specifically for EJB deployment. Meta-data about the EJB, the EJB's type information, and the EJB's class information are all defined in the deployment descriptor file. The file is used along with compiled versions of the EJB's classes and interfaces to create an EJB JAR module. The EJB JAR module is then encapsulated within an EAR file, which is deployed to a J2EE-compliant EJB container/server.

J2EE Application Client Configuration and Deployment

We make reference to the use of a J2EE application client on occasion throughout this book. As discussed earlier in this chapter, you can think of a J2EE application client as akin to a regular J2SE-based application client, but one that runs inside a special J2EE container. This J2EE container does not offer all the services provided by J2EE Web or EJB containers, but it does offer a base set of services that enable a Java-based application client to utilize basic J2EE configuration and deployment features, as well as better guarantee client-side library interoperability with server-side J2EE applications. J2EE application clients are used mostly when hosting an EJB client that must talk with an EJB server.

J2EE Application Client Packaging

A J2EE application client is associated with a special standard `application-client.xml` deployment descriptor file. Meta-data about the client and any EJB reference information are both defined in this file for the client. This file is used along with a compiled version of the client classes to create a client JAR module. A vendor of a particular J2EE application client container will often provide a command-line or GUI-based approach to generating such deployment descriptors and packaging the client inside of a JAR file. The `application-client.xml` file is placed beneath a `META-INF/` directory inside of the client JAR file. A `Main-Class` attribute added to the manifest file of the client JAR file specifies the class name of the client class that provides the `main()` method implementation to be executed at startup as exemplified here:

```
Manifest-Version: 1.0
Main-Class: ejava.ejb.session.creditmgr.CreditManagerClient
```

Most commonly, the client JAR file is then launched by a special J2EE application client launcher program, which starts the client inside of a lightweight J2EE application client container process. The J2EE reference implementation uses a special `runclient` launcher program to start a J2EE application client inside of a managed container environment. As exemplified here, a `MyApClient` J2EE application client is invoked inside of such a managed environment with client code stored in a `MyApClient.ear` file and client stubs stored inside of a `MyStubs.jar` file:

```
runclient -client MyApClient.ear -stubs MyStubs.jar -name MyApClient
```

J2EE Application Client Deployment (`<application-client>`)

The XML schema defining the J2EE application client's deployment descriptor is provided at `http://java.sun.com/xml/ns/j2ee/application-client_1_4.xsd`. Subsequent chapters illustrate the basic premise behind using J2EE application clients for EJB client development. Furthermore, all (except for one) of the J2EE application client deployment descriptor elements are also used inside of J2EE EJB and Web component deployment descriptors. Hence, we present only the top-level elements of a J2EE application client deployment descriptor here. Some of the elements have already been defined in the chapters preceding this one. We defer discussion of the remaining element details as relevant examples in subsequent chapters warrant. The top-level elements of a J2EE application client deployment descriptor are defined this way:

- `<application-client>`: The root element of a J2EE application client deployment for a single client JAR file containing a sequence of the elements that follow here.
- `<description>`: Generally used to describe its containing element (zero or more).
- `<display-name>`: Generally used as a name for display by tools (zero or more).
- `<icon>`: Contains an optional `<small-icon>` sub-element defining the name for a small 16×16-pixel GIF or JPG file, and an optional `<large-icon>` sub-element defining the name for a large 32×32-pixel GIF or JPG file (zero or more).
- `<env-entry>`: Defines an application environment configuration value (zero or more).

- `<ejb-ref>`: Defines information used by the client to reference an EJB (zero or more).
- `<service-ref>`: Defines information used by the client to reference a Web service (zero or more).
- `<resource-ref>`: Defines information used by the client to reference an external resource such as JDBC resource connection information (zero or more).
- `<resource-env-ref>`: Defines information used by the client to reference a resource administered by the client's environment (zero or more).
- `<message-destination-ref>`: Defines information used by the client to reference a destination for an asynchronous message (zero or more).
- `<callback-handler>`: Defines a JAAS `javax.security.auth.callback.CallbackHandler` derived class used to collect authentication information from the client (optional).
- `<message-destination>`: Defines a logical message destination (zero or more).

J2EE application client module deployment descriptors defined according to the preceding top-level format must also include a reference to the standard XML schema being used. The basic top-level structure of J2EE application client deployment descriptor thus follows the sample form as exemplified here:

```
<application-client
          xmlns="http://java.sun.com/xml/ns/j2ee"
          xmlns:xsi="http://www.w3.org/2001/XMLSchema-instance"
          xsi:schemaLocation="http://java.sun.com/xml/ns/j2ee
          http://java.sun.com/xml/ns/j2ee/application-client_1_4.xsd"
          version="1.4">
  <description> ... </description>
  <display-name> ... </display-name>
  <icon>
    <small-icon> ... </small-icon>
    <large-icon> ... </large-icon>
  </icon>
  <ejb-ref>...</ejb-ref>
  <service-ref>...</service-ref>
  <resource-ref>...</resource-ref>
  <resource-env-ref>...</resource-env-ref>
  <message-destination-ref>...</message-destination-ref>
  <callback-handler>...</callback-handler>
  <message-destination>...</message-destination>
</application-client>
```

J2EE Enterprise Application Configuration and Deployment

As we have continued to discuss throughout this chapter, one or more different types of "modules" may be packaged together to compose a J2EE enterprise application. Such modules may be of the Web or J2EE application client module ilk that we've seen thus far. Subsequent chapters in this part of the book describe how to create EJB modules in greater detail. As we'll also see in Chapter 29, "EJB Integration and Management," a special resource adapter module may also be included within a deployed J2EE enterprise application. Although all such modules may be deployed independently, this section describes how such modules may also be logically assembled to compose a cohesive J2EE enterprise application.

J2EE Enterprise Application Packaging

As is the case with J2EE modules, a J2EE enterprise application is packaged inside of a JAR file format. A J2EE enterprise application's JAR file is referred to as an enterprise archive (EAR) file and has a `.ear` filename extension. Generally speaking, an EAR file will contain a collection of J2EE module JAR files, deployment descriptors, and a JAR manifest file. A `Manifest.mf` file and deployment descriptors associated with the EAR file are stored beneath a `META-INF/` directory. The deployment descriptors include a standard J2EE enterprise application deployment descriptor called `application.xml` and any vendor-specific deployment descriptors.

Optional J2EE Packaging

In addition to the standard way to package a particular J2EE JAR file, a JAR file can also refer to other files (for example, classes or text files) outside of a particular JAR file. This is allowed only if the external files are inside of another JAR file and included within the same EAR file or are already installed inside of the J2EE container. This is accomplished by referring to such external files via a `Class-Path` entry inside of the referencing JAR's manifest file. For example, a particular `Manifest.mf` file may contain the following:

```
Class-Path: foo.jar,bar.jar,ati.jar
```

The standards surrounding such package specifications are part of the standard J2SE JAR packaging standards defined at `java.sun.com/j2se/1.4/docs/guide/extensions` and `java.sun.com/j2se/1.4/docs/guide/jar/jar.html`.

J2EE Enterprise Application Deployment (`<application>`)

A J2EE enterprise application's standard deployment descriptor, `application.xml`, contains elements (one for each module) that define where to locate a module relative to the top level of an associated EAR file. The top-level element of the `application.xml` file is defined here:

- `<application>`: The root element of a J2EE enterprise application deployment for a single EAR file containing a sequence of the elements that follow here.
- Description group: A collection of optional description-related elements, including `<description>`, `<display-name>`, and `<icon>` (optional).

- <module>: Indicates where you can find a module's JAR file relative to the root directory of the containing EAR file (one or more).
- <security-role>: Identifies those security roles defined for enterprise applications with sub-elements defined as described in Chapter 28 (zero or more).

The XML schema defining the J2EE enterprise application's deployment descriptor is provided at http://java.sun.com/xml/ns/j2ee/application_1_4.xsd. The common J2EE schema types used by this XML schema are defined at http://java.sun.com/xml/ns/j2ee. Such schema locations must be referenced at the top of the application.xml file as exemplified here:

```
<?xml version="1.0" encoding="UTF-8"?>
<application
    xmlns="http://java.sun.com/xml/ns/j2ee"
    xmlns:xsi="http://www.w3.org/2001/XMLSchema-instance"
    xsi:schemaLocation="http://java.sun.com/xml/ns/j2ee
    http://java.sun.com/xml/ns/j2ee/application_1_4.xsd"
    version="1.4">
  <display-name>Bla bla bla</display-name>
  <module>...</module>
  <module>...</module>
  <module>...</module>
  <module>...</module>
</application>
```

J2EE Enterprise Application Module Deployment (<module>)

A particular <module> element contains a set of sub-elements that indicate where you can locate a module's JAR file within a particular EAR file. URIs are defined relative to the EAR file's top-level directory. The <module> file is defined as detailed here:

- <module>: Indicates where you can find a module's JAR file relative to the root directory of the containing EAR file via sub-elements that follow here.
- Module type-specific element: This first sub-element of the <module> element is associated with a URI referencing a particular archive file type and having an element name that is a function of the particular module type, such as (a) <connector> for a resource adapter archive (RAR) file, (b) <ejb> for an EJB JAR file, (c) <java> for a J2EE application client JAR file, or (d) <web> containing sub-elements that define a WAR file URI and context root for a Web application.
- <alt-dd>: Defines an alternative path name for the location of a deployment descriptor associated with a particular module and thus overrides the default location per each module's packaging scheme and standard deployment descriptor name convention (optional).

The <web> element is used within a <module> specification to define the location and root context of a J2EE Web application as shown here:

- <web>: Encapsulates a WAR file URI and context root for a Web application with sub-elements defined as described here.
- <web-uri>: Defines a URI path name for a Web application archive (WAR) file.
- <context-root>: Defines the context root of the Web application.

As an example, a J2EE Web application module and EJB module may be deployed as a cohesive J2EE enterprise application as exemplified here:

```
<?xml version="1.0" encoding="UTF-8"?>
<application ...>
      ...
  <module>
    <ejb>BeeShirtsEJBs.jar</ejb>
  </module>

  <module>
    <web>
      <web-uri>BeeShirtsWeb.war</web-uri>
      <context-root>beeshirts</context-root>
    </web>
  </module>

</application>
```

Application Service Management

In addition to the ease with which enterprise application components can be built and with which clients can connect to these components, application servers also make it easy for enterprise application components to tap various enterprise services. Service mechanisms include data connectivity, communications enabling, security, availability, enterprise application integration, and more. Some of these services are transparently provided using declarative configuration parameters in a deployment descriptor file. Other services have their API exposed to the enterprise application component by the application server. Regardless of how the component accesses these services, the application server often creates, allocates, destroys, and generally manages the life cycle of all underlying service-related objects.

J2EE-based servers are no different. For example, security and transaction management are provided as services to the EJB (as well as Web components) in a declarative fashion using configurable deployment descriptor properties. Access to such services can also be provided programmatically via exposed APIs. JDBC is another example in which the J2EE container/server will manage the creation and destruction of connections and the allocation of connections to J2EE components from a JDBC connection pool. J2EE components can then utilize the JDBC connection and statement APIs as usual.

We close the chapter here with a brief list of those core services commonly managed by application servers with specific focus on EJB-based servers and how such service management is provided:

- *Distributed Communications Services:* Application servers transparently provide distributed communication support for server-side components. For example, EJB containers provide handler code for calls to server-side skeletons from client-side stubs. These handlers then delegate calls to EJB server component instances pulled from an EJB pool of instances and are allocated to their own thread, which is also often retrieved from a pool of threads. Thus, EJB server components can be implemented without worrying about managing server-side resources or threads.
- *State Management:* Application servers often handle the resolution of particular client requests to the state managed for that client on the server side. EJB stateful session objects provide a means to resolve requests from a particular client to particular server-side object instances. The passivation and activation of such state are also managed by the EJB container/server.
- *Database Connectivity:* Application servers often provide handles to pooled database connections via an API and may also provide object-relational data mapping services. EJBs provide direct access to the JDBC API from components with the capability to configure database resources via deployment descriptors. Although the JDBC API may be exposed, EJB servers handle the creation, destruction, and allocation of database connections from a pool. EJB containers also provide an object-to-relational means for specifying how fields of an object automatically map to columns in a database table or view. Such mappings allow for a more object-oriented interface to EJBs, with the container handling the actual relational database inserts, deletes, queries, and updates.
- *Configuration Services:* Application servers also provide ways to define properties of an application that can be read from configuration files. JNDI is used in EJB application server environments for looking up environment configuration information specified in deployment descriptors. Component-specific initialization parameters can also be specified in deployment descriptors for the automatic initialization of components during activation.
- *Security:* Security in application servers can be specified declaratively and programmatically. Declarative security parameters in J2EE deployment descriptors can define required authentication mechanisms and authorization parameters. Security roles and how they map to groups and users can all be specified declaratively to implement the access-control decision logic for defining who can access which EJB. Additionally, programmatic security interfaces provide for more sophisticated and application-specific access control when the limited J2EE security model does not suffice.

- *Availability:* Availability of service in application servers is provided primarily as a function of proper thread management, resource management, transaction management, and state management. J2EE-based servers provide both declarative and programmatic means for managing JTA/JTS-based transactions from within EJB server components and from within a few EJB client types. Additionally, EJB servers provide thread, resource, and state management to enable the capability to build scalable enterprise applications. Additionally, some application servers provide clustering and failover mechanisms.
- *Enterprise Application Integration and Connectivity:* Many application server products realize the importance of not only connecting to back-end enterprise data, but also connecting to back-end enterprise business logic. The J2EE Connector Architecture provides a standard means for connecting to back-end enterprise applications from within J2EE environments. EJBs can also utilize technologies such as CORBA and Web Services for integrating with enterprise applications.

Conclusions

The term *Enterprise Application Platform* may mean different things to different people depending on their concept of what an enterprise application comprises. In general, enterprise application platforms provide a set of services to enterprise applications often in a transparent and configurable fashion or via well-defined and higher-level APIs. The services provided are infrastructure services that reduce the amount of hand-coding by developers for creating such services and allow a developer to focus on the business logic of an enterprise application. We examined the evolution of generic enterprise application frameworks from TP monitors to OTMs, as well as from Web servers, from database servers, and even from operating systems (that is, Microsoft). We've also discussed the advantages and disadvantages of many application-specific frameworks and explored the basic features of enterprise application management service frameworks.

In this chapter, you were also provided a glimpse of how application server architectures partition the problem of building enterprise applications by decomposing an enterprise architecture into elements whose providers can encapsulate the proper level of knowledge needed to create those elements. Enterprise application container and server providers can thus focus on what they know best, which is to provide infrastructure and domain-independent services, and enterprise application component developers can focus on what they know best, which is the business logic and data specific to a particular domain. We discussed how EJB makes implementing such enterprise application server components a simple task. EJB clients talk to EJBs using standard interface patterns and can also operate inside of their own J2EE application client container environment. Finally, application servers and EJB can make configuring and deploying components and providing management services for components a simple matter of declaring properties in an XML file. Although standalone enterprise applications will still be key components of an enterprise system solution, enterprise application servers and EJB can provide your enterprise with a central hub to rapidly deploy the lion's share of your enterprise system's business logic and data handling.

24

EJB Basics

J2EE ENTERPRISE JAVABEANS (EJB) PROVIDES A MODEL for developing server-side enterprise application components that can make building portable and distributed enterprise applications an easier task than is required for building standalone enterprise applications. EJB containers/servers provide distributed communications-enabling services, data-enabling services, common distributed communication services, and systems assurance services for EJB components with minimal effort on the part of a developer to utilize these services. This chapter introduces the basic architecture and concepts behind the Enterprise JavaBeans architecture. EJB architecture, basic EJB types, and development steps for creating EJBs are all covered in this chapter. Basic EJB configuration and deployment steps are also defined in this chapter.

In this chapter, you will learn:

- An overview of EJB and its basic features.
- The basic architecture behind EJB servers and clients, including both remote and local EJB client types.
- The basic architecture behind the new EJB timer service for inducing timed event callbacks onto EJBs.
- An introduction to the basic types of EJBs, including session, entity, and message-driven beans.
- The basic steps involved in developing an EJB.
- The common approach for configuring and deploying all types of EJBs.

EJB Introduction

Enterprise JavaBeans represents a powerful component model for building distributed, server-side, and Java-based enterprise application components. The Enterprise JavaBeans model can be starkly contrasted with the regular JavaBeans model described in Appendix B, "JavaBeans." The JavaBeans model defines a means for building Java-based components for use in containers that have a nondistributed nature, have many client-side GUI semantics associated with them, and do not define standard operations to enable sophisticated life-cycle management of JavaBean components. The Enterprise JavaBeans model, on the other hand, defines a means for building Java-based components for use in containers that do offer distributed client connectivity, have exclusive server-side semantics associated with them, and define various standard operations to enable sophisticated life-cycle management of Enterprise JavaBean components.

EJBs, in fact, have the following key features:

- Provide a model for defining server-side components.
- Provide a model for defining distributed client interfaces to the services provided by these components.
- Provide standard operations and semantics for allowing a container to create, destroy, allocate, persist, activate, and invoke component instances.
- Provide a standard model for defining a component that maintains a conversational session with a client with session management handled by the container.
- Provide a standard model for defining a component that encapsulates a data source (for example, database) entry with object-to-relational data mapping being handled by the container.
- Provide a standard model for defining a component that encapsulates an asynchronous message consumer with messaging service interactions being handled by the container.
- Provide a standard model for defining a component that encapsulates a Web service with SOAP messaging interactions being handled by the container.
- Provide a standard for defining configuration and deployment characteristics of a component independent of its implementation.
- Provide a standard model for declaratively defining the security attributes of a component.
- Provide a standard model for declaratively defining the transactions attributes of a component.
- Provide a standard component interface contract such that components can run in any vendor-compliant container/server which implements that standard interface contract.

The EJB component model is thus a very powerful model for building enterprise applications and is the focal point of the J2EE architecture. The J2EE v1.4 requires that all EJB v.2.1 APIs and implementations be included within J2EE EJB containers and that EJB v2.1 client APIs and implementations be included with J2EE Web containers and J2EE application clients. EJB v2.1 represents a significant advancement over earlier EJB versions. EJB v2.1 compliance includes session, entity, message-driven, and Web service enabled beans; includes a special timer feature for timed event invocations of beans; includes sophisticated object-relational mapping container support; and adopts

XML-based deployment descriptors described via XML Schema, among other relatively new features.

EJB Architecture

Figure 24.1 depicts the basic architecture of EJB-based client-server enterprise applications. The client side of an EJB architecture contains the EJB interfaces needed for invoking business-specific methods on an EJB, as well as for managing handles to server-side objects. The server side of an EJB architecture contains the instances of the actual EJB component implementation, as well as the container code that maps calls to and from clients and EJBs after appropriate service management infrastructure logic has been executed. RMI remote interface semantics are currently implied by these interfaces and enable RMI/IIOP mappings to be used as the interface mechanism. As you'll see in subsequent chapters, support for SOAP over HTTP and enhanced CORBA interoperability is also enabled via underlying J2EE v1.4 container support.

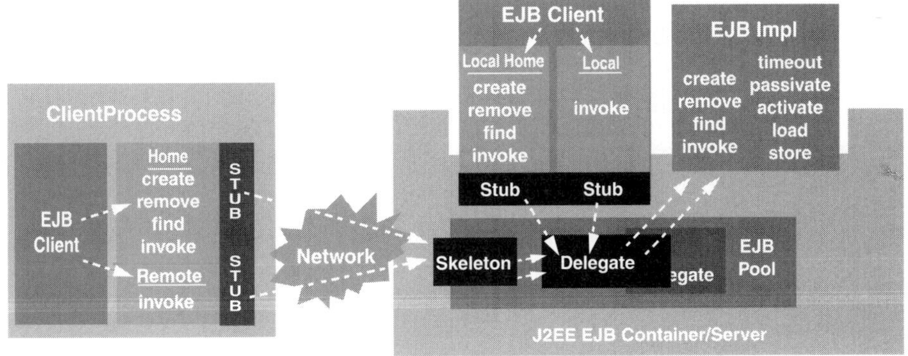

Figure 24.1 The EJB architecture.

The primary elements of these application-specific elements of an EJB architecture as depicted in the diagram are listed here:

- *EJB Clients:* EJB client applications utilize JNDI to look up references to EJB interfaces in order to communicate with EJB server functionality either in a distributed fashion or from within the same EJB container process.
- *EJB Home Interfaces:* EJB home interfaces provide distributed operations for clients to create, remove, and find handles to EJB remote interface objects, as well as to invoke general static business methods independent of a particular EJB instance. Underlying stubs marshal home interface requests and unmarshal home interface responses for the client.
- *EJB Remote Interfaces:* EJB remote interfaces provide the business-specific client interface methods defined for a particular EJB. Underlying stubs marshal remote interface requests and unmarshal remote interface responses for the client.

- *EJB Local Home Interfaces:* EJB local home interfaces provide operations for clients to create, remove, and find handles to EJB local interface objects inside of the same container as the EJB implementation, as well as to invoke general static business methods independent of a particular EJB instance. Underlying stubs route home interface requests and responses for the client within the EJB container without the need for marshaling or unmarshaling invocations.
- *EJB Local Object Interfaces:* EJB local object interfaces provide the business-specific client interface methods defined for a particular EJB. Underlying stubs route local object interface requests and responses for the client within the EJB container without the need for marshaling or unmarshaling invocations.
- *EJB Implementations:* EJB implementations are the actual EJB application components implemented by developers to provide any application-specific business method invocation, creation, removal, finding, timeout callbacks, activation, passivation, database storage, and database loading logic.
- *Container EJB Implementations:* The container manages the distributed communication skeletons used to marshal and unmarshal data sent to and from the client. Containers also may store EJB implementation instances in a pool and use delegates to perform any service management operations related to a particular EJB before calls are delegated to the EJB implementation instance. Local home and object requests do not have to be marshaled or unmarshaled by the container and can instead route directly between EJB local client stubs and EJB implementation delegates.

EJB Server Architecture

Figure 24.2 provides a more detailed picture of the server-side architecture behind constructing EJBs. A developer provides an implementation of an EJB, `MyEJBImpl`, which adheres to a set of interface rules established by the EJB specification and `javax.ejb` package. In such a way, the EJB container can know how to make callbacks onto the interface standards-compliant EJB implementation (via a delegate class). An EJB implementation can also communicate directly with its EJB container context via an `EJBContext` object. The container exposes access and management of security information, client home interfaces, a special timer service, and transaction information via this EJB context.

EJB Remote Client Architecture

Figure 24.3 provides a more detailed picture of the client-side architecture behind constructing remote interfaces to EJBs. A remote EJB client, `MyRemoteEJBClient`, interfaces with a JNDI context to look up handles to remote EJB home interfaces. A concrete EJB home interface, `MyEJBHome`, ultimately extends a standard `EJBHome` interface. An EJB home interface defines a set of methods specific to a particular EJB that allow the EJB client to create, look up, and remove EJB remote object associations. An

EJB home interface also allows an EJB client to obtain a persisted version of the home interface via a `HomeHandle` object as well as meta-data about the remote EJB via an `EJBMetaData` object. An underlying stub actually implements such home interfaces to handle marshaling requests to and unmarshaling responses from the remote EJB server implementation.

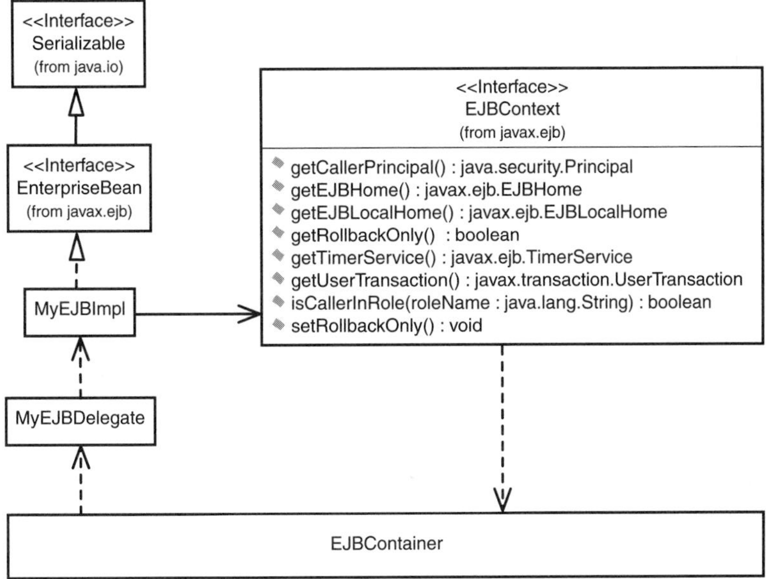

Figure 24.2 EJB server architecture.

An EJB client uses an EJB home interface to obtain a reference to a concrete remote EJB object, `MyEJBRemote`. The concrete EJB remote interface contains business-specific methods that the EJB server exposes to distributed EJB clients. The EJB client uses the EJB remote interface to invoke the operations on the distributed EJB implementation. A base standard `EJBObject` interface also defines methods that allow the client to cross-reference the EJB home interface and obtain a persisted version of the remote interface via a `Handle` object. An underlying stub actually implements such remote interfaces to handle marshaling requests to and unmarshaling responses from the remote EJB server implementation.

EJB Local Client Architecture

Figure 24.4 provides a more detailed picture of the client-side architecture behind constructing local interfaces to EJBs. A local EJB client, `MyLocalEJBClient`, interfaces with a JNDI context to look up handles to local EJB home interfaces. A concrete EJB local home interface, `MyEJBLocalHome`, ultimately extends a standard `EJBLocalHome` interface. Similar to the EJB remote home interface, an EJB local home interface defines a set of methods specific to a particular EJB that allow the EJB client to create, look up, and remove EJB object associations. However, such operations occur within the same EJB container process as opposed to remotely. An underlying stub actually implements such local home interfaces to handle delegating requests and responses between the EJB client and the EJB server implementation.

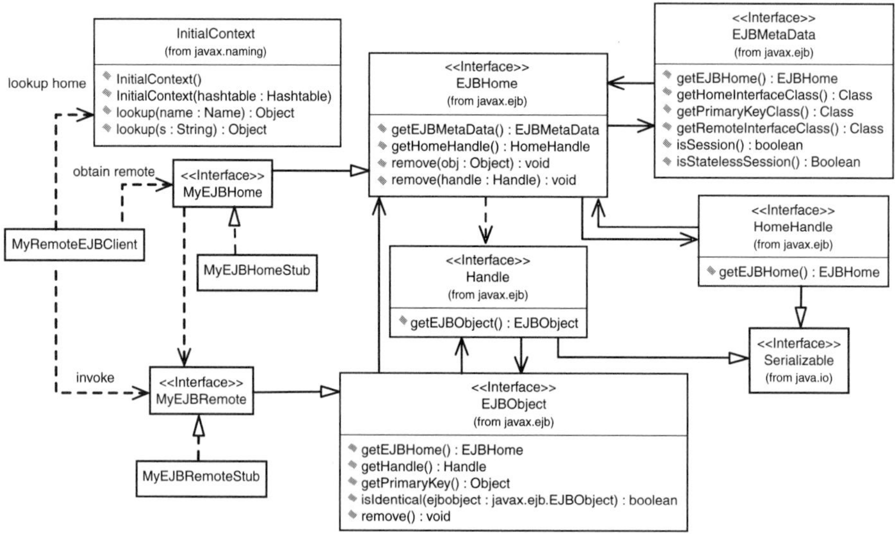

Figure 24.3 EJB remote client architecture.

An EJB client uses an EJB local home interface to obtain a reference to a concrete local EJB object, `MyEJBLocalObject`, that extends a standard `EJBLocalObject` interface. The concrete EJB local interface contains the business-specific methods that the EJB server exposes to EJB clients within a local EJB container. The EJB client then uses the EJB local interface to invoke the operations on the local EJB implementation. An underlying stub actually implements such local object interfaces to handle delegating requests and responses between the EJB client and the EJB server implementation.

EJB Exceptions

Because EJB interfaces imply RMI semantics, all distributed EJB client interfaces extend from `java.rmi.Remote` and throw the `java.rmi.RemoteException` from each of their methods. In addition to `RemoteException` objects and application-specific exceptions, EJBs can also throw other EJB-specific exceptions that relate to error and failure scenarios resulting from the invocation of EJB operations. Figure 24.5 depicts this EJB exception hierarchy:

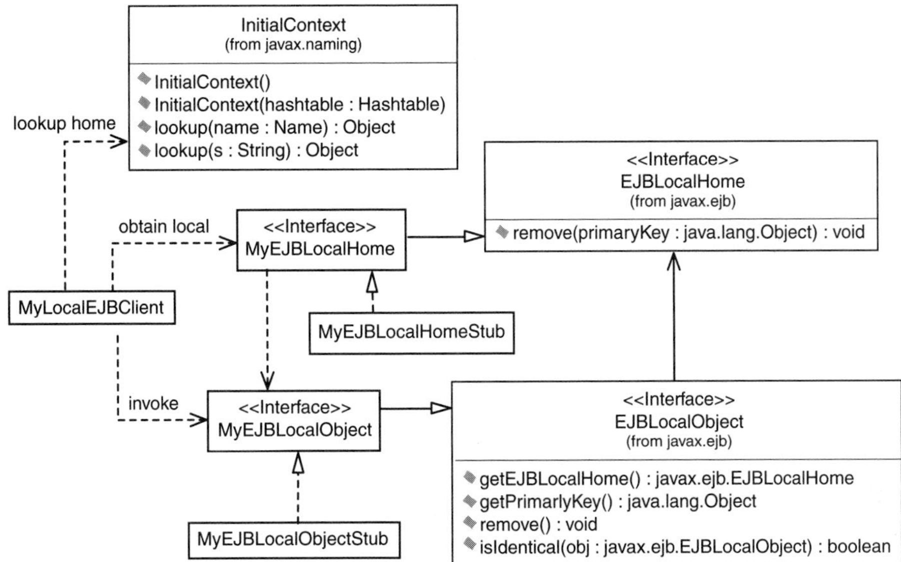

Figure 24.4 EJB local client architecture.

- `CreateException`: This exception is thrown when a particular EJB cannot be created.
- `DuplicateKeyException`: This exception is thrown when a particular EJB cannot be created when objects with the same unique identity key already exist.
- `FinderException`: This exception is thrown when a collection of one or more EJBs cannot be found.
- `ObjectNotFoundException`: This exception is thrown when a singular EJB object cannot be found.
- `RemoveException`: This exception is thrown when an error occurs while attempting to remove an EJB.
- `EJBException`: This exception is thrown by an EJB when a runtime business method invocation cannot be completed.
- `AccessLocalException`: This exception is thrown when a local EJB client is not allowed access (that is, no permission) to invoke a particular method.
- `NoSuchEntityException`: This exception is thrown by an EJB when a particular EJB does not exist.
- `NoSuchObjectException` and `NoSuchObjectLocalException`: These exceptions are thrown when a client attempts to invoke a non-existent method on either a remote or local interface, respectively.

- `TransactionRequiredException` and `TransactionRequiredLocalException`: These exceptions are thrown when a client did not propagate a transaction context even though it was required for either a remote or local interface, respectively.
- `TransactionRolledbackException` and `TransactionRolledbackLocalException`: These exceptions are thrown when a client invokes a method and a transaction has rolled back for either a remote or local interface, respectively.

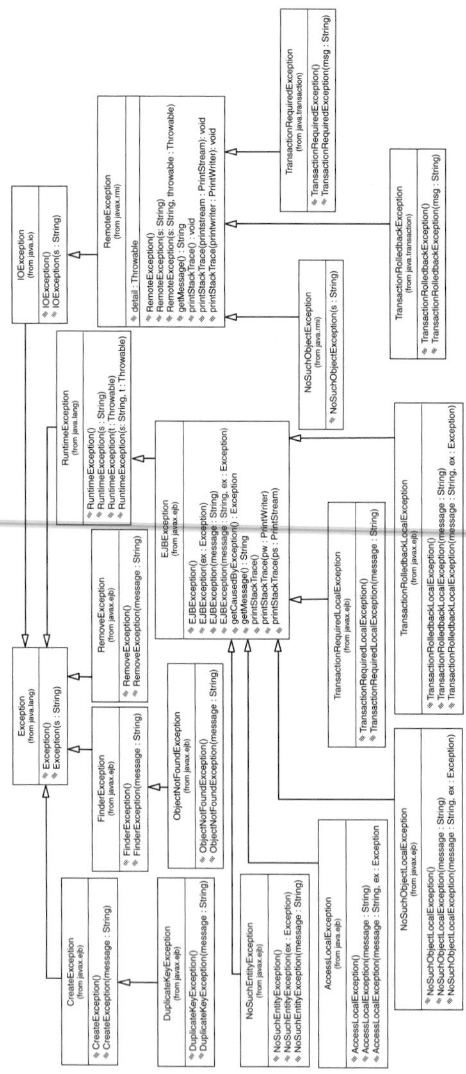

Figure 24.5 EJB exceptions.

EJB Timer Service

Thus far in this chapter, we have discussed the basic and general architecture of EJB-based clients and servers. Subsequent chapters describe the specific EJB interfaces used to construct each specific type of EJB client and server available using the EJB v2.1 programming model. As a result, the specific semantics behind the creation, finder, removal, and other operations on EJB client interfaces and EJB implementations will be most apparent in the context of each specific EJB type. However, the EJB timer service introduced in EJB v2.1 is relatively independent of each such type. As a result, we introduce the basic architecture of the EJB timer service here and explain how to use it with each EJB type in subsequent chapters. The EJB timer service essentially provides a means for EJB objects to receive callbacks from the container defined based on some timed event.

Figure 24.6 depicts the EJB timer service architecture. Here we see that an EJB implementation object designates its cooperation with the EJB container by implementing the `TimedObject` interface. When a timed event has occurred, the container invokes the `ejbTimeout()` method on the EJB implementation object and passes it a `Timer` object. The `Timer` object contains information related to the timed event that occurred.

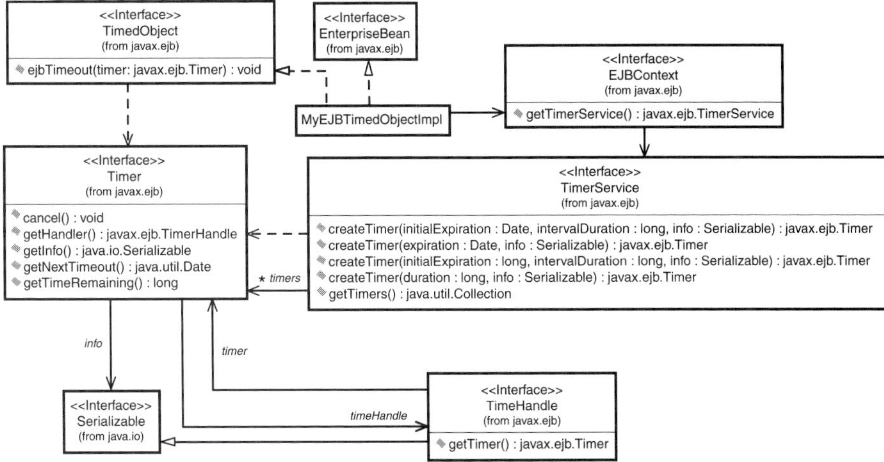

Figure 24.6 EJB timer service.

Among the information provided to the EJB implementation object by the `Timer` object, the time at which the next timed event will occur can be gleaned. The `getNextTimeout()` and `getTimeRemaining()` methods respectively provide the `java.util.Date` at which the next timed event will occur and the milliseconds remaining before the next timed event. The timer may be cancelled by invoking its `cancel()` method. A serialized form of the `Timer` (that is, `TimerHandle`) may be gotten by invoking the getHandle() method, which then may be used to persist the state of the timer.

Perhaps the main method of interest, however, is the Timer.getInfo() method, which returns a serializable representation of the information associated with a timed event. Such information is presented to the container when the timer was created. Timers can programmatically be created via one of the createTimer() methods defined on the TimerService interface. The various createTimer() methods take not only the serializable information object associated with the timed event but also additional information indicating the following:

- *Initial duration single action timer:* Timed event occurs after a certain number of milliseconds (long) pass.
- *Initial duration and periodic timer:* Timed event occurs after a certain number of milliseconds (long) pass and continues to occur on a periodic basis every specified number of milliseconds (long).
- *Initial specific date single action timer:* Timed event occurs after a certain date (Date) occurs.
- *Initial specific date and periodic timer:* Timed event occurs after a certain date (Date) occurs and continues to occur on a periodic basis every specified number of milliseconds (long).

An EJB implementation may obtain a handle to a TimerService object by invoking getTimerService() on its EJBContext. In addition to calling createTimer() on the TimerService, a Collection of the Timer objects associated with the EJB may also then be retrieved by invoking the TimerService.getTimers() method. We cover specific usage of the EJB timer service as appropriate in subsequent chapters as they are used by the specific EJB types.

Types of EJBs

The EJB architecture described thus far provides a general view of the services offered by EJB containers and components. The actual features and services available to EJB components are really a function of their EJB type. Subsequent chapters describe the EJB types and their specific construction in detail. However, taking another, broader point of view for this chapter's introductory purposes, EJBs may be categorized according to the following criteria:

- *Object Type:* An EJB may be distinguished as representing either a controller or an entity type of object. That is, a controller type object may be typically responsible for receiving requests, orchestrating how to route such a request, performing some sophisticated business logic function, and generating a response. An entity type object is typically only a passive repository of data stored in object form.
- *Synchronicity Type:* An EJB may also be distinguished as to whether it is synchronous or asynchronous. A synchronous EJB represents an object receiving

synchronous requests and generating responses while the client blocks. An asynchronous EJB represents a message consumer object that receives asynchronous requests from a message producer.

- *Message Protocol:* The underlying message format and protocol may also affect how the EJB is constructed. That is, a binary message format using IIOP as the underlying protocol may distinguish one class of EJBs most suited for intra-enterprise communications. An XML-based message format using SOAP over HTTP as the underlying protocol may distinguish an EJB as one most suited for inter-enterprise communications via Web services. Similarly, a tailored MOM-based message format over some MOM-specific profile may also distinguish an EJB for a particular inter- or intra-enterprise usage.

The EJB v2.1 standard in fact defines three general EJB roles that can be distinguished according to the general criteria defined previously. By partitioning EJBs into roles, the programmer can develop an EJB according to a more focused programming model than would be the case if such roles were not distinguished. Such roles also allow the EJB container to determine how to best manage a particular EJB based on its programming model type. These are the three main EJB types:

- *Session Beans:* Session beans are synchronous EJBs that are created to perform some action on the enterprise system and possibly return results to the client. Session beans correspond to the controllers of a system exposed for manipulation to clients. Session beans may thus be thought of as the "verbs" of a particular problem domain for which they are implemented to solve. Session beans are particularly well suited to encapsulate coarse-grained "frontline" service entry points into the system. The creation of fine-grained session bean service points is discouraged due to potential resource limitations when such applications must scale. Session beans primarily operate atop IIOP in J2EE-compliant containers but can also operate atop SOAP/HTTP in order to expose the bean as a Web service.
- *Entity Beans:* Entity beans are synchronous EJBs that are created to encapsulate some data contained by the enterprise system. Such data may be created, removed, or found by clients. Data may also be retrieved and updated by clients with EJB containers determining how any updates occur based on the transaction semantics for a particular entity bean. Entity beans also have special primary key classes defined for them that relate to the primary keys of an associated entity stored in the database. Entity beans correspond to some enterprise system entity. Entity beans may thus be thought of as the "nouns" of a particular problem domain for which they are implemented to solve. Because clients could potentially hold many entity references as the result of a find operation, many effective EJB designs will provide access to entity beans only from session beans and limit how many entity bean handles are returned to a client. Scalability can become severely taxed if an excessive number of entity bean remote object references are doled out to clients. Entity beans primarily operate atop IIOP in J2EE-compliant containers.

- *Message-Driven Beans:* Message-driven beans are asynchronous EJBs that offer an asynchronous means by which EJBs can receive requests and act as messaging consumers. A message-driven bean's life cycle is managed by the container in a manner similar to the container's management of a stateless session bean. Hence, the same general controller object type principles behind constructing stateless session beans apply to message-driven beans. However, the distinction is that message-driven beans act solely in an asynchronous mode and the underlying message format is dictated by the particular MOM-based messaging protocol being used.

Within the realm of session beans, two further distinctions may be made:

- *Stateless Session Beans:* Stateless session beans represent those session EJBs created with no regard for the maintenance of any state between subsequent calls by a client. Stateless session beans thus represent pure input and output engines.
- *Stateful Session Beans:* Stateful session beans represent those session EJBs created to maintain state for a particular client between subsequent calls before some maximum amount of time has expired. Stateful session beans thus represent input and output engines that can utilize the state created by a client from a previous invocation.

Within the realm of entity beans, two distinctions also apply:

- *Bean-Managed Persistence (BMP) Entity Beans:* BMP entity beans represent those entity EJBs in which all code dealing with the insert, delete, querying, and update of data to a relational data source (for example, a database) is performed by the entity EJB developer.
- *Container-Managed Persistence (CMP) Entity Beans:* CMP entity beans represent those entity EJBs in which all code dealing with the insert, delete, querying, and update of data to a relational data source (for example, a database) is provided by the container EJB implementations. Containers primarily provide such an implementation by using deployment descriptor–based information to map EJB class fields to relational data table columns and then subsequently generate the SQL code using these mappings.

EJB Development

The steps to developing EJBs may be partitioned along two main lines: server-side and client-side development. Although server-side development of distributed communications servers, such as CORBA and RMI, may take on a somewhat complicated nature at times, server-side development of EJBs is simplified because much of the communications, state management, resource allocation, and thread management infrastructure coding is provided by the container. These are the main steps employed for server-side EJB development:

1. *Implement EJB Standard Interfaces:* Any interfaces required by the standard EJB component model to enable container-based management of the EJB should be implemented.
2. *Implement EJB Business-Specific Interfaces:* Any business-specific interfaces provided by your EJB and any supporting helper and utility classes should be implemented.
3. *Create Client Object Interfaces:* The remote and local object interface for your EJB that defines all business-specific interfaces to the EJB should be created.
4. *Create Client Home Interfaces:* The remote and local home interface for your EJB that defines the application-specific methods for creating your EJB, as well as application-specific methods for finding your EJB, should be created.
5. *Compile EJB Code:* The EJB implementation, home interface, and remote interface should be compiled.
6. *Configure Module Deployment Descriptors:* The standard EJB deployment descriptor should be configured to define the specific structural characteristics and dependencies of your EJB. Any deployment descriptors needed by your container/server provider should also be configured.
7. *Package EJB into EJB JAR Module:* The standard EJB deployment descriptor, any vendor-specific deployment descriptors, and one or more of your compiled EJB class files should be packaged into an EJB JAR module.
8. *(Optional) Configure Application Deployment Descriptor:* A standard J2EE deployment descriptor may be configured for a cohesive collection of J2EE modules.
9. *(Optional) Package EJB Modules into J2EE EAR Application:* The standard J2EE deployment descriptor and one or more EJB JAR files may be packaged into a J2EE EAR application.
10. Deploy the J2EE Application: The EJB JAR or J2EE EAR application should be deployed to a J2EE-compliant application container/server environment.

On the client side, clients must simply be designed to utilize the proper EJB client interfaces and libraries. EJB client development proceeds along the following lines:

1. *Standard Client Library Verification:* The proper EJB client libraries must be utilized, including correct versions of JNDI, EJB client, RMI/IIOP, JMS, and JDBC libraries.
2. *EJB Client Interface Generation:* The properly compiled interfaces and stubs specific to a particular EJB must also be provided to an EJB client.
3. *Client Implementation:* The EJB client may be implemented to utilize any interfaces as appropriate.
4. *Client Code Compilation:* The EJB client code should be compiled.
5. *(Optional) Configure Application Client Deployment Descriptors:* Any standard J2EE application client deployment descriptor may be configured to define the specific configuration properties of your EJB client.

6. *(Optional) Package Client into Application Client JAR:* A standard J2EE Application Client deployment descriptor and compiled EJB client class files may then be packaged into a J2EE application client JAR.
7. (Optional) Launch the J2EE Application Client: A J2EE application client may be launched within a special J2EE application client container environment.

EJB Configuration and Deployment

As discussed throughout this book, J2EE enterprise applications are composed of one or more individual J2EE modules. J2EE modules have deployment descriptors specific to the module type, and J2EE enterprise applications also have their own deployment descriptor format. We have already described the J2EE Web application module deployment descriptor in Chapter 19, "Java Servlets," and the J2EE enterprise application deployment descriptor in Chapter 23, "Enterprise Application Services." In this chapter we introduce the EJB application module deployment descriptor. We introduce the basics for understanding EJB deployment descriptors, deployed archives, and deployment procedures in this section.

EJB Deployment Descriptor Top-Level Elements

J2EE EJB application module deployment descriptors are defined in XML files named `ejb-jar.xml`. Because configuring EJB deployment descriptors is more involved than configuring Web component deployment descriptors, we take a slightly different tack in describing the format and use of the EJB deployment descriptor. We in fact describe elements of the EJB deployment descriptor as they become relevant to the topic at hand throughout this chapter and the subsequent chapters on EJB. We thus carve out pieces of the EJB module's XML schema and describe them as the elements they define become relevant. If you are the type who can't wait and absolutely must digest the entire EJB v2.1 deployment descriptor structure, you can find the XML schema definition at `http://java.sun.com/xml/ns/j2ee/ejb-jar_2_1.xsd`. A set of schema elements common across the J2EE v1.4 are referenced from within the EJB v2.1 schema located at `http://java.sun.com/xml/ns/j2ee/j2ee_1_4.xsd`.

The top-level XML schema elements of an EJB deployment descriptor are containers used to define EJB application meta-data, EJB structure, information about relationships between EJBs, EJB assembly information, and the archive filename for any EJB client files. The top-level elements of an EJB deployment descriptor are defined here:

- `<ejb-jar>`: The root element of EJB deployment for a single EJB JAR file containing a sequence of the elements that follow here.
- Description group: A collection of optional description-related elements including `<description>`, `<display-name>`, and `<icon>` (optional).

- `<enterprise-beans>`: Container for one or more `<session>`, `<entity>`, and `<message-driven>` bean descriptors.
- `<relationships>`: Describes relationships among container-managed persistence entity EJBs (optional).
- `<assembly-descriptor>`: Contains definitions for security and transaction semantics associated with the application in the `ejb-jar` file (optional).
- `<ejb-client-jar>`: Specifies a JAR file URL containing the client stub and interface classes needed by EJB clients to use the EJBs in the `ejb-jar` file (optional).

EJB application module deployment descriptors defined according to the preceding top-level format must also include a reference to the standard XML schema being used. The basic top-level structure of an EJB deployment descriptor thus follows the sample form as exemplified here:

```
<?xml version='1.0' encoding='UTF-8'?>
<ejb-jar
          xmlns="http://java.sun.com/xml/ns/j2ee"
          xmlns:xsi="http://www.w3.org/2001/XMLSchema-instance"
          xsi:schemaLocation="http://java.sun.com/xml/ns/j2ee
          http://java.sun.com/xml/ns/j2ee/ejb-jar_2_1.xsd"
          version="2.1">
  <description> This is my BeeShirts.com EJB Application </description>
  <display-name> BeeShirts.com Application Service </display-name>
  <icon>
    <small-icon> beeshirtsSmall.jpg </small-icon>
    <large-icon> beeshirtsLarge.jpg </large-icon>
  </icon>
  <enterprise-beans>
    <session> ... </session>
    <session> ... </session>
    <entity> ... </entity>
    <entity> ... </entity>
    <message-driven> ... </message-driven>
      ...
  </enterprise-beans>
  <relationships>
    ...
  </relationships>
  <assembly-descriptor>
    ...
  </assembly-descriptor>
  <ejb-client-jar> beeshirtsClient.jar </ejb-client-jar>
</ejb-jar>
```

EJB JAR Files

An EJB JAR file represents the deployable JAR library that contains the server-side code and configuration of the EJB module. During deployment, the `ejb-jar.xml` file is placed under the `META-INF` directory of the EJB JAR file. Any entity and session beans defined within the `ejb-jar.xml` file must have the `.class` files for their implementations, remote and local home interfaces, remote and local object interfaces, and any dependent classes archived inside of the EJB JAR file. As you'll see in subsequent chapters, the `ejb-jar.xml` file can be used to define references from EJBs defined in its associated EJB JAR file to other EJBs inside of other EJB JAR files. If the `Class-Path` attribute in the EJB JAR file's `Manifest.mf` file includes any auxiliary EJB JAR file library URLs, then the current EJB JAR file does not need to include any EJB client stubs or interfaces from any associated auxiliary EJBs that its EJBs are dependent on.

Any client stub and interface classes needed to access the EJBs in a particular EJB JAR file can be placed in a separate EJB client JAR file. The URL of this EJB client JAR file can then be specified in the `ejb-jar.xml` file's `<ejb-client-jar>` element. Any EJB clients of the EJBs in the associated server-side EJB JAR file can then automatically receive downloaded interface and stub classes as they are needed if the EJB client's class loader can reach the URL defined within the `<ejb-client-jar>` element. If no automatic class downloading mechanism is supported or used by the client, the EJB client JAR libraries should be installed on the EJB client's machine.

EJB Deployment Procedures

The process for deploying J2EE applications involves establishing environment variables, configuring server properties, compiling Java code, creating XML-based deployment descriptors, packaging archive files, and deploying archives to a J2EE server environment. We focus on the deployment of our J2EE-based EJB applications in this section. Appendix A, "Software Configuration," provides detailed instructions for how to install and perform the basic configuration of both a J2EE reference implementation server and a BEA WebLogic Server used to deploy our J2EE-based EJB applications. However, the general procedure for deploying J2EE-based EJB applications assumes the following general steps, with optional steps for packaging the EJB module into a J2EE application indicated:

1. *Set J2EE Server Environment Variables:* Environment variables must be set for running a J2EE server environment and will vary per vendor implementation and operating-system platform.
2. *Configure J2EE Server Properties:* Configuration properties for most J2EE server implementations can be set to suit your particular network and operating environment.
3. *Compile J2EE EJB Application Code:* All J2EE EJB implementation, home interfaces, object interfaces, and dependent utility code must be compiled using a standard Java compiler.

4. *Create a J2EE EJB Application Deployment Descriptor:* An XML-based deployment descriptor is created according to the EJB application XML schema defined throughout this chapter and subsequent chapters. Many products create this file for you from a GUI-based configuration tool.
5. *Create Vendor-Specific Deployment Descriptors:* Vendor-specific deployment descriptors are required to perform various container-specific properties and for customizing the deployment behavior of EJBs within the vendor's container. Vendors often provide a GUI-based means to configure these files.
6. *Package J2EE EJB Application Code:* The EJB deployment descriptors, all compiled J2EE EJB implementation classes, all compiled J2EE EJB implementation interfaces, and all other compiled classes dependent on your EJBs need to be packaged into an EJB JAR file with a `.jar` extension. J2EE-based products may supply command-line and/or GUI-based utilities for this purpose.
7. *Start the J2EE Server:* The J2EE-compliant server must generally be started or already be started at this stage. The exact mechanism for starting a server is often vendor dependent but can be as simple as invoking a single startup command from the command line.
8. *(Optional) Create a J2EE Application Deployment Descriptor:* A J2EE application deployment descriptor may be created to collect one or more Web, EJB, and application client modules into a cohesive J2EE application. Many products will create this file for you automatically or via a GUI-based configuration tool.
9. *(Optional) Package J2EE Application Code:* The J2EE application deployment descriptor, Web applications, EJB applications, and application clients may then be packaged into an enterprise archive (EAR) file with a `.ear` extension. Many products also create this archive for you automatically or via GUI-based development tools.
10. *Deploy the EJB or J2EE Enterprise Application Code:* Finally, the individual EJB module or integrated J2EE application is deployed to the J2EE server environment for access by enterprise application clients. This step is also often automated via GUI tools.

Conclusions

Enterprise JavaBeans provides a standard component model for developing distributed enterprise applications as components that operate inside of an EJB container environment. EJBs are architected to allow the EJB container to make callbacks onto EJB components such that the container can manage certain enterprise resource services and the EJB life cycle on behalf of the EJB. In such a way, the EJB component developer can focus most of his energy on implementing business logic and leave a significant amount of resource management work to the container. The steps to develop, configure, and deploy EJBs are also simplified. Standard XML-based deployment descriptors define how an EJB is to behave inside of an EJB container. Design-wise, the EJB developer has to choose between session, entity, and message-driven beans. The next three chapters (Chapters 25 through 27) cover those three models in depth and provide examples. The three chapters after that (Chapters 28 through 30) provide detailed discussions on EJB security, transactions, Web tier integration, and Web services integration, among other advanced EJB topics.

25

Session EJB

SESSION BEANS ARE EJB COMPONENTS DESIGNED to perform some action on the enterprise system on behalf of the client. Session beans are often designed to serve as the entry points or "frontline" EJBs for EJB clients. EJB clients interact with session beans in order to be provided with the functional behavior and services of the enterprise system that the clients desire to utilize. This chapter describes how to create session beans and session bean clients, as well as how to configure and deploy such components into an EJB container.

In this chapter, you will learn:

- How to build stateless session EJB components.
- How to build stateful session EJB components.
- How to build EJB clients to remotely access session beans.
- How to build EJB clients to locally access session beans inside the same container process.
- How to build session EJB components that can receive timed event callbacks by the EJB container.
- How to configure and deploy session beans.

Stateless Session Beans

This section describes how to create session bean component implementations that adhere to the EJB component-container model contract that enables them to operate inside of an EJB container to expose its services to session bean clients. We specifically present the rules and approach for building stateless session beans in this section. Stateless session bean components are implemented assuming that no state will be maintained for a particular client between subsequent invocations on that bean over time. Stateless session bean implementations thus provide pure input-output request and response behavior for their clients.

Stateless session beans are designed not to require the preservation of state within the EJB that is specific to a particular EJB client. This does not imply that the EJB does not actually maintain any state within its fields or associated objects. However, it does imply that the state it maintains is not required to be accessed or utilized for a specific EJB client later.

Such a designation allows an EJB container some flexibility in maximizing the efficiency in management of such EJBs. Because use of stateless session bean components implies that any of their instances created by the container can be used by any client at any time, the container can maintain a pool of such instances that are allocated to clients on an as-needed basis without regard to which instance belongs to which client. Containers can also easily create and destroy bean instances as needed to adjust for scalability and resource demands. Thus, although stateless session beans can have state, no assumptions are to be made by the programmer about the validity of that state between successive uses of that bean instance. EJB containers may create, destroy, and allocate stateless session beans for use as they please.

Stateless Session Bean Logical Component Architecture

Figure 25.1 depicts the basic architecture involved in creating stateless session bean components. At the top of the diagram is the `javax.ejb.EnterpriseBean` marker interface, which is the base interface for all EJBs. The `EnterpriseBean` interface is extended by the `javax.ejb.SessionBean` interface, which is required to be implemented by all session EJB classes. Public, nonfinal, and non-abstract stateless session bean EJBs, such as `MyStatelessSessionEJBean` as shown in the diagram, must implement the `SessionBean` interface. Stateless session bean EJBs implement public, nonfinal, and nonstatic business-specific methods, such as `someMethod()` and `anotherMethod()` shown in the diagram. Session bean implementations must also have a public parameterless constructor and should not implement the `finalize()` method. Because a session bean can be a subclass of some other class, if all of its required methods are not implemented by the session EJB implementation class itself, they must be implemented by one of the session bean's superclasses.

Stateless Session Bean Context Setting

The `setSessionContext()` method defined on a stateless session bean is used to pass an instance of a `SessionContext` object to the EJB. It is also the first method defined on the `SessionBean` interface that is called by the container. A `SessionContext` object encapsulates an interface to the EJB session container context. The `SessionContext` interface extends a more generic `EJBContext` interface and provides hooks for session beans to access client interfaces to the EJB, transaction information, timed object information, and security information. We have more to say about client interfaces and timed objects later in this chapter and discuss EJB transactions and security in Chapter 28, "EJB Assurance Services."

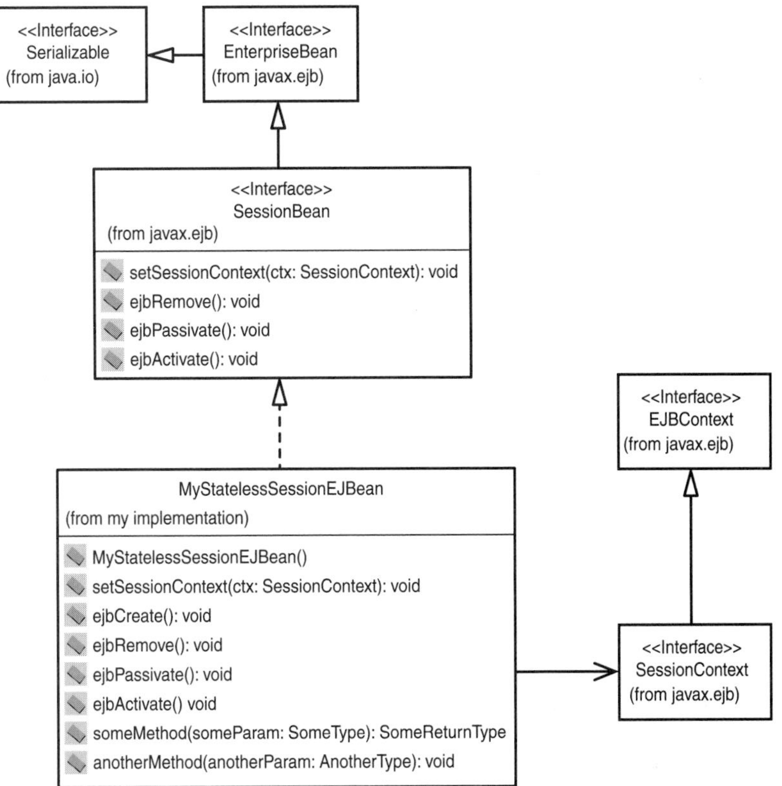

Figure 25.1 Stateless session EJBs.

Stateless Session Bean Creation and Removal

A key operation required by a custom stateless session bean, such as `MyStatelessSessionEJBean`, but not defined within the `SessionBean` interface is the `ejbCreate()` method. A single public, nonfinal, nonstatic, and parameterless `ejbCreate()` method must be defined on stateless session bean implementations with a `void` return type. This method is called by the EJB container when the container decides to create an instance of the stateless session EJB. The container may decide to do this when it wants to create an initial pool of bean instances, or it may do this when it receives a client's request. The `ejbCreate()` method is thus akin to a special type of constructor or initialization method implemented by EJBs.

The `ejbRemove()` method is called by a container on a session bean object when the container is about to decommission the bean instance from handling any more client requests. For stateless session beans, the container is solely responsible for determining when it will call `ejbRemove()` on a particular session bean instance. It is not bound in any way to the EJB client.

Stateless Session Bean Passivation and Activation

Because no assumptions are made about the importance of state in a stateless session bean, there is no assumed need to passivate and activate stateless session beans. That is, containers do not assume that a stateless session bean must close any open resources when it is to be removed from active memory (that is, passivated) and do not need to re-create any connections to open resources when brought back into active memory from persistent memory (that is, activated). Thus, the implementations for `ejbPassivate()` and `ejbActivate()` methods for stateless session beans may simply be empty implementations. Such methods, in fact, are not invoked on stateless session beans by the EJB container.

Stateless Session Bean Component Interface Rules Summary

The life cycle of a stateless session bean is implied by the methods it must support. The life cycle of a stateless session bean as managed by its EJB container proceeds according to these basic general guidelines:

1. *Instantiate EJB:* The container calls `Class.newInstance()` with the name of your EJB to create a new instance of the stateless session bean when the container decides it is necessary.
2. *Set Context:* The container calls `setSessionContext()` on the EJB with a container managed `SessionContext` object.
3. *Call* `ejbCreate()`*:* The container then calls `ejbCreate()` on the EJB.
4. *Add EJB to Pool:* The container may now add the EJB to a pool of stateless session beans.
5. *Delegate Client Calls:* The container delegates EJB client calls on the stateless session bean to a stateless session bean instance it selects from a pool. Calls are delegated from a distributed skeleton layer to the actual EJB implementation object.
6. *Call* `ejbRemove()`*:* The container calls `ejbRemove()` on the EJB when the container wants to destroy the stateless session bean that sits in the pool.

Stateless session beans are thus extremely simple EJBs to create. An EJB applications developer needs to worry only about implementing the rather simple `SessionBean` interface and creating business-specific methods. The standard operations of concern are the `setSessionContext()`, parameterless `ejbCreate()`, `ejbRemove()`, empty `ejbPassivate()`, and empty `ejbActivate()` methods. Stateless session bean implementations must simply receive a request via one of their business-specific methods, implement some functionality when that method is invoked, and return any response via any return type from that method call.

EJB containers for stateless session beans take care of the actual bean's instance creation and destruction, as well as determining when to allocate the bean to a client request. The container ensures that only one thread associated with a client's request is allowed to execute a bean instance's method at any instant. Thus, you should be careful to design your session beans such that concurrent calls from different threads don't attempt to access the same bean instance. This could happen, for example, if your session bean itself or one of the objects associated with it attempts to use the same remote or local object interface instance to that session bean and thus results in a loopback call to the bean instance.

If for some reason, a second client request does make its way to attempt access to the session bean instance while that instance is processing another client request, the container must handle this situation to ensure that concurrent access does not occur. The container may throw a `java.rmi.RemoteException` exception in the case of a remote client, may throw a `javax.ejb.EJBException` exception in the case of a local client, or may choose to queue and serialize the concurrent requests of the clients. Although properly designed EJB clients will not ever be in such a situation, the container is required at least to protect the integrity of your server-side session bean instance against such breaches of client etiquette.

Stateless Session Bean Example

We have created a back-end enterprise application serving framework for our BeeShirts.com example using EJBs. Such example EJBs are described throughout this chapter and the subsequent EJB chapters. Because our sample code is moderately large for inclusion in this book, we cannot insert all the source code in the chapter text but will provide core listings and snippets from such code as relevant topics are introduced.

> **Note**
>
> All the sample code strewn throughout this chapter may be located as described in Appendix A and is extracted beneath the `examples\src\ejava\ejb` directory, `examples\src\ejava\ejb\session` subdirectories, and `examples\src\ejava\ejb\timer` directory. Because the session EJB-related code represents a moderately large amount of BeeShirts.com enterprise application component code, we do not present all the code in this chapter. Rather, we describe the basic structure of such code and present snippets from that code germane to chapter topics as they are discussed. Also note that this code depends on some of the code from Chapter 19, "Java Servlets," extracted to the `examples\src\ejava\servlets` directory, and code from Chapter 26, "Entity EJB," extracted to the `examples\src\ejava\ejb\entity` subdirectories. Appendix A describes how to build and deploy such code.

Listing 25.1 presents a stateless session bean example in the form of those core snippets from the `BrowseEJBean` implementation of a stateless session bean that are germane to our discussion here. No standard `ejbXXX()` methods need special implementation for this bean, but a public `queryShirts()` method is provided for business-specific logic.

Essentially, the `BrowseEJBean` represents a front-line session EJB that can be used to query for `TShirt`-related products at the BeeShirts.com Web site.

Listing 25.1 **Stateless Session Bean Example (`BrowseEJBean.java`)**

```
package ejava.ejb.session.browse;
  ...
public class BrowseEJBean implements SessionBean {
  // EJB session context
  private SessionContext sessionContext;
  // Home interface to a TShirt entity bean
  private TShirtLocalHome tshirtHome;

  // Standard session EJB interfaces implemented
  public void setSessionContext(SessionContext aCtx)
    throws RemoteException {
    sessionContext = aCtx;
    try {
      lookupTShirtHome();
    } catch (NamingException ne) {
      throw new RemoteException(ne.getMessage());
    }
  }
  public void ejbCreate() { /* no creation logic */ }
  public void ejbRemove() { /* no removal logic */  }
  public void ejbPassivate() { /* no state persistence */ }
  public void ejbActivate() { /* no state activation */ }

  /** Finds the TShirt Home Object */
  private void lookupTShirtHome() throws NamingException {
    if (tshirtHome == null) {
      InitialContext context = new InitialContext();
      Object tshirtHomeRef = context.lookup(EJBHelper.TSHIRT_REFNAME);
      tshirtHome =
        (TShirtLocalHome) PortableRemoteObject.narrow(
          tshirtHomeRef,
          ejava.ejb.entity.tshirt.TShirtLocalHome.class);
      context.close();
    }
  }

  /** Find TShirt entity beans and create Serialized versions */
  public Vector queryShirts(String size, String color)
    throws RemoteException {
    // Create collections for entity beans and serialized objects
    Collection queriedShirts = null;
```

Listing 25.1 **Continued**

```
    Vector returnedShirts = new Vector();

    try {
      // Find a collection of TShirt entity beans in the database
      queriedShirts = tshirtHome.findBySizeAndColor(size, color);
      Iterator iterator = queriedShirts.iterator();
      // While cycling through TShirt entity object collection...
      while (iterator.hasNext()) {
        // Get TShirt entity bean
        ejava.ejb.entity.tshirt.TShirtLocal beanShirt =
          (ejava.ejb.entity.tshirt.TShirtLocal) iterator.next();

        // Create Serialized TShirt object from entity bean data
        TShirt clientShirt =
          new TShirt(
            beanShirt.getShirtID().intValue(),
            beanShirt.getShirtSize(),
            beanShirt.getColor(),
            beanShirt.getDesignFront(),
            beanShirt.getDesignBack(),
            beanShirt.getPictureFront(),
            beanShirt.getPictureBack(),
            beanShirt.getUnitPrice());

        // Add the TShirt object to a return vector
        returnedShirts.addElement(clientShirt);
      }
    } catch (FinderException finderException) {
      finderException.printStackTrace();
    }

    // Return the Vector of Serialized TShirt objects
    return returnedShirts;
  }
}
```

The `BrowseEJBean.queryShirts()` method first looks up a reference to the `TShirt` entity bean home interface from within `lookupTShirtHome()` and then uses that interface to query for a collection of `TShirt` entity beans that match the shirt size and color query parameters. We describe how to build entity beans in the next chapter, but suffice it to say that a `Collection` of `TShirt` entity bean remote interface objects is returned. For each entity bean in the `Collection`, the `queryShirts()` method creates an associated `Serializable` `TShirt` object instance and returns a `Vector` of these `Serializable` `TShirt` objects.

In addition to the BrowseEJBean, three other stateless session beans are included with the example EJB code. We don't describe each bean in detail here but will occasionally refer to such beans and demonstrate snippets from such beans throughout the EJB chapters in this book. These are the other stateless session EJBs:

- ejava.ejb.session.customermgr.CustomerManagerEJBean: A stateless session bean serving as a front-line interface to manage BeeShirts.com customer-related information. The creation of new customer accounts and retrieval of customer information is managed through this bean. Such customer-related information is associated with the Customer entity bean and its related beans.
- ejava.ejb.session.creditmgr.CreditManagerEJBean: A stateless session bean serving as a front-line interface to manage BeeShirts.com customer credit-related information. The creation of new credit-card accounts is managed through this bean. Such credit-related information is associated with the Credit entity bean. A J2EE application client in the same package, CreditManagerClient, is used to communicate with the CreditManagerEJBean.
- ejava.ejb.session.ordermgr.OrderManagerEJBean: A stateless session bean serving as a front-line interface to manage BeeShirts.com order-related information. The creation of new orders and retrieval of order information is managed through this bean. Such order-related information is primarily associated with the Order entity bean and its related beans.

Stateful Session Beans

This section describes how to create stateful session bean component implementations that adhere to the EJB component-container model contract. We specifically present the rules and approach for building stateful session beans in this section. Stateful session beans assume that a client may revisit the same bean instance later and that the state preserved for that bean relates to a particular client's prior interaction with the bean. Stateful session bean implementations thus provide a stateful object interaction behavior to be utilized within the request and response behavior provided to their clients.

Stateful session beans are session beans that preserve some state within the EJB specifically associated with its EJB client. The state (aka conversational state) of a stateful session bean refers to the data stored within the fields (that is, variables) of the bean instance, as well as within any objects the bean holds and those objects' fields and objects, and so on. When an EJB client accesses a stateful session bean at one instant and changes the state of the bean instance, that state must be preserved and assumed by the bean instance at some later instant in which the bean is accessed.

When a session bean that is stateful is created, the container must assume more responsibility and care in how it manages the bean, as opposed to the case with stateless session beans. For one, stateful session bean instances are associated with the clients that create them and therefore cannot simply be plucked at random from a pool to service client requests. In fact, the creation and removal of a stateful session bean by a client is directly related to the creation and removal of stateful session bean instances on the server side. Furthermore, when resources become limited, a container may decide to serialize (aka passivate) one or more stateful session beans to persistent storage. As resources become available or perhaps upon client request, the passivated bean must be activated and brought into active memory. In light of such behavior within an EJB container, stateful session beans require additional special design considerations on the part of the bean developer.

Stateful Session Bean Logical Component Architecture

Figure 25.2 depicts the basic architecture involved in creating stateful session bean components. Public, nonfinal, and non-abstract stateful session bean implementations, such as `MyStatefulSessionEJBean`, must implement the `SessionBean` interface, which in turn extends the `EnterpriseBean` interface. Stateful session EJBs also implement public, nonfinal, and nonstatic business-specific methods, such as the `someMethod()` and `anotherMethod()` sample methods shown in the diagram. Session bean implementations must also have a public parameterless constructor and should not implement the `finalize()` method. Because a session bean can be a subclass of some other class, if all of its required methods are not implemented by the session EJB implementation class itself, they must be implemented by one of the session bean's superclasses.

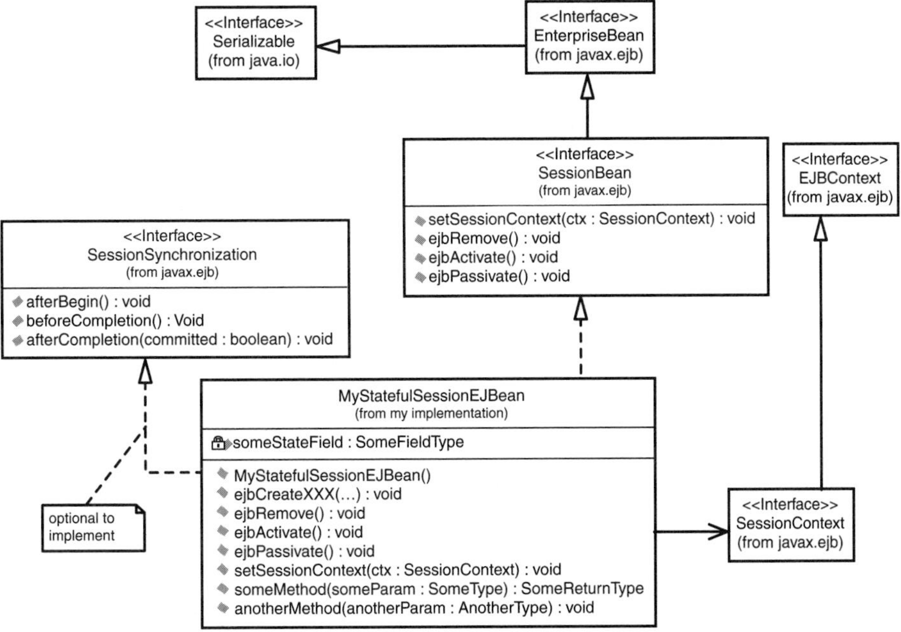

Figure 25.2 Stateful session EJBs.

Optionally, stateful session beans may implement the `javax.ejb.SessionSynchronization` interface to enable the bean to be notified of certain transaction management events. We defer discussion of most EJB transaction management issues until Chapter 28.

Stateful Session Bean Creation and Removal

Because the maintenance of state is of primary importance to stateful session beans, the initial state in which such a bean is created may be important. Thus, stateful session beans can be defined with one or more public, nonfinal, and nonstatic `ejbCreateXXX(...)` methods that take zero or more input parameters and return a `void` type. The exact parameters that are passed into such methods are application specific, but the name of the method must be `ejbCreateXXX` whereby the developer can name the method with any valid method name identifiers substituted for the *XXX* as long as the method name is prefixed by `ejbCreate`. Unlike the `ejbCreate()` invocation on a stateless session bean, stateful session bean `ejbCreateXXX()` method invocations are directly bound to the EJB client that created the instance and that will continue to use that specific instance. Note also that before any `ejbCreateXXX()` method is called, the container calls `setSessionContext()` on the stateful session bean, as was the case with the stateless session bean.

The invocation of an `ejbRemove()` method implemented by a session bean indicates that the client to which this session belongs has requested that the stateful session bean be prohibited from servicing any more requests. The container may also invoke `ejbRemove()` on a bean when a configurable session maximum timeout has expired. However, because there is no guarantee that `ejbRemove()` will always be called in the event of a server failure or after certain critical exceptions, an auxiliary method to periodically attempt the cleanup of any unclosed resources may need to be provided by the applications developer.

Stateful Session Bean Passivation and Activation

Perhaps the most significant things to consider when designing a stateful session bean are the ramifications of passivation and activation on your bean. As stated earlier, a container passivates your session bean by serializing its contents and writing this information to some persistent storage mechanism (for example, to the local server file system). A container does this when active memory resources are becoming scarce and usually employs some sort of least-recently-used algorithm to determine which specific bean instances should be passivated (although the actual algorithm used is vendor specific). Before a container passivates your bean instance, it will call `ejbPassivate()` on your bean, which your bean must implement.

The implementation of `ejbPassivate()` implementation must clean up any resources that cannot be serialized and persisted, such as database connections and open file handles. Any objects that remain unclosed after `ejbPassivate()` completes must be passivatable by the container. Passivatable objects include fundamental types,

`Serializable` objects, objects set to null, or a collection of special enterprise Java object references. The special enterprise Java object references that are passivatable and that must also not be specified as transient objects in a session bean are EJB home and object references (be they local or remote), JNDI and session contexts, and `UserTransaction` references.

When a request for a passivated bean is made or perhaps when resources are again freed up, the container will activate the bean. That is, the container will deserialize the persisted state of the bean and reconstruct the bean in active memory with the state in which it was originally persisted. After the bean state is reconstructed, the container will call `ejbActivate()` on the stateful session bean implementation, which should reconstruct any resources that were closed during the call to `ejbPassivate()`. Alternatively, if a certain amount of time has expired while the bean was in persistent storage, the container vendor implementation may elect to remove the bean from persistent storage given some configurable time limit.

Stateful Session Bean Component Interface Rules Summary

Much like the stateless session bean, the life cycle of a stateful session bean is also implied by the methods it must support. However, because of its stateful nature, issues such as passivation and activation must be considered by the container. We present here the basic guidelines that a container for a stateful session bean must consider (sans transaction management):

1. *Instantiate EJB:* The container calls `Class.newInstance()` with the name of your EJB to create a new instance of the stateful session bean when the EJB client induces the creation of such a bean.
2. *Set Context:* The container calls `setSessionContext()` on the EJB with a container-managed `SessionContext` object.
3. *Call* `ejbCreateXXX(...)`*:* The container then calls the appropriate `ejbCreateXXX(...)` on the EJB depending on the call that the EJB client used to create the EJB instance.
4. *Add EJB to Cache:* The container may now cache the stateful session EJB in memory.
5. *Delegate Client Calls:* The container delegates EJB client calls to the stateful session bean whose reference is associated with the client. Calls from a client pass from client stub to the container's skeleton representation of the EJB and then to the EJB implementation itself.
6. *Call* `ejbPassivate()`*:* The container may decide to passivate the stateful session bean according to some container-specific policy (for example, least-recently-used algorithm). The container first calls `ejbPassivate()` and then serializes the state of the session bean to persistent storage.

7. *Retire Passive Beans:* The container may remove from persistent storage a session bean that has been passivated for an amount of time exceeding some configurable limit.
8. *Call* `ejbActivate()`*:* The container will activate any passivated beans when a client attempts to access such beans. Activated beans are brought from persistent storage into the active cache memory. The container first deserializes the state of the session bean and then calls `ejbActivate()` on the bean.
9. *Call* `ejbRemove()`: The container calls `ejbRemove()` on the EJB when the client attempts to remove the bean.

Stateful session beans thus require more design considerations than do stateless session beans. Aside from implementing the `SessionBean` interface, a collection of `ejbCreateXXX(...)` methods can be specified to provide initial state to the bean. Furthermore, passivation and activation must be taken into consideration when defining the field objects of a stateful session bean, as well as when implementing the `ejbPassivate()` and `ejbActivate()` methods.

Finally, as is the case for stateless session beans, EJB containers for stateful session beans ensure that only one thread associated with an EJB client request is allowed to execute a bean instance's method at any moment. Hence, you should also be careful to design your stateful session beans such that concurrent calls from different threads don't attempt to access the same bean instance. In the event of a concurrent invocation from another client thread, the EJB container may throw a `java.rmi.RemoteException` to a remote client, may throw a `javax.ejb.EJBException` exception to a local client, or may choose to queue and serialize the concurrent client request.

Stateful Session Bean Example

Listing 25.2 presents a stateful session bean example in the form of those core snippets from the `ShoppingCartEJBean` implementation of a stateful session bean that specifically relate to our discussion here. The complete code listing can be downloaded as described in Appendix A. Most standard `ejbXXX()` methods are not needed for this bean. An `ejbCreate(Hashtable)` method is defined, however, to populate the session bean with initial shopping-cart data. Furthermore, the `addAnItemToTheCart()`, `getSelectedItemsInTheCart()`, and `checkOut()` public business-specific methods do contain component logic and will be exposed to EJB clients.

Listing 25.2 **Stateful Session Bean Example (`ShoppingCartEJBean.java`)**

```
package ejava.ejb.session.shoppingcart;
    ...
public class ShoppingCartEJBean implements SessionBean {
  // Session context
  private SessionContext sessionContext;
  // Local entity bean home interfaces
```

Listing 25.2 **Continued**

```
private CMRTShirtLocalHome tshirtHome;
private OrderManagerLocalHome orderManagerHome;
private CMRCustomerLocalHome customerHome;
// Shopping cart items (stateful client specific state)
private Hashtable itemsInTheCart;
// Time duration constants
private static final long FIVE_DAYS = 432000000;
private static final long THIRTY_DAYS = FIVE_DAYS * 6;

// Standard interfaces
public void setSessionContext(SessionContext aCtx) {
  sessionContext = aCtx;
  try {
    lookupCustomerHome();
    lookupTShirtHome();
    lookupOrderManagerHome();
  } catch (NamingException ne) {
    throw new EJBException(ne.getMessage());
  }
}
public void ejbCreate() { /* no creation logic */}
public void ejbRemove() { /* no removal logic */}
public void ejbPassivate() { /* no state persistence */}
public void ejbActivate() { /* no state activation */}
public void ejbCreate(Hashtable initialCart) // Initial cart data
{
  itemsInTheCart = initialCart;
}

/** Lookup Customer Home object */
private void lookupCustomerHome() throws NamingException {...}
/** Lookup TShirt Home object */
private void lookupTShirtHome() throws NamingException {...}
/** Lookup Order Home object */
private void lookupOrderManagerHome() throws NamingException {...}

/** Add a particular item identified by ID and quantity to session */
public void addAnItemToTheCart(int shirtID, int quantity) {
  // If no Hashtable created make one
  if (itemsInTheCart == null) {
    itemsInTheCart = new Hashtable();
  }
  try {
    // Put the item ID and quantity into Hashtable (session state)
    itemsInTheCart.put(new Integer(shirtID), new Integer(quantity));
```

Listing 25.2 **Continued**

```
    } catch (Exception exception) {
      exception.printStackTrace();
    }
  }

  /** For each item in session, return Vector of associated TShirts */
  public Vector getSelectedItemsInTheCart() {
    // Create return Vector
    Vector returnItemsInTheCart = new Vector();

    // For each ID in Hashtable (session state)
    Enumeration shirtIDs = itemsInTheCart.keys();
    while (shirtIDs.hasMoreElements()) {
      Integer shirtID = (Integer) shirtIDs.nextElement();
      Integer quantity = (Integer) itemsInTheCart.get(shirtID);

      try {
        // Find an associated TShirt entity bean
        ejava.ejb.entity.tshirt.CMRTShirtLocal beanShirt =
          tshirtHome.findByPrimaryKey(shirtID);
        // Create and initialize a Serializable TShirt object
        //    with data from TShirt entity bean.
        TShirt clientShirt =
          new TShirt(
            beanShirt.getShirtID().intValue(),
            beanShirt.getShirtSize(),
            beanShirt.getColor(),
            beanShirt.getDesignFront(),
            beanShirt.getDesignBack(),
            beanShirt.getPictureFront(),
            beanShirt.getPictureBack(),
            beanShirt.getUnitPrice());
        clientShirt.setQuantity(quantity.intValue());
        clientShirt.setTotalPrice(
          quantity.intValue() * beanShirt.getUnitPrice());
        // Add Serializable TShirt object to return vector
        returnItemsInTheCart.addElement(clientShirt);
      } catch (FinderException fe) {
        fe.printStackTrace();
        throw new EJBException(fe.getMessage());
      }
    }

    // Return Vector of Serializable TShirt objects
    return returnItemsInTheCart;
```

Listing 25.2 **Continued**

```
}

/**
 * Set default order shipping information and
 * create an order based on customer ID
 * and cart information.
*/
private Order fillDefaultOrderInformation(
  int customerID,
  String shipInstruction,
  double shipWeight,
  double shipCharge)
  throws FinderException {
  Order order = new Order();
  // Default date to order is created
  order.setOrderDate(new Date(System.currentTimeMillis()));
  // Default date to be paid
  order.setPaidDate(
    new Date(System.currentTimeMillis() + THIRTY_DAYS));
  // Default date to be shipped
  order.setShippingInstructions(shipInstruction);
  order.setShipWeight(shipWeight);
  order.setShipCharge(shipCharge);
  order.setShipDate(new Date(System.currentTimeMillis() + FIVE_DAYS));
  // Set customer info for order being created
  Customer customer = getCustomerInfo(customerID);
  order.setCustomer(customer);
  order.setBillingAddress(customer.getAddress());
  order.setShippingAddress(customer.getAddress());
  // Retrieve items from shopping cart session info
  Vector itemsInTheCart = getSelectedItemsInTheCart();
  // Create items in the cart as array of items
  TShirt[] items = new TShirt[itemsInTheCart.size()];
  for (int i = 0; i < itemsInTheCart.size(); i++) {
    items[i] = (TShirt) itemsInTheCart.elementAt(i);
  }
  // Set items onto order
  order.setItems(items);
  return order;
}

/** Get Customer object based on customer ID */
private Customer getCustomerInfo(int customerID)
  throws FinderException {
  CMRCustomerLocal customerLocal =
```

Listing 25.2 **Continued**

```
      customerHome.findByPrimaryKey(new Integer(customerID));
    Customer customer = fillReturnCustomer(customerLocal);
    customer.setCustomerID("" + customerID);
    return customer;
  }

  /** Get Customer object from local EJB interface */
  private Customer fillReturnCustomer(CMRCustomerLocal customerLocal) {
    Address address =
      new Address(
        customerLocal.getAddress_1(),
        customerLocal.getAddress_2(),
        customerLocal.getCity(),
        customerLocal.getState(),
        customerLocal.getZipCode());
    Customer customer =
      new Customer(
        customerLocal.getFirstName(),
        customerLocal.getLastName(),
        customerLocal.getMiddleName(),
        address,
        customerLocal.getPhone(),
        customerLocal.getEmail(),
        null);
    return customer;
  }

  /** Checkout based on cart information */
  public Order checkOut(Order orderInformation) {
    try {
      // Get Vector of items from the shopping cart
      Vector itemsInTheCart = getSelectedItemsInTheCart();
      // Create items in the cart as array of items
      TShirt[] items = new TShirt[itemsInTheCart.size()];
      for (int i = 0; i < itemsInTheCart.size(); i++) {
        items[i] = (TShirt) itemsInTheCart.elementAt(i);
      }
      // Set items from cart into order information
      orderInformation.setItems(items);
      // Return new order as created with order manager
      return createAnOrder(orderInformation);
    } catch (CreateException ce) {
      throw new EJBException(ce.getMessage());
    }
  }
```

Listing 25.2 **Continued**

```
  /** Checkout based on cart information. Set default shipping */
  public Order checkOut(int customerID) {
    try {
      // Now create and set default order information...
      // Default shipping instruction
      String shippingInstruct = "Leave package at door.";
      // Default max shipping weight
      double shipWeight = 5.0;
      // Default shipping charge
      double shipCharge = 1.95;
      // Default max paid date
      java.sql.Date paidDate =
        new java.sql.Date(System.currentTimeMillis() + THIRTY_DAYS);
      // Get default order information
      Order defaultOrder =
        fillDefaultOrderInformation(
          customerID,
          shippingInstruct,
          shipWeight,
          shipCharge);
      // Return new order as created with order manager
      return createAnOrder(defaultOrder);
    } catch (CreateException ce) {
      throw new EJBException(ce.getMessage());
    } catch (FinderException fe) {
      throw new EJBException(fe.getMessage());
    }

  }

  /**
   * Create an order using order manager and get order ID
   */
  private Order createAnOrder(Order order) throws CreateException {
    OrderManagerLocal orderManager = this.orderManagerHome.create();
    Integer newOrderID = orderManager.createNewOrder(order);
    order.setOrderID(newOrderID.intValue());
    return order;
  }
}
```

The state variable of interest to clients in this example is the `Hashtable` variable called `itemsInTheCart`. The `addAnItemToTheCart()` method adds an entry to the `itemsInTheCart Hashtable` given an item ID and quantity. A subsequent call to the bean instance by a client on a method such as `getSelectedItemsInTheCart()` will utilize the `itemsInTheCart Hashtable`. After the `TShirt` entity bean is looked up based on each item ID in the `itemsInTheCart Hashtable`, a `Serializable TShirt` object is created and added to a `Vector` returned to the client. The `checkout(Order)` method also uses the stateful `itemsInTheCart Hashtable` by creating an `Order` entity bean and returning a `Serializable Order` object based on the items that have been added to the client's shopping-cart information stored in the `itemsInTheCart`.

Session Bean Remote Client Interfaces

Now that we have seen how to build session bean components on the server side, let's explore how distributed clients can tap the services provided by these components. Two main types of distributed interfaces exist for client interfacing to a session bean: a session bean home interface and a session bean remote interface. The session bean home interface is used primarily as a factory to create references to session bean objects. The session bean remote interface then provides the client-side interface to the distributed session bean object's application-specific operations. Additionally, both home and remote interfaces provide a means to destroy client object references.

We describe how to build such interfaces and how clients access these interfaces in this section. We also describe the slightly different rules and semantics that exist for defining and using these interfaces as applied to both stateless and stateful session beans. Many of the concepts and abstractions described here also apply to entity bean interfacing, and we describe those similarities and the differences in the next chapter.

Session Bean Remote Interfaces

A session bean remote interface defines the set of application-specific distributed operations that can be invoked on a particular session bean. Remote interfaces describe the client's view of the EJB akin to the way RMI remote interfaces describe the client's view of an RMI server. In fact, remote interfaces are essentially defined using RMI/IIOP semantics. A CORBA mapping to such interfaces also exists, as we discuss in Chapter 29, "EJB Integration and Management." This section describes how to build and use session bean remote interfaces.

Session Bean Remote Interface Logical Architecture

Figure 25.3 depicts the basic logical architecture for building and using remote EJB client interfaces to distributed session EJBs. All application-specific interfaces to distributed EJB objects, such as `MySessionEJB` shown in the diagram, must extend the `javax.ejb.EJBObject` interface. `EJBObject` in turn extends `java.rmi.Remote`, which adds the distributed RMI semantics to remote EJB interfaces. Under the hood, remote interfaces make use of some container-provided stub implementation on the client side that handles the marshaling of calls to the distributed server-side skeleton. EJB container skeletons and delegates in turn delegate calls to the actual server-side EJB component implementation such as the `MySessionEJBean` shown in the diagram. Runtime EJB containers are ultimately responsible for managing which bean instance is used and how calls are routed on the server side, but the result is that calls from an EJB client to application-specific EJB remote interface methods ultimately result in the invocation of an associated application-specific method on the server-side EJB component instance.

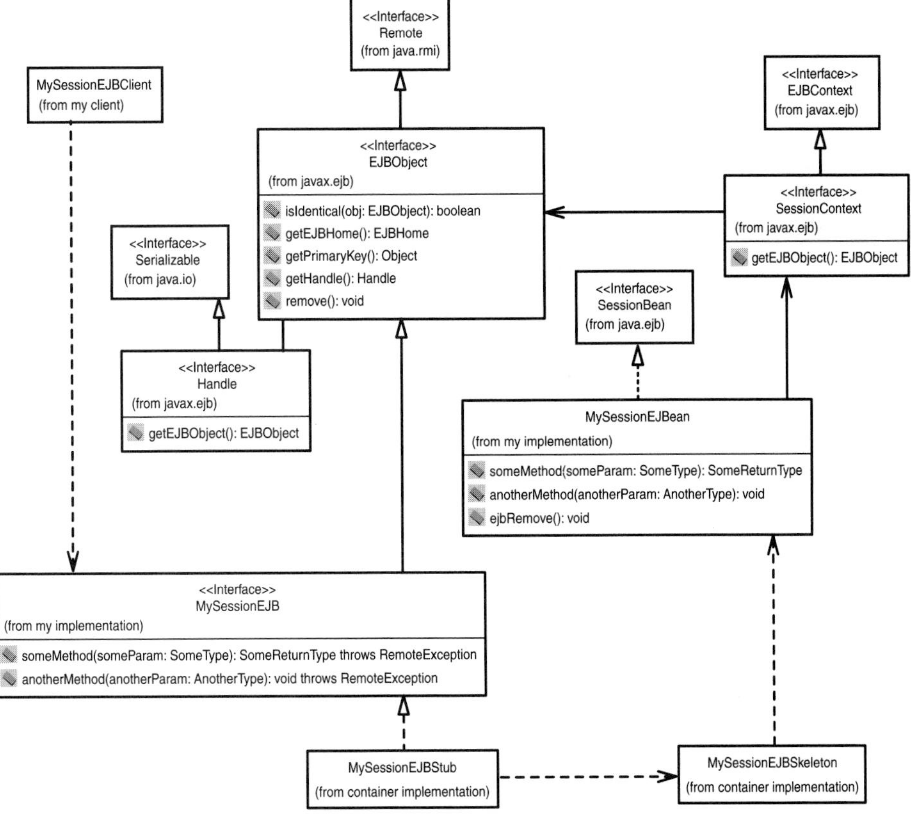

Figure 25.3 The session bean remote interface architecture.

Session Bean Application-Specific Remote Interfaces

An application-specific remote EJB interface must be created for EJB components wanting to be accessed remotely. This interface provides the distributed interface usable by EJB clients to invoke the application-specific logic of EJB components. For each distributable application-specific method on an EJB server-side component, such as `MySessionEJBean.someMethod()`, an associated application-specific method must be defined on the EJB client-side remote interface, such as `MySessionEJB.someMethod()`. As a side effect of their distributable nature, each distributed method in the application-specific remote interface should also declare that it can throw a `java.rmi.RemoteException`. Of course, such rules apply only to those server-side component methods you want to be made distributable.

Session Bean Generic Remote Interfaces

In addition to application-specific interfaces on an EJB remote interface, a set of methods inherited from `EJBObject` can be invoked on a remote EJB object. In situations in which clients want to determine whether one remote EJB object is identical to another, the `EJBObject.isIdentical()` method can be called. The `EJBObject.getEJBHome()` method returns a handle to the home interface object that is used to create remote interface objects. Because session EJBs do not have primary keys, calling `EJBObject.getPrimaryKey()` on a remote interface for a session bean will result in a `RemoteException` being thrown.

The `EJBObject.getHandle()` method returns an object that implements the `javax.ejb.Handle` interface. The `Handle` object encapsulates a persistent reference to a distributed remote EJB object. Because the `Handle` object is serializable, it can be serialized and persisted by the client and then reactivated later to obtain a reference to the remote EJB object via the call to `Handle.getEJBObject()`.

The `EJBObject.remove()` method is used by clients to destroy their reference to the remote EJB object. This method definitively destroys EJB object resources only on the client side. Containers will call `ejbRemove()` on a server-side stateful session bean instance when such a call is made. However, the invocation of `remove()` from the client side on a remote stateless session bean object does not necessarily induce the container to invoke `ejbRemove()` on a server-side bean instance because containers reuse stateless session bean instances for different client invocations.

As a final note, on the server side, a session bean can obtain a reference to an `EJBObject` with which it is associated by calling `getEJBObject()` on its `SessionContext` object. Bean components may want to obtain such a reference for use as input or output parameters in their application-specific methods. Be aware of the fact, however, that the `EJBObject` will be valid only between the time when `ejbCreateXXX()` is called and the time when `ejbRemove()` is called on the bean instance. Also be aware that direct access to `EJBObject` references should be passed around with care. This is because no more than one client thread can utilize a single server-side bean instance at a time lest it induce a `RemoteException`. Thus, EJB server objects should pass around `EJBObject` instances that have been bound to server-side bean instances only when they can be certain that one client will utilize the `EJBObject` reference at a time.

Session Bean Remote Interface Examples

The remote interfaces of properly designed session beans should naturally imply the stateless or stateful session of the bean for an application. Our `Browse` remote interface shown in Listing 25.3 defines the single distributable operation exposed by the `BrowseEJBean` described in Listing 25.1. Note that no state to be maintained by the bean is implied by the very nature of its business-specific semantics. This stateless session bean call thus simply takes input from a client and returns output.

Listing 25.3 **Stateless Session Bean Remote Interface Example (`Browse.java`)**

```
package ejava.ejb.session.browse;
   ...
public interface Browse extends EJBObject {
  /** Return Vector of Serializable TShirt objects
      based on queried shirt size and color */
  public Vector queryShirts(String size, String color)
    throws RemoteException;
}
```

The `ShoppingCartSession` remote interface, shown in Listing 25.4, relates to the distributed interfaces provided by the `ShoppingCartEJBean` presented in Listing 25.2. Note that statefulness is implied by the application-specific business logic of these methods. Thus, a stateful session bean was indeed best suited for this bean implementation.

Listing 25.4 **Stateful Session Bean Remote Interface Example (`ShoppingCart.java`)**

```
package ejava.ejb.session.shoppingcart;
   ...
public interface ShoppingCart extends EJBObject {
  /** Add an item to this shopping session with an ID and quantity */
  public void addAnItemToTheCart(int shirtID, int quantity)
    throws RemoteException;
  /** Obtain a Vector of Serializable TShirt objects for the
      items stored in this shopping session */
  public Vector getSelectedItemsInTheCart() throws RemoteException;
  /** Check out of this shopping session by creating and returning
      an order for the items associated with this shopping session.
      Input order contains order information.
      Return order contains order w/assigned order ID.
    */
  public Order checkOut(Order order) throws RemoteException;
  /** Check out of this shopping session by creating and returning
      an order for the items associated with this shopping session.
      Input customer ID associated with order for address
      information lookup. Other default shipping information is used.
      Return order contains order w/assigned order ID.
    */
  public Order checkOut(int customerID) throws RemoteException;
}
```

Session Bean Home Interfaces

Session bean clients use distributed home interfaces to create initial references to session beans, as well as remove these references. These references are, of course, implemented via the remote session bean interface objects. Clients should always use home interfaces to create references to EJBs. Home interfaces enable the container to manage how to allocate EJB bean instance resources. Furthermore, if a client bypasses use of home interfaces and uses an `EJBObject` handle retrieved via some other means, it runs the risk of causing a threading problem. This is again because no more than one client thread can utilize a single server-side bean instance.

Session Bean Home Interface Logical Architecture

Figure 25.4 depicts the architecture behind creating session bean home interfaces and how clients may use these interfaces. JNDI is used to obtain handles to application-specific EJB home interface objects, such as `MySessionEJBHome`, which must extend the standard `javax.ejb.EJBHome` interface. Application-specific EJB home interface objects are also implemented on the client side by stubs, which communicate with server-side skeletons, and the container, which creates, destroys, and delegates calls to session bean instances as appropriate. Home interfaces can also be used for persisting their handles for later reconstruction and for obtaining meta-data about the EJBs they serve to create.

Session Bean Home Object Lookup

An EJB client must first obtain a handle to an EJB's home interface when it wants to create a new reference to the EJB. This task is accomplished via JNDI. Clients that operate inside of a J2EE container environment can utilize the default parameterless constructor of the `InitialContext` object and simply look up a handle to an EJB's home interface with a call to `InitialContext.lookup()`. The J2EE container handles establishing the system properties that should be assumed by the `InitialContext` object. The name passed to an `InitialContext.lookup()` can refer to an `<ejb-ref>` element in the client's XML-based deployment descriptor. The `<ejb-ref>` element defines the reference name that will be used in creating the name passed to `InitialContext.lookup()`, the type of EJB being referenced, the home information, the remote information, and the linking information according to the following deployment descriptor elements:

- `<ejb-ref>`: Top-level element that defines a reference to an EJB from a particular J2EE component.
- `<description>`: Description of the reference (optional).
- `<ejb-ref-name>`: Provides a name to refer to an EJB, typically prefixed with `ejb/`.
- `<ejb-ref-type>`: Specifies the type of referenced EJB: `Entity`, `Session`.
- `<home>`: Fully qualified referenced home interface name.
- `<remote>`: Fully qualified referenced remote interface name.

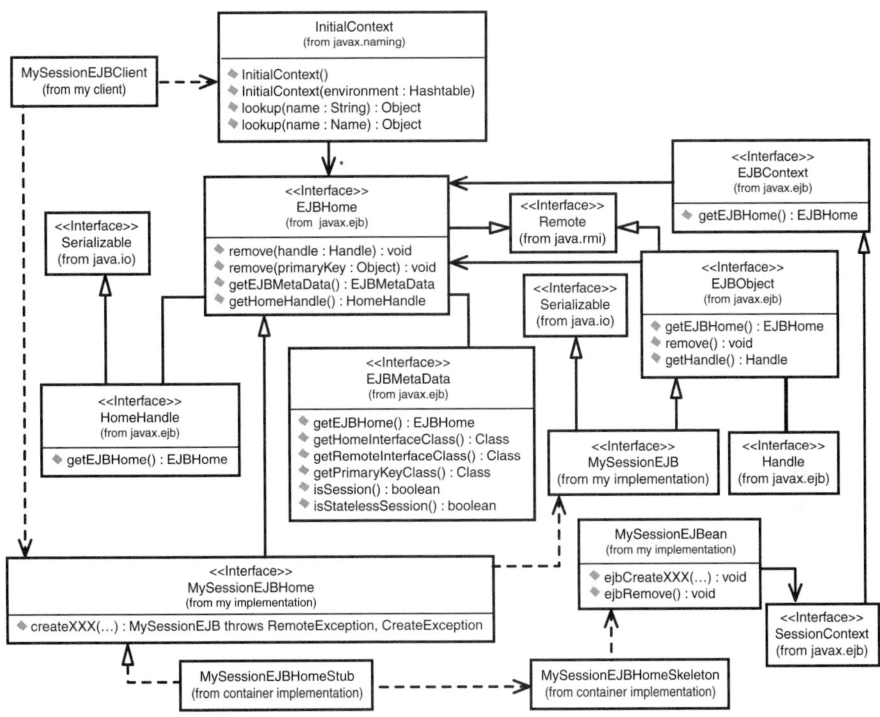

Figure 25.4 The session bean home interface architecture.

- `<ejb-link>`: Specifies an `ejb-name` of an EJB to which this reference is linked (optional). The other EJB may be in the same JAR file or in another JAR file that is in the same J2EE enterprise application. The relative path name of the EJB JAR file followed by a # character may be prepended to the `ejb-name` in order to explicitly indicate which EJB in which JAR file is referenced.

Such `<ejb-ref>` elements can be embedded inside of a referencing EJB's deployment descriptor element, a referencing Web component's deployment descriptor element, or perhaps a J2EE application client's deployment descriptor element. As an example, the `ejava.ejb.session.creditmgr.CreditManagerClient` class serves as a J2EE application client. It acts as an EJB client that remotely accesses the stateless session `CreditManagerEJBean` via the bean's `CreditManagerHome` and `CreditManager` remote interfaces. Thus, the `CreditManagerClient` defines its reference to such a bean via its J2EE application client deployment descriptor, `application-client.xml`, as illustrated here:

```
<application-client>
  <display-name>CreditManagerClient</display-name>
  <ejb-ref>
    <ejb-ref-name>ejb/CreditManager</ejb-ref-name>
```

```
    <ejb-ref-type>Session</ejb-ref-type>
    <home>ejava.ejb.session.creditmgr.CreditManagerHome</home>
    <remote>ejava.ejb.session.creditmgr.CreditManager</remote>
    <ejb-link>CreditManager.jar#CreditManagerEJB</ejb-link>
  </ejb-ref>
</application-client>
```

Thus, our `CreditManagerClient` acts as an EJB client to the `CreditManager` EJB. The `CreditManagerClient` looks up a reference to the `CreditManagerHome` interface object from within the `runJ2EEClient()` method as shown here:

```
public void runJ2EEClient() {
  try {
    // Get initial context using container provided context
    Context context = new InitialContext();
    // Look up server reference using EJB reference
    //   from the XML deployment descriptor
    Object object = context.lookup("java:comp/env/ejb/CreditManager");
    // Now run common client code
    runCommonClientBody(object);
  } catch (Exception exception) {
    exception.printStackTrace();
  }
}
```

The returned `CreditManagerHome` object is then used after being properly cast from within the `runCommonClientBody()` method as illustrated here:

```
private void runCommonClientBody(Object creditManagerHomeRef)
  throws Exception {
  System.out.println(
    "Class Type :" + creditManagerHomeRef.getClass().getName());
  // Narrow to credit manager reference
  CreditManagerHome creditManagerHome =
    (CreditManagerHome) PortableRemoteObject.narrow(
                  creditManagerHomeRef,
                  ejava.ejb.session.creditmgr.CreditManagerHome.class);
  // Create handle to server object now using home factory
  CreditManager creditManager = creditManagerHome.create();
  // Solicit user information from input and send to CreditManager
  processCreditRecordsOnRemote(creditManager);
}
```

Tip

Note that use of the RMI/IIOP `javax.rmi.PortableRemoteObject.narrow()` call semantics on the returned home and remote interface is required to guarantee portability with all EJB container/server implementations, as opposed to simply casting returned objects.

EJB clients that operate outside of a J2EE container environment also use JNDI to create an `InitialContext`. In fact, the `TestClient` classes associated with the various EJB examples inside of the `ejava.ejb.*` packages operate as standalone EJB clients. Additionally, the `CreditManagerClient` itself can also act in standalone mode when it is executed with the flag `-standalone`. Its `runStandaloneClient()` method is called when run in standalone mode and is illustrated here:

```
public void runStandaloneClient() {
  try {
    // Get initial context for standalone client using
    //   system environment variables for context parameters
    Context context = new InitialContext();

    // Look up server reference using raw JNDI name
    Object object = context.lookup("CreditManagerHome");

    // Now run common client code
    runCommonClientBody(object);
  } catch (Exception exception) {
    exception.printStackTrace();
  }
}
```

Such standalone clients must use the raw JNDI name when looking up the registered EJB home interface. Because the mapping of EJB reference names to JNDI names is container specific, the mapping is performed inside of a vendor-specific property file. The vendor-specific property file simply maps the logical `ejb-name` used to a valid JNDI name for that container (for example, defined inside of a `jndi-name` element associated with the `ejb-name`).

Session Bean Application-Specific Home Interfaces

After looking up an EJB home object, a handle to a remote object must be created. A series of one or more `create`*`XXX`*`(...)` methods are defined on the custom home interface to represent the different ways in which the associated remote EJB object can be created. A single `create`*`XXX`*`(...)` method must be defined on the home interface for each `ejbCreate`*`XXX`*`(...)` method defined on the EJB implementation that will be used for remote EJB object creation. Each version of a `create`*`XXX`*`(...)` method returns an instance of the EJB's remote interface (for example, `MySessionEJB`) and contains zero or more input parameters related to the specific types of initialization parameters needed by the associated `ejbCreate`*`XXX`*`(...)` methods. Each `create`*`XXX`*`(...)` method must also be defined to throw a `java.rmi.RemoteException` and `javax.ejb.CreateException`. Additionally, each `create`*`XXX`*`(...)` method must be defined to throw any application-specific exceptions that have been defined for its associated `ejbCreate`*`XXX`*`(...)` method. Because stateless session beans define only one parameterless `ejbCreate()` method, stateless session bean home interfaces can define only one parameterless `create()` method. Invoking `create()` on stateless session beans only induces a container to pull a bean instance from the pool and does not necessarily cause the container to call `ejbCreate()` on the bean at that moment. However, stateful session beans do induce the container to call `ejbCreateXXX(...)` on a bean instance with any parameters passed into an associated home interface `createXXX(...)` method.

Session Bean Generic Home Interfaces

As you saw in the preceding section, after a handle to an EJB object is obtained, a client can invoke `EJBObject.remove()` to release its hold on a particular session EJB. Clients can also call `remove(Handle)` inherited from `EJBHome` by the home interface object. The `Handle`, of course, needs to relate to the particular `EJBObject` that is to be removed. The specific rules for removal of stateless and stateful session beans are the same here as they were when `EJBObject.remove()` was being called. The `EJBHome.remove(Object)`, which takes a primary key as a parameter, is not valid for session home objects and will throw a `RemoteException` when invoked.

Much like an `EJBObject` object can persist its reference in a `Handle` object, `EJBHome` objects can persist their references in `javax.ejb.HomeHandle` objects. A call to `EJBHome.getHomeHandle()` will return this `Serializable HomeHandle` object. When a `HomeHandle` is persisted and later brought into active memory, the `HomeHandle.getEJBHome()` call can be used to return a reference to the reconstructed `EJBHome` object.

The `EJBHome.getEJBMetaData()` method is called to obtain a handle to a `javax.ejb.EJBMetaData` object, which provides a mechanism for clients to discover certain information about an EJB. `EJBMetaData.getEJBHome()` simply returns a reference to the home interface again. The `getHomeInterfaceClass()` and `getRemoteInterfaceClass()` methods return `Class` objects associated with the EJB's home and remote interfaces, respectively. The `getPrimaryKeyClass()` is useful only for entity beans. Finally, the `isSession()` method can be used to determine whether the EJB is a session bean or an entity bean, and the `isStatelessSession()` can be used to determine whether the EJB is a stateless session bean. If `isSession()` returns `true` and `isStatelessSession()` returns `false`, you may assume that the EJB is a stateful session bean.

As a final note, on the server side, a session bean can obtain a reference to an `EJBHome` object with which it is associated by calling `getEJBHome()` on its `SessionContext` object (as inherited from `EJBContext`). Bean components may want to obtain such a reference for the creation of their own beans.

Session Bean Home Interface Examples

The home interfaces of session beans are typically simple interfaces. Our `BrowseHome` home interface shown in Listing 25.5 defines only a single parameterless `create()` method because it is a stateless session bean.

Listing 25.5 **Stateless Session Bean Home Interface Example (`BrowseHome.java`)**

```
package ejava.ejb.session.browse;
    ...
public interface BrowseHome extends EJBHome
{
  /** Parameterless creation of session bean */
  Browse create() throws CreateException, RemoteException;
}
```

The `ShoppingCartHome` home interface shown in Listing 25.6 defines a parameterless `create()` method that results in the invocation of `ShoppingCartEJBean.ejbCreate()`. A `create(Hashtable)` method is also defined to provide initial shopping-cart state to the `ShoppingCartEJBean.ejbCreate(Hashtable)` method.

Listing 25.6 **Stateful Session Bean Home Interface Example (`ShoppingCartHome.java`)**

```
package ejava.ejb.session.shoppingcart;
    ...
public interface ShoppingCartHome extends EJBHome {
  /** Create session bean with default initial state */
  public ShoppingCart create() throws CreateException, RemoteException;
  /** Create session bean with initial shopping cart data */
  public ShoppingCart create(java.util.Hashtable initialCart)
    throws CreateException, RemoteException;
}
```

Session Bean Local Client Interfaces

The preceding section described remote interfaces to session beans such that session bean implementations can be accessed in a distributed fashion. This section describes local interfaces to a session bean such that session bean implementations can be more efficiently accessed by EJB clients that reside within the same physical process as the session bean implementation instance. The reason for such added efficiency is that the EJB container can ensure that when such local interfaces are used, no parameter copying, marshaling, and unmarshaling of data needs to take place because the EJB client and server instance are in the same process. Because such parameters are not passed over the wire, no such EJB container parameter handling needs to take place to account for transmission of the parameters over the network.

However, because the EJB container does not have to perform such "network-aware" parameter handling, there are some additional design constraints that must be considered by the EJB developer when exposing a session EJB's interfaces for local access. In fact, object parameters passed over a local interface are passed by reference. More accurately, the input and output parameters of local interface methods have their object references passed by value, as is the case with other Java objects passed around inside of the same JVM process. Thus, most often, additional design care must be taken to ensure that an EJB which passes objects back to an EJB client are not stored by that EJB client and instead are simply used within the same scope of the EJB client's invocation. Of course, if such objects are to be stored and modified by the client, the EJB server implementation may explicitly make a copy of the object before it returns the local object parameter to the client.

Such design considerations that reflect the EJB container's distinction between local and remote interfaces often result in EJB designs in which the remote interfaces are designed for more course-grained operations whereas the local interfaces are designed for finer-grained operations. These local interface design considerations can leverage the advantages of in-process object passing-by-reference. Thus, local interfaces are most often used when the particular interface methods are required to be accessed frequently by the same clients, reference fine-grained discrete data, or reference large in-memory objects. Regardless of such distinction by design, a particular EJB implementation's methods can be exposed for both remote and local access. This section describes how local object and local home interfaces are implemented for session beans.

Session Bean Local Object Interfaces

A session bean local object interface defines the set of application-specific local in-process operations that can be invoked on a particular session bean. Local object interfaces describe the client's view of the EJB akin to the way any regular Java interface defines the operations available to other in-process Java objects. Accordingly, the input and output objects of such interface methods are passed by reference (that is, Java object references passed-by-value). This section describes how to build and use session bean local object interfaces.

Session Bean Local Object Interface Logical Architecture

Figure 25.5 depicts the basic logical architecture for building and using local EJB client interfaces to local session EJBs. All application-specific interfaces to local EJB objects, such as `MySessionEJBLocal` shown in the diagram, must extend the `javax.ejb.EJLocalObject` interface. Local interfaces make use of a stub implementation that implements the actual calls made to the EJB component implementation such as the `MySessionEJBean` shown in the diagram. Runtime EJB containers are ultimately responsible for managing which bean instance is used and how calls are routed, but the result is that calls from an EJB client to application-specific EJB interface methods ultimately result in the invocation of an associated application-specific method on the EJB component instance.

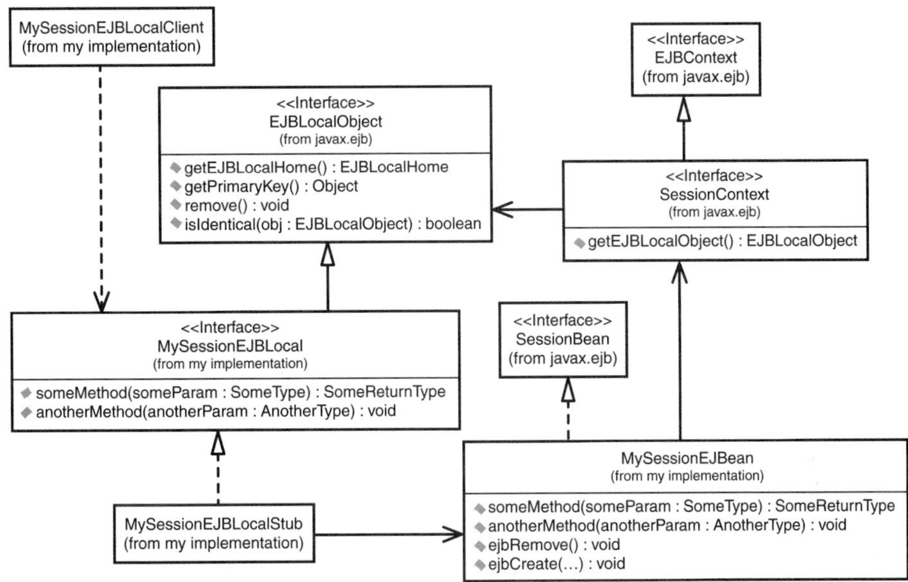

Figure 25.5 The session bean local object interface architecture.

Session Bean Application-Specific Local Object Interfaces

An application-specific local object interface must be created for EJB components wanting to be accessed in a local fashion. This interface provides the local interface usable by EJB clients to invoke the application-specific logic of EJB components. For each local application-specific method on an EJB server-side component, such as `MySessionEJBean.someMethod()`, an associated application-specific method must be defined on the EJB client-side local object interface, such as `MySessionEJBLocal.someMethod()`. Of course, such rules apply only to those EJB component methods you want to be made accessible locally within the same container process as the client.

Session Bean Generic Local Object Interfaces

In addition to application-specific interfaces on an EJB local object interface, a set of methods inherited from `EJBLocalObject` can be invoked on a local EJB object. Most of these methods are identical to those defined on the remote `EJBObject` interface defined earlier. That is, the `isIdentical()`, `remove()`, and `getPrimaryKey()` methods defined on the `EJBLocalObject` all provide functionality similar to those defined on the `EJBObject` interface. One distinction is the `EJBLocalObject.getEJBLocalHome()` method. This method returns a handle to the home interface object that is used to create local interface objects.

A session bean implementation can obtain a reference to an `EJBLocalObject` with which it is associated by calling `getEJBLocalObject()` on its `SessionContext` object. Similar to the reason for why bean components obtain handles to `EJBObject` references, bean components may want to obtain such a reference for use as input or output parameters in their application-specific methods. Thusly, handling of `EJBLocalObject` references by an EJB implementation must be performed with care as is the case with handling `EJBObject` references.

Session Bean Local Object Interface Example

Our `BrowseLocal` local object interface shown in Listing 25.7 defines the single locally accessible operation exposed by the `BrowseEJBean` described in Listing 25.1. Akin to the `Browse` remote interface described in Listing 25.3, no state to be maintained by the bean is implied by the nature of its business-specific semantics. In fact, aside from the base interface that is extended, the only difference between the `BrowseLocal` and `Browse` interface defined earlier is that the `Browse` interface method throws a `RemoteException`, whereas as the `BrowseLocal` interface does not.

Listing 25.7 **Session Bean Local Object Interface Example (`BrowseLocal.java`)**

```
package ejava.ejb.session.browse;
   ...
public interface BrowseLocal extends EJBLocalObject
{
  /** Return Vector of Serializable TShirt objects
      based on queried shirt size and color */
  public Vector queryShirts(String size, String color);
}
```

Session Bean Local Home Interfaces

Session bean clients use local home interfaces to create initial references to session beans, as well as remove these references. These references are implemented via the local session bean interface objects. As with remote clients, local clients should always use local home interfaces to create references to EJBs because these provide the container with the opportunity it needs to manage how to allocate EJB bean instance resources.

Session Bean Home Interface Logical Architecture

Figure 25.6 depicts the architecture behind creating session bean local home interfaces and how clients may use these interfaces. As with remote home interface lookups, JNDI is used to obtain handles to application-specific EJB local home interface objects, such as `MySessionEJBLocalHome`, which must extend the standard `javax.ejb.EJBLocalHome` interface. Application-specific EJB local home interface objects are also implemented by stubs, which communicate with server-side implementations, and the container, which creates, destroys, and delegates calls to session bean instances as appropriate.

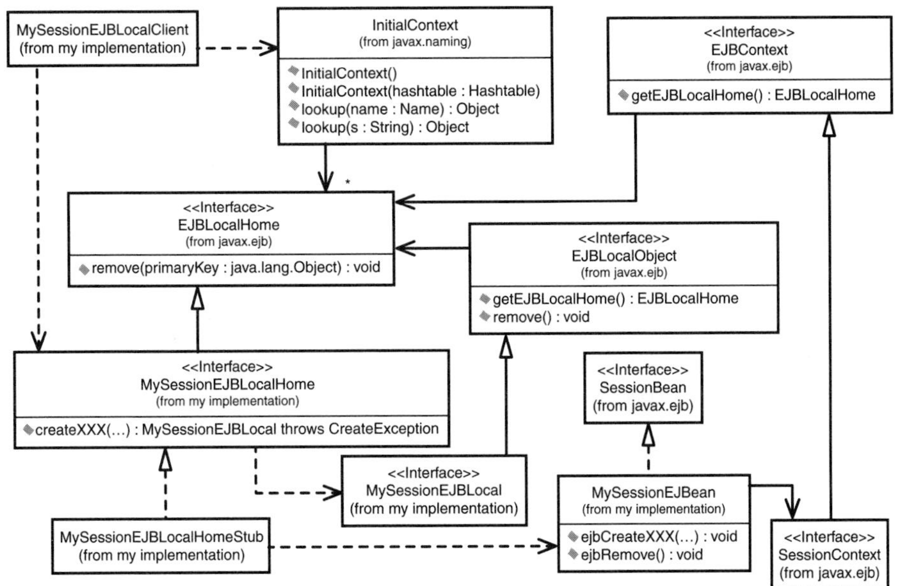

Figure 25.6 The session bean local home interface architecture.

Session Bean Local Home Object Lookup

A local EJB client must first obtain a handle to an EJB's local home interface when it wants to create a new local reference to the EJB. Clients that operate inside of a J2EE container environment can utilize the default parameterless constructor of the `InitialContext` object and simply look up a handle to an EJB's local home interface with a call to `InitialContext.lookup()`. The name passed to an `InitialContext.lookup()` can refer to an `<ejb-local-ref>` element in the client's XML-based deployment descriptor. The `<ejb-local-ref>` element defines the reference name that will be used in creating the name passed to `InitialContext.lookup()`, the type of EJB being referenced, the local home information, the local object information, and the linking information in a fashion nearly identical to the `<ejb-ref>` element described earlier in this chapter. The only difference is that the `<ejb-local-ref>` element contains a `<local-home>` and `<local>` element to define the fully qualified referenced local home and local object interfaces, respectively. The `<local-home>` and `<local>` elements in the `<ejb-local-ref>` element thus are used in a manner similar to the `<home>` and `<remote>` elements used in the `<ejb-ref>` element.

The <ejb-local-ref> elements can be embedded inside of a referencing EJB's deployment descriptor element, a referencing Web component's deployment descriptor element, or a J2EE application client's deployment descriptor element. As an example, the `ejava.ejb.session.shoppingcart.ShoppingCartEJBean` class of Listing 25.2 is an EJB acting as an EJB client that locally accesses the stateless session `OrderManagerEJBean` via the bean's `OrderManagerLocalHome` and `OrderManagerLocal` local interfaces. Thus, the `ShoppingCartEJBean` defines its reference to such a bean via its EJB deployment descriptor, `ejb-jar.xml`, as illustrated here:

```
<ejb-jar>
    ...
  <enterprise-beans>
        ...
   <session>
        ...
     <ejb-name>ShoppingCartEJB</ejb-name>
          ...
      <ejb-local-ref>
          <ejb-ref-name>ejb/ordermgr</ejb-ref-name>
          <ejb-ref-type>Session</ejb-ref-type>
          <local-home>
            ejava.ejb.session.ordermgr.OrderManagerLocalHome
          </local-home>
          <local>
            ejava.ejb.session.ordermgr.OrderManagerLocal
          </local>
          <ejb-link>Cart.jar#OrderManagerEJB</ejb-link>
     </ejb-local-ref>
   </session>
  </enterprise-beans>
   ...
</ejb-jar>
```

The `ShoppingCartEJBean` looks up a reference to the `OrderManagerLocalHome` interface object from within the `lookupOrderManagerHome()` method as shown here:

```
private void lookupOrderManagerHome() throws NamingException {
  if (orderManagerHome == null) {
    InitialContext context = new InitialContext();
    orderManagerHome = (OrderManagerLocalHome) context.lookup(
                                 EJBHelper.ORDER_MANAGER_REFNAME);
    context.close();
  }
}
```

The `EJBHelper.ORDER_MANAGER_REFNAME` is defined inside the `EJBHelper` class in this way:

```
public static String ORDER_MANAGER_REFNAME
                  = "java:comp/env/ejb/ordermgr";
```

Session Bean Application-Specific Local Home Interfaces

As with the remote home interface, a series of one or more `create`*`XXX`*`(...)` methods are defined on the custom local home interface to represent the different ways in which the associated local EJB object can be created. A single `create`*`XXX`*`(...)` method must be defined on the local home interface for each `ejbCreate`*`XXX`*`(...)` method defined on the EJB implementation that will be used for local EJB object creation. Each version of a `create`*`XXX`*`(...)` method returns an instance of the EJB's local object interface (for example, `MySessionLocalEJB`) and contains zero or more input parameters related to the specific types of initialization parameters needed by the associated `ejbCreate`*`XXX`*`(...)` methods. Each `create`*`XXX`*`(...)` method must also be defined to throw a `javax.ejb.CreateException`. Additionally, each `create`*`XXX`*`(...)` method must be defined to throw any application-specific exceptions that have been defined for its associated `ejbCreate`*`XXX`*`(...)` method. For stateless session beans allowing local access, a single parameterless `create()` method must be defined on the local home interface.

Session Bean Generic Local Home Interfaces

Only one generic method is defined on the `EJBLocalHome` interface. However, it is in fact a method that is invalid for local home interfaces associated with session beans. The `EJBLocalHome.remove(Object)`, which takes a primary key as a parameter, is not valid for session local home objects and will throw an `EJBException` when invoked.

Session Bean Local Home Interface Example

The local home interfaces of session beans are typically very simple interfaces. Our `BrowseLocalHome` home interface shown in Listing 25.8 in fact defines only a single parameterless `create()` method because it is a stateless session bean.

Listing 25.8 **Session Bean Local Home Interface Example (`BrowseLocalHome.java`)**

```
package ejava.ejb.session.browse;
   ...
public interface BrowseLocalHome extends EJBLocalHome
{
  /** Parameterless creation of session bean */
  BrowseLocal create() throws CreateException;
}
```

Timed Session Bean Objects

The preceding chapter describes the new EJB timer service and its API architecture. A stateless session bean acts as a timed object as described in the preceding chapter and depicted in Figure 24.6. Thus, in addition to the `SessionBean` interface, a stateless session bean designates its interaction with the EJB timer service by implementing the `TimedObject` interface as well. Thus, the session bean implementation must simply implement the `ejbTimeout()` method in addition to the other methods it must implement to satisfy its contract with the EJB container.

As an example, Listing 25.9 shows a timed object stateless session bean. The `ejbTimeout()` method is implemented to look up every customer in the BeeShirts.com database, print a message indicating that an email is being sent for each customer, and then resets the timer with a default duration value of 30 days from the current date. An EJB client may interact with this EJB and invoke the `resetTimerDuration()` or `resetDuration()` methods, which both create timers based on a specified duration value. The `resetDuration()` method, however, also cancels all current timers before setting a timer.

Listing 25.9 **Session Bean Timed Object Implementation Example (`SessionTimerEJBean.java`)**

```
package ejava.ejb.timer;
   ...
public class SessionTimerEJBean implements SessionBean, TimedObject {
  // Local attributes
  private SessionContext sessionContext;
  private CustomerLocalHome customerHome;
  private static final int N_DAYS = 30;
  private long defaultDuration = -1;

  // Standard session bean interfaces
  public void setSessionContext(SessionContext aCtx)
    throws RemoteException {
    sessionContext = aCtx;

    // lookup customer home
    try {
      lookupCustomerHome();
    } catch (NamingException ne) {
      ne.printStackTrace();
    }
  }
  public void ejbCreate() { /* no removal logic */
  }
  public void ejbRemove() { /* no removal logic */
  }
```

Listing 25.9 **Continued**

```
public void ejbPassivate() { /* no state persistence */
}
public void ejbActivate() { /* no state activation */
}

/**
 * Timed object method implementation.
 * Prints out email delivery message info and resets
 * the timer duration.
 */
public void ejbTimeout(Timer timer) {
  System.out.println("SessionTimerEJBean: ejbTimeout  Called! ");
  System.out.println(
    " I will start sending email now!:" + System.currentTimeMillis());
  try {
    // Print out email to Every customer.
    sendEmailToEveryCustomer();
    // Reset timer to default Duration
    resetTimerDuration(getDuration());
  } catch (FinderException fe) {
    fe.printStackTrace();
  }
}

/**
 * Implements the public exposed EJB method.
 * This gets the timer service and creates a timer
 * using the duration passed into the method.
 */
public void resetTimerDuration(long duration) {
  System.out.println("SessionTimerEJBean: start resetTimer ");
  TimerService timerService = sessionContext.getTimerService();
  System.out.println("Current Timer Service is : " + timerService);
  Timer timer = timerService.createTimer(duration, "Email Timer");
  System.out.println("New Timer is :" + timer);
}

/**
 * Implements the public exposed EJB method.
 * First cancels all existing timers.
 * It then gets the timer service and creates a timer
 * using the duration passed into the method.
 */
public void resetTimer(long duration) {
  System.out.println("SessionTimerEJBean: start createTimer ");
```

Listing 25.9 **Continued**

```
    // Cancel Existing Timers
    cancelExistingTimers();
    // create new timer with new duration
    resetTimerDuration(duration);
  }



  /**
   * Gets the timers from the timer service and
   * cancels every one of them.
   */
  private void cancelExistingTimers() {
    TimerService timerService = sessionContext.getTimerService();
    Iterator timers = timerService.getTimers().iterator();
    while (timers.hasNext()) {
      Timer timer = (Timer) timers.next();
      timer.cancel();
    }
  }

  /**
   * Get email for each customer in the database.
   * Indicate that you are sending them an email.
   * For heaven's sake, we're not actually going to
   * do that for this example!!!!
   * Thus...we just print a message here.
   */
  private void sendEmailToEveryCustomer() throws FinderException {
    Iterator iterator = customerHome.findAll().iterator();
    while (iterator.hasNext()) {
      CustomerLocal customer = (CustomerLocal) iterator.next();
      String emailAddress = customer.getEmail();
      System.out.println(
        "Sending Email to :"
          + customer.getFirstName()
          + ","
          + customer.getLastName());
    }
  }

  /** Lookup Customer Home object */
  private void lookupCustomerHome() throws NamingException {
    if (customerHome == null) {
      InitialContext context = new InitialContext();
      customerHome =
```

Listing 25.9 **Continued**

```
        (CustomerLocalHome) context.lookup(EJBHelper.CUSTOMER_REFNAME);
      context.close();
    }
  }

  /** Get duration of 30 days from now */
  private long getDuration(){
    // Set a default timer duration as 30 days from now
    Calendar time = Calendar.getInstance();
    time.add(Calendar.DATE, N_DAYS);
    return time.getTimeInMillis();
  }
}
```

The `SessionTimer` remote and `SessionTimerHome` home interfaces for this bean are used by the `TestClient` class defined inside the same `ejava.ejb.timer` example package. The `TestClient` simply looks up the EJB's home interface, creates a new remote interface handle, and then creates a timer for the bean to go off in 30 seconds, as illustrated here:

```
Context context = new InitialContext();
Object objectRef =
    context.lookup(EJBHelper.TIMER_HOME);

SessionTimerHome timerHome =
   (SessionTimerHome)PortableRemoteObject.narrow(objectRef,
                                       SessionTimerHome.class);

SessionTimer sessionTimer = timerHome.create();
sessionTimer.resetTimerDuration(THIRTY_SECS);
```

Session Bean Configuration and Deployment

In the preceding chapter, we introduced the basic top-level structure of an EJB application module deployment descriptor. The root `<ejb-jar>` element contained an `<enterprise-beans>` element, which could in turn contain a collection of `<session>` elements. Each `<session>` element is used to describe the configuration and deployment of an individual session bean. The `<session>` bean element deployment descriptor structure defines session bean meta-data, a unique name in the EJB JAR file, the bean's class and interface names, the type of session bean, configuration parameters, references to other EJBs and database connections, security semantics, and EJB assurance properties. The top-level structure of the `<session>` deployment descriptor element is defined here:

- <session>: Top-level element used to collect the following elements that describe a session bean's deployment.
- Description group: A collection of description-related elements, including <description>, <display-name>, and <icon> (optional).
- <ejb-name>: Logical name for the session bean.
- <home>: Fully qualified remote home interface name (optional).
- <remote>: Fully qualified remote interface name (optional).
- <local-home>: Fully qualified local home interface name (optional).
- <local>: Fully qualified local interface name (optional).
- <service-endpoint>: Fully qualified JAX-RPC–compliant Web service endpoint interface name (optional).
- <ejb-class>: Fully qualified EJB implementation class.
- <session-type>: Indication of the session bean type: Stateless or Stateful.
- <transaction-type>: Indication of whether the EJB or the container manages this bean's transactions: Bean or Container.
- <env-entry>: Composed of <description>, <env-entry-name>, <env-entry-type>, and <env-entry-value> elements, which contain configuration environment variables as described in Chapter 19 (zero or more).
- <ejb-ref>: Composed of information related to referencing remote EJBs by this EJB as described earlier in this chapter (zero or more).
- <ejb-local-ref>: Composed of information related to referencing local EJBs by this EJB as described earlier in this chapter (zero or more).
- <service-ref>: Composed of information related to referencing Web services by this EJB as described in Chapter 22 and Chapter 30 (zero or more).
- <resource-ref>: Used to define information used by the client to reference an external resource such as JDBC resource connection information (zero or more). Sub-elements of this element are described in Chapter 26.
- <resource-env-ref>: Used to define information used by the client to reference a resource administered by the client's environment (zero or more). Sub-elements of this element are described in Chapter 29.
- <message-destination-ref>: Used to define information used by the client to reference a destination for an asynchronous message (zero or more). Sub-elements of this element are described in Chapter 27.
- <security-role-ref>: Used within the EJB to reference a particular secure role using an EJB security role-name (zero or more). Sub-elements of this element are described in Chapter 28.

- `<security-identity>`: Used to define how the security identity of the caller is used (optional). Sub-elements of this element are described in Chapter 28.

As an example, the session-related elements of our stateless session `Browse` bean's EJB v2.1–compliant deployment descriptor are shown in Listing 25.10. You'll note that in addition to standard meta-data and structural information about the EJB, it has defined an `<ejb-local-ref>` element for the entity EJB it accesses as a client to that bean.

Listing 25.10 **Example of EJB Session Bean Deployment Descriptor Information**

```
<?xml version="1.0" encoding="UTF-8"?>
<ejb-jar
  version="2.1"
  xmlns="http://java.sun.com/xml/ns/j2ee"
  xmlns:xsi="http://www.w3.org/2001/XMLSchema-instance"
  xsi:schemaLocation="http://java.sun.com/xml/ns/j2ee
                     http://java.sun.com/xml/ns/j2ee/ejb-jar_2_1.xsd">
  <display-name>BrowseSessionEJB</display-name>
  <enterprise-beans>
    <session>
      <display-name>BrowseEJB</display-name>
      <ejb-name>BrowseEJB</ejb-name>
      <home>ejava.ejb.session.browse.BrowseHome</home>
      <remote>ejava.ejb.session.browse.Browse</remote>
      <ejb-class>ejava.ejb.session.browse.BrowseEJBean</ejb-class>
      <session-type>Stateless</session-type>
      <transaction-type>Container</transaction-type>
      <ejb-local-ref>
        <ejb-ref-name>ejb/tshirt</ejb-ref-name>
        <ejb-ref-type>Entity</ejb-ref-type>
        <local-home>ejava.ejb.entity.tshirt.TShirtLocalHome</local-home>
        <local>ejava.ejb.entity.tshirt.TShirtLocal</local>
        <ejb-link>Browse.jar#TShirtEJB</ejb-link>
      </ejb-local-ref>
    </session>
        ...
  </enterprise-beans>
     ...
</ejb-jar>
```

Vendor-specific deployment descriptor files to configure and deploy session beans are also needed and are provided with the examples associated with this chapter. Developers most often use GUI-based deployment tools provided by vendors to develop such files, but we wanted to explicitly provide you with a sense of what they contain with our sample code.

Conclusions

Session EJB types include simple request and response handlers known as stateless session beans and also include stateful session beans to maintain state within a component on behalf of a particular client over time. A particular application design indicates which session bean type to utilize for each of your front-line controller type application components. Session EJBs can also be designed to expose themselves to clients using either remote or local interfaces. A stateless session bean can also be implemented as a timed object such that the EJB container will invoke the EJB on a timed event basis. The overarching runtime behavior of session beans can be controlled using deployment descriptor elements specific to describing a session bean's deployment. The next chapter begins to complete the painting of the EJB picture by describing entity beans and how they interact with session beans.

26

Entity EJB

ENTITY BEANS PROVIDE THE J2EE DEVELOPER with the means to represent and encapsulate passive repositories of data inside of their applications. That is, an entity bean serves as an object-oriented representation of some business-specific entity information inside of an enterprise application such as an order or a customer. The EJB developer can use entity beans to encapsulate such information and allow the container to manage the resources associated with that object. The EJB developer can choose to implement the object-to-relational mappings themselves or allow the container to perform such mappings with some additional information provided inside of the entity bean deployment descriptors.

In this chapter, you will learn:

- The basic means by which EJBs can use JDBC to access information in a database.
- The basic services provided to server-side entity bean components by the EJB container.
- The steps required for building server-side bean-managed persistence (BMP) entity bean components requiring the developer to write database access code.
- The steps required for building server-side container-managed persistence (CMP) entity bean components whereby the container is left to generate the database access code.
- The steps required for building remote EJB clients to entity beans.
- The steps required for building local in-process EJB clients to entity beans.
- The structure and semantics behind the Enterprise JavaBeans Query Language (EJB QL) for describing how CMP entity beans formulate database queries.
- The steps required to configure and deploy entity beans.

EJB Database Connectivity

The need to connect to databases from within EJBs is clearly one of the most significant features of interest to EJB developers. All J2EE-based components may need to talk with a database, and J2EE provides support for this need via JDBC. Vendors and a future J2EE specification may allow the use of SQLJ (discussed in Chapter 2, "Enterprise Data") to provide database connectivity. However, our primary approach advocated in this book and assumed here is the use of JDBC. J2EE-compliant environments provide access to the JDBC API and a convenient means for configuring JDBC resources via the XML-based deployment descriptor and for connecting to JDBC resources via JNDI.

JDBC driver configuration and data-source identification are accomplished via the XML-based deployment descriptor for J2EE modules. The `<resource-ref>` element can be defined for individual J2EE EJB session and entity beans, J2EE servlets and JSPs, and J2EE application clients. Zero or more JDBC resources may be configured per EJB, servlet, JSP, or application client within the J2EE deployment descriptor. The top-level structure of the `<resource-ref>` element is defined here:

- `<resource-ref>`: Top-level element to define the reference to an external resource (such as a JDBC resource) and composed of the sub-elements that follow.
- `<description>`: Description of the reference (optional).
- `<res-ref-name>`: Defines the logical name of the external resource factory reference.
- `<res-type>`: Fully qualified class name of the external resource connection factory.
- `<res-auth>`: Indicates whether the J2EE component will programmatically or the container will declaratively perform authentication with the external resource: `Application` or `Container`.
- `<res-sharing-scope>`: Indicates whether external resource connections can be shared: `Shareable` or `Unshareable` (optional).

Here's an example of JDBC resource configuration for entity EJBs as extracted from the `ejb-xml.jar` file for our BeeShirts.com `Credit` entity bean:

```
<ejb-jar>
  ...
  <enterprise-beans>
    ...
    <entity>
      ...
      <resource-ref>
         <res-ref-name>jdbc/ejavaPool</res-ref-name>
         <res-type>javax.sql.DataSource</res-type>
         <res-auth>Container</res-auth>
      </resource-ref>
```

```
    </entity>
    ...
  </enterprise-beans>
  ...
</ejb-jar>
```

Utilizing such a data source from within an EJB is then a simple matter of looking up the named data source from within the EJB and obtaining a handle to a `javax.sql.DataSource` object. The `DataSource` object, as described in Chapter 6, "Advanced JDBC," can then be used to obtain a `java.sql.Connection` object. The underlying container is responsible for determining how this `Connection` object is to be allocated to your bean and will most likely maintain a pool of connections. From that point on, the bean can use the `Connection` object to create JDBC statements and obtain results as usual. For example, the `ejava.ejb.EJBHelper` class provides a method to return a `Connection` object using the configured `DataSource` reference as shown here:

```
public static String BEESHIRTS_DATA_SOURCE
                              = "java:comp/env/jdbc/ejavaPool";

/** Get database Connnection for BeeShirts.com data source */
public static Connection getDBConnection()
  throws SQLException,  NamingException
{
  // Create initial context
  InitialContext initialContext = new InitialContext();
  // Look up DataSource object
  DataSource dataSource = (DataSource)
        initialContext.lookup(EJBHelper.BEESHIRTS_DATA_SOURCE);
  // Request Connection object from pool managed by DataSource
  Connection connection = dataSource.getConnection();
  // Close context
  initialContext.close();
  // Return Connection object
  return connection;
}
```

Because bean-managed entity beans must manage their own connectivity to the database, a means for connecting to a database via Java must be employed. Although we use JDBC resources only from within bean-managed persistence entity beans in this chapter, JDBC resources can also be explicitly accessed from session beans, Java Servlets, and JSPs. Session bean access to JDBC resources configured inside of zero or more `<resource-ref>` elements is located within the `<session>` sub-element of the `<enterprise-beans>` element in an EJB deployment descriptor and within the `<web-app>` element in the Web deployment descriptor. However, we tend to stray away from direct access to enterprise data stored in databases from Java Servlets and JSPs as a general design philosophy to avoid security problems and to maintain the Web server tier as a scalable presentation layer. Inside of the application-serving tier, we also avoid any direct database access from within session EJBs because that is the primary role filled by entity EJBs. However, the option is still available, and the means by which such resources are configured and accessed is the same.

Entity Bean Server Components

An entity bean is a class that generally serves as a logical representation of data in a database. An entity bean class contains fields that map to elements of a database schema definition. Entity bean fields most easily map directly to columns of a database table, and the entity bean itself may be likened to one or more actual database tables. Relations among entity beans may thus be analogous to relations among tables.

Entity bean instances that contain populated values within their fields correspond to an actual entry within a data source. Thus, an entity bean instance may correspond to a particular row within a table or perhaps be related to the single result of a table join query. For example, our `Customer` BeeShirts.com entity bean class that encapsulates a customer directly relates to a `CUSTOMER` table in our sample database. Fields of the `Customer` entity bean directly relate to columns of the `CUSTOMER` database. An instance of a `Customer` entity bean contains the data for a particular customer whose field values directly correspond to the column values in the `CUSTOMER` table for a row associated with that customer.

Entity bean components can be developed in one of two ways by developers. Bean-managed persistence (BMP) entity beans contain code (typically JDBC code) created by developers to manage all database inserts, deletions, querying, and updates associated with a particular entity bean. Container-managed persistence (CMP) entity beans are defined in such a way by developers that the EJB containers can automatically provide all the code required for managing all database inserts, deletions, querying, and updates associated with the entity bean. Developers opt to use BMP entity beans most often when their container does not support CMP entity beans when a particular data source is too complex to enable effective CMP entity bean mapping, or when the developer desires more control over how the data should be managed. Otherwise, CMP entity beans can significantly reduce the amount of hand-coding required to data-enable enterprise applications.

Entity Bean Pooling

A particular server-side instance from a container's point of view may not always correspond to a particular data-source entry (for example, a row in a table) at all times. Entity bean container implementations often pool a limited number of server-side entity bean instances belonging to the same type in order to preserve resources and provide a scalable EJB client base. When the number of entity bean instances exceeds some maximum value, the container may begin to passivate and persist the state of some instances in order to reuse those instances to populate them with the state of other data-source entries. Thus, from a container's perspective, server-side entity bean instances may be viewed as hosts for data from particular data-source entries. These server-side instances can be distinguished from the distributed client-side instance stubs for such entity beans, which are of course under the management of the client application.

How a container manages server-side entity bean instance pooling is very much transparent to the entity bean developer. An entity bean developer designs a bean under the assumption that any actions on the bean relate to the state it contains and therefore relate to the particular data-source entry to which that state maps. When properly designed and when adhering to the specified entity bean component interface contract, the container will manage when and how instances of entity beans actually get allocated to particular data-source entries throughout the operation of the system.

Primary Keys

Although EJB containers may pool entity beans and reuse server-side entity bean instances to encapsulate different data-source entries at different times, there must be a way to uniquely identify a particular data-source entry. If the client-side handle were to simply refer to the server-side entity bean instance directly, there would be no guarantee that the instance is actually related to the correct data-source entry given the EJB container instance pooling and reuse policies.

Entity beans thus utilize the concept of a primary key. A primary key uniquely identifies the data-source entries associated with a particular entity bean instance. That is, although a particular entity bean instance can be allocated with different data-source entry values at different times by a container, the primary key provides a way to identify the particular data-source entry that should underlie an entity bean instance. When EJB clients create or look up particular data-source entries using entity bean interfaces, the container then associates a primary key with the EJB entity bean handle(s) returned to the client. Thus, for example, if a customer entity bean has a customer first and last name that represents a primary key for a customer entity bean, those two values should uniquely identify a row in a customer table for the container. From the programmer's point of view, however, it maps to a unique entity bean instance.

Timed Entity Bean Objects

Chapter 24, "EJB Basics," describes the new EJB timer service API. The preceding chapter provided an example implementation of the `TimedObject` interface by a session bean. Entity beans may also optionally implement the `TimedObject` interface, and the method by which this service is used is in fact nearly identical to the way it is used for session beans. That is, an EJB container will invoke an entity bean's `ejbTimeout()` method implementation when a timed event associated with the `TimerService` expires. The entity bean implements any responses to such a timeout inside of the `ejbTimeout()` method.

The EJB container will first look for an entity bean instance available to service the timed event. If no instance is available, the container will activate an instance so that it can service the request. Of course, because such timed events occur within an EJB container process, the EJB implementation must not expose access to the timed event information or `ejbTimeOut()` interface via a remote interface.

BMP Entity Beans

This section describes how to build entity beans using BMP entity bean component semantics. Many of the concepts and techniques used here also apply to CMP entity beans. However, BMP entity beans, as you will see, require a significant amount of hand-coding. In a certain sense, there is not much difference between using BMP entity beans and creating homegrown JDBC-based components. The difference lies in how the implementation of such JDBC logic is encapsulated. Specifically, standard methods on a BMP entity bean imply which JDBC statement types should be created and processed. Additionally, BMP entity beans can inherit the declarative transactional and security aspects of EJBs, as described in Chapter 28, "EJB Assurance Services."

BMP Entity Bean Logical Component Architecture

Figure 26.1 introduces the basic elements needed to construct a BMP entity bean. Public, nonfinal, and non-abstract entity bean implementations, such as `MyBeanManagedEntityEJBean`, must ultimately implement the `javax.ejb.EntityBean` interface, which in turn extends the `EnterpriseBean` marker interface. The `EntityBean` interface defines a set of operations that must be implemented by an entity bean to support the life-cycle management contract required by the EJB container. Bean-managed entity EJBs can also implement public, nonfinal, and nonstatic business-specific methods, such as the `someMethod()` and `anotherMethod()` sample methods shown in the diagram. A bean-managed entity bean will also typically define some state in the form of field variables that contain cached versions of the data-source entry values. Entity bean implementations must also have a public parameterless constructor and should not implement the `finalize()` method. Because an entity bean can be a subclass of some other class, if all of its required methods are not implemented by the entity EJB implementation class itself, they must be implemented by one of the entity bean's superclasses.

> **Note**
>
> In what follows, we discuss the particular rules for implementing the methods defined in Figure 26.1. However, it should be noted that the same convention used throughout this book for describing methods applies to the method names ending with *XXX* in the diagram. That is, for example, as the method naming convention "ejbCreate*XXX*" implies, the developer may also name these types of methods with any words substituted for the *XXX* as long as the method name is prefixed by `ejbCreate`.

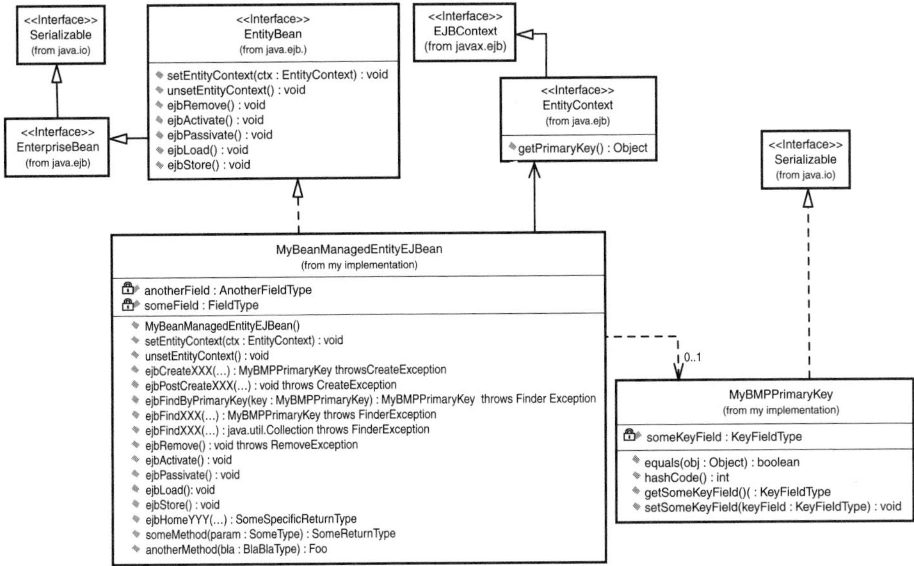

Figure 26.1 Bean-managed persistence entity EJBs.

BMP Entity Bean Primary Key

In general, an entity bean's primary key class must be serializable, must be an RMI/IIOP value type, must implement the `equals()` method, and must implement the `hashCode()` method, as is illustrated with the `MyBMPPrimaryKey` class in Figure 26.1. The value type requirement placed on the primary key simply means that the primary key must be transferable over the wire in a distributed fashion via RMI/IIOP and thus must be serializable and have valid IIOP value types (see Chapter 8, "CORBA Communications," and Chapter 9, "RMI Communications," for more details).

BMP Entity Bean Context Setting and Unsetting

The `javax.ejb.EntityContext` interface is implemented by a container object that provides a handle to an entity bean's runtime context. `EntityContext` extends the more generic `EJBContext` and defines a method for obtaining a reference to a remote EJB interface handle, as well as for obtaining a reference to the bean instance's primary key. The `setEntityContext()` method on an `EntityBean` implementation is invoked by a container immediately after an instance of the bean is constructed. The bean should save this value in a field variable for later use. An entity bean may also find calling the `getPrimaryKey()` method useful in determining the primary key that this particular entity bean instance identifies.

An `unsetEntityContext()` method is also required to be implemented by entity bean implementations. A container will call this method when the entity bean instance is to be decoupled from the container context. That is, the container is about to terminate this bean instance from memory, and the bean should take care to close any resources that were opened during a call to `setEntityContext()`.

BMP Entity Bean Finding

Whenever a client desires to locate particular existing entity bean instances that correspond to particular existing data-source entries, the container will invoke one of the `ejbFindXXX(...)` methods on the entity bean. The `ejbFindXXX(...)` methods fill a role similar to a SQL `SELECT` statement in database functionality. As the method naming convention "ejbFind*XXX*" implies, the developer may name these type of methods with any words substituted for the *XXX* as long as the method name is prefixed by `ejbFind`.

The `ejbFindByPrimaryKey()` method must be defined on all entity beans. An implementation of this method must take the primary key of an entity bean as an input parameter, verify that the associated data-source entry identified by the primary key exists in the database, and then return the primary key to the container. If the requested data-source entry does not exist, a BMP implementation may throw a `FinderException` or one of its subclasses to indicate that the requested object could not be found. Most likely, a BMP entity bean will formulate a `SELECT` statement query to issue to the database via JDBC to implement this method to verify that the data with the primary key exists in the database.

Zero or more additional `ejbFindXXX(...)` methods may also be defined that take zero or more business-specific input parameters and must attempt to locate any associated data-source entries in the database. If the method is designed to return a single object, the primary key for that object may be returned. If the method is designed to return a collection of objects, then for each located entry a collection of primary keys associated with each entry should be returned from the `ejbFindXXX()` method. The collection may be returned in one of two forms. For JDK 1.1 and above compatibility, a `java.util.Enumeration` of primary key objects can be returned (not shown in the diagram). For Java 2.0 and above compatibility, a `java.util.Collection` of primary key objects can be returned. A BMP implementation of these methods can utilize the JDBC API to issue a SQL `SELECT` statement as a function of the input parameters and bean type and then use the results to create a collection of associated primary key objects. If the underlying query results in no primary keys to return, an empty collection should be returned.

BMP Entity Bean Creation and Removal

Zero or more `ejbCreateXXX(...)` methods with zero or more parameters may be defined on an entity bean. The optional `ejbCreateXXX()` methods perform a function akin to database `INSERT` statements in that they create an entry in the data source associated with this entity bean type and populate it with any data established within the entity bean. Data can be established within the bean via the initialization of any field variables during construction, as well as by using any values passed as parameters to an `ejbCreateXXX(...)` method. A container calls `ejbCreateXXX(...)` on an entity bean due to a client-induced creation event on the bean. The `ejbCreateXXX(...)` methods must return an application-specific Java `Object` that represents the primary key for this newly created entity bean.

BMP entity beans must implement the necessary database connectivity logic to perform the database SQL `INSERT` within the `ejbCreateXXX(...)` methods. The primary mechanism to accomplish this task is via the JDBC API, which can be configured via XML-based data-source configuration parameters. BMP entity beans may throw the `CreateException` to indicate that an entity bean cannot be created for some reason. BMP entity beans may also throw the `DuplicateKeyException` subclass of `CreateException` if an entity bean could not be created due to the existence of a data-source entry with the same primary key.

For each `ejbCreateXXX(...)` method defined, the entity bean must also define an `ejbPostCreateXXX(...)` method using the same input parameters. The `ejbPostCreateXXX()` method is called by the container after it calls `ejbCreateXXX()` and after the container associates an instance of the entity bean with the client reference. Thus, any initial actions your entity bean desires to perform using a fully associated entity bean instance can be done when this method is called. The `ejbPostCreateXXX(...)` methods may also throw a `CreateException` to indicate an application error that has occurred during this method call.

When a client induces a remove action on an entity bean, the container calls the `ejbRemove()` method. The `ejbRemove()` method for an entity bean means that the associated data-source entry should be deleted from the database akin to a SQL `DELETE` statement in functionality. A BMP entity bean will need to obtain a handle to the primary key using its entity context's `getPrimaryKey()` method and then use the JDBC API to formulate a SQL `DELETE` statement for this particular data-source entry. A BMP implementation of `ejbRemove()` may also throw the `RemoveException` to indicate a general exception that has occurred during the attempted deletion operation.

BMP Entity Bean Passivation and Activation

The `ejbPassivate()` and `ejbActivate()` methods must be implemented for entity beans as they were for stateful session beans. The `ejbPassivate()` method is called by the container before it returns the entity bean to the pool of bean instances. This is most likely to occur when the bean has been inactive for some period and perhaps will be selected for passivation according to a least-recently-used algorithm. The entity bean should clean up any resources and states that cannot be serialized to a passive persistent store. None of the bean's field values that relate to data-source entry elements should be persisted within this method, though.

The `ejbActivate()` method generally performs the inverse operations of `ejbPassivate()`. A container calls `ejbActivate()` when it needs to bring the state of a previously passivated bean into active memory due to some client demand on that bean. The BMP implementation must reestablish any resources that were closed during the call to `ejbPassivate()` and populate any data that was serialized during the call to `ejbPassivate()`. This data does not include the bean's field values that relate to data-source entry elements, however.

BMP Entity Bean Storing and Loading

Whereas `ejbPassivate()` and `ejbActivate()` relate to closing and opening any non–data-source related resources, the `ejbLoad()` and `ejbStore()` methods explicitly deal with the data-source information. A container will call `ejbStore()` and `ejbLoad()` on an entity bean whenever it wants the bean to synchronize the state of the database field data in the bean with the state of the associated data actually stored in the data source.

A container calls `ejbStore()` on a bean when it wants the bean instance to update the associated data-source entry with the state of the data in the bean instance. This operation thus satisfies a function similar to that of a SQL `UPDATE` in the database. However, the determination of when this update is performed is a function of the container's decision-making logic. A container will also call `ejbStore()` right before it makes a call to `ejbPassivate()`. BMP implementations will typically use JDBC to implement SQL `UPDATE` statements when `ejbStore()` is invoked.

A container calls `ejbLoad()` on a bean when it wants the bean instance to be updated with the latest state values of the associated data-source entry in the database. This operation thus updates the in-memory bean instance representation of the database entry. A BMP implementation will typically call `getPrimaryKey()` on the associated entity context to first determine the specific data-source entry associated with this bean instance. The BMP implementation will then query the data-source entry's element values using JDBC and update the state of the bean. A container determines when `ejbLoad()` is called as a function of transaction management and also calls `ejbLoad()` before calls to `ejbRemove()` and after calls to `ejbActivate()`.

BMP Entity Bean Home Business Methods

A relatively recent addition to the EJB standard is the introduction of entity bean home business methods. Home business methods correspond to those methods defined on an entity bean that allow the bean to perform some business-specific functionality related to the particular entity bean type. This is different from business-specific methods such as the `someMethod()` and `anotherMethod()` examples of Figure 26.1. Those business-specific methods relate to functionality performed by a particular bean instance. Home business methods relate to functionality performed by a particular bean type. Using an analogy, business-specific methods on an entity bean are like nonstatic methods on a regular Java class, whereas home business methods on an entity bean are like static methods on a regular Java class. That is, the home business methods perform functionality that is appropriate to be performed on behalf of all of that entity bean's instances.

The naming convention for such home business methods requires that each method be named with the prefix `ejbHome`. Thus, various `ejbHome`*YYY*`()` methods may exist on an entity bean and can take zero or more input parameters and optionally return an output parameter. Because home business methods do not correspond to any particular bean instance, care must be taken when designing a bean's home business method.

BMP Entity Bean Component Interface Rules Summary

The life cycle of an entity bean is significantly more complicated than that of a session bean and relies heavily on transaction management. Such complexity is part of the reason why entity bean support was not required by EJB v1.0–compliant implementations to lower the barrier for entry into the EJB marketplace. Although we defer discussion of transaction management with EJBs until Chapter 28, we present here the basic steps that a container for an entity bean must follow (without transaction management):

1. *Instantiate EJB:* The container calls `Class.newInstance()` with the name of your EJB to create a new instance of the entity bean when the container decides it needs an entity bean instance for its pool of entity beans.
2. *Set Context:* The container calls `setEntityContext()` on the EJB with a container-created `EntityContext` object.
3. *Add EJB to Pool:* The container may now add the entity bean to a pool of server-side entity bean instances of this same type. Note that these server-side instances are not yet related to a client-side reference.
4. *Call* `ejbHome`*YYY*`(...)`*:* The container may use any available bean instance from the pool to implement the functionality of a home business method as induced by a client.
5. *Call* `ejbFind`*XXX*`(...)`*:* The container may use any available bean instance from the pool to implement the functionality of a select method as induced by a client. The returned primary key or keys are used to create delegates of entity beans but are not instances of server-side entity beans themselves. Client-side references are associated with these delegates.
6. *Call* `ejbCreate`*XXX*`(...)` *and* `ejbPostCreate`*XXX*`(...)`*:* The container may use a bean instance's implementation of these methods to insert a new database entry into the database as induced by a client.
7. *Call* `ejbActivate()`*:* The container calls `ejbActivate()` whenever a client demands that a particular database entry be accessed in memory and requires the bean to allocate any needed resources.
8. *Call* `ejbLoad()`*:* A container calls `ejbLoad()` when it wants to synchronize the state of database-related fields with the field values of an entity bean instance.

9. *Delegate Client Calls:* The container delegates EJB client calls to the entity bean whose reference is associated with the client. Calls from a client pass from the client stub to the container's skeleton representation of the EJB and then to the server-side bean instance implementation itself.
10. *Call* `ejbStore()`*:* The container calls `ejbStore()` when it wants to synchronize the state of the entity bean's database-related fields with the database by means of a database update operation.
11. *Call* `ejbPassivate()`*:* The container calls `ejbPassivate()` whenever it wants to release the resources consumed by an entity bean so that the bean instance can be used to encapsulate another database entry.
12. *Call* `ejbRemove()`*:* A container calls `ejbRemove()` when a client induces the deletion of an associated database entry. This does not remove the bean instance from the pool, though.
13. *Unset Context:* A container calls `unsetEntityContext()` when a bean instance is about to be removed from memory as determined by the container's memory management policy.

BMP entity beans thus require a significant amount of hand-coding to accomplish the desired effects of database connectivity. BMP entity beans provide implementations for the management of bean instance state and resources, as well as for the management of database data and connectivity. BMP entity beans manage bean instance state and resources through business-specific methods and home business methods (via `ejbHome`*`YYY`*), as well as through the implementation of standard methods that effect resource closing (via `ejbPassivate`), resource opening (via `ejbActivate`), and state management (via `setEntityContext` and `unsetEntityContext`). BMP entity beans manage database data and connectivity through the implementation of standard methods that effect database entry querying (via `ejbFind`*`XXX`*), insertion (via `ejbCreate`*`XXX`*), post-insertion (via `ejbPostCreate`*`XXX`*), deletion (via `ejbRemove`), synchronization updates (via `ejbStore`), and in-memory synchronization (via `ejbLoad`). BMP entity beans provide this functionality through the use of a Java enterprise technology such as JDBC. BMP entity beans thus may be viewed as providing standard interfaces for JDBC-based code that want to operate inside of the J2EE EJB container environment.

BMP Entity Bean Example

The only example of a BMP entity bean in our BeeShirts.com application is the `Credit` EJB. Only the core snippets from this `CreditEJBean` BMP entity bean are shown in Listing 26.1. The database entity creation, removal, finding, and updating logic of the `CreditEJBean` largely delegates to a helper class in this bean's directory called `CreditDBAccess`. Each `ejb`*`XXX`*`()` call that must perform some database-related activity first obtains a connection from our `EJBHelper` class, sets this connection onto `CreditDBAccess`, and then instructs `CreditDBAccess` to perform an insert, delete, select, or update operation, depending on the `ejbXXX()` method invoked on `CreditEJBean`. All credit information associated with the credit entity is stored in the `CreditEJBean` object's `creditInformation Hashtable` with key names taken from the `CreditDefinition` interface's constant names. Additionally, a `CreditPrimaryKey` class, shown in Listing 26.2, defines the primary key for this bean, which includes a customer ID, an order ID, and a card number.

Note

All the sample code strewn throughout this chapter may be located as described in Appendix A, "Software Configuration," and is extracted beneath the `examples\src\ejava\ejb\entity` subdirectories. Because the entity EJB-related code represents a moderately large amount of BeeShirts.com enterprise application component code, we do not present all the code in this chapter. Rather, we describe the basic structure of such code and present snippets from that code germane to chapter topics as they are discussed. Also note that this code depends on some of the code from Chapter 19, "Java Servlets," extracted to the `examples\src\ejava\servlets` directory and code from Chapter 25, "Session EJB," extracted to the `examples\src\ejava\ejb` directory. Appendix A describes how to build and deploy such code.

Listing 26.1 **BMP Entity Bean Example (`CreditEJBean.java`)**

```
package ejava.ejb.entity.credit;
   ...
public class CreditEJBean  implements EntityBean
{
  private EntityContext entityContext;
  private Hashtable creditInformation; // Stores credit information

  /** Create CREDIT table entry based on initial creditInformation */
  public CreditPrimaryKey ejbCreate(Hashtable creditInformation)
    throws CreateException {
    CreditDBAccess dbAccess = new CreditDBAccess();
    Connection connection = null;
       ...
      // Get connection, set on CreditDBAccess, and perform INSERT
      connection = EJBHelper.getDBConnection();
      dbAccess.setConnection(connection);
      dbAccess.insert(creditInformation);
      this.creditInformation = creditInformation;

       ...
    // Create primary key and return
    CreditPrimaryKey primaryKey = new CreditPrimaryKey();
    primaryKey.customerID =
      ((Integer) creditInformation.get(CreditDefinition.CUSTOMER_ID))
        .intValue();
```

Listing 26.1 **Continued**

```
    primaryKey.orderID =
      ((Integer) creditInformation.get(CreditDefinition.ORDER_ID))
        .intValue();
    primaryKey.cardNumber =
      ((String) creditInformation.get(CreditDefinition.CARD_NUMBER));
    return primaryKey;
  }

  /** No need for post creation semantics */
  public void ejbPostCreate(Hashtable creditInformation)
    throws CreateException {}

  /** No need for activation semantics */
  public void ejbActivate() {}

  /** No need for passivation semantics */
  public void ejbPassivate() {}

  /** Verify that primary key for Credit exists */
  public CreditPrimaryKey ejbFindByPrimaryKey(CreditPrimaryKey primaryKey)
    throws FinderException {
    if ((primaryKey == null)) {
      throw new FinderException("PrimaryKey should not be null");
    }
    // Throws exception if cannot load based on this key
    loadCreditData(primaryKey);
    return primaryKey;
  }

  /** Look up all primary keys for Credit objects with customer ID */
  public Collection ejbFindByCustomerID(int customerID)
    throws FinderException {
    Connection connection = null;
    CreditDBAccess dbAccess = new CreditDBAccess();
        ...
      // Get/set connection, SELECT credit info from database
      connection = EJBHelper.getDBConnection();
      dbAccess.setConnection(connection);
      Vector results = dbAccess.select(customerID);
      // Return results Vector
      return results;
        ...
  }

  /** Look up primary keys for Credit with customer ID and order ID */
```

Listing 26.1 **Continued**

```
public Collection ejbFindByCustomerIDAndOrderID(
  int customerID,
  int orderID)
  throws FinderException {

  Connection connection = null;
  CreditDBAccess dbAccess = new CreditDBAccess();
      ...
    // Get/Set connection, SELECT credit information
    connection = EJBHelper.getDBConnection();
    dbAccess.setConnection(connection);
    Vector results = dbAccess.select(customerID, orderID);
    // Return Credit info Hashtables
    return results;
      ...
}

/** Remove data source entry associated with this bean from DBMS */
public void ejbRemove() {
  Connection connection = null;
  CreditDBAccess dbAccess = new CreditDBAccess();
      ...
    // Get/Set Connection, DELETE this credit info from DB
    connection = EJBHelper.getDBConnection();
    dbAccess.setConnection(connection);
    dbAccess.delete((CreditPrimaryKey) entityContext.getPrimaryKey());
      ...
}

/** Store EJB data to database */
public void ejbStore() {
  Connection connection = null;
  CreditDBAccess dbAccess = new CreditDBAccess();
      ...
    // Get/Set connection, UPDATE credit info in DB
    connection = EJBHelper.getDBConnection();
    dbAccess.setConnection(connection);
    dbAccess.update(creditInformation);
      ...
}

/** Load EJB data from database */
public void ejbLoad() {
  // Get primary key
  CreditPrimaryKey primaryKey =
```

Listing 26.1 **Continued**

```
      (CreditPrimaryKey) entityContext.getPrimaryKey();
    System.out.println("ejbLoad called :");
    // Now load the actual data based on primary key
    loadCreditData(primaryKey);
    System.out.println(primaryKey);
  }

  /** Private method to load credit data into bean using primary key */
  private void loadCreditData(CreditPrimaryKey primaryKey) {
    Connection connection = null;
    CreditDBAccess dbAccess = new CreditDBAccess();

        ...
      // Get Connection, set connection, SELECT credit info
      connection = EJBHelper.getDBConnection();
      dbAccess.setConnection(connection);
      creditInformation =
        dbAccess.select(
          primaryKey.customerID,
          primaryKey.orderID,
          primaryKey.cardNumber);
        ...
  }

  /** Sets the EntityContext for the EJBean. */
  public void setEntityContext(EntityContext entityContext) {
    this.entityContext = entityContext;
  }

  /** Unsets the EntityContext for the EJBean. */
  public void unsetEntityContext() {
    entityContext = null;
  }

  /** Set credit information onto bean */
  public void setCreditInformation(Hashtable creditInformation) {
    this.creditInformation = creditInformation;
  }

  /** Retrieve credit info from bean. */
  public Hashtable getCreditInformation() {
    System.out.println("Sending Before :" + this.creditInformation);
    return creditInformation;
  }
}
```

Listing 26.2 **Primary Key Example (`CreditPrimaryKey.java`)**

```
package ejava.ejb.entity.credit;

import java.io.Serializable;

public class CreditPrimaryKey implements Serializable {
  public int customerID;
  public int orderID;
  public String cardNumber;

  public int hashCode() {
    return (orderID + cardNumber + customerID).hashCode();
  }

  public boolean equals(Object object) {
    if (object instanceof CreditPrimaryKey) {
      CreditPrimaryKey otherKey = (CreditPrimaryKey) object;
      if (otherKey.orderID == orderID
        && otherKey.customerID == customerID
        && otherKey.cardNumber.equals(cardNumber)) {
        return true;
      } else {
        return false;
      }
    } else {
      return false;
    }
  }

  public int getCustomerID() {
    return customerID;
  }

  public int getOrderID() {
    return orderID;
  }

  public String getCardNumber() {
    return cardNumber;
  }

  public void setCustomerID(int customerID) {
    this.customerID = customerID;
  }

  public void setOrderID(int orderID) {
```

Listing 26.2 **Continued**

```
    this.orderID = orderID;
  }

  public void setCardNumber(String cardNumber) {
    this.cardNumber = cardNumber;
  }
}
```

We do not list the `CreditDBAccess` code here because it is rather long and contains only JDBC code not germane to the topic of EJB. We encourage you to take a look at the `CreditDBAccess` class associated with this chapter's code, however. `CreditDBAccess` wraps all the actual JDBC calls to be performed by the `CreditEJBean`. Using the schema names from the `CreditDefinition` interface and data passed into its particular methods, it makes the appropriate JDBC calls joining both the `CREDIT_TABLE` and the `CHARGE_CARD_TYPE` database entities. The `CreditDBAccess` method has `select()`, `insert()`, `delete()`, and `update()` methods to perform the relational database operations related to these method names. A `Hashtable` used by these methods whose elements are named according to the `CreditDefinition` class identify both `CreditEJBean` data elements and database columns. The `Hashtable` is used during `CreditDBAccess` calls to `insert()` and `update()` and is returned from one of the `select()` calls. Additional `select()` calls return a `Vector` of `CreditPrimaryKey` objects. The `CreditDBAccess.delete()` call is invoked only with the `CreditPrimaryKey`.

CMP Entity Beans

As you have just seen, creating BMP entity beans can be quite a chore. Although the amount of hand-coding may be equivalent to what you would expect for implementing JDBC-based connectivity to access your enterprise data, EJB also provides a means to simplify the amount of effort required to create entity beans via its container-managed persistence (CMP) entity bean standards. With CMP, the container implements all the JDBC database access logic for you. The container thus handles the object-to-relational mapping necessary to transfer data from your EJB entity object to relational database entities and from the relational database entities to your EJB entity object. We describe how to create CMP entity bean components in this section. We primarily focus on those aspects of developing CMPs that differ from the development of BMPs and avoid reiterating discussion of the common concepts shared by CMPs and BMPs.

CMP Entity Bean Logical Component Architecture

Figure 26.2 depicts the basic architecture behind creating CMP entity bean components. A public and abstract CMP entity bean implementation, such as

MyContainerManagedEntityEJBean, must ultimately implement the EntityBean interface. CMP entity EJBs can also implement public, nonfinal, and nonstatic business-specific methods, such as the someMethod() and anotherMethod() sample methods shown in the diagram. Also note that entity bean implementations must have a public parameterless constructor and should not implement the finalize() method. Because an entity bean can be a subclass of some other class, if all of its required methods are not implemented by the entity EJB implementation class itself, they must be implemented by one of the entity bean's superclasses.

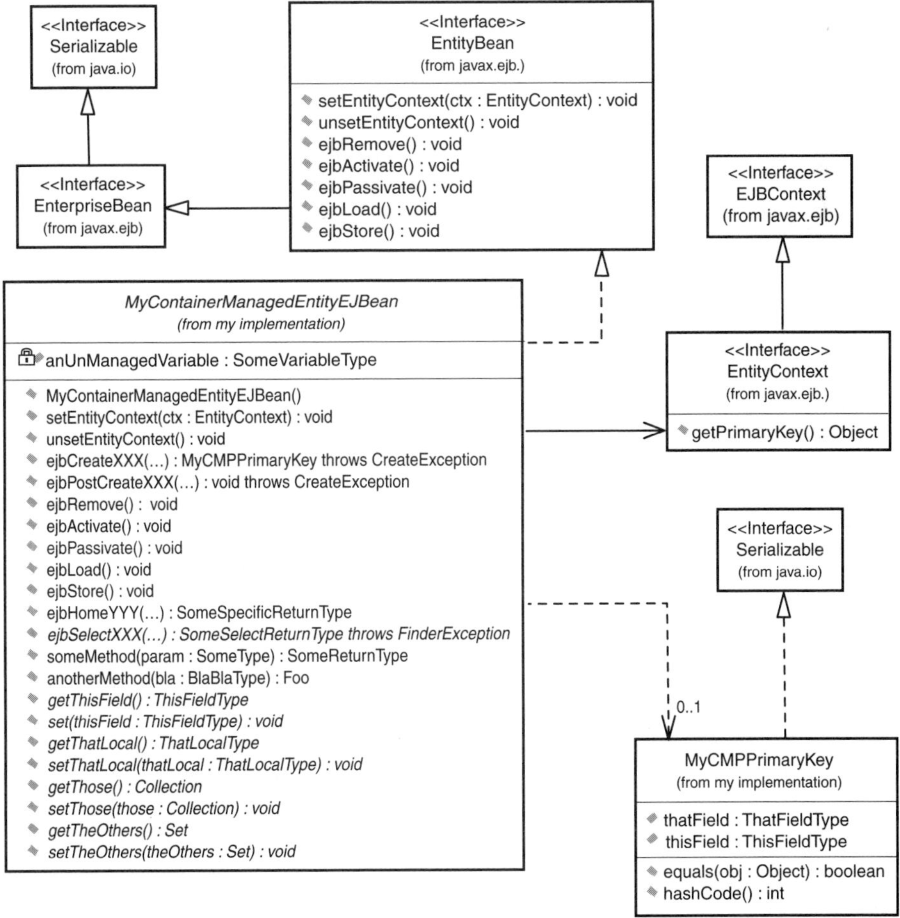

Figure 26.2 Container-managed persistence EJBs.

CMP Entity Bean Fields and Accessors

Fields associated with an entity bean represent those attributes and objects contained or related to the bean. Those persistent fields contained by the bean correspond to its most primitive data. Such field information is simply contained by the entity bean and used to compose the entity bean's state. Relationships associated with an entity bean correspond to more sophisticated relations with other entity beans. Such relationships may be one-to-one, one-to-many, or many-to-many. Furthermore, such relationships may be unidirectional or bidirectional.

Persistent fields contained by a CMP entity bean correspond to primitive types or `Serializeable` value types. Relationship fields associated with a CMP entity bean correspond to local entity bean interface types or collections of local entity bean interface types. The collections are represented by either `java.util.Collection` or `java.util.Set` objects.

With EJB v2.1, such contained persistent and relationship fields do not physically exist as attributes of the CMP entity bean class implementation. Hence you do not see any such attributes defined in Figure 26.2 on `MyContainerManagedEntityEJBean`. Such fields do exist virtually, however. That is, to the CMP entity bean developer, the bean is designed only to assume that such fields exist. The container will provide the concrete implementation of the abstract `MyContainerManagedEntityEJBean` class and create such physical field implementations transparent to the bean developer.

The bean is developed, however, to define accessor methods on the CMP entity bean implementation that correspond to the manipulation of such fields. Such accessor methods are implemented to be public and abstract getters and setters according to the standard JavaBeans rules for such getters and setters. The basic types of field accessor methods are described here for the different CMP entity bean field types:

- *Persistent Field Attributes:* Individual persistent field types (primitive or `Serializeable` value types) can be gotten and set using `get`*`XXX`*`()` and `set`*`XXX`*`()` JavaBeans method naming semantics, as illustrated in Figure 26.2 with the `getThisField()` and `setThisField()` example abstract methods.
- *Relationship Field Attributes:* Individual relationship field types (local entity bean interfaces) can be gotten and set using `get`*`XXX`*`()` and `set`*`XXX`*`()` JavaBeans method naming semantics, as illustrated in Figure 26.2 with the `getThatLocal()` and `setThatLocal()` example abstract methods.
- *Relationship Field Collections:* Collections of relationship field types (`Collection` or `Set` collections of local entity bean interface objects) can be gotten and set using `get`*`XXX`*`()` and `set`*`XXX`*`()` method naming semantics, as illustrated in Figure 26.2 with the `getThose()`, `setThose()`, `getTheOthers()`, and `setTheOthers()` example abstract methods.

CMP Entity Bean Primary Key

As was the case with BMP entity beans, a CMP entity bean's primary key class must be serializable, must be an RMI/IIOP value type, must implement the `equals()` method, and must implement the `hashCode()`. However, for CMP entity beans, additional constraints are placed on the primary key. For one, any fields of the primary key must map to persistent fields on the CMP entity bean. If the primary key has a single field, then as we'll see, it must be specified in the deployment descriptor and map to a persistent field for the CMP entity bean. Hence, the type of the primary key must be either a primitive type or value type as permitted to be defined for persistent fields. If the primary key maps to multiple CMP entity bean fields, then the implementation of the primary key must be such that its fields are public and map to JavaBeans-compliant persistent field accessors defined on the entity bean implementation. Certain container environments may also allow a primary key to be created and defined at deployment time by the container itself.

CMP Entity Bean Context Setting and Unsetting

Setting and unsetting the `EntityContext` associated with a CMP entity bean is accomplished using the `setEntityContext()` and `unsetEntityContext()` methods, respectively. Containers call these methods on CMP entity beans for the same reasons and during the same phases of a bean's life cycle as they do for BMP entity beans. However, CMP entity beans may not be as interested in using the `EntityContext` for its capability to return the bean's primary key because the container handles the resolution of data-source entry to bean instance. CMPs may, however, decide to manage the allocation and closing of resources tied to a bean instance from within the entity context setting and unsetting method.

CMP Entity Bean Finding

CMP entity beans relieve the programmer from having to define and write `ejbFind`*`XXX`*`(...)` methods. Rather, the container deduces how to implement such methods for the CMP entity bean by reading special Enterprise JavaBeans Query Language configuration information from the EJB deployment descriptors. The implementation of these methods is thus transparent to the developer. These methods may be implemented by EJB vendor products within subclasses of the CMP entity bean or by separate entities to which the calls are delegated and results received. Regardless of the underlying implementation, the CMP bean developer does not write any code to support these operations. Rather, as you'll soon see, the developer either explicitly specifies or uses a vendor-supplied tool to generate EJB QL information used to formulate the queries that underlie such method implementations.

CMP Entity Bean Creation and Removal

The bean developer need not worry about implementing the actual database `INSERT` related code to support any `ejbCreateXXX(...)` methods defined. Rather, the developer need only ensure that each container-managed field value is properly initialized with any default values and with values passed in as parameters to the `ejbCreateXXX(...)` method. The bean developer accomplishes this initialization within the `ejbCreateXXX(...)` method by implementing invocations of the abstract field accessors defined for the entity bean. The bean developer should implement `ejbCreateXXX(...)` methods to declare a primary key as the return type but actually return a `null` value for the primary key from this method. The container implementation of the CMP entity bean will handle the actual creation and return of a primary key.

The container will initialize all container-managed field values to the Java language defaults (for example, `0` and `null`) before it calls this method. Such default value initialization may be all that is needed for a particular EJB and thus not require any special `ejbCreateXXX(...)` implementation on the part of the bean developer. However, not defining any `ejbCreateXXX(...)` methods for the bean means that the EJB client will not be able to use the entity bean to perform database inserts.

CMP bean providers must also define `ejbPostCreate(...)` methods that match `ejbCreate(...)` methods in terms of parameters. The `ejbPostCreate()` method is called by the container after it calls `ejbCreate()` and after the container associates an instance of the entity bean with the client reference. Thus, any initial actions your entity bean desires to perform using a fully associated entity bean instance can be done when this method is called. Containers handle all primary key resolutions and throwing of EJB exceptions as appropriate.

The container calls `ejbRemove()` on a CMP right before it deletes associated data from the database. The bean developer need only focus on any actions that must be performed before the data is deleted from the database. The container implements all database deletion code and throws any EJB exceptions as appropriate.

For entity beans with relationships, the container will also handle how such related entity beans will be deleted. The container ensures that a removed entity bean will be removed from any relationships in which that entity bean was associated. For example, if a particular order is removed, then a customer having a collection of orders, one of which was the removed order, will have its order collection relationship updated to reflect the removed order. As you'll also see later in this chapter, the deployment descriptor for an entity bean can be used to specify whether a deletion of one entity bean should be cascaded to delete related entity beans. For example, if a customer entity bean is deleted, the decision to cascade this deletion and remove the orders contained in the customer's order collection relationship can also be performed by the container. Regardless of the bean's relationships, whenever the entity bean is removed, the container will invoke `ejbRemove()` on that instance.

CMP Entity Bean Passivation and Activation

The `ejbPassivate()` and `ejbActivate()` methods must be implemented by CMP entity bean developers as they were for BMP entity bean developers. Developers must thus clean up any non–data-source entry related resources within an `ejbPassivate()` method implementation. Developers must also reestablish any non–data-source entry related resources within an `ejbActivate()` method implementation.

CMP Entity Bean Storing and Loading

The container for CMP entity beans also handles most of the work that was previously implemented inside of `ejbLoad()` and `ejbStore()` BMP entity bean method calls. Containers manage the actual storage of data that was previously implemented within the `ejbStore()` call on a BMP entity bean. CMP entity bean developers need worry only about readying any field values for persistence to the database, such as deriving any recent updates that need to be reflected in the field values before they are persisted. CMP developers similarly need to worry only about reflecting any changes that were made to a bean's field values within the `ejbLoad()` method implementation. After a container handles updating the field values, the `ejbLoad()` method is called and the CMP entity bean implementation of this method may need to derive any changes to other states that result from this synchronization with the database. For CMP persistent field values, the abstract field accessor methods will need to be used to get and set any such values. For unmanaged and transient state of the bean, the bean can, of course, access such variables directly.

CMP Entity Bean Home Business Methods

As with BMP entity beans, CMP entity beans may also leverage use of home business methods. Home business methods correspond to those methods defined on an entity bean that allow the bean to perform some business-specific functionality related to the particular entity bean type. The naming convention for such home business methods requires that each method be named with the prefix `ejbHome`. Thus, various `ejbHome`*`YYY`*`()` methods may exist on an entity bean and can take zero or more input parameters and optionally return an output parameter. Because home business methods do not correspond to any particular bean instance, care must be taken when designing a bean's home business method.

CMP Entity Bean Select Methods

A CMP entity bean may also define a series of `ejbSelect`*`XXX`*`(...)` methods. These methods are defined to perform special queries used within business methods of the CMP entity bean, but not exposed to the entity bean's clients. Such methods thus serve as special helper methods useful to the bean's business logic implementation. The bean developer simply defines abstract `ejbSelect`*`XXX`*`(...)` methods with input and output parameters corresponding to the querying functionality desired by such methods and refers to such methods from within the bean's business-specific methods. These `ejbSelectXXX(...)` methods should also be defined to throw a `FinderException`.

As with other abstract methods defined on a CMP entity bean, these methods are not physically implemented by the bean developer. Rather, the container automatically generates the underlying method implementation. In fact, for `ejbSelectXXX(...)` methods, the container will generate the underlying implementation at deployment time based on EJB QL configuration information specified in the deployment descriptor. Thus, the `ejbSelectXXX(...)` methods are abstract methods and, as you'll see later in this chapter, have their functionality completely implemented by specification of EJB QL syntax in the entity bean's deployment descriptor.

CMP Entity Bean Component Interface Rules Summary

The life cycle of CMP entity beans is essentially identical to that of BMP entity beans. Thus, we do not reiterate the entity bean component life-cycle guidelines here. The only difference is in who implements the functionality embedded inside of the entity bean life-cycle methods. For CMP entity beans, the container implements much of this functionality, and for BMP entity beans, it is the bean developer's job.

CMP entity beans thus alleviate a significant amount of the hand-coding that was required by BMP entity beans to accomplish the desired effects of database access. CMP entity bean providers simply ready beans for container-managed persistence operations within calls to the `ejbCreateXXX()`, `ejbPostCreateXXX()`, `ejbRemove()`, `ejbLoad()`, and `ejbStore()` methods. CMP entity bean developers should, however, manage bean instance state and resources through business-specific and home business methods, as well as through the implementation of standard methods that effect resource closing (via `ejbPassivate`), resource opening (via `ejbActivate`), and state management (via `setEntityContext` and `unsetEntityContext`). Most often, the coding performed within such methods is either extremely minimal or nonexistent. CMP entity beans thus may be viewed as providing standard interfaces for enabling a J2EE EJB container to implement object-relational mapping for an EJB and for providing the underlying database connectivity solution.

CMP Entity Bean Example

Listing 26.3 and Listing 26.4 contain the core portions from our `Order` CMP entity bean implementation. Listing 26.3 is for an `OrderEJBean`, which is a CMP entity bean; it implements all the standard entity bean interfaces plus the abstract getters and setters for the bean's persistent fields. Listing 26.4 is for a `CMROrderEJBean`, which simply extends the `OrderEJBean` to define abstract getters and setters for relationships associated with the `Order` entity bean, defines special create methods assuming such relationships, defines special helper `ejbSelectXXX()` methods, and defines a few `ejbHomeXXX()` business methods. As you can see, CMP entity bean code implementations can be tremendously more simple than BMP entity bean code implementations. In fact, the code by and large focuses simply on method definitions and any business-specific method implementations. However, we will have to specify more information about the CMP entity bean in its XML-based deployment descriptors, as you'll see in a subsequent section of this chapter.

Listing 26.3 **CMP Entity Bean Example with Persistent Fields (`OrderEJBean.java`)**

```
package ejava.ejb.entity.order;
  ...
public abstract class OrderEJBean implements EntityBean {
  private EntityContext entityContext;

  /**
   * Abstract getters and setters for CMP entity
   * bean persistent fields.
   */
  public abstract void setOrderID(Integer orderID);
  public abstract Integer getOrderID();

  public abstract void setCustomerID(Integer customerID);
  public abstract Integer getCustomerID();

  public abstract void setOrderDate(Date orderDate);
  public abstract Date getOrderDate();

  public abstract String getShippingInstructions();
  public abstract void setShippingInstructions(String shippingInstructions);

  public abstract void setShipDate(Date shipDate);
  public abstract Date getShipDate();

  public abstract void setShipWeight(double shipWeight);
  public abstract double getShipWeight();

  public abstract void setShipCharge(double shipCharge);
  public abstract double getShipCharge();

  public abstract void setPaidDate(Date paidDate);
  public abstract Date getPaidDate();

  /** Set and unset the EntityContext for the EJB */
  public void setEntityContext(EntityContext entityContext) {
    this.entityContext = entityContext;
  }
  public void unsetEntityContext() {
    entityContext = null;
  }

  /**
   * Standard ejbCreate() method for setting initial state.
```

Listing 26.3 **Continued**

```
   * Requires special linking ID for customer relationship.
   */
  public Integer ejbCreate(
    Integer orderID,
    Integer customerID,
    Date orderDate,
    String shippingInstructions,
    Date shipDate,
    double shipWeight,
    double shipCharge,
    Date paidDate)
    throws CreateException {
    this.setOrderID(orderID);
    this.setCustomerID(customerID);
    this.setOrderDate(orderDate);
    this.setShippingInstructions(shippingInstructions);
    this.setShipDate(shipDate);
    this.setShipWeight(shipWeight);
    this.setShipCharge(shipCharge);
    this.setPaidDate(paidDate);
    return null;
  }

  /**
   * Corresponding ejbPostCreate() for ejbCreate() method.
   */
  public void ejbPostCreate(
    Integer orderID,
    Integer customerID,
    Date orderDate,
    String shippingInstructions,
    Date shipDate,
    double shipWeight,
    double shipCharge,
    Date paidDate)
    throws CreateException {
  }

  /** No impl needed for these standard method calls. */
  public void ejbActivate() {}
  public void ejbPassivate() {}
  public void ejbRemove() {}
  public void ejbLoad() {}
  public void ejbStore() {}
}
```

Listing 26.4 **CMP Entity Bean Example with Relationship Fields (`CMROrderEJBean.java`)**

```
package ejava.ejb.entity.order;
  ...
public abstract class CMROrderEJBean extends OrderEJBean {
  private CMRCustomerLocalHome customerHome = null;

  /**
   * Abstract relationship accessors for one to many
   * relationship between an Order and Item bean.
   */
  public abstract Collection getItems();
  public abstract void setItems(Collection items);

  /**
   * Abstract relationship accessors for many to one
   * relationship between an Order and Customer bean.
   */
   public abstract CMRCustomerLocal getCustomer();
  public abstract void setCustomer(CMRCustomerLocal customer);

  /**
   * Abstract relationship accessors for one to many
   * relationship between an Order and Address bean.
   */
  public abstract Collection getAddresses();
  public abstract void setAddresses(Collection addresses);

  /**
   * Abstract ejbSelectXXX() helper method for selecting
   * a collection of items in an order.
   */
  public abstract Collection ejbSelectItemsInAnOrder(Integer orderID)
    throws FinderException;

  /**
   * Abstract ejbSelectXXX() helper method for selecting
   * a collection of orders for a customer.
   */
  public abstract Collection ejbSelectOrdersOfACustomer(Integer customerID)
    throws FinderException;

  /**
   * An ejbHomeXXX() home business method for returning the number
   * of items associated with an order.
   */
```

Listing 26.4 **Continued**

```
public int ejbHomeNumberOfItemsInAnOrder(Integer orderID)
  throws FinderException {
  return ejbSelectItemsInAnOrder(orderID).size();
}

/**
 * An ejbHomeXXX() home business method for returning the average
 * order value of a particular customer.
 */
public float ejbHomeAverageOrderValue(Integer customerID)
  throws FinderException {
  System.out.println("Inside ejbHomeAverageOrderValue");
  int nItems = 0;
  float totalValue = 0.0f;

  // Iterate through collection of orders for a customer
  Collection orders = ejbSelectOrdersOfACustomer(customerID);
  Iterator ordersIterator = orders.iterator();
  while (ordersIterator.hasNext()) {
    // Iterate through collection of items per order
    Collection items =
      ((CMROrderLocal) ordersIterator.next()).getItems();
    Iterator iterator = items.iterator();
    while (iterator.hasNext()) {
      // Accumulate item price and increment item count
      CMRItemLocal item = (CMRItemLocal) iterator.next();
      nItems++;
      totalValue += item.getTotalPrice();
      System.out.println(
        "ejbHomeAverageOrderValue: currentTotal:" + totalValue);
    }
  }
  // Return average price of items for the customer
  float returnValue = 0.0f;
  if (nItems > 0)
    returnValue = totalValue / nItems;
  return returnValue;
}

/**
 * Standard ejbCreate() method for setting initial state.
 * Does not require special linking ID for customer relationship
 * since relationship is implied by the CMP relationship field.
 */
public Integer ejbCreate(
```

Listing 26.4 **Continued**

```
    Integer orderID,
    Date orderDate,
    String shippingInstructions,
    Date shipDate,
    double shipWeight,
    double shipCharge,
    Date paidDate)
    throws CreateException {
    this.setOrderID(orderID);
    this.setOrderDate(orderDate);
    this.setShippingInstructions(shippingInstructions);
    this.setShipDate(shipDate);
    this.setShipDate(shipDate);
    this.setShipWeight(shipWeight);
    this.setShipCharge(shipCharge);
    this.setPaidDate(paidDate);
    return null;
  }

  /**
   * Corresponding ejbPostCreate() for ejbCreate() method.
   */
  public void ejbPostCreate(
    Integer orderID,
    Date orderDate,
    String shippingInstructions,
    Date shipDate,
    double shipWeight,
    double shipCharge,
    Date paidDate)
    throws CreateException {
  }
}
```

Note

For our CMP entity bean examples beneath the `examples/ejava/ejb/entity` directory, we take the same approach for each in structuring the bean implementation. That is, one bean implementation class is defined with the standard methods and persistent field accessor methods implemented. A separate bean implementation defining the relationship field accessor methods and methods associated with such relationships is provided to extend the base CMP entity bean implementation.

Note that this is not a requirement imposed by the EJB specification. We simply take this approach here in the book to decouple the container-managed relationship implementation from the base CMP entity bean

> implementation. The main reason behind this approach is that deploying and testing the base CMP entity beans is much faster and unit test demonstration is easier. Thus, our approach is simply for pedagogic and demonstration purposes. The build and deployment scripts associated with the session beans that use these entity beans illustrate the end-to-end usage of such beans. Thus, by taking this approach, you have the flexibility and option of deploying and testing each CMP entity bean individually or deploying and testing the CMP entity beans with relationships and front-end session beans as a cohesive unit.
>
> Also note that a special `ADDRESS` database table exists in the example database and is used with the code examples for this chapter. The `ADDRESS` table enables a more sophisticated EJB CMP relationship structure to be demonstrated between the address and order entity beans.

In addition to the CMP entity bean defined in the `ejava.ejb.entity.order` package, five other CMP entity beans are included with the example EJB code. We don't describe each bean in detail here but will occasionally refer to such beans and demonstrate snippets from such beans throughout the EJB chapters in this book. The other CMP entity beans are in the following packages and have the following roles:

- `ejava.ejb.entity.tshirt`: Contains a CMP entity bean encapsulating BeeShirts.com T-shirt product information. A `TShirt` is part of order `Item` information. The `BrowseManagerEJBean` session bean utilizes this `TShirt` information and its relationships.
- `ejava.ejb.entity.item`: Contains a CMP entity bean encapsulating BeeShirts.com order item information. An `Item` has many `TShirt` products associated with it and belongs to a single `Order`. The `OrderManagerEJBean` session bean utilizes this `Item` information and its relationships.
- `ejava.ejb.entity.address`: Contains a CMP entity bean encapsulating BeeShirts.com order address information. An `Address` is part of `Order` information, such as a billing address and shipping address. The `OrderManagerEJBean` session bean utilizes this `Address` information and its relationships.
- `ejava.ejb.entity.authentication`: Contains a CMP entity bean encapsulating BeeShirts.com customer authentication information. `Authentication` information is related to a particular `Customer`. The `CustomerManagerEJBean` session bean utilizes this `Authentication` information.
- `ejava.ejb.entity.customer`: Contains a CMP entity bean encapsulating BeeShirts.com customer information. A `Customer` is related to its `Authentication` information and one or more `Order` beans. The `CustomerManagerEJBean`, `ShoppingCartEJBean`, and `OrderManagerEJBean` session beans utilize this `Customer` information and its relationships.

Entity Bean Remote Client Interfaces

Building and using home and remote client interfaces for entity beans is very similar to building and using home and remote client interfaces for session beans. In fact, except for an additional type of finder method and home business method that can to be added to the entity bean home interface definition, only a few subtle semantic differences exist. In this section we describe how to build entity bean interfaces and how clients access these interfaces.

Perhaps the most significant difference between remote entity bean interfaces and remote session bean interfaces is that remote entity bean interfaces are often used less by design. That is, the very nature of entity beans renders their interfaces laden with methods that access discrete data elements. Such discrete element access is often far too fine-grained for most designs. Rather, one most often opts to expose access to entity beans from behind the wall of a session bean or perhaps via a coarser-grained set of entity bean business methods exposed as remote interfaces. Despite such design considerations, the option to expose an entity bean via remote interfaces exists, and this section describes the mechanism by which you do this.

Entity Bean Remote Interfaces

Entity bean remote interfaces encapsulate the client's view of an entity bean. The approach by which entity bean remote interfaces are developed is very similar to that of session bean remote interfaces. Entity bean interfaces typically consist of getters and setters for retrieving and establishing data to be associated with an entity bean, but they can also have other arbitrary application-specific interfaces defined for them. This subsection describes how to build and use entity bean remote interfaces.

Entity Bean Remote Interface Logical Architecture

Figure 26.3 depicts the basic logical architecture for building and using remote EJB client interfaces to distributed entity EJBs. All application-specific interfaces to distributed EJB objects, such as `MyEntityEJB` shown in the diagram, must ultimately extend the `javax.ejb.EJBObject` interface. As with session beans, entity beans also employ underlying stubs, skeletons, and container management services for implementing distributed and managed access to server-side entity EJBs from client-side interfaces. The only real difference between entity bean and session bean remote interfaces lies in a few subtle semantic differences, as we discuss next.

Entity Bean Application-Specific Remote Interfaces

As with session bean remote interfaces, an application-specific remote EJB interface must be implemented for each entity bean component. This interface provides the distributed interface used by remote entity bean clients to invoke the application-specific logic of entity beans. For each distributable application-specific method on an entity bean server-side component, such as `MyEntityEJBean.someMethod()`, an associated application-specific method must be defined on the EJB client-side remote interface, such as `MyEntityEJB.someMethod()`. As a side effect of their distributable nature, each method in the application-specific remote interface should also declare that it could throw a `java.rmi.RemoteException`. Of course, such rules apply only to those server-side component methods you want to be made distributable. Those methods defined on the entity bean implementation that return or take local interface objects as parameters should not be exposed in a distributed fashion.

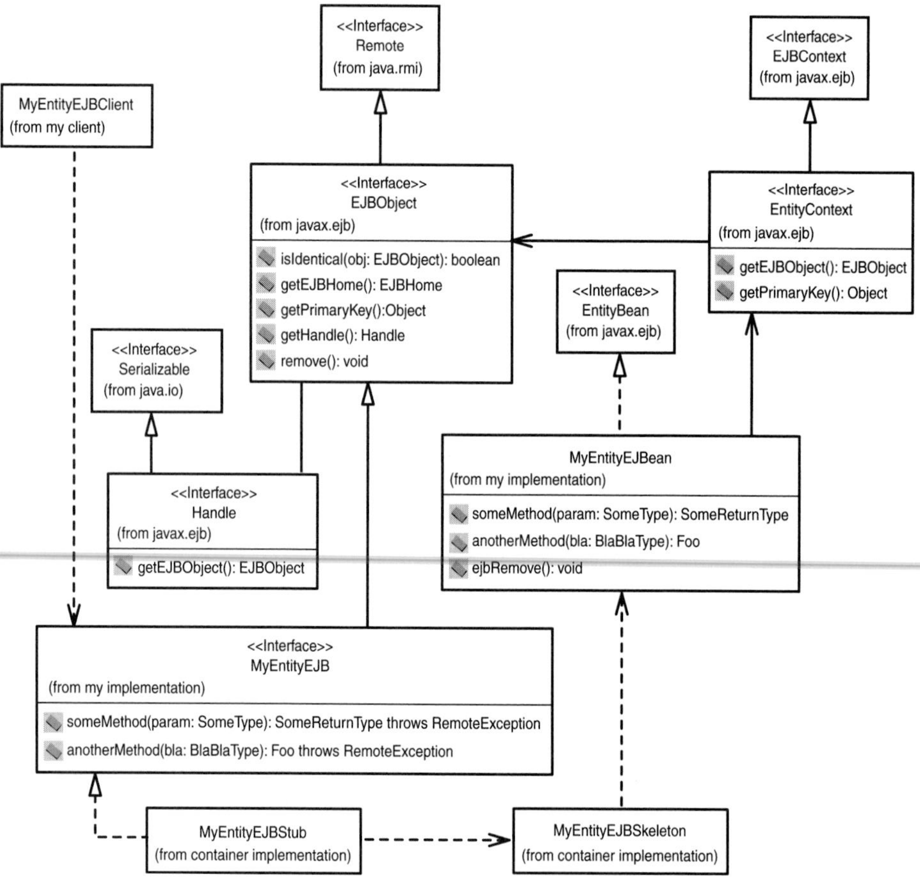

Figure 26.3 Entity bean remote interface architecture.

Entity Bean Generic Remote Interfaces

In addition to application-specific interfaces on an EJB remote interface, a set of methods inherited from `EJBObject` can also be invoked on a remote entity bean object.

When clients want to determine whether EJB objects are identical to others, the `EJBObject.isIdentical()` method can be called. The `EJBObject.getEJBHome()` method returns a handle to the entity bean's home interface object that is used to create remote interface objects. The `EJBObject.getHandle()` method returns an object that implements the `javax.ejb.Handle` interface for serializing and persisting `EJBObject` references. On the server side, an entity bean can obtain a reference to an `EJBObject` with which it is associated by calling `getEJBObject()` on its `EntityContext` object. Bean components may want to obtain such a reference for use as input or output parameters in their application-specific methods.

All such invocations are akin to the session bean's interface support. However, unlike session bean clients, entity bean clients can make a valid call to `EJBObject.getPrimaryKey()` on a remote interface to obtain the primary key object associated with the entity bean object.

Another very important difference between session bean client interface and entity bean client interface semantics is the implication of calling the `EJBObject.remove()` method. For session beans, this method cleans up client references and possibly destroys a server-side stateful session object. For entity beans, a call to `remove()` will result in the deletion of an associated data-source entry from the database, removal of the server-side object from any related entity beans, and potentially cascading the removal of contained entity beans. Thus, entity bean clients must be particularly careful when using this method and must make sure that they intend for the data to be deleted and not the object reference.

Entity Bean Remote Interface Examples

Our sample remote interfaces corresponding to the two types of entity beans presented earlier really convey no new information beyond what was conveyed for session bean remote interfaces. Nevertheless, Listing 26.5 is presented to show you the `Credit` remote interface for our BMP `CreditEJBean` entity bean described in Listing 26.1. Listing 26.6 presents the `Order` remote interface for our CMP `OrderEJBean` entity bean that was presented in Listing 26.3.

Listing 26.5 **BMP Entity Bean Remote Interface Example** (`Credit.java`)

```
package ejava.ejb.entity.credit;
  ...
public interface Credit extends EJBObject {
  /** Set credit information onto the bean using key names
      taken from the CreditDefinition interface */
  public void setCreditInformation(Hashtable creditInformation)
    throws RemoteException;
  /** Get credit information from the bean accessible with key
      names from CreditDefinition interface. */
  public Hashtable getCreditInformation() throws RemoteException;
}
```

Listing 26.6 **CMP Entity Bean Remote Interface Example (`Order.java`)**

```
package ejava.ejb.entity.order;
   ...
public interface Order extends EJBObject {

  /**
   * Exposing getters and setters for CMP entity
   * bean persistent fields in a remote fashion.
   */
  public Integer getOrderID() throws RemoteException;

  public void setCustomerID(Integer customerID) throws RemoteException;
  public Integer getCustomerID() throws RemoteException;

  public void setOrderDate(Date orderDate) throws RemoteException;
  public Date getOrderDate() throws RemoteException;

  public void setShippingInstructions(String shippingInstructions)
    throws RemoteException;
  public String getShippingInstructions() throws RemoteException;

  public void setShipDate(Date shipDate) throws RemoteException;
  public Date getShipDate() throws RemoteException;

  public void setShipWeight(double shipWeight) throws RemoteException;
  public double getShipWeight() throws RemoteException;

  public void setShipCharge(double shipCharge) throws RemoteException;
  public double getShipCharge() throws RemoteException;

  public void setPaidDate(Date paidDate) throws RemoteException;
  public Date getPaidDate() throws RemoteException;
}
```

As you can see from Listing 26.6, for example purposes, we demonstrate exposing access to most of the getters and setters defined for the `OrderEJBean` implementation's persistent field accessors in a distributed fashion. Notice also that we do not define a setter for the primary key field in Listing 26.6 because we want only the container to set such a field. We do not and cannot expose access to the getters and setters defined for the `CMROrderEJBean` implementation's relationship field accessors in a distributed fashion. This is of course because such accessors on the `CMROrderEJBean` implementation involve the getting and setting of in-process local interface objects that are not allowed to be gotten or set by a distributed EJB client.

Entity Bean Home Interfaces

Entity bean clients use home interfaces to create, find, and remove entity beans. Creation of entity beans actually relates to the insertion of new entries into a data source (for example, a new row in a database table). Interfaces for finding entity beans provide a mechanism for querying for data-source entries with results returned in an object-oriented fashion (that is, in terms of entity bean objects). Removing an entity bean relates to the deletion of its associated data-source entries in the database. This subsection describes how to create and utilize entity bean interfaces to perform these basic functions as well as additional supporting functionality.

Entity Bean Home Interface Logical Architecture

Figure 26.4 depicts the architecture behind creating entity bean home interfaces and how clients may use these interfaces. To obtain handles to application-specific EJB home interface objects, such as `MyEntityEJBHome`, which must ultimately extend the standard `javax.ejb.EJBHome` interface, we use JNDI to look up named home references. Server-side skeletons and the container handle mapping calls from entity bean client stubs that implement application-specific home interfaces onto a particular entity bean instance. Home interfaces can also be used to persist their handles for later reconstruction and for obtaining meta-data about the EJBs they serve to create.

Entity Bean Home Object Lookup

The means by which entity bean home objects are looked up by clients is identical to the means by which session bean home objects are looked up. JNDI is used whether your client operates inside of a J2EE container or outside of a container in a standalone fashion. If a client operates inside of a J2EE container, `<ejb-ref>` elements can be used to refer to EJB home interfaces during lookup. Entity beans that want to act as clients to other EJBs define `<ejb-ref>` elements within their `<entity>` element definition inside of an `ejb-jar.xml` file.

Entity Bean Application-Specific Home Interfaces

A series of one or more `create`*`XXX`*`(...)` methods are defined on the custom home interface to represent the different ways in which the associated entity bean data-source entry can be created. A single `create`*`XXX`*`(...)` method must be defined on the home interface for each `ejbCreate`*`XXX`*`(...)` method defined on the entity bean implementation. Each version of a `create`*`XXX`*`(...)` method returns an object instance implementing the entity bean's remote interface (for example, `MyEntityEJB`) and contains zero or more input parameters related to the specific types of initialization parameters needed by the associated `ejbCreate`*`XXX`*`(...)` methods. Each `create`*`XXX`*`(...)` method must also be defined to throw a `java.rmi.RemoteException` and `javax.ejb.CreateException`. Additionally, each `create`*`XXX`*`(...)` method must be defined to throw any application-specific exceptions that have been defined for its associated `ejbCreate`*`XXX`*`(...)` method.

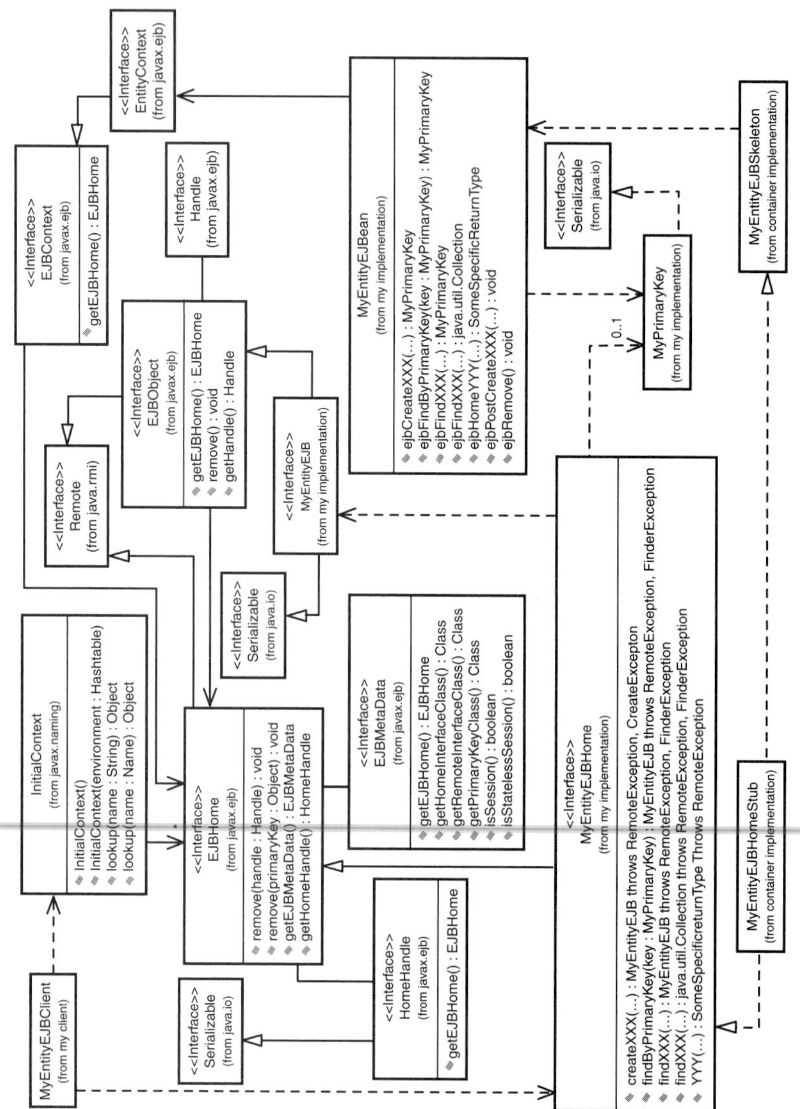

Figure 26.4 Entity bean home interface architecture.

The `createXXX()` methods are not the only application-specific methods that can be defined on an entity bean home interface. A collection of finder methods are also defined that enable the client to query for existing entity beans. A `findXXX(...)` method on the entity bean home interface must exist for each `ejbFindXXX(...)` method that exists on the entity bean implementation. For CMP entity beans, because no `ejbFindXXX(...)` methods are explicitly defined on an entity bean implementation, the valid `findXXX(...)` methods can be determined from the entity bean deployment descriptor (as we'll cover in a subsequent section). Each `findXXX(...)` method defined on the entity bean client home interface should also declare that `RemoteException` and `FinderException` objects can be thrown back to the client.

All entity bean home interfaces must define at least one `findByPrimaryKey()` method because all entity beans must define an `ejbFindByPrimaryKey()` method. The `findByPrimaryKey()` method must be defined such that it returns a reference to an entity bean remote object (for example, `MyEntityEJB`). The container handles associating the primary key returned from the `ejbFindByPrimaryKey()` entity bean method to an actual bean instance and returned entity bean client remote interface stub. Similarly, `findXXX(...)` methods must also be defined to return a reference to an entity bean remote interface object for each `ejbFindXXX(...)` method implementing an individual entity finder that returns a primary key from within the entity bean implementation.

The other `findXXX(...)` methods must also be defined to match each associated `ejbFindXXX(...)` method and should have the same input and output parameters. The difference on the client side is that the `Collection` (or `Enumeration`) object returned from `findXXX(...)` contains implementations of entity bean remote objects as opposed to primary keys contained in the collections returned from associated `ejbFindXXX(...)` methods on server-side entity bean implementations.

Finally, any home business methods defined on the entity bean that you want to be exposed in a distributed fashion must be specified within the home interface. Any `ejbHomeYYY(...)` method defined on the entity bean implementation that you want to expose for distributed access must have a corresponding `YYY(...)` method defined on the home interface method and must also indicate that a `RemoteException` may be thrown. The input and output parameters for the bean implementation's version of the home business method and the home interface's version of the home business method must match.

Entity Bean Generic Home Interfaces

In addition to calling `EJBObject.remove()` on a remote entity bean object to delete an associated data-source entry, entity bean clients can also call `remove(Handle)` inherited from `EJBHome` by the home interface object. The `Handle`, of course, needs to relate to the particular `EJBObject` that is to be removed. Entity bean objects may also be removed by passing the primary key object associated with a particular entity bean to the `remove(Object)` method defined at the `EJBHome` level.

As with session beans, the `EJBHome.getEJBMetaData()` method is called to obtain a handle to an `EJBMetaData` object that provides a mechanism for clients to discover certain information about an entity bean. Entity bean `EJBMetaData` methods provide the same semantics as they do for session beans when calling `getEJBHome()` to return the home object, `getHomeInterfaceClass()` to return the home interface `Class`, getRemoteInterfaceClass() to return the remote interface Class, and isSession() to determine whether it is a session or an entity EJB. Additionally, the getPrimaryKeyClass() method can be called to return the Class object that represents the entity bean's primary key class. A call to isStatelessSession() always returns false for entity beans.

On the server side, an entity bean can extract a handle for its EJBHome object with a call to getEJBHome() on its EntityContext object (as inherited from EJBContext). Bean components may want to obtain such a reference for creating, finding, and removing entity beans of their own type.

Entity Bean Home Interface Examples

In addition to creation methods, our entity bean home interface examples include finder method definitions in them according to the way in which the entity bean objects can be selected. Listing 26.7 depicts the CreditHome BMP entity bean home interface associated with the CreditEJBean of Listing 26.1. Here, our create() method is mapped by the container to a call to our CreditEJBean.ejbCreate() method, and the find*XXX*(...) methods map to calls to associated CreditEJBean.ejbFind*XXX*(...) methods.

Listing 26.7 **BMP Entity Bean Home Interface Example (CreditHome.java)**

```
package ejava.ejb.entity.credit;
  ...
public interface CreditHome extends EJBHome {
  /**
   * Create a Credit entity given credit information whose
   *  keys are defined according to names from CreditDefinition.
   */
  public Credit create(Hashtable creditInformation)
    throws CreateException, RemoteException;

  /**
   * Find a Credit entity given its primary key.
   */
  public Credit findByPrimaryKey(CreditPrimaryKey primaryKey)
    throws FinderException, RemoteException;

  /**
   * Find a collection of Credit entities associated
   * with the given customer ID.
   */
  public Collection findByCustomerID(int customerID)
    throws FinderException, RemoteException;

  /** Find a collection of Credit entities given an associated
```

Listing 26.7 **Continued**

```
   * customer ID and order ID.
   */
  public Collection findByCustomerIDAndOrderID(
    int customerID,
    int orderID)
    throws FinderException, RemoteException;
}
```

Listing 26.8 presents the `OrderHome` CMP home interface for the `OrderEJBean` of Listing 26.3. Although it is apparent that the `create(...)` method maps to the `OrderEJBean.ejbCreate()` method, just how the `findXXX(...)` methods are mapped or even defined may not be so apparent to you just yet. No `ejbFindXXX(...)` methods are defined on our `OrderEJBean`. In a section later in this chapter, we discuss how the container implements such methods after appropriate hints are given to the container using EJB QL during configuration and deployment of the CMP entity bean.

Listing 26.8 **CMP Entity Bean Home Interface Example (**`OrderHome.java`**)**

```
package ejava.ejb.entity.order;
  ...
public interface OrderHome extends EJBHome {

  /**
   * Standard ejbCreate() method for setting initial state.
   * Requires special linking ID for customer relationship.
   */
  public Order create(
    Integer orderID,
    Integer customerID,
    Date orderDate,
    String shippingInstruct,
    Date shipDate,
    double shipWeight,
    double shipCharge,
    Date paidDate)
    throws CreateException, RemoteException;

  /**
   * Given an order ID primary key, this method will return a
   * handle to the associated remote Order object if the
   * order exists in persistent storage.
   */
  public Order findByPrimaryKey(Integer orderID)
    throws FinderException, RemoteException;
```

Listing 26.8 **Continued**

```
    /**
     * Given a customer ID, this method will find any orders
     * associated with that customer and return a Collection
     * of remote Order entity bean object references.
     */
    public Collection findByCustomerID(Integer customerID)
      throws FinderException, RemoteException;
}
```

Entity Bean Local Client Interfaces

In the preceding chapter we described EJB local interfaces as they applied to session beans. The same basic rules and principles behind constructing and using such interfaces apply here for entity beans. Perhaps the most significant difference is that entity bean home interfaces also allow local entity bean clients to invoke finder and home business methods. Local interfaces are also more heavily used inside of entity bean designs. The fine-grained and discrete nature of entity bean business methods typically dictates that such methods be invoked in-process and behind the wall of a coarser-grained remote session or entity bean interface. Of course, entity bean methods that pass handles to local interface objects as return parameters cannot be exposed as distributed interfaces. It is for these reasons that the entity bean developer must carefully determine what methods should be exposed in a local fashion and how to design the entity bean such that the EJB client can interface with such beans in the most meaningful and efficient manner. This section explores how to create entity bean local object and home interfaces.

Entity Bean Local Object Interfaces

An entity bean local object interface defines the set of application-specific local in-process operations that can be invoked on a particular entity bean. An entity bean client views a local interface as it would most other in-process Java object interfaces. Entity bean local interfaces most often also expose access to other local entity bean objects via an implied set of relationships among such entity beans. This subsection describes how to build and use entity bean local object interfaces.

Entity Bean Local Object Interface Logical Architecture

Figure 26.5 depicts the basic logical architecture for building and using local EJB client interfaces to local entity EJBs. All application-specific interfaces to local EJB objects, such as `MyEntityEJBLocal` shown in the diagram, must ultimately extend the `javax.ejb.EJBLocalObject` interface. Local interfaces make use of a stub implementation that implements the actual calls made to the EJB component implementation such as the `MyEntityEJBBean` shown in the diagram. Runtime EJB containers are ultimately responsible for managing which bean instance is used and how calls are routed, but the result is that calls from an EJB client to application-specific EJB interface methods ultimately result in the invocation of an associated application-specific method on the EJB component instance.

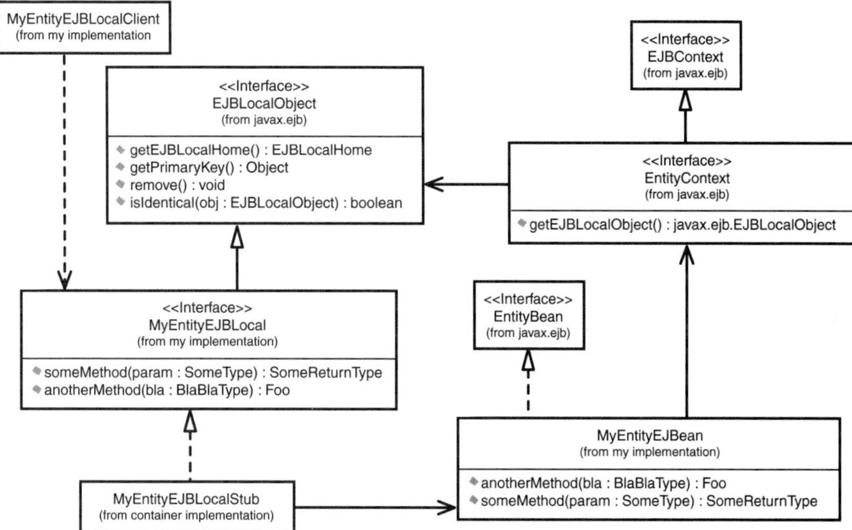

Figure 26.5 The entity bean local object interface architecture.

Entity Bean Application-Specific Local Object Interfaces

An application-specific local object interface must be created for entity bean components that need to be accessed in a local fashion. This interface provides the local interface usable by entity bean clients to invoke the application-specific logic of entity bean. For each local application-specific method on an entity bean implementation, such as `MyEntityEJBean.someMethod()`, an associated application-specific method must be defined on the entity bean local object interface, such as `MyEntityEJBLocal.someMethod()`. Of course, such rules apply only to those entity bean methods you want to be made accessible locally within the same container process as the client. The definition and use of such local interfaces is most common among CMP entity beans that are part of relationships with other entity beans.

Entity Bean Generic Local Object Interfaces

In addition to application-specific interfaces on an entity bean local object interface, a set of methods inherited from `EJBLocalObject` can be invoked on a local EJB object. We have covered these methods in the context of both session bean interfaces and remote `EJBObject` entity bean interfaces defined earlier. That is, the `isIdentical()`, remove(), and getPrimaryKey() methods defined on the EJBLocalObject all provide functionality similar to that of the methods defined on the EJBObject interface. An entity bean implementation can obtain a reference to an EJBLocalObject with which it is associated by calling getEJBLocalObject() on its EntityContext object. The EJBLocalObject.getEJBLocalHome() method returns a reference to the home interface object that is used to create local interface objects.

Entity Bean Local Object Interface Example

Listing 26.9 presents the OrderLocal local object interface that exposes local access to the persistent field getters and setters defined on the OrderEJBean of Listing 26.3. Listing 26.10 presents the CMROrderLocal local object interface that extends OrderLocal to expose local access to the relationship field getters and setters defined on the CMROrderEJBean of Listing 26.4. Thus the OrderLocal interface can be used when it is desired to access the order entity bean abstraction sans consideration for any relationships in a manner not dissimilar (aside from distributed access) to the functionality offered by the remote Order interface defined in Listing 26.6. The CMROrderLocal interface simply extends this functionality to expose local access to the local entity bean relationships defined on the CMP order entity bean.

Listing 26.9 **Entity Bean Local Object Interface to Persistent Fields Example (OrderLocal.java)**

```
package ejava.ejb.entity.order;
    ...
public interface OrderLocal extends EJBLocalObject {
  /**
   * Exposing getters and setters for CMP entity
   * bean persistent fields in a local fashion.
   */
  public Integer getOrderID();

  public void setCustomerID(Integer customerID);
  public Integer getCustomerID();

  public void setOrderDate(Date orderDate);
  public Date getOrderDate();

  public void setShippingInstructions(String shippingInstructions);
  public String getShippingInstructions();

  public void setShipDate(Date shipDate);
  public Date getShipDate();

  public void setShipWeight(double shipWeight);
  public double getShipWeight();
```

Listing 26.9 **Continued**

```
  public void setShipCharge(double shipCharge);
  public double getShipCharge();

  public void setPaidDate(Date paidDate);
  public Date getPaidDate();
}
```

Listing 26.10 **Entity Bean Local Object Interface to Relationship Fields Example (`CMROrderLocal.java`)**

```
package ejava.ejb.entity.order;
  ...
public interface CMROrderLocal extends OrderLocal {
  /**
   * Local relationship accessors for one to many
   * relationship between an Order and Item.
   */
  public Collection getItems();
  public void setItems(Collection items);

  /**
   * Local relationship accessors for many to one
   * relationship between an Order and Customer.
   */
  public CMRCustomerLocal getCustomer();
  public void setCustomer(CMRCustomerLocal customer);

  /**
   * Local relationship accessors for one to many
   * relationship between an Order and Address.
   */
  public Collection getAddresses();
  public void setAddresses(Collection addresses);
}
```

Entity Bean Local Home Interfaces

As with session bean clients, entity bean clients use local home interfaces to create initial references to EJBs as well as remove these references. For entity beans, these references are implemented via the local entity bean interface objects. As with remote clients, local clients should always use local home interfaces to create references to EJBs because these provide the container with the opportunity it needs to manage how to allocate EJB bean instance resources.

Entity Bean Home Interface Logical Architecture

Figure 26.6 depicts the architecture behind creating entity bean local home interfaces and how entity bean clients may use these interfaces. JNDI is used to obtain handles to application-specific entity bean local home interface objects, such as `MyEntityEJBLocalHome`, which must extend the standard `javax.ejb.EJBLocalHome` interface. Application-specific entity bean local home interface objects are also implemented by stubs, which communicate with server-side implementations, and the container, which creates, destroys, and delegates calls to entity bean instances as appropriate.

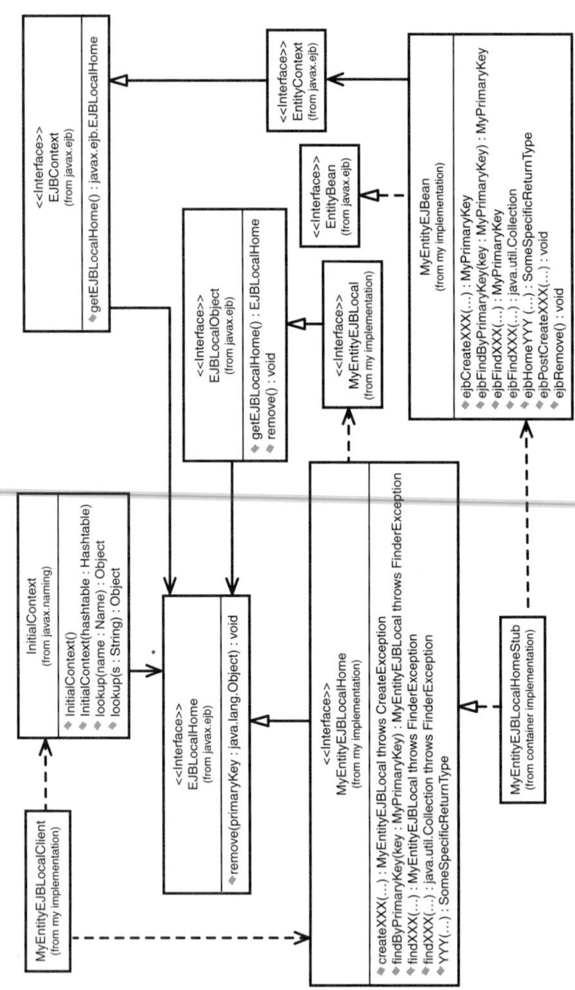

Figure 26.6 The entity bean local home interface architecture.

Entity Bean Local Home Object Lookup

A local entity bean client must first obtain a handle to an entity bean's local home interface when it wants to create a new local reference to the entity bean. Clients that operate inside of a J2EE container environment utilize the default parameterless constructor of the `InitialContext` object and simply look up a handle to an entity bean's local home interface with a call to `InitialContext.lookup()`. As with session bean local home interface lookups, the name passed to an `InitialContext.lookup()` can refer to an `<ejb-local-ref>` element in the client's XML-based deployment descriptor. The `<ejb-local-ref>` element defines the reference name that will be used in creating the name passed to `InitialContext.lookup()`, the type of EJB being referenced, the local home information, the local object information, and the linking information.

As an example, the `ejava.ejb.session.ordermgr.OrderManagerEJBean` class included with the code for this book's EJB chapters is an EJB acting as an EJB client. It locally accesses the CMP entity bean `CMROrderEJBean` via the bean's `CMROrderLocalHome` and `CMROrderLocal` local interfaces. The `OrderManagerEJBean` defines its reference to such a bean as well as other CMP entity beans via its EJB deployment descriptor, `ejb-jar.xml`, as illustrated here:

```
<ejb-jar ...>
    ...
   <enterprise-beans>
       ...
      <session>
         <display-name>OrderManagerEJB</display-name>
         <ejb-name>OrderManagerEJB</ejb-name>
             ...
         <ejb-local-ref>
            <ejb-ref-name>ejb/order</ejb-ref-name>
            <ejb-ref-type>Entity</ejb-ref-type>
            <local-home>
              ejava.ejb.entity.order.CMROrderLocalHome
            </local-home>
            <local>ejava.ejb.entity.order.CMROrderLocal</local>
            <ejb-link>OrderManager.jar#OrderEJB</ejb-link>
         </ejb-local-ref>
         <ejb-local-ref>
            <ejb-ref-name>ejb/customer</ejb-ref-name>
            <ejb-ref-type>Entity</ejb-ref-type>
            <local-home>
              ejava.ejb.entity.customer.CMRCustomerLocalHome
            </local-home>
            <local>ejava.ejb.entity.customer.CMRCustomerLocal</local>
            <ejb-link>OrderManager.jar#CustomerEJB</ejb-link>
         </ejb-local-ref>
```

```
          <ejb-local-ref>
             <ejb-ref-name>ejb/address</ejb-ref-name>
             <ejb-ref-type>Entity</ejb-ref-type>
             <local-home>
               ejava.ejb.entity.address.CMRAddressLocalHome
             </local-home>
             <local>ejava.ejb.entity.address.CMRAddressLocal</local>
             <ejb-link>OrderManager.jar#AddressEJB</ejb-link>
          </ejb-local-ref>
          <ejb-local-ref>
             <ejb-ref-name>ejb/item</ejb-ref-name>
             <ejb-ref-type>Entity</ejb-ref-type>
             <local-home>
               ejava.ejb.entity.item.CMRItemLocalHome
             </local-home>
             <local>ejava.ejb.entity.item.CMRItemLocal</local>
             <ejb-link>OrderManager.jar#ItemEJB</ejb-link>
          </ejb-local-ref>
            ...
       </session>
    </enterprise-beans>
     ...
</ejb-jar>
```

As you can see, the OrderManagerEJBean defines local EJB client references to the order, customer, address, and item CMP entity beans.

The OrderManagerEJBean looks up a reference to the CMROrderLocalHome interface object from within the lookupOrderHome() method as shown here:

```
private void lookupOrderHome() throws NamingException {
  if (orderHome == null) {
    InitialContext context = new InitialContext();
    orderHome =
         (CMROrderLocalHome) context.lookup(EJBHelper.ORDER_REFNAME);
    context.close();
  }
}
```

The EJBHelper.ORDER_REFNAME is defined inside the EJBHelper class as shown here:

```
public static String ORDER_REFNAME = "java:comp/env/ejb/order";
```

Entity Bean Application-Specific Local Home Interfaces

A series of one or more create*XXX*(...) methods are defined on a custom entity bean local home interface to represent the different ways in which the associated local entity bean object can be created. A single `createXXX(...)` method must be defined on the local home interface for each `ejbCreateXXX(...)` method defined on the entity bean implementation that will be used for local entity bean object creation. Each version of a `createXXX(...)` method returns an instance of the entity bean's local object interface (for example, `MyEntityLocalEJB`) and contains zero or more input parameters related to the specific types of initialization parameters needed by the associated `ejbCreateXXX(...)` methods. Each `createXXX(...)` method must also be defined to throw a `javax.ejb.CreateException`. Additionally, each `createXXX(...)` method must be defined to throw any application-specific exceptions that have been defined for its associated `ejbCreateXXX(...)` method.

As with entity bean remote home interfaces, a collection of finder methods may also be defined on entity bean local home interfaces that enable the client to query for existing entity beans. The rules for such definition are almost identical with the exception that local home interfaces don't throw a `RemoteException`. That is, a `findXXX(...)` method on the entity bean home interface must exist for each `ejbFindXXX(...)` method that exists on the entity bean implementation. CMP entity beans have their `ejbFindXXX(...)` methods defined virtually via deployment descriptor information, but the local home interface must nonetheless explicitly indicate those finder interfaces that are accessible locally via a corresponding `findXXX(...)` method.

Any home business methods defined on the entity bean that are to be exposed in a local fashion must be specified within the local home interface. Any `ejbHomeYYY(...)` method defined on the entity bean implementation that you want to be accessed locally must have a corresponding `YYY(...)` method defined on the local home interface method.

Entity Bean Generic Local Home Interfaces

Only one generic method is defined on the `EJBLocalHome` interface. This `remove(Object)` method can be used to remove an entity bean based on a primary key passed in as a parameter. If the entity bean client is not allowed to invoke this operation, a `RemoveException` will be thrown.

Entity Bean Local Home Interface Example

Listing 26.11 presents the `OrderLocalHome` interface exposing local home interface methods defined on the `OrderEJBean` of Listing 26.3. The `OrderLocalHome` interface simply exposes the `OrderEJBean` entity bean's create and finder operations for access by a client locally. Because the `OrderEJBean` represents a basic entity bean with no container-managed relationships, the exposed `create()` method requires the client to provide an explicit customer identifier that will be used to relate the bean to a customer. The `OrderEJBean` is a CMP entity bean, however, and as such can expose access to a set of virtual finder methods that will be defined inside of the EJB implementation's deployment descriptor.

Listing 26.11 **Non-CMR Entity Bean Local Home Interface Example (`OrderLocalHome.java`)**

```
package ejava.ejb.entity.order;
   ...
public interface OrderLocalHome extends EJBLocalHome {

  /**
   * Standard create() method for setting initial state.
   * Requires special linking ID for customer relationship.
   */
  public OrderLocal create(
    Integer orderID,
    Integer customerID,
    Date orderDate,
    String shippingInstruct,
    Date shipDate,
    double shipWeight,
    double shipCharge,
    Date paidDate)
    throws CreateException;

  /**
   * Given an order ID primary key, this method will
   * return an OrderLocal object reference if the bean
   * can be found.
   */
  public OrderLocal findByPrimaryKey(Integer orderID)
    throws FinderException;

  /**
   * Given a customer ID this method will return a collection
   * of OrderLocal object references if any such beans
   * can be found.
   */
  public Collection findByCustomerID(Integer customerID)
    throws FinderException;
}
```

Listing 26.12 presents the `CMROrderLocalHome` interface exposing local home interface methods defined on the `CMROrderEJBean` of Listing 26.4. The `CMROrderLocalHome` exposes those interfaces to the `CMROrderEJBean` that extend the `OrderEJBean` to provide access to container-managed relationships with the bean. Special create, finder, and home business methods are all exposed by this local home interface.

Listing 26.12 **CMR Entity Bean Local Home Interface Example (`CMROrderLocalHome.java`)**

```
package ejava.ejb.entity.order;
   ...
public interface CMROrderLocalHome extends EJBLocalHome {

  /**
   * Standard create() method for setting initial state.
   * Does not require special linking ID for customer relationship
   * since relationship is implied by the CMP relationship field.
   */
  public CMROrderLocal create(
    Integer orderID,
    Date orderDate,
    String shippingInstructions,
    Date shipDate,
    double shipWeight,
    double shipCharge,
    Date paidDate)
    throws CreateException;

  /**
   * Given an order ID primary key, this method will
   * return a CMROrderLocal object reference if the bean
   * can be found.
   */
  public CMROrderLocal findByPrimaryKey(Integer orderID)
    throws FinderException;

  /**
   * Given a customer ID this method will return a collection
   * of CMROrderLocal object references if any such beans
   * can be found.
   */
  public Collection findByCustomerID(Integer customerID)
    throws FinderException;

  /**
   * Find a collection of CMROrderLocal object references
   * that fall within a particular order range of values.
   */
  public Collection findAllOrdersInRange(
    double startValue,
    double endVlaue)
    throws FinderException;
```

Listing 26.12 **Continued**

```
  /**
   * A home business method for returning the number
   * of items associated with an order.
   */
  public int numberOfItemsInAnOrder(Integer orderID)
    throws FinderException;

  /**
   * A home business method for returning the average
   * order value of a particular customer.
   */
  public float averageOrderValue(Integer customerID)
    throws FinderException;
}
```

EJB QL

The Enterprise JavaBeans Query Language (EJB QL) is a language used to specify how CMP entity beans' `findXXX(...)` and `ejbSelectXXX(...)` methods are implemented. You'll recall from earlier in this chapter that for CMP entity beans, no concrete implementation of such methods was ever defined. Yet CMP entity bean clients invoked the respective finder methods, and CMP entity bean business methods invoked the respective select methods fully expecting to induce a query and receive a result. EJB QL is the intermediate language used by the EJB container to describe how such methods are implemented. Although EJB container vendors most often will provide GUI-based tools to automatically generate EJB QL for you when building CMP entity beans, it nonetheless can be important to understand EJB QL in order to better understand how your entity bean queries perform and how they are constructed.

When one first looks at EJB QL, it has a familiar look and feel but at the same time has a syntax that is not completely intuitive and easy to immediately digest. The reason for the familiar look and feel is that EJB QL is somewhat similar to SQL by its basic structure. That is, the basic structure of an EJB QL statement is as follows:

```
SELECT ... FROM ... WHERE ... ORDER BY
```

Thus, an EJB QL statement indicates the following akin to SQL:

- `SELECT`: Specifies the resultant values selected to be returned from the query (required).
- `FROM`: Specifies the domain of types from which the query may yield results (required).

- `WHERE`: Specifies conditional expressions wherein the query results must satisfy (optional).
- `ORDER BY`: Specifies the order by which the query results are returned (optional).

However, because EJB QL statements are defined to refer to abstract representations of CMP entity bean fields and relationships, EJB QL statements are defined in terms of objects and their attributes. SQL statements, on the other hand, are defined in terms of tables and their columns. The syntax involved with describing EJB QL statements thus stops short of being similar with SQL via its basic structure. In this section we describe the structure and semantics of EJB QL statements. In the section following this section, we describe how EJB QL and other configuration data is embedded into entity bean deployment descriptors to render entity beans alive and functional.

EJB QL Types

Before we describe the structure of an EJB QL statement, it is important to understand a little bit about the valid types that are used from within EJB QL statements. As with any programmatic language, a type is fundamental in identifying the set of valid interfaces and attributes that can be associated with a particular data structure or object. EJB QL is no different in needing to identify types. In EJB QL, types are often referred to as "abstract schema types." Such types are "abstract" because they do not exist and only model objects in some abstract form.

Valid abstract schema types in EJB QL directly relate to CMP entity bean types and their field types. For a particular CMP entity bean type, it has its own abstract schema type and is associated with a particular logical name. This "abstract schema name" thus has a one-to-one mapping to the CMP entity bean's home interface type. Such type names are referred to inside of EJB QL statements.

EJB QL statements are defined to describe the underlying functionality of CMP entity bean finder and select methods. The Java return types from such methods thus must map to logical names used to describe such return types in EJB QL statements. The return type mappings from EJB QL types to Java types are defined here:

- *Finders returning remotes:* Query result from a remote finder method maps from an EJB QL abstract schema type to a Java entity bean remote interface type or collection thereof.
- *Finders returning locals:* Query result from a local finder method maps from an EJB QL abstract schema type to a Java entity bean local interface type or collection thereof.
- *Selects returning remotes:* Query result from a select method maps from an EJB QL abstract schema type to a Java entity bean remote interface type if the select method is designated as returning a remote type mapping in the deployment descriptor.

- *Selects returning locals:* Query result from a select method maps from an EJB QL abstract schema type to a Java entity bean local interface type if the select method is designated as returning a local type mapping in the deployment descriptor.
- *Selects returning persistent fields:* Query result from a select method maps from an EJB QL abstract schema type persistent field to an entity bean's corresponding persistent field Java type or collection thereof.
- *Selects returning primitive types:* Query result from a select method maps from an EJB QL abstract schema type field to an entity bean's corresponding persistent field Java primitive type or a collection of the Java wrapper objects for such primitive types.
- *Selects returning aggregate value types:* Query result from a select method maps from an EJB QL aggregate function (that is, sum, count, average, min, max) return type (that is, numeric, string, character, or date) to a corresponding Java primitive type or a collection of the Java wrapper objects for such primitive types.

As stated, an EJB QL statement is used to define the implementation of a CMP entity bean's finder and select methods. Such EJB QL statements are inserted inside of an entity bean's deployment descriptor and can reference only those abstract schema types related to the CMP entity beans in the deployment descriptor.

As a final note on types, EJB QL types can also assume `NULL` values. EJB QL type values can also be compared if they are of the same type or if they are numerically compatible for comparison.

EJB QL Variables

As with any programmatic type, *variables* represent the instances that adhere to such types and that are used in programmatic statements. Because EJB QL uses special abstract types, variables of those types can be used inside of EJB QL statements. Because EJB QL types map to CMP entity bean types and fields, EJB QL variables map to variables of CMP entity beans, collections of CMP entity beans, or persistent fields of CMP entity beans.

EJB QL variables can be dereferenced using the dot (`.`) separator. That is, if you have some EJB QL variable `order` and it contains or is related to another variable `customer`, then you may dereference the variable as `order.customer`. Such dereferencing in fact can be used in a continuous fashion to dereference each variable that has another variable or relates to another variable, such as in `order.customer.address.city`. Because such variables map to entity beans, collections of entity beans, or persistent fields of entity beans, this dereferencing cannot occur past a dereferenced persistent field.

The means to represent such variables is accomplished in a few discrete ways inside of EJB QL statements. Some of the more common and basic ways to represent abstract variables and how they map to their CMP entity bean equivalents are described here with example fragments:

- *Single valued identifier:* An identifier may be used that is of a single abstract schema type. Such a variable thus maps to a single CMP entity bean type. As an example, a variable may refer to an order type:

  ```
  someOrder
  ```

- *Single valued variable:* A variable may be dereferenced using the `.` character and refer to a single type associated with a particular abstract schema type. Such a type maps to a CMP entity bean type. As an example, a variable may refer to a customer associated with an order:

  ```
  someOrder.customer
  ```

- *Collection variable:* A variable may refer to a collection associated with a particular abstract schema type. Such a collection maps to a collection of CMP entity bean types. As an example, a variable may refer to a collection of items associated with an order:

  ```
  someOrder.items
  ```

- *Persistent field variable:* A variable may refer to a persistent field associated with a particular abstract schema type. Such an abstract persistent field maps to a persistent field on a CMP entity bean. As an example, a variable may refer to a shipping charge persistent field associated with an order:

  ```
  someOrder.shipCharge
  ```

EJB QL `FROM` Clause

The EJB QL `FROM` clause identifies the domain of abstract schema types to be considered in executing a particular query. The `FROM` clause also defines a set of variable names mapped to a particular domain of types. Such variable names are then used in other parts of the EJB QL statement to identify a particular domain of types to which the query fragment is limited.

A variable name may map to an abstract schema type name for an entity bean. In one form of declaration, an identifier variable can be declared to map to a particular abstract schema name (and therefore an entity bean type) as shown next (wherein the `AS` keyword is optional):

```
Order AS o
```

This fragment thus indicates that the single valued identifier `o` relates to an `Order` abstract schema type name. As you'll see, this abstract schema type name `Order` is then mapped to a particular entity bean type inside of the deployment descriptor.

A variable name can be declared to map to an abstract schema type name inside of a collection relationship for an entity bean type as shown here (again the `AS` keyword is optional):

```
IN(o.items) AS i
```

This fragment indicates that the variable `i` relates to the type inside of the `Order` type's `items` collection. In our CMP entity bean example, such a type is an `Item` and relates to our item entity bean.

Given such a means to evaluate variables and specify a domain of types to which a query applies, an associated `FROM` clause would look as follows:

```
FROM Order AS o, IN(o.items) AS i
```

The `FROM` clause is evaluated from left to right so any variables used within the `FROM` clause itself must be defined to the left of that variable's use in the `FROM` clause. A `FROM` clause can have an arbitrarily long set of comma-delimited variable mappings along the following exemplary lines:

```
FROM Bla AS b, Foo AS f, IN(f.bars) AS bs, ...
```

EJB QL `WHERE` Clause

The optional EJB QL `WHERE` clause delineates a conditional expression that establishes the constraints on type values that must be satisfied by any resultant values returned from the EJB QL query. An EJB QL `WHERE` clause uses variables that were declared inside of the `FROM` clause to express such conditions. As with `FROM` clauses, `WHERE` clauses may use variables and the `.` separator to dereference such variables as needed to identify the entity bean field of interest inside of the conditional expression.

Conditional expressions defined inside of `WHERE` clauses follow the intuitive and standard conventions for expressing conditional statements. Standard operator evaluation precedence and operators are employed. Furthermore, some additional conditional expression elements are also defined for EJB QL expressions. The set of valid operators and conditional expression elements are defined here with example fragments as appropriate:

- *Literals:* Single quotes are used to delineate string literals and numbers are expressed as in the Java programming language.

  ```
  'USA'          20          45.3          -651E3
  ```

- *Brackets:* `(` and `)` are used to group conditional expressions.
- *Comparison operators:* Equals =, greater than >, greater than or equals to >=, less than <, less than or equals to <=, and not equals to <>.

  ```
  WHERE employee.income <= employee.minimumWage
  ```

- *Arithmetic operators:* Unary + and -, addition +, subtraction -, multiplication *, and division /.

  ```
  WHERE ((employee.income * employee.taxRate) + employee.ira) > 100000
  ```

- *Logical operators:* `NOT`, `AND`, `OR`.

  ```
  WHERE (NOT employee.hired) AND employee.hasStapler
  ```

- *Input parameters:* Identify the input parameters to an associated finder or select method by their positional number inside of the method and preceded by a `?`.

```
WHERE employee.income >= ?1 and employee.income <= ?2
```

- *Between expressions:* `BETWEEN` and `NOT BETWEEN` are used to indicate whether an identification variable falls within a range of values.

```
WHERE employee.yearsEmployed BETWEEN 10 AND 20
```

- *In expressions:* `IN` and `NOT IN` are used to indicate whether an identification variable is within a defined set of values.

```
WHERE employee.state NOT IN ('VA') AND employee.country IN ('USA')
```

- *Like expressions:* `LIKE` and `NOT LIKE` are used to indicate whether an identification variable matches a particular pattern using `%` to indicate any sequence of characters, _ to indicate a single character, and any other sequence of characters. An escape character used inside the pattern string is defined after the pattern string with the word `ESCAPE` preceding the escape character.

```
WHERE employee.email LIKE '%\_%@beeshirts.com' ESCAPE '\'
```

- *Null comparison expressions:* `IS NULL` and `IS NOT NULL` can be used to indicate null or not null values.

```
WHERE employee IS NOT NULL
```

- *Empty collection comparison expressions:* `IS EMPTY` and `IS NOT EMPTY` can be used to indicate whether a particular collection is empty.

```
WHERE employees IS NOT EMPTY
```

- *Collection member expressions:* `MEMBER OF` and `NOT MEMBER OF` can be used to indicate whether a particular element is a member of a collection.

```
WHERE employee MEMBER OF board.members
```

In addition to such operators and conditional expression elements, `WHERE` clauses can also make use of a set of built-in string and arithmetic functions as defined here:

- *Concatenation string function:* `CONCAT(String, String)` concatenates a `String` and returns a `String`.
- *Sub-string function:* `SUBSTRING(String, start, length)` returns the `String` starting at the `start` index of the input `String` up until the `length` of the input `String`.
- *Locate string function:* `LOCATE(String, String)` searches a `String` for a particular `String` value and returns the index of the located `String` as an `int` if found or `-1` if not.

- *Length string function:* `LENGTH(String)` returns the length of the input `String` as an `int`.
- *Absolute number function:* `ABS(number)` returns the absolute value of the input number (that is, `int`, `float`, or `double`) value.
- *Square root number function:* `SQRT(double)` returns the square root of the input value as a `double`.
- *Modulus number function:* `MOD(int, int)` returns the modulus of one `int` by another `int` and returns the resulting `int`.

EJB QL SELECT Clause

The EJB QL `SELECT` clause defines the scope of resultant information values and determines the return type from the query. Such queries must map to results from CMP entity bean finder or select methods. The `SELECT` clause contains an `OBJECT(singleValuedIdentifier)` operator when it wants to indicate that a particular domain of object types having the type associated with a single valued identifier is to be returned from the query. As an example fragment:

```
SELECT OBJECT(o) FROM Order AS o WHERE ...
```

The `SELECT` clause may instead contain a dereferenced single valued variable that maps to a single abstract schema type such as the following example fragment:

```
SELECT o.customer FROM Order AS o WHERE ...
```

The keyword `DISTINCT` is used after the `SELECT` keyword to indicate that the values returned from the query must be unique within the returned collection of values as exemplified here:

```
SELECT DISTINCT OBJECT(c) FROM Customer AS c WHERE ...
```

A series of built-in aggregate functions may also be applied to `SELECT` clauses associated with CMP entity bean `ejbSelectXXX(...)` methods. The following aggregate functions may be used inside of a `SELECT` clause:

- `COUNT()`: Returns the count of the results returned based on a variable passed into the `COUNT()` function.

  ```
  SELECT COUNT(i) FROM Order AS o, IN(o.items) AS i WHERE ...
  ```

- `AVG()`: Returns the average amount based on a persistent field variable having a numeric value.

  ```
  SELECT AVG(i.totalPrice) FROM Order AS o, IN(o.items) AS i WHERE ...
  ```

- `SUM()`: Returns the sum total amount based on a persistent field variable having a numeric value.

  ```
  SELECT SUM(i.totalPrice) FROM Order AS o, IN(o.items) AS i WHERE ...
  ```

- `MIN()`: Returns the minimum value based on a persistent field variable having an orderable nature such as numeric, string, character, and date types.

  ```
  SELECT MIN(i.totalPrice) FROM Order AS o, IN(o.items) AS i WHERE ...
  ```

- `MAX()`: Returns the maximum based on a persistent field variable having an orderable nature such as numeric, string, character, and date types.

  ```
  SELECT MAX(i.totalPrice) FROM Order AS o, IN(o.items) AS i WHERE ...
  ```

As you can see and as mentioned before, the type returned from a `SELECT` clause is an abstract schema type, persistent field type, or aggregate function value type. Such EJB QL types respectively map to CMP entity bean interface types, CMP entity bean persistent field types, or Java-equivalents for EJB QL aggregate functional return values (that is, numeric, string, character, or date types).

EJB QL `ORDER BY` Clause

The optional EJB QL `ORDER BY` clause can be used to indicate an order by which the resultant query values are returned. A persistent field variable is used with the `ORDER BY` clause to indicate a persistent field by which to order the result. For example:

```
SELECT OBJECT(i) FROM Order AS o, IN(o.items) AS i
➥ WHERE ... ORDER BY i.totalPrice
```

Although the default ordering is by ascending order, this may be made explicit by the `ASC` keyword as illustrated here:

```
SELECT OBJECT(i) FROM Order AS o, IN(o.items) AS i
➥ WHERE ... ORDER BY i.totalPrice ASC
```

One may also specify descending order by using the `DESC` keyword as illustrated here:

```
SELECT OBJECT(i) FROM Order AS o, IN(o.items) AS i
➥ WHERE ... ORDER BY i.totalPrice DESC
```

More than one ordering criterion may be specified as well, with ordering importance decreasing from left to right. For example, to order by descending total price and then by ascending quantity, we might have this:

```
SELECT OBJECT(i) FROM Order AS o, IN(o.items) AS i
➥ WHERE ... ORDER BY i.totalPrice DESC, i.quantity ASC
```

Entity Bean Configuration and Deployment

For the deployment of EJBs, we have already presented the basic top-level deployment descriptor in Chapter 24, "EJB Basics," and the session bean deployment descriptor elements in Chapter 25, "Session EJB." As we discussed, the root `<ejb-jar>` element contained an `<enterprise-beans>` element, which in turn contained a collection of `<session>` elements. In addition to `<session>` elements, the `<enterprise-beans>` element can also contain a collection of `<entity>` elements. Each `<entity>` element is used to describe the configuration and deployment of an individual entity bean. The <entity> bean element structure defines entity bean meta-data; a unique name in the EJB JAR file; the bean's class, interface, and primary key names; the type of entity bean; configuration parameters; references to other EJBs and database connections; security semantics; and elements to assist in the object-relational mapping for CMP entity beans.

Entity Bean (<entity>) Deployment Structure

As stated, the <entity> element serves as the top-level element to describe the deployment properties of a particular entity bean. Multiple <entity> elements can exist within the <enterprise-beans> element. The top-level structure of the <entity> element is described here:

- <entity>: Top-level element used to collect the following elements that describe an entity bean's deployment.
- Description group: A collection of optional description-related elements, including <description>, <display-name>, and <icon> (optional).
- <ejb-name>: Logical name for the entity bean.
- <home>: Fully qualified remote home interface name (optional).
- <remote>: Fully qualified remote interface name (optional).
- <local-home>: Fully qualified local home interface name (optional).
- <local>: Fully qualified local interface name (optional).
- <ejb-class>: Fully qualified EJB implementation class.
- <persistent-type>: Indicates whether this is a BMP or CMP entity bean: `Bean` or `Container`.
- <prim-key-class>: Fully qualified class name of the primary key class or `java.lang.Object` if class type is determined at deployment time.
- <reentrant>: Indicates whether the entity bean is reentrant: `true` or `false`. This element is described in more detail in Chapter 28.
- <cmp-version>: Indicates the version of CMP supported by this entity bean: 1.x or 2.x (optional). We of course focus on EJB v2.1 and thus 2.x-compliant CMP entity beans in this chapter.
- <abstract-schema-name>: Specifies a logical name for a CMP entity bean's abstract schema type as referenced in EJB QL statements (optional).
- <cmp-field>: Top-level element to describe a persistent field that is managed by the container for a CMP entity bean (zero or more).
- <primkey-field>: Name of the container-managed primary key field if the primary key maps to a single persistent field on the CMP entity bean (optional). The name begins with a lowercase letter and is the name to which "get" and "set" are prepended in the bean's primary key field accessors. If the primary key maps to

multiple fields on the CMP entity bean, then this element is not used and the standard rules for defining the primary key's fields as being public and matching the entity bean's fields apply.

- <env-entry>: Composed of <description>, <env-entry-name>, <env-entry-type>, and <env-entry-value> elements that contain configuration environment variables as described in Chapter 19 (zero or more).
- <ejb-ref>: Composed of information related to referencing remote EJBs by this EJB as described in Chapter 25 (zero or more).
- <ejb-local-ref>: Composed of information related to referencing local EJBs by this EJB as described in Chapter 25 (zero or more).
- <service-ref>: Composed of information related to referencing Web services by this EJB as described in Chapter 22 and Chapter 30 (zero or more).
- <resource-ref>: Used to define information used by the client to reference an external resource such as JDBC resource connection information as described earlier in this chapter (zero or more).
- <resource-env-ref>: Used to define information used by the client to reference a resource administered by the client's environment (zero or more). Sub-elements of this element are described in Chapter 29.
- <message-destination-ref>: Used to define information used by the client to reference a destination for an asynchronous message (zero or more). Sub-elements of this element are described in Chapter 27.
- <security-role-ref>: Used within the EJB to reference a particular secure role using a EJB security role-name (zero or more). Sub-elements of this element are described in Chapter 28.
- <security-identity>: Used to define how the security identity of the caller is used (optional). Sub-elements of this element are described in Chapter 28.
- <query>: A sequence of elements that map the finder and select methods defined on this CMP entity bean to their corresponding EJB QL statements implementing the methods (zero or more).

Persistent Field (<cmp-field>) Deployment

For CMP entity beans, additional elements inside of the <entity> element must also be defined in greater detail. The <cmp-field> elements within the <entity> element identifying the persistent fields in a CMP entity bean are defined here:

- <cmp-field>: Top-level element defined inside of an <entity> element to describe a persistent field that is managed by the container for that entity bean and using the elements that follow.
- <description>: Description of the container-managed persistent field (zero or more).

- `<field-name>`: Name of the container-managed persistent field. The name begins with a lowercase letter and is the name to which "get" and "set" are prepended in the bean's persistent field accessors.

EJB QL (`<query>`) Deployment

Also for a CMP entity bean, the queries that implement the functionality behind the finder and select methods must be defined. The `<query>` elements within the `<entity>` element accomplish this as detailed here:

- `<query>`: Top-level element defined inside of an `<entity>` element that maps a finder or select method defined on a CMP entity bean to its corresponding EJB QL statement that implements the method. Sub-elements of `<query>` follow here.
- `<description>`: Description of the container-managed persistent field (zero or more).
- `<query-method>`: Identifies a finder or select method on the associated CMP entity bean.
- `<result-type-mapping>`: Identifies whether an abstract schema type returned from a select query should be mapped to an EJB local or remote interface object: `Local` or `Remote` (optional).
- `<ejb-ql>`: Contains the specification of an EJB QL string.

EJB QL Method Identification (`<query-method>`) Deployment

The specific finder or select method associated with a query is identified by the `<query-method>` element as shown here:

- `<query-method>`: Top-level element defined inside of a `<query>` element that identifies a finder or select method on a CMP entity bean with sub-elements that follow.
- `<method-name>`: The name of a `find`*`XXX`*`(...)` or `ejbSelect`*`XXX`*`(...)` method associated with a CMP entity bean.
- `<method-params>`: Contains a sequence of zero or more `<method-param>` sub-elements, each of which defines the fully qualified class name or a primitive type of a parameter to a method.

Entity Bean Relationships (`<relationships>`) Deployment Structure

Recall also from Chapter 24 that a special `<relationships>` element was defined at the top-level beneath the `<ejb-jar>` element. This element is used with CMP entity beans to describe the various container-managed relationships among such beans. The `<relationship>` element is defined this way:

- <relationships>: Top-level element within the <ejb-jar> element used to describe relationships among CMP entity beans with sub-elements that follow.
- <description>: Description of the container-managed relationships (zero or more).
- <ejb-relation>: Describes the two roles involved with a relationship between two entity beans (one or more).

Specific Relationship (<ejb-relation>) Deployment

The identification of specific and individual EJB relationships is accomplished via the <ejb-relation> element within this <relationships> element as shown here:

- <ejb-relation>: Top-level element within the <relationships> element that describes the two roles involved with a relationship between two entity beans and identifies the entity beans as well as their behavior in such roles with sub-elements to follow.
- <description>: Describes this relationship between two entity beans (zero or more).
- <ejb-relation-name>: A logical name for the relationship unique within the associated EJB JAR file (optional).
- <ejb-relationship-role>: Identifies one end of a role within a relationship between two entity beans.
- <ejb-relationship-role>: Identifies the other end of a role within a relationship between two entity beans.

Specific EJB Role (<ejb-relationship-role>) Deployment

The identification of a specific entity bean involved in this particular EJB relationship and the role of the bean in that relationship is accomplished via the <ejb-relationship-role> element within the <ejb-relation> element:

- <ejb-relationship-role>: Top-level element within an <ejb-relation> element that identifies a role within a relationship between two entity beans with sub-elements that follow.
- <description>: Description of this relationship role (zero or more).
- <ejb-relationship-role-name>: Logical name for a role inside of a relationship (optional).
- <multiplicity>: Describes the multiplicity of the role in the relationship: One or Many.
- <cascade-delete/>: Empty element indicating that the lifetime of the entity beans for this role in the relationship are to be deleted if the entity bean in the other role of this relationship is deleted (optional). This element is valid only if the multiplicity of the other role in this relationship is One.

- `<relationship-role-source>`: Composed of zero or more `<description>` sub-elements and an `<ejb-name>` element that indicates the logical name of the entity bean associated with this role in the relationship.
- `<cmr-field>`: Describes a relationship field that is managed by the container for this entity bean (optional).

Relationship Field (`<cmr-field>`) Deployment

The specific field within an entity bean that is involved with a particular relationship is identified by the `<cmr-field>` element within the `<ejb-relationship-role>` element as shown here:

- `<cmr-field>`: Top-level element defined inside of an `<ejb-relationship-role>` element to describe a relationship field that is managed by the container for that entity bean and using the elements that follow.
- `<description>`: Description of the container-managed relationship field (zero or more).
- `<cmr-field-name>`: Name of the container-managed relationship field. The name begins with a lowercase letter and is the name to which "get" and "set" are prepended in the bean's relationship field accessors.
- `<cmr-field-type>`: Defines the fully qualified class name of the collection type used if this relationship field is a collection: `java.util.Collection` or `java.util.Set` (optional).

BMP Entity Bean Deployment Example

As an example of entity bean deployment, we first will take a look at the deployment of a BMP entity bean because it is simpler to deploy than CMP entity beans. As our example, we have selected the `ejb-jar.xml` file from the `ejava/ejb/session/creditmgr` directory as illustrated in Listing 26.13. Although this deployment descriptor is associated with the `CreditManagerEJBean` session bean in that directory, it also illustrates the deployment of the `CreditEJBean` BMP entity bean along with that session bean. You'll note that the `CreditEJBean` is deployed as a `Bean` inside the `<persistence-type>` element, indicating that it is a BMP entity bean. The `CreditEJBean` exposes its local interfaces via the `<local>` and `<local-home>` elements, and the `CreditManagerEJBean` references such interfaces from within its `<ejb-local-ref>` element. The `CreditEJBean` also defines its custom primary key class from within the `<prim-key-class>` element.

Listing 26.13 **BMP Entity Bean Deployment Descriptor Example (`ejava/ejb/session/creditmgr/ejb-jar.xml`)**

```
<?xml version="1.0" encoding="UTF-8"?>
<ejb-jar
  version="2.1"
  xmlns="http://java.sun.com/xml/ns/j2ee"
  xmlns:xsi="http://www.w3.org/2001/XMLSchema-instance"
  xsi:schemaLocation="http://java.sun.com/xml/ns/j2ee
                      http://java.sun.com/xml/ns/j2ee/ejb-jar_2_1.xsd">
  <enterprise-beans>
    <session>
      <description>Credit Manager EJB</description>
      <display-name>CreditManagerEJB</display-name>
      <ejb-name>CreditManagerEJB</ejb-name>
      <home>ejava.ejb.session.creditmgr.CreditManagerHome</home>
      <remote>ejava.ejb.session.creditmgr.CreditManager</remote>
      <ejb-class>
         ejava.ejb.session.creditmgr.CreditManagerEJBean
      </ejb-class>
      <session-type>Stateless</session-type>
      <transaction-type>Container</transaction-type>
      <env-entry>
        <env-entry-name>Handler</env-entry-name>
        <env-entry-type>java.lang.Boolean</env-entry-type>
        <env-entry-value>true</env-entry-value>
      </env-entry>
      <ejb-local-ref>
         <ejb-ref-name>ejb/credit</ejb-ref-name>
         <ejb-ref-type>Entity</ejb-ref-type>
         <local-home>
            ejava.ejb.entity.credit.CreditLocalHome
         </local-home>
         <local>ejava.ejb.entity.credit.CreditLocal</local>
         <ejb-link>CreditManager.jar#CreditEJB</ejb-link>
      </ejb-local-ref>
    </session>
    <entity>
      <description/>
      <display-name>CreditEJB</display-name>
      <ejb-name>CreditEJB</ejb-name>
      <local-home>ejava.ejb.entity.credit.CreditLocalHome</local-home>
      <local>ejava.ejb.entity.credit.CreditLocal</local>
      <ejb-class>ejava.ejb.entity.credit.CreditEJBean</ejb-class>
      <persistence-type>Bean</persistence-type>
      <prim-key-class>
          ejava.ejb.entity.credit.CreditPrimaryKey
```

Listing 26.13 **Continued**

```
      </prim-key-class>
      <reentrant>false</reentrant>
       <resource-ref>
         <res-ref-name>jdbc/ejavaPool</res-ref-name>
         <res-type>javax.sql.DataSource</res-type>
         <res-auth>Container</res-auth>
      </resource-ref>
    </entity>
  </enterprise-beans>
    ...
</ejb-jar>
```

As another point to note, the `CreditEJBean` also defines its reference to the database via the `<resource-ref>` element because the `CreditEJBean` is a BMP entity bean and must use JDBC directly. The `CreditEJBean` establishes a connection with the database when it invokes the `EJBHelper` class's `getDBConnection()` method as shown here:

```
public static Connection getDBConnection()
  throws SQLException, NamingException {
  // Create initial context
  InitialContext initialContext = new InitialContext();

  // Look up DataSource object
  DataSource dataSource =
    (DataSource) initialContext.lookup(
        EJBHelper.BEESHIRTS_DATA_SOURCE);

  // Request Connection object from pool managed by DataSource
  Connection connection = dataSource.getConnection();

  // Close context
  initialContext.close();

  // Return Connection object
  return connection;
}
```

The `EJBHelper` references the data source via the following `static String` mapping to the `<res-ref-name>` element in the deployment descriptor:

```
public static String BEESHIRTS_DATA_SOURCE
                     = "java:comp/env/jdbc/ejavaPool";
```

CMP Entity Bean Deployment Example

As you would expect, CMP entity bean deployment is a bit more involved. The `ejb-jar.xml` file in the `ejava/ejb/session/ordermgr` examples directory is associated with the `OrderManagerEJBean`. This session bean interacts with various CMP entity beans and provides a good example of how to deploy a lattice of CMP entity beans with various inter-relationships. Listing 26.14 only provides a few core snippets from that deployment descriptor because it is rather large and the intention here is to simply provide examples for the EJB QL and other CMP entity bean deployment discussions we've had throughout this book.

Listing 26.14 **CMP Entity Bean Deployment Descriptor Example (`ejava/ejb/session/ordermgr/ejb-jar.xml`)**

```
<?xml version="1.0" encoding="UTF-8"?>
<ejb-jar
  version="2.1"
  xmlns="http://java.sun.com/xml/ns/j2ee"
  xmlns:xsi="http://www.w3.org/2001/XMLSchema-instance"
  xsi:schemaLocation="http://java.sun.com/xml/ns/j2ee
                      http://java.sun.com/xml/ns/j2ee/ejb-jar_2_1.xsd">
   <display-name>OrderManagerEJB</display-name>
   <enterprise-beans>
      <entity>
         <display-name>CustomerEJB</display-name>
         <ejb-name>CustomerEJB</ejb-name>
         <local-home>
            ejava.ejb.entity.customer.CMRCustomerLocalHome
         </local-home>
         <local>ejava.ejb.entity.customer.CMRCustomerLocal</local>
         <ejb-class>
            ejava.ejb.entity.customer.CMRCustomerEJBean
         </ejb-class>
            ...
         <abstract-schema-name>Customer</abstract-schema-name>
            ...
      </entity>
      <entity>
         <display-name>TShirtEJB</display-name>
         <ejb-name>TShirtEJB</ejb-name>
         <local-home>
            ejava.ejb.entity.tshirt.CMRTShirtLocalHome
         </local-home>
         <local>ejava.ejb.entity.tshirt.CMRTShirtLocal</local>
         <ejb-class>ejava.ejb.entity.tshirt.CMRTShirtEJBean</ejb-class>
            ...
```

Listing 26.14 **Continued**

```
        <abstract-schema-name>TShirt</abstract-schema-name>
            ...
    </entity>
    <entity>
        <display-name>ItemEJB</display-name>
        <ejb-name>ItemEJB</ejb-name>
        <local-home>
            ejava.ejb.entity.item.CMRItemLocalHome
        </local-home>
        <local>ejava.ejb.entity.item.CMRItemLocal</local>
        <ejb-class>ejava.ejb.entity.item.CMRItemEJBean</ejb-class>
            ...
        <abstract-schema-name>Item</abstract-schema-name>
            ...
    </entity>
    <entity>
        <display-name>AuthenticationEJB</display-name>
        <ejb-name>AuthenticationEJB</ejb-name>
        <local-home>
            ejava.ejb.entity.authentication.AuthenticationLocalHome
        </local-home>
        <local>
            ejava.ejb.entity.authentication.AuthenticationLocal
        </local>
        <ejb-class>
            ejava.ejb.entity.authentication.AuthenticationEJBean
        </ejb-class>
            ...
        <abstract-schema-name>Authentication</abstract-schema-name>
            ...
    </entity>
    <entity>
        <display-name>OrderEJB</display-name>
        <ejb-name>OrderEJB</ejb-name>
        <local-home>
            ejava.ejb.entity.order.CMROrderLocalHome
        </local-home>
        <local>ejava.ejb.entity.order.CMROrderLocal</local>
        <ejb-class>ejava.ejb.entity.order.CMROrderEJBean</ejb-class>
        <persistence-type>Container</persistence-type>
        <prim-key-class>java.lang.Integer</prim-key-class>
         <reentrant>false</reentrant>
        <cmp-version>2.x</cmp-version>
        <abstract-schema-name>Order</abstract-schema-name>
        <cmp-field>
```

Listing 26.14 **Continued**

```
                <field-name>orderID</field-name>
            </cmp-field>
            <cmp-field>
                <field-name>customerID</field-name>
            </cmp-field>
            <cmp-field>
                <field-name>orderDate</field-name>
            </cmp-field>
            <cmp-field>
                <field-name>shippingInstructions</field-name>
            </cmp-field>
            <cmp-field>
                <field-name>shipDate</field-name>
            </cmp-field>
            <cmp-field>
                <field-name>shipWeight</field-name>
            </cmp-field>
            <cmp-field>
                <field-name>shipCharge</field-name>
            </cmp-field>
            <cmp-field>
                <field-name>paidDate</field-name>
            </cmp-field>
            <primkey-field>orderID</primkey-field>
            <query>
                <query-method>
                    <method-name>findByCustomerID</method-name>
                    <method-params>
                        <method-param>java.lang.Integer</method-param>
                    </method-params>
                </query-method>
                <ejb-ql>
                  <![CDATA[
                        SELECT OBJECT(o) FROM Order AS o
                          WHERE o.customer.customerID = ?1
                  ]]>
                </ejb-ql>
            </query>
            <query>
                <query-method>
                    <method-name>findAllOrdersInRange</method-name>
                    <method-params>
                        <method-param>double</method-param>
                        <method-param>double</method-param>
                    </method-params>
```

Listing 26.14 **Continued**

```
        </query-method>
        <ejb-ql>
          <![CDATA[
            SELECT DISTINCT OBJECT(o) FROM Order  o, IN(o.items) i
              WHERE i.totalPrice >=  ?1 AND i.totalPrice <= ?2
          ]]>
        </ejb-ql>
    </query>
    <query>
        <query-method>
           <method-name>ejbSelectItemsInAnOrder</method-name>
           <method-params>
              <method-param>java.lang.Integer</method-param>
           </method-params>
        </query-method>
        <ejb-ql>
          <![CDATA[
              SELECT OBJECT(i) FROM Order  o, IN(o.items) i
                WHERE o.orderID = ?1
          ]]>
        </ejb-ql>
    </query>
<query>
        <query-method>
           <method-name>ejbSelectOrdersOfACustomer</method-name>
           <method-params>
              <method-param>java.lang.Integer</method-param>
           </method-params>
        </query-method>
        <ejb-ql>
          <![CDATA[
              SELECT OBJECT(o) FROM Order AS o
                WHERE o.customer.customerID = ?1
          ]]>
        </ejb-ql>
    </query>
</entity>
<entity>
  <display-name>AddressEJB</display-name>
  <ejb-name>AddressEJB</ejb-name>
  <local-home>
     ejava.ejb.entity.address.CMRAddressLocalHome
  </local-home>
  <local>ejava.ejb.entity.address.CMRAddressLocal</local>
  <ejb-class>
```

Listing 26.14 **Continued**

```
        ejava.ejb.entity.address.CMRAddressEJBean
      </ejb-class>
        ...
      <abstract-schema-name>Address</abstract-schema-name>
        ...
    </entity>
    <session>
      <display-name>OrderManagerEJB</display-name>
      <ejb-name>OrderManagerEJB</ejb-name>
      <home>ejava.ejb.session.ordermgr.OrderManagerHome</home>
      <remote>ejava.ejb.session.ordermgr.OrderManager</remote>
      <ejb-class>
        ejava.ejb.session.ordermgr.OrderManagerEJBean
      </ejb-class>
      <session-type>Stateless</session-type>
      <transaction-type>Container</transaction-type>
      <ejb-local-ref>
        <ejb-ref-name>ejb/order</ejb-ref-name>
        <ejb-ref-type>Entity</ejb-ref-type>
        <local-home>
          ejava.ejb.entity.order.CMROrderLocalHome
        </local-home>
        <local>ejava.ejb.entity.order.CMROrderLocal</local>
        <ejb-link>OrderManager.jar#OrderEJB</ejb-link>
      </ejb-local-ref>
        ...
    </session>
  </enterprise-beans>
  <relationships>
      ...
    <ejb-relation>
      <ejb-relation-name>Customer-Order</ejb-relation-name>
      <ejb-relationship-role>
        <ejb-relationship-role-name>
          Customer-Has-Orders
        </ejb-relationship-role-name>
        <multiplicity>One</multiplicity>
        <relationship-role-source>
          <ejb-name>CustomerEJB</ejb-name>
        </relationship-role-source>
        <cmr-field>
          <cmr-field-name>orders</cmr-field-name>
          <cmr-field-type>java.util.Collection</cmr-field-type>
        </cmr-field>
      </ejb-relationship-role>
```

Listing 26.14 **Continued**

```
      <ejb-relationship-role>
        <ejb-relationship-role-name>
          Order-Belongs-to-A-Customer
        </ejb-relationship-role-name>
        <multiplicity>Many</multiplicity>
        <relationship-role-source>
          <ejb-name>OrderEJB</ejb-name>
        </relationship-role-source>
        <cmr-field>
          <cmr-field-name>customer</cmr-field-name>
        </cmr-field>
      </ejb-relationship-role>
    </ejb-relation>
    <ejb-relation>
      <ejb-relation-name>Order-Address</ejb-relation-name>
      <ejb-relationship-role>
        <ejb-relationship-role-name>
          Order-Has-Addresses
        </ejb-relationship-role-name>
        <multiplicity>One</multiplicity>
        <relationship-role-source>
          <ejb-name>OrderEJB</ejb-name>
        </relationship-role-source>
        <cmr-field>
          <cmr-field-name>addresses</cmr-field-name>
          <cmr-field-type>java.util.Collection</cmr-field-type>
        </cmr-field>
      </ejb-relationship-role>
      <ejb-relationship-role>
        <ejb-relationship-role-name>
          Address-Belongs-to-An-Order
        </ejb-relationship-role-name>
        <multiplicity>Many</multiplicity>
        <relationship-role-source>
          <ejb-name>AddressEJB</ejb-name>
        </relationship-role-source>
        <cmr-field>
          <cmr-field-name>order</cmr-field-name>
        </cmr-field>
      </ejb-relationship-role>
    </ejb-relation>
    <ejb-relation>
      <ejb-relation-name>Order-Item</ejb-relation-name>
      <ejb-relationship-role>
        <ejb-relationship-role-name>
```

Listing 26.14 **Continued**

```
            Order-Has-Items
          </ejb-relationship-role-name>
          <multiplicity>One</multiplicity>
          <relationship-role-source>
            <ejb-name>OrderEJB</ejb-name>
          </relationship-role-source>
          <cmr-field>
            <cmr-field-name>items</cmr-field-name>
            <cmr-field-type>java.util.Collection</cmr-field-type>
          </cmr-field>
        </ejb-relationship-role>
        <ejb-relationship-role>
          <ejb-relationship-role-name>
            Item-Belongs-to-An-Order
          </ejb-relationship-role-name>
          <multiplicity>Many</multiplicity>
          <relationship-role-source>
            <ejb-name>ItemEJB</ejb-name>
          </relationship-role-source>
          <cmr-field>
            <cmr-field-name>order</cmr-field-name>
          </cmr-field>
        </ejb-relationship-role>
      </ejb-relation>
    </relationships>
      ...
</ejb-jar>
```

Listing 26.14 fully lists the CMROrderEJBean CMP entity bean's (that is, <persistence-type> as Container) deployment descriptor elements and the salient elements of interest associated with the other CMP entity beans, as well as the OrderManagerEJBean session bean. The <abstract-schema-name> for this CMROrderEJBean is Order. As you can see, the various <query> elements that implement the finders and select methods on the CMROrderEJBean refer to such an abstract schema type name from within the EJB QL inside of the <ejb-ql> elements. The <cmp-field> elements defined for the CMROrderEJBean also factor into the EJB QL defined inside of the <ejb-ql> element definitions.

Listing 26.14 also provides a full listing of the <ejb-relation> elements that relate to the CMROrderEJBean. Such elements define the container-managed relationship structure of this bean with other entity beans. The multiplicities, related beans, field types, and field names are all defined inside of these elements. Such information enables the container to manage the CMROrderEJBean and the relationships in which it participates.

Vendor-Specific Entity Bean Deployment

Vendor-specific deployment descriptor files to configure and deploy entity beans inside a particular vendor's EJB container are also needed. As you might imagine, a significant amount of information is also provided inside of these deployment descriptors in order to map from generic J2EE deployment descriptor information to concrete server and database information. That is, while EJB QL, for example, defines the queries for finder and select methods in an abstract fashion, some means to map these abstract queries into concrete database queries (for example, SQL statements inside of JDBC calls) must be performed. Vendor-specific deployment descriptors and deployment tools must perform these mappings.

Developers will most often use GUI-based deployment tools provided by vendors to develop such mappings. However, vendor-specific deployment descriptor files for the J2EE reference implementation and the BEA WebLogic Server are included with the examples in this book. Appendix A describes how to configure such examples to be run inside each vendor-specific EJB container.

Conclusions

Although JDBC provides enterprise Java developers with an API that may be used to access a database, entity beans may be used to augment such capabilities by easily imbuing your enterprise application components with life-cycle and resource management services. As such, one of the most commonly utilized and critical aspects of building an enterprise system (that is, data access) can reap the benefits of added assurance and more rapid application development offered by implementing data access using entity beans. You can still use JDBC with BMP entity beans to perform such data access, but you must design your data access components in such a way that the EJB container can make entity bean callbacks onto that component to allow for better memory and database access management. CMP entity beans further enable rapid application development by leaving the actual implementation of database access calls to your EJB container. A CMP entity bean developer simply focuses on properly defining the interface contract for the entity bean to ensure that the container can implement database access functionality. The CMP entity developer, however, does have to do more work to define how such access is implemented by specifying additional configuration information and defining EJB QL statements inside of the bean's deployment descriptor or by using a vendor-supplied deployment tool.

27

Message-Driven EJB

THE EJBs THAT WE'VE EXAMINED THUS far have all required a synchronous communications interface between EJB client and server components. EJB v2.0 introduced support for asynchronous communications that allow an EJB component to expose itself as an asynchronous consumer of messages via the message-driven bean type. Whereas EJB v2.0 previously required all message-driven beans to expose themselves as JMS message receivers, EJB v2.1 now allows one to define a message-driven bean that can implement other messaging service paradigms as well. This chapter explores how to create message-driven beans and deploy them inside of EJB containers.

In this chapter, you will learn:

- The conceptual overview of message-driven beans
- The steps required for building server-side message-driven EJB components acting as message consumers
- The steps required for building clients acting as message producers to message-driven beans
- The basic approach for implementing timed message-driven bean components
- The steps required to configure and deploy message-driven beans

Message-Driven Bean Overview

Chapter 15, "Messaging Services with JMS and JAXM," explored messaging services as a means for passing messages between distributed applications in a reliable, asynchronous, loosely coupled, language-independent, platform-independent, and configurable fashion. Messaging services accomplish this task by encapsulating messages that are sent between a sender and a receiver, and by providing a software layer that sits between distributed messaging clients. A messaging service also provides an interface for messaging clients to use that isolates the underlying message service implementation so that heterogeneous clients can communicate using a programmer-friendly interface.

Chapter 15 explored the Java Message Service (JMS) v1.1 as a Java API that defines how messaging clients can interface with underlying messaging service providers in a standard fashion. Messaging consumers use the JMS API to asynchronously receive messages, and messaging producers use the JMS API to asynchronously send messages. Chapter 15 also explored the Java API for XML Messaging (JAXM) v1.1 as a Java API that defines how messaging producers and consumers can asynchronously send and receive XML- and SOAP-based messages in a Web services paradigm. Although J2EE v1.4 requires JMS v1.1, it does not require JAXM. Nevertheless, the EJB v2.1 specification gives consideration for how one might expose an EJB as a JMS, a JAXM, or another asynchronous messaging consumer type.

In the EJB v2.0 specification, a new type of EJB was defined that allows JMS message receivers to be implemented as EJBs. EJB v2.1 loosens this limitation and allows this new type of EJB to implement other messaging types as well. This new type of EJB is referred to as a message-driven EJB. A message-driven EJB simply implements an interface that allows the EJB to receive and process messages sent asynchronously by message producers.

Message producers to the message-driven bean are constructed in the same fashion as they would be if the message consumer was implemented in some other way. Thus, for example, the EJB client to a message-driven bean implemented using JMS may be implemented simply as a JMS message producer. Such message producers do not know that the consumer of the message is implemented as an EJB. With this new style of EJB implementation, EJB developers have a new means for EJBs to asynchronously receive messages. Such features open up your world to a whole new class of applications when you want to create business logic that must scale within an EJB container yet is loosely coupled to the client applications by a message-oriented middleware service.

Message-Driven Bean Components

Figure 27.1 depicts the basic architecture involved in creating message-driven bean components. At the top of the diagram, we have the `javax.ejb.EnterpriseBean` marker interface, which is the base interface for all EJBs. The `EnterpriseBean` interface is extended by the `javax.ejb.MessageDrivenBean` interface, which is required to be implemented by all message-driven bean classes. Public, nonfinal, and non-abstract message-driven beans, such as `MyMessageDrivenEJBean` as shown in the diagram, must ultimately implement the `MessageDrivenBean` interface. Message-driven bean implementations must have a public parameterless constructor and should not implement the `finalize()` method. Because a message-driven bean can be a subclass of some other class, if all of its required methods are not implemented by the message-driven bean implementation class itself, they must be implemented by one of the bean's superclasses.

Message-Driven Bean Generic Interfaces

The `setMessageDrivenContext()` method defined on a message-driven bean is used to pass an instance of a `MessageDrivenContext` object to the EJB. It is also the first method defined on the MessageDrivenBean interface that is called by the container. A MessageDrivenContext object encapsulates an interface to the EJB message-driven container context and thereby extends the EJBContext interface.

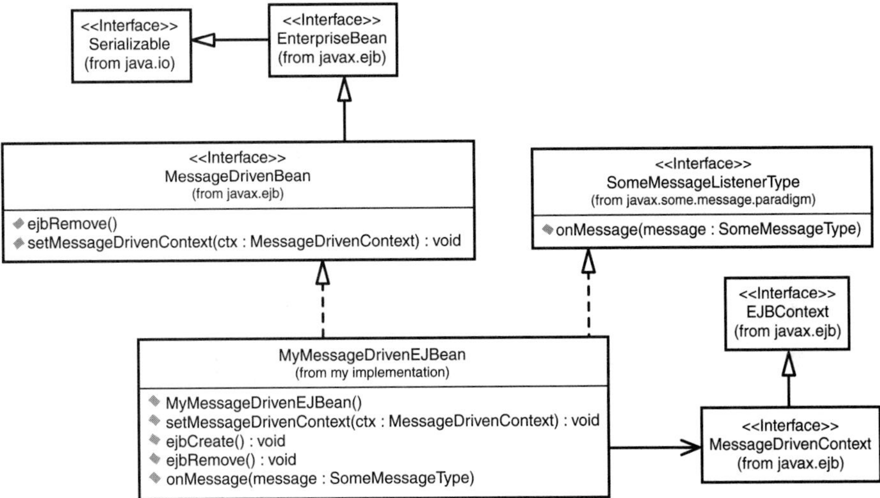

Figure 27.1 Message-driven EJBs.

One key operation that must be implemented by custom message-driven beans is the parameterless ejbCreate() method. This method is called by the EJB container when the container decides to create an instance of the message-driven bean. The container might decide to do this when it wants to create an initial pool of bean instances, or it might do this when it receives a client's request. Like EJB creation methods on other beans, the ejbCreate() method is akin to a special type of constructor or initialization method implemented by EJBs.

The ejbRemove() method is called by a container on a message-driven bean object when the container is about to decommission the bean instance from handling any more client requests. The container is solely responsible for determining when it will call ejbRemove() on a particular message-driven bean instance. It is not bound in any way to the EJB client. Be aware, however, that ejbRemove() is not guaranteed to be invoked by the container. Under normal operational circumstances, the container should call ejbRemove(), but when system exceptions are thrown from the message-driven bean implementation back to the container, there is no guarantee that ejbRemove() will be invoked. As such, the bean implementer must ensure that any resources allocated by the bean are periodically checked and cleaned up.

Message-Driven Bean Message Listening Interfaces

Unlike other EJBs, message-driven beans do not expose business-specific methods to a client; they are concerned only with adhering to those interface requirements of the EJB container and as required by some messaging paradigm specific interface. That is, message-driven beans must implement whatever interface is required by its messaging paradigm, such as implementing the example `SomeMessageListenerType` interface shown in Figure 27.1. As Figure 27.2 illustrates, these types will vary depending on whether the messaging listener is a JMS type, a one-way listener JAXM type, a request-response listener JAXM type, or perhaps some other messaging paradigm specific type.

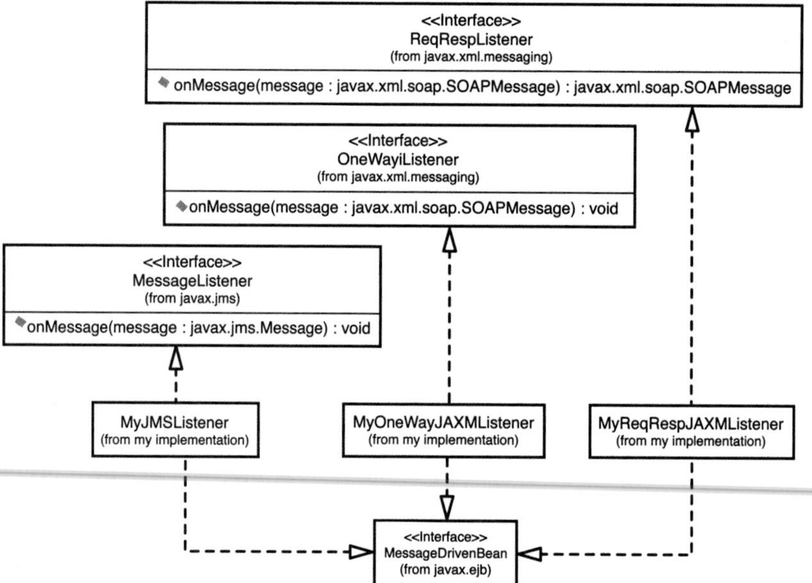

Figure 27.2 Message-driven EJB types.

Thus, for the case of JMS, a particular message-driven bean implementation must implement the `javax.jms.MessageListener` interface in addition to the `javax.ejb.MessageDrivenBean` interface. The business-specific functionality of the message-driven bean is implemented inside of the `onMessage()` method. The container invokes the `onMessage()` method when it receives a message asynchronously and passes it onto the message-driven bean implementation for handling. Thus, the message-driven bean developer simply implements the `onMessage()` method as he would for a JMS or JAXM messaging consumer.

EJB Messaging Paradigm Support

Although message-driven beans can support different messaging paradigm types, JMS is still by far the most widely used type for message-driven beans in EJB v2.1 containers. In fact, the EJB v2.1 specification is relatively undeveloped for consideration of how other non-JMS types of messaging services integrate with EJB containers. Nevertheless, the specification has made a first step in keeping the standard more open and flexible for future enhancements and vendor-supplied features.

Although the interfaces for JMS- and JAXM-based message-driven beans define only one method on their interfaces, the EJB v2.1 specification does not require that only one method be defined per messaging interface type. In fact, a particular messaging interface type may require more than one method with more than one argument per method to be implemented. In such cases, an underlying J2EE Connector Architecture resource adapter determines how these methods are invoked. We discuss the J2EE Connector Architecture in Chapter 29, "EJB Integration and Management."

Message-Driven Bean Component Interface Rules Summary

The life cycle of a message-driven bean is implied by the methods it must support. The life cycle of a message-driven bean as managed by its EJB container proceeds according to these basic general guidelines

1. *Instantiate EJB:* The container calls `Class.newInstance()` with the name of your EJB to create a new instance of the message-driven bean when the container decides it is necessary.
2. *Set Context:* The container calls `setMessageDrivenContext()` on the EJB with a container managed `MessageDrivenContext` object.
3. *Call* `ejbCreate()`*:* The container then calls `ejbCreate()` on the EJB.
4. *Add EJB to Pool:* The container may now add the EJB to a pool of message-driven beans.
5. *Delegate Message Handling:* The container hands off messages received asynchronously to a message-driven bean instance that it selects from a pool.
6. *Call* `ejbRemove()`*:* The container calls `ejbRemove()` on the EJB when the container wants to destroy the message-driven bean that sits in the pool.

Given that message-driven beans are stateless by design, they are also as simple to create as stateless session beans. An EJB applications developer needs to worry only about implementing the `MessageDrivenBean` interface, implementing an `ejbCreate()` method, and implementing the business-specific message handling method (for example, `onMessage()`). Message-driven bean implementations must simply receive a message via their business-specific message handling method and implement some functionality when that method is invoked.

EJB containers for message-driven beans take care of the actual bean's instance creation and destruction, as well as determining when to allocate the bean to a message handling event. The container ensures that a particular message-driven bean instance handles only one client request at a time. However, no guarantee is made that a particular sequence of messages will be handled in the proper order by the container for a series of message-driven beans.

Message-Driven Bean Example

Listing 27.1 provides an example of a basic message-driven bean that serves as a JMS listener. The `BatchOrderEJBean` uses the `ejbCreate()` method to implement a lookup to an `OrderManagerHome` interface. Recall from Chapter 25, "Session EJB," that the order manager stateless session bean provides a means to manage and create orders associated with the BeeShirts.com Web site. The `onMessage()` method of the `BatchOrderEJBean` in fact simply plucks an `Order` object from the received JMS message and delegates an order creation call to the order manager bean via its local EJB interface.

Note

All the sample code strewn throughout this chapter may be located as described in Appendix A, "Software Configuration," and is extracted beneath the `examples\src\ejava\ejb\mdb` directory. Note that this code depends on some of the code from Chapter 19, "Java Servlets," extracted to the `examples\src\ejava\servlets` directory; code from Chapter 25, "Session EJB," extracted to the `examples\src\ejava\ejb\session` subdirectories, `examples\src\ejava\ejb\timer` directory, and `examples\src\ejava\ejb` directory; and code from Chapter 26, "Entity EJB," extracted to the `examples\src\ejava\ejb\entity` directory. Appendix A describes how to build and deploy such code.

Listing 27.1 **Message-Driven Bean Example (`BatchOrderEJBean.java`)**

```
package ejava.ejb.mdb;
  ...
public class BatchOrderEJBean
  implements MessageDrivenBean, MessageListener {

  // Message-driven context
  private MessageDrivenContext messageDrivenContext;
  // Handle to the order manager home interface (local)
  private OrderManagerLocalHome orderManagerHome;

  /**
   * Standard ejbCreate() method. Simply print out a message
   * and look up a handle to a local order manager home
   * interface.
   */
  public void ejbCreate() {
    System.out.println("MDB: ejbCreate called");
```

Listing 27.1 **Continued**

```
    try {
      lookupOrderManagerHome();
    } catch (NamingException ne) {
      ne.printStackTrace();
    }
  }

  /**
   * Standard ejbRemove() method. Simply print out a message.
   */
  public void ejbRemove() {
    System.out.println("MDB: ejbRemove called");
  }

  /**
   * Standard setMessageDrivenContext() method. Simply print
   * out a message.
   */
  public void setMessageDrivenContext(MessageDrivenContext ctx) {
    System.out.println("MDB: setMessageDrivenContext called");
    this.messageDrivenContext = ctx;
  }

  /**
   * Receives an ObjectMessage, gets the order from the
   * JMS message, and then delegates the call to the
   * OrderManager session bean for creating the order.
   */
  public void onMessage(Message receivedMessage) {
    try {
      // If an object message is received...
      if (receivedMessage instanceof ObjectMessage) {
        ObjectMessage message = (ObjectMessage) receivedMessage;
        System.out.println("MDB: onMessage called");
        // Get the order from the message and create an order
        Order order = (Order) message.getObject();
        createAnOrder(order);
      } else {
        System.out.println(
          "This bean can consume only ObjectMessage types");
      }
    } catch (JMSException ex) {
      ex.printStackTrace();
    } catch (CreateException ce) {
      ce.printStackTrace();
```

Listing 27.1 **Continued**

```
      System.out.println("Failed to Create Order:");
    }
  }

  /**
   * This private method creates a new order object by
   * inducing the OrderManager session bean to create the order.
   */
  private Order createAnOrder(Order order) throws CreateException {
    System.out.println("creating order...");
    OrderManagerLocal orderManager = this.orderManagerHome.create();
    Integer newOrderID = orderManager.createNewOrder(order);
    order.setOrderID(newOrderID.intValue());
    System.out.println("Newly Created Order ID :" + newOrderID);
    return order;
  }

  /** Look up OrderManagerHome object */
  private void lookupOrderManagerHome() throws NamingException {
    if (orderManagerHome == null) {
      InitialContext context = new InitialContext();
      orderManagerHome =
        (OrderManagerLocalHome) context.lookup(
          EJBHelper.ORDER_MANAGER_REFNAME);
      context.close();
    }
  }
}
```

Message-Driven Bean Client Interfaces

Unlike other EJBs, the client of a message-driven bean does not interface with any EJB client APIs. In fact, the client of a message-driven bean does not know that an EJB will actually handle the message on the receiving end. Instead, a message-driven bean client is constructed as a messaging producer in whatever messaging paradigm is being used. For message-driven beans that implement JMS consumer behavior, the messaging producer is implemented as a JMS producer. For message-driven beans that implement JAXM consumer behavior, the messaging producer is implemented as a JAXM producer.

Because such messaging producers were covered in Chapter 15, we don't cover them here. However, we do provide a concrete example of a JMS client, shown in Listing 27.2, to the JMS-based message-driven bean shown in Listing 27.1. The JMS `BatchOrderClient` class's `main()` method takes a JMS connection factory name and JMS queue name as arguments and uses them to construct a `BatchOrderClient` instance. The `BatchOrderClient` constructor simply uses this information to look up a JMS connection factory and JMS queue that are ultimately used to create a JMS connection. The `main()` method then invokes the `writeMessage()` method to create an `Order` object associated with an `ObjectMessage` that is then sent to the JMS queue for delivery to the message-driven bean.

Listing 27.2 **Message-Driven Bean Client Example (`BatchOrderClient.java`)**

```
package ejava.ejb.mdb;
   ...
public class BatchOrderClient {
  // Client JMS producer interfaces
  private QueueConnection connection;
  private QueueSession requesterSession;
  private QueueSender requester;
  private Queue requesterQueue;

  /**
   * Client constructor does the following standard
   * operations for a JMS producer:
   *     - Get JNDI context
   *     - Look up JMS connection factory from JNDI
   *     - Create JMS connection
   *     - Create JMS session
   *     - Look up JMS queue name from JNDI
   *     - Create a JMS sender on the queue
   *     - Set local JMS producer variables
   *     - Start the JMS connection
   */
  public BatchOrderClient(
    String connectionFactoryName,
    String queueName)
    throws Exception {
    InitialContext context = new InitialContext();
    QueueConnectionFactory queueConnectionFactory =
      (QueueConnectionFactory) context.lookup(connectionFactoryName);
    QueueConnection connection =
      queueConnectionFactory.createQueueConnection();
    QueueSession requesterSession =
      connection.createQueueSession(false, Session.AUTO_ACKNOWLEDGE);
    Queue requesterQueue = (Queue) context.lookup(queueName);
    QueueSender requester =
      requesterSession.createSender(requesterQueue);
    set(connection, requesterSession, requester, requesterQueue);
    connection.start();
  }
```

Listing 27.2 **Continued**

```
/** Set local JMS producer variables */
private void set(
  QueueConnection connection,
  QueueSession senderSession,
  QueueSender sender,
  Queue senderQueue) {
  this.connection = connection;
  this.requesterSession = senderSession;
  this.requester = sender;
  this.requesterQueue = senderQueue;
}

/**
 * Create an ObjectMessage, create an Order,
 * set the Order onto the ObjectMessage, then
 * send the message over the JMS producer interface.
 */
protected void writeMessage() throws JMSException {
  // Create a Message
  ObjectMessage message = requesterSession.createObjectMessage();
  // Create an Order
  Order order = createNewOrder();
  // Set the message body
  message.setObject(order);
  System.out.println("Sending Order :");
  // Produce message
  this.requester.send(message);
}

/* Create an example order */
private Order createNewOrder() {
  Order order = new Order();
  // Order is created today and paid today and shipped today.
  order.setOrderDate(new Date());
  order.setPaidDate(new Date());
  order.setShippingInstructions("Leave at Door");
  order.setShipWeight(10.8);
  order.setShipCharge(32.54);
  order.setShipDate(new Date());
  // The customer info for the order is created
  Customer customer = new Customer();
  int aCustomerID = 101;
  customer.setCustomerID("" + aCustomerID);
  order.setCustomer(customer);
  order.setBillingAddress(createAnAddress());
  order.setShippingAddress(createAnAddress());
```

Listing 27.2 **Continued**

```
    order.setItems(createItems());
    return order;
  }

  /* Create an example address */
  private Address createAnAddress() {
    Address address = new Address();
    address.setAddress_1(" 2.1 EJB Way");
    address.setAddress_2(" 1");
    address.setCity(" J2EE ");
    address.setState("CA");
    address.setZipCode("14000");
    return address;
  }

  /* Create an example set of order items */
  private TShirt[] createItems() {
    TShirt itemOne = new TShirt();
    itemOne.setQuantity(2);
    itemOne.setTotalPrice(21.0);
    itemOne.setSize("XL");
    itemOne.setColor("White");
    itemOne.setUnitPrice(10.5);

    TShirt itemTwo = new TShirt();
    itemTwo.setQuantity(2);
    itemTwo.setTotalPrice(21.0);
    itemTwo.setSize("L");
    itemTwo.setColor("White");
    itemTwo.setUnitPrice(10.5);
    TShirt[] createdItems = { itemOne, itemTwo };
    return createdItems;
  }

  /**
   * Create a new client object with a JMS connection factory
   * name, and queue name passed in from the command line.
   *
   * Then write a message to the consumer after user hits
   * the "enter" key on the command line.
   */
  public static void main(String[] args) throws Exception {
    if (args.length < 1)
      System.out.println("Queue missing");
    BatchOrderClient sender = new BatchOrderClient(args[0], args[1]);
    BufferedReader commandLineReader =
```

Listing 27.2 **Continued**

```
      new java.io.BufferedReader(new InputStreamReader(System.in));
    sender.writeMessage();
  }
}
```

Timed Message-Driven Bean Objects

In Chapter 24, "EJB Basics," we introduced the new EJB timer service API. In Chapter 25, "Session EJB," we saw an example of a stateless session bean that implemented the `TimedObject` interface. Message-driven beans can also implement the `TimedObject` interface in the same way. In fact, the exact same APIs and behavior that a stateless session bean may tap and exhibit as a `TimedObject` may also be tapped and exhibited by a message-driven bean. Thus, a message-driven bean must simply implement the `TimedObject` interface and provide a concrete implementation for the `ejbTimeout()` method in addition to the other interfaces and methods it must implement.

The `ejava.ejb.timer.MessageTimerEJBean` class included with this chapter's examples provides an example of a message-driven bean implementing the `TimedObject` interface. The functionality of this bean is in fact identical to the functionality of the `ejava.ejb.timer.SessionTimerEJBean` presented in Listing 25.9 of Chapter 25. The primary difference is that the `MessageTimerEJBean` implements its timer reset functionality inside of its `onMessage()` method.

The basic structure of the `MessageTimerEJBean` is shown here:

```
package ejava.ejb.timer;

   ...

public class MessageTimerEJBean
  implements MessageDrivenBean, MessageListener, TimedObject {
      ...
  public void ejbRemove() {...}
  public void ejbCreate() {...}
  public void setMessageDrivenContext(MessageDrivenContext ctx) {...}

  public void ejbTimeout(Timer timer) {
     // Implement business-specific timed event handling
  }

  /**
   * Receives a TextMessage and resets the timer duration
   * passed via the message.
   */
  public void onMessage(Message receivedMessage) {
         ...
      TextMessage message = (TextMessage) receivedMessage;
```

```
        System.out.println("Received Duration :" + message.getText());
        long duration = Long.parseLong(message.getText());
        resetTimerDuration(duration);
            ...
    }
}
```

The `ejava.ejb.timer.MessageTimerClient` acts as a simple message producer to this bean akin to how the `ejava.ejb.timer.TestClient` acts as a client to the `ejava.ejb.timer.SessionTimerEJBean`. The `MessageTimerClient`, however, implements its timer reset request via a message produced from within its `writeMessage()` method as shown here:

```
protected void writeMessage() throws JMSException {
  // Create a Message
  TextMessage message = requesterSession.createTextMessage();
  // Create a message body
  message.setText("" + resetDuration);
  System.out.println("Sending Reset Duration :" + resetDuration);
  // Send the message using a QueueSender (requester variable)
  this.requester.send(message);
}
```

Message-Driven Bean Configuration and Deployment

We've already seen how session and entity beans can be deployed in this book thus far. An individual EJB's configuration and deployment is defined inside of a singular element containing sub-elements. The `<ejb-jar>` element contains an `<enterprise-beans>` element that contains a collection of elements, each of which defines the configuration and deployment of a particular EJB. Message-driven beans are no different. This section describes how to configure and deploy individual message-driven beans inside of an EJB v2.1 container.

Message Destination (`<message-destination>`) Deployment Structure

The first thing you might consider when working with message-driven beans, and for that matter any components that tap the features of a messaging service, is the `<assembly-descriptor>` element defined beneath the top-level `<ejb-jar>` element. This element is primarily used to describe security and transactional properties of the EJBs inside the EJB JAR file. However, a series of `<message-destination>` sub-elements of the `<assembly-descriptor>` may also be defined to deal with the messaging behavior of your EJB application. Zero or more `<message-destination>` elements occur within an `<assembly-descriptor>` element with its location relative to other `<assembly-descriptor>` sub-elements as illustrated here:

```
<ejb-jar>
  ...
  <assembly-descriptor>
     <security-role> ...0 or more... </security-role>
     <method-permission> ...0 or more... </method-permission>
     <container-transaction> ...0 or more... </container-transaction>
     <message-destination> ...0 or more... </message-destination>
     <exclude-list> ...0 or 1... </exclude-list>
  </assembly-descriptor>
  ...
</ejb-jar>
```

Each `<message-destination>` element identifies a logical messaging destination. This logical messaging destination information is then ultimately mapped to physical messaging destination information by vendor-specific deployment descriptors. Nevertheless, the `<message-destination>` element defines that standard information that may be used as a logical messaging destination reference by other standard deployment descriptor elements. The `<message-destination>` element and its sub-elements are defined here:

- `<message-destination>`: Identifies a logical messaging destination via the sub-elements that follow.
- Description group: A collection of optional description-related elements, including `<description>`, `display-name>`, and `<icon>` (optional).
- `<message-destination-name>`: Defines a logical name for a messaging destination that must be unique per this deployment descriptor file.

Message-Driven Bean (`<message-driven>`) Deployment Structure

Chapter 24, "EJB Basics," presented the top-level structure of an EJB application module deployment descriptor. The root `<ejb-jar>` element contained an `<enterprise-beans>` element, which could in turn contain a collection of `<message-driven>` elements. Each `<message-driven>` element is used to describe the configuration and deployment of an individual message-driven bean. The `<message-driven>` bean element deployment descriptor structure defines message-driven bean meta-data, a unique name of the bean, the bean's class name, configuration parameters, security semantics, transaction semantics, and identification of the particular messaging model implied by the bean. The top-level structure of the `<message-driven>` deployment descriptor element is defined here:

- `<message-driven>`: Top-level element used to collect the following elements that describe a message-driven bean's deployment.
- Description group: A collection of optional description-related elements including `<description>`, `<display-name>`, and `<icon>` (optional).

- `<ejb-name>`: Logical name for the message-driven bean.
- `<ejb-class>`: Fully qualified EJB implementation class.
- `<messaging-type>`: Indicates the messaging paradigm type used by specifying the fully qualified name of the message listener interface type (optional). The default type `javax.jms.MessageListener` is assumed if this element is not present.
- `<transaction-type>`: Indication of whether the EJB or the container manages this bean's transactions: `Bean` or `Container`.
- `<message-destination-type>`: Fully qualified interface type name for the type of messaging destination to which messages will be delivered and received by this bean, such as `javax.jms.Queue` or `javax.jms.Topic` (optional).
- `<message-destination-link>`: Specifies the name of the destination for which this bean acts as a consumer corresponding to a `<message-destination-name>` element either in the same EJB JAR file or in another file with the EJB JAR file name followed by a # prepended to the `<message-destination-name>` element value (optional).
- `<activation-config>`: Has sub-elements that specify a collection of configuration property name/value pairs that are specific to a particular messaging paradigm type (optional).
- `<env-entry>`: Composed of `<description>`, `<env-entry-name>`, `<env-entry-type>`, and `<env-entry-value>` elements that contain configuration environment variables as described in Chapter 19 (zero or more).
- `<ejb-ref>`: Composed of information related to referencing remote EJBs by this EJB as described in Chapter 25 (zero or more).
- `<ejb-local-ref>`: Composed of information related to referencing local EJBs by this EJB as described in Chapter 25 (zero or more).
- `<service-ref>`: Composed of information related to referencing Web services by this EJB as described in Chapter 22 and Chapter 30 (zero or more).
- `<resource-ref>`: Used to define information used by the bean to reference an external resource such as JDBC resource connection information as described in Chapter 26 (zero or more).
- `<resource-env-ref>`: Used to define information used by the bean to reference a resource administered by the bean's environment (zero or more). Sub-elements of this element are described in Chapter 29.
- `<message-destination-ref>`: Has sub-elements that define information used by this bean to reference a destination to which this bean sends asynchronous messages (zero or more).
- `<security-identity>`: Used to define how the security identity of the caller is used (optional). Sub-elements of this element are described in Chapter 28.

Messaging Configuration Property (`<activation-config>`) Deployment

Different messaging paradigms as well as different messaging services within those paradigms have different configuration parameters that may be set. For example, recall from Chapter 15, "Messaging Services with JMS and JAXM," that JMS had various ways in which the underlying service provider could be configured. The primary JMS configuration properties and corresponding description of values for message-driven beans are listed here (see Chapter 15 for details):

- `acknowledgeMode`: Indicates the JMS message acknowledgment mode for a bean as either `Auto-acknowledge` or `Dups-ok-acknowledge`.
- `messageSelector`: Defines criteria to filter which messages are received by the bean according to JMS message selector syntax.
- `destinationType`: Indicates whether the destination is a JMS `javax.jms.Queue` or `javax.jms.Topic` type.
- `subscriptionDurability`: Indicates the durability of a Topic destination type as either `Durable` or `NonDurable`.

Such configuration properties are defined as a set of name-value pairs inside of the message-driven bean's deployment descriptor. The `<activation-config>` sub-element of the `<message-driven>` element can define such properties as shown here:

- `<activation-config>`: Specifies a collection of configuration property name-value pairs that are specific to a particular messaging paradigm type according to the sub-elements that follow.
- `<description>`: Description of the activation configuration properties for this message-driven bean (zero or more).
- `<activation-config-property>`: A name-value pair contained within an `<activation-config-property-name>` sub-element and an `<activation-config-property-value>` sub-element pair that encapsulate a configuration property specific to the messaging paradigm being used (one or more). For example, as describe previously, JMS messaging types may define configuration properties with names such as `acknowledgeMode`, `messageSelector`, `destinationType`, and `subscriptionDurability` along with their corresponding values.

Messaging Destination Reference (`<message-destination-ref>`) Deployment

In addition to acting as a messaging consumer, message-driven beans may also act as a producer of messages to other asynchronous messaging consumers. In fact, session and entity beans can act as messaging producers as well. It is for this reason that all such EJB types allow for the definition of zero or more `<message-destination-ref>` elements within their outermost bean element (that is, within `<message-driven>`, `<session>`, or `<entity>` elements). The `<message-destination-ref>` elements describe a logical reference to a messaging destination to which any EJB type may produce messages. Additionally, message-driven beans can act as consumers of messages from such destinations. The `<message-destination-ref>` element is described here:

- `<message-destination-ref>`: Used to define information used by the client to reference a destination for an asynchronous message as defined by the subelements that follow.
- `<description>`: Description of the message destination references for this message-driven bean (zero or more).
- `<message-destination-ref-name>`: Defines a unique (to the local EJB JAR file) logical name that may be used to reference a messaging destination and as usually prepended with `java:comp/env/` when performing a JNDI lookup of this message destination reference.
- `<message-destination-type>`: Fully qualified interface type name for the type of messaging destination to which messages will be sent and/or received by the referencing component, such as `javax.jms.Queue` or `javax.jms.Topic`.
- `<message-destination-usage>`: Indicates whether this destination is to be used by the referencing component to consume messages, produce messages, or both consume and produce messages: `Consumes`, `Produces`, or `ConsumesProduces`.
- `<message-destination-link>`: Specifies the name of the destination for which this bean acts as a consumer and/or producer corresponding to a `<message-destination-name>` element either in the same EJB JAR file or in another file with the EJB JAR filename followed by a # prepended to the `<message-destination-name>` element value (optional).

Message-Driven Bean Deployment Example

As an example of a message-driven bean deployment descriptor, Listing 27.3 depicts the key elements associated with the deployment of the `BatchOrderEJBean` message-driven bean described in this chapter. Here we see that the bean indicates that it implements the `javax.jms.MessageListener` in the `<messaging-type>` element and thus indicates that it is a JMS message listener. The messaging destination type is a `javax.jms.Queue` as defined in the `<message-destination-type>` element. Because this message-driven bean delegates its calls to the `OrderManageEJBean`, it also must define an EJB reference to the local interfaces for such a bean.

Listing 27.3 **Message-Driven Bean Deployment Descriptor Example (`ejava/ejb/mdb/ejb-jar.xml`)**

```
<?xml version="1.0" encoding="UTF-8"?>
<ejb-jar
  version="2.1"
  xmlns="http://java.sun.com/xml/ns/j2ee"
```

Listing 27.3 **Continued**

```
  xmlns:xsi="http://www.w3.org/2001/XMLSchema-instance"
  xsi:schemaLocation="http://java.sun.com/xml/ns/j2ee
                     http://java.sun.com/xml/ns/j2ee/ejb-jar_2_1.xsd">
   <enterprise-beans>
      <message-driven>
         <ejb-name>BatchOrderEJB</ejb-name>
         <ejb-class>ejava.ejb.mdb.BatchOrderEJBean</ejb-class>
         <messaging-type>javax.jms.MessageListener</messaging-type>
         <transaction-type>Container</transaction-type>
         <message-destination-type>
            javax.jms.Queue
         </message-destination-type>
         <ejb-local-ref>
            <ejb-ref-name>ejb/ordermgr</ejb-ref-name>
            <ejb-ref-type>Session</ejb-ref-type>
            <local-home>
                ejava.ejb.session.ordermgr.OrderManagerLocalHome
            </local-home>
            <local>ejava.ejb.session.ordermgr.OrderManagerLocal</local>
            <ejb-link>BatchOrder.jar#OrderManagerEJB</ejb-link>
         </ejb-local-ref>
      </message-driven>
         ...
      <session>
         <display-name>OrderManagerEJB</display-name>
         <ejb-name>OrderManagerEJB</ejb-name>
         <local-home>
            ejava.ejb.session.ordermgr.OrderManagerLocalHome
         </local-home>
         <local>ejava.ejb.session.ordermgr.OrderManagerLocal</local>
         <ejb-class>
            ejava.ejb.session.ordermgr.OrderManagerEJBean
         </ejb-class>
         <session-type>Stateless</session-type>
             ...
      </session>
   </enterprise-beans>
         ...
</ejb-jar>
```

Vendor-Specific Message-Driven Bean Deployment

Vendor-specific deployment descriptor files are needed to bridge the gap between the many logical references defined in the standard `ejb-jar.xml` file and the physical references implemented by the vendor's EJB server. That is, for message-driven beans, a means must be provided to map the logical messaging destination names to names that are registered with the vendor's JNDI service that map to physical messaging destination object references. While most vendor offerings may allow you to manually create such files in a reasonably simple fashion, many vendors will also provide a GUI interface for you to construct such files. Nevertheless, vendor-specific deployment descriptor files for the J2EE reference implementation and the BEA WebLogic Server are included with the examples in this book. Appendix A describes how to configure such examples to be run inside each vendor-specific EJB container.

Conclusions

Message-driven beans provide a simple way to expose the services of an EJB as an asynchronous consumer of messages. Clients to such EJBs are implemented similarly as a client to a messaging service would be implemented. That is, if the message-driven bean is implemented as a JMS message consumer listener, then the client to that bean may be implemented as a JMS message producer. Such clients are simply JMS clients and have no knowledge of whether the message consumer is an EJB. Message-driven beans are deployed in a fashion not unlike how other EJB types are deployed. Message-driven beans thus provide a simple means to implement and deploy a scalable messaging service consumer application allowing the underlying EJB container and messaging service provider to manage the resources for such beans and thus further alleviate low-level development concerns of developers.

28

EJB Assurance Services

As discussed in Chapter 17, "Assurance and Security Services," when building enterprise systems, one must consider an infrastructure and approach not only for enabling rapid development but also imbued with systems assurance for scalability, reliability, maintainability, availability, and security. One of the primary reasons often espoused for using Enterprise JavaBeans (EJB) technology is the inherent and transparent benefits it provides for enhancing systems assurance. Despite the significance often ascribed to EJB assurance features, the consideration and proper utilization of such features is often overlooked or put on the back burner in favor of taking advantage of EJB's rapid development benefits and layering in new functionality. This chapter focuses on describing the specific EJB assurance features and how to leverage their use in constructing enterprise systems. Specifically, this chapter discusses EJB transactions, security, clustering, and other EJB features that can be used to infuse scalability, reliability, maintainability, availability, and security into enterprise systems built with EJB.

In this chapter, you will learn:

- How to define and utilize transactions with EJB.
- How to utilize J2EE EJB container features for building scalable and available EJB applications.
- How to utilize EJB security features for building secure EJB applications.
- How to utilize JAAS for building secure J2EE and EJB applications.

EJB Transactions

We explored a wide range of Java-related transaction management concepts and services in Chapter 14, "Transaction Services with JTA and JTS." Transactions are critical to ensure the reliability of your enterprise applications. Without atomicity, consistency, isolation, and durability (ACID) principles embodied by transactions, the reliability of your applications is tremendously affected.

Transaction services for EJB components are implemented within the confines of the EJB container/server environment. EJBs can use such services either declaratively or programmatically. Declarative transaction management (aka container-managed transaction demarcation) involves the specification of transaction attributes associated with EJBs via deployment descriptor parameters. Programmatic transaction management (aka bean-managed transaction demarcation) involves using JTA APIs to manage transactions associated with EJBs. This section describes the means for using transactions with EJBs according to both models of transaction demarcation, as well as general considerations for providing transactions for EJBs.

General EJB Transaction Considerations

A few general facts must be considered and absorbed before we describe how to use transactions with EJBs. For one, the basic model employed by transactions with EJBs is the flat transaction model as described in Chapter 14. Nested transactions are not specifically required to be supported by vendors but may be incorporated into a future EJB specification. In addition to the basic transaction model, a basic set of APIs must be supported. The JTA is required to be supported, but the JTS for interoperability between different application servers is not required to be supported. The J2EE connector transaction-related APIs, discussed in the next chapter, however, are required.

In general, when an EJB client invokes the services of an EJB via one of its interfaces, the EJB container intercepts such an invocation before it delegates the call to an appropriate EJB instance. The container first assesses what method call is being made on what bean. The container then assesses what transaction attributes apply to that method to determine the transactional behavior of the method. Depending on the transaction attribute, the container may suspend any transaction context passed from the client, propagate any transaction context passed from the client, create a new transaction context, throw any exceptions associated with improper transaction context propagation, or neither propagate nor define any transaction context.

The container will make sure transaction context is propagated appropriately to other beans within the same container environment as needed. The container may also propagate the context to other EJB containers or perhaps to other distributed application servers via JTS. The container will also interact with a resource manager and transaction manager to coordinate and synchronize with such resources to ensure that distributed transaction processing can occur effectively. Chapter 2, "Enterprise Data," discussed such transaction management as it applied to databases as resource managers, and Chapter 14, discussed such transaction management as it applies in general.

EJB Transaction Attributes

Chapter 14 also presented the core types of transaction attributes and their meaning. Figure 28.1 depicts the types of transaction attributes and how their specification affects the propagation of transaction context to an EJB instance. The transaction attribute types are listed, followed by an indication as to whether a transaction associated with that transaction attribute type must ultimately be associated with the bean instance. The three columns following such information in Figure 28.1 depict from what source the transaction context may be propagated (that is, client or container), as well as whether and how it propagates to the EJB instance. An arrow with a circle at its beginning indicates that the transaction must propagate from that source, whereas an arrow without such a circle indicates that it may optionally propagate from that source.

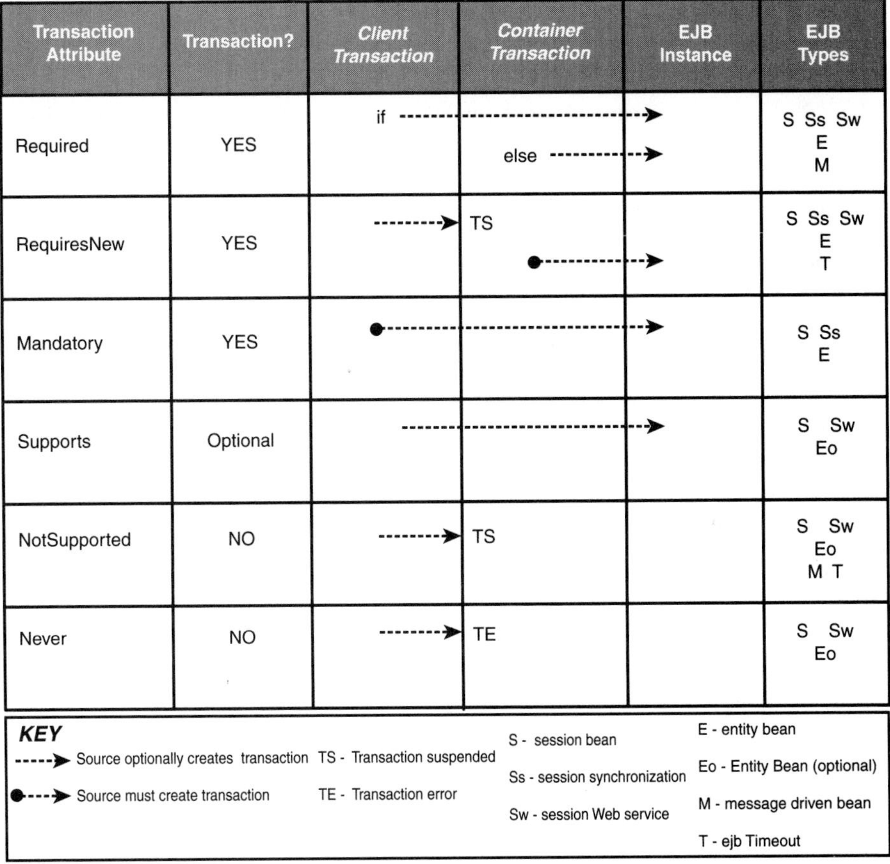

Transaction Attribute	Transaction?	Client Transaction	Container Transaction	EJB Instance	EJB Types
Required	YES	if	else		S Ss Sw E M
RequiresNew	YES		TS		S Ss Sw E T
Mandatory	YES				S Ss E
Supports	Optional				S Sw Eo
NotSupported	NO		TS		S Sw Eo M T
Never	NO		TE		S Sw Eo

Figure 28.1 EJB transaction attributes.

If the container stops a client's transaction from propagating, a "TS" indicates that it suspends the transaction and resumes that transaction after the bean instance method invocation returns. A "TE" indicates that the transaction is halted and an error condition is returned to the client. In such a case, the container will throw a `RemoteException` if the client is a remote EJB client or an `EJBException` if the client is a local client. If a transaction attribute is `Mandatory` and a transaction has not propagated from the client, then the container will throw a `TransactionRequiredException` to a remote client and a `TransactionRequiredLocalException` to a local client. Finally, Figure 28.1 also defines those EJB types (with identifiers mapping to the EJB types indicated in the figure's key) to which each transaction attribute may apply.

EJB Concurrency

As can be inferred from Figure 28.1, not all EJB types have the same transactional behavior ascribed to them. In fact, different bean types dictate how the container will process transactions for that bean, as well as how the container processes concurrent requests to such beans. This section describes these considerations in more detail.

Table 28.1 provides a mapping for the different concurrency scenarios that may be associated with an EJB and how transactions affect the behavior of the container in dealing with these scenarios. The primary two column groupings indicate what view is being considered for the concurrency scenario—that is, whether or not the view is from the EJB client or container's perspective.

Table 28.1 **Concurrent EJB Access**

	Concurrent Calls	Concurrent Calls at Server View	
Bean Type	**by Client View**	**Same Tx**	**Different Tx**
Stateless Session Beans	Incorrect to do	Impossible to happen	
Stateful Session Beans	Incorrect to do	Throw exception or Serialize access	
Entity Beans	Allowed to do	Non-reentrant-throw exception or Reentrant-program around	Create multiple instances or Serialize access
Message Driven Beans	Impossible to do	Impossible to happen	

Session Bean Concurrency

From an EJB client's perspective, if more than one client thread concurrently accesses a particular session bean's object interface, this is to be viewed as an application error. If the session bean is a stateless session bean, the client should simply use the bean's home interface to obtain a handle to a new object interface. If the session bean is a stateful session bean, this is generally regarded as an application error because the conversational state associated with the client by the server is supposed to be with respect to one client session.

From the container's perspective, the story is a little different. Here we have a situation in which a container receives a client request and must determine how to select and deliver that request to an EJB instance capable of handling the request. In the case of stateless session beans, a container will simply select an EJB from a pool of beans for that bean type and delegate the client request to that instance for handling. There is no concurrency issue because the container has complete control over which bean instance will service the request.

However, consider the case of a concurrent request on a stateful session bean instance from the server's perspective. Suppose first that a request comes in for a particular stateful session bean instance and the container will handle this by delegating the invocation to the appropriate bean instance as usual. Now suppose that another concurrent request comes in for the same bean instance before the existing method invocation has had a chance to service the request. In such a case, the container should generally throw a `RemoteException` if the client is a remote EJB client or an `EJBException` if the client is a local client. In some circumstances, the container may alternatively elect to handle both requests by serializing the request from the second client and allowing it to execute after the existing method invocation returns. This can lead to unpredictable behavior, however, and clients should not rely on this being offered by your EJB container.

Message-Driven Bean Concurrency

For message-driven beans, it is impossible for clients to reference the same bean's client view because the clients are message consumers that simply produce messages to a particular topic or queue. The messaging service and EJB container deal with the delivery of such messages. In the case of message-driven beans, from the container's point of view it will simply select a message-driven bean from a pool of beans to deliver the message to for handling. There is also no concurrency issue for message-driven beans because the container has complete control over which bean instance will service the request as it did for stateless session beans.

Entity Bean Concurrency with Different Transaction Contexts

For entity beans, it is actually quite natural for EJB clients to try to talk to the same entity bean view. For example, more than one EJB client may be attempting to access and update a particular user account entity bean. The EJB clients, however, obtain handles to such beans most often via the home interface for such beans.

For entity beans, the concurrency story is somewhat different from the container's perspective. If a concurrent request comes in for a particular entity bean instance and the requests are associated with different transaction contexts, the container generally is left with determining how to handle the situation. A container may serialize access to the bean instance or it may create multiple bean instances, one for each request. In the case of serialized access to the instance, the container generally will obtain an exclusive lock on the associated data in the database. With such an exclusive lock on the associated database data, the instance does not need to have its state synchronized with the database every time a new transaction begins and is associated with the instance.

In the case in which multiple bean instances are created to handle requests, the resource manager (that is, database) is left with the chore of synchronizing the concurrent access when such calls result in database access calls. The container may either return such instances to the pool or cache them in some way when the instances are finished with their transactions. In either case, when another transaction is begun and associated with such instances, the container must invoke `ejbLoad()` on the instances to load their state and ensure that they are in sync with the database. When such instances are being updated inside of a transaction, the container might acquire a temporary exclusive lock on the database while the instance's method under the transaction is being processed. This, of course, could lead to a deadlock situation if concurrent locks are sought by different transactions. Alternatively, the container can wait to update the database with any updates to the bean instance as the container attempts to commit the transaction. The situation to consider in this case, however, is that such an update at commit time may result in a rollback of the transaction.

Entity Bean Concurrency with the Same Transaction Context

In the case in which an entity bean instance is accessed concurrently by clients and the same transaction context is associated with both client requests, this generally is considered an application error. However, in some situations it may be allowed. Such situations are sometimes referred to as "loopback" calls. Loopback calls are best described via a simple illustration as shown in Figure 28.2. Here we see an EJB client that invokes a method `foo()` on some entity bean A's interface. This call is then delegated to the bean A's instance, which in turn invokes a method `bar()` on some other entity bean B's interface. That call is delegated to entity bean B's instance, which in turn calls some method `naboo()` on entity A's interface and is then delegated to that bean's instance. This situation, when occurring within the same transaction context, is referred to as a loopback call because entity bean A's instance has in effect been invoked twice within the same transaction.

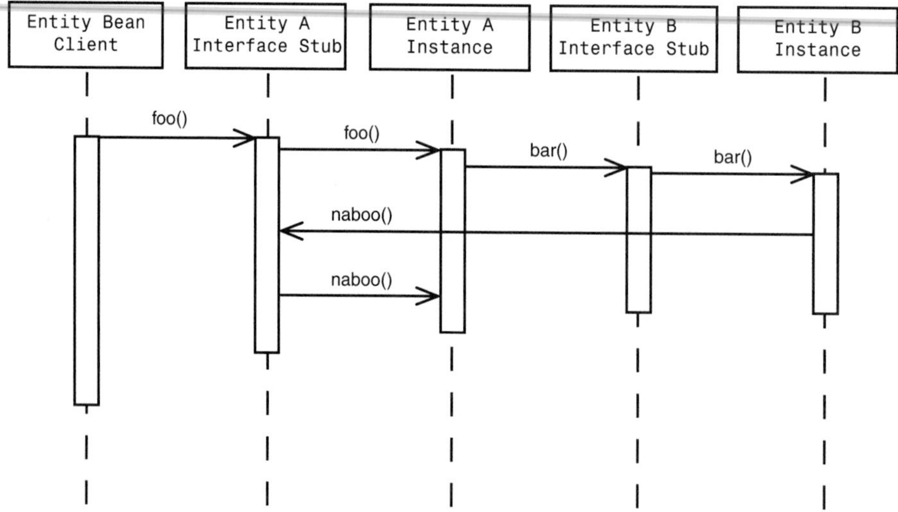

Figure 28.2 EJB loopback calls.

Such a scenario, of course, happens only by design of your entity beans. If you've designed your beans in such a way that this situation is possible, you must also consider designing your beans to allow for such behavior without affecting the integrity and correctness of processing. If you cannot create your beans to properly handle this situation, but the situation can indeed occur, then your entity bean is considered "nonreentrant." When an entity bean is nonreentrant and indicated as such to the container, the container will throw a `RemoteException` to remote clients and an `EJBException` to local clients attempting to access the same bean instance while it is still processing another method invocation invoked inside the same transaction. If you have been able to design your bean to handle such loopback calls, your bean is considered reentrant and you can indicate to the container that it may handle such situations as a reentrant bean.

If such concurrent requests to the same bean instance come from clients in different and external processes, the container may elect to throw a `RemoteException` to the client regardless of whether the bean is reentrant. Alternatively, an EJB container environment may attempt to handle such a distributed situation by creating one instance of the entity bean in one container process and routing all requests to that one instance, by creating the instance in multiple container processes but always calling `ejbLoad()` and `ejbStore()` at the beginning and end of each business method to ensure synchronicity of data, or by perhaps using a distributed lock manager on instances across the container environment.

Bean-Managed Transaction Demarcation

Only session beans and message-driven beans can take advantage of programmatic bean-managed transaction demarcation through the use of a `javax.transaction.UserTransaction` object, as well as through JDBC objects retrievable from the container environment. Entity beans must use container-managed demarcation, described in the next section. Session and message-driven beans must indicate their bean-managed as opposed to container-managed transaction demarcation preference via setting the `<transaction-type>` element inside of its `<session>` or `<message-driven>` EJB deployment descriptor to a value of `Bean` (as opposed to `Container`). Bean-managed transaction demarcation enables beans to explicitly indicate where a transaction must begin, commit, and potentially roll back via calls to `UserTransaction` from within their methods. EJBs can obtain handles to `UserTransaction` objects from the EJB container by calling `getUserTransaction()` on its `SessionContext` or `MessageDrivenContext` object (as inherited from `EJBContext`).

> **Note**
>
> This section contains a few simple code snippets that can be found beneath the `examples/src/ejava/ejb/transactions` directory for the code associated with this chapter located as described in Appendix A, "Software Configuration." Such code snippets are merely for purposes of illustrating various transaction management approaches and JTA API usage from within EJBs.

Alternatively, an EJB can also obtain a handle to a `UserTransaction` object from the EJB container via a JNDI lookup using the name `java:comp/UserTransaction` as shown here:

```
// Acquire handle to JNDI context from container environment
Context jndiCtx = new InitialContext();

// Look up UserTransaction from container environment
UserTransaction transaction
    = (UserTransaction) jndiCtx.lookup("java:comp/UserTransaction");
```

> **Tip**
>
> Despite what the EJB specification indicates, some vendor implementations may register the `UserTransaction` handle under a different JNDI name such as via the name `javax.transaction.UserTransaction`.

With a `UserTransaction` object in hand, calls to `begin()`, `commit()`, and `rollback()` can be used to programmatically demarcate transaction boundaries as you saw in Chapter 14. Between the boundaries of a `begin()` and `commit()`, all JDBC calls and calls to other resource managers that need to occur in an atomic, consistent, isolated, and durable fashion should be implemented. Given the flat transaction model required of EJBs, after a transaction is begun in such a fashion, another transaction should not be started until the current transaction is committed or rolled back. If an EJB client propagates a transaction to a bean-managed entity bean, the container will suspend the transaction and resume the transaction for the client only after the bean returns from its method call.

Furthermore, whereas stateful session beans can keep a transaction uncompleted across multiple calls on the same bean instance, stateless session beans and message-driven beans must commit or roll back the transaction before the bean method in which it was invoked returns from the call. Those EJBs implemented using the timer services (that is, `TimedObject` beans) must also begin and commit any transactions within the scope of their `ejbTimeout()` method calls. If a transaction is begun before a prior one has been completed, a `javax.transaction.NotSupportedException` must be thrown by the container. If a stateless session bean, message-driven bean, or `ejbTimeout()` method does not commit before its transactional method is returned, the container must discard the associated instance, log an error, roll back, and throw an exception (`RemoteException` or `EJBException`).

As described in Chapter 14, a transaction's isolation level defines how and when changes made to data within a transaction are visible to other applications accessing that data. Manipulating transaction isolation levels from within an EJB is specific to a particular resource manager. For JDBC, the transaction isolation level can be gotten and set with calls to a `java.sql.Connection` object via `getTransactionIsolation()` and `setTransactionIsolation()` calls, respectively. Recall from the earlier chapters that JDBC `Connection` objects are obtained from calls to `getConnection()` on `javax.sql.DataSource` objects, which are in turn retrieved from JNDI lookups using `<resource-ref>` defined names.

For example, we might attempt to demarcate transactions within a session bean that periodically handles resolving data between a BeeShirts.com orders database and a separate database used to store orders sent to suppliers as shown here:

```
public class MySessionEJBean implements SessionBean {
  private SessionContext ejbContext;
    ...
  public void setSessionContext(SessionContext aCtx) {
    ejbContext = aCtx;
  }

  public void resolveOrders(String supplierName) {

    // Get UserTransaction
    UserTransaction transaction = ejbContext.getUserTransaction();

    try {
      // Get context and data sources and connections
      InitialContext jndiCtx = new InitialContext();
      DataSource ordersDatabase =
        (DataSource) jndiCtx.lookup("java:comp/env/jdbc/Orders");
      DataSource suppliersDatabase =
        (DataSource) jndiCtx.lookup("java:comp/env/jdbc/Suppliers");
      Connection ordersConnection = ordersDatabase.getConnection();
      Connection suppliersConnection =
        suppliersDatabase.getConnection();

      // Possibly set isolation level for a connection
      suppliersConnection.setTransactionIsolation(
        Connection.TRANSACTION_READ_COMMITTED);

      // Begin transaction
      transaction.begin();

      // Do work...
      // 1) Create JDBC statements from connections.
      // 2) Do a bunch of JDBC update-related work on statements.

      // If error occurs while doing work...
      transaction.rollback();

      // Else if all is OK when done...end Transaction
      transaction.commit();
```

```
      // Close any connection and statements
    } catch (Exception e) {
      // Error occurred while doing work...
      try {
        transaction.rollback();
      } catch (SystemException se) {
        se.printStackTrace();
      }
      e.printStackTrace();
    }
  }
  ...
}
```

As an example of a stateful session bean that begins a transaction when an order is placed via one method and subsequently notifies the supplier in another method before the transaction is completed, we have the following:

```
public class MySessionEJBean implements SessionBean {
  private SessionContext ejbContext;
  private DataSource ordersDatabase = null;
  private DataSource suppliersDatabase = null;
  private Connection ordersConnection = null;
  private Connection suppliersConnection = null;

  public void setSessionContext(SessionContext aCtx) {
    ejbContext = aCtx;
  }

  public void placeOrder(String orderID, Object orderInfo) {
    // Get UserTransaction
    UserTransaction transaction = ejbContext.getUserTransaction();

    try {
      // Get context and data sources and connections
      InitialContext jndiCtx = new InitialContext();
      ordersDatabase =
        (DataSource) jndiCtx.lookup("java:comp/env/jdbc/Orders");
      ordersConnection = ordersDatabase.getConnection();

      // Begin transaction
      transaction.begin();

      // Do work...
      // 1) Create JDBC statements from connections.
      // 2) Update order database.
    } catch (Exception e) {
      // Error occurred while doing work...
```

```
      try {
        transaction.rollback();
      } catch (SystemException se) {
        se.printStackTrace();
      }
      e.printStackTrace();
    }
  }

  public void notifySupplier(String supplierName, String orderID) {
    // Get UserTransaction
    UserTransaction transaction = ejbContext.getUserTransaction();

    try {
      // Get context and data sources and connections
      InitialContext jndiCtx = new InitialContext();
      suppliersDatabase =
        (DataSource) jndiCtx.lookup("java:comp/env/jdbc/Suppliers");
      suppliersConnection = suppliersDatabase.getConnection();

      // Possibly set isolation level for a connection
      suppliersConnection.setTransactionIsolation(
        Connection.TRANSACTION_READ_COMMITTED);

      // Do work...
      // 1) Create JDBC statements from connections.
      // 2) Do a bunch of JDBC update-related work on
      //     order and suppliers database statements.

      // If error occurs while doing work...
      transaction.rollback();

      // Else if all is OK when done...end Transaction
      transaction.commit();

      // Close any connection and statements
    } catch (Exception e) {
      // Error occurred while doing work...
      try {
        transaction.rollback();
      } catch (SystemException se) {
        se.printStackTrace();
      }
      e.printStackTrace();
    }
  }
  ...
}
```

Container-Managed Transaction Demarcation

Session, entity, and message-driven beans can all take advantage of declarative container-managed transaction management services. Such services are automatically provided by the container environment based on information configured in the EJB's deployment descriptors. Container-managed transaction demarcation in fact is a requirement for entity beans. To use container-managed transactions, a session or message-driven bean must specify the value of `Container` in its `<transaction-type>` element within the `<session>` or `<message-driven>` element in an EJB deployment descriptor, but no such option even exists for entity beans.

Container Transaction Configuration (`<container-transaction>`)

The means by which a container determines how to demarcate transactions for a bean is via establishment of zero or more `<container-transaction>` elements within an `<assembly-descriptor>` element. Recall that this `<assembly-descriptor>` element can be optionally defined within the root `<ejb-jar>` element for an EJB module as discussed in Chapter 24, "EJB Basics." The top-level structure of the `<container-transaction>` element is defined as explained here:

- `<container-transaction>`: Associates a transaction attribute with one or more EJB methods with sub-elements that follow.
- `<description>`: Describes this transaction management specification (zero or more).
- `<method>`: Identifies particular method(s) for which this transaction management specification applies (one or more).
- `<trans-attribute>`: Specifies the transaction attribute for the method(s) on a particular EJB that are associated with this attribute. The valid types are `Required`, `RequiresNew`, `Mandatory`, `Supports`, `NotSupported`, and `Never`.

Method Deployment Configuration (`<method>`)

The `<method>` element is further decomposed to identify those methods to which the specification applies as shown here:

- `<method>`: Identifies particular method(s) for which a containing specification applies with sub-elements that follow.
- `<description>`: Describes the method identified by this `<method>` element (zero or more).
- `<ejb-name>`: Identifies the EJB name to which this specification applies.
- `<method-intf>`: Indicates the type of interface on the EJB to which this specification applies: `Home`, `Remote`, `LocalHome`, `Local`, or `ServiceEndpoint` (optional).
- `<method-name>`: Identifies the EJB method(s) to which this specification applies. If an asterisk (`*`) is used, this particular specification applies to all methods on the

EJB. If another container-transaction is specified for this EJB with a specific name, the properties specific to that method override those defined by an `*`.

- `<method-params>`: Used to specify fully qualified parameter types associated with an EJB method to which this specification applies (optional). Providing this information uniquely identifies a particular EJB method and overrides any generic specification for a particular group of overloaded methods or for the whole EJB. Contains one or more `<method-param>` elements that define the fully qualified type for a method parameter.

Thus, if an `*` is used for a method name, the element specification associated with this setting becomes the default for all methods associated with that bean. If a method name is provided, such a method name's associated element specification overrides the `*` setting and the element specification associated with this setting becomes the default for all methods of that name. If a method name and its fully qualified parameter types are defined, the associated element specification overrides any other settings for that method. The `<method-intf>` element is used in those cases in which a particular method and operation signature is identically defined on two or more of the bean's interfaces.

Methods identified by such elements have transactions managed for them by the container according to the specified transaction attribute type. A session bean using such declarative transaction specifications must have all of its business-specific remote interface methods associated with a particular transaction attribute. An entity bean needs both its business-specific remote interface methods and its home interface methods associated with a transaction attribute. A message-driven bean using such declarative transactions must have its messaging listener interface method associated with a particular transaction attribute. If no transaction attributes are specified for the EJB, such attributes must be defined either by default or manually at deployment time.

Container-Managed Demarcation Example

As an example, suppose that we've defined the following transaction-unaware bean for which we want to allow a container to manage transaction demarcation:

```
package ejava.ejb.transactions;

import javax.ejb.*;
import java.rmi.*;

public class MyEntityEJBean  implements EntityBean
{
  public void myMethod(){ /* Do something...*/  }
  public void myMethod(String foo){ /* Do something...*/ }
  public void myMethod(String foo, Object bar) {/* Do something...*/ }

  public void myOtherMethod(){ /* Do something...*/  }
  public void myOtherMethod(String foo){ /* Do something...*/ }
  ...
}
```

Now suppose that during assembly time, we decide the following about this bean's transaction semantics:

- All remote methods should have a `Required` transactional attribute by default. That is, the container will demarcate a transaction if the client does not.
- The remote `myMethod(String, Object)` method should have a `RequiresNew` transactional attribute associated with it. That is, the container will suspend any client transaction and create its own for the bean.
- Both remote `myOtherMethod()` methods should have a `Mandatory` transactional attribute associated with them. That is, the container will not demarcate transactions, but requires that the client does.

Given such transactional semantics, we might define our `ejb-jar.xml` file for this bean according to the basic structure shown here:

```
<?xml version="1.0" encoding="UTF-8"?>
<ejb-jar
  version="2.1"
  xmlns="http://java.sun.com/xml/ns/j2ee"
  xmlns:xsi="http://www.w3.org/2001/XMLSchema-instance"
  xsi:schemaLocation="http://java.sun.com/xml/ns/j2ee
  http://java.sun.com/xml/ns/j2ee/ejb-jar_2_1.xsd">
   ...
  <enterprise-beans>
     ...
    <entity>
      <description>Transaction-unaware Bean</description>
      <display-name>MyEntityEJBean</display-name>
      <ejb-name>MyEntityEJBean</ejb-name>
      <home>ejava.ejb.transactions.MyEntityHome</home>
      <remote>ejava.ejb.transactions.MyEntity</remote>
      <ejb-class>ejava.ejb.transactions.MyEntityEJBean</ejb-class>
      <persistence-type>Container</persistence-type>
      <prim-key-class>java.lang.String</prim-key-class>
      <reentrant>false</reentrant>
        ...
    </entity>
  </enterprise-beans>

  <assembly-descriptor>

    <container-transaction>
      <method>
        <description>
          Required transaction for all methods as default.
        </description>
```

```
      <ejb-name>MyEntityEJBean</ejb-name>
      <method-intf>Remote</method-intf>
      <method-name>*</method-name>
    </method>
    <trans-attribute>Required</trans-attribute>
  </container-transaction>

  <container-transaction>
    <method>
      <description>
        Require new transaction for myMethod(String, Object).
      </description>
      <ejb-name>MyEntityEJBean</ejb-name>
      <method-intf>Remote</method-intf>
      <method-name>myMethod</method-name>
      <method-params>
        <method-param>java.lang.String</method-param>
        <method-param>java.lang.Object</method-param>
      </method-params>
    </method>
    <trans-attribute>RequiresNew</trans-attribute>
  </container-transaction>

  <container-transaction>
    <method>
      <description>
        Mandatory transaction for myOtherMethod(...).
      </description>
      <ejb-name>MyEntityEJBean</ejb-name>
      <method-intf>Remote</method-intf>
      <method-name>myOtherMethod</method-name>
    </method>
    <trans-attribute>Mandatory</trans-attribute>
  </container-transaction>

 </assembly-descriptor>

</ejb-jar>
```

Interface Calls with Container-Managed Demarcation Beans

Although bean implementations should not attempt to perform any transaction demarcation or isolation setting themselves under container-managed demarcation, beans can call `getRollbackOnly()` and `setRollbackOnly()` on their `EJBContext` object. `EJBContext.setRollbackOnly()` is used to set the current transaction state such that it can only roll back and never commit. The `EJBContext.getRollbackOnly()`

method can be called to return a `boolean` value indicating whether such a state was already set. Setting a transaction to roll back is useful only to inform the container that an application error has occurred within the current transaction, and that the state of the system affected by this transaction should thus be considered invalid. The container will then roll back the transaction when it is appropriate.

Stateful session beans can also be made a tad more transaction aware when they implement the `javax.ejb.SessionSynchronization` interface as shown in Figure 25.2 of Chapter 25, "Session EJB." Stateful session beans that implement the `SessionSynchronization` interface's `afterBegin()`, `beforeCompletion()`, and `afterCompletion(boolean)` methods can be informed when the container has just begun a transaction, is about to complete a transaction, or has just completed the transaction with a `true` status if it committed, respectively.

Vendor-Specific Transaction Demarcation

On a final note, vendors will also define their own specific transaction semantics for EJBs. For example, the BEA WebLogic Server's `weblogic-ejb-jar.xml` deployment descriptor contains a `<transaction-descriptor>` element that contains a `<trans-timeout-seconds>` element to define the maximum time in seconds a transaction may exist between its beginning and completion. If this time expires before the transaction can be completed, the transaction will be rolled back.

Vendor-specific deployment descriptors may also define a transaction isolation level in a vendor-specific fashion. BEA WebLogic's `weblogic-ejb-jar.xml` deployment descriptor, in fact, defines such information inside of a `<transaction-isolation>` element according to the following basic structure with isolation levels defined as in Chapter 14:

```
<transaction-isolation>
 <isolation-level>TransactionSerializable</isolation-level>
    <method>
        <description>
           Describe the method to which this isolation
           level applies here.
        </description>
        <ejb-name>MyEntityEJBean</ejb-name>
        <method-intf>Remote</method-intf>
        <method-name>myMethod</method-name>
        <method-params>
          <method-param>java.lang.String</method-param>
          <method-param>java.lang.Object</method-param>
        </method-params>
    </method>
</transaction-isolation>
```

J2EE and EJB Availability and Scalability

EJB-based applications may represent large-scale enterprise applications encapsulating business logic and operations that are crucial to an enterprise's health, success, and growth. Chapter 17 discussed some of the reasons enterprise applications often need to be highly available and scale to meet the demands of users. EJB-based applications are where some of the more critical needs for scalability and availability are required. This section discusses just a few facets of this complex problem and how to apply solutions to EJB-based applications.

Redundant Server Overview

The core principle involved with providing highly scalable and highly available enterprise applications is the principle of redundancy. Redundant servers involve running more than one physical server instance in an operational environment. Redundant servers may be used for two primary purposes affecting the scalability and availability of your system:

- *Load Balancing:* Requests from clients may be distributed in some fashion across multiple server instances. This helps ensure that excessive client load doesn't reduce the throughput of your servers and thus affect availability by virtue of reduced capability to satisfy client demands.
- *Fail-over:* In the event of a failure of one server process, a means to fail-over to another server process is provided with minimal to no disruption to the client's session.

In J2EE environments, multiple types of objects may need to be made redundant in order to achieve the goals of load balancing and fail-over. These include J2EE components such as EJB, Java Servlet, and JSP components. These may also include J2EE resources such as JMS, JDBC, and distributed communication resource connections. The remainder of this section discusses load balancing and fail-over management generally in J2EE environments and then focuses on its more complicated application to EJB servers.

J2EE Clusters

Figure 28.3 depicts a basic redundant unit associated with J2EE servers. This unit is only one example of a J2EE cluster. A J2EE cluster, as we define it here, is basically a collection of physical servers that are aware of one another in some way such that they can expose themselves as a high-assurance platform used by distributed clients. Clients communicate with the servers as a unit and generally remain unaware of the fact that they are talking to a clustered server environment. From the client's perspective, they are communicating with a server process that just happens to rarely if ever "go down." As shown in the diagram, every candidate physical tier of the clustered environment is replicated and redundant. Any number of servers within each tier, of course, may be built out so that a particular tier could have two, three, or more servers. Furthermore, the diagram of Figure 28.3 simply intends to convey the core components of a highly available and scalable J2EE cluster. The services offered by each tier (to be discussed next) in fact may be collapsed and collocated within the same physical process.

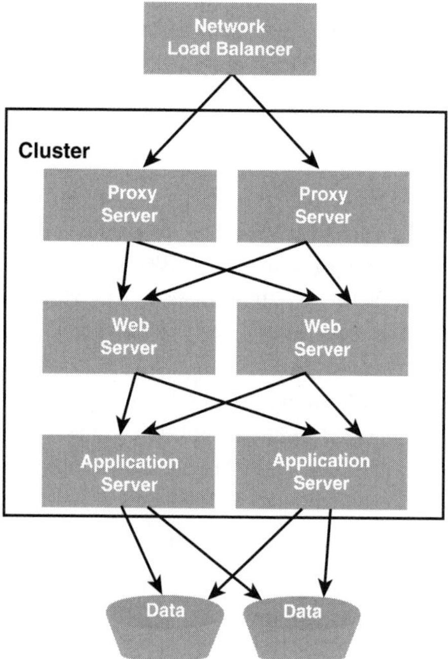

Figure 28.3 J2EE cluster.

J2EE EJB and Web Servers in a Cluster

Although it is not a requirement, physically separate J2EE Web server and EJB tiers may be employed by such a clustered architecture environment. In such a configuration, Java Servlets and JSP components run inside of Web server processes to expose themselves to Web clients, whereas EJBs run inside of application server processes to expose themselves to the Web tier and perhaps to thick clients operating inside the enterprise firewall. Such an approach provides demilitarized zones (DMZ) that keep access to the database secured behind the wall of the application server tier.

Proxy Servers in a Cluster

Additionally, a proxy tier may be provided inside of a J2EE cluster. These servers act as lightweight Web Servers whose primary function is to provide another DMZ and perhaps make use of a special plug-in to load balance across J2EE Web servers, as well as pin requests to particular servers. Such a plug-in may be needed to inform the proxy server how to read and recognize session and server information baked into URLs or cookies. The server identifiers baked into such URLs or cookies indicate which back-end Web server a particular request is to be routed to. If a request comes in and the proxy server reads the URL or cookie and understands that it should pin the request to a particular server, and that server happens to be down, then the proxy server will route the request to one of the backup servers perhaps identified in the request's URL or cookie.

Of course, a particular J2EE vendor's offering may also offer other configurations whereby proxy, Web, and application servers may be co-located as a collapsed redundant tier. Or the servers might be configured in such a way that they share all of their state with all other servers in their tier of the cluster. In such a way, a proxy server would not require any special plug-in to determine how to route a particular request in the event of a failure. Rather, the proxy server would be able to route the request to any Web server in the cluster because it can be assured that all servers in that cluster have shared their state and can act as a "hot" backup server for any client. The disadvantage of such a configuration, however, is that there would need to be increased communications overhead between the servers in a tier to ensure that all servers in that tier have replicated state of one another. In the situation in which the proxy servers use a special plug-in to read URLs and cookies, they are able to know which specific servers act as backups for other servers, and hence the need for replicated state across an entire cluster tier is not needed. Another approach would be to have the servers define one particular cluster policy indicating which servers act as backups for which servers and where to route requests in the event of failures as a general policy.

Network Load Balancers in a Cluster

Also depicted in Figure 28.3 is the concept of a network load-balancing mechanism. In high-assurance operational Web environments, a front-end means to balance incoming requests across multiple proxy servers may be employed. This is because proxy servers, though relatively simply servers, are still prone to failure due to the inherent complexity of processing software on a general computing platform. Hence, a hardware-based product that balances incoming requests across proxy servers may be employed. Many network load balancers operate by examining low-level source and destination IP address headers to determine how to allocate requests across servers.

In high-assurance operational Web environments, a single IP address is used to indicate the target address for a clustered server environment. The network load balancer is configured to map this address to the target proxy server addresses. The network load balancer then picks that server, rewrites the IP destination address header, and delivers the request to the selected proxy server. Any subsequent requests may be pinned to that selected proxy server based on the incoming IP address. If the proxy server fails, the IP load balancer may route the request to another proxy server. Alternatively, the IP load balancer may simply load balance requests indiscriminately across the bank of proxy servers without any session pinning.

One issue may arise if the incoming address is changed in mid-session for the client. This may happen if the client requests are coming through a particular ISP that happens to balance client sessions itself across different servers. Thus, for example, if a client request is coming through a particular ISP and its IP address (from the IP load balancer's perspective) is one value at one particular instant, the ISP may change that address and it then looks like another potentially new client session. Hence the network load balancer may send that request to a different proxy server. In the case of Figure 28.3, this is not a problem because the proxy servers simply use the information baked into URLs or cookies to determine how to route requests to the intended servers. When multiple clusters are used, however, a request may be routed by the IP load balancer to a server in a different cluster. Because it is presumed that redundancy communication between servers occurs only within the confines of a cluster, this would result in a lost client session.

Multiple J2EE Clusters

Multiple J2EE clusters may be needed in situations in which a site needs to operate at nearly 100% availability. In these scenarios, to update software on the server, to upgrade versions of Web and application servers, or perhaps to upgrade a database server in some way, particular servers may need to be brought down to perform these updates and upgrades. Multiple clusters can be used such that the sessions in one cluster are slowly "bled" from the servers by telling the network load balancer to stop allocating new requests to the proxy servers in one of the clusters. After all the sessions in that cluster are finished, the servers in that cluster may be shut down and upgraded. While this is occurring, the servers in the other cluster may be servicing requests.

As was indicated, network load balancers may route requests to different proxy servers if the incoming IP addresses change. Of course, if a different target address and port combination is received (such as the case when switching between secure and nonsecure ports), then the network load balancer may also route the request to a different proxy server. For one, session pinning must be supported by the network load balancer to even allow for this functionality to pin requests to particular proxy servers by the network load balancer. However, in the anomalous situations of changing source and destination addresses, the network load balancer can still route the requests to different servers in different clusters. Particular design approaches may be undertaken to resolve this situation. One might create a Web server plug-in or J2EE Web component handler that redirects the first request from a Web client back to a host name associated with the cluster as a whole. The network load balancer then routes requests to that host name to those proxy servers associated with that cluster.

J2EE Web Component Clustering

Clustering Web servers can be rather straightforward. After configuring any network load balancing and proxy tier servers, the J2EE Web servers run as they would in a standalone fashion, except for a few additional configuration parameters. The state that must be preserved in order to enable Web tier clustering is luckily largely localized to one general physical area: the HTTP session. Because of such localization and because most Web designs (at least those designed well) don't store a lot of information inside of HTTP session memory on the server, it is relatively easy to make such information redundant. This is often accomplished in one of two basic ways:

- *HTTP Session Backup:* Whenever state is written to an HTTP session object, at least one backup server for the Web server is communicated this state update. In the event of a failure, the backup server is used to host the client's session.
- *Persisted HTTP Sessions:* Whenever state is written to an HTTP session object, this state is persisted in some way. In the event of a failure, the persisted form of the session is read by a backup server.

The efficacy and performance of how such clustering occurs will be a function of your particular vendor's server and configuration options. For example, if your vendor requires that all servers in a tier be broadcast the session updates, this may be inefficient if your cluster architecture employs a large number of servers and hence requires an excessive amount of inter-server communications. If you use an approach whereby session information is persisted, you'll want to consider how such information is persisted and how often the information is persisted in order to assess whether an extraordinary amount of overhead will be involved with such operations. Regardless, the basic Web tier clustering options available to you, the different policy options and parameters for such clustering available to you, and your particular Web tier design all must be taken into consideration on a vendor-specific and design-specific basis.

J2EE EJB Clustering

Configuring servers to cluster on a Web tier is relatively straightforward compared to the options available to you in the application server tier. Because EJBs are often longer-lived and coarser-grained components than Web tier components, their operational demand is greater. This section discusses the basic options often available to a developer in vendor-provided EJB clustering environments. Not all options discussed in this section are available in all vendor EJB server configurations. This is because such features are not required by the J2EE or EJB standards. However, this section does aim to arm you with the most common features available and concepts involved so that you can more rapidly hone in on how to employ such features with your particular EJB application server.

General Design Considerations

In the event of a failure, the state that is contained by EJBs may be more likely to be preserved if the client also held that state or if it was persisted in some way. That is, when using value objects to pass information between EJB client and server, the client may have references to such value objects and utilize them to re-issue a request to another server in the event of a failure. If the state inside an EJB is persisted and a failure arises, the client may also re-issue a request to an EJB that can reconstruct its state prior to the failure.

Although such design guidelines are common sense, it doesn't really much help the developer who wants to assume that he's using a server environment that is highly assured in a fashion transparent to the client. Furthermore, the EJBs themselves must also be designed with such value object or state persistence logic in mind.

Cluster-Aware EJB Interface Stubs

When clustering EJBs, generally some form of special stubs needs to be used by EJB clients so that they know how to communicate with the clustered server environment. The stubs may be distinguished as to whether they are stubs for home interfaces or stubs for remote object interfaces. Because clustering functionality is implemented in a vendor-specific fashion, a vendor-specific tool must be provided to generate such cluster-aware stubs. Hence, EJB clients that communicate with clustered EJBs need to be provided with such stubs. Because EJB utilizes RMI underneath the hood, as discussed in Chapter 9, "RMI Communications," such stubs may be dynamically downloaded by the client. The EJB client does not need to be recompiled to work with such stubs because the standard EJB client interface may be used with a cluster-aware stub being referenced transparently to the EJB client.

Home interface stubs that are cluster-aware must contain information that is used to determine to which server in a cluster a particular home interface operation is to be directed. That is, when an EJB create, remove, finder, or home business method is invoked, a means for directing that request to an appropriate server in the cluster must be baked into the logic of the home interface stub.

For load-balancing purposes, the stub may be constructed to route a home interface request to a different server in the cluster according to a particular load-balancing policy baked into the stub. Vendors offering different policies for load balancing generally allow the specification of which load-balancing policy is to be employed on a per-EJB-type basis in a vendor-specific deployment descriptor. Of course, whether or not a particular home interface type is clusterable should also be configurable via vendor-specific deployment descriptors. If a vendor allows for an extensible way to define new load-balancing policies, a GUI interface may be provided or custom class extension mechanism may be provided that allows for you to specify your own parameters and algorithms used in the selection of a server used when load balancing. The more common load-balancing policies that may be provided to you or that you may build include the following:

- *Round robin:* Servers are selected one after the other in a cyclic list (for example, server-1, server-2, server-3, server-1, server-2,...).
- *Random:* Servers are selected on a random basis.
- *Weighting:* Servers are weighted according to how often they should receive requests according to a random selection distribution (for example, server-1 50% of the time, server-2 10% of the time, server-3 40% of the time).
- *Affinity:* Server selection preferences are determined according to whether the client already has a connection established with that server.

Home interface stubs that are aware of multiple servers in a cluster for load-balancing purposes may also use such information for fail-over purposes. Thus, if a particular server is attempted to be accessed via a home interface invocation and that server does not respond, the home interface stub may indicate that such a server has failed and direct the request to another server in the cluster. The stub may also be implemented to transparently request updated information from a server in a cluster regarding which servers have failed and which have come alive. This information may then be used to update the list of available servers to access inside the client's interface stub.

After a home interface is used to create an instance of an object on one of the servers in a cluster, a special remote object stub implementation associated with that EJB may also be returned to the EJB client. This cluster-aware remote interface stub can also be used for load-balancing and fail-over purposes. The particular nature of such is a function of a particular EJB type.

Clustered Session Beans

The interface stub for a stateless session bean can route requests to any server in the cluster. Different requests to the stateless session interface by the client can be routed to different servers in the cluster. This is because the state of a stateless session bean is not bound to a particular EJB client session. Of course, in addition to the load-balancing opportunity such an interface stub type allows, another server may be selected for a stateless session bean interface request if the original server to which a request was directed failed.

Stateful session beans must have their state preserved for a particular EJB client's session with the bean. The means by which such support is provided may be similar to that provided for HTTP session preservation with Web components. That is, a stateful session bean may be clustered this way:

- *Stateful Session Backup:* Whenever state is updated in a stateful session bean instance, one or more backup servers for the Web server are communicated this state update. In the event of a failure, the backup server is used to reconstruct a stateful server bean instance with this state.
- *Persisted Stateful Sessions:* Whenever state is updated in a stateful session bean instance, this state is persisted in some way. In the event of a failure, the persisted form of the stateful session bean's state is read by a backup server and used to reconstruct a new stateful session bean instance.

The decision for how and when to replicate the state to a backup session bean or storage is up to the EJB container vendor. Generally, after a transaction, state should be updated to the backup session bean state. For nontransactional calls, the state should be updated after a method invocation. In the rare event of a failure after primary state is updated but before backup state can be updated, or in the event of a failure of both primary and backup state preservation mechanisms, the integrity of a stateful session bean may be compromised.

Clustered Entity Beans

Entity beans have advantages in that their state is persisted to a database, transactional, and hence more easily reconstructed. EJB container vendors may allow you to configure the nature of entity bean clustering and persistence frequency with the database, however. The more common entity bean clustering policies include the following:

- *Read-Write Entity Beans*: An interface stub for the bean is pinned to a particular server containing the associated entity bean instance. The bean's `ejbLoad()` method is invoked to load the bean's state from the database before each transaction is begun and invoke the `ejbStore()` method to store the bean's state to the database on commit of a transaction.
- *Read-Only Entity Beans*: An interface stub for the bean load balances across entity bean instances in multiple servers across the cluster. Hence, the state associated with such beans is cached inside every server in the cluster.

EJB Idempotence

Although all such clustering approaches work well for fail-over situations whereby a failure occurs between method invocations, if a failure occurs during a method invocation, then special considerations must be made. If a bean is designed to be "idempotent," this essentially means that multiple method invocations can be made on the bean any number of times and not result in any updates made to persistent or cached state of the bean that affects the behavior of the application. You simply have to think about the case when a bean has one of its methods invoked more than once. If the two invocations affect the state of the system in such a way that would be different if the method were invoked only once, then the bean's method is not idempotent.

For example, in the case of a shopping cart, when we add items to the cart, clearly the methods to insert an item into the cart change the state of the system and hence multiple invocations are different than a single invocation. Thus, such a method is not idempotent. If a bean is a simple content browser that reads product items from the database, multiple invocations of the bean do not result in state updates, thus allowing us to classify such a bean's associated methods as idempotent.

Some vendors require that you indicate whether a particular bean is idempotent because that information will allow the container to manage how to fail-over in those situations in which a failure occurs during processing of a particular method. A vendor may also allow the specification of idempotence at the level of an entire bean and/or individual method level. In some cases during such failure types involving non-idempotent beans, nothing can be done and the EJB client simply needs to be made aware of the fact, perhaps via some exception to handle.

EJB Security

As with any distributed object used in security-critical enterprise applications, EJBs must be secured. However, EJB components operate inside of a container environment and rely on the container to provide distributed connectivity to an EJB, to create and destroy EJB instances, to passivate and activate EJB instances, to invoke business methods on EJBs, and to generally manage the life cycle of an EJB. Because such control is relinquished to an EJB container/server environment, securing the EJB also relies heavily on the support provided by the EJB container environment. Security mechanisms can be distinguished by standard mechanisms required by the J2EE and EJB specifications, mechanisms that are EJB container/server vendor-specific, and mechanisms that may be hand-coded by the EJB developer.

Figure 28.4 illustrates the basic architecture required for securing EJBs. Standard security mechanisms defined for EJBs are currently largely focused around providing a minimal set of constructs for role-based EJB access control. Standard mechanisms for determining role-based permissions to access EJB methods may be tapped by EJB components programmatically via a few interfaces to the EJB container context as exposed by the EJB API. Standard EJB method access control mechanisms can also be defined declaratively via a set of standard XML elements contained in a standard EJB deployment descriptor. Additionally, a few vendor-specific access control features are needed to support the mapping of security roles defined in standard deployment descriptors to principal identities managed by the operational environment.

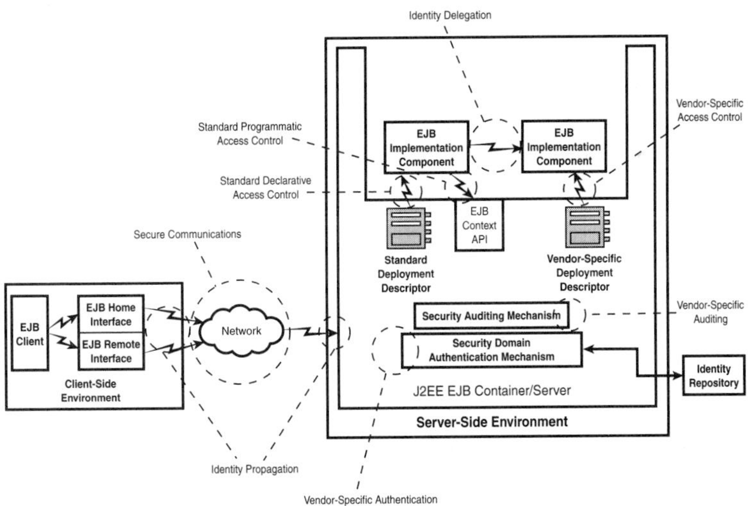

Figure 28.4 EJB security architecture.

Although a mechanism for authenticating a user is implied by virtue of the fact that a particular user must be granted access to a particular EJB method, no standard means for authenticating a user is explicitly required in the EJB v2.1 and the J2EE v1.4 specifications. However, the JAAS, now part of the underlying J2SE v1.4, represents the primary option for implementation of authentication in a standard fashion. Nevertheless, some form of identity propagation from client-to-server and principal authentication with an identity repository must be provided by an EJB container/server vendor for practical EJB enterprise security. The policy for delegating principal identity between EJBs must also be defined by an EJB container/server vendor. Furthermore, the security of the communications session between EJB client and server must be provided by a vendor in an interoperable fashion for practical enterprise deployment scenarios. Vendors may also provide a means for auditing security-critical EJB events.

Standard Programmatic EJB Access Controls

Although the programmatic implementation of security access control logic within EJB components is discouraged in favor of container-managed security features by the EJB specification, in many practical cases it may be inevitable. A minimal set of standard methods is provided by the EJB API to enable programmatic access control from within your EJB. As illustrated in Figure 28.5, two primary EJB hooks for obtaining security information from the EJB container environment are provided by the `javax.ejb.EJBContext` object (with two other EJB v1.0 methods deprecated). Other non–security-related `EJBContext` methods are not shown in this diagram. Note that message-driven beans are not shown in this diagram because message-driven beans do not have a client security context. The container in fact throws an `IllegalStateException` if a message-driven bean attempts to invoke the methods defined on the `EJBContext` shown in Figure 28.5.

A handle to an `EJBContext` object will be available to an EJB implementation object when the EJB container sets the context object onto a bean instance after the bean instance has been created by the container. For session bean implementations, such as `MySessionBean` shown in Figure 28.5, the EJB container will call `setSessionContext()` on the bean with a `javax.ejb.SessionContext` object. For entity bean implementations, such as `MyEntityBean` shown in Figure 28.5, the EJB container will call `setEntityContext()` on the bean with a `javax.ejb.EntityContext` object. After a context is set onto a bean, security-related calls to the `EJBContext` object are callable only from within the context of a business-specific method on the EJB. Otherwise, a `java.lang.IllegalStateException` will be thrown by the container to indicate that no security context exists.

The `EJBContext.getCallerPrincipal()` method is invoked by an EJB to obtain a handle to a `java.security.Principal` object. The `Principal` represents the particular principal identity on behalf of which the invoking EJB client is acting. A call to `Principal.getName()` by the bean can return a `String` object that can be used for business-specific security checking logic decision making. The deprecated `EJBContext.getCallerIdentity()` method may still be supported by your container, but a vendor may choose to throw an exception or return `null` from this method.

The `EJBContext.isCallerInRole(String)` method is used to ask the EJB environment whether the current principal associated with this security context is a member of the role passed in as a `String` to this method. A `boolean` return value indicates whether the caller is indeed in this role. The deprecated `EJBContext.isCallerInRole(Identity)` method may still be supported by your container, but a vendor may choose to throw an exception from this method.

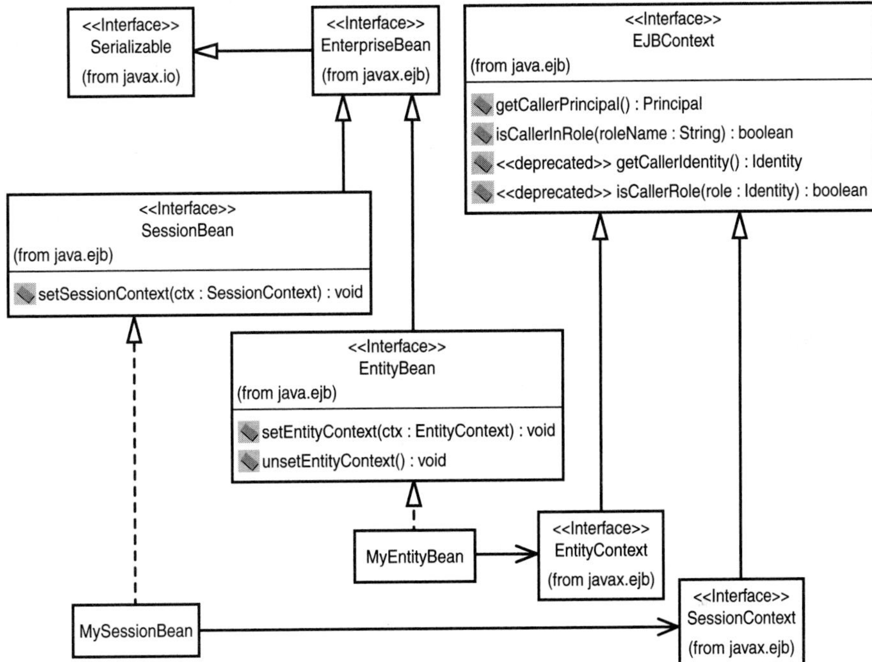

Figure 28.5 EJB security APIs.

> **Note**
>
> This section contains a few simple code snippets as well as working example code that can be found beneath the `examples/src/ejava/ejb/security/basic` directory for the code associated with this chapter and located as described in Appendix A. Note that the examples in that directory related to bean-managed programmatic security are simply snippets used for illustrative purposes in the text that follows. The examples related to container-managed declarative security for this chapter are working code examples integrated with the EJB code of Chapter 25 (and that chapter's dependent code). Hence, you will need the code from Chapters 19, 25, and 26 to run this chapter's declarative security examples.

As an example, the `SecureOrderManagerEJBean` class of Listing 28.1 extends the `ejava.ejb.session.ordermgr.OrderManagerEJBean` discussed throughout our EJB examples in previous chapters. Here we see that the

SecureOrderManagerEJBean overrides the queryOrders() method to perform programmatic security checking before it allows the client to invoke the method.

Listing 28.1 **Programmatic EJB Access Control (SecureOrderManagerEJBean.java)**

```
package ejava.ejb.security.basic;
   ...
public class SecureOrderManagerEJBean extends OrderManagerEJBean {

  /**
   * Get customer username (i.e., email) based on customer ID
   */
  private String getUserName(int customerID){
    String userName = "";
    try{
      CustomerLocal customer
        = getCustomerHome().findByPrimaryKey(new Integer(customerID));
      userName = customer.getEmail();
    }catch(Exception e){
      System.out.println("Username not found " + e.getMessage());
    }
    return userName;
  }

  /**
   * Query for the orders in the DBMS and return them.
   */
  public Vector queryOrders(int customerID) {
    Vector orders = null;
    try {
      // Get a username associated with this customer ID
      String customerUserName = this.getUserName(customerID);

      // Get the EJB context for this bean
      EJBContext ejbContext = this.getSessionContext();

      // Get principal from context and principal name
      java.security.Principal caller = ejbContext.getCallerPrincipal();
      String callerUserName = caller.getName();

      // If not in manager role and not the user associated with
      //   this order, then deny access...
      if ((ejbContext.isCallerInRole("manager") == true)
        || (callerUserName.equalsIgnoreCase(customerUserName))) {
```

Listing 28.1 **Continued**

```
        // Allow access to do security-critical stuff here...
        //    ...which in this case is to call superclass method
        orders = super.queryOrders(customerID);
      } else {
        // Access denied. Audit this event and return...
        System.out.println("**** ILLEGAL ACCESS ATTEMPT ****"
                         + "\n  OrderManager.queryOrders(int)"
                         + "\n  Caller Name; " + callerUserName
                         + "\n  Customer Name " + customerUserName);
      }
    } catch (Exception e) {
      e.printStackTrace();
    }
    return orders;
  }
}
```

The `queryOrders()` method first looks up a username for a given customer ID which essentially returns the email address for that customer used as the customer's username. Calls to the `EJBContext` security methods are then performed to retrieve the username for the user attempting to call this bean's method. If the caller username matches the username for the customer whose order is being examined, or if the caller is in the `manager` role, then the superclass's unprotected `queryOrders()` method is invoked. Otherwise, the event is audited as a security-critical event.

EJB Security Role References (`<security-role-ref>`)

Whenever a call to `EJBContext.isCallerInRole()` is made from within EJB code, an associated `<security-role-ref>` should be identified in the EJB's standard deployment descriptor for that bean. The `<security-role-ref>` element is defined within an `<entity>` element for entity beans and within a `<session>` element for session beans. The `<security-role-ref>` element has the following definition:

- `<security-role-ref>`: Identifies a security role reference for the containing EJB with sub-elements that follow.
- `<description>`: Describes this security role reference (zero or more).
- `<role-name>`: Identifies a logical role name that this EJB uses.
- `<role-link>`: References a role defined in a `<security-role>` element.

As an example, if we have defined a standard `ejb-jar.xml` file for our `SecureOrderManagerEJBean` session bean that implements the `queryOrders()` method as defined in Listing 28.1, then we would want to define a `<security-role-ref>` entry for the referenced `Managers` role as illustrated in Listing 28.2.

Listing 28.2 **EJB Security Role Reference**

```
<ejb-jar...>
   ...
  <enterprise-beans>
   <session>
     <display-name>SecureOrderManagerEJB</display-name>
     <ejb-name>SecureOrderManagerEJB</ejb-name>
     <home>ejava.ejb.session.ordermgr.OrderManagerHome</home>
     <remote>ejava.ejb.session.ordermgr.OrderManager</remote>
     <ejb-class>
         ejava.ejb.security.basic.SecureOrderManagerEJBean
     </ejb-class>
     <session-type>Stateless</session-type>
        ...
     <security-role-ref>
        <description>This bean references Managers role.</description>
        <role-name>manager</role-name>
      </security-role-ref>
   </session>
  </enterprise-beans>
    ...
</ejb-jar>
```

It is the responsibility of EJB developers to define in a deployment descriptor those security roles that their EJB implementations programmatically reference. However, it is up to the EJB assembler and deployer to map such roles to security roles and users in the operational deployment environment. The next section illustrates how such a mapping occurs in the context of standard declarative EJB access controls.

Standard Declarative EJB Access Controls

Standard declarative EJB access control mechanisms are defined as XML elements in the standard EJB deployment descriptor file. In addition to the `<role-name>` element, a `<role-link>` element may also be defined within an EJB's `<security-role-ref>` element. This element value is defined during EJB assembly to reference a role name specified by an individual (that is, EJB assembler) cognizant of the security roles assumed by a particular deployment environment. Thus, an EJB assembler might modify the standard `ejb-jar.xml` file to map a programmatic role name identified by the `<role-name>` element to an assembly-specific role name identified by a `<role-link>` element.

As an example, our `SecureOrderManagerEJBean` bean's deployment descriptor may be modified to incorporate an assembly-specific `<role-link>` element as illustrated in Listing 28.3.

> **Note**
>
> Because Listing 28.2 and Listing 28.3 are simply illustrative examples, the actual example deployment descriptor is named `ejb-jar-bean.xml` in the `examples/src/ejava/ejb/security/basic` directory.

Listing 28.3 **EJB Security Role Reference with Role Link** (`ejb-jar-bean.xml`)

```
<ejb-jar...>
   ...
  <enterprise-beans>
   <session>
     <display-name>SecureOrderManagerEJB</display-name>
     <ejb-name>SecureOrderManagerEJB</ejb-name>
        ...
     <security-role-ref>
        <description>This bean references Managers role.</description>
        <role-name>manager</role-name>
        <role-link>Managers</role-link>
      </security-role-ref>
   </session>
  </enterprise-beans>
     ...
</ejb-jar>
```

EJB Security Role Declarations (`<security-role>`)

The `<role-link>` element within an EJB's `<security-role-ref>` element may be defined during EJB assembly to refer to a `<role-name>` defined within a particular `<security-role>` element. All logical security roles defined for a particular EJB module are identified by `<security-role>` elements that sit within an `<assembly-descriptor>` element, which in turn can optionally be defined within the root `<ejb-jar>` element for an EJB module. The `<security-role>` element is defined as shown here:

- `<security-role>`: Identifies those security roles defined for an EJB module with sub-elements that follow.
- `<description>`: Describes this logical security role (zero or more).
- `<role-name>`: Identifies a logical role name that this EJB module uses.

As an example, an EJB assembler would define a `<security-role>` element for the `Managers` role linked by our `SecureOrderManagerEJBean` bean as illustrated in Listing 28.4.

Listing 28.4 **EJB Security Role** (`ejb-jar-bean.xml`)

```
<ejb-jar...>
   ...
  <enterprise-beans>
   <session>
     <display-name>SecureOrderManagerEJB</display-name>
     <ejb-name>SecureOrderManagerEJB</ejb-name>
        ...
     <security-role-ref>
        <description>This bean references Managers role.</description>
        <role-name>manager</role-name>
        <role-link>Managers</role-link>
      </security-role-ref>
   </session>
  </enterprise-beans>

  <assembly-descriptor>
      <security-role>
        <description>
          Only managers can have this role.
        </description>
        <role-name>Managers</role-name>
      </security-role>
  </assembly-descriptor>
</ejb-jar>
```

Although such `<security-role>` elements can be defined to link from `<security-role-ref>` elements defined for EJBs that use programmatic EJB security features, these `<security-role>` elements can also be defined for EJBs that make exclusive use of declarative EJB security features. That is, EJBs using declarative EJB security features do not rely on programming security checks as the `SecureOrderEJBean` of Listing 28.1 demonstrated. Rather, an EJB can solely rely on specifying security properties in the EJB's deployment descriptors. This is exemplified in Listing 28.5 by redefining the `ejb-jar.xml` file for our original `OrderManagerEJBean` class having no programmatic security features.

Listing 28.5 **EJB Declarative Security** (`ejb-jar.xml`)

```
<?xml version="1.0" encoding="UTF-8"?>
<ejb-jar
  version="2.1"
  xmlns="http://java.sun.com/xml/ns/j2ee"
  xmlns:xsi="http://www.w3.org/2001/XMLSchema-instance"
  xsi:schemaLocation="http://java.sun.com/xml/ns/j2ee
  http://java.sun.com/xml/ns/j2ee/ejb-jar_2_1.xsd">
```

Listing 28.5 **Continued**

```
<display-name>OrderManagerEJB</display-name>
<enterprise-beans>
     ...
   <session>
      <display-name>OrderManagerEJB</display-name>
      <ejb-name>OrderManagerEJB</ejb-name>
      <home>ejava.ejb.session.ordermgr.OrderManagerHome</home>
      <remote>ejava.ejb.session.ordermgr.OrderManager</remote>
      <ejb-class>
        ejava.ejb.session.ordermgr.OrderManagerEJBean
      </ejb-class>
      <session-type>Stateless</session-type>
         ...
      <security-identity>
        <description>
          Use caller identity in access control decisions
         </description>
         <use-caller-identity/>
      </security-identity>
   </session>
</enterprise-beans>
<relationships>
   ...
</relationships>
<assembly-descriptor>

   <security-role>
     <description>
       Every authenticated user can have this base role.
     </description>
     <role-name>EveryUser</role-name>
   </security-role>

   <security-role>
     <description>
       Only managers can have this role.
     </description>
     <role-name>Managers</role-name>
   </security-role>

   <method-permission>
     <description>
       Managers can invoke all Order Manager methods by default.
     </description>
     <role-name>Managers</role-name>
```

Listing 28.5 **Continued**

```
        <method>
          <ejb-name>OrderManagerEJB</ejb-name>
          <method-name>*</method-name>
        </method>
      </method-permission>

      <method-permission>
        <description>
          No access control is required to
          create a handle to an OrderManager.
        </description>
        <unchecked/>
        <method>
          <ejb-name>OrderManagerEJB</ejb-name>
          <method-name>create</method-name>
        </method>
      </method-permission>

      <method-permission>
        <description>
          Every authenticated user can create a new order.
        </description>
        <role-name>EveryUser</role-name>
        <method>
          <ejb-name>OrderManagerEJB</ejb-name>
          <method-name>createNewOrder</method-name>
        </method>
      </method-permission>
      ...
       <exclude-list>
        <description>
          These methods should not be accessed at all.
        </description>
        <method>
          <ejb-name>OrderManagerEJB</ejb-name>
          <method-name>getCustomer</method-name>
        </method>
      </exclude-list>
  </assembly-descriptor>
     ...
</ejb-jar>
```

EJB Method Permissions (<method-permission>)

Listing 28.5 demonstrates two security roles being defined for our application. The Managers and EveryUser roles respectively correspond to those users who are managers and are authenticated users of a system. Special deployment descriptor elements can then be defined that dictate those security roles that can access particular methods on an EJB. Zero or more <method-permission> elements defined within an <assembly-descriptor> element are used to provide such role-to-method access control mappings. A <method-permission> element is defined as shown here:

- <method-permission>: Maps methods on an EJB to the roles allowed access to such methods or indicates that such methods are to be unchecked for authorization with sub-elements that follow.
- <description>: Describes the method permissions for an EJB (zero or more).
- <role-name>: Contains role name values that have been defined in a <role-name> element contained by the <security-role> elements defined previously (zero or more). Either zero or more <role-name> elements or an <unchecked/> element may be specified within the <method-permission> element, but not both.
- <unchecked/>: Is an empty element indicating that the associated method(s) are not checked for authorization. If it is indicated elsewhere in the deployment descriptor that a method is to be checked for authorization, the <unchecked/> element takes precedence and the method will not be checked. Either zero or more <role-name> elements or the <unchecked/> element may be specified within the <method-permission> element, but not both.
- <method>: Identifies particular EJB method(s) for which this access control specification applies (zero or more). The specification for a <method> element is identical to that defined for transactions described earlier in this chapter.

As an example, Listing 28.5 identifies three method access control specifications. The access control checking rules that apply to this specification for the OrderManagerEJB (mapped to the OrderManagerEJBean) are defined here:

- All methods allow users in the Managers role access by default.
- The create() method, however, is not checked for authorization to invoke it.
- The createNewOrder() method is allowed access by those users in the EveryUser role in addition to those in the Managers role.

EJB Method Exclusion List (<exclude-list>)

There may be scenarios in which an assembler and a deployer determine that regardless of whether a method is defined in a home or object interface for access by clients, the method should simply not be invoked. Thus, regardless of whether the method uses access control to determine whether a user in a particular role may invoke it, the optional <exclude-list> element defined within an <assembly-descriptor> element may identify such methods. The <exclude-list> element is defined here:

- <exclude-list>: Identifies those EJB methods that are not allowed to be invoked at all by EJB clients. If it is indicated elsewhere in the deployment descriptor that a method is to be checked or not checked for authorization, the <exclude-list> element takes precedence and the methods will not be invoked. The <exclude-list> element has the following sub-elements.
- <description>: Describes the method exclusion list for an EJB (zero or more).
- <method>: Identifies particular EJB method(s) for which this exclusion list specification applies (zero or more). The specification for a <method> element is identical to that defined for transactions described earlier in this chapter.

Listing 28.5 presented such an example in which the `getCustomer()` method defined for the `OrderManagerEJB` (mapped to the `OrderManagerEJBean`) is not allowed to be accessed by clients of the bean.

Such declarative EJB security access control checking mechanisms provide a codeless way for determining whether a particular user in a particular role is allowed access to a particular method on a particular EJB. However, some enterprise applications may need to provide access control checking functionality in which access to a particular EJB method should be allowed based on some business-specific state and logic of the system associated with that user. For example, it may not simply be valid to say that all users belonging to a particular `employee` role have access or do not have access to particular getter and setter methods on some `TimeSheet` EJB that encapsulates employee timesheets in an enterprise human resource management application. Rather, you may want to implement a security checking mechanism that provides access control to such `TimeSheet` EJB getter and setter methods based on whether the identity of the invoking client matches some `employeeID` field state of the `TimeSheet` EJB. Although bean developers can use the standard programmatic EJB security access control checking mechanisms to implement the needed logic, some EJB container vendors may provide additional access control mechanisms to implement such features.

Standard EJB Principal Identification and Delegation

Thus far we've discussed the logical model involved with defining access control for EJBs. Such access control involved defining those methods on EJBs that can be accessed by users in particular roles. The role of a user is different from the identity defined by the user's security principal representation. As we saw, the principal identity of a user that is attempting to access an EJB can be gotten via a call to the `EJBContext` class's `getCallerPrincipal()` method. The identity used during access control decisions by the EJB container, however, can be different.

EJB Invocation Security Identity (<security-identity>)

A <security-identity> element defined within a <session>, <entity>, or <message-driven> bean element definition indicates what identity is used during access control decisions as explained here:

- <security-identity>: Defines the identity type to be used by the container when making access control decisions on the enclosed EJB with sub-elements that follow.
- <description>: Describes the security identification scheme for an EJB (zero or more).
- <use-caller-identity/>: Is an empty element to indicate that the principal identity of the user (that is, caller) should be used in access control decision making by the container. Either the <use-caller-identity/> element or a <run-as-identity> element is used inside of a <security-identity> element, but not both.
- <run-as-identity>: Contains zero or more <description> elements and a <role-name> element identifying that role which should be used in access control decision making by the container. Either the <use-caller-identity/> element or the <run-as-identity> element is used inside of a <security-identity> element, but not both.

Listing 28.5, in fact, illustrates the fact that any access control decisions made by the container for access to any methods on the OrderManagerEJB should use the caller's principal identity in those decisions. The caller identity must, of course, map to a valid role by the EJB container. As of EJB v2.1, this mapping is done in a vendor-specific fashion.

Alternatively, if we desired to deploy the OrderManagerEJB such that the container assumed that every user access attempt was made via the Managers role, we might have the following for the bean's <security-identity>:

```
<session>
   <display-name>OrderManagerEJB</display-name>
   <ejb-name>OrderManagerEJB</ejb-name>
        ...
   <security-identity>
     <description>
       Use Managers role for access control decisions.
     </description>
     <run-as>Managers</run-as>
   </security-identity>
</session>
```

Because no caller identity is associated with message-driven or TimedObject beans, the <use-caller-identity> element must never be specified for such bean types. Rather, the <run-as> identity must be defined or rely upon a container default value.

Such <security-identity> specifications are used only by the container when it is performing access control checking for an EJB. The principal identity returned from the EJBContext.getCallerPrincipal() method is that of the caller regardless of any <run-as> specification for the bean. Similarly, the EJBContext.isCallerInRole() method uses the caller identity versus any <run-as> security identity. If no authentication takes place, an anonymous user identity as defined by the container must be returned from getCallerPrincipal() and used in the isCallerInRole() decision making.

EJB Security Identity Delegation

Finally, if an EJB calls the services of another EJB, which calls the services of another EJB, and so on, then a means for principal identity delegation must be defined. The container defines this principal identity delegation in a vendor-specific fashion. However, the capability to allow principal identity to propagate as either the caller identity or the run-as identity value must be allowed by the container. This enables EJB developers to design their applications with such principal delegation schemes in mind.

Vendor-Specific EJB Access Controls

Although the roles specified by an assembler in the <security-role> elements of an ejb-jar.xml file define logical roles assumed by an EJB application, the container and EJB deployers must map these roles to actual user groups and/or users in the operational system. Additionally, the container and EJB deployers must manage how these roles relate to particular security domains from the operational system. Such mappings from logical security role to operational environment groups/users may be performed in an automated fashion by vendor tools without requiring the development of vendor-specific code.

As an example of a vendor-specific mapping tool, the BEA WebLogic Server comes equipped with a GUI administration console tool. The administration console can be used to map standard J2EE EJB defined role names to principal names that have meaning in an operational BEA WebLogic Server environment. The standard EJB security application roles that are stored in <security-role> elements for an EJB module must be mapped to valid groups used within a WebLogic security realm. The administration console then allows operational principal names to be mapped to the standard J2EE role names (exactly how such principal names are made available is described in the next section).

When performing such a mapping, the administration console populates a vendor-specific weblogic-ejb-jar.xml file. The weblogic-ejb-jar.xml file contains zero or more <security-role-assignment> elements which contain a standard EJB <role-name> element that maps to one or more WebLogic-specific <principal-name> elements. As an example included with this chapter's code, we specify that our standard Managers role name maps to an ejavaManager WebLogic username and that our standard EveryUser role name maps to an ejavaUser

WebLogic username in an operational WebLogic Server environment. The example mapping yields the following `weblogic-ejb-jar.xml` file snippet:

```
<weblogic-ejb-jar>
    ...
  <security-role-assignment>
    <role-name>
      Managers
    </role-name>
    <principal-name>
      ejavaManager
    </principal-name>
  </security-role-assignment>

  <security-role-assignment>
    <role-name>
      EveryUser
    </role-name>
    <principal-name>
      ejavaUser
    </principal-name>
  </security-role-assignment>
</weblogic-ejb-jar>
```

As another example, the J2EE reference implementation also provides similar tools to perform such mappings. The vendor-specific `sun-j2ee-ri.xml` file included with this chapter's example yields the following mapping:

```
<j2ee-ri-specific-information>
  <rolemapping>
    <role name="Managers">
      <principals>
        <principal>
          <name>ejavaManager</name>
        </principal>
      </principals>
      <groups>
        <group name="ejavagroup"/>
      </groups>
    </role>

    <role name="EveryUser">
      <principals>
        <principal>
          <name>ejavaUser</name>
        </principal>
      </principals>
```

```
      <groups>
        <group name="ejavagroup"/>
      </groups>
    </role>
  </rolemapping>
    ...
</j2ee-ri-specific-information>
```

Vendor-Specific EJB Authentication

Vendor-specific mappings from logical security role to operational environment groups/users may not require any vendor-specific code, but the exact means for how your container manages the access, addition, and removal of the operational groups/users within its auspices may indeed require vendor-specific code. That is, we saw the vendor-specific means for mapping standard EJB security roles to principal names in the preceding section, but how do we customize our vendor's server environment to be cognizant of such valid principal names? For example, if your enterprise manages principal information in a database, a vendor-specific means to access that information via custom JDBC calls may be required. However, you may also decide to use whatever means are provided by your particular vendor to automatically manage such information, which may or may not require specialized coding. Such methods might include a means to specify principal information in a simple text file, an XML file, or an LDAP structure.

Vendor-Specific Authentication Classes

Some vendors may use a simple text-based configuration file as the default means for storing usernames and passwords. User information may be added to such a file in the form of name/value entries as shown here:

```
security.password.userName=userPassword
```

Similarly, groups may be added to the file in the following form:

```
security.group.groupName=userName1,userName2,userName3,...
```

Configuring principal information using static configuration files, however, will be infeasible for most medium- to large-scale applications. Thus, many vendors will also provide a means to manage identities stored in alternative principal identification repositories (that is, security domains or realms). An alternative realm may be designated in a configuration file by setting a special property equal to a fully qualified class name representing the alternative realm. Such classes may then implement vendor-specific interfaces that enable the vendor's server environment to invoke operations on such class instances during operational processing of security-related events.

Realm types from a vendor might include means for authenticating users via information stored in a database, an LDAP server, or operating system–specific security directory services. Some vendors may also allow you to create a custom realm that enables you to create a special realm class that implements methods to retrieve and modify user, group, and access control information. Thus, user profile information may be stored in a repository of your choice and managed in a business-specific fashion by these interface implementations. Although use of such vendor-specific authentication techniques may provide a lot of flexibility in how you implement operational user profiles, your operational environment-specific implementations of these interfaces will be based entirely on vendor-specific interfaces.

EJB Client Authentication with JNDI

A principal identity name and set of credentials must somehow propagate from EJB client to EJB server for authentication to occur. One way vendors may accomplish this is via setting of `javax.naming.Context.SECURITY_PRINCIPAL` and `javax.naming.Context.SECURITY_CREDENTIALS` properties onto a `javax.naming.InitialContext` during initial connectivity with the EJB server from the client. As an example for the BEA WebLogic Server, the `ejava.ejb.session.ordermgr.TestClient` EJB client wanting access to the previously secured `OrderManagerEJB` may pass username and credential information to the EJB server when obtaining an initial JNDI context. The `TestClient` is shown in Listing 28.6.

Listing 28.6 **EJB Test Client (`TestClient.java`)**

```
package ejava.ejb.session.ordermgr;
   ...
public class TestClient {
  private static String userName;
  private static String password;
  private static int queryCustomerID = 101;
  private static int queryOrderID = 1001;

  public static void printOrder(Order order) {
    System.out.println("ID :" + order.getOrderID());
    System.out.println("orderDate :" + order.getOrderDate());
    System.out.println(
      "shipInstruct :" + order.getShippingInstructions());
    System.out.println("shipDate :" + order.getShipDate());
    System.out.println("shipWeight :" + order.getShipWeight());
    System.out.println("paidDate :" + order.getPaidDate());
  }

  private static Integer createNewOrder(OrderManager orderManager)
    throws RemoteException {
    Order order = new Order();
    // Order is created today and paid today and shipped today.
    order.setOrderDate(new Date());
    order.setPaidDate(new Date());
```

Listing 28.6 **Continued**

```
    order.setShippingInstructions("Leave at Door");
    order.setShipWeight(10.8);
    order.setShipCharge(32.54);
    order.setShipDate(new Date());
    // The customer info the order is being created for
    Customer customer = new Customer();
    customer.setCustomerID("" + queryCustomerID);
    order.setCustomer(customer);
    order.setBillingAddress(createAnAddress());
    order.setShippingAddress(createAnAddress());
    order.setItems(createItems());
    return orderManager.createNewOrder(order);
  }

  private static Address createAnAddress() {
    Address address = new Address();
    address.setAddress_1(" 2.1 EJB Way");
    address.setAddress_2(" 1");
    address.setCity(" J2EE ");
    address.setState("CA");
    address.setZipCode("14000");
    return address;
  }

  private static TShirt[] createItems() {
    TShirt itemOne = new TShirt();
    itemOne.setQuantity(2);
    itemOne.setTotalPrice(21.0);
    itemOne.setSize("XL");
    itemOne.setColor("White");
    itemOne.setUnitPrice(10.5);

    TShirt itemTwo = new TShirt();
    itemTwo.setQuantity(2);
    itemTwo.setTotalPrice(21.0);
    itemTwo.setSize("L");
    itemTwo.setColor("White");
    itemTwo.setUnitPrice(10.5);
    TShirt[] createdItems = { itemOne, itemTwo };
    return createdItems;
  }

  public static void main(String[] args) {
    try {
      // Create initial context
```

Listing 28.6 **Continued**

```
Context context = new InitialContext();
System.out.println(
  " looking for :"
    + EJBHelper.ORDER_MANAGER_HOME
    + " context:"
    + context);

// Look up order manager home reference
Object objectRef = context.lookup(EJBHelper.ORDER_MANAGER_HOME);
OrderManagerHome orderManagerHome =
  (OrderManagerHome) PortableRemoteObject.narrow(
    objectRef,
    ejava.ejb.session.ordermgr.OrderManagerHome.class);

// Create an order manager handle reference
OrderManager orderManager = orderManagerHome.create();

// Create a new order
Integer newOrderID = createNewOrder(orderManager);
System.out.println("New Order ID :" + newOrderID);

// Query for number of items in the order
int nItems = orderManager.numberOfItemsInAnOrder(queryOrderID);
System.out.println(" Number of Items in an Order :" + nItems);

// Query for orders based on customer ID
Vector orders = orderManager.queryOrders(queryCustomerID);
System.out.println("Received Orders :" + orders.getClass());
for (int i = 0; i < orders.size(); i++) {
  Order order = (Order) orders.elementAt(i);
  System.out.println("Received Order : " + i + ": Order Detail");
  printOrder(order);
}

// Get the average order value for a customer
float avgValue =
  orderManager.averageOrderValueOfACustomer(queryCustomerID);
System.out.println(
  " Average Order Value of a Customer :" + avgValue);

// Get a customer associated with an order
Customer customer
  = orderManager.getCustomer(newOrderID.intValue());
System.out.println(
  " Customer email address :" + customer.getEmail());
```

Listing 28.6 **Continued**

```
    } catch (Exception exception) {
      exception.printStackTrace();
    }
  }
}
```

Note that the `TestClient` uses the parameterless form of the `InitialContext` constructor, which means that it is getting the properties used to construct an initial context from the system properties. The `runClient`, `runClientEveryUser`, and `runClientManager` scripts generated by the ANT scripts for these examples (that is, in the `examples/config/execscripts/ejava/ejb/security/basic` directory) pass a `CONTEXT_FACTORY` and `PROVIDER_URL` to the `TestClient` class's JVM as system properties. The `runClientEveryUser` and `runClientManager` example scripts additionally pass `CONTEXT_PRINCIPAL` and `CONTEXT_CREDENTIALS` properties to the JVM. The `CONTEXT_FACTORY` and `PROVIDER_URL` properties are established by the ANT script using the properties set in the example's `ejava/ejb/build.properties` file:

```
# JNDI Properties - when using WebLogic
jndi.factory=weblogic.jndi.WLInitialContextFactory
jndi.provider.url=t3://localhost:7001/

# JNDI Properties - when using the J2EE Reference Implementation
#jndi.factory=com.sun.enterprise.naming.SerialInitContextFactory
#jndi.provider.url=iiop://localhost:1050/
```

The `CONTEXT_PRINCIPAL` and `CONTEXT_CREDENTIALS` properties are ultimately read in from the example's `ejava/ejb/security/basic/build.properties` file as shown here:

```
# Everyuser principal
everyuser_role_principal=ejavaUser

# Everyuser credentials
everyuser_role_credentials=ejavaUser

# Manager role user principal
manager_role_principal=ejavaManager

# Manager role user credentials
manager_role_credentials=ejavaManager
```

Thus, when executing the respective `runClientXXX` scripts for this example, you should see the following behavior depending on which script is run:

- `runClient`: Runs with no username and password. Hence should be able to create an order manager, but that's all it has permissions to do.
- `runClientEveryUser`: Runs with the `everyuser.role.principal` username and `everyuser.role.credentials` password properties defined previously. Hence should be able to create an order manager and create a new order but nothing else.
- `runClientManager`: Runs with the `manager.role.principal` username and `manager.role.credentials` password properties defined previously. Hence should be able to invoke every operation on the order manager with the exception of the `getCustomer()` method because that is in the exclude list for the bean.

On the EJB server side, if a vendor-specific realm is being used, special callbacks onto the realm implementation class are made to pass such principal and credential information to enable your code to provide authentication of such users with the system. A vendor-specific object returned within the vendor's container representing an authenticated user of the system is then associated with a server-side thread handler for the client. When subsequent requests are made from that same client associated with the thread, the client's credentials from its thread handler then can be used in the process of providing access control for EJBs.

Thus, if the EJB client that was previously authenticated during an initial JNDI context creation operation can access the system, it may attempt to look up EJB home references and invoke operations on those EJBs as usual. If an EJB's methods have been restricted using the standard and vendor-specific access control mechanisms defined previously, the security-critical EJB operations will be checked by the server during runtime operation. Running the `TestClient` of Listing 28.6 illustrates this behavior.

EJB Connection Security

The EJB client authentication sequence defined in the preceding section passed user credential information into a JNDI context object with no guarantee about the secured nature of the client-to-server connection. Thus, the client's credential information could very well have been transferred to the server in the clear. For certain types of EJB clients and application scenarios, this may be acceptable. For example, if the EJB client is a Java Servlet or JavaServer Page, and the Web server sits behind the same trusted computing base and firewall as the EJB application server, this may be acceptable for certain applications. However, for other enterprise applications, the connection between EJB client and EJB server needs to operate over some secured socket mechanism.

The means for securing the connection between EJB client and server is described in the EJB v2.1 specification such that interoperability may be assured. EJB uses IIOP for communications and secure communications interoperability is defined within the OMG's Common Security Interoperability v2 specification. EJB servers must adhere to conformance level 0 of that specification to ensure interoperability of security context information passed between client and server, as well as between servers.

One basic implication of this specification on an EJB server is that SSL v3.0 and TLS v1.0 are required as encryption standards for transport-level security. X.509 certificates, Kerberos, and a set of standard cipher suites are all delineated as standards within this encryption security umbrella. Furthermore, the SSL host and port information of a server is required to be baked into the home or remote EJB interface stub IOR so that the client knows how to connect with a server via SSL. If authentication information isn't passed around at this secured transport level, such information is passed inside of the IIOP messages themselves.

EJB Principal Delegation

The default means for propagating principal identity should allow principal identity to propagate from one EJB to another EJB. Thus, in a chain of calls made from one EJB to another, the principal identity associated with the original EJB client that initiated the call sequence will be propagated. Exactly how principal identity is propagated from the initial EJB client to the EJB server is left up to the vendor. An EJB vendor must provide a means during deployment for selecting which identity propagation policy should be employed. As a minimum requirement, the EJB client's principal identity used to connect to the EJB server will be able to be used as the principal identity to be delegated to other EJBs within the EJB server environment. The run-as identity may also be used and propagated across an EJB call chain.

EJB Security Auditing

EJB server vendors may also provide a means for auditing security-critical events. Security-critical events may include logging the generation of any security-related exceptions, successful and failed authentication attempts, and failed EJB access attempts. Vendors, for example, may enable you to implement a vendor-specific auditing class. A special security auditing configuration property in the vendor's specific configuration files might then be set to this class name. The vendor's server may then invoke methods on this class when an attempted authentication occurs, an authorization request is made, or an invalid user certificate is propagated to the server.

J2EE and EJB Security with JAAS

In the discussion thus far, an underlying vendor-specific means to authenticate a user was assumed to be used on the EJB server side. Although such vendor-specific means can be employed with minimal effects to your code base, a core principle of J2EE is to enable you to build enterprise applications that are portable across servers. A reliance on a vendor-specific authentication mechanism or custom realm will somewhat tie you to that vendor's EJB container.

The EJB v2.1 and J2EE v1.4 specifications do not explicitly require a vendor to support the standard security and authentication offerings for Java. Chapter 17 briefly introduced the Java Authentication and Authorization Service (JAAS) as a means for limiting access to security-critical resources based on an authenticated user identity. With JAAS, APIs for login and logout provide a standard technique for authenticating users and passing around secure context and credential information. Different underlying authentication and authorization models can be plugged into the JAAS service provider interface model while enabling API users to have a stable and standard interface. Although JAAS is now included with the J2SE v1.4, there is no explicit requirement in the EJB and J2EE specifications that EJB containers must use JAAS to provide server-side authentication services.

Nevertheless, many vendors are slowly embracing JAAS for server-side EJB authentication, and a future specification may require more wholehearted support of JAAS if it becomes a popular means for providing such services. This section discusses JAAS in detail and specifically describes how it may be used in EJB environments. We take the approach in this section of first describing the basic mechanisms of JAAS for authentication and authorization so that you can best understand and focus on the JAAS APIs and how they may be used in various J2EE container environments. We then discuss how JAAS may be integrated with EJB environments so that you can understand how JAAS would be most commonly used and how it can offer you a vendor-independent authentication and authorization approach.

JAAS Subjects

The core abstractions involved with JAAS that are common to both authentication and authorization are depicted in Figure 28.6. An abstraction for a subject must exist to enable both the authentication of a subject with the system and the authorization of a subject's access to valued resources. Because a subject can have more than one principal name, a subject abstraction must also encapsulate a collection of principal objects. Furthermore, a subject can also have one or more public and private credentials to present to a system for authentication. Credential objects may be of any form and can implement special interfaces that signify the fact that they can be refreshed for an extended validity period or signify that they can be destroyed from the system.

The `javax.security.auth.Subject` class is a `Serializable` and `final` class used to encapsulate an entity that wants to utilize some security-critical aspect of a system. Such an entity may correspond to a person, another system, or perhaps a group of people or systems. Because subjects can have multiple ways to identify themselves as a unit, the `Subject` class maintains a collection of one or more `java.security.Principal` objects in a standard `java.util.Set` collection. Thus, for example, if the `Subject` does correspond to a person, `Prinicpal` objects may be associated with the `Subject` for that person's name, employee identification number, Social Security number, and so on.

`Subject` objects may also be associated with credentials that define information used to validate such principal identities. Credential objects associated with a `Subject` are also stored in `java.util.Set` collections but have no required type except for being basic `java.lang.Object` types. Credentials may be either public or private and thus are managed in different collections. Public credentials, such as public certificates, can be shared with other users of a system, whereas private credentials, such as private keys, should not be made accessible to anyone but the owning subject.

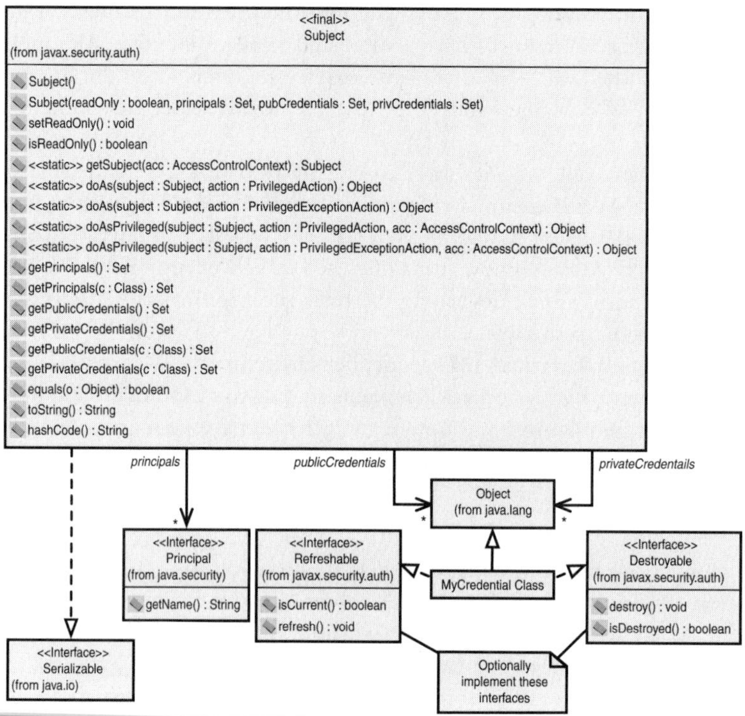

Figure 28.6 Core JAAS abstractions.

Creating Subjects

Although a default `Subject` constructor is provided, the `Subject(boolean, Set, Set, Set)` constructor is used primarily as the means to create a subject with a set of principals, set of public credentials, and a set of private credentials. A `boolean` value is also passed into this constructor to indicate whether the `Subject` object is read-only. As an example, we might have this:

```
// Create a principal and credentials hash sets
HashSet principals = new HashSet();
HashSet privateCredentials = new HashSet();
HashSet publicCredentials = new HashSet();

// Add initial elements to the sets
principals.add(new MyPrincipal("edison"));
publicCredentials.add("publicPassword");
```

```
privateCredentials.add("privatePassword");

// Create a Subject
Subject subject = new Subject(false, principals,
                              publicCredentials, privateCredentials);
```

Manipulating Subject Attributes

After a handle to a `Subject` object is either created or received, the principal objects and credential objects may be retrieved. The `getPrincipals()`, `getPublicCredentials()`, and `getPrivateCredentials()` methods all return a `Set` object containing the associated object types. Any updates performed on the `Set` objects from a non–read-only `Subject` will result in the `Set` object associated with the `Subject` being updated as well. Here's an example:

```
// Retrieve the public credential
String publicCredential =
   (String) ((subject.getPublicCredentials()).iterator()).next();
System.out.println("Public credential = " + publicCredential);

// Retrieve the private credential
String privateCredential =
   (String) ((subject.getPrivateCredentials()).iterator()).next();
System.out.println("Private credential = " + privateCredential);

// Retrieve a principal and display its value
//    and number of principals in Subject (currently has one)
MyPrincipal principal =
   (MyPrincipal) ((subject.getPrincipals()).iterator()).next();
System.out.println("Principal object in Subject = " + principal.getName());
System.out.println("Number of Principal objects in Subject = "
                   + subject.getPrincipals().size());

// Modify the principal (is OK)
principal.setName("watson");
// Modify the set (is also OK)
try{
  subject.getPrincipals().add(new MyPrincipal("joe"));
}
catch(IllegalStateException ex){
  System.out.println("This statement won't be called");
  ex.printStackTrace();
}

// See number of principals in Subject (now has two)
System.out.println("Number of Principal objects in Subject = "
                   + subject.getPrincipals().size());
```

Alternatively, the getPrincipals(Class), getPublicCredentials(Class), and getPrivateCredentials(Class) methods all return a Set object containing the associated object types whose class type is a subclass or is the type of class specified by the Class input parameter. Because these method calls return copies of the Set objects that they return, updates made to the Set objects do not affect the state of the Subject object. However, any updates made to the individual elements within the Set object will affect the Subject object state. For example:

```
// Modify the set (only modifies the copy and not the Subject)
try{
  Set mySetCopy = subject.getPrincipals(MyPrincipal.class);
  mySetCopy.add(new MyPrincipal("bart"));
}
catch(IllegalStateException ex){
  System.out.println("This statement won't be called");
  ex.printStackTrace();
}

// See number of principals in Subject (still has two)
System.out.println("Number of Principal objects in Subject = "
                   + subject.getPrincipals().size());
```

If a Subject is set to be read-only, then attempted modifications to the Subject object's principal Set, public credentials Set, and private credentials Set will not be permitted and will result in the throwing of an IllegalStateException. The read-only nature of the Subject can be determined from Subject.isReadOnly(). The Subject.setReadOnly() can be used to set a Subject to be read-only, but there is no way to make a Subject writable after it has been set to read-only. Here's an example:

```
// Set the Subject to read-only
subject.setReadOnly();

// Modify the principal value (is still OK)
principal.setName("sam");
// Modify the set (is NOT OK and will throw IllegalStateException)
try{
  subject.getPrincipals().add(new MyPrincipal("marcus"));
}
catch(IllegalStateException ex2){
  System.out.println("This statement WILL be called");
  ex2.printStackTrace();
}
```

The Subject class also defines a getSubject() method, two doAs() methods, and two doAsPrivileged() methods. These methods involve authorization concepts and are covered later in this section.

Specializing Subject Credentials

As a final note, two interfaces, javax.security.auth.Refreshable and javax.security.auth.Destroyable, may also be used with credential objects associated with a Subject. If a particular credential class implements the Refreshable interface, such a class designates that the credential can have its validity period extended (that is, refreshed). If a credential class implements the Destroyable interface, the credential information contained by that class can be wiped from memory.

Authentication with JAAS

Authentication in JAAS involves a client application that communicates with a login context to present any principal credential information to JAAS, as well as perform login and logout operations. The login context communicates with a modular login module service provider interface to interact with any underlying authentication-specific technologies. Such an architecture follows the pattern employed by the Pluggable Authentication Module (PAM) framework for shielding applications from the underlying authentication technologies. Login modules used by an application are configured using a special configuration abstraction that determines how to load and initialize the login modules. Figure 28.7 depicts the basic set of JAAS abstractions involved with authentication.

Login Context Construction

The javax.security.auth.login.LoginContext class is the primary class utilized by clients to the JAAS API. A LoginContext provides the interfaces necessary for subjects to log in and log out of the system. The LoginContext class shields JAAS clients from the underlying authentication mechanisms.

Clients first create an instance of a LoginContext object using one of four constructor options. The LoginContext(String) constructor is used to create a LoginContext for a particular named authentication configuration. The authentication configuration name is simply used to identify particular methodologies for logging into the application and particular parameters associated with those methodologies. All LoginContext() constructors require an authentication configuration name to be supplied. Because no Subject is associated with the LoginContext(String) constructor call, the LoginContext will create one for the user and expects to receive principal and credential information via an alternative mechanism. The LoginContext(String, Subject) method creates a handle to a named authentication configuration with a particular Subject to be authenticated. As an example, we might have this:

```
// Get our dummy Subject ("edison")
Subject subject = ...

// Create LoginContext
LoginContext loginContext = null;
```

```
try{
  loginContext = new LoginContext("PasswordExample", subject);
}
catch(LoginException loginException){
  loginException.printStackTrace();
  System.exit(1);
}
```

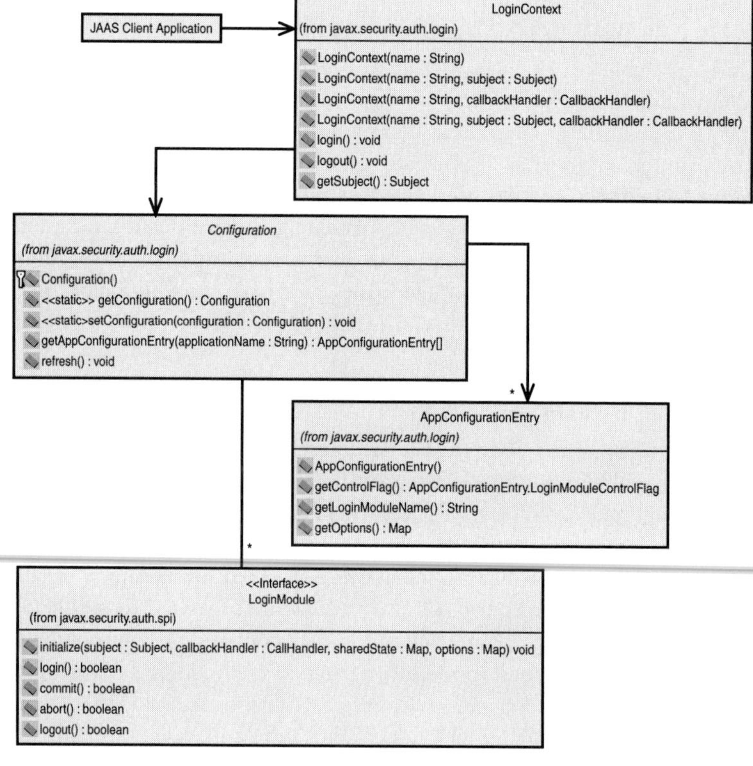

Figure 28.7 JAAS authentication abstractions.

Login Module Configuration

During construction time, the `LoginContext` object consults a `javax.security.auth.login.Configuration` object to load the login modules associated with the application. The `Configuration` object determines which login modules should be loaded and the order in which they should be loaded. Because

`Configuration` is an abstract class, a concrete subclass must be specified somewhere for your JAAS applications to run properly. To override the default `Configuration` implementation, you must alter your J2SE `<JAVA_HOME>/jre/lib/security/java.security` file such that a `login.configuration.provider` property points to a fully qualified `Configuration` subclass name. Otherwise, the default `Configuration` implementation class assumes that a special file for configuring login modules is defined according to the following form:

```
AuthenticationConfigurationName
{
  ModuleName AuthenticationFlag ModuleOptions;
  ModuleName AuthenticationFlag ModuleOptions;
    ...
};

AuthenticationConfigurationName
{
  ModuleName AuthenticationFlag ModuleOptions;
  ModuleName AuthenticationFlag ModuleOptions;
    ...
};

...

other
{
  ModuleName AuthenticationFlag ModuleOptions;
  ModuleName AuthenticationFlag ModuleOptions;
    ...
};
```

Each *`AuthenticationConfigurationName`* identifies one or more login modules that should be used to authenticate users for the application that desires to use this particular configuration. Each login module entry corresponds to a class that implements the `javax.security.auth.spi.LoginModule` interface. The `ModuleName` entry thus relates to a fully qualified `LoginModule` implementation class name. The default `Configuration` class implementation will proceed down the list for the *`AuthenticationConfigurationName`* and attempt any authentication with a `LoginModule` based on its ordered entry in the list. If no *`AuthenticationConfigurationName`* is found for the application, the default `other` application configuration will be used.

Each login module entry also defines an *`AuthenticationFlag`* value that defines how the authentication proceeds with the login modules configured for this authentication configuration. The basic values that can be specified for the *AuthenticationFlag* are listed here:

- `Required`: The associated login module must succeed with authenticating the subject for authentication to be considered successful. The authentication process still continues down the list for other login modules, however.
- `Requisite`: The associated login module must succeed for authentication to be considered successful. The authentication process terminates as failed if a failed login occurs.
- `Sufficient`: The associated login module's successful authentication is sufficient and the authentication may terminate as successful if a successful login occurs. If a `Sufficient` flag is configured, the `Required` and `Requisite` modules preceding this module only must have succeeded.
- `Optional`: The associated login module's capability to authenticate the subject is not required. The authentication process still continues down the list for other login modules. At least one `Optional` or one `Sufficient` module must have succeeded if no `Required` or `Requisite` modules are configured.

Finally, the *ModuleOptions* entry per login module is used to define any configuration parameters that can be passed to the associated `LoginModule` implementation during initialization. Such parameters are defined as a series of *name=value* pairs.

As an example, we might define an example `jaas.config` file for an example application as shown here:

```
PasswordExample
{
   ejava.jaas.AuthenticationExampleModule Required
➥ fileName=credentials.properties;
};
```

Thus, our call to new `LoginContext("PasswordExample", subject)` as illustrated earlier will induce the default `Configuration` implementation to configure our application to make use of the `PasswordExample` authentication configuration information defined in the example `jaas.config` file. A special `ejava.jaas.AuthenticationExampleModule` class (to be defined soon) serves as an example required login module implementation to be used for authenticating subjects. Note that the example `AuthenticationExampleModule` class also utilizes a special `fileName` module option during its initialization process.

Login Module Configuration File Location

The location of the `jaas.config` file can be specified for our application in one of three ways. From the command line, we can set a special system property named `java.security.auth.login.config` to the location of our authentication configuration file. Thus, if the `jaas.config` file is in our current directory, we might execute the example like this:

```
java -Djava.security.auth.login.config=jaas.config
➥ ejava.jaas.AuthenticationExample
```

We can also define a series of `login.config.url.`*n* properties in the `<JAVA_HOME>/jre/lib/security/java.security` file to point to the location of authentication configuration files. The order in which configuration files are loaded is implied by the numeric value associated with the *n* in `login.config.url.`*n*. For example:

```
login.config.url.1=file:C:/ejava/jaas/certificate.config
login.config.url.2=file:C:/myb2c/config/b2c.config
login.config.url.3=file:C:/myb2b/config/b2b.config
```

If no location is specified via the system property or from the `java.security` file, JAAS will attempt to load configuration information from the default `<USER_HOME>/.java.login.config` file.

Login Module Initialization

After loading and instantiating any objects that implement the `LoginModule` interface, the `Configuration` class invokes the `initialize()` method on each `LoginModule` object. The `initialize()` method takes as input parameters the `Subject` to be authenticated, any `CallbackHandler` object for interacting with the end user (to be described shortly), a `Map` of any data shared with other `LoginModule` objects, and a `Map` of module-specific options for this `LoginModule` (such as those read from the *`ModuleOptions`* entry described earlier). Although application developers most often utilize off-the-shelf `LoginModule` implementations, such as those defined at `http://java.sun.com/products/jaas/`, we demonstrate a simple `LoginModule` here to better illustrate the authentication process involved with JAAS. The example `ejava.jaas.AuthenticationExampleModule` class implements a simple `LoginModule` that we will use to authenticate users based on credential information stored in a properties file.

The `AuthenticationExampleModule.initialize()` method stores some basic information in addition to the name of the credential properties file as shown here:

```
package ejava.jaas;
  ...
public class AuthenticationExampleModule implements LoginModule
{
  private Subject subject = null;
  private String credentialFileName = null;
  private CallbackHandler callbackHandler = null;
  private Map otherState = null;
  private boolean loginSucceeded = false;
```

```
  public void initialize(Subject aSubject,
                         CallbackHandler aCallbackHandler,
                         Map sharedState, Map options) {

    // Get Subject, callback handler, and shared state
      subject = aSubject;
    callbackHandler = aCallbackHandler;
    otherState = sharedState;

    // Get filename of credential file
    credentialFileName = (String) options.get("fileName");

    // Print out info
    System.out.println("Start AuthenticationExampleModule with file "
                       + credentialFileName);
  }
  ...
}
```

The Authentication Process

After each `LoginModule` is initialized, user authentication may proceed. A JAAS client will induce the authentication process to begin by invoking the `LoginContext.login()` method. The `LoginContext.login()` method will in turn invoke the `login()` method on each `LoginModule` object configured for this application. The exact nature of the `login()` implementation is a function of the particular authentication technique to be employed by the `LoginModule` implementation. During this first phase of authentication, our `AuthenticationExampleModule` implementation reads credential information from a file and then simply compares it with the established credential information passed in with the `Subject` as shown here:

```
public boolean login() throws LoginException
  {
    // First dynamically load credentials file
    Properties credentialsInfo = this.loadCredentialsFile();

    // Get principal list
    Iterator principals = (subject.getPrincipals()).iterator();

    // For each principal, attempt login
    while(principals.hasNext()){
      // Get principal and print out info
      Principal principal = (Principal) principals.next();
      String name = principal.getName();
      System.out.println("Attempting login for " + name);
```

```
      // If principal is in the credentials file...
      if(credentialsInfo.containsKey(name)){
        // Get and print out password (since is just a test program)
        String password = (String) credentialsInfo.get(name);
        System.out.println(name + " password is " + password);
        Set privateCreds = subject.getPrivateCredentials();
        if(privateCreds.contains(password)){
          System.out.println("Success in login");
          loginSucceeded = true;
          return true;
        }
      }
      else{
        System.out.println("Fail in login");
        loginSucceeded = false;
        throw new LoginException("Not a valid subject");
      }
    }

    System.out.println("Fail in login");
    loginSucceeded = false;
    return false;
}

private Properties loadCredentialsFile() throws LoginException
{
    // Throw exception if no credentials file
    if(credentialFileName == null){
      System.out.println("Fail in login");
      loginSucceeded = false;
      throw new LoginException("No credentials file");
    }

    // Load the properties
    Properties properties = new Properties();
    try{
      FileInputStream fin = new FileInputStream(credentialFileName);
      properties.load(fin);
    }
    catch(Exception e){
      System.out.println("Fail in login");
      loginSucceeded = false;
      throw new LoginException("No credentials file");
    }

    return properties;
}
```

If the subject was successfully authenticated during the overall authentication process, a second phase of the authentication process results in the `commit()` method being invoked on each `LoginModule` implementation object. If a particular `LoginModule` successfully authenticated the subject, it should associate any `Principal` and credential objects with the `Subject` contained by this `LoginModule`. For our `AuthenticationExampleModule`, we assume that a populated `Subject` object will be associated with the `LoginModule` during initialization and thus there is no need to re-associate any `Prinicpal` or credential information with the `Subject`. When a `LoginContext` constructor is called with no `Subject`, the application logic of the invoked `LoginModule` implementations will have to retrieve the principal and credential information from a user via some other mechanism (such as callbacks) and associate this information with a `Subject` during the call to `LoginModule.commit()`. If the authentication for this `LoginModule` failed, the `LoginModule` implementation must destroy any saved state. A value of `true` is returned from `commit()` if the method succeeded.

If the subject was not successfully authenticated during the overall authentication process, the second phase of the authentication process results in the `abort()` method being invoked on each `LoginModule` implementation object. This method implementation must destroy any saved state. A value of `true` is returned from `abort()` if the method succeeded.

The JAAS client application may invoke `getSubject()` on the `LoginContext` object anytime after authentication succeeded and obtain a handle to the authenticated `Subject` object. If authentication failed, the `getSubject()` method returns `null`.

Finally, when the JAAS client application invokes `logout()` on a `LoginContext` object, the `LoginContext` object will invoke `logout()` on each `LoginModule` configured for this application. Each `LoginModule` should destroy any `Principal` and credential state stored. A value of `true` is returned from `LoginModule.logout()` if the method succeeded.

Callback Handling

Callbacks provide a means for JAAS application clients to be notified of certain events during the authentication process and to provide data to the authentication process. Figure 28.8 depicts the basic structure for implementing callbacks in JAAS. A special `javax.security.auth.callback.CallbackHandler` interface is implemented by JAAS applications that want to be consulted during the authentication process. A `CallbackHandler.handle()` method is implemented by JAAS application clients to receive a collection of `javax.security.auth.callback.Callback` objects when a `LoginModule` is performing the login process. Such callback objects contain information relevant to the particular type of authentication being performed. JAAS application clients then retrieve and provide any necessary information via `Callback` objects for authentication to proceed.

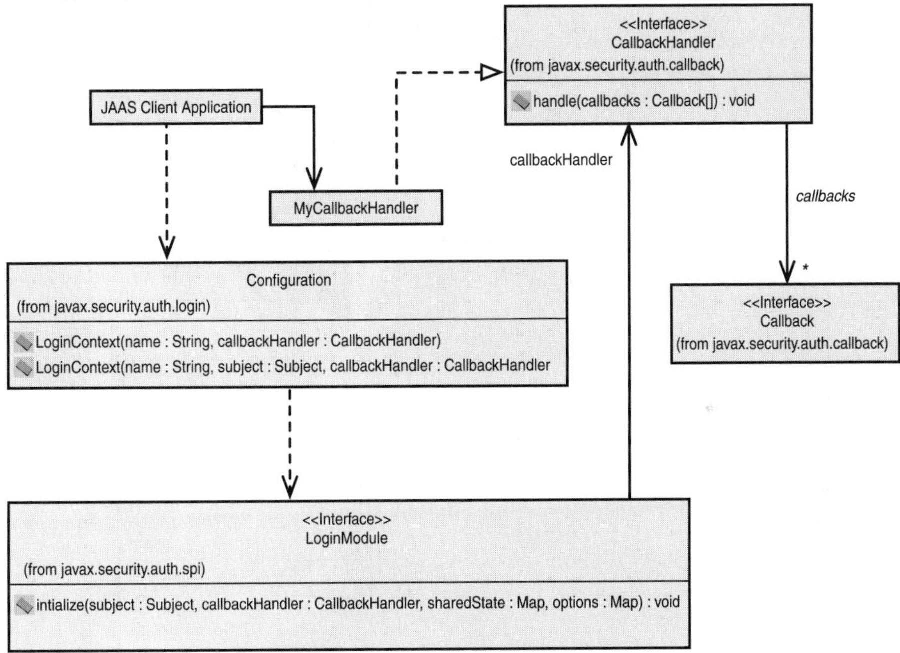

Figure 28.8 Basic JAAS callback handling.

`CallbackHandler` objects are registered with a `LoginContext` via one of two constructors shown in Figure 28.8. `LoginModule` implementations may save such `CallbackHandler` references for later use when a call to `LoginModule.initialize()` is made. A `LoginModule` may then invoke the services of the `CallbackHandler` object during the authentication process via a call to `CallbackHandler.handle()`. The actual `Callback` objects passed into the `handle()` method is a function of the particular type of authentication being performed. Figure 28.9 depicts the basic collection of `Callback` implementations equipped with JAAS included with the J2SE v1.4.

Although we will not go into a detailed description of each `Callback` mechanism here, we should point out the fact that the basic callback types shown in Figure 28.9 have the following general roles:

- `ChoiceCallback`: Used to retrieve a list of choices available during authentication and enable the client application to select particular authentication options.
- `ConfirmationCallback`: Used to retrieve authentication confirmation information and for clients to establish particular confirmation information to drive the authentication process.
- `LanguageCallback`: Used to get and set geographic and regional locale information during authentication.

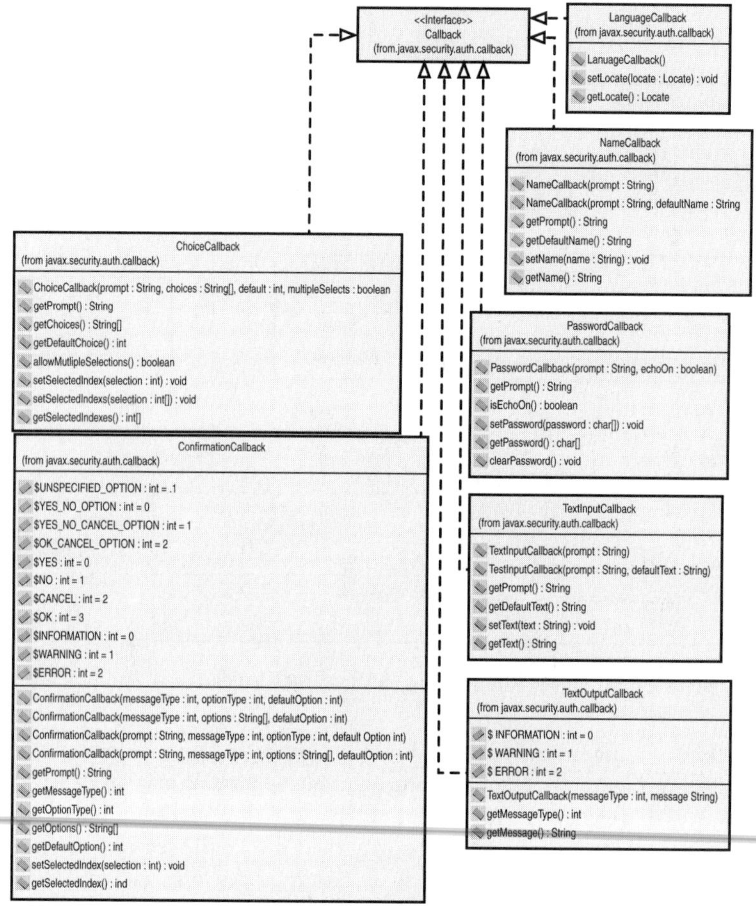

Figure 28.9 Standard JAAS callback implementations.

- `NameCallback`: Used to get and set any username information used during authentication.
- `PasswordCallback`: Used to get and set any user password information used during authentication.
- `TextInputCallback`: Used to provide any general text input to the authentication process.
- `TextOutputCallback`: Used to receive any general textual output messages from the authentication process.

As a general example, if a `LoginModule` wants to receive username and password information from a user during authentication, we might have the following inside of a `login()` method implementation of a `LoginModule`:

```
// If have no callback handler...cannot login
if (callbackHandler == null){
  throw new LoginException("No handler available");
}

// Create a username and password callback
NameCallback nameCallback = new NameCallback(" Enter Username ");
PasswordCallback passwordCallback =
                 new PasswordCallback(" Enter Password ", false);

// Create the callback array for the CallbackHandler
Callback callbacks[] = new Callback[2];
callbacks[0] = nameCallback;
callbacks[1] = passwordCallback;

// Invoke handler() on the CallbackHandler
try{
  callbackHandler.handle(callbacks);
}
catch(Exception ex){
  ex.printStackTrace();
  loginSucceeded = false;
  throw new LoginException(" Cannot login.");
}

// Now should have the username and password
String userName = nameCallback.getName();
char [] password = passwordCallback.getPassword();
```

On the JAAS client application side, the handling of this callback will be application specific. That is, the username and password may be obtained from a GUI, via some distributed object call, or via some other mechanism. However, a basic skeleton for such a `handle()` implementation might follow as shown here:

```
public void handle(Callback[] callbacks)
    throws UnsupportedCallbackException, IOException
{

    // Get callbacks
    NameCallback nameCallback = (NameCallback) callbacks[0];
    PasswordCallback passwordCallback = (PasswordCallback) callbacks[1];
```

```
    // Get username prompt
    String prompt = nameCallback.getPrompt();
    // Get name from user (ap-specific)...
    String userName = ...
    // Now set name
    nameCallback.setName(userName);

    // Get password prompt
    passwordCallback.getPrompt();
    // Get password from user (ap-specific)...
    char [] password = ...
    // Now set password
    passwordCallback.setPassword(password);

    ...
}
```

Authorization with JAAS

After successfully authenticating a subject, the authorization features unique to JAAS may be employed to limit access to valued resources based on the authenticated subject information. By virtue of incorporating JAAS within the J2SE, the JAAS authorization model resulted in the extension of the Java 2 security model to include additional access control decision-making logic based on the subject requesting access.

The `Subject.doAs()` and `Subject.doAsPrivileged()` methods may be used to perform security-critical actions as a particular `Subject`. These static methods (as shown in Figure 28.6) have a role similar to the `AccessController.doPrivileged()` methods. However, these methods also require an additional `Subject` object input parameter. Fine-grained access control for such `Subject.doXXX()` calls are defined in the Java security policy file.

Java Security Policies with Subjects

In the default implementation of Java security policy management, a security policy is defined in an ASCII text file. Recall from Chapter 17 that the Java security policy file has the following general form:

```
grant codebase "URL", SignedBy "list of names",
      Principal [principal_class_name] "principal_name",
      Principal ...
{
    permission permission_class_name [ "target name" ] [, "actions"]
                                     [, SignedBy "list of names"];
    permission ...
};
```

As discussed in Chapter 17, the basic policy file includes the specification of a security domain beginning with the `grant` keyword and contains one or more permission definitions for the particular domain of protection. Each permission entry begins with the `permission` keyword and is followed by the fully qualified permission `class_name`. Permission target names and a comma-separated list of actions also follow a permission designation. The `SignedBy` field following the permission is provided with a comma-separated list of alias names that indicate who must have signed the Java code for the permissions class. Each grant entry delimiting a domain of protection can also contain a `SignedBy` field designating the fact that code being executed in the JVM associated with the grant entry must be signed by the named signers. A `CodeBase` field may also be associated with a grant entry to relate a set of permissions with a resource location from where the code is loaded.

Java security policy files may also specify one or more principal identification values associated with each grant entry. A fully qualified principal class name identifies the type of `Principal` object associated with valid principals to which the associated permissions apply. The actual principal name must also be supplied. Thus, any `Subject` to which the associated permissions apply must have all the specified principal values associated with the Java security policy entry.

We thus define the following simple entry in a Java security file for the example `AuthenticationExample` application:

```
grant codebase "file:authaction.jar",
      Principal ejava.jaas.MyPrincipal "edison"
{
   permission java.io.FilePermission "myLogFile.txt", "write";
};
```

Thus, our `AuthenticationExample` will only allow write permissions to a `myLogFile.txt` file for an authenticated subject containing the principal name of `edison`. Furthermore, the codebase for this permission is associated with code loaded from an `authaction.jar` file.

Performing Security-Critical Actions

The security-critical action to be performed by our example application attempts to write to a file named `myLogFile.txt`. We will encapsulate this security-critical operation within a `PrivilegedAction` class as can be done with other standard Java 2 security-critical actions. We then compile and insert this security-critical action class into the `authaction.jar` file as referenced by our Java security policy file described previously. The definition of this `PrivilegedAction` class is rather simple for our demonstration purposes and is encapsulated with an `AuthorizationAction` class as shown here:

```
package ejava.jaas;

import java.security.PrivilegedAction;
import java.io.*;
```

```
public class AuthorizationAction implements PrivilegedAction
{
  public Object run()
  {
    try{
      FileOutputStream fout = new FileOutputStream("myLogFile.txt");
      DataOutputStream dout = new DataOutputStream(fout);
      dout.writeChars("Attempted log!");
    }
    catch(Exception e){
      e.printStackTrace();
    }

    return null;
  }
}
```

The invocation of this privileged action by our `AuthenticationExample` occurs after our subject has been authenticated by the system. Thus, we might simply attempt to perform this security-critical action as shown here:

```
// Get our subject after authentication
Subject mySubject = loginContext.getSubject();

// Now perform the security-critical authorization action
Subject.doAs(mySubject, new AuthorizationAction());
```

JAAS Security Authorization Permissions

Upon integration of JAAS with the J2SE, the `java.security.ProtectionDomain` class was extended to define a `ProtectionDomain(CodeSource, PermissionCollection, ClassLoader, Principal[])` constructor. This allows a `ProtectionDomain` to be defined to associated with one or more principals as required by subject-oriented authorization to incorporate subjects into a Java security policy grant entry. The `java.security.Policy` class was also extended to define a `getPermissions(ProtectionDomain)` method that returns a `PermissionCollection` object associated with a particular `ProtectionDomain` which could include subjects associated with a Java security policy grant entry.

A few permissions are also defined in the `javax.security.auth` package to define permissions related to JAAS-oriented authentication. The `javax.security.AuthPermission` class encapsulates authentication permissions that have a target name (but no action lists) that can be used to grant permissions for access to `Subject`, `LoginContext`, and `Configuration` objects. The target names of an `AuthPermission` may be one of the following:

- `doAs`: Allows for the invocation of `Subject.doAs()` methods.
- `doAsPrivileged`: Allows for the invocation of `Subject.doAsPrivileged()` methods.

- getSubject: Allows for the invocation of Subject.getSubject() methods to obtain a handle to a Subject object for the current thread.
- getSubjectFromDomainCombiner: Allows for the invocation of the SubjectDomainCombiner.getSubject() method. The javax.security.auth.SubjectDomainCombiner class extends the java.security.DomainCombiner class to update protection domains with subject permissions defined with the Java security policy.
- setReadOnly: Allows for permission to set the Subject to be read-only.
- modifyPrincipals: Allows for permission to modify a Set containing a Subject object's principals.
- modifyPublicCredentials: Allows for permission to modify a Set containing a Subject object's public credentials.
- modifyPrivateCredentials: Allows for permission to modify a Set containing a Subject object's private credentials.
- refreshCredential: Allows for permission to invoke the Refreshable.refresh() method in order to refresh a credential object's state.
- destroyCredential: Allows for permission to invoke the Destroyable.destroy() method to destroy a credential object's state.
- CreateLoginContext.{name}: Allows for permission to create a LoginContext object with the specified name or * for any name.
- getLoginConfiguration: Allows for permission to retrieve the login Configuration.
- setLoginConfiguration: Allows for permission to set the login Configuration.
- refreshLoginConfiguration: Allows for permission to refresh the login Configuration.

The javax.security.auth.PrivateCredentialPermission class is used to grant or limit access to private credential objects that are associated with a Subject. The basic format for specifying such a permission in a Java security policy file is as follows:

```
permission javax.security.auth.PrivateCredentialPermission
➥ "CredentialClassName PrincipalClassName \"principal_name\"",
➥ "read";
```

As an example, we must grant permission to the principal name edison for access to their private credentials with our AuthenticationExample using the following Java security permission in a Java security policy file:

```
permission javax.security.auth.PrivateCredentialPermission
    "java.lang.String ejava.jaas.MyPrincipal \"edison\"", "read";
```

Alternatively, an asterisk, `*`, may be used in place of the *`CredentialClassName`* to indicate that this permission applies to all credential class types. Furthermore, an asterisk may also be used in place of the *`principal_name`* to indicate that this permission applies to all principals with the associated *`PrincipalClassName`* as a principal class type. If the *`PrincipalClassName`* is also specified with an asterisk, the permission applies to any principal class type. As a final note, additional *`PrincipalClassName`* and *`principal_name`* pairs can be specified within the same permission.

Java Security Policies with Authentication Permissions

As we have previously mentioned, our example application also requires that we configure additional Java security policies in order to execute our example application. Specifically, the `AuthenticationExample` application creates a `LoginContext` object, attempts to read private credentials for our user named `edison`, attempts to perform a privileged action associated with a `Subject`, attempts to read a properties file from the local file system, and attempts to write a security log file to the local file system. Our Java policy file thus utilized by our example application must have the following additional grant entries:

```
grant codebase "file:example.jar"
{
   permission javax.security.auth.AuthPermission "createLoginContext";
   permission javax.security.auth.PrivateCredentialPermission
    "java.lang.String ejava.jaas.MyPrincipal \"edison\"", "read";
   permission javax.security.auth.AuthPermission "doAs";
   permission java.io.FilePermission "credentials.properties", "read";
   permission java.io.FilePermission "myLogFile.txt", "write";
};
```

As just shown, our authentication example code is packaged into a local `example.jar` file referenced by the codebase in this standard Java security policy file.

Thus, we may then execute our example with the following command whereby all such referenced configuration and policy files are contained in the local directory:

```
java -Djava.security.auth.login.config=jaas.config
➥ -Djava.security.manager
➥ -Djava.security.policy=security.policy
➥ ejava.jaas.AuthenticationExample
```

Because our `security.policy` file also included an entry defined earlier to allow `edison` to write to a log file, the example should execute with no security exceptions. If we were to alter the `security.policy` file to assume a different principal name for `myLogFile.txt` file write permission and execute the application, a `FilePermission` failure for `edison`'s permission to write to the `myLogFile.txt` file would occur.

Using JAAS with EJB

Although the JAAS API previously described can apply to standalone J2SE and container-based J2EE environments alike, the most common usage for JAAS is expected to be in the context of EJB container environments. There are a few reasons to expect this. First, enterprise applications represent the most common application type used with Java. Second, security-critical enterprise applications are often constructed in a demilitarized zone that naturally leverage use of an EJB container/server environment. Hence, a standard means for authentication and authorization in such environments is crucial. This is where JAAS may step in and provide the greatest help.

EJB Clients and JAAS

An EJB client first must obtain information that it will use to authenticate itself with the server. This information may be gotten in various ways, including from a command line, a GUI, or perhaps a local store of credential information.

The EJB client may choose to implement a `CallbackHandler` object as previously described to retrieve login information from a user. A client uses the `LoginContext` abstraction to associate such a `CallbackHandler` with the client-side JAAS authentication process. A custom or vendor-supplied class that implements the `LoginModule` interface must then be set by the `LoginContext` with the `CallbackHandler`. The custom or vendor-supplied `LoginModule` is then responsible for transferring authentication information stored in the `CallbackHandler` to the EJB server transparent to the EJB client. The EJB client simply uses standard JAAS interfaces and specifies the configuration of the custom or vendor-specific `LoginModule` via the JAAS configuration file. The EJB client has no need to talk directly with the `LoginModule` implementation class.

> **Note**
>
> An example EJB client using JAAS is associated with the code for this chapter located as described in Appendix A. The code is extracted to the `examples/src/ejava/ejb/security/jaas` directory. A `TestClient` class in that directory represents a JAAS client that talks to the `OrderManagerEJB` session bean deployed to the EJB server. The `TestClient` uses a `TestCallbackHandler` for authentication. Note that this example assumes that you are running the BEA WebLogic Server and needs to make use of a vendor-specific `URLCallback` class. Such a vendor binding was necessary at the time of this writing due to the early stages of integration of JAAS with J2EE. A `TestAction` associated with these examples performs `PrivilegedAction` operations on the `OrderManagerEJB` that requires security-critical access control decision making.

J2EE application clients may also specify a special `<callback-handler>` element inside of their `application-client.xml` deployment descriptor as defined in Chapter 23, "Enterprise Application Services." This element is defined with a fully qualified class name of a `CallbackHandler` implementation as illustrated here:

```
<application-client ...>
    ...
  <callback-handler>
    ejava.ejb.security.jaas.TestCallbackHandler
  </callback-handler>
    ...
</application-client>
```

The `<callback-handler>` element references a `CallbackHandler` interface implementation with a parameterless constructor. The J2EE application client's container uses this callback handler to extract authentication from the client at runtime before the client is allowed to interact with a security-critical EJB.

EJB Servers and JAAS

On the server side, the EJB server makes any vendor-specific calls to the server's underlying authentication mechanisms. The EJB server vendor may use JAAS on the server side as well to transform authentication information into concrete `CallbackHandler` objects usable by that vendor's EJB container. JAAS may be used to initialize a `LoginModule` implementation on the server side with the `CallbackHandler` associated with the client's authentication information. The `LoginModule` implementation may be provided by your EJB container vendor or it may be a custom `LoginModule`. If your EJB container vendor allows you to implement your own custom JAAS `LoginModule` classes, you may generally implement them in a vendor-independent fashion by adhering to the JAAS standard interfaces. Thus, you'll be able to use those custom `LoginModule` implementations in other J2EE containers supporting JAAS.

> **Custom JAAS *`LoginModule`* Classes**
>
> Custom `LoginModule` classes may be needed if your vendor's supplied `LoginModule` implementations cannot work with your particular credential storage mechanism. For example, you may store legacy credential information in a database that uses a proprietary encryption algorithm to decrypt passwords. In such a case, even if your EJB vendor supplies you with some generic `LoginModule` implementation for retrieving information from a database, it may not be able to support the decryption algorithm needed for your custom authentication process.

The EJB server then uses JAAS to induce a login that performs the `LoginModule` class-specific authentication process. If a successful login occurs, the JAAS subject information is associated on the server side with the client's thread or by some other security context association means. One means is to sign the principal information associated with an authenticated `Subject`. Such signed "security tokens" may then be returned to the EJB client as security context information. The server can then check such security tokens in a much more efficient fashion whenever subsequent security-critical EJB operations are attempted by the client.

Conclusions

Thinking about the reliability, availability, scalability, and security of your EJB applications means thinking about EJB assurance. This chapter described some of the most core technologies available to you from within J2EE as well as provided by vendors to help you build assured EJB applications. Use of transactions with EJB can be done in either a programmatic or a declarative form and helps guarantee the reliability of your EJBs in distributed enterprise environments. The scalability and availability of your EJB applications is largely a function of what clustering features your EJB container provides to support fail-over and load balancing. Securing your EJBs involves the most consideration. Standard provisions for EJB security largely revolve around programmatic and declarative access control mechanisms. Although JAAS may be used to help provide standard authentication mechanisms, other vendor-specific authentication and security mechanisms may be employed. Regardless, this chapter leaves you with the basis to think about how to approach infusing assurance into your EJB applications and how you might do this leveraging J2EE standards as much as possible.

29

EJB Integration and Management

THE INTEGRATION OF AUXILIARY AND LEGACY enterprise applications with your Java enterprise applications is a problem that is generally addressed by enterprise application integration (EAI) solutions. EAI involves providing tools, techniques, and technologies for integrating enterprise data and application logic among disparate systems. EAI can be partitioned into those integration efforts internal to an enterprise and those inter-enterprise efforts that extend beyond a single enterprise into more business-to-business (B2B) specific arenas. EAI can also be distinguished according to whether your enterprise application seeks to tap the services of another application, expose its own services to other applications, or both. Finally, in J2EE environments, the J2EE container itself may seek to integrate with services provided external to the container. This chapter describes those key J2EE technologies available to enable the integration and management of J2EE components and containers with services external to themselves.

In this chapter, you will learn:

- An overview of enterprise application integration and management concepts.
- A basic approach for integrating J2EE Web components and EJBs with BeeShirts.com serving as an integrated example.
- A basic approach for exposing EJBs to CORBA clients.
- The means by which a J2EE container manages resources and how J2EE components use such resources.
- A basic approach for integrating J2EE applications with distributed communication services.
- The architecture and usage of the J2EE Connector Architecture standard for integrating J2EE components and containers with an enterprise information system (EIS).
- A basic overview of the Java Authorization Contract for Containers (JACC) standard used in integrating security service providers with J2EE containers.

- A basic overview of the J2EE Management and Java Management Extension (JMX) standards used in integrating enterprise application management tools with J2EE containers.
- A basic overview of the J2EE Deployment standard used in integrating enterprise application configuration and deployment tools with J2EE containers.

Enterprise Application Integration and Management Overview

Although this book has focused on how to build new enterprise applications, many enterprise application development problems also involve integrating with auxiliary or legacy enterprise applications. A significant portion of overall development time can, in fact, revolve around integration with other enterprise applications. Integration may take place with a particular Java component as a client or server to the legacy or auxiliary enterprise application. Figure 29.1 depicts a very simplified view of the problem and enterprise application integration solution. On the right side of the diagram, we see a legacy/auxiliary enterprise application that we want to integrate with our Java enterprise applications. EAI involves solving the problem regarding how to integrate the data and logic of such legacy/auxiliary systems into the framework of your current and future-generation Java enterprise systems.

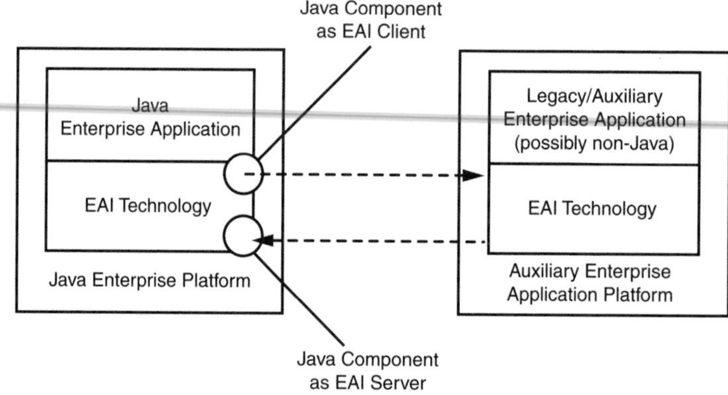

Figure 29.1 Enterprise application integration.

When legacy/auxiliary enterprise applications are internally managed by an enterprise, we have an internal EAI problem that can offer more flexibility and controllability over how a solution may be provided. When legacy/auxiliary enterprise applications sit external to an enterprise, these external EAI problems can become significantly more complicated because multiple enterprise organizations must agree and come to some consensus on how their systems will integrate. Such, however, are often the problems of business-to-business (B2B) applications that must decide how to exchange enterprise data.

In J2EE architectures, EJBs serve as the centerpiece for enterprise applications. Hence, most EAI problems involve use of EJBs as clients to legacy or auxiliary enterprise applications or perhaps involve exposing EJBs in such a way that auxiliary applications can tap their services. Thus far in this book, we have already discussed how EJBs can expose themselves to standalone Java and J2EE application clients. We've also seen how EJBs can act as message consumers via use of message-driven beans. This chapter also explores how to expose EJBs to a Web tier and thus enable Web clients to access EJBs. The means for exposing EJBs to CORBA clients perhaps implemented in other programming languages will also be briefly discussed. The next chapter is dedicated to a detailed description of how EJBs can be exposed as Web services offering next-generation capabilities for bringing EJBs into the limelight as the engines driving Web services.

We also explore how EJBs can be used to integrate with legacy and auxiliary applications whereby EJBs act as clients to such services. In this context we describe EJBs' use of container-managed connections to such auxiliary resources. We've in fact already seen how EJBs can reference and make use of JDBC connections and JMS messaging destinations managed by an EJB container. This chapter expands on such concepts further and discusses how EJBs can integrate with other distributed communication and resource services. New standard means for J2EE containers themselves to integrate with such services are also briefly highlighted.

EJB Web Client Integration

Throughout this book, we have presented numerous examples of how to create both standalone Java clients and J2EE application clients to an EJB. We've also seen how to make one EJB serve as a client to another EJB. But you also may be wondering how one makes the business logic and data encapsulated behind a wall of EJBs accessible via the Web. One significant means for doing this is to use Java Servlets or JSPs as EJB clients. As you'll discover, because Java Servlets and JSPs operate inside of a J2EE container environment, turning them into EJB clients is very similar to the process in which J2EE application clients and EJBs are turned into EJB clients. Furthermore, the next chapter also discusses how to expose EJBs directly to the Web via Web services implemented as EJBs.

BeeShirts.com Integrated J2EE Web and EJB E-commerce Application

Given the BeeShirts.com J2EE JSPs of Chapter 20, "JavaServer Pages (JSP)," and the J2EE EJBs of Chapters 25 through 27, we have integrated these two J2EE component tiers together and provide a downloadable version of this integrated code. Figure 29.2 depicts the architecture of this fully integrated BeeShirts.com e-commerce enterprise application.

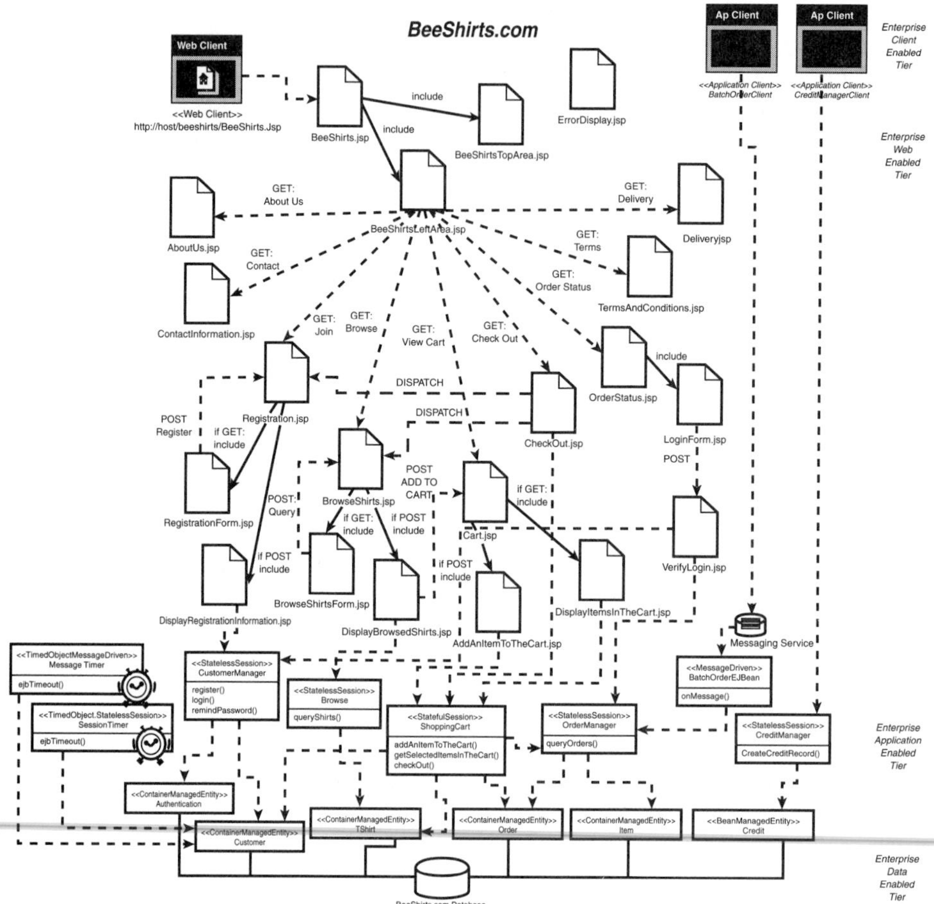

Figure 29.2 BeeShirts.com e-commerce enterprise application.

The architecture of Figure 29.2 can be partitioned into four primary tiers:

- *Enterprise Data Enabled Tier:* Our enterprise data tier contains all BeeShirts.com enterprise data in a database accessed by JDBC from BMP entity beans and via an EJB container for CMP entity beans. Much of our BeeShirts.com data schema was introduced in Chapter 5 and Chapter 6.
- *Enterprise Application Enabled Tier:* Our BeeShirts.com application business logic and data are encapsulated by EJBs at this tier. Our EJB infrastructure was introduced in Chapters 25 through 27.
- *Enterprise Web Enabled Tier:* Our Web presentation layer is composed of JSPs as described primarily in Chapter 20. All BeeShirts.com Web requests and responses

are handled at this layer, delegating business logic and data requests to the EJB layer.

- *Enterprise Client Enabled Tier:* The primary interface to our BeeShirts.com application is the Web interface described in Chapters 19 through 21. Through this interface, BeeShirts.com customers browse for T-shirts, add shirts to a shopping cart, register, place orders, and learn about BeeShirts.com business practices. A simple credit manager client to add customer credit-card information using a credit manager bean demonstrates a simple J2EE application client that interacts with our enterprise application tier directly. A simple batch order client sending messages to a queue received by our batch order message-driven bean demonstrates a simple message producer whose message is delivered to a batch order message-driven bean. Two timed object beans are also used to access customer information in order to formulate a message based on some timed event.

To integrate the BeeShirts.com Web and EJB tiers, we had to slightly reengineer the Web tier JSPs to delegate calls to and receive responses from the EJBs. The points of BeeShirts.com integration between the Web and EJB tier are described here:

- *Customer Registration:* The `DisplayRegistrationInformation` JSP was engineered to now invoke the `CustomerManager` EJB's `register()` method with a `Serializable Customer` object before the user is officially registered with the system and added to the database.
- *T-Shirt Browsing:* The `DisplayBrowsedShirts` JSP was engineered to invoke the `Browse` EJB's `queryShirts()` method to query for actual T-shirt data in the database.
- *Shopping-Cart Item Addition:* The `AddAnItemToTheCart` JSP was engineered to create a `ShoppingCart` EJB and add it to the JSP's session, if none was currently in the JSP session. The `AddAnItemToTheCart` JSP was then engineered to invoke the `ShoppingCart` EJB's `addAnItemToTheCart()` method to add selected item data to the shopping session.
- *Shopping-Cart Item Retrieval:* The `DisplayItemsInTheCart` JSP was engineered to use the `ShoppingCart` EJB stored in the JSP session to invoke that EJB's `getSelectedItemsInTheCart()` method for retrieving cart items from this shopping session.
- *Shopping-Cart Checkout:* The `Checkout` JSP was engineered to invoke the `ShoppingCart` EJB's `checkOut()` method to create an order for the customer based on the shopping cart session items and then display this order for the customer.
- *Customer Login:* The `VerifyLogin` JSP was engineered to invoke the `CustomerManager` EJB's `login()` method to effect a login and receive a serialized `Customer` object when a Login button is clicked.

- *Order Query:* The `VerifyLogin` JSP (included from the `OrderStatus` JSP) was engineered to invoke the `OrderManager` EJB's `queryOrders()` method to retrieve a collection of orders for this customer that will be displayed. Note that this occurs only if the customer can successfully log in.
- *Customer Password Reminding:* The `VerifyLogin` JSP was engineered to invoke the `CustomerManager` EJB's `remindPassword()` method to effect the emailing of a customer's password when a Remind button is clicked.

EJB Web Client Integration Approach and Examples

Now that we've seen *what* was integrated between our BeeShirts.com Web and EJB components, let's explore *how* this is accomplished. Whether from within a Java Servlet, from a JSP scriptlet, or from a helper class invoked from a JSP, the application code for looking up EJB home interface object handles is very straightforward. After a parameter-less `javax.naming.InitialContext` object is created, a `lookup()` is performed on that context given an EJB reference name. EJB reference names follow the general form of `java:comp/env/ejb/`*`MyEJBRefName`*.

> **Note**
>
> The reengineered JSP code for talking with the EJBs can be located as described in Appendix A, "Software Configuration," and is extracted beneath the `examples/src/ejava/integration/web` directory. Note that we insert snippets from such code in this section. Also note that this code depends on some of the code from Chapter 19 extracted to the `examples/src/ejava/servlets` directory and code from Chapters 25 through 27 extracted beneath the `examples/src/ejava/ejb` directory. Appendix A describes how to build and deploy this code.

We have created a `WebHelper` class for this chapter's code that is similar to the `JSPHelper` class from Chapter 20. The `WebHelper` also defines a series of methods to assist with creating handles to EJBs, as well as to invoke EJBs. For example, this new `ejava.integration.web.WebHelper` class looks up various EJB home objects and invokes the methods of EJBs as shown here for the `BrowseLocalHome` and `BrowseLocal` objects:

```
package ejava.integration.web;
  ...
public class WebHelper{
   ...
  private static String BROWSE_REFNAME = "java:comp/env/ejb/browse";
  ...
  public static BrowseLocalHome getBrowseHome() {
    if (browseHome == null) {
      try {
        InitialContext ctx = new InitialContext();
        browseHome = (BrowseLocalHome) ctx.lookup(BROWSE_REFNAME);
```

```
        ctx.close();
        System.out.println("Got Browse Manager Home :" + browseHome);
      } catch (NamingException ne) {
        ne.printStackTrace();
      }
    }
    return browseHome;
  }
   ...
  public static Vector queryShirts(String size, String color)
    throws CreateException{
    // Create a return value and look up Browse home interface
    Vector returnValue = null;
    if (browseHome == null) {
      getBrowseHome();
    }

    // Create the Browse local interface
    System.out.println("Browse Session ");
    BrowseLocal browseLocal = browseHome.create();

    // Induce the Browse interface to return a Vector of shirts
    System.out.println("Browse Session Created ");
    returnValue = browseLocal.queryShirts(size, color);
    return returnValue;
  }
  ...
}
```

Our `DisplayBrowsedShirts` JSP invokes the `WebHelper.queryShirts()` method from within the JSP. At the top of the JSP, this `queryShirts()` method is called to receive and display a `Vector` of `Serializable TShirt` objects. The `DisplayBrowsedShirts` JSP reengineered to invoke the `Browse` EJB's `queryShirts()` method to query for actual T-shirt data in the database is shown here:

```
<%
  System.out.println(" Displaying :"+WebHelper.SERVER_INFO);
  String postToPage =
   application.getAttribute(WebHelper.SERVER_INFO)+WebHelper.CART_PAGE;
  System.out.println(" Displaying :1");
  String queriedSize = request.getParameter(SHIRT_SIZE);
  String queriedColor = request.getParameter(SHIRT_COLOR);
  System.out.println(" Displaying :2"+queriedSize+queriedColor);
  Vector browsedShirts =
    WebHelper.queryShirts(queriedSize,queriedColor);
  int resultItemsCount = browsedShirts.size();
  System.out.println(" Displaying :3"+browsedShirts);
```

```
  session.setAttribute(WebHelper.BROWSED_SHIRTS, browsedShirts);
%>
<TD VALIGN=TOP>
<TABLE  bgcolor="#CCCC99" cellpadding="1" cellspacing="0" border="1">
<%
  if(browsedShirts.size() == 0){
%>
  <TR> <TD><STRONG> NO Shirts Match Your Query Criteria
       </STRONG> </TD> </TR>
<%
  }
%>

<TR> <TD COLSPAN=2> Queried For :</TD> </TR>
<TR> <TD> SHIRT_SIZE : </TD> <TD> <%=queriedSize%></TD> </TR>
<TR> <TD> "SHIRT_COLOR ": </TD> <TD> <%=queriedColor%></TD> </TR>
<TR> </TR>
<TR> </TR>
<TR> </TR>
<%
    for(int i = 0; i< browsedShirts.size(); i++){
      TShirt tShirt = (TShirt)browsedShirts.elementAt(i);
      out.println("<TR> <TD VALIGN=TOP COLSPAN=2> "+
        tShirt.getTShirtAsHTMLTableForBrowing(postToPage)+
        "</TD></TR>");
    }
%>
</TABLE>
</TD>
```

The means by which EJB reference names are mapped to point to the correct EJBs is a function of configuring your `web.xml` file for the JSP or Java Servlet, as well as a function of deployment time mapping of EJB names to JNDI names. Recall that the `web.xml` file has an `<ejb-ref>` element under the root `<web-app>` element. At a minimum, the `<ejb-ref>` element defines the EJB reference name, the type of EJB being referenced, the home or home local interface class name, and the remote or local interface class name.

As an example, an EJB reference to the `Browse` bean utilized in the preceding code snippets is defined within the `web.xml` file for these examples this way:

```
<web-app...>
   ...
   <ejb-local-ref>
      <ejb-ref-name>ejb/browse</ejb-ref-name>
      <ejb-ref-type>Session</ejb-ref-type>
      <local-home>ejava.ejb.session.browse.BrowseLocalHome</local-home>
      <local>ejava.ejb.session.browse.BrowseLocal</local>
```

```
      <ejb-link>BeeShirtsEJBs.jar#BrowseEJB</ejb-link>
   </ejb-local-ref>
   ...
</web-app>
```

> **Note**
>
> The deployment descriptors and ANT build script for creating the Web client module and for building the enterprise application for this integrated BeeShirts.com application are contained in the `examples/src/ejava/integration/web` directory. The `web.xml` file contains the standard Web module descriptor. Vendor-specific deployment descriptors for deploying the Web tier are also defined in this directory. Appendix A describes how to deploy J2EE applications in the context of different vendor implementations.
>
> Additionally, an `examples/src/ejava/integration/web/buildejbs` directory contains an ANT build script for building and deploying the EJBs invoked by the Web tier. This build script is invoked when you run the ANT build script in the `examples/src/ejava/integration/web/buildejbs` directory. The Web tier WAR file and EJB JAR file are both incorporated into an enterprise application defined inside of an EAR file built for this chapter's example.

You'll note that the `web.xml` file refers to the EJBs packaged inside of the EJB JAR file. The Web tier is built and packaged inside of a `BeeShirtsWeb.war` file, whereas the EJBs are built and packaged inside of a `BeeShritsEJBs.jar` file for this chapter's example. The WAR file and EJB JAR file are deployed as part of a cohesive J2EE enterprise application defined via the `application.xml` file as shown here:

```
<application...>
  <display-name>BeeshirtsApplication</display-name>
  <module>
    <ejb>BeeShirtsEJBs.jar</ejb>
  </module>
  <module>
    <web>
      <web-uri>BeeShirtsWeb.war</web-uri>
      <context-root>beeshirts</context-root>
    </web>
  </module>
</application>
```

EJB CORBA Client Integration

For maximum interoperability, one must consider how to expose EJBs as CORBA servers. That is, how does one create an EJB and expose it as a CORBA server to CORBA clients such that the clients have no idea they are talking with a CORBA server implemented as an EJB or via some other means? Despite the fact that EJB uses IIOP as the underlying wire-level protocol, exposing an EJB as a pure CORBA server is a nontrivial if not somewhat impractical proposal. Because J2EE-compliant EJB containers do not allow EJBs to create their own server sockets in order to enable the container to be able to manage system resources, EJBs cannot create and register their own CORBA servers. Rather, EJB developers must rely on the capability to offer CORBA interfaces to their EJB components to be provided by the container/server provider. This section briefly discusses the approach one must consider to create CORBA clients and servers with J2EE-compliant EJBs.

The EJB v2.1 specification defines the standards that must be followed by EJB container/server vendors wanting to provide interoperable CORBA interfaces to EJBs. The EJB specification defines a standard means for EJB server environments to be able to better interoperate with other server environments because standard CORBA communication protocols, naming, transaction context propagation, and security context propagation are scoped within the specification.

Two main types of clients can access such CORBA-enabled EJB servers. An EJB/CORBA client is a Java-based client that uses JNDI for EJB home lookups, relies on RMI/IIOP, and uses the JTA `UserTransaction` API for any client-side transaction demarcation. A pure CORBA client implemented in any language can use CosNaming for EJB home lookups, relies on CORBA/IIOP and IDL-based interfaces, and uses the OTS for any client-side transaction demarcation. CORBA-compliant J2EE EJB servers provide support for these two types of clients in the following four key ways:

- *CORBA Distribution:* J2EE EJB servers provide support for pure CORBA v2.3.1 IIOP v1.2 communication protocols. Remote and home interfaces for EJBs are mapped from Java to IDL in a standard fashion. Clients thus utilize such IDL to interact with CORBA-enabled EJB components narrowing any references as necessary. IDL mappings exist for all standard client-related abstractions in a `javax::ejb` module, such as `EJBHome`, `EJBObject`, `Handle`, `HomeHandle`, and `EJBMetaData`. IDL mappings must also exist for `Enumeration`, `Collection`, `Iterator`, and standard exceptions. Furthermore, IDL mappings must also be generated for any application-specific EJB home and remote interfaces and application-specific exceptions.
- *CORBA Naming:* A CosNaming-compliant naming service must be provided by a J2EE EJB server for clients to look up handles to `EJBHome` interface objects. EJB/CORBA clients can access this naming service via JNDI with a CosNaming SPI plug-in. Pure CORBA clients use the CosNaming service directly. When EJB JAR files are deployed to a server, they are deployed specifying the root CosNaming context from which the names defined in their `ejb-jar.xml` file are relative. Exactly how such a root context is defined is vendor specific.
- *CORBA Transactions:* A CORBA Object Transaction Service (OTS) v1.2 implementation must be provided by a J2EE EJB server to enable support for CORBA clients to propagate their transaction context during client-managed transaction demarcation. Transaction context information is baked inside of IIOP messages according to the format defined inside of the `CosTranactions::PropagationContext` IDL description.

- *CORBA Security:* As discussed in Chapter 28, conformance level 1 of the OMG's Common Security Interoperability v2 (CSIv2) specification must be employed for security interoperability. SSLv3.0 and TLS v1.0 must also be used at the transport level.

After a CORBA-compliant J2EE EJB server is used that adheres to the preceding requirements, EJB developers can deploy their beans to such servers and let the platform handle all CORBA connectivity. Developers can generate the IDL for their application-specific client interfaces using a standard Java-to-IDL mapping tool. From the client side, CORBA client development proceeds as usual with the proper IDL files in hand.

Container Managed Resources

The recommended means for J2EE components to reference resources external or internal to the J2EE container is through resource references. For EJBs, resource references are stored in a JNDI tree per deployed EJB type rooted with the JNDI name `java:comp/env/`. Objects located beneath that JNDI context are associated with the calling EJB's environment. This section introduces those container-managed resources that an EJB may reference, how they might reference such resources, and how such resources are specified in the bean's deployment descriptor (that is, within a `<session>`, `<entity>`, or `<message-driven>` element).

Managed Resources References (`<resource-ref>`)

In Chapter 26, "Entity EJB," we described and saw examples for how EJBs could connect to databases using JDBC. The `<resource-ref>` deployment descriptor elements were used to define references to JDBC resources. The EJB then referred to such resources using a logical resource reference name, which was then mapped to a physical resource name by the EJB container. Besides references to JDBC connection factories, such a methodology for referencing external resources applies to other managed resource types as well. An EJB container may provide a wide-variety of managed resource types. However, four standard managed resource types, their reference naming convention, and the types returned from JNDI lookups via reference names are defined here:

- *JDBC Connections:* References JDBC connection resources. JDBC connection factories are stored by convention in the JNDI namespace beginning with `java:comp/env/jdbc/` and return `javax.sql.DataSource` types. For example:

```
DataSource resource
  = (DataSource) ctx.lookup("java:comp/env/jdbc/jdbcPool");
```

- *JMS Destinations:* References JMS destination resources. JMS destination connection factories are stored by convention in the JNDI namespace beginning with `java:comp/env/jms/` and return `javax.jms.QueueConnectionFactory`, `javax.jms.TopicConnectionFactory`, or `javax.jms.ConnectionFactory`, types. For example:

```
QueueConnectionFactory resource  = (QueueConnectionFactory )
    ctx.lookup("java:comp/env/jms/ejavaQueues");
```

- *JavaMail Connections:* References JavaMail connection resources. JavaMail connection factories are stored by convention in the JNDI namespace beginning with `java:comp/env/mail/` and return `javax.mail.Session` types. For example:

```
Session resource
  = (Session) ctx.lookup("java:comp/env/mail/emailSource");
```

- *URL Connections:* References URL connection resources. URL connection factories are stored by convention in the JNDI namespace beginning with `java:comp/env/url/` and return `java.net.URL` types. For example:

```
URL resource
  = (URL) ctx.lookup("java:comp/env/url/remoteURL");
```

In addition to simply identifying the resources inside `<resource-ref>` deployment descriptor elements, a few other options are available to indicate how the container should manage those resources. For one, a `<res-auth>` sub-element may be defined as either `Application` or `Container`. When `Container` is used, the container is left with determining how it will authenticate itself with the remote resource on the J2EE component's behalf. Most often the J2EE container vendor will allow you to specify such authentication information inside of a vendor-specific deployment descriptor or configuration file. When `Application` is used as the `<res-auth>` element value, the J2EE component must programmatically use whatever resource type specific methods are offered to allow the component to authenticate itself with the resource.

Finally, if a `<res-sharing-scope>` element is defined within a `<resource-ref>` element, the container may be informed if the component wants to share the connections returned from the factory for the component (that is, `Shareable`) or if it wants its own connection for exclusive use (that is, `Unshareable`). By default, all connections are defined as `Shareable` in order to allow the container to manage connections in a pool.

As a refresher example of JDBC resource configuration for entity EJBs as extracted, we have this:

```
<ejb-jar>
  ...
  <enterprise-beans>
    ...
    <entity>
      ...
      <resource-ref>
         <description>This bean hogs its own connection.</description>
         <res-ref-name>jdbc/ejavaPool</res-ref-name>
         <res-type>javax.sql.DataSource</res-type>
         <res-auth>Container</res-auth>
```

```
        <res-sharing-scope>Unshareable</res-sharing-scope>
      </resource-ref>
    </entity>
    ...
  </enterprise-beans>
  ...
</ejb-jar>
```

Administered Object Resource References (<resource-env-ref>)

In addition to references to resources associated directly with connections to external resource managers, an EJB may also have a need to interact with administered objects managed by the container and associated with an EJB's environment. Such administered objects may ultimately map to resources external to the container, but typically require additional management services provided by the container above and beyond pure connection pooling. Hence, the administered object represents the resource itself versus a connection factory used to generate a connection to the resource. For example, a messaging service may be integrated directly with an EJB container and require that JMS destinations act as administered objects.

The means by which EJBs identify such objects is accomplished in an almost identical to the way it is accomplished for connection factory resources. In fact, a <resource-env-ref> element is used to configure such environment resource connectivity akin to the <resource-ref> element. The top-level structure of the <resource-env-ref> element is defined here:

- <resource-env-ref>: Top-level element to define the reference to a resource managed within the same environment as the J2EE component and composed of the sub-elements that follow.
- <description>: Description of the reference (optional).
- <resource-env-ref-name>: Defines the logical name of the environment resource.
- <resource-env-type>: Fully qualified class name of the environment resource administered object type.

Hence, an administered resource may be defined as accessible by an EJB via the following example deployment descriptor entries:

```
<ejb-jar>
  ...
  <enterprise-beans>
    ...
    <session>
      ...
      <resource-env-ref>
         <description>This bean uses a JMS queue.</description>
```

```
        <resource-env-ref-name>jms/myQueue</resource-env-ref-name>
        <resource-env-type>javax.jms.Queue</resource-env-type>
      </resource-env-ref>
    </session>
    ...
  </enterprise-beans>
  ...
</ejb-jar>
```

The bean would then access such a resource directly as illustrated here:

```
Queue queue = (Queue) jndiContext.lookup("java:comp/env/jms/myQueue");
```

EJB JavaMail Resource References

We explored the JavaMail style of asynchronous messaging in Chapter 16, "JavaMail." JavaMail provides APIs to send email via a messaging transport and retrieve email from a message store. JavaMail support is in fact required for J2EE v1.4 EJB, Web, and application client containers.

As mentioned previously, the `<resource-ref>` elements defined within a bean's element definition may be used to configure handles to JavaMail `Session` objects that serve as factory objects for `Transport` objects. EJBs can use JNDI to look up handles to these `Session` objects after they're configured.

> **Note**
>
> This section contains a few simple code snippets that can be found in the EJB code associated with Chapter 25, "Session EJB," contained within the `examples/src/ejava/ejb/session/customermgr` directory.

Our example `CustomerManagerEJBean` bean, in fact, defines a JavaMail factory reference from within its `ejb-jar.xml` file (both in its `examples/src/ejava/ejb/session/customermgr` directory and the Web client integration example in the `examples/src/ejava/integration/web/buildejbs` directory) as shown here:

```
<ejb-jar>
  ...
  <enterprise-beans>
    <session>
      ...
      <resource-ref>
        <description>Mail Session Reference</description>
        <res-ref-name>mail/BeeShirtsMailSession</res-ref-name>
        <res-type>javax.mail.Session</res-type>
        <res-auth>Container</res-auth>
      </resource-ref>
      ...
    </session>
```

```
  </enterprise-beans>
    ...
</ejb-jar>
```

The `remindPassword()` method implementation on our `CustomerManagerEJBean` class first finds a `Customer` entity bean based on an email address `String`, finds an `Authentication` entity bean based on a customer ID from `Customer`, and then invokes a `sendMail()` method on a special `MailSender` helper class as shown here:

```
public void remindPassword(String email) {
    try {
      System.out.println("Sending email to: " + email);

      // Look up local interface and password
      CMRCustomerLocal customerBean = customerHome.findByEmail(email);
      String password = customerBean.getAuthentication().getPassword();

      // Send mail using MailSender utility given email and password
      MailSender.sendMail(email, password);
    } catch (FinderException finderException) {
      finderException.printStackTrace();
    }
}
```

Finally, the `MailSender.sendMail()` utility method handles the `Session` lookup from the J2EE environment, creating the email message and sending it to the customer as shown here:

```
package ejava.ejb.session.customermgr;
...
public class MailSender {

  /**
   * send email to the user to remind them of their password
   */
  public static void sendMail(String toAddress, String password) {
    // Look up JavaMail Session reference
    Session session = null;
    try {
      InitialContext context = new InitialContext();
      session =
        (Session) context.lookup(
          "java:comp/env/mail/BeeShirtsMailSession");

      System.out.println("Mail Session :" + session);
      session.setDebug(true);
      context.close();
    } catch (NamingException namingException) {
      namingException.printStackTrace();
```

```
    }

    // Get Mail Session and Send Email
    try {
      // Create Email Message
      Message message = new MimeMessage(session);
      message.setFrom(new InternetAddress("contact@beeshirts.com"));
      InternetAddress[] address = { new InternetAddress(toAddress)};
      message.setRecipients(Message.RecipientType.TO, address);
      message.setSubject("Password Reminder");
      message.setSentDate(new Date());
      message.setText("Your BeeShirts.com password :" + password);
      System.out.println("Sending message :");

      // Send Email Message
      Transport.send(message);
    } catch (MessagingException messagingException) {
      messagingException.printStackTrace();
    }
  }
}
```

EJB Enterprise Communications Integration

Some enterprise environments, as illustrated in Figure 29.3, demand distributed access to services provided by particular auxiliary enterprise applications. Many of the distributed enterprise communications enabling paradigms described in Part III, "Enterprise Communications Enabling," will thus become applicable when such needs arise. Furthermore, a few of these distributed communication approaches can be implemented directly from the vantage point of a J2EE EJB component, as discussed earlier in this chapter. This section briefly explains those approaches and considerations for using distributed enterprise communication paradigms when providing EAI connectivity between auxiliary or legacy enterprise applications and your Java enterprise applications.

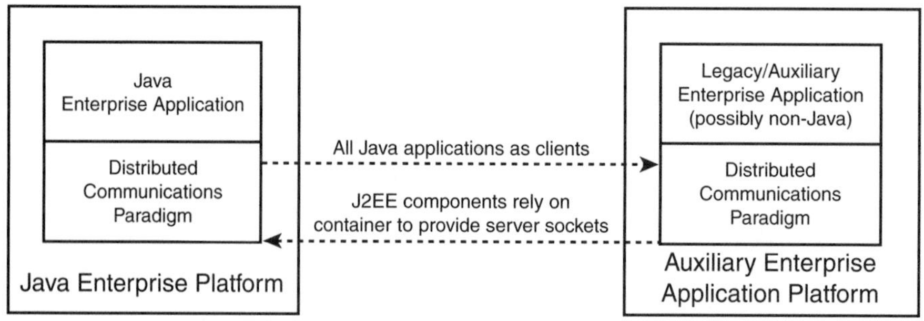

Figure 29.3 EAI with distributed communication paradigms.

EAI with TCP/IP

As you are probably aware or might infer by reading Appendix D, "TCP/IP Communications," use of TCP/IP in Java enterprise environments can be a costly solution in terms of time spent coding, but it may be the only distribution mechanism possible for certain environments. It is thus at least important to consider how TCP/IP can be used to connect auxiliary enterprise applications to your Java enterprise applications.

An auxiliary or legacy application may already provide or be adaptable to support a TCP/IP-based interface for tapping its services. However, a non-Java–based language may have been used to implement the auxiliary application. In such cases, the Java Native Interface (JNI) with Java-based TCP/IP or the native language with native socket libraries may be used to implement the auxiliary enterprise application distributed TCP/IP interface. In either case, any Java enterprise application, J2EE or standalone, can act as a TCP/IP client to this distributed auxiliary enterprise application interface using the `java.net` libraries described in Appendix D. J2EE EJB components, however, would not be able to support a socket callback mechanism if it were needed without any container-provided support for such a feature (which is highly unlikely to be offered as a "feature").

In addition to EJB restrictions, TCP/IP-based EAI has plenty of other limitations. One notable limitation relates to the significant amount of hand-coding that often must be performed to implement custom marshaling and unmarshaling and other high-level protocol features. In general, TCP/IP will be useful only when the distributed auxiliary application requires a simple interface or when limited COTS makes employing an auxiliary distributed component technology impossible.

EAI with HTTP

Although HTTP has a focused Web-based applicability, HTTP can be useful in low-cost EAI solutions as well. Of course, any low-level programming of request and response handling via HTTP begins to lose its low-cost appeal if the EAI solution is anything but simple. Nevertheless, certain EAI solutions are indeed simple. In such cases, creating simple HTTP servers to implement `GET` functionality can be very straightforward.

Using the `java.net` libraries described in Appendix E, "HTTP Communications," a simple homegrown HTTP server can be made that creates a single `ServerSocket` object to block for incoming client requests using `accept()`. The returned client `Socket` objects can then be handed off to a custom server `Thread`, and the listener can go about its business listening for more incoming socket requests. The custom server `Thread`, however, can read HTTP request data from the client using the `InputStream` returned from `Socket.getInputStream()` and send any HTTP response data back to the client via an `OutputStream` returned from `Socket.getOutputStream()`. The custom server `Thread` must parse any HTTP request data and submit it to the legacy/auxiliary application and transform any response from the legacy/auxiliary application into HTTP response data. Thus, the custom server `Thread` must have intimate knowledge of how to parse HTTP request data and generate HTTP response data at the byte level, which is largely why such custom HTTP serving will often be practical only in the simplest of EAI cases. Of course, one of the COTS-based Web-enabling solutions of Part V, "Enterprise Web Enabling," may also be used on the legacy/auxiliary application end to offer EAI via HTTP.

On the HTTP client end of EAI, many options are available to our Java enterprise applications. Because HTTP and simple HTTP client abstractions are built into the J2SE, both standalone Java applications and J2EE-based components can easily tap the services of a legacy/auxiliary application integrated with HTTP. As defined in Appendix E, the standard `java.net.HttpUrlConnection` and `java.net.URL` classes can be used as the basis for building basic Web client functionality into Java applications. Connections can be created, HTTP requests can be issued, and HTTP responses can be received using these two abstractions.

J2EE container environments have life a little easier because managed handles to `java.net.URL` factories for URL connections can be obtained directly from JNDI using resource references. That is, say that we have a URL factory defined inside of a J2EE XML-based deployment descriptor as shown here:

```
<resource-ref>
  <description> My URL Connection Factory </description>
  <res-ref-name>url/MyHttpEAIServer</res-ref-name>
  <res-type>java.net.URL</res-type>
  <res-auth>Container</res-auth>
</resource-ref>
```

Then we can obtain a handle to such factories as shown here:

```
InitialContext ctx = new InitialContext();
java.net.URL myHttpEAIServer
    = (java.net.URL) ctx.lookup("java:comp/env/url/MyHttpEAIServer");
```

Of course, a container-specific way to map such logical URL factory references to remote host addresses and ports must also be provided. After that, your EJBs and J2EE Web components are in business for integrating with a remote application over HTTP.

EAI with CORBA

One of the more significant techniques for implementing EAI over a distributed communications paradigm is via CORBA. As described in Chapter 8, "CORBA Communications," CORBA is a language- and platform-independent solution for enabling distributed communications. Thus, providing CORBA-based interfaces to auxiliary and legacy applications enables a very high level of EAI with other applications. On the legacy/auxiliary enterprise application side, a native language CORBA wrapper implementation around the application may be provided with distributed interfaces defined via CORBA IDL. Alternatively, JNI with Java can be used to bridge the auxiliary application locally with the distributed CORBA interface implemented via Java IDL or a commercial Java-based CORBA ORB implementation.

Regardless of whether Java is used as a bridging technology on the auxiliary enterprise application side, the interface to the application is via IDL. Therefore, we can speak to such applications from within standalone Java applications using Java IDL or a commercial ORB, and we can also speak to the auxiliary applications from a J2EE EJB or Web component. J2EE components, however, cannot implement any sort of CORBA server callback mechanism due to the restrictions on creating server sockets in J2EE environments by a component. Of course, in order to serve up EJBs as CORBA services, as described earlier in this chapter, a CORBA-enabled EJB can be defined in J2EE container environments that support CORBA-to-EJB mappings.

EAI with RMI

RMI, as described in Chapter 9, "RMI Communications," can also be used as a distributed EAI-enabling paradigm in certain cases. The strong case for RMI on the Java enterprise application side is that maximum interoperability is guaranteed with all J2EE EJB environments because RMI/IIOP is the standard EJB interface technology. Callbacks to EJBs over RMI are thus a matter of implementing regular EJB client interfacing on the legacy/auxiliary application side. RMI on the legacy/auxiliary application end means that JNI bridging will be needed if the application is implemented in another language.

EAI with Web Services

Perhaps the most significant technology development in the past few years has been the birth and growth of Web services. Because Web services were created as a means for achieving interoperability across applications, Web services are inherently excellent candidates for EAI. Chapter 10, "Web Service Communications," described SOAP, WSDL, and Web services RPC. Chapter 10 also discussed the J2EE APIs such as SAAJ and JAX-RPC involved with implementing Web services and Web service clients. Chapter 22, "Web Services with Web Components," demonstrated how to deploy J2EE Web components as Web services. The next chapter closes the book with a discussion on how EJBs can also be exposed as Web services, as well as how they can act as Web service clients. All of these various ways for using Web services inside of J2EE applications thus provide key hooks not only for communicating with remote Web services from within J2EE components but also for exposing J2EE components themselves as Web services.

EAI with JMS

The distributed communication paradigms used for EAI all depend on the capability to make synchronous calls onto the legacy/auxiliary enterprise applications that are to be integrated. Such an approach to EAI may be best suited for particular internal EAI projects as opposed to external EAI or B2B projects. When the need arises to perform external EAI, an asynchronous messaging scheme is almost always the best option. As described in Chapter 15, "Messaging Services with JMS and JAXM," asynchronous messaging schemes allow for a greater level of decoupling between systems and also allow for the centralized management of reliable and robust message queuing by the messaging service provider. Of course, within J2EE and Java enterprise environments, JMS is the messaging service technology of choice. Although Chapter 15 describes how to implement standalone JMS consumers and producers, Chapter 27, "Message-Driven EJB," describes how EJBs may be implemented as messaging consumers and discusses how EJBs can also act as messaging producers. Finally, earlier in this chapter, we also discussed how a container can manage JMS-related resources for an EJB and how an EJB may obtain references to such resources.

J2EE Connector Architecture

Although a technology such as JDBC defines a means to interact with external resource managers, JDBC is defined with relational database access in mind. To interface with more generic resource managers, a more generic API is needed. The J2EE Connector Architecture v1.5 required by the J2EE v1.4 defines such a standard. Above and beyond the generic API for interacting with such external resource managers, the J2EE Connector Architecture in fact defines a standard and generic way to interface with legacy/auxiliary applications of a broad range of types as well as how such systems can plug into a J2EE container to enable interoperable resource management.

J2EE Connector Architecture Overview

The J2EE Connector Architecture, as illustrated in Figure 29.4, defines a standard connector Service Provider Interface (SPI) to be implemented by legacy/auxiliary enterprise application vendors (aka enterprise information system or "EIS" vendors). EIS vendors provide resource adapters implementing the connector SPI to provide connectivity between the management services of a J2EE-based container/server and the vendor's EIS. By providing such resource adapters implementing standard SPIs, J2EE container providers can properly manage the services provided by EIS vendors using an interface that does not need to vary per vendor EIS. EIS vendors can also be guaranteed that their products will easily plug into various J2EE-compliant server products.

The connector SPI defines the following main interface types that can be implemented by EIS vendors to properly integrate with J2EE containers:

- *Life-Cycle Management:* Allows a J2EE container to manage the life cycle of a resource adapter via mechanisms such as interfaces for startup, shutdown, deployment, or undeployment.
- *Connection Management:* Allows a J2EE container to manage the connections associated with an EIS.
- *Communications Management:* Allows a resource adapter to process messages and requests from the EIS to the J2EE container and components. Includes a model and interfaces for inbound requests, handling incoming asynchronous messages, and for delegating invocations onto EJBs.

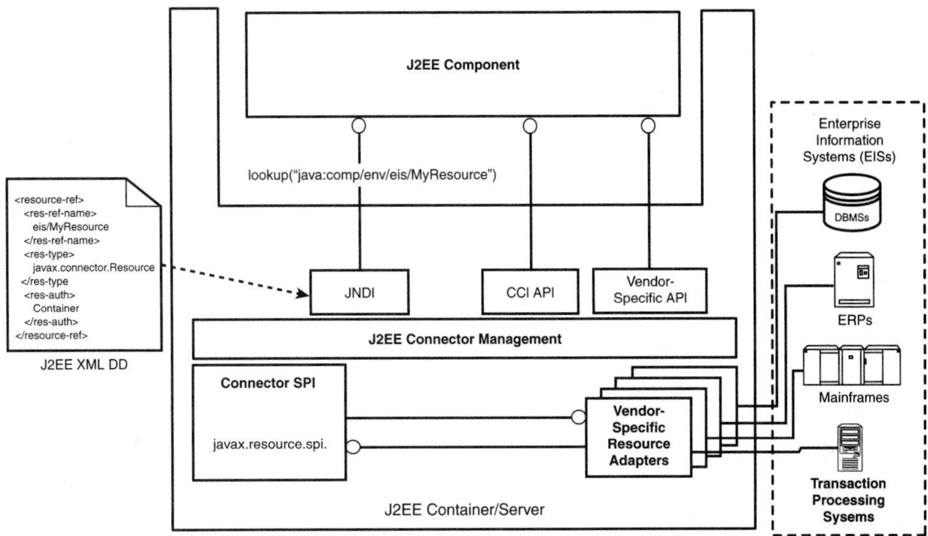

Figure 29.4 J2EE connector architecture.

- *Transaction Management:* Allows a J2EE container to manage the transactions associated with a resource adapter as well as to receive transactions from the EIS.
- *Security Management:* Allows a J2EE container to manage the security identity propagation and authentication associated with an EIS.
- *Work Management:* Allows an EIS and resource adapter to perform some unit of work perhaps with J2EE components and inside of container-managed threads by invoking methods exposed by the J2EE container.

Common Client Interface (CCI)

In addition to the set of standard system interfaces between the J2EE container and resource adapter, a standard interface contract also exists between the J2EE components and resource adapters known as the Common Client Interface (CCI). Although connector adapter vendors are not required to offer such an interface, it is highly recommended in the specification. Although vendors may be inclined to want J2EE component developers to make full use of their vendor-specific interfaces, the CCI is also defined to integrate easily with development and deployment tools. That is, the CCI adopts a JavaBeans interface convention such that resource adapter vendors may open the market for integration of vendor-supplied resource adapters with third-party development tools.

Although the CCI is geared for use in JavaBeans-based development environments, it does represent the one interface source that J2EE developers may be interested in tapping. It is thus the approach of this section to focus our attention on the CCI. The CCI defines a simple interface that allows J2EE component developers access to EIS functionality. J2EE applications establish connections and interactions with EIS applications in order to issue functional calls given a generic set of input records and receiving a generic set of output records. The generic input records, output records, and interaction interfaces map to concrete resource adapter specific types by a resource adapter vendor implementation. As you'll see, not only is such a model and API similar in part to the JDBC model and API, but it also is usable with databases akin to the JDBC API.

Resource Adapter Packaging

A resource adapter is packaged as a J2EE module inside of its own JAR file type. This JAR file type is a Resource Archive (RAR) file, which has the extension `.rar`. This RAR file may then be deployed as its own J2EE module or packaged along with other J2EE modules associated with an EAR file. Thus, one or more EJB and J2EE Web modules may be deployed with a resource module.

EIS Resource Connection Factories

Recall from Chapter 11, "Naming Services with JNDI," that JNDI provided a `javax.naming.Referenceable` interface used to encapsulate a means to obtain a reference (that is, a `javax.naming.Reference`) to an object that sat outside of a naming system. Such a reference was obtained via a `getReference()` method. The `javax.resource.Referenceable` interface depicted in Figure 29.5 extends that interface to allow for the registration of a `Reference` object into a naming service's namespace. With J2EE connectors, the referenceable object of interest is a `ConnectionFactory` object that extends the `javax.resource.Referenceable` interface as shown in Figure 29.5.

> **Note**
>
> The example J2EE connector architecture code snippets used in this section can be located as described in Appendix A and are extracted beneath the `examples/src/ejava/integration/jca` directory. Note that we insert snippets from such code throughout this section. Appendix A describes how to build and deploy this code.

The `ConnectionFactory` provides a means for J2EE components to obtain handles to `Connection` objects. A J2EE component looks up a handle to a `ConnectionFactory` object via JNDI using the recommended naming convention for a connection factory prefixed with `java:comp/env/eis/`. Here is an example lookup:

```
// Create JNDI initial context
InitialContext initialContext = new InitialContext();

// Look up ConnectionFactory object
String factoryName = "java:comp/env/eis/ejavaConnector";
ConnectionFactory connectionFactory
```

```
  = (ConnectionFactory) initialContext.lookup(factoryName);

// Close JNDI context
initialContext.close();
```

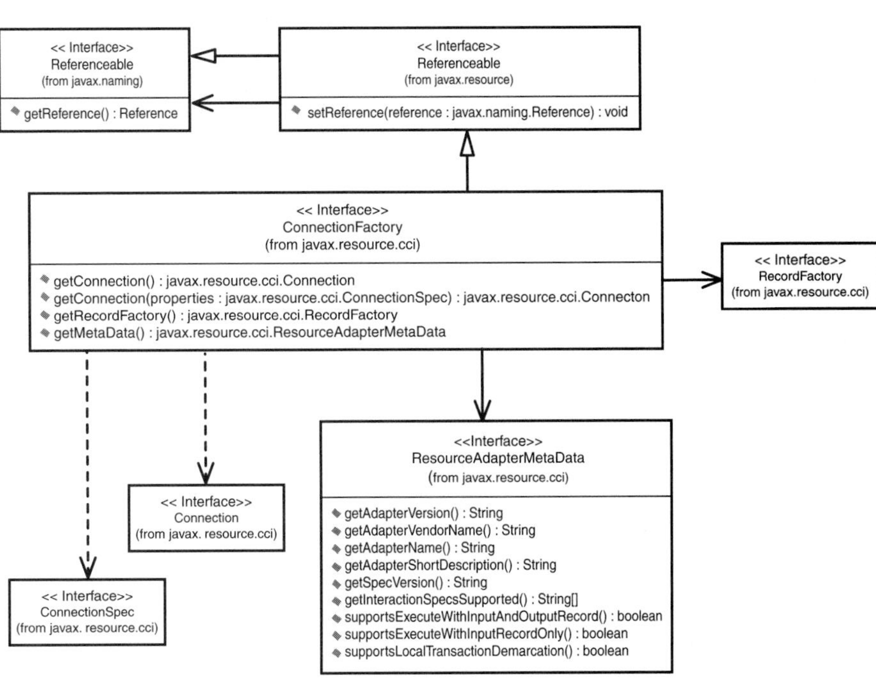

Figure 29.5 EIS resource connection factories.

The logical name for such a connector connection factory is defined inside of a `<resource-ref>` element for the EJB in its standard `ejb-jar.xml` file as illustrated here:

```
<ejb-jar...>
  <enterprise-beans>
   <session>
     <ejb-name>ConnectorSampleEJB</ejb-name>
     <home>ejava.integration.jca.ConnectorSampleHome</home>
     <remote>ejava.integration.jca.ConnectorSample</remote>
     <ejb-class>ejava.integration.jca.ConnectorSampleEJBean</ejb-class>
     <session-type>Stateless</session-type>
     <transaction-type>Container</transaction-type>
     <resource-ref>
        <res-ref-name>eis/ejavaConnector</res-ref-name>
        <res-type>javax.resource.cci.ConnectionFactory</res-type>
        <res-auth>Container</res-auth>
```

```
      </resource-ref>
    </session>
  </enterprise-beans>
    ...
</ejb-jar>
```

The logical resource name must of course be mapped to a physical resource in the particular EJB container vendor environment. This is accomplished in a vendor-specific fashion typically involving the mapping inside of a vendor-specific deployment descriptor, as well as vendor-specific configuration files or GUI input. As an example, the J2EE reference implementation's `sun-j2ee-ri.xml` deployment descriptor for our example looks as follows:

```
<j2ee-ri-specific-information>
      ...
  <enterprise-beans>
    <module-name>ConnectorSample.jar</module-name>
    <unique-id>0</unique-id>
    <ejb>
      <ejb-name>ConnectorSampleEJB</ejb-name>
      <jndi-name>ConnectorSampleHome</jndi-name>
      <resource-ref>
        <res-ref-name>eis/ejavaConnector</res-ref-name>
        <jndi-name>eis/ejavaConnector</jndi-name>
        <default-resource-principal>
          <name>TSHIRTS</name>
          <password>TSHIRTS</password>
        </default-resource-principal>
      </resource-ref>
    </ejb>
  </enterprise-beans>
</j2ee-ri-specific-information>
```

After a `ConnectionFactory` handle is obtained, the J2EE component can then obtain a handle to a `Connection` object. This is accomplished by invoking the `getConnection()` method on the factory which assumes that the container will pass on any required authentication information needed by the EIS. Alternatively, a `getConnection(ConnectionSpec)` method can be invoked that takes a `ConnectionSpec` marker interface used to define any JavaBean-style properties to be associated with the `Connection` to be created. When J2EE components create connections using such a class, they typically must use a connector-specific API to handle such `ConnectionSpec` information. However, a `ConnectionSpec` must at least support `UserName` and `Password` JavaBean properties with appropriately named getters and setters. As example of creating a connection, we might have this:

```
// Get connection spec object (vendor-specific)
ConnectionSpec connectionSpec = new CciConnectionSpec();
```

```
// Could get authenticating version above too as follows...
// ConnectionSpec connectionSpec
//   = new CciConnectionSpec(userName, password);

// Get the connection from the factory with a connection spec
Connection connection
  = connectionFactory.getConnection(connectionSpec);
```

J2EE components may obtain a better understanding of the services offered by the underlying resource adapter by invoking the `ConnectionFactory` object's `getMetaData()` method. The `ResourceAdapterMetaData` object returned can be used to obtain information about the resource adapter (that is, not the EIS itself) via invocation of appropriately named methods to return a displayable adapter name, a brief description of the adapter, the name of the adapter vendor, the adapter version number, the connector architecture specification version supported, and an array of fully qualified names for supported `InteractionSpec` types (to be described shortly). Furthermore, support for executing actions with the EIS using input and output records, input only records, or with local transaction optimization may also be determined via a `ResourceAdapterMetaData` object.

EIS Resource Connections

Figure 29.6 depicts the basic abstractions involved with a `Connection`. After obtaining a handle to a `Connection` from the `ConnectionFactory`, a J2EE component uses the `Connection` to start an interaction with the EIS via a call to the `createInteraction()` method. If the J2EE component wants to demarcate transaction boundaries internal to a resource manager, it may call the `getLocalTransaction()` method to obtain a `LocalTransaction` object used to begin, commit, and rollback transactions as appropriate. After a J2EE component is done with a connection, it will typically call `close()` on the `Connection` object to allow the container to return the connection to a managed pool.

Certain meta-data associated with a `Connection` may also be gotten via a call to `getMetaData()`. The returned `ConnectionMetaData` object provides information about the underlying EIS such as its product name, its product version, and the username associated with the underlying active connection. Furthermore, as you'll see shortly, `ResultSet` objects may be returned after the execution of certain operations with the EIS. Meta-data about the nature of such results may be obtained by calling `getResultSetInfo()` on the `Connection` object. Appropriately named methods on the returned `ResultSetInfo` object indicate support for updates, inserts, and deletes. A `ResultSetInfo` object can also be used to indicate what result set types may be invoked using `java.sql.ResultSet` type and concurrency identifiers as input parameters to such methods.

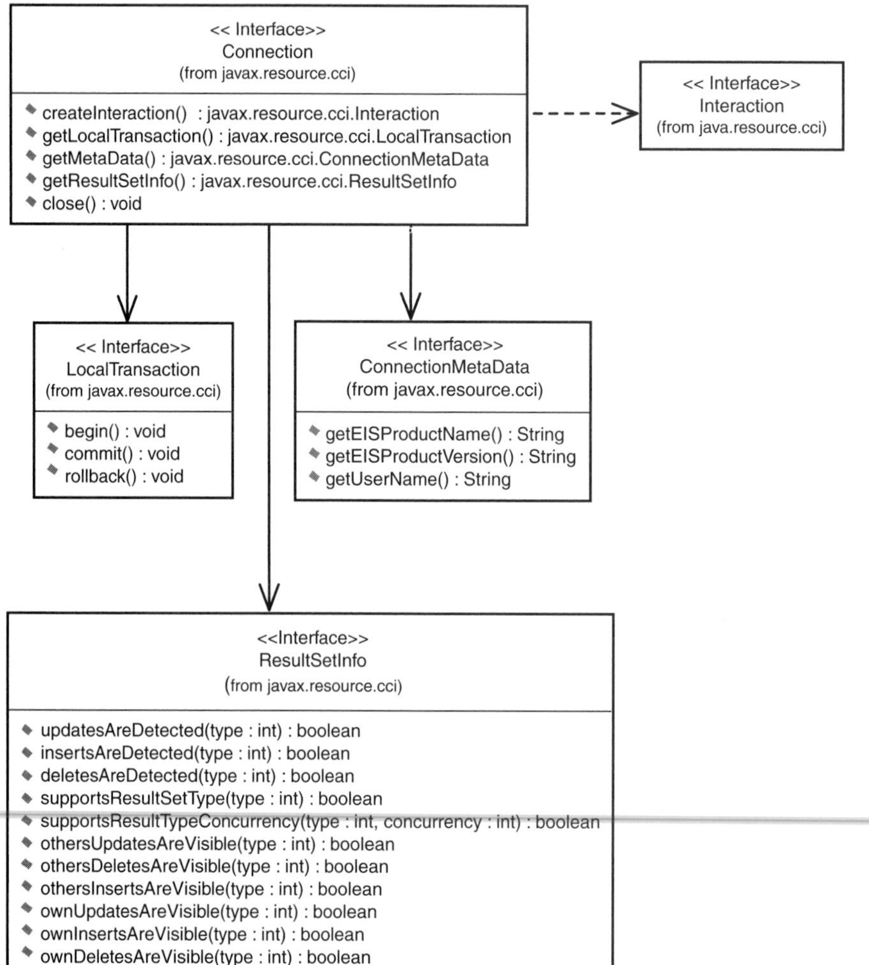

Figure 29.6 EIS resource connections.

EIS Records

The base class encapsulating an input to or output from an EIS is the `Record` interface depicted in Figure 29.7. The minimal required attributes associated with a `Record` are its name and a brief description, which may be gotten or set via the `Record` interface. A concrete `Record` type generally assumes one of the four basic forms:

- `IndexedRecord`: Encapsulates an ordered `java.util.List Record` of elements involved with an EIS interaction.
- `MappedRecord`: Encapsulates a key-based `java.util.Map Record` of elements involved with an EIS interaction.

- `ResultSet`: Encapsulates a cursor-based relational `java.sql.ResultSet` `Record` of elements returned from an EIS interaction.
- `JavaBean`: Encapsulates a custom JavaBean type representation of elements involved with an EIS interaction.

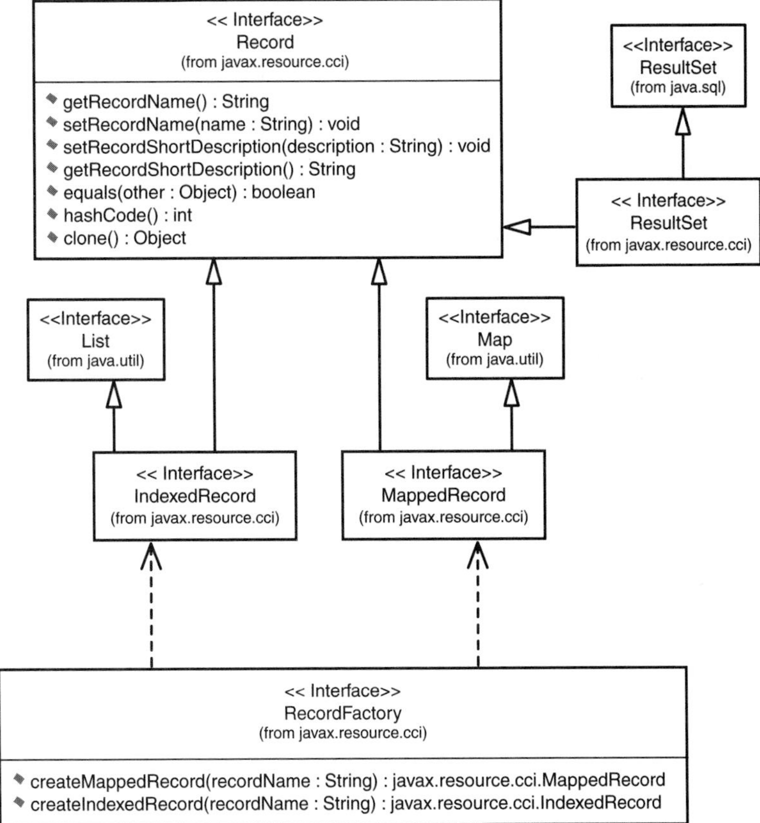

Figure 29.7 EIS records.

As depicted in Figure 29.7, the `RecordFactory` abstraction may be used to create instances of `IndexedRecord` or `MappedRecord` objects that may be sent as inputs to an EIS interaction given the names for such records. A handle to a `RecordFactory` object is obtained from the `ConnectionFactory` abstraction's `getRecordfactory()` method as depicted in Figure 29.5.

As an example, suppose, we have defined the following function as a stored procedure in a database:

```
CREATE OR REPLACE
FUNCTION getTotalPriceForOrder (vorder_id IN NUMBER )
RETURN NUMBER
```

```
  IS
      vtotal_value NUMBER;
  BEGIN
      SELECT I.total_price INTO vtotal_value
      FROM orders O,item I
      WHERE O.order_id =vorder_id AND O.order_id = I.order_id_fk;
    RETURN vtotal_value;
END;
```

Now suppose that an `orderID` represents the `IN` parameter and a `totalValue` represents the `OUT` parameter for such a function. If we then want to create an `IndexedRecord` named "`InputRecord`" that will be used to contain an `orderID` EIS interaction input parameter of an `Integer` type, we might have this:

```
// Get a record factory
RecordFactory recordFactory =
  connectionFactory.getRecordFactory();

// Create and set the input record values
IndexedRecord inputRecord =
  recordFactory.createIndexedRecord("InputRecord");
inputRecord.add(orderID);
```

EIS Interactions

The `Interaction` abstraction depicted in Figure 29.8, created via a `Connection` object, serves as the encapsulation of an interaction with an EIS. An `InteractionSpec` marker interface is a JavaBean type object with properties that define the parameters to be associated with a particular EIS interaction. When J2EE components establish interactions using such a class, they typically must use a connector-specific API to contain such `InteractionSpec` information. However, an `InteractionSpec` must at least support a JavaBeans-style `FunctionName` string property defining the EIS function name to invoke, an `ExecutionTimeout` integer property defining the number of milliseconds to wait for timeout on an EIS interaction, and an `InteractionVerb` integer property defining the EIS interaction mode (that is, send, received, send and receive) via one of the `static public` constants defined on the `InteractionSpec` interface.

As an example of defining an `InteractionSpec` for the EIS `getTotalPriceForOrder` function described earlier, using a vendor-specific `InteractionSpec` object, we might have this:

```
// Create an interaction spec (vendor-specific)
InteractionSpec interactionSpec = new CciInteractionSpec();

// Set the function name
interactionSpec.setFunctionName("GETTOTALPRICEFORORDER");

// Set other example JavaBean properties for schema & catalog
interactionSpec.setSchema("TSHIRTS");
interactionSpec.setCatalog(null);
```

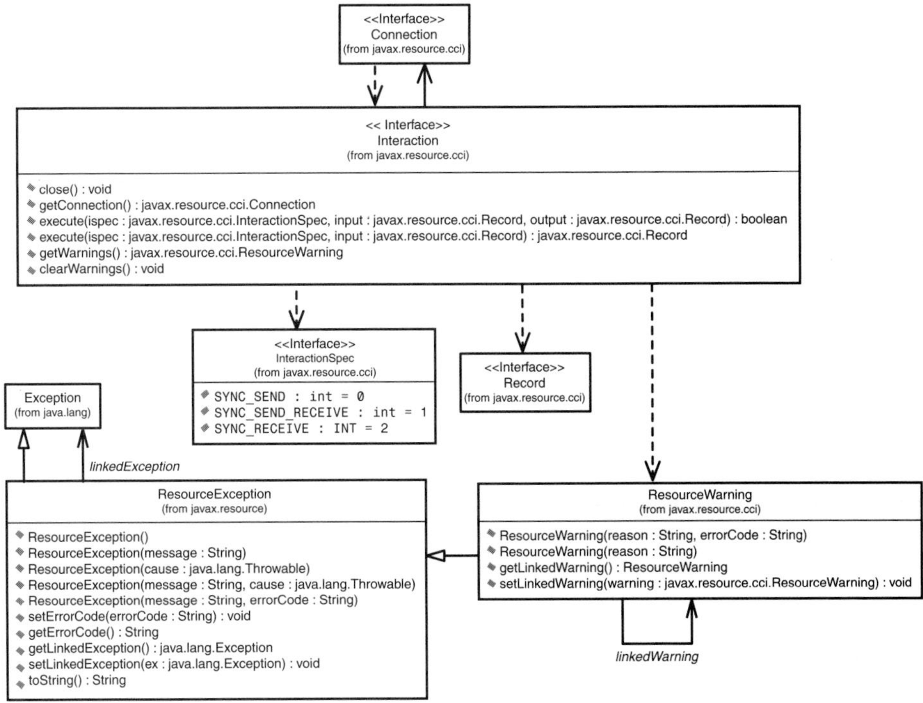

Figure 29.8 EIS interactions.

The `Interaction` object's `execute(InteractionSpec, Record)` method may be then invoked to pass an input record and receive an output as a returned `Record` object. Alternatively, the `execute(InteractionSpec, Record, Record)` method may be invoked with an output `Record` added to the method signature whereby the output `Record` object is updated with any results along with a `boolean` value returned to indicate the success status of the execution. After an interaction is induced, the EIS interaction may be closed by invoking the `Interaction.close()` method. As an example, if we desired to now execute the interaction we've established thus far and traverse the results for a resulting total order value, we might have the following:

```
// Create an interaction and execute the function
Interaction interaction = connection.createInteraction();
Record outRecord =
  interaction.execute(interactionSpec, inputRecord);

// Get and traverse the output record result (one for order ID)
Iterator iterator = ((IndexedRecord) outRecord).iterator();
while (iterator.hasNext()) {
  Object value = iterator.next();
  totalValue = ((BigDecimal)value).doubleValue();
```

```
}

// Now close the interaction and EIS connection
interaction.close();
connection.close();
```

On a final note, we should also mention that in the event of any warnings that occur during the processing of an interaction, the EIS will return them as a chain of `ResourceWarning` exception types via an invocation of the `Interaction` object's `getWarning()` method. The `ResourceWarning` class and base `ResourceException` class are depicted in Figure 29.8.

Java Authorization Contract for Containers (JACC)

The Java Authorization Contract for Containers defines a set of interfaces between J2EE containers and vendors providing security service implementations. Such security service implementations assumed by the JACC architecture largely revolve around authorization and security policy product integration. Such an interface contract enables third-party security service implementations to more easily integrate with J2EE containers. The J2EE v1.4 requires incorporation of the JACC v1.0.

Because the JACC is an interface contract between J2EE container vendors and third-party security service providers, a J2EE developer will typically have little need to understand the JACC interfaces. Nevertheless, we present Figure 29.9 here so that you can better understand how use of JACC-compliant containers and providers can help you leverage incorporation of third-party security service providers inside of your J2EE container environments. Figure 29.9 depicts the basic class architecture of the JACC (with method signatures excluded for simplicity). A J2EE container interfaces with the JACC abstractions implemented by a JACC provider. The core abstractions provided and implemented via JACC are defined here:

- `PolicyConfiguration`: Implemented by JACC providers to allow J2EE containers to manage the security policies implemented by the provider.
- `PolicyConfigurationFactory`: Used in the construction of `PolicyConfiguration` objects.
- `PolicyContextHandler`: Implemented by JACC providers to encapsulate the context information for a security policy decision.
- `PolicyContext`: Used to manage a collection of `PolicyContextHandler` objects.
- `*XXX*Permission`: A set of `java.security.Permission` objects used to define access control permissions associated with EJB and J2EE Web components.

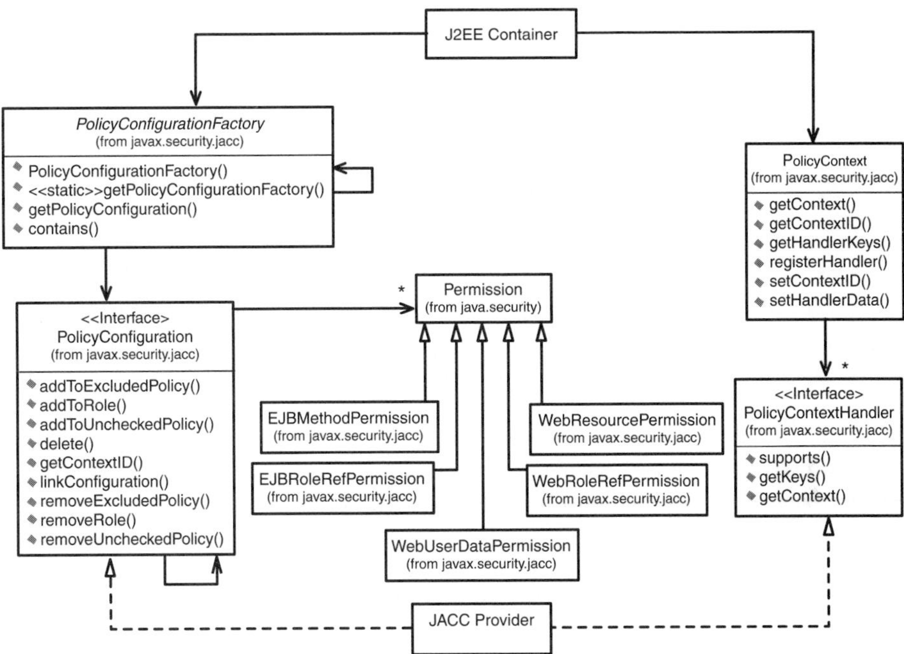

Figure 29.9 JACC architecture.

J2EE Management and JMX

Enterprise application management deals with the management of enterprise applications across a heterogeneous distributed network for applications that range from scalable distributed applications to embedded enterprise applications. The management of such applications is greatly facilitated when they can be configured, monitored, shut down, restarted, and updated using remote administration tools.

Although a few key standard network management frameworks exist, Sun and a few industry leaders have developed a Java-based standard via the Java Community Process. The Java Management Extension (JMX) specification defines a framework, a set of APIs, and services for managing distributed network services. An instrumentation-level standard defines a means for making any Java-based object resource capable of being managed by the JMX framework. An agent-level standard defines a means for building distributed agent containers of instrumented Java-based object resources. Agents provide services to such resources and communicate with distributed network management servers defined at a management-level standard. JMX also defines APIs to enable use of existing network management standards.

The J2EE Management API defines a means for enterprise application management tools to interface with J2EE containers for externally observing the state of and controlling the behavior of resources operating inside of the container. The J2EE Management v1.0 API is incorporated as part of J2EE v1.4 and includes some components from the JMX v1.2 standard. Hence, the JMX is not incorporated in its entirety by the J2EE, but is partially incorporated by virtue of the J2EE Management API.

Given the nature of services that observe and control the behavior of applications, enterprise application management tools thus may require some instrumentation considerations when building your enterprise applications. This is due to the need for such objects to be managed by a distributed network management framework such as JMX. Some J2EE vendor environments indeed have long provided a means to manage Java Servlets, JSPs, and EJBs via a user-friendly GUI-based management interface. However, effective use of such services historically resulted in nonstandard instrumentation and management of J2EE components. With the J2EE Management API, a J2EE container's integration with distributed resource management tools further enhances interoperability and selectivity between J2EE containers and J2EE management tools.

As depicted in Figure 29.10, the J2EE Management specification defines a standard interface model between containers and management tools enabling the management of J2EE components. A special J2EE Management EJB (MEJB) is specified which provides a standard management home and remote EJB interface usable by Java applications that aim to manage a J2EE environment. J2EE Management also provides optional mappings to other industry enterprise application management standards. Such other industry standards include the Common Information Model (CIM) and SNMP Management Information Base (MIB). Although J2EE developers may rarely implement services that observe and control the behavior of a J2EE environment via the J2EE Management API, they can at least leverage the management tools integration advantages and enhanced interoperability offered by yet another J2EE standard.

J2EE Deployment

The J2EE Deployment API defines an interface contract between a J2EE container and tools used to deploy J2EE components and applications. A deployment tool vendor implements these standard interfaces to enable the deployment of applications to J2EE containers in a standard fashion. A J2EE container vendor can enable their container product to integrate with a deployment tool adhering to the J2EE Deployment API. Hence, the J2EE Deployment API provides another standard interface between potential discrete service providers involved with providing an enterprise application platform.

By defining such an API, a deployment tool vendor can be better guaranteed that its operational configuration and deployment services integrate with various J2EE container offerings. Likewise, J2EE container vendors are better guaranteed that they can integrate with various J2EE operation configuration and deployment tools. The J2EE v1.4 container vendors can elect to incorporate the J2EE Deployment v1.1 standard with their product offerings to enable greater interoperability.

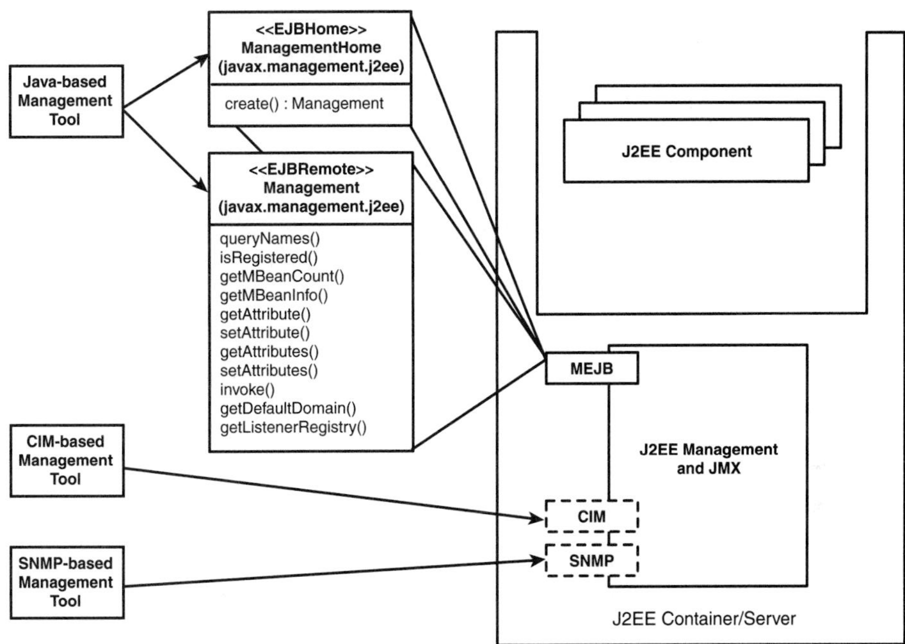

Figure 29.10 J2EE Management architecture.

Figure 29.11 depicts the basic architecture of the J2EE Deployment standard interfaces. A set of standard interfaces defined within the `javax.enterprise.deploy.model` package may be implemented by deployment tool providers in order to be integrated with a J2EE container/server environment. Standard interfaces defined within and beneath a set of `javax.enterprise.deploy.spi.*` packages may be implemented by a J2EE product provider allowing for the deployment of J2EE components by third-party deployment tools. The deployment tool provider and J2EE product provider interface implementations both make use of standard common deployment abstractions encapsulated within and beneath a set of `javax.enterprise.deploy.shared.*` packages.

Although a deployment tool may be tightly integrated with a J2EE container/server environment, it will often be physically located outside of the J2EE server process. J2EE Deployment interfaces provide a way for the J2EE server to discover and connect to an external deployment tool process. With such an interface contract, as illustrated in Figure 29.11, a J2EE product provider and deployment tool provider can thus be loosely coupled and interoperate. J2EE product providers thus can reap the benefit of integrating with various deployment tools that provide a simple deployment tool provider model implementation. Likewise, deployment tool providers can reap the benefit of integrating with various J2EE product environments that support J2EE product provider deployment implementations.

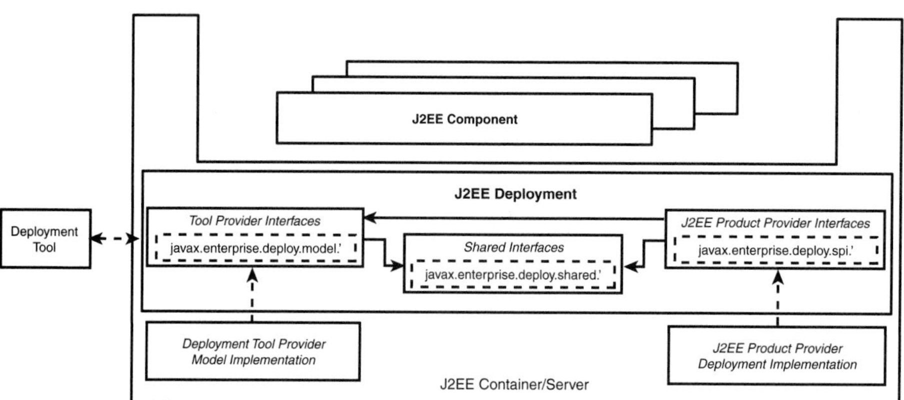

Figure 29.11 J2EE Deployment architecture.

Conclusions

This chapter described the various means by which J2EE components can interface with and tap the services of enterprise applications and systems external to their J2EE container. The support provided by the container in managing connections and interactions with such services was also discussed. In addition to integrating J2EE components with such services, various standard interface contracts defined between a J2EE container itself and such services were defined. Such system-level interface contracts enable greater levels of integration between vendors of J2EE containers and vendors of other enterprise application services. This chapter also described the various means by which EJBs can expose their services to clients via standard enterprise communications paradigms such as the Web and CORBA. The next chapter concludes this line of discussion by describing how EJBs can now also expose themselves via Web services and thus paving the way for even greater integration possibilities for J2EE applications.

30

Web Services with EJB

THE CHAPTERS THUS FAR IN PART VI, "Enterprise Applications Enabling," have focused on describing how to build and use Enterprise JavaBeans (EJB). Earlier in this book, you also saw how to build Java-based Web service applications and how to expose J2EE Web components as Web services. This chapter builds on this material to describe how EJBs may be deployed such that their services are exposed as Web services.

In this chapter, you will learn:

- An overview of how EJBs can expose themselves as Web services.
- How EJBs are implemented as Web services.
- How to configure EJB deployment descriptors to be Web service ready.
- How to configure EJBs as Web services.
- How to configure EJBs to reference other Web services.
- How to package and deploy EJBs as Web services.

EJBs as Web Services Overview

As you saw in Chapter 22, "Web Services with Web Components," much of the work involved with deploying J2EE Web components as Web services involved configuring deployment descriptors to enable such processing. The same truth holds for deploying EJBs as Web services. That is, various deployment descriptors must be configured in order to define the behavior of the EJB inside of an EJB container that can expose the bean as a Web service.

We already examined how EJBs operate inside of an EJB container in Chapters 24 through 29. Chapter 10, "Web Service Communications," described how to construct JAX-RPC Web service clients and service implementations. J2EE v1.4 now requires that compliant EJB containers include a JAX-RPC runtime to allow stateless session beans to be exposed as Web services. Specifically, a J2EE v1.4 EJB container (that is, EJB v2.1 compliant) must provide a JAX-RPC v1.1 runtime environment. The implication of this fact means that the EJB container must perform the following general sequence of events when handling Web service requests mapped to stateless session beans:

1. *Receive Request:* Listen for incoming SOAP/HTTP requests on a predefined port or at the URL defined inside of the deployed Web service's WSDL file.
2. *Identify Endpoint Type:* Map the SOAP message's target information into an intended stateless session bean implementing a Web service endpoint according to J2EE deployment descriptor information.
3. *Unmarshal Request:* Unmarshal and deserialize the SOAP request message into Java type representations according to the JAX-RPC standards for such type mapping.
4. *Delegate Request:* Delegate the resulting Java type input parameters to a stateless session bean instance of the appropriate type.
5. *Receive Response:* Receive any Java type response parameters from the stateless session bean.
6. *Marshal Response:* Marshal and serialize any Java response object to a SOAP response message according to the JAX-RPC standards for such type mapping.
7. *Deliver Response:* Pack the SOAP message into an HTTP response and deliver back to the client.

The remainder of this chapter describes how to construct the stateless session beans operating inside of such a container environment, as well as how to configure and deploy such EJBs as Web services.

Web Service EJB Implementations

Much like the implementation of a J2EE Web component as a Web service is straightforward, so too is the implementation using a stateless session bean. Figure 30.1 depicts the basic requirements for implementing a stateless session bean as a Web service. You'll note that this diagram should seem like a merger between Figure 10.16 of Chapter 10 illustrating a general Web service implementation and Figure 25.1 of Chapter 25 illustrating a stateless session bean implementation. This is because that is in essence what a stateless session bean as a Web service is supposed to be.

Because we already discussed how to create Web services and stateless session beans in this book, we won't rehash all the rules for their construction here. However, a summarized form of the rules expressed in terms of the merging of the two technologies is defined here for a stateless session bean implemented as a Web service:

- Must be a public, final, and non-abstract class.
- Must have a parameterless constructor.
- Must not define a `finalize()` method.
- Must implement the method signatures defined by the service endpoint interface. Although it technically does not have to indicate that it is implementing the

service endpoint interface, it is a good idea from a design perspective to do so. The stateless session bean is not implemented to throw a `RemoteException`, however.

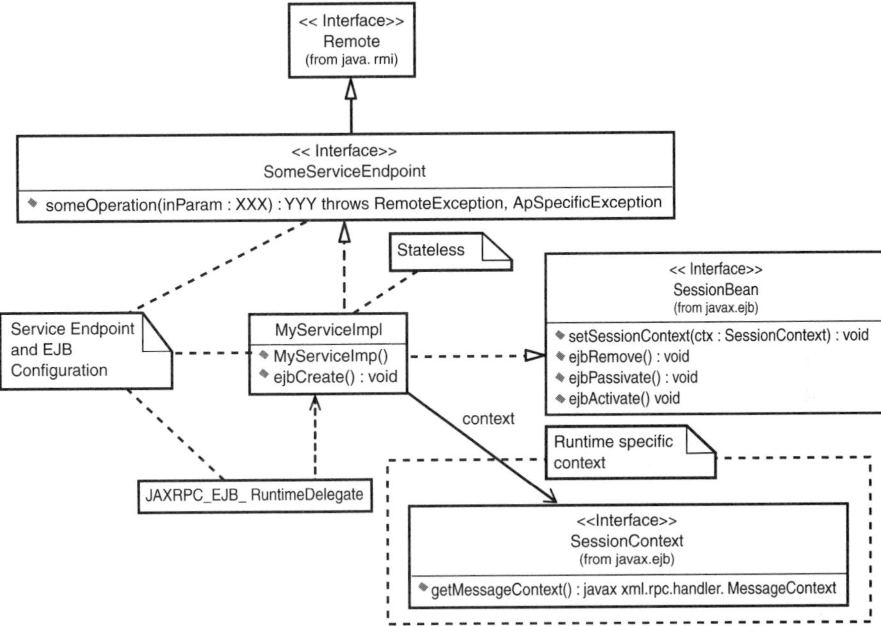

Figure 30.1 Web service EJB implementation.

- Must be implemented as a stateless session bean component.
- Must implement the `javax.ejb.SessionBean` interface.
- Must implement the `ejbCreate()` and `ejbRemove()` methods with any creation and removal logic inserted as needed.
- Must provide an empty implementation for the `ejbActivate()` and `ejbPassivate()` method signatures, although such methods are not invoked by the container.
- May obtain a handle to a `javax.ejb.SessionContext` interface as its context inside of a J2EE EJB container.

As with J2EE Web components implemented as Web services, there is no support for custom JAX-RPC serializers and deserializers with EJBs implemented as Web services. However, unlike J2EE Web components implemented as Web services as illustrated in Figure 10.16, there is no need for stateless session beans implemented as a Web service to implement the `ServiceLifecycle` interface. This is because a stateless session bean receives its context from the standard EJB `setSessionContext()` method, has its instance created via the `ejbCreate()` method, and has its instance destroyed via the `ejbRemove()` method. Thus, a stateless session bean already has methods equivalent to those defined on the `ServiceLifecycle` that are invoked on it by the EJB container.

Handlers for EJBs

You'll notice that the `SessionContext` interface of Figure 30.1 defines a `getMessageContext()` method enabling the stateless session bean to obtain a handle to a JAX-RPC `MessageContext` object. In the case of SOAP/HTTP, this context is a `javax.xml.rpc.handler.soap.SOAPMessageContext` type. Recall from Chapter 10 that such a context can be used to access the message context and SOAP messages shared with any handlers.

Thus, it should be apparent that stateless session beans can use JAX-RPC handlers as described in Chapter 10. Such handlers can be created to preprocess SOAP requests before they are unmarshaled and make their way to the stateless session bean. Handlers can also be created to post-process responses after the response from the stateless session bean is marshaled into a SOAP response.

EJB containers, however, will often perform some processing on a message before handing it off to a JAX-RPC handler. Such processing for EJBs may involve method level security checking and other container servicing. Thus, the handler for an EJB in fact cannot process such information used by the container in a portable manner. If such a handler modifies the information embedded into a SOAP header in any way, the container is required to generate a SOAP fault back to the client indicating this event.

Web Service EJB Example

As with our J2EE Web component example of Chapter 22, the `ejava.webservices.rpc.QueryServerImpl` class described in Chapter 10 serves as the basis for this chapter's example. The `QueryServerImpl` class provides the implementation for all the Web service–specific processing required by our example stateless session bean. The only modifications we make here are to implement the standard stateless session bean interfaces required by the EJB container.

Note

The example code in this chapter makes significant use of the code provided for Chapter 10 and extracted beneath the `examples\src\ejava\webservices\rpc` directory. Additional code elements for this chapter are located as described on this book's CD in Appendix A, "Software Configuration," and extracted to the `examples\src\ejava\ejb\webservices` directory.

This code also make use of an `ejava.ejb.EJBHelper` class associated with Chapter 25's code and extracted to the `examples\src\ejava\ejb` directory.

Note that an `examples\src\ejava\ejb\webservices\client` directory is also extracted for this chapter's example containing deployment descriptors related to a J2EE application client.

The `ejava.ejb.webservices.QueryServiceEJBean` class of Listing 30.1 extends the `QueryServerImpl` class. Note that the functionality for creating and deleting a database connection used by the example's super class is accomplished by the `QueryServiceEJBean` class's `ejbCreate()` and `ejbRemove()` methods, respectively. This may be contrasted to similar functionality provided by the `WebQueryServerImpl` class's use of the `init()` and `destroy()` methods, as shown in Listing 22.1.

Listing 30.1 **Web Services EJB Example (`QueryServiceEJBean.java`)**

```
package ejava.ejb.webservices;
   ...
public class QueryServiceEJBean
  extends ejava.webservices.rpc.QueryServerImpl
  implements javax.ejb.SessionBean
{
  // Session bean & Web services context
  private SessionContext sessionContext;

  /**
   * Public default constructor
   */
  public QueryServiceEJBean(){
      super();
  }

  /**
   * Set standard context
   */
  public void setSessionContext(SessionContext aCtx){
    sessionContext = aCtx;
  }

  /**
   * Standard ejbCreate() method impl
   * Creates and sets connection for parent class
   */
  public void ejbCreate(){
    System.out.println("ejbCreate called");
    try{
      super.setConnection(EJBHelper.getDBConnection());
    }catch(Exception exception){
      System.out.println("Failed to create connection");
      exception.printStackTrace();
    }
  }
```

Listing 30.1 **Continued**

```
  /**
   * Standard ejbRemove() method impl
   * Deletes connection for parent class
   */
  public void ejbRemove(){
    System.out.println("ejbRemove called");
    try{
      super.getConnection().close();
    }catch(Exception exception){
      System.out.println("Failed to close connection");
      exception.printStackTrace();
    }
  }

  // Standard session bean methods not invoked
  public void ejbPassivate(){ }
  public void ejbActivate(){ }

  // Super class Web service life cycle methods not invoked
  public void init(Object context){ }
  public void destroy(){ }
}
```

Web Service EJB Clients

Clients to Web services implemented as stateless session beans can be implemented as any client to any Web service would be implemented. The Web service client has no need to understand how the Web service is implemented, nor does it need to know that the Web service is implemented using a stateless session bean. The Web service client simply communicates with the Web service using SOAP/HTTP and is provided interoperability with the service by virtue of the SOAP protocol and messaging format, as well as the underlying HTTP transport protocol. This is why one of our client examples associated with this chapter can use the `ejava.webservices.rpc.QueryClient` class described in Chapter 10.

As another simple example, the `ejava.ejb.webservices.QueryJ2EEAppClient` class in Listing 30.2 serves as a simple client class that queries the services of the `QueryServiceEJBean` from within a J2EE application client container process. The `QueryJ2EEAppClient` serves to illustrate how a client to a J2EE-based Web service can invoke such a Web service when that client itself operates inside of a J2EE container. The primary point here is simply that the client uses JNDI to look up a reference to the Web service. The same lookup methodology would apply if this client were operating inside of a J2EE Web container (that is, client as a J2EE Web component) or EJB container (that is, client as an EJB).

Listing 30.2 **Web Services J2EE Client Example** (QueryJ2EEAppClient.java)

```
package ejava.ejb.webservices;
   ...
public class QueryJ2EEAppClient
{
   public static void main(String[] args){
    try{
      // Logical service reference JNDI name
      String serviceNameContext =
          "java:comp/env/service/QueryService";

      // Use JNDI to look up QueryService handle
      //  -- Note that QueryService is a generated interface
      InitialContext ic = new InitialContext();
      QueryService queryService =
        (QueryService)ic.lookup(serviceNameContext);

      // Use the QueryService to get a QueryServer handle
      QueryServer  queryServerPort =
          queryService.getQueryServerPort();

      // Invoke the QueryServer's ping() method
      System.out.println("<QueryServer.ping() via AppClient>:\n" +
      queryServerPort.ping() + "\n");

      // Invoke the QueryServer's findOrder() method
      int orderID = 1002;
      System.out.println("<QueryServer.findOrder() via AppClient>:\n"
                + queryServerPort.findOrder(orderID) + "\n");
    }catch(Exception e){
      e.printStackTrace();
    }
  }
}
```

In addition to exposing itself as a Web service, a stateless session bean may also define remote and local interfaces for usage by remote and local EJB clients. Of course, when defining those methods that you plan to expose in a remote, local, or Web service fashion, you must obey the set of rules associated with the valid input types passed over such interfaces. The material discussed throughout this book on RMI/IIOP, JAX-RPC, EJB remote, and EJB local interfaces addresses such interface definition constraints in detail.

EJB Deployment Configuration (ejb-jar.xml)

When exposing a stateless session bean as a Web service, you must identify this fact in that bean's ejb-jar.xml deployment descriptor. After the stateless session bean's remote and local interfaces are optionally identified for the bean, a `<service-endpoint>` interface may be defined that provides the full-qualified class name of the bean's service endpoint interface. Listing 30.3 demonstrates this definition for our example `QueryServiceEJBean` class's `ejb-jar.xml` file. Because our bean extends the `QueryServerImpl` class, its service endpoint interface is simply that class's implemented `QueryServer` interface.

Listing 30.3 **J2EE EJB Deployment Descriptor** (`ejb-jar.xml`)

```
<?xml version="1.0" encoding="UTF-8"?>
<ejb-jar
  version="2.1"
  xmlns="http://java.sun.com/xml/ns/j2ee"
  xmlns:xsi="http://www.w3.org/2001/XMLSchema-instance"
  xsi:schemaLocation="http://java.sun.com/xml/ns/j2ee
  http://java.sun.com/xml/ns/j2ee/ejb-jar_2_1.xsd">

  <enterprise-beans>
    <session>
      <display-name>QueryeServiceEJB</display-name>
      <ejb-name>QueryServiceEJB</ejb-name>
      <service-endpoint>
          ejava.webservices.rpc.QueryServer
      </service-endpoint>
      <ejb-class>ejava.ejb.webservices.QueryServiceEJBean</ejb-class>
      <session-type>Stateless</session-type>
      <transaction-type>Bean</transaction-type>
      <resource-ref>
         <res-ref-name>jdbc/ejavaPool</res-ref-name>
         <res-type>javax.sql.DataSource</res-type>
         <res-auth>Container</res-auth>
      </resource-ref>
    </session>
  </enterprise-beans>
    ...
</ejb-jar>
```

Listing 30.3 demonstrates the fact that our `QueryServiceEJBean` service implementation class is to be deployed by the container as a stateless session bean with the EJB name `QueryServiceEJB`. Note also that the `QueryServiceEJBean` class is configured with a `<resource-ref>` element for fetching a JDBC connection. Recall that the JDBC connection is fetched using the `EJBHelper` class's `getDBConnection()`, as illustrated with the following code snippets:

```
public class EJBHelper{
    ...
  public static String BEESHIRTS_DATA_SOURCE =
```

```
        "java:comp/env/jdbc/ejavaPool";
    ...
  public static Connection getDBConnection()
    ...
    InitialContext initialContext = new InitialContext();
    DataSource dataSource = (DataSource)
              initialContext.lookup(EJBHelper.BEESHIRTS_DATA_SOURCE);
     ...
  }
    ...
}
```

Web Services EJB Deployment Configuration (`webservices.xml` and `java-wsdl-mapping.xml`)

Recall from Chapter 22 that a new standard deployment descriptor is used to define those deployment and configuration characteristics associated with a Web service deployed using J2EE components. This deployment descriptor is defined inside of a `webservices.xml` file. For J2EE EJB deployed as Web services, this file must always accompany the `ejb-jar.xml` file used to deploy those EJBs into an EJB container. Chapter 22 also described the `java-wsdl-mapping.xml` deployment descriptor (or other appropriately named and referenced type mapping file) used as a standard means for describing the mapping between Java types and WSDL types. Because Chapter 22 described these deployment descriptors in detail, we won't reiterate their composition here. However, we will point out one subtle difference in the material that follows.

Web Service EJB Port Component Deployment (`<port-component>`)

Recall that the `<webservice-description>` element associated with a `webservices.xml` file defines those standard elements common across the various port components that compose the Web service such as its WSDL file and type mappings between Java types and WSDL types. It does this via one or more `<port-component>` elements. Each `<port-component>` element in turn can contain a `<servlet-impl-bean>` element. The `<servlet-impl-bean>` element can contain a `<servlet-link>` element that references a `<servlet-name>` value as defined in the `web.xml` file associated with a WAR module. For stateless session beans deployed as Web services, an `<ejb-link>` element is used instead of this `<servlet-link>` element. The `<ejb-link>` element references an `<ejb-name>` value as defined in the `ejb-jar.xml` file associated with the JAR module for the EJB.

Web Service Deployment Configuration Example

Listing 30.4 provides an example `webservices.xml` deployment descriptor used to deploy our `QueryServiceEJBean` class. A single Web service is deployed within the

<webservice-description> element. A single port component is also defined and associated with the QueryServiceEJB logical name defined in the ejb-jar.xml file as our example <ejb-name> and identified in the webservices.xml file via the <service-impl-bean> element's <ejb-link> element value.

Listing 30.4 **J2EE Web Services EJB Deployment Descriptor** (webservices.xml)

```
<?xml version="1.0" encoding="ISO-8859-1"?>

<webservices xmlns="http://java.sun.com/xml/ns/j2ee"
  xmlns:xsi="http://www.w3.org/2001/XMLSchema-instance"
  xsi:schemaLocation="http://java.sun.com/xml/ns/j2ee
  http://www.ibm.com/webservices/xsd/j2ee_web_services_1_1.xsd"
  version="1.1">

  <description>EJB Web Service</description>
  <webservice-description>
    <webservice-description-name>
      QueryServer as an EJB Web Service
    </webservice-description-name>

    <wsdl-file>QueryService.wsdl</wsdl-file>
    <jaxrpc-mapping-file>java-wsdl-mapping.xml</jaxrpc-mapping-file>

    <port-component>
      <port-component-name>QueryServerPort</port-component-name>
      <wsdl-port>
        <namespaceURI>http://ws.beeshirts.com/wsdl</namespaceURI>
        <localpart>QueryServerPort</localpart>
      </wsdl-port>

      <service-endpoint-interface>
          ejava.webservices.rpc.QueryServer
      </service-endpoint-interface>
      <service-impl-bean>
        <ejb-link>QueryServiceEJB</ejb-link>
      </service-impl-bean>

      <handler>
        <description> User security handler example </description>
        <handler-name>AdminHandler</handler-name>
        <handler-class>
           ejava.webservices.rpc.AdminHandler
        </handler-class>
        <init-param>
           <param-name>username</param-name>
           <param-value>sysop</param-value>
```

Listing 30.4 **Continued**

```
        </init-param>
        <init-param>
           <param-name>password</param-name>
           <param-value>btgllyra</param-value>
        </init-param>
        <init-param>
           <param-name>headerNamespace</param-name>
           <param-value>
              http://ws.beeshirts.com/wsdl/QueryService
           </param-value>
        </init-param>
        <init-param>
           <param-name>headerName</param-name>
           <param-value>Security</param-value>
        </init-param>
        <init-param>
           <param-name>headerPrefix</param-name>
           <param-value>beeshirts</param-value>
        </init-param>
      </handler>
    </port-component>
  </webservice-description>
</webservices>
```

Note that the `AdminHandler` is also defined in the `webservices.xml` file for use by this EJB. A series of `<init-param>` values are defined and used by the `AdminHandler` class and its base `SecurityHandler` class as presented in Chapter 10.

Web Services EJB References

Chapter 22 presented a basic means for any J2EE component to reference a Web service as a client via its deployment descriptor. If an EJB wants to tap the services of a Web service, it must define a reference to that service from within its deployment descriptor. This is accomplished using the `<service-ref>` element as described in Chapter 22. For EJBs, the `<service-ref>` element is similarly defined but contained, of course, inside of the `ejb-jar.xml` file relatively positioned inside of an individual EJB's element declaration as illustrated here:

```
<ejb-jar ...>
  <enterprise-beans>
       ...
    <session>
       ...
      <env-entry> ... </env-entry>
```

```
      <ejb-ref> ... </ejb-ref>
      <ejb-local-ref> ... </ejb-local-ref>
      <service-ref> ... </service-ref>
      <resource-ref> ... </resource-ref>
       ...
    </session>
       ...
    <entity>
       ...
      <service-ref> ... </service-ref>
       ...
    </entity>
       ...
    <message-driven>
       ...
      <service-ref> ... </service-ref>
       ...
    </message-driven>
       ...
  </enterprise-beans>
</ejb-jar>
```

Zero or more of such `<service-ref>` elements can be defined within an EJB's element definition. The contents of the `<service-ref>` element are the same here as defined in Chapter 22.

Of course, any J2EE component defines a `<service-ref>` element in a similar fashion in order to reference a Web service. For example, the `QueryJ2EEAppClient` described earlier, in Listing 30.2, requires that it be deployed with the deployment descriptor as shown in Listing 30.5. Here we see that the `service/QueryService` logical name can be used by the `QueryJ2EEAppClient` to look up a handle to the `QueryServiceEJBean` class's service endpoint, as Listing 30.2 demonstrated.

> **Note**
>
> The deployment descriptor of Listing 30.5 and other deployment descriptors for this chapter's J2EE application client example are contained beneath the `examples\src\ejava\ejb\webservices\client` directory.

Listing 30.5 **Web Services J2EE Client Deployment Descriptor (`application-client.xml`)**

```
<?xml version="1.0" encoding="UTF-8"?>
<application-client version="1.4"
  xmlns="http://java.sun.com/xml/ns/j2ee"
```

Listing 30.5 **Continued**

```
  xmlns:xsi="http://www.w3.org/2001/XMLSchema-instance"
  xsi:schemaLocation="http://java.sun.com/xml/ns/j2ee
  http://java.sun.com/xml/ns/j2ee/application-client_1_4.xsd">

  <display-name>QueryServiceAppClient</display-name>
  <service-ref>
      <description>Query Service Reference</description>
      <service-ref-name>service/QueryService</service-ref-name>
      <service-interface>
        ejava.webservices.rpc.QueryService
      </service-interface>
      <wsdl-file>QueryService.wsdl</wsdl-file>
      <jaxrpc-mapping-file>
          java-wsdl-mapping-appclient.xml
      </jaxrpc-mapping-file>
  </service-ref>
</application-client>
```

Web Services EJB Deployment

This last section describes the steps remaining to deploy an EJB as a Web service. Thus far, you've seen those standard deployment descriptor files needed and Java classes needed to construct an EJB-based Web service. In addition to the standard deployment descriptors, a set of vendor-specific deployment descriptors must also be generated. The various compiled classes and deployment descriptors are then packaged inside of an EJB JAR module file. Finally, the EJB JAR file is deployed into an EJB container with a JAX-RPC runtime.

Vendor-Specific Deployment Configuration

The standard deployment descriptors described in this chapter enable you to specify the bulk of deployment configuration parameters involved with deploying a stateless session bean as a Web service. Additionally, vendor EJB container implementations also require other deployment descriptors to complete the deployment configuration process. Vendor-specific deployment descriptors map logical names in the standard deployment descriptors to physical process-related names associated with the vendor's EJB server. These vendor-specific and standard deployment descriptor files are often generated by either command line or GUI tools. It does, however, behoove you to be aware of such deployment descriptors specific to your vendor's deployment environment in order to better understand the runtime deployment behavior associated with your EJB applications.

> **Note**
>
> The example in this chapter is deployable to J2EE v1.4–compliant environments supporting Web services with EJB. The J2EE v1.4 reference implementation is of course one such environment. Appendix A provides more detailed information on how to configure and deploy the example in this chapter. Appendix A also provides a link to a Web site to which additional supported configuration profiles will be posted as more vendors begin to support J2EE v1.4–compliant Web services.
>
> The J2EE reference implementation uses a `sun-j2ee-ri.xml` file to configure EJB component information such as mapping the JDBC connection pool logical name to a physical JNDI name. The `config.xml` and `config-client.xml` files included with this chapter's examples are also needed and respectively associated with configuring the JAX-RPC runtime on the server side and client side.

Web Service EJB Packaging

Chapter 24, "EJB Basics," described how to package and deploy EJBs using EJB JAR files. The packaging of an EJB as a Web service is nearly identical. The only new fact is that the `webservices.xml` file must be packaged beneath the `META-INF` directory of the EJB JAR file. Furthermore, the JAX-RPC type-mapping file (for example, `java-wsdl-mapping.xml`) must be located and named according to the `<jaxrpc-mapping-file>` element contained beneath a `<webservice-description>` element defined in the `webservices.xml` file. Alternatively, `java-wsdl-mapping.xml` may be located relative to the root of the EJB jar file if not specified by the `<jaxrpc-mapping-file>` element.

After placing the files in their appropriate directory structure, the WSDL file and any Web service skeletons may be generated using a vendor's compilation tool. An EJB JAR file for the EJBs implemented as Web services may then be constructed as described in Chapter 24. A J2EE enterprise application file may also be constructed to cohesively combine one or more EJB JAR files, as well as other J2EE module archive files, into the same enterprise application, as described in Chapter 23, "Enterprise Application Services." Finally, a vendor-specific deployment tool is then used to deploy the EJB application to a running EJB container/server process.

> **Note**
>
> Different J2EE vendor implementations provide different types of tools for generating Web service skeletons and WSDL files, as well as for deploying J2EE applications. The J2EE reference implementation uses a program called `ws-compile` to generate WSDL files from Java-based Web services and any skeletons to implement such service. The J2EE reference implementation uses a program called `deploy-tool` to deploy J2EE applications.
>
> Appendix A describes the configuration instructions associated with deploying the example for this chapter. Appendix A also provides a link to a Web site that may be referenced for additional J2EE v1.4–compliant Web service configuration instructions as they become available.

Conclusions

Stateless session beans may be deployed as Web services using a J2EE v1.4–compliant EJB container. As you've seen in this chapter, exposing an EJB as a Web service is rather straightforward. Most new concepts involved with such a task revolve around specifying your deployment descriptors appropriately. Furthermore, as you have seen, the deployment of an EJB as a Web service is very similar to the deployment of a J2EE Web component as a Web service. Standard `ejb-jar.xml` deployment descriptors are configured and used to deploy the service implementation as stateless session beans. Standard `webservices.xml` and `java-wsdl-mapping.xml` deployment descriptors are used to configure the component to expose itself as a Web service and enable the container to map between Java and WSDL types. J2EE v1.4 thus provides you the enterprise developer a methodology for constructing Web services that are portable across hardware, operating system, Web server, and application server platforms, offering you unparalleled reusability and selectability for deploying Web services never before seen in industry.

Congratulations! You've just completed the most comprehensive and cohesive treatise on modern enterprise software development.

Appendixes (on CD-ROM)

Index

Symbols

A

B

C

E

F

G

H

I

J

K

L

M

Q

S

U

V

W

X - Y - Z

Sun Microsystems, Inc.

Binary Code License Agreement

READ THE TERMS OF THIS AGREEMENT AND ANY PROVIDED SUPPLEMENTAL LICENSE TERMS (COLLECTIVELY "AGREEMENT") CAREFULLY BEFORE OPENING THE SOFTWARE MEDIA PACKAGE. BY OPENING THE SOFTWARE MEDIA PACKAGE,YOU AGREE TO THE TERMS OF THIS AGREEMENT. IF YOU ARE ACCESSING THE SOFTWARE ELECTRONICALLY, INDICATE YOUR ACCEPTANCE OF THESE TERMS BY SELECTING THE "ACCEPT" BUTTON AT THE END OF THIS AGREEMENT. IF YOU DO NOT AGREE TO ALL THESE TERMS, PROMPTLY RETURN THE UNUSED SOFTWARE TO YOUR PLACE OF PURCHASE FOR A REFUND OR, IF THE SOFTWARE IS ACCESSED ELECTRONICALLY, SELECT THE "DECLINE" BUTTON AT THE END OF THIS AGREEMENT.

1. **LICENSE TO USE.** Sun grants you a non-exclusive and non-transferable license for the internal use only of the accompanying software and documentation and any error corrections provided by Sun (collectively "Software"), by the number of users and the class of computer hardware for which the corresponding fee has been paid.
2. **RESTRICTIONS.** Software is confidential and copyrighted. Title to Software and all associated intellectual property rights is retained by Sun and/or its licensors. Except as specifically authorized in any Supplemental License Terms, you may not make copies of Software, other than a single copy of Software for archival purposes. Unless enforcement is prohibited by applicable law, you may not modify, decompile, or reverse engineer Software. Licensee acknowledges that Licensed Software is not designed or intended for use in the design, construction, operation or maintenance of any nuclear facility. Sun Microsystems, Inc. disclaims any express or implied warranty of fitness for such uses. No right, title or interest in or to any trademark, service mark, logo or trade name of Sun or its licensors is granted under this Agreement.
3. **LIMITED WARRANTY.** Sun warrants to you that for a period of ninety (90) days from the date of purchase, as evidenced by a copy of the receipt, the media on which Software is furnished (if any) will be free of defects in materials and workmanship under normal use. Except for the foregoing, Software is provided "AS IS". Your exclusive remedy and Sun's entire liability under this limited warranty will be at Sun's option to replace Software media or refund the fee paid for Software.
4. **DISCLAIMER OF WARRANTY.** UNLESS SPECIFIED IN THIS AGREEMENT, ALL EXPRESS OR IMPLIED CONDITIONS, REPRESENTATIONS AND WARRANTIES, INCLUDING ANY IMPLIED WARRANTY OF

MERCHANTABILITY, FITNESS FOR A PARTICULAR PURPOSE OR NON-INFRINGEMENT ARE DISCLAIMED, EXCEPT TO THE EXTENT THAT THESE DISCLAIMERS ARE HELD TO BE LEGALLY INVALID.

5. **LIMITATION OF LIABILITY.** TO THE EXTENT NOT PROHIBITED BY LAW, IN NO EVENT WILL SUN OR ITS LICENSORS BE LIABLE FOR ANY LOST REVENUE, PROFIT OR DATA, OR FOR SPECIAL, INDIRECT, CONSEQUENTIAL, INCIDENTAL OR PUNITIVE DAMAGES, HOWEVER CAUSED REGARDLESS OF THE THEORY OF LIABILITY, ARISING OUT OF OR RELATED TO THE USE OF OR INABILITY TO USE SOFTWARE, EVEN IF SUN HAS BEEN ADVISED OF THE POSSIBILITY OF SUCH DAMAGES. In no event will Sun's liability to you, whether in contract, tort (including negligence), or otherwise, exceed the amount paid by you for Software under this Agreement. The foregoing limitations will apply even if the above stated warranty fails of its essential purpose.
6. **Termination.** This Agreement is effective until terminated. You may terminate this Agreement at any time by destroying all copies of Software. This Agreement will terminate immediately without notice from Sun if you fail to comply with any provision of this Agreement. Upon Termination, you must destroy all copies of Software.
7. **Export Regulations.** All Software and technical data delivered under this Agreement are subject to US export control laws and may be subject to export or import regulations in other countries. You agree to comply strictly with all such laws and regulations and acknowledge that you have the responsibility to obtain such licenses to export, re-export, or import as may be required after delivery to you.
8. **U.S. Government Restricted Rights.** If Software is being acquired by or on behalf of the U.S. Government or by a U.S. Government prime contractor or subcontractor (at any tier), then the Government's rights in Software and accompanying documentation will be only as set forth in this Agreement; this is in accordance with 48 CFR 227.7201 through 227.7202-4 (for Department of Defense (DOD) acquisitions) and with 48 CFR 2.101 and 12.212 (for non-DOD acquisitions).
9. **Governing Law.** Any action related to this Agreement will be governed by California law and controlling U.S. federal law. No choice of law rules of any jurisdiction will apply.
10. **Severability.** If any provision of this Agreement is held to be unenforceable, this Agreement will remain in effect with the provision omitted, unless omission would frustrate the intent of the parties, in which case this Agreement will immediately terminate.
11. **Integration.** This Agreement is the entire agreement between you and Sun relating to its subject matter. It supersedes all prior or contemporaneous oral or written

communications, proposals, representations and warranties and prevails over any conflicting or additional terms of any quote, order, acknowledgment, or other communication between the parties relating to its subject matter during the term of this Agreement. No modification of this Agreement will be binding, unless in writing and signed by an authorized representative of each party.

JAVA™ 2 SOFTWARE DEVELOPMENT KIT (J2SDK), STANDARD

EDITION, VERSION 1.4.1_X

SUPPLEMENTAL LICENSE TERMS

These supplemental license terms ("Supplemental Terms") add to or modify the terms of the Binary Code License Agreement (collectively, the "Agreement"). Capitalized terms not defined in these Supplemental Terms shall have the same meanings ascribed to them in the Binary Code License Agreement. These Supplemental Terms shall supersede any inconsistent or conflicting terms in the Binary Code License Agreement, or in any license contained within the Software.

1. **Software Internal Use and Development License Grant.** Subject to the terms and conditions of this Agreement, including, but not limited to Section 4 (Java Technology Restrictions) of these Supplemental Terms, Sun grants you a non-exclusive, non-transferable, limited license without fees to reproduce internally and use internally the binary form of the Software complete and unmodified for the sole purpose of designing, developing, testing, and running your Java applets and applications intended to run on Java-enabled general purpose desktop computers and servers ("Programs").
2. **License to Distribute Software.** Subject to the terms and conditions of this Agreement, including, but not limited to Section 4 (Java Technology Restrictions) of these Supplemental Terms, Sun grants you a non-exclusive, non-transferable, limited license without fees to reproduce and distribute the Software, provided that (i) you distribute the Software complete and unmodified (unless otherwise specified in the applicable README file) and only bundled as part of, and for the sole purpose of running, your Programs, (ii) the Programs add significant and primary functionality to the Software, (iii) you do not distribute additional software intended to replace any component(s) of the Software (unless otherwise specified in the applicable README file), (iv) you do not remove or alter any proprietary legends or notices contained in the Software, (v) you only distribute the Software subject to a license agreement that protects Sun's interests consistent with the terms contained in this Agreement, and (vi) you agree to defend and indemnify Sun and its

licensors from and against any damages, costs, liabilities, settlement amounts and/or expenses (including attorneys' fees) incurred in connection with any claim, lawsuit or action by any third party that arises or results from the use or distribution of any and all Programs and/or Software. (vi) include the following statement as part of product documentation (whether hard copy or electronic), as a part of a copyright page or proprietary rights notice page, in an "About" box or in any other form reasonably designed to make the statement visible to users of the Software: "This product includes code licensed from RSA Security, Inc.", and (vii) include the statement, "Some portions licensed from IBM are available at `<http://oss.software.ibm.com/icu4j/>`".

3. **License to Distribute Redistributables.** Subject to the terms and conditions of this Agreement, including but not limited to Section 4 (Java Technology Restrictions) of these Supplemental Terms, Sun grants you a non-exclusive, non-transferable, limited license without fees to reproduce and distribute those files specifically identified as redistributable in the Software "README" file ("Redistributables") provided that: (i) you distribute the Redistributables complete and unmodified (unless otherwise specified in the applicable README file), and only bundled as part of Programs, (ii) you do not distribute additional software intended to supersede any component(s) of the Redistributables (unless otherwise specified in the applicable README file), (iii) you do not remove or alter any proprietary legends or notices contained in or on the Redistributables, (iv) you only distribute the Redistributables pursuant to a license agreement that protects Sun's interests consistent with the terms contained in the Agreement, (v) you agree to defend and indemnify Sun and its licensors from and against any damages, costs, liabilities, settlement amounts and/or expenses (including attorneys' fees) incurred in connection with any claim, lawsuit or action by any third party that arises or results from the use or distribution of any and all Programs and/or Software, (vi) include the following statement as part of product documentation (whether hard copy or electronic), as a part of a copyright page or proprietary rights notice page, in an "About" box or in any other form reasonably designed to make the statement visible to users of the Software: "This product includes code licensed from RSA Security, Inc.", and (vii) include the statement, "Some portions licensed from IBM are available at `<http://oss.software.ibm.com/icu4j/>`".
4. **Java Technology Restrictions.** You may not modify the Java Platform Interface ("JPI", identified as classes contained within the "java" package or any subpackages of the "java" package), by creating additional classes within the JPI or otherwise causing the addition to or modification of the classes in the JPI. In the event that you create an additional class and associated API(s) which (i) extends the functionality of the Java platform, and (ii) is exposed to third party software developers for the purpose of developing additional software which invokes such additional API, you must promptly publish broadly an accurate specification for such API for free use by all developers. You may not create, or authorize your licensees to create,

additional classes, interfaces, or subpackages that are in any way identified as "java", "javax", "sun" or similar convention as specified by Sun in any naming convention designation.

5. **Notice of Automatic Software Updates from Sun.** You acknowledge that the Software may automatically download, install, and execute applets, applications, software extensions, and updated versions of the Software from Sun ("Software Updates"), which may require you to accept updated terms and conditions for installation. If additional terms and conditions are not presented on installation, the Software Updates will be considered part of the Software and subject to the terms and conditions of the Agreement.

6. **Notice of Automatic Downloads.** You acknowledge that, by your use of the Software and/or by requesting services that require use of the Software, the Software may automatically download, install, and execute software applications from sources other than Sun ("Other Software"). Sun makes no representations of a relationship of any kind to licensors of Other Software. TO THE EXTENT NOT PROHIBITED BY LAW, IN NO EVENT WILL SUN OR ITS LICENSORS BE LIABLE FOR ANY LOST REVENUE, PROFIT OR DATA, OR FOR SPECIAL, INDIRECT, CONSEQUENTIAL, INCIDENTAL OR PUNITIVE DAMAGES, HOWEVER CAUSED REGARDLESS OF THE THEORY OF LIABILITY, ARISING OUT OF OR RELATED TO THE USE OF OR INABILITY TO USE OTHER SOFTWARE, EVEN IF SUN HAS BEEN ADVISED OF THE POSSIBILITY OF SUCH DAMAGES.

7. **Distribution by Publishers.** This section pertains to your distribution of the Software with your printed book or magazine (as those terms are commonly used in the industry) relating to Java technology ("Publication"). Subject to and conditioned upon your compliance with the restrictions and obligations contained in the Agreement, in addition to the license granted in Paragraph 1 above, Sun hereby grants to you a non-exclusive, nontransferable limited right to reproduce complete and unmodified copies of the Software on electronic media (the "Media") for the sole purpose of inclusion and distribution with your Publication(s), subject to the following terms: (i) You may not distribute the Software on a stand-alone basis; it must be distributed with your Publication(s); (ii) You are responsible for downloading the Software from the applicable Sun web site; (iii) You must refer to the Software as Java™ 2 Software Development Kit, Standard Edition, Version 1.4.1; (iv) The Software must be reproduced in its entirety and without any modification whatsoever (including, without limitation, the Binary Code License and Supplemental License Terms accompanying the Software and proprietary rights notices contained in the Software); (v) The Media label shall include the following information: Copyright 2002, Sun Microsystems, Inc. All rights reserved. Use is subject to license terms. Sun, Sun Microsystems, the Sun logo, Solaris, Java, the Java Coffee Cup logo, J2SE , and all trademarks and logos based on Java are trademarks or registered trademarks of Sun Microsystems, Inc. in the U.S. and other countries.

This information must be placed on the Media label in such a manner as to only apply to the Sun Software; (vi) You must clearly identify the Software as Sun's product on the Media holder or Media label, and you may not state or imply that Sun is responsible for any third-party software contained on the Media; (vii) You may not include any third party software on the Media which is intended to be a replacement or substitute for the Software; (viii) You shall indemnify Sun for all damages arising from your failure to comply with the requirements of this Agreement. In addition, you shall defend, at your expense, any and all claims brought against Sun by third parties, and shall pay all damages awarded by a court of competent jurisdiction, or such settlement amount negotiated by you, arising out of or in connection with your use, reproduction or distribution of the Software and/or the Publication. Your obligation to provide indemnification under this section shall arise provided that Sun: (i) provides you prompt notice of the claim; (ii) gives you sole control of the defense and settlement of the claim; (iii) provides you, at your expense, with all available information, assistance and authority to defend; and (iv) has not compromised or settled such claim without your prior written consent; and (ix) You shall provide Sun with a written notice for each Publication; such notice shall include the following information: (1) title of Publication, (2) author(s), (3) date of Publication, and (4) ISBN or ISSN numbers. Such notice shall be sent to Sun Microsystems, Inc., 4150 Network Circle, M/S USCA12-110, Santa Clara, California 95054, U.S.A , Attention: Contracts Administration.

8. **Trademarks and Logos.** You acknowledge and agree as between you and Sun that Sun owns the SUN, SOLARIS, JAVA, JINI, FORTE, and iPLANET trademarks and all SUN, SOLARIS, JAVA, JINI, FORTE, and iPLANET-related trademarks, service marks, logos and other brand designations ("Sun Marks"), and you agree to comply with the Sun Trademark and Logo Usage Requirements currently located at http://www.sun.com/policies/trademarks. Any use you make of the Sun Marks inures to Sun's benefit.

9. **Source Code.** Software may contain source code that is provided solely for reference purposes pursuant to the terms of this Agreement. Source code may not be redistributed unless expressly provided for in this Agreement.

10. **Termination for Infringement.** Either party may terminate this Agreement immediately should any Software become, or in either party's opinion be likely to become, the subject of a claim of infringement of any intellectual property right.

For inquiries please contact: Sun Microsystems, Inc., 4150 Network Circle, Santa Clara, California 95054, U.S.A
(LFI#120080/Form ID#011801)

What's on the CD-ROM

The companion CD-ROM contains Sun Microsystem's Java Software Development Kit (SDK) version 1.4.1; MySQL; Apache Ant; Apache Tomcat; the entire book in electronic format, including bonus appendixes; plus the source code from the book.

Windows Installation Instructions

1. Insert the disc into your CD-ROM drive.
2. From the Windows desktop, double-click on the My Computer icon.
3. Double-click on the icon representing your CD-ROM drive.
4. Double-click on the icon titled `start.html` to launch a web-based guide to installing the CD-ROM contents.

Linux, Mac OS X, and Unix Installation Instructions

1. Insert the disc into your CD-ROM drive.
2. If you have a volume manager on your Unix workstation, the disc will be automatically mounted. If you do not have a volume manager, you need to manually mount the CD-ROM. For example, if you were mounting the CD-ROM on a Linux workstation, you would type

   ```
   mount -tiso9660 /dev/cdrom /mnt/cdrom
   ```

3. Follow the instructions in `start.html` to install the software components.

NOTE

The mount point on your Unix workstation must exist before mounting the CD-ROM to it. The mount point in the example is the usual mount point for a CD-ROM, but you can use any existing directory as a mount point. If you are having difficulty or insufficient permission rights to mount a CD-ROM, please review the man page for mount or talk to your system administrator.